Annual Conference of the Nations of the Americas Chapter of the Association for Computational Linguistics (NAACL 2025)

Student Research Workshop

Albuquerque, New Mexico, USA
30 April - 1 May 2025

ISBN: 979-8-3313-1907-6

Printed from e-media with permission by:

Curran Associates, Inc.
57 Morehouse Lane
Red Hook, NY 12571

Some format issues inherent in the e-media version may also appear in this print version.

Association for Computational Linguistics
209 N. Eighth Street
Stroudsburg, Pennsylvania 18360

Phone: 1-570-476-8006
Fax: 1-570-476-0860

acl@aclweb.org

Additional copies of this publication are available from:

Curran Associates, Inc.
57 Morehouse Lane
Red Hook, NY 12571 USA
Phone: 845-758-0400
Fax: 845-758-2633
Email: curran@proceedings.com
Web: www.proceedings.com

NAACL 2025

The 2025 Conference of the Nations of the Americas Chapter of the Association for Computational Linguistics

Proceedings of the Student Research Workshop

April 30 - May 1, 2025

The NAACL organizers gratefully acknowledge the support from the following sponsors.

Sponsors

Order copies of this and other ACL proceedings from:

Association for Computational Linguistics (ACL)
317 Sidney Baker St. S
Suite 400 - 134
Kerrville, TX 78028
USA
Tel: +1-855-225-1962
acl@aclweb.org

Introduction

Welcome to the NAACL 2025 Student Research Workshop.

The Student Research Workshop (SRW) is a workshop for student researchers in computational linguistics and natural language processing, and provides a unique opportunity for student participants to present their work and receive valuable feedback from the research community.

Continuing the tradition of previous student research workshops, we offer archival and non-archival tracks, and accept both research papers as well as thesis proposals in each track. The research paper track welcomes submissions from Ph.D. students, Masters students, and advanced undergraduate or high school students. Additionally, the thesis proposal submissions caters to advanced Masters and Ph.D. students who have identified their thesis topic, offering them a platform to receive feedback on their proposal and guidance on potential future avenues for their research.

This year, we received a record 169 submissions in total. Of the 145 valid submissions, we accepted 89 total, resulting in an acceptance rate of 61%. Out of the 89 accepted papers, 48 were archival research papers, 29 were non-archival research papers, 6 were archival thesis proposals, and 6 were non-archival thesis proposals.

Another core aspect of the SRW is mentoring. In line with previous years, we had a pre-submission mentoring program before the submission deadline. A total of 28 papers participated in the pre-submission mentoring program. This program offered students the opportunity to receive comments from an experienced researcher to improve the writing style and presentation of their submissions. We are incredibly grateful to all researchers who volunteered as mentors, particularly due the considerable increase in student requests this year.

We are immensely grateful to the Association for Computational Linguistics for their sponsorship. Their support has played a significant role in ensuring the success of the conference and has allowed a large number of students to publish their work and attend the conference. We also express our sincere gratitude to the program committee members for their thorough reviews of each paper. We are also deeply appreciative of the NAACL 2025 organizing committee for their ongoing support, and our faculty advisors Maria Pacheco and Shira Wein, for their valuable guidance which was invaluable to organizing this year's workshop. Lastly, we thank all the student authors for submitting their work and participating in the 2025 edition of the NAACL SRW.

Organizing Committee

Student Chairs

Abteen Ebrahimi, University of Colorado Boulder
Emmy Liu, Carnegie Mellon University
Samar Haider, University of Pennsylvania

Faculty Advisors

Maria Leonor Pacheco, University of Colorado Boulder
Shira Wein, Amherst College

Program Committee

Mentors

Valerio Basile
David Chiang
Brian Davis
Chris Develder
Luis Espinosa-Anke
Dipesh Gautam
Daphne Ippolito
Najoung Kim
Mascha Kurpicz
Kaixin Ma
Archita Pathak
Philip Resnik
Carolyn Rose
Richard Sproat
Andrea Varga
Bonnie Webber

Reviewers

Hadi Abdi Ghavidel, Noor Abo Mokh, Rodrigo Agerri, Dareen Safar Alharthi, Miguel A. Alonso, Tatiana Anikina, Stéphane Aroca-Ouellette

S R Balasundaram, Tadesse Destaw Belay, Peter Belcak, Samuel Belkadi, Lamia Benhiba, Himanshu Beniwal, Gabriel Bernier-Colborne, Steven Bethard, Henrike Beyer, Atharva Bhargude, Gagan Bhatia, Abari Bhattacharya, Chris Biemann, Nimet Beyza Bozdag, Sabur Butt

Allen Chang, Khaoula Chehbouni, David Chiang, Young Min Cho, Javier Conde

Zhongdongming Dai, Samvit Dammalapati, Brian Davis, Jacob Devasier, Chris Develder, Kaustubh Dhole, Cecilia Domingo, Ritam Dutt, Upasana Dutta

Carlos Escolano, Luis Espinosa-Anke, Shaun Esua-Mensah

Martin Fajčík, Amany Fashwan, Virginia K. Felkner, Dayne Freitag, Yicheng Fu, Richard Futrell

Manas Gaur, Dipesh Gautam, Kshitish Ghate, Kripabandhu Ghosh, Dhiman Goswami, Nidhi Goyal, Qiming Guo, Abhay Gupta

Kevin Han, Lifeng Han, Peitao Han, Chandler Haney, Youssef Al Hariri, Truong-Son Hy, Truong-Son Hy, Mika Hämäläinen

Helen Jin, Ashvini Kumar Jindal, Abhinav Joshi

Pritam Kadasi, Tomoyuki Kajiwara, Katikapalli Subramanyam Kalyan, Hidetaka Kamigaito, Sudipta Kar, Daisuke Kawahara, Lemlem Eyob Kawo, Danush Khanna, Lev Kharlashkin, Grigorii

Khvatskii, Philipp Koehn, Zhanibek Kozhirbayev, Mascha Kurpicz-Briki

Alexandra Lavrentovich, Yongjia Lei, Bryan Li, Lei Li, Lixiang Li, Austen Liao, Jasy Suet Yan Liew, Constantine Lignos, Jinhyeong Lim, Peerat Limkonchotiwat, Xuye Liu, Yijun Liu, Zhu Liu, Josh Magnus Ludan

Bolei Ma, Wolfgang Maass, Yunho Maeng, Valentin Malykh, Ali Marashian, John Philip McCrae, Nicolo Micheletti, Filip Miletić, Filip Miletić, Negar Mokhberian

Sachin Narayan Nagargoje, Atharva Naik, Shoichi Naito, Nihal V. Nayak, Hamada Nayel, Lilian Ngweta

Yusuke Oda, Atul Kr. Ojha, Şaziye Betül Özateş

Artemis Panagopoulou, Alexander Panchenko, Tanmay Parekh, Hyeyoung Park, Namyong Park, Ajay S Patil, Xin Peng, Lis Pereira, Vladia Pinheiro, Adithya Pratapa, Gabriele Prato, Priyanshu Priya, Rifki Afina Putri

Sree Harsha Ramesh, Philip Resnik, Enora Rice, Anthony Rios, João Victor Pessoa Rocha, Elisei Rykov

Ahmed Sabir, Parisa Safikhani, Harshita Sahijwani, Yusuke Sakai, Jonathan Sakunkoo, Ahnaf Mozib Samin, Prajvi Saxena, Michael Saxon, Rajiv Ratn Shah, Vishal Shah, Wan Jou She, Sina Sheikholeslami, Andrii Shportko, Chenglei Si, Afroz Ahamad Siddiqui, Harman Singh, Aryan Singhal, Thamar Solorio, Yejin Son, Yueqi Song, Richard Sproat, Yirong Sun, Sathya Krishnan Suresh, Nikita Sushko

Savannah Jennifer Thais, Uthayasanker Thayasivam, Nicholas Tomlin

Takehito Utsuro

Sowmya Vajjala, Andrea Varga, Prasoon Varshney, Ishwara Vasista, Supriti Vijay

Wenlu Wang, Yimu Wang, Yu Wang, Taro Watanabe, Bonnie Webber, Adam Wiemerslage, Steven R Wilson, Zach Wood-Doughty, Jian Wu, Yulong Wu

Yiqing Xie, Xi Xu

Ivory Yang, Ziyu Yao, Haotian Ye, Aditya Yedetore

Haiqi Zhang, Haoran Zhang, Chenyang Zhao, Xingmeng Zhao, Yang Zhong, Andrew Zhu, Yuqicheng Zhu, Zhengyuan Zhu

Keynote Talk

Philip Resnik
Unversity of Maryland, College Park

Bio: Philip Resnik is MPower Professor at University of Maryland with joint appointments in the Department of Linguistics and the Institute for Advanced Computer Studies. He earned his bachelor's in Computer Science at Harvard and his PhD in Computer and Information Science at the University of Pennsylvania, and does research in computational linguistics. Prior to joining UMD, he was an associate scientist at BBN, a graduate summer intern at IBM T.J. Watson Research Center (subsequently awarded an IBM Graduate Fellowship) while at UPenn, and a research scientist at Sun Microsystems Laboratories. In 2020 he was designated a Fellow of the Association for Computational Linguistics. Philip's most recent research has focused in two areas. One is the computational cognitive neuroscience of language, where he has been using computational modeling in connection with brain imaging to look at the role of context and predictive processing during online language comprehension. The other is computational social science, with an emphasis on connecting the signal available in people's language use with underlying mental state – this has applications in computational political science, particularly in connection with ideology, framing, and beliefs, and in mental health, focusing on the ways that linguistic behavior may help to identify and monitor depression, schizophrenia, and suicidality. Philip is a scientific advisor for NORC at the University of Chicago (a non-partisan, independent social research organization). In entrepreneurial life he was a technical co-founder of CodeRyte (NLP for electronic health records, acquired by 3M in 2012), and is an advisor to FiscalNote (machine learning and analytics for government relations, went public in 2022), and Trustible (a leading technology provider of responsible AI governance).

Table of Contents

Fine-Grained and Multi-Dimensional Metrics for Document-Level Machine Translation

Yirong Sun[1], **Dawei Zhu**[2], **Yanjun Chen**[1,3], **Erjia Xiao**[4], **Xinghao Chen**[1,3], **Xiaoyu Shen**[1*]
[1] Digital Twin Institute, Eastern Institute of Technology, Ningbo, China
[2] Saarland University, Saarland Informatics
[3] Department of Computing, The Hong Kong Polytechnic University
[4]The Hong Kong University of Science and Technology (Guangzhou)
win1282467298@gmail.com {xyshen}@eitech.edu.cn

Abstract

Large language models (LLMs) have excelled in various NLP tasks, including machine translation (MT), yet most studies focus on sentence-level translation. This work investigates the inherent capability of instruction-tuned LLMs for document-level translation (docMT). Unlike prior approaches that require specialized techniques, we evaluate LLMs by directly prompting them to translate entire documents in a single pass. Our results show that this method improves translation quality compared to translating sentences separately, even without document-level fine-tuning. However, this advantage is not reflected in BLEU scores, which often favor sentence-based translations. We propose using the LLM-as-a-judge paradigm for evaluation, where GPT-4 is used to assess document coherence, accuracy, and fluency in a more nuanced way than n-gram-based metrics. Overall, our work demonstrates that instruction-tuned LLMs can effectively leverage document context for translation. However, we caution against using BLEU scores for evaluating docMT, as they often provide misleading outcomes, failing to capture the quality of document-level translation.[1]

1 Introduction

Large language models (LLMs) have demonstrated exceptional performance across a wide range of natural language processing tasks (Radford et al., 2019; Brown et al., 2020; Touvron et al., 2023; Dubey et al., 2024). In the realm of machine translation (MT), recent findings also suggest that LLM-based models rival dedicated commercial systems like Google Translate, particularly in translating high-resource languages (Hendy et al., 2023; Peng et al., 2023; Jiao et al., 2023; Zhu et al., 2024a,b). Nonetheless, most research has focused only on sentence-level translation. While some studies have begun to explore document-level translation (docMT) with LLMs, there is a prevailing belief that directly applying instruction-tuned LLMs to docMT performs poorly without specialized training and prompting techniques, largely due to the limited availability of document-level content in instruction-tuning datasets (Wu et al., 2024; Cui et al., 2024; Li et al., 2024). However, their conclusions are frequently drawn from n-gram-based metrics without thorough analysis to substantiate the models' true performance.

In this work, we conduct an in-depth investigation into the *inherent* capabilities of instruction-tuned LLMs in handling docMT tasks. Unlike previous studies that explore special tricks, such as multi-turn inference (Wang et al., 2023), we directly prompt LLMs to translate entire documents in a single pass. Comparing this method to a simpler baseline that translates individual sentences separately and then stitches them together, we can evaluate whether instruction-tuned LLMs can leverage their inherent ability to incorporate document-level context and improve translation quality.

A key challenge in our research is the evaluation of document-level machine translation (docMT). Traditional metrics[2] like BLEU[3], ChrF, and TER (Papineni et al., 2002; Popović, 2015; Snover et al., 2006), though widely used, often poorly correlate with human judgment (Freitag et al., 2022), especially in docMT, where maintaining coherence and logical flow across a document is essential—something n-gram overlap struggles to capture. Metrics like CTT, AZPT, and BLONDE (Jiang et al., 2021; Wang et al., 2023)

*Corresponding authors.

[1]Our code and the outputs from GPT4-as-a-judge are available at https://github.com/EIT-NLP/BLEUless_DocMT

[2]While COMET (Rei et al., 2020) is more reliable than BLEU for sentence-level translation, it is trained exclusively on sentence-level data. As a result, using COMET to evaluate docMT can be unreliable, since out-of-distribution.

[3]Although we do not want to use BLEU based metric, it remains a common metric in existing/recent research, despite its limitations.

Proceedings of the 2025 Conference of the Nations of the Americas Chapter of the Association for Computational Linguistics: Human Language Technologies (Volume 4: Student Research Workshop), pages 1–17

address specific aspects such as terminology consistency and zero-pronoun accuracy, but still rely heavily on word matching and symbolic statistics. We argue that an ideal docMT metric should be (1) context-aware—capturing document-level coherence and accuracy, (2) structured—evaluating aspects such as fluency, accuracy, and coherence separately, and (3) interpretable—explicitly identifying translation errors for clear, objective human evaluation. To this end, we design a GPT-4-based evaluation pipeline to provide deeper insights into the docMT capabilities of LLMs.

- We show that translating entire documents yields better results than translating sentences independently then merging them, even without document-level fine-tuning.
- We propose using the LLM-as-a-judge paradigm with multiple prompts that assess different aspects of translated text to achieve a more targeted and accurate evaluation.
- We recommend against using d-BLEU scores for docMT, as they fail to capture discourse-level phenomena and can often provide misleading results.

2 Problem Settings

Given a document containing l source sentences $\mathbf{X} = \{x^1, \cdots, x^l\}$, the goal of docMT is to generate its translation $\mathbf{Y} = \{y^1, \cdots, y^{l'}\}$ as a sequence of sentences in the target language. In this work, we explore two approaches for generating translations using instruction-tuned LLMs:

- ST[k]: We concatenate k source sentences into a chunk, input each chunk into the LLM for translation, and then concatenate the translated chunks together to form the full document translation.
- DOC: We instruct the LLM to directly translate the entire document in one pass.

The DOC approach is designed to capture inter-sentence dependencies by considering the full document context, potentially leading to more coherent and accurate translations. However, this approach requires the LLM to process and generate longer sequences of text, which can increase the risk of cumulative errors, especially if the model has not been explicitly optimized for document-level translation.

3 BLEU-based Evaluation

Document-level BLEU (d-BLEU, Liu et al., 2020) is widely used for evaluating translations in DocMT. However, we notice that it is sensitive to overly lengthy generation, which can be problematic as LLMs sometimes overgenerate. We find that even minor overgeneration can significantly affect the final d-BLEU score.[4] We argue that documents are generally independent units, so they should be weighted equally in the evaluation. We, therefore, propose an alternative, AvgBLEU, defined as:

$$\text{AvgBLEU} = \frac{1}{N}\sum_{i=1}^{N} \text{BLEU}\left(Y_i^{\text{ref}}, Y_i^{\text{pred}}\right)$$

Here, N is the number of documents, and $\mathbf{Y}^{\text{ref}}$ and $\mathbf{Y}^{\text{pred}}$ represent the reference document translations and the predicted translations, respectively. This allows us to calculate the average BLEU score (AvgBLEU) for the entire dataset, providing a comprehensive measure of translation quality.

	Number of Sentences	Avg. Document Length
zh-en	1142	252
en-zh	1696	219
de-en	1899	204
en-de	1780	231
Total	6517	225

Table 1: Statistics of our test set. The document length is measured by the token count using Vicuna's tokenizer.

Evaluation Setup. For evaluation, we use the test set from WMT22 (Kocmi et al., 2022), which includes sentence-level reference translations along with annotated document boundaries. Document-level references are obtained by concatenating the corresponding sentence translations. We cover four translation directions in our evaluation: German (de) and Chinese (zh) translated to and from English (en). Specific dataset statistics are presented in Table 1. We evaluate five instruction-tuned LLMs: Vicuna-7B/13B (Zheng et al., 2023), their -16K versions and Mistral-instruct-7B (Jiang et al., 2023), all of which have very limited document-level content in their instruction-tuning datasets.

Results. Table 2 presents the comparison between the two document-level translation approaches. ST[k] consistently achieves higher AvgBLEU scores across all models and nearly all translation directions, with zh-en using Vicuna-7B and

[4]For completeness, we report results using the standard d-BLEU in Appendix B.

Model	Eval Type	Translation Direction			
		zh-en	en-zh	de-en	en-de
Vicuna-7B	ST1	19.70	30.97	29.42	20.82
	ST2	19.69	31.65	**29.56**	22.10
	ST3	19.62	**32.14**	29.22	**22.53**
	DOC	**20.50**	31.70	29.15	21.94
Vicuna-7B-16K	ST1	**20.26**	28.08	28.16	21.11
	ST2	20.05	31.17	28.78	**22.99**
	ST3	19.99	**31.64**	**28.89**	22.93
	DOC	20.20	30.77	28.65	21.57
Vicuna-13B	ST1	**22.40**	36.22	30.50	25.03
	ST2	21.01	35.82	**30.89**	25.46
	ST3	21.13	**36.24**	30.84	**25.66**
	DOC	21.83	34.93	30.60	25.59
Vicuna-13B-16K	ST1	21.07	35.55	29.87	25.22
	ST2	20.97	**36.76**	30.47	24.87
	ST3	20.79	36.46	**30.71**	**25.58**
	DOC	**21.07**	34.97	30.62	25.14
Mistral-7B	ST1	**19.82**	26.24	29.23	21.28
	ST2	18.89	26.84	**29.86**	21.44
	ST3	18.78	**26.87**	29.82	**21.74**
	DOC	18.61	24.31	28.98	21.09

Table 2: AvgBLEU scores with different translation approaches across four translation directions. The best scores are in bold, with red/blue shading indicating the highest score paradigm, respectively. In most cases, merged sentence translations yield higher BLEU scores than direct document translations.

Vicuna-13B-16K as the only two exceptions. The specific value of k that yields the highest AvgBLEU score varies depending on the translation direction, however, on average, ST3 achieves the highest score overall. While independently translated sentences yield better AvgBLEU scores than document translations done in one pass by LLMs, manual inspection reveals that ST[k] translations often contain more redundancy, literal translations, and disjointed phrasing. While these translations may achieve higher AvgBLEU scores, we find that DOC translations result in more fluent, readable, and cohesive output. This raises concerns about how much AvgBLEU can be trusted as a metric for evaluating docMT.

4 LLM-as-a-judge Evaluation

Maruf et al. (2021) outlines various discourse phenomena that should be considered when evaluating document-level translations, such as cohesion and the use of discourse connectives. In the past, automatic evaluation of these aspects was difficult due to the need for deep semantic understanding, and evaluations typically focused on one aspect at a time using specialized test sets (Hardmeier and Federico, 2010; Gong et al., 2015; Jwalapuram et al., 2019). Inspired by the "LLM-as-a-judge" approach (Zheng et al., 2023), we aim to assess multiple aspects simultaneously using a strong LLM.

Evaluation Setup. We design four (sub) metrics: (1) **Fluency**, (2) Content Errors (**CE**), (3) Lexical Cohesion Errors (**LE**), and (4) Grammatical Cohesion Errors (**GE**). All metrics are measured using prompts provided to GPT-4. See Appendix C for details on prompt design.

Fluency is rated on a scale of 1 to 5, with higher being better. Since fluency can be evaluated solely based on the translated text, we present only the model's outputs to GPT-4 for this assessment, decoupling fluency from metrics that require consideration of source and reference texts.

Content Errors refer to translation mistakes such as mistranslations, omissions, or additions. We instruct GPT-4 (`gpt-4-0613`) to output a list containing all identified mistakes. The CE score is determined by the length of this list, and report the average CE score over the test set.[5]

Cohesion Errors are further divided into two subcategories: lexical (LE) and grammatical (GE), which affect text connection and the logic flow, respectively. LE includes incorrect vocabulary usage, missing synonyms, or overuse of certain terms that disrupt the flow. GE includes pronouns, conjunctions, and sentence-linking structure mistakes. Similar to CE, we prompt GPT-4 to generate a list of identified errors, with the score corresponding to the length of the list.

Other settings, such as translation directions and the models of interest, remain consistent with Section 3. Due to the cost associated with using GPT-4, we sample 70 documents per translation direction from the WMT22 dataset for our evaluation.

Results. The results with `en-zh` are shown in Table 3. Although ST3 scores higher than DOC on AvgBLEU, DOC consistently outperforms ST3 in Fluency. Additionally, DOC generally exhibits fewer CE, also known as content errors. For cohesion errors, the results are mixed: DOC shows better LE with vicuna-7B and its -16K version, and Mistral-7B, while Vicuna-13B and its -16K version yield higher LE. As for GE, DOC performs better with -16K models and Mistral-7B while others are mostly comparable. We also observe that the -16K versions perform similarly to their original counterparts in fluency but demonstrate notable improvements in CE reduction. This pattern is

[5]For simplicity, all mistake types are equally weighted, but our approach is flexible and can easily use different weights if certain types are considered more severe than others.

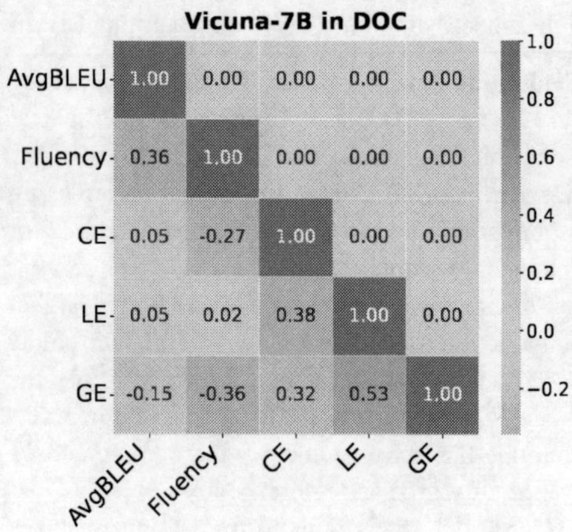

Figure 1: PCC Heatmaps among AvgBLEU, Fluency, CE, LE and GE for Vicuna-7B under DOC evaluation type in the en-zh translation direction.

consistent across all translation directions, with full results provided in Appendix D. Overall, our approach enables a more detailed evaluation of translation quality in DocMT. It clearly shows that instruction-tuned LLMs, even without fine-tuning for document-level MT tasks, are effective at capturing long-context information for DocMT.

To gain a deeper understanding of how these metrics correlates with each other, we compute the Pearson Correlation Coefficients (PCC) among those metrics and visualize them in Figure 1, as well as translation directions, showing that BLEU score has poor correlation with those discourse-level phenomena metrics. Other translation directions also exhibit low correlation results in Appendix E. Therefore, we suggest not using BLEU score for docMT since it fails to account for discourse-level phenomena, and even worse, it often produces misleading results—such as suggesting that sentence translations are better.

Human Agreement. While some judgments by the LLM-as-a-judge may appear reasonable, certain nuances may still be misinterpreted due to unique human perspectives. To validate the alignment between our LLM-as-a-judge paradigm and human evaluations, we conducted experiments to assess agreement. For each model in both ST3 and DOC, we used 10 samples per translation direction and asked human evaluators to respond with a simple "yes" or "no" regarding their agreement with the LLM-as-a-judge's assessments according to our metrics.

Model	Eval Type	AvgBLEU↑	Fluency↑	CE↓	LE↓	GE↓
Vicuna-7B	ST3	**33.44**	3.64	4.97	2.55	**1.21**
	DOC	28.48	**4.04**	**4.40**	**2.31**	1.25
Vicuna-7B-16K	ST3	**31.30**	3.08	5.30	2.22	1.71
	DOC	30.80	**3.97**	**4.72**	**2.17**	**1.15**
Vicuna-13B	ST3	**37.44**	3.78	**4.82**	**1.70**	**1.14**
	DOC	35.58	**4.12**	4.87	2.02	1.14
Vicuna-13B-16k	ST3	**38.66**	2.98	4.21	**1.84**	1.02
	DOC	34.25	**4.10**	**4.15**	2.04	**0.95**
Mistral-7B	ST3	**26.82**	2.80	6.77	4.08	2.62
	DOC	23.27	**3.11**	**5.98**	**3.71**	**2.51**

Table 3: Evaluation results (en-zh) by GPT-4 for Vicuna-7B, Vicuna-13B, their -16K versions and Mistral-7B under ST3 and DOC, showing metrics AvgBLEU, fluency, content errors, lexical cohesion errors, and grammatical cohesion errors. Best performances are in bold, with red/blue shading indicating the winning paradigm, respectively.

Our manual evaluation confirmed a strong alignment between human judgments and the LLM-as-a-judge paradigm. As shown in Table 4, GPT-4-as-a-judge achieved approximately 95% agreement with human evaluations across all languages and evaluation types (ST3 and DOC), indicating robust concordance with human judgment across translation directions and metrics. This high level of agreement further validates GPT-4-as-a-judge as a reliable metric for document-level translation quality.

	AFluency↑	ACE↑	ALE↑	AGE↑
zh-en	0.96	0.95	0.94	0.96
en-zh	0.97	0.98	0.96	0.96
de-en	0.98	0.96	0.94	0.95
en-de	0.96	0.96	0.95	0.97

Table 4: Human agreement percentage on GPT4-as-a-judge with our metrics in WMT22. Each judgment is independently reviewed three times by different annotators and consensus results are recorded. AFluency, ACE, ALE, and AGE denote human agreement on the metrics of Fluency, CE, LE, and GE.

Case Study. To inspect the advantages of LLMs in docMT, we present two pairs of samples from Vicuna-7B and Vicuna-7B-16K(zh-en), covering beginning, middle, and end of each sample.

On the right side of first case in Box 2, the translation of "Hunan" remains consistent throughout the document, illustrating the LLM's capability to leverage context and capture inter-sentence dependencies. Conversely, on the left side, we see an

Comparison Cases in ST3 and DOC

Model: Vicuna-7B

Prediction in ST3:
The 13th Provincial Tea Expo opened today... This morning, the 13th Hunan Tea Industry Expo and... were held in the Hunan International Convention...
At the opening ceremony, the provincial leaders awarded the fourth batch of enterprises with the right to use the Lake South Red Tea trademark. New Hope held the Lake Red Source. The Chaozhou tea industry warmly welcomed the arrival of the new spring.

Prediction in DOC:
The 13th Hunan Tea Industry Expo opened today at the Hunan International Convention...
At the opening ceremony, Hunan's provincial leaders awarded the fourth batch of enterprises with the right to use the Hunan Red Tea trademark... The Hunan Red Tea is red in color and has injected the cultural connotation of tea into it, making it popular and lively, and the Hunan tea industry is looking forward to a new spring.

Model: Vicuna-7B-16K

Prediction in ST3:
Color: As shown in the picture (please avoid shooting to avoid color difference...
Therefore, girls who can't drive should not complain about their clothes being old...
2021.6.11部分圈中售出。看好编号下单，古董物品售出不退不换。购买须知The products sold at this store are non-refundable... The store does not accept styles that are different from what is imagined, and size and style cannot be used as reasons for refunds or exchanges...

Prediction in DOC:
Color: As shown in the picture (Please note that the color difference may not be avoided due to shooting...
So, some girls who can't drive vintage clothing should not say that the clothes are old-fashioned, but that you are not suitable for it!...
If the item is not suitable for personal reasons, such as not fitting or not liking it, you can ask the store owner to transfer it to the shelf, and once it is sold, it cannot be exchanged or refunded. Part of the circle in the middle was sold on June 11, 2021...

Box 2: Comparison of Vicuna-7B and Vicuna-7B-16K translations under ST3 and DOC evaluation types in the en-zh translation direction.

erroneous translation where "Hunan" is rendered as "Lake South" in "Lake South Red Tea" and simply as "Lake" in "Lake Red Source". Notably, the model in ST3 correctly translates "Hunan" in other parts of the text. In this case, although ST3 achieves a BLEU score approximately 11.88 points higher than DOC, it is evident that DOC provides more coherent wording and aligns better with natural human expression.

We present another case in Box 2: ST3 translates "color difference is inevitable in the photos" as "please avoid shooting to avoid color difference," resulting in a significant change in meaning. Additionally, a description about some girls' struggles with a style is mistranslated as "girls who can't drive" where "drive" is incorrectly used as an intransitive verb. In contrast, DOC accurately translates this as "some girls who can't drive vintage clothing" preserving the intended meaning while employing the same words in different contexts. Furthermore, the statement "once it is sold, it cannot be exchanged or refunded. Part of the circle in the middle was sold on June 11, 2021" is correctly translated in DOC, while ST3 reject translating this segment entirely. These cases explicitly demonstrate that instruction-tuned LLMs can effectively capture inter-sentence dependencies by considering the entire document context, leading to a deeper understanding of the text and fewer content errors.

Thus, we advocate against using BLEU as an evaluation metric for docMT, as it fails to detect the true advantages of LLMs in this context and can yield misleading results.

5 Conclusion

In this work, we investigate the performance of instruction-tuned LLMs in document-level machine translation (docMT), comparing the translation of entire documents in a single pass to translating individual sentences that are then concatenated. Our findings show that translating entire documents yields better results, as the model can capture inter-sentence dependencies and maintain discourse coherence, even without explicit fine-tuning for docMT tasks. However, evaluating these improvements is challenging. Traditional metrics like d-BLEU fail to consider discourse-level phenomena, often favoring sentence-level translations and producing misleading results. To address this limitation, we propose the LLM-as-a-judge approach, utilizing GPT-4 to assess specific aspects of discourse through tailored prompts. This method enhances interpretability and can be adapted for evaluating translation quality in other domains.

Limitations

Translation Directions. We evaluate only high-resource language pairs, which limits the generalizability of our findings for low-resource languages. Due to data availability constraints, our experiments focus on well-resourced translation directions. Future research should explore whether instruction-tuned LLMs translating entire documents yield better results than translating sentences independently in low-resource languages.

Model Size and Diversity. We focus exclusively on small-scale LLMs. Future work should investigate larger models to observe whether instruction-tuned LLMs continue to perform better in docMT, and whether BLEU would work.

Max Length. A small fraction ($\sim 2\%$) of documents in WMT22, including both their source texts and translations, exceed 2048 tokens. Thus, we focus solely on samples within the model's context length (2048 tokens), as these instruction-tuned LLMs are primarily trained on text within this limit. In future work, we will evaluate LLMs with longer context lengths, examine -16K models, and investigate whether long conversation instruction-tuned will help and whether those phenomena persist when translating text that exceeds the models' context length.

Ethical Considerations

Our study aims to investigate the docMT reliability of instruction-tuned LLMs without fine-tuning for docMT, concerned by the potential for accumulating errors during decoding, which may lead to increased hallucinations. We expect minimal social risks associated with our efforts.

References

Tom Brown, Benjamin Mann, Nick Ryder, Melanie Subbiah, Jared D Kaplan, Prafulla Dhariwal, Arvind Neelakantan, Pranav Shyam, Girish Sastry, Amanda Askell, et al. 2020. Language models are few-shot learners. In *Advances in Neural Information Processing Systems*.

Menglong Cui, Jiangcun Du, Shaolin Zhu, and Deyi Xiong. 2024. Efficiently exploring large language models for document-level machine translation with in-context learning. In *Findings of the Association for Computational Linguistics ACL 2024*, pages 10885–10897, Bangkok, Thailand and virtual meeting. Association for Computational Linguistics.

Abhimanyu Dubey, Abhinav Jauhri, Abhinav Pandey, Abhishek Kadian, Ahmad Al-Dahle, Aiesha Letman, Akhil Mathur, Alan Schelten, Amy Yang, Angela Fan, et al. 2024. The llama 3 herd of models. *arXiv preprint arXiv:2407.21783*.

Markus Freitag, Ricardo Rei, Nitika Mathur, Chi-kiu Lo, Craig Stewart, Eleftherios Avramidis, Tom Kocmi, George Foster, Alon Lavie, and André F. T. Martins. 2022. Results of WMT22 metrics shared task: Stop using BLEU – neural metrics are better and more robust. In *Proceedings of the Seventh Conference on Machine Translation (WMT)*, pages 46–68, Abu Dhabi, United Arab Emirates (Hybrid). Association for Computational Linguistics.

Zhengxian Gong, Min Zhang, and Guodong Zhou. 2015. Document-level machine translation evaluation with gist consistency and text cohesion. In *Proceedings of the Second Workshop on Discourse in Machine Translation*, pages 33–40, Lisbon, Portugal. Association for Computational Linguistics.

Michael Alexander Kirkwood Halliday and Ruqaiya Hasan. 2014. *Cohesion in english*. Routledge.

Christian Hardmeier and Marcello Federico. 2010. Modelling pronominal anaphora in statistical machine translation. In *Proceedings of the 7th International Workshop on Spoken Language Translation: Papers*, pages 283–289, Paris, France.

Amr Hendy, Mohamed Abdelrehim, Amr Sharaf, Vikas Raunak, Mohamed Gabr, Hitokazu Matsushita, Young Jin Kim, Mohamed Afify, and Hany Hassan Awadalla. 2023. How good are GPT models at machine translation? A comprehensive evaluation. *CoRR*, abs/2302.09210.

Albert Q. Jiang, Alexandre Sablayrolles, Arthur Mensch, Chris Bamford, Devendra Singh Chaplot, Diego de Las Casas, Florian Bressand, Gianna Lengyel, Guillaume Lample, Lucile Saulnier, Lélio Renard Lavaud, Marie-Anne Lachaux, Pierre Stock, Teven Le Scao, Thibaut Lavril, Thomas Wang, Timothée Lacroix, and William El Sayed. 2023. Mistral 7b. *CoRR*, abs/2310.06825.

Yuchen Eleanor Jiang, Tianyu Liu, Shuming Ma, Dongdong Zhang, Jian Yang, Haoyang Huang, Rico Sennrich, Ryan Cotterell, Mrinmaya Sachan, and Ming Zhou. 2021. Blonde: An automatic evaluation metric for document-level machine translation. *arXiv preprint arXiv:2103.11878*.

Wenxiang Jiao, Wenxuan Wang, Jen-tse Huang, Xing Wang, Shuming Shi, and Zhaopeng Tu. 2023. Is chatgpt a good translator? yes with gpt-4 as the engine. *arXiv preprint arXiv:2301.08745*.

Prathyusha Jwalapuram, Shafiq Joty, Irina Temnikova, and Preslav Nakov. 2019. Evaluating pronominal anaphora in machine translation: An evaluation measure and a test suite. In *Proceedings of the 2019 Conference on Empirical Methods in Natural Language*

Processing and the 9th International Joint Conference on Natural Language Processing (EMNLP-IJCNLP), pages 2964–2975, Hong Kong, China. Association for Computational Linguistics.

Tom Kocmi, Rachel Bawden, Ondřej Bojar, Anton Dvorkovich, Christian Federmann, Mark Fishel, Thamme Gowda, Yvette Graham, Roman Grundkiewicz, Barry Haddow, Rebecca Knowles, Philipp Koehn, Christof Monz, Makoto Morishita, Masaaki Nagata, Toshiaki Nakazawa, Michal Novák, Martin Popel, and Maja Popović. 2022. Findings of the 2022 conference on machine translation (WMT22). In *Proceedings of the Seventh Conference on Machine Translation (WMT)*, pages 1–45, Abu Dhabi, United Arab Emirates (Hybrid). Association for Computational Linguistics.

Yachao Li, Junhui Li, Jing Jiang, and Min Zhang. 2024. Enhancing document-level translation of large language model via translation mixed-instructions. *arXiv preprint arXiv:2401.08088*.

Yinhan Liu, Jiatao Gu, Naman Goyal, Xian Li, Sergey Edunov, Marjan Ghazvininejad, Mike Lewis, and Luke Zettlemoyer. 2020. Multilingual Denoising Pre-training for Neural Machine Translation. *Transactions of the Association for Computational Linguistics*, 8:726–742.

Sameen Maruf, Fahimeh Saleh, and Gholamreza Haffari. 2021. A survey on document-level neural machine translation: Methods and evaluation. *ACM Computing Surveys (CSUR)*, 54(2):1–36.

Kishore Papineni, Salim Roukos, Todd Ward, and Wei-Jing Zhu. 2002. Bleu: a method for automatic evaluation of machine translation. In *Proceedings of the 40th Annual Meeting on Association for Computational Linguistics*, ACL '02, page 311–318, USA. Association for Computational Linguistics.

Keqin Peng, Liang Ding, Qihuang Zhong, Li Shen, Xuebo Liu, Min Zhang, Yuanxin Ouyang, and Dacheng Tao. 2023. Towards making the most of chatgpt for machine translation. In *Findings of the Association for Computational Linguistics: EMNLP 2023, Singapore, December 6-10, 2023*, pages 5622–5633. Association for Computational Linguistics.

Maja Popović. 2015. chrF: character n-gram F-score for automatic MT evaluation. In *Proceedings of the Tenth Workshop on Statistical Machine Translation*, pages 392–395, Lisbon, Portugal. Association for Computational Linguistics.

Alec Radford, Jeffrey Wu, Rewon Child, David Luan, Dario Amodei, Ilya Sutskever, et al. 2019. Language models are unsupervised multitask learners. OpenAI blog.

Ricardo Rei, Craig Stewart, Ana C. Farinha, and Alon Lavie. 2020. COMET: A neural framework for MT evaluation. In *Proceedings of the 2020 Conference on Empirical Methods in Natural Language Processing, EMNLP 2020, Online, November 16-20, 2020*, pages 2685–2702. Association for Computational Linguistics.

Matthew Snover, Bonnie Dorr, Richard Schwartz, Linnea Micciulla, and John Makhoul. 2006. A study of translation edit rate with targeted human annotation. In *Proceedings of the 7th Conference of the Association for Machine Translation in the Americas: Technical Papers*, pages 223–231.

Hugo Touvron, Louis Martin, Kevin Stone, Peter Albert, Amjad Almahairi, Yasmine Babaei, Nikolay Bashlykov, Soumya Batra, Prajjwal Bhargava, Shruti Bhosale, Dan Bikel, Lukas Blecher, Cristian Canton-Ferrer, Moya Chen, Guillem Cucurull, David Esiobu, Jude Fernandes, Jeremy Fu, Wenyin Fu, Brian Fuller, Cynthia Gao, Vedanuj Goswami, Naman Goyal, Anthony Hartshorn, Saghar Hosseini, Rui Hou, Hakan Inan, Marcin Kardas, Viktor Kerkez, Madian Khabsa, Isabel Kloumann, Artem Korenev, Punit Singh Koura, Marie-Anne Lachaux, Thibaut Lavril, Jenya Lee, Diana Liskovich, Yinghai Lu, Yuning Mao, Xavier Martinet, Todor Mihaylov, Pushkar Mishra, Igor Molybog, Yixin Nie, Andrew Poulton, Jeremy Reizenstein, Rashi Rungta, Kalyan Saladi, Alan Schelten, Ruan Silva, Eric Michael Smith, Ranjan Subramanian, Xiaoqing Ellen Tan, Binh Tang, Ross Taylor, Adina Williams, Jian Xiang Kuan, Puxin Xu, Zheng Yan, Iliyan Zarov, Yuchen Zhang, Angela Fan, Melanie Kambadur, Sharan Narang, Aurélien Rodriguez, Robert Stojnic, Sergey Edunov, and Thomas Scialom. 2023. Llama 2: Open foundation and fine-tuned chat models. *CoRR*, abs/2307.09288.

Longyue Wang, Chenyang Lyu, Tianbo Ji, Zhirui Zhang, Dian Yu, Shuming Shi, and Zhaopeng Tu. 2023. Document-level machine translation with large language models. In *Proceedings of the 2023 Conference on Empirical Methods in Natural Language Processing*, pages 16646–16661, Singapore. Association for Computational Linguistics.

Minghao Wu, Yufei Wang, George Foster, Lizhen Qu, and Gholamreza Haffari. 2024. Importance-aware data augmentation for document-level neural machine translation. In *Proceedings of the 18th Conference of the European Chapter of the Association for Computational Linguistics (Volume 1: Long Papers)*, pages 740–752, St. Julian's, Malta. Association for Computational Linguistics.

Lianmin Zheng, Wei-Lin Chiang, Ying Sheng, Siyuan Zhuang, Zhanghao Wu, Yonghao Zhuang, Zi Lin, Zhuohan Li, Dacheng Li, Eric Xing, Hao Zhang, Joseph E Gonzalez, and Ion Stoica. 2023. Judging llm-as-a-judge with mt-bench and chatbot arena. In *Advances in Neural Information Processing Systems*, volume 36, pages 46595–46623. Curran Associates, Inc.

Dawei Zhu, Pinzhen Chen, Miaoran Zhang, Barry Haddow, Xiaoyu Shen, and Dietrich Klakow. 2024a. Fine-tuning large language models to translate: Will a touch of noisy data in misaligned languages suffice? *arXiv preprint arXiv:2404.14122*.

Dawei Zhu, Sony Trenous, Xiaoyu Shen, Dietrich Klakow, Bill Byrne, and Eva Hasler. 2024b. A preference-driven paradigm for enhanced translation with large language models. In *Proceedings of the 2024 Conference of the North American Chapter of the Association for Computational Linguistics: Human Language Technologies (Volume 1: Long Papers)*, pages 3385–3403, Mexico City, Mexico. Association for Computational Linguistics.

A Evaluation Metrics Shortcoming Analysis

While COMET has been shown to provide more reliable evaluations than BLEU in many cases, it is primarily trained on sentence-level translations and, as such, is not well-suited for docMT. Given that COMET lacks specific training to capture the complexities of inter-sentence dependencies and discourse-level phenomena, it is not an ideal metric for evaluating the true capabilities of LLMs in docMT tasks. Therefore, in this work, we opted to explore more appropriate evaluation methods tailored to document-level translation challenges.

Similarly, metrics like ChrF (Popović, 2015), ChrF2, and TER have made incremental progress by incorporating word-level matching mechanisms that extend beyond simple token overlap, but they still fundamentally rely on surface-level statistics. Like BLEU, these metrics do not adequately account for deeper discourse relationships, cohesion, and the broader context required for accurate docMT assessment. As a result, their limitations become more apparent when evaluating LLMs on longer texts, where capturing the overall document structure is essential.

While metrics such as cTT and aZPT are designed to address specific issues like terminology consistency and zero pronoun accuracy, they remain grounded in automatic identified lexical alignment. These metrics operate under the assumption that the presence of specific terminology or pronouns directly correlates with translation quality. However, in practice, meaning can be conveyed in multiple ways without strictly adhering to these surface-level features. This makes cTT and aZPT limited in scope, as they are unable to fully assess translation quality when alternative phrasing or omitted pronouns still preserve meaning accurately.

Blonde represents a more sophisticated approach by categorizing and analyzing discourse coherence using linguistic features such as verb tense (e.g., VBD for past tense verbs). While this is a step toward capturing discourse-level phenomena, Blonde is still constrained by symbolic statistical methods. Its reliance on predefined linguistic categories means that it struggles to account for the full range of discourse phenomena that can arise in real-world documents. As a result, these metrics, despite their improvements, remain insufficient for capturing the nuances of document-level translation in its entirety.

To address these limitations, we propose leveraging LLM-as-a-judge for evaluating docMT. By employing GPT-4 with specifically designed judging prompts, we can define and assess discourse phenomena in a more abstract and flexible manner, similar to how human evaluators would approach the task. This method avoids the need to predefine all possible linguistic cases and allows for a more holistic evaluation of translation quality, ensuring that complex discourse relationships and contextual dependencies are properly recognized. In doing so, we provide more reliable and interpretable metrics and prompts for evaluating document-level translations, moving beyond the restrictive frameworks of traditional metrics.

B d-BLEU Performance

We observe that the trend in Table 5 remains consistent with Table 2, and the BLEU score shows an even stronger preference for translations that are processed separately and concatenated. It is worth to Notice that the red data point in Table 5 is influenced by the sensitivity of BLEU, where a certain generated translation contains a long-repeated incorrect token toward the end, thus lowering the overall score. When calculating the BLEU score for this sample, we find that the document receives a score near zero, despite the fact that the earlier part of the translation is mostly accurate. This sensitivity is one of the reasons why BLEU should not be used in docMT.

C GPT4-as-a-judge Evaluation Prompts

C.1 Fluency

Fluency refers to the naturalness and smoothness of a text in the target language, without awkward or unnatural phrasing. In machine translation evaluation, fluency is crucial for assessing the readability and linguistic quality of the output, which is often not fully captured by traditional metrics like BLEU. While BLEU focuses on n-gram overlap between the translation and reference text, it does not di-

Model	Eval Type	Translation Direction			
		zh-en	en-zh	de-en	en-de
Vicuna-7B	ST1	18.75	32.43	30.00	21.96
	ST2	19.99	33.52	**30.87**	23.35
	ST3	**20.52**	**33.92**	30.68	**23.96**
	DOC	19.93	32.40	30.27	22.90
Vicuna-7B-16K	ST1	19.54	28.45	29.75	21.49
	ST2	20.38	32.52	**30.60**	**24.27**
	ST3	**20.43**	**33.15**	30.56	23.95
	DOC	19.50	30.87	16.58	21.34
Vicuna-13B	ST1	21.33	37.62	31.98	26.24
	ST2	21.26	37.70	**32.16**	**27.19**
	ST3	**21.89**	**37.97**	32.15	26.94
	DOC	21.63	35.87	31.22	26.31
Vicuna-13B-16K	ST1	21.22	37.29	31.48	26.21
	ST2	21.99	**37.93**	31.78	26.53
	ST3	**22.61**	37.83	**32.02**	**26.98**
	DOC	21.84	35.01	31.60	26.03
Mistral-7B	ST1	18.69	25.75	29.50	22.37
	ST2	**19.29**	**26.83**	30.02	21.98
	ST3	18.82	26.81	**30.11**	**22.60**
	DOC	13.70	17.54	27.50	21.98

Table 5: d-BLEU score with different translation paradigms. More explanations about not using d-BLEU and about the red data point in the Table are stated in Appendix B

rectly evaluate how natural the translation sounds or whether it adheres to syntactic rules. Fluency, in contrast, provides a more nuanced evaluation of the model's ability to produce human-like text.

In this task, we assess fluency on a scale of 1 to 5, with higher scores indicating more fluent translations. Evaluators are instructed to analyze the text and assign a score based solely on the naturalness and grammatical correctness of the model's output.

Importantly, the fluency evaluation is conducted in isolation, decoupled from cohesion, with only inference text input, to ensure a clear focus on the text's immediate readability. Cohesion, which refers to the grammatical and lexical connectivity between text units (Halliday and Hasan, 2014), is considered separately to avoid confounding the two metrics, as fluency and cohesion could be correlated, as it is common sense that if a text is cohesive, its flow is naturally better. See the correlation heatmaps like Figure 1 which show that our prompt design successfully decouples these two metrics.

The evaluation is supported by specific examples and justifications for the assigned score. Below is the prompt used to guide the evaluation:

> *Please evaluate the fluency of the following text in the target language (English, Chinese, or German).*
>
> **Instructions:**
>
> - **Task**: Evaluate the fluency of the text.
> - **Scoring**: Provide a score from 1 to 5, where:
>   - **5**: The text is highly fluent, with no grammatical errors, unnatural wording, or stiff syntax.
>   - **4**: The text is mostly fluent, with minor errors that do not impede understanding.
>   - **3**: The text is moderately fluent, with noticeable errors that may slightly affect comprehension.
>   - **2**: The text has low fluency, with frequent errors that hinder understanding.

- **1**: The text is not fluent, with severe errors that make it difficult to understand.

- **Explanation**: Support your score with specific examples to justify your evaluation.

Output Format:

Provide your evaluation in the following JSON format:
{ "Fluency": { "Score": "<the score>", "Explanation": "<your explanation on how you made the decision>" } }

Text to Evaluate:

"inference text"

C.2 Content Errors

Unlike fluency, which assesses the naturalness and grammatical correctness of the output, accuracy focuses on the semantic alignment between the translated text and the original reference. The evaluator's task is to identify and categorize errors that affect the translation's fidelity, such as mistranslations, omissions, or additions.

Rather than relying on simple n-gram matching, the evaluation emphasizes meaning preservation. The evaluator compares the translation with the reference text, identifying instances where the translation deviates in meaning. However, if the translated text conveys the same information as the reference but uses different words or phrasing, it is not considered an error, since we suspect that this phenomenon could happen in LLMs in document-level translation task. This approach ensures that the model's output is evaluated based on its ability to faithfully represent the source content, capturing specific issues like mistranslations or information loss, and ensuring semantic integrity. The accuracy evaluation prompt is structured as follows:

Please evaluate the accuracy of the following text by comparing it to the reference text provided.

Instructions:

- **Task**: Compare the text to the reference text.
- **Identify Mistakes**: List all mistakes related to accuracy.
  - **Mistake Types**:
    * **Wrong Translation**: Incorrect meaning or misinterpretation leading to wrong information.
    * **Omission**: Missing words, phrases, or information present in the reference text.
    * **Addition**: Extra words, phrases, or information not present in the reference text.
    * **Others**: Mistakes that are hard to define or categorize.
- **Note**: If the text expresses the same information as the reference text but uses different words or phrasing, it is **not** considered a mistake.
- **Provide a List**: Summarize all mistakes without repeating the exact sentences. Provide an empty list if there are no mistakes.

Output Format:

{ "Accuracy": { "Mistakes": ["<list of all mistakes in the text, provide an empty list if there are no mistakes>"] }

Text to Evaluate:

"inference text"

C.3 Cohesion Errors

Cohesion is a critical aspect of machine translation evaluation as it ensures that the various parts of the text are well-connected and that the overall flow is logical. Unlike metrics such as fluency or accuracy, cohesion specifically examines how sentences are linked together through lexical (lexical cohesion) and grammatical (grammatical cohesion) means (Maruf et al., 2021). This is particularly important in document-level translation, where the consistency of vocabulary and the logical connection of grammatical structures across a longer text are challenging for models to maintain.

In the context of translations produced using the ST3 and DOC paradigms, evaluating cohesion allows us to assess whether the model effectively leverages contextual information to maintain consistency across the text. By decoupling cohesion from fluency, our evaluation framework enables evaluators to focus specifically on identifying lexical cohesion mistakes—such as incorrect vocabulary usage, missing synonyms, or overuse of certain terms that disrupt the flow—and grammatical cohesion mistakes—such as errors in pronouns, conjunctions, or sentence-linking structures.

The evaluator is asked to identify any mistakes related to cohesion and categorize them as either lexical or grammatical cohesion issues. The evaluation prompt is structured as follows:

> *Please evaluate the cohesion of the following text by comparing it to the reference text.*
>
> **Instructions:**
>
> - **Task**: Evaluate the cohesion of the text.
> - **Definition**: Cohesion refers to how different parts of a text are connected using language structures like grammar and vocabulary. It ensures that sentences flow smoothly and the text makes sense as a whole.
> - **Identify Mistakes**: List all mistakes related to cohesion.
>   - **Lexical Cohesion Mistakes**: Issues with vocabulary usage, incorrect or missing synonyms, or overuse of certain words that disrupt the flow.
>   - **Grammatical Cohesion Mistakes**: Problems with pronouns, conjunctions, or grammatical structures that link sentences and clauses.
> - **Provide Lists**: Provide separate lists for lexical cohesion mistakes and grammatical cohesion mistakes. Provide empty lists if there are no mistakes.

Output Format:

> { "Cohesion": { "Lexical Cohesion Mistakes": ["<list of all mistakes in the text, provide an empty list if there are no mistakes>"], "Grammatical Cohesion Mistakes": ["<list of all mistakes in the text, provide an empty list if there are no mistakes>"] } }

Text to Evaluate:
"inference text"

D GPT4-as-a-judge Evaluation Performance

Model	Eval Type	AvgBLEU↑	Fluency↑	CE↓	LE↓	GE↓
Vicuna-7B	ST3	**20.25**	**4.27**	**3.06**	1.46	0.96
	DOC	19.36	4.20	3.24	**1.40**	**0.67**
Vicuna-7B-16K	ST3	20.07	4.24	3.50	1.20	0.77
	DOC	**21.14**	**4.38**	**3.24**	**1.18**	**0.67**
Vicuna-13B	ST3	22.46	4.09	3.31	1.57	1.07
	DOC	**23.46**	**4.34**	**3.04**	**1.04**	**0.59**
Vicuna-13B-16K	ST3	21.80	4.21	3.27	0.90	0.65
	DOC	**22.22**	**4.48**	**2.82**	**0.80**	**0.41**
Mistral-7B	ST3	18.84	3.96	4.41	1.47	1.10
	DOC	**19.50**	**4.34**	**3.50**	**1.30**	**0.83**

Table 6: Evaluation results (zh-en) by GPT-4 for Vicuna-7B, Vicuna-13B, and Mistral-7B under ST3 and DOC evaluation types, showing metrics AvgBLEU, Fluency, Content Errors(CE), Lexical Cohesion Errors(LE), and Grammatical Cohesion Errors(GE).

Model	Eval Type	AvgBLEU↑	Fluency↑	CE↓	LE↓	GE↓
Vicuna-7B	ST3	**24.53**	3.23	7.31	**3.73**	3.00
	DOC	21.18	**3.61**	**6.46**	3.76	**2.87**
Vicuna-7B-16K	ST3	26.02	**4.21**	2.88	1.17	0.77
	DOC	**26.95**	4.11	**2.84**	**0.98**	**0.67**
Vicuna-13B	ST3	26.76	3.59	6.84	3.79	2.39
	DOC	**27.32**	**3.90**	**5.23**	**3.34**	**1.96**
Vicuna-13B-16K	ST3	28.15	4.32	2.67	**0.78**	**0.42**
	DOC	**28.54**	**4.45**	**2.28**	0.95	0.45
Mistral-7B	ST3	**22.32**	3.16	6.83	4.64	**2.93**
	DOC	21.46	**3.17**	**6.63**	**4.51**	2.96

Table 7: Evaluation results (en-de) by GPT-4 for Vicuna-7B, Vicuna-13B, and Mistral-7B under ST3 and DOC evaluation types, showing metrics AvgBLEU, Fluency, Content Errors(CE), Lexical Cohesion Errors(LE), and Grammatical Cohesion Errors(GE).

Model	Eval Type	AvgBLEU↑	Fluency↑	CE↓	LE↓	GE↓
Vicuna-7B	ST3	**26.82**	4.11	4.01	**1.23**	1.11
	DOC	25.64	**4.31**	**3.14**	1.67	**0.66**
Vicuna-7B-16k	ST3	**23.56**	**3.61**	**5.74**	3.52	2.52
	DOC	21.71	3.54	5.81	**3.47**	**2.21**
Vicuna-13B	ST3	27.23	4.30	**3.06**	**1.13**	0.66
	DOC	**28.44**	**4.33**	3.36	1.33	**0.60**
Vicuna-13B-16K	ST3	**26.55**	4.15	5.47	**2.72**	**1.91**
	DOC	26.28	**4.18**	**4.7**	2.91	1.92
Mistral-7B	ST3	**26.09**	4.10	**4.73**	1.49	1.37
	DOC	25.68	**4.33**	4.89	**1.26**	**0.80**

Table 8: Evaluation results (de-en) by GPT-4 for Vicuna-7B, Vicuna-13B, and Mistral-7B under ST3 and DOC evaluation types, showing metrics AvgBLEU, Fluency, Content Errors(CE), Lexical Cohesion Errors(LE), and Grammatical Cohesion Errors(GE).

E Correlation Visualizations

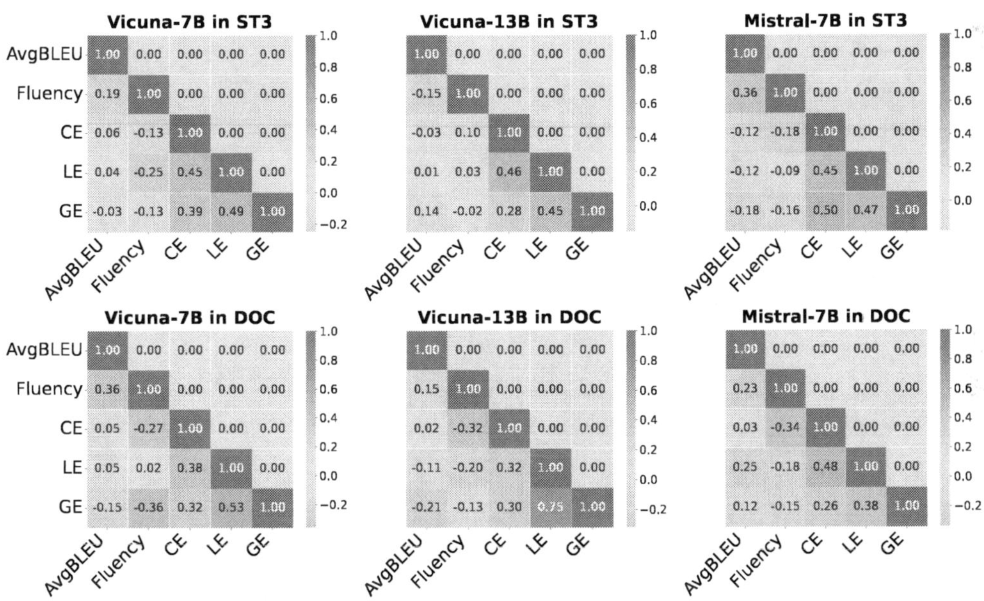

Figure 3: PCC Heatmaps among AvgBLEU, Fluency, CE, LE, GE for Vicuna-7B, Vicuna-13B, and Mistral-7B under ST3 and DOC evaluation types in translation direction of en-zh.

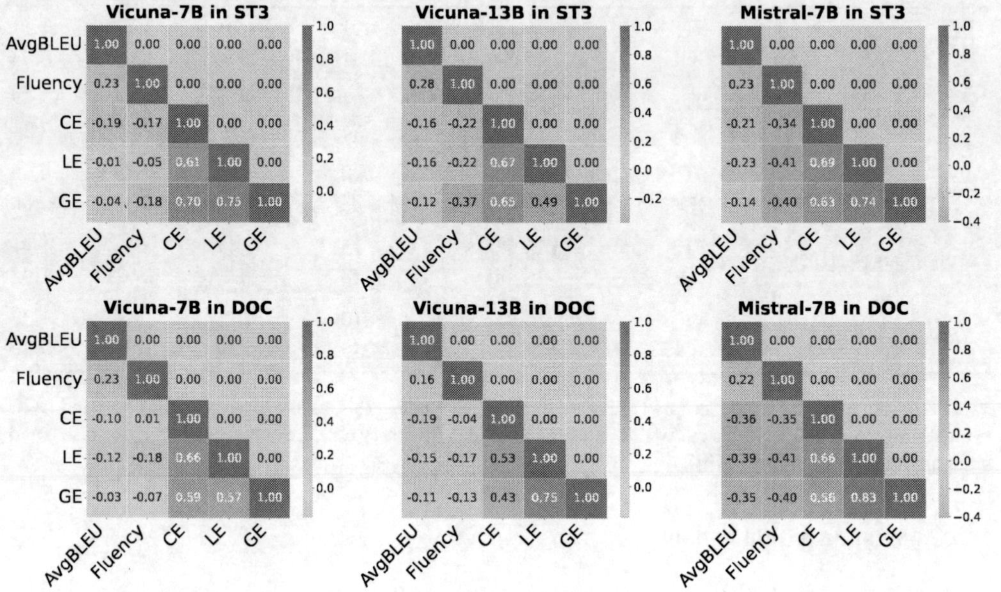

Figure 4: PCC Heatmaps among AvgBLEU, Fluency, CE(Content Errors), LE(Lexical Cohesion errors), GE(Grammatical Cohesion Errors) for Vicuna-7B, Vicuna-13B, and Mistral-7B under ST3 and DOC evaluation types in translation direction of zh-en.

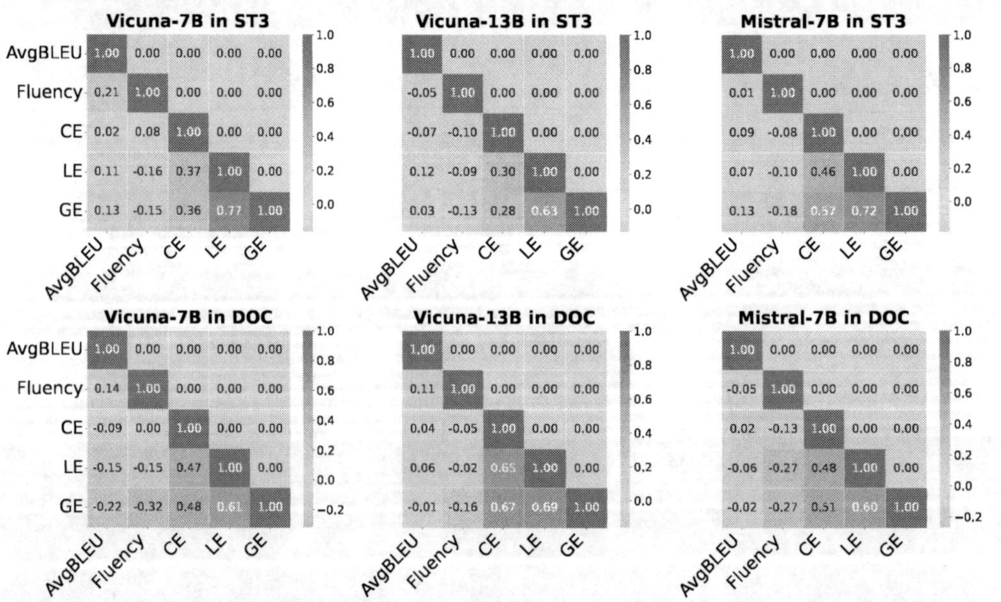

Figure 5: PCC Heatmaps among AvgBLEU, Fluency, CE(Content Errors), LE(Lexical Cohesion errors), GE(Grammatical Cohesion Errors) for Vicuna-7B, Vicuna-13B, and Mistral-7B under ST3 and DOC evaluation types in translation direction of de-en.

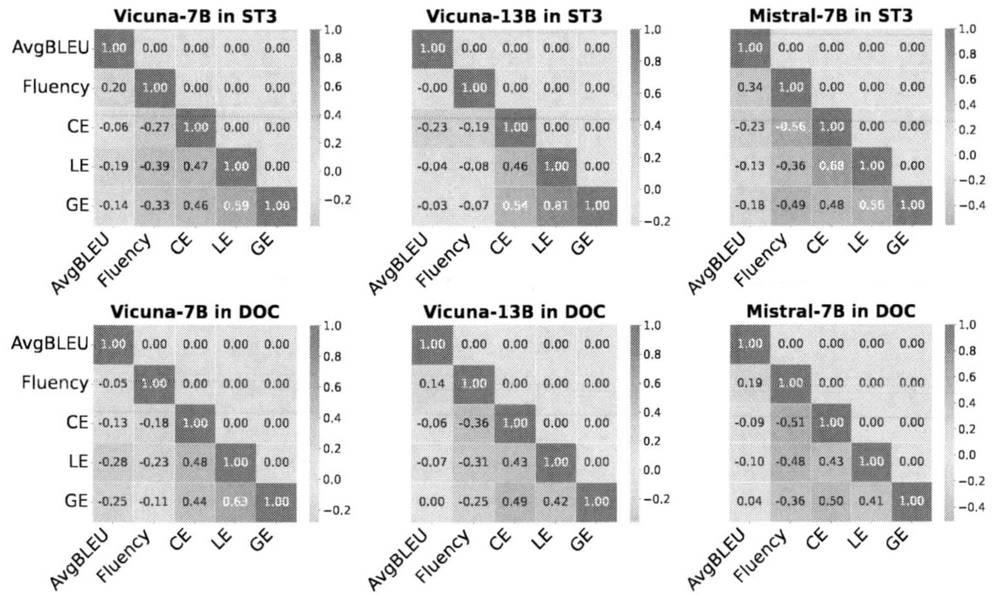

Figure 6: PCC Heatmaps among AvgBLEU, Fluency, CE(Content Errors), LE(Lexical Cohesion errors), GE(Grammatical Cohesion Errors) for Vicuna-7B, Vicuna-13B, and Mistral-7B under ST3 and DOC evaluation types in translation direction of en-de.

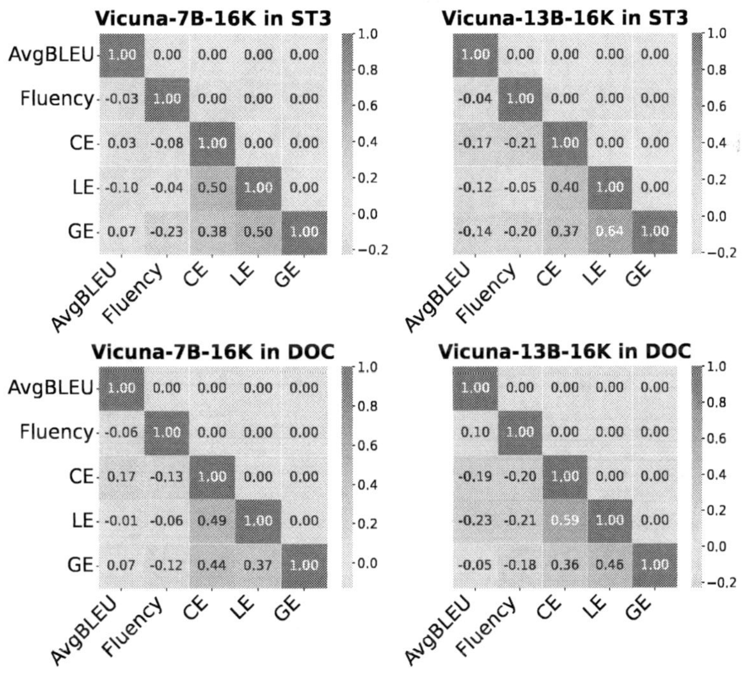

Figure 7: PCC Heatmaps among AvgBLEU, Fluency, CE, LE, GE for Vicuna-7B-16K and Vicuna-13B-16K under ST3 and DOC evaluation types in translation direction of en-zh.

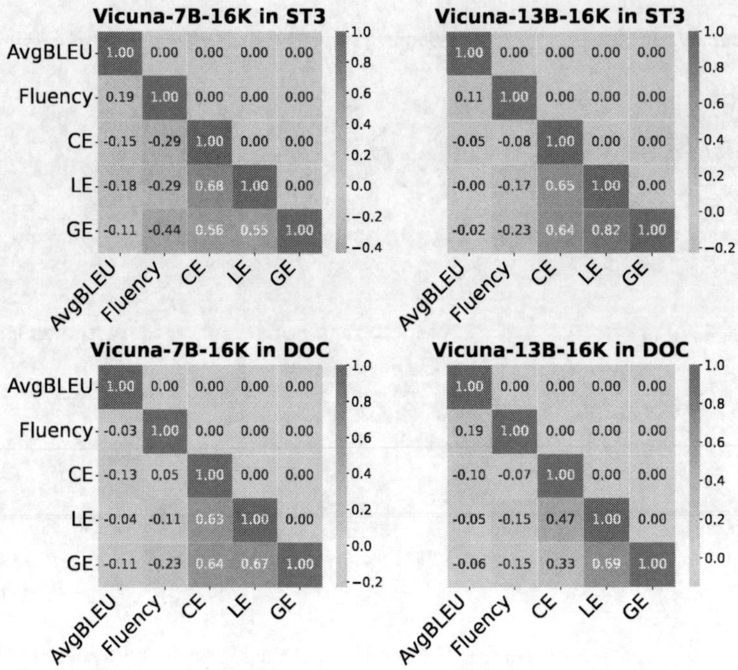

Figure 8: PCC Heatmaps among AvgBLEU, Fluency, CE(Content Errors), LE(Lexical Cohesion errors), GE(Grammatical Cohesion Errors) for Vicuna-7B-16K and Vicuna-13B-16K under ST3 and DOC evaluation types in translation direction of zh-en.

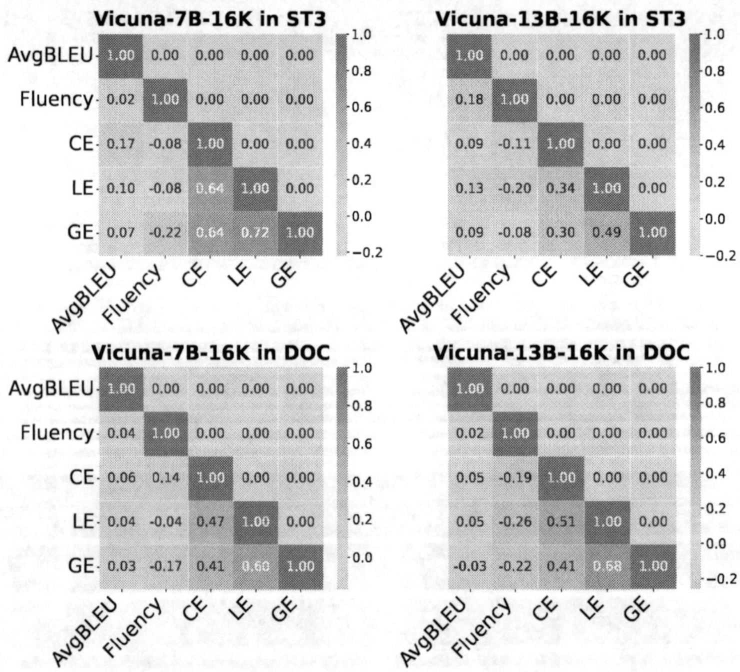

Figure 9: PCC Heatmaps among AvgBLEU, Fluency, CE(Content Errors), LE(Lexical Cohesion errors), GE(Grammatical Cohesion Errors) for Vicuna-7B-16K and Vicuna-13B-16K under ST3 and DOC evaluation types in translation direction of de-en.

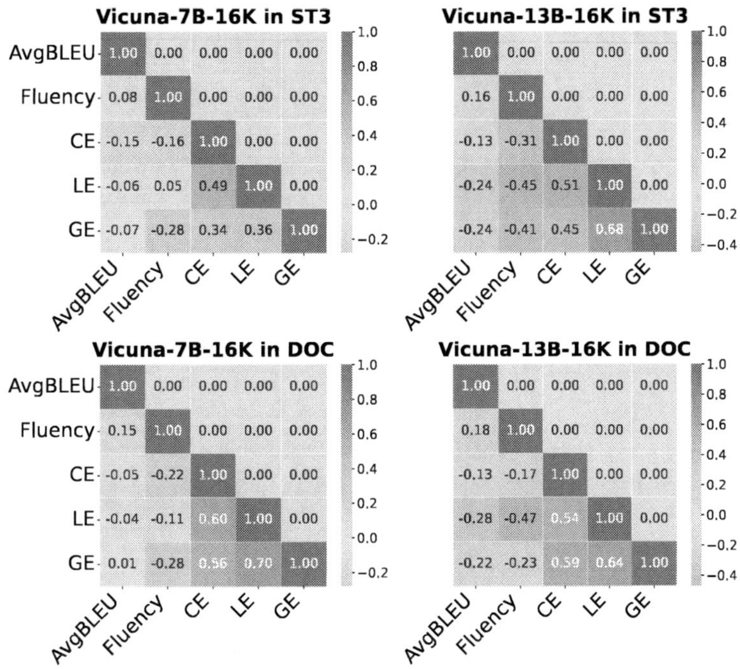

Figure 10: PCC Heatmaps among AvgBLEU, Fluency, CE(Content Errors), LE(Lexical Cohesion errors), GE(Grammatical Cohesion Errors) for Vicuna-7B-16K and Vicuna-13B-16K under ST3 and DOC evaluation types in translation direction of en-de.

InsightBuddy-AI: Medication Extraction and Entity Linking using Pre-Trained Language Models and Ensemble Learning

Pablo Romero
MMU
Oxford Rd
Greater Manchester, UK
pablo2004romero@gmail.com

Lifeng Han*
LIACS & LUMC
Leiden University, NL
University of Manchester, UK
l.han@lumc.nl

Goran Nenadic
University of Manchester
Oxford Rd
Greater Manchester, UK
g.nenadic@manchester.ac.uk

* *corresponding author*

Abstract

This paper presents our system, InsightBuddy-AI, designed for extracting medication mentions and their associated attributes, and for linking these entities to established clinical terminology resources, including SNOMED-CT, the British National Formulary (BNF), ICD, and the Dictionary of Medicines and Devices (dm+d). To perform medication extraction, we investigated various ensemble learning approaches, including stacked and voting ensembles (using first, average, and max voting methods) built upon eight pre-trained language models (PLMs). These models include general-domain PLMs—BERT, RoBERTa, and RoBERTa-Large—as well as domain-specific models such as BioBERT, BioClinicalBERT, BioMedRoBERTa, ClinicalBERT, and PubMedBERT. The system targets the extraction of drug-related attributes such as adverse drug effects (ADEs), dosage, duration, form, frequency, reason, route, and strength. Experiments conducted on the n2c2-2018 shared task dataset demonstrate that ensemble learning methods outperformed individually fine-tuned models, with notable improvements of 2.43% in Precision and 1.35% in F1-score. We have also developed cross-platform desktop applications for both entity recognition and entity linking, available for Windows and macOS. The InsightBuddy-AI application is freely accessible for research use at https://github.com/HECTA-UoM/InsightBuddy-AI.

1 Introduction

Extracting information about medications and their associated attributes is a crucial task in natural language processing (NLP) for the clinical domain, particularly to enhance digital healthcare solutions. Traditionally, clinicians and healthcare professionals have manually performed clinical coding to translate medical events—such as diseases, medications, and treatments—into standardised terminologies like ICD and SNOMED. This manual process is often labour-intensive and prone to human error, potentially compromising accuracy. Automating the extraction of medication-related information paves the way for automatic mapping of these terms to existing medical terminologies, enabling automated clinical coding. Given the potential of this approach, numerous NLP models have been applied in recent years to tasks such as medication mining and clinical coding—though typically in isolation. In this study, we unify these tasks by 1) developing a pipeline that integrates medication and attribute extraction (including dosage, route, strength, adverse effects, frequency, duration, form, and reason) with automated clinical coding. Furthermore, 2) we explore ensemble learning techniques—specifically Stacking and Voting—across a diverse set of NLP models fine-tuned for named entity recognition (NER). These include general-domain models like BERT, RoBERTa, and RoBERTa-L, as well as clinical-domain models such as BioBERT, BioClinicalBERT, BioMedRoBERTa, ClinicalBERT, and PubMedBERT. Our approach allows practitioners to bypass the challenge of selecting individual models for clinical NER tasks; instead, they can incorporate newer models into the ensemble framework to evaluate their effectiveness.

2 Literature Review and Related Work

Named Entity Recognition (**NER**) plays a vital role in extracting essential information from unstructured texts, such as medical correspondence. The inherent complexity and context sensitivity of medical language make accurate entity extraction particularly challenging. Traditional NER methods, including rule-based approaches, have had limited success in capturing the rich contextual details required for clinical applications (Nadeau and Sekine, 2007). The introduction of deep learning methods, notably Long Short-Term Memory (LSTM) net-

Proceedings of the 2025 Conference of the Nations of the Americas Chapter of the Association for Computational Linguistics: Human Language Technologies (Volume 4: Student Research Workshop), pages 18–27
April 30 - May 1, 2025

works, led to considerable improvements in NER performance (Graves and Schmidhuber, 2005), particularly through their capacity to model long-range dependencies in text. Nevertheless, these models continued to face difficulties with infrequent entities and intricate contextual relationships commonly found in **clinical notes**. The emergence of BERT (Bidirectional Encoder Representations from Transformers) (Devlin et al., 2019) brought a major breakthrough across multiple NLP tasks, including NER. BERT leverages masked language modelling on extensive corpora to learn rich token-level representations, which can then be fine-tuned with an added classification layer for token-level predictions. However, since BERT is pre-trained on general-domain corpora (Wikipedia and books), its effectiveness on specialised medical texts has been constrained. This limitation has spurred the development of **domain-specific** BERT variants. Examples include BioBERT (Lee et al., 2019), trained on large biomedical datasets; ClinicalBERT (Wang et al., 2023), fine-tuned on electronic health records from three million patients following pre-training on 1.2 billion words across various disease contexts; and Med-BERT (Rasmy et al., 2021), all of which have shown improved results for medical NER tasks due to their focused training in the healthcare domain. Other notable versions of ClinicalBERT include (Huang et al., 2019) and (Alsentzer et al., 2019), both trained on data from the Medical Information Mart for Intensive Care III (MIMIC-III) dataset (Johnson et al., 2016).

Despite these advancements, **single-model solutions** still encounter obstacles due to the inherent variability and complexity in clinical language, as demonstrated in the comparative evaluation in (Belkadi et al., 2023), which tested models including BERT, ClinicalBERT, BioBERT, and custom-trained Transformers. To mitigate these limitations, **ensemble** techniques have gained traction. Successfully applied in other areas such as computer vision (Lee et al., 2018), ensemble methods combine multiple models to exploit their complementary strengths and reduce their individual shortcomings. In the NER domain, ensembling has led to improved outcomes, as evidenced by (Naderi et al., 2021), who demonstrated significant performance gains by applying ensemble strategies to health and life sciences corpora. Naderi et al. (2021) employed max voting across models for word-level data in biology, chemistry, and medicine. However, their work focused on French for the clinical/medical NER domain using the DEFT benchmark, while English data were only utilised for the biology and chemistry domains. Among ensemble methods, two of the most widely adopted are voting and stacked ensembles: 1) **Maximum voting**, where each model has equal influence on the final decision—as used in (Naderi et al., 2021)—selects the label with the most votes. 2) **Stacking**, a more advanced method introduced by Wolpert (1992), involves training a meta-model on the outputs of base models to learn complex relationships between predictions. For instance, (Saleh et al., 2022) showed that stacking, when implemented with a support vector machine (SVM), improved sentiment analysis performance. In our work, we opt for a simple feed-forward network that maps the ensemble outputs to final predictions. Additional examples of stacking can be found in (Mohammed and Kora, 2022; Güneş et al., 2017). While ensemble strategies have shown promise across various NER applications, their applicability to clinical NER—especially with complex datasets like n2c2 2018 (Henry et al., 2020)—has yet to be thoroughly explored. This study **seeks to bridge that gap** by examining whether ensemble approaches, particularly stacking and voting, can enhance NER performance on clinical texts and help overcome the challenges associated with individual model limitations.

3 Methodologies

The overall architecture of INSIGHTBUDDY is illustrated in Figure 1, which outlines the base models used from both general and clinical domains. From the general domain, we included 1) BERT (Devlin et al., 2019), RoBERTa (Liu et al., 2019), and RoBERTa-Large; and from biomedical/clinical domains, 2) BioBERT (Lee et al., 2019), BioClinicalBERT (Alsentzer et al., 2019), BioMedRoBERTa (Gururangan et al., 2020), ClinicalBERT (Wang et al., 2023), and PubMedBERT (Gu et al., 2020). All eight models were fine-tuned using the same hyperparameters and training set from the n2c2-2018 shared task, following data pre-processing. The performance of each model was first evaluated individually using the n2c2-2018 test set, providing a baseline comparison. Subsequently, ensemble learning was applied to the outputs of all models. We then introduced an **entity linking** component to map the extracted medical entities into standardised clinical terminologies. Initially, we

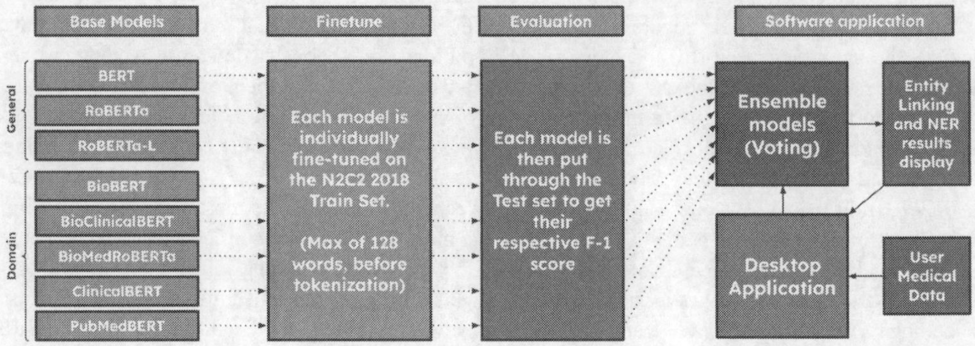

Figure 1: INSIGHTBUDDY Framework Pipeline: This diagram illustrates the full pipeline, including individual NER model fine-tuning, ensemble integration, entity linking, and desktop applications in both Windows and Mac systems. The base models are drawn from two domains: general and biomedical. Data pre-processing involves splitting the input sequence either at the first full stop (".") occurring after the 100th word or, if none is found, truncating at 128 words. Fine-tuning is carried out using identical hyperparameter settings across all eight models. Ensembling is performed using various strategies, which are detailed in Figure 3. Entity linking connects extracted entities to clinical knowledge bases (KBs), specifically BNF and SNOMED CT.

used **SNOMED-CT and BNF** as our knowledge bases (KB), which were further aligned with ICD and dm+d.

For pre-processing, the input text was segmented into chunks of up to 128 tokens. If a full stop (".") appeared between the 100th and 128th word, the chunk was cut at that punctuation mark. To explain our ensemble-learning approach, we present the InsightBuddy ensemble diagram in Figure 3. The initial outputs from each of the eight fine-tuned NER models are in sub-word format, as per their tokenisation strategy. For example, the word "Paracetamol" may be tokenised as "Para ##ce ##tam ##ol". Therefore, our first step is to **reconstruct** words from sub-word tokens for practical usage and voting. However, since each sub-word receives a potentially different label, discrepancies often occur within the same word. To resolve this, we implemented three grouping strategies: first-token voting, max-token voting, and average voting. In the *first-token voting* method, the label of the first sub-word is applied to the entire word. For instance, if "Para" is labelled as "B-Drug", then "Paracetamol" will be assigned the same label, regardless of labels on subsequent sub-words. In the *max-token voting* method, the label with the highest logit score among the sub-words is assigned to the word—reflecting the model's highest confidence in that prediction. The *average voting* approach computes the mean of logits across all sub-words, from which the label for the full word is derived. Regarding **word-level ensemble** learning, we explore a classical **voting** approach with two specific strategies: The ">=4 or O" strategy assigns the majority label if at least four models agree. If no majority exists, the label "O" (non-entity) is used by default to signify context words. The max-voting strategy selects the most frequently predicted label, regardless of how many models it came from (e.g. 2, 3, or 4 votes). In cases of a tie (e.g. two labels each receiving three votes from six models), we resolve it either alphabetically or randomly.

We also depict the STACKED-ENSEMBLE approach in Figure 2. During training, the data is split into 80% for training and 20% for testing the ensemble model. Output data from base models is only used when at least two models assign a label other than "O"; otherwise, "O" is kept and the token is excluded from stacked training data. For the stacked model's input, we convert each model's output logits into one-hot encoded vectors, then concatenate them alongside the true label of each token. As we use eight models, the training input consists of eight one-hot vectors and one label. Each vector is of length 19 (representing 19 possible labels), containing a single '1' at the predicted label's index and '0' elsewhere. As a result, each training sample contains 8 vectors × 19 values = 152 values, with exactly eight '1's and the remaining 144 being '0's. We choose to use

Voting Average Ensemble word level (BIO)			
Metric	P	R	F1
accuracy	0.9796		
macro avg	0.8253	0.8256	0.8227
weighted avg	0.9807	0.9796	0.9798
Voting First logit Ensemble word level (BIO)			
Metric	P	R	F1
accuracy	0.9796		
macro avg	0.8255	**0.8260**	0.8229
weighted avg	0.9807	0.9796	0.9798
Voting Max logit Ensemble word level (BIO)			
Metric	P	R	F1
accuracy	0.9796		
macro avg	0.8261	0.8259	**0.8232**
weighted avg	0.9807	0.9796	0.9798
Stacked Ensemble first logit word level (BIO)			
Metric	P	R	F1
accuracy	0.9796		
macro avg	**0.8351**	0.8065	0.8156
weighted avg	0.9800	0.9796	0.9794
Non-BIO-only-word ensemble			
Metric	P	R	F1
accuracy	0.9839		
macro avg	***0.8844***	***0.8830***	***0.8821***
weighted avg	0.9840	0.9839	0.9838

Table 1: Word-level ensemble grouping results: While all three logit aggregation methods—max, first, and average—produce similar scores, max-logit voting slightly outperforms the others. The **stacked** ensemble achieves the highest **Precision**, but at the cost of lower Recall, resulting in a reduced F1 score overall. The lower section of the table presents word-level evaluation results without differentiating between B- and I-labels, based on the n2c2 2018 test dataset.

one-hot encoding instead of raw logits to reduce the risk of *overfitting*, since models often produce highly confident predictions on the data they were trained on. We provide evaluation outcomes when using "raw logits" for stacked-ensemble in Figure 7 (evaluation scores) and 8 (confusion matrix) using word-level grouping ensemble using max logit, stacked ensemble, non-one-hot encoding, where they showed lower performances. One-hot vectors help regularise training by removing this overconfidence and ensuring a more generalisable stacked model.

4 Experimental Evaluations

We employed the dataset from the n2c2-2018 shared task, which focuses on named entity recognition (NER) of adverse drug events and associated medical attributes (Henry et al., 2020). The data includes annotated labels such as ADE, Dosage, Drug, Duration, Form, Frequency, Reason, Route, and Strength in BIO tagging format, resulting in a total of 19 possible tags: 2 (B/I) for each of the 9 classes, plus 1 (O). The original dataset comprises 303 training letters and 202 testing letters. Following the data split approach by Belkadi et al. (2023), we divided the training set into a 9:1 ratio for training and validation purposes. We evaluate the models using Precision, Recall, and F1-score under both "macro" and "weighted" averaging schemes, along with overall Accuracy. The "**macro**" average gives equal importance to each class, regardless of how often it appears in the dataset, whereas the "**weighted**" average scales scores according to label frequency. We begin by reporting the results from individual fine-tuned models (sub-word level), followed by evaluations of ensemble models using various strategies (word level).

4.1 Individual Models: sub-word level

The performance of individual models post fine-tuning is presented in Table 2. Among general-domain models, RoBERTa-Large achieved the highest macro Precision (0.8489), Recall (0.8606), and F1-score (0.8538), even outperforming domain-specific models. BioMedRoBERTa emerged as the top performer among domain-specific models, with macro Precision, Recall, and F1 scores of 0.8482, 0.8477, and 0.8468, respectively. When compared to the results reported by Belkadi et al. (2023), whose ClinicalBERT-Apt model achieved macro averages of 0.842, 0.834, and 0.837, our fine-tuned ClinicalBERT model delivered comparable results (0.848, 0.825, 0.834), validating the effectiveness of our fine-tuning. Notably, our BioMedRoBERTa model outperforms theirs with macro scores. Furthermore, RoBERTa-Large achieved even higher macro scores and Accuracy of 0.9782 (Figure 4). Both BioMedRoBERTa and RoBERTa-Large thus surpass the best-performing model reported in Belkadi et al. (2023), namely ClinicalBERT-CRF, which scored 0.85, 0.829, and 0.837 with Accuracy of 0.976. Building on this, our work transitions to a focus on **word-level** evaluation, which contrasts with the sub-word emphasis seen in Belkadi et al. (2023).

4.2 Ensemble: word-level grouping (logits)

We evaluated three strategies for aggregating sub-word predictions into word-level labels: **first** logit voting, **max** logit voting, and **average** logit voting. Their results are displayed in the upper section of Table 1. The first-logit method produced a higher Recall (0.8260), while max-logit voting yielded the highest Precision (0.8261) and F1-score (0.8232),

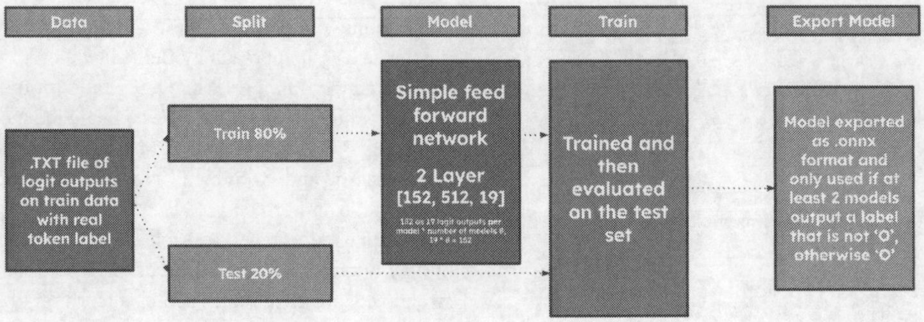

Figure 2: STACKEDENSEMBLE: training strategy.

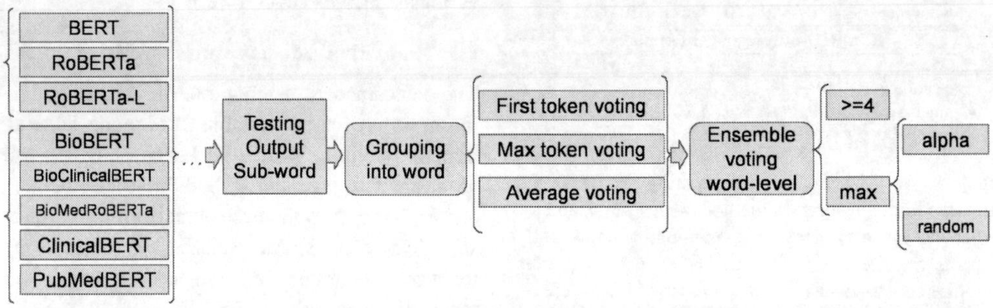

Figure 3: INSIGHTBUDDY Voted Ensemble Pipeline: Each individual NER model is fine-tuned to produce predictions at the token or sub-word level. (Note: "Logits" refer to the neural network outputs prior to applying the activation function.) The first step involves aggregating sub-word tokens into complete words using one of three strategies: selecting the label of the first sub-word, applying max-token voting, or averaging logits across sub-words. According to our results (see Table 1), the first-token approach yields higher Recall, while the other two methods slightly favour Precision. However, all three produce nearly identical F1 scores. Based on these findings, we adopt the first-token label method for further processing. For the word-level ensemble across all eight models, two voting strategies are explored: 1) majority voting—if four or more models assign the same label, it is selected; otherwise, the label defaults to "O", and 2) max voting—selecting the most frequently predicted label, regardless of count. In the case of ties (e.g. 3,3,2), we experimented with resolving ties either alphabetically or randomly. Our findings indicate that the ">=4 or O" strategy performs comparably to max + alphabetical", while "max + random" shows slightly reduced performance.

following the trend: *Max > First > Average*, based on macro F1 (0.8232, 0.8229, 0.8227). Given the marginal performance differences, we selected the first-logit voting output for the next ensemble step for its computational efficiency.

4.3 Ensemble: Voting vs Stacked (one-hot)

The Stacked Ensemble approach, which uses one-hot encoded vectors, is shown in the middle part of Table 1. It achieved a higher Precision (0.8351) compared to the best from voting ensembles (0.8261). However, its macro Recall dropped to 0.8065, whereas voting ensembles reached 0.8260. This suggests that while stacking reduced false positives, it also increased false negatives—indicating a more conservative prediction style when identifying positive cases.

4.4 Ensemble Models: BIO-span vs non-strict word-level

Up to this point, evaluations have been based on strict BIO tagging—treating labels like B-Drug and I-Drug as distinct, with mismatches considered incorrect. However, in practice, the distinction between B and I tags may not be necessary for all use cases. As shown in Table 1, when we ignore the B/I prefix and evaluate based on the 9 core label types, the ensemble model at the word level significantly

Model	Macro P	Macro R	Macro F	Accuracy	Tokens(sub-words)
BERT	0.8336	0.8264	0.8283	0.9748	756798
ROBERTa	0.8423	0.8471	0.8434	0.9770	756014
ROBERTa-L	**0.8489**	**0.8606**	**0.8538**	**0.9782**	756014
PubMedBERT	0.8324	0.8381	0.8339	**0.9783**	681211
ClinicalBERT	**0.8482**	0.8245	0.8341	0.9753	*796313*
BioMedRoBERTa	**0.8482**	**0.8477**	**0.8468**	0.9775	756014
BioClinicalBERT	0.8440	0.8405	0.8406	0.9751	791743
BioBERT	0.8365	0.8444	0.8393	0.9750	791743

Table 2: INSIGHTBUDDY individual sub-word level model eval on n2c2-2018 test set. The first group: normal domain PLM; The second group: biomedical PLM. The different numbers of Support are due to the different tokenizers they used – ROBERTa and ROBERTa-L use the same tokenizers, BioClinicalBERT and BioBERT use the same tokenizers, and other models all use different tokenizers; PubMedBERT generated the least number of sub-words/tokens 681,211 while ClinicalBERT generated the largest number of tokens 796,313.

improves. Macro Precision reaches 0.8844, Recall 0.8830, and F1 0.8821—well above the macro F1 of 0.8232 (voting-max-logit) and 0.8156 (stacked-first-logit) under strict BIO conditions.

4.5 Word-level: voting ensembles vs individual fine-tuned

As reported in Table 3, the BioMedRoBERTa model, when evaluated individually using max-logit grouping, achieved macro averages of P/R/F1 (0.8065, 0.8224, 0.8122). In contrast, the max-voting ensemble delivered (0.8261, 0.8259, 0.8232). This represents an improvement of 2.43% in Precision and 1.35% in F1-score. These gains confirm the success of ensemble voting, which enhances Precision—thus reducing the number of *false positive* predictions—while maintaining Recall, thereby preserving true positive detections.

5 Entity Linking: BNF and SNOMED

To integrate the recognised named entities with a clinical knowledge base, we utilised the existing mapping resources provided by the British National Formulary (BNF), which establish links between SNOMED-CT, BNF, dm+d, and ICD codes (available at `https://www.nhsbsa.nhs.uk/prescription-data/understanding-our-data/bnf-snomed-mapping`). We began by reducing the full set of 377,834 SNOMED codes to 10,804 entries through pre-processing, eliminating duplicate mappings between SNOMED and BNF. Additionally, we filtered out non-drug terms found in the text. This included removing items that contained words such as ['system', 'ostomy', 'bag', 'filter', 'piece', 'closure'], as these typically refer to medical equipment rather than pharmaceuticals. For mapping to SNOMED CT, we applied a fuzzy string-matching technique on the refined list, using drug names as search queries. When a match was found, the associated SNOMED CT code was appended and used to generate a direct link to the SNOMED CT online portal. In contrast, the BNF mapping process relied on a keyword-based search to retrieve matching entries from the BNF website. This approach was necessary due to differences in how the BNF site handles search queries compared to the SNOMED CT platform. Depending on their needs or preferences, users can choose to utilise either of these two clinical knowledge bases (KBs), as illustrated in Figure 9.

6 Discussion and Conclusion

This paper presented a pilot investigation into the application of Stacked and Voting Ensemble techniques for medical named entity recognition, utilising eight pre-trained language models (PLMs) drawn from both general-purpose and biomedical/clinical domains. Our experimental results demonstrate that the best-performing fine-tuned individual models surpassed the state-of-the-art results on the standard n2c2-2018 shared task dataset. Moreover, by incorporating ensemble approaches—specifically using output logits and one-hot encoded vectors—we achieved further performance gains, with a 2.43% improvement in Precision and a 1.35% increase in F1-score. In addition, we developed a desktop tool and user interface for our fine-tuned models, which includes an entity linking and normalisation feature that maps recognised entities to the BNF and SNOMED CT clinical knowledge bases. This tool, named INSIGHTBUDDY-AI, is publicly accessible at `https://github.com/HECTA-UoM/InsightBuddy-AI`.

Limitations

Ensemble approaches—particularly those involving large-scale models—can be demanding in terms of computational resources. During both training and inference, we encountered challenges related to hardware limitations. Future directions include reducing the computational load associated with ensemble learning, investigating alternative ensemble strategies, model *quantisation*, model output *significance* testing, and extending the approach to additional datasets. At present, the desktop applications support the deployment of all individual fine-tuned NER models, including any Hugging Face-compatible models. However, ensemble-based models are not yet integrated. Future work may focus on embedding ensemble learning directly into the application workflow, rather than requiring it as a separate, manual process.

Ethics

To use the n2c2 shared task data, the authors have carried out CITI training (`https://physionet.org/settings/credentialing/`) and gained the access to the data with user agreement.

Acknowledgements

We thank the reviewers' valuable comments, which have made our work much better. LH and GN are grateful for the support from the grant "Assembling the Data Jigsaw: Powering Robust Research on the Causes, Determinants and Outcomes of MSK Disease", and the grant "Integrating hospital outpatient letters into the healthcare data space" (EP/V047949/1; funder: UKRI/EPSRC). LH is grateful for the 4D Picture EU project (`https://4dpicture.eu/`) on supporting the journey of cancer patients. PR was supported by the University of Manchester Urenco Internships grant as part of an outreach programme.

References

Emily Alsentzer, John Murphy, William Boag, Wei-Hung Weng, Di Jindi, Tristan Naumann, and Matthew McDermott. 2019. Publicly available clinical BERT embeddings. In *Proceedings of the 2nd Clinical Natural Language Processing Workshop*, pages 72–78, Minneapolis, Minnesota, USA. Association for Computational Linguistics.

Samuel Belkadi, Lifeng Han, Yuping Wu, and Goran Nenadic. 2023. Exploring the value of pre-trained language models for clinical named entity recognition. In *2023 IEEE International Conference on Big Data (BigData)*, pages 3660–3669.

Jacob Devlin, Ming-Wei Chang, Kenton Lee, and Kristina Toutanova. 2019. BERT: Pre-training of deep bidirectional transformers for language understanding. In *Proceedings of the 2019 Conference of the North American Chapter of the Association for Computational Linguistics: Human Language Technologies, Volume 1 (Long and Short Papers)*, pages 4171–4186, Minneapolis, Minnesota. Association for Computational Linguistics.

Alex Graves and Jürgen Schmidhuber. 2005. Framewise phoneme classification with bidirectional lstm and other neural network architectures. *Neural Networks*, 18(5):602–610. IJCNN 2005.

Yu Gu, Robert Tinn, Hao Cheng, Michael Lucas, Naoto Usuyama, Xiaodong Liu, Tristan Naumann, Jianfeng Gao, and Hoifung Poon. 2020. Domain-specific language model pretraining for biomedical natural language processing.

Funda Güneş, Russ Wolfinger, and Pei-Yi Tan. 2017. Stacked ensemble models for improved prediction accuracy. In *Proc. Static Anal. Symp*, pages 1–19.

Suchin Gururangan, Ana Marasović, Swabha Swayamdipta, Kyle Lo, Iz Beltagy, Doug Downey, and Noah A. Smith. 2020. Don't stop pretraining: Adapt language models to domains and tasks. In *Proceedings of ACL*.

Sam Henry, Kevin Buchan, Michele Filannino, Amber Stubbs, and Ozlem Uzuner. 2020. 2018 n2c2 shared task on adverse drug events and medication extraction in electronic health records. *Journal of the American Medical Informatics Association*, 27(1):3–12.

Kexin Huang, Jaan Altosaar, and Rajesh Ranganath. 2019. Clinicalbert: Modeling clinical notes and predicting hospital readmission. *CoRR*, abs/1904.05342.

Alistair EW Johnson, Tom J Pollard, Lu Shen, Li-wei H Lehman, Mengling Feng, Mohammad Ghassemi, Benjamin Moody, Peter Szolovits, Leo Anthony Celi, and Roger G Mark. 2016. Mimic-iii, a freely accessible critical care database. *Scientific data*, 3(1):1–9.

Jinhyuk Lee, Wonjin Yoon, Sungdong Kim, Donghyeon Kim, Sunkyu Kim, Chan Ho So, and Jaewoo Kang. 2019. BioBERT: a pre-trained biomedical language representation model for biomedical text mining. *Bioinformatics*, 36(4):1234–1240.

Jinsu Lee, Sang-Kwang Lee, and Seong-Il Yang. 2018. An ensemble method of cnn models for object detection. In *2018 International Conference on Information and Communication Technology Convergence (ICTC)*, pages 898–901.

Yinhan Liu, Myle Ott, Naman Goyal, Jingfei Du, Mandar Joshi, Danqi Chen, Omer Levy, Mike Lewis, Luke Zettlemoyer, and Veselin Stoyanov. 2019.

Roberta: A robustly optimized BERT pretraining approach. *CoRR*, abs/1907.11692.

Ammar Mohammed and Rania Kora. 2022. An effective ensemble deep learning framework for text classification. *Journal of King Saud University - Computer and Information Sciences*, 34(10, Part A):8825–8837.

David Nadeau and Satoshi Sekine. 2007. A survey of named entity recognition and classification. *Lingvisticae Investigationes*, 30(1):3–26.

Nona Naderi, Julien Knafou, Jenny Copara, Patrick Ruch, and Douglas Teodoro. 2021. Ensemble of deep masked language models for effective named entity recognition in health and life science corpora. *Frontiers in research metrics and analytics*, 6:689803.

Laila Rasmy, Yang Xiang, Ziqian Xie, Cui Tao, and Degui Zhi. 2021. Med-bert: pretrained contextualized embeddings on large-scale structured electronic health records for disease prediction. *NPJ digital medicine*, 4(1):86.

Hager Saleh, Sherif Mostafa, Lubna Abdelkareim Gabralla, Ahmad O. Aseeri, and Shaker El-Sappagh. 2022. Enhanced arabic sentiment analysis using a novel stacking ensemble of hybrid and deep learning models. *Applied Sciences*, 12(18).

Guangyu Wang, Xiaohong Liu, Zhen Ying, Guoxing Yang, Zhiwei Chen, Zhiwen Liu, Min Zhang, Hongmei Yan, Yuxing Lu, Yuanxu Gao, et al. 2023. Optimized glycemic control of type 2 diabetes with reinforcement learning: a proof-of-concept trial. *Nature Medicine*, 29(10):2633–2642.

David H. Wolpert. 1992. Stacked generalization. *Neural Networks*, 5(2):241–259.

A InsightBuddy-AI Desktop Application

For **Clinical Coding** (entity linking) options, the desktop application can currently directly link the extracted entities to BNF and SNOMED-CT, as in Figure 9 from the screenshots. The INSIGHTBUDDY-AI software supports both Mac and Windows systems.

B Diagrams and Scoring Tables

B.1 Sub-word level diagrams

Sub-word level BioMedRoBERTa confusion matrix, RoBERTa-L evaluation and confusion matrix are shown in Figure 6, 4, and 5.

B.2 Word-level Ensemble: Stacked using output logits (non one-hot)

When we used the 'output logits' instead of 'one-hot encoding' for stacked ensemble, as we discussioned in the methodology section, it will lead to overfitting issues. We use the Max logit stacked ensemble as an example, in figure 7, which shows that the Stacked Ensemble using output logits produced much lower evaluation scores macro avg (0.6863 0.7339 0.6592) than the voting mechanism macro avg (0.8261 0.8259 0.8232) for (P, R, F1). The corresponding confusion matrix from the stacked ensemble using the max logit is shown in Figure 8 with more errors spread in the image, the coloured numbers outside the diagonal line.

B.3 Individual vs Ensemble Models

The word-level performance comparisons from individual models and voting max-logit ensembles are presented in Table 3.

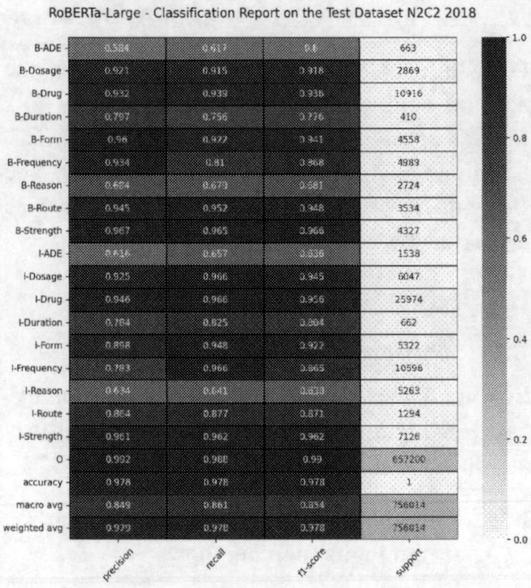

Figure 4: RoBERTa-L Eval at Sub-word Level on n2c2 2018 test data.

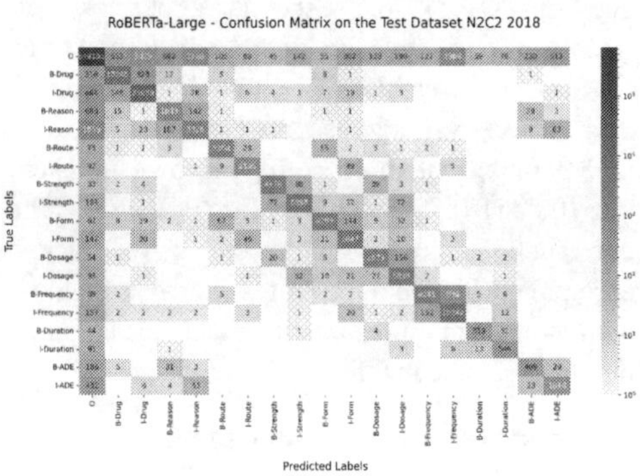

Figure 5: RoBERTa-L Eval Confusion Matrix at Sub-word Level on n2c2 2018 test data.

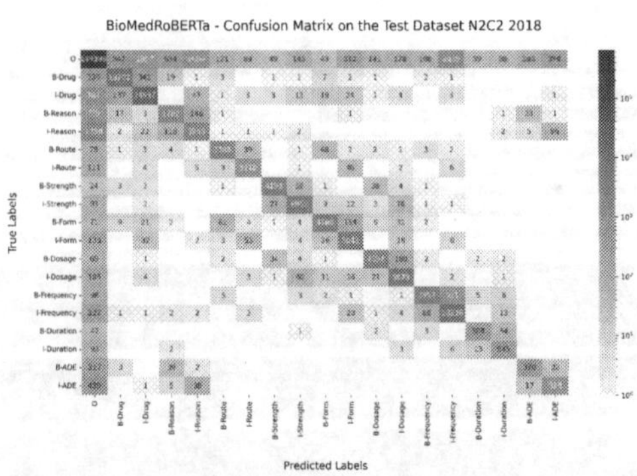

Figure 6: BioMedRoBERTa Eval Confusion Matrix at Sub-word Level on n2c2 2018 test data.

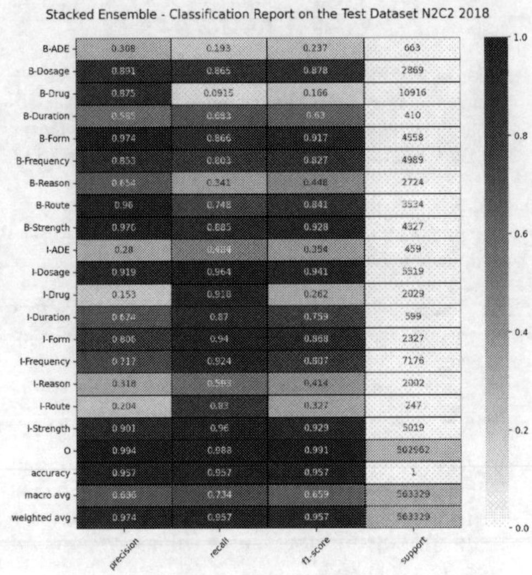

Figure 7: word-level grouping ensemble, max logit (logits, non-one-hot): stacked ensemble Eval on n2c2 2018 test data, which is much lower than the max voting.

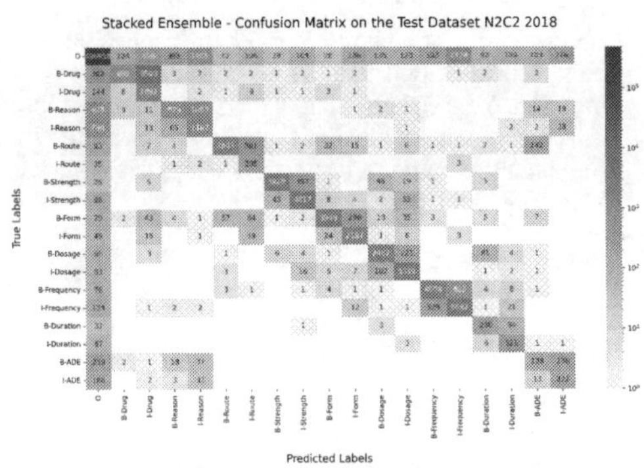

Figure 8: word-level grouping ensemble, max logit: stacked ensemble confusion matrix Eval on n2c2 2018 test data, which is much worse than the max voting.

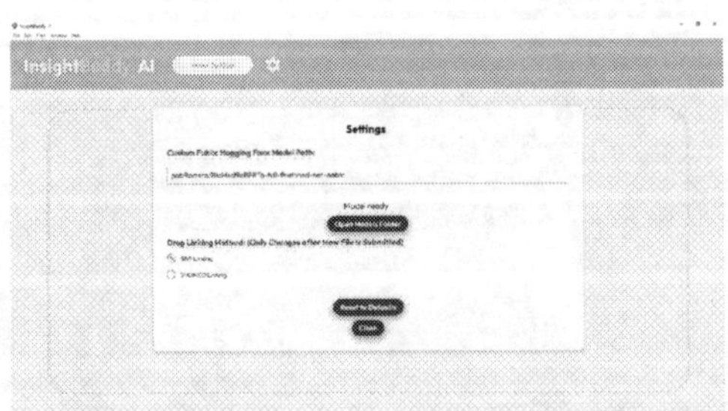

Figure 9: INSIGHTBUDDY-AI coding: Choice of BNF and SNOMED-CT Linking

Individual models max-logit grouping (word)			
Metric	**P**	**R**	**F1**
BERT			
accuracy	0.9773		
macro avg	0.7942	0.7965	0.7928
weighted avg	0.9784	0.9773	0.9775
RoBERTa			
accuracy	0.9780		
macro avg	0.8029	0.8201	0.8094
weighted avg	0.9795	0.9780	0.9784
RoBERTa-Large			
accuracy	0.9788		
macro avg	0.8091	0.8351	0.8202
weighted avg	0.9802	0.9788	0.9792
ClinicalBERT			
accuracy	0.9780		
macro avg	0.8087	0.7916	0.7964
weighted avg	0.9785	0.9780	0.9779
BioBERT			
accuracy	0.9776		
macro avg	0.7972	0.8131	0.8027
weighted avg	0.9787	0.9776	0.9779
BioClinicalBERT			
accuracy	0.9776		
macro avg	0.7999	0.8090	0.8017
weighted avg	0.9788	0.9776	0.9779
BioMedRoBERTa			
accuracy	0.9783		
macro avg	0.8065	0.8224	0.8122
weighted avg	0.9797	0.9783	0.9786
PubMedBERT			
accuracy	0.9784		
macro avg	0.8087	0.8292	0.8166
weighted avg	0.9800	0.9784	0.9788
Voting Max logit ensemble word level			
accuracy	0.9796		
macro avg	**0.8261**	0.8259	**0.8232**
weighted avg	0.9807	0.9796	0.9798

Table 3: Word-level individual model (grouping using max-logit) vs ensemble using max-logit, Eval on n2c2 2018 test data

Linguistic Features in German BERT: The Role of Morphology, Syntax, and Semantics in Multi-Class Text Classification

Henrike Beyer[1] **& Diego Frassinelli**[2]
[1]Centre for Argument Technology, University of Dundee, UK
[2]Center for Information and Language Processing, LMU Munich, Germany
2579207@dundee.ac.uk, frassinelli@cis.lmu.de

Abstract

Most studies on the linguistic information encoded by BERT primarily focus on English. Our study examines a monolingual German BERT model using a semantic classification task on newspaper articles, analysing the linguistic features influencing classification decisions through SHAP values. We use the TüBa-D/Z corpus, a resource with gold-standard annotations for a set of linguistic features, including POS, inflectional morphology, phrasal, clausal, and dependency structures. Semantic features of nouns are evaluated via the GermaNet ontology using shared hypernyms. Our results indicate that the features identified in English also affect classification in German but suggests important language- and task-specific features as well.

1 Introduction

Even today, with large language models (LLMs) like GPT-4 (OpenAI et al., 2023), Llama (Touvron et al., 2023), or Mistral (Jiang et al., 2023) representing the de facto state-of-the-art systems for most NLP tasks in English, the exploration of BERT-like models still provides extremely useful insights for low-resource and non-English scenarios (Brookshire and Reiter, 2024; Sivanaiah et al., 2024; Bressem et al., 2024), often offering more efficient and lightweight solutions.

Despite the extensive research evaluating the linguistic knowledge encoded in various English versions of BERT (Devlin et al., 2019) using interpretative methods like attention analysis (Jawahar et al., 2019; Goldberg, 2019; Kalouli et al., 2022), monolingual models pre-trained on languages other than English have received considerably less attention. Given that languages can differ quite significantly in their morphological, syntactic, and semantic complexity, it is crucial to identify which behaviours observed for English translate to other languages and which, instead, are language-specific.

For example, Jawahar et al. (2019) found that different types of linguistic information are distributed across different layers of English BERT; surface-level information like phrasal structure is processed by layers closer to the input, syntactic information by the middle layers, and semantic information by the layers closer to the output. The ability of BERT-like models to process syntactic information has been evaluated by assessing their performance on subject-verb agreement in English (Goldberg, 2019). More recently, Kalouli et al. (2022) assessed the quality of the semantic representations for general function words (e.g. negations, coordinating conjunctions, and quantification terms) in these models. Their findings suggest that BERT-like models struggle to accurately complete sentences based on these function words alone, often relying on other indicators, like Named Entities (NEs), for their predictions.

Our work investigates which morphological, syntactic, and semantic features are the strongest predictors in an eight-class text classification task for a German BERT model. Building on evidence from English, we analyse similarities and differences, particularly exploring how the richer inflectional morphology of German (Eisenberg, 2020) affects model performance. Former studies on German have analysed morphological or syntactic features separately (Zaczynska et al., 2020; Guarasci et al., 2021). Claeser (2022) conducts a study on the same corpus we use in this work, but considers only the influence of morphology with regard to CNNs. Our study covers a larger selection of morphological, syntactic, and semantic features and focuses on BERT.[1]

[1]Additional information for reproducibility can be found at: https://github.com/CoPsyN/ling-in-German-BERT

Proceedings of the 2025 Conference of the Nations of the Americas Chapter of the Association for Computational Linguistics: Human Language Technologies (Volume 4: Student Research Workshop), pages 28–39

2 Materials and Methodology

2.1 Corpus Selection

For our analysis, we use the *Tübinger Baumdatenbank Deutsch/Zeitungskorpus* (TüBa-D/Z; Telljohann et al. (2004)). This corpus contains 3,642 newspaper articles (1,782,129 tokens; 153,990 types) from the German newspaper *Die Tageszeitung* and includes gold-standard annotations for inflectional morphology, part-of-speech tags, and syntax, along with automatically generated dependency structures. In addition, we use the semantic annotation layer by Claeser (2022), that categorizes the articles into eight topics with varying levels of coverage across the corpus: culture (kultur; 24%), politics (politik; 22%), miscellaneous (panorama; 17%), conflicts abroad (konflikteausland; 11%), economy (wirtschaft; 9%), crime (kriminalität; 8%), sport (sport; 5%), and environment (umwelt, 4%). This corpus offers consistent, rich, high-quality annotations on all layers. In addition, the text classification task covers a broad range of topics, allowing for good generalisability. To make the text compatible with BERT, we split the available text into 6,674 chunks of approximately 500 tokens each, ensuring that only full sentences are included. We ensured that there is no different in performance between chunks of the same text throughout our experiments.

2.2 Model Fine-Tuning

We fine-tune a monolingual BERT-base German-cased model (Chan et al., 2020) for 5 epochs with a batch-size of 8, a learning-rate of 5e-5 and AdamW as optimizer on the 8-way classification task mentioned above. We use a 10-fold-cross-validation design on the multi-class classification task described above. Due to the corpus' relatively small size and class imbalance, the fine-tuning of each fold is repeated five times with a new random initialization of the model. The classifier achieves an average F1-score of 0.72±0.01. Table 1 reports the accuracy scores per class, showing considerable differences (0.59 for "environment" vs. 0.90 for "sport"). Such differences should be considered when interpreting the results in the following analyses.

2.3 SHAP Value Calculation

To determine the importance of specific words in the classification task, we use the KernelSHAP algorithm (Lundberg and Lee, 2017) through the TransSHAP library (Kokalj et al., 2021). SHapley Additive exPlanations (SHAP) (Lundberg and Lee, 2017) have been successfully applied to various NLP tasks (Chakravarthi et al., 2023; Jang et al., 2023; Tang et al., 2024; Rizinski et al., 2024). For our analysis, we calculate the SHAP values, which reflect the importance of each token in a text to the classification decision for the whole text.

class	**percentage**	**accuracy**
culture	24%	$0.82 \pm .06$
politics	22%	$0.70 \pm .04$
miscellaneous	17%	$0.60 \pm .03$
conflicts abroad	11%	$0.68 \pm .06$
economy	9%	$0.65 \pm .09$
crime	8%	$0.73 \pm .06$
sport	5%	$0.90 \pm .06$
environment	4%	$0.59 \pm .11$

Table 1: Distribution of semantic text classification categories in the 500-word chunk version of the corpus and the validation accuracy.

3 Results and Discussion

All steps in the following analysis focus on the top 10% tokens with positive SHAP values in correctly classified texts; in this way we inspect only words that positively contribute to the correct classification decision. In addition to the usual quantitative analysis of SHAP values, we run a statistical analysis to identify which features significantly affect model performance. We make this decision to ensure that all reported effects are significant above chance, which is especially important for less frequent features. As null hypothesis, we assume that the distribution of each SHAP feature within a category matches its original distribution in the corpus for the same category. Positive contributions are reported when values significantly exceed the null hypothesis, and negative contributions when they are significantly lower (refer to Appendix A for more details). To reduce data sparsity and increase generalizability, we group all linguistic features into coarse-grained categories (e.g., "verbs" would include all types of verbs; refer to Appendix B for the detailed mapping).

3.1 POS Analysis

The outcome of the POS analysis in Figure 1 depicts the null hypothesis as the red central line,

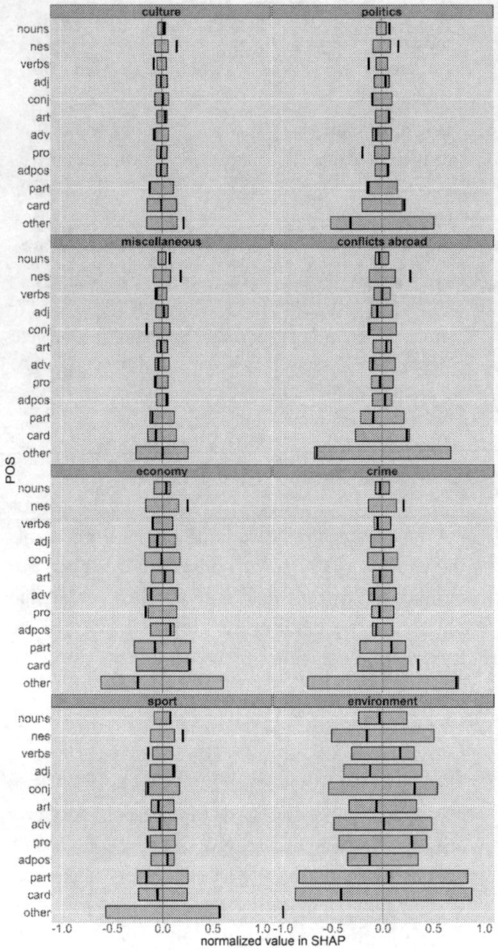

Figure 1: Distribution of POS per classification category, normalized against its category distribution. POS label groups are explained in Table 3 in Appendix B.

with a two standard deviations confidence interval.[2] The black vertical line represents the observed frequency of each POS among SHAP values. Values to the right of the red line indicate that a specific feature has a positive contribution in the SHAP values compared to its corpus distribution, while those to the left that it is has a negative contribution. Significance is reached when the black line is outside the confidence interval.

Among the noun POS-tags analysed, named entities (nes) have a significant positive impact on the predictions across all categories except for "environment". This finding perfectly mirrors the results by Kalouli et al. (2022) on English. Additionally, cardinal numbers (card) strongly predict categories related to factual content, such as "politics", "conflicts abroad", "economy", and "crime". Likely due to data sparsity (see Section 2.1), "environment" is the only category where no features reach significance.

3.2 Inflectional Morphology

We analyse morphological features for nouns, adjectives, and verbs. Figure 2 shows that for the classes "politics" and "conflicts abroad", nouns in nominative are significantly more present than in the overall distribution, while nouns in accusative are significantly less present. For "miscellaneous", only accusative reaches significance as a negative predictor. These differences are surprising given the many syncretisms between nominative and accusative in German, leading to identical surface forms. Possibly, the distinction mainly comes from their roles as subjects and objects.

For the number feature, plural is a negative predictor in "economy" and a positive one in "environment". This result is not straightforward to interpret and may hint to category-specific preferences.

For adjectives only the underspecification of case reaches positive significance in "politics", "miscellaneous", "culture", "crime", and "sport". In addition, accusative is a significant negative predictor in "politics" and genitive in "miscellaneous". For number, there are no significant predictors.

For verbs, the subjunctive is a significant negative predictor in "politics", "miscellaneous", "economy", and "crime". Given that the German subjunctive differs strongly in its morphology from

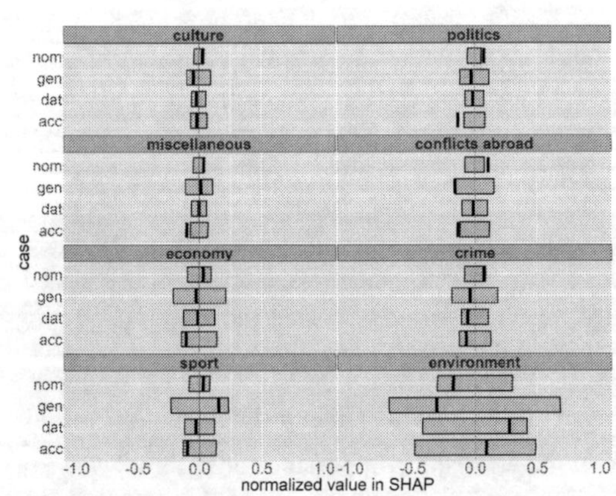

Figure 2: Normalized distribution of **case** (nominative, genitive, accusative, dative) for nouns.

[2]The main text includes only the most relevant figures for each step of the analysis, while the full set of plots supporting the discussion is provided in Appendix C.

the more commonly used indicative forms, BERT likely considers these less frequent forms as less important for the classification decision. In addition, it needs to be mentioned that the subjunctive in German has two morphological forms. Among the two, the *subjunctive 1* is used more commonly in German newspaper texts (as present in the TüBa corpus) compared to more casual forms of written German as it can be found in social media posts or the rest of the internet.

For the inflectional degree, tense, and person, only one significant negative predictor is found for infinitive and past forms in "conflicts abroad" and 1st person in "culture". For number only plural is a significant positive predictor for "environment". These observations hint to a class-specific phenomenon rather than a generalisable behaviour of the assessed model.

3.3 Syntactic Analysis

We study phrase, clause, complement, and dependency relations between the words in a sentence based on the annotation layers in the TüBa-corpus.

In the analysis of phrases, noun phrases and determiner phrases are significant positive predictors in "miscellaneous", while prepositional phrases are in "sport". Significant negative predictors are finite verb phrases in "miscellaneous", finite verb phrases in "politics", "miscellaneous", "conflicts abroad", "crime", and "sport", and determiner phrases in "politics". The analysis on the distribution of nouns across different phrase types reveals no significant results. Since our analysis considers the full 12 layer models, the results of the phrasal analysis do not contradict Jawahar et al. (2019), who claims that phrasal information tends to be more diluted in the lower layers of BERT.

With regard to the higher-order phrase levels, relative clauses (R-SIMPX) are significant negative predictors for most categories (except "economy"). Other subordinate types are not very important for the classification task.

The analysis of complements shows subjects as significant positive predictors in "politics" and "miscellaneous", while objects are significant negative predictors in "culture". This perfectly aligns with our previous discussion on the nominative case. We do not observe a clear preference for any other complement tags.

Dependency relations[3] provide a perspective on the relations between the words in a sentence. Figure 3 shows the result for dependencies.

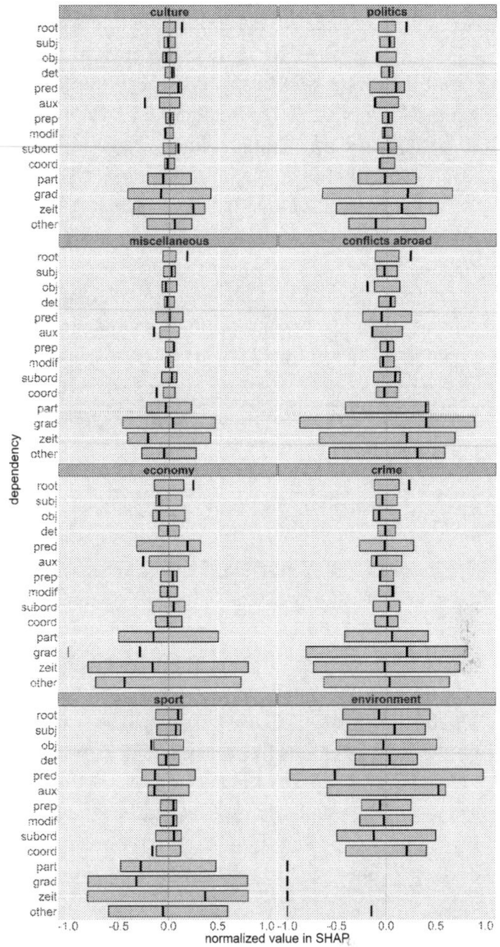

Figure 3: Normalized distribution of dependency labels for a dependency-grammar perspective on syntax. The labels are grouped according to Table 5 in Appendix B.

The multi-head attention mechanism in BERT allows the model to establish direct inter-token relationships similar to dependency relations. Similarly to the analysis of complements, the dependency analysis indicates that objects are strong negative predictors for "conflicts abroad", "politics", and "sport". However, this is not true for subjects. This variability has two possible explanations. First, the analysis relies on semi-automatically generated labels, increasing the probability of annotation errors. Second, complements and dependency relations differ in their theoretical definitions, leading

[3]Based on semi-automatically generated Hamburg Dependency Treebank (Foth et al., 2014) annotations from the 2010 version of the TüBa corpus.

to slight differences in the resulting annotation.

The initial word in a dependency structure ("root" tag) is a significant positive predictor for "culture", "politics", "miscellaneous", "conflicts abroad", "economy", and "crime". The additional results for significant positive and negative predictors are rather wide-spread over categories and relations, indicating possibly class-specific preferences.

Overall, the results from the dependency analysis are able to reproduce objects as a significant negative predictor, found in clausal representations and suggested in the morphological analysis of case for nouns. Further, the model seems to prefer the initial word in a dependency structure.

In a last step, we test whether the model is more likely to consider a pair of tokens because they are in a dependency relation. Since we cannot measure a reference value from the full corpus data because the corpus contains already the full dependency structure, we estimate the expected value for this observation to be $\approx 1,392$ tokens (calculated based on Equation 2 in Appendix A). This step considers for the set of top 10% of positive SHAP values the binary decision of a token and its governing token, which is approximately Poisson distributed. The observed value of 5,360 is nearly four times higher than expected, indicating the model gives disproportionate importance to words connected by a dependency relation.

A closer look at the types of dependencies linking these tokens reveals some general (yet non significant; probably due to data sparsity) tendencies for tokens connected by a subject, subordinate, particle or modifier dependency relation.

Overall, these results suggest that the model does not favour a specific type of dependency. Instead, it appears to group different tokens based on their connections through specific dependency relations, such as subject, particle, modifier, or subordinate relations. This could indicate that the model considers words within smaller syntactic clusters, linking them according to their dependency relations.

3.4 Semantic Analysis

To assess the influence of semantic features on the classification task, we use GermaNet.[4] The semantic ontology includes information on verbs, adjectives and nouns. Since the results for POS on both verbs and adjectives do not yield significant results, the following analysis focuses uniquely on the same nouns as considered in the previous sections. The semantic analysis exploits the tree-like structure of the ontology. We pair each noun[5] in the category with every other noun in the same category and identify the closest shared hypernym for each pair. We then count the number of shared hypernyms in each category and normalize this by the frequency of each hypernym in the corpus. This allows us to identify hypernyms that are generally uncommon across categories, but very distinctive to a specific one. Finally, we rank these hypernyms by category, analyse the top 20, and manually select only those that are associated to the category. Table 2 reports the count of selected hypernyms appearing in the top 5, 10, 15, and 20 most frequent hypernyms and the percentage in the top 20 for each category.

class	top 5	top 10	top 15	top 20	percent
culture	1	2	4	5	10%
politics	0	0	0	1	4%
miscellaneous	0	0	0	0	0%
conflicts abroad	0	0	0	0	0%
economy	0	0	0	0	0%
crime	0	1	1	1	4%
sport	0	2	4	7	33%
environment	0	0	0	1	100%

Table 2: Analysis of class related hypernyms in top 5-20 hypernyms with the highest weighted mean. The last column reports the percentage of all class-related hypernyms present in the top 20.

In this ranking of counts of shared hypernyms (weighted by general hypernym frequency), we can assess which class has an exceptionally high number of hypernyms related to its topic. For, "culture" and "sport", a higher percentage of class-related concepts in the most frequent shared hypernyms correlates with a higher classification accuracy (cf. Table 1). The high number of class-related shared hypernyms indicates that the words that are important to the classification decision are more likely to be hyponyms of rather class-specific concepts. This outcome indicates a closer semantic cluster making it easier to for the model to discriminate the category.

Overall, this suggests that not only the class-size is decisive for the classification accuracy, but also that a smaller category may benefit from a higher semantic proximity of its characteristic words.

[4]Accessed using the provided Germanetpy API (https://github.com/Germanet-sfs/germanetpy).

[5]Pairs of identical nouns and named entities were excluded.

4 Conclusion

This work investigates the role of linguistic information in a monolingual German BERT model for a multi-class classification task. It replicates prior findings on the dilution of phrasal information in a full 12-layer model (Jawahar et al., 2019) and BERT's preference for NEs (Kalouli et al., 2022).

The results suggest that German BERT's syntactic representation prioritizes dependency relations over clausal or phrasal ones by focusing on word clusters in dependency relations, showing opportunities for further research. Additionally, German noun inflection has a minor influence, with a preference for nominative over accusative, possibly due to the syntactic function outweighing its morphological form.

The semantic analysis shows that classification accuracy depends not only on class size but also on smaller categories forming a coherent semantic space, and consequently, increasing their distinctiveness.

Overall, this study indicates some cross-linguistic consistency in BERT's linguistic representations while emphasizing the need for further analyses of language-specific phenomena, especially in low-resource contexts.

5 Limitations

When interpreting the results of this study, it is important to note that only one model (BERT), one corpus domain (news), and one specific semantic classification task was analysed. Therefore, the findings may reflect the specific distributions of the assessed corpus and task; yet high generalisability is expected given the broad nature of the chosen task. Some results are not straightforward to interpret, but we offer explanations based on the most reasonable assumptions.

Finally, the study does not specifically analyse the full complexity of inflectional morphology and syntax. A more detailed analysis of nouns could provide further insights into the model's preferences. Similarly, more research is needed to understand how structural simplifications impact syntactic complexity and the contribution of specific words to this process.

6 Ethics statement

We do not anticipate any ethical concerns with this work. We used open-sourced data and models, which have been appropriately cited.

7 Acknowledgements

We would like to thank the Fraunhofer Institute for Communication, Information Processing and Ergonomics (FKIE) for supporting this research, particularly Daniel Claeser and Albert Pritzkau for their valuable guidance. Additionally, we acknowledge the Volkswagen Stiftung for partially funding this work under grant 98 543. We also appreciate the resources provided by the Department of Linguistics at the University of Konstanz, which facilitated some of our experiments. Finally, we thank Jonathan Pampel for insightful discussions on the mathematical aspects of this paper.

References

Keno K. Bressem, Jens-Michalis Papaioannou, Paul Grundmann, Florian Borchert, Lisa C. Adams, Leonhard Liu, Felix Busch, Lina Xu, Jan P. Loyen, Stefan M. Niehues, Moritz Augustin, Lennart Grosser, Marcus R. Makowski, Hugo J.W.L. Aerts, and Alexander Löser. 2024. medbert.de: A comprehensive german bert model for the medical domain. *Expert Systems with Applications*, 237:121598.

Patrick Brookshire and Nils Reiter. 2024. Modeling moravian memoirs: Ternary sentiment analysis in a low resource setting. In *Proceedings of the 8th Joint SIGHUM Workshop on Computational Linguistics for Cultural Heritage, Social Sciences, Humanities and Literature (LaTeCH-CLfL 2024)*, pages 91–100, St. Julians, Malta. Association for Computational Linguistics.

Bharathi Raja Chakravarthi, Ruba Priyadharshini, Shubanker Banerjee, Manoj Balaji Jagadeeshan, Prasanna Kumar Kumaresan, Rahul Ponnusamy, Sean Benhur, and John Philip McCrae. 2023. Detecting abusive comments at a fine-grained level in a low-resource language. *Natural Language Processing Journal*, 3:100006.

Branden Chan, Stefan Schweter, and Timo Möller. 2020. German's Next Language Model. In *Proceedings of the 28th International Conference on Computational Linguistics*, pages 6788–6796, Barcelona, Spain (Online). International Committee on Computational Linguistics.

Daniel Benedikt Claeser. 2022. *Zur Rolle der Flexionsmorphologie in der automatischen Klassifikation deutschsprachiger Textdokumente*. Ph.D. thesis, Rheinische Friedrich-Wilhelms-Universität Bonn.

Jacob Devlin, Ming-Wei Chang, Kenton Lee, and Kristina Toutanova. 2019. BERT: Pre-training of Deep Bidirectional Transformers for Language Understanding. In *Proceedings of the 2019 Conference of the North American Chapter of the Association for Computational Linguistics: Human Language Technologies, Volume 1 (Long and Short Papers)*, pages

4171–4186, Minneapolis, Minnesota. Association for Computational Linguistics.

Peter Eisenberg. 2020. *Grundriss der deutschen Grammatik: Das Wort*. J.B. Metzler.

Kilian A. Foth, Arne Köhn, Niels Beuck, and Wolfgang Menzel. 2014. Because Size Does Matter: The Hamburg Dependency Treebank. In *Proceedings of the Ninth International Conference on Language Resources and Evaluation (LREC'14)*, pages 2326–2333, Reykjavik, Iceland. European Language Resources Association (ELRA).

Yoav Goldberg. 2019. Assessing bert's syntactic abilities. *CoRR*, abs/1901.05287.

Raffaele Guarasci, Stefano Silvestri, Giuseppe De Pietro, Hamido Fujita, and Massimo Esposito. 2021. Assessing bert's ability to learn italian syntax: a study on null-subject and agreement phenomena. *Journal of Ambient Intelligence and Humanized Computing*, 14(1):289–303.

Hyewon Jang, Qi Yu, and Diego Frassinelli. 2023. Figurative Language Processing: A Linguistically Informed Feature Analysis of the Behavior of Language Models and Humans. *Findings of the Association for Computational Linguistics: ACL 2023*, pages 9816–9832.

Ganesh Jawahar, Benoît Sagot, and Djamé Seddah. 2019. What Does BERT Learn about the Structure of Language? In *Proceedings of the 57th Annual Meeting of the Association for Computational Linguistics*, pages 3651–3657, Florence, Italy. Association for Computational Linguistics.

Albert Q. Jiang, Alexandre Sablayrolles, Arthur Mensch, Chris Bamford, Devendra Singh Chaplot, Diego de las Casas, Florian Bressand, Gianna Lengyel, Guillaume Lample, Lucile Saulnier, Lélio Renard Lavaud, Marie-Anne Lachaux, Pierre Stock, Teven Le Scao, Thibaut Lavril, Thomas Wang, Timothée Lacroix, and William El Sayed. 2023. Mistral 7b. *arXiv preprint*.

Aikaterini-Lida Kalouli, Rita Sevastjanova, Christin Beck, and Maribel Romero. 2022. Negation, Coordination, and Quantifiers in Contextualized Language Models. In *Proceedings of the 29th International Conference on Computational Linguistics*, pages 3074–3085, Gyeongju, Republic of Korea. International Committee on Computational Linguistics.

Enja Kokalj, Blaž Škrlj, Nada Lavrač, Senja Pollak, and Marko Robnik-Šikonja. 2021. BERT meets Shapely: Extending SHAP Explanations to Transformer based Classifiers. In *Proceedings of the EACL Hackashop on News Media Content Analysis and Automated Report Generation*, pages 16–21. Association for Computational Linguistics.

Scott M Lundberg and Su-In Lee. 2017. A Unified Approach to Interpreting Model Predictions. In I. Guyon, U. V. Luxburg, S. Bengio, H. Wallach, R. Fergus, S. Vishwanathan, and R. Garnett, editors, *Advances in Neural Information Processing Systems 30*, pages 4765–4774. Curran Associates, Inc.

OpenAI, Josh Achiam, et al. 2023. Gpt-4 technical report. *arXiv preprint*.

Maryan Rizinski, Hristijan Peshov, Kostadin Mishev, Milos Jovanovik, and Dimitar Trajanov. 2024. Sentiment analysis in finance: From transformers back to explainable lexicons (xlex). *IEEE Access*, 12:7170–7198.

Rajalakshmi Sivanaiah, Subhankar Suresh, Sushmithaa Pandian, and Angel Deborah Suseelan. 2024. Bridging the language gap: Transformer-based bert for fake news detection in low-resource settings. In *Speech and Language Technologies for Low-Resource Languages*, pages 398–411, Cham. Springer Nature Switzerland.

Xiaoyi Tang, Hongwei Chen, Daoyu Lin, and Kexin Li. 2024. Incorporating fine-grained linguistic features and explainable ai into multi-dimensional automated writing assessment. *Applied Sciences*, 14(10).

Heike Telljohann, Erhard Hinrichs, and Sandra Kübler. 2004. The Tüba-D/Z Treebank: Annotating German with a Context-Free Backbone. In *Proceedings of the Fourth International Conference on Language Resources and Evaluation (LREC'04)*, Lisbon, Portugal. European Language Resources Association (ELRA).

Heike Telljohann, Erhard W. Hinrichs, Sandra Kübler, Heike Zinsmeister, and Kathrin Beck. Stylebook for the Tübingen Treebank of Written German (TüBa-D/Z).

Hugo Touvron, Thibaut Lavril, Gautier Izacard, Xavier Martinet, Marie-Anne Lachaux, Timothée Lacroix, Baptiste Rozière, Naman Goyal, Eric Hambro, Faisal Azhar, Aurelien Rodriguez, Armand Joulin, Edouard Grave, and Guillaume Lample. 2023. Llama: Open and efficient foundation language models. *arXiv preprint*.

Karolina Zaczynska, Nils Feldhus, Robert Schwarzenberg, Aleksandra Gabryszak, and Sebastian Möller. 2020. Evaluating german transformer language models with syntactic agreement tests.

A Statistical Analysis

The statistical analysis in this paper highlights the significance of specific linguistic features in the text classification task. We compare the distribution of each feature in the SHAP values to its distribution in the same category within the TüBa corpus. Both distributions are normalized based on the total number of words per category in the SHAP values and in the entire corpus, respectively. As shown in Equation 1, the null hypothesis ($H0$) assumes that the two distributions are identical:

$$H0 : \frac{k}{n} = \frac{K}{N} \tag{1}$$

where k is the count of the feature in the category in the SHAP values, n is the total number of words in the top 10% positive SHAP values for the category, K is the count of the feature in the category within the corpus, and N is the total number of words in the category in the corpus.

The statistical analysis (two-sided t-test) identifies features in SHAP that have a significantly higher or lower contribution to model performance compared to their actual distribution in the corpus.

The analysis for the co-occurrence of tokens with their governing token in a dependency relation requires to estimate an expected value as reference under the assumption that the dependency-related tokens end up in the SHAP values based on a random selection. A random selection assumes in this case that there is a binary criterion of a token and its governing token being in the SHAP values or not. Under this assumption, Equation 2 approximates the question whether two dependency-related tokens end up in the SHAP values as a Poisson Distribution.

$$\begin{aligned} A &:= P_{\text{gov. token of last word in SHAPS}} \\ &= \frac{n_{SHAPs}}{n_{Tueba}} \\ &= \frac{46043}{1523384} \\ E_{\text{gov. tokens in SHAPs}} &= n_{SHAPs} \cdot A \\ &= \frac{n_{SHAPs}^2}{n_{Tueba}} \\ &= \frac{46043^2}{1523384} \\ &\approx \underline{\underline{1392}} \end{aligned} \tag{2}$$

B Labels Mapping

Here, we document the mapping between the fine-grained labels in the corpus, based on the Stuttgart-Tübingen-Tagset (STTS), complement labels and the dependency labels according to the Hamburg Dependency Treebank. Table 3 documents POS tags, Table 4 complement labels, and Table 5 the dependency labels.

Grouped Tag	Abbreviation	STTS Tag
nouns	nouns	NN
named entities (NEs)	nes	NE
adjectives	adj	ADJA, ADJD
cardinal numbers	card	CARD
verbs	verbs	VMFIN, VAFIN, VVFIN, VAIMP, VVIMP, VVINF, VAINF, VMINF, VVIZU, VVPP, VMPP, VAPP
articles	art	ART
pronouns	pro	PPER, PRF, PPOSAT, PPOSS, PDAT, PDS, PIAT, PIDAT, PIS, PRELAT, PRELS, PWAT, PWS, PWAV, PAV
adverbs	adv	ADV
conjunctions	conj	KOUI, KOUS, KON, KOKOM
particle	part	PTKZU, PTKNEG, PTKVZ, PTKA, PTKANT
other	other	ITJ, TRUNC, XY, FM

Table 3: Mapping between fine-grained STTS labels and the coarse-grained labels used in the **POS** analysis.

Grouped Tag	Abbreviation	Complement Tag
subject	subj	ON
object	obj	OD, OA, OG, OS, OPP, OADVP, OADJP
predicate	pred	PRED
verbal objects	ov	OV
facultative prepositional object	fopp	FOPP
apposition	app	APP

Table 4: Grouping of **complement labels** for the analysis. For the original labels, see (Telljohann et al.).

Grouped Tag	Abbreviation	Dependency Tag
root node of dependency structure	root	ROOT
subject	subj	SUBJ, SUBJC, EXPL
object	obj	OBJA, OBJI, OBJG, OBJC, OBJD
subordination	subord	APP, NEB, REL, PAR, S, gmod-app
determiner	det	DET
predicative complement	pred	PRED
auxiliary	aux	AUX
prepositions	prep	PP, PN, OBJP
modifier	modif	ADV, ATTR, GMOD, PART, KOM
subordordination	subord	REL, NEB, PAR
coordination	coord	CJ, KONJ, KON, koord
participles	part	AVZ, PART
time information	zeit	ZEIT
gradual (indicating a measure)	grad	GRAD
other	other	left over punctuation signs, -UNKNOWN-

Table 5: Grouping of **dependency labels** for the analysis based on the labels from the Hamburg Dependency Treebank (Foth et al., 2014).

C Feature Analysis: Additional Plots

Below, we present the additional plots supporting the complete feature analysis as documented in the main text for the morphological features of nouns (Figure 4), adjectives (Figures 5 and 6), and verbs (Figures 7, 9, 8, 10, and 11), followed by the syntactic analysis for phrasal (Figures 12, 13, and 14), clausal (Figure 15), and dependency (Figure 16) features. As discussed in Section 3.1, the red central line indicates the null hypothesis surrounded by the $2\sigma(95\%)$ confidence interval in light blue. The black vertical line represents the observed frequency of each feature among SHAP values. Values to the right of the red line indicate that a specific feature is over-represented in the SHAP values compared to its corpus distribution, while those to the left that it is under-represented. Significance is reached when the black line is outside the confidence interval.

C.1 Morphology Plots

C.2 Morphology: Nouns

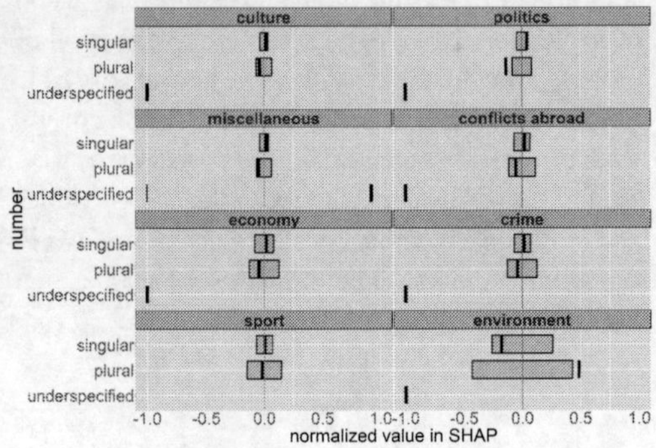

Figure 4: Normalized distribution of **number** (singular, plural, underspecified) for nouns.

C.2.1 Morphology: Adjectives

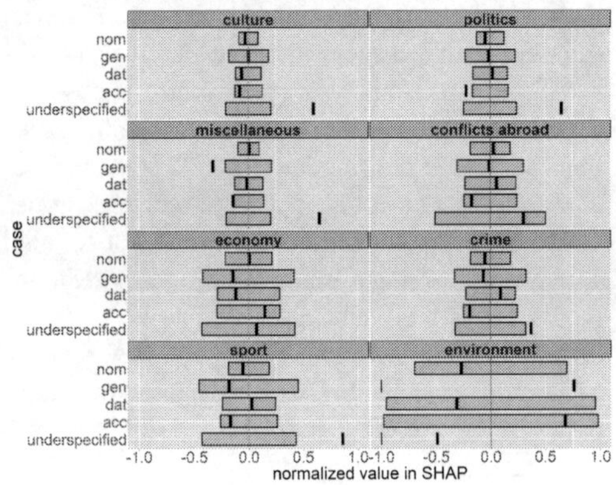

Figure 5: Normalized distribution of **case** (nominative, genitive, dative, accusative, underspecified) for adjectives.

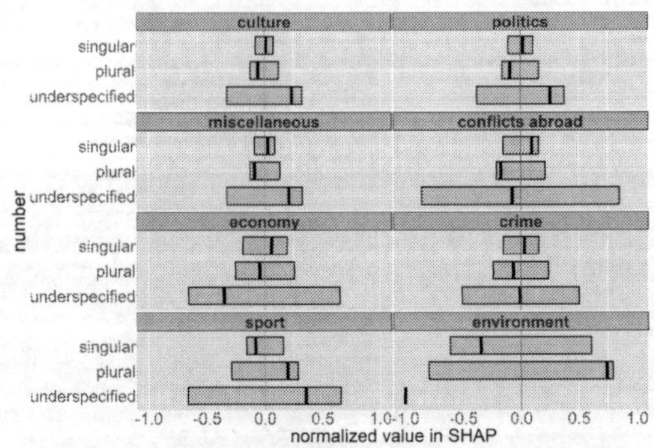

Figure 6: Normalized distribution of **number** (singular, plural, underspecified) for adjectives.

C.2.2 Morphology: Verbs

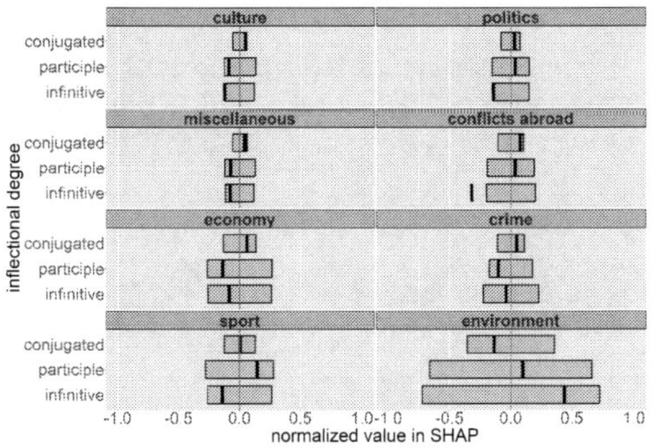

Figure 7: Normalized distribution of **inflectional degree** (infinitive, participle, inflected) for verbs.

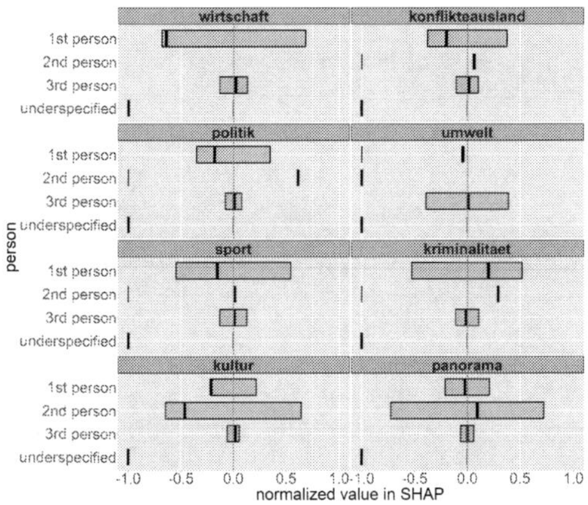

Figure 8: Normalized distribution of **grammatical person** (1st, 2nd, 3rd, underspecified) for verbs.

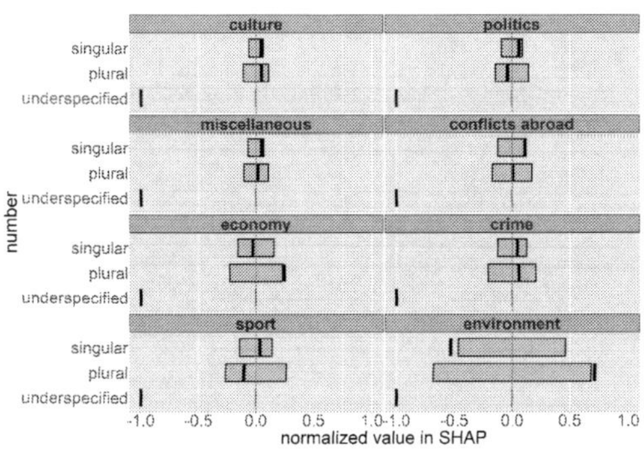

Figure 9: Normalized distribution of **number** (singular, plural, underspecified) for verbs.

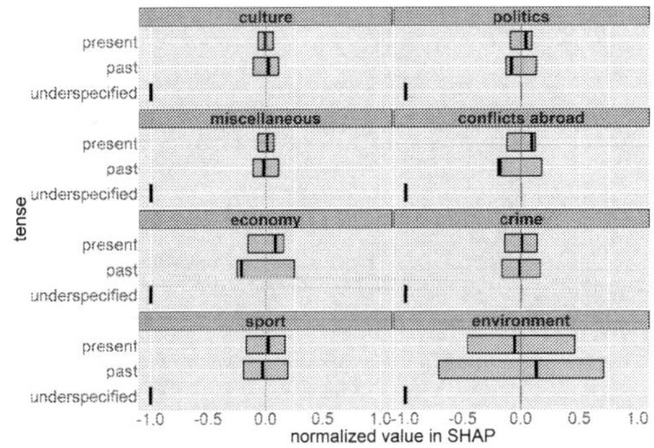

Figure 10: Normalized distribution of **tense** (present, past, underspecified) for verbs.

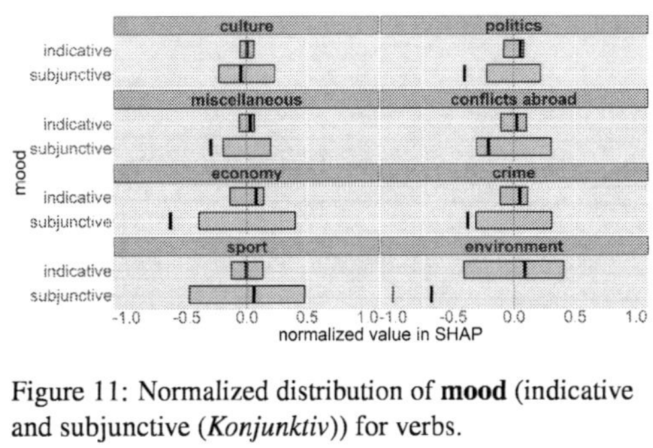

Figure 11: Normalized distribution of **mood** (indicative and subjunctive (*Konjunktiv*)) for verbs.

C.3 Syntactic analysis

C.3.1 Phrasal analysis

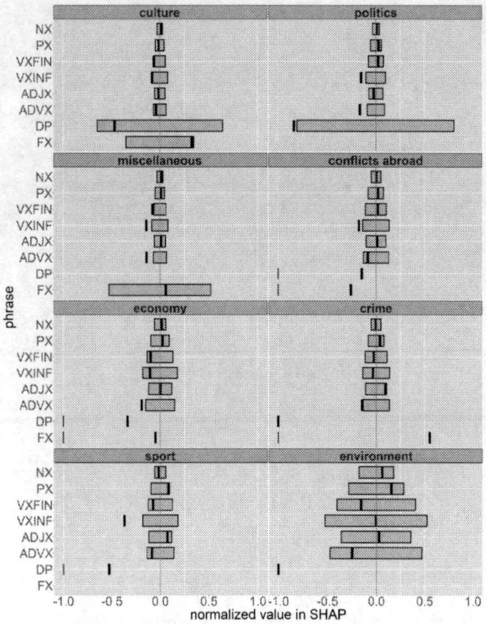

Figure 12: Normalized distribution of phrase labels.

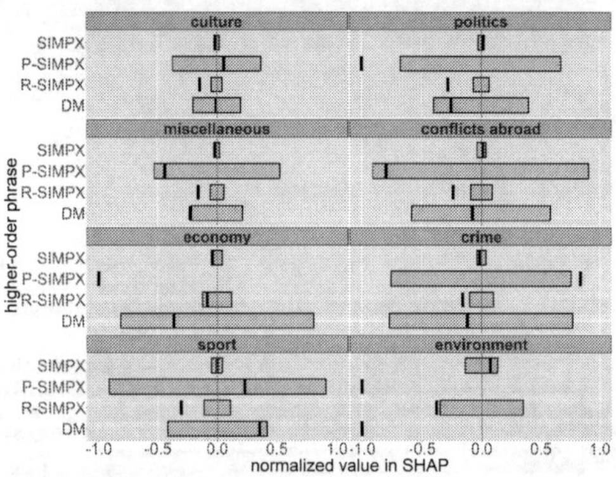

Figure 13: Normalized distribution of higher-order phrase labels.

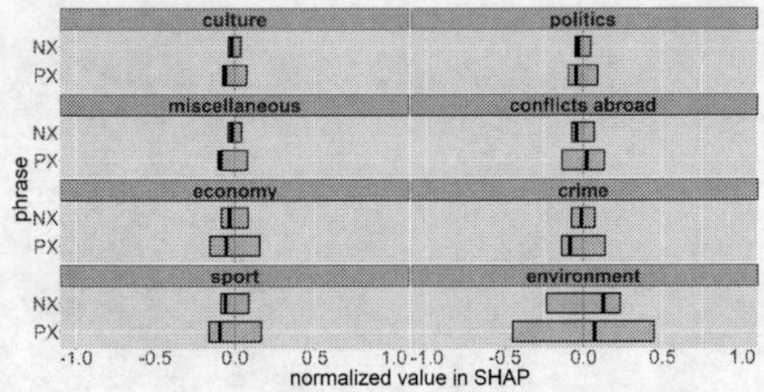

Figure 14: Normalized distribution of phrase labels for nouns to assess whether the phrasal attachment of a noun influences the classification.

C.3.2 Clausal Analysis

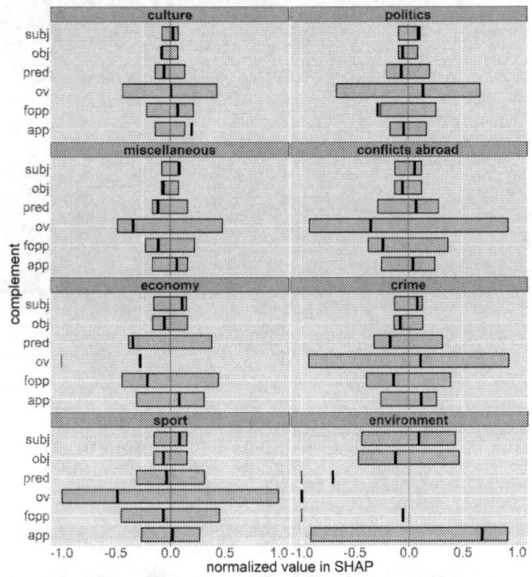

Figure 15: Normalized distribution of complement labels. The grouping of the labels can be found in 4.

C.3.3 Dependency Analysis

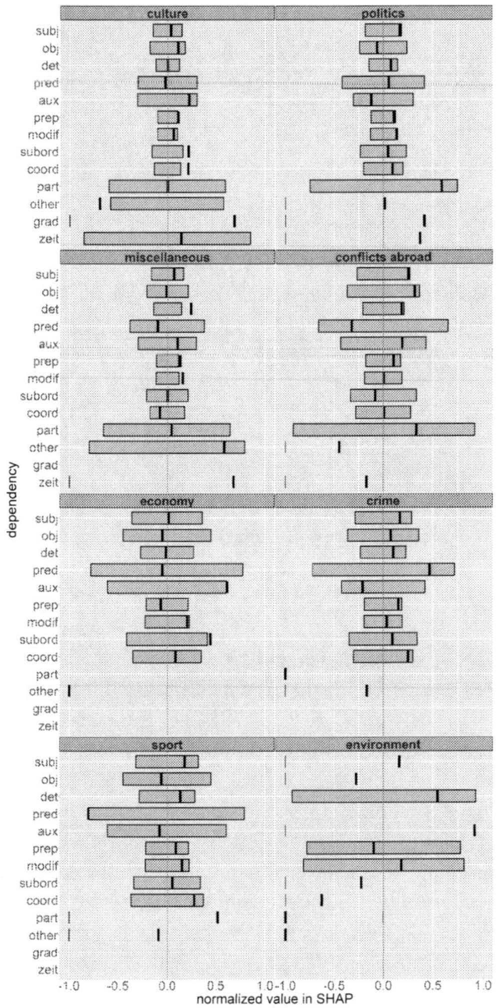

Figure 16: Normalized distribution of dependency relations between tokens, where both tokens appear in the SHAP values. This aims to reveal whether specific tokens are important to the classification task due to their dependency relations.

Thesis Proposal: Uncertainty in Knowledge Graph Embeddings

Yuqicheng Zhu
Bosch Center for Artificial Intelligence, Germany
University of Stuttgart, Germany
Yuqicheng.Zhu@de.bosch.com

Abstract

Knowledge Graph Embedding (KGE) methods are widely used to map entities and relations from knowledge graphs (KGs) into continuous vector spaces, enabling non-classical reasoning over knowledge structures. Despite their effectiveness, the uncertainty of KGE methods has not been extensively studied in the literature. This gap poses significant challenges, particularly when deploying KGE models in high-stakes domains like medicine, where reliability and risk assessment are critical. This dissertation seeks to investigate various types of uncertainty in KGE methods and explore strategies to quantify, mitigate, and reason under uncertainty effectively. The outcomes of this research will contribute to enhancing the reliability of KGE methods, providing greater confidence in their use beyond benchmark datasets, and supporting their application in real-world, high-stakes domains.

1 Introduction

Knowledge graphs (KGs) encode factual knowledge about real-world entities and their relationships, represented as triples <*head entity*, *predicate*, *tail entity*>. These structures provide semantically rich information, playing a crucial role in advancing intelligent systems (Lenat and Feigenbaum, 2000). Ontologies and logic rules, as standard knowledge representation formalisms, are commonly used to reason about the semantics in KGs (Hogan et al., 2021). However, management and updating of rules can be cumbersome and the inherently symbolic nature of such systems complicates their integration with machine learning tasks.

Knowledge graph embedding (KGE) methods map entities and predicates into numerical vectors (a.k.a embeddings), providing non-classical reasoning capability by exploiting similarities and analogies over knowledge structure (Wang et al., 2017; Zhu et al., 2024a). While KGE methods have demonstrated effectiveness in various downstream tasks, including triple classification (Socher et al., 2013), link prediction (Bordes et al., 2013; Nickel et al., 2011) and recommendation (Liu et al., 2019), the uncertainty of KGE methods remains largely under-explored.

Handling uncertainty in KGE methods is critical because KGE models often encounter significant uncertainty in their predictions (*predictive uncertainty*) (Zhu et al., 2024a,b). This predictive uncertainty can stem from several procedures throughout the KGE pipeline shown in Figure 1. During KG construction, noise and errors may arise from inconsistent or ambiguous data aggregated from multiple sources (Zhou et al., 2022), or from inaccurate automated knowledge extraction processes (Zhou et al., 2021). Additionally, some knowledge is inherently uncertain, such as molecular interactions, which are random process by nature (Szklarczyk et al., 2016). This uncertainty, associated with KGs before training the KGE model, is referred to as *knowledge uncertainty*. Furthermore, *algorithmic uncertainty* can emerge during model development, caused by randomness and variability in the KGE training process.

Understanding and dealing with these types of uncertainty is especially critical in high-stakes domains such as medicine, where reliable predictions and robust risk assessment are imperative. Despite the relevance, research on uncertainty in KGE methods remains limited. For instance, studies by He et al. (2015); Xiao et al. (2015); Wang et al. (2022) model algorithmic uncertainty and predictive uncertainty using probabilistic embeddings. While these approaches have improved overall accuracy, the quality of the modeled uncertainty has not been systematically studied. Moreover, these methods often demand additional parameters, incur high computational costs due to the need for calculating distance between probability distribution, and are challenging to adapt to other KGE methods

Proceedings of the 2025 Conference of the Nations of the Americas Chapter of the Association for Computational Linguistics: Human Language Technologies (Volume 4: Student Research Workshop), pages 40–47

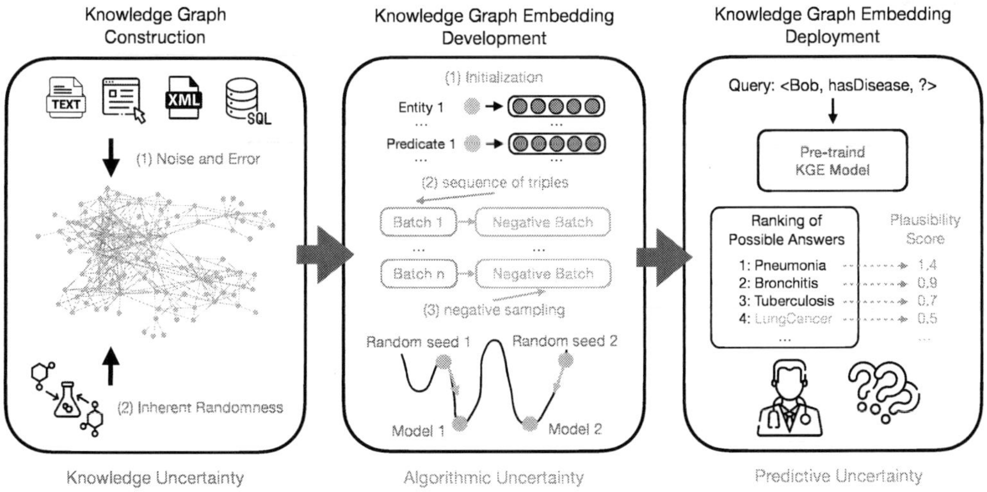

Figure 1: This figure illustrates the three key stages in the KGE pipeline and their associated uncertainties: (1) *Knowledge Uncertainty* arises during knowledge graph construction due to noise, errors, and inherent randomness in the knowledge sources; (2) *Algorithmic Uncertainty* is introduced during KGE development through randomized initialization, batch sampling, and negative sampling, leading to variations in the resulting models; and (3) *Predictive Uncertainty*, which occurs in the deployment of a pre-trained KGE model, refers to the model's confidence in its predictions for a given query.

without substantial modifications.

To address these gaps, this dissertation plans to systematically explore various types of uncertainty in KGE methods and aim to propose model-agnostic and easy-to-implement approaches to deal with uncertainty. The remainder of this dissertation proposal is structured as follows: Section 2 provides an overview of KGE methods and related work relevant to this research. Section 3 details the research questions and the proposed methodologies to address them. Section 4 concludes the proposal and outlines the anticipated contributions.

2 Background

2.1 Knowledge Graph Embedding

A KG $\mathcal{G}$ is a labelled directed graph, which can be viewed as a set of triples $\mathcal{T} \subseteq \mathcal{E} \times \mathcal{R} \times \mathcal{E}$, where $\mathcal{E}$ is the set of entities, and $\mathcal{R}$ is the set of predicates. An entity represents a real-world object. Often the labels of entities and predicates are chosen to be URIs or IRIs (Internationalised Resource Identifiers). The elements in $\mathcal{G}$ are called triples and denoted as $\langle h, r, t \rangle$, where $h \in \mathcal{E}$ is the subject, $r \in \mathcal{R}$ is the predicate, and $t \in \mathcal{E}$ is the object.

A KGE model $M_\theta : \mathcal{E} \times \mathcal{R} \times \mathcal{E} \rightarrow \mathbb{R}$ assigns a score to each triple, measuring the plausibility that the triple holds. Concretely, there are three key components of a KGE model: *embedding mapping*, *score function* and *embedding training* (Cao et al., 2022).

Embedding Mapping. In the embedding mapping process, entities and predicates are mapped into vector representations. For example, TransE (Bordes et al., 2013) map them into Euclidean space, while others map them into alternative mathematical spaces, such as complex space (Sun et al., 2019) or hyperbolic space (Balazevic et al., 2019; Xiong et al., 2022). Let $\mathbf{h}$, $\mathbf{r}$ and $\mathbf{t}$ denote the vector representation of entities and predicates in a triple.

Score Function. The score function, denoted as $s(\mathbf{h}, \mathbf{r}, \mathbf{t})$, then calculates a plausibility score for the triple based on the vector representations. For example, the translation-based scoring function $s(\mathbf{h}, \mathbf{r}, \mathbf{t}) = -||\mathbf{h} + \mathbf{r} - \mathbf{t}||_{1/2}$ is widely used to measure the plausibility that a triple is positive (Bordes et al., 2013). More scoring functions are summarized in Table 1.

Embedding Training. The parameters θ are learned to let M_θ assign higher plausibility scores to positive triples (real facts) while assigning lower plausibility scores to negative triples (false facts). Training begins with random initialization of θ and then minimizes a loss function, such as *margin-based ranking loss* (Bordes et al., 2013) or *cross-entropy loss* (Nickel et al., 2011; Dettmers et al.,

	Score Function $s(\langle \mathbf{h}, \mathbf{r}, \mathbf{t} \rangle)$
TransE (Bordes et al., 2013)	$-\|\|\mathbf{h} + \mathbf{r} - \mathbf{t}\|\|_{1/2}$
RotatE (Sun et al., 2019)	$-\|\|\mathbf{h} \circ \mathbf{r} - \mathbf{t}\|\|_{p}$
RESCAL (Nickel et al., 2011)	$\mathbf{h}^T \mathbf{M}_r \mathbf{t}$
DistMult (Yang et al., 2015)	$\mathbf{h}^T diag(\mathbf{r})\mathbf{t}$
ComplEx (Trouillon et al., 2016)	$Re(\mathbf{h}^T diag(\mathbf{r})\overline{\mathbf{t}})$
ConvE (Dettmers et al., 2018)	$f(vec(f([\overline{\mathbf{h}}; \overline{\mathbf{r}}] * \omega))\mathbf{W})\mathbf{t}$

Table 1: The score function of KGE models, where $\circ$ denotes Hadamard product. $\bar{\cdot}$ refers to conjugate for complex vectors in ComplEx, and 2D reshaping for real vectors in ConvE. $*$ is operator for 2D convolution. ω is the filters and W is the parameters for 2D convolutional layer.

2018). Since ground truth negative triples are typically unavailable in KGs, they are generated by corrupting positive triples during training. A common approach involves replacing the head or tail entity in an observed triple with a random entity sampled from $\mathcal{E}$.

2.2 Downstream Tasks and Evaluation

The quality of learned embeddings is commonly assessed through two primary tasks: *triple classification* and *link prediction* (Bordes et al., 2013), with their performance measured using specific evaluation metrics.

Triple Classification. The goal of triple classification is to determine whether a given triple is true or false. The model uses the learned embeddings to compute plausibility scores and classify triples accordingly. Performance is evaluated using standard binary classification metrics, such as accuracy, precision, recall, and F1 score.

Link Prediction. Link prediction is essentially a ranking task aimed at answering a given query, such as $\langle h, r, ? \rangle$ or $\langle ?, r, t \rangle$. The model ranks potential triples $\langle h, r, e \rangle$ or $\langle e, r, t \rangle$, where $e \in \mathcal{E}$, based on their plausibility scores. Positive triples are expected to rank higher than negative ones. Ranking-based metrics are used to evaluate performance:

- Mean Rank (MR): The average rank of the true entity in the model's predictions.
- Mean Reciprocal Rank (MRR): The average reciprocal rank of the true entity.
- Hits@K: The proportion of test triples where the true entity is ranked within the top-K predictions.

Beyond these tasks, KG embeddings are used to answer more complex queries (He et al., 2023, 2024a,b).

2.3 Related Work

Several works embed entities and relations from deterministic KGs as probabilistic distributions rather than single numerical vectors to model uncertainty in the embeddings (He et al., 2015; Xiao et al., 2015; Wang et al., 2022). These methods typically learn distribution parameters by minimizing the KL-divergence between the probability distribution of the difference between head and tail entities and that of the relation, adhering to the translational paradigm of KGE models. While this line of work captures both algorithmic and predictive uncertainty through prior and posterior distributions in the vector representations, the evaluation primarily focuses on accuracy, leaving the quality of the uncertainty modeling largely unexplored. To the best of our knowledge, Loconte et al. (2023) is the only study that evaluates uncertainty quality using calibration diagrams and empirical calibration error, as detailed in Loconte et al. (2023, Appendix F.5.3).

Other approaches represent knowledge uncertainty by associating facts or axioms with a confidence score or probability (Chen et al., 2019, 2021b,a; Zhu et al., 2023, 2024c). These methods aim to learn embeddings that incorporate both KG structure and input data uncertainty. For instance, UKGE (Chen et al., 2019) extends DistMult (Yang et al., 2014) by predicting confidence scores for facts. It computes the plausibility of triples as the product of embedding vectors and maps this plausibility to a confidence score in the range $[0, 1]$. To enrich the training data, UKGE employs probabilistic soft logic to infer confidence scores for a subset of unseen triples. Subsequent work enhances these methods through improved negative sampling strategies via semi-supervised learning (Chen et al., 2021b) and by increasing the robustness and expressiveness of UKGE using entity representations as boxes and affine transformations for relations (Chen et al., 2021a).

Explicit studies on predictive uncertainty in triple classification have also been conducted. Research by Tabacof and Costabello (2020) and Safavi et al. (2020a) applies off-the-shelf calibration techniques, such as Platt scaling and isotonic regression, to KGE models. These techniques convert uncalibrated plausibility scores into probabilities by minimizing the negative log-likelihood on a validation set. However, these approaches are sensitive to the quality of the validation set and lack formal guarantees for the generated probabilities.

3 Research Questions

The primary objective of this dissertation is to systematically investigate various types of uncertainty in KGE methods and to develop model-agnostic approaches for effectively managing them. Specifically, this work focuses on the following research questions:

> RQ1: For the reducible component of predictive uncertainty caused by algorithmic uncertainty, how can we effectively reduce it?
>
> RQ2: For the irreducible component of predictive uncertainty, how can we reliably quantify it with statistical guarantees?
>
> RQ3: When knowledge uncertainty is explicitly present in the input KGs, how can KGE methods effectively and efficiently reason under such uncertainty?

In this section, I will elaborate on each research question, introduce sub-research questions, outline tentative solutions, and describe the preliminary results or the expected contributions for each.

3.1 Reducing Uncertainty

The training process for KGE models, described in Section 2.1, introduces randomness through various sources, such as randomized embedding initialization, randomized sequences of training triples, and randomized negative sampling. Due to the non-convex nature of the training process, identical configurations (including the training KG, KGE algorithm, and hyperparameters) can result in different KGE models that converge to different local minima.

Among the possible KGE models trained under the same configuration, some may achieve similar accuracy on the training KG but differ significantly in their vector representations of entities and predicates, capturing distinct patterns. This phenomenon, known as model multiplicity in machine learning (Breiman, 2001; Marx et al., 2020; Black et al., 2022b,a), poses a significant obstacle to reliably training models that behave as expected during deployment (D'Amour et al., 2022). An extreme example involves two models with both 50% accuracy but mutually contradictory predictions on the validation set, which creates challenges for model selection. Randomly selecting models based on accuracy alone fails to justify decision-making, especially in high-stakes domains such as loan approval or medical diagnosis (Black et al., 2022b).

Model multiplicity is a specific form of algorithmic uncertainty that contributes to predictive uncertainty by producing conflicting predictions under identical training configurations. To better understand and address model multiplicity in KGE methods, this research investigates the following sub-questions:

- RQ1.1: How can model multiplicity in KGE methods be formally defined?
- RQ1.2: How can model multiplicity in KGE methods be measured?
- RQ1.3: What are the key factors influencing model multiplicity in KGE methods?
- RQ1.4: How can model multiplicity in KGE methods be alleviated to reduce predictive uncertainty?

Although model multiplicity is known to be ubiquitous in gradient-based optimization (D'Amour et al., 2022), we explore strategies to mitigate the predictive uncertainty it induces. A promising approach involves ensembling models trained with different random seeds. Such ensembles, inspired by voting methods from social choice theory (Brandt et al., 2016), can combine predictions to reduce the impact of single model's error, thereby effectively reducing predictive uncertainty (Black et al., 2022a; Potyka et al., 2024).

Our preliminary results in (Zhu et al., 2024a) contribute in the following aspects:

- Development of suitable evaluation metrics to quantify and analyze model multiplicity in the context of KGE methods.
- Theoretical insights into model multiplicity in KGE methods.
- Design of a novel ensemble-based strategy to effectively reduce predictive uncertainty caused by model multiplicity.

3.2 Quantifying Uncertainty

Once a KGE model is deployed, the reliability of its predictions becomes a critical concern. Current KGE models generate plausibility scores for triples, which are used to differentiate positive triples from negative ones. However, these scores lack probabilistic interpretation and do not reflect the true likelihood of a triple being correct (Tabacof and Costabello, 2019; Safavi et al., 2020b).

Previous studies (Tabacof and Costabello, 2019; Safavi et al., 2020b) have attempted to calibrate these plausibility scores using techniques that convert them into probabilities. However, this calibration relies on high-quality negative triples in the validation set, which are often unavailable. Furthermore, the calibration process, which minimizes negative log-likelihood on the validation set, is sensitive to the distribution of validation triples and offers no theoretical guarantees for the calibrated probabilities. Consequently, practitioners lack a reliable framework to assess when predictions can be trusted.

To address this issue, the following subquestions are explored:

- RQ2.1: Can the uncertainty of KGE methods be quantified without relying on ground-truth negative triples?
- RQ2.2: Is it possible to provide statistical guarantees for the quantified uncertainty?

Conformal prediction (Vovk et al., 2005), a general framework for generating prediction sets that include the ground truth with predefined probabilistic guarantees, is a good candidate to provide statistically rigorous uncertainty estimates.

In Zhu et al. (2024b), we first assess whether the assumptions of conformal prediction, particularly the exchangeability of triples between the training and test sets, are satisfied in the context of KGE. We then establish theoretical guarantees for the coverage probability and empirically verify them through comprehensive evaluations.

The contributions of this work include:

- Development of a novel uncertainty quantification methods with statistical guarantees.
- An efficient implementation of the approach.

3.3 Reasoning under Uncertainty

Most existing KGE methods assume deterministic KGs as input, where every fact is treated as unequivocally true. However, real-world knowledge is often uncertain due to noise, acquisition errors, or the uncertain nature of knowledge itself. Reasoning under such knowledge uncertainty remains an under-explored area.

Recent studies (Chen et al., 2019, 2021b,a) have extended KGE methods to uncertain KGs by modifying the loss function and incorporating probabilistic reasoning techniques such as probabilistic soft logic (Chen et al., 2019) and semi-supervised learning (Chen et al., 2021b). However, these approaches produce only point estimates for predictions, failing to capture the inherent variance associated with uncertainty.

Given the complexity of modeling deterministic KGs, reasoning under knowledge uncertainty presents additional challenges in capturing the uncertainty associated with triples. This motivates the following research questions:

- RQ3.1: What is the variance in predictions made by existing uncertain KGE methods when the training process is repeated?
- RQ3.2: How can prediction intervals be estimated to reliably reflect the uncertainty of predictions instead of relying solely on point estimates?

Conformal prediction, also commonly used for regression task to provide prediction intervals with guarantees (Vovk et al., 2005; Lei et al., 2018), is planed to be applied to develop an approach for reasoning under knowledge uncertainty with reliable uncertainty estimates. The expected contributions are as follows:

- Systematical analysis of the variance of point estimates produced by existing uncertain KGE methods.
- Development of a novel uncertain KGE approach with reliable uncertainty estimates.

4 Conclusion

In summary, this research seeks to address the critical yet underexplored challenge of uncertainty in KGE methods. By investigating knowledge, algorithmic, and predictive uncertainty, the dissertation aims to enhance the reliability of KGE methods, particularly in high-stakes applications. The anticipated contributions include novel methodologies and theoretical insights for reducing, quantifying and reasoning under uncertainty. These advancements will not only bridge significant gaps in current research but also support the deployment of more reliable KGE systems in real-world scenarios.

5 Acknowledgements

The authors thank the International Max Planck Research School for Intelligent Systems (IMPRS-IS) for supporting Yuqicheng Zhu. The work was partially supported by EU Projects Graph Massivizer (GA 101093202), enRichMyData (GA 101070284) and SMARTY (GA 101140087).

References

Ivana Balazevic, Carl Allen, and Timothy Hospedales. 2019. Multi-relational poincaré graph embeddings. *Advances in Neural Information Processing Systems*, 32.

Emily Black, Klas Leino, and Matt Fredrikson. 2022a. Selective ensembles for consistent predictions. In *ICLR*. OpenReview.net.

Emily Black, Manish Raghavan, and Solon Barocas. 2022b. Model multiplicity: Opportunities, concerns, and solutions. In *Proceedings of the 2022 ACM Conference on Fairness, Accountability, and Transparency*, pages 850–863.

Antoine Bordes, Nicolas Usunier, Alberto Garcia-Duran, Jason Weston, and Oksana Yakhnenko. 2013. Translating embeddings for modeling multi-relational data. *Advances in neural information processing systems*, 26.

Felix Brandt, Vincent Conitzer, Ulle Endriss, Jérôme Lang, and Ariel D. Procaccia, editors. 2016. *Handbook of Computational Social Choice*. Cambridge University Press.

Leo Breiman. 2001. Statistical modeling: The two cultures (with comments and a rejoinder by the author). *Statistical science*, 16(3):199–231.

Jiahang Cao, Jinyuan Fang, Zaiqiao Meng, and Shangsong Liang. 2022. Knowledge graph embedding: A survey from the perspective of representation spaces. *arXiv preprint arXiv:2211.03536*.

Xuelu Chen, Michael Boratko, Muhao Chen, Shib Sankar Dasgupta, Xiang Lorraine Li, and Andrew McCallum. 2021a. Probabilistic box embeddings for uncertain knowledge graph reasoning. *arXiv preprint arXiv:2104.04597*.

Xuelu Chen, Muhao Chen, Weijia Shi, Yizhou Sun, and Carlo Zaniolo. 2019. Embedding uncertain knowledge graphs. In *Proceedings of the AAAI conference on artificial intelligence*, volume 33, pages 3363–3370.

Zhu-Mu Chen, Mi-Yen Yeh, and Tei-Wei Kuo. 2021b. Passleaf: a pool-based semi-supervised learning framework for uncertain knowledge graph embedding. In *Proceedings of the AAAI Conference on Artificial Intelligence*, volume 35, pages 4019–4026.

Alexander D'Amour, Katherine Heller, Dan Moldovan, Ben Adlam, Babak Alipanahi, Alex Beutel, Christina Chen, Jonathan Deaton, Jacob Eisenstein, Matthew D Hoffman, et al. 2022. Underspecification presents challenges for credibility in modern machine learning. *Journal of Machine Learning Research*, 23(226):1–61.

Tim Dettmers, Pasquale Minervini, Pontus Stenetorp, and Sebastian Riedel. 2018. Convolutional 2d knowledge graph embeddings. In *Proceedings of the AAAI conference on artificial intelligence*, volume 32.

Shizhu He, Kang Liu, Guoliang Ji, and Jun Zhao. 2015. Learning to represent knowledge graphs with gaussian embedding. In *Proceedings of the 24th ACM international on conference on information and knowledge management*, pages 623–632.

Yunjie He, Daniel Hernandez, Mojtaba Nayyeri, Bo Xiong, Yuqicheng Zhu, Evgeny Kharlamov, and Steffen Staab. 2024a. Generating $sroi^{-}$ ontologies via knowledge graph query embedding learning. *arXiv preprint arXiv:2407.09212*.

Yunjie He, Mojtaba Nayyeri, Bo Xiong, Yuqicheng Zhu, Evgeny Kharlamov, and Steffen Staab. 2023. Can pattern learning enhance complex logical query answering? In *ISWC (Poster/Demos/Industry)*.

Yunjie He, Bo Xiong, Daniel Hernández, Yuqicheng Zhu, Evgeny Kharlamov, and Steffen Staab. 2024b. Dage: Dag query answering via relational combinator with logical constraints. *arXiv preprint arXiv:2410.22105*.

Aidan Hogan, Eva Blomqvist, Michael Cochez, Claudia d'Amato, Gerard De Melo, Claudio Gutierrez, Sabrina Kirrane, José Emilio Labra Gayo, Roberto Navigli, Sebastian Neumaier, et al. 2021. Knowledge graphs. *ACM Computing Surveys (Csur)*, 54(4):1–37.

Jing Lei, Max G'Sell, Alessandro Rinaldo, Ryan J Tibshirani, and Larry Wasserman. 2018. Distribution-free predictive inference for regression. *Journal of the American Statistical Association*, 113(523):1094–1111.

Douglas Lenat and E Feigenbaum. 2000. On the thresholds of knowledge. *Artificial Intelligence: Critical Concepts*, 2:298.

Chan Liu, Lun Li, Xiaolu Yao, and Lin Tang. 2019. A survey of recommendation algorithms based on knowledge graph embedding. In *2019 IEEE International Conference on Computer Science and Educational Informatization (CSEI)*, pages 168–171. IEEE.

Lorenzo Loconte, Nicola Di Mauro, Robert Peharz, and Antonio Vergari. 2023. How to turn your knowledge graph embeddings into generative models via probabilistic circuits. *arXiv preprint arXiv:2305.15944*.

Charles T. Marx, Flávio P. Calmon, and Berk Ustun. 2020. Predictive multiplicity in classification. In *ICML*, volume 119 of *Proceedings of Machine Learning Research*, pages 6765–6774. PMLR.

Maximilian Nickel, Volker Tresp, and Hans-Peter Kriegel. 2011. A three-way model for collective learning on multi-relational data. In *ICML*, pages 809–816. Omnipress.

Nico Potyka, Yuqicheng Zhu, Yunjie He, Evgeny Kharlamov, and Steffen Staab. 2024. Robust knowledge extraction from large language models using social choice theory. In *Proceedings of the 23rd International Conference on Autonomous Agents and Multiagent Systems*, AAMAS '24, page 1593–1601, Richland, SC. International Foundation for Autonomous Agents and Multiagent Systems.

Tara Safavi, Danai Koutra, and Edgar Meij. 2020a. Evaluating the calibration of knowledge graph embeddings for trustworthy link prediction. In *EMNLP (1)*, pages 8308–8321. Association for Computational Linguistics.

Tara Safavi, Danai Koutra, and Edgar Meij. 2020b. Evaluating the calibration of knowledge graph embeddings for trustworthy link prediction. *arXiv preprint arXiv:2004.01168*.

Richard Socher, Danqi Chen, Christopher D Manning, and Andrew Ng. 2013. Reasoning with neural tensor networks for knowledge base completion. *Advances in neural information processing systems*, 26.

Zhiqing Sun, Zhi-Hong Deng, Jian-Yun Nie, and Jian Tang. 2019. Rotate: Knowledge graph embedding by relational rotation in complex space. In *ICLR (Poster)*. OpenReview.net.

Damian Szklarczyk, John H Morris, Helen Cook, Michael Kuhn, Stefan Wyder, Milan Simonovic, Alberto Santos, Nadezhda T Doncheva, Alexander Roth, Peer Bork, et al. 2016. The string database in 2017: quality-controlled protein–protein association networks, made broadly accessible. *Nucleic acids research*, page gkw937.

Pedro Tabacof and Luca Costabello. 2019. Probability calibration for knowledge graph embedding models. *arXiv preprint arXiv:1912.10000*.

Pedro Tabacof and Luca Costabello. 2020. Probability calibration for knowledge graph embedding models. In *ICLR*. OpenReview.net.

Théo Trouillon, Johannes Welbl, Sebastian Riedel, Éric Gaussier, and Guillaume Bouchard. 2016. Complex embeddings for simple link prediction. In *International conference on machine learning*, pages 2071–2080. PMLR.

Vladimir Vovk, Alexander Gammerman, and Glenn Shafer. 2005. *Algorithmic learning in a random world*, volume 29. Springer.

Feiyang Wang, Zhongbao Zhang, Li Sun, Junda Ye, and Yang Yan. 2022. Dirie: knowledge graph embedding with dirichlet distribution. In *Proceedings of the ACM Web Conference 2022*, pages 3082–3091.

Quan Wang, Zhendong Mao, Bin Wang, and Li Guo. 2017. Knowledge graph embedding: A survey of approaches and applications. *IEEE transactions on knowledge and data engineering*, 29(12):2724–2743.

Han Xiao, Minlie Huang, Yu Hao, and Xiaoyan Zhu. 2015. Transg: A generative mixture model for knowledge graph embedding. *arXiv preprint arXiv:1509.05488*.

Bo Xiong, Shichao Zhu, Mojtaba Nayyeri, Chengjin Xu, Shirui Pan, Chuan Zhou, and Steffen Staab. 2022. Ultrahyperbolic knowledge graph embeddings. In *Proceedings of the 28th ACM SIGKDD Conference on Knowledge Discovery and Data Mining*, pages 2130–2139.

Bishan Yang, Wen-tau Yih, Xiaodong He, Jianfeng Gao, and Li Deng. 2014. Embedding entities and relations for learning and inference in knowledge bases. *arXiv preprint arXiv:1412.6575*.

Bishan Yang, Wen-tau Yih, Xiaodong He, Jianfeng Gao, and Li Deng. 2015. Embedding entities and relations for learning and inference in knowledge bases. In *ICLR (Poster)*.

Dongzhuoran Zhou, Baifan Zhou, Jieying Chen, Gong Cheng, Egor Kostylev, and Evgeny Kharlamov. 2021. Towards ontology reshaping for kg generation with user-in-the-loop: applied to bosch welding. In *Proceedings of the 10th International Joint Conference on Knowledge Graphs*, pages 145–150.

Dongzhuoran Zhou, Baifan Zhou, Zhuoxun Zheng, Ahmet Soylu, Gong Cheng, Ernesto Jimenez-Ruiz, Egor V Kostylev, and Evgeny Kharlamov. 2022. Ontology reshaping for knowledge graph construction: applied on bosch welding case. In *International Semantic Web Conference*, pages 770–790. Springer.

Yuqicheng Zhu, Nico Potyka, Mojtaba Nayyeri, Bo Xiong, Yunjie He, Evgeny Kharlamov, and Steffen Staab. 2024a. Predictive multiplicity of knowledge graph embeddings in link prediction. In *Findings of the Association for Computational Linguistics: EMNLP 2024*, pages 334–354.

Yuqicheng Zhu, Nico Potyka, Jiarong Pan, Bo Xiong, Yunjie He, Evgeny Kharlamov, and Steffen Staab. 2024b. Conformalized answer set prediction for knowledge graph embedding. *arXiv preprint arXiv:2408.08248*.

Yuqicheng Zhu, Nico Potyka, Bo Xiong, Trung-Kien Tran, Mojtaba Nayyeri, Evgeny Kharlamov, and Steffen Staab. 2024c. Approximating probabilistic inference in statistical el with knowledge graph embeddings. *arXiv preprint arXiv:2407.11821*.

Yuqicheng Zhu, Nico Potyka, Bo Xiong, Trung-Kien Tran, Mojtaba Nayyeri, Steffen Staab, and Evgeny Kharlamov. 2023. Towards statistical reasoning with ontology embeddings. In *ISWC (Poster/Demos/Industry)*.

Detecting Sexism in Tweets: A Sentiment Analysis and Graph Neural Network Approach

Diana P. Madera-Espíndola[1], **Zoe Caballero-Domínguez**[1], **Valeria J. Ramírez-Macías**[1], **Sabur Butt**[1,2], **Hector G. Ceballos**[1,2]

[1]Tecnológico de Monterrey, [2]Institute for the Future of Education

A01025835@tec.mx, A01747247@tec.mx, A01636965@tec.mx

saburb@tec.mx, ceballos@tec.mx

Abstract

In the digital age, social media platforms like Twitter serve as an extensive repository of public discourse, including instances of sexism. It is important to identify such behavior since radicalized ideologies can lead to real-world violent acts. This project aims to develop a deep learning-based tool that leverages a combination of BERT (both English and multilingual versions) and GraphSAGE, a Graph Neural Network (GNN) model, alongside sentiment analysis and natural language processing (NLP) techniques. The tool is designed to analyze tweets for sexism detection and classify them into five categories.

1 Introduction

In today's digital age, social media platforms such as Twitter have become central to public discourse, providing users with a space to express their thoughts and opinions, while also serving as a powerful tool for activism (ElSherief et al., 2017). However, while social media can empower victims to share their experiences, it also enables the spread of harmful ideologies such as sexism and Gender-Based Violence (GBV) (Martínez et al., 2021).

Peter Glick and Susan Fiske introduced a theory in 1996 that explains how power imbalances and mutual dependence between men and women give rise to two interconnected forms of sexist attitudes (Bareket and Fiske, 2023). The first, hostile sexism (HS), is marked by overtly attitudes, including aggression, resentment, objectification, sexual violence, and misogyny. In contrast, benevolent sexism (BS) praises women who conform to traditional roles, offering protection and admiration. However, this attitude is based on the belief that women are inherently weaker, reinforcing harmful stereotypes and gender inequality (Rodríguez-Sánchez et al., 2024).

This dynamic of sexism is not limited to interpersonal interactions but extends to digital platforms, where it takes on new forms and reaches broader audiences. Twitter, with its 280-character limit, often amplifies the problem of hate speech, including gender-based violence and sexism, by encouraging more aggressive and sensational content compared to platforms like Facebook (Founta et al., 2018). Therefore, systems that accurately detect hate speech are crucial for proactive moderation (Davidson et al., 2017).

Sentiment analysis techniques are commonly employed to extract insights about the public sentiment on a wide range of topics, including sexism (Caruccio et al., 2022; Anna Maria Górska and Jemielniak, 2023). When it comes to this classification task, a variety of approaches have been explored, incorporating both machine learning (Sreekumar et al., 2024) and deep learning tools (Castorena et al., 2021; Al-Garadi et al., 2022; Kalra and Zubiaga, 2021). A popular advancement in text representation involves the use of transformers, like BERT, which capture deep, bidirectional contextual information, significantly enhancing the understanding of language complexities (Magnossão et al., 2021; Butt et al., 2021).

However, despite its strengths, these techniques often struggle to capture the complex relationships and structures within texts, such as dependencies between words and tend to underperform when dealing with long-range dependencies. To address these limitations, Graph Neural Networks (GNNs) have been applied in text classification tasks, as they are capable of modeling relationships and dependencies between nodes by propagating information along edges (Khosravi et al., 2024; Utku et al., 2023; Singh and Singh, 2024). Additionally, to further enhance performance, recent approaches have sought to combine BERT embeddings with GNNs (Liu et al., 2025). Our approach builds on this by leveraging BERT's capacity to understand complex language contexts alongside GraphSAGE, a GNN model chosen for its ability to generate

Proceedings of the 2025 Conference of the Nations of the Americas Chapter of the Association for Computational Linguistics: Human Language Technologies (Volume 4: Student Research Workshop), pages 48–54
April 30 - May 1, 2025 ©2025 Association for Computational Linguistics

node representations by aggregating features from neighboring nodes (Lu et al., 2024).

Then the contributions of this research in addressing the sexism classification task are summarized as follows:

- The use of representation embeddings combined with GraphSAGE, a GNN model, for detecting and classifying sexism in social media text.

- A competitive tool's accuracy in classifying instances of sexism through a binary classification.

- A comparative study of our proposal against some relevant models in the EXIST 2021 competition.

The rest of the paper is structured with Section 2 covering the dataset and methodology of the proposed model, Section 3 presenting the results, and Section 4 discussing the findings.

2 Method and Data

2.1 Data Description

The dataset used in our study was sourced from the 2021 edition of the sEXism Identification in Social neTworks (EXIST) contest (Rodríguez-Sánchez et al., 2021; Montes et al., 2021), which aims to promote the automatic identification of sexism by providing a benchmark dataset. This dataset includes data from Twitter and Gab.com in both English and Spanish [1]. This distinction highlights the challenge of training a model on one type of structure (tweets) while testing it on a different structure (gabs) to evaluate its adaptability. For this work, we used only the English dataset, which contains 3,436 tweets for training and 2,208 for testing.

The classification task consists of two main subtasks. Task 1 is a binary classification problem, where automated systems must determine whether a message is sexist or non-sexist, as illustrated in Figure 1. The second subtask, shown in Figure 2, involves categorizing a message that has been identified as sexist according to the type of sexism it conveys, such as ideological and inequality, stereotyping and dominance, objectification, sexual violence, and misogyny or non-sexual violence.

[1] https://nlp.uned.es/exist2021/

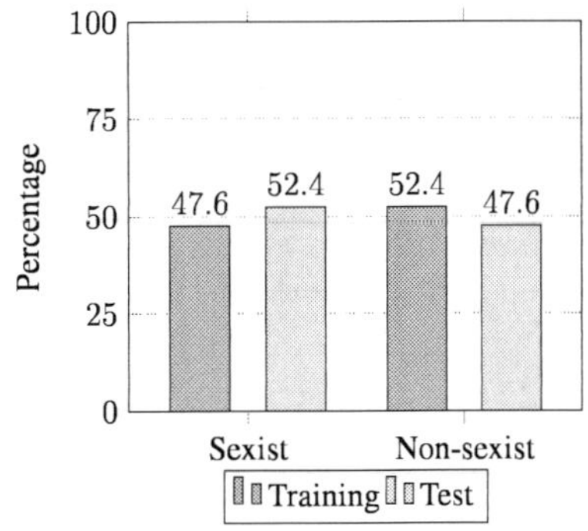

Figure 1: Proportion of Training and Test Datasets for Binary Classification for the EXIST dataset

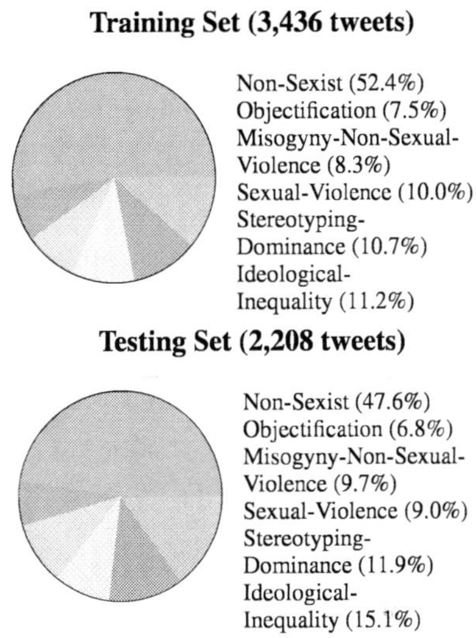

Figure 2: Comparative Class Distribution for English tweets in the EXIST dataset

2.2 Data Processing

In order to enhance the performance of the GraphSAGE. The cleaning process involved:

- Converting text to lowercase

- Removing HTTP links

- Removing Twitter mentions (@username)

- Removing punctuation marks

- Eliminating repeated consecutive letters to at most two consecutive letters

- Removing stop words

2.3 Graph Definition

GraphSAGE is a framework for inductive representation learning on large graphs. It is particularly useful for generating low-dimensional vector representations for nodes, especially in graphs with rich node attribute information (Hamilton et al., 2017). In our case, the graph captures relationships between tweets based on the similarity of their content. First, let us define a graph G as a tuple $G = (V, E)$, where V is the set of nodes (in this case, tweets) of the graph, and E is the set of edges (connections between similar tweets).

For the text numerical representation, we decided to experiment with both the English and Multilingual versions of Bidirectional Encoder Representations from Transformers (BERT and mBERT, respectively). We tested the multilingual version of mBERT to to assess its effectiveness in handling the complexities of multilingual examples, as social media content often contains tokens in multiple languages (Magnossão et al., 2021). Additionally, we included a sentiment polarity attribute because, as noted by (Raees and Fazilat, 2024), it is a key factor in identifying the positive or negative sentiment of a tweet.

Therefore in our graph, each node representing a tweet T_i was associated with four attributes: an embedding vector e_i generated by the pre-trained model, the sentiment polarity score, and two labels. The first label was a binary encoded label, while the second was a multiclass encoded label. Regarding the graph connections, we chose four metrics to appropriately weigh the edges, with the goal of forming a composite weight. Two of these metrics, include cosine similarity between the tweet embeddings and cosine similarity between TF-IDF vector representations (Nakajima and Sasaki, 2023). We decided to incorporate the vector representation TF-IDF to complement the embeddings, as it is a statistical measure used to evaluate the importance of a word in a document relative to a corpus (Khosravi et al., 2024).

For the remaining two metrics that contribute to the composite weight, we chose semantic similarity and sentiment agreement. For semantic similarity, we used the NLP model en-core-web-md from $SpaCy$, which computes the similarity between the embeddings of the tweets. For sentiment agreement, we used the sentiment polarity score from $TextBlob$ to calculate the sentiment of each tweet. The sentiment agreement is then determined by calculating

$$1 - abs(sent1, sent2) \tag{1}$$

where $sent1$ and $sent2$ represent the sentiment polarity scores of the two tweets being compared.

To identify the optimal weights for each metric, we conducted two experiments on the training set. One experiment used nodes generated by BERT, while the other used nodes generated by mBERT. For each pair of nodes, we calculated four key metrics: cosine similarity between embeddings, cosine similarity between TF-IDF vectors, semantic similarity, and sentiment agreement. To optimize memory usage, the training dataset was divided into smaller chunks during computation.

After calculating the four metrics, they were normalized to ensure compatibility with the Louvain algorithm. This algorithm partitions a network into communities by first assigning each node to its own community, then iteratively merging nodes or communities to maximize modularity. By optimizing modularity, the algorithm identifies clusters where nodes are more strongly connected to each other than to those outside the cluster (Kim and Sayama, 2019).

We tested 15 random weight combinations, each prioritizing a specific metric, to assess its impact on community formation. This approach enabled us to evaluate the importance of each metric in creating meaningful communities. Finally, we analyzed the results to determine the weight combination that produced the most cohesive community structure, using modularity as the evaluation criterion. Based on the experiment with the highest modularity score, we assigned the following weights:

$$\begin{aligned} \text{composite weight} = &\text{cosine similarity TF-IDF} \times 0.1 \\ &+ \text{semantic similarity} \times 0.8 \\ &+ \text{sentiment agreement} \times 0.1 \end{aligned} \tag{2}$$

Additionally, to reduce noise and avoid computational problems due to a very dense graph, we established a threshold of 0.7, ensuring that only edges with a similarity score above this threshold are created. Furthermore, we limited the number of connections per node to a maximum of 5. Finally, we construct the graph by creating an Adjacency matrix A, where each entry A_{i_j} corresponds to the edge between tweets T_i and T_j.

2.4 GraphSAGE

Unlike previous approaches that require all nodes to be available during the training of embeddings,

GraphSAGE leverages node feature information to create effective representations even for unseen nodes. This inductive property allows the algorithm to generalize beyond the trained data (Hamilton et al., 2017). As demonstrated by (Lu et al., 2024), integrating BERT into the GraphSAGE framework significantly improves generalization ability and classification accuracy compared to traditional graph-based and BERT-based models. While their study focused on classification within a citation network, they also tested their model on sentiment analysis for movie reviews, which motivated us to explore this GNN model for our task.

For Task 1, we used two layers with ReLU activation and a Sigmoid function for the output layer. The Adam optimizer was employed, with Binary Cross-Entropy as the loss function. For Task 2, we also used two layers with ReLU activation, but applied the argmax function for the output. The Adam optimizer was retained, and the loss function was changed to Cross-Entropy for multiclass classification. To address class imbalance, we assigned higher weights to less frequent classes, ensuring the model focused more on these during training.

2.5 Hyperparameter Optimization

We used Optuna (Akiba et al., 2019), a framework for hyperparameter optimization, targeting validation accuracy, which allowed the framework to iteratively test various configurations and select the best. The key hyperparameters optimized were hidden channels, dropout rate, learning rate, weight decay, and epochs. These were selected because hidden channels enhance feature learning, dropout rate helps reduce overfitting, learning rate and weight decay balance convergence and regularization, and epochs control the training depth and efficiency.

We tested two different graphs for both tasks: one with BERT embeddings, and another one with mBERT embeddings. We ran 100 Optuna trials for each one of the four models. Table 1 show the obtained best configurations for the hyperparameters. An important note is that we used a transductive training approach, where the training, validation, and test sets are part of the same graph but segmented through attribute-based masking. This setting enables us to leverage all available node information within the graph structure (Li et al., 2021).

Task	Hyperparameter	BERT graph	mBERT graph
Task 1	**Hidden channels**	62	62
Task 1	**Dropout rate**	0.178	0.1837
Task 1	**Learning rate**	0.0032	0.00078
Task 1	**Weight decay**	0.0049	0.0056
Task 1	**Epochs**	76	102
Task 2	**Hidden channels**	128	128
Task 2	**Dropout rate**	0.4170	0.5009
Task 2	**Learning rate**	9.1012	9.9856
Task 2	**Weight decay**	0.0061	0.0052
Task 2	**Epochs**	320	300

Table 1: Best hyperparameter configuration obtained by Optuna for both graphs in Task 1 (binary classification) and Task 2 (multiclass classification)

Task	Model	Accuracy	F1
Task 1	BERT	0.7020	0.7303
	mBERT	0.6359	0.6271
Task 2	BERT	0.5308	0.3783
	mBERT	0.5231	0.2981

Table 2: Performance Comparison of Both Models

3 Results

Results of both tasks are presented in Table 2 showing a comparison of the main metrics obtained on Task 1 (binary) between the first proposed model, which uses embeddings generated with BERT, and the second model, which uses embeddings generated with mBERT. It is important to note that the primary metric we are using to measure the success of our model is the F1-score.

Actual	Predicted	
	Sexist	Not Sexist
Sexist	True Positive 840	False Negative 318
Not Sexist	False Positive 340	True Negative 710

Table 3: Confusion Matrix for BERT Embeddings Model on Task 1

The BERT graph exhibited strong performance in distinguishing sexist tweets from non-sexist ones, achieving an accuracy of 0.702 and an F1 score of 0.731. In contrast, mBERT produced lower results for both metrics, highlighting the superiority of BERT over mBERT on this task. Table 3, presents the confusion matrix for the BERT model in this binary classification, showing similar error rates for false positives and false negatives. Although, the model slightly favors non-sexist classification, with 318 false negatives compared to 340 false positives, indicating a relatively balanced performance.

Act. \ Pred.	NS	II	SD	OBJ	SV	MNSV
NS	413	172	150	104	118	93
II	56	203	38	13	14	9
SD	45	62	87	28	25	15
OBJ	15	5	31	70	20	9
SV	16	24	22	25	82	29
MNSV	29	36	34	27	24	65

Table 4: Confusion Matrix for BERT Embeddings Model on Task 2. NS: Non Sexist, II: Ideological Inequality, SD: Stereotyping Dominance, OBJ: Objectification, SV: Sexual Violence, MNSV: Misogyny Non Sexual Violence

For Task 2, both embeddings showed lower performance overall; however, BERT continued to demonstrate its advantage over mBERT with an accuracy of 0.5308 and an F1 score of 0.3783. Table 4, displays the confusion matrix for BERT in this multiclass classification task, revealing the highest confusion between the Non-Sexist (NS) and Ideological Inequality (II) classes, with 172 instances of II misclassified as NS. There was also significant confusion between NS and Stereotyping Dominance (SD), with 150 misclassifications. Overall, the model shows a bias toward classifying instances as NS but performs best at identifying the Ideological Inequality (II) class, with a precision of 61.0%. It struggles the most with the MNSV (30.2% precision) and SD (33.2% precision) classes.

4 Discussion and Related Work

The application of GNNs, such as GraphSAGE, to text classification, remains relatively unexplored but holds considerable promise. Our model demonstrated competitive performance on Task 1. However, it requires improvements for Task 2.

The first-place team in the EXIST contest (Magnossão et al., 2021) created a second version of both BERT and mBERT by translating some instances from Spanish to English to enhance the training data. They also implemented ensemble strategies, combining predictions from individual models, which consistently outperformed the single mBERT and BERT models. Therefore, integrating some data strategies and an ensemble of GraphSAGE networks could be a worthy experiment for future research. Nonetheless, this entry was not the only using data augmentation strategies. Butt et al. (Butt et al., 2021) used a 'Back Translation' strategy, where they input the text in the source language, translate it to another second language, and finally back to the source language. Furthermore, data augmentation strategies can also be utilized to mitigate the class imbalance problem of Task 2.

Among the models reviewed by the contestants, MB-Courage (Wilkens and Ognibene, 2021) was the model most closely aligned with our proposed approach, as it also utilizes GNN for identifying sexism. However, while MB-Courage employs Graph Convolutional Neural Networks (GCN), we use GraphSAGE, a distinct variation of GNN. In terms of performance, our model outperformed MB-Courage's best proposal on F1-score for Task 1. Regarding Task 2, our best proposal proved to be the least effective among the compared models showed in Table 5. We attribute the low performance in this second task to class imbalance and the model's difficulty in understanding the context of statements. This explains why it can generalize for two classes but struggles to adapt to multiclass classification.This would also explain why proposal that performed data augmentation performed well. By adding more examples of each class, the class imbalance could be lessen and, in turn, the model may enough data to distinguish the different classes.

As a final point, exploring alternative text similarity metrics such as emotion detection, Latent Dirichlet Allocation (LDA) topic modeling, or ConceptNet similarity, could provide valuable insights for defining the graph structure, leading to improved performance in second tasks. Moreover, improved text preprocessing and experimenting with different embedding models could help preserve higher-quality information.

Conclusion and future work

Our best model archived an F1 score of 0.7331 on Task 1, which demonstrates competitive performance, as this would have placed us 29th out of

Task	Model	Accuracy	F1 Score
Task 1	**mBERT & GraphSAGE**	0.636	0.627
Task 1	**BERT & GraphSAGE**	0.702	0.730
Task 1	**Ensemble Model**	0.789	0.780
Task 1	**GCN**	0.715	0.715
Task 1	**BERT & Data Augmentation**	0.728	0.727
Task 2	**BERT & GraphSAGE**	0.531	0.378
Task 2	**mBERT & GraphSAGE**	0.523	0.298
Task 2	**Ensemble Model**	0.658	0.579
Task 2	**GCN**	0.595	0.459
Task 2	**BERT & Data Augmentation**	0.553	0.491

Table 5: Accuracy and F1 scores of our models for Task 1 (binary classification) and Task 2 (multiclass classification), compared to those reported by Magnossão de Paula et al., Wilkens & Ognibene, and Butt et al.

72 participants in the competition, and also outperforms the only Graph Neural Network proposal used in the competition. This performance shows the potential of using Graph Neural Networks for sexism in text settings.

However, further enhancements can be made to improve upon these results, especially in Task 2, where our model only managed an F1 score of 0.378 (56th place out of 72). Exploring data augmentation techniques and incorporating an ensemble of GraphSAGE networks could be valuable, particularly for tasks like Task 2, where class imbalance was a significant factor. Additionally, experimenting with different text similarity metrics and enhancing data pre-processing approaches could lead to better performance.

References

Takuya Akiba, Shotaro Sano, Toshihiko Yanase, Takeru Ohta, and Masanori Koyama. 2019. Optuna: A next-generation hyperparameter optimization framework. In *Proceedings of the 25th ACM SIGKDD International Conference on Knowledge Discovery and Data Mining*.

Mohammed Ali Al-Garadi, Sangmi Kim, Yuting Guo, Elise Warren, Yuan-Chi Yang, Sahithi Lakamana, and Abeed Sarker. 2022. Natural language model for automatic identification of intimate partner violence reports from twitter. *Array*, 15:100217.

Karolina Kulicka Anna Maria Górska and Dariusz Jemielniak. 2023. Men not going their own way: a thick big data analysis of #mgtow and #feminism tweets. *Feminist Media Studies*, 23(8):3774–3792.

Orly Bareket and Susan T Fiske. 2023. A systematic review of the ambivalent sexism literature: Hostile sexism protects men's power; benevolent sexism guards traditional gender roles. *Psychological bulletin*.

Sabur Butt, Noman Ashraf, Grigori Sidorov, and Alexander F Gelbukh. 2021. Sexism identification using bert and data augmentation-exist2021. In *IberLEF@ SEPLN*, pages 381–389.

Loredana Caruccio, Stefano Cirillo, Vincenzo Deufemia, Giuseppe Polese, and Roberto Stanzione. 2022. Data analytics on twitter for evaluating women inclusion and safety in modern society. In *itaDATA*.

Carlos M. Castorena, Itzel M. Abundez, Roberto Alejo, Everardo E. Granda-Gutiérrez, Eréndira Rendón, and Octavio Villegas. 2021. Deep neural network for gender-based violence detection on twitter messages. *Mathematics*, 9(8).

Thomas Davidson, Dana Warmsley, Michael Macy, and Ingmar Weber. 2017. Automated hate speech detection and the problem of offensive language. *Preprint*, arXiv:1703.04009.

Mai ElSherief, Elizabeth Belding, and Dana Nguyen. 2017. #NotOkay: Understanding gender-based violence in social media. *Proceedings of the International AAAI Conference on Web and Social Media*, 11(1).

Antigoni-Maria Founta, Constantinos Djouvas, Despoina Chatzakou, Ilias Leontiadis, Jeremy Blackburn, Gianluca Stringhini, Athena Vakali, Michael Sirivianos, and Nicolas Kourtellis. 2018. Large scale crowdsourcing and characterization of twitter abusive behavior. *Preprint*, arXiv:1802.00393.

Will Hamilton, Zhitao Ying, and Jure Leskovec. 2017. Inductive representation learning on large graphs. *Advances in neural information processing systems*, 30.

Amikul Kalra and Arkaitz Zubiaga. 2021. Sexism identification in tweets and gabs using deep neural networks. *arXiv preprint*.

Asal Khosravi, Zahed Rahmati, and Ali Vefghi. 2024. Relational graph convolutional networks for sentiment analysis. *arXiv preprint*.

Minjun Kim and Hiroki Sayama. 2019. The power of communities: A text classification model with automated labeling process using network community detection.

Chen Li, Xutan Peng, Hao Peng, Jianxin Li, and Lihong Wang. 2021. Textgtl: Graph-based transductive learning for semi-supervised text classification via structure-sensitive interpolation. In *Proceedings of the Thirtieth International Joint Conference on Artificial Intelligence*, page 2680–2686, Montreal, Canada. International Joint Conferences on Artificial Intelligence Organization.

Qi Liu, Kejing Xiao, and Zhaopeng Qian. 2025. A hybrid re-fusion model for text classification. *Scientific Reports*, 15(1):9333.

Junwen Lu, Lingrui Zheng, and Moudong Zhang. 2024. Application of bert-graphsage model in text and paper classification tasks. In *Advanced Data Mining and Applications: 20th International Conference, ADMA 2024, Sydney, NSW, Australia, December 3–5, 2024, Proceedings, Part V*, page 315–327, Berlin, Heidelberg. Springer-Verlag.

Angel Felipe Magnossão, Roberto Fray da Silva, and Ipek Baris Schlicht. 2021. Sexism prediction in spanish and english tweets using monolingual and multilingual bert and ensemble models. *CoRR*, arXiv:2111.04551.

Fátima Martínez, Carolina Pacheco, and Marco Galicia. 2021. The #metoo movement in twitter: Fighting gender-based violence. In *Information Technology and Systems*, pages 36–44, Cham. Springer International Publishing.

M. Montes, P. Rosso, J. Gonzalo, E. Aragón, R. Agerri, M.A. Álvarez Carmona, E. Álvarez Mellado, J. Carrillo-de Albornoz, L. Chiruzzo, L. Freitas, H. Gómez Adorno, Y. Gutiérrez, S.M. Jiménez-Zafra, S. Lima, F.M. Plaza-del Arco, and M. Taulé. 2021. In *Proceedings of the Iberian Languages Evaluation Forum (IberLEF 2021)*.

Hiromu Nakajima and Minoru Sasaki. 2023. Text classification based on the heterogeneous graph considering the relationships between documents. *Big Data and Cognitive Computing*, 7(4).

Muhammad Raees and Samina Fazilat. 2024. Lexicon-based sentiment analysis on text polarities with evaluation of classification models. *Preprint*, arXiv:2409.12840.

Francisco Rodríguez-Sánchez, Jorge Carrillo-de Albornoz, and Laura Plaza. 2024. Detecting sexism in social media: an empirical analysis of linguistic patterns and strategies. *Applied Intelligence*, 54(21):10995–11019.

Francisco Rodríguez-Sánchez, Laura Plaza Jorge Carrillo-de Albornoz, Julio Gonzalo, Paolo Rosso, Miriam Comet, and Trinidad Donoso. 2021. Overview of exist 2021: sexism identification in social networks. *Procesamiento del Lenguaje Natural*, 67(0):195–207.

Loitongbam Gyanendro Singh and Sanasam Ranbir Singh. 2024. Sentiment analysis of tweets using text and graph multi-views learning. *Knowledge and Information Systems*, 66(5):2965–2985.

Murari Sreekumar, Shreyas Karthik, Durairaj Thenmozhi, Shriram Gopalakrishnan, and Krithika Swaminathan. 2024. Sexism identification in tweets using machine learning approaches. In *Conference and Labs of the Evaluation Forum*.

Anıl Utku, Can Umit, and Aslan Serpil. 2023. Detection of hateful twitter users with graph convolutional network model. *Earth Science Informatics*, 16(1):329–343.

Rodrigo Souza Wilkens and Dimitri Ognibene. 2021. Mb-courage @ exist: Gcn classification for sexism identification in social networks. In *IberLEF@SEPLN*.

Towards Codec-LM Co-design for Neural Codec Language Models

Shih-Lun Wu* [1,2] **Aakash Lahoti** [1,3] **Arjun Desai** [1] **Karan Goel** [1]
Chris Donahue† [3] **Albert Gu**† [1,3]

[1] Cartesia AI [2] MIT [3] CMU

* Work done during internship at Cartesia AI † Co-senior author **Correspondence:** slseanwu@mit.edu

Abstract

Neural codec language models (or *codec LMs*) are emerging as a powerful framework for audio generation tasks like text-to-speech (TTS). These models leverage advancements in language modeling and residual vector quantization (RVQ)-based audio codecs, which compress audios into discrete codes for LMs to process. Despite the close interdependence of codecs and LMs in these systems, research on codecs and LMs has largely remained siloed. In this work, we propose three techniques for better codec-LM co-design: (i) a *frame-wise codec encoder* that improves both LM log-likelihood and end-to-end TTS metrics, (ii) *LM codebook level dropout*, a method to efficiently navigate a portion of the codec-LM design space by training a single LM, and (iii) *increased codec frame duration*, which we show can accelerate inference while maintaining end-to-end performance. Our experiments demonstrate that combining all three co-design techniques results in doubled inference speed, and improvements in intelligibility, audio quality, and speaker control in TTS relative to a siloed baseline.

1 Introduction

Neural codec language models (or codec LMs) (van den Oord et al., 2017; Wu et al., 2024) have recently emerged as a prominent framework for text-to-speech (TTS) (Tan et al., 2021; Wang et al., 2023; Yang et al., 2024) and general audio generation tasks (van den Oord et al., 2016; Copet et al., 2023; Borsos et al., 2023; Yang et al., 2024), replacing autoregressive methods that model continuous raw waveforms (van den Oord et al., 2016; Kalchbrenner et al., 2018; Goel et al., 2022). The success of codec LMs can be attributed to improvements in the architecture, scaling, and efficiency of language models (LMs) (Vaswani et al., 2017; Brown et al., 2020; Dao et al., 2022; Gu and Dao, 2023), as well as increasingly high-fidelity convolutional audio codecs that employ the residual vector quantization (RVQ) technique (Zeghidour et al., 2021; Défossez et al., 2023; Kumar et al., 2023), bridging continuous-domain audio generation tasks with LM methods that model discrete tokens.

Although the codec and the LM are closely coupled, they represent relatively isolated research areas. Research on codecs (Zeghidour et al., 2021; Défossez et al., 2023; Kumar et al., 2023; Ahn et al., 2024) primarily focuses on achieving higher compression rates (i.e., lower bandwidths) while maintaining reconstruction quality. Conversely, research on codec-based LMs (Borsos et al., 2023; Wang et al., 2023; Copet et al., 2023; Yang et al., 2024) typically treats the codec as a fixed module and explores how to best model the codec tokens. (We defer more detailed Related Work to Appendix A.) While the design space of codecs and LMs combined is too large to explore exhaustively, considering each in isolation may be suboptimal when the goal is to improve the end-to-end performance.

In this work, we aim to break the isolation and uncover co-design principles between the codec and the LM. We identify several aspects that play a key role in the interactions between the two, and substantially impact the end-to-end generation quality and/or efficiency. Leveraging these co-design insights, we propose actionable interventions which can improve the performance and efficiency (both at training and inference) of end-to-end audio generation systems. Our technical contributions are:

- Considering the different impacts of receptive field overlaps in the RVQ codec encoder and decoder, we introduce a **framewise codec encoder** (Sec. 3.1), which encodes each frame (i.e., non-overlapping chunks in input audio) independently. We find that this leads to improvements in the LM log-likelihood (>8% higher), and all end-to-end TTS metrics (Table 1).
- Observing that the end-to-end generation per-

Proceedings of the 2025 Conference of the Nations of the Americas Chapter of the Association for Computational Linguistics: Human Language Technologies (Volume 4: Student Research Workshop), pages 55–65

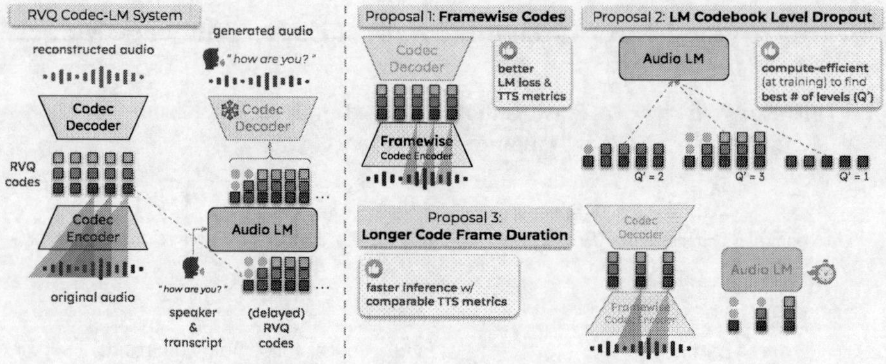

Figure 1: Overview of an RVQ-based codec-LM system for TTS (left), our contributions (right, **Proposals 1, 2 & 3**), and associated benefits. (Shaded triangles are receptive fields per code frame.)

formance is heavily influenced by number of RVQ codebook levels modeled by the LM, we propose **LM codebook level dropout** (Sec. 3.2), which allows practitioners to efficiently tune this salient hyperparameter of the codec-LM design space in a single LM training run (Fig. 2).

- As codec frame duration is inversely proportional to LM sequence length, we show that using **longer frame durations** (Sec. 3.3), while tuning other codec hyperparameters accordingly, can accelerate end-to-end TTS inference, and preserve TTS metrics (Table 2).

A schematic diagram of our end-to-end audio generation system and proposed techniques can be found in Fig. 1. Our experiments are based on a streamable (i.e., causal) variant of the DAC codec (Kumar et al., 2023), and we implement our changes (i.e., framewise encoder, and longer frame duration) without altering its architecture. We then train *Delay*-pattern LMs (Copet et al., 2023) for TTS, where LM codebook level dropout is applied, on the RVQ codes from our codecs. We finally demonstrate that combining all three co-design techniques doubles the end-to-end TTS inference speeds while *improving* all end-to-end TTS metrics (Table 3) concerning intelligibility, audio quality, and speaker control.

We open source our implementation of the framewise and causal DAC (Kumar et al., 2023) codecs at `https://github.com/slSeanWU/descript-audio-codec/tree/main`.

2 Technical Background

Residual vector quantization (RVQ)-based audio codecs. An RVQ-based audio codec compresses a continuous *waveform* $w \in \mathbb{R}^{\mathrm{Tf_s}}$, where T is the duration (in seconds) and $\mathrm{f_s}$ is the sampling rate (in Hz) of the waveform, into discrete *codes* $\boldsymbol{x} \in \mathcal{V}^{\mathrm{Tf_x} \times Q}$. Here, $\mathcal{V} := \{1, 2, \dots, |\mathcal{V}|\}$ represents the *codebook*, $\mathrm{f_x}$ (typically much smaller than $\mathrm{f_s}$) is the *frame rate* (in Hz) of the codec, and Q is the number of *codebook levels* used to represent each frame. We also call downsampling rate of the codec, i.e., $\mathrm{f_s}/\mathrm{f_x}$, the *frame size* (an integer number of audio *samples*) and $1/\mathrm{f_x}$ the *frame duration* (in seconds). The term *residual* refers to how the Q codebook levels are structured to progressively refine the quantization (Zeghidour et al., 2021). Let the unquantized representation (i.e., the codec encoder output) for the i-th frame be denoted by $\boldsymbol{h}_i^{(1)} \in \mathbb{R}^D$, where D is the codec encoder's output dimension. The RVQ process works iteratively for each level $q \in \{1, \dots, Q\}$ on a frame-by-frame basis, quantizing the residual information from preceding levels using a level-wise learned codebook $\mathcal{C}^{(q)} : \mathcal{V} \to \mathbb{R}^D$. The operations at each level are:

$$x_{i,q} := \arg\min_{\tilde{x} \in \mathcal{V}} \|\boldsymbol{h}_i^{(q)} - \mathcal{C}^{(q)}(\tilde{x})\|_2^2 \quad (1)$$

$$\boldsymbol{h}_i^{(q+1)} := \boldsymbol{h}_i^{(q)} - \mathcal{C}^{(q)}(x_{i,q}) \,, \quad (2)$$

where $x_{i,q} \in \mathcal{V}$ is an element in the code sequence $\boldsymbol{x}$, and $\mathcal{C}^{(q)}(x_{i,q}) \in \mathbb{R}^D$ is the quantized representation corresponding to $x_{i,q}$. The level-wise quantized representations are summed frame-by-frame, i.e., $\sum_q^Q \mathcal{C}^{(q)}(x_{i,q})$; $\forall i \in \{1, \dots, \mathrm{Tf_x}\}$, and sent to the decoder to reconstruct the original waveform.

Typically, during RVQ codec training, *quantizer dropout* (Zeghidour et al., 2021; Kumar et al., 2023) is applied, which sometimes performs Eqn. (1) and (2) for $Q_{\mathrm{trunc}} < Q$ levels. This enables the codec to encode and reconstruct audio waveforms at all Q possible RVQ level counts.

Language modeling with *Delay* pattern of RVQ codes. We can construct an end-to-end audio generative model by training an LM on the RVQ codes $\boldsymbol{x} \in \mathcal{V}^{\mathrm{Tf_x} \times Q'}$, where $Q' \in \{1, \ldots, Q\}$ is a subset of the RVQ levels to model. To model such 2D-structured codes, we adopt the *Delay* pattern proposed in (Copet et al., 2023), which makes a good tradeoff between the efficiency and efficacy of modeling the RVQ codes $\boldsymbol{x}$. Instead of naively flattening $\boldsymbol{x}$ to a sequence of $\mathrm{Tf_x} \times Q'$ elements, it shifts the q-th level of $\boldsymbol{x}$ to the right by q positions, creating a shifted code sequence $\boldsymbol{x}^{(\text{delay})} \in \mathcal{V}^{(\mathrm{Tf_x}+Q'-1) \times Q'}$, where each frame is $\boldsymbol{x}_t^{(\text{delay})} := [x_{t-q+1,\,q}]_{q=1}^{Q'}$. Then, the LM models:

$$p(\boldsymbol{x}) = p(\boldsymbol{x}^{(\text{delay})}) := \prod_{t=1}^{\mathrm{Tf_x}+Q'-1} p(\boldsymbol{x}_t^{(\text{delay})} \mid \boldsymbol{x}_{<t}^{(\text{delay})}), \tag{3}$$

predicting the elements in each frame $\boldsymbol{x}_t^{(\text{delay})}$ in parallel. Though omitted in Eqn. (3), the LM is typically trained with conditions $\boldsymbol{y}$ expected from the user, e.g., text transcripts and speaker characteristics. Bringing all components together, our codec-LM audio generation system models:

$$p(\boldsymbol{w}, \boldsymbol{x} \mid \boldsymbol{y}) := \underbrace{p(\boldsymbol{w} \mid \boldsymbol{x})}_{\text{learned by codec}} \cdot \underbrace{p(\boldsymbol{x} \mid \boldsymbol{y})}_{\text{learned by LM}}, \tag{4}$$

where conditional independence between waveform $\boldsymbol{w}$ and user inputs $\boldsymbol{y}$ is assumed given codes $\boldsymbol{x}$. We note that $p(\boldsymbol{w} \mid \boldsymbol{x})$ is typically a deterministic mapping parameterized by the RVQ codec decoder.

3 Method

3.1 Codes with non-overlapping receptive fields (*Framewise codec encoder*)

Most common RVQ audio codecs (Zeghidour et al., 2021; Défossez et al., 2023; Kumar et al., 2023) set the stride size of each 1D convolutional layer to be smaller than the filter size. This way the neighboring outputs (along the time dimension) have overlapping receptive fields. When we consider the entire codec encoder, where multiple convolutional layers are stacked, this overlapping property at each layer causes the receptive field of each code frame $\boldsymbol{x}_t$ to overlap with those of preceding code frames $[\boldsymbol{x}_{t-k}, \ldots, \boldsymbol{x}_{t-1}]$, assuming the codec is causal.[1] A similar property also holds in the codec decoder, i.e., each sample in the reconstructed waveform $\hat{\boldsymbol{w}}$ is influenced by multiple code frames.

[1]For example, for the architecture of DAC (Kumar et al., 2023), the extent of overlap is $k = 8$.

If we reason about the frame-level overlaps, it is intuitive that they benefit the decoder, as the mutual information between multiple code frames can be leveraged for improved reconstruction. On the other hand, whether these overlaps are advantageous on the encoder side is less clear. They may provide the opportunity for the codec to pack information in high-complexity waveform segments (e.g., fast speech with frequent intonation changes) into neighboring code frames corresponding to low-information segments (e.g., silence), hence improving audio reconstruction. However, this could be detrimental for the downstream LM as each code frame may hold varying amounts of (confounding) information from preceding frames.

Therefore, we propose a setup where the codes are encoded *framewise*, i.e., each code frame $\boldsymbol{x}_t$ has a receptive field covering only $\mathrm{f_s}/\mathrm{f_x}$ waveform samples, without overlapping with other code frames. Operationally, this is achieved by reshaping the waveform (i.e., the inital input to the codec encoder) from $(B, \mathrm{Tf_s}, 1)$, where the dimensions represent (batch, sequence, channels), to $(B\mathrm{Tf_x},\ \mathrm{f_s}/\mathrm{f_x},\ 1)$. Since the downsampling rate of the entire encoder is precisely $\mathrm{f_s}/\mathrm{f_x}$, the final encoder output is of shape $(B\mathrm{Tf_x}, 1, D)$, which we then reshape back to $(B, \mathrm{Tf_x}, D)$ before quantization as in normal codecs with frame-level overlaps. Note that no architectural changes are required.

This setup with *encoder-framewise* and *decoder-overlapping* receptive fields retains desirable properties such as leveraging mutual information between code frames for reconstruction, Also, the information unique to each frame of waveform samples is encoded *distinctly* into one code frame, instead of spilling over multiple code frames, which we anticipate might benefit the downstream LM.

3.2 LM Codebook level dropout (*CL drop*)

Here we propose a novel method designed to increase the efficiency of hyperparameter tuning for the number of codec RVQ levels Q' used when training the downstream LM. The choice of the hyperparameter Q' can have a substantial impact on the end-to-end audio generation performance of the codec LM system. While increasing Q' monotonically improves codec audio reconstruction due to a wider information bottleneck, its impact on the combined codec LM system is ambiguous. Using too low of a Q' value in the LM could result in poor audio quality, while using too high of a value could be detrimental as modeling finer-grained lev-

Codec setting	Framewise Enc. ?	Codec Recons. Mel-L1↓	Text-to-Speech NLL↓	WER↓	NISQA↑	Spk. sim.↑	Uncond. Music NLL↓	FAD↓
Causal	✗	**.846**	5.46±.00	4.12±.35	4.35±.01	80.2±.1	6.06±.01	18.7±1.2
Proposed	✓	.873	**4.97**±.02	**3.71**±.19	**4.37**±.02	**80.7**±.2	**5.16**±.00	**17.1**±0.8

Table 1: Codec encoder receptive field settings vs. end-to-end TTS & music generation performance. Our proposed **framewise codec encoder** (Sec. 3.1) consistently beats the commonly used streamable setting (i.e., *Causal*) both on LM likelihood (cf. NLL) and all end-to-end metrics. Stdev over 5 runs follow ±.

els may: (i) present information that is too stochastic for the LM to process effectively, or (ii) shift the LM's capacity away from the coarser-grained levels which contain more crucial structural or semantic information about the audio.[2]

However, naively training $\mathcal{O}(Q)$ LMs to tune Q' is computationally expensive. Thus, we propose *codebook level dropout* (CL drop), which trains just a single LM that allows evaluation/inference at all possible level counts up to Q, analogous to the quantizer dropout method used to train the codec. To perform CL drop, we first define a *dropout distribution* $\mathcal{P}(q)$ over the all levels $q \in \{1, \dots, Q\}$, and then during LM training, we truncate inputs $\boldsymbol{x}^{(\text{delay})}$ along the level dimension according to $\mathcal{P}(q)$. The LM's training objective can hence be written as:

$$\min_{\theta} \mathbb{E}_{(\boldsymbol{x},\boldsymbol{y})\sim\mathcal{D},Q'\sim\mathcal{P}(q)} \left[-\log p_\theta \left(\boldsymbol{x}^{(\text{delay})}_{:,:Q'} \mid \boldsymbol{y} \right) \right] \quad (5)$$

where $\mathcal{D}$ is the LM training set with paired conditions $\boldsymbol{y}$ and RVQ codes $\boldsymbol{x}$ for the desired audio, and θ is the set of the LM's trainable parameters.

For CL drop to be effective in determining the best Q', its end-to-end performance profile across different level counts should closely mirror the trends without CL drop (i.e., the 'end-to-end TTS' curve in Fig. 3). Intuitively, the choice of $\mathcal{P}(q)$ is critical in preserving the trends, as it governs how much the LM's focus is shifted toward the lower (coarser-grained) levels.[3]

3.3 Navigating other codec hyperparameters

In addition to the number of RVQ levels (Q), there are two additional hyperparameters that affect the compression factor of the codec: (i) the codec's frame duration ($1/\text{f}_\text{x}$), and (ii) the codebook size ($|\mathcal{V}|$). The bitrate of the codec, equal to $Q\text{f}_\text{x}\log_2(|\mathcal{V}|)$ bits per second, is a function of these three factors and directly impacts the reconstruction quality. In siloed codec design, these three factors can be traded off freely to optimize for higher reconstruction quality at some fixed bitrate. However, in a co-design context, the LM's behavior can be impacted by different tradeoffs even when the codec's bitrate is kept fixed.

Here we make several observations about frame duration and codebook size respectively in the context of codec-LM co-design. From Eqn. (3), we can observe that the Delay LM sequence length is inversely proportional to frame duration. Thus, increasing it by a factor of two can roughly halve sequence length, resulting in efficiency gains and reduced inference latency. (Note that either $|\mathcal{V}|$ or Q should be increased accordingly to preserve audio quality.)

On the other hand, increasing the codebook size $|\mathcal{V}|$ may have mixed impacts on the LM. On the positive side, assuming the frame duration and bitrate are controlled, using a larger codebook (and hence fewer RVQ levels) reduces the extent of packing information from multiple (i.e., Q') code frames into one Delay LM timestep $\boldsymbol{x}^{(\text{delay})}_t$. However, increasing only $|\mathcal{V}|$ while holding Q constant leads to an exponential growth in the LM's vocabulary size (and embedding parameters) relative to a linear increase in bitrate. This growth can inflate the LM's memory footprint and introduce potential modeling challenges. Thus, while our CL drop technique can efficiently find the best Q' given a fixed $|\mathcal{V}|$, finding the optimal $|\mathcal{V}|$ still requires trial and error.

4 Experiments and Discussion

We first conduct experiments specifically for each proposed technique (i.e., Sec 3.1, 3.2, and 3.3) to elucidate their individual effects, and finally combine them to show their collective benefits. We use word error rate (WER), NISQA (Mittag et al., 2021), and cosine similarity of speaker embeddings (Jung et al., 2022) to evaluate the *intelligibility*, *audio quality*, and *speaker control* of end-to-end TTS generations. For music generation, we use Fréchet audio distance (FAD) (Kilgour et al., 2019) to capture overall quality. More experimental setups are deferred to Appendix C.

[2] Experiments on the impact Q' are in Appendix B.

[3] Experiments on different $\mathcal{P}(q)$'s are in Appendix D.

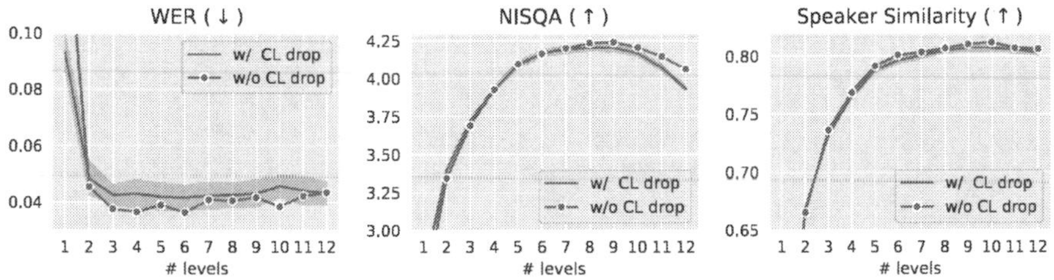

Figure 2: Number of RVQ codebook levels used by LM vs. end-to-end TTS metrics. Training one LM with **codebook level dropout** (**'CL drop'**, Sec. 3.2) leads to performance trends that closely follow training $Q = 12$ LMs w/o CL drop at each $Q' \in \{1, \ldots, 12\}$. Note that practitioners can then train a second LM at the found optimal level count w/o CL drop for best possible performance. Shaded bands represent stdev over 3 runs.

Codec Config				*Codec Recons.*	*Text-to-Speech*			*Efficiency*
Frame dur.	$\log_2(\lvert\mathcal{V}\rvert)$	Q'	Rel. bitrate	Mel-L1↓	WER↓	NISQA↑	Spk. sim.↑	Inf. speedup↑
11ms	10	9	1.00×	.873	3.71 $\pm$.19	4.37 $\pm$.02	80.7 $\pm$.2	1.00×
11ms	15	6	1.00×	.874	3.73 $\pm$.28	4.33 $\pm$.01	80.4 $\pm$.1	1.01×
22ms	10	16	0.89×	.888	4.21 $\pm$.33	**4.42** $\pm$.01	**81.0** $\pm$.1	1.94×
22ms	15	11	0.92×	.876	**3.55** $\pm$.36	4.33 $\pm$.01	79.3 $\pm$.1	2.00×
44ms	10	32	0.89×	.875	6.73	4.14	76.7	3.20×
44ms	15	20	0.83×	.871	4.53	3.65	73.2	**3.77**×

Table 2: Effects of using **longer frame durations** (Sec. 3.3), holding audio reconstruction quality approximately constant by varying codebook size $|\mathcal{V}|$ and/or # of RVQ levels Q'. We measure the actual inference time (LM & codec decoding combined) over 50 samples with batch size 1 and treat the first row as the baseline for the 'Inf. speedup' column. In general, using a 2× frame duration (22ms) strikes best balance between performance and efficiency. Stdev over 5 runs follow $\pm$. First row is the default configuration inherited from DAC.

Framewise codec encoder. Table 1 presents a comparison of audio reconstruction and downstream TTS (and music) generation performance with and without the use of our proposed framewise codec encoder. Here, we adopt the default DAC (Kumar et al., 2023) codec configurations.[4] Our framewise codec encoder setting **outperforms** the default streamable *causal* setting consistently, both **on LM likelihood** (>8% lower NLL) **and all end-to-end TTS and music generation metrics**. Notably, it is slightly worse on Mel-L1, underscoring the fact that **better audio reconstruction does not always translate to better end-to-end performance**. Due to its advantage, we conduct all subsequent experiments with framewise codec encoders, unless otherwise specified.

LM codebook level dropout (CL drop). Results of training the LM with codebook level dropout (see Sec. 3.2) are presented in Fig. 2. To examine how end-to-end performance evolves in the higher-bitrate regime, we use 15-bit codebooks ($\log_2(|\mathcal{V}|) = 15$) and codebook levels $Q = 12$ for the codec.[5] We experiment with various dropout distributions $\mathcal{P}(q)$ (see App. D for details) and conclude that it is best to train at the full level count (i.e., 12 in this case) for 90% of the steps and uniformly distribute the remaining 10% to all lower level counts. The curves in Fig. 2 show that training a single LM with CL drop produces a performance profile closely aligned with training 12 separate LMs without CL drop. This demonstrates that **CL drop is a reliable method for practitioners to efficiently optimize for the level count Q' with significantly reduced training compute**. Besides, the curves also show that WER, which focuses on (coarser) word-level information, reaches the best early at 3∼4 levels, while NISQA and speaker similarity, which are tied more closely to the fine-grained details, peak at around 9 levels. Though different metrics behave differently w.r.t. level count, we find that **choosing the best level count based on FAD** (shown in Fig. 3, which uses the same codec as here and would suggest using 9 levels) **achieves a balanced performance between all the TTS metrics** we consider.

[4]Frame duration $(1/f_x) = 11$ms; number of RVQ levels (Q and Q') $= 9$; codebook size per level ($|\mathcal{V}|$) $= 2^{10}$.

[5]amounting to a max bitrate that is 2× that of official DAC.

Proposals			*Codec Config*			*Text-to-Speech Metrics*			*Efficiency*
#1	**#2**	**#3**	Frame dur.	$\log_2(\lvert\mathcal{V}\rvert)$	$Q' : Q$	WER↓	NISQA↑	Spk. sim.↑	Inf. speedup↑
✗	✗	✗	11ms	10	9 : 9	4.12 ±.35	4.35 ±.01	80.2 ±.1	1.00×
✓	✗	✗	11ms	10	9 : 9	**3.71** ±.19	4.37 ±.02	80.7 ±.2	1.01×
✓	✗	✓	22ms	10	16:16	4.21 ±.33	*4.42* ±.01	**81.0** ±.1	*1.95*×
✓	✓	✓	22ms	10	14:16	*3.86* ±.19	**4.43** ±.01	*80.8* ±.2	**2.01**×

Table 3: Combined improvements from using multiple proposed techniques—**#1**: Framewise codec encoder; **#2**: CL drop; **#3**: Longer frame duration. Q' denotes the # of levels the LM is trained with for end-to-end TTS, while Q denotes the RVQ codec's full # of levels. We *italicize* the second best setting for each metric. Compared to the baseline using a causal codec (1st row), applying all of our proposed techniques (last row) improves both the efficiency and all end-to-end TTS metrics.

Longer frame duration. Table 2 displays the effects of using longer frame durations ($\{1\times, 2\times, 4\times\}$ that of default DAC), and wider codebooks (2^{10} (default) or 2^{15} codewords per level). Here, we use the number of levels Q' (in this set of experiments, $Q' = Q$) as a variable to roughly control for audio reconstruction quality (i.e., Mel-L1). In general, **using a 22ms frame duration** (i.e., $2\times$ that of default DAC) **preserves or improves TTS performance and enjoys a $2\times$ inference speedup** at the same time. Increasing the frame duration to 44ms leads to substantially worse TTS metrics despite further efficiency gains. However, whether to increase the codebook size $|\mathcal{V}|$ from the default 2^{10} to accommodate longer frame durations remains unclear (better on WER, worse on other metrics), warranting a more fine-grained exploration (e.g., a dense sweep over 10- to 15-bit codebooks) in future work.

Combining all techniques. Table 3 illustrates the cumulative impact of progressively integrating our proposed techniques. In the last row, we apply LM codebook level dropout to a (22ms, 10-bit, 16-level) codec, identifying the optimal level count $Q' = 14$ using FAD on end-to-end TTS. Comparing the streamable baseline (1st row) and the final model with all our techniques (last row), we achieve substantial improvements across all end-to-end TTS metrics, while doubling inference speed.

Future work. Our work may be extended to: (i) study the theory of why framewise compressed representations improve language modeling, (ii) develop RVQ codecs that have flexibility also in codebook size and frame duration such that our LM codebook level dropout can be applied to multiple key hyperparameters altogether, and (iii) uncover the scaling properties (Hoffmann et al., 2022) of the optimal codec settings w.r.t. larger models and more training data.

References

Andrea Agostinelli, Timo I Denk, Zalán Borsos, Jesse Engel, Mauro Verzetti, Antoine Caillon, Qingqing Huang, Aren Jansen, Adam Roberts, Marco Tagliasacchi, et al. 2023. MusicLM: Generating music from text. *arXiv preprint arXiv:2301.11325*.

Sunghwan Ahn, Beom Jun Woo, Min Hyun Han, Chanyeong Moon, and Nam Soo Kim. 2024. HILCodec: High fidelity and lightweight neural audio codec. *arXiv preprint arXiv:2405.04752*.

Dmitry Bogdanov, Minz Won, Philip Tovstogan, Alastair Porter, and Xavier Serra. 2019. The MTG-Jamendo dataset for automatic music tagging. In *Proc. Workshop on Machine Learning for Music Discovery (ML4MD)*.

Zalán Borsos, Raphaël Marinier, Damien Vincent, Eugene Kharitonov, Olivier Pietquin, Matt Sharifi, Dominik Roblek, Olivier Teboul, David Grangier, Marco Tagliasacchi, et al. 2023. AudioLM: a language modeling approach to audio generation. *IEEE/ACM Trans. on Audio, Speech, and Language Processing (T-ASLP)*.

Tom Brown, Benjamin Mann, Nick Ryder, Melanie Subbiah, Jared D Kaplan, Prafulla Dhariwal, Arvind Neelakantan, Pranav Shyam, Girish Sastry, Amanda Askell, Sandhini Agarwal, Ariel Herbert-Voss, Gretchen Krueger, Tom Henighan, Rewon Child, Aditya Ramesh, Daniel Ziegler, Jeffrey Wu, Clemens Winter, Chris Hesse, Mark Chen, Eric Sigler, Mateusz Litwin, Scott Gray, Benjamin Chess, Jack Clark, Christopher Berner, Sam McCandlish, Alec Radford, Ilya Sutskever, and Dario Amodei. 2020. Language models are few-shot learners. *Advances in Neural Information Processing Systems (NeurIPS)*.

Yu-An Chung, Yu Zhang, Wei Han, Chung-Cheng Chiu, James Qin, Ruoming Pang, and Yonghui Wu. 2021. W2v-bert: Combining contrastive learning and masked language modeling for self-supervised speech pre-training. In *Proc. Automatic Speech Recognition and Understanding Workshop (ASRU)*.

Jade Copet, Felix Kreuk, Itai Gat, Tal Remez, David Kant, Gabriel Synnaeve, Yossi Adi, and Alexandre Défossez. 2023. Simple and controllable music generation. *Advances in Neural Information Processing Systems (NeurIPS)*.

Tri Dao, Dan Fu, Stefano Ermon, Atri Rudra, and Christopher Ré. 2022. Flashattention: Fast and memory-efficient exact attention with io-awareness. *Advances in Neural Information Processing Systems (NeurIPS)*.

Tri Dao and Albert Gu. 2024. Transformers are SSMs: Generalized models and efficient algorithms through structured state space duality. In *Proc. Int. Conf. on Machine Learning (ICML)*.

Michaël Defferrard, Kirell Benzi, Pierre Vandergheynst, and Xavier Bresson. 2017. FMA: A dataset for music analysis. In *Proc. Int. Soc. for Music Information Retrieval Conf. (ISMIR)*.

Alexandre Défossez, Jade Copet, Gabriel Synnaeve, and Yossi Adi. 2023. High fidelity neural audio compression. *Transactions on Machine Learning Research (TMLR)*.

Alexandre Défossez, Laurent Mazaré, Manu Orsini, Amélie Royer, Patrick Pérez, Hervé Jégou, Edouard Grave, and Neil Zeghidour. 2024. Moshi: a speech-text foundation model for real-time dialogue. Technical report, Kyutai.

Jacob Devlin, Ming-Wei Chang, Kenton Lee, and Kristina Toutanova. 2019. BERT: Pre-training of deep bidirectional transformers for language understanding. In *Proc. NAACL*.

Chris Donahue, Julian McAuley, and Miller Puckette. 2019. Adversarial audio synthesis. In *Proc. Int. Conf. on Learning Representations (ICLR)*.

Jort F Gemmeke, Daniel PW Ellis, Dylan Freedman, Aren Jansen, Wade Lawrence, R Channing Moore, Manoj Plakal, and Marvin Ritter. 2017. Audio set: An ontology and human-labeled dataset for audio events. In *Proc. Int. Conf. on Acoustics, Speech and Signal Processing (ICASSP)*.

Karan Goel, Albert Gu, Chris Donahue, and Christopher Ré. 2022. It's raw! audio generation with state-space models. In *Proc. Int. Conf. on Machine Learning (ICML)*.

Ian Goodfellow, Jean Pouget-Abadie, Mehdi Mirza, Bing Xu, David Warde-Farley, Sherjil Ozair, Aaron Courville, and Yoshua Bengio. 2014. Generative adversarial nets. *Advances in Neural Information Processing Systems (NeurIPS)*.

Albert Gu and Tri Dao. 2023. Mamba: Linear-time sequence modeling with selective state spaces. *arXiv preprint arXiv:2312.00752*.

Ali Hatamizadeh and Jan Kautz. 2024. Mambavision: A hybrid mamba-transformer vision backbone. *arXiv preprint arXiv:2407.08083*.

Shawn Hershey, Sourish Chaudhuri, Daniel PW Ellis, Jort F Gemmeke, Aren Jansen, R Channing Moore, Manoj Plakal, Devin Platt, Rif A Saurous, Bryan Seybold, et al. 2017. CNN architectures for large-scale audio classification. In *Proc. Int. Conf. on Acoustics, Speech and Signal Processing (ICASSP)*.

Jordan Hoffmann, Sebastian Borgeaud, Arthur Mensch, Elena Buchatskaya, Trevor Cai, Eliza Rutherford, Diego de Las Casas, Lisa Anne Hendricks, Johannes Welbl, Aidan Clark, et al. 2022. Training compute-optimal large language models. *arXiv preprint arXiv:2203.15556*.

Wei-Ning Hsu, Benjamin Bolte, Yao-Hung Hubert Tsai, Kushal Lakhotia, Ruslan Salakhutdinov, and Abdelrahman Mohamed. 2021. Hubert: Self-supervised speech representation learning by masked prediction of hidden units. *IEEE/ACM Trans. on Audio, Speech, and Language Processing (T-ASLP)*.

Shengpeng Ji, Minghui Fang, Ziyue Jiang, Rongjie Huang, Jialung Zuo, Shulei Wang, and Zhou Zhao. 2024. Language-Codec: Reducing the gaps between discrete codec representation and speech language models. *arXiv preprint arXiv:2402.12208*.

Jee-weon Jung, You Jin Kim, Hee-Soo Heo, Bong-Jin Lee, Youngki Kwon, and Joon Son Chung. 2022. Pushing the limits of raw waveform speaker recognition. In *Proc. Interspeech*.

Nal Kalchbrenner, Erich Elsen, Karen Simonyan, Seb Noury, Norman Casagrande, Edward Lockhart, Florian Stimberg, Aaron Oord, Sander Dieleman, and Koray Kavukcuoglu. 2018. Efficient neural audio synthesis. In *Proc. Int. Conf. on Machine Learning (ICML)*.

Kevin Kilgour, Mauricio Zuluaga, Dominik Roblek, and Matthew Sharifi. 2019. Fréchet audio distance: A reference-free metric for evaluating music enhancement algorithms. In *Proc. Interspeech*.

Jaehyeon Kim, Keon Lee, Seungjun Chung, and Jaewoong Cho. 2024. CLam-TTS: Improving neural codec language model for zero-shot text-to-speech. In *Proc. Int. Conf. on Learning Representations (ICLR)*.

Yuma Koizumi, Heiga Zen, Shigeki Karita, Yifan Ding, Kohei Yatabe, Nobuyuki Morioka, Michiel Bacchiani, Yu Zhang, Wei Han, and Ankur Bapna. 2023. LibriTTS-R: A restored multi-speaker text-to-speech corpus. In *Proc. Interspeech*.

Jungil Kong, Jaehyeon Kim, and Jaekyoung Bae. 2020. HiFi-GAN: Generative adversarial networks for efficient and high fidelity speech synthesis. *Advances in Neural Information Processing Systems (NeurIPS)*.

Kundan Kumar, Rithesh Kumar, Thibault De Boissiere, Lucas Gestin, Wei Zhen Teoh, Jose Sotelo, Alexandre De Brebisson, Yoshua Bengio, and Aaron C Courville. 2019. MelGAN: Generative adversarial networks for conditional waveform synthesis. *Advances in Neural Information Processing Systems (NeurIPS)*.

Rithesh Kumar, Prem Seetharaman, Alejandro Luebs, Ishaan Kumar, and Kundan Kumar. 2023. High-fidelity audio compression with improved RVQGAN. *Advances in Neural Information Processing Systems (NeurIPS)*.

Ilya Loshchilov and Frank Hutter. 2018. Decoupled weight decay regularization. In *Proc. Int. Conf. on Learning Representations (ICLR)*.

Gabriel Mittag, Babak Naderi, Assmaa Chehadi, and Sebastian Möller. 2021. NISQA: A deep cnn-self-attention model for multidimensional speech quality prediction with crowdsourced datasets. In *Proc. Interspeech*.

Gautham J Mysore. 2014. Can we automatically transform speech recorded on common consumer devices in real-world environments into professional production quality speech?—a dataset, insights, and challenges. *IEEE Signal Processing Letters*.

Alec Radford, Jong Wook Kim, Tao Xu, Greg Brockman, Christine McLeavey, and Ilya Sutskever. 2023. Robust speech recognition via large-scale weak supervision. In *Proc. Int. Conf. on Machine Learning (ICML)*.

Zafar Rafii, Antoine Liutkus, Fabian-Robert Stöter, Stylianos Ioannis Mimilakis, and Rachel Bittner. 2017. The MUSDB18 corpus for music separation.

Xu Tan, Tao Qin, Frank Soong, and Tie-Yan Liu. 2021. A survey on neural speech synthesis. *arXiv preprint arXiv:2106.15561*.

Aaron van den Oord, Sander Dieleman, Heiga Zen, Karen Simonyan, Oriol Vinyals, Alex Graves, Nal Kalchbrenner, Andrew Senior, Koray Kavukcuoglu, et al. 2016. Wavenet: A generative model for raw audio. *arXiv preprint arXiv:1609.03499*.

Aaron van den Oord, Oriol Vinyals, et al. 2017. Neural discrete representation learning. *Advances in Neural Information Processing Systems (NeurIPS)*.

Ashish Vaswani, Noam Shazeer, Niki Parmar, Jakob Uszkoreit, Llion Jones, Aidan N. Gomez, Łukasz Kaiser, and Illia Polosukhin. 2017. Attention is all you need. *Advances in Neural Information Processing Systems (NeurIPS)*.

Roger Waleffe, Wonmin Byeon, Duncan Riach, Brandon Norick, Vijay Korthikanti, Tri Dao, Albert Gu, Ali Hatamizadeh, Sudhakar Singh, Deepak Narayanan, et al. 2024. An empirical study of mamba-based language models. *arXiv preprint arXiv:2406.07887*.

Chengyi Wang, Sanyuan Chen, Yu Wu, Ziqiang Zhang, Long Zhou, Shujie Liu, Zhuo Chen, Yanqing Liu, Huaming Wang, Jinyu Li, et al. 2023. Neural codec language models are zero-shot text to speech synthesizers. *arXiv preprint arXiv:2301.02111*.

Haibin Wu, Xuanjun Chen, Yi-Cheng Lin, Kai-wei Chang, Ho-Lam Chung, Alexander H Liu, and Hung-yi Lee. 2024. Towards audio language modeling–an overview. *arXiv preprint arXiv:2402.13236*.

Dongchao Yang, Jinchuan Tian, Xu Tan, Rongjie Huang, Songxiang Liu, Haohan Guo, Xuankai Chang, Jiatong Shi, Sheng Zhao, Jiang Bian, Zhou Zhao, Xixin Wu, and Helen M. Meng. 2024. UniAudio: Towards universal audio generation with large language models. In *Proc. Int. Conf. on Machine Learning (ICML)*.

Neil Zeghidour, Alejandro Luebs, Ahmed Omran, Jan Skoglund, and Marco Tagliasacchi. 2021. Soundstream: An end-to-end neural audio codec. *IEEE/ACM Trans. on Audio, Speech, and Language Processing (T-ASLP)*.

Xin Zhang, Dong Zhang, Shimin Li, Yaqian Zhou, and Xipeng Qiu. 2024. SpeechTokenizer: Unified speech tokenizer for speech large language models. In *Int. Conf. on Learning Representations (ICLR)*.

A Related Work

Neural audio codecs. Compressing and quantizing long, continuous audio waveforms into shorter discrete codes using a convolutional autoencoder was first proposed by van den Oord et al. (2017). Their proposed VQ-VAE method involves online K-Means for quantizing latent representations and a reconstruction objective on the decoder's output. Later, SoundStream (Zeghidour et al., 2021) introduced the 2D-structured Residual Vector Quantization (RVQ) to such codecs. This work also integrated a mixture of discriminators, a technique adoped from GAN-based audio synthesis (Goodfellow et al., 2014; Donahue et al., 2019; Kumar et al., 2019; Kong et al., 2020), on top of the decoder to enhance the perceptual quality of reconstructed waveforms—this RVQ-GAN setup has since been a norm for neural audio codecs. EnCodec (Défossez et al., 2023) and DAC (Kumar et al., 2023) further advanced the RVQ-GAN architecture with optimized discriminator setup, activation function, and (low) latent dimensionality. HILCodec (Ahn et al., 2024) showed that layer-wise variance constraining helps with the depth scaling of lightweight RVQ-GAN codecs. Overall, research in neural audio codecs has focused on achieving higher compression (i.e., lower bitrates) while maintaining audio reconstruction quality, rather than downstream audio generation, and often involved detailed architectural designs and tuning. In contrast, our work approaches codec design from an end-to-end audio generation practitioners' perspective, exploring codec hyperparameters that are both easily configurable and influential to the end-to-end system.

LM-based end-to-end audio generation. Autoregressive modeling of compressed discrete codes for audio waveforms was first proposed alongside VQ-VAE (van den Oord et al., 2017). AudioLM (Borsos et al., 2023) introduced a hierarchical LM approach that first generates *semantic tokens* (Hsu et al., 2021; Chung et al., 2021), derived from BERT-like pretraining (Devlin et al., 2019) on audio data, followed by RVQ codes (or *acoustic tokens*), resulting in better long-term coherence in generated audios. To navigate the efficiency-quality tradeoff given an RVQ codec, VALL-E (Wang et al., 2023) proposed non-autoregressive modeling for all RVQ levels except the coarsest one, and MusicGen (Copet et al., 2023) introduced the *Delay* pattern, dramatically shortening the sequence length while preserving key autoregressive dependencies. UniAudio (Yang et al., 2024) unified tokenization schemes for text, phonemes, audio, and symbolic music to build an LM for a wide range of audio generation tasks. Despite these advancements, all aforementioned work treated the audio codec, which is upstream from the LM, as a fixed component, leaving out the potential gains from a co-design between the codec and the LM.

Co-design of audio codecs and LMs. Compared to the two previously discussed areas, designing codecs with the goal of improving end-to-end audio generations is a relatively nascent direction. SpeechTokenizer (Zhang et al., 2024) proposed to distill information in semantic tokens (Hsu et al., 2021) into the first (coarsest) level of the RVQ codec, alleviating the need of using two LMs (Borsos et al., 2023; Agostinelli et al., 2023) in tandem for semantic and acoustic RVQ tokens. Moshi (Défossez et al., 2024), a work conducted concurrently with ours, adopted this technique and used a causal codec setup to enable low-latency, streamable real-time voice conversations. Language-Codec (Ji et al., 2024) proposed to arrange the RVQ levels in a first-parallel, then-sequential fashion to distribute information more evenly among the RVQ levels. While the methods above improved the latency and/or quality of end-to-end generations, they focused on single, and highly specific, modifications to the codec. Meanwhile, our work investigate the downstream impact of multiple general RVQ codec hyperparameters in combination, painting a more complete picture for end-to-end system practitioners.

B Impact of RVQ levels on reconstruction vs. on end-to-end generation

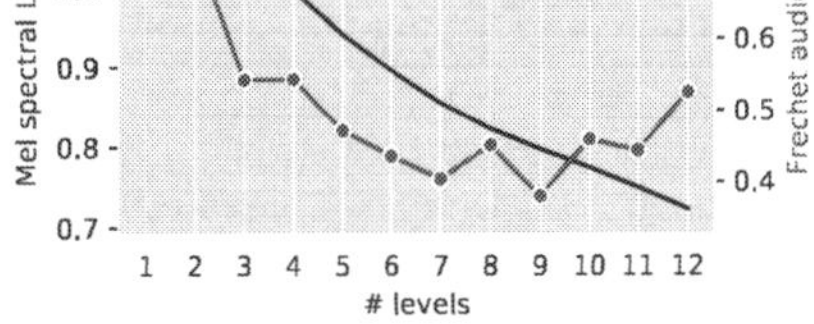

Figure 3: Impacts of # of codebook levels Q' are different on codec-only *audio reconstruction* vs. *end-to-end TTS* involving both the codec and the LM. (frame duration $1/f_x = 11$ms; codebook size $|\mathcal{V}| = 2^{15}$.)

We train a single RVQ codec on speech data

with $Q = 12$ levels and train 12 LMs for text-to-speech (TTS) using each possible value of $Q' \in \{1, \ldots, 12\}$. In Fig. 3, we first plot the codec audio reconstruction performance as measured by Mel-spectral L1 distance. We also plot the end-to-end codec LM system performance as measured by Fréchet audio distance (FAD) (Kilgour et al., 2019), an end-to-end metric for audio generation. We observe that end-to-end performance improves as the number of levels increases towards a global minima at 9 levels and deteriorates afterwards, as opposed to the monotonically improving curve of audio reconstruction.

C Experimental Setup

Datasets for codec. For TTS, we collect 1.7K hours of YouTube podcast data in-house to train the codec. For music experiments, we use the *medium* version of FMA dataset (Defferrard et al., 2017) containing 200 hours of multitrack music. To evaluate audio reconstruction of our codecs, we follow DAC (Kumar et al., 2023) and create a dataset of 3K 10-second audios comprising speech (Mysore, 2014), music (Rafii et al., 2017) and general sounds (Gemmeke et al., 2017) (1K each).

Datasets for LM. For TTS, we use the 550-hour LibriTTS-R (Koizumi et al., 2023) for LM training, and its *test-clean* split (8 hours, 4.7K samples) for evaluation. For unconditional music generation, we train our LMs on 1.5K hours of multitrack music from MTG-Jamendo dataset (Bogdanov et al., 2019). We exclude examples with vocals using the associated metadata, and and hold out 1.5K examples for evaluation.

Codec model specifics. We utilize the open-source code of DAC (Kumar et al., 2023) and implement our changes on top. Our codecs have 76~84M non-codebook parameters due to various frame durations. We train our codecs for 300K steps with an effective batch size of 75 seconds of audio. We use the AdamW (Loshchilov and Hutter, 2018) optimizer with 10^{-4} initial learning rate and exponential decay. The training process takes about 25 hours on 4 NVidia H100 (80G) GPUs.

LM model specifics. Following recent validation that a hybrid of state-space model (SSM) and attention outperforms either approach alone (Waleffe et al., 2024; Hatamizadeh and Kautz, 2024), we use 24 layers of stacked Mamba2 (Dao and Gu, 2024) and Transformer decoder blocks (Vaswani et al., 2017), totaling 400M non-embedding parameters. We prepend the conditioning information for TTS (i.e., $\boldsymbol{y}$, which includes text transcripts and speaker embedding) to the RVQ audio codes $\boldsymbol{x}^{(\text{delay})}$. The text transcript is transformed into character embeddings, while the speaker embedding is extracted using a raw waveform-based speaker recognition model (Jung et al., 2022).

We train our LMs for 30K steps with a batch size equivalent to 500 seconds of audio. We use the AdamW optimizer (Loshchilov and Hutter, 2018) with a peak learning rate of 4×10^{-4}, and 10% warmup steps followed by cosine decay. Training takes 12 hours on 8 H100 (80G) GPUs. For inference, we use pure sampling from the LM's output logits.

Evaluation for audio reconstruction (codec). We follow (Kumar et al., 2023) and compute the L1 distance between the log-scaled Mel spectrograms of the original and reconstructed waveforms to measure reconstruction at the signal level. We abbreviate this metric as ***Mel-L1*** hereafter.

Evaluation for end-to-end audio generation (codec + LM). To evaluate our end-to-end TTS system involving both the codec and the LM, we consider the following three aspects:

- **Intelligibility:** Following (Wang et al., 2023), we measure the word error rate (WER, in %) between the given text transcript and automatically transcribed text by Whisper (Radford et al., 2023) (v3 large) model from the generated speech.
- **Audio quality:** We leverage NISQA (Mittag et al., 2021) overall quality score, which is predicted by a CNN-Transformer model trained on pairs of speech audios and human-labeled quality scores in the range of $[1, 5]$. NISQA has been shown to correlate well (Pearson's $r \geq 0.9$) with human judgments of speech audio quality.
- **Speaker control:** Following (Wang et al., 2023; Kim et al., 2024), we compute the cosine similarity ($\in [-1, 1]$, reported in %) between the given speaker embedding and that extracted from the generated speech, using the same speaker recognition model (Jung et al., 2022).

For experiments on unconditional music generation, following (Copet et al., 2023; Agostinelli et al., 2023), we report Fréchet audio distance

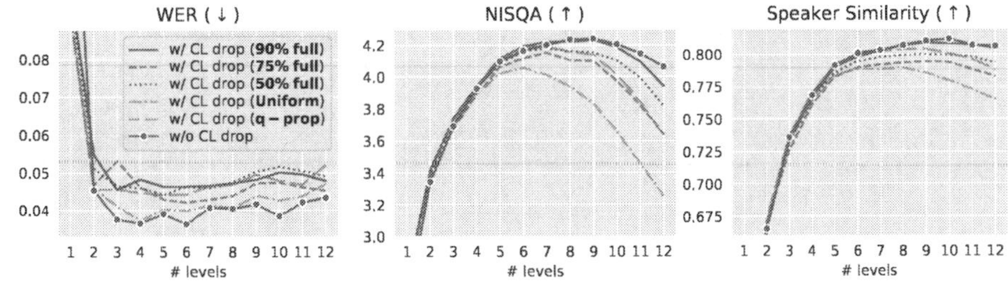

Figure 4: Effects of using different dropout distributions, i.e., $\mathcal{P}(q)$, for LM codebook level dropout. The curves of 'w/ CL drop' settings are the closer to those of 'w/o CL drop' the better.

(FAD) (Kilgour et al., 2019) computed on audio embeddings from the VGGish (Hershey et al., 2017) audio classification model. FAD captures how realistic the generations are at the dataset level (i.e., all generations vs. all reference inputs) using feature-wise covariances estimated from all audio embeddings of the generated/reference set.

D Choosing A Good $\mathcal{P}(q)$ for LM Codebook Level Dropout

For LM codebook level dropout (i.e., CL drop) to be effective in determining the optimal level count, its performance profile w.r.t. the level count should trend as closely as possible to that resulting from training LMs without CL drop at every possible number of levels. Here, we find that the choice of dropout distribution $\mathcal{P}(q)$, which determines the fraction of training steps allocated to each level count, to be critical. We experiment with a total of 5 different $\mathcal{P}(q)$'s detailed below:

- **Uniform:** $\mathcal{P}(q) := \frac{1}{Q}$; $\forall q \in \{1, \dots, Q\}$, i.e., every level count gets equal attention.
- ***q*-proportional (or *q-prop*):** $\mathcal{P}(q) := \frac{q}{Z(Q)}$; $\forall q \in \{1, \dots, Q\}$, where the normalization constant $Z(Q) := \sum_{q'=1}^{Q} q'$, i.e., the fraction for each level count q is proportional to q.
- **50% full:** $\mathcal{P}(q) := 0.5$ for $q = Q$, and $\mathcal{P}(q) := \frac{1-0.5}{Q-1}$; $\forall q \in \{1, \dots, Q-1\}$, i.e., the full level count Q gets 50% of the steps, and all the lower level counts share the remaining 50% uniformly.
- **75% full:** $\mathcal{P}(q) := 0.75$ for $q = Q$, and $\mathcal{P}(q) := \frac{1-0.75}{Q-1}$; $\forall q \in \{1, \dots, Q-1\}$, which is similar to **50% full** but focuses more on the full level count Q.
- **90% full:** $\mathcal{P}(q) := 0.9$ for $q = Q$, and $\mathcal{P}(q) := \frac{1-0.9}{Q-1}$; $\forall q \in \{1, \dots, Q-1\}$, which puts even more focus on $q = Q$ than **75% full**.

The performance profiles resulting from these $\mathcal{P}(q)$'s are shown in Fig. 4. The NISQA (which evalutes *audio quality*) and speaker similarity profiles suggest that **90% full** is the best choice among the five $\mathcal{P}(q)$'s. Other choices all peak at relatively lower level counts, and **Uniform**, which is the most straightforward option, appears to be the worst of the five.

The reasons behind why allocating only 10% to lower level counts leads to metrics that track most closely those from training separate LMs for each level count are left for further investigation. Our intuition is that, training with Q levels already includes modeling all the lower levels, and hence the LM only needs a small number of steps to adapt to the scenarios where the finer-grained information in higher levels is absent.

Low-resource Machine Translation for Code-switched Kazakh-Russian Language Pair

Maxim Borisov[1], Zhanibek Kozhirbayev[2], Valentin Malykh[3,4,5]
[1]ITMO University, Saint-Petersburg, Russia;
[2]Nazarbayev University, Astana, Kazakhstan;
[3]MTS AI, Moscow, Russia;
[4]ISP RAS Research Center for Trusted Artificial Intelligence, Moscow, Russia;
[5]IITU University, Almaty, Kazakhstan

Abstract

Machine translation for low-resource language pairs is a challenging task. This task could become extremely difficult once a speaker uses code switching. We present the first code-switching Kazakh-Russian parallel corpus. Additionally, we propose a method to build a machine translation model for code-switched Kazakh-Russian language pair with no labeled data. Our method is basing on generation of synthetic data. This method results in a model beating an existing commercial system by human evaluation.

1 Introduction

Code-switching presents a significant challenge in Natural Language Processing due to its unpredictability, variability, and the lack of available corpora, especially for low-resource languages. There were no publicly available code-switched Kazakh-Russian parallel dataset, thus we present one in this work. The sample from the dataset is presented in Tab. 1. This dataset contains only 618 parallel sentences, so it can be used only for evaluation and not for training. We propose a method for training a machine translation model for code-switching task. In our method we use several publicly available Kazakh-Russian datasets, but since these datasets do not address code-switching problem, we generate additional training data by translating relevant monolingual corpus and show the effectiveness of this approach. We augment the data to address challenge of code-switching. To do so we developed a novel text transformation method based on SimAlign (Sabet et al., 2020). We train several machine translation models on the augmented dataset resulting in 3.09 Likert score for the best baseline model, while Yandex commercial model shows 2.80 Likert score. These experimental results suggest that our method is able to improve the performance of machine translation systems on real code-switching data and jump start for those language pairs that do not have collected code-switched data.

The following paper is structured as follows: section 2 describes the work on code-switching done for other language pairs alongside with studies devoted to Russian-Kazakh language pair; section 3 presents the description of the existing public datasets for the mentioned language pair and the description of a newly introduced dataset with code-switching phenomenon captured; section 4 contains the details regarding our proposed augmentation method; section 5 describes the baselines, their training process, and the achieved results, while section 9 concludes the paper.

The contribution of this work is three-fold: (i) we present the first Kazakh-Russian code-switching dataset;[1] (ii) we present an evaluation of the existing models on this dataset; (iii) we propose a novel data augmentation for not code-switched datasets, which allowed us to fine-tune the existing open models achieving almost on par performance with an available commercial system.

2 Related Work

Recent progress in NLP has spurred the development of technologies capable of handling code-switched data. Despite the initiation of Code-Switching research several years ago, progress within the research community has been sluggish. The primary challenge to address this issue arises from the insufficient availability of data (Winata et al., 2023). A limited number of languages, such as Spanish-English

[1]KRCS dataset could be accessed here: https://github.com/madrugado/KRCS.

Proceedings of the 2025 Conference of the Nations of the Americas Chapter of the Association for Computational Linguistics: Human Language Technologies (Volume 4: Student Research Workshop), pages 66–76

Original	казахстанский гендерлік теңдік саласындағы 12 халықаралық құжаттарды бекітті .	фискал көзқарастан гөрі либералдандыру жақсы
Corrected	Қазақстан гендерлік теңдік саласындағы 12 халықаралық құжаттарды бекітті .	Фискалдық көзқарастан гөрі либералдандыру жақсы
Russian	Казахстаном ратифицировано 12 международных документов в сфере гендерного равенства .	Лучше либерализация , чем фискальный подход
Augmented	Қазақстан гендерного теңдік саласындағы 12 халықаралық құжаттарды бекітті .	Фискалдық подход гөрі либералдандыру

Table 1: Sample sentence triplet from KRCS dataset accompained with cs-5 augmentation of a Russian one.

(Weller et al., 2022; Xu and Yvon, 2021), Hindi-English (Appicharla et al., 2021; Jadhav et al., 2022), or Chinese-English (Li et al., 2012), dominate research and resources in code switching. Nevertheless numerous countries and cultures that extensively use code switching remain underrepresented in NLP research.

A common feature of natural interactions among bilingual speakers is the spontaneous and continuous switching between the Kazakh and Russian languages. It is worth noting that the field still faces challenges, particularly due to the scarcity of code-switched data and the colloquial characteristic of code-switching. To our knowledge, only a few research papers have been published on this matter. In the context of Kazakh-Russian code-switching, a study by Ubskii et al. (2020) attempted to determine the benefit of bilingual training on matrix language (Kazakh) and embedded language (Russian) monolingual data (Myers-Scotton, 1997), as opposed to training on code-switched data only. The study made use of two datasets: Kazakh speech with code-switching and Russian speech with no code-switching. The main objective of the experiments was to compare the performance of a model trained on code-switched speech with that of a model trained on full utterances in both languages. Experimental results suggested that bilingual training improves the model's performance on matrix words, and greatly improves its performance on embedded words. Another study by Zharkynbekova and Chernyavskaya (2022) discussed the ethnic bilingual practice in Kazakhstan. The focus was on code-switching or, in other term, code-mixing in the Kazakh-Russian and Russian-Kazakh bilingualism. The bi- and multilingualism is characteristic for Kazakhstan and is caused by multi-ethnicity of the republic. The study analyzed 300 contexts that show the Kazakh-Russian code-mixing in everyday and internet communication, and in modern Kazakh films reflecting the typical code-mixing practice.

3 Datasets

Training Datasets consist of a dataset collected by Nazarbayev University and described in (Kozhirbayev and Islamgozhayev, 2023), we refer to this dataset as NU below; a dataset collected by Al Farabi University and described in (Balzhan et al., 2015) (KazNU); translated domain adaptation dataset, which is based on Russian tweet corpus described in (Рубцова, 2012) (RTC). We provide more details on domain adaptation in section 8. These three datasets are the main sources of training data, in addition we use several smaller datasets. To acquire these datasets we used MTData tool described in (Gowda et al., 2021). We combine all the datasets in a single one and apply deduplication. We call this dataset "all data" below. We provide the statistics for all the training datasets in Appendix B.

Evaluation Dataset We use Kazakh-Russian Code-Switching dataset (KRCS) as our evaluation dataset. The KRCS dataset consists of 618 colloquial Kazakh sentences from social media which include some Russian phrases with corresponding ground truth translations to grammatically correct Kazakh and Russian labeled by annotators. We had two annotators, both of them were natively bilingual in Kazakh and Russian, both of them are working in academia. The annotation were done as part of their academic duties.

Number of sentences	618
# in an original Kazakh sentence	11.95
Russian # in an original sentence	2.77
# in a corrected Kazakh sentence	12.27
# in a Russian sentence	13.64

Table 2: KRCS dataset statistics. # stands for average number of tokens.

The descriptive statistics of the collected corpus is provided in Tab. 2. In Tab. 1 we provide a sample from KRCS dataset.

4 Dataset Augmentation

Code-Switching Emulation Method In the previous section we described the training datasets, nevertheless we need to state clearly that that datasets are not consider code-switching phenomenon and thus cannot be used effectively in our setup. Therefore we decided to make code-switching data artificially, using specific techniques for data augmentation.

First, we prepare the data. For it we follow the M2M100 recipe provided in fairseq repository which is an official implementation of (Ott et al., 2019). Namely, we filter out sentences with more than 50% of punctuation, remove the duplicates, and discard sentences with more than 50% of symbols that are not common for a given language.

Next, we take Kazakh processed sentences and augment them. We chose cs-5 method for augmentation: Replace a Kazakh word with a Russian word aligned using SimAlign (Sabet et al., 2020). Preliminary, we tried several augmentation techniques, their description and evaluation can be found in section 7.

For cs-5 Minimal Aligned Units (MAU) are extracted following an approach described in (Xu and Yvon, 2021): the small billingual phrase pairs (a, b) extracted from symmetrical alignment such that for every word in a there exists a link to word in b and vise versa.

Next, we replace 15% of tokens/MAUs in the Kazakh sentence at random[2]. Sentences with length of less than 7 tokens have one replacement following (Anwar, 2023). We provide a sample of augmented sentence in Tab. 1. We also provide additional linguistic analysis and justification for each method in Appendix D.

[2]The exact percentage is inspired by Masked Language Modeling approach firstly introduced in (Devlin et al., 2018)

5 Evaluation

Baselines There are several baselines which are used in our experiments. We use **identity** baseline, which simply copying its input to the output. This baseline is obviously not trained.

There are two trained from scratch baselines, namely, the first one is **transformer-600**, which is described below. The architecture of the model follows NLLB one, specifically the 600M parameters variant. The details of implementation can be found in Appendix A.

The second trained from scratch baseline is a reproduced approach from (Kozhirbayev and Islamgozhayev, 2023). We call this baseline **transformer-NU**.

The next three baselines are using pre-trained machine translation models and fine-tune them on our training data. These baselines are **mBART**, a model family described in (Liu et al., 2020), we use specifically mbart-large-50-many-to-many-mmt variant; **M2M100**, a model family described in (Fan et al., 2020), specifically facebook/m2m100_1.2B; and **NLLB-600**, a model family described in (Costa-jussà et al., 2022), specifically facebook/nllb-200-distilled-600M.

The last fine-tuned baseline is **NLLB-3.3B** from the same model family as the previous one, but it is facebook/nllb-200-3.3B variant. We do not fully fine-tune this model, instead we use PiSSA (Meng et al., 2024), a PEFT approach.

Metrics In our work we are using three standard metrics: BLEU score (Papineni et al., 2002), which is basically a token accuracy; ChrF++ score (Popović, 2017), which is character level F-score; and COMET score (Rei et al., 2020), which is a Transformer-based model trained to compare translations. For the last metric we use specifically Unbabel/wmt22-cometkiwi-da model, described in (Rei et al., 2022).

6 Results

For this evaluation we use all the baselines with cs-5 augmentation, since it is the best in our setup as it shown in previous section. In

Model	w/o training	trained
identity	7.55 / 25.10 / **0.56**	N/A
transformer-NU	7.87 / 31.99 / 0.50	11.31 / 35.35 / 0.53
transformer-600	N/A	12.49 / 36.44 / 0.54
mBART	4.62 / 17.83 / **0.56**	12.08 / 34.31 / 0.53
M2M100	5.37 / 21.59 / 0.42	12.50 / 36.44 / 0.53
NLLB-600	12.26 / 36.67 / 0.53	12.95 / 36.44 / 0.54
NLLB-3.3B	**15.23** / **39.68** / **0.56**	**16.48** / **42.27** / **0.56**
Commercial APIs		
Yandex MT[2]	22.24 / 47.13 / 0.67	N/A
Google MT	24.14 / 47.84 / 0.64	N/A

Table 3: The comparison of baseline models in BLEU / ChrF++ / COMET on KRCS dataset.

addition, we provide results for two commercial machine translation systems, namely Yandex MT and Google MT. The results are provided in Tab. 3. As one can see, the best results are achieved by NLLB-3.3B model. This is not surprising, once it is the biggest model in comparison. What is interesting in this setup is that our approach allows to achieve good results with all the trained models, and the best trained model once achieved a score close to Yandex MT system[3]. Another point worth mentioning that COMET scores are close for identity baseline, mBART model, and NLLB-3.3B model.

Human Evaluation We have done human evaluation for our best model (chosen by BLEU score) and two commercial APIs. We asked our assessors to use Likert scale and averaged their scores for 100 random sentences from KRCS. The results are provided in Tab. 4. As can be seen, the results are a bit unexpected. Despite the automatic metrics scoring the Yandex MT system higher than NLLB-3.3B model, human evaluation showed the opposite. Also, it is worth noting that even the best commercial system is pretty far from ground truth translation in this domain.

We also evaluated the naturalness of augmentation in Kazakh. We chose 100 random sentences with cs-5 augmentation and asked our assessors again to use Likert scale. The achieved result is 2.62, which could be considered acceptable.

[3]We provide current scores for Yandex MT system at 15th of June. When the work has been started the score for Yandex MT was **16.72** BLEU.

	Mean	Std.
Ground Truth	4.75	0.68
NLLB-3.3B	3.09	1.13
Yandex MT	2.80	1.17
Google MT	3.49	1.14

Table 4: The human evaluation results.

7 Augmentation Study

We experiment with 5 augmentation types, namely: **cs-1:** Replace a Kazakh word with a Russian one in normal form; **cs-2:** Replace a Kazakh word with a Russian one's stem with Kazakh ending, extracted from a Kazakh word by excluding stem from it; **cs-3:** Replace a Kazakh word with a Russian one in random form; **cs-4:** Replace a Kazakh word with a Russian word aligned using fastalign (Dyer et al., 2013); **cs-5:** Replace a Kazakh word with a Russian word aligned using SimAlign (Sabet et al., 2020).

For cs-1, cs-2, and cs-3 we employ a publicly available Kazakh-Russian dictionary from work (Rakhimova, 2020). For cs-4 Minimal Aligned Units are extracted as for cs-5. For all augmentation methods, the replacement is done as for cs-5. We provide samples for all the augmentation types in Tab. 5.

7.1 Augmentation Evaluation

In this section we provide a comparison for the models trained on different augmentation types. We train our transformer-600 model on cs-1, cs-

kk	Қазақстан гендерлік теңдік саласындағы 12 халықаралық құжаттарды бекітті .	Фискалдық көзқарастан гөрі либералдандыру жақсы
cs-1	казахстанский гендерлік теңдік саласындағы 12 халықаралық құжаттарды бекітті .	фискал көзқарастан гөрі либералдандыру жақсы
cs-2	казахстансктан гендерлік теңдік саласындағы 12 халықаралық құжаттарды бекітті .	фискадық көзқарастан гөрі либералдандыру жақсы
cs-3	Қазақстан гендерлік теңдік саласындағы 12 международной құжаттарды бекітті .	Фискалдық көзқарастан скорейших либералдандыру жақсы
cs-4	Қазақстан гендерлік теңдік саласындағы 12 халықаралық құжаттарды бекітті .	Фискалдық көзқарастан гөрі либерализация жақсы
cs-5	Қазақстан гендерного теңдік саласындағы 12 халықаралық құжаттарды бекітті .	Фискалдық подход гөрі либералдандыру
ru	Казахстаном ратифицировано 12 международных документов в сфере гендерного равенства .	Лучше либерализация , чем фискальный подход

Table 5: Examples of code-switching augmentations.

Data	NU	CS-1	CS-2	CS-3	CS-4	CS-5	KRCS
all data (AD)	36.03	33.10	33.41	33.00	29.64	35.16	12.25
AD + cs-1	35.07	**34.34**	33.60	**33.67**	30.51	34.25	10.20
AD + cs-2	35.54	33.78	**35.17**	33.49	30.03	34.52	11.65
AD + cs-3	34.24	33.37	32.94	33.25	29.53	33.42	10.22
AD + cs-4	35.58	32.87	33.10	32.74	**33.69**	37.03	11.38
AD + cs-5	**36.83**	33.68	34.18	33.63	32.96	**39.05**	**12.49**

Table 6: The BLEU scores for transformer-600 model on differently augmented datasets.

2, cs-3, cs-4 and cs-5 augmented datasets. We evaluate the trained models on testing subset of NU dataset, and its augmented versions. A version of NU test set augmented with cs-1 is called CS-1, the other types are called in the same manner. More importantly we evaluate the models on KRCS dataset. The results are presented in Tables 6.

Interesting, that the only augmentation type which helps to improve the baseline results is cs-5. All other types are leading to decrease in quality. For all the types, except cs-3, the evaluation on corresponding augmented testset is the best. For cs-3 the best result is achieved by a model trained on CS-1, this result is not surprising since the cs-3 augmentation is just a random choice between cs-1 and cs-2 augmentations. Another interesting point is that cs-5 augmentation allowed a model to achieve the best performance on the original testset. We hypothesize that this augmentation produces the closest data distribution to the spoken Kazakh language, thus effectively extending the trainset.

8 Domain Adaptation

As one can conclude from section 3, there is a domain mismatch for the available training data and collected evaluation data. We provide a visualization of this mismatch in Fig. 1. It is a tSNE projection of LaBSE embeddings (Feng et al., 2020) of the Kazakh sentences from the training datasets and Russian sentences from Russian Tweet Corpus. One can see that centroid of Russian Tweet Corpus is closer to the centroid of KRCS dataset than any other one of another dataset. This observation drove us to conclusion that we might need a domain adaptation.

Since Russian Tweet Corpus is a monolingual Russian language dataset, we translated it to Kazakh using publicly available machine translation model nllb-200-distilled-600M from

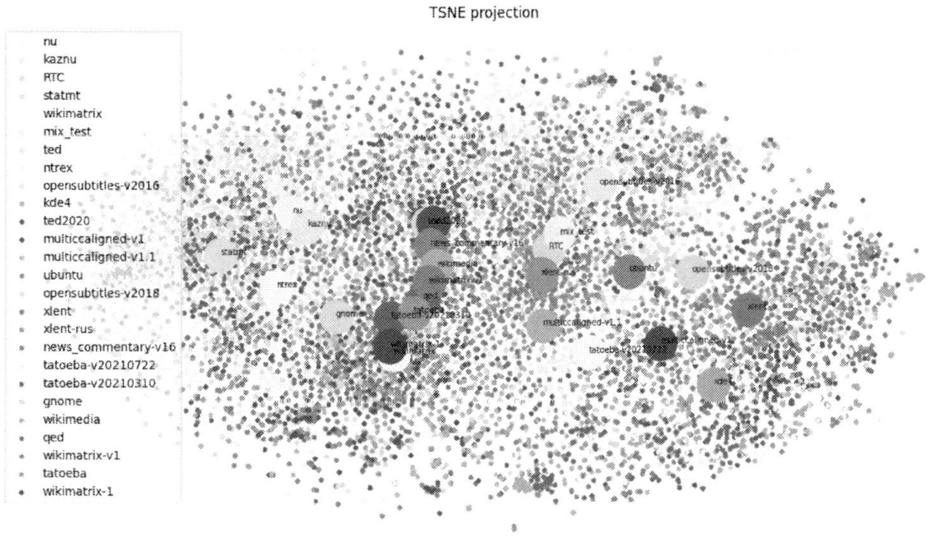

Figure 1: Sentence embedding visualization with dataset centroids.

NLLB model family described in (Costa-jussà et al., 2022). Our choice of the model was driven by the fact that it shows the best quality in standard Russian-Kazakh translation.

8.1 Domain Adaptation Evaluation

We decided to evaluate the importance of domain adaptation corpus which is extend our training dataset. We trained our transformer baseline model in three setups, namely: whole training data, including RTC, whole training data, *ex*cluding RTC, and RTC only. The experiments show that domain adaptation is indeed important, but the single domain adaptation data is not enough to achieve high performance in code switching task. These results are in Tab. 7.

Data	KRCS
all data	12.25 / 37.10 / 0.52
all data w/o RTC	11.64 / 35.58 / 0.49
RTC only	10.86 / 34.76 / 0.52

Table 7: The results of training on different datasets.

9 Conlusion

In conclusion, the proposed method demonstrates a viable approach to tackling machine translation challenges for low-resource, code-switched language pairs, specifically Kazakh-Russian. By utilizing synthetic data generation, the method circumvents the need for labeled training data, which is typically scarce for such language pairs.

Furthermore, the introduction of the first code-switching Kazakh-Russian parallel corpus represents a significant contribution to the field, providing a valuable resource for future research and development. The empirical results indicate that the system's performance surpasses that of an existing commercial translation system, as evidenced by superior human evaluation outcomes. This highlights the effectiveness and potential of the proposed approach for improving machine translation in similar low-resource, code-switched contexts.

10 Limitations

Synthetic Data Dependence: The approach relies heavily on the generation of synthetic data, which may not perfectly capture the nuances and complexities of natural code-switching in Kazakh-Russian speech.

Evaluation Scope: While achieving a BLEU score of 16.48 is promising, the evaluation is limited to specific criteria and doesn't necessarily account for all aspects of translation quality, such as fluency and contextual accuracy.

Corpus Size and Diversity: The newly presented code-switching Kazakh-Russian parallel corpus may still be limited in size and diversity, potentially impacting the generalizability of the model to broader linguistic contexts or different dialects.

Commercial System Comparison: The performance comparison to an existing commercial system is based on certain benchmarks and human evaluations, which might not cover all practical use cases and scenarios where the commercial system might excel.

Scalability and Adaptability: The method's scalability to other low-resource, code-switched language pairs is not addressed, raising questions about its broader applicability and adaptability to different linguistic environments.

Long-term Sustainability: There is no discussion on the long-term sustainability and maintenance of the synthetic data generation process and how it might evolve with changes in the language pair dynamics or increased data availability.

By acknowledging these limitations, future research can focus on addressing these gaps to further enhance the robustness and applicability of machine translation models for code-switched languages.

Acknowledgments

The authors are grateful to Zhannura Manapbekova who did the initial collection and annotation of KRCS corpus. The work of Valentin Malykh was supported by a grant for research centers in the field of artificial intelligence, provided by the Analytical Center for the Government of the Russian Federation in accordance with the subsidy agreement (agreement identifier 000000D730321P5Q0002) and the agreement with the Ivannikov Institute for System Programming of the Russian Academy of Sciences dated November 2, 2021 No. 70-2021-00142.

References

Mohamed Anwar. 2023. The effect of alignment objectives on code-switching translation. *arXiv preprint arXiv:2309.05044*.

Ramakrishna Appicharla, Kamal Kumar Gupta, Asif Ekbal, and Pushpak Bhattacharyya. 2021. IITP-MT at CALCS2021: English to Hinglish neural machine translation using unsupervised synthetic code-mixed parallel corpus. In *Proceedings of the Fifth Workshop on Computational Approaches to Linguistic Code-Switching*, pages 31–35, Online. Association for Computational Linguistics.

Abduali Balzhan, Zhadyra Akhmadieva, Saule Zholdybekova, Ualsher Tukeyev, and Diana Rakhimova. 2015. Study of the problem of creating structural transfer rules and lexical selection for the kazakh-russian machine translation system on apertium platform. In *PROCEEDINGS OF THE INTERNATIONAL CONFERENCE" TURKIC LANGUAGES PROCESSING" TurkLang-2015*, pages 5–9.

Marta R Costa-jussà, James Cross, Onur Çelebi, Maha Elbayad, Kenneth Heafield, Kevin Heffernan, Elahe Kalbassi, Janice Lam, Daniel Licht, Jean Maillard, et al. 2022. No language left behind: Scaling human-centered machine translation. *arXiv preprint arXiv:2207.04672*.

Jacob Devlin, Ming-Wei Chang, Kenton Lee, and Kristina Toutanova. 2018. Bert: Pre-training of deep bidirectional transformers for language understanding. *arXiv preprint arXiv:1810.04805*.

Chris Dyer, Victor Chahuneau, and Noah A Smith. 2013. A simple, fast, and effective reparameterization of ibm model 2. In *Proceedings of the 2013 Conference of the North American Chapter of the Association for Computational Linguistics: Human Language Technologies*, pages 644–648.

Angela Fan, Shruti Bhosale, Holger Schwenk, Zhiyi Ma, Ahmed El-Kishky, Siddharth Goyal, Mandeep Baines, Onur Celebi, Guillaume Wenzek, Vishrav Chaudhary, et al. 2020. Beyond english-centric multilingual machine translation. *arXiv preprint arXiv:2010.11125*.

Fangxiaoyu Feng, Yinfei Yang, Daniel Cer, Naveen Arivazhagan, and Wei Wang. 2020. Language-agnostic bert sentence embedding. *arXiv preprint arXiv:2007.01852*.

Thamme Gowda, Zhao Zhang, Chris Mattmann, and Jonathan May. 2021. Many-to-English machine translation tools, data, and pretrained models. In *Proceedings of the 59th Annual Meeting of the Association for Computational Linguistics and the 11th International Joint Conference on Natural Language Processing: System Demonstrations*, pages 306–316, Online. Association for Computational Linguistics.

Ishali Jadhav, Aditi Kanade, Vishesh Waghmare, Sahej Singh Chandok, and Ashwini Jarali. 2022. Code-mixed hinglish to english language translation framework. In *2022 International Conference on Sustainable Computing and Data Communication Systems (ICSCDS)*, pages 684–688.

Diederik P Kingma and Jimmy Ba. 2014. Adam: A method for stochastic optimization. *arXiv preprint arXiv:1412.6980*.

Zhanibek Kozhirbayev and Talgat Islamgozhayev. 2023. Cascade speech translation for the kazakh language. *Applied Sciences*, 13(15):8900.

Ying Li, Yue Yu, and Pascale Fung. 2012. A Mandarin-English code-switching corpus. In *Proceedings of the Eighth International Conference on Language Resources and Evaluation (LREC'12)*, pages 2515–2519, Istanbul, Turkey. European Language Resources Association (ELRA).

Yinhan Liu, Jiatao Gu, Naman Goyal, Xian Li, Sergey Edunov, Marjan Ghazvininejad, Mike Lewis, and Luke Zettlemoyer. 2020. Multilingual denoising pre-training for neural machine translation. *Transactions of the Association for Computational Linguistics*, 8:726–742.

Fanxu Meng, Zhaohui Wang, and Muhan Zhang. 2024. Pissa: Principal singular values and singular vectors adaptation of large language models. *arXiv preprint arXiv:2404.02948*.

Carol Myers-Scotton. 1997. *Duelling languages: Grammatical structure in codeswitching*. Oxford University Press.

Myle Ott, Sergey Edunov, Alexei Baevski, Angela Fan, Sam Gross, Nathan Ng, David Grangier, and Michael Auli. 2019. fairseq: A fast, extensible toolkit for sequence modeling. *arXiv preprint arXiv:1904.01038*.

Kishore Papineni, Salim Roukos, Todd Ward, and Wei-Jing Zhu. 2002. Bleu: a method for automatic evaluation of machine translation. In *Proceedings of the 40th annual meeting of the Association for Computational Linguistics*, pages 311–318.

Maja Popović. 2017. chrf++: words helping character n-grams. In *Proceedings of the second conference on machine translation*, pages 612–618.

Diana R Rakhimova. 2020. Normalization of kazakh language words. *Journal Scientific and Technical Of Information Technologies, Mechanics and Optics*, 128(4):545–551.

Ricardo Rei, José GC De Souza, Duarte Alves, Chrysoula Zerva, Ana C Farinha, Taisiya Glushkova, Alon Lavie, Luisa Coheur, and André FT Martins. 2022. Comet-22: Unbabel-ist 2022 submission for the metrics shared task. In *Proceedings of the Seventh Conference on Machine Translation (WMT)*, pages 578–585.

Ricardo Rei, Craig Stewart, Ana C Farinha, and Alon Lavie. 2020. Comet: A neural framework for mt evaluation. In *Proceedings of the 2020 Conference on Empirical Methods in Natural Language Processing (EMNLP)*, pages 2685–2702.

Masoud Jalili Sabet, Philipp Dufter, François Yvon, and Hinrich Schütze. 2020. Simalign: High quality word alignments without parallel training data using static and contextualized embeddings. In *EMNLP 2020*, pages 1627–1643.

Christian Szegedy, Vincent Vanhoucke, Sergey Ioffe, Jon Shlens, and Zbigniew Wojna. 2016. Rethinking the inception architecture for computer vision. In *Proceedings of the IEEE conference on computer vision and pattern recognition*, pages 2818–2826.

Dmitrii Ubskii, Yuri Matveev, and Wolfgang Minker. 2020. Impact of using a bilingual model on kazakh-russian code-switching speech recognition. In *CEUR Workshop Proceedings*, pages 1–6.

Orion Weller, Matthias Sperber, Telmo Pires, Hendra Setiawan, Christian Gollan, Dominic Telaar, and Matthias Paulik. 2022. End-to-end speech translation for code switched speech. In *Findings of the Association for Computational Linguistics: ACL 2022*, pages 1435–1448, Dublin, Ireland. Association for Computational Linguistics.

Genta Winata, Alham Fikri Aji, Zheng Xin Yong, and Thamar Solorio. 2023. The decades progress on code-switching research in NLP: A systematic survey on trends and challenges. In *Findings of the Association for Computational Linguistics: ACL 2023*, pages 2936–2978, Toronto, Canada. Association for Computational Linguistics.

Jitao Xu and François Yvon. 2021. Can you traducir this? machine translation for code-switched input. In *Proceedings of the Fifth Workshop on Computational Approaches to Linguistic Code-Switching*, pages 84–94, Online. Association for Computational Linguistics.

Sholpan K Zharkynbekova and Valeria E Chernyavskaya. 2022. Kazakh-russian bilingual practice: Code-mixing as a resource in communicative interaction. *RUDN Journal of Language Studies, Semiotics and Semantics*, 13(2):468–482.

Ю Рубцова. 2012. Автоматическое построение и анализ корпуса коротких текстов (постов микроблогов) для задачи разработки и тренировки тонового классификатора. *Инженерия знаний и технологии семантического веба*, 1:109–116.

A Baseline Implementation Details

Transformer-600 is implemented in fairseq framework (Ott et al., 2019). The model has 6 encoder layers and 6 decoder layers with hidden size of 512. Feed forward network hidden dimension is 4096, there are 8 attention heads for encoder and for decoder. Layer normalization before each encoder and decoder block is applied. For regularization we apply dropout of 0.3, Attention dropout of 0.2 and ReLU dropout of 0.2 (which in a dropout probability after ReLU in FFN). The embedding matrices for encoder input, decoder input and decoder output are all shared. The model was optimized using Adam (Kingma and Ba, 2014) with betas of (0.9, 0.98) and epsilon $1e^{-0.6}$. Scheduler is inverse square root with initial learning rate of $3e^{-0.5}$ and warmup of 2500 updates. Max tokens per batch is 2048. Maximum number of updates is 500000. Criterion is label smoothed cross entropy with smoothing factor of 0.2 following (Szegedy et al., 2016). The hyperparameters of the Transformer-600 model are presented in Tab. 8.

Number of layers	6
Hidden size	512
FFN hidden dimension	4096
Attention heads	8
LN before blocks	True
Max Tokens	2048
Criterion	label smoothed CE
Label smoothing	0.2
Optimizer	adam
Adam epsilon	1e-06
Adam betas	(0.9, 0.98)
Lr scheduler	inverse sqrt
Lr	3e-05
Warmup updates	2500
Dropout	0.3
ReLU dropout	0.2
Attention dropout	0.2
Share all embeddings	True
Max update	500000

Table 8: Model Hyperparameters. LN stands for Layer Normalization. CE stands for Cross-Entropy.

B Train Datasets

The statistics for the training datasets is presented in Tab. 9. For Russian Tweet Corpus we report number of Kazakh tokens for the generated translation.

C Additional Scores

The additional statistics for the baseline evaluation on augmented datasets is presented in Tab. 10.

D Augmentation Analysis

cs-1: Replace a Kazakh word with a Russian one in normal form Linguistic

Soundness: This approach is straightforward and resembles natural code-switching seen in everyday speech, where speakers often insert words from another language in their base form, especially nouns and technical terms.

Examples: In Kazakh media and daily conversations, you might hear sentences like "Мен жаңа ручка сатып алдым" ("I bought a new pen"), where "ручка" is a Russian-origin word used in its normal form.

Usage Contexts: Such patterns are common in informal speech, especially when referring to modern or technical terms for which there might be no direct equivalent in Kazakh.

cs-2: Replace a Kazakh word with a Russian word's stem with Kazakh ending

Linguistic Soundness: This is somewhat less natural, as it involves morphologically adapting Russian stems with Kazakh endings, which does not always fit the natural phonological or morphological rules of Kazakh. However, speakers often perform such blending to maintain grammatical consistency within a sentence.

Examples: This is occasionally seen in youth slang or creative language use in social media where Kazakh speakers playfully adapt Russian words. For instance, "жазать" (from Russian "писать" but adapted to sound more Kazakh) might appear in informal texts, though not formally accepted.

Usage Contexts: This type of adaptation is mostly informal, often perceived as a playful or creative linguistic exercise rather than standard usage

Dataset Name	#Sentences	#Ave. Tokens	Domain
NU (Kozhirbayev and Islamgozhayev, 2023)	895372	20.58	Juridical docs
KazNU (Balzhan et al., 2015)	80627	20.74	Off. press-releases
Russian tweet corpus (Рубцова, 2012)	12752816	7.88	Social media
Statmt-news_commentary-15-kaz-rus	11735	19.43	News
Statmt-news_commentary-14-kaz-rus	9204	19.15	News
Statmt-news_commentary-16-kaz-rus	13224	19.42	News
Facebook-wikimatrix-1-kaz-rus	165109	10.09	Web docs
OPUS-tatoeba-v2-kaz-rus	2010	8.59	General
OPUS-wikimatrix-v1-kaz-rus	32807	10.47	Wikipedia
OPUS-tatoeba-v20190709-kaz-rus	2390	8.27	General
OPUS-tatoeba-v20210310-kaz-rus	2401	8.26	General
OPUS-tatoeba-v20210722-kaz-rus	2417	8.24	General
OPUS-multiccaligned-v1-kaz-rus	1841440	4.94	Web docs
OPUS-xlent-v1.1-kaz-rus	87167	2.05	Software doc-n
OPUS-kde4-v2-kaz-rus	68014	4.70	Software doc-n
OPUS-qed-v2.0a-kaz-rus	5125	10.74	Software doc-n
OPUS-opensubtitles-v2016-kaz-rus	1246	4.55	Subtitles
OPUS-ubuntu-v14.10-kaz-rus	235	4.13	Software doc-n
OPUS-wikimedia-v20210402-kaz-rus	40714	16.41	Wikipedia
OPUS-tatoeba-v20200531-kaz-rus	2400	8.26	General
OPUS-multiccaligned-v1.1-kaz-rus	431952	12.04	Web docs
OPUS-ted2020-v1-kaz-rus	9484	12.05	Subtitles
OPUS-opensubtitles-v2018-kaz-rus	2223	4.21	Subtitles
OPUS-news_commentary-v14-kaz-rus	9163	19.12	News
OPUS-news_commentary-v16-kaz-rus	9163	19.03	News
OPUS-tatoeba-v20220303-kaz-rus	2418	8.59	General
OPUS-xlent-v1-kaz-rus	307929	2.05	Software doc-n
OPUS-gnome-v1-kaz-rus	20550	3.07	Software doc-n
OPUS-tatoeba-v20201109-kaz-rus	2401	8.26	General
all data (dedup.)	20424090		Mixed

Table 9: Train datasets statistics.

Data	NU	CS-1	CS-2	CS-3	CS-4	CS-5	KRCS
all data (AD)	61.28 / 0.82	59.58 / 0.76	59.44 / 0.76	58.96 / 0.75	56.73 / 0.69	61.78 / 0.78	**37.10** / 0.52
AD + cs-1	60.64 / 0.81	**60.13 / 0.77**	59.67 / 0.77	59.51 / 0.76	56.95 / 0.69	60.47 / 0.77	34.52 / 0.51
AD + cs-2	61.09 / 0.82	59.67 / 0.77	**60.85 / 0.78**	59.53 / 0.76	56.76 / 0.69	61.12 / 0.77	36.02 / 0.52
AD + cs-3	60.33 / 0.81	59.62 / 0.77	59.50 / 0.77	**59.59 / 0.76**	56.18 / 0.69	59.82 / 0.77	33.72 / 0.50
AD + cs-4	59.81 / 0.81	58.16 / 0.74	58.33 / 0.74	58.16 / 0.74	**59.15 / 0.69**	62.56 / 0.77	34.81 / 0.51
AD + cs-5	**61.63 / 0.82**	59.22 / 0.75	59.68 / 0.75	59.20 / 0.74	58.81 / 0.69	**64.27 / 0.79**	36.44 / **0.54**

Table 10: The ChrF++ and COMET scores for transformer-600 model on differently augmented datasets.

cs-3: Replace a Kazakh word with a Russian one in random form

Linguistic Soundness: This approach might lack naturalness as it disregards context, grammar, and sentence flow. The randomness can introduce syntactic or morphological anomalies.

Examples: You might hear mismatched forms in spontaneous bilingual speech, particularly among less proficient speakers who switch languages mid-sentence without full grammatical integration. For example, "Мен пошел домой" ("I went home" mixing Kazakh and Russian), where the Russian verb form is not conjugated correctly according to Kazakh syntax.

Usage Contexts: Common in highly informal settings, such as among bilingual children or learners who are not fully competent in both languages.

cs-4: Replace a Kazakh word with a Russian word aligned using FastAlign *Linguistic Soundness:* Using statistical alignments like FastAlign generally improves the naturalness of word replacements because it considers contextual word pairs frequently appearing together in parallel corpora.

Examples: News broadcasts or bilingual podcasts often use consistent patterns of switching, aligning with how FastAlign might map Kazakh-Russian sentence structures. For example, "Менің ойымша, это не совсем правильно" ("I think this is not quite right") frequently occurs.

Usage Contexts: Seen in media content where consistent patterns in code-switching reflect translation or repeated bilingual interactions.

cs-5: Replace a Kazakh word with a Russian word aligned using SimAlign

Linguistic Soundness: SimAlign uses contextual embeddings, making this approach more linguistically sound as it considers sentence-level semantics for alignment. This tends to produce contextually appropriate and grammatically fitting replacements.

Examples: In digital content, such as YouTube videos or podcasts with bilingual speakers, there are instances like "Бұл өте интересно тақырып" ("This is a very interesting topic"), where alignment mirrors natural bilingual communication.

Usage Contexts: Common in both formal and informal settings, particularly where speakers frequently shift between languages without disrupting the overall meaning.

Generative Product Recommendations for Implicit Superlative Queries

Kaustubh D. Dhole[α*], **Nikhita Vedula**[β], **Saar Kuzi**[β], **Giuseppe Castellucci**[β]
Eugene Agichtein[α*], **Shervin Malmasi**[β]
[α]Emory University, Atlanta, GA [β]Amazon.com Inc., Seattle, WA, USA
kdhole@emory.edu, {veduln,skuzi,giusecas,eugeneag,malmasi}@amazon.com

Abstract

In recommender systems, users often seek the *best* products through indirect, vague, or under-specified queries, such as *"best shoes for trail running"*. Such queries, also referred to as implicit superlative queries, pose a significant challenge for standard retrieval and ranking systems as they lack an explicit mention of attributes and require identifying and reasoning over complex attributes. We investigate how Large Language Models (LLMs) can generate implicit attributes for ranking as well as reason over them to improve product recommendations for such queries. As a first step, we propose a novel four-point schema for annotating the best product candidates for superlative queries called **SUPERB**, paired with LLM-based product annotations. We then empirically evaluate several existing retrieval and ranking approaches on our new dataset, providing insights and discussing their integration into real-world e-commerce production systems.

1 Introduction

Superlative queries are common in product search as users seek products with the highest degree of one or more attributes to satisfy their needs. While some superlative queries can be handled by existing retrieval systems (Kumar et al., 2024; Zhang et al., 2015) through attribute-based filtering (e.g., "the largest M2 Pro with 32 GB RAM"), others can pose challenges to the existing solutions.

Specifically, in this paper, we study the problem of product ranking and recommendation for *implicit superlative queries*, where the desired product attributes are not explicitly stated. These queries often involve aspects that require common sense knowledge of the product (Bos and Nissim, 2006; Scheible, 2007). This problem is further compounded by users creating vague and under specified search queries, either due to a lack of knowledge about certain entity features or the search spanning implicit dimensions, frequently leading to query-product mismatches. For example, a query such as ***"the best toy for a 3 year old girl"*** requires gauging the best products across several implicit attributes. To effectively serve such a query, product recommendations should consider popular toy standards like ASTM F963, quality, non-toxic materials, and bright, engaging colors — attributes that are often unknown to end users. With a plethora of product options available on e-commerce platforms, identifying the best products to meet customer needs requires additional product category and world knowledge.

Queries	Query Type	Ranking Criteria
toys	Expecting Relevant Products	No Superlative criteria.
highest rated toy for 3-year olds	Objective Superlative	*Single Objective Criteria:* highest rating
best toy for my 3-year nephew who loves the Flintstones	Implicit Superlative	*Multiple & Implicit Criteria:* highly-rated, overall positively-reviewed, suitable for a male child, likes Flintstones, dinosaurs, etc.

Table 1: Types of Queries along with the criteria of each. **SUPERB** focuses on implicit superlative queries.

Existing ranking pipelines (Reddy et al., 2022) rely on traditional relevance labels like 'Highly Relevant' vs 'Irrelevant' or ESCI (Exact, Substitute, Complement, Irrelevant), and are typically designed for highly objective queries. They do not capture the nuances of product quality and the subjective expectations of "best" products for a given need. In such a scenario, Large Language Models (LLMs) trained on vast amounts of data from diverse sources can act as sources of common-sense knowledge. They have been exposed to extensive text sources and have demonstrated success in modeling global opinions in various domains (Santurkar et al., 2023) and predicting user preferences (Kang et al., 2023). LLMs can leverage this knowledge to offer expert insights beyond the basic product descriptions, thereby enabling search and ranking based on external knowledge.

*Work done at Amazon.

Proceedings of the 2025 Conference of the Nations of the Americas Chapter of the Association for Computational Linguistics: Human Language Technologies (Volume 4: Student Research Workshop), pages 77–91
April 30 - May 1, 2025

We hypothesize that LLMs possess the capability to perform multi-objective optimization over implicit attributes that match user preferences. Hence, LLMs could play a pivotal role in recommending products for superlative queries by (i) offering comprehensive knowledge across multiple product dimensions and (ii) addressing the inherent subjectivity associated with such queries.

Our work aims to investigate the research question: ***Can LLMs effectively rank and recommend the "best" products?*** To that end, we propose a four-level labeling scheme for superlative queries – **SUPERB** with LLM-based annotations, and evaluate retrieval effectiveness across multiple traditional and LLM-based ranking pipelines. To our knowledge, this is the first work to explore implicit superlative queries for product recommendation. Specifically, we make the following contributions:

- We investigate the challenges in answering superlative queries, and define a four-level labeling scheme for relevance ratings.
- We introduce **SUPERB**,[1] **Super**latives with **B**est relevance annotations, a schema of superlative queries and pair them with LLM-based annotations using four different ranking approaches i.e., **pointwise**, **pairwise**, **listwise** and **deliberated** prompting.
- We evaluate the retrieval effectiveness of multiple ranking pipelines against **SUPERB**.

Our contributions highlight the importance of addressing superlative queries in recommendation systems, an area that has been largely overlooked.

2 Related Work

We now discuss related work to place our contributions in context.

2.1 LLMs for Ranking and Recommendation

LLMs have been successfully applied for ranking and recommendation (Yue et al., 2023). Early pointwise ranking approaches (Nogueira et al., 2019) fine-tuned BERT (Devlin et al., 2019) and T5 (Raffel et al., 2020) with query-document pairs, and showed improved performance across a variety of benchmarks (Craswell et al., 2021; Thakur et al.). Pointwise approaches (Ma et al., 2024) ranked items based on scores predicted for individual documents, while pairwise approaches (Qin et al., 2024) prompted models with the query and two documents to compare and rank. Others (Pradeep et al., 2023a,b; Sun et al., 2023) explored a listwise ranking strategy by prompting with a list of documents and generating a ranked list of document IDs.

2.2 LLMs for Relevance Labelling

After showing promise in predicting searcher preferences (Thomas et al., 2024), LLMs have been extensively used in generating relevance labels (Faggioli et al., 2023; Yan et al., 2024; MacAvaney and Soldaini, 2023; Mehrdad et al., 2024; Dhole and Agichtein, 2024a; Dhole et al., 2025). As compared to human evaluation, automated relevance labeling is faster and more scalable.

2.3 Prompting Approaches

Apart from standard prompting approaches, deliberative prompting (Li et al., 2023; Zheng et al., 2024) approaches like Chain-of-Thought (Wei et al., 2022) and scaling inference time compute (Snell et al., 2024; Guo et al., 2025) have successfully improved the performance of LLMs. These methods involve the model generating related information, such as reasoning chains or explanations, to elucidate the reasoning process before arriving at an answer. Our deliberated prompting approach, discussed in Section 5.2 is on similar lines, where we seek to regurgitate implicit attributes so as to make them explicit and help in arriving at the appropriate best label.

2.4 Superlative Search Queries

Much of the research related to superlatives has focused on applications in question answering, opinion mining, and sentiment analysis. A recent study (Kumar et al., 2024) focused on ranking over objective superlatives where the dimensions to compare against (also referred to as the comparison set (Pyatkin et al., 2024)) are often explicitly provided. However, superlative queries often have implicit, vague and complex dimensions.

3 Implicit Superlative Queries

We now formalize the type of superlative queries that we seek to address. We define implicit superlative queries as those which (i) *seek the highest degree of one or more attributes or features of a product*; and (ii) *are implicit in nature*. These queries involve preferences which are generally popular, subjective, and not just based on quantifiable attributes. E.g., the superlative query "best toy

[1] https://github.com/emory-irlab/SUPERB

for my 3-year nephew who loves the Flintstones" – requires an implicit understanding that the user might be looking for a good quality toy which is well-rated and reviewed, reasonably priced, age appropriate, and relates to characters or properties of the show "The Flintstones". Addressing such implicit superlative queries would require (i) inferring hidden attributes, (ii) world knowledge or a general understanding of concepts, and (iii) being able to reason and compare across different related products and ensure that the necessary attributes are of the highest degree. Table 1 shows a summary and examples of targeted queries.

4 The SUPERB Relevance Scheme

We design a novel four-category relevance taxonomy to rank, recommend, and evaluate the retrieved product candidates for superlative queries.

- ***Overall Best (3)***: reserved for products that excel across a broad spectrum of parameters including quality, user experience, value for money, innovation, aesthetics, and environmental impact, among others. Products in this category represent the best of what is available in the market, meeting or exceeding all the expected criteria.
- ***Almost Best (2)***: includes products that perform exceptionally well for most criteria but may fall short in one or a few aspects. These products are generally considered top-tier but lack one or more elements that would elevate them to the Overall Best status.
- ***Relevant but Not the Best (1)***: captures products that are suitable for certain contexts or specific needs but do not represent the best available option across the board.
- ***Not Relevant (0)***: products that do not align well with the user's query or fail to meet the basic standards expected in their category, making them generally not recommended.

We design such a fine-grained system for multiple reasons. Fine-grained labels have been found to be more advantageous than simplistic binary choices (Zhuang et al., 2024). In addition, they facilitate nuanced evaluations and provide comprehensive feedback. For example, differentiating between **Overall Best** and **Almost Best** might be less obvious when purchasing standard office supplies, where basic functionality is adequate. However, this distinction becomes essential when selecting infant car seats, where the highest safety and technology standards are vital.

5 Dataset Construction

We now describe how we generate superlative queries and pair them with products labeled with annotations from our schema.

5.1 Creation of Superlative Queries

For generating superlative queries, we employ the Amazon Shopping Queries dataset (Reddy et al., 2022), which consists of search queries each annotated with up to 40 potential items with ESCI relevance judgements.[2]

Inspired by LLM-based reformulation approaches (Yang et al., 2023; Dhole and Agichtein, 2024b; Dhole et al., 2024), we prompt `Claude-Sonnet` (Anthropic, 2024b) with tailored few-shot instructions, to reformulate these shopping queries into their superlative counterparts. We select queries paired with at least five products with the **Exact** ESCI label. We consider all the products of such queries for subsequent **SUPERB** annotations.[3] We generate a total of 35,651 superlative queries from 1,825 original queries. The complete prompt is shown in Appendix Table 6 and some of the generated queries are shown in Table 2.

Query	Superlative Queries
"running shoes"	*"best running shoes for flat feet"* *"best running shoes for rocky terrain"*
"diaper backpack"	*"best diaper backpack for twins", "most comfortable diaper backpack for back pain"*

Table 2: Examples of generated superlative queries.

5.2 Creating Relevance Annotations

We adopt four methods for annotating the retrieved product candidates with an LLM: **pointwise, pairwise, listwise** and **deliberated** prompting. In the **pointwise** approach, we prompt the model with a superlative query q and the description of a product p_1, to generate a single annotation label b_1 that corresponds to a category in our schema, along with an explanation E (Eq. 1).

$$(q, p_1) \rightarrow \mathbf{M} \rightarrow b_1 + E \quad (1)$$

[2]Exact (3), Substitute (2), Complement (1), Irrelevant (0)

[3]Products of the highest relevance might not necessarily be the **Overall Best** option.

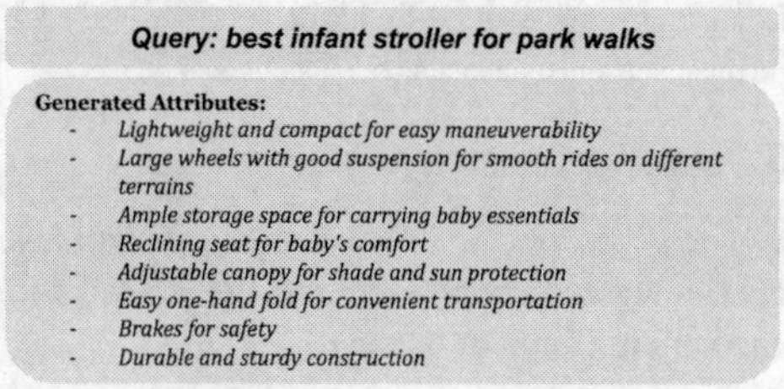

Figure 1: Attributes generated through deliberated prompting for a superlative query.

In the **pairwise** approach, we want the model **M** to compare a product p_1 to another product p_2. Hence, we prompt **M** with the additional description p_2 and force it to generate two labels b_1 and b_2 for both products as shown (Eq. 2).

$$(q, p_1, p_2) \rightarrow \mathbf{M} \rightarrow b_1\, b_2 + E \tag{2}$$

In the **listwise** approach, we expand the context to $N-1$ additional products. We hypothesize that providing a context of other products would help the model make accurate judgements in inferring the necessary attributes. Besides, it is more efficient as compared to the pointwise approach as it can process multiple products simultaneously and generate category labels for each (Eq. 3).

$$(q, p_1, \ldots, p_N) \rightarrow \mathbf{M} \rightarrow b_1\, b_2 \ldots b_N + E \tag{3}$$

The pairwise and listwise approaches allow gauging the properties of other related product(s) for generating the category label of a product. We do not explicitly force the model to select the highest category (i.e., Overall Best) in these scenarios.

$$q \rightarrow \mathbf{M} \rightarrow a_q \tag{4}$$

$$(q, a_q, p_1) \rightarrow \mathbf{M} \rightarrow b_1 + E \tag{5}$$

We also employ a two-step **deliberated prompting** strategy inspired by previous studies (Wei et al., 2022; Li et al., 2023; Zheng et al., 2024), which asks the model to deliberate and reason before generating the final answer. We first generate a set of attributes a_q characterizing the best features of products, and then use them to prompt the model to generate the final taxonomy label (Eq. 4-5). These attributes serve as potential dimensions for the model to compare against in the subsequent pointwise step. Figure 2 shows an example of the label generation process with deliberated prompting.

In each of the methods, we also force the model to generate an explanation to improve model performance (Wei et al., 2022) and also aid human evaluation. Figure 1 shows sample generated attributes for a superlative query. We describe the corresponding instructions in Table 13 in the Appendix.

Queries	Best Annotations
2,230	29,218
Best Label	**Number of Examples**
Overall Best	8,564
Almost Best	10,100
Relevant But Not the Best	8,342
Not Relevant	2,212

Table 3: Category label distribution of **SUPERB**.

We use deliberated prompting to generate a large number of `(query, product, best-label)` triplets, which we refer to as **SUPERB**. We generate a total of 29,218 triplets corresponding to 2,230 randomly sampled unique superlative queries. The label distribution is shown in Table 3. Most of the labels are concentrated in the **Almost Best** and **Relevant But Not the Best** categories, with fewer in the **Not Relevant** category. This is expected as annotations were performed over products that were human-rated as **Exact**, albeit with respect to the original non-superlative queries.

6 Methods

We perform our analysis in a constrained setting where the item description is limited to 512 tokens in length. This is useful for low latency applications. We then use **SUPERB** for evaluating the following ranking pipelines:
(i) **BM25**: We use BM25 as our baseline.
(ii) **RM3**: We also employ a pseudo-relevance feedback baseline RM3 (Abdul-Jaleel et al., 2004).
(iii) **BM25/RM3 + Listwise Re-ranking**: Here, we re-rank the results of the first stage BM25 and RM3 through a listwise ranking approach. We force the model to generate a ranked list of product IDs in the style of RankGPT (Sun et al., 2023) (Eq. 6).

$$(q, p_1, \ldots, p_N) \rightarrow \mathbf{M} \rightarrow r_1 \ldots r_N + E \tag{6}$$

where r_j is the index of a product ranked j.
(iv) **BM25/RM3 + Deliberated Pointwise Re-ranking**: Here, the model is forced to generate a schema label for each item along with a confidence score, when given a query and estimated product attributes. The final ranked list is obtained by first sorting using the labels, and resolving ties first by confidence scores, and then by the BM25 scores.

Retrieval Pipeline	P@5	P@10	P@20	nDCG@5	nDCG@10	nDCG@20
BM25	.206	.163	.125	.219	.213	.235
RM3	.214	.180	.139	.219	.219	.243
BM25 Top K + Pointwise Reranking	.226	.163	-	.205	.198	-
RM3 Top K + Pointwise Reranking	.208	.180	-	.199	.210	-
BM25 Top K + Listwise Reranking	**.262**$^{\alpha}$	.192$^{\alpha}$	.125	**.278**$^{\alpha}$	**.259**$^{\alpha}$	**.264**$^{\alpha}$
RM3 Top K + Listwise Reranking	.248	**.201**$^{\alpha}$	**.140**	.245	.241	.254

Table 4: Performance metrics for different ranking pipelines. α denotes significant improvements (paired t-test with Holm-Bonferroni (Holm, 1979) correction, $p < 0.05$) over BM25.

Retrieval Pipeline	P@10	P@50	nDCG@10	nDCG@50
BM25-Top 100	.154	.079	.205	.279
BM25-Top 100 + Window (5, 2)	**.185**$^{\alpha}$	**.084**$^{\alpha}$	**.241**$^{\alpha}$	**.309**$^{\alpha}$
BM25-Top 100 + Window (20, 10)	.198$^{\alpha}$	.082$^{\alpha}$	.240	.302$^{\alpha}$
BM25-Top 200	.196	.079	.205	.279
BM25-Top 200 + Window (20, 10)	**.262**	**.088**	**.259**	**.328**

Table 5: Comparing different retrieval pipelines for the long context setting. α denotes significant improvements (paired t-test with Holm-Bonferroni (Holm, 1979) correction, $p < 0.05$) over BM25.

This can also be seen as a black-box counterpart of pointwise ranking approaches which provide confidence through logit probabilities. The confidence scores range between 1 and 9 (Eq. 7-8).

$$q \rightarrow \mathbf{M} \rightarrow a_q \quad (7)$$

$$(q, p_1, a_q) \rightarrow \mathbf{M} \rightarrow b_1 + c_1 + E \quad (8)$$

We choose the `Claude-Haiku` (Anthropic, 2024a) model for our experiments since it is beneficial to evaluate smaller models for production pipelines. We use the PyTerrier (Macdonald and Tonellotto, 2020) library with the PyTerrier-GenRank (Dhole, 2024) plugin for designing the retrieval and re-ranking pipelines, and computing `precision` and `nDCG` metrics.

Analysis on Longer Context: We also analyze the case where we use **longer product descriptions**, and when there are a **large number of products in the context**. In that case, employing a listwise strategy can be detrimental as LLMs have been known to show bias towards specific positions of text in the context (Liu et al., 2024), while employing a pointwise strategy would involve excessive inference calls. Also, in practice, we found that LLMs find it hard to generate 100 or 200 item IDs at once hindering their ability to rerank items properly. We hence evaluate such queries using (v) a **BM25 + Sliding-window** approach introduced in RankGPT (Sun et al., 2023).

7 Results and Analysis

As shown in Table 4, we find that the listwise ranking approach is able to rank the best products significantly better as compared to other approaches across all metrics. The listwise scores are better for queries with larger `nDCG` values of BM25 meaning they benefit from an initial ranked list as shown in Appendix Figure 4. Pointwise approaches also help marginally with `P@10` compared to BM25.

We also show the results for top-100 and top-200 items with long descriptions in Table 5. We find that employing a listwise approach in a sliding window fashion significantly improves retrieval effectiveness over the baseline BM25 retrieval across all metrics. In some cases, we observed modest improvements compared to BM25, highlighting the difficulty of handling superlative queries, which is inherently challenging due to ambiguities and the need for extensive world knowledge. This complexity underscored the hardness of the task, as it requires more than traditional retrieval models.

7.1 Error Analysis

By analyzing queries where the methods perform well or poorly, we can gain insights into the model's behavior. The relative performance by nDCG@10 is summarized in Figure 4 in the Appendix.

Both BM25 and LLM perform well: Queries like "most versatile baby carrier for all terrains" (nDCG@10 of 0.756 and 0.756, respectively) and "Best of montreal album for summer road trips" (0.787, 0.951) show strong performance for both approaches. These queries are specific, and the attributes are commonly matched both lexically and semantically to product descriptions.

Both BM25 and LLM perform poorly: For queries such as "Most durable kids plates not plastic" (nDCG@10 of 0.024 and 0.016, respectively) and "most gentle water wipes for baby's skin" (nDCG 0.066 and 0.054, respectively), both approaches struggled. In these cases, challenges like negation, tokenization errors, and specific attributes may contribute to poor performance.

LLM outperforms BM25: Queries like "most modern LG refrigerators to complement minimalist kitchen decor" or "most stylish child safety harness to match toddler's outfits" involve interpreting nuances related to style, versatility, and aesthetics, where LLMs arguably excel i.e. recognizing global preferences and broader contexts, enabling them to rerank products with less tangible attributes.

BM25 outperforms LLM: Many of the BM25-favored queries have clear, well-defined criteria, such as "safest bottle warmer for preserving nutrients" (nDCG 0.508 vs. 0.264); "most flexible rv caulking sealant for easy application" (nDCG 0.619 vs. 0.474). We speculate that BM25 excels with queries containing specific product terms and common words, as it performs well without advanced reasoning, while LLMs might over-generalize.

8 Conclusion

This work studied superlative queries with implicit attributes, which are typically more complex compared to other query types since ranking products for them requires inferring attributes, placing other products in context, and using commonsense knowledge to determine the best ones. Our analysis shows that LLMs can rank the best items, improve ranking when provided with initial ranked lists, and can also be sensitive to them. In addition, our methods are applicable to rank superlative queries in other item and document ranking settings.

We present the **SUPERB**, **4-point schema** and propose **pointwise, deliberated pointwise, pairwise, and listwise** methods to label superlative queries over it and re-rank retrieved products, using an LLM as the backbone. The listwise approach is preferable for lower budgets, while the deliberated point-wise approach can be preferred for better quality annotations. We believe that our study can drive further research on superlative search queries.

Our work highlights key considerations for deploying an LLM-based product ranking system into production. While a listwise approach effectively ranks multiple items at once, it can be inefficient due to lengthy item descriptions. In contrast, a pointwise approach is faster, especially with parallel processing. Sliding window methods and query reformulation are also viable alternatives. Generating attributes and explanations clarifies label assignments, boosting user trust and satisfaction.

Addressing superlative queries in product recommendation systems is essential, particularly for the next generation of interactive shopping assistants (Vedula et al., 2024; Li et al., 2025) and generative recommender systems (Senel et al., 2024). This becomes even more relevant as information-seeking and product search system grow closer together (Kuzi and Malmasi, 2024). These superlative queries capture user intent to find the best possible items, an aspect often overlooked in current systems. Introducing **SUPERB** allows for the development and assessment of recommendation pipelines capable of handling high-expectation queries, helping systems address this unmet need.

Limitations

LLMs have a tendency to average out preferences and often aligning to the majority of the users making them apt for our use case, as shoppers frequently tend to buy the best products unanimously for instance, following viral trends or popular recommendations provided by bloggers.

However, there are other types of superlative queries that could be subjective and depend on user preferences. It would be interesting to see how such user preferences could be incorporated in ranking the best. We envisage various ways our work could be extended to achieve this – through traditional techniques like relevance feedback, conversational interactions, and understanding cultural contexts (Dhole, 2023; Mitchell et al., 2025). Besides, users often make use of public reviews, blogs and ephemeral trends to guide their purchase decision (Hsu et al., 2013; Wilson et al., 2024). Hence incorporating public reviews, and external information through retrieval augmentation could be an interesting line of subsequent study.

Acknowledgments

The authors would like to thank Dhineshkumar Ramasubbu for helping with the annotations and the anonymous reviewers for their helpful feedback.

References

Nasreen Abdul-Jaleel, James Allan, W Bruce Croft, Fernando Diaz, Leah Larkey, Xiaoyan Li, Mark D Smucker, and Courtney Wade. 2004. Umass at trec 2004: Novelty and hard. *Computer Science Department Faculty Publication Series*, page 189.

Anthropic. 2024a. Claude 3 haiku: our fastest model yet. Accessed: 2024-07-10.

Anthropic. 2024b. Introducing claude 3.5 sonnet. Accessed: 2024-07-10.

Johan Bos and Malvina Nissim. 2006. An empirical approach to the interpretation of superlatives. In *Proceedings of the 2006 conference on empirical methods in natural language processing*, pages 9–17.

Nick Craswell, Bhaskar Mitra, Emine Yilmaz, Daniel Campos, and Jimmy Lin. 2021. Ms marco: Benchmarking ranking models in the large-data regime. In *Proceedings of the 44th international ACM SIGIR conference on research and development in information retrieval*, pages 1566–1576.

Jacob Devlin, Ming-Wei Chang, Kenton Lee, and Kristina Toutanova. 2019. Bert: Pre-training of deep bidirectional transformers for language understanding. In *Proceedings of the 2019 Conference of the North American Chapter of the Association for Computational Linguistics: Human Language Technologies, Volume 1 (Long and Short Papers)*, pages 4171–4186.

Kaustubh Dhole. 2023. Large language models as sociotechnical systems. In *Proceedings of the Big Picture Workshop*, pages 66–79.

Kaustubh Dhole and Eugene Agichtein. 2024a. Llm judges for retrieval augmented argumentation.

Kaustubh D Dhole. 2024. Pyterrier-genrank: The pyterrier plugin for reranking with large language models.

Kaustubh D Dhole and Eugene Agichtein. 2024b. Genqrensemble: Zero-shot llm ensemble prompting for generative query reformulation. In *European Conference on Information Retrieval*, pages 326–335. Springer.

Kaustubh D Dhole, Ramraj Chandradevan, and Eugene Agichtein. 2024. Generative query reformulation using ensemble prompting, document fusion, and relevance feedback. *arXiv preprint arXiv:2405.17658*.

Kaustubh D. Dhole, Kai Shu, and Eugene Agichtein. 2025. ConQRet: Benchmarking fine-grained evaluation of retrieval augmented argumentation with LLM judges. In *Proceedings of the 2025 Annual Conference of the Nations of the Americas Chapter of the Association for Computational Linguistics*, Albuquerque, New Mexico. Association for Computational Linguistics.

Guglielmo Faggioli, Laura Dietz, Charles LA Clarke, Gianluca Demartini, Matthias Hagen, Claudia Hauff, Noriko Kando, Evangelos Kanoulas, Martin Potthast, Benno Stein, et al. 2023. Perspectives on large language models for relevance judgment. In *Proceedings of the 2023 ACM SIGIR International Conference on Theory of Information Retrieval*, pages 39–50.

Daya Guo, Dejian Yang, Haowei Zhang, Junxiao Song, Ruoyu Zhang, Runxin Xu, Qihao Zhu, Shirong Ma, Peiyi Wang, Xiao Bi, et al. 2025. Deepseek-r1: Incentivizing reasoning capability in llms via reinforcement learning. *arXiv preprint arXiv:2501.12948*.

Sture Holm. 1979. A simple sequentially rejective multiple test procedure. *Scandinavian journal of statistics*, pages 65–70.

Chin-Lung Hsu, Judy Chuan-Chuan Lin, and Hsiu-Sen Chiang. 2013. The effects of blogger recommendations on customers' online shopping intentions. *Internet research*, 23(1):69–88.

Wang-Cheng Kang, Jianmo Ni, Nikhil Mehta, Maheswaran Sathiamoorthy, Lichan Hong, Ed Chi, and Derek Zhiyuan Cheng. 2023. Do llms understand user preferences? evaluating llms on user rating prediction. *arXiv preprint arXiv:2305.06474*.

Nitesh Kumar, Usashi Chatterjee, and Steven Schockaert. 2024. Ranking entities along conceptual space dimensions with llms: An analysis of fine-tuning strategies. *arXiv preprint arXiv:2402.15337*.

Saar Kuzi and Shervin Malmasi. 2024. Bridging the Gap Between Information Seeking and Product Search Systems: Q&A Recommendation for E-Commerce. *SIGIR Forum*, 58(1):1–10.

Bei Li, Rui Wang, Junliang Guo, Kaitao Song, Xu Tan, Hany Hassan, Arul Menezes, Tong Xiao, Jiang Bian, and JingBo Zhu. 2023. Deliberate then generate: Enhanced prompting framework for text generation. *arXiv preprint arXiv:2305.19835*.

Xiangci Li, Zhiyu Chen, Jason Ingyu Choi, Nikhita Vedula, Besnik Fetahu, Oleg Rokhlenko, and Shervin Malmasi. 2025. Wizard of shopping: Target-oriented e-commerce dialogue generation with decision tree branching.

Nelson F. Liu, Kevin Lin, John Hewitt, Ashwin Paranjape, Michele Bevilacqua, Fabio Petroni, and Percy Liang. 2024. Lost in the middle: How language models use long contexts. *Transactions of the Association for Computational Linguistics*, 12:157–173.

Xueguang Ma, Liang Wang, Nan Yang, Furu Wei, and Jimmy Lin. 2024. Fine-tuning llama for multi-stage text retrieval. In *Proceedings of the 47th International ACM SIGIR Conference on Research and Development in Information Retrieval*, SIGIR '24, page 2421–2425, New York, NY, USA. Association for Computing Machinery.

Sean MacAvaney and Luca Soldaini. 2023. One-shot labeling for automatic relevance estimation. In *Proceedings of the 46th International ACM SIGIR Conference on Research and Development in Information Retrieval*, SIGIR '23, page 2230–2235, New York, NY, USA. Association for Computing Machinery.

Craig Macdonald and Nicola Tonellotto. 2020. Declarative experimentation ininformation retrieval using pyterrier. In *Proceedings of ICTIR 2020*.

Navid Mehrdad, Hrushikesh Mohapatra, Mossaab Bagdouri, Prijith Chandran, Alessandro Magnani, Xunfan Cai, Ajit Puthenputhussery, Sachin Yadav, Tony Lee, ChengXiang Zhai, et al. 2024. Large language models for relevance judgment in product search. *arXiv preprint arXiv:2406.00247*.

Margaret Mitchell, Giuseppe Attanasio, Ioana Baldini, Miruna Clinciu, Jordan Clive, Pieter Delobelle, Manan Dey, Sil Hamilton, Timm Dill, Jad Doughman, Ritam Dutt, Avijit Ghosh, Jessica Zosa Forde, Carolin Holtermann, Lucie-Aimée Kaffee, Tanmay Laud, Anne Lauscher, Roberto L Lopez-Davila, Maraim Masoud, Nikita Nangia, Anaelia Ovalle, Giada Pistilli, Dragomir Radev, Beatrice Savoldi, Vipul Raheja, Jeremy Qin, Esther Ploeger, Arjun Subramonian, Kaustubh Dhole, Kaiser Sun, Amirbek Djanibekov, Jonibek Mansurov, Kayo Yin, Emilio Villa Cueva, Sagnik Mukherjee, Jerry Huang, Xudong Shen, Jay Gala, Hamdan Al-Ali, Tair Djanibekov, Nurdaulet Mukhituly, Shangrui Nie, Shanya Sharma, Karolina Stanczak, Eliza Szczechla, Tiago Timponi Torrent, Deepak Tunuguntla, Marcelo Viridiano, Oskar van der Wal, Adina Yakefu, Aurélie Névéol, Mike Zhang, Sydney Zink, and Zeerak Talat. 2025. SHADES: Towards a multilingual assessment of stereotypes in large language models. In *Proceedings of the 2025 Annual Conference of the Nations of the Americas Chapter of the Association for Computational Linguistics*, Mexico City, Mexico. Association for Computational Linguistics.

Rodrigo Nogueira, Wei Yang, Kyunghyun Cho, and Jimmy Lin. 2019. Multi-stage document ranking with bert. *arXiv preprint arXiv:1910.14424*.

Ronak Pradeep, Sahel Sharifymoghaddam, and Jimmy Lin. 2023a. Rankvicuna: Zero-shot listwise document reranking with open-source large language models. *arXiv preprint arXiv:2309.15088*.

Ronak Pradeep, Sahel Sharifymoghaddam, and Jimmy Lin. 2023b. Rankzephyr: Effective and robust zero-shot listwise reranking is a breeze! *arXiv preprint arXiv:2312.02724*.

Valentina Pyatkin, Bonnie Webber, Ido Dagan, and Reut Tsarfaty. 2024. Superlatives in context: Explicit and implicit domain restrictions for superlative frames. *arXiv preprint arXiv:2405.20967*.

Zhen Qin, Rolf Jagerman, Kai Hui, Honglei Zhuang, Junru Wu, Le Yan, Jiaming Shen, Tianqi Liu, Jialu Liu, Donald Metzler, Xuanhui Wang, and Michael Bendersky. 2024. Large language models are effective text rankers with pairwise ranking prompting. In *Findings of the Association for Computational Linguistics: NAACL 2024*, pages 1504–1518, Mexico City, Mexico. Association for Computational Linguistics.

Colin Raffel, Noam Shazeer, Adam Roberts, Katherine Lee, Sharan Narang, Michael Matena, Yanqi Zhou, Wei Li, and Peter J Liu. 2020. Exploring the limits of transfer learning with a unified text-to-text transformer. *Journal of machine learning research*, 21(140):1–67.

Chandan K. Reddy, Lluís Màrquez, Fran Valero, Nikhil Rao, Hugo Zaragoza, Sambaran Bandyopadhyay, Arnab Biswas, Anlu Xing, and Karthik Subbian. 2022. Shopping queries dataset: A large-scale ESCI benchmark for improving product search.

Shibani Santurkar, Esin Durmus, Faisal Ladhak, Cinoo Lee, Percy Liang, and Tatsunori Hashimoto. 2023. Whose opinions do language models reflect? In *International Conference on Machine Learning*, pages 29971–30004. PMLR.

Silke Scheible. 2007. Towards a computational treatment of superlatives. In *Proceedings of the ACL 2007 Student Research Workshop*, pages 67–72, Prague, Czech Republic. Association for Computational Linguistics.

Lütfi Kerem Senel, Besnik Fetahu, Davis Yoshida, Zhiyu Chen, Giuseppe Castellucci, Nikhita Vedula, Jason Choi, and Shervin Malmasi. 2024. Generative Explore-Exploit: Training-free Optimization of Generative Recommender Systems using LLM Optimizers. In *Proceedings of ACL 2024 (Research Track)*.

Charlie Snell, Jaehoon Lee, Kelvin Xu, and Aviral Kumar. 2024. Scaling llm test-time compute optimally can be more effective than scaling model parameters. *arXiv preprint arXiv:2408.03314*.

Weiwei Sun, Lingyong Yan, Xinyu Ma, Shuaiqiang Wang, Pengjie Ren, Zhumin Chen, Dawei Yin, and Zhaochun Ren. 2023. Is chatgpt good at search? investigating large language models as re-ranking agents. In *Proceedings of the 2023 Conference on Empirical Methods in Natural Language Processing*, pages 14918–14937.

Nandan Thakur, Nils Reimers, Andreas Rücklé, Abhishek Srivastava, and Iryna Gurevych. Beir: A heterogeneous benchmark for zero-shot evaluation of information retrieval models.

Paul Thomas, Seth Spielman, Nick Craswell, and Bhaskar Mitra. 2024. Large language models can accurately predict searcher preferences. In *Proceedings of the 47th International ACM SIGIR Conference on Research and Development in Information Retrieval*, SIGIR '24, page 1930–1940, New York, NY, USA. Association for Computing Machinery.

Nikhita Vedula, Oleg Rokhlenko, and Shervin Malmasi. 2024. Question suggestion for conversational shopping assistants using product metadata. In *Proceedings of the 47th International ACM SIGIR Conference on Research and Development in Information Retrieval*, SIGIR '24, page 2960–2964, New York, NY, USA. Association for Computing Machinery.

Jason Wei, Xuezhi Wang, Dale Schuurmans, Maarten Bosma, Fei Xia, Ed Chi, Quoc V Le, Denny Zhou, et al. 2022. Chain-of-thought prompting elicits reasoning in large language models. *Advances in neural information processing systems*, 35:24824–24837.

George Wilson, Oliver Johnson, and William Brown. 2024. The influence of digital marketing on consumer purchasing decisions.

Le Yan, Zhen Qin, Honglei Zhuang, Rolf Jagerman, Xuanhui Wang, Michael Bendersky, and Harrie Oosterhuis. 2024. Consolidating ranking and relevance predictions of large language models through post-processing. *arXiv preprint arXiv:2404.11791*.

Dayu Yang, Yue Zhang, and Hui Fang. 2023. Zero-shot query reformulation for conversational search. In *Proceedings of the 2023 ACM SIGIR International Conference on Theory of Information Retrieval*, pages 257–263.

Zhenrui Yue, Sara Rabhi, Gabriel de Souza Pereira Moreira, Dong Wang, and Even Oldridge. 2023. Llamarec: Two-stage recommendation using large language models for ranking. *arXiv preprint arXiv:2311.02089*.

Sheng Zhang, Yansong Feng, Songfang Huang, Kun Xu, Zhe Han, and Dongyan Zhao. 2015. Semantic interpretation of superlative expressions via structured knowledge bases. In *Proceedings of the 53rd Annual Meeting of the Association for Computational Linguistics and the 7th International Joint Conference on Natural Language Processing (Volume 2: Short Papers)*, pages 225–230.

Huaixiu Steven Zheng, Swaroop Mishra, Xinyun Chen, Heng-Tze Cheng, Ed H. Chi, Quoc V Le, and Denny Zhou. 2024. Take a step back: Evoking reasoning via abstraction in large language models. In *The Twelfth International Conference on Learning Representations*.

Honglei Zhuang, Zhen Qin, Kai Hui, Junru Wu, Le Yan, Xuanhui Wang, and Michael Bendersky. 2024. Beyond yes and no: Improving zero-shot llm rankers via scoring fine-grained relevance labels. In *Proceedings of the 2024 Conference of the North American Chapter of the Association for Computational Linguistics: Human Language Technologies (Volume 2: Short Papers)*, pages 358–370.

Appendix

Given a query, generate multiple diverse superlative versions of the same which require common sense inference. The reformulated superlative queries should provide additional context for which common sense knowledge is required. The context should be related to the item in the original query in various ways and should seek the highest degree of some related aspects. For instance, if a user is looking for a mouse pad, she might be interested in the best one which best complements the color of her laptop, or may require the most suitable one for painful wrists, etc. The context should require generally understood knowledge and common sense and it should not depend on objective criteria like highest rated or cheapest. Some examples of superlative queries are "Best booster chairs to make mealtime hassle-free for my toddler", "most user-friendly diaper pail to make my life as a new mom easier", "most suitable lawnmover for rocky areas", "most stylish and modern changing table pad to complement my nursery decor","Smoothest-riding 2 seater stroller for twin toddlers","Best diaper genie for sparking a child's creativity","Highest quality epoxy resin for creating stunning wood art pieces", You should not try to change the type of the product which the user is asking for. Only if the product explicitly mentions a single product, you should change it to make it more generalized (for instance, Amazon $100 gift card can be changed to $100 gift card and so on). Do not generate anything else except for one body of JSON and do not explain yourself. Do not include double quotes while generating the superlatives.
Provide your output in the form of a JSON.
Input Query: LEGO kit

```
{{
    "superlatives" : [
        "best LEGO kit for chess players",
        "best lego kits for marvel fans",
        "most impressive lego kits for my friend who is fascinated about India",
        "best lego kit to encourage my toddler to learn astronomy",
        ]
}}
```

Input Query: black halter beaded satin long gowns sequin

```
{{
    "superlatives": [
        "Trendiest black halter beaded satin long gowns with sequins for an Afro-themed fashion parade",
        "Best halter beaded satin long gowns to match my husband's black silk coat",
        "Most casual black halter satin long gowns with sequins helpful ",
        "most suitable black halter beaded satin long gowns sequin for a date night"
        ]
}}
```

Input Query: armani exchange glasses

```
{{
    "superlatives": [
        "best glasses with bold and trendy frames",
        "best glasses which can be used for office and at parties",
        "best retro look armani exchange glasses",
        "most suitable armani exchange glasses for travelling to dubai and mexico" ,
        "best armani exchange glasses that blend seamlessly with my red jeans",
        ]
}}
```

Input Query: {query}

Table 6: Prompt used for Superlative Query Generation

Based on the item description and some of its reviews, your internal knowledge about all the features of such types of items, and a user's given shopping query, you should classify the item into one of the taxonomy categories: User Query: {query} Item Description: Title: {title} Description: {description} User Query: {query} Categories: 3. Overall Best: The item meets the following criteria: The item is overall best in its category on various parameters – excellence in quality, user experience, value for money, innovation, aesthetics, environmental impact, market position, safety, versatility, processing speed, user rating, etc.. 2. Almost Best: The item scores high on most or majority of the parameters except for a few. Most users would consider this as item as the best.. 1. Relevant But Not Best: The item is suitable in certain contexts but not the best option.. 0. Not Relevant: The item is generally not recommended as it is not relevant to the user's query.. Please classify the item into one of the four types. You should return a number between between 3 (Overall Best) and 0 (Not Relevant) followed by an explanation on the next line justifying why that category of best is suitable.

Table 7: Pointwise Prompt Used For Best Annotations

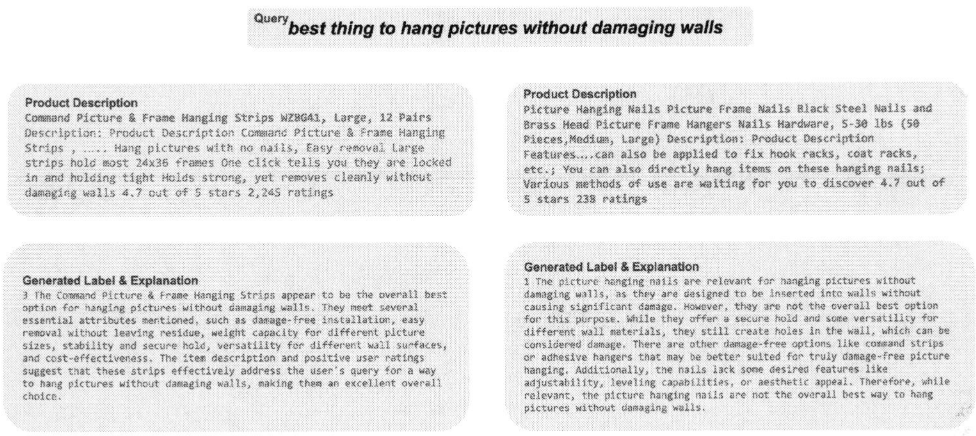

Figure 2: Sample generated label and explanation using the deliberated pointwise approach.

A Evaluating the Best Product Judgements

To evaluate the efficacy of the **SUPERB** labels from the above methods, we perform a human evaluation to record the agreement with the model's labels. In-house domain experts performed the annotation. For each superlative query, the product descriptions, the corresponding category labels and their explanations from the pointwise, pairwise and listwise methods are presented to the annotator, who may agree with none, some, or all of the LLM generated labels.

As shown in Table 8, in our first phase of human evaluation, we find that the pointwise approach is more often preferred over listwise and pairwise approaches. During the process of annotation, we find that the pairwise approach tends to narrow its focus on attributes presented in the single product in the context, often misjudging necessary attributes. In the pointwise and listwise approaches, this seems to be less of a concern.

In the second phase of human evaluation, we use the best strategy of the first phase, i.e., pointwise, and measure the effects of deliberation over a separate set of queries. We find that deliberated prompting is preferred more often than its non-deliberated counterpart, as shown in Table 9, and making the attributes explicit helps assign better quality annotations.

	Pointwise	Pairwise	Listwise
Agreement Rate	**66.36%**	44.86%	60.75%

Table 8: Comparing the three best labelling approaches over 107 random superlative queries.

	Without	With Deliberation
Agreement Rate	75.23%	**78.90%**

Table 9: Effect of deliberation on pointwise prompting for 109 random superlative queries.

Effect of Increasing the Number of Products: We measure the listwise ranking performance while increasing the number of input products K. As shown in Figure 3, we find that the listwise approach increases the likelihood of picking the best product as we provide more products in the context, and then tends to stagnate after a large K. The pointwise approach's performance remains almost the same.

As shown in Table 10, we also shuffle the product order from the first stage retriever and evaluate how sensitive the listwise re-ranker is to the initial order. Shuffling the top-20 products in three different random orders causes drastic performance drops in each, i.e. listwise re-ranking benefits from an initial ranked list and improves upon it.

Listwise	BM25	seed1	seed2	seed3	RM3
nDCG@10	.259	.147	.143	.141	.241

Table 10: Listwise reranking performance when the top-20 products are placed in context with initial rankings from BM25, random and RM3 orderings. The listwise re-ranker is highly sensitive to the order provided by the first stage retriever.

B Effect of Query Reformulation

To reduce inference latency for such scenarios, we also investigate incorporating LLM-based reformulation i.e. employing the LLM during query generation rather than during reranking. Specifically, we introduce (vi) two types of **query reformulations** to generate i) ***keywords***: this is accomplished by generating generic query expansion terms which are related to the query ii) ***attributes***: we use the above estimated ideal attributes for expanding the query.

Results: We also find that employing keyword and attribute-based reformulated queries helps improve overall retrieval effectiveness, as compared to the original queries. Attribute-based reformulation improves recall and MAP across all retrieval settings.

We find that by employing keyword and attribute based reformulated queries helps improve overall retrieval effectiveness, as compared to the original queries. Attribute based reformulation improves recall and MAP across all retrieval settings. Table 11 presents the details.

Based on the following descriptions of multiple items and a user's shopping query, you need to classify each item into one of the taxonomy categories:

User Query: {query}
Item 1 Description: Title: {Title 1} Description: {Item Description 1}
Item 2 Description: Title: {Title 2} Description: {Item Description 2}
...
...
Item N-1 Description: Title: {Title N-1} Description: {Item Description N-1}
Item N Description: Title: {Title N} Description: {Item Description N}
User Query: {query}

Classification Categories:

3. Overall Best: The item meets the following criteria: The item is overall best in its category on various parameters – excellence in quality, user experience, value for money, innovation, aesthetics, environmental impact, market position, safety, versatility, processing speed, has been rated highly, etc..
2. Almost Best: The item scores high on most or majority of the parameters except for a few. Most users would consider this as item as the best..
1. Relevant But Not Best: The item is suitable in certain contexts but not the best option..
0. Not Relevant: The item is generally not recommended as it is not relevant to the user's query..

Please rank each item into one of the four types. First, return the rankings as numbers separated by ' ' where each number ranges between between 3 (Overall Best) and 0 (Not Relevant). And then provide a short explanation as to why you assigned the best categories. You should start your answer with only the rankings (i.e. 3 2 2 0 and so on) and not a description. Ensure that the number of rankings is equal to the number of items shown i.e. exactly 25.

Table 12: Listwise Prompt Used For Best Annotations – Provides multiple additional items as context

Given a user seeking the best item, define the ideal requirements for satisfying the user query by returning a list of attributes which are essential for that item. For instance, if the user is seeking the best laptop for his 15 year old son, the attributes could be a large RAM, the best GPUs (maybe from NVIDIA or AMD), good speakers etc. You should try to come up attributes which are essential for the perfect or the best item as well as which satisfy the user query. Return your output as a json. Do not generate anything else. {query}

Table 13: Deliberation Step used for Generating Attributes

Based on the following descriptions of two items, their reviews, and a user's shopping query, you need to rank each item into one of the taxonomy categories:

User Query: {query}
Item 1 Description: Title: {Title 1} Description: {Item Description 1}
Item 2 Description: Title: {Title 2} Description: {Item Description 2}
User Query: {query}

Categories:
3. Overall Best: The item meets the following criteria: The item is overall best in its category on various parameters – excellence in quality, user experience, value for money, innovation, aesthetics, environmental impact, market position, safety, versatility, processing speed, has been rated highly, etc..
2. Almost Best: The item scores high on most or majority of the parameters except for a few. Most users would consider this as item as the best..
1. Relevant But Not Best: The item is suitable in certain contexts but not the best option..
0. Not Relevant: The item is generally not recommended as it is not relevant to the user's query..

Please rank each item into one of the four types. First, return two numbers separated by ' ' where each number ranges between between 3 (Overall Best) and 0 (Not Relevant). And then briefly explain why the category of best is suitable.

Table 14: Pairwise Prompt Used For Best Annotations – Provides one additional item as context

Based on the following descriptions of two items, their reviews, and a user's shopping query, you need to rank each item into one of the taxonomy categories:
User Query: {query}
The best item would possibly possess many of such attributes: {Predicted Attributes}
Item 1 Description: Title: {title} Description: {Item Description}
User Query: {query}
Categories:
3. Overall Best: The item meets the following criteria: The item is overall best in its category on various parameters – excellence in quality, user experience, value for money, innovation, aesthetics, environmental impact, market position, safety, versatility, processing speed, has been rated highly, etc..
2. Almost Best: The item scores high on most or majority of the parameters except for a few. Most users would consider this as item as the best..

1. Relevant But Not Best: The item is suitable in certain contexts but not the best option..
0. Not Relevant: The item is generally not recommended as it is not relevant to the user's query..

Please rank each item into one of the four types. First, return two numbers separated by ' ' where each number ranges between between 3 (Overall Best) and 0 (Not Relevant). And then briefly explain why the category of best is suitable.

Table 15: Deliberated Pointwise Prompt Used For Best Annotations – Predicted attributes are provided as context

Based on the item description and some of its reviews, your internal knowledge about all the features of such types of items, and a user's given shopping query, you should classify the item into one of the taxonomy categories and provide a confidence score for your prediction:

User Query: {`query`}
The best item would possibly possess many of such attributes: {Predicted Attributes}
Item Description: Title: {`title`} Description: {`description`}
User Query: {`query`}

Categories:
3. Overall Best: The item meets the following criteria: The item is overall best in its category on various parameters – excellence in quality, user experience, value for money, innovation, aesthetics, environmental impact, market position, safety, versatility, processing speed, user rating, etc..
2. Almost Best: The item scores high on most or majority of the parameters except for a few. Most users would consider this as item as the best..
1. Relevant But Not Best: The item is suitable in certain contexts but not the best option..
0. Not Relevant: The item is generally not recommended as it is not relevant to the user's query..

You should return a number between between 3 (Overall Best) and 0 (Not Relevant) followed by the confidence of your prediction between 1 to 9 and an explanation on the next line justifying why that category of best is suitable. Your output should look something like this: 2 8 some explanation or 3 4 some explanation. If you are fully confident, then your confidence should have high values like 7, 8 upto 9. If you are not sure, then you should assign low confidence values like 1, 2 or 3. If you are partially confident, then assign other values.

Table 16: Deliberated Pointwise Prompt Used For Ranking for generating labels and confidence scores.

Based on the following descriptions of multiple items and a user's shopping query, you need to rank the items using the below taxonomy:

User Query: {`query`}
Item 1 Description: Title: {`Title 1`} Description: {`Item Description 1`}
Item 2 Description: Title: {`Title 2`} Description: {`Item Description 2`}
...
...
Item N-1 Description: Title: {`Title N-1`} Description: {`Item Description N-1`}
Item N Description: Title: {`Title N`} Description: {`Item Description N`}
User Query: {`query`}

Classification Categories:
3. Overall Best: The item meets the following criteria: The item is overall best in its category on various parameters – excellence in quality, user experience, value for money, innovation, aesthetics, environmental impact, market position, safety, versatility, processing speed, has been rated highly, etc..
2. Almost Best: The item scores high on most or majority of the parameters except for a few. Most users would consider this as item as the best..
1. Relevant But Not Best: The item is suitable in certain contexts but not the best option..
0. Not Relevant: The item is generally not recommended as it is not relevant to the user's query..

The 'Overall Best' item(s) should be ranked higher, followed by the 'Almost Best' item(s), the 'Relevant But not the best' and then the 'not relevant' ones. You should return the item ids separated by ' ' something like 8 3 9 1 2... You should start your answer with only the rankings and not a description. Ensure that each item id is present in the list. Ensure that the number of rankings is equal to the number of items shown i.e. exactly K.

Table 17: Listwise Prompt Used For Ranking

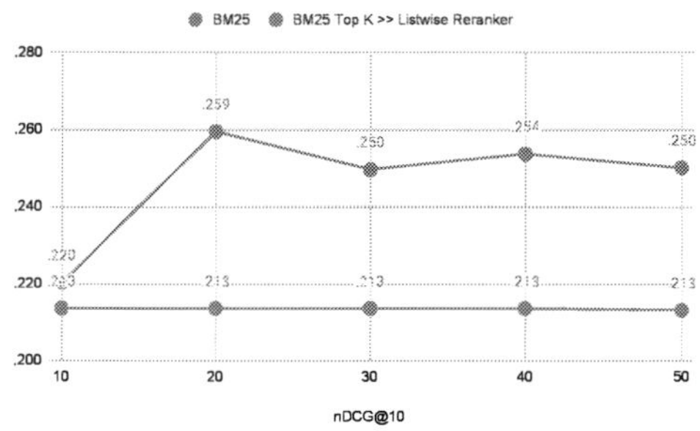

Figure 3: Listwise ranking consistently improves best ranking for different values of K.

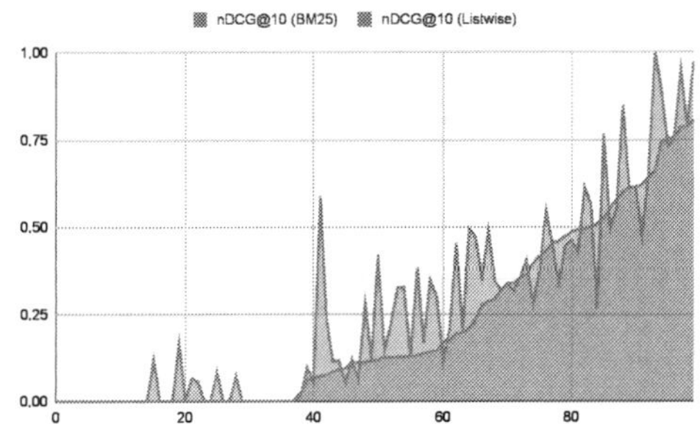

Figure 4: Listwise scores rank better than BM25 for almost all queries. Moreover, LLMs when employed in a listwise fashion benefit from an initial ranked list as queries with higher BM25 scores tend to get better improvements from the listwise approach.

	BM25			BM25 + Window (20,10)		
Queries	MAP	R@50	**nDCG@50**	MAP	R@50	**nDCG@50**
SUPERB (Raw)	.152	.358	.279	.168	.372	.302
+ Keyword based QR	.155	.371	**.291**	.172	.383	.31
+ Attribute based QR	**.156**	**.382**	**.291**	**.176**	**.389**	**.311**

Table 11: Comparison of Query Reformulation with BM25 over superlative queries.

ConQuer: A Framework for Concept-Based Quiz Generation

Yicheng Fu[1], **Zikui Wang**[1], **Liuxin Yang**[1], **Meiqing Huo**[1], **and Zhongdongming Dai**[2]
[1]Stanford University, CA, USA
[2]University of California San Diego, CA, USA
{easonfu, zikuiw, lyang822, meiqing7}@stanford.edu[1]
z1dai@ucsd.edu[2]

Abstract

Quizzes play a crucial role in education by reinforcing students' understanding of key concepts and encouraging self-directed exploration. However, compiling high-quality quizzes can be challenging and require deep expertise and insight into specific subject matter. Although LLMs have greatly enhanced the efficiency of quiz generation, concerns remain regarding the quality of these AI-generated quizzes and their educational impact on students. To address these issues, we introduce **ConQuer**, a concept-based quiz generation framework that leverages external knowledge sources. We employ comprehensive evaluation dimensions to assess the quality of the generated quizzes, using LLMs as judges. Our experiment results demonstrate a 4.8% improvement in evaluation scores and a 77.52% win rate in pairwise comparisons against baseline quiz sets. Ablation studies further underscore the effectiveness of each component in our framework. Code available at `https://github.com/sofyc/ConQuer`.

1 Introduction

Quizzes are a widely used tool in modern education, serving as a means to test students' understanding of material and providing opportunities for reflection (Cheong et al., 2013; Evans et al., 2021). Well-designed quizzes can enhance active learning, provide valuable feedback, and stimulate curiosity (Malandrino et al., 2014; Mukaromah et al., 2019). However, the process of creating quizzes is often labor intensive, requiring subject matter expertise, careful consideration of key concepts, and understanding of students' knowledge levels (Gorin, 2006). This challenge becomes even more pronounced in fields where content is updated frequently or where educators need to generate quizzes on a scale.

In recent years, the emergence of Large Language Models has provided a promising solution to these challenges. LLMs can quickly generate quizzes that cover a wide range of topics. Elkins et al. (2023) demonstrated that the LLM-generated quizzes are promising for widespread use in the classroom. Although this approach offers significant efficiency gains, it also raises concerns about the quality and relevance of the generated quizzes (Lodovico Molina et al., 2024). Specifically, there are questions about whether the quizzes accurately reflect key concepts in a given domain and whether they are grounded in reliable sources of knowledge (Zhang et al., 2023).

To address these concerns, we propose a concept-based quiz generation method grounded in external knowledge corpora, such as Wikipedia and ConceptNet (Speer et al., 2017). Using concepts instead of keywords to search for relevant information enables the capture of knowledge points that may not be explicitly mentioned in students' questions. By anchoring quiz generation in well-established knowledge bases, our approach ensures that quizzes are not only relevant but also comprehensive, covering critical concepts that learners must grasp.

We employ comprehensive evaluation dimensions to assess various aspects of quiz quality. Our concept-based approach achieves a 4.8% improvement in evaluation scores compared to traditional LLM-generated quizzes. In pairwise evaluations, our method consistently outperforms other alternatives,with 77.52% of evaluations favoring our method over LLM-generated quizzes. Additionally, ablation studies reveal the critical contributions of the concept extraction module, knowledge source, and summary module in enhancing the overall effectiveness of our framework.

In summary, our key contributions are as follows:

- We present **ConQuer**, a novel concept-based quiz generation framework that significantly improves the quality of LLM-generated

Proceedings of the 2025 Conference of the Nations of the Americas Chapter of the Association for Computational Linguistics: Human Language Technologies (Volume 4: Student Research Workshop), pages 92–104
April 30 - May 1, 2025

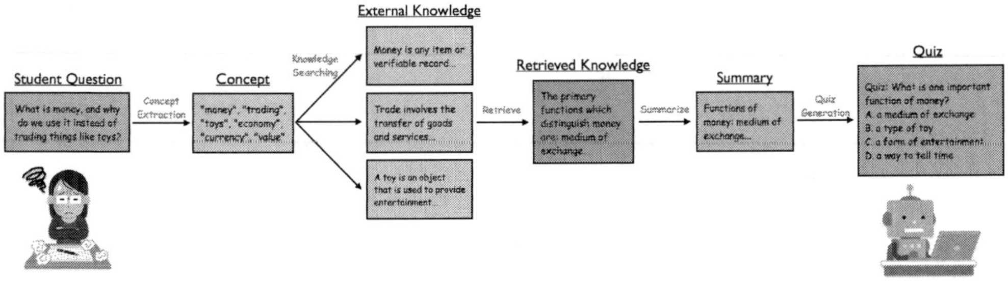

Figure 1: The ConQuer Framework. First, key concepts are extracted from student questions, followed by retrieving relevant information from external knowledge sources based on semantic similarity. Finally, the main topics are summarized to generate personalized quizzes.

quizzes. A diagram of our framework is shown in Figure 1.

- We conduct a detailed ablation study with qualitative analysis, revealing that each component of our framework plays a crucial role in improving the quality of quiz generation.
- We release our student question dataset and quiz generation pipeline code as open-source resources to facilitate future research.

2 Related Work

Retrieval-Augmented Generation While LLMs have demonstrated strong performance in various understanding and reasoning tasks, their ability to generate reliable and factually accurate text remains a challenge, particularly in knowledge-intensive tasks (Kandpal et al., 2023). This often leads to hallucinations, where models produce incorrect or fabricated information (Zhang et al., 2023). Retrieval-Augmented Generation (RAG) (Lewis et al., 2020) has been proposed to address this issue by integrating LLMs with retrieval mechanisms, allowing models to refer to external databases and improve the factuality and credibility of their outputs. RAG has shown promising results in QA tasks such as SQuAD (Rajpurkar et al., 2018) and HotpotQA (Yang et al., 2018), as well as in personal planning applications (Fu et al., 2024b), where external knowledge is essential for generating accurate and contextually relevant responses.

Quiz Generation Quizzes are Widely recognized as an effective tool to promote active learning and improve knowledge retention (Evans et al., 2021; Mukaromah et al., 2019). Recent studies have explored how large language models (LLMs) can be used to improve the quality of generated quiz content. For instance, Vu et al. (2024) investigates interactive prompting strategies for designing question banks, while Hasan et al. (2024) combines LLMs with structured resources to enhance factual accuracy and contextual relevance in quiz generation. Additionally, Gabajiwala et al. (2022) explores keyword extraction to generate better quizzes. Biancini et al. (2024) proposes to generate quizzes by Injecting external knowledge into LLM prompts. These approaches typically rely on pre-identified topic and keyword-based techniques. In contrast, our ConQuer framework tackles scenarios where Students may lack awareness of the concepts they need to learn, requiring a focus on deeper concept identification rather than surface-level keyword-based methods.

3 Task

Previous studies have explored quiz generation based on predefined topics (Song and Zhao, 2016; Vu et al., 2024). However, Such topic-centered approaches often fails to capture the complexities of real-world educational settings. In practice, students Frequently ask vague or incomplete question, sometimes without fully grasping the underlying concepts they are struggling with (Commeyras, 1995). Research in education has shown that students' questions can reflect their thought processes and serve as a valuable resource to enhance learning (Cuccio-Schirripa and Steiner, 2000; Chin and Osborne, 2008). Inspired by this, our approach shifts from relying on predefined topics for LLM-based quiz generation. Instead, we focus on generating questions that mirror the types of inquiries students might pose to instructors, capturing their authentic learning challenges. The task then becomes generating quizzes that effectively support students with limited information about their current knowledge level.

To enhance the diversity of student questions and broaden the framework's applicability across a wide audience, we selected 30 subject areas from the MMLU dataset (Hendrycks et al., 2020) and considered three educational levels: primary school, high school, and PhD. For each subject and educational level, we tasked GPT-4o (Hurst et al., 2024) with generating five representative questions that students would typically ask. This approach yields a dataset of 450 questions, which we compiled into a comprehensive question set for experiment. The quiz generation task involves generating three quizzes for each student question, where each quiz consists of one question, one correct answer, and three incorrect options, with the correct answer always positioned as option A. We believe that a single quiz may only provide a limited perspective on the topic, and a set of quizzes offers a more comprehensive approach, thereby enhancing students' overall understanding of the subject matter.

To verify that the difficulty of the student questions varies appropriately across different education levels, we tasked the LLM with assessing the reasoning difficulty and knowledge depth required to answer each student question, assigning a score on a scale of 1 to 5. The results are presented in Figures 2 and 3. As anticipated, the difficulty remains consistent within subject areas but increases progressively with the educational level, aligning with our goal for the dataset. Example student questions can be found in the Appendix A.

4 Framework

The proposed framework ConQuer operates as follows. The system receives three inputs: the student's question, their educational level, and the subject area. We first use an LLM to extract key concepts from the question. For example, given the question, "What happens to a plant when it doesn't get enough sunlight or water?", we identify several potentially relevant key concepts such as "plant", "sunlight", "water", "photosynthesis", "growth", "stress", "environment".

After extracting the relevant concepts, we retrieve relevant information from a knowledge source based on these concepts. In this work, we primarily use Wikipedia, which provides a wealth of information on a wide range of topics. To locate the most relevant content, we utilize Sentence-BERT (Reimers, 2019) to compute cosine similarity scores. This allows the system to pinpoint the most contextually appropriate sections of text. Subsequently, an LLM-based summarization module condenses the retrieved information into its key points. These summarized details are then passed to the quiz generator, which creates tailored quizzes based on the content.

5 Experiments

5.1 Evaluation

To evaluate the quality of the generated quizzes, we propose 5 evaluation dimensions:

- **Educational Value**: Whether the quizzes enhance learning and help students acquire new knowledge.
- **Diversity**: Whether the quizzes cover a broad range of important topics and concepts.
- **Area Relevance**: How well the quizzes align with the student's query and the specific subject area they are trying to learn.
- **Difficulty Appropriateness**: Whether the quiz difficulty matches the student's education and knowledge level.
- **Comprehensiveness**: Whether the quizzes cover the topic's key concepts thoroughly.

We leverage LLM-as-a-judge for evaluation, with GPT-4o (Hurst et al., 2024) serving as the judge model in all our evaluations. The model is instructed to assign a score on a scale of 1 to 5, with detailed prompts provided in Appendix B. To further compare quiz quality, we perform pairwise comparisons, prompting the judge model to select the better quiz set based on each of the five criteria outlined above. To mitigate any potential ordering bias, pairwise comparisons are conducted in both orders, and the average win rate is computed.

5.2 Experiment Setup

We use GPT-4o-mini (Hurst et al., 2024) and Gemini-2.0-flash (Team et al., 2023) as LLMs to complete the task. For information retrieval, we employ the text-embedding-3-large model for embeddings, with a chunk size of 128, a chunk overlap of 50, and retrieve the top 3 results. Detailed prompts are provided in the Appendix B.

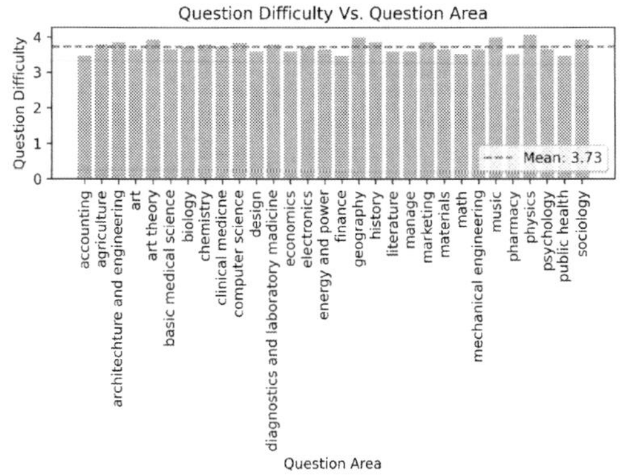

Figure 2: Student Question Difficulty Vs. Area

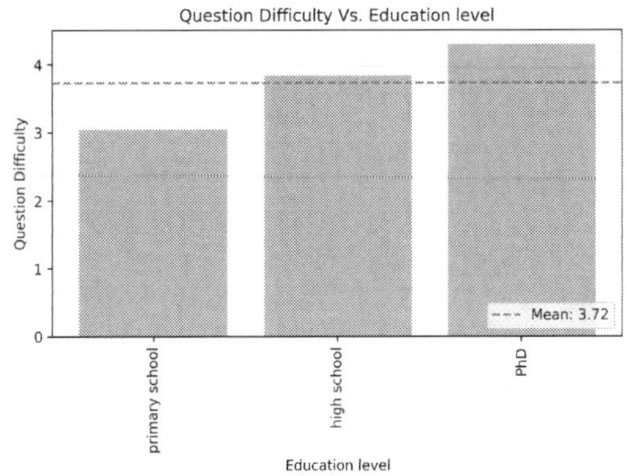

Figure 3: Student Question Difficulty Vs. Education Level

5.3 Ablation Study

To evaluate the contribution of each component in our framework, we conduct three ablation studies.

- **Concept Extraction Module:** We remove the concept extraction module and rely solely on the pure words from the sentence after removing stop words and punctuation to search for relevant information in Wikipedia.
- **Knowledge Source:** Instead of retrieving information from Wikipedia, we rely on ConceptNet (Speer et al., 2017) to gather related concepts and their relational descriptions in sentence format. Unlike Wikipedia, which provides detailed introductions to each term, ConceptNet only includes simple relational descriptions between words like "Find [[a money]] in [[a bank]]".
- **Summarization Module:** We remove the summarization module and directly feed all the information retrieved from Wikipedia into the quiz generator without any further processing.

6 Results

We compare the performance of our ConQuer framework against a baseline, where the quiz is generated directly from the student's question without utilizing any external materials or concepts. The evaluation score for quizzes generated by GPT-4o-mini is shown in Figure 4, and the win rate of ConQuer in pairwise comparison is presented in Figure 5. For clarity, the evaluation score has been scaled to 100, and the win rate is expressed as a percentage. Additional results for Gemini-2.0-flash can be found in the Appendix C.

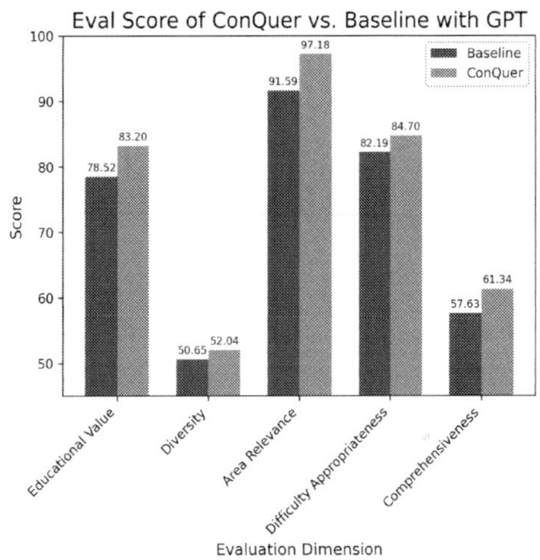

Figure 4: Evaluation score comparison between the baseline and ConQuer with GPT-4o-mini. The evaluation score has been normalized to a scale of 100.

Our results, based on both evaluation score and pairwise comparison win rates, demonstrate that ConQuer consistently outperforms the baseline across all five evaluation dimensions. Although the average score improvement across these five dimensions is only 4.8%, ConQuer achieves a significant win rate of 77.52% in the pairwise comparison. We hypothesize that both ConQuer and the baseline produce quizzes that appear well-constructed when considered in isolation, leading to high evaluation scores for both. However, when evaluated together, ConQuer significantly outperforms the baseline because its quizzes are grounded in high-

Source	EV	Diversity	AR	DA	Comprehensiveness	Avg	Δ
ConQuer	**83.22**	52.04	**97.18**	**84.70**	**61.34**	**75.70**	—
- Concept Extraction	80.31	52.13	93.24	83.36	59.42	73.69	-2.66%
ConceptNet	80.36	**53.06**	93.60	83.40	59.91	74.07	-1.32%
- Summary	77.49	52.39	88.28	81.88	57.94	71.60	-5.42%

Table 1: Ablation Study Results. EV, AR, and DA stand for Educational Value, Area Relevance, and Difficulty Appropriateness, respectively.

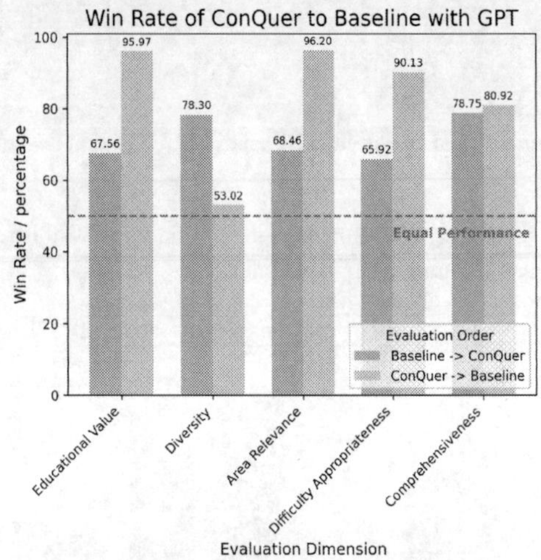

Figure 5: Win rate from pairwise comparison between the baseline and ConQuer with GPT-4o-mini

quality knowledge sources that are closely aligned with key concepts. We have observed that the LLM judge tends to prefer the second candidate, except in the diversity dimension. This preference may be attributed to the fact that the second candidate is closer to answer tokens, prompting the model to allocate more attention weights to it. In the diversity dimension, however, the model identifies more repeated content in the second candidate, as it has already seen all the quizzes from the first candidate. Correlation analysis of the five evaluation dimensions can be found in Appendix E.

6.1 Results of Ablation Studies

The results of ablation study are in Table 1. We observe that removing any of the three components leads to a decrease in performance, except in the diversity dimension. Although the performance drop is minimal, as noted in the previous analysis, it may represent a significant reduction in quality when compared to the original quiz. The diversity score remains largely unaffected, likely because the task only requires generating three quizzes, making it relatively easy to ensure variety. A qualitative analysis of each ablation experiment is provided in the Appendix D.

Removing the concept extraction module leads to the loss of important concepts that may not be explicitly mentioned in the sentence. For example, in the student question, "What happens to a plant when it doesn't get enough sunlight or water?", the key concept "Photosynthesis" is missing, resulting in the omission of vital information.

Using ConceptNet as the knowledge source reduces the richness and quality of the retrieved information, although this is not as apparent in the three-quiz scenario since the retrieved information is still sufficient to generate distinct quizzes.

Removing the summarization module causes the most significant drop in scores. This likely happens because the model is overwhelmed by the excessive information and struggles to focus on the key elements.

7 Conclusion

We introduced ConQuer, a concept-based framework for generating conceptually grounded and educationally effective quizzes. By prioritizing key concepts over surface-level keywords, ConQuer ensures alignment with essential learning objectives. Our evaluations show a 4.8% improvement in quiz quality and a 77.52% win rate in pairwise comparisons, highlighting the superiority of our approach. Ablation studies emphasize the importance of each component in driving these improvements.

ConQuer offers a scalable, accurate, and pedagogically valuable tool for quiz generation across diverse educational contexts. Future work could extend knowledge sources, refine quiz generation for adaptive difficulty, and personalize learning path. ConQuer represents a step forward in automating quiz creation while ensuring the accuracy and relevance that are critical to effective learning.

Limitations

While ConQuer demonstrates significant improvements over the baseline in several aspects, there are key limitations to our evaluation. One notable limitation is that it is evaluated for generating only three multiple-choice quizzes, limiting its generalizability to other quiz formats or larger-scale quiz settings.

Another limitation is that our evaluation relies solely on LLMs for assessing quiz quality, without human input, which may undermine its validity by omitting human values and preferences. Additionally, the lack of feedback assessment limits the practical usefulness of the quizzes. Future research should explore the impact of personalized quiz generation based on student profiles, such as learning history and preferences.

In interactive learning environments, students often expect quizzes to be generated rapidly; however, the inherent latency of LLMs can hinder this expectation. Addressing this challenge may require integrating supplementary LLM serving systems with adaptive computing strategies, as proposed in (Fu et al., 2024a).

Finally, while concept extraction plays a crucial role, it is not without its flaws. Critical concepts may be overlooked or misinterpreted, particularly when questions are ambiguous or contain implicit ideas, potentially compromising quiz quality and relevance.

References

Giorgio Biancini, Alessio Ferrato, and Carla Limongelli. 2024. Multiple-choice question generation using large language models: Methodology and educator insights. In *Adjunct Proceedings of the 32nd ACM Conference on User Modeling, Adaptation and Personalization*, page 584–590.

Christopher Cheong, France Cheong, and Justin Filippou. 2013. Quick quiz: A gamified approach for enhancing learning.

Christine Chin and Jonathan Osborne. 2008. Students' questions: a potential resource for teaching and learning science. *Studies in science education*, 44(1):1–39.

Michelle Commeyras. 1995. What can we learn from students' questions? *Theory into practice*, 34(2):101–106.

Santine Cuccio-Schirripa and H Edwin Steiner. 2000. Enhancement and analysis of science question level for middle school students. *Journal of Research in Science Teaching: The Official Journal of the National Association for Research in Science Teaching*, 37(2):210–224.

Sabina Elkins, Ekaterina Kochmar, Iulian Serban, and Jackie CK Cheung. 2023. How useful are educational questions generated by large language models? In *International Conference on Artificial Intelligence in Education*, pages 536–542. Springer.

Tanya Evans, Barbara Kensington-Miller, and Julia Novak. 2021. Effectiveness, efficiency, engagement: Mapping the impact of pre-lecture quizzes on educational exchange. *Australasian Journal of Educational Technology*, 37(1):163–177.

Yichao Fu, Junda Chen, Siqi Zhu, Zheyu Fu, Zhongdongming Dai, Aurick Qiao, and Hao Zhang. 2024a. Efficiently serving llm reasoning programs with certaindex. *arXiv preprint arXiv:2412.20993*.

Yicheng Fu, Raviteja Anantha, and Jianpeng Cheng. 2024b. Camphor: Collaborative agents for multi-input planning and high-order reasoning on device. *arXiv preprint arXiv:2410.09407*.

Ebrahim Gabajiwala, Priyav Mehta, Ritik Singh, and Reeta Koshy. 2022. Quiz maker: Automatic quiz generation from text using nlp. In *Futuristic Trends in Networks and Computing Technologies: Select Proceedings of Fourth International Conference on FTNCT 2021*, pages 523–533. Springer.

Joanna S Gorin. 2006. Test design with cognition in mind. *Educational measurement: Issues and practice*, 25(4):21–35.

ASM Hasan, Md Alvee Ehsan, Kefaya Benta Shahnoor, and Syeda Sumaiya Tasneem. 2024. *Automatic question & answer generation using generative Large Language Model (LLM)*. Ph.D. thesis, Brac University.

Dan Hendrycks, Collin Burns, Steven Basart, Andy Zou, Mantas Mazeika, Dawn Song, and Jacob Steinhardt. 2020. Measuring massive multitask language understanding. *arXiv preprint arXiv:2009.03300*.

Aaron Hurst, Adam Lerer, Adam P Goucher, Adam Perelman, Aditya Ramesh, Aidan Clark, AJ Ostrow, Akila Welihinda, Alan Hayes, Alec Radford, et al. 2024. Gpt-4o system card. *arXiv preprint arXiv:2410.21276*.

Nikhil Kandpal, Haikang Deng, Adam Roberts, Eric Wallace, and Colin Raffel. 2023. Large language models struggle to learn long-tail knowledge. In *International Conference on Machine Learning*, pages 15696–15707. PMLR.

Patrick Lewis, Ethan Perez, Aleksandra Piktus, Fabio Petroni, Vladimir Karpukhin, Naman Goyal, Heinrich Küttler, Mike Lewis, Wen-tau Yih, Tim Rocktäschel, et al. 2020. Retrieval-augmented generation for knowledge-intensive nlp tasks. *Advances in Neural Information Processing Systems*, 33:9459–9474.

Ivo Lodovico Molina, Valdemar Švábenský, Tsubasa Minematsu, Li Chen, Fumiya Okubo, and Atsushi Shimada. 2024. Comparison of large language models for generating contextually relevant questions. In *European Conference on Technology Enhanced Learning*, pages 137–143. Springer.

Delfina Malandrino, Ilaria Manno, Giuseppina Palmieri, Vittorio Scarano, and Giovanni Filatrella. 2014. How quiz-based tools can improve students' engagement and participation in the classroom. In *2014 International Conference on Collaboration Technologies and Systems (CTS)*, pages 379–386. IEEE.

Dyah Mukaromah, Anisa Mutoharoh, A Pramudwiatmoko, S Tsutoh, G Gutmann, A Konagaya, YE Putri, S Wiryono, Y Nainggolan, and TD Cahyono. 2019. Digital quiz as media to review material for english education students. *Script Journal: Journal of Linguistic and English Teaching*, 4(2):88–100.

Pranav Rajpurkar, Robin Jia, and Percy Liang. 2018. Know what you don't know: Unanswerable questions for squad. *arXiv preprint arXiv:1806.03822*.

N Reimers. 2019. Sentence-bert: Sentence embeddings using siamese bert-networks. *arXiv preprint arXiv:1908.10084*.

Linfeng Song and Lin Zhao. 2016. Domain-specific question generation from a knowledge base. *arX-iv.*

Robyn Speer, Joshua Chin, and Catherine Havasi. 2017. Conceptnet 5.5: An open multilingual graph of general knowledge. In *Proceedings of the AAAI conference on artificial intelligence*, volume 31.

Gemini Team, Rohan Anil, Sebastian Borgeaud, Jean-Baptiste Alayrac, Jiahui Yu, Radu Soricut, Johan Schalkwyk, Andrew M Dai, Anja Hauth, Katie Millican, et al. 2023. Gemini: a family of highly capable multimodal models. *arXiv preprint arXiv:2312.11805*.

Sinh Trong Vu, Huong Thu Truong, Oanh Tien Do, Tu Anh Le, and Tai Tan Mai. 2024. A chatgpt-based approach for questions generation in higher education. In *Proceedings of the 1st ACM Workshop on AI-Powered Q&A Systems for Multimedia*, pages 13–18.

Zhilin Yang, Peng Qi, Saizheng Zhang, Yoshua Bengio, William W Cohen, Ruslan Salakhutdinov, and Christopher D Manning. 2018. Hotpotqa: A dataset for diverse, explainable multi-hop question answering. *arXiv preprint arXiv:1809.09600*.

Yue Zhang, Yafu Li, Leyang Cui, Deng Cai, Lemao Liu, Tingchen Fu, Xinting Huang, Enbo Zhao, Yu Zhang, Yulong Chen, et al. 2023. Siren's song in the ai ocean: a survey on hallucination in large language models. *arXiv preprint arXiv:2309.01219*.

A Example student question

Example questions of biology area can be found below. The question difficulty across the three educational levels shows a clear progression. For primary school, questions focus on basic understanding of natural phenomena and straightforward cause-and-effect relationships, requiring minimal specialized knowledge. At the high school level, questions become more complex, involving scientific methods, deeper concepts like genetic variation and the impacts of human activities, and a higher demand for critical thinking. For PhD-level questions, the focus shifts to advanced research topics, such as methodologies in studying microbiomes and the ethical implications of genetic manipulation.

Example Student Questions

Primary School:

- What are the ways plants and animals adapt to their environments to survive?
- How do some animals use camouflage to protect themselves from predators?
- What happens to a plant when it doesn't get enough sunlight or water?
- Why do some animals migrate long distances, and how do they find their way?
- How do different animal habitats, like forests and deserts, affect the types of species that live there?

High School:

- What are the various methods scientists use to study ecosystems, and what challenges do they face in collecting data?
- How do genetic variations within a population contribute to natural selection and evolution?
- What role do enzymes play in biochemical reactions, and how can temperature and pH affect their activity?
- In what ways do human activities impact biodiversity, and what strategies can be employed to mitigate these effects?
- How do different types of symbiotic relationships (like mutualism and parasitism) influence ecological balance?

PhD:

- What are the current methodologies used in studying the microbiome's influence on human health, and how do they differ in their approaches?
- How does epigenetic modification play a role in the adaptation of organisms to their environments over generations?
- What are the key differences in the mechanisms of action between CRISPR technologies and traditional gene editing techniques?
- In studying evolutionary biology, how do we measure and interpret the rate of speciation in various ecosystems?
- What ethical considerations arise in the manipulation of genetic material in research, particularly regarding biodiversity conservation?

B Prompts

Here is the prompts we use as baseline method

Baseline Prompt

You are a quiz generator. The students are currently studying {area} at the {level} level and have asked a question. Your task is to create 3 quizzes that help the student better understand the question. The quiz should consist of one question, one correct answer, and three incorrect options. The correct answer must always be placed in option A.

Example:

Student Question: Where is Beijing located?
[Quiz]
Quiz: What is the capital city of China?
A. Beijing
B. Chengdu

C. Shanghai
D. Hangzhou

[Quiz]
Quiz: What continent is Beijing located?
A. Asia
B. Europe
C. Africa
D. North America

Now, please generate 3 quizzes following the format, each quiz should follow the sign of [Quiz]:
Student Question: {question}

Here is the prompt we use with WikiPedia knowledge:

ConQuer Prompt

You are a quiz generator. The students are currently studying {area} at the {level} level and have asked a question. Your task is to create 3 quizzes that helps the student better understand the question. You have access to summarized reference information from Wikipedia. The quizzes should accurately reflect reference information, and the correct answer must be well-supported by reference information. The quiz should consist of one question, one correct answer, and three incorrect options. The correct answer must always be placed in option A.

Example:

Student Question: Where is Beijing located?
[Quiz]
Quiz: What is the capital city of China?
A. Beijing
B. Chengdu
C. Shanghai
D. Hangzhou

[Quiz]
Quiz: What continent is Beijing located?
A. Asia
B. Europe
C. Africa
D. North America

Now, please generate 3 quizzes following the format, each quiz should follow thw sign of [Quiz]:

Reference Wikipedia Information:
{summary}
Student Question: {question}

Here is the prompt we use to evaluate the overall quality of quiz set:

Prompt for Quiz Quality Evaluation

A student studying {area} at the {level} level is asking a question: "{question}". Based on the following quiz set related to the question, I need you to evaluate the educational quality of the quiz set. For each of the following criteria, assign a score from 1 to 5 for the entire quiz set:

1. Educational Value: Do you think these quizzes are educational? Will students learn more by taking these quizzes?
- 1: Not educational at all, no learning value.
- 2: Minimally educational, little learning value.
- 3: Moderately educational, some learning value.
- 4: Very educational, strong learning value.
- 5: Highly educational, great learning value.

2. Diversity: Do you think these quizzes are diverse? Are the quizzes covering a broad range of topics, or do they all focus on the same concept?
- 1: Very repetitive, covers a narrow area.
- 2: Some diversity, but mostly focuses on one concept.
- 3: Fairly diverse, covers a few different topics.
- 4: Quite diverse, covers multiple relevant topics.
- 5: Extremely diverse, covers a broad range of topics.

3. Area Relevance: Are these quizzes

relevant to the student's question and the concepts they're trying to learn? Are the quizzes tailored to the subject area being studied?
- 1: Not relevant to the question or subject at all.
- 2: Minimally relevant, some connection to the question/subject.
- 3: Moderately relevant, fairly aligned with the question/subject.
- 4: Highly relevant, strongly aligned with the question/subject.
- 5: Perfectly relevant, directly tied to the question/subject.

4. Difficulty Appropriateness: Do you think these quizzes match the student's current education level? Would these quizzes be too easy or too difficult for a student at this level?
- 1: Too easy or too difficult, not appropriate for the level.
- 2: Slightly mismatched, quizzes may be too easy or too hard.
- 3: Moderately appropriate, quizzes are somewhat aligned with the level.
- 4: Mostly appropriate, quizzes are well-suited for the level.
- 5: Perfectly suited to the student's education level.

5. Comprehensiveness: Do these quizzes cover the depth and breadth of the topic? Are they thorough in addressing key concepts and details?
- 1: Very superficial, only scratches the surface of the topic.
- 2: Somewhat incomplete, misses important aspects.
- 3: Moderately comprehensive, covers the basics but lacks depth.
- 4: Quite comprehensive, addresses most key aspects with reasonable depth.
- 5: Highly comprehensive, thoroughly covers the topic in great depth and detail.

Here is the quiz set related to the question:
{quiz_set}

Please start by providing a step-by-step reasoning analysis of the quiz set, then return your evaluation as a JSON object in the following format:

```json
{
"Educational Value": score,
"Diversity": score,
"Area Relevance": score,
"Difficulty Appropriateness": score,
"Comprehensiveness": score
}
```

Here is the prompt we use to do pairwise comparisons of quality of quiz set:

Prompt for Pairwise Comparison

A student studying {area} at the {level} level has asked the following question: "{question}". You are given two quiz sets that aim to help the student better understand the question. Please choose the quiz set that best address this question. Please evaluate and compare the educational quality of these quiz sets based on the criteria listed below. For each criterion, select the quiz set that performs better by outputting 1 or 2.

1. Educational Value: Which quiz set offers greater learning potential? Which set will help students gain a deeper understanding of the topic?
2. Diversity: Which quiz set covers a broader range of topics? Does it explore a variety of concepts or focus narrowly on a single idea?
3. Area Relevance: Which quiz set is more aligned with the student's question and the key concepts they are studying? How well is it tailored to the specific subject area?
4. Difficulty Appropriateness: Which quiz set is better suited to the student's current educational level, neither too simple nor too advanced?
5. Comprehensiveness: Which quiz set provides greater depth and breadth? Which one is more thorough in addressing key concepts and details?

Here is the quiz set 1:

```
{quiz_set_1}

Here is the quiz set 2:
{quiz_set_2}

Please start by providing a step-by-step reasoning analysis of the quiz sets, then return your evaluation as a JSON object in the following format:
'''json
{
"Educational Value": choice,
"Diversity": choice,
"Area Relevance": choice,
"Difficulty Appropriateness": choice,
"Comprehensiveness": choice
}'''
```

C Additioanl Experimental Results with Gemini

To further demonstrate the generalizability of ConQuer across different LLMs, we conducted experiments using Gemini-2.0-flash (Team et al., 2023). The corresponding results are presented in Figures 6 and 7. On average, ConQuer achieved a 3.1% improvement across five evaluation dimensions, with a win rate of 66.32%. While this performance is slightly lower than that of GPT-4o-mini, it clearly demonstrates the effectiveness of the ConQuer framework in generating high-quality quizzes.

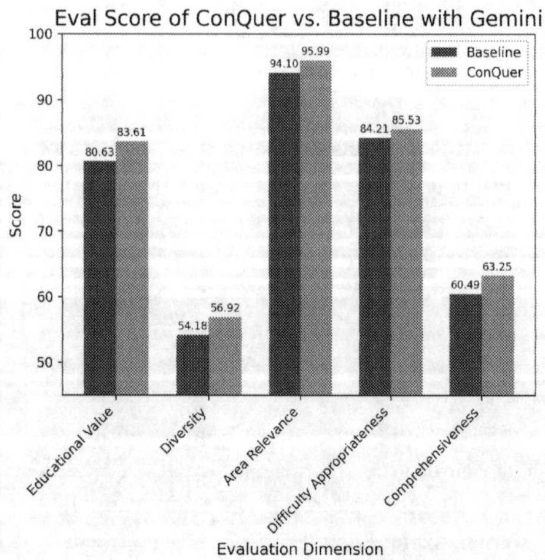

Figure 6: Evaluation score comparison between the baseline and ConQuer with Gemini-2.0-flash

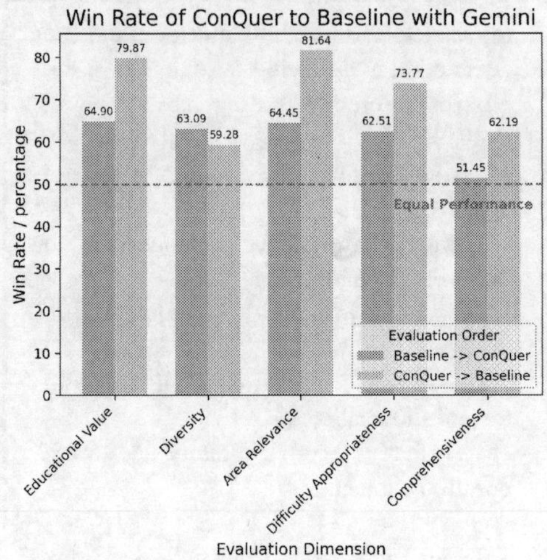

Figure 7: Win rate from pairwise comparison between the baseline and ConQuer with Gemini-2.0-flash

D Qualitative Analysis of Ablation Study

In this section, we provide a qualitative analysis of the quizzes generated by ConQuer and compare them to quizzes generated with different modules removed, as shown in Table 2. For clarity, we select representative quizzes from the quiz set and only present a subset of the results.

Removing the concept extraction module significantly impacts the quiz's ability to capture the underlying concept behind the student's question. In the example related to plant growth, the quiz generated without this module fails to mention photosynthesis, which is essential for the student's understanding of the process and its importance for plants.

When the knowledge source is altered, the generated quiz becomes overly simplistic, essentially repeating basic concepts without depth. In contrast, the quiz generated by ConQuer, utilizing a more comprehensive knowledge base like Wikipedia, incorporates richer details, such as explaining how Earth's mass and distance influence gravity.

Finally, when the summarization module is removed, the resulting quiz deviates from the student's original question, likely due to the model's failure to focus on the key information. On the other hand, the quiz generated by ConQuer maintains a close alignment with the student's question, demonstrating its ability to stay on topic and provide relevant information.

Ablation Module	Student Question	Quiz Generated without Ablation Module	Quiz Generated by ConQuer
Concept Extraction Module	What happens to a plant when it doesn't get enough sunlight or water?	Nothing about photosynthesis	Quiz: Which process do plants struggle with when they do not get enough sunlight? A. Photosynthesis B. Respiration C. Digestion D. Germination
Wikipedia Knowledge Source	How does gravity affect the way objects move on Earth and in space?	Quiz: What force pulls objects toward each other on Earth? A. Gravity B. Magnetism C. Friction D. Electricity	Quiz: What determines the strength of Earth's gravitational field at a given location? A. The mass of Earth and the distance from its center B. The temperature of the air C. The speed of sound in water D. The color of the sky
Summarization Module	What role does childhood development play in shaping adult behavior and personality?	Quiz: Which of the following attachment styles was NOT identified by Mary Ainsworth in her strange situation experiment? A. Independent B. Secure C. Ambivalent D. Avoidant	Quiz: What term is often used to describe personality in children? A. Temperament B. Mood C. Character D. Disposition

Table 2: Ablation Study Result

E Analysis of Correlation of Evaluation Dimensions

Given the range of evaluation dimensions employed in this study, it is essential to examine the relationships between them. To facilitate this, we present a heatmap illustrating the correlation between the scores of each evaluation dimension.

The heatmap reveals several dimensions with strong positive correlations. For instance, Educational Value, Difficulty Appropriateness, and Comprehensiveness are closely related. These correlations can be explained by the fact that a more comprehensive quiz tends to cover a broader range of topics, thereby enhancing its educational value. Similarly, a difficulty level aligned with the student's abilities tends to improve both educational value and comprehension by appropriately challenging the learner.

On the other hand, some metrics exhibit little to no correlation. For example, Diversity and Area Relevance show near-zero or even negative corre-

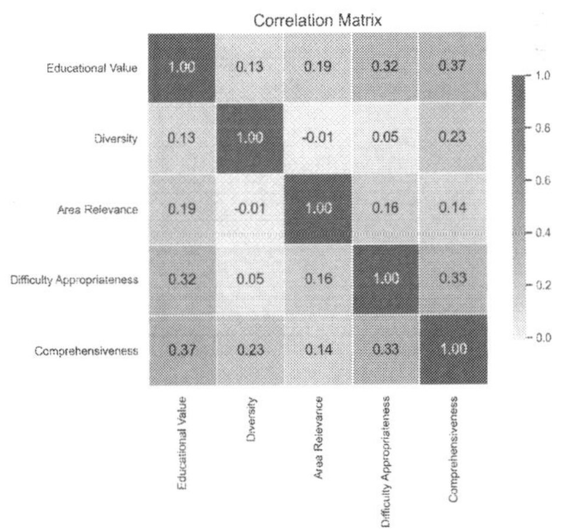

Figure 8: Correlation of scores in each evaluation dimension.

lations. This may occur because increasing the diversity of content often necessitates expanding the scope of topics, which could inadvertently reduce the focus on a specific subject area.

What is it?
Towards a Generalizable Native American Language Identification System

Ivory Yang **Weicheng Ma**
Carlos Guerrero Alvarez **William Dinauer** **Soroush Vosoughi**
Department of Computer Science, Dartmouth College
{Ivory.Yang.GR, Soroush.Vosoughi}@dartmouth.edu

Abstract

This paper presents a research thesis proposal to develop a generalizable Native American language identification system. Despite their cultural and historical significance, Native American languages remain entirely unsupported by major commercial language identification systems. This omission not only underscores the systemic neglect of endangered languages in technological development, but also highlights the urgent need for dedicated, community-driven solutions. We propose a two-pronged approach: (1) systematically curating linguistic resources across all Native American languages for robust training, and (2) tailored data augmentation to generate synthetic yet linguistically coherent training samples. As proof of concept, we extend an existing rudimentary Athabaskan language classifier by integrating Plains Apache, an extinct Southern Athabaskan language, as an additional language class. We also adapt a data generation framework for low-resource languages to create synthetic Plains Apache data, highlighting the potential of data augmentation. This proposal advocates for a community-driven, technological approach to supporting Native American languages.

1 Introduction

Language is more than a means of communication; it is a vessel of culture, history, and identity (Miller and Hoogstra, 1992; Bucholtz and Hall, 2004; Sirbu, 2015). For many Indigenous communities, the loss of a language represents not just linguistic erosion but the disappearance of traditions, worldviews, and ways of knowing (Grenoble and Whaley, 1998; Khawaja, 2021). Despite increasing efforts in computational linguistics to support low-resource languages (Ranathunga et al., 2023; Singh et al., 2024), the landscape remains starkly imbalanced. Google's LangID (Caswell et al., 2020), one of the most commercialized language identification systems, covers over 200 languages, but overlooks almost all North American Native languages.

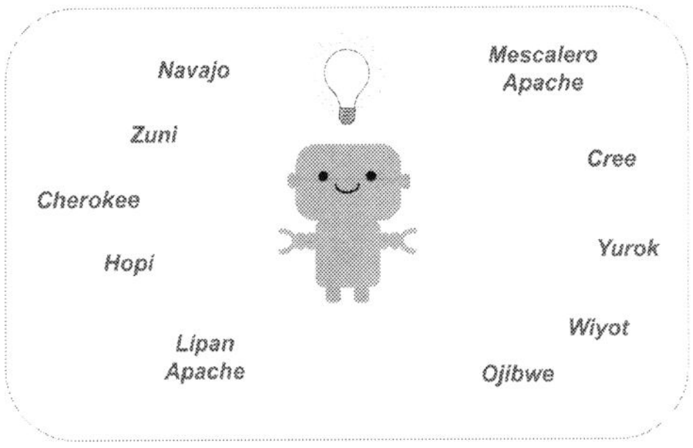

Figure 1: A simplified, stylized rendition of the proposed generalizable Native American Language identification system.

This exclusion is an alarming reflection of how centralized language technologies systematically marginalize Indigenous voices (Khubchandani, 2016; Yim, 2024).

The state of New Mexico (NM) stands as a crucial focal point in this discussion. Home to eight Native American languages[1] (New Mexico Secretary of State, 2025), the state exemplifies both the resilience and fragility of Indigenous linguistic heritage. While computational linguistics has explored the most-widely spoken Navajo to some extent (Liu et al., 2021; Yang et al., 2025b), progress remains constrained by the scarcity of accessible linguistic data (Meek, 2012; Goswami et al., 2024). To address the current gap in commercialized language technologies, we propose a research agenda to build a generalizable Native American language identification system, the first of its kind, as exemplified in Figure 1.

Our approach consists of two key initiatives: (1) Data Resource Aggregation: A comprehensive, systematic effort to manually collect and curate linguistic datasets across all available Native Amer-

[1]The eight languages are Tiwa, Tewa, Keres, Towa, Zuni, Navajo, Mescalero Apache and Jicarilla Apache. There are eleven New Mexico counties with Native American lands.

Proceedings of the 2025 Conference of the Nations of the Americas Chapter of the Association for Computational Linguistics: Human Language Technologies (Volume 4: Student Research Workshop), pages 105–111

ican languages, ensuring high-quality, representative training data. (2) Synthetic Data Generation: Applying an established data augmentation framework for endangered languages to expand existing data, particularly for languages with few or no remaining fluent speakers. For proof of concept, we manually curated a small dataset of 25 Plains Apache sentences, an extinct Southern Athabaskan language, and successfully integrated it into an existing rudimentary Athabaskan language classifier (Yang et al., 2025b). We then adapted a data generation framework for low-resource languages (Yang et al., 2025a) to create 5 syntactically-coherent new Plains Apache sentences, displaying the promise of our approach. **This paper serves as both a research thesis proposal and a call to action, working towards a future where Native American languages are not only included but actively supported by commercialized language technologies.**

2 Related Work

Efforts to develop Natural Language Processing (NLP) technologies for endangered languages are hindered by scarce datasets (Maimaiti et al., 2022) and non-specialized model architectures (Lin et al., 2018). This section reviews emergent research in two key areas: Native American language classification, and synthetic data generation for endangered languages.

2.1 Native American Language Classification

Yang et al. (2025b) exposed the shortcomings of centralized NLP systems in handling Native American languages. Google's LangID system (Caswell et al., 2020), despite covering over 100 languages, failed to include any Native American languages, even the most widely spoken Navajo (Palakurthy, 2022). To address this gap, they developed a Random Forest classifier (Ho, 1995) trained on Navajo and 20 of its most frequently confused languages, achieving a near-perfect accuracy (97-100%). Further experiments revealed that the classifier generalized well to other Athabaskan languages[2] under the same family tree, suggesting potential scalability across related language families. However, while this work introduced a novel approach to Native American language identification, its scope was limited, covering only five languages. Expanding its applicability requires broader generalization across diverse linguistic groups.

[2]The languages tested with the Navajo classifier were Western Apache, Mescalero Apache, Jicarilla Apache and Lipan Apache, which are all Southern Athabaskan languages.

2.2 Synthetic Data Generation for Endangered Languages

Data scarcity is a persistent challenge in low-resource NLP (Ghafoor et al., 2021; Adimulam et al., 2022), particularly for languages with few or no fluent speakers (Bansal et al., 2021). Yang et al. (2025a) demonstrated the effectiveness of synthetic data augmentation for endangered languages on Nüshu, a near-extinct ancient Chinese script (Congrong, 2024). Using a language-specific data generation framework, they produced a novel dataset of 98 linguistically coherent synthetic sentences in Nüshu, demonstrating a viable approach to language revitalization.

Applying this approach to Native American languages presents both opportunities and challenges. Unlike Nüshu's text-to-text structure (Di, 2024), many Indigenous languages require careful handling of phonetic, morphological, and orthographic variation (Link et al., 2021). Still, a synthetic data pipeline remains a promising strategy for expanding training resources, especially for those on the verge of extinction.

2.3 Towards a Unified Approach

Building on prior work, this paper proposes a hybrid approach that combines language classification and synthetic data generation to create a scalable Native American language identification system. Unlike previous efforts that addressed classification or data expansion in isolation, we argue that both are essential for developing a truly generalizable, resource-efficient, and community-driven model. By integrating rigorous classifier development with targeted augmentation, we aim to surpass existing limitations and advance linguistic inclusivity in commercialized language technologies.

3 Native American Language Landscape

Native American languages form a vast and diverse linguistic ecosystem (Oberg and Olsen-Harbich, 2022), reflecting centuries of cultural, historical, and geographical significance (Clements, 2021). While many of these languages once flourished across North America, colonization (Huang, 2024), forced assimilation policies (Ellinghaus, 2022), and systemic marginalization (Sear and Turin, 2021)

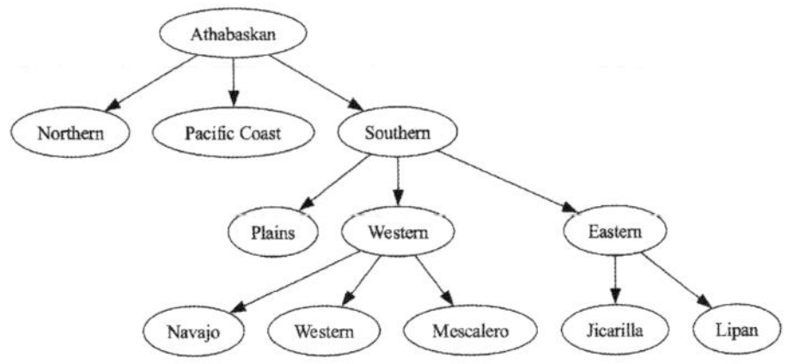

Figure 2: Family Tree for Athabaskan Languages

have led to widespread language loss. Today, their survival depends on urgent and deliberate revitalization efforts (De Costa, 2021), including the development of computational tools for language preservation and accessibility.

3.1 Statistics

At the time of European contact, over 300 Native American languages were spoken across North America (Williams, 2022), belonging to numerous distinct language families (Sutton, 2021). These languages exhibited immense structural diversity, with some featuring polysynthetic morphology (e.g., Mohawk, Inuktitut) (Arkadiev, 2023), complex tone systems (e.g., Athabaskan languages) (Uchihara, 2023), or elaborate evidential marking (e.g., Quechua) (Kalt, 2021). In present-day United States, about 175 Native American languages are still spoken (Antoine, 2021). While some languages like Cherokee and Navajo are better documented, with existing text corpora (Zhang et al., 2021; Goldhahn et al., 2012), many others have little to no surviving linguistic records (Leonard, 2023).

3.2 Endangered Status and Language Loss

The vast majority of Native American languages in the United States are either moribund (Dorzheeva et al., 2021), where they are spoken only by the elderly, or critically endangered (Estrada et al., 2022), where fewer than 100 speakers remain. The statistics are stark: Only about 20 Native American languages are being acquired by children as a first language (Clifton, 2021), and by 2050, at least 90% of Native American languages are predicted to become extinct (Yerian and Halima, 2024).

These figures highlight an accelerating crisis - one driven not only by natural language shift but by centuries of forced assimilation policies, including residential schools that punished Indigenous children for speaking their native tongues (Lomawaima and McCarty, 2025). Even today, Native American communities face systemic barriers to language transmission, from limited access to bilingual education (McCarty and Brayboy, 2021) to the shortage of digital language tools that support continued learning and usage (Meighan, 2021). Without deliberate investment in technological solutions tailored to Indigenous languages, these languages risk further exclusion from digital spaces, thus accelerating their decline.

4 Language Detection Experiments

To demonstrate the feasibility of our proposed approach mentioned in Section 2.3, we conduct a small-scale experiment using Plains Apache (Saxon, 2023), an extinct member of the Southern Athabaskan language family. This proof of concept serves as as a preliminary step in our broader effort to build a generalizable Native American language identification system.

4.1 Why Plains Apache?

Plains Apache presents a unique case study for two key reasons. Firstly, the Athabaskan language classifier proposed by Yang et al. (2025b) covered nearly all Southern Athabaskan languages except Plains Apache. Given its linguistic proximity to Navajo and other Apache languages, as shown in Figure 2, incorporating it into the classifier offers a straightforward and scalable expansion. Secondly, unlike Navajo, which still has thousands of speakers, Plains Apache is extinct (Tellmann, 2021), with no known fluent speakers. This makes it an ideal candidate for synthetic data augmentation using the text generation framework for endangered languages proposed by Yang et al. (2025a). If successful, this experiment could serve as a blueprint for generating linguistically sound training data for other highly endangered or extinct Native American languages. By implementing the classifier expansion and synthetic data pipeline with the Plains Apache language, we aim to evaluate the feasibility of our broader research approach on a small scale before scaling to a multi-language setting.

4.2 Manually Gathering Plains Apache Data

Due to the absence of publicly available digital corpora for Plains Apache, we manually scraped and transcribed sentences from various linguistic sources (Wikipedia, 2025; Morgan, 2012). As an

1. *Dèènáá kóó ʔíłbééš*
2. *Séé míídžǫ́ʔdą́ʔ dàyìɣíníít*
3. *bíč'èèčą́ą́ bìzèèdą́ yìč'į̀ʔ dáágòłčìʔ*
4. *bìč'èèčą́ą́ bìzèèdą́ yìč'į̀ʔ dáágòłčìʔ*
5. *'ʔééšdòòʔ šį́ į́ dàɣą́ą́ šìlížǫ́ǫ́*

Figure 3: Sample sentences of manually curated Plains Apache text

initial effort, we curated 25 Plains Apache sentences in CSV format, with a small sample shown in Figure 3. This manually curated dataset underscores the challenges of working with endangered and extinct Indigenous languages, highlighting the urgent need for automated, scalable solutions such as data augmentation.

4.3 Integration into Athabaskan Classifier

Integrating Plains Apache as an additional language class into the Random Forest classifier yielded interesting results. With all other training weights of the original classifier unchanged, Plains Apache sentences were classified as Navajo with 100% likelihood, as shown in Table 1. In the original experiments conducted by Yang et al. (2025b), Western Apache and Mescalero Apache had the highest classification rates as Navajo at 96.00% and 100%, respectively, while Jicarilla Apache and Lipan Apache performed lower at 92.32% and 62.16%. This disparity was previously attributed to subgroup distinctions, as Jicarilla and Lipan Apache belong to the Eastern branch of Southern Athabaskan, whereas Navajo, Western Apache, and Mescalero Apache fall under the Western subgroup, as illustrated in Figure 2. However, Plains Apache, despite being its own distinct subgroup, exhibited classification behavior identical to Mescalero Apache. This raises new questions about the lexical and syntactic relationships among the Southern Athabaskan subgroups, warranting further analysis.

4.4 Synthetic Data Generation for Plains Apache

We applied the framework introduced by Yang et al. (2025a) to expand our Plains Apache text. Originally developed for the endangered Nüshu language, this approach combines few-shot prompting with language-specific tailoring to generate new synthetic data. Using the GPT-4o model, we provided a dataset of 25 Plains Apache sentences and prompted the model to generate 5 new artificial sentences, which it successfully produced[3]. While this represents a small-scale test, it highlights the potential of synthetic augmentation for highly endangered Indigenous languages, even in cases of extreme data scarcity. Moving forward, this methodology could be extended to other extinct or moribund Native American languages, significantly increasing the amount of available data for classification, modeling, and revitalization efforts.

Language	Classified as Navajo	Total Sentences
Western Apache	96.00%	25
Mescalero Apache	100.00%	32
Jicarilla Apache	92.31%	13
Lipan Apache	62.16%	37
Plains Apache	100.00%	25

Table 1: Classification Results for Apache Languages: Percentage of sentences classified as Navajo and total number of sentences examined for each Apache language, with the addition of Plains Apache, highlighted in pink.

5 Conclusion

This paper presents a long-term research vision for developing a generalizable Native American language identification system, addressing the critical absence of Indigenous languages in commercial language technologies. By building on existing work in Native American language classification and synthetic data generation, we propose a unified approach that leverages both to bridge this gap. Our small-scale experiments integrating Plains Apache demonstrate the promise and feasibility of this method. Beyond its technical contributions, this work serves as a call to action for the broader NLP community to invest in decentralized, community-driven language technologies that prioritize linguistic diversity. Through collective efforts, we can ensure that these languages are not only preserved, but actively recognized and used in the digital age.

[3]These generated sentences have not yet been rigorously validated beyond a visual review; we propose this as a viable method for data augmentation rather than asserting complete accuracy.

Limitations

While this study lays the groundwork for Native American language identification, limitations remain. The Plains Apache experiment, though informative, is constrained by scarce natural data, and while synthetic augmentation mitigates this, it cannot fully replicate the depth of naturally spoken language. Our focus on Athabaskan languages also raises questions about the broader applicability of this approach to other linguistic families. Additionally, reliance on synthetic data poses risks of capturing artifacts rather than true linguistic features. Beyond identification, future work must explore applications like translation and speech recognition for meaningful impact. Expanding datasets, refining augmentation techniques, and engaging Indigenous communities will be essential to ensuring these technologies support both linguistic and cultural preservation.

Ethics Statement

Ethical considerations are important when developing technologies for Native American languages, which have a big role in cultural, spiritual, and historical settings. This study recognizes that these languages are not only tools for communication but also symbols of culture and heritage. Thus, the development of language technologies for Native American languages should happen in close collaboration with community members and leaders to ensure language preservation rather than cultural homogenization and appropriation. We are actively engaging with the Native American and Indigenous Languages department at our institution to ensure this project is conducted in a thoughtful, respectful, and community-centered manner.

References

Thejaswi Adimulam, Swetha Chinta, and Suprit Kumar Pattanayak. 2022. Transfer learning in natural language processing: Overcoming low-resource challenges. *International Journal of Enhanced Research In Science Technology & Engineering*, 11:65–79.

Jurgita Antoine. 2021. New grant to support aihec's native languages program. *Tribal College*, 33(2):1–2.

Peter Arkadiev. 2023. Polysynthesis: lessons from northwest caucasian languages. In *Mediterranean Morphology Meetings*, volume 13, pages 1–26.

Rachit Bansal, Himanshu Choudhary, Ravneet Punia, Niko Schenk, Émilie Pagé-Perron, and Jacob Dahl. 2021. How low is too low? a computational perspective on extremely low-resource languages. In *Proceedings of the 59th Annual Meeting of the Association for Computational Linguistics and the 11th International Joint Conference on Natural Language Processing: Student Research Workshop*, pages 44–59.

Mary Bucholtz and Kira Hall. 2004. Language and identity. *A companion to linguistic anthropology*, 1:369–394.

Isaac Caswell, Theresa Breiner, Daan van Esch, and Ankur Bapna. 2020. Language id in the wild: Unexpected challenges on the path to a thousand-language web text corpus. In *Proceedings of the 28th International Conference on Computational Linguistics*, pages 6588–6608.

William M Clements. 2021. *Native American verbal art: Texts and contexts*. University of Arizona Press.

PYE Clifton. 2021. Documenting the acquisition of indigenous languages. *Journal of Child Language*, 48(3):454–479.

Li Congrong. 2024. History, characteristics, and modern vitality of nüshu: A cultural anthropology perspective. *Anthropological Explorations of Gender, Identity, and Economics*, 85.

Peter I De Costa. 2021. Indigenous language revitalization: how education can help reclaim "sleeping" languages. *Journal of Language, Identity & Education*, 20(5):355–361.

Ming Di. 2024. The other mother tongues and minority writing in china. *Mother Tongues and Other Tongues: Creating and Translating Sinophone Poetry*, 53:224.

Victoria Vladimirovna Dorzheeva et al. 2021. Preservation of indigenous languages in the united states. legislation and challenges. *European Proceedings of Social and Behavioural Sciences*.

Katherine Ellinghaus. 2022. *Blood will tell: Native Americans and assimilation policy*. U of Nebraska Press.

Alejandro Estrada, Paul A Garber, Sidney Gouveia, Álvaro Fernández-Llamazares, Fernando Ascensão, Agustin Fuentes, Stephen T Garnett, Christopher Shaffer, Júlio Bicca-Marques, Julia E Fa, et al. 2022. Global importance of indigenous peoples, their lands, and knowledge systems for saving the world's primates from extinction. *Science advances*, 8(31):eabn2927.

Abdul Ghafoor, Ali Shariq Imran, Sher Muhammad Daudpota, Zenun Kastrati, Rakhi Batra, Mudasir Ahmad Wani, et al. 2021. The impact of translating resource-rich datasets to low-resource languages through multi-lingual text processing. *IEEE Access*, 9:124478–124490.

Dirk Goldhahn, Thomas Eckart, and Uwe Quasthoff. 2012. Building large monolingual dictionaries at the Leipzig corpora collection: From 100 to 200 languages. In *Proceedings of the Eighth International Conference on Language Resources and Evaluation.*

Dhiman Goswami, Sharanya Thilagan, Kai North, Shervin Malmasi, and Marcos Zampieri. 2024. Native language identification in texts: A survey. In *Proceedings of the 2024 Conference of the North American Chapter of the Association for Computational Linguistics: Human Language Technologies (Volume 1: Long Papers)*, pages 3149–3160.

Lenore A Grenoble and Lindsay J Whaley. 1998. *Endangered languages: Language loss and community response.* Cambridge University Press.

Tin Kam Ho. 1995. Random decision forests. In *Proceedings of 3rd International Conference on Document Analysis and Recognition.*

Yi-Wen Huang. 2024. Language loss and translingual identities near the navajo land. *International Journal of Language Studies*, 18(2).

Susan E Kalt. 2021. Acquisition, loss and innovation in chuquisaca quechua—what happened to evidential marking? *Languages*, 6(2):76.

Masud Khawaja. 2021. Consequences and remedies of indigenous language loss in canada. *Societies*, 11(3):89.

Lachman Mulchand Khubchandani. 2016. The relationship between language and culture is interwoven in a unique manner in different traditions. one of the major consequences of technology-driven globalization has been the increasing marginalization of less-populated language communities and the intimidating hegemony of larger socio-economic networks. this phenomenon acquires more vis. *The Language Loss of the Indigenous*, page 183.

Wesley Y Leonard. 2023. Challenging "extinction" through modern miami language practices. In *Global Language Justice*, pages 126–165. Columbia University Press.

Ying Lin, Shengqi Yang, Veselin Stoyanov, and Heng Ji. 2018. A multi-lingual multi-task architecture for low-resource sequence labeling. In *Proceedings of the 56th Annual Meeting of the Association for Computational Linguistics (Volume 1: Long Papers)*, pages 799–809.

Adrianna Link, Abigail Shelton, and Patrick Spero. 2021. *Indigenous languages and the promise of archives.* U of Nebraska Press.

Ling Liu, Zach Ryan, and Mans Hulden. 2021. The usefulness of bibles in low-resource machine translation. In *Proceedings of the Workshop on Computational Methods for Endangered Languages*, volume 1, pages 44–50.

K Tsianina Lomawaima and Teresa L McCarty. 2025. *" To remain an Indian": Lessons in democracy from a century of Native American education.* Teachers College Press.

Mieradilijiang Maimaiti, Yang Liu, Huanbo Luan, and Maosong Sun. 2022. Data augmentation for low-resource languages nmt guided by constrained sampling. *International Journal of Intelligent Systems*, 37(1):30–51.

Teresa L McCarty and Bryan McKinley Jones Brayboy. 2021. Culturally responsive, sustaining, and revitalizing pedagogies: Perspectives from native american education. In *The Educational Forum*, volume 85, pages 429–443. Taylor & Francis.

Barbra A Meek. 2012. *We are our language: An ethnography of language revitalization in a Northern Athabaskan community.* University of Arizona Press.

Paul J Meighan. 2021. Decolonizing the digital landscape: The role of technology in indigenous language revitalization. *AlterNative: An International Journal of Indigenous Peoples*, 17(3):397–405.

Peggy J Miller and Lisa Hoogstra. 1992. Language as tool in the socialization and apprehension of cultural meanings. *New directions in psychological anthropology*, 3:83–101.

Juliet Liane Morgan. 2012. *Classificatory Verbs in Plains Apache.* Ph.D. thesis, University of Oklahoma.

New Mexico Secretary of State. 2025. Native american languages in new mexico.

Michael Leroy Oberg and Peter Jakob Olsen-Harbich. 2022. *Native America: a history.* John Wiley & Sons.

Kayla Palakurthy. 2022. New speakers and language change in diné bizaad (navajo). *International Journal of Bilingualism*, 26(5):601–619.

Surangika Ranathunga, En-Shiun Annie Lee, Marjana Prifti Skenduli, Ravi Shekhar, Mehreen Alam, and Rishemjit Kaur. 2023. Neural machine translation for low-resource languages: A survey. *ACM Computing Surveys*, 55(11):1–37.

Leslie Saxon. 2023. 39 dene–athabaskan. *The Languages and Linguistics of Indigenous North America: A Comprehensive Guide, Vol. 2*, 13:875.

Victoria Sear and Mark Turin. 2021. Locating criticality in the lexicography of historically marginalized languages. *history of humanities*, 6(1):237–259.

Gurinder Singh, Astha Gupta, Pranay Verma, Naina Chaudhary, Rajneesh Kler, and Ayush Thakur. 2024. Catalyzing multilingual nlp: New methods for low-resource language support. In *2024 4th International Conference on Technological Advancements in Computational Sciences (ICTACS)*, pages 67–75. IEEE.

Anca Sirbu. 2015. The significance of language as a tool of communication. *Scientific Bulletin" Mircea cel Batran" Naval Academy*, 18(2):405.

Mark Q Sutton. 2021. *An introduction to native North America*. Routledge.

Bryce D Tellmann. 2021. *The Great Plains and the Available Means of Regionalism*. The Pennsylvania State University.

Hiroto Uchihara. 2023. 3 tone. *The Languages and Linguistics of Indigenous North America: A Comprehensive Guide, Vol 1*, 13:63.

Wikipedia. 2025. Plains apache language.

Roger Williams. 2022. *A Key Into the Language of America: The Help to the Language of the Natives in That Part of America Called New-England*. DigiCat.

Ivory Yang, Weicheng Ma, and Soroush Vosoughi. 2025a. Nüshurescue: Reviving the endangered nüshu language with ai. In *Proceedings of the 31st International Conference on Computational Linguistics*, pages 7020–7034.

Ivory Yang, Weicheng Ma, Chunhui Zhang, and Soroush Vosoughi. 2025b. Is it navajo? accurate language detection in endangered athabaskan languages. *arXiv preprint arXiv:2501.15773*.

Keli Yerian and Bibi Halima. 2024. Language endangerment and revitalization. *Learning How to Learn Languages*.

Thomas Yim. 2024. Technology's dual role in language marginalization and revitalization. *GRACE: Global Review of AI Community Ethics*, 2(1).

Shiyue Zhang, Benjamin Frey, and Mohit Bansal. 2021. Chrentranslate: Cherokee-english machine translation demo with quality estimation and corrective feedback. In *Proceedings of the 59th Annual Meeting of the Association for Computational Linguistics and the 11th International Joint Conference on Natural Language Processing: System Demonstrations*, pages 272–279.

A Exploration with Support Vector Machines

While not discussed in detail in this paper, we also explored Support Vector Machines (SVM) as a potential alternative or complement to the proposed Random Forest classifier. We initialized an SVM classifier with a linear kernel and probability outputs, using `GridSearchCV` with cross-validation on the F1 score for hyperparameter tuning. Due to the computational demands of SVM training, we leveraged research computing resources, setting `n_jobs` to 32 for parallel processing. Initial results were largely coherent, though further investigation is needed to assess its comparative effectiveness.

Med-CoDE: Medical Critique based Disagreement Evaluation Framework

Mohit Gupta[*]**, Akiko Aizawa**[+]**, Rajiv Ratn Shah**[*]
[*]Indraprastha Institute of Information Technology Delhi, India,
[+]National Institute of Informatics, Tokyo, Japan
{mohit22112, rajivratn}@iiitd.ac.in[*]
aizawa@nii.ac.jp[+]

Abstract

The emergence of large language models (LLMs) has significantly influenced numerous fields, including healthcare, by enhancing the capabilities of automated systems to process and generate human-like text. However, despite their advancements, the reliability and accuracy of LLMs in medical contexts remain critical concerns. Current evaluation methods often lack robustness and fail to provide a comprehensive assessment of LLM performance, leading to potential risks in clinical settings. In this work, we propose Med-CoDE, a specifically designed evaluation framework for medical LLMs to address these challenges. The framework leverages a critique-based approach to quantitatively measure the degree of disagreement between model-generated responses and established medical ground truths. This framework captures both accuracy and reliability in medical settings. The proposed evaluation framework aims to fill the existing gap in LLM assessment by offering a systematic method to evaluate the quality and trustworthiness of medical LLMs. Through extensive experiments and case studies, we illustrate the practicality of our framework in providing a comprehensive and reliable evaluation of medical LLMs.

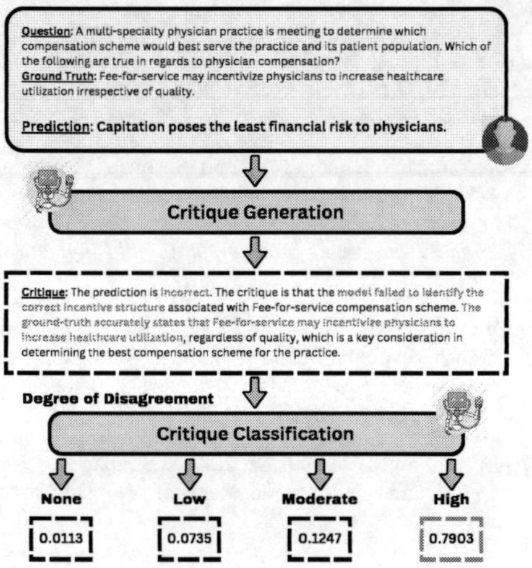

Figure 1: Med-Code Framework

1 Introduction

Medical Question Answering systems based on Large Language Models represent a significant leap in leveraging artificial intelligence for healthcare. These systems are designed to process and respond to medical queries. The primary aim of Medical QA LLMs is to provide accurate, reliable, and timely information to support clinicians, researchers, and patients. Evaluating the performance of these LLMs is crucial to ensure their reliability and effectiveness in real-world medical applications. Performance evaluation typically involves assessing the accuracy, relevance, and coherence of the generated responses compared to established medical standards or expert opinions.

Traditional methods for evaluating text generation, such as string similarity metrics (e.g., METEOR, BLEU, ROUGE), have been used widely across various domains. These metrics compare the overlap between generated and reference text-based on the n-gram matching, synonymy, and paraphrasing. While effective in general text generation tasks, these metrics pose significant limitations in the medical QA domain. Medical texts often require precise and contextually accurate responses where minor discrepancies can lead to substantial misunderstandings or clinical errors. Traditional metrics fail to capture the nuanced medical context, thereby providing an inadequate measure of LLM performance in this sensitive field.

To address the shortcomings of traditional evaluation methods, researchers have started exploring the use of LLMs themselves for evaluating other

Proceedings of the 2025 Conference of the Nations of the Americas Chapter of the Association for Computational Linguistics: Human Language Technologies (Volume 4: Student Research Workshop), pages 112–119

LLMs. Frameworks such as Harness (Gao et al., 2023), DeepEval[1], MLFlow[2] represent this shift towards LLM-assisted evaluation. These frameworks aim to provide more contextual and comprehensive evaluations by leveraging the advanced capabilities of LLMs to understand the generated responses. Despite these advancements, the current LLM-assisted evaluation methods still lack a structured approach to quantifying disagreement and assessing reliability.

This research paper presents an reliable evaluation framework tailored for Medical QA LLMs. Drawing inspiration from the work of (Wang et al., 2023), our framework introduces a critique-based methodology that quantitatively assesses the discrepancies between model-generated responses and established medical ground truths. By employing a critique model, we analyzed the differences in LLM outputs and provide a comprehensive evaluation of their accuracy and reliability. The visual representation of Med-Code framework is shown in Fig. 1.

The contributions of this work are as follows.

- We curated a specialized medical critique dataset, incorporating medical Q&A pairs from benchmark datasets such as Medqa (Zhang et al., 2018), Medmcqa (Pal et al., 2022). etc. The dataset includes responses from various medical language models (LLMs) and a degree of disagreement label between the ground-truth answers and the models' responses.

- We developed an advanced evaluation pipeline based on the Shepherd model (Wang et al., 2023), where we fine-tuned the Phi-3 model for generating critiques and employed a BERT model for classifying them.

- To demonstrate the effectiveness of our evaluation framework, we conducted comprehensive experiments across four medical benchmark datasets, utilizing diverse evaluation techniques to ensure robust validation.

2 Related Work

This section discusses related work in the field of evaluation, highlighting previous contributions. Our motivation stems from the Shepherd Model (Wang et al., 2023), which introduces a large language model designed to generate critiques of model responses to given prompts. We extend this work by using critiques to evaluate discrepancies between model responses and ground truth.

Recent studies have shown that traditional metrics such as METEOR (Banerjee and Lavie, 2005), ROUGE (Lin, 2004) and BLEUScore (Zhang et al., 2020) are inadequate for accurately evaluating open-ended generation tasks due to their reliance on reference text (Chiang and Lee, 2023; Gu et al., 2021; Guan et al., 2021; Polišenská et al., 2020; Wu et al., 2021). Advances have led to new research using LLMs as evaluators, demonstrating their potential to overcome these limitations (Kim et al., 2024; Kocmi and Federmann, 2023; Liu et al., 2024b,c). Notably, approaches employing powerful LLMs like GPT-4 have achieved remarkable performance (Fu et al., 2024; Liu et al., 2023). However, current LLM-based evaluators exhibit shortcomings in robustness, as their performance is highly sensitive to prompts, leading to instability in the evaluation process. Recent studies have sought to address these challenges by generating explanations for evaluation outputs (Chiang and Lee, 2023), but this approach does not inherently improve robustness or reliability due to issues such as hallucinations (Xu et al., 2023).

In the context of medical AI, where accuracy and reliability are crucial, several research efforts propose strategies to evaluate LLM responses. An automatic evaluation metric and algorithm for LLMs' clinical capabilities is proposed in (Liu et al., 2024a), featuring a multi-agent framework with Retrieval-Augmented Evaluation (RAE) to assess the behaviors of a doctor agent. (Awasthi et al., 2023) propose a structured method for comprehensive human evaluation of LLM outputs, introducing the HumanELY guidance and tool. (Liao et al., 2024) introduce the Automated Interactive Evaluation (AIE) framework, which provides a dynamic, realistic platform for assessing LLMs through multi-turn doctor-patient simulations.

3 Methodology

In this section, we discuss the process of creating a fine-tuning dataset for the medical domain critique model, the approach we used for fine-tuning the LLM, and the development of classification model.

[1]https://docs.confident-ai.com/
[2]https://mlflow.org/

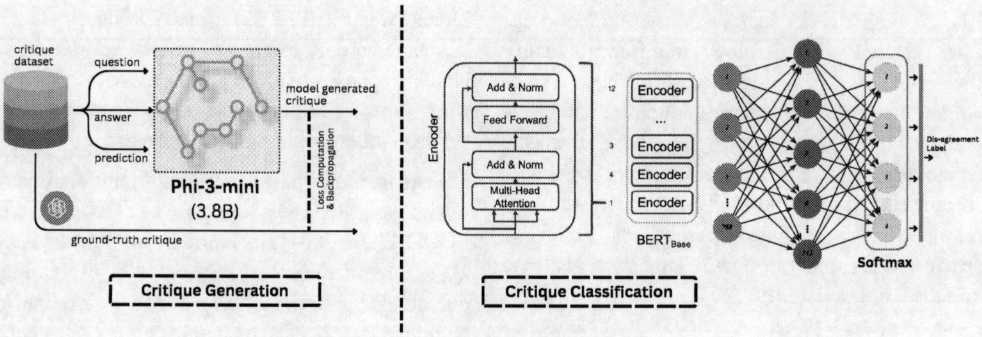

Figure 2: The overall Fine-tuning pipeline for Critique Generator & Classifier.

3.1 Dataset

In this research, we curated a specialized dataset using the OpenAI GPT-4 model to build a fine-tuning dataset for our critique generation model. Our final critique dataset comprises *38,819* samples, with an average critique length of *58.95* words. This dataset enables us to assess how well LLM responses align with ground-truth answers and to measure the degree of disagreement, providing a robust foundation for evaluating the performance of medical QA LLMs.

For medical domain data, we selected and combined small random subsets from standard medical QA datasets including Medqa (Zhang et al., 2018), Medmcqa (Pal et al., 2022), MMLU (Hendrycks et al., 2021), and Pubmedqa (Jin et al., 2019). These datasets encompass medical question-answer pairs from various medical fields, covering different levels of difficulty and types of questions. This comprehensive combination ensures that our critique model can effectively evaluate both objective and subjective questions.

```
<|user|>
You are a expert ai assistant. You are given a question, its ground-truth answer and the prediction from a model. Your task is to generate critique for the given prediction with respect to the given question, and ground-truth. This is very important and crucial task. While generating the critique, please keep the critique precise, clear and short.

### Question: {sample['question']}
### Ground-Truth: {sample['ground-truth']}
### Prediction: {sample['prediction']}

Only return the helpful answer below and nothing else.<|end|>
<|assistant|>
```

Figure 3: Critique Generation Prompt Template

After merging the random subsets, we employed SOTA medical domain LLMs, such as Meditron-7B (Chen et al., 2023), SelfBioRAG-7B (Jeong et al., 2024), to generate answers for each question. Each response was then critically evaluated using OpenAI GPT-4, which assigned a disagreement label from one of four categories: None, Low, Medium, and High. A High disagreement label indicates that the model-generated response is entirely incorrect and does not align with the ground truth in any aspect, whereas a None disagreement label signifies that the response is accurate and fully aligns with the ground truth without any extraneous information. In Low disagreement label the response is mostly accurate with minor additional details or slight deviations from the ground truth, lastly, the Moderate disagreement label, the response contains a mix of correct and incorrect information, with significant deviations from the ground truth, meaning the model is hallucinating.

3.2 Models

To build this lightweight evaluation framework, we employed two small models: ***Phi-3 3.8B*** (Abdin et al., 2024) for generating critiques & ***BERT*** (Devlin et al., 2019) for classifying the critiques. Although larger models with superior text generation capabilities and understanding are available, our objective was to create a domain-specific model tailored for a single task. Hence, these models were chosen. The visual representation of fine-tuning model architectures is shown in Fig. 2. This integrated pipeline proved efficient across all aspects, including computation, speed, and accuracy.

4 Experiments

In this section, we will delve into the experiment setup we have used for building this framework. It is divided into two subsections, first is for the critique generation model, and second is for the critique classification model.

4.1 Critique Generation Model

The objective of this model is to generate critiques based on a given question, its ground-truth answer, and the model's response. For this purpose, we employed the phi-3-mini model, which contains 3.8 billion parameters.

The hyperparameters configured for fine-tuning include *5* epochs, a batch size of *128*, a learning rate of *1.41e-5*, and the AdamW 8-bit optimizer. We utilized the LORA technique for efficient fine-tuning, with a rank parameter $r = 16$. The training process consumed an average of *20* GBs VRAM and required approximately *4-5* hours of GPU time. The data set was split into *30,000* samples for training, *4,409* for testing, and *4,410* for validation. The prompt template used in the fine-tuning and inference is given in Fig. 3.

Examples for each class of disagreement are provided in Fig. 4. These examples illustrate that the critiques generated by the model are highly precise and clear in identifying discrepancies between the ground-truth answers and the model's predictions, thereby supporting the efficacy of the fine-tuning process. To evaluate the quality of the dataset, we conducted a quality assessment on a small subset, as detailed in Section 5.1.

4.2 Critique Classification Model

For the critique classification model, we utilized the BERT base model, which contains *110M* parameters. This model is lightweight yet offers a deep bidirectional understanding of context, effectively capturing nuanced language patterns. The architecture of the entire classification network is depicted in Fig. 2.

Framework	Accuracy
GPT-3.5	78.12
Med-Code	71.72

Table 1: Human Evaluation Results of Disagreement Classification

The hyperparameters configured for fine-tuning are *25* epochs, a learning rate of *1e-3*, a dropout rate of *0.3*, a batch size of *16*, and a maximum sequence length of *208* tokens. The fine-tuning process employed a weighted average of all classes, with class weights specified as [*5.96, 1.34, 0.83, 0.52*]. The divergence function used is the Negative Log Likelihood. The total GPU utilization for fine-tuning this network is *2,771* MiB with *1* hour of GPU time. The data split used in this model training is *27,173* samples for training, *5,823* samples for validation, and *5,823* samples for testing.

We conducted a performance analysis of OpenAI's GPT-3.5 and our proposed framework, Med-Code, on a human labeled subset of 265 randomly selected samples. Each model received a question, a ground-truth answer, and the model's prediction, and we evaluated their accuracy in disagreement classification based on the critiques they generated. As shown in Table. 1, GPT-3.5 correctly classified approximately 207 out of 265 samples, and our proposed Med-Code framework produced results comparable to those of GPT-3.5 which is around 190 samples.

5 Results & Analysis

To assess the effectiveness of evaluating responses from large language models, we conducted experiments on four medical benchmark datasets: Medqa (Zhang et al., 2018), Medmcqa (Pal et al., 2022), Pubmedqa (Jin et al., 2019), and Mmlu (Hendrycks et al., 2021). These datasets are widely used in medical benchmarking and consist of objective-type questions. Our analysis focused on the test sets of these datasets using three LLMs: LLaMA-3 (AI@Meta, 2024), Mistral (Jiang et al., 2023), and BioMistral (Labrak et al., 2024). We selected these LLMs due to their demonstrated superior performance on general tasks and medical benchmarks.

We utilized Meteor and Rouge-L scores for automatic evaluation, the LLaMA-3 model for LLM-assisted evaluation, and our Med-Code framework to analyze LLM performance comprehensively. Med-Code categorizes responses into four degrees of disagreement, where an ideal model would show the highest average probability for "None" disagreement and the lowest for "High" disagreement. Detailed descriptions of each disagreement label are provided in the Section 3.1.

In Table 2, LLaMA-3, BioMistral, and Mistral models were used for inference. LLaMA-3 performed best on the MMLU dataset, achieving high scores in both automatic and LLM-assisted evaluations. Med-Code results showed that the "None" disagreement probability was the highest, indicating strong alignment between the model's responses and the ground-truth answers. Conversely, the "High" disagreement probability was the lowest, supporting the model's accuracy.

Dataset	Automatic Evaluation		LLM-Accuracy	Dis-agreement Evaluation			
	Meteor	Rouge-L		None ↑↑	Low ↑	Moderate ↓	High ↓↓
Results for LLaMA-3							
MEDQA USMLE	0.51	0.52	0.69	0.53	0.22	0.13	0.12
MEDMCQA	0.12	0.26	0.53	0.47	0.32	0.13	0.07
PUBMEDQA	0.11	0.12	0.39	0.55	0.30	0.10	0.05
MMLU	0.71	0.71	0.70	0.57	0.31	0.09	0.04
Results for BioMistral 7B							
MEDQA USMLE	0.14	0.07	0.74	0.44	0.29	0.16	0.11
MEDMCQA	0.16	0.08	0.61	0.35	0.39	0.18	0.08
PUBMEDQA	0.21	0.16	0.73	0.54	0.30	0.11	0.05
MMLU	0.33	0.19	0.70	0.32	0.41	0.19	0.07
Results for Mistral 7B v2.0							
MEDQA USMLE	0.16	0.12	0.68	0.47	0.28	0.15	0.01
MEDMCQA	0.56	0.11	0.56	0.33	0.38	0.20	0.08
PUBMEDQA	0.21	0.19	0.68	0.60	0.26	0.09	0.05
MMLU	0.37	0.25	0.65	0.36	0.37	0.19	0.07

Table 2: Evaluation Results for LLaMA-3, BioMistral 7B and Mistral 7B v2.0

The automatic evaluation results for BioMistral, a medical domain-specific LLM, did not convey significant information due to its poor string/semantic matching. However, BioMistral outperformed Mistral in LLM-assisted evaluation accuracy across all datasets, which was expected.

There was a strong positive correlation between accuracy and "None" disagreement probability, demonstrating that Med-Code effectively identified correct responses. Additionally, there is a positive correlation between METEOR scores and a 'Low' disagreement probability, suggesting that the low semantic relation between ground truth and model predictions. The low positive correlation between LLM-assisted accuracy and both 'Moderate' and 'High' disagreement probabilities confirmed instances where the models hallucinated or produced incorrect results.

When examining the correlation between automatic evaluation scores like METEOR and ROUGE-L scores and LLM accuracy, the correlation is inconsistent across different LLMs. This inconsistency may be due to the fact that automatic metrics are based on string matching, while LLM-assisted accuracy relies on the model's knowledge and logic. For example,

"If the model generates medicine X for disease D, but the ground truth answer lists medicine Y for the same disease, the automatic evaluation scores might be low. However, the LLM-assisted accuracy could still be correct because the model knows that X is equivalent to Y for disease D."

5.1 Human Evaluation

To assess the quality of the critique data generated by the OpenAI model for fine-tuning purposes, we conducted a thorough evaluation on a randomly selected subset of 265 samples. Each sample was manually reviewed to determine how effectively the model understood the relationship between the ground-truth answer and the model's prediction, and whether it could accurately identify minute discrepancies and details within the predictions.

Upon analysis, we found that approximately 240 out of the 265 samples (about *91%*) were accurately critiqued. The generated critiques successfully highlighted the flaws and discrepancies between the ground-truth and the predictions, demonstrating the model's capability to provide precise and detailed feedback. This quality assessment validates the reliability of the generated data for fine-tuning the critique generation model. The ground-truth critiques are noted for their clarity and precision,

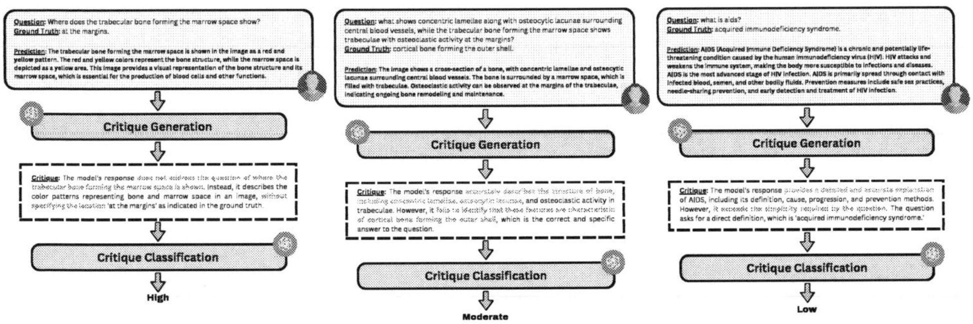

Figure 4: Critique data samples with different dis-agreement Labels

effectively pinpointing subtle differences between the ground-truth answers and the model's predictions. This ensures that the data can be effectively used for fine-tuning the critique generation model, allowing it to learn and adapt with high accuracy and precision.

6 Conclusion

In this work, we introduce Med-CoDE, an evaluation framework designed to assess the performance of Medical LLMs using critiques and degrees of disagreement. Med-CoDE excels in identifying subtle discrepancies between ground-truth answers and model predictions, offering a nuanced evaluation with four levels of disagreement. These levels provide insights into the model's behavior, such as hallucinations, accuracy, and adherence to the question. Our framework aids researchers in pinpointing areas where LLMs fall short, enabling targeted improvements. Extensive experiments on standard medical benchmark datasets demonstrate Med-CoDE's effectiveness in thoroughly and efficiently analyzing model behavior. This robust evaluation method is crucial for advancing the reliability and safety of AI-driven healthcare solutions. This evaluation framework is adaptable for assessing large language models across various domain-specific tasks as well as general tasks, simply by modifying the critique dataset.

7 Limitations

In this paper, we assess both automatic and human evaluation. Despite experimenting with a substantial number of data examples and utilizing human annotators to the best of our financial capabilities, there is room for further enhancement. Limited access to the costly OpenAI APIs meant that we used these resources judiciously, focusing on crucial areas. Additionally, computational constraints restricted the scope of our experiments. Nonetheless, these limitations highlight opportunities for future work to expand and refine the proposed framework with more extensive experimental analysis and resource allocation.

8 Ethical Considerations

The Med-CoDE framework, designed to assess the reliability and accuracy of medical LLMs, operates within a domain where the potential consequences of errors are particularly significant, given the direct impact on patient care and treatment outcomes.

In this work, only the publicly available standard benchmark medical QA datasets are used for training and evaluations. The Med-CoDE framework aims to enhance the evaluation of LLMs to ensure they meet rigorous standards of accuracy and reliability. However, it is essential to recognize that even well-evaluated models are not infallible and should not replace human judgment. Instead, they should be used as tools to support healthcare professionals, who must remain the final arbiters in clinical decision-making.

By addressing these ethical considerations, the Med-CoDE framework can contribute to the responsible development and deployment of medical LLMs, ultimately supporting safer and more effective healthcare solutions.

9 Acknowledgments

This work was supported by Cross-ministerial Strategic Innovation Promotion Program (SIP) on "Integrated Health Care System" Grant Number JPJ012425.

References

Marah I Abdin, Sam Ade Jacobs, Ammar Ahmad Awan, Jyoti Aneja, Ahmed Awadallah, Hany Hassan Awadalla, Nguyen Bach, Amit Bahree, Arash Bakhtiari, Harkirat Behl, Alon Benhaim, Misha Bilenko, Johan Bjorck, Sébastien Bubeck, Martin Cai, Caio César Teodoro Mendes, Weizhu Chen, Vishrav Chaudhary, Parul Chopra, Allie Del Giorno, Gustavo de Rosa, Matthew Dixon, Ronen Eldan, Dan Iter, Abhishek Goswami, Suriya Gunasekar, Emman Haider, Junheng Hao, Russell J. Hewett, Jamie Huynh, Mojan Javaheripi, Xin Jin, Piero Kauffmann, Nikos Karampatziakis, Dongwoo Kim, Mahmoud Khademi, Lev Kurilenko, James R. Lee, Yin Tat Lee, Yuanzhi Li, Chen Liang, Weishung Liu, Xihui (Eric) Lin, Zeqi Lin, Piyush Madan, Arindam Mitra, Hardik Modi, Anh Nguyen, Brandon Norick, Barun Patra, Daniel Perez-Becker, Thomas Portet, Reid Pryzant, Heyang Qin, Marko Radmilac, Corby Rosset, Sambudha Roy, Olli Saarikivi, Amin Saied, Adil Salim, Michael Santacroce, Shital Shah, Ning Shang, Hiteshi Sharma, Xia Song, Olatunji Ruwase, Xin Wang, Rachel Ward, Guanhua Wang, Philipp Witte, Michael Wyatt, Can Xu, Jiahang Xu, Weijian Xu, Sonali Yadav, Fan Yang, Ziyi Yang, Donghan Yu, Chengruidong Zhang, Cyril Zhang, Jianwen Zhang, Li Lyna Zhang, Yi Zhang, Yunan Zhang, and Xiren Zhou. 2024. Phi-3 technical report: A highly capable language model locally on your phone.

AI@Meta. 2024. Llama 3 model card.

Raghav Awasthi, Shreya Mishra, Dwarikanath Mahapatra, Ashish Khanna, Kamal Maheshwari, Jacek Cywinski, Frank Papay, and Piyush Mathur. 2023. Humanely: Human evaluation of llm yield, using a novel web-based evaluation tool.

Satanjeev Banerjee and Alon Lavie. 2005. METEOR: An automatic metric for MT evaluation with improved correlation with human judgments. In *Proceedings of the ACL Workshop on Intrinsic and Extrinsic Evaluation Measures for Machine Translation and/or Summarization*, pages 65–72, Ann Arbor, Michigan. Association for Computational Linguistics.

Zeming Chen, Alejandro Hernández Cano, Angelika Romanou, Antoine Bonnet, Kyle Matoba, Francesco Salvi, Matteo Pagliardini, Simin Fan, Andreas Köpf, Amirkeivan Mohtashami, Alexandre Sallinen, Alireza Sakhaeirad, Vinitra Swamy, Igor Krawczuk, Deniz Bayazit, Axel Marmet, Syrielle Montariol, Mary-Anne Hartley, Martin Jaggi, and Antoine Bosselut. 2023. Meditron-70b: Scaling medical pretraining for large language models. *Preprint*, arXiv:2311.16079.

Cheng-Han Chiang and Hung-yi Lee. 2023. Can large language models be an alternative to human evaluations? In *Proceedings of the 61st Annual Meeting of the Association for Computational Linguistics (Volume 1: Long Papers)*, pages 15607–15631, Toronto, Canada. Association for Computational Linguistics.

Jacob Devlin, Ming-Wei Chang, Kenton Lee, and Kristina Toutanova. 2019. BERT: Pre-training of deep bidirectional transformers for language understanding. In *Proceedings of the 2019 Conference of the North American Chapter of the Association for Computational Linguistics: Human Language Technologies, Volume 1 (Long and Short Papers)*, pages 4171–4186, Minneapolis, Minnesota. Association for Computational Linguistics.

Jinlan Fu, See-Kiong Ng, Zhengbao Jiang, and Pengfei Liu. 2024. GPTScore: Evaluate as you desire. In *Proceedings of the 2024 Conference of the North American Chapter of the Association for Computational Linguistics: Human Language Technologies (Volume 1: Long Papers)*, pages 6556–6576, Mexico City, Mexico. Association for Computational Linguistics.

Leo Gao, Jonathan Tow, Baber Abbasi, Stella Biderman, Sid Black, Anthony DiPofi, Charles Foster, Laurence Golding, Jeffrey Hsu, Alain Le Noac'h, Haonan Li, Kyle McDonell, Niklas Muennighoff, Chris Ociepa, Jason Phang, Laria Reynolds, Hailey Schoelkopf, Aviya Skowron, Lintang Sutawika, Eric Tang, Anish Thite, Ben Wang, Kevin Wang, and Andy Zou. 2023. A framework for few-shot language model evaluation.

Jing Gu, Qingyang Wu, and Zhou Yu. 2021. Perception score: A learned metric for open-ended text generation evaluation. *Proceedings of the AAAI Conference on Artificial Intelligence*, 35(14):12902–12910.

Jian Guan, Zhexin Zhang, Zhuoer Feng, Zitao Liu, Wenbiao Ding, Xiaoxi Mao, Changjie Fan, and Minlie Huang. 2021. OpenMEVA: A benchmark for evaluating open-ended story generation metrics. In *Proceedings of the 59th Annual Meeting of the Association for Computational Linguistics and the 11th International Joint Conference on Natural Language Processing (Volume 1: Long Papers)*, pages 6394–6407, Online. Association for Computational Linguistics.

Dan Hendrycks, Collin Burns, Steven Basart, Andy Zou, Mantas Mazeika, Dawn Song, and Jacob Steinhardt. 2021. Measuring massive multitask language understanding. *Proceedings of the International Conference on Learning Representations (ICLR)*.

Minbyul Jeong, Jiwoong Sohn, Mujeen Sung, and Jaewoo Kang. 2024. Improving medical reasoning through retrieval and self-reflection with retrieval-augmented large language models. *Preprint*, arXiv:2401.15269.

Albert Q. Jiang, Alexandre Sablayrolles, Arthur Mensch, Chris Bamford, Devendra Singh Chaplot, Diego de las Casas, Florian Bressand, Gianna Lengyel, Guillaume Lample, Lucile Saulnier, Lélio Renard Lavaud, Marie-Anne Lachaux, Pierre Stock, Teven Le Scao, Thibaut Lavril, Thomas Wang, Timothée Lacroix, and William El Sayed. 2023. Mistral 7b. *Preprint*, arXiv:2310.06825.

Qiao Jin, Bhuwan Dhingra, Zhengping Liu, William Cohen, and Xinghua Lu. 2019. PubMedQA: A dataset for biomedical research question answering. In *Proceedings of the 2019 Conference on Empirical Methods in Natural Language Processing and the 9th International Joint Conference on Natural Language Processing (EMNLP-IJCNLP)*, pages 2567–2577, Hong Kong, China. Association for Computational Linguistics.

Seungone Kim, Jamin Shin, Yejin Cho, Joel Jang, Shayne Longpre, Hwaran Lee, Sangdoo Yun, Seongjin Shin, Sungdong Kim, James Thorne, and Minjoon Seo. 2024. Prometheus: Inducing fine-grained evaluation capability in language models. *Preprint*, arXiv:2310.08491.

Tom Kocmi and Christian Federmann. 2023. Large language models are state-of-the-art evaluators of translation quality. In *Proceedings of the 24th Annual Conference of the European Association for Machine Translation*, pages 193–203, Tampere, Finland. European Association for Machine Translation.

Yanis Labrak, Adrien Bazoge, Emmanuel Morin, Pierre-Antoine Gourraud, Mickael Rouvier, and Richard Dufour. 2024. BioMistral: A collection of open-source pretrained large language models for medical domains. In *Findings of the Association for Computational Linguistics: ACL 2024*, pages 5848–5864, Bangkok, Thailand. Association for Computational Linguistics.

Yusheng Liao, Yutong Meng, Yuhao Wang, Hongcheng Liu, Yanfeng Wang, and Yu Wang. 2024. Automatic interactive evaluation for large language models with state aware patient simulator. *Preprint*, arXiv:2403.08495.

Chin-Yew Lin. 2004. ROUGE: A package for automatic evaluation of summaries. In *Text Summarization Branches Out*, pages 74–81, Barcelona, Spain. Association for Computational Linguistics.

Lei Liu, Xiaoyan Yang, Fangzhou Li, Chenfei Chi, Yue Shen, Shiwei Lyu, Ming Zhang, Xiaowei Ma, Xiangguo Lv, Liya Ma, Zhiqiang Zhang, Wei Xue, Yiran Huang, and Jinjie Gu. 2024a. Towards automatic evaluation for llms' clinical capabilities: Metric, data, and algorithm. In *Proceedings of the 30th ACM SIGKDD Conference on Knowledge Discovery and Data Mining*, KDD '24, page 5466–5475, New York, NY, USA. Association for Computing Machinery.

Minqian Liu, Ying Shen, Zhiyang Xu, Yixin Cao, Eunah Cho, Vaibhav Kumar, Reza Ghanadan, and Lifu Huang. 2024b. X-eval: Generalizable multi-aspect text evaluation via augmented instruction tuning with auxiliary evaluation aspects. In *Proceedings of the 2024 Conference of the North American Chapter of the Association for Computational Linguistics: Human Language Technologies (Volume 1: Long Papers)*, pages 8560–8579, Mexico City, Mexico. Association for Computational Linguistics.

Yang Liu, Dan Iter, Yichong Xu, Shuohang Wang, Ruochen Xu, and Chenguang Zhu. 2023. G-eval: NLG evaluation using gpt-4 with better human alignment. In *Proceedings of the 2023 Conference on Empirical Methods in Natural Language Processing*, pages 2511–2522, Singapore. Association for Computational Linguistics.

Yuxuan Liu, Tianchi Yang, Shaohan Huang, Zihan Zhang, Haizhen Huang, Furu Wei, Weiwei Deng, Feng Sun, and Qi Zhang. 2024c. Calibrating LLM-based evaluator. In *Proceedings of the 2024 Joint International Conference on Computational Linguistics, Language Resources and Evaluation (LREC-COLING 2024)*, pages 2638–2656, Torino, Italia. ELRA and ICCL.

Ankit Pal, Logesh Kumar Umapathi, and Malaikannan Sankarasubbu. 2022. Medmcqa: A large-scale multi-subject multi-choice dataset for medical domain question answering. In *Proceedings of the Conference on Health, Inference, and Learning*, volume 174 of *Proceedings of Machine Learning Research*, pages 248–260. PMLR.

Kamila Polišenská, Shula Chiat, and Jakub Szewczyk. 2020. Effects of semantic plausibility, syntactic complexity and n-gram frequency on children's sentence repetition.

Tianlu Wang, Ping Yu, Xiaoqing Ellen Tan, Sean O'Brien, Ramakanth Pasunuru, Jane Dwivedi-Yu, Olga Golovneva, Luke Zettlemoyer, Maryam Fazel-Zarandi, and Asli Celikyilmaz. 2023. Shepherd: A critic for language model generation. *Preprint*, arXiv:2308.04592.

Haiyan Wu, Zhiqiang Zhang, and Qingfeng Wu. 2021. Exploring syntactic and semantic features for authorship attribution.

Wenda Xu, Danqing Wang, Liangming Pan, Zhenqiao Song, Markus Freitag, William Wang, and Lei Li. 2023. INSTRUCTSCORE: Towards explainable text generation evaluation with automatic feedback. In *Proceedings of the 2023 Conference on Empirical Methods in Natural Language Processing*, pages 5967–5994, Singapore. Association for Computational Linguistics.

Tianyi Zhang, Varsha Kishore, Felix Wu, Kilian Q. Weinberger, and Yoav Artzi. 2020. Bertscore: Evaluating text generation with bert. *Preprint*, arXiv:1904.09675.

Xiao Zhang, Ji Wu, Zhiyang He, Xien Liu, and Ying Su. 2018. Medical exam question answering with large-scale reading comprehension. In *Proceedings of the Thirty-Second AAAI Conference on Artificial Intelligence and Thirtieth Innovative Applications of Artificial Intelligence Conference and Eighth AAAI Symposium on Educational Advances in Artificial Intelligence*, AAAI'18/IAAI'18/EAAI'18. AAAI Press.

Sentimatic: Sentiment-guided Automatic Generation of Preference Datasets for Customer Support Dialogue System

Suhyun Lee, Changheon Han
Hanyang University, Seoul, Republic of Korea
{su7561632, datajedi23}@hanyang.ac.kr

Abstract

Supervised Fine-tuning (SFT) and preference optimization (PO) are key methods for enhancing language models and aligning them with human preferences. However, scaling preference datasets for PO training is challenging, leading AI customer support systems to rely on SFT. To address this, we propose the **Senti**ment-guided Auto**matic** Generation of Preference Datasets (**Sentimatic**) methodology to automatically generate customer preference datasets without human intervention using a publicly available dataset constructed for SFT. Our approach classifies responses by sentiment, fine-tunes models on them, and applies advanced sampling and evaluation techniques to ensure diversity and quality. Ultimately, we generated 1,174 customer preference datasets based on 357 test datasets, and through experiments, we confirmed that the AI customer support system trained on these datasets is capable of carefully considering customer emotions and generating professional and appropriate responses.

1 Introduction

Previous studies have used the SFT approach primarily to train AI models for customer service (Xu et al., 2017; Golchha et al., 2019; He et al., 2022). However, SFT focuses solely on the accuracy of individual tokens generated by the model, failing to adequately reflect the overall quality of conversations. This limitation can lead to inefficiencies in performance evaluation and optimization. In contrast, PO addresses these issues by evaluating the quality of the entire response generated by the model (Hua et al., 2024).

However, the preference datasets required for PO training are created through response comparisons, which require the involvement of human annotators. This dependency significantly increases the time and cost of large-scale data collection, posing challenges to the widespread adoption of PO. To address these challenges, AI-based feedback approaches that utilize large language models (LLMs) have been proposed to minimize human intervention (Cui et al., 2024; Bai et al., 2022). However, these approaches still rely on human-authored evaluation criteria for practical application. In the customer service domain, where providing responses that align with customer preferences and mitigate negative emotions is critical, the ambiguity of the evaluation criteria further highlights the limitations of existing methods.

To overcome these challenges, this study proposes a novel methodology for generating customer preference datasets without human intervention. This methodology provides a foundation for the efficient construction and scalability of PO datasets, enabling a wider adoption of PO in AI customer support systems. The proposed methodology consists of the following three key steps:

1. Sentiment Analysis: Model pool is used to analyze emotional changes before and after a response. Responses showing positive emotional changes are considered aligned with customer preferences and included in the positive dataset, while those showing negative emotional changes are included in the negative dataset.

2. Completion Sampling: Positive and negative datasets are used to fine-tune separate models. These models generate pairs of positive and negative responses for the test dataset. To ensure diversity and scalability, N responses are generated for each input by repeating the sampling process.

3. Preference Classification: BERTScore (Zhang et al., 2020) are calculated for the generated response pairs by comparing them with reference responses. High-quality responses are filtered based on a defined threshold.

Proceedings of the 2025 Conference of the Nations of the Americas Chapter of the Association for Computational Linguistics: Human Language Technologies (Volume 4: Student Research Workshop), pages 120–128

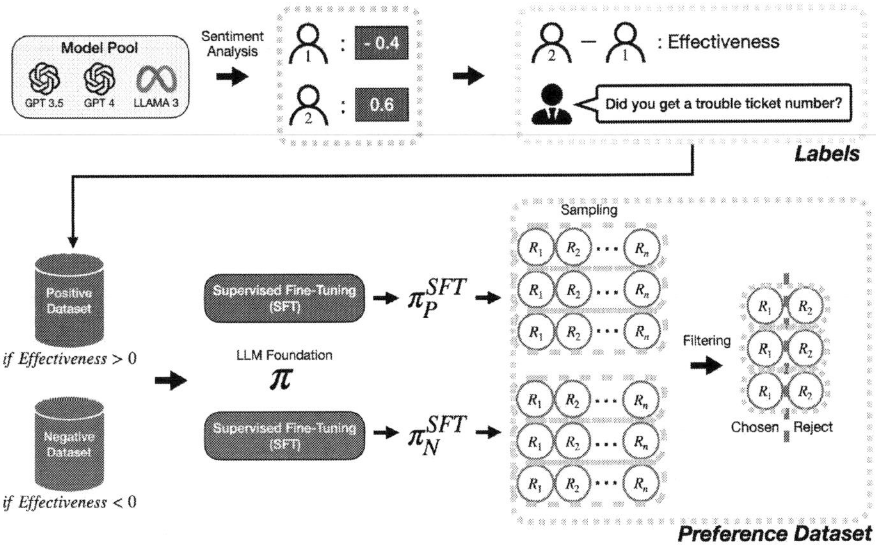

Figure 1: An overview of the Sentimatic methodology. A model pool (GPT-4 (OpenAI et al., 2024), GPT-3.5 (Ouyang et al., 2022), and LLaMA 3 (Grattafiori et al., 2024)) analyzes customer conversations to compute scalar sentiment scores. Responses showing positive emotional shifts are labeled as aligned with customer preferences, while those with negative shifts are not. These labeled datasets are used to fine-tune models for generating aligned and non-aligned responses. Diverse sampling techniques (beam search (Freitag and Al-Onaizan, 2017), top-k (Fan et al., 2018), top-p (Holtzman et al., 2020)) are employed to generate multiple responses per input. BERTScore is then calculated to validate response quality.

2 Methods

2.1 Overview

We adopt an AI-based feedback approach that leverages LLMs with scalability in mind. However, defining "responses aligned with customer preferences" poses a significant challenge. Therefore, instead of following the conventional approach (Cui et al., 2024; Bai et al., 2022) of designing prompts based on human-defined criteria for inference, we opted to fine-tune models separately to learn the responses patterns that align with customer preferences and those that do not.

Specifically, to distinguish between responses aligned with customer preferences and those that are not, we utilized a model pool to obtain sentiment scores for the initial customer conversation and the response, then calculated the difference between them. Responses that demonstrated a positive emotional shift were identified as aligned with customer preferences, while those that showed a negative emotional shift were classified as not aligned with customer preferences, forming the respective datasets.

We then fine-tuned two separate large-language models using the respective datasets. One model was trained on the Positive Dataset to generate responses aligned with customer preferences, while the other was trained on the Negative Dataset to learn patterns of non-aligned responses. Next, we used the fine-tuned models to repeatedly sample responses, generating N responses for the same input to ensure diversity. Finally, we calculate the BERTScore for the generated responses and classify high-quality comparison pairs based on a defined threshold. In the following section, we introduce the Sentimatic methodology in detail.

2.2 Curated Dataset

First, we selected the TWEETSUMM dataset (Feigenblat et al., 2021). This dataset contains real conversations between customer service agents and dissatisfied customers on Twitter, making it suitable for learning linguistic patterns and interaction styles in the customer service domain. Originally, TWEETSUMM is a multi-turn dataset, but we restructured it to focus on initial responses. Conversations were organized based on tweet IDs and transformed into single-turn interactions. Each conversation begins with the initial message from the

Table 1: Dataset Overview. "P" and "N" in the Sentimatic dataset indicate positive and negative preference labels, respectively.

	Sentimatic dataset		TWEETSUMM
Dialog	P	N	Multi-turn
# Train	1,530	1,129	879
# Test	211	146	110
# Valid	192	127	110

Table 2: Quality Evaluation of Completion Sampling (#: Number of samples, C: Chosen average BERTScore, R: Rejected average BERTScore, Δ: Difference average Between Chosen and Rejected Scores)

Sampling	α	β	#	C	R	Δ
Beam Search	0.78	0.2	1174	0.825	0.729	0.096
	0.8	0.2	952	0.834	0.762	0.064
	0.82	0.2	707	0.841	0.730	0.111
Top-K	0.78	0.2	1174	0.825	0.729	0.096
	0.8	0.2	952	0.834	0.762	0.064
	0.82	0.2	707	0.841	0.730	0.111
Top-P	0.78	0.2	1174	0.825	0.729	0.096
	0.8	0.2	952	0.834	0.762	0.064
	0.82	0.2	707	0.841	0.730	0.111

customer (c_1), followed by the agent's response, and ends with the customer's reply text after the agent's response (c_2).

Next, we used various models (GPT-4, GPT-3.5, LLaMA3) to perform a sentiment analysis on the customer's initial text (c_1) and the customer's reply text after the agent's response (c_2), assigning the average score as the numerical sentiment score. The prompt used for sentiment analysis can be found in Appendix 6. In this process, if any of the models produced a score of 0, indicating that the model failed to detect positive or negative sentiment tendencies for the given data, the result of that model was excluded. To determine the direction of the change in sentiment, we calculated the difference between the sentiment score of c_1 (s_1) and c_2 (s_2), selecting only responses that showed a positive change (+). Through this process, we collected 1,530 response data points aligned with customer preferences and 1,129 response data points not aligned with customer preferences. A summary of the dataset can be found in Table 1.

2.3 Completion Sampling

LLMs are trained on large-scale datasets to achieve generalization capabilities across various tasks. However, this training approach may not capture the nuances and specific knowledge required in certain domains. Previous studies have shown that fine-tuning in specific domains, such as legal document processing, medical diagnosis, and financial analysis, can lead to significant performance improvements (Dominguez-Olmedo et al., 2025; Ismail et al., 2024; Parker et al., 2022).

Therefore, after fine-tuning the LLMs with a curated dataset, we ensure that the collected responses are diverse and evenly distributed by repeating the various sampling processes (beam-search, top-k, top-p) multiple times to generate N responses for the same input. Specifically, we fine-tune the input-output pairs (x, y) of the selected data set to obtain initial parameters π^{SFT}. Using π^{SFT}, we then generate N responses $y_1, y_2,...$ and y_N:

$$(y_1, \ldots, y_N) \sim \pi^{\text{SFT}}(y|x) \tag{1}$$

The prompt used for fine-tuning can be found in Appendix 7. For inference, only the Instruction and Input parts of the same prompt were used.

2.4 Quality Evaluation

To ensure contextual relevance and prevent excessive deviation from the dialogue flow, we calculated the BERTScore by comparing the generated responses with the responses from the original data set as references. Specifically, we compute the BERTScore as follows:

$$S_{\text{BERT}}(y, r) = \frac{1}{N} \sum_{i=1}^{N} \cos(\mathbf{h}_i^y, \mathbf{h}_i^r) \tag{2}$$

where y represents the generated response, r is the original reference response from the dataset, and $\mathbf{h}_i^y$, $\mathbf{h}_i^r$ are the contextual embeddings of each token in y and r, respectively. The final score is obtained by averaging the cosine similarities across all token embeddings.

We use this score to classify high-quality response pairs applying a threshold α, filtering out responses that deviate significantly from the original context. Furthermore, we define a threshold β for the difference in the BERTScore between the chosen and rejected responses to maintain semantic diversity within the dataset. The statistics of the dataset based on α and β are reported in Table 2

3 Experiments

3.1 Response Generation Model

To validate the effectiveness of the Sentimatic methodology, we compare two versions of the Re-

Table 3: Evaluation of different LLM judges on contextual relevance, problem-solving approach, and handling of negative emotions.

Judge	Model	Contextual Relevance	Problem-Solving Approach	Handling Negative Emotions
GPT-4o	T5 + SFT	7.35%	9.45%	15.49%
	T5 + ORPO w/Sentimatic	**67.72%**	**48.29%**	**50.39%**
ChatGPT	T5 + SFT	18.64%	**17.59%**	18.90%
	T5 + ORPO w/Sentimatic	**66.93%**	**62.99%**	**64.30%**
GPT-o3	T5 + SFT	43.83%	46.98%	13.12%
	T5 + ORPO w/Sentimatic	**52.49%**	46.98%	**81.63%**

sponse Generation Model: 1) the SFT version trained on the existing TWEETSUMM dataset based on T5 (Wu et al., 2023) and 2) the Sentimatic version trained with PO using the dataset generated through the proposed methods.

Evaluation Methodology We evaluate the quality of generated responses using the LLM-as-a-judge approach, which follows a win/tie/lose framework judged by multiple LLMs (GPT-4o, ChatGPT, GPT-o3). In particular, we focus on three key aspects that are critical in Customer Support Dialogue Systems: contextual relevance, problem-solving approach, and handling of negative emotions. Each judge compares the responses generated by the two models and selects a preferred one, resulting in the win rate percentages shown in Table 3.

The LLM-as-a-judge methodology has been validated in prior work (Zheng et al., 2023), where strong LLMs such as GPT-4 demonstrated over 80% agreement with human preferences in both controlled and crowdsourced settings. This evaluation framework enables scalable and interpretable estimation of human-like preferences while significantly reducing the cost and effort associated with human evaluation. The used prompt can be found in Appendix 8

Setup We used 1,174 pairs of training data and 319 pairs of validation data, performing 3 fine-tuning iterations. The value of α was set to 0.78 and the value of β was set to 0.2. The ORPO (Hong et al., 2024) method was used as part of the PO approach. For fine-tuning, we utilized the AdamW optimizer with a learning rate of 0.0005 and a linear learning rate scheduler. The batch size per GPU was 8, and the training was performed on a single A6000 GPU.

Result As shown in Table 3, across all three evaluation axes and for all LLM judges, the Sentimatic-enhanced model (T5 + ORPO w/Sentimatic) consistently outperformed the baseline (T5 + SFT). Notably:

- GPT-4o judge: Sentimatic achieved a 67.72% win rate in contextual relevance, 48.29% in problem-solving, and 50.39% in handling negative emotions.
- ChatGPT judge: Sentimatic scored 66.93%, 62.99%, and 64.30% respectively.
- GPT-o3 judge: Sentimatic led with 52.49% for contextual relevance and a striking 81.63% win rate in handling negative emotions.

These results strongly suggest that Sentimatic improves response generation in both contextual understanding and emotional sensitivity, validated by multiple independent LLM judges.

3.2 Qualitative analysis

Table 4 presents representative examples that compare the responses generated by the SFT version and the Sentimatic-enhanced version of the model. We analyze responses along three key axes: contextual relevance, problem solving approach, and handling of negative emotions. Generally,the Sentimatic model demonstrates clear qualitative improvements across all three dimensions, reflecting its effectiveness in producing emotionally intelligent, contextually appropriate, and support-driven responses.

Contextual Relevance The Sentimatic model consistently demonstrates greater contextual awareness in its responses. For example, in row (b-1), the agent acknowledges the user's concern and explicitly refers to the situation ("Can you tell us more about what's going on?"), showing an intention to engage more deeply. In contrast, the SFT version in (a-1) offers a shallow suggestion ("Have you tried restarting your MacBook?") without confirming the actual problem of the user. Additionally, in (b-2), the Sentimatic model tailors the request by asking for specific details, while the SFT version (a-2) provides a generic, less targeted reply. These differences highlight how Sentimatic better aligns its responses with the intent and content of the customer's message.

Table 4: Examples of Model Inference Results

(a) Example 1: SFT version

1.	
Customer:	*@SpotifyCares hey, any explanation why the "Create similar playlist" function doesn't work anymore for me? MacBook, v1.0.64.399.g4637b02a*
Agent:	*@267878 I'm sorry to hear that. Have you tried restarting your MacBook?*
2.	
Customer:	*@AskAmex When is interest charged on Charge Cards with Pay Over Time, Sign and Travel, etc. From the Due Date or from the Closing Date?*
Agent:	*@261778 I'm sorry, I cannot provide an answer to that question as it requires additional information. Please provide the details of the Charge Cards you are interested in.*
3.	
Customer:	*@Delta I just sent it @Delta Thank you, that was excellent resolution, glad I sent that tweet just in time while I still had a window to change the itinerary without a fee.*
Agent:	*@261715 Hi, I'm sorry to hear that. We're glad to hear that you're happy with the resolution. We'll send you a link to the new itinerary.*

(b) Example 2: Sentimatic version

1.	
Customer:	*@SpotifyCares hey, any explanation why the "Create similar playlist" function doesn't work anymore for me? MacBook, v1.0.64.399.g4637b02a.*
Agent:	*@179244 Hi there, thanks for getting back to us. Can you tell us more about what's going on? We're here to help anyway we can.*
2.	
Customer:	*@AppleSupport I did not understood what do you mean by DM my iPhone*
Agent:	*Understood, please provide me with your full name, email address, and postcode. I'll be happy to take a closer look.*
3.	
Customer:	*@airtelcare xxx you, your company, your CEO and even COO. you will fold up and run into loss as u have caused me pains,weeks n counting.*
Agent:	*@179244 Hi there, thanks for getting back to us. We've made a note of this and passed over your feedback to our Developers JB*

Problem-Solving Approach Sentimatic responses generally adopt a more structured and cooperative problem solving approach. For example, (b-2) asks for the customer's full name, email, and postcode in order to assist further—this kind of information gathering is essential in real customer support workflows. However, the SFT response in (a-2) defers the assistance entirely without providing a concrete next step. Similarly, in (b-1), the Sentimatic version attempts to diagnose the problem by requesting more context, whereas the SFT model prematurely offers a potential fix. These examples demonstrate how Sentimatic responses are more proactive and service-oriented in resolving customer issues.

Handling of Negative Emotions Sentimatic shows a significant improvement in emotionally sensitive scenarios. The most striking example is (b-3), where the customer expresses frustration with harsh language. The Sentimatic model remains calm, professional and empathetic, acknowledging the message without escalating the tone, and assuring the user that feedback has been passed to the relevant team. In contrast, the SFT model in similar scenarios, such as (a-3), provides a flat, impersonal response that misses the opportunity to acknowledge the user's sentiment. This suggests that the Sentimatic model is better at defusing negative sentiment and maintaining a respectful tone, even in high-stress conversations.

3.3 AI Feedback Model Specialized for the Customer Support Domain

To develop a scalable method for collecting preference data without relying on public datasets in the customer support domain, we designed an AI feedback model based on LaMini-Flan-T5. This model is configured as a text-to-text task, generating scalar scores representing the quality of responses along with the corresponding textual critiques, allowing a single model to produce both outputs.

The difference between the emotion scores s_1 and s_2, along with c_2, is mapped to a template to generate a scalar score that reflects the change in customer emotion and the expected response.

To validate the effectiveness of the pipeline, two versions of the model were developed. The SFT version was trained using SFT with the mapped text and the initial customer text (y, c_1), while the Sentimatic version was trained using PO on a preference dataset generated through the pipeline. Notably, this process does not aim to create a preference

Table 5: Quality of Text Generation for Customers' Next Response and Score Prediction Error

Model + Method	MSE	BLEU	ROUGE1	ROUGE2	ROUGEL	METEOR
LaMini-Flan-T5-77M + SFT	0.63	32.70	0.46	0.36	0.45	0.49
LaMini-Flan-T5-77M + Sentimatic	**0.55**	28.62	0.52	0.43	0.51	0.49
LaMini-Flan-T5-783M + SFT	0.45	32.92	0.48	0.37	0.46	0.50
LaMini-Flan-T5-783M + Sentimatic	**0.44**	32.48	0.46	0.35	0.44	0.49

dataset itself. Instead of explicitly separating Positive and Negative data, the pipeline expands the dataset using sampling techniques after SFT training. Subsequently, BERTScore is utilized to filter the data, and responses with higher and lower scores are paired to form pairs of 'Chosen' and 'Reject'.

Setup We used 2,852 pairs of training data and performed 30 fine-tuning iterations. The ORPO method was applied as part of the Preference Optimization (PO) approach. For fine-tuning, we employed the AdamW optimizer with a learning rate of 0.0005 and a linear learning rate scheduler. The batch size per GPU was set to 8, and training was performed on a single A6000 GPU.

To evaluate the quality of the Response Generation Model, we used four widely recognized metrics: BLEU(Papineni et al., 2002) , ROUGE(Lin, 2004), and METEOR(Banerjee and Lavie, 2005). Furthermore, the mean squared error (MSE) metric was used to assess the accuracy of the prediction of 'score'.

Result Table 5 presents the performance metrics for different methods in predicting emotion scores and generating customer responses. The LaMini-Flan-T5-77M model, when fine-tuned with the Sentimatic methodology, achieved an MSE of 0.55, indicating a 12.7% improvement compared to the application of SFT alone (MSE 0.63). Similarly, the LaMini-Flan-T5-783M model demonstrated an MSE of 0.44, marking a 2.22% improvement over the SFT-only model (MSE 0.45).

Figure 2 illustrates the distribution of predicted effectiveness scores between models. The SFT-only model shows a high concentration of scores around -0.5, suggesting that the model frequently generates similar emotion scores that deviate from the true values. In contrast, Sentimatic methodology results in a wider distribution of scores, demonstrating the ability to predict a broader range of emotions that align more closely with actual values.

Conclusion

This study proposed a novel methodology for constructing a preference dataset for Preference Optimization (PO) using publicly available customer support data without human intervention. As a result, we generated 1,174 customer preference datasets based on 357 test data instances. The model trained through the proposed data construction pipeline demonstrated effective improvements in the quality of customer support dialogue responses. In particular, we empirically validated that the model can be trained to better meet user expectations without relying on costly human annotations. Across the three key evaluation criteria: contextual relevance, problem solving approach, and handling of negative emotions, the Sentimatic-enhanced model consistently outperformed the baseline model trained by supervised fine-tuning (SFT). These results were reliably validated through the LLM-as-a-judge evaluation framework, involving independent LLM judges including GPT-4o, ChatGPT, and GPT-o3.Overall, the proposed method is scalable, cost-efficient, and readily applicable to real-world customer service scenarios, offering a promising direction for developing emotionally aware and user-centered AI agents.

Limitation

The proposed methodology has certain limitations, depends on multiple LLMs for sentiment detection, which can introduce bias or inaccuracies, and focuses primarily on Twitter-based complaints. To overcome these limitations, future research will evaluate the performance of Sentimatic methodology in general conversation by comparing it with human feedback-based datasets. In addition, ensemble modeling and complementary evaluation techniques will be introduced to minimize bias in large-language models.

References

Yuntao Bai et al. 2022. Training a helpful and harmless assistant with reinforcement learning from human feedback. *Preprint*, arXiv:2204.05862.

Satanjeev Banerjee and Alon Lavie. 2005. Meteor: An automatic metric for mt evaluation with improved correlation with human judgments. In *Proceedings of the acl workshop on intrinsic and extrinsic evaluation measures for machine translation and/or summarization*, pages 65–72.

Ganqu Cui et al. 2024. Ultrafeedback: Boosting language models with scaled ai feedback. In *Forty-first International Conference on Machine Learning*.

Ricardo Dominguez-Olmedo, Vedant Nanda, Rediet Abebe, Stefan Bechtold, Christoph Engel, Jens Frankenreiter, Krishna P. Gummadi, Moritz Hardt, and Michael Livermore. 2025. Lawma: The power of specialization for legal annotation. In *The Thirteenth International Conference on Learning Representations*.

Angela Fan, Mike Lewis, and Yann Dauphin. 2018. Hierarchical neural story generation. In *Proceedings of the 56th Annual Meeting of the Association for Computational Linguistics (Volume 1: Long Papers)*, pages 889–898, Melbourne, Australia. Association for Computational Linguistics.

Guy Feigenblat, Chulaka Gunasekara, Benjamin Sznajder, Sachindra Joshi, David Konopnicki, and Ranit Aharonov. 2021. Tweetsumm–a dialog summarization dataset for customer service. *arXiv preprint arXiv:2111.11894*.

Markus Freitag and Yaser Al-Onaizan. 2017. Beam search strategies for neural machine translation. In *Proceedings of the First Workshop on Neural Machine Translation*, pages 56–60, Vancouver. Association for Computational Linguistics.

Hitesh Golchha, Mauajama Firdaus, Asif Ekbal, and Pushpak Bhattacharyya. 2019. Courteously yours: Inducing courteous behavior in customer care responses using reinforced pointer generator network. In *Proceedings of the 2019 Conference of the North American Chapter of the Association for Computational Linguistics: Human Language Technologies, Volume 1 (Long and Short Papers)*, pages 851–860.

Aaron Grattafiori et al. 2024. The llama 3 herd of models. *Preprint*, arXiv:2407.21783.

Keqing He, Jingang Wang, Chaobo Sun, and Wei Wu. 2022. Unified knowledge prompt pre-training for customer service dialogues. In *Proceedings of the 31st ACM International Conference on Information & Knowledge Management*, pages 4009–4013.

Ari Holtzman, Jan Buys, Li Du, Maxwell Forbes, and Yejin Choi. 2020. The curious case of neural text degeneration. *Preprint*, arXiv:1904.09751.

Jiwoo Hong, Noah Lee, and James Thorne. 2024. Orpo: Monolithic preference optimization without reference model. *Preprint*, arXiv:2403.07691.

Ermo Hua, Biqing Qi, Kaiyan Zhang, Yue Yu, Ning Ding, Xingtai Lv, Kai Tian, and Bowen Zhou. 2024. Intuitive fine-tuning: Towards simplifying alignment into a single process. *arXiv preprint arXiv:2405.11870*.

Amelia Ritahani Ismail, Amira Shazleen Aminuddin, Afiqa Nurul, Noor Azura Zakaria, and Wafa Haussain Nasser Fadaaq. 2024. A fine-tuned large language model for domain-specific with reinforcement learning. In *2024 3rd International Conference on Creative Communication and Innovative Technology (ICCIT)*, pages 1–6. IEEE.

Chin-Yew Lin. 2004. Rouge: A package for automatic evaluation of summaries. In *Text summarization branches out*, pages 74–81.

OpenAI, Josh Achiam, et al. 2024. Gpt-4 technical report. *Preprint*, arXiv:2303.08774.

Long Ouyang et al. 2022. Training language models to follow instructions with human feedback. *Advances in neural information processing systems*, 35:27730–27744.

Kishore Papineni, Salim Roukos, Todd Ward, and Wei-Jing Zhu. 2002. Bleu: a method for automatic evaluation of machine translation. In *Proceedings of the 40th annual meeting of the Association for Computational Linguistics*, pages 311–318.

Brydon Parker, Alik Sokolov, Mahtab Ahmed, Matt Kalebic, Sedef Akinli Kocak, and Ofer Shai. 2022. Domain specific fine-tuning of denoising sequence-to-sequence models for natural language summarization. *arXiv preprint arXiv:2204.09716*.

Minghao Wu, Abdul Waheed, Chiyu Zhang, Muhammad Abdul-Mageed, and Alham Fikri Aji. 2023. Lamini-lm: A diverse herd of distilled models from large-scale instructions. *arXiv preprint arXiv:2304.14402*.

Anbang Xu, Zhe Liu, Yufan Guo, Vibha Sinha, and Rama Akkiraju. 2017. A new chatbot for customer service on social media. In *Proceedings of the 2017 CHI conference on human factors in computing systems*, pages 3506–3510.

Tianyi Zhang, Varsha Kishore, Felix Wu, Kilian Q. Weinberger, and Yoav Artzi. 2020. Bertscore: Evaluating text generation with bert. *Preprint*, arXiv:1904.09675.

Lianmin Zheng, Wei-Lin Chiang, Ying Sheng, Siyuan Zhuang, Zhanghao Wu, Yonghao Zhuang, Zi Lin, Zhuohan Li, Dacheng Li, Eric P. Xing, Hao Zhang, Joseph E. Gonzalez, and Ion Stoica. 2023. Judging llm-as-a-judge with mt-bench and chatbot arena. *Preprint*, arXiv:2306.05685.

A Appendix

Instruction	The conversation consists of three sequential segments: {c1} (customer's utterance before the agent's response), {agent} (agent's response), and {c2} (customer's utterance following the agent's response). Please analyze the emotions in the conversation. Calculate the change in emotion using the formula: (c2's emotional score - c1's emotional score). Respond with a single float number only, within the range of -2 to 2. Do not include any explanation or additional text.
Input Data	{c1: [Customer's utterance before agent's response], agent: [Agent's response], c2: [Customer's utterance after agent's response]}

Table 6: Example of Prompt Template used for scoring

Instruction	You are a customer service chatbot. Generate a agent's response to the following customer message.
Inputs	Customer said: `{customer_inquiry}`
Labels	Agent said: `{agent_reply}`

Table 7: Example of Prompt Template used for Completion Sampling

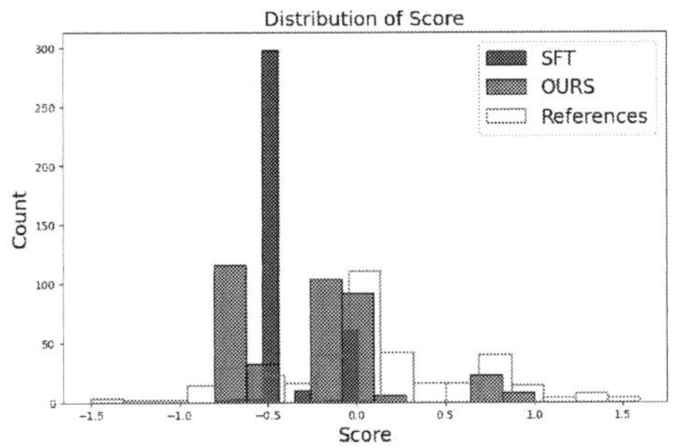

Figure 2: Score Distributions

Instruction	Given a customer message, compare two agent responses. `customer`: {customer} `response_A`: {response_A} `response_B`: {response_B} Evaluate the responses according to the following criteria: 1. Context appropriateness 2. Problem-solving effectiveness 3. Handling of negative emotions Select the better response for each criterion. If one response is clearly superior, label it as "A wins" or "B wins". If both are equivalent, label it as "Draw". Return your judgment in the following JSON format: `{"Context appropriateness": "A wins", "Problem-solving effectiveness": "Draw", "Handling of negative emotions": "B wins"}` No further explanation is required.
Input Data	{customer: [Customer message], response_A: [Response generated by T5 + ORPO w/ Sentimatic], response_B: [Response generated by T5 + SFT]}

Table 8: Prompt template used for comparative response evaluation

Privacy-Preserving Federated Learning for Hate Speech Detection

Ivo de Souza Bueno Júnior[1*] **Haotian Ye**[12] **Axel Wisiorek**[12] **Hinrich Schütze**[12]

[1]Center for Information and Language Processing, LMU Munich
[2]Munich Center for Machine Learning (MCML)
ivosb.junior@gmail.com

Abstract

This paper presents a federated learning system with differential privacy for hate speech detection, tailored to low-resource languages. By fine-tuning pre-trained language models, ALBERT emerged as the most effective option for balancing performance and privacy. Experiments demonstrated that federated learning with differential privacy performs adequately in low-resource settings, though datasets with fewer than 20 sentences per client struggled due to excessive noise. Balanced datasets and augmenting hateful data with non-hateful examples proved critical for improving model utility. These findings offer a scalable and privacy-conscious framework for integrating hate speech detection into social media platforms and browsers, safeguarding user privacy while addressing online harm.

1 Introduction

Protecting personal data while enabling effective machine learning is a critical challenge, especially in low-resource languages where data scarcity compounds the difficulty of detecting hate speech. Traditional models primarily focus on high-resource languages, leaving underrepresented languages unsupported. Federated learning (FL) with differential privacy (DP) offers a solution by enabling collaborative model training without sharing sensitive data. However, the trade-off between privacy and performance in low-resource settings remains a significant concern. This paper investigates the use of privacy-preserving FL for hate speech detection in low-resource languages, specifically Afrikaans and Russian, which are considered low-resource with regard to labeled hate speech resources, addressing three research questions:

- **(RQ1)** Can privacy-preserving methods effectively support federated hate speech detection models in low-resource languages?
- **(RQ2)** What is the trade-off between privacy and model accuracy in this context?
- **(RQ3)** How minimal can low-resource data be while still ensuring user privacy?

The main contribution of this work is the adaptation of differential privacy within a federated learning framework for hate speech detection in a low-resource environment, and the understanding of the challenges imposed by such systems.

2 Related Work

Hate speech detection has primarily focused on high-resource languages like English. Efforts to address low-resource languages include Ranasinghe and Zampieri (2021), who applied transfer learning to fine-tune transformer models for Arabic, Bengali, and Hindi, showing that pre-trained BERT-based models, like ALBERT, work well in these contexts. Fine-tuning pre-trained models remains a dominant approach, with studies like Geet d'Sa et al. (2020) and Wullach et al. (2021) demonstrating its effectiveness. However, BERT fine-tuning can be unstable, particularly with small datasets, as noted by Mosbach et al. (2021).

Privacy concerns, driven by regulations like the EU's GDPR (of the European Union, 2016), have led to federated learning adoption for decentralized data processing. While early work like Zampieri et al. (2024) showed FL's promise, vulnerabilities in shared model weights have been identified, as seen in Geiping et al. (2020). Differential privacy, introduced by Dwork (2006), mitigates such risks by adding noise to gradients, ensuring privacy while enabling collaborative learning. Both global (Wei et al., 2020) and local (Truex et al., 2020) DP methods in federated learning have shown effectiveness and limitations, as reviewed by Ouadrhiri and Abdelhadi (2022). While recent approaches, such as Ye et al. (2024), leverage FL for few-shot hate speech detection in low-resource languages, this

Proceedings of the 2025 Conference of the Nations of the Americas Chapter of the Association for Computational Linguistics: Human Language Technologies (Volume 4: Student Research Workshop), pages 129–141
April 30 - May 1, 2025

paper adapts DP to further enhance model security and evaluate its impact on performance.

3 Methods

Dataset. For our experiments, we used hate speech data from two low-resource languages: Afrikaans and Russian. The Afrikaans dataset includes statements targeting black people and LGBTQ+ individuals, while the Russian dataset focuses on hate speech directed at war-affected groups and LGBTQ+ individuals. The datasets were created by native speakers between June 2023 and March 2024 as part of the Respond2Hate research project (Ye et al., 2024). Hate speech examples were inspired by anonymized content from social media and news outlets and were carefully adapted to ensure privacy and cultural relevance. The merged dataset consisted of 1,543 sentences, with 865 (56%) labeled as hateful and 678 (44%) as non-hateful.

Of the 1,543 sentences, 309 were randomly selected as a test set, and the rest were used for fine-tuning. Each client in the federated system received a distinct set of sentences, ensuring non-overlapping data.

Models. Multiple `BERT`-based models were used for various experiments conducted in this work. They are: `BERT Base uncased`, `BERT Large uncased` (Devlin et al., 2019), `HateBERT` (Caselli et al., 2021), `ALBERT Base`, `ALBERT Large`, `ALBERT XLarge`, `ALBERT XXLarge` (Lan et al., 2020), `BERT Base Multilingual uncased` (Devlin et al., 2019), `XLM-RoBERTa Base`, `XLM-RoBERTa Large` (Conneau et al., 2020), and `DistilBERT Base Multilingual cased` (Sanh et al., 2020) More information on the selected models can be seen in Appendix A.

Federated Learning and Differential Privacy Implementation. Federated learning was implemented using the Flower framework (Beutel et al., 2020), which facilitates communication and aggregation between the server and clients. Flower was selected for its support of manual client training steps. Differential privacy was implemented using Opacus (Yousefpour et al., 2021), a PyTorch (Paszke et al., 2019) library that enables DP by adding noise to model gradients. Opacus automatically calculates the noise scale σ based on (ϵ, δ)-DP and the $\mathcal{L}_2$ norm clipping threshold C. PyTorch was used for model fine-tuning, and pre-trained models were sourced from Hugging-Face (Wolf et al., 2020).

4 Experiments and Results

4.1 Experimental Setup

The `ALBERT Base` model from Hugging Face was selected for fine-tuning due to its strong performance, as explored in the Model Comparison experiment described below, and seen in Table 1, and efficient fine-tuning times. Privacy parameters were set to $\epsilon = 5$ and $\delta = 10^{-5}$, with a clipping threshold C of 0.5, clipping 1% of the highest gradient values.

The training setup involved one server and eight clients, each receiving 50 balanced sentences (25 hateful, 25 non-hateful). Fine-tuning used a batch size of 1, cross-entropy loss, and the Adam optimizer with a learning rate of 10^{-4} to maintain stability with DP. Baseline experiments included versions without DP ("No DP") and without fine-tuning ("No FT"). For "No DP," the learning rate was reduced to 2×10^{-5} to prevent divergence. All experiments ran for 10 FL rounds.

The weighted F1-score, which is calculated separately for each class, and returned as the weighted sum, was used as the primary evaluation metric due to slight dataset imbalance. Each experiment was run five times, with metrics averaged across clients to minimize variability and account for fine-tuning instabilities. The following experiments were conducted:

Model Comparison. This experiment evaluated the performance of various models fine-tuned with FL and DP for low-resource hate speech detection. Several pre-trained models were tested, but `BERT Large uncased` and `XLM-RoBERTa Large` were excluded due to communication timeouts in FL, likely caused by their large number of parameters. The Flower framework could not handle the computational overhead for these models. No other hyperparameter modifications were made.

Level of Privacy Comparison. The privacy-utility trade-off was tested by fine-tuning the model with various values of ϵ, δ, and clipping threshold C. ϵ values tested ranged from 100 (weak privacy) to 0.1 (strong privacy), with corresponding C values chosen to clip gradients at various percentages: $C = 100$ (no clipping), $C = 0.5$ (1%), $C = 0.1$ (10%), $C = 0.05$ (25%), and $C = 0.01$ (50%). These C values were selected based on observed gradient ranges after initial training rounds. The default $\delta = 10^{-5}$ was used, and `ALBERT Base` and

BERT Base Multilingual models were compared, keeping all other hyperparameters unchanged.

Additionally, different δ values (10^{-3}, 10^{-5}, 10^{-7}) were tested on ALBERT Base with $\epsilon = 5$ to assess their impact on the privacy-utility trade-off. For each δ value, various C values were also tested, with all other hyperparameters kept at their defaults.

Dataset Size Comparison. This test evaluated how the model responded to FL with DP fine-tuning using varying dataset sizes per client. Each client fine-tuned the model with datasets starting at 10 sentences (5 hateful, 5 non-hateful), increasing in increments of 10 up to 130 sentences (65 hateful, 65 non-hateful). All other hyperparameters were kept at their default values and the ALBERT Base model was used.

Dataset Composition Comparison. This experiment tested how different data compositions affected model performance. Three compositions were tested: an "unchanged" composition with the natural imbalance of 56% hateful and 44% non-hateful sentences, a "balanced" composition with 50% hateful and 50% non-hateful sentences, and a "hate-only" composition with only hateful sentences. The "hate-only" composition was tested to simulate a federated system where users report only hateful sentences, and the data is not augmented with negative samples. All other hyperparameters were kept at their default values and the ALBERT Base model was used.

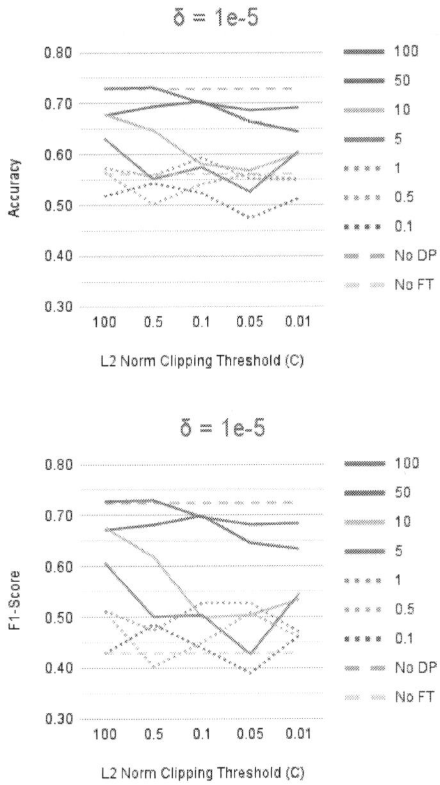

Figure 1: Accuracy and F1-score comparison of different values of ϵ for $\delta = 10^{-5}$.

4.2 Results and Analysis

Model	No Diff. Priv.		Diff. Priv.	
	ACC	F1	ACC	F1
BERT Base	0.762	0.762	0.511 (-0.251)	0.395 (-0.367)
HateBERT	0.770	0.770	0.532 (-0.238)	0.415 (-0.355)
ALBERT Base	0.728	0.725	**0.602** (-0.126)	**0.542** (-0.183)
ALBERT Large	0.710	0.707	0.513 (-0.197)	0.385 (-0.322)
ALBERT XLarge	0.668	0.663	0.510 (-0.158)	0.353 (-0.310)
ALBERT XXLarge	0.714	0.710	**0.587** (-0.127)	**0.551** (-0.159)
BERT Base Multilingual	**0.819**	**0.819**	0.490 (-0.329)	0.403 (-0.416)
XLM-RoBERTa Base	**0.847**	**0.847**	0.489 (-0.358)	0.327 (-0.520)
DistilBERT Base	0.807	0.807	0.524 (-0.283)	0.405 (-0.402)

Table 1: Model comparison between different models fine-tuned by using FL with and without DP. The utility loss between the private and the non-private fine-tuning is shown in red.

Model Comparison. Table 1 shows the results of the model comparison, with best scores marked in bold and utility loss with DP highlighted in red. Multilingual models (BERT Base Multilingual and XLM-RoBERTa Base) performed best in accuracy and F1-score without DP, even in low-resource settings, as they were pre-trained on data containing the low-resource languages used. However, these models suffered the greatest utility loss with DP.

In contrast, ALBERT models maintained high utility under DP, with ALBERT Base and ALBERT XXLarge showing the lowest utility loss. Their fewer layers (12) compared to the other two ALBERT models (24 layers) likely contributed to this performance. Notably, model size did not significantly affect the privacy-utility trade-off, as ALBERT XXLarge exhibited the lowest utility loss, while XLM-RoBERTa Base showed the highest.

Level of Privacy Comparison. Two experiments assessed the impact of privacy levels on model performance. The first experiment evaluated different ϵ values with $\delta = 10^{-5}$ (Figure 1). As ϵ decreased, indicating stronger privacy, accuracy and F1-scores degraded compared to non-private fine-tuning (No DP). For $\epsilon = 100$ and $\epsilon = 50$,

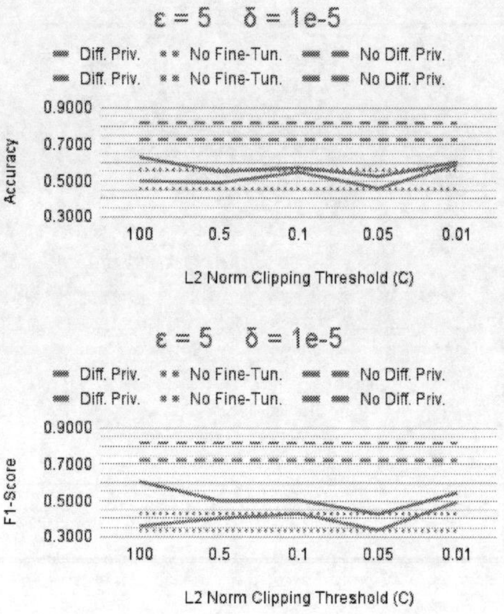

Figure 2: Accuracy and F1-score comparison of BERT (blue) and ALBERT (red) at the same level of privacy ($\epsilon = 5, \delta = 10^{-5}$).

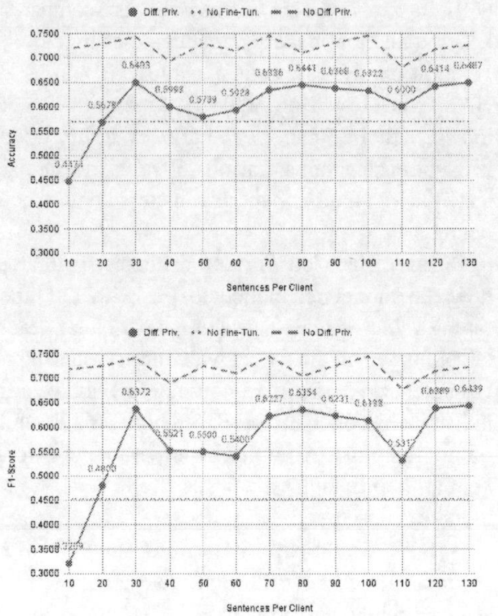

Figure 3: Accuracy (blue, above), and F1-score (red, below), for models fine-tuned with FL clients with different sizes of datasets.

utility loss was moderate but represented weak privacy. Real-world applications typically use $\epsilon < 10$, where performance steeply declined, especially with gradient clipping ($C = 0.5$). At $\epsilon \leqslant 1$, accuracy fell below non-fine-tuned (No FT) levels, and results became noisier. Higher clipping thresholds did not consistently improve scores, particularly at lower ϵ. Similar experiments for $\delta = 10^{-3}$ and $\delta = 10^{-7}$ are shown in Appendix B.

The second experiment evaluated the impact of privacy on fine-tuning ALBERT and BERT for $\epsilon = 5$ and $\delta = 10^{-5}$ (Figure 2). Additional comparisons for other ϵ values are in Appendix C. Without privacy, BERT outperformed ALBERT, but the opposite was true for models without fine-tuning. Both models exhibited similar trends under privacy constraints, hovering near non-fine-tuned levels, with ALBERT achieving higher accuracy and F1-scores than BERT. Notably, BERT showed greater fine-tuning instability, with 29% of runs (51/175) failing to improve after the first FL round, compared to 11% (19/175) for ALBERT.

Varying δ values for a fixed ϵ value offered no relevant insights. These results are in Appendix D.

Dataset Size Comparison. Figure 3 shows the results of the dataset size comparison, with accuracy (blue) and F1-scores (red). As a baseline, we evaluated on the test set by using a model fine-tuned without DP and a model without fine-tuning. The x-axis represents the number of sentences per client during FL.

The model fine-tuned without DP outperforms the one fine-tuned with it, as expected due to the noise introduced by DP. When fine-tuning with very small datasets (10–20 sentences per client), the model performs slightly worse than the non-fine-tuned baseline. This occurs because the noise added by DP is not proportional to the dataset size, leading to parameter updates dominated by noise rather than data.

In this experiment, model performance peaks at 30 sentences per client, achieving an accuracy of 0.64 and an F1-score of 0.63. A similar peak is observed in the non-private fine-tuning version. Figure 4 highlights the difference in accuracy and F1-scores between models fine-tuned with and without DP. A logarithmic interpolation was applied, yielding the best fit with $R^2 = 0.683$ for accuracy and $R^2 = 0.701$ for F1-score, compared to other interpolation methods. The results indicate that as the dataset size increases, the performance of the private model approaches that of the non-private model. However, this trend is not linear and stabilizes eventually, demonstrating that while larger

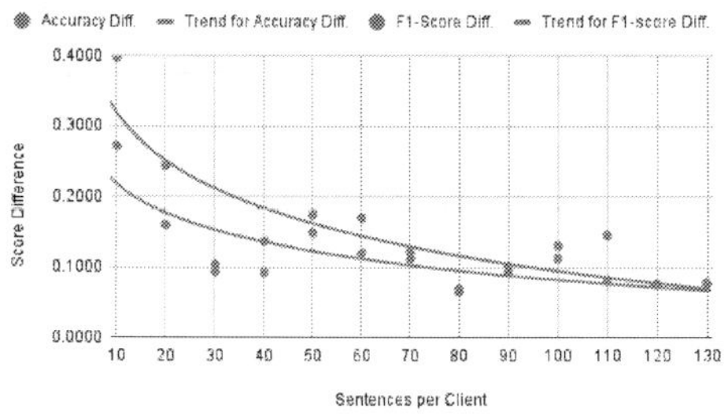

Figure 4: Accuracy (blue) and F1-score (red) difference between models fine-tuned with and without differential privacy, at different dataset sizes.

datasets mitigate the effects of DP noise, they cannot fully eliminate its impact.

Dataset Composition Comparison. Table 2 presents accuracy and F1-scores for different dataset compositions. Results are provided for models evaluated without fine-tuning (No Fine-Tun.) and fine-tuned with (Diff. Priv.) or without differential privacy (No Diff. Priv.). The best metric in each category is highlighted in bold, with utility loss and gain compared to DP fine-tuning marked in red and green, respectively.

The table reveals minimal differences in accuracy between the unchanged and balanced dataset compositions. While the balanced dataset yields higher F1-scores without DP, this advantage disappears under DP fine-tuning. The unchanged dataset composition delivers the best scores and privacy-utility trade-off when fine-tuning with DP, which could point out that having a slight imbalance towards hateful sentences might be advantageous.

As expected, fine-tuning exclusively on hateful sentences, regardless of DP, performs worse in both accuracy and F1-scores than skipping fine-tuning altogether.

Data Comp.	Accuracy		
	Diff. Priv.	No Fine-Tun.	No Diff. Priv.
Unchanged	**0.608**	**0.561** (-0.047)	0.721 (0.113)
Balanced	0.604	**0.561** (-0.043)	**0.742** (0.138)
Hate-Only	0.553	**0.561** (0.008)	0.553 (0.000)
	F1-Score		
	Diff. Priv.	No Fine-Tun.	No Diff. Priv.
Unchanged	**0.565**	**0.429** (-0.136)	0.719 (0.154)
Balanced	0.558	**0.429** (-0.129)	**0.741** (0.183)
Hate-Only	0.406	**0.429** (0.023)	0.396 (-0.010)

Table 2: Dataset composition comparison.

5 Discussion

This paper investigates federated learning with differential privacy for hate speech detection in low-resource environments. Results show that this approach is feasible for fine-tuning models, even with limited data, but models react differently to added noise. ALBERT models (Base and XXLarge) performed the best due to parameter sharing, which might have mitigated the noise. Deeper and multilingual models experienced greater utility loss, though further research is needed to confirm these findings.

Achieving strong privacy guarantees remains challenging. At $\epsilon \leqslant 1$, performance dropped below the non-fine-tuned baseline, highlighting the difficulty of selecting optimal ϵ values, which depend on the model, dataset, and parameter interactions.

More local data per client improved results, with 50 sentences per client showing consistent gains. However, limited data hampers effective learning under differential privacy. Balanced datasets are critical, but a slight imbalance towards hateful sentences helped overcome the noise added by differential privacy. Sampling non-hateful examples is crucial for effective training. Despite challenges, federated learning with differential privacy remains advantageous where privacy is paramount.

Addressing the research questions:

- **(RQ1)** Privacy-preserving federated learning for hate speech detection in low-resource languages is feasible, but may not meet strong privacy standards without sufficient data.
- **(RQ2)** The privacy-utility trade-off is significant, with better results achievable at lower privacy levels.
- **(RQ3)** For minimal data, 50 sentences per client suffice for moderate privacy, though more data reduces degradation and stabilizes training.

6 Conclusion

This paper explored federated learning with differential privacy for hate speech detection in low-resource settings. Fine-tuning a pre-trained ALBERT model showed improved performance at moderate privacy levels. Key findings included the importance of nearly-balanced datasets and the impact of differential privacy parameters (ϵ, δ, and C), with ALBERT outperforming other BERT-based models.

The results addressed the research questions, highlighting both strengths and areas for improvement.

In conclusion, despite challenges in low-resource environments, federated learning with differential privacy can effectively detect hate speech while ensuring user privacy.

7 Limitations

This paper has several limitations. Training required each client to store a local model, limiting experiments to eight clients, and the use of smaller, BERT-based models, instead of LLMs, due to memory constraints. Future work could explore varying client numbers and adaptive clipping thresholds, which were untested due to fixed C values in Opacus. Adaptive methods, as proposed by Andrew et al. (2021), could improve performance. Additionally, non-BERT models like GPT or LLaMA were not evaluated. Finally, the number of federated learning rounds and epochs was not varied, but exploring these hyperparameters may impact model performance.

Acknowledgements

The data used in this research was created within the ERC Proof of Concept project Respond2Hate, funded by the European Research Council (ERC) under Grant No. 101100870.

References

Galen Andrew, Om Thakkar, Brendan McMahan, and Swaroop Ramaswamy. 2021. Differentially private learning with adaptive clipping. In *Advances in Neural Information Processing Systems*, volume 34, pages 17455–17466. Curran Associates, Inc.

Daniel J. Beutel, Taner Topal, Akhil Mathur, Xinchi Qiu, Javier Fernandez-Marques, Yan Gao, Lorenzo Sani, Kwing Hei Li, Titouan Parcollet, Pedro Porto Buarque de Gusmão, and Nicholas D. Lane. 2020. Flower: A friendly federated learning research framework. *arXiv*, abs/2007.14390.

Tommaso Caselli, Valerio Basile, Jelena Mitrović, and Michael Granitzer. 2021. HateBERT: Retraining BERT for abusive language detection in English. In *Proceedings of the 5th Workshop on Online Abuse and Harms (WOAH 2021)*, pages 17–25, Online. Association for Computational Linguistics.

Alexis Conneau, Kartikay Khandelwal, Naman Goyal, Vishrav Chaudhary, Guillaume Wenzek, Francisco Guzmán, Edouard Grave, Myle Ott, Luke Zettlemoyer, and Veselin Stoyanov. 2020. Unsupervised cross-lingual representation learning at scale. In *Proceedings of the 58th Annual Meeting of the Association for Computational Linguistics*, pages 8440–8451, Online. Association for Computational Linguistics.

Jacob Devlin, Ming-Wei Chang, Kenton Lee, and Kristina Toutanova. 2019. BERT: Pre-training of deep bidirectional transformers for language understanding. In *Proceedings of the 2019 Conference of the North American Chapter of the Association for Computational Linguistics: Human Language Technologies, Volume 1 (Long and Short Papers)*, pages 4171–4186, Minneapolis, Minnesota. Association for Computational Linguistics.

Cynthia Dwork. 2006. Differential privacy. In *International colloquium on automata, languages, and programming*, ICALP'06, pages 1–12, Berlin, Heidelberg. Springer.

Ashwin Geet d'Sa, Irina Illina, and Dominique Fohr. 2020. Classification of Hate Speech Using Deep Neural Networks. *Revue d'Information Scientifique & Technique*, 25(01).

Jonas Geiping, Hartmut Bauermeister, Hannah Dröge, and Michael Moeller. 2020. Inverting gradients - how easy is it to break privacy in federated learning? In *Advances in Neural Information Processing Systems*, volume 33, pages 16937–16947. Curran Associates, Inc.

Zhenzhong Lan, Mingda Chen, Sebastian Goodman, Kevin Gimpel, Piyush Sharma, and Radu Soricut. 2020. ALBERT: A lite BERT for self-supervised learning of language representations. In *International Conference on Learning Representations*, ICLR2020.

Marius Mosbach, Maksym Andriushchenko, and Dietrich Klakow. 2021. On the stability of fine-tuning BERT: Misconceptions, explanations, and strong baselines. In *International Conference on Learning Representations*, ICLR2021.

Official Journal of the European Union. 2016. Regulation (eu) 2016/679 of the european parliament and of the council of 27 april 2016 on the protection of natural persons with regard to the processing of personal data and on the free movement of such data, and repealing directive 95/46/ec (general data protection regulation) (text with eea relevance). `https://eur-lex.europa.eu/eli/reg/2016/679/oj`. [Accessed 27-06-2024].

Ahmed El Ouadrhiri and Ahmed Abdelhadi. 2022. Differential privacy for deep and federated learning: A survey. *IEEE Access*, 10:22359–22380.

Adam Paszke, Sam Gross, Francisco Massa, Adam Lerer, James Bradbury, Gregory Chanan, Trevor Killeen, Zeming Lin, Natalia Gimelshein, Luca Antiga, Alban Desmaison, Andreas Kopf, Edward Yang, Zachary DeVito, Martin Raison, Alykhan Tejani, Sasank Chilamkurthy, Benoit Steiner, Lu Fang,

Junjie Bai, and Soumith Chintala. 2019. Pytorch: An imperative style, high-performance deep learning library. In *Advances in Neural Information Processing Systems 32*, pages 8024–8035. Curran Associates, Inc.

Tharindu Ranasinghe and Marcos Zampieri. 2021. Multilingual offensive language identification for low-resource languages. *ACM Trans. Asian Low-Resour. Lang. Inf. Process.*, 21(1).

Victor Sanh, Lysandre Debut, Julien Chaumond, and Thomas Wolf. 2020. DistilBERT, a distilled version of BERT: smaller, faster, cheaper and lighter. *arXiv*, abs/1910.01108.

Stacey Truex, Ling Liu, Ka-Ho Chow, Mehmet Emre Gursoy, and Wenqi Wei. 2020. LDP-Fed: federated learning with local differential privacy. In *Proceedings of the Third ACM International Workshop on Edge Systems, Analytics and Networking*, EdgeSys '20, page 61–66, New York, NY, USA. Association for Computing Machinery.

Kang Wei, Jun Li, Ming Ding, Chuan Ma, Howard H. Yang, Farhad Farokhi, Shi Jin, Tony Q. S. Quek, and H. Vincent Poor. 2020. Federated learning with differential privacy: Algorithms and performance analysis. *IEEE Transactions on Information Forensics and Security*, 15:3454–3469.

Thomas Wolf, Lysandre Debut, Victor Sanh, Julien Chaumond, Clement Delangue, Anthony Moi, Pierric Cistac, Tim Rault, Remi Louf, Morgan Funtowicz, Joe Davison, Sam Shleifer, Patrick von Platen, Clara Ma, Yacine Jernite, Julien Plu, Canwen Xu, Teven Le Scao, Sylvain Gugger, Mariama Drame, Quentin Lhoest, and Alexander Rush. 2020. Transformers: State-of-the-art natural language processing. In *Proceedings of the 2020 Conference on Empirical Methods in Natural Language Processing: System Demonstrations*, pages 38–45, Online. Association for Computational Linguistics.

Tomer Wullach, Amir Adler, and Einat Minkov. 2021. Fight fire with fire: Fine-tuning hate detectors using large samples of generated hate speech. In *Findings of the Association for Computational Linguistics: EMNLP 2021*, pages 4699–4705, Punta Cana, Dominican Republic. Association for Computational Linguistics.

Haotian Ye, Axel Wisiorek, Antonis Maronikolakis, Özge Alaçam, and Hinrich Schütze. 2024. A federated approach to few-shot hate speech detection for marginalized communities. *arXiv*, abs/2412.04942.

Ashkan Yousefpour, Igor Shilov, Alexandre Sablayrolles, Davide Testuggine, Karthik Prasad, Mani Malek, John Nguyen, Sayan Ghosh, Akash Bharadwaj, Jessica Zhao, Graham Cormode, and Ilya Mironov. 2021. Opacus: User-friendly differential privacy library in PyTorch. *arXiv*, abs/2109.12298.

Marcos Zampieri, Damith Premasiri, and Tharindu Ranasinghe. 2024. A federated learning approach to privacy preserving offensive language identification. In *Proceedings of the Fourth Workshop on Threat, Aggression & Cyberbullying @ LREC-COLING-2024*, pages 12–20, Torino, Italia. ELRA and ICCL.

A Model Information

- BERT Base uncased (Devlin et al., 2019) (110M parameters), and BERT Large uncased (336M parameters), both trained with monolingual English data.
- A BERT-based model trained on hate speech data: HateBERT (Caselli et al., 2021) (110M parameters, monolingual English).
- ALBERT Base (Lan et al., 2020) (11M parameters), Large (17M parameters), XLarge (58M parameters), and XXLarge (223M parameters), all trained with monolingual English data.
- BERT Base Multilingual uncased (Devlin et al., 2019) (110M parameters), pre-trained using multilingual data from Wikipedia in 102 languages, including Afrikaans and Russian.
- XLM-RoBERTa Base (Conneau et al., 2020) (270M parameters), and XLM-RoBERTa Large (550M parameters), both pre-trained using multilingual data from CommonCrawl in 100 languages, including Afrikaans and Russian.
- DistilBERT Base Multilingual cased (Sanh et al., 2020) (134M parameters), which is a distilled version of BERT Base Multilingual Cased, which was pre-trained using multilingual data from Wikipedia in 104 languages, including Afrikaans and Russian.

B Privacy comparison with different values of ϵ, for the model ALBERT Base.

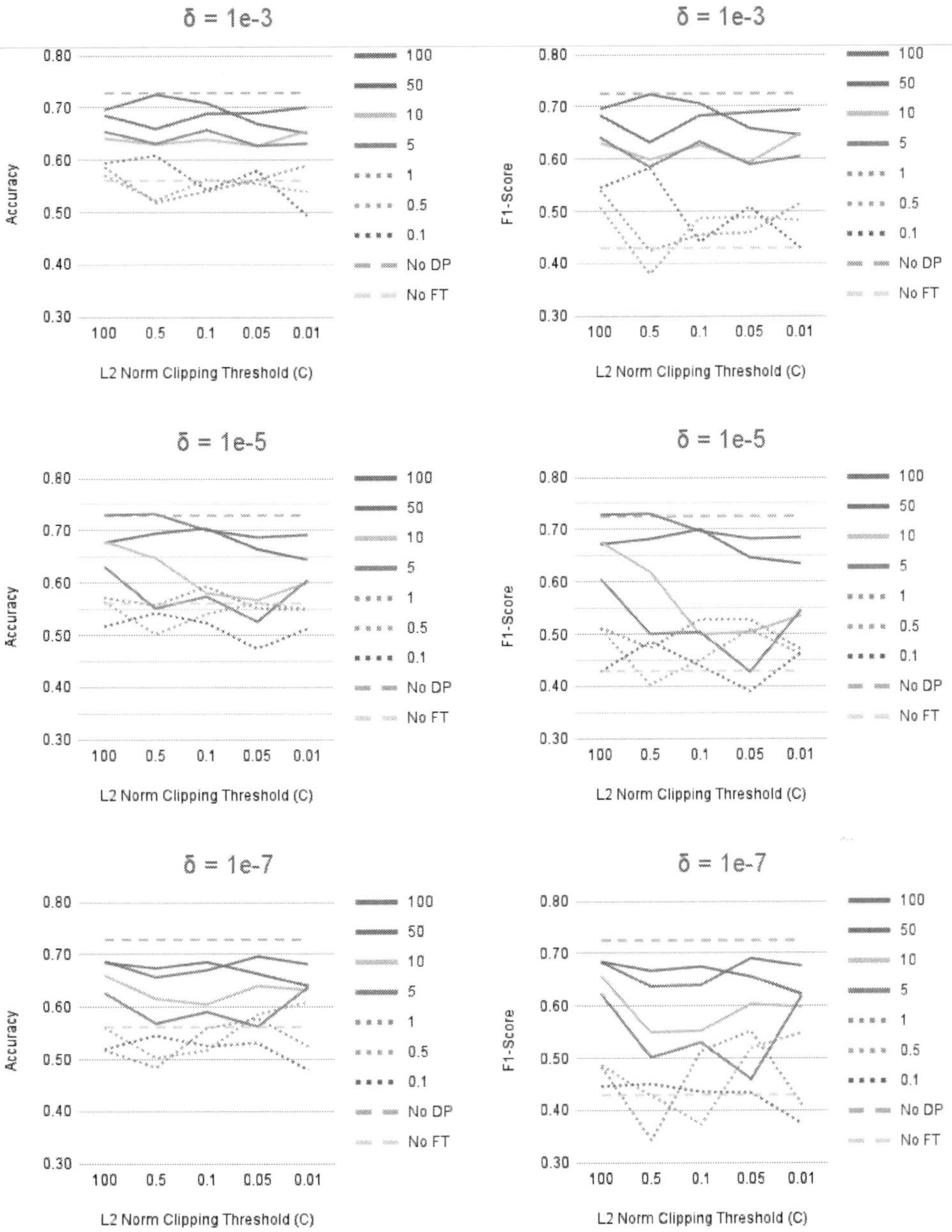

Figure 5: Accuracy (left) and F1-score (right) comparison of different values of ϵ for $\delta \in \{10^{-3}, 10^{-5}, 10^{-7}\}$.

C BERT and ALBERT comparison with different levels of privacy.

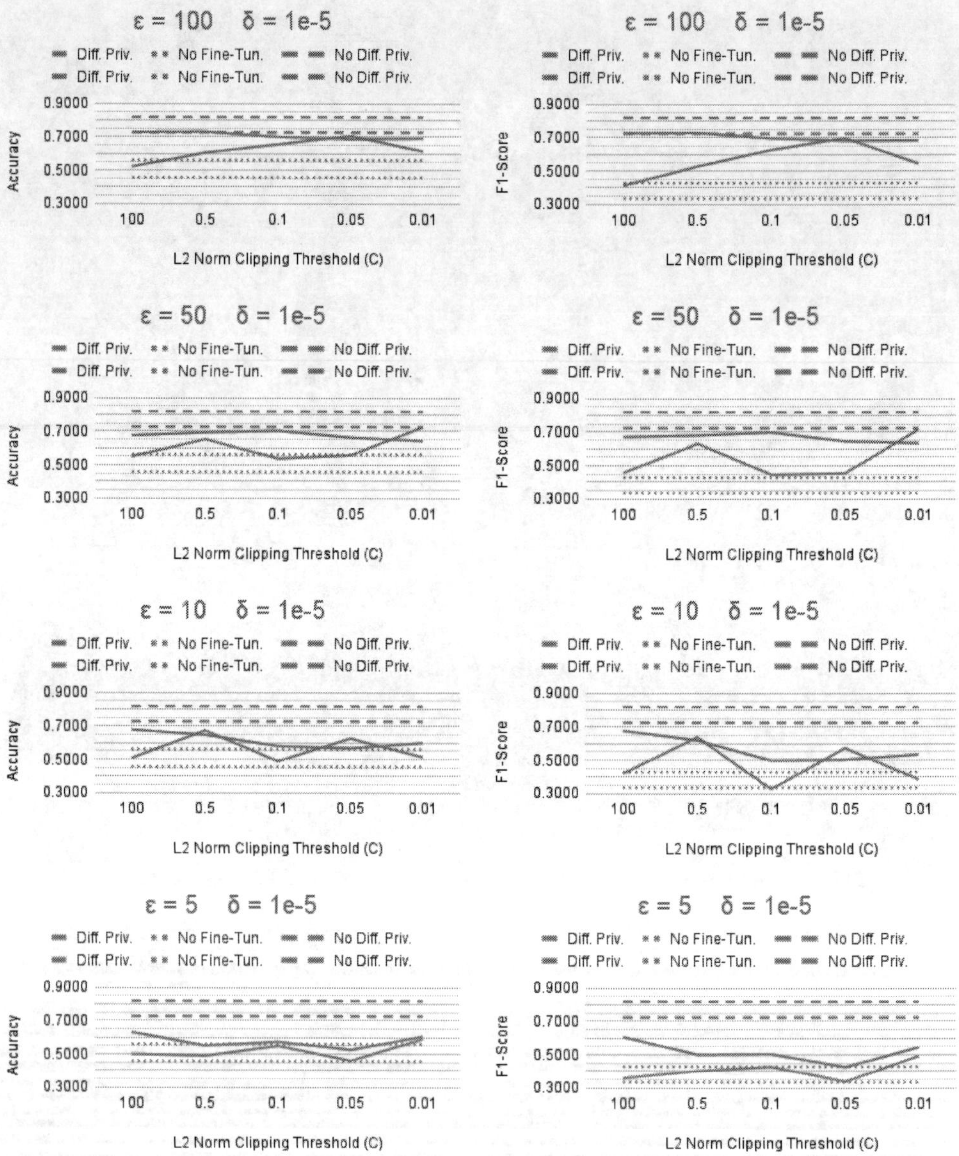

Figure 6: Accuracy (left) and F1-score (right) comparison of BERT (blue) and ALBERT (red) at the different levels of privacy ($\epsilon \in \{100, 50, 10, 5\}$, $\delta = 10^{-5}$).

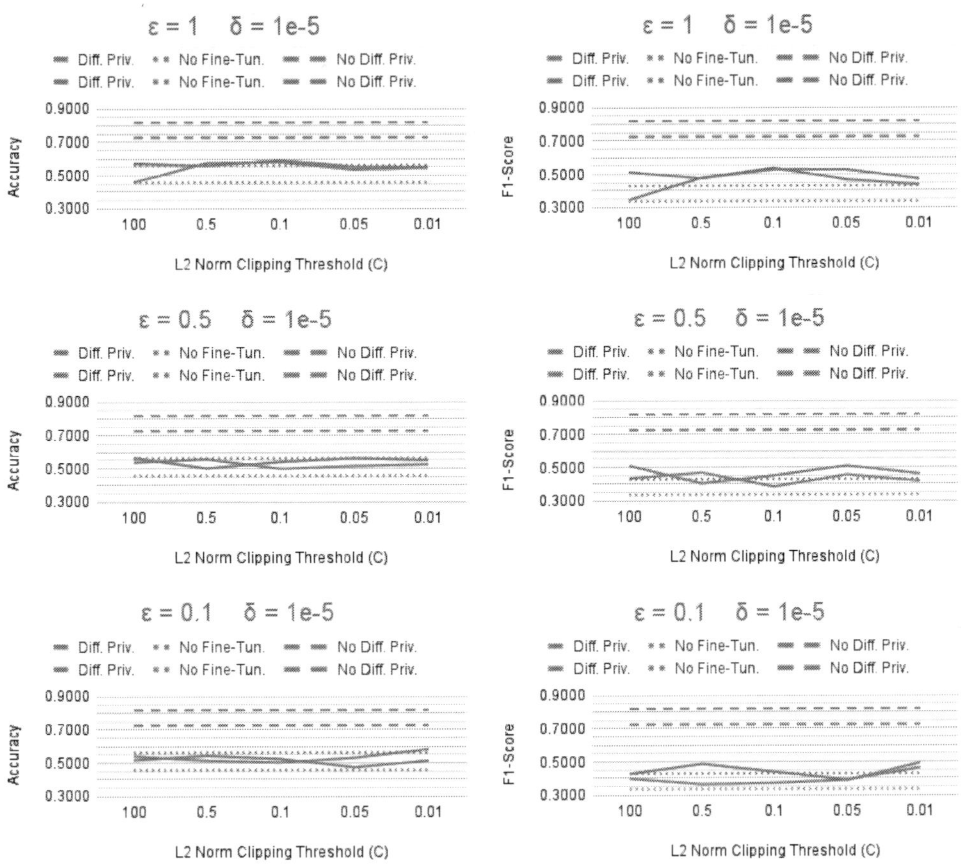

Figure 7: Accuracy (left) and F1-score (right) comparison of BERT (blue) and ALBERT (red) at the different levels of privacy ($\epsilon \in \{1, 0.5, 0.1\}$, $\delta = 10^{-5}$).

D Privacy comparison with different values of δ, for the model ALBERT Base.

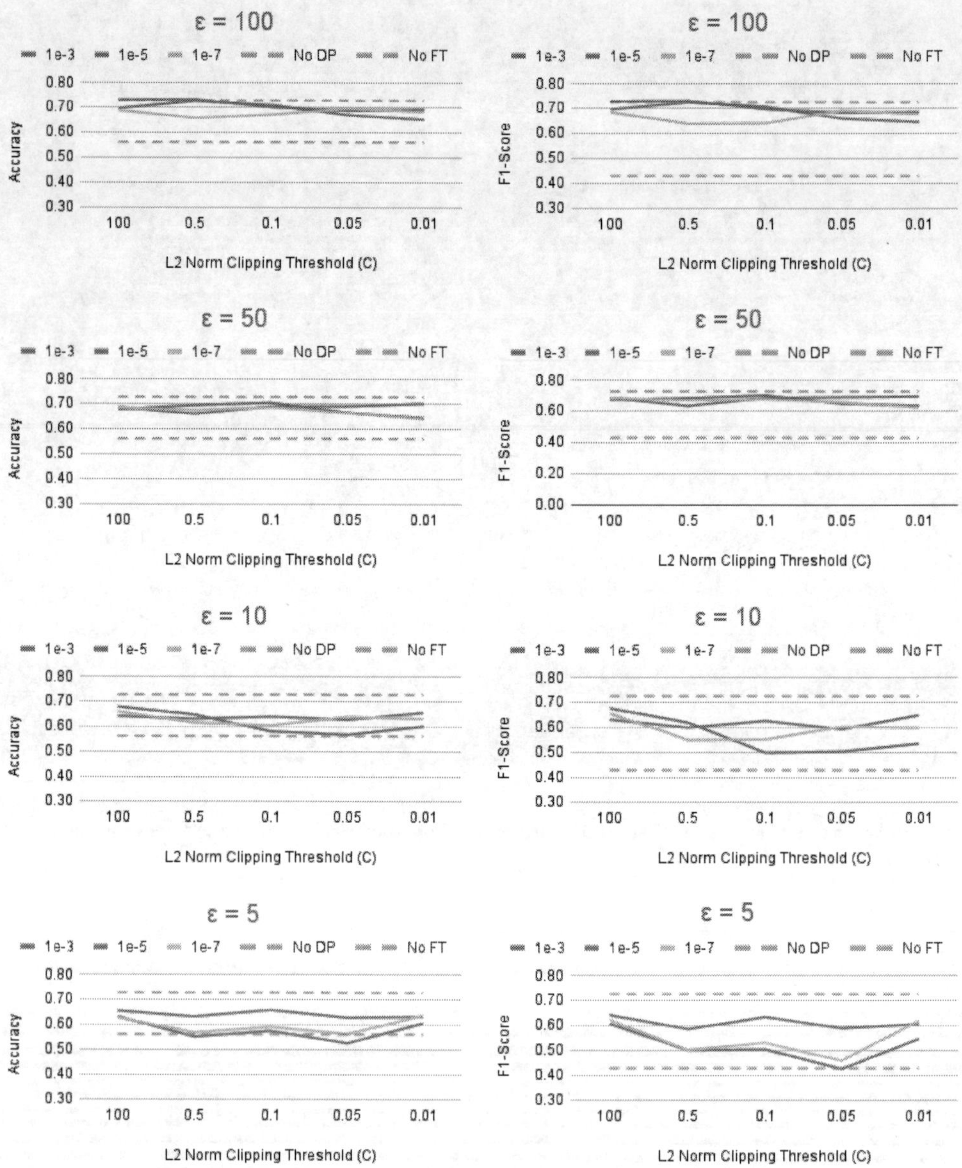

Figure 8: Accuracy (left) and F1-score (right) comparison of different values of δ for $\epsilon \in \{100, 50, 10, 5\}$.

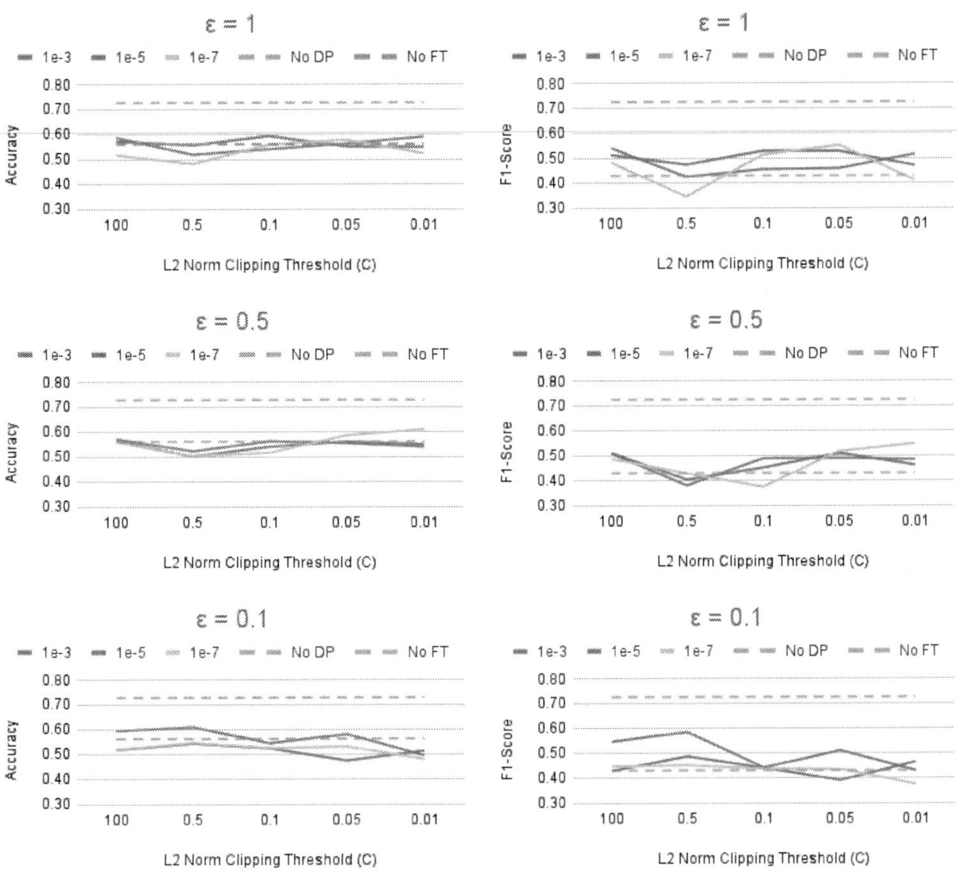

Figure 9: Accuracy (left) and F1-score (right) comparison of different values of δ for $\epsilon \in \{1, 0.5, 0.1\}$.

From Annotation to Adaptation: Metrics, Synthetic Data, and Aspect Extraction for Aspect-Based Sentiment Analysis with Large Language Models

Nikita Neveditsin[1], Pawan Lingras[1], Vijay Mago[2]
[1]Saint Mary's University, Halifax, Canada
[2]York University, Toronto, Canada

Abstract

This study examines the performance of Large Language Models (LLMs) in Aspect-Based Sentiment Analysis (ABSA), with a focus on implicit aspect extraction in a novel domain. Using a synthetic sports feedback dataset, we evaluate open-weight LLMs' ability to extract aspect-polarity pairs and propose a metric to facilitate the evaluation of aspect extraction with generative models. Our findings highlight both the potential and limitations of LLMs in the ABSA task.

1 Introduction

ABSA is a nuanced form of sentiment analysis that focuses on identifying sentiments related to specific aspects within a text (Pontiki et al., 2014). Researchers have decomposed ABSA into various subtasks, such as aspect extraction, sentiment classification, aspect category detection, and opinion term extraction, each contributing to a comprehensive understanding of the problem. Table 1 summarizes these subtasks as discussed in the literature. Combining these tasks allows the extraction of ABSA-related entities in the form of tuples, triples, or quadruples from sentences or documents, resulting in a wide range of compound ABSA solutions.

LLMs with their in-context learning (ICL) capabilities (Brown et al., 2020) and parameter-efficient fine-tuning methods, such as Low-Rank Adaptation (LoRA) with quantization (Dettmers et al., 2024; Hu et al., 2021), offer straightforward yet effective approaches for complex ABSA tasks. These approaches facilitate the extraction of *implicit aspects*, which are aspects that are not explicitly stated in the text but can be inferred based on context, sentiment, or background knowledge.

This study examines the performance of LLMs in extracting aspect-polarity pairs within the underexplored and unanticipated domain of sports feedback. This domain poses unique challenges for ABSA due to its reliance on implicit references and domain-specific terminology. By evaluating LLMs in this context, we provide critical insights into their capacity to adapt to novel data.

Moreover, recognizing the linguistic variability involved in expressing implicit aspects, we propose an evaluation metric that calculates precision and recall while accounting for this variability in settings with a high prevalence of implicit aspects. We also demonstrate the broader applicability of this metric, showing its utility in assessing generative LLMs on classic ABSA datasets. Finally, we explore various strategies for adapting LLMs to domain-specific datasets, highlighting key challenges and offering insights for future research.

2 Related Work

Aspect-Based Sentiment Analysis

Traditional approaches to ABSA, extensively reviewed in the literature (Nazir et al., 2020; Brauwers and Frasincar, 2022; Zhang et al., 2023b), primarily utilize bidirectional encoders (Dos Santos et al., 2021; Zhang et al., 2023a), recurrent networks (Xu et al., 2020), graph networks (Zhou et al., 2020; Wu et al., 2022; Wang et al., 2024b), sequence-to-sequence models (Ma et al., 2019), and ensembles of models (Yang et al., 2023). Various techniques have recently been proposed to improve accuracy, precision, and recall in ABSA-related tasks, for example, context denoising (Tian et al., 2024), abstract meaning representation (Ma et al., 2023), and global semantic features (Zhou et al., 2024). These methods have achieved robust results in within-domain explicit aspect extraction and polarity classification (Meng et al., 2019; Meškelė and Frasincar, 2020; Wang et al., 2020).

Recent studies have investigated the ability of LLMs to perform ABSA tasks on both traditional (Šmíd et al., 2024) and more complex datasets

Proceedings of the 2025 Conference of the Nations of the Americas Chapter of the Association for Computational Linguistics: Human Language Technologies (Volume 4: Student Research Workshop), pages 142–161

Table 1: ABSA Subtasks.

Subtask Names	Extracted Entity
Aspect Extraction (Liu, 2012), Opinion Target Expression Extraction (Pontiki et al., 2015), Aspect Term Extraction (ATE) (Pontiki et al., 2014; Scaria et al., 2024)	Aspect (e.g., "restaurant atmosphere", "technical support")
Aspect Sentiment Classification (Liu, 2012), Sentiment Polarity Classification (Pontiki et al., 2015), Aspect Term Polarity Classification (Pontiki et al., 2014)	Polarity (e.g., "positive", "negative", "neutral")
Aspect Category Detection (Pontiki et al., 2014)	Category (e.g., "food")
Opinion Term Extraction (Zhang et al., 2023b)	Opinion Phrase (e.g, "could be better")

(Deng et al., 2023; Krugmann and Hartmann, 2024), highlighting the potential of generative models in key ABSA subtasks (Kheiri and Karimi, 2023; Scaria et al., 2024; Yang et al., 2024). Nevertheless, challenges persist in effectively capturing implicit aspects, particularly in low-resource domains, where difficulties in data collection and annotation further exacerbate the problem (Tubishat et al., 2018; Wankhade et al., 2022; Cai et al., 2021; Zhang et al., 2023b).

Data Creation and Annotation for ABSA

Advancing ABSA research can benefit from quality datasets. Recent work by Chebolu et al. (2024) demonstrated that human annotation of ABSA datasets involving implicit aspects is challenging and laborious. Generative LLMs have been successfully utilized to create and annotate synthetic datasets, leveraging their capacity to generate creative and contextually rich text (Meyer et al., 2022; Bao et al., 2023; Eldan and Li, 2023; Mirowski et al., 2023). Although LLMs may not always match human annotators in accuracy, studies have shown that their annotations can be valuable, particularly when combined with human expertise (Goel et al., 2023; Gray et al., 2023; Mohta et al., 2023; He et al., 2024; Liyanage et al., 2024).

Moreover, leveraging synthetic data has been explored to enhance the performance of downstream models in various NLP tasks, including ABSA (Kramchaninova and Defauw, 2022; Yu et al., 2023; Deng et al., 2023; Wang et al., 2024a).

3 Datasets

3.1 Novel dataset

We introduce a novel dataset of artificially generated feedback from volunteers at sports event, a domain not yet represented in existing ABSA datasets. This domain poses unique challenges due to its specific terminology and the abundance of implicit aspects. The dataset facilitates an out-of-domain evaluation of the ABSA capabilities of open-weight LLMs against baseline solutions. Notably, at least 35% of its content comprises implicit aspects[1]. Additionally, the dataset's domain specificity provides an opportunity to test the generalization capabilities of ABSA solutions beyond their usual training contexts, contributing to a deeper understanding of their real-world applicability.

We chose two state-of-the-art models[2] for dataset generation: GPT-4 and Gemini 1.0 Ultra. The novel dataset comprises 480 documents, with an average of 222 characters per document. Most of the dataset (75%) was generated using GPT-4, acknowledging its superior reported results for major benchmarks such as MMLU (OpenAI, 2023). Additionally, we employed Gemini 1.0 Ultra to generate 25% of the dataset, introducing some diversity of content. Appendix A provides examples of prompts and generated text, illustrating the models' ability to produce mixed-emotion and diverse style feedback.

The dataset annotation process, illustrated in Figure 1, involved three steps, integrating both LLMs and human annotators. First, LLMs generated initial annotation drafts to alleviate the cognitive and time burden on the expert. Next, volunteers selected the better draft from two options. Finally, the expert revised and refined the selected draft.

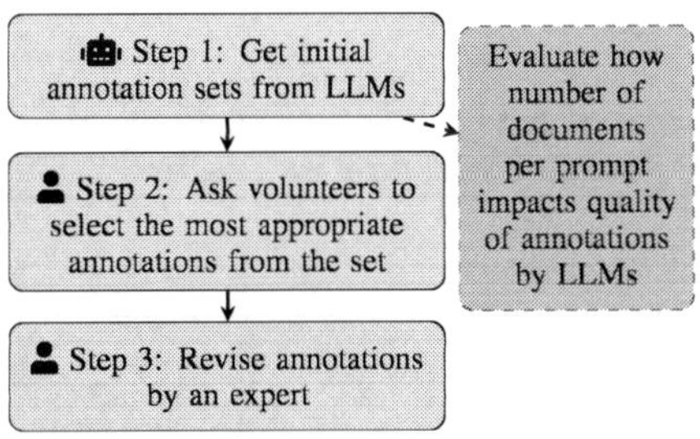

Figure 1: Workflow of the Annotation Process.

Appendix B provides a detailed description of the dataset annotation process. We make the dataset and the prompts used for its generation publicly

[1]Aspects that do not exactly match any part of a document.

[2]As of March 2024, when the dataset was generated and annotated

available[3] and publish the Datasheet for the dataset, as proposed by Gebru et al. (2021), in the same repository.

3.2 Existing Datasets

For this study, we specifically selected existing datasets that are well-suited for the joint task of detection of aspects and the classification of their polarities. While numerous other datasets are available (Chebolu et al., 2023; Zhang et al., 2023b), we restricted our choices to those documented in published, peer-reviewed papers to ensure higher annotation quality. Table 2 summarizes these datasets and includes statistics for the novel dataset we introduce in this paper in the last row. Appendix E provides additional characteristics of the datasets.

Table 2: Datasets Used for Experiments.

	Train	Test	Implicit Aspects
SemEval-14-Laptop (Pontiki et al., 2014)	1482	422	0%
SemEval-14-Restaurant (Pontiki et al., 2014)	2019	606	0%
MAMS (Jiang et al., 2019)	4297	500	0%
Twitter (Dong et al., 2014)	6248	692	3.5%
Composite	14046	2220	0.88%
Sports Feedback (Novel)	96	384	35%

4 Metrics

Automated evaluation of models for the aspect detection subtask faces several challenges. First, documents may contain implicit aspects that do not directly match with individual words. For example, the sentence from our dataset:

> *I found that some locations had multiple volunteers that didn't appear to be overly busy and could have been useful at other locations where there were shortages.*

This sentence alludes to the aspect 'allocation of volunteers' without explicitly stating it in the text. Moreover, the definition of what constitutes an aspect is often fuzzy: in the cited example, 'placement of volunteers' could also be interpreted as a valid aspect.

Second, when LLMs are used for aspect extraction instead of traditional span-based approaches, relying on exact matches to compute metrics such as precision, recall, and F-score without accounting for linguistic variation can be problematic.

[3] https://github.com/neveditsin/absa-sport

To address these evaluation challenges, we propose a generalized method for assessing precision (P) and recall (R) inspired by the work of Euzenat (2007) on ontology alignment. Specifically, to account for partial matches and linguistic variation between predicted and true aspect sets, we define precision and recall as follows. For a given document, we define S_d as the set of detected aspects and S_g as the set of true (gold) aspects. The function ι, parameterized by a threshold $\theta \in [0, 1]$, returns the set of partial matches between S_d and S_g. Figure 2 illustrates the concept of the intersection ι between the two sets of aspects.

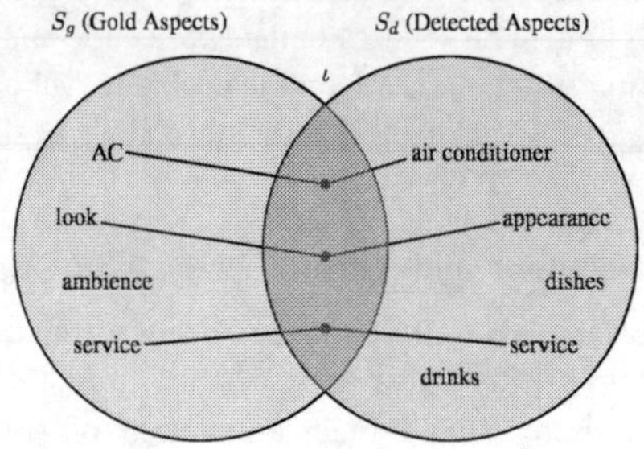

Figure 2: Intersection ι of Gold Aspects (S_g) and Detected Aspects (S_d).

The threshold θ serves as a filter for the minimal similarity required between pairs of matching aspects. In the special case where $\theta = 1$, the function $\iota(S_d, S_g)$ reduces to the intersection of the two sets, enforcing exact aspect matches. Conversely, when $0 \leq \theta \ll 1$, it permits the matching of semantically unrelated pairs, making values of θ close to zero impractical. For the purpose of experiments in this study, we set $\theta = 0.95$. An empirical analysis of the impact of θ on matching errors in the context of this study is provided in Appendix F.

With these definitions, the generalized precision, denoted as P^θ, is given by:

$$P^\theta = \frac{|\iota(S_d, S_g, \theta)|}{|S_d|} \tag{1}$$

Similarly, the generalized recall, denoted as R^θ, is formulated as:

$$R^\theta = \frac{|\iota(S_d, S_g, \theta)|}{|S_g|} \tag{2}$$

The F_1^θ score, defined as the harmonic mean of precision P^θ and recall R^θ, effectively captures the balance between these metrics within this framework.

Algorithm 1 provides the implementation of the function $\iota(S_g, S_d, \theta)$ used in this study. A similarity measure $\sigma : s_1 \times s_2 \to [0, 1]$ quantifies the resemblance between individual elements from the sets, resulting in a similarity matrix with values ranging from 0 to 1. To avoid false positive matches, values below a specified threshold θ are set to zero. The similarity matrix is then converted into a cost matrix, and the linear sum assignment problem is solved to determine the optimal pairing of elements between the sets, minimizing the total cost. This procedure yields a set of optimal element pairs, $\mathcal{I}$.

Algorithm 1 Algorithm for Finding Intersection ι

Require: Two finite sets of aspects S_g and S_d; similarity measure $\sigma : s_1 \times s_2 \to [0, 1]$; similarity threshold θ
Ensure: Optimal pairing set $\mathcal{I}$ of index pairs (i, j)
Initialize similarity matrix M of size $|S_g| \times |S_d|$
for each $s_{1i} \in S_g$ **do**
  for each $s_{2j} \in S_d$ **do**
    $M_{ij} \leftarrow \sigma(s_{1i}, s_{2j})$
  end for
end for
for each element M_{ij} in M **do**
  if $M_{ij} < \theta$ **then**
    $M_{ij} \leftarrow 0$
  end if
end for
Define cost matrix C where $C_{ij} \leftarrow 1 - M_{ij}$
Solve the linear sum assignment problem using C to obtain optimal pairing set $\mathcal{I}$
return $\mathcal{I}$

For this study, we use the algorithm described by Crouse (2016) to solve the linear sum assignment problem and implement the function $\sigma(s_1, s_2)$ as the scaled cosine similarity between the embeddings of s_1 and s_2.

5 Models

We evaluated two open-weight models, Mistal 7B Instruct (Jiang et al., 2023) and LLaMA-3 8B Instruct (Bhatt et al., 2024), against the baseline PyABSA (Yang et al., 2023) on the Aspect-Polarity Pair Extraction (ASPE) task. The selection of the open-weight models was motivated by their state-of-the-art performance within the parameter range[4], ease of deployment, and computational efficiency. Their relatively compact sizes (7–8 billion parameters) allow local deployment without reliance on external computational resources, a material factor for practical applications.

PyABSA is an actively maintained, ensemble-based framework trained on publicly available datasets. It serves as a reliable baseline representing traditional yet robust ABSA methodologies.

For measuring phrase similarity, we selected Sentence-T5 (Large) (Ni et al., 2021). Despite its smaller size compared to more recent large-scale models, Sentence-T5 demonstrates strong performance on text embedding benchmarks (Muennighoff et al., 2023), making it well-suited for experiments with limited computational resources.

6 Evaluation of Open-Weight Models

Our experiments aim to address the following research questions:

1. Can open-weight LLMs outperform the baseline without fine-tuning?
2. How do in-context learning examples affect the performance of LLMs on the ASPE task?
3. Does fine-tuning on (i) similar data or (ii) data from a different domain with a large fraction of implicit aspects improve the performance of the selected LLMs on the joint task compared to the baseline and non-fine-tuned models?

For the experiments, we organized the datasets from Table 2 into two categories: (i) the *Novel dataset*, introduced in this paper, and (ii) the *Composite dataset*, assembled by aggregating the previously published datasets listed in Table 2. For model evaluation, we used the test sets from both datasets: 2,220 samples from the Composite dataset and 384 samples from the Novel dataset.

For model fine-tuning, we utilized:

1. The training portion of the Composite dataset, containing 14,046 samples.
2. The training portion of the Novel dataset, consisting of 96 samples. Due to its limited size, we allocated 80% of the Novel dataset to testing and 20% to training.
3. A blended dataset obtained by combining the training portion of the Novel dataset (96 samples) with 96 randomly selected samples from each of the existing datasets listed in Table 2, resulting in a total of 480 samples.

Appendix G provides the complete set of fine-tuning hyperparameters and lists the hardware and software used for the experiments.

For ICL examples, we uniformly sampled documents along with their associated sets of aspect-polarity pairs from the training subset of the re-

[4] As of July 2024

spective dataset: when evaluating on the Novel dataset, we sampled from its training subset, and when evaluating on the Composite datasets, we sampled from its training portion. For each polarity in $\mathcal{P} = \{\text{positive, neutral, negative}\}$, two documents were selected to ensure compatibility with the model's context window during inference.

Table 3 compares the performance of fine-tuned models, generic ICL (using the same predefined prompt with arbitrary examples presented to the models; see Appendix H for reference), ICL with sampling, and a baseline on the aspect extraction subtask. The evaluation employs macro-averaged metrics with a threshold $\theta = 0.95$. This threshold, empirically chosen to accommodate variations in aspect phrasing while minimizing errors, is analyzed in detail in Appendix F.

Table 3: Experimental Results for Aspect Extraction.

Model	Fine-Tuning / ICL	Composite Dataset			Novel Dataset		
		$P^{.95}$	$R^{.95}$	$F_1^{.95}$	$P^{.95}$	$R^{.95}$	$F_1^{.95}$
Mistral	Generic ICL	0.35	0.59	0.44	0.21	0.44	0.29
LLaMA-3	Generic ICL	0.49	0.59	0.53	0.33	0.51	0.40
Mistral	ICL with sampling	0.68	0.63	0.65	0.52	0.50	0.51
LLaMA-3	ICL with sampling	0.65	0.63	0.64	0.45	0.54	0.49
Mistral	FT Composite	0.81	0.82	0.82	0.35	0.45	0.39
LLaMA-3	FT Composite	0.87	0.85	0.86	0.35	0.33	0.34
Mistral	FT Novel	0.46	0.42	0.44	0.55	0.54	0.55
LLaMA-3	FT Novel	0.47	0.43	0.45	0.54	0.54	0.54
Mistral	FT Blended	0.76	0.77	0.77	0.49	0.53	0.51
LLaMA-3	FT Blended	0.77	0.74	0.76	0.52	0.54	0.53
PyABSA	-	0.77	0.75	0.76	0.33	0.27	0.30

We employed a paired bootstrap test, following the methodology of Berg-Kirkpatrick et al. (2012), with 10^5 iterations to compute p-values. Results were deemed statistically significant for comparisons where $p < 0.05$.

Open-weight LLMs' performance varies by dataset when used without fine-tuning. They performed worse than the PyABSA baseline on the Composite dataset (which matches PyABSA's training data), but outperformed it on the Novel dataset (which differs in domain and implicit aspect frequency). Using ICL with sampling significantly improved performance across both datasets, showing that providing relevant examples is an effective way to enhance LLMs' aspect extraction abilities.

Fine-tuning effectiveness depends on the similarity between training and evaluation data. When fine-tuned on the Composite dataset, both LLaMA-3 and Mistral showed significant performance gains on Composite samples compared to their non-fine-tuned versions, but their performance on Novel samples declined, falling below that of ICL with sampling. The reverse held true when fine-tuning on the Novel dataset: while significant improvements were observed on Novel samples, performance on Composite samples degraded below that of ICL with sampling. In contrast, fine-tuning on a mixed dataset combining both Novel and Composite samples yielded consistent performance gains across both dataset classes. Appendix I presents detailed experimental results for individual datasets on the aspect extraction task, evaluated using both adjusted metrics $\theta = 0.95$ and exact match criteria.

Table 4 presents the experimental results for aspect sentiment classification (ASC) using standard precision (P), recall (R), and F_1 metrics, as generalized metrics are unnecessary for this task.

Table 4: Experimental Results for Aspect Sentiment Classification.

Model	Fine-Tuning / ICL	Composite Dataset			Novel Dataset		
		P	R	F_1	P	R	F_1
Mistral	Generic ICL	0.55	0.33	0.41	0.56	0.28	0.37
LLaMA-3	Generic ICL	0.53	0.33	0.38	0.59	0.36	0.43
Mistral	ICL with sampling	0.56	0.36	0.44	0.58	0.38	0.41
LLaMA-3	ICL with sampling	0.55	0.35	0.43	0.59	0.36	0.44
Mistral	FT Composite	0.58	0.48	0.52	0.49	0.22	0.30
LLaMA-3	FT Composite	0.60	0.52	0.56	0.46	0.15	0.23
Mistral	FT Novel	0.52	0.24	0.31	0.60	0.33	0.43
LLaMA-3	FT Novel	0.49	0.24	0.30	0.69	0.31	0.42
Mistral	FT Blended	0.58	0.46	0.51	0.65	0.31	0.42
LLaMA-3	FT Blended	0.57	0.44	0.49	0.67	0.29	0.39
PyABSA	-	0.61	0.46	0.52	0.52	0.14	0.21

ASC performance depends on successful aspect extraction, since only correctly identified aspects count toward recall and overall results. The patterns mirror aspect extraction findings: fine-tuning on a different dataset degrades model performance, whereas fine-tuning on similar data improves it. However, ICL with sampling showed no major improvement on the Novel dataset.

7 Discussion and Further Research

Our study reveals several key findings and corresponding future research directions. SOTA LLMs demonstrated effectiveness in generating initial annotations for the proposed dataset, despite inherent limitations like restricted context windows and occasional inaccuracies. The implemented multi-step annotation process, combining automated LLM-generated annotations with human validation, successfully streamlined the traditionally labor-intensive workflow while maintaining annotation quality through human oversight.

The employment of ICL with sampling proved effective for enhancing LLM performance in extracting ABSA pairs, offering advantages over fine-tuning approaches that can lead to overfitting and reduced generalizability. To build upon this success, future research should explore more sophisticated ICL strategies, such as retrieval-augmented ICL (Milios et al., 2023), which could further enhance the extraction of aspect-sentiment pairs.

Our proposed metric for generalized precision and recall captures model performance on the aspect extraction task while accounting for linguistic variability. Future work should focus on developing methods for automatic determination of the optimal threshold θ value, investigating its relationship with various semantic similarity models. Additionally, implementing error detection methods could enable dynamic θ adjustment, ensuring accurate performance measurement across both explicit and implicit aspect extraction scenarios.

Finally, adopting multi-step reasoning approaches like chain-of-thought prompting (Wei et al., 2022) or iterative refinement (Madaan et al., 2024) presents a promising direction for improving both data annotation and pair extraction processes, potentially reducing the need for human intervention while maintaining output quality.

Conclusion

This study serves as a proof of concept, demonstrating the applicability of our proposed approach in a challenging domain characterized by domain-specific terminology and a high prevalence of implicit aspects. While the dataset and findings are currently domain-specific, the methods introduced, such as the tailored evaluation metric and annotation framework, are designed to be adaptable to other contexts.

Limitations

A significant drawback of employing LLMs for ABSA is the substantial computational resources required, particularly in terms of GPU usage. This demand can limit accessibility and scalability for practitioners with limited resources. However, as technological advancements continue to optimize hardware and algorithms, we anticipate a reduction in these computational barriers, potentially making LLM-based approaches the standard in ABSA.

The novel dataset is limited to a single domain and language (English), which may restrict its representativeness across other domains and languages. Additionally, it may not fully capture the richness and variability of natural language. Since it is generated by an LLM, it may exhibit limitations such as reduced lexical diversity and reliance on common phrasing patterns. Moreover, LLM-generated content may lack the contextual depth needed to capture implicit sentiment, aspect-specific variations, and the diversity of real-world expressions.

Annotation of datasets remains a considerable challenge. Identifying implicit aspects is a time-consuming and cognitively demanding task for human annotators. When aspects are abstract rather than concrete objects, inter-annotator agreement tends to decrease, affecting the reliability of the annotations. This highlights the need for improved annotation methodologies or assistance tools to better capture implicit aspects.

Moreover, we acknowledge that fine-tuning large language models on a small dataset, such as the 96 samples used in this study (25% of the novel dataset), may not yield reliable or generalizable results. This limitation likely contributed to the observed decline in F_1 scores on the composite dataset and the improvement on the novel dataset, suggesting potential overfitting. The large parameter space of LLMs necessitates substantial data for effective fine-tuning. To address this, future research should not only explore fine-tuning with larger, more diverse datasets, including those beyond peer-reviewed venues, but also incorporate regularization techniques such as dropout, weight decay, and early stopping.

Finally, the proposed metric for detecting aspects relies on the quality of the similarity scores, which may affect its consistency across different datasets.

Ethics Statement

This research was conducted in accordance with the principles outlined in the ACL Code of Ethics, emphasizing honesty, transparency, and integrity throughout all stages of the study, from data collection to analysis and reporting. All data utilized in this study are publicly available and documented following best practices.

We acknowledge the potential biases introduced by using LLMs for data generation in creating this novel dataset. To ensure the quality of the synthetic dataset, an expert with a background in natural language processing conducted a comprehensive review of the generated content. This review focused on identifying potential biases introduced by the LLMs, including the over-representation of certain sentiment polarities, repetitive patterns in aspect phrasing, and cultural or linguistic biases. Based on the findings, approximately 6% of the generated sentences were removed to address these concerns. Given the dataset's intended use in Aspect-Based Sentiment Analysis, we do not foresee significant risks of harm, affirming its utility for ethically advancing sentiment analysis research. Importantly, this dataset is not designed for tasks beyond ABSA.

Although large language models were employed in the initial data annotation step, subsequent steps were conducted by human annotators experienced in ABSA tasks and ethical considerations. This multi-step approach ensured a rigorous and ethically sound annotation process.

References

Jianzhu Bao, Rui Wang, Yasheng Wang, Aixin Sun, Yitong Li, Fei Mi, and Ruifeng Xu. 2023. A synthetic data generation framework for grounded dialogues. In *Proceedings of the 61st Annual Meeting of the Association for Computational Linguistics (Volume 1: Long Papers)*, pages 10866–10882, Toronto, Canada. Association for Computational Linguistics.

Taylor Berg-Kirkpatrick, David Burkett, and Dan Klein. 2012. An empirical investigation of statistical significance in NLP. In *Proceedings of the 2012 Joint Conference on Empirical Methods in Natural Language Processing and Computational Natural Language Learning*, pages 995–1005, Jeju Island, Korea. Association for Computational Linguistics.

Manish Bhatt, Sahana Chennabasappa, Yue Li, Cyrus Nikolaidis, Daniel Song, Shengye Wan, Faizan Ahmad, Cornelius Aschermann, Yaohui Chen, Dhaval Kapil, David Molnar, Spencer Whitman, and Joshua Saxe. 2024. Cyberseceval 2: A wide-ranging cybersecurity evaluation suite for large language models.

Gianni Brauwers and Flavius Frasincar. 2022. A survey on aspect-based sentiment classification. *ACM Comput. Surv.*, 55(4).

Tom B. Brown, Benjamin Mann, Nick Ryder, Melanie Subbiah, Jared Kaplan, Prafulla Dhariwal, Arvind Neelakantan, Pranav Shyam, Girish Sastry, Amanda Askell, Sandhini Agarwal, Ariel Herbert-Voss, Gretchen Krueger, Tom Henighan, Rewon Child, Aditya Ramesh, Daniel M. Ziegler, Jeffrey Wu, and Clemens Winter et al. 2020. Language models are few-shot learners. *CoRR*, abs/2005.14165.

Hongjie Cai, Rui Xia, and Jianfei Yu. 2021. Aspect-category-opinion-sentiment quadruple extraction with implicit aspects and opinions. In *Proceedings of the 59th Annual Meeting of the Association for Computational Linguistics and the 11th International Joint Conference on Natural Language Processing (Volume 1: Long Papers)*, pages 340–350.

Siva Uday Sampreeth Chebolu, Franck Dernoncourt, Nedim Lipka, and Thamar Solorio. 2023. Survey of aspect-based sentiment analysis datasets.

Siva Uday Sampreeth Chebolu, Franck Dernoncourt, Nedim Lipka, and Thamar Solorio. 2024. OATS: A challenge dataset for opinion aspect target sentiment joint detection for aspect-based sentiment analysis. In *Proceedings of the 2024 Joint International Conference on Computational Linguistics, Language Resources and Evaluation (LREC-COLING 2024)*, pages 12336–12347, Torino, Italia. ELRA and ICCL.

David F. Crouse. 2016. On implementing 2d rectangular assignment algorithms. *IEEE Transactions on Aerospace and Electronic Systems*, 52(4):1679–1696.

Xiang Deng, Vasilisa Bashlovkina, Feng Han, Simon Baumgartner, and Michael Bendersky. 2023. Llms to the moon? reddit market sentiment analysis with large language models. In *Companion Proceedings of the ACM Web Conference 2023*, pages 1014–1019.

Tim Dettmers, Artidoro Pagnoni, Ari Holtzman, and Luke Zettlemoyer. 2024. Qlora: Efficient finetuning of quantized llms. *Advances in Neural Information Processing Systems*, 36.

Li Dong, Furu Wei, Chuanqi Tan, Duyu Tang, Ming Zhou, and Ke Xu. 2014. Adaptive recursive neural network for target-dependent twitter sentiment classification. In *Proceedings of the 52nd annual meeting of the association for computational linguistics (volume 2: Short papers)*, pages 49–54.

Brucce Neves Dos Santos, Ricardo Marcondes Marcacini, and Solange Oliveira Rezende. 2021. Multi-domain aspect extraction using bidirectional encoder representations from transformers. *IEEE Access*, 9:91604–91613.

Ronen Eldan and Yuanzhi Li. 2023. Tinystories: How small can language models be and still speak coherent english?

Jérôme Euzenat. 2007. Semantic precision and recall for ontology alignment evaluation. In *Proc. 20th International Joint Conference on Artificial Intelligence (IJCAI)*, pages 348–353. AAAI Press.

Timnit Gebru, Jamie Morgenstern, Briana Vecchione, Jennifer Wortman Vaughan, Hanna Wallach, Hal Daumé Iii, and Kate Crawford. 2021. Datasheets for datasets. *Communications of the ACM*, 64(12):86–92.

Akshay Goel, Almog Gueta, Omry Gilon, Chang Liu, Sofia Erell, Lan Huong Nguyen, Xiaohong Hao, Bolous Jaber, Shashir Reddy, Rupesh Kartha, Jean Steiner, Itay Laish, and Amir Feder. 2023. Llms accelerate annotation for medical information extraction. In *Proceedings of the 3rd Machine Learning for Health Symposium*, volume 225 of *Proceedings of Machine Learning Research*, pages 82–100. PMLR.

Morgan Gray, Jaromir Savelka, Wesley Oliver, and Kevin Ashley. 2023. Can gpt alleviate the burden of annotation? In *Legal Knowledge and Information Systems*, pages 157–166. IOS Press.

Zeyu He, Chieh-Yang Huang, Chien-Kuang Cornelia Ding, Shaurya Rohatgi, and Ting-Hao Kenneth Huang. 2024. If in a crowdsourced data annotation pipeline, a gpt-4. In *Proceedings of the 2024 CHI Conference on Human Factors in Computing Systems*, CHI '24, New York, NY, USA. Association for Computing Machinery.

Edward J. Hu, Yelong Shen, Phillip Wallis, Zeyuan Allen-Zhu, Yuanzhi Li, Shean Wang, Lu Wang, and Weizhu Chen. 2021. Lora: Low-rank adaptation of large language models.

Albert Q. Jiang, Alexandre Sablayrolles, Arthur Mensch, Chris Bamford, Devendra Singh Chaplot, Diego de las Casas, Florian Bressand, Gianna Lengyel, Guillaume Lample, Lucile Saulnier, Lélio Renard Lavaud, Marie-Anne Lachaux, Pierre Stock, Teven Le Scao, Thibaut Lavril, Thomas Wang, Timothée Lacroix, and William El Sayed. 2023. Mistral 7b.

Qingnan Jiang, Lei Chen, Ruifeng Xu, Xiang Ao, and Min Yang. 2019. A challenge dataset and effective models for aspect-based sentiment analysis. In *Proceedings of the 2019 Conference on Empirical Methods in Natural Language Processing and the 9th International Joint Conference on Natural Language Processing (EMNLP-IJCNLP)*, pages 6280–6285, Hong Kong, China. Association for Computational Linguistics.

Kiana Kheiri and Hamid Karimi. 2023. Sentimentgpt: Exploiting gpt for advanced sentiment analysis and its departure from current machine learning. *arXiv preprint arXiv:2307.10234*.

Alina Kramchaninova and Arne Defauw. 2022. Synthetic data generation for multilingual domain-adaptable question answering systems. In *Proceedings of the 23rd Annual Conference of the European Association for Machine Translation*, pages 151–160.

Jan Ole Krugmann and Jochen Hartmann. 2024. Sentiment analysis in the age of generative ai. *Customer Needs and Solutions*, 11(1):3.

Bing Liu. 2012. *Sentiment Analysis and Opinion Mining*. Synthesis Lectures on Human Language Technologies. Springer.

Chandreen R Liyanage, Ravi Gokani, and Vijay Mago. 2024. Gpt-4 as an x data annotator: Unraveling its performance on a stance classification task. *PloS one*, 19(8):e0307741.

Dehong Ma, Sujian Li, Fangzhao Wu, Xing Xie, and Houfeng Wang. 2019. Exploring sequence-to-sequence learning in aspect term extraction. In *Proceedings of the 57th annual meeting of the association for computational linguistics*, pages 3538–3547.

Fukun Ma, Xuming Hu, Aiwei Liu, Yawen Yang, Shuang Li, Philip S. Yu, and Lijie Wen. 2023. AMR-based network for aspect-based sentiment analysis. In *Proceedings of the 61st Annual Meeting of the Association for Computational Linguistics (Volume 1: Long Papers)*, pages 322–337, Toronto, Canada. Association for Computational Linguistics.

Aman Madaan, Niket Tandon, Prakhar Gupta, Skyler Hallinan, Luyu Gao, Sarah Wiegreffe, Uri Alon, Nouha Dziri, Shrimai Prabhumoye, Yiming Yang, et al. 2024. Self-refine: Iterative refinement with self-feedback. *Advances in Neural Information Processing Systems*, 36.

Wei Meng, Yongqing Wei, Peiyu Liu, Zhenfang Zhu, and Hongxia Yin. 2019. Aspect based sentiment analysis with feature enhanced attention cnn-bilstm. *IEEE Access*, 7:167240–167249.

Selina Meyer, David Elsweiler, Bernd Ludwig, Marcos Fernandez-Pichel, and David E Losada. 2022. Do we still need human assessors? prompt-based gpt-3 user simulation in conversational ai. In *Proceedings of the 4th Conference on Conversational User Interfaces*, pages 1–6.

Donatas Meškelė and Flavius Frasincar. 2020. Aldonar: A hybrid solution for sentence-level aspect-based sentiment analysis using a lexicalized domain ontology and a regularized neural attention model. *Information Processing and Management*, 57(3):102211.

Aristides Milios, Siva Reddy, and Dzmitry Bahdanau. 2023. In-context learning for text classification with many labels. In *GenBench: The first workshop on generalisation (benchmarking) in NLP*, page 173.

Piotr Mirowski, Kory W. Mathewson, Jaylen Pittman, and Richard Evans. 2023. Co-writing screenplays and theatre scripts with language models: Evaluation by industry professionals. In *Proceedings of the 2023 CHI Conference on Human Factors in Computing Systems*, CHI '23, New York, NY, USA. Association for Computing Machinery.

Jay Mohta, Kenan Ak, Yan Xu, and Mingwei Shen. 2023. Are large language models good annotators? In *Proceedings on "I Can't Believe It's Not Better: Failure Modes in the Age of Foundation Models" at NeurIPS 2023 Workshops*, volume 239 of *Proceedings of Machine Learning Research*, pages 38–48. PMLR.

Niklas Muennighoff, Nouamane Tazi, Loic Magne, and Nils Reimers. 2023. MTEB: Massive text embedding benchmark. In *Proceedings of the 17th Conference of the European Chapter of the Association for Computational Linguistics*, pages 2014–2037, Dubrovnik, Croatia. Association for Computational Linguistics.

Ambreen Nazir, Yuan Rao, Lianwei Wu, and Ling Sun. 2020. Issues and challenges of aspect-based sentiment analysis: A comprehensive survey. *IEEE Transactions on Affective Computing*, 13(2):845–863.

Jianmo Ni, Gustavo Hernández Ábrego, Noah Constant, Ji Ma, Keith B. Hall, Daniel Cer, and Yinfei Yang. 2021. Sentence-t5: Scalable sentence encoders from pre-trained text-to-text models.

OpenAI. 2023. Gpt-4 technical report.

Maria Pontiki, Dimitris Galanis, Haris Papageorgiou, Suresh Manandhar, and Ion Androutsopoulos. 2015. SemEval-2015 task 12: Aspect based sentiment analysis. In *Proceedings of the 9th International Workshop on Semantic Evaluation (SemEval 2015)*, pages 486–495, Denver, Colorado. Association for Computational Linguistics.

Maria Pontiki, Dimitris Galanis, John Pavlopoulos, Harris Papageorgiou, Ion Androutsopoulos, and Suresh Manandhar. 2014. SemEval-2014 task 4: Aspect based sentiment analysis. In *Proceedings of the 8th International Workshop on Semantic Evaluation (SemEval 2014)*, pages 27–35, Dublin, Ireland. Association for Computational Linguistics.

Kevin Scaria, Himanshu Gupta, Siddharth Goyal, Saurabh Sawant, Swaroop Mishra, and Chitta Baral. 2024. InstructABSA: Instruction learning for aspect based sentiment analysis. In *Proceedings of the 2024 Conference of the North American Chapter of the Association for Computational Linguistics: Human Language Technologies (Volume 2: Short Papers)*, pages 720–736, Mexico City, Mexico. Association for Computational Linguistics.

Jakub Šmíd, Pavel Priban, and Pavel Kral. 2024. LLaMA-based models for aspect-based sentiment analysis. In *Proceedings of the 14th Workshop on Computational Approaches to Subjectivity, Sentiment, & Social Media Analysis*, pages 63–70, Bangkok, Thailand. Association for Computational Linguistics.

Yuanhe Tian, Chang Liu, Yan Song, Fei Xia, and Yongdong Zhang. 2024. Aspect-based sentiment analysis with context denoising. In *Findings of the Association for Computational Linguistics: NAACL 2024*, pages 3083–3095, Mexico City, Mexico. Association for Computational Linguistics.

Mohammad Tubishat, Norisma Idris, and Mohammad A.M. Abushariah. 2018. Implicit aspect extraction in sentiment analysis: Review, taxonomy, oppportunities, and open challenges. *Information Processing and Management*, 54(4):545–563.

Haining Wang, Kang He, Bobo Li, Lei Chen, Fei Li, Xu Han, Chong Teng, and Donghong Ji. 2024a. Refining and synthesis: A simple yet effective data augmentation framework for cross-domain aspect-based sentiment analysis. In *Findings of the Association for Computational Linguistics ACL 2024*, pages 10318–10329.

Kai Wang, Weizhou Shen, Yunyi Yang, Xiaojun Quan, and Rui Wang. 2020. Relational graph attention network for aspect-based sentiment analysis.

Zhihao Wang, Bo Zhang, Ru Yang, Chang Guo, and Maozhen Li. 2024b. DAGCN: Distance-based and aspect-oriented graph convolutional network for aspect-based sentiment analysis. In *Findings of the Association for Computational Linguistics: NAACL 2024*, pages 1863–1876, Mexico City, Mexico. Association for Computational Linguistics.

Mayur Wankhade, Annavarapu Chandra Sekhara Rao, and Chaitanya Kulkarni. 2022. A survey on sentiment analysis methods, applications, and challenges. *Artificial Intelligence Review*, 55(7):5731–5780.

Jason Wei, Xuezhi Wang, Dale Schuurmans, Maarten Bosma, Fei Xia, Ed Chi, Quoc V Le, Denny Zhou, et al. 2022. Chain-of-thought prompting elicits reasoning in large language models. *Advances in neural information processing systems*, 35:24824–24837.

Haiyan Wu, Zhiqiang Zhang, Shaoyun Shi, Qingfeng Wu, and Haiyu Song. 2022. Phrase dependency relational graph attention network for aspect-based sentiment analysis. *Knowledge-Based Systems*, 236:107736.

Borun Xu, Xiaoxiao Wang, Bo Yang, and Zhongfeng Kang. 2020. Target embedding and position attention with lstm for aspect based sentiment analysis. In *Proceedings of the 2020 5th International Conference on Mathematics and Artificial Intelligence*, pages 93–97.

Heng Yang, Chen Zhang, and Ke Li. 2023. Pyabsa: A modularized framework for reproducible aspect-based sentiment analysis. In *Proceedings of the 32nd ACM International Conference on Information and Knowledge Management*, CIKM '23, page 5117–5122, New York, NY, USA. Association for Computing Machinery.

Songhua Yang, Xinke Jiang, Hanjie Zhao, Wenxuan Zeng, Hongde Liu, and Yuxiang Jia. 2024. Faima: Feature-aware in-context learning for multi-domain aspect-based sentiment analysis.

Jianfei Yu, Qiankun Zhao, and Rui Xia. 2023. Cross-domain data augmentation with domain-adaptive language modeling for aspect-based sentiment analysis. In *Proceedings of the 61st Annual Meeting of the Association for Computational Linguistics (Volume 1: Long Papers)*, pages 1456–1470.

Mao Zhang, Yongxin Zhu, Zhen Liu, Zhimin Bao, Yunfei Wu, Xing Sun, and Linli Xu. 2023a. Span-level aspect-based sentiment analysis via table filling. In *Proceedings of the 61st Annual Meeting of the Association for Computational Linguistics (Volume 1: Long Papers)*, pages 9273–9284, Toronto, Canada. Association for Computational Linguistics.

Wenxuan Zhang, Xin Li, Yang Deng, Lidong Bing, and Wai Lam. 2023b. A survey on aspect-based sentiment analysis: Tasks, methods, and challenges. *IEEE TRANSACTIONS ON KNOWLEDGE AND DATA ENGINEERING*, 35(11):11019–11038.

Jie Zhou, Jimmy Xiangji Huang, Qinmin Vivian Hu, and Liang He. 2020. Sk-gcn: Modeling syntax and knowledge via graph convolutional network for aspect-level sentiment classification. *Knowledge-Based Systems*, 205:106292.

Ting Zhou, Ying Shen, and Yinghui Li. 2024. GC-Net: Global-and-context collaborative learning for aspect-based sentiment analysis. In *Proceedings of the 2024 Joint International Conference on Computational Linguistics, Language Resources and Evaluation (LREC-COLING 2024)*, pages 7570–7580, Torino, Italia. ELRA and ICCL.

A Examples of Prompts and Generated Feedback

Prompt 1

You are a human who participated as a volunteer in New Brunswick sport games for minorities (the event is called NBMSG). You are invited to take a survey. Generate 10 naturally sounding diverse responses with variable length (from 5 to 10 sentences with average of 6-7 sentences, try to provide longer responses). Try to be informal and use a lot of slang.

Chunk Of The Model Response (Gemini)

1. Sure ya! I'd be happy to answer some questions about NBMSG. Those games were AWESOME! Met so many cool ppl and really felt like the volunteers were appreciated. Although, maybe next time a bit more info on what to expect beforehand woulda been helpful.
2. Hey yeah, I can totally do a survey! NBMSG was a blastt - so glad I volunteered. It was tiring at times, but seeing those kids faces light up made it all worth it. Defo considering doing it again next year!
3. Absolutely, hit me with that survey! Being a volunteer at NBMSG was an amazing experience. It was so inspiring to see how passionate everyone was about sports and inclusion. Just a suggestion, maybe a little more organization with scheduling would be good? But overall, 10/10 would volunteer again!
4. Ya ofc I'll do the survey! Those NBMSG games were lit. I volunteered at the concession stand and it was craaazy busy at times, but the teamwork between us volunteers was awesome . Definitely recommend volunteering there if you get the chance!

Prompt 2

You are a human who participated as a volunteer in New Brunswick sport games for minorities (the event is called NBMSG). You are invited to take a survey. Generate 20 naturally sounding diverse responses with variable length (from 1 to 5 sentences with average of 3-5 sentences, try to provide longer responses). Use a lot of typos, grammatical errors, slang, emojis, etc.. Be negative.

Chunk Of The Model Response (Gemini - Emojis Removed)

1. Ugh, finally got around to this NBMSG survey. Took forever to find the time between work and everything, and let's just say it wasn't the best volunteer experience. Not sure what I expected, but maybe a bit more organization next time?
2. Fine, here's my survey response about NBMSG. Honestly, kind of disappointed. The description made it sound way more fun and impactful than it actually was. Definitely not what I signed up for.
3. **NBMSG survey**... Not sure what I was thinking volunteering there. Felt kinda lost and confused most of the time. Barely any training, and nobody seemed to know what was going on half the time. Doubt I'll be back next year.
4. Ugh, this NBMSG survey is taking foreverrrrrrr. Get on with it already! Look, I volunteered my time, the least they could do is make this quick and painless.

Prompt 3

You are a human who participated as a volunteer in New Brunswick sport games for minorities (the event is called NBMSG). You are invited to take a survey. Generate 20 naturally sounding diverse responses with variable length (from 1 to 10 sentences with average of 4-6 sentences, try to provide longer responses). Focus on negative sentiment towards various aspects. Be emotional and creative. Don't hesitate to use slang.

Chunk Of The Model Response (GPT-4)

1. "The IT setup was a hot mess – like, seriously? In the age of tech, how are we dealing with systems crashing left and right? Made it impossible to keep up with schedules and scores. Frustrating doesn't even start to cover it."
2. "Food options were straight-up disappointing. With such a rich tapestry of cultures, I expected a feast for the senses. Instead, we got the same old, same old. Missed opportunity to showcase the diversity we were all there to celebrate."
3. "Weather threw us for a loop, and it felt like the organizers hadn't even glanced at the forecast. Events got cancelled and shuffled around with hardly any heads-up. Chaos isn't even the word for it."
4. "Volunteer coordination was a joke. Half the time, I didn't know where I was supposed to be or what I was supposed to be doing. It was like trying to solve a puzzle without the picture. Super frustrating."

Prompt 4

You are a human who participated as a volunteer in New Brunswick sport games for minorities (the event is called NBMSG). You are invited to take a survey. Generate 20 naturally sounding diverse responses with variable length (from 1 to 10 sentences with average of 4-6 sentences, try to provide longer responses). Focus on positive and neutral sentiment towards various aspects. The style of comments should reflect the following person: 35-50 years old, education: university degree

Chunk Of The Model Response (GPT-4)

1. "Volunteering at NBMSG provided a wonderful opportunity to meet people from various backgrounds and professions. The diversity among the volunteers alone was a testament to the inclusive nature of the event. It was an enriching experience that I believe contributed positively to the community spirit."
2. "Participating as a volunteer at NBMSG was an eye-opening experience. It was refreshing to see such a wide range of ages, backgrounds, and abilities come together in celebration of sport and culture. The positive atmosphere was contagious and made the hard work worthwhile."
3. "The event's use of digital platforms for scheduling and updates was a forward-thinking approach, though not without its challenges. As we become increasingly reliant on technology, it's essential for events like NBMSG to continue improving their digital infrastructure to enhance the experience for all involved."
4. "The logistical coordination of NBMSG, while complex, was handled with notable effort and dedication by the organizers. As a volunteer, I felt supported and appreciated, which in turn motivated me to contribute my best to the event's success. It was a valuable learning experience."

B Dataset Annotation Process

In the first step of dataset annotation, both GPT-4 and Gemini 1.0 Ultra were tasked with annotating the data. Appendix C provides sample annotation prompts and responses from the models.

As an auxiliary step (indicated by the blue box in Figure 1 of the main text), we experimented with varying the number of documents per prompt, ranging from 20 to 120, to assess how this variation affects annotation quality. The results indicated that the quality of annotations for both models substantially decreased as the number of documents per prompt increased. To quantify this, we asked both models to evaluate the annotation sets produced with 20, 40, 60, and 120 documents per prompt using a scale from 1 to 10. This scale was chosen to provide a sufficiently granular assessment while maintaining simplicity for quantitative interpretation. Notably, the models were unaware of both the number of documents per prompt and which model had provided the annotations. Figure 3 illustrates the evaluation scores for different numbers of documents per prompt (20, 40, 60, 120). The y-axis shows the score distribution for GPT-4 (green boxplots) and Gemini (red boxplots), while the x-axis represents the annotations provided by the models, with the corresponding number of documents per prompt indicated in parentheses. The mean Fleiss' Kappa, calculated across four binned labels, is 0.62.

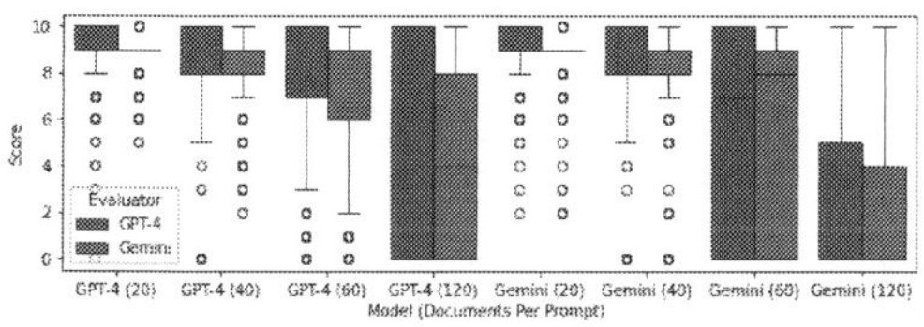

Figure 3: Impact of Document Quantity on Annotation Quality: Evaluation Scores from GPT-4 and Gemini Models.

The second step involved refining the annotations. Two annotation sets were selected for this purpose: one from GPT-4 and another from Gemini, each generated with 20 documents per prompt. Three undergraduate student volunteers, familiar with ABSA tasks, were tasked with selecting the most suitable annotation from each set based on the accuracy of identified aspects and their polarities. This evaluation yielded a Fleiss' Kappa score of 0.3, reflecting the inherent difficulty of implicit aspect identification and the subjective nature of interpreting subtle or context-dependent aspects. This highlights the importance of the third step involving thorough expert review to ensure the quality of the final annotations. Appendix D provides the written instructions given to volunteers, along with details of the training sessions provided.

The third step involved revision and adjustment by an expert[5], who selected the annotations based on the volunteers' feedback and their own judgment, particularly in cases with low volunteer agreement. Adjustments were required for 12.5% of the documents.

[5]Holds MSc in Computer Science

C Examples of Annotation Prompts and Generated Annotations

Annotation Prompt 1

Follow the instructions precisely. Provide answers as directed in the example below (key-value pairs in curly braces, separated by comma, do not reprint sentences and do not provide any additional information). Do not divide answers into categories, just follow the sequence of sentences.
Given the following feedback from volunteers of an event called NBMSG, perform aspect-based sentiment analysis: identify aspects and polarities (Positive, Negative, Neutral) as in the examples below.
Note: the empty dictionary for the third example indicates that there are no aspects or polarities associated with the text:
1 "I like school but the organization of the art classes needs improvement."
1 {"school":"Positive","organization of art classes":"Negative"}
2 "Dog drinks water."
2 {}
3 "Volunteers could be allocated better, but at least everyone seemed to be fine with that."
3 {"Allocation of volunteers":"Neutral"}
Feedback:
1. "The organization was a total mess, honestly. They had us running around with barely any direction. And when you ask for help, it's like no one knew what was going on either."
2. "I was really excited to help out, but the weather totally ruined it for me. It was like they didn't even check the forecast. We were all soaked and miserable."
3. "The sign-up process was a nightmare. The website kept crashing, and when it didn't, it was super slow. They really need to get their IT stuff together."
4. "Food there was just sad. Like, if you're gonna have us there all day, at least provide something decent to eat. The options were super limited and way overpriced."
5. "Nobody mentioned anything about the parking situation. I ended up parking a mile away and walking. They should've sent out some info or something."
6. "They said there'd be Wi-Fi, but I couldn't connect the whole time I was there. Made it impossible to post anything or stay updated."
7. "I felt really unprepared. They didn't give us enough info before the event, so I was kinda just winging it the whole time. Not cool."
8. "It's like they didn't even think about the weather. We were out in the sun with no shade for hours. I got a wicked sunburn."
9. "The equipment was pretty outdated. It's supposed to be a sports event, right? Shouldn't they have decent gear for the athletes?"
10. "I was hyped to help out, but the lack of organization just killed the vibe. Waited around a lot for someone to tell me what to do."
11. "The schedule was a joke. Everything was running late or overlapping. Made it impossible to catch the events I wanted to see."
12. "There was literally nowhere to get water unless you wanted to buy overpriced bottles. For an outdoor event, that's just irresponsible."
13. "Communication was a major issue. Half the time, the announcements were so muffled you couldn't understand anything."
14. "They promised some cool activities, but a bunch got canceled last minute. Super disappointing for everyone looking forward to them."
15. "I wanted to contribute, but the disorganization made it so stressful. At one point, I just sat down because I had no clue where I was needed."
16. "The volunteer shirts were ugly and uncomfortable. It's a small thing, but if I'm wearing it all day, at least make it bearable."
17. "The medical tent was hard to find, and when you did, they seemed really unprepared for any serious issues. That's worrying at a sports event."
18. "They were super strict about bringing your own food, which wouldn't have been a problem if their food wasn't so bad. I was starving by the end."
19. "I felt like there was a lack of appreciation for the volunteers. A simple 'thank you' would have gone a long way."
20. "The event was supposed to be about inclusivity, but it felt like they missed the mark on several fronts. From accessibility issues to lack of diversity in food choices."

Model Response (GPT-4)

1. {"Organization":"Negative"}
2. {"Weather preparedness":"Negative"}
3. {"Sign-up process":"Negative", "Website functionality":"Negative"}
4. {"Food quality":"Negative", "Food pricing":"Negative"}
5. {"Parking information":"Negative"}
6. {"Wi-Fi availability":"Negative"}
7. {"Pre-event information":"Negative"}
8. {"Weather preparedness":"Negative", "Sun protection":"Negative"}
9. {"Equipment quality":"Negative"}
10. {"Organization":"Negative"}
11. {"Schedule":"Negative"}
12. {"Water availability":"Negative"}
13. {"Communication clarity":"Negative"}
14. {"Activity fulfillment":"Negative"}
15. {"Organization":"Negative"}
16. {"Volunteer shirts":"Negative"}
17. {"Medical preparedness":"Negative"}
18. {"Food policy":"Negative", "Food quality":"Negative"}
19. {"Volunteer appreciation":"Negative"}
20. {"Inclusivity":"Negative", "Accessibility":"Negative", "Food diversity":"Negative"}

Model Response (Gemini)

1. {"organization": "Negative", "direction": "Negative", "help": "Negative"}
2. {"weather": "Negative", "forecast": "Negative"}
3. {"sign-up process": "Negative", "website": "Negative", "IT": "Negative"}
4. {"food": "Negative", "options": "Negative", "overpriced": "Negative"}
5. {"parking situation": "Negative", "info": "Negative"}
6. {"Wi-Fi": "Negative"}
7. {"preparation": "Negative", "info": "Negative"}
8. {"weather": "Negative", "shade": "Negative", "sunburn": "Negative"}
9. {"equipment": "Negative"}
10. {"organization": "Negative", "vibe": "Negative"}
11. {"schedule": "Negative"}
12. {"water": "Negative", "irresponsible": "Negative"}
13. {"communication": "Negative", "announcements": "Negative"}
14. {"activities": "Negative", "canceled": "Negative"}
15. {"disorganization": "Negative", "stressful": "Negative"}
16. {"volunteer shirts": "Negative"}
17. {"medical tent": "Negative", "unprepared": "Negative"}
18. {"food policy": "Negative", "their food": "Negative"}
19. {"appreciation for volunteers": "Negative"}
20. {"inclusivity": "Negative", "accessibility": "Negative", "diversity in food choices": "Negative"}

D Instructions for Volunteers

You will be provided with feedback and two sets of annotations. Your task is to choose the annotation set that best captures the feedback based on the following criteria:

1. Assess whether the set clearly identifies **most of** the relevant aspects *without introducing irrelevant or redundant ones.*

2. Assess if the sentiment (positive, negative, or neutral) attached to each aspect correctly reflects the feedback's tone.

Instructions for Selecting the Set:

- If you prefer **Set 1**, mark your choice as **1**.

- If you prefer **Set 2**, mark your choice as **2**.

- If **both** sets represent the same aspects and associated polarities, mark your choice as **0**.

Example 1:

Feedback: "The food stalls, despite some limitations, did a fantastic job of offering a taste of home to many attendees. It was a nice touch that added to the overall welcoming atmosphere of the event".

Annotation Sets:

- Set 1: {'Food stalls': 'Positive'}

- Set 2: {'food stalls': 'Positive', 'atmosphere': 'Positive'}

Analysis:

- **Aspects**:
  - Set 1 captures 'Food stalls', which is one valid aspect, but it misses the other key aspect, 'atmosphere'.
  - Set 2 captures both 'food stalls' and 'atmosphere', both of which are valid aspects.

- **Sentiment**:
  - Both sets correctly classify the polarity as positive for the aspects they capture.

- **Conclusion**:
  - Set 1 identifies only 'Food stalls', which is relevant but misses the additional positive aspect related to 'atmosphere', while Set 2 provides a more complete annotation, identifying both 'food stalls' and 'atmosphere', which are relevant to the feedback and add no redundant aspects. Thus, in this case, based on the refined criteria, you would select **2**

Example 2:

Feedback: "The food and beverage situation was disappointing, not only in variety but also in accommodating different cultural preferences. It's a basic aspect that should be given more thought in an event celebrating diversity".

Annotation Sets:

- Set 1: {'Food and beverage diversity': 'Negative'}

- Set 2: {'food and beverage': 'Negative', 'variety': 'Negative', 'cultural preferences': 'Negative'}

Analysis:

- **Aspects**:
  - Set 1 captures 'Food and beverage diversity', which concisely summarizes the feedback and directly reflects the core complaint.
  - Set 2 introduces 'variety', which feels disconnected from 'food and beverage' and may add confusion by not clearly aligning with the broader point. It also includes 'cultural preferences', which, although mentioned in the feedback, seems redundant because it is disconnected from the major idea.

- **Sentiment**:
  - Both sets correctly identify the sentiment as negative for the aspects they capture.

- **Conclusion**:
  - Set 1 offers a concise and relevant summary by capturing 'Food and beverage diversity', without introducing any irrelevant or redundant information, while Set 2 introduces additional aspects ('variety' and 'cultural preferences') that seem disconnected or redundant, making the annotation less relevant and more complicated. Thus, in this case, based on the refined criteria, you would select **1**.

E Additional Characteristics of Datasets

Table 5: Additional Characteristics of Datasets.

	Total Documents	Total Aspects	Unique Aspects	Avg Aspects/Doc	Total Positive	Total Negative	Total Neutral/ Conflicting	Total Sentences	Avg Sentences/Doc
SemEval-14-Restaurant	2625	4785	1545	1.82	2871	986	824	2660	1.01
SemEval-14-Laptop	1904	2950	1194	1.55	1308	964	619	1932	1.01
MAMS	4797	12522	2659	2.61	3780	3093	5649	4841	1.01
Twitter	6940	6940	117	1.00	1734	1733	3473	12526	1.80
Composite	16266	27197	4880	1.67	9693	6776	10565	21959	1.35
Sports Feedback (Novel)	480	938	491	1.95	405	501	32	1409	2.94

[1] The number of sentences was obtained using the **sent_tokenize** function of **nltk** (version 3.8.1).

F Empirical Selection of θ and Metric Analysis

The proposed metric is parameterized by the value of θ. To select the optimal value of θ, we established the criterion of maximizing the number of correct aspect pairings while ensuring minimal incorrect aspect pairings.

To evaluate the validity of our proposed metric with the chosen threshold θ, we conducted the following analyses on a combined dataset, created by merging the test subset of the Novel dataset and a test portion of the Composite dataset:

1. Compile a set $\mathcal{D}$ consisting of the detected aspect sets from all model variations listed in Table 3. The total number of unique detected aspects across all subsets in $\mathcal{D}$ is given by $\left|\bigcup_{D_i \in \mathcal{D}} D_i\right| = 10856$.

2. For each detected aspect set D_i in $\mathcal{D}$ and its corresponding gold aspect set G_i, compute the set difference:
$$I_i = i(D_i, G_i, \theta) \setminus \{(d, g) \mid d \in D_i,\ g \in G_i,\ d = g\}.$$
Then, define $\mathcal{I}$ as the union of these sets over all i:
$$\mathcal{I} = \bigcup_i I_i.$$
This results in $\mathcal{I}$, the set of all aspect pairs identified by our metric $i(D_i, G_i, \theta)$ across all data, but not captured by a simple case-insensitive intersection.

3. Manually examine all aspect pairs in $\mathcal{I}$ to assess their validity in relation to the original documents from which they were derived.

Since θ is a real-valued parameter, determining its precise optimal value is infeasible largely due to the requirement for manual analysis of all aspect pairs in $\mathcal{I}$. Therefore, in this study, we adopt a practical approach by restricting the search space to increments of 0.025 within the interval (0, 1]. Figure 4 illustrates the effect of θ on $|\mathcal{I}|$ and the fraction of errors introduced by lower θ values.

Manual examination of the pairs in $\mathcal{I}$ revealed no instances of incorrect aspect pairings for $\theta = 0.95$, except in 2% of cases where detected compound aspects were matched with a single gold aspect or vice versa. For example, if *"tomato and onions"* appears as a gold aspect while *"tomato"* and *"onions"*

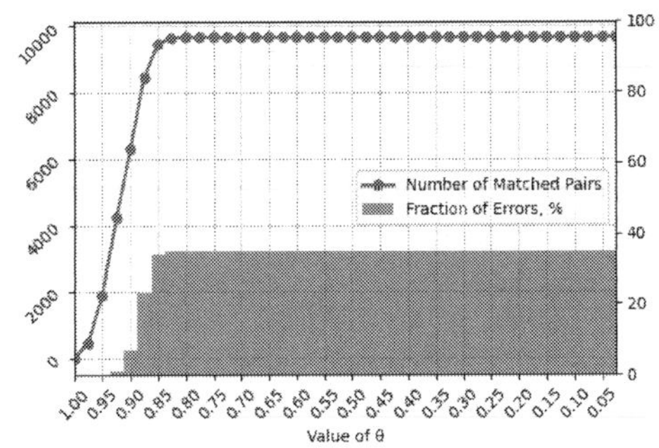

Figure 4: Impact of θ on $|\mathcal{I}|$ and the Fraction of Errors.

are detected as separate aspects by one of the models, the $i(D_i, G_i, 0.95)$ approach pairs the gold aspect with *"tomato"*. Despite these exceptions, the proposed metric successfully identified matches not captured by a simple case-insensitive intersection, including the following cases:

1. Orthographic Errors: Typographical discrepancies between terms, e.g., *"NBMSG"* and *"NSBG"*, *"atmoshere"* and *"atmosphere"*.

2. Paraphrastic Variants: Implicit aspects where rearranged word order corresponds to the same concept, such as *"Event variety"* and *"Variety of events"*.

3. Contextual Elaborations: Aspects identified with additional contextual information, for example, *"Athlete registration"* and *"Athlete registration process"*, *"patties"* and *"full sized patties"*, *"Seagate Momentus XT hybrid drives"* versus *"Two Seagate Momentus XT hybrid drives"*.

4. Lexical Substitutions: Rephrased aspects demonstrating semantic equivalence, such as *"Food options diversity"* and *"variety of food options"*.

5. Synonymy: Use of synonyms to express similar concepts, exemplified by *"looks"* and *"appearance"*.

6. Acronymy: Representation of terms through acronyms, e.g., *"OS"* for *"Operating System"*, *"AC"* for *"Air Conditioning"*.

Decreasing θ to 0.925 introduces a 1% error rate. These errors primarily stem from terms that are related through a shared context but are not true synonyms. Examples include: *"Alicia Keys"* and *"Aaliyah"*, *"Stephen Colbert"* and *"Jon Stewart"*,

"Barack Obama" and *"Hillary Clinton"*, *"Xbox"* and *"PlayStation"*, *"Bill Gates"* and *"Microsoft"*, *"iPhone"* and *"WiFi"*, and *"lamb"* and *"chicken"*.

Further decreasing θ sharply increases the error rate, making it impractical. Thus, we conclude that $\theta = 0.95$ allows the proposed metric to effectively evaluate model performance taking linguistic variation into account while minimizing false-positive pairings.

G Experimental Setup

Table 6: Summary of fine-tuning hyperparameters.

Hyperparameter	Value
LoRA Attention Dimension (r)	128
LoRA Alpha	32
LoRA Dropout	0.1
Bias	none
Task Type	CAUSAL_LM
Per-Device Batch Size	8
Gradient Accumulation Steps	1
Learning Rate	1×10^{-4}
Optimizer	paged_adamw_32bit
Max Training Steps	varies based on dataset used
Warmup Steps	2
Mixed Precision (fp16)	True
4-bit Precision	True
4-bit Double Quantization	True
4-bit Quantization Type	nf4
4-bit Compute Data Type	bfloat16
Additional Note	We saved the model's weights after every 200 steps and selected the checkpoint just before the validation loss began to increase to avoid overfitting

Table 7: Hardware and Software Used For Experiments.

Component	Specification
Hardware	
GPU	NVIDIA A100 80GB
CPU	AMD EPYC 7552
System Memory	128GB DDR4 RAM
Software	
Operating System	Ubuntu 22.04.3 LTS
Python	3.10.12
Transformers	4.46.1
PyTorch	2.5.1+cu124
Datasets	2.14.7
bitsandbytes	0.43.0
flash-attn	2.6.3
PyABSA	2.3.4

H Generic ICL

Generic Prompt

Given a text, identify aspects and polarities (Positive, Negative, Neutral) as in the examples below.
Note: the empty dictionary for the third example indicates that there are no aspects or polarities associated with the text:
TEXT: "I like school but the organization of the art classes needs improvement"
ASPECTS AND POLARITIES: {"school":"Positive","organization of art classes":"Negative"}
TEXT: "Dog drinks water"
ASPECTS AND POLARITIES: {}
TEXT: "Fall is OK season"
ASPECTS AND POLARITIES: {"fall":"Neutral"}

I Detailed Experimental Results

Table 8: Detailed Results for Aspect Extraction Using Adjusted Metrics ($\theta = 0.95$) vs Exact Match Evaluation.

Dataset	Model	Method	$P^{.95}$	$R^{.95}$	$F_1{}^{.95}$	P	R	F_1
Laptop-14	LLaMA-3	FT Blended	0.72	0.52	0.60	0.65	0.47	0.54
Laptop-14	LLaMA-3	FT Composite	0.91	0.72	0.81	0.88	0.70	0.78
Laptop-14	LLaMA-3	FT Novel	0.43	0.42	0.42	0.34	0.33	0.34
Laptop-14	LLaMA-3	Generic ICL	0.18	0.25	0.21	0.16	0.22	0.19
Laptop-14	LLaMA-3	ICL with sampling	0.62	0.78	0.69	0.58	0.72	0.64
Laptop-14	Mistral	FT Blended	0.79	0.74	0.76	0.75	0.70	0.72
Laptop-14	Mistral	FT Composite	0.85	0.80	0.83	0.81	0.77	0.79
Laptop-14	Mistral	FT Novel	0.49	0.50	0.50	0.40	0.41	0.41
Laptop-14	Mistral	Generic ICL	0.33	0.60	0.43	0.25	0.46	0.33
Laptop-14	Mistral	ICL with sampling	0.67	0.70	0.68	0.61	0.63	0.62
Laptop-14	PyABSA	-	0.86	0.82	0.84	0.80	0.76	0.78
Restaurant-14	LLaMA-3	FT Blended	0.72	0.58	0.64	0.66	0.54	0.59
Restaurant-14	LLaMA-3	FT Composite	0.88	0.77	0.82	0.84	0.73	0.78
Restaurant-14	LLaMA-3	FT Novel	0.43	0.36	0.39	0.37	0.31	0.34
Restaurant-14	LLaMA-3	Generic ICL	0.19	0.39	0.25	0.17	0.35	0.23
Restaurant-14	LLaMA-3	ICL with sampling	0.72	0.81	0.77	0.68	0.76	0.72
Restaurant-14	Mistral	FT Blended	0.80	0.85	0.83	0.75	0.80	0.77
Restaurant-14	Mistral	FT Composite	0.85	0.90	0.87	0.81	0.85	0.83
Restaurant-14	Mistral	FT Novel	0.63	0.58	0.60	0.55	0.51	0.53
Restaurant-14	Mistral	Generic ICL	0.41	0.70	0.52	0.35	0.60	0.45
Restaurant-14	Mistral	ICL with sampling	0.78	0.79	0.79	0.71	0.73	0.72
Restaurant-14	PyABSA	-	0.88	0.88	0.88	0.82	0.82	0.82
Twitter	LLaMA-3	FT Blended	0.65	0.55	0.59	0.62	0.53	0.57
Twitter	LLaMA-3	FT Composite	0.96	0.86	0.91	0.96	0.85	0.90
Twitter	LLaMA-3	FT Novel	0.16	0.26	0.20	0.14	0.23	0.17
Twitter	LLaMA-3	Generic ICL	0.13	0.33	0.19	0.12	0.29	0.17
Twitter	LLaMA-3	ICL with sampling	0.75	0.85	0.80	0.70	0.79	0.74
Twitter	Mistral	FT Blended	0.80	0.83	0.81	0.79	0.82	0.80
Twitter	Mistral	FT Composite	0.92	0.92	0.92	0.91	0.91	0.91
Twitter	Mistral	FT Novel	0.21	0.37	0.27	0.18	0.33	0.24
Twitter	Mistral	Generic ICL	0.15	0.52	0.23	0.12	0.44	0.19
Twitter	Mistral	ICL with sampling	0.65	0.80	0.72	0.60	0.74	0.66
Twitter	PyABSA	-	0.43	0.32	0.37	0.32	0.23	0.27
MAMS	LLaMA-3	FT Blended	0.67	0.46	0.54	0.62	0.42	0.50
MAMS	LLaMA-3	FT Composite	0.74	0.69	0.71	0.69	0.65	0.67
MAMS	LLaMA-3	FT Novel	0.32	0.22	0.26	0.24	0.16	0.19
MAMS	LLaMA-3	Generic ICL	0.19	0.32	0.24	0.16	0.28	0.21
MAMS	LLaMA-3	ICL with sampling	0.54	0.62	0.58	0.50	0.57	0.53
MAMS	Mistral	FT Blended	0.68	0.72	0.70	0.63	0.67	0.65
MAMS	Mistral	FT Composite	0.71	0.76	0.73	0.67	0.71	0.69
MAMS	Mistral	FT Novel	0.41	0.27	0.33	0.32	0.22	0.26
MAMS	Mistral	Generic ICL	0.33	0.46	0.39	0.27	0.37	0.31
MAMS	Mistral	ICL with sampling	0.50	0.51	0.50	0.44	0.45	0.45
MAMS	PyABSA	-	0.77	0.83	0.80	0.74	0.80	0.77
Novel (ABSA-Sport)	LLaMA-3	FT Blended	0.52	0.54	0.53	0.37	0.39	0.38
Novel (ABSA-Sport)	LLaMA-3	FT Composite	0.35	0.33	0.34	0.27	0.26	0.26
Novel (ABSA-Sport)	LLaMA-3	FT Novel	0.54	0.54	0.54	0.37	0.38	0.37
Novel (ABSA-Sport)	LLaMA-3	Generic ICL	0.33	0.51	0.40	0.23	0.35	0.27
Novel (ABSA-Sport)	LLaMA-3	ICL with sampling	0.45	0.54	0.49	0.35	0.42	0.38
Novel (ABSA-Sport)	Mistral	FT Blended	0.49	0.53	0.51	0.35	0.38	0.36
Novel (ABSA-Sport)	Mistral	FT Composite	0.35	0.45	0.39	0.26	0.34	0.30
Novel (ABSA-Sport)	Mistral	FT Novel	0.55	0.54	0.55	0.38	0.38	0.38
Novel (ABSA-Sport)	Mistral	Generic ICL	0.21	0.44	0.29	0.14	0.30	0.19
Novel (ABSA-Sport)	Mistral	ICL with sampling	0.52	0.50	0.51	0.41	0.39	0.40
Novel (ABSA-Sport)	PyABSA	-	0.33	0.27	0.30	0.23	0.19	0.21

Developing Japanese CLIP Models Leveraging an Open-weight LLM for Large-scale Dataset Translation

Issa Sugiura[♣,‡], **Shuhei Kurita**[◇,‡], **Yusuke Oda**[‡],
Daisuke Kawahara[♠,‡], **Naoaki Okazaki**[♡,‡]
[♣]Kyoto University, [‡]NII LLMC, [◇]National Institute of Informatics,
[♠]Waseda University, [♡]Institute of Science Tokyo
sugiura.issa.q29@kyoto-u.jp, {skurita, odashi}@nii.ac.jp
dkw@waseda.jp, okazaki@c.titech.ac.jp

Abstract

CLIP is a foundational model that bridges images and text, widely adopted as a key component in numerous vision-language models. However, the lack of large-scale open Japanese image-text pairs poses a significant barrier to the development of Japanese vision-language models. In this study, we constructed a Japanese image-text pair dataset with 1.5 billion examples using machine translation with open-weight LLMs and pre-trained Japanese CLIP models on the dataset. The performance of the pre-trained models was evaluated across seven benchmark datasets, achieving competitive average scores compared to models of similar size without the need for extensive data curation. However, the results also revealed relatively low performance on tasks specific to Japanese culture, highlighting the limitations of translation-based approaches in capturing cultural nuances. Our dataset[1], models[2], and code[3] are publicly available.

1 Introduction

Contrastive Language-Image Pre-training (CLIP) (Radford et al., 2021) has emerged as a powerful framework for aligning images and text within a shared embedding space. By leveraging contrastive learning, CLIP has demonstrated remarkable capability in bridging visual and textual modalities, thereby being adopted in numerous multimodal models such as visual-language models and diffusion models (Liu et al., 2023; Lin et al., 2024; Ramesh et al., 2022).

While the size and quality of the pre-training dataset is critical for CLIP's performance (Cherti et al., 2023; Xu et al., 2024), the availability of large-scale, high-quality Japanese image-text pairs remains limited, posing challenges for advancing research of Japanese vision-language models. As of this writing, the largest publicly available Japanese dataset is the Japanese subset of ReLAION-5B (Schuhmann et al., 2022), comprising approximately 120 million image-text pairs. This size is smaller than the 2.1 billion image-text pairs available in the English subset of ReLAION-5B, highlighting a gap in data size. Moreover, while the English subset is filtered using OpenAI's CLIP, which has high performance, the Japanese subset is filtered using mCLIP (Chen et al., 2023a), where the filtering quality may be suboptimal due to mCLIP's lower performance on Japanese.

To construct large-scale Japanese image-text pair datasets, there are two primary approaches: web crawling using resources such as Common Crawl (Schuhmann et al., 2022) and translating existing English datasets. However, web crawling presents challenges due to the relatively small proportion of Japanese web pages in Common Crawl, which account for only about 5% compared to the about 43% occupied by English pages[4], indicating a nearly ninefold disparity. Consequently, machine translation emerges as a viable alternative.

In this paper, we constructed a dataset of 1.5 billion Japanese image-text pairs by leveraging open-weight LLMs for translation. We also pre-trained Japanese CLIP models using the constructed dataset to assess its effectiveness. Our experimental evaluations demonstrate that our models achieve competitive performance across various benchmark datasets, compared to other models of similar size. However, the performance on tasks related to Japanese culture was relatively low, highlighting the limitations of translation-based approaches in effectively enhancing understanding of Japanese culture.

[1] https://huggingface.co/llm-jp/relaion2B-en-research-safe-japanese-translation
[2] https://huggingface.co/llm-jp/llm-jp-clip-vit-base-patch16, https://huggingface.co/llm-jp/llm-jp-clip-vit-large-patch14
[3] https://github.com/llm-jp/clip-eval
[4] https://commoncrawl.github.io/cc-crawl-statistics

Proceedings of the 2025 Conference of the Nations of the Americas Chapter of the Association for Computational Linguistics: Human Language Technologies (Volume 4: Student Research Workshop), pages 162–170
April 30 - May 1, 2025

English Caption	Japanese Caption
Iron Man Movie Poster	アイアンマン映画ポスター
Unique 14k Gold Yellow and Blue Diamond Engagement Ring 2.64ct.	ユニークな14金イエローゴールドとブルーダイヤの婚約指輪 2.64ct.
Hot Chocolate With Marshmallows, Warm Happiness To Soon Follow	マシュマロ入りホットチョコレート、まもなく幸せが訪れる。
Herd of cows on alpine pasture among mountains in Alps, northern Italy. Stock Photo	アルプス北部、イタリアのアルプス山脈の山々の中にある高地草地に群れでいる牛の写真

Table 1: Examples of original English captions of ReLAION-5B and their Japanese translations by gemma.

2 Constructing a Japanese Image-Text Pair Dataset

To construct a Japanese image-text pair dataset, we translated the captions of the English subset of ReLAION-5B[5] into Japanese using gemma-2-9b-it[6], a high-performance open-weight LLM. ReLAION-5B is a refined version of LAION-5B (Schuhmann et al., 2022), with Child Sexual Abuse Material (CSAM) removed. It is a large-scale dataset of image-text pairs, where images and their corresponding IMG-alt text are collected from Common Crawl and filtered using existing CLIP models. The dataset is divided into three subsets: English, multilingual, and no-language.

To enable the rapid translation of large datasets, we developed `text2dataset`[7], a translation tool for LLMs. This tool utilizes `vLLM` (Kwon et al., 2023), a fast LLM inference library, to efficiently translate large-scale English datasets into Japanese.

Prompt To translate text using LLMs, it is crucial to provide both the text for translation and a clear instruction prompt (Zhu et al., 2024). In this study, we used the following prompt:

```
You are an excellent English-
Japanese translator. Please
translate the following sentence
into Japanese.\n You must output
only the translation.\n Sentence
:{passage}\n Translation:
```

The `{passage}` is replaced with the source text for translation. The LLM is then expected to generate the translated text based on this prompt.

[5]https://laion.ai/blog/relaion-5b
[6]https://huggingface.co/google/gemma-2-9b-it
[7]https://github.com/llm-jp/text2dataset

Translation Results We translated the entire captions of the English subset of ReLAION-5B, consisting of 2,097,693,557 examples. This process was completed in about 9 days using 32 NVIDIA A100 40GB GPUs.

Table 1 shows translated examples. It is evident that the English captions were successfully translated into Japanese. However, a manual check of the first 10,000 examples revealed some translation issues. Despite explicitly specifying the target language in the prompt, there were examples where the translation was incorrectly performed into Chinese or Korean, which accounted for about 1% of the cases. Additionally, a phenomenon specific to instruction-tuned LLMs was observed: for example, an expression like "`Please let me know if you have any questions.`" was added at the end of the translated text, which accounts for about 0.1% of the examples. These issues could be improved by utilizing higher-performance translation LLMs or applying post-processing to the translation results. We leave them as future work.

We used `img2dataset` (Beaumont, 2021) to download images. Due to issues such as broken URL links or preprocessing failures, the success rate of downloading was approximately 70%, resulting in a final dataset of 1,451,957,221 Japanese image-text pairs.

3 Training CLIP

We describe the training settings of llm-jp-clip-ViT-B/16 as our default model in this section.

We pre-trained CLIP models using the constructed dataset. In this study, we used ViT-B/16 (Dosovitskiy et al., 2021) as the image encoder and $\text{RoBERTa}_{\text{BASE}}$ (Liu et al., 2019) as the text encoder. The output dimension of each encoder was set to 512, and both were trained from

English Template	Japanese Template
a photo of the {}	{}の写真
a sketch of a {}	{}のスケッチ
a photo of the cool {}	かっこいい{}の写真

Table 2: Examples of prompt template.

Dataset	Examples	Classes	Language
Image Classification			
ImageNet	50,000	1,000	En
Recruit	7,654	161	Ja
CIFAR10	10,000	10	En
CIFAR100	10,000	100	En
Food101	25,250	101	En
Caltech101	8,677	101	En
Image-Text Retrieval			
XM3600	3,600	–	En, Ja, etc

Table 3: Details of evaluation datasets.

scratch. We used the `llm-jp-tokenizer`[8] as the base tokenizer and applied custom modifications tailored for CLIP. The text encoder's maximum context length was set to 76 tokens. The image resolution was set to 224 × 224.

For optimization, we used AdamW with hyperparameters of $\beta_1 = 0.9$, $\beta_2 = 0.98$, and $\epsilon = 10^{-6}$. Learning rate scheduling consisted of 2,000 steps of linear warmup followed by cosine decay, with a peak learning rate of 5.0×10^{-4} and a minimum learning rate of 0.0. We trained the model for 9 epochs, processing a total of 13 billion examples.

We employed the contrastive loss function proposed by Radford et al. (2021). The batch size was set to 8,192, with gradient accumulation over four steps. Notably, the accumulated loss differs from the contrastive loss computed directly with a batch size of 32,768.

We used `OpenCLIP` (Ilharco et al., 2021) as the training framework and trained the model on 16 NVIDIA H100 80GB GPUs, requiring two weeks for training.

4 Evaluation

We evaluated the performance of our models by comparing it with Japanese and multilingual baseline CLIP models on zero-shot image classification and image-text retrieval tasks.

4.1 Evaluation Settings

Zero-shot Image Classification We followed the evaluation methodology proposed by Radford et al. (2021) for zero-shot image classification. First, we convert class labels corresponding to the target images into natural language sentences using prompt templates. For example, a label will be inserted into the placeholder `{label}` in a template "`a photo of a {label}`" to convert the label into a natural sentence. Next, we compute the similarity scores between images and texts, and the label with the highest similarity is selected as the predicted class for the image. In this study, we used Japanese prompt templates provided by `japanese-clip` (Shing et al., 2022). Table 2 shows examples of the Japanese templates used in this experiment. For evaluation, we used accuracy@1 as the metric.

Zero-shot Image-Text Retrieval Image-text retrieval involves two main tasks: text-to-image retrieval and image-to-text retrieval. In text-to-image retrieval, the goal is to find the most relevant images based on a textual query by computing the similarity between the text embedding and the embeddings of all candidate images, then ranking the images accordingly. In contrast, image-to-text retrieval aims to retrieve the most relevant textual descriptions for a given image query. For evaluation, we used recall@1 as the metric.

Evaluation Datasets Table 3 provides details of the evaluation datasets used in our experiments.

In zero-shot image classification task, we used ImageNet-1K (Deng et al., 2009), Recruit[9], CIFAR10 (Krizhevsky, 2009), CIFAR100 (Krizhevsky, 2009), Food101 (Bossard et al., 2014), and Caltech101 (Li et al., 2022). For ImageNet, we used Japanese class labels from `japanese-clip`. Recruit consists of four image classification tasks related to concepts and objects unique to Japan: jafood101, jaflower30, jafacility20, and jalandmark10, with 7,586 images successfully retrieved from 7,654. For CIFAR10, CIFAR100, Food101, and Caltech101, class labels were translated into Japanese using DeepL.

In zero-shot image-text retrieval task, we used CrossModal-3600 (XM3600) (Thapliyal et al., 2022). XM3600 is a dataset containing multilingual annotations for 3,600 images. In this exper-

[8] https://github.com/llm-jp/llm-jp-tokenizer

[9] https://huggingface.co/datasets/recruit-jp/japanese-image-classification-evaluation-dataset

Model	# Params (M)	Image Classification						Retrieval		Avg.
		ImageNet	Recruit	CIFAR10	CIFAR100	Food101	Caltech101	XM3600 I→T	XM3600 T→I	
Japanese CLIP										
Rinna ViT-B/16	196	50.6	39.9	90.7	64.0	53.2	84.6	53.8	54.0	61.4
Rinna ViT-B/16 cloob	196	54.6	41.6	88.2	60.3	57.2	80.2	53.4	53.4	61.1
LY ViT-B/16	196	52.0	**83.8**	96.3	76.7	73.9	**88.4**	**76.9**	**78.0**	**78.3**
llm-jp-clip-ViT-B/16	248	54.2	59.4	91.8	69.2	82.2	85.6	73.6	72.7	73.6
StabilityAI ViT-L/16	414	**62.4**	70.5	97.6	**84.1**	74.0	86.7	67.3	66.0	76.1
llm-jp-clip-ViT-L/14	467	59.5	62.9	96.4	77.0	**88.2**	87.8	74.1	74.1	77.5
Multilingual CLIP										
SigLIP B/16-256 multi	370	51.9	71.2	92.4	65.8	78.6	85.6	45.9	43.0	66.8
jina-clip-v2	865	35.8	48.1	95.1	58.3	52.0	69.4	67.3	66.4	61.6
LAION ViT-H/14 multi	1193	53.0	74.5	**97.9**	78.4	74.3	85.1	75.0	72.0	76.3

Table 4: Performance of each model in zero-shot image classification and image-text retrieval tasks. **Bold** indicates first place, and underline indicates second place.

Model	# Params (M)	Recruit				
		jafacility20	jafood101	jaflower30	jalandmark10	Overall
Japanese CLIP						
Rinna ViT-B/16	196	63.0	28.4	56.5	60.3	39.9
Rinna ViT-B/16 cloob	196	61.5	27.3	63.5	69.4	41.6
LY ViT-B/16	196	**82.0**	**83.8**	**90.5**	**91.8**	**83.8**
llm-jp-clip-ViT-B/16	248	72.4	52.7	67.0	82.2	59.4
StabilityAI ViT-L/16	414	70.8	65.1	89.0	78.6	70.5
llm-jp-clip-ViT-L/14	467	75.3	55.8	73.5	84.7	62.9
Multilingual CLIP						
SigLIP B/16-256 multi	370	64.9	70.7	88.5	68.0	71.2
jina-clip-v2	865	80.0	47.1	44.0	48.5	48.1
LAION ViT-H/14 multi	1193	80.5	69.1	85.4	89.1	74.5

Table 5: Performance of each model in zero-shot image classification across each subtask of Recruit.

iment, we used the first Japanese annotations assigned to each image.

Baseline Models To compare the performance of our models, we used Japanese CLIP and multilingual CLIP models. For Japanese CLIP models, we used Rinna ViT-B/16 (Sawada et al., 2024), Rinna ViT-B/16 cloob (Sawada et al., 2024), LY ViT-B/16 (Shuhei et al., 2024), and StabilityAI ViT-L/16 (Shing and Akiba, 2023). For multilingual CLIP models, we used SigLIP B/16-256 multi (Zhai et al., 2023), jina-clip-v2 (Koukounas et al., 2024), and LAION ViT-H/14 multi (Schuhmann et al., 2022). Details of the baseline models can be found in Appendix A.

4.2 Results

The performance of each model is shown in Table 4. Our llm-jp-clip-ViT-B/16 model achieves the second highest average score among Japanese CLIP models of similar size, following LY ViT-B/16. On ImageNet, a key benchmark dataset for CLIP, llm-jp-clip-ViT-B/16 achieved a high score of 54.2, second only to Rinna ViT-B/16 cloob's 54.6 among models of similar size. However, Rinna ViT-B/16 cloob, which was trained on the relatively small CC12M (Changpinyo et al., 2021) dataset, shows limited generalization performance outside ImageNet. We suspect that this is due to the limited diversity and scale of CC12M, which restricts the ability of the Rinna ViT-B/16 cloob to generalize

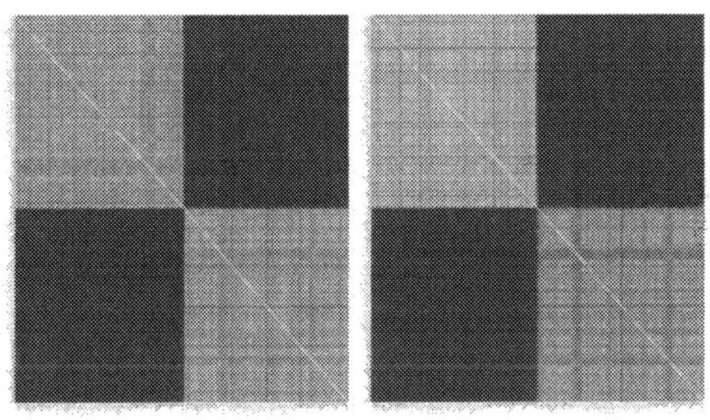

Figure 1: Cosine similarity matrices of text and image embeddings. Left: LY ViT-B/16. Right: llm-jp-clip-ViT-B/16. The top-left block represents similarities among text embeddings, the bottom-right block represents similarities among image embeddings, and the top-right/bottom-left blocks represent similarities between text and image embeddings. Brighter colors indicate higher similarity.

Image Encoder	ImageNet	XM3600	
		I → T	T → I
Full Scratch	**54.2**	**73.6**	**72.7**
Continued	52.9	71.6	71.7
LiT	52.7	71.7	70.9

Table 6: Effect of training settings of image encoders.

beyond ImageNet.

On Recruit, which contains images specific to Japanese culture, its score was more than 30 points lower compared to LY ViT-B/16. The performance of each model in zero-shot image classification across each subtask of Recruit is shown in Table 5. We can observe that llm-jp-clip-ViT-B/16 significantly underperforms compared to LY ViT-B/16 on jafood101.

To investigate the cause of this performance gap, we visualized and analyzed the embeddings of LY ViT-B/16 and llm-jp-clip-ViT-B/16. We calculated the cosine similarities between all combinations of text and image embeddings for each class within jafood101. The similarity matrices for both models are shown in Figure 1. We can observe that LY ViT-B/16 separates positive and negative text embeddings more clearly than llm-jp-clip-ViT-B/16. This performance gap may be due to the lack of examples specific to Japanese culture in the translation data, leading to poor results on Recruit, which contains images specific to Japanese such as "交番" (police station), "おでん" (oden, a Japanese fishcake stew), and "鎌倉大仏" (the Great Buddha of Kamakura).

4.3 Ablation Study on Image Encoder

We performed several ablation studies to determine the optimal configuration of the image encoder.

Effect of Training Settings We experimented with the following three training settings for the image encoder: (1) Training from scratch, (2) Continued pre-training, and (3) Pre-training only the text encoder with a frozen pre-trained image encoder (Locked-image Tuning; LiT (Zhai et al., 2022)). For the continued pre-training and LiT settings, we initialized the weights of the image encoder model using the LAION's CLIP[10]. For all settings, the text encoder was trained from scratch. To prevent loss spikes in both the continued pre-training and LiT settings, the peak learning rate was reduced to 1.0×10^{-4}. Figure 2 shows the accuracy curve of ImageNet for each setting, and Table 6 reports the final performance. Similarly to previous research (Zhai et al., 2022), LiT exhibited a significant performance improvement in the early stages of training, but subsequent improvements were gradual. Although the initial performance of ImageNet was low when training from scratch, substantial performance improvements were observed as training progressed, surpassing both continued training and LiT settings in the end.

[10]https://huggingface.co/laion/CLIP-ViT-B-16-laion2B-s34B-b88K/tree/main

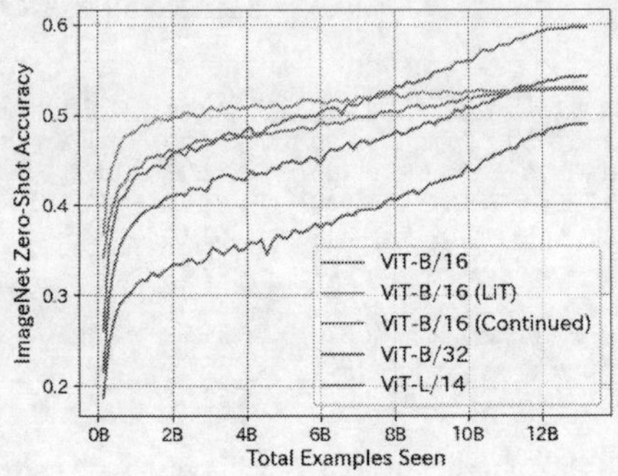

Figure 2: Accuracy curve of ImageNet zero-shot image classification.

Effect of Model Size We compared the performance of ViT-B/16 and ViT-L/14. All settings other than the image encoder were kept the same. The results are shown in Table 4. In all tasks, ViT-L/14 outperformed ViT-B/16. This reconfirmed that increasing the model size leads to better performance, as observed in the previous study (Cherti et al., 2023).

Effect of Patch Size We examined the performance differences on ImageNet caused by different patch size settings in the image encoder. In this study, we evaluated ViT-B/32 and ViT-B/16. For ViT-B/32, the batch size was set to 16,384, with gradient accumulation over two steps, and the peak learning rate set to 1.0×10^{-3}. Other settings were kept the same as those for ViT-B/16. The results of accuracy curve on ImageNet are shown in Figure 2. ViT-B/16 consistently outperformed ViT-B/32, aligning with previous findings (Radford et al., 2021), where smaller patch sizes yielded better performance.

5 Conclusion

In this study, we constructed a large-scale Japanese image-text dataset using translation with open-weight LLMs and pre-trained Japanese CLIP models on the dataset. The results demonstrated competitive performance in the average score across the benchmark datasets compared to models of similar size. However, the performance on tasks related to Japanese culture was relatively low, highlighting the limitations of translation-based approaches in capturing cultural nuances. Future work includes building more diverse and high-quality Japanese image-text datasets and further improving the performance of Japanese CLIP models.

Limitations

In this study, we used open-weight LLMs for translation. While these models require GPUs, making large-scale processing costly, recent advancements have enabled access to smaller, high-performing LLMs that offer a more cost-effective alternative. For instance, assuming an average caption length of 50 characters, translating 2.1 billion examples with DeepL would cost approximately 260M JPY. In contrast, using an open-weight LLM reduced the cost to just 500K–1M JPY.

Acknowledgments

In this research work, we used the "mdx: a platform for building data-empowered society".

References

Romain Beaumont. 2021. img2dataset: Easily turn large sets of image urls to an image dataset.

Lukas Bossard, Matthieu Guillaumin, and Luc Van Gool. 2014. Food-101 – mining discriminative components with random forests. In *Computer Vision – ECCV 2014*, pages 446–461.

Soravit Changpinyo, Piyush Sharma, Nan Ding, and Radu Soricut. 2021. Conceptual 12m: Pushing web-scale image-text pre-training to recognize long-tail visual concepts. In *2021 IEEE/CVF Conference on Computer Vision and Pattern Recognition (CVPR)*, pages 3557–3567.

Guanhua Chen, Lu Hou, Yun Chen, Wenliang Dai, Lifeng Shang, Xin Jiang, Qun Liu, Jia Pan, and Wenping Wang. 2023a. mCLIP: Multilingual CLIP via cross-lingual transfer. In *Proceedings of the 61st Annual Meeting of the Association for Computational Linguistics (Volume 1: Long Papers)*, pages 13028–13043. Association for Computational Linguistics.

Xi Chen, Xiao Wang, Soravit Changpinyo, AJ Piergiovanni, Piotr Padlewski, Daniel Salz, Sebastian Goodman, Adam Grycner, Basil Mustafa, Lucas Beyer, Alexander Kolesnikov, Joan Puigcerver, Nan Ding, Keran Rong, Hassan Akbari, Gaurav Mishra, Linting Xue, Ashish Thapliyal, James Bradbury, Weicheng Kuo, Mojtaba Seyedhosseini, Chao Jia, Burcu Karagol Ayan, Carlos Riquelme, Andreas Steiner, Anelia Angelova, Xiaohua Zhai, Neil Houlsby, and Radu Soricut. 2023b. Pali: A jointly-scaled multilingual language-image model. *Preprint*, arXiv:2209.06794.

Mehdi Cherti, Romain Beaumont, Ross Wightman, Mitchell Wortsman, Gabriel Ilharco, Cade Gordon, Christoph Schuhmann, Ludwig Schmidt, and Jenia Jitsev. 2023. Reproducible scaling laws for contrastive language-image learning. In *2023 IEEE/CVF Conference on Computer Vision and Pattern Recognition (CVPR)*, pages 2818–2829.

Jia Deng, Wei Dong, Richard Socher, Li-Jia Li, Kai Li, and Li Fei-Fei. 2009. ImageNet: A large-scale hierarchical image database. In *2009 IEEE Conference on Computer Vision and Pattern Recognition*, pages 248–255.

Alexey Dosovitskiy, Lucas Beyer, Alexander Kolesnikov, Dirk Weissenborn, Xiaohua Zhai, Thomas Unterthiner, Mostafa Dehghani, Matthias Minderer, Georg Heigold, Sylvain Gelly, Jakob Uszkoreit, and Neil Houlsby. 2021. An image is worth 16x16 words: Transformers for image recognition at scale. In *International Conference on Learning Representations*.

Alex Fang, Albin Madappally Jose, Amit Jain, Ludwig Schmidt, Alexander Toshev, and Vaishaal Shankar. 2023. Data filtering networks. *Preprint*, arXiv:2309.17425.

Samir Yitzhak Gadre, Gabriel Ilharco, Alex Fang, Jonathan Hayase, Georgios Smyrnis, Thao Nguyen, Ryan Marten, Mitchell Wortsman, Dhruba Ghosh, Jieyu Zhang, Eyal Orgad, Rahim Entezari, Giannis Daras, Sarah Pratt, Vivek Ramanujan, Yonatan Bitton, Kalyani Marathe, Stephen Mussmann, Richard Vencu, Mehdi Cherti, Ranjay Krishna, Pang Wei W Koh, Olga Saukh, Alexander J Ratner, Shuran Song, Hannaneh Hajishirzi, Ali Farhadi, Romain Beaumont, Sewoong Oh, Alex Dimakis, Jenia Jitsev, Yair Carmon, Vaishaal Shankar, and Ludwig Schmidt. 2023. Datacomp: In search of the next generation of multimodal datasets. In *Advances in Neural Information Processing Systems*, volume 36, pages 27092–27112.

Gabriel Ilharco, Mitchell Wortsman, Ross Wightman, Cade Gordon, Nicholas Carlini, Rohan Taori, Achal Dave, Vaishaal Shankar, Hongseok Namkoong, John Miller, Hannaneh Hajishirzi, Ali Farhadi, and Ludwig Schmidt. 2021. OpenCLIP.

Andreas Koukounas, Georgios Mastrapas, Bo Wang, Mohammad Kalim Akram, Sedigheh Eslami, Michael Günther, Isabelle Mohr, Saba Sturua, Scott

Martens, Nan Wang, and Han Xiao. 2024. jina-clip-v2: Multilingual multimodal embeddings for text and images. *Preprint*, arXiv:2412.08802.

Alex Krizhevsky. 2009. Learning multiple layers of features from tiny images.

Woosuk Kwon, Zhuohan Li, Siyuan Zhuang, Ying Sheng, Lianmin Zheng, Cody Hao Yu, Joseph Gonzalez, Hao Zhang, and Ion Stoica. 2023. Efficient memory management for large language model serving with pagedattention. In *Proceedings of the 29th Symposium on Operating Systems Principles*, page 611–626.

Fei-Fei Li, Marco Andreeto, Marc'Aurelio Ranzato, and Pietro Perona. 2022. Caltech 101.

Ji Lin, Hongxu Yin, Wei Ping, Pavlo Molchanov, Mohammad Shoeybi, and Song Han. 2024. VILA: On pre-training for visual language models. In *2024 IEEE/CVF Conference on Computer Vision and Pattern Recognition (CVPR)*, pages 26679–26689.

Tsung-Yi Lin, Michael Maire, Serge Belongie, James Hays, Pietro Perona, Deva Ramanan, Piotr Dollár, and C. Lawrence Zitnick. 2014. Microsoft COCO: Common objects in context. In *Computer Vision – ECCV 2014*, pages 740–755.

Haotian Liu, Chunyuan Li, Qingyang Wu, and Yong Jae Lee. 2023. Visual instruction tuning. In *Advances in Neural Information Processing Systems*, volume 36, pages 34892–34916.

Yinhan Liu, Myle Ott, Naman Goyal, Jingfei Du, Mandar Joshi, Danqi Chen, Omer Levy, Mike Lewis, Luke Zettlemoyer, and Veselin Stoyanov. 2019. RoBERTa: A robustly optimized bert pretraining approach. *Preprint*, arXiv:1907.11692.

Alec Radford, Jong Wook Kim, Chris Hallacy, Aditya Ramesh, Gabriel Goh, Sandhini Agarwal, Girish Sastry, Amanda Askell, Pamela Mishkin, Jack Clark, Gretchen Krueger, and Ilya Sutskever. 2021. Learning transferable visual models from natural language supervision. In *Proceedings of the 38th International Conference on Machine Learning*, volume 139, pages 8748–8763.

Aditya Ramesh, Prafulla Dhariwal, Alex Nichol, Casey Chu, and Mark Chen. 2022. Hierarchical text-conditional image generation with clip latents. *Preprint*, arXiv:2204.06125.

Kei Sawada, Tianyu Zhao, Makoto Shing, Kentaro Mitsui, Akio Kaga, Yukiya Hono, Toshiaki Wakatsuki, and Koh Mitsuda. 2024. Release of pre-trained models for the Japanese language. In *Proceedings of the 2024 Joint International Conference on Computational Linguistics, Language Resources and Evaluation (LREC-COLING 2024)*, pages 13898–13905.

Christoph Schuhmann, Romain Beaumont, Richard Vencu, Cade W Gordon, Ross Wightman, Mehdi Cherti, Theo Coombes, Aarush Katta, Clayton Mullis, Mitchell Wortsman, Patrick Schramowski, Srivatsa R Kundurthy, Katherine Crowson, Ludwig Schmidt, Robert Kaczmarczyk, and Jenia Jitsev. 2022. LAION-5B: An open large-scale dataset for training next generation image-text models. In *Thirty-sixth Conference on Neural Information Processing Systems Datasets and Benchmarks Track*.

Makoto Shing and Takuya Akiba. 2023. Japanese Stable CLIP ViT-L/16.

Makoto Shing, Tianyu Zhao, and Kei Sawada. 2022. japanese-clip.

Yokoo Shuhei, Okada Shuntaro, Zhu Peifei, Nishimura Shuhei, and Takayama Naoki. 2024. CLIP Japanese Base.

Ashish V. Thapliyal, Jordi Pont Tuset, Xi Chen, and Radu Soricut. 2022. Crossmodal-3600: A massively multilingual multimodal evaluation dataset. In *Proceedings of the 2022 Conference on Empirical Methods in Natural Language Processing*, pages 715–729.

Bart Thomee, David A. Shamma, Gerald Friedland, Benjamin Elizalde, Karl Ni, Douglas Poland, Damian Borth, and Li-Jia Li. 2016. YFCC100M: the new data in multimedia research. *Commun. ACM*, 59(2):64–73.

Hu Xu, Saining Xie, Xiaoqing Tan, Po-Yao Huang, Russell Howes, Vasu Sharma, Shang-Wen Li, Gargi Ghosh, Luke Zettlemoyer, and Christoph Feichtenhofer. 2024. Demystifying CLIP data. In *The Twelfth International Conference on Learning Representations*.

Xiaohua Zhai, Basil Mustafa, Alexander Kolesnikov, and Lucas Beyer. 2023. Sigmoid loss for language image pre-training. In *2023 IEEE/CVF International Conference on Computer Vision (ICCV)*, pages 11941–11952.

Xiaohua Zhai, Xiao Wang, Basil Mustafa, Andreas Steiner, Daniel Keysers, Alexander Kolesnikov, and Lucas Beyer. 2022. LiT: Zero-shot transfer with locked-image text tuning. In *2022 IEEE/CVF Conference on Computer Vision and Pattern Recognition (CVPR)*, pages 18102–18112.

Wenhao Zhu, Hongyi Liu, Qingxiu Dong, Jingjing Xu, Shujian Huang, Lingpeng Kong, Jiajun Chen, and Lei Li. 2024. Multilingual machine translation with large language models: Empirical results and analysis. In *Findings of the Association for Computational Linguistics: NAACL 2024*, pages 2765–2781.

A Details of Baseline Models

Table 7 shows the details of the baseline models: Rinna ViT-B/16[11], Rinna ViT-B/16 cloob[12], LY ViT-B/16[13], StabilityAI ViT-L/16[14], SigLIP B/16-256 multi[15], jina-clip-v2[16], and LAION ViT-H/14 multi[17].

[11]https://huggingface.co/rinna/japanese-clip-vit-b-16

[12]https://huggingface.co/rinna/japanese-cloob-vit-b-16

[13]https://huggingface.co/line-corporation/clip-japanese-base

[14]https://huggingface.co/stabilityai/japanese-stable-clip-vit-l-16

[15]https://huggingface.co/google/siglip-base-patch16-256-multilingual

[16]https://huggingface.co/jinaai/jina-clip-v2

[17]https://huggingface.co/laion/CLIP-ViT-H-14-frozen-xlm-roberta-large-laion5B-s13B-b90k

Model	# Params (M)	Training Dataset
Japanese CLIP		
Rinna ViT-B/16	196	CC12M (Changpinyo et al., 2021)
Rinna ViT-B/16 cloob	196	CC12M
LY ViT-B/16	196	CC12M, YFCC100M (Thomee et al., 2016), Common Crawl†
StabilityAI ViT-L/16	414	CC12M, MS-COCO (Lin et al., 2014)
Multilingual CLIP		
SigLIP B/16-256 multi	370	WebLI† (Chen et al., 2023b)
jina-clip-v2	865	DFN (Fang et al., 2023), CommonPool (Gadre et al., 2023)
LAION ViT-H/14 multi	1193	LAION-5B (Schuhmann et al., 2022)

Table 7: Details of the baseline models used in the experiment. Datasets marked with † are not publicly available. We report only the primary dataset used by the developers.

Self-Vocabularizing Training for Neural Machine Translation

Pin-Jie Lin[♠] **Ernie Chang**[♦] **Yangyang Shi**[♦] **Vikas Chandra**[♦]
[♠]Virginia Tech
[♦]Meta
pinjie@vt.edu, erniecyc@meta.com

Abstract

Past vocabulary learning techniques identify relevant vocabulary before training, relying on statistical and entropy-based assumptions that largely neglect the role of model training. Empirically, we observe that trained translation models are induced to use a byte-pair encoding (BPE) vocabulary subset distinct from the original BPE vocabulary, leading to performance improvements when retrained with the induced vocabulary. In this paper, we analyze this discrepancy in neural machine translation by examining vocabulary and entropy shifts during self-training—where each iteration generates a labeled dataset by pairing source sentences with the model's predictions to define a new vocabulary. Building on these insights, we propose *self-vocabularizing training*, an iterative method that self-selects a smaller, more optimal vocabulary, yielding up to a 1.49 BLEU improvement. Moreover, we find that deeper model architectures lead to both an increase in unique token usage and a 6–8% reduction in vocabulary size.

1 Introduction

Vocabulary construction, also known as vocabularization, is essential for many natural language processing tasks that involve neural networks, including neural machine translation (MT), as highlighted in various studies (Mikolov et al., 2013; Vaswani et al., 2017; Gehrmann et al., 2018; Zhang et al., 2018; Devlin et al., 2019). However, past vocabulary learning techniques rely on corpus statistics such as entropy (Xu et al., 2020) or frequency counts (Sennrich et al., 2016), without considering contextual information or the model's ability to represent it.

Despite the success of vocabularization in improving MT model efficiency (Xu et al., 2020), we observe a discrepancy between the original byte-pair encoding (BPE) vocabulary (Gage, 1994) (V_0), derived from the initial training data, and the BPE vocabulary induced from pseudo-labeled data (V_1) (see Figure 1). This discrepancy is surprising, as it suggests that MT models implicitly learn a pseudo-"optimal" vocabulary (V_1) that is substantially different from the original vocabulary (V_0) and is also smaller in size. For instance, on the IWSLT14 DE-EN dataset, $|V_1|$ is approximately 20% smaller than $|V_0|$. Moreover, MT models retrained with the pseudo vocabulary V_1 outperform those trained on the original vocabulary set. This suggests a need to re-examine the assumptions underlying vocabulary learning techniques such as byte-pair encoding and the marginal utility of vocabularization (Xu et al., 2020), as existing methods may overlook model-data interactions, leaving key optimization factors unaccounted for.

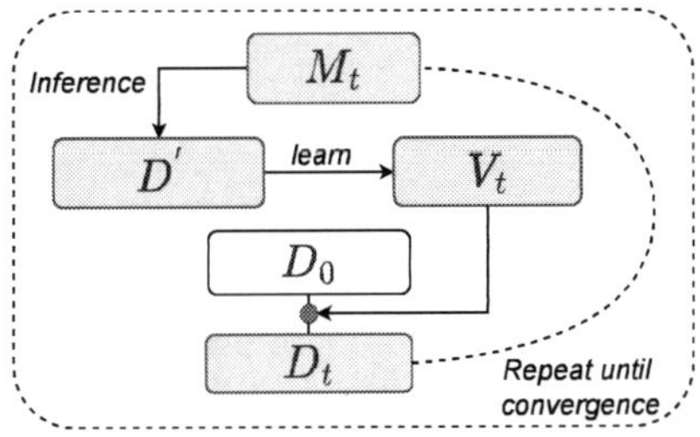

Figure 1: Illustration of self-vocabularizing training: At each iteration, the original dataset D_0 is segmented using vocabulary V_t to form the training set D_t. D_t is then used to train model M_t, which generates a pseudo dataset D'. A new vocabulary set V_{t+1} is derived from D', completing the training loop. This process repeats until no further improvements are observed.

In this paper, we aim to understand this discrepancy in neural machine translation models by analyzing shifts in vocabulary and entropy during self-training. To this end, we conduct experiments on two language tasks, comparing the vocabulary sets learned from the original training data and the pseudo-labeled data. Our results suggest limited overlap between the two vocabularies and that pseudo data induces a more optimal vocabulary,

Proceedings of the 2025 Conference of the Nations of the Americas Chapter of the Association for Computational Linguistics: Human Language Technologies (Volume 4: Student Research Workshop), pages 171–177

enabling further improvements. Furthermore, our findings indicate that the decoder has a limited impact on this vocabulary shift, whereas encoder-based interactions play a crucial role in entropy reduction. This suggests that future vocabulary induction methods should focus more on the cross-attention module. Finally, our study has implications for defining an optimal vocabulary set in language generation.

This preliminary study also introduces a simple yet effective technique: iterative self-training to self-select a more optimal vocabulary set for performance gains.

In summary, this paper makes the following contributions: (1) We identify a discrepancy between the optimal and pseudo-labeled vocabulary derived from MT models. (2) We analyze shifts in vocabulary and entropy during self-training. (3) We propose a simple approach to obtain a competitive vocabulary set and introduce a self-vocabularizing training algorithm that improves performance.

2 Iterative Self-Vocabularization

Current vocabularization techniques adopt two contrasting perspectives: (1) Focusing on frequency or entropy statistics to avoid the computational cost of trial training (Xu et al., 2020), which often neglects important parameters and interactions in the process. (2) Obtaining a more optimal vocabulary set through training (Salesky et al., 2020), but at a higher computational cost. This work combines both perspectives by adopting an entropy-based vocabularization approach while utilizing self-training.

In self-training, a base model M_t is trained on the dataset to generate predictions for input sequences, which are then used to update the next iteration of the base model M_{t+1}. This process is repeated iteratively with the supervised loss $\mathcal{L}$ from labeled instances (He et al., 2019), where x and y are the source and target texts, respectively:

$$\mathcal{L} = -\mathbb{E}_{\mathbf{x}\sim p(\mathbf{x})}\mathbb{E}_{\mathbf{y}\sim p_{\theta^*}(\mathbf{y}|\mathbf{x})} \log p_\theta(\mathbf{y}|\mathbf{x}), \quad (1)$$

where $p(\mathbf{x})$ is the empirical data distribution approximated with samples from D, and $p_\theta(\mathbf{y}|\mathbf{x})$ is the conditional distribution defined by the model. The parameter θ^* is randomly initialized at every iteration. For each training iteration at $t+1$, we relearn the BPE vocabulary using the *original source* and the *pseudo target* generated with M_t (i.e., $D' = \{(\mathbf{x}, f_\theta(\mathbf{x}))|\mathbf{x} \in U\}$). Then, M_{t+1} is trained on D_{t+1}, segmented with the newly derived vocabulary V_{t+1}.

Measuring Vocabulary Shifts Subword-based approaches like byte-pair encoding are widely used and have demonstrated strong empirical performance (Sennrich et al., 2016; Al-Rfou et al., 2019; Costa-jussà and Fonollosa, 2016; Lee et al., 2017; Ding et al., 2019; Liu et al., 2020; Ott et al., 2018; Kudo and Richardson, 2018; Wang et al., 2020). These methods construct vocabulary by selecting high-probability subword units.

Following Xu et al. (2020), we define the vocabulary shift as the negative change in entropy normalized by vocabulary size:

$$\frac{-(\mathcal{H}_{M_{t+1}(\mathbf{x})} - \mathcal{H}_{M_t(\mathbf{x})})}{|V_t|}, \quad (2)$$

where $M_{t+1}(\mathbf{x}) \rightarrow V_{t+1}$ and $M_t(\mathbf{x}) \rightarrow V_t$ represent vocabularies from two consecutive training iterations, with sizes $|V_{t+1}|$ and $|V_t|$. The ratio $|V_{t+1}|/|V_t|$ reflects compression in vocabulary size.

Corpus entropy $\mathcal{H}_v$ with vocabulary V is defined as the sum of token entropy, normalized by the average token length:

$$\mathcal{H}_v = -\frac{1}{l_v}\sum_{j\in V} p(j) \log p(j), \quad (3)$$

where $p(j)$ represents the relative frequency of token j in the training corpus, and l_v is the average token length (i.e., the number of characters per token).

3 Experimental Settings

For our experiments, we used the IWSLT14 German-English parallel corpus for both German-to-English (DE-EN) and English-to-German (EN-DE) translation tasks. We preprocessed the data using `MOSES` (Bollmann et al., 2021) and applied byte-pair encoding (BPE) (Sennrich et al., 2016) to construct the vocabulary set.

We trained a transformer-based NMT model using the `fairseq` library (Ott et al., 2019), with six layers, four attention heads, and a hidden size of 1024 dimensions. The Adam optimizer was used with a learning rate of 0.0002 and a batch size of 64. Training lasted for 50 epochs, with exponential learning rate decay and early stopping based on the validation set.

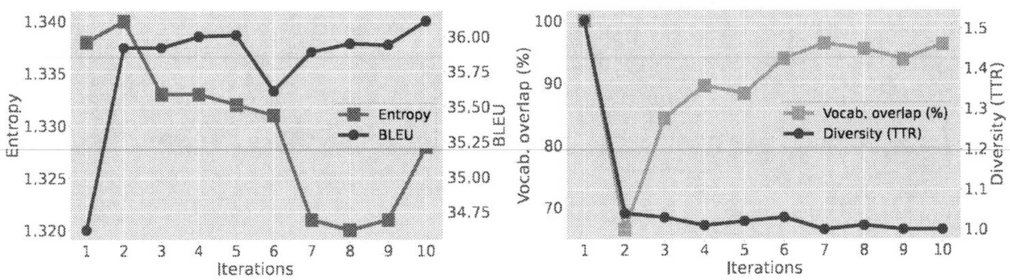

Figure 2: Entropy and performance across self-vocabularizing training iterations. **(Left)** BLEU score (blue) consistently improves across iterations. Meanwhile, the self-learned vocabulary reduces corpus entropy (teal), indicating a better estimation of token distribution. **(Right)** Vocabulary shift measured by vocabulary overlap (orange) between consecutive vocabularies V_t and V_{t-1}, showing that the model initially selects a broad set of subwords before consolidating onto a subset of V_{t-1}[1]. The type-token ratio (TTR) (purple) reflects the diversity of learned semantic units, reported on the training corpus scaled by 1000.

We evaluated model performance using BLEU scores on the test set, comparing against the baseline and other comparable models. For self-training, we ran each iteration until performance converged. In each iteration i, the model was trained from scratch in the self-training step (*ST-i*) for analysis purposes. Results were averaged over three initialization runs with different θ^*.

3.1 Main Results

We first compared the performance of MT models trained with two different approaches: one using a fixed output vocabulary and the other refining the output vocabulary through self-training iterations. As shown in Table 1 and Figure 3, the MT model trained with the self-trained output vocabulary gradually improves with each newly derived vocabulary, achieving up to a 1.3 BLEU point increase after a single iteration. Table 1 further confirms a consistent trend across both language tasks: self-training improves model performance and reduces vocabulary entropy, leading to enhanced fluency and correctness while decreasing vocabulary size.

Beyond translation quality, we also observe lower overall corpus entropy and a smaller vocabulary in the self-trained model (see Figure 2). This suggests that self-training not only enhances translation accuracy but also results in a more efficient model with a compact, more targeted vocabulary—potentially enabling faster and more memory-efficient deployment.

[1]Vocabulary overlaps at firs iteration leverages the identical vocabulary where $V_0 = V_1$.

	BLEU	|V|	Overlap (%)	Fluency	Adequacy
ST-0	34.62	10000	-	2.89	3.21
ST-1	35.92	8950	66.42	3.13	3.46
ST-5	36.01	8892	88.27	3.42	3.87
ST-10	**36.11**	8702	96.19	3.95	4.21

Table 1: Performance comparison of BLEU, vocabulary size ($|V|$), vocabulary overlap (%), fluency, and adequacy on the IWSLT14 DE-EN translation task for **ST-0**, **ST-1**, **ST-5**, and **ST-10** models. Fluency and adequacy scores are segment-level averages on 100 random outputs, rated on a 1-5 scale (5 being the most fluent or correct) (Koehn and Monz, 2006; Freitag et al., 2021). Scores were assigned by three raters and then averaged. Detailed results for IWSLT14 EN-DE are provided in Appendix A.1.

4 Ablations of Self-Vocabularization

4.1 Shifts Across Iterations

In text generation, self-training can enhance the quality of the generated output. However, the impact of the number of self-training iterations on output entropy (i.e., the randomness or unpredictability of the generated text) is not straightforward and depends on the specifics of the model and training data. We therefore examine: (1) corpus entropy and (2) subword-based overlap between the original and self-trained BPE vocabulary.

Corpus Entropy. Increasing the number of self-training iterations allows the model to learn from a progressively smaller set of labeled examples, potentially leading to more coherent and accurate outputs with reduced diversity. In the left plot of Figure 3, we observe that, in general, as entropy gradually decreases, self-training performance improves until the rate of change in both entropy and BLEU slows. Surprisingly, even at the 10th iteration, the model continues to improve its BLEU

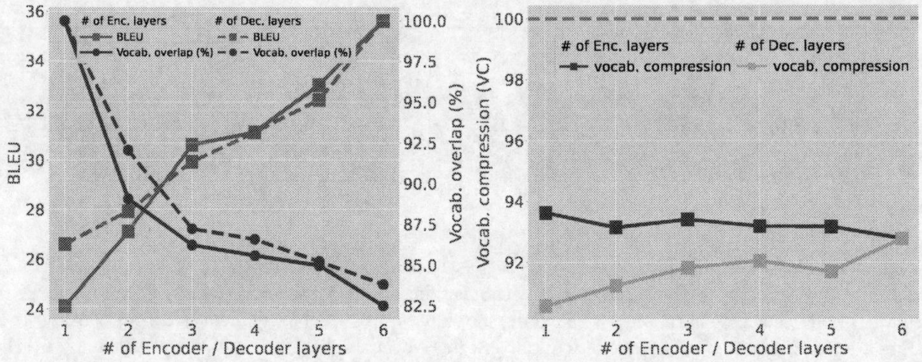

Figure 3: Performance and vocabulary overlap across models with different encoder and decoder depths. (**Left**) As the number of encoder (teal -) or decoder (teal - -) layers increases, BLEU scores consistently improve. However, vocabulary overlap decreases for deeper encoder (blue -) or decoder (blue - -) layers, indicating that deeper models tend to use more unique tokens. (**Right**) Vocabulary compression (VC) across models with varying depths. All models trained with self-vocabularizing training effectively compress the token set. Notably, deeper encoder models (purple) exhibit a smoother reduction in VC rates, whereas deeper decoder models (orange) require more tokens for inference. VC is reported on the test set using models of different depths in either the encoder or decoder, with a single round of self-vocabularizing training.

score.

Vocabulary Overlap ($V_O \cap V_P$). The original BPE vocabulary consists of subword units created by applying BPE to the training data, serving as a fixed vocabulary during training and inference. While the number of self-training iterations does not directly alter the BPE vocabulary (as it is predefined before training), fine-tuning on additional labeled examples can improve model performance, leading to more accurate and diverse outputs that better align with the original BPE vocabulary. Additionally, vocabulary size consistently decreases across iterations. We observe an initial sharp drop of approximately 10% after the first iteration, followed by a gradual reduction in BPE vocabulary size until the 5th iteration (see Figure 2).

4.2 Ablations on Model Architecture

Deeper Model Depth Contributes to Lower Vocabulary Overlap. The number of encoder and decoder layers in a neural network plays a crucial role in determining output coherence and accuracy, which in turn affects the model's output token set. As shown in Figure 3, increasing encoder or decoder layers generally improves BLEU scores. Additionally, vocabulary overlap gradually decreases to approximately 93% as the number of layers increases, following a similar trend observed in Figure 2 at the first iteration. This suggests that deeper architectures allow the model to implicitly select more unique tokens compared to shallow models, with encoders playing a particularly important role in vocabulary selection.

Vocabulary Compression. *Vocabulary compression (VC)* is defined as the ratio of the number of tokens used in the inference output to the number of tokens in the original test set, i.e., $\frac{|V|^{inf.}}{|V|^{test}}$ Figure 3 illustrates the relationship between the number of encoder/decoder layers and VC. All models achieve significant token set compression, reducing vocabulary size by 6% to 8%. Notably, increasing encoder depth results in a smaller token set, whereas increasing decoder depth leads to a larger token set. We conjecture that deeper encoders have a stronger ability to process source sentences and represent them as fixed-length context vectors, enabling the decoder to use fewer subword units for translation.

5 Conclusions and Findings

In this paper, we investigated the discrepancy between the "optimal" vocabulary set identified prior to training a translation model and the vocabulary actually used by the trained model. We found that the trained model diverged from the original BPE vocabulary and that a single iteration of self-training was sufficient to generate a competitive vocabulary set. Additionally, we examined the relationship between the self-vocabularizing process and the encoder-decoder architecture, demonstrating that deeper models favor the selection of rarer tokens while reducing vocabulary size, whereas decoders have a lesser influence on vocabularization.

Limitations

While self-vocabularizing training is simple and provides significant improvements over baseline training, it remains time-consuming. Moreover, further analysis is needed to better understand vocabulary shifts and how to efficiently determine the optimal set without requiring costly training iterations. This analysis should include an examination of token types and subword granularity, such as how subword segmentation evolves across training iterations.

In addition, our findings have yet to be verified across multiple language pairs, leaving this as an avenue for future work. Overall, this study highlights the need to incorporate vocabulary relearning during self-training and suggests that new vocabulary construction techniques could bridge the gap between model training and text interactions.

Ethics Statement

Vocabularization with model training has significantly improved machine translation performance. To minimize potential negative impacts, we conduct our experiments on publicly available datasets commonly used in machine translation research. However, if this method is applied to sensitive data, such as medical records, privacy-preserving policies should be strictly considered.

Additionally, while deeper model architectures promote the use of unique tokens, they also increase computational demands. The potential environmental impact of large-scale model training should be carefully evaluated when scaling this approach.

References

Rami Al-Rfou, Dokook Choe, Noah Constant, Mandy Guo, and Llion Jones. 2019. Character-level language modeling with deeper self-attention. In *The Thirty-Third AAAI Conference on Artificial Intelligence, AAAI 2019, The Thirty-First Innovative Applications of Artificial Intelligence Conference, IAAI 2019, The Ninth AAAI Symposium on Educational Advances in Artificial Intelligence, EAAI 2019, Honolulu, Hawaii, USA, January 27 - February 1, 2019*, pages 3159–3166. AAAI Press.

Marcel Bollmann, Rahul Aralikatte, Héctor Murrieta Bello, Daniel Hershcovich, Miryam de Lhoneux, and Anders Søgaard. 2021. Moses and the character-based random babbling baseline: CoAStaL at AmericasNLP 2021 shared task. In *Proceedings of the First Workshop on Natural Language Processing for Indigenous Languages of the Americas*, pages 248–254, Online. Association for Computational Linguistics.

Marta R. Costa-jussà and José A. R. Fonollosa. 2016. Character-based neural machine translation. In *Proceedings of the 54th Annual Meeting of the Association for Computational Linguistics, ACL 2016, August 7-12, 2016, Berlin, Germany, Volume 2: Short Papers*. The Association for Computer Linguistics.

Jacob Devlin, Ming-Wei Chang, Kenton Lee, and Kristina Toutanova. 2019. BERT: pre-training of deep bidirectional transformers for language understanding. In *Proceedings of the 2019 Conference of the North American Chapter of the Association for Computational Linguistics: Human Language Technologies, NAACL-HLT 2019, Minneapolis, MN, USA, June 2-7, 2019, Volume 1 (Long and Short Papers)*, pages 4171–4186. Association for Computational Linguistics.

Shuoyang Ding, Adithya Renduchintala, and Kevin Duh. 2019. A call for prudent choice of subword merge operations in neural machine translation. In *Proceedings of Machine Translation Summit XVII Volume 1: Research Track, MTSummit 2019, Dublin, Ireland, August 19-23, 2019*, pages 204–213. European Association for Machine Translation.

Markus Freitag, George Foster, David Grangier, Viresh Ratnakar, Qijun Tan, and Wolfgang Macherey. 2021. Experts, errors, and context: A large-scale study of human evaluation for machine translation. *Transactions of the Association for Computational Linguistics*, 9:1460–1474.

Philip Gage. 1994. A new algorithm for data compression. *C Users Journal*, 12(2):23–38.

Sebastian Gehrmann, Yuntian Deng, and Alexander M. Rush. 2018. Bottom-up abstractive summarization. In *Proceedings of the 2018 Conference on Empirical Methods in Natural Language Processing, Brussels, Belgium, October 31 - November 4, 2018*, pages 4098–4109. Association for Computational Linguistics.

Junxian He, Jiatao Gu, Jiajun Shen, and Marc'Aurelio Ranzato. 2019. Revisiting self-training for neural sequence generation. In *International Conference on Learning Representations*.

Philipp Koehn and Christof Monz. 2006. Manual and automatic evaluation of machine translation between European languages. In *Proceedings on the Workshop on Statistical Machine Translation*, pages 102–121, New York City. Association for Computational Linguistics.

Taku Kudo and John Richardson. 2018. Sentencepiece: A simple and language independent subword tokenizer and detokenizer for neural text processing. In *Proceedings of the 2018 Conference on Empirical Methods in Natural Language Processing, EMNLP*

2018: System Demonstrations, Brussels, Belgium, October 31 - November 4, 2018, pages 66–71. Association for Computational Linguistics.

Jason Lee, Kyunghyun Cho, and Thomas Hofmann. 2017. Fully character-level neural machine translation without explicit segmentation. *Transactions of the Association for Computational Linguistics*, 5:365–378.

Xiaodong Liu, Kevin Duh, Liyuan Liu, and Jianfeng Gao. 2020. Very deep transformers for neural machine translation. *CoRR*, abs/2008.07772.

Tomas Mikolov, Ilya Sutskever, Kai Chen, Gregory S. Corrado, and Jeffrey Dean. 2013. Distributed representations of words and phrases and their compositionality. In *Advances in Neural Information Processing Systems 26: 27th Annual Conference on Neural Information Processing Systems 2013. Proceedings of a meeting held December 5-8, 2013, Lake Tahoe, Nevada, United States*, pages 3111–3119.

Myle Ott, Sergey Edunov, Alexei Baevski, Angela Fan, Sam Gross, Nathan Ng, David Grangier, and Michael Auli. 2019. fairseq: A fast, extensible toolkit for sequence modeling. In *Proceedings of the 2019 Conference of the North American Chapter of the Association for Computational Linguistics (Demonstrations)*, pages 48–53, Minneapolis, Minnesota. Association for Computational Linguistics.

Myle Ott, Sergey Edunov, David Grangier, and Michael Auli. 2018. Scaling neural machine translation. In *Proceedings of the Third Conference on Machine Translation: Research Papers, WMT 2018, Belgium, Brussels, October 31 - November 1, 2018*, pages 1–9. Association for Computational Linguistics.

Elizabeth Salesky, Andrew Runge, Alex Coda, Jan Niehues, and Graham Neubig. 2020. Optimizing segmentation granularity for neural machine translation. *Machine Translation*, pages 1–19.

Rico Sennrich, Barry Haddow, and Alexandra Birch. 2016. Neural machine translation of rare words with subword units. In *Proceedings of the 54th Annual Meeting of the Association for Computational Linguistics, ACL 2016, August 7-12, 2016, Berlin, Germany, Volume 1: Long Papers*. The Association for Computer Linguistics.

Ashish Vaswani, Noam Shazeer, Niki Parmar, Jakob Uszkoreit, Llion Jones, Aidan N. Gomez, Lukasz Kaiser, and Illia Polosukhin. 2017. Attention is all you need. In *Advances in Neural Information Processing Systems 30: Annual Conference on Neural Information Processing Systems 2017, 4-9 December 2017, Long Beach, CA, USA*, pages 5998–6008.

Changhan Wang, Kyunghyun Cho, and Jiatao Gu. 2020. Neural machine translation with byte-level subwords. In *The Thirty-Fourth AAAI Conference on Artificial Intelligence, AAAI 2020, The Thirty-Second Innovative Applications of Artificial Intelligence Conference, IAAI 2020, The Tenth AAAI Symposium on Educational Advances in Artificial Intelligence, EAAI 2020, New York, NY, USA, February 7-12, 2020*, pages 9154–9160. AAAI Press.

Jingjing Xu, Hao Zhou, Chun Gan, Zaixiang Zheng, and Lei Li. 2020. Vocabulary learning via optimal transport for neural machine translation. *arXiv preprint arXiv:2012.15671*.

Lei Zhang, Shuai Wang, and Bing Liu. 2018. Deep learning for sentiment analysis: A survey. *Wiley Interdisciplinary Reviews: Data Mining and Knowledge Discovery*, 8(4).

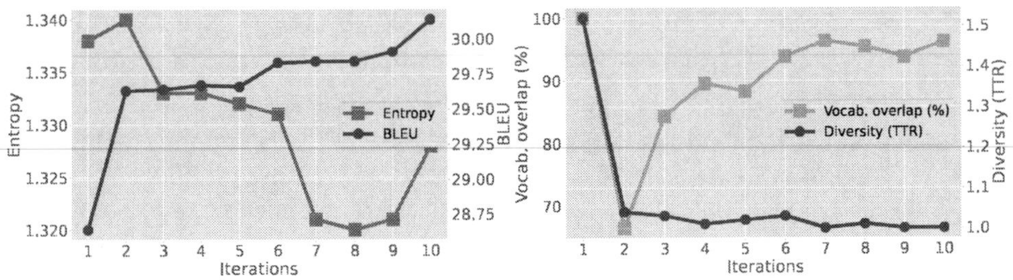

Figure 4: Impact of self-vocabularizing training on IWSLT14 EN-DE. (**Left**) BLEU scores improve consistently across iterations, while corpus entropy decreases, indicating more stable and predictable token distributions. (**Right**) Vocabulary overlap reduces as the model gradually refines its subword selection, while the type-token ratio (TTR) reflects evolving semantic diversity.

A Detailed Results

A.1 IWSLT14 EN-DE

We present results for MT models trained with self-vocabularizing on the IWSLT14 EN-DE dataset over 10 iterations. We report performance for the baseline model (**ST-0**) and models trained with self-vocabularizing at iterations 1, 5, and 10. As shown in Table 2, all self-trained models outperform the fixed-vocabulary baseline (**ST-0**), with a 2.4-point increase in BLEU after 10 iterations. Additionally, vocabulary size decreases with each iteration, leading to a more compact vocabulary.

	BLEU	|V|	Overlap (%)
ST-0	28.64	10000	-
ST-1	29.63	8969	66.42
ST-5	29.66	8892	88.27
ST-10	30.14	8863	93.91

Table 2: BLEU scores, vocabulary size ($|V|$), and overlap (%) on the IWSLT14 EN-DE translation task for **ST-0**, **ST-1**, **ST-5**, and **ST-10** models.

Figure 4 illustrates the impact of self-vocabularizing training on corpus entropy, performance, vocabulary overlap, and diversity for the IWSLT14 EN-DE dataset. We observe a consistent decrease in corpus entropy and vocabulary overlap, alongside performance improvements with increasing training iterations. This confirms the effectiveness of self-vocabularizing training on the EN-DE translation task. Notably, the EN-DE translation exhibits lower diversity than the DE-EN task, which aligns with expectations since German shares more semantic units than English.

CCT-Code: Cross-Consistency Training for Multilingual Clone Detection and Code Search

Nikita Sorokin[1, 4*], Anton Tikhonov[1, 3*], Dmitry Abulkhanov[8], Ivan Sedykh[1], Irina Piontkovskaya[2], Sergey Nikolenko[5, 6], Valentin Malykh[1, 6, 7]

[1]MTS AI, Moscow, Russia; [2]Luzin Research Center, Moscow, Russia;
[3]ITMO University, Saint-Petersburg, Russia; [4]Higher School of Economics, Moscow, Russia;
[5]St. Petersburg Department of the Steklov Institute of Mathematics, Saint-Petersburg, Russia;
[6]ISP RAS Research Center for Trusted Artificial Intelligence, Moscow, Russia;
[7]IITU University, Almaty, Kazakhstan; [8]Independent Researcher

Abstract

We consider the well-known and important tasks of clone detection and information retrieval for source code. The most standard setup is to search clones inside the same language code snippets. But it is also useful to find code snippets with identical behaviour in different programming languages. Nevertheless multi- and cross-lingual clone detection has been little studied in literature. We present a novel training procedure, cross-consistency training (CCT) leveraging cross-lingual similarity, that we apply to train language models on source code in various programming languages. We show that this training is effective both for encoder- and decoder-based models. The trained encoder-based CCT-LM model achieves a new state of the art on POJ-104 (monolingual C++ clone detection benchmark) with 96.73% MAP and AdvTest (monolingual Python code search benchmark) with 47.18% MRR. The decoder-based CCT-LM model shows comparable performance in these tasks. In addition, we formulate the multi- and cross-lingual clone detection problem and present XCD, a new benchmark dataset produced from CodeForces submissions.

1 Introduction

Clone detection is crucial in software development for identifying semantically similar code, aiding in unification, refactoring, and side effect control. Originally formulated for C/C++ by Mou et al. (2016), the task has since expanded to other languages, with the next step being multilingual clone detection. This work introduces a new multilingual dataset XCD and establishes baseline models.

Early clone detection relied on algorithmic methods (Baker, 1993; Krinke, 2001), later evolving into machine learning-based approaches (Li et al., 2017; Thaller et al., 2020; Gotmare et al., 2021) that embed code snippets for similarity-based retrieval. We propose CCT, a novel training technique that enhances code embeddings, achieving state-of-the-art results on both POJ-104 (Mou et al., 2016) and our new XCD dataset. Additionally, we demonstrate that CCT-LM, trained with CCT, is also effective for code search, as formulated by Lu et al. (2021b).

Main Contributions CCT – A pretraining method for aligning multilingual code snippets. XCD – A novel multilingual clone detection dataset from CodeForces. State-of-the-art results on POJ-104 and XCD with CCT-LM. CCT-LM achieves state-of-the-art on *AdvTest* for code search.

*Equal contribution.

2 Related Work

Our methods are inspired by natural language processing, thus related work includes both pure NLP and source code processing.

Datasets. Husain et al. (2019) presented the *CodeSearchNet* dataset constructed from a *GitHub* dump where the authors split method bodies into the code itself and a description. This dataset contains 2 million code snippet-description pairs in 6 programming languages, including *Python*. This dataset was partially used by Hasan et al. (2021) who combined *CodeSearchNet* and three other datasets into a larger one. From *CodeSearchNet* they used the *Java* part and *Python* part translated automatically into *Java*. The resulting dataset contains 4 million code snippet-description pairs. There are two main datasets for clone detection: POJ-104 (Mou et al., 2016) and *BigCloneBench* (Wang et al., 2020). POJ-104 represents a comparatively small corpus of C++ solutions from a student judging system. *BigCloneBench* comprises a vast dataset containing automatically mined data in the Java language.

Code Search. Gu et al. (2018) introduced

Proceedings of the 2025 Conference of the Nations of the Americas Chapter of the Association for Computational Linguistics: Human Language Technologies (Volume 4: Student Research Workshop), pages 178–185

dense vector representations for code search, training two recurrent neural networks for source code and text. Feng et al. (2020) used a language model to produce these representations. Gotmare et al. (2021) employed three Transformer-based models for hierarchical encoding but found parameter sharing reduced quality. In contrast, our model uses a single Transformer decoder to embed queries and documents, omitting the classifier.

Clone Detection. One of the first successful deep learning approaches was CClearner (Li et al., 2017) that used text extracted from a program and its AST features and had a simplistic multilayer perceptron architecture for clone classification on a closed code base. More recent deep learning models include graph neural networks on ASTs (Wang et al., 2020) and employ pretrained language models Villmow et al. (2022).

Language models for source code. BERT-like models, initially successful in natural language processing, have been adapted for programming languages. Several pre-trained models have emerged, including CodeBERT (Feng et al., 2020), a bimodal model trained on masked language modeling (MLM) and replaced token detection; GraphCodeBERT (Guo et al., 2021), which incorporates abstract syntax trees for training; and SynCoBERT (Wang et al., 2021), which leverages multimodal contrastive learning with identifier and AST edge prediction. More recently, autoregressive decoder models like DeepSeek-Coder (Guo et al., 2024) have gained prominence, focusing on source code generation tasks such as code completion and documentation generation.

3 Datasets

In this work we use two kinds of datasets, one for clone detection and another for code search.

Code Search. For code search we use the *CodeSearchNet* dataset introduced by Husain et al. (2019). The original version of *CodeSearchNet* consists of natural language queries paired with most relevant code snippets in six programming languages. Each snippet represents the code of a function collected from *GitHub* open source code.

CodeSearchNet AdvTest

AdvTest is a Python-only dataset derived from the *CodeSearchNet* corpus by Lu et al. (2021b), pairing functions with text where the first documentation paragraph serves as the query (Husain et al., 2019).

Lu et al. (2021b) found that normalizing function and variable names significantly reduces Mean Reciprocal Rank (MRR) scores, dropping from 0.809 to 0.419 for RoBERTa (Liu et al., 2019) and 0.869 to 0.507 for CodeBERT (Feng et al., 2020). They improved dataset quality by filtering unparsable code, overly short/long documents, special tokens, and non-English or empty texts, resulting in 251 820 training, 9 604 validation, and 19 210 test examples.

To assess generalization, *AdvTest* normalizes function and variable names in the development and test sets, replacing them with generic tokens (e.g., *func*, *arg_i*). Unlike prior works (Husain et al., 2019; Feng et al., 2020), which evaluated on 1 000 candidates per query, *AdvTest* uses the entire test set, increasing difficulty. The training data, derived from the filtered CodeSearchNet (Husain et al., 2019), retains raw code and applies language-specific tokenization. Performance is measured using Mean Reciprocal Rank (MRR).

Clone Detection. In the clone detection task, the problem is to retrieve semantically similar codes given a code as the query. To train and test models for clone detection, we use the **POJ-104** dataset introduced by Mou et al. (2016). It comes from a pedagogical programming open judge (OJ) system that automatically judges the validity of submitted source code for specific problems by running the code. The POJ-104 dataset consists of 104 problems and includes 500 student-written C/C++ programs for each problem. The clone detection here is, given a program's source code, to retrieve other programs that solve the same problem. The problems are grouped into three sets with 64/16/24 problems for training, validation, and testing respectively. The default metric for the POJ-104 dataset is Mean Average Precision (MAP), where the average precision (AP) is defined as $\text{AP} = \sum_{i=1}^{100}(R_i - R_{i-1}) \cdot P_i$, where R_i and P_i are the precision and recall at threshold i, i.e., computed taking into account only top i items from the candidate list. MAP is the mean AP over all queries. It is important to mention that for POJ-104 the maximal possible i is 499 since there are only 500 candidates in total.

3.1 XCD Dataset

Existing works have not thoroughly explored the multilingual capabilities of code language models. To address this gap, we introduce XCD, a new multilingual clone detection and code retrieval dataset. The dataset supports three evaluation settings: full comparison (binary classification like BUCC (Xu et al., 2018)), **retrieval-style clone detection** (similar to POJ-104 (Mou et al., 2016)), and a hybrid approach

We constructed XCD using CodeForces submissions, selecting 110 problems with 100 accepted solutions per problem in five languages (Python, Java, C#, C++, C), totaling 55,000 snippets.

Evaluation Setups Full Comparison Binary classification of test set pairs (n^2 comparisons). Each pair is positive if solving the same problem, otherwise negative. Evaluated using F1-score (Sasaki et al., 2007).

Retrieval Style Tasked with retrieving 100 snippets per language solving the same problem from 11,000 positive snippets. Evaluated using MAP@100 (Mou et al., 2016).

Hybrid Evaluation Includes all snippets in the same language, making it more challenging (similar to *AdvTest*). Evaluated using MRR@R (Lu et al., 2021b).

Cross-Lingual Evaluation Extends all setups across multiple languages to assess cross-lingual code understanding.

Additional Labeling Beyond solution status (Accepted/Not Accepted), we also mined error statuses from 97M code snippets across 10+ programming languages. CodeForces provides 15 verdicts, which we categorized into four groups:

1. Defect – Runtime errors (e.g., division by zero, stack overflow).
2. Skip – Judging errors (e.g., rejected due to unclear reasons).
3. Accepted – Passed all tests.
4. Wrong – Failed tests or constraints (e.g., time/memory limit exceeded).

This additional labeling enhances dataset utility for error prediction and robust code retrieval.

4 Method

In this section, we introduce our pre-training approach CCT (Cross-Consistency Training). Its goal is to robustly learn the embedding space of code snippets and create a *strong* alignment between snippets solving the same problems across programming languages. The difference between strong and weak alignment is illustrated in Fig. 1: in a weakly aligned embedding space, the nearest neighbor might be a semantically similar snippet from a different language but generally most neighbors are in the same language, while in a strongly aligned space the similarity is purely semantic and does not care about the language at all.

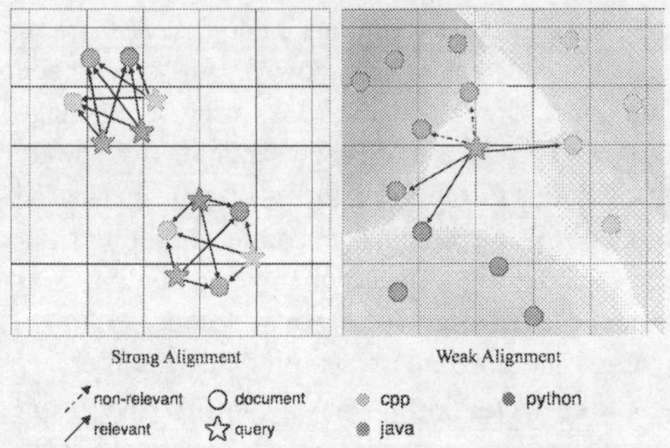

Figure 1: Strong and weak cross-lingual alignment.

To achieve strong alignment, we employ a contrastive learning objective $\mathcal{L}_{\text{XCD}}$: for a randomly code snippet, we train the vector representations of the source code tokens in such a way that their aggregation, for example, averaging or last token, is closer to the source code, which solves the same problem regardless of the programming language. This ensures that the embeddings of the source code differentiates between related snippets and random or similar but different (hard negative) snippets effectively.

Noise-contrastive estimation and losses. To learn a language-agnostic cross-lingual representation space, we propose a training procedure based on noise contrastive estimation (NCE). Let $\mathcal{X}$ and $\mathcal{Z}$ be some finite sets and $s_{\boldsymbol{\theta}} : \mathcal{X} \times \mathcal{Z} \to \mathbb{R}$ be a relevance score function differentiable in $\boldsymbol{\theta} \in \mathbb{R}^d$. The goal is to learn $\boldsymbol{\theta}$ such that the classifier $\mathbf{x} \mapsto \arg\max_{\mathbf{z} \in \mathcal{Z}} s_{\boldsymbol{\theta}}(\mathbf{x}, \mathbf{z})$ has the optimal expected loss. This leads to conditional density estimation: for every $\mathbf{x} \in \mathcal{X}$

$$p_{\boldsymbol{\theta}}(\mathbf{z}|\mathbf{x}) = \frac{e^{s_{\boldsymbol{\theta}}(\mathbf{x},\mathbf{z})}}{\sum_{\mathbf{z}^- \in \mathcal{Z}} e^{s_{\boldsymbol{\theta}}(\mathbf{x},\mathbf{z}^-)}} \quad (1)$$

with $\boldsymbol{\theta}^* = \arg\min_{\boldsymbol{\theta}} \mathbb{E}_{\mathbf{x},\mathbf{z}} [-\log p_{\boldsymbol{\theta}}(\mathbf{z}|\mathbf{x})]$ being the optimum. In practice, optimizing this objective directly is infeasible: if $\mathcal{Z}$ is large the normalization term in (1) is intractable. Therefore, NCE uses subsampling, so (1) becomes

$$\pi_{\boldsymbol{\theta}}(\mathbf{z}|\mathbf{x}) = \frac{e^{s_{\boldsymbol{\theta}}(\mathbf{x},\mathbf{z})}}{\sum_{\mathbf{z}^- \in \mathcal{B}_{\mathbf{x},\mathbf{z}}} e^{s_{\boldsymbol{\theta}}(\mathbf{x},\mathbf{z}^-)} + e^{s_{\boldsymbol{\theta}}(\mathbf{x},\mathbf{z})}}, \quad (2)$$

where $\mathcal{B}_{\mathbf{x},\mathbf{z}} = \{\mathbf{z}_1^-, \mathbf{z}_2^-, \ldots, \mathbf{z}_n^-\}$ is a set of *negatives* sampled from $\mathcal{Z}$ that do not match the *pos itive* answer $\mathbf{z}^+$ for this $\mathbf{x}$. NCE also often uses objectives similar to (2) but with $\pi_{\boldsymbol{\theta}}(\hat{\mathbf{z}}|\mathbf{z})$ where $\mathbf{z}$ and $\hat{\mathbf{z}}$ come from the same space, and the objective corresponds to some similarity function.

Cross-lingual objective. Contrastive learning frequently employs pretext tasks to learn data representations without the need for labeled examples. In the context of learning from a multilingual set of documents, a possible pretext task would be to train a network to differentiate between documents with similar content but written in different languages (positive pairs) and those with dissimilar content (negative pairs). This leads to the loss function:

$$\mathcal{L}_{\text{XCD}}(\boldsymbol{\theta}) = \mathbb{E}_{(\hat{\mathbf{z}},\mathbf{z})\sim\mathcal{W}_{\text{XCD}}}\left[-\log \pi_{\boldsymbol{\theta}}(\hat{\mathbf{z}}|\mathbf{z})\right], \quad (3)$$

where $\mathcal{W}_{\text{XCD}}$ is a distribution on the set of pairs of submissions in different programming languages from the XCD dataset (Section 3) that shows if the submissions are solving the same problem or not.

Hard negative mining. Previous works on contrastive learning show the importance of training on hard negative samples (Qu et al., 2021; Izacard and Grave, 2020). They used iterative training to get hard negatives, but our data already contains strong negative examples as preliminary solutions from the same users that solve the same problems but fail some tests (that is why a user would submit an updated solution to get the "Accepted" verdict). Thus, we mine hard negative examples as failed solutions from the same user; if there are none we use failed solutions from random users, and only if there are none (e.g., for an unpopular problem) we use a random submission for a random problem.

5 Experiments

In this section, we describe the details about data pre-training and our CCT pipeline for multilingual clone detection and code search tasks.

Pretraining. We train two models, one is encoder-based, which is initialized with pretrained $\text{GraphCodeBERT}_{\text{base}}$ (Guo et al., 2021); we call the resulting model $\text{CCT-LM}_{\text{enc}}$. Another one is decoder-based, which is initilized with a pretrained DeepSeek-Coder-1.3B model (Guo et al., 2024); we call the resulting model $\text{CCT-LM}_{\text{dec}}$. Similarity scores are calculated based on dot products of the last token vector representations, but we also researched using various types of poolings and allowing bidirectional attention.

Hyperparameters. We use the AdamW optimizer with learning rate 5e-5, weight decay 0.01, and linear learning rate decay. We use gradient accumulation for pretraining with an effective batch size of 2000.

	Clone detection (MAP)	Code search (MRR)
Endcoder-only		
RoBERTa-base (Liu et al., 2019)	76.67	18.33
CodeBERT (Feng et al., 2020)	82.67	27.19
SynCoBERT (Wang et al., 2021)	88.24	38.10
CodeRoBERTa	—	42.35
GraphCodeBERT (Guo et al., 2021)	85.16	—
CasCode (Gotmare et al., 2021)	—	43.98
Villmow et al. (2022)	91.34	—
$\text{CCT-LM}_{\text{enc}}$	**96.73**	**47.18**
Decoder-only		
CodeGen (Nijkamp et al., 2023)	89.68	—
CodeGPT (Lu et al., 2021a)	87.96	—
SantaCoder (Allal et al., 2023)	83.98	—
Phi-1 (Gunasekar et al., 2023)	92.72	—
$\text{CCT-LM}_{\text{dec}}$	**95.84**	37.61

Table 1: Results on code clone detection on the POJ-104 dataset and code search on the *AdvTest* dataset.

Monolingual Results. Tab. 1 presents the results of CCT-LM models compared to existing approaches, showing that CCT-LM outperform all previous models by a large margin in this monolingual setting. Thus, strong alignment enforced by CCT pretraining is not only helpful for multilingual transfer but also improves the latent space structure in general. It is important to mention, that CCT pretraining works for both encoder- and decoder-based models, improving the results.

5.1 Multi- and Cross-lingual Evaluation

For these types of evaluation on XCD we use several setups described in Sec. 3.1. Since these setups are computationally intensive we work only with encoder-based models.

Multilingual Results

The top half of Tab. 2 presents multilingual results on the proposed XCD dataset. Interestingly, knowledge transfer from the POJ-104 dataset does not improve performance, and metrics remain low. However, CCT-LM significantly outperforms others, likely due to its multilingual pretraining approach. BM25 is not evaluated in this setup, as it is unsuitable for document comparison.

For retrieval-based evaluation, CCT-LM_{enc} outperforms all baselines, providing a viable solution, while GraphCodeBERT fails across all programming languages. BM25, a strong baseline for nat-

	Python	Java	C#	Ruby	JS	Haskell	PHP	OCaml	Perl	Avg
Multilingual setting										
Full Comparison, F_1 measure										
$\text{GraphCodeBERT}_{\text{base}}$	0.02	0.05	0.00	0.04	0.00	0.02	0.01	0.03	0.01	0.02
$\text{GraphCodeBERT}_{\text{base}}^{\text{POJ}}$	0.04	0.00	0.01	0.06	0.07	0.08	0.06	0.06	0.06	0.05
$\text{CCT-LM}_{\text{enc}}$	**22.24**	**18.39**	**17.33**	**23.33**	**10.46**	**17.64**	**21.43**	**17.01**	**16.40**	**18.24**
Retrieval Style, MAP@100										
BM25	0.00	0.00	0.00	0.00	0.00	0.00	0.00	0.00	0.00	0.00
$\text{GraphCodeBERT}_{\text{base}}$	7.21	9.25	1.33	4.28	1.59	5.78	6.08	2.90	10.37	5.42
$\text{GraphCodeBERT}_{\text{base}}^{\text{POJ}}$	30.12	24.63	23.54	32.78	36.64	24.45	37.21	33.94	45.33	32.07
$\text{CCT-LM}_{\text{enc}}$	**87.42**	**55.99**	**65.35**	**72.12**	**74.32**	**81.05**	**83.21**	**71.53**	**71.89**	**73.65**
Hybrid, MRR@20										
BM25	0.00	0.00	0.00	0.00	0.00	0.00	0.00	0.00	0.00	0.00
$\text{GraphCodeBERT}_{\text{base}}$	2.08	5.42	0.22	2.59	0.80	1.99	2.90	1.40	5.23	2.51
$\text{GraphCodeBERT}_{\text{base}}^{\text{POJ}}$	27.10	20.04	19.44	30.98	28.37	19.70	32.89	30.08	39.98	27.62
$\text{CCT-LM}_{\text{enc}}$	**74.97**	**62.08**	**58.77**	**80.60**	**74.56**	**62.27**	**81.21**	**72.64**	**79.16**	**71.80**
Cross-lingual setting										
Full Comparison, F_1 measure										
$\text{GraphCodeBERT}_{\text{base}}$	0.01	0.01	0.00	0.01	0.00	0.01	0.01	0.01	0.01	0.01
$\text{GraphCodeBERT}_{\text{base}}^{\text{POJ}}$	0.01	0.00	0.01	0.01	0.01	0.01	0.01	0.01	0.01	0.01
$\text{CCT-LM}_{\text{enc}}$	**8.92**	**9.46**	**4.78**	**6.01**	**7.33**	**5.82**	**6.47**	**5.33**	**3.56**	**6.40**
Retrieval Style, MAP@100										
BM25	0.00	0.00	0.00	0.00	0.00	0.00	0.00	0.00	0.00	0.00
$\text{GraphCodeBERT}_{\text{base}}$	3.18	5.24	0.23	1.77	1.15	3.38	3.12	1.90	16.27	4.02
$\text{GraphCodeBERT}_{\text{base}}^{\text{POJ}}$	12.83	14.75	9.33	12.78	17.16	15.94	19.53	16.01	23.88	15.80
$\text{CCT-LM}_{\text{enc}}$	**44.82**	**20.34**	**23.33**	**35.01**	**32.57**	**40.07**	**43.36**	**36.66**	**37.80**	**34.88**
Hybrid, MRR@20										
BM25	0.00	0.00	0.00	0.00	0.00	0.00	0.00	0.00	0.00	0.00
$\text{GraphCodeBERT}_{\text{base}}$	1.24	2.42	0.34	1.28	0.82	0.93	1.43	0.76	2.15	1.26
$\text{GraphCodeBERT}_{\text{base}}^{\text{POJ}}$	20.12	13.08	10.37	17.28	12.62	19.70	14.31	18.08	18.33	15.98
$\text{CCT-LM}_{\text{enc}}$	**30.83**	**22.77**	**19.32**	**32.66**	**31.64**	**20.80**	**31.59**	**40.42**	**39.40**	**29.93**

Table 2: Multilingual clone detection in two evaluation setups on the XCD dataset.

ural language information retrieval, does not work for clone detection, as it relies on identical tokens, which are often sparse even in similar code snippets.

The hybrid evaluation setup confirms these findings: BM25 remains ineffective, code language models demonstrate some knowledge transfer across solutions, and training on POJ-104 clone detection leads to a noticeable performance boost. However, CCT-LM_{enc} consistently outperforms all methods, establishing a new benchmark for multilingual code-related tasks.

Cross-lingual Results. Our results in this setting are presented in the bottom half of Tab. 2. All conclusions derived for the multilingual case (above) apply here too, but in comparison to the multilingual setting, cross-lingual tasks are significantly harder and all values are lower. We suggest that the difference in the results across programming languages could be caused by the imbalance in the pretraining dataset.

6 Conclusion

Understanding semantic similarity is crucial for language processing, enabling solutions for various tasks in natural and programming languages. In this work, we presented CCT-LM, a new method that enhances this capability via a novel CCT pretraining approach, demonstrating its effectiveness in clone detection and code search. We introduced a novel task of multilingual clone detection and the XCD dataset for multilingual source code analysis, formalized in two evaluation setups.

The proposed CCT-LM models (encoder- and decoder-based) outperformed strong baselines in clone detection and code search. CCT-LM_{enc} excelled across all setups for multi- and cross-lingual evaluation, showing that CCT pretraining improves semantic similarity understanding in language models.

We hope our method benefits other source code processing tasks, left for future work, and believe modifications of our approach could aid NLP and other machine learning fields.

7 Limitations

We have studied several programming languages, including Python and Java, in our XCD setup; although all our methods seem to be language-agnostic, a further study for other languages would be interesting, especially since all considered languages are interpreted rather than compiled (like C/C++). Many inputs exceed 512 tokens; we used standard truncation for evaluation (taking into consideration only the beginning of the code), which may be suboptimal, and more suitable input representations could be found. We expect our model to improve with training on long documents. We also suppose that the model would benefit from increasing the batch size by using more powerful hardware with more memory. Note also that while CCT-LM significantly improved state of the art in clone detection and code search.

Acknowledgments

The work of Sergey Nikolenko and Valentin Malykh was supported by a grant for research centers in the field of artificial intelligence, provided by the Analytical Center for the Government of the Russian Federation in accordance with the subsidy agreement (agreement identifier 000000D730321P5Q0002) and the agreement with the Ivannikov Institute for System Programming of the Russian Academy of Sciences dated November 2, 2021 No. 70-2021-00142.

References

Loubna Ben Allal, Raymond Li, Denis Kocetkov, Chenghao Mou, Christopher Akiki, Carlos Munoz Ferrandis, Niklas Muennighoff, Mayank Mishra, Alex Gu, Manan Dey, Logesh Kumar Umapathi, Carolyn Jane Anderson, Yangtian Zi, Joel Lamy Poirier, Hailey Schoelkopf, Sergey Troshin, Dmitry Abulkhanov, Manuel Romero, Michael Lappert, Francesco De Toni, Bernardo García del Río, Qian Liu, Shamik Bose, Urvashi Bhattacharyya, Terry Yue Zhuo, Ian Yu, Paulo Villegas, Marco Zocca, Sourab Mangrulkar, David Lansky, Huu Nguyen, Danish Contractor, Luis Villa, Jia Li, Dzmitry Bahdanau, Yacine Jernite, Sean Hughes, Daniel Fried, Arjun Guha, Harm de Vries, and Leandro von Werra. 2023. Santacoder: don't reach for the stars!

Brenda S Baker. 1993. A program for identifying duplicated code. *Computing Science and Statistics*, pages 49–49.

Zhangyin Feng, Daya Guo, Duyu Tang, Nan Duan, Xiaocheng Feng, Ming Gong, Linjun Shou, Bing Qin, Ting Liu, Daxin Jiang, and Ming Zhou. 2020. CodeBERT: A Pre-Trained Model for Programming and Natural Languages. In *Findings of the Association for Computational Linguistics: EMNLP 2020*, pages 1536–1547, Online. Association for Computational Linguistics.

Akhilesh Deepak Gotmare, Junnan Li, Shafiq Joty, and Steven CH Hoi. 2021. Cascaded fast and slow models for efficient semantic code search. *arXiv preprint arXiv:2110.07811*.

Xiaodong Gu, Hongyu Zhang, and Sunghun Kim. 2018. Deep code search. In *2018 IEEE/ACM 40th International Conference on Software Engineering (ICSE)*, pages 933–944. IEEE.

Suriya Gunasekar, Yi Zhang, Jyoti Aneja, Caio César Teodoro Mendes, Allie Del Giorno, Sivakanth Gopi, Mojan Javaheripi, Piero Kauffmann, Gustavo de Rosa, Olli Saarikivi, Adil Salim, Shital Shah, Harkirat Singh Behl, Xin Wang, Sébastien Bubeck, Ronen Eldan, Adam Tauman Kalai, Yin Tat Lee, and Yuanzhi Li. 2023. Textbooks are all you need.

Daya Guo, Shuo Ren, Shuai Lu, Zhangyin Feng, Duyu Tang, Shujie Liu, Long Zhou, Nan Duan, Alexey Svyatkovskiy, Shengyu Fu, Michele Tufano, Shao Kun Deng, Colin Clement, Dawn Drain, Neel Sundaresan, Jian Yin, Daxin Jiang, and Ming Zhou. 2021. GraphCodeBERT: Pre-training Code Representations with Data Flow. In *ICLR*.

Daya Guo, Qihao Zhu, Dejian Yang, Zhenda Xie, Kai Dong, Wentao Zhang, Guanting Chen, Xiao Bi, Y. Wu, Y. K. Li, Fuli Luo, Yingfei Xiong, and Wenfeng Liang. 2024. Deepseek-coder: When the large language model meets programming – the rise of code intelligence.

Masum Hasan, Tanveer Muttaqueen, Abdullah Al Ishtiaq, Kazi Sajeed Mehrab, Md Mahim Anjum Haque, Tahmid Hasan, Wasi Ahmad, Anindya Iqbal, and Rifat Shahriyar. 2021. Codesc: A large code–description parallel dataset. In *Findings of the Association for Computational Linguistics: ACL-IJCNLP 2021*, pages 210–218.

Hamel Husain, Ho-Hsiang Wu, Tiferet Gazit, Miltiadis Allamanis, and Marc Brockschmidt. 2019. CodeSearchNet Challenge: Evaluating the State of Semantic Code Search.

Gautier Izacard and Edouard Grave. 2020. Distilling knowledge from reader to retriever for question answering.

J. Krinke. 2001. Identifying similar code with program dependence graphs. In *Proceedings Eighth Working Conference on Reverse Engineering*, pages 301–309.

Liuqing Li, He Feng, Wenjie Zhuang, Na Meng, and Barbara Ryder. 2017. Cclearner: A deep learning-based clone detection approach. In *2017 IEEE International Conference on Software Maintenance and Evolution (ICSME)*, pages 249–260. IEEE.

Yinhan Liu, Myle Ott, Naman Goyal, Jingfei Du, Mandar Joshi, Danqi Chen, Omer Levy, Mike Lewis, Luke Zettlemoyer, and Veselin Stoyanov. 2019. Roberta: A robustly optimized bert pretraining approach. *arXiv preprint*.

Shuai Lu, Daya Guo, Shuo Ren, Junjie Huang, Alexey Svyatkovskiy, Ambrosio Blanco, Colin Clement, Dawn Drain, Daxin Jiang, Duyu Tang, Ge Li, Lidong Zhou, Linjun Shou, Long Zhou, Michele Tufano, Ming Gong, Ming Zhou, Nan Duan, Neel Sundaresan, Shao Kun Deng, Shengyu Fu, and Shujie Liu. 2021a. Codexglue: A machine learning benchmark dataset for code understanding and generation.

Shuai Lu, Daya Guo, Shuo Ren, Junjie Huang, Alexey Svyatkovskiy, Ambrosio Blanco, Colin Clement, Dawn Drain, Daxin Jiang, Duyu Tang, et al. 2021b. Codexglue: A machine learning benchmark dataset for code understanding and generation. In *Thirty-fifth Conference on Neural Information Processing Systems Datasets and Benchmarks Track (Round 1)*.

Lili Mou, Ge Li, Lu Zhang, Tao Wang, and Zhi Jin. 2016. Convolutional neural networks over tree structures for programming language processing.

Erik Nijkamp, Bo Pang, Hiroaki Hayashi, Lifu Tu, Huan Wang, Yingbo Zhou, Silvio Savarese, and Caiming Xiong. 2023. Codegen: An open large language model for code with multi-turn program synthesis.

Yingqi Qu, Yuchen Ding, Jing Liu, Kai Liu, Ruiyang Ren, Xin Zhao, Daxiang Dong, Hua Wu, and Haifeng Wang. 2021. Rocketqa: An optimized training approach to dense passage retrieval for open-domain question answering. *ArXiv*, abs/2010.08191.

Yutaka Sasaki et al. 2007. The truth of the f-measure. 2007. *URL: https://www. cs. odu. edu/mukka/cs795sum09dm/Lecturenotes/Day3/F-measure-YS-26Oct07. pdf [accessed 2021-05-26]*, 49.

Hannes Thaller, Lukas Linsbauer, and Alexander Egyed. 2020. Towards semantic clone detection via probabilistic software modeling. In *2020 IEEE 14th International Workshop on Software Clones (IWSC)*, pages 64–69. IEEE.

Johannes Villmow, Viola Campos, Adrian Ulges, and Ulrich Schwanecke. 2022. Addressing leakage in self-supervised contextualized code retrieval. *arXiv preprint*.

Wenhan Wang, Ge Li, Bo Ma, Xin Xia, and Zhi Jin. 2020. Detecting code clones with graph neural network and flow-augmented abstract syntax tree. In *2020 IEEE 27th International Conference on Software Analysis, Evolution and Reengineering (SANER)*, pages 261–271. IEEE.

Xin Wang, Yasheng Wang, Fei Mi, Pingyi Zhou, Yao Wan, Xiao Liu, Li Li, Hao Wu, Jin Liu, and Xin Jiang. 2021. SynCoBERT: Syntax-Guided Multi-Modal Contrastive Pre-Training for Code Representation. *arXiv preprint*. Number: arXiv:2108.04556 arXiv:2108.04556 [cs].

Ruochen Xu, Yiming Yang, Naoki Otani, and Yuexin Wu. 2018. Unsupervised cross-lingual transfer of word embedding spaces. In *Proceedings of the 2018 Conference on Empirical Methods in Natural Language Processing*, pages 2465–2474, Brussels, Belgium. Association for Computational Linguistics.

	Java	Ruby	PHP	Go	JS	Avg
CodeBERT$_{\text{base}}$	46.37	50.65	37.83	50.65	50.48	47.19
GraphCodeBERT$_{\text{base}}$	47.33	59.95	37.47	60.28	**52.04**	51.41
CCT-LM$_{enc}$	**48.71**	**62.25**	**42.78**	**61.44**	51.06	**53.24**

Table 3: Zero-shot retrieval; F_1 score, *CodeSearchNet*.

GraphCodeBERT	Clone Detection (MAP)	Code Search (MRR)	Defect detection (Acc)
Base	85.16	45.80	62.51
Base + $\mathcal{L}_{\text{XCD}}$	95.92	29.93	61.05
Base + $\mathcal{L}_{\text{XCD}}$ + $\mathcal{L}_{\text{LM}}$	95.67	47.18	63.68
Base + $\mathcal{L}_{\text{XCD}}$ + $\mathcal{L}_{\text{LM}}$	96.03	45.22	64.91
Base + $\mathcal{L}_{\text{XCD}}$ + $\mathcal{L}_{\text{LM}}$ + SL	96.46	47.33	-
Base + $\mathcal{L}_{\text{XCD}}$ + $\mathcal{L}_{\text{LM}}$ + $\mathcal{L}_{\text{err}}$ + SL	**96.73**	**47.57**	**65.58**

Table 4: GraphCodeBERT variations: clone detection on POJ-104, code search on *AdvTest*, defect detection on *Devign*; SL denotes the size limit.

Table 5: A comparison of DeepSeek-Coder 1.3b variations: clone detection on POJ-104, code search on *AdvTest*

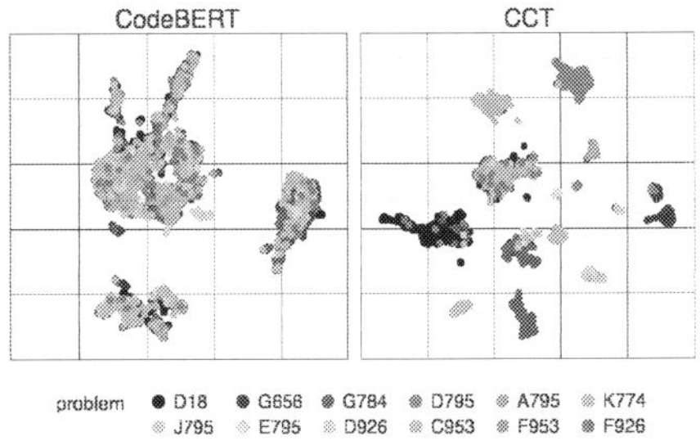

(a) Projected embeddings of 12 coding problems.

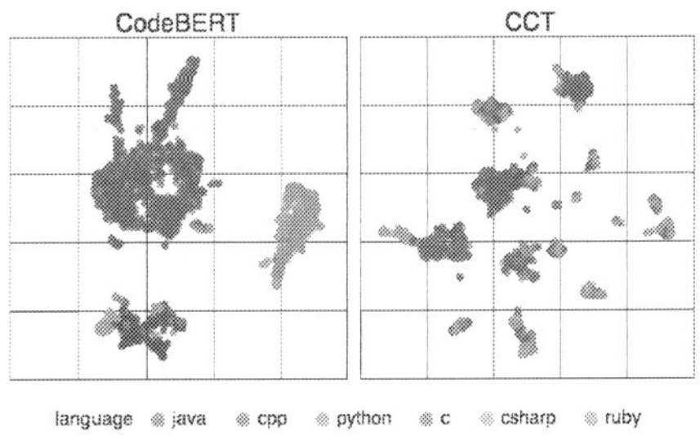

(b) The same embeddings by programming language.

Figure 2: Sample multilingual embeddings.

A Analysis

Zero-shot Results. We investigated zero-shot transfer from Python to Java, Ruby, PHP, Go, and JavaScript on the *CodeSearchNet* dataset for previously introduced code language models and our CCT-LM. The zero-shot results are presented in Table 3. As evidence for the power of pretrained language models, we see that existing approaches show rather good results even though they have not been trained on the retrieval task. By leveraging its multilingual ability, CCT-LM improves over the baselines in the zero-shot setup for all languages except *JavaScript* (JS).

Latent space structure. Figure 1 showed an abstract representation of the basic CCT idea of semantically aligned language-agnostic embedding space. Figure 2 turns this theory into practice with projections of actual embeddings for sample code snippets before and after CCT training. The snippets represent solutions for 12 sample tasks in six programming languages. We see that after CCT, representations of code snippets are not aligned by language but rather by problem (Fig. 2b), while their alignment had been language-dependent before CCT (Fig. 2a).

This illustrates that CCT training significantly improves the multilingual latent space for code snippets, making it semantic and language-agnostic.

Ablation Study. In this section, we study the effects of various parts of CCT. Table 5 shows the results of several DeepSeek-Coder-based models on clone detection, code search tasks. We compare the DeepSeek-Coder base model with different pretraining poolings and attention types.

Text Compression for Efficient Language Generation

David Gu
ETH Zurich
david.gu@inf.ethz.ch

Peter Belcak
NVIDIA
pbelcak@nvidia.com

Roger Wattenhofer
ETH Zurich
wattenhofer@ethz.ch

Abstract

We challenge the prevailing assumption that LLMs must rely fully on sub-word tokens for high-quality text generation. To this end, we propose the "Generative Pretrained Thoughtformer" (GPTHF), a hierarchical transformer language model capable of text generation by compressing text into sentence embeddings and employing a sentence attention mechanism. GPTHF retains GPT's architecture, modifying only token interactions via dynamic sparse attention masks.

Our experiments show that GPTHF achieves an up to an order of magnitude improvement in FLOPs efficiency and a threefold increase in runtime speed compared to equally-sized GPT models in the low-size regime. This is achieved through a unique generation method that caches and reuses sentence embeddings, allowing significant portions of the input to bypass large parts of the network.

1 Introduction

The development of LLMs has garnered substantial interest due to their impressive capabilities in NLP tasks. The dominant paradigm for improving LLMs has been *scaling*, with models scaling from hundreds of millions (e.g. BERT, Devlin et al. (2018)) to over a trillion parameters (e.g. Switch Transformer, Fedus et al. (2022)) in a span of four years. While these massive scales unlock remarkable performance across NLP tasks (Naveed et al., 2023), they come with substantial costs in hardware, energy, and time (Strubell et al., 2019; Patterson et al., 2021), requiring the exploration for more efficient methods.

Efforts to improve efficiency include pruning (Augasta and Kathirvalavakumar, 2013), quantization (Hubara et al., 2018), and knowledge distillation (Gou et al., 2021). Mixture of experts models (Shazeer et al., 2017; Fedus et al., 2022) further reduced inference costs while preserving capacity. However, one area remains under explored: the reliance of LLMs on sub-word tokens, each requiring embeddings several kilobytes in size. This raises the question of whether more condensed text representations could offer similar performance with greater efficiency. Models like the Funnel-Transformer (Dai et al., 2020) hint at potential gains through compressing and subsequently decompressing hidden states.

Going one step further, we introduce GPTHF, a hierarchical transformer that compresses entire sentences into fixed-size embeddings. We explore whether such representations still carry sufficient semantic payload to maintain generation quality, thereby asking if sub-word tokens could possibly be eliminated for greater computational efficiency. Experimental results show that GPTHF achieves strong perplexity scores, follows scaling laws in the low-parameter regime, and operates at a significantly reduced FLOPs cost and inference time.

Contributions. 1. We propose GPTHF, a transformer language model that generates text by compressing sentences into one fixed-size embedding and employing sentence-level attention, with minimal modifications to GPT. 2. We introduce a generation method that caches and reuses sentence embeddings, yielding linear efficiency improvements with context size, achieving up to 10x FLOP reductions and 3x runtime speedup.

2 Related Work

A new line of research explored the idea of a "hierarchical transformer," a transformer operating on variable-size embeddings within different layers of the network. Early examples include the models of Yang et al. (2016) and Montero et al. (2021). The Funnel Transformer (Dai et al., 2020) compressed token sequences via incremental pooling, with inter-layer skip connections allowing later layers to access pre-compressed information. When re-investing the saved FLOPs, the Funnel Transformer outperformed previous state-of-the-art models with comparable computational resources.

Proceedings of the 2025 Conference of the Nations of the Americas Chapter of the Association for Computational Linguistics: Human Language Technologies (Volume 4: Student Research Workshop), pages 186–192

Nawrot et al. (2021) expanded this idea to generative transformers with their "Hourglass" model, demonstrating improved perplexity on a Wikipedia dataset. Other examples include Sentence-BERT (Reimers and Gurevych, 2019) and Sentence-GPT (Muennighoff, 2022), focus on generating sentence embeddings for downstream tasks.

Our work differs from all of the above in several ways. Instead of compressing a fixed-size group of tokens, we compress a sentence – a unit of higher semantic value in language – into one embedding. We focus on leveraging these embeddings to improve computational efficiency, not on the embeddings themselves.

3 Methodology

3.1 Architecture

The GPTHF model consists of two main components: a word-level transformer encoder (`wlt_encoder`) and a sentence-level transformer body (`slt_body`). The encoder compresses each sentence into a single embedding while preserving essential information. The `slt_body` contextualizes these sentence embeddings and generates the next-token prediction.

During the forward pass (see Figure 2), the input tokens $x_1, \cdots, x_n$ are first processed by the `wlt_encoder`, producing contextualized sub-word embeddings. The `wlt_encoder` uses block attention masks, which will be explained below. Fetching the last token of each sentence s_i yields an embedding $e_i, i \in [m]$:

$$e_i = \text{Pooling}(\texttt{wlt\_encoder}(x_1, ..., x_n)),$$

where m is the number of sentences. These embeddings are then processed by the `slt_body`:

$$\hat{e_i} = \texttt{slt\_body}(e_1, ..., e_n)), i \in [m].$$

Finally, $\hat{e_m}$ is fed into the language modeling head to predict the next token.

Block attention masks. To ensure sentence embeddings capture only intra-sentence information, we use a localized attention mechanism that restricts token attention to within the same sentence. This is enforced via a dynamically computed (for each input) block attention mask, defined by a *sentence index vector* at tokenization time. Each block corresponds to a sentence, preventing cross-sentence interactions (see Figure 1).

Model sizes and Details. A summary of the model sizes and other hyperparameters are provided in Table 1. Through empirical experimentation, a relatively large encoder is found beneficial.

$$\begin{pmatrix} 1 & 1 & 0 & 0 & 0 \\ 1 & 1 & 0 & 0 & 0 \\ 0 & 0 & 1 & 1 & 1 \\ 0 & 0 & 1 & 1 & 1 \\ 0 & 0 & 1 & 1 & 1 \end{pmatrix} \quad \begin{pmatrix} 1 & 0 & 0 & 0 & 0 \\ 1 & 1 & 0 & 0 & 0 \\ 0 & 0 & 1 & 0 & 0 \\ 0 & 0 & 1 & 1 & 0 \\ 0 & 0 & 1 & 1 & 1 \end{pmatrix}$$

(a) (b)

Figure 1: Visualization of block attention masks for a text with sentence index vector $[0, 0, 1, 1, 1]$. (a) A block matrix allowing attention within sentences. (b) Block lower triangular matrix allowing attention to previous tokens within sentences during training.

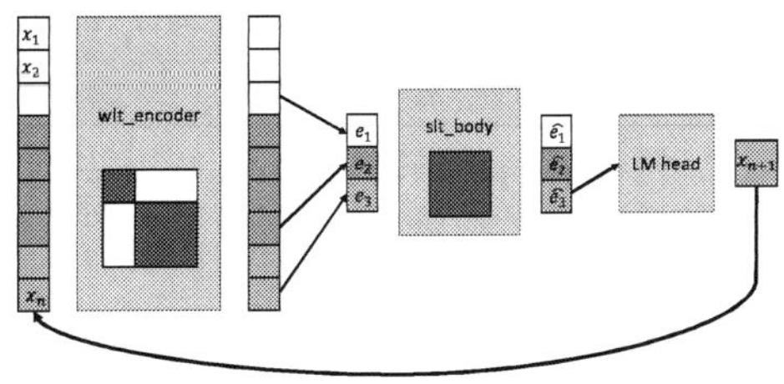

Figure 2: Overview of the Generative THF (GPTHF) Architecture during inference. The boxes in the models indicate the type of attention masks used. The attention masks are explained in Figure 1.

We decide on the following modifications over the vanilla transformer (Vaswani et al., 2017), mostly inspired by Llama-1 (Touvron et al., 2023) and Geiping and Goldstein (2023), who proposed architectural changes when training language models in low-compute settings.

First, we replace an absolute positional embedding layer with rotary positional embeddings (RoPE, Su et al. (2024)) at each attention layer of the network. We use SwiGLU activation (Shazeer, 2020) with a dimension of 2/3 4d. Moreover we use pre-normalization layers with RMSNorm (Zhang and Sennrich, 2019). Finally, we disable all QKV biases in the transformer attention layers and linear layers.

3.2 Pre-training

We use the next token prediction objective common in auto-regressive models. To prepare GPTHF for token prediction while enabling efficient parallel training, we again employ specialized attention masks (Figure 4). The target is the next token in the sequence (Figure 3).

Interestingly, training GPT and GPTHF differs only in replacing full triangular attention matrices with dynamically computed sparse ones, with no architectural changes.

Name	Params	d	n_{heads}	l_{enc}	l_{body}	lr
GPTHF-8-4	151M	768	12	8	4	6e-4
GPTHF-16-8	454M	1024	16	16	8	4e-4

Table 1: Model sizes and hyperparameters for GPTHF models.

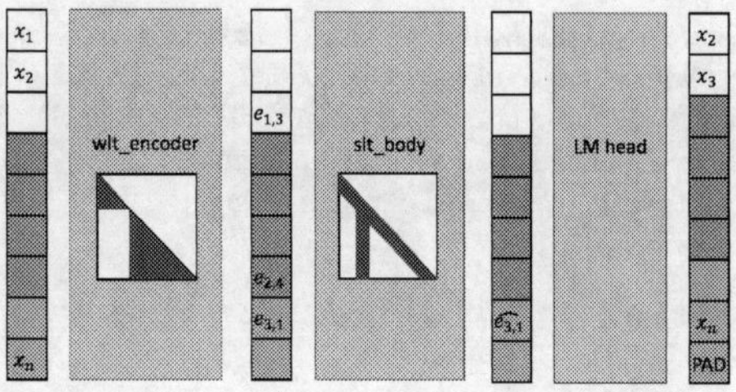

Figure 3: Overview of the pre-training procedure. The boxes in the models indicate the type of attention masks used. The attention masks are explained in Figure 4.

Data. Our training corpus incorporates OpenWebText, Wikipedia and ArXiv. OpenWebText forms the backbone due to its large size and diverse internet content. Wikipedia is known for its vast coverage of general knowledge. Finally, ArXiv augments our corpus with scientific and technical texts. We use the standard GPT-2 tokenizer, inheriting its handling of vocabulary size and unknown words, while introducing an "end-of-sentence" token. This token is crucial in the design of a fast generation method, a cornerstone of this work.

Details. We use the Adam optimizer with weight decay of 0.01, $\beta_1 = 0.9$, $\beta_2 = 0.98$ and $\epsilon = 10^{-8}$. We maintain gradient clipping with a value of 0.5. As our learning rate scheduler we use linear decay with 10000 warmup steps. The peak learning rates are provided in Table 1. We keep the batch size scheduler from (Geiping and Goldstein, 2023), starting batch size at 64 and linearly ramping up to 4096, reaching this peak at 60% of the training duration. Lastly, we eliminate dropout during training. Our models undergo only a single pass or less over the pre-training corpus, which mitigates the risk of overfitting.

$$\begin{pmatrix} 1 & 0 & 0 & 0 & 0 \\ 1 & 1 & 0 & 0 & 0 \\ 0 & 0 & 1 & 0 & 0 \\ 0 & 0 & 1 & 1 & 0 \\ 0 & 0 & 1 & 1 & 1 \end{pmatrix}$$

(a) Encoder attention matrix

$$\begin{pmatrix} 1 & 0 & 0 & 0 & 0 \\ 0 & 1 & 0 & 0 & 0 \\ 0 & 1 & 1 & 0 & 0 \\ 0 & 1 & 0 & 1 & 0 \\ 0 & 1 & 0 & 0 & 1 \end{pmatrix}$$

(b) Body attention matrix

Figure 4: Attention masks during pre-training for an input with the sentence index vector [0,0,1,1,1]: The left matrix is the "block triangular mask" as in Section 3.1. After going through the encoder, every token represents the compressed prefix of its sequence up to itself, and is only allowed to attend to itself and compressions of previous sequences (right).

3.3 Fast generation

The insight that enables a faster generation algorithm to be mathematically equivalent to regular token generation is the design of our block-wise attention matrix. During the generation loop, when generating a token in sentence j, only tokens in sentence j are affected – tokens in previous sentences remain unchanged. Since the feed-forward layers operate element-wise, there is no operation within the transformer layer that alters the compressed embeddings $e_1, e_2, \cdots, e_{j-1}$. The core idea is to cache these embeddings, allowing the encoder to process only the current sentence j to compute e_j. The body then processes the concatenation of the cached embeddings $e_1, e_2, \cdots, e_{j-1}$ and the updated e_j. For an illustration, see Figure 5.

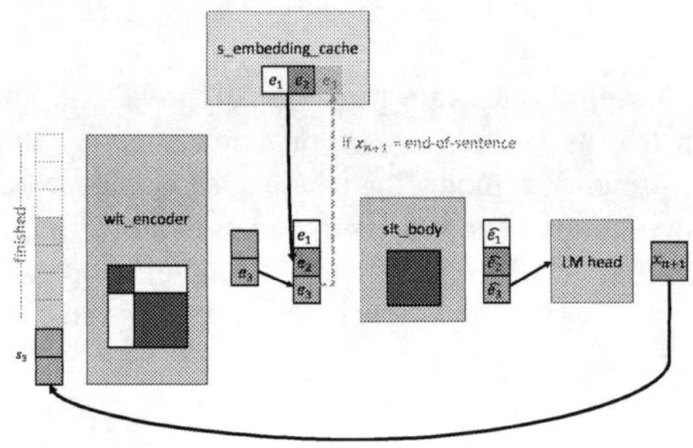

Figure 5: Illustration of the Fast Generation Algorithm. Having finished s_1 and s_2 in the context, any subsequent token mathematically cannot influence e_1, e_2. The Fast Generation Algorithm caches them and feeds them directly to the `slt_body`, together with e_3.

4 Experiments

4.1 Setup

We evaluate GPTHF against GPT-style baselines of comparable size, using validation perplexity and efficiency metrics (FLOPs and runtime). Due to computational constraints, the training data is limited to 10 billion tokens, divided into 320'000 micro-batch steps of size 64 with a context size of 512 tokens. All models are pre-trained on the same datasets.

Baselines. We trained a 12-layer baseline named "Baseline-12" and a 24-layer "Baseline-24" with the same architecture and size as their GPTHF

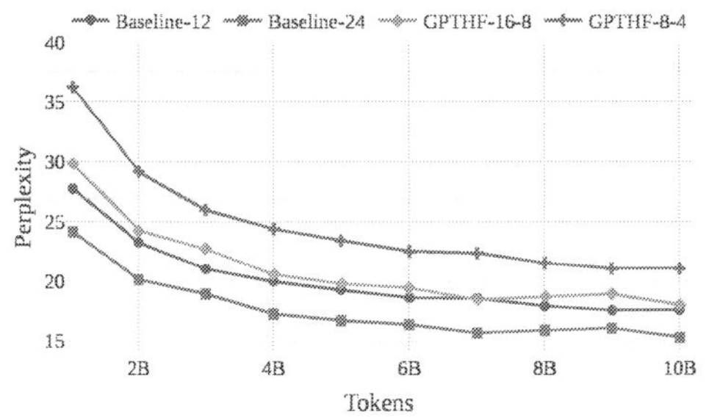

Figure 6: Validation perplexity of pre-trained models and baselines. Lower values indicate better performance.

counterparts. The only difference was that they were trained using full triangular masks for both encoder and body, as opposed to the masks in Figure 4. As remarked in Section 3.2, the baselines can be regarded as equivalent to conventional GPTs.

4.2 Perplexity

Validation perplexities after training are presented in Figure 6. They were calculated on a hold-out validation dataset comprising 16 million tokens.

Scaling Laws Hold in the Low-Compute Setting. GPTHF models have higher perplexity than baselines but follow scaling laws in the low-parameter regime. Both show a ~5-point perplexity drop when scaling from 12 to 24 layers after 10B tokens. GPTHF-16-8 and the 12-layer baseline perform on par, setting a basis for further comparisons: If GPTHF-16-8 achieves higher generation efficiency and/or speed than a 12-layer GPT, training a larger model capable of compression might be worthwhile.

4.3 FLOPs

The speedup from our fast generation algorithm (Section 3.3) depends on token distribution across sentences as opposed to only the shape of the input. Intuitively, more sentences help by caching completed ones to skip the encoder. Since theoretical FLOPs analysis is impractical, we measure empirically using OpenWebText samples with varying prompt lengths (n) and token counts (k), leveraging the tool from Li. All numbers in Table 2 exclude KV-caching (Pope et al., 2023), as adapting our approach to it requires significant additional effort.

Efficiency Gain Increases With Prompt Length. The results show that efficiency improves with larger n, but surprisingly decreases with higher k. A closer examination reveals that our models generate few relevant tokens, often repeating them without generating end-of-sentence tokens. This occurs in both GPTHF models and baselines, indicating that it likely stems from insufficient scale or training rather than compression. Since the fast algorithm relies on completed sentences, generation quality directly affects efficiency. This explains a) the small gains 100-prompt/250-generation tokens, and b) strong efficiency gains (up to 10x) for 500-prompt/20-generation tokens. We hypothesize that a model capable of correctly terminating sentences achieves greater efficiency gains than reported in Table 2, increasing with both n and k.

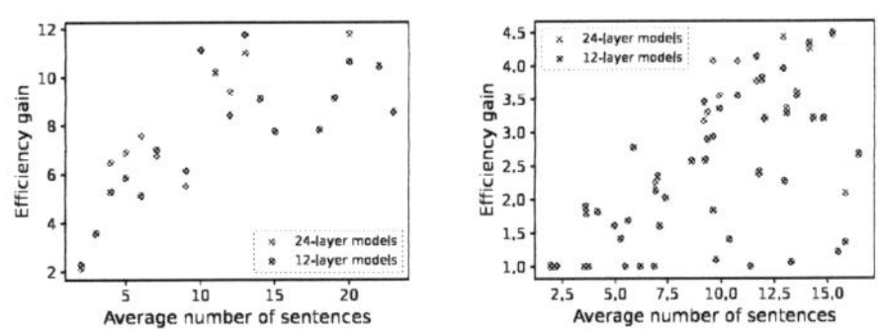

(a) Batch size = 1 (b) Batch size = 32

Figure 7: Scatter plots showing the average number of sentences (x-axis) versus the efficiency gain (y-axis) of GPTHF over GPT when generating 20 tokens.

Sentences vs Efficiency. Figure 7 shows scatter plots of the average sentence count (x-axis) versus efficiency gain (y-axis). We see that the efficiency gain increases *linearly* with the average number of sentences. For batched data, the efficiency gain is lower likely due to larger variety (which can be observed from the increased variance) in tokens, leading to more padding tokens being processed, which slows the fast generation algorithm.

4.4 Inference Time

While we save many FLOPs, not all translate to faster runtime due to GPU inefficiencies from non-trivial and conditional executions. We measure actual inference times to account for this, using an identical setup (see Table 3).

Speedup Increases With Context. Similar to the FLOP experiment, increasing up to 25% for unbatched data as k grows. Batched data shows gains with larger n but not k, which we attribute to the same sentence-termination limitations.

Latency vs. Throughput. We attribute the significant speedup differences between unbatched and batched data to latency vs. throughput. For unbatched data with small contexts, the GPU remains idle. This limits the runtime by latency, which primarily depends on model size. Batched data utilizes GPUs better, converting efficiency gains in

	Batch size 1					Batch size 32				
$n, k =$	100,100	100,250	250,100	250,250	500,20	100,100	100,250	250,100	250,250	500,20
Baseline-12	2.38T	9.1T	4.88T	15.7T	1.56T	2.46T	9.62T	4.96T	16.0T	1.7T
GPTHF-8-4	0.95T	4.16T	0.80T	4.31T	0.17T	1.90T	7.72T	2.53T	9.32T	0.58T
Efficiency	2.51x	2.19x	6.10x	3.64x	**9.18x**	1.29x	1.25x	1.96x	1.72x	**2.93x**
Baseline-24	8.30T	31.4T	17.0T	53.9T	5.45T	8.52T	32.7T	17.2T	54.9T	5.95T
GPTHF-16-8	2.99T	17.4T	2.97T	17.5T	0.56T	6.11T	25.6T	8.39T	31.3T	2.04T
Efficiency	2.78x	1.81x	5.72x	3.08x	**9.73x**	1.39x	1.28x	2.05x	1.75x	**2.92x**

Table 2: Empirical FLOP count per sample for varying prompt lengths n and generated token counts k. Lower values indicate better efficiency. Bold values highlight highest speedup for each batch size. The mean over 50 batches is reported. Efficiency is calculated as the inverse of the FLOP reduction of the GPTHF model compared to its respective baseline.

	Batch size 1					Batch size 32				
$n, k =$	100,100	100,250	250,100	250,250	500,20	100,100	100,250	250,100	250,250	500,20
Baseline-12	1.73s	4.44s	1.82s	4.77s	0.44s	0.17s	0.57s	0.28s	0.88s	0.093s
GPTHF-8-4	1.77s	4.46s	1.77s	4.48s	0.41s	1.90T	0.50s	0.18s	0.56s	0.041s
Speedup	0.98x	1.00x	1.03x	1.06x	**1.07x**	1.13x	1.14x	1.56x	1.57x	**2.27x**
Baseline-24	3.40s	8.88s	3.73s	9.85s	0.84s	0.40s	1.42s	0.73s	2.34s	0.26s
GPTHF-16-8	3.32s	8.43s	3.32s	8.44s	0.67s	0.35s	1.24s	0.37s	1.29s	0.087s
Speedup	1.02x	1.05x	1.12x	1.17x	**1.25x**	1.14x	1.15x	1.97x	1.81x	**2.99x**

Table 3: Empirical generation time in seconds per sample for different prompt lengths n and number of tokens generated k. Lower values are better. Bold values indicate highest speedup for each batch size. The mean over 50 batches executed on a single NVIDIA RTX A6000 is reported. Speedup is calculated as the inverse time reduction of our model in comparison to the baseline.

FLOPs into higher throughput. Moreover, speedup increases with model size, resulting in up to triple the speedup when comparing GPTHF with equal-sized baselines and slightly faster when comparing GPTHF 16-8 with the 12-layer baseline.

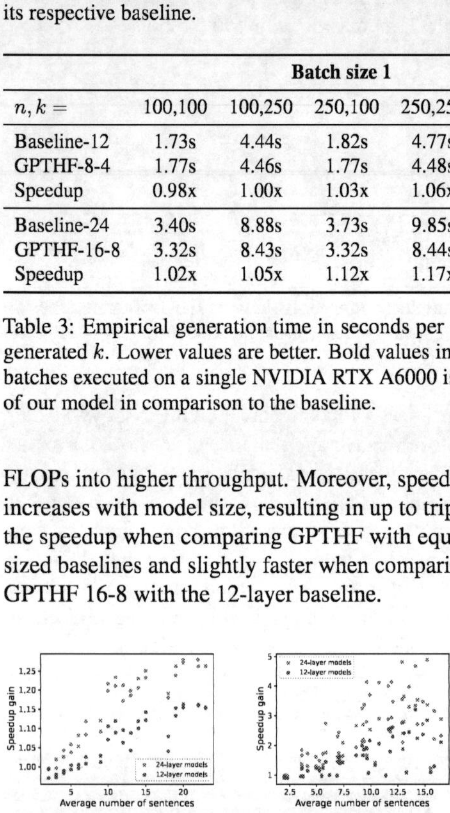

(a) Batch size = 1 (b) Batch size = 32

Figure 8: Scatter plots showing the average number of sentences (x-axis) versus the speedup gain (y-axis) of GPTHF over GPT when generating 20 tokens.

Sentences vs. Speedup. Figure 8 plots average sentence count (x-axis) against runtime speedup (y-axis). The figure highlights a *linear* relationship between the number of sentences and the speedup, with a larger constant for a larger model size.

4.5 Discussion

Our experiments show that compression results in a notable performance drop. Switching from a baseline/GPT to a GPTHF increases perplexity by 5 points after 10B tokens of training, similar to reducing a 24-layer GPT to 12 layers.

However, GPTHF models exhibit promising scaling behavior and significant efficiency improvements. Our method achieves speedups of up to 10x in FLOPs and 3x in runtime, scaling linearly with context size. For both our method and the baseline, KV-caching was excluded. Future work might want to explore KV cache integration to evaluate the effectiveness of our approach over state-of-the-art implementations.

Evaluating the overall tradeoff, we compare the GPTHF-16-8 and the 12-layer baseline, which perform on par (Figure 6). When processing 500 tokens of context, GPTHF-16-8 uses $\sim 1/3$ of the FLOPs for unbatched data and is slightly faster (7%) for batched data. Larger prompt lengths and batch sizes are expected to amplify these gains, making the tradeoff worthwhile at low compute scales.

These results suggest that sentence embeddings **could replace sub-word tokens in low-compute settings** while maintaining reasonable perplexity, but whether they remain competitive at larger scales is still open.

5 Limitations

A central question remains in whether transformers can generate high-quality text using only compressed sentence embeddings with sufficient size and training. While smaller GPTHF models follow scaling laws similar to GPTs, their inability to reliably finish sentences highlights challenges tied to either scale or the compression method itself. Further training on larger models is necessary to determine if this limitation is inherent to compression or surmountable via scaling.

Future work should evaluate these models on downstream tasks to assess practical utility beyond perplexity. Additionally, integrating GPTHF with existing optimizations like KV-caching could yield better speedups, though diminishing returns are a potential challenge. Comprehensive ablation studies focusing on key parameters like hidden size could offer deeper insights into performance. Alternative approaches, such as directly generating sentence embeddings and subsequently decompressing, warrant exploration to enhance or complement current methods.

References

M Augasta and Thangairulappan Kathirvalavakumar. 2013. Pruning algorithms of neural networks—a comparative study. *Open Computer Science*, 3(3):105–115.

Zihang Dai, Guokun Lai, Yiming Yang, and Quoc Le. 2020. Funnel-transformer: Filtering out sequential redundancy for efficient language processing. *Advances in neural information processing systems*, 33:4271–4282.

Jacob Devlin, Ming-Wei Chang, Kenton Lee, and Kristina Toutanova. 2018. Bert: Pre-training of deep bidirectional transformers for language understanding. *arXiv preprint arXiv:1810.04805*.

William Fedus, Barret Zoph, and Noam Shazeer. 2022. Switch transformers: Scaling to trillion parameter models with simple and efficient sparsity. *Journal of Machine Learning Research*, 23(120):1–39.

Jonas Geiping and Tom Goldstein. 2023. Cramming: Training a language model on a single gpu in one day. In *International Conference on Machine Learning*, pages 11117–11143. PMLR.

Jianping Gou, Baosheng Yu, Stephen J Maybank, and Dacheng Tao. 2021. Knowledge distillation: A survey. *International Journal of Computer Vision*, 129(6):1789–1819.

Itay Hubara, Matthieu Courbariaux, Daniel Soudry, Ran El-Yaniv, and Yoshua Bengio. 2018. Quantized neural networks: Training neural networks with low precision weights and activations. *Journal of Machine Learning Research*, 18(187):1–30.

Cheng Li. flops-profiler. `https://pypi.org/project/flops-profiler/`.

Ivan Montero, Nikolaos Pappas, and Noah A Smith. 2021. Sentence bottleneck autoencoders from transformer language models. *arXiv preprint arXiv:2109.00055*.

Niklas Muennighoff. 2022. Sgpt: Gpt sentence embeddings for semantic search. *arXiv preprint arXiv:2202.08904*.

Humza Naveed, Asad Ullah Khan, Shi Qiu, Muhammad Saqib, Saeed Anwar, Muhammad Usman, Nick Barnes, and Ajmal Mian. 2023. A comprehensive overview of large language models. *arXiv preprint arXiv:2307.06435*.

Piotr Nawrot, Szymon Tworkowski, Michał Tyrolski, Łukasz Kaiser, Yuhuai Wu, Christian Szegedy, and Henryk Michalewski. 2021. Hierarchical transformers are more efficient language models. *arXiv preprint arXiv:2110.13711*.

David Patterson, Joseph Gonzalez, Quoc Le, Chen Liang, Lluis-Miquel Munguia, Daniel Rothchild, David So, Maud Texier, and Jeff Dean. 2021. Carbon emissions and large neural network training. *arXiv preprint arXiv:2104.10350*.

Reiner Pope, Sholto Douglas, Aakanksha Chowdhery, Jacob Devlin, James Bradbury, Jonathan Heek, Kefan Xiao, Shivani Agrawal, and Jeff Dean. 2023. Efficiently scaling transformer inference. *Proceedings of Machine Learning and Systems*, 5.

Nils Reimers and Iryna Gurevych. 2019. Sentence-bert: Sentence embeddings using siamese bert-networks. *arXiv preprint arXiv:1908.10084*.

Noam Shazeer. 2020. Glu variants improve transformer. *arXiv preprint arXiv:2002.05202*.

Noam Shazeer, Azalia Mirhoseini, Krzysztof Maziarz, Andy Davis, Quoc Le, Geoffrey Hinton, and Jeff Dean. 2017. Outrageously large neural networks: The sparsely-gated mixture-of-experts layer. *arXiv preprint arXiv:1701.06538*.

Emma Strubell, Ananya Ganesh, and Andrew McCallum. 2019. Energy and policy considerations for deep learning in nlp. *arXiv preprint arXiv:1906.02243*.

Jianlin Su, Murtadha Ahmed, Yu Lu, Shengfeng Pan, Wen Bo, and Yunfeng Liu. 2024. Roformer: Enhanced transformer with rotary position embedding. *Neurocomputing*, 568:127063.

Hugo Touvron, Thibaut Lavril, Gautier Izacard, Xavier Martinet, Marie-Anne Lachaux, Timothée Lacroix, Baptiste Rozière, Naman Goyal, Eric Hambro, Faisal Azhar, et al. 2023. Llama: Open and efficient foundation language models. *arXiv preprint arXiv:2302.13971*.

Ashish Vaswani, Noam Shazeer, Niki Parmar, Jakob Uszkoreit, Llion Jones, Aidan N Gomez, Łukasz Kaiser, and Illia Polosukhin. 2017. Attention is all you need. *Advances in neural information processing systems*, 30.

Zichao Yang, Diyi Yang, Chris Dyer, Xiaodong He, Alex Smola, and Eduard Hovy. 2016. Hierarchical attention networks for document classification. In *Proceedings of the 2016 conference of the North American chapter of the association for computational linguistics: human language technologies*, pages 1480–1489.

Biao Zhang and Rico Sennrich. 2019. Root mean square layer normalization. *Advances in Neural Information Processing Systems*, 32.

Multilingual Native Language Identification with Large Language Models

Dhiman Goswami[1], Marcos Zampieri[1], Kai North[2]
Shervin Malmasi[3], Antonios Anastosopoulos[1]

[1]George Mason University, USA, [2]Cambium Assessment, USA
[3]Amazon.com, Inc. USA

dgoswam@gmu.edu

Abstract

Native Language Identification (NLI) is the task of automatically identifying the native language (L1) of individuals based on their second language (L2) production. The introduction of Large Language Models (LLMs) with billions of parameters has renewed interest in text-based NLI, with new studies exploring LLM-based approaches to NLI on English L2. The capabilities of state-of-the-art LLMs on non-English NLI corpora, however, have not yet been fully evaluated. To fill this important gap, we present the first evaluation of LLMs for multilingual NLI. We evaluated the performance of several LLMs compared to traditional statistical machine learning models and language-specific BERT-based models on NLI corpora in English, Italian, Norwegian, and Portuguese. Our results show that fine-tuned GPT-4 models achieve state-of-the-art NLI performance.

1 Introduction

Individuals proficient in a language have the ability to identify accent patterns in non-native speech (Major, 2007). Automatically identifying a speaker's native language (L1) when speaking a second language (L2) on the basis of pronunciation, stress, and prosodic patterns has been substantially explored in speech-based NLI (Krishna et al., 2019). Similarly, in text-based NLI, linguistic patterns common to an individual's L1 such as word choices, syntax, and spelling, can be recognized in texts written in a given L2. Computational models can be then trained on texts authored by non-native speakers to learn distinctive properties of their L1, aiming to identify the writer's mother tongue (Malmasi, 2016).

The underlying assumption in NLI is that the native language influences Second Language Acquisition (SLA) and production, a phenomenon known as cross-linguistic influence or language transfer (Krashen, 1981; Ellis, 2015). Language transfer results in L1 features manifesting in L2 production, allowing computational models to recognize patterns shared by speakers of the same L1 when communicating in a given L2. Text-based NLI has numerous important applications such as serving as a corpus-driven approach for SLA (Jarvis and Crossley, 2012) and enabling the development of effective L2 teaching materials and computer-aided language learning (CALL) software. Additionally, NLI has been shown to improve NLP systems dealing with texts from non-native speakers, contributing to tasks like author profiling, forensics, spam and phishing detection (Malmasi et al., 2017).

As evidenced by a recent survey (Goswami et al., 2024), traditional statistical models such as Support Vector Machines (SVMs) trained on n-grams as features have historically delivered the best performance for text-based NLI. A few recent studies (Zhang and Salle, 2023; Ng and Markov, 2024), however, have shown that fine-tuned LLMs such as GPT-4 deliver state-of-the-art performance for English NLI. A key limitation of these studies, as discussed by Ng and Markov (2024) is the lack of evaluation of LLMs for languages other than English. To address this important gap in the literature, we propose the first multilingual evaluation of LLMs in NLI. We evaluate various LLMs, in a zero-shot and fine-tuned setting, on corpora containing English, Italian, Norwegian, and Portuguese L2 production.

We investigate two research questions (RQs):

- **RQ1:** How effectively can LLMs identify L1s across NLI datasets in English and other languages?
- **RQ2:** To what extent does task-specific fine-tuning improve the performance of LLMs compared to zero-shot prompting across different languages?

Proceedings of the 2025 Conference of the Nations of the Americas Chapter of the Association for Computational Linguistics: Human Language Technologies (Volume 4: Student Research Workshop), pages 193–199

2 Related Work

The aforementioned survey by Goswami et al. (2024) presents a comprehensive account of text-based NLI, covering more than 100 papers on the topic. It describes studies that use a variety of features such as word n-grams (Gebre et al., 2013), part-of-speech tags (Wong et al., 2012), and syntactic features (Wong and Dras, 2011; Mechti et al., 2020). The survey also covers computational models widely employed in text-based NLI from statistical classifiers like SVMs (Jarvis et al., 2013; Goutte et al., 2013) and Logistic Regression (Tsvetkov et al., 2013; Popescu and Ionescu, 2013; Gupta, 2018) to deep learning architectures (Ajees and Idicula, 2018; Lotfi et al., 2020; Uluslu and Schneider, 2022) and LLMs (Zhang and Salle, 2023). In addition, it reviews shared tasks organized on the topic that provided important benchmark text-based datasets (Tetreault et al., 2013; Malmasi et al., 2017; Soman, 2018).

The findings described in Goswami et al. (2024) reveal that until recently, approaches that combined statistical classifiers with feature engineering achieved state-of-the-art performance on text-based NLI while deep learning architectures achieved limited success. Recent studies, however, have showed that the latest generation of LLMs, most notably GPT-4, are able to outperform statistical and previous neural models (Zhang and Salle, 2023) particularly when such models are fined-tuned for text-based NLI (Ng and Markov, 2024).

The majority of studies referenced here, including recent studies on LLM architectures (Ng and Markov, 2024), only address English NLI. This is due to the wider availability of English L2 corpora compared to other languages including widely-used learner corpora such as ICLE (Granger et al., 2009), TOEFL11 (Blanchard et al., 2013), and ICNALE (Ishikawa, 2011). Multiple multilingual studies have been conducted that describe data and approaches to text-based NLI in other L2s. This includes studies on Arabic (Malmasi and Dras, 2014a; Ionescu, 2015; Bassas and Kübler, 2024), Chinese (Malmasi and Dras, 2014b), Czech (Tydlitátová, 2016), Finish (Malmasi and Dras, 2014c), Norwegian (Malmasi et al., 2015), Portuguese (Malmasi et al., 2018; del Río, 2020), and Turkish (Uluslu and Schneider, 2023).

To the best of our knowledge, all text-based NLI studies on L2 other than English employed traditional machine learning models combined with feature engineering or early deep learning approaches. The use of LLMs for L2s other than English remains unexplored. Our work fills this gap by presenting the first multilingual evaluation of LLMs in text-based NLI on four languages and five datasets.

3 Data

In this study we use five NLI corpora in English, Italian, Norwegian, and Portuguese. NLI corpora, and learner corpora in general, are only available for English and a few other high-resource languages (Malmasi, 2016; Goswami et al., 2024) which limits the choice of languages we can study. With the goal of carrying out a multilingual evaluation, we choose Italian, Norwegian, and Portuguese due to the availability of suitable corpora.

Data Splits For TOEFL11 and NLI-PT we follow pre-defined training, development, and testing split from prior work (Tetreault et al., 2012; Malmasi et al., 2018). For all other corpora, we use a random label wise 80%-10%-10% split for training, development, and testing. To ensure comparability of results, we use the same splits across the different experiments presented in the paper. Brief descriptions of the five corpora are presented next.

English - FCE and TOEFL11 For L2 English, we use FCE and TOEFL11. FCE contains 1,244 exam scripts extracted from the Cambridge Learner Corpus (CLC) and written by candidates who took the Cambridge ESOL First Certificate in English (FCE) in 2000 and 2001 (Malmasi, 2016). It includes the following L1s: Spanish, French, Korean, Russian, Japanese, Turkish, Polish, Italian, Greek, German, Portuguese, Chinese, Catalan, Thai, Swedish, and Dutch. TOEFL 11 (Tetreault et al., 2012) is a dataset of essays written by speakers of 11 L1s: Arabic, German, French, Hindi, Italian, Japanese, Korean, Spanish, Telugu, Turkish and Chinese. Following the split by Tetreault et al. (2012) we use 1,100 essays for each L1 with 900 for training, 100 for development, and 100 for testing.

Italian - VALICO For Italian, we use VALICO (Corino et al., 2017), the *Varieta di Apprendimento deLlla Lingua Italiana Corpus Online*, i.e. Online Corpus of Learner Varieties of Italian. VALICO contains 2,531 texts written by L1 speakers of Albanian, Chinese, Czech, English, French, German, Hindi, Japanese, Polish, Portuguese, Romanian, Russian, Serbian, Spanish.

Norwegian - ASK For Norwegian, we use ASK (Tenfjord et al., 2006), the *Andrespråkskorpus*, i.e. Second Language Corpus. It features essays written in Norwegian Bokmål as part of an exam in Norwegian as a second language. It covers 2,158 essays written by L1 speakers of Albanian, Dutch, English, German, Polish, Russian, Serbian, Somali, Spanish, and Vietnamese.

Portuguese - NLI-PT For Portuguese, we acquire NLI-PT (del Río et al., 2018). NLI-PT is a corpus collected from three learner corpora of Portuguese: (i) COPLE2; (ii) Leiria corpus, and (iii) PEAPL2. It contains written productions from learners of European Portuguese with different proficiency levels and L1s. We use 1,075 texts written by L1 speakers of Chinese, Spanish, English, Italian, and German and the same train, development, and test split as in Malmasi et al. (2018).

4 Models

Statistical Machine Learning Ensemble We trained a Logistic Regression (LR) and an SVM classifier on POS n-grams of $n \in [1, 4]$. The data was normalized and its dimensionality was reduced using TruncatedSVD and PCA. We then combine the LR and SVM models in a majority voting ensemble (Malmasi and Dras, 2017). We refer to this model as ML Ensemble.

Transformers We fine-tune two multilingual models for the four languages, namely mBERT (Devlin et al., 2019) and XLM-R (Conneau et al., 2020). We also fine-tune several language specific models. For English we use BERT (Devlin et al., 2019) and RoBERTa (Liu et al., 2019), for Italian we use italianBERT (Dbmdz, 2020), for Norwegian we use norBERT (Samuel et al., 2023), and for Portuguese we use BERTimbau (Souza et al., 2020). We use learning rate 1e-5 for all models. The hyperparameters for the transformer models for all corpora are presented in Table 1.

Dataset	Epochs	Batch Size
FCE	5	8
TOEFL11	3	16
VALICO	10	16
ASK	5	16
NLI-PT	5	8

Table 1: Hyperparameters for BERT-based transformers and Flan-T5.

LLM Prompting We use FLAN-T5 (Chung et al., 2024) and GPT-4 (Achiam et al., 2023) for zero-shot prompting. We also carried out preliminary experiments with various 7 billion parameter models (e.g., Mistral-7B (Jiang et al., 2023)) which obtained much lower performance overall and therefore have not been included in our experiments. A sample LLM prompt used in our experiments is presented below.

```
Role (system): You are a forensic linguistics expert that reads <L2 Language> texts written by non-native authors in order to classify the native language of the author as one of: <List of L1s>. The output will be the short form of the languages in this list - <label>. Use clues such as spelling errors, word choice, syntactic patterns, and grammatical errors to decide. DO NOT USE ANY OTHER CLASS.
IMPORTANT: Do not classify any input as <L2 Language>. <L2 Language> is an invalid choice.
Role (user): <a text written by a non-native speaker>
```

LLM Fine-tuning We further fine-tune FLAN-T5 and GPT-4 for all datasets. For FLAN-T5, we have used the same epochs and batch size presented in Table 1. For GPT-4, we use the API provided OpenAI.[1] The data gets validated and an optimal set of hyperparameters are automatically fixed for fine-tuning. The hyperparameters of GPT-4 fine-tuning for all the datasets are given in Table 2 while the learning rate for all languages is 2e-5.

Dataset	Epochs	Batch Size
FCE	3	2
TOEFL11	2	16
VALICO	3	4
ASK	3	3
NLI-PT	3	2

Table 2: Hyperparameter for GPT-4 Fine-Tuning.

5 Results

We present the results for all languages in terms of accuracy and Macro F1, which is the standard in prior work (Malmasi, 2016; Goswami et al., 2024). The results are presented along with a random and a majority class baseline for comparison. Finally, to ensure a fair and comparable analysis across all

[1] https://platform.openai.com/finetune/

experiments, we evaluate all models on the same test sets for each particular corpus.

5.1 English

The results for English are presented in Table 3. We observe that all models achieve performance significantly higher than the two baselines provided. The results across the two NLI datasets demonstrate that LLMs, and in particular GPT-4, achieve state-of-the-art performance in text-based NLI when fine-tuned for the task. As shown in Table 3, fine-tuned GPT-4 achieves the highest F1 scores on both corpora with 0.82 for FCE and 0.92 for TOEFL11.

It is also worth noting that the the GPT-4 prompting results for TOEFL11 are unusually high compared to the results obtained by this model on the other four corpora. This is in line with the results reported by (Zhang and Salle, 2023) on TOEFL11. The high results suggest that model may have seen instances from this dataset indicating potential data contamination.

	FCE		TOEFL11	
Models	**Acc.**	**F1**	**Acc.**	**F1**
Random Baseline	0.06	0.06	0.10	0.10
Majority Baseline	0.14	0.04	0.09	0.02
ML Ensemble	0.47	0.46	0.84	0.82
BERT	0.25	0.25	0.68	0.68
mBERT	0.27	0.27	0.67	0.66
RoBERTa	0.29	0.28	0.71	0.71
XLM-R	0.33	0.32	0.63	0.62
FLAN T5 Prompt	0.38	0.36	0.32	0.32
GPT-4 Prompt	0.39	0.39	0.83	0.83
FLAN-T5 FT	0.37	0.36	0.73	0.73
GPT-4 FT	**0.83**	**0.82**	**0.92**	**0.92**

Table 3: Model results and baselines for English in terms of Accuracy (Acc.) and Macro F1 (F1). "Prompt" indicates zero-shot prompting, "FT" indicates fine-tuning.

Another key finding is that LLM fine-tuning outperforms all other models by a substantial margin. The ML ensemble, achieves 0.82 F1 for TOEFL11 lagging significantly behind the fine-tuned GPT-4 model. Another notable trend is that fine-tuning drastically improve LLM performance over zero-shot prompting. For example, on TOEFL11, while GPT-4 zero-shot gets 0.83 F1, fine-tuning boosts the performance to 0.92 F1. Finally, when comparing multilingual and language-specific transformer models, we obtain mixed results. On TOEFL11, monolingual models like RoBERTa outperform multilingual ones, while on FCE, multilingual XLM-R performs better than RoBERTa.

5.2 Italian, Norwegian, and Portuguese

Results for Italian, Norwegian, and Portuguese are presented in Table 4. Similarly to what we observed for English, we see a significant effect of task fine-tuning over zero-shot prompting on the LLMs performance. This is evidenced by the GPT-4 performance which, for Italian, achieves 0.78 F1 score when fine-tuned and 0.31 F1 when prompting. A similar trend is observed for Norwegian and Portuguese. We observe that the zero-shot results are much lower for Italian, Norwegian, and Portuguese when compared to English. This is somewhat expected as LLMs have shown to possess greater capabilities for English compared to all other languages (Minaee et al., 2024).

We see that the ML Ensemble outperforms all of the Transformer-based small LMs for all languages. This confirms the findings of related studies as discussed in a recent survey (Goswami et al., 2024). Finally, with the exception of norBERT for Norwegian, we see that language-specific transformers such as italianBERT and BERTimbau outperform the multilingual models mBERT and XLM-R. The reinforces the mixed results on language-specific vs. multilingual transformer models we described for English.

6 Conclusion and Future Work

This paper presented the first evaluation of LLMs on multilingual text-based NLI, experimenting with four languages and five corpora. Our results indicate that larger task fine-tuned LLMs, such as GPT-4, deliver state-of-the-art performance for text-based NLI in the four languages studied. This finding is in line with prior results obtained for English NLI (Ng and Markov, 2024).

We further observed that for non-English languages, zero-shot LLM prompting approaches are generally outperformed by BERT-based and statistical ML approaches. This is likely a limitation of the LLMs we leveraged here, as they are mostly focused on English.

We conclude the paper by revisiting the two RQs below and presenting avenues for future work.

RQ1: How effectively can LLMs identify L1s across NLI datasets in English and other languages?

Model	Italian		Norwegian		Portuguese	
	Accuracy	F1	Accuracy	F1	Accuracy	F1
Random Baseline	0.09	0.10	0.10	0.11	0.13	0.14
Majority Baseline	0.16	0.04	0.13	0.03	0.27	0.11
ML Ensemble	0.66	0.63	0.76	0.76	0.59	0.59
italianBERT	0.45	0.42	-	-	-	-
norBERT	-	-	0.67	0.67	-	-
BERTimbau	-	-	-	-	0.56	0.55
mBERT	0.48	0.44	0.43	0.40	0.57	0.57
XLM-R	0.43	0.36	0.42	0.39	0.32	0.30
FLAN T5 Prompt	0.28	0.27	0.37	0.36	0.30	0.29
GPT-4 Prompt	0.31	0.31	0.52	0.51	0.45	0.36
FLAN T5 FT	0.62	0.57	0.73	0.72	0.45	0.42
GPT-4 FT	**0.79**	**0.78**	**0.92**	**0.92**	**0.86**	**0.86**

Table 4: Model results and baselines for Italian, Norwegian and Portuguese in terms of Accuracy and Macro F1 (F1). "Prompt" indicates zero-shot prompting while "FT" indicates fine-tuning.

RQ1 Results: Our evaluation of LLM zero-shot prompting indicates that LLMs have very little knowledge of NLI for the four languages and five corpora explored. A notable exception is TOEFL11, the most popular NLI corpus available, for which the results obtained using GPT-4 were very high using zero-shot prompting. This seems to indicate potential data contamination. When fine-tuned, we observed that LLM results have significantly increased (see RQ2 Results). Finally, for all languages, statistical ML classifiers obtained performance superior to several transformers and LLM prompting.

RQ2: To what extent does task-specific fine-tuning improve the performance of LLMs compared to zero-shot prompting across different languages?

RQ2 Results: When fine-tuned to the task, GPT-4 achieves state-of-the-art performance for all four languages and five corpora explored. Furthermore, we observe that the performance gap between zero-shot and fine-tuning is much smaller for English compared to the other three languages. This provides further evidence of the ability of LLMs to better deal with English data compared to all other languages.

In future work, we would like to use the output of these classifiers to carry out a cross-lingual study of L1 to L2 transfer. This has been done extensively in the past using statistical classifiers (Jarvis and Crossley, 2012; Bykh and Meurers, 2014; Malmasi, 2016). We believe that the models used in our experiments may reveal interesting linguistic patterns being transferred from L1 that may generalize to various L2s in terms of spelling, word choices, and syntax.

Limitations

We hope the results presented in this paper motivate further research in multilingual NLI. The limitations of this work are related to the choice of languages and models. With respect to the languages, there are unfortunately very few corpora available for NLI which limits the choice of languages we can study. We hope our findings motivate researchers to create new NLI corpora for languages other than English and, in particular, for low-resource languages. All four languages that we studied are considered to be high-resourced. Finally, with respect to the models, we would like to investigate the performance of recently released LLMs such as Gemma, as in Ng and Markov (2024), on multilingual text-based NLI.

Acknowledgments

We thank the anonymous reviewers for the feedback provided. We further thank the creators of the five datasets used in this study for making the data available to the community. Antonios Anastasopoulos is generously supported by the National Science Foundation under award IIS-2327143.

References

Josh Achiam, Steven Adler, Sandhini Agarwal, Lama Ahmad, Ilge Akkaya, Florencia Leoni Aleman, Diogo Almeida, Janko Altenschmidt, Sam Altman, Shyamal Anadkat, et al. 2023. Gpt-4 technical report. *arXiv preprint arXiv:2303.08774*.

AP Ajees and Sumam Mary Idicula. 2018. Inli@ fire-2018: A native language identification system using convolutional neural networks. In *FIRE (Working Notes)*.

Yasmeen Bassas and Sandra Kübler. 2024. Investigating linguistic features for arabic nli. In *Proceedings of ArabicNLP*.

Daniel Blanchard, Joel Tetreault, Derrick Higgins, Aoife Cahill, and Martin Chodorow. 2013. Toefl11: A corpus of non-native english. *ETS Research Report Series*.

Serhiy Bykh and Detmar Meurers. 2014. Exploring syntactic features for native language identification: A variationist perspective on feature encoding and ensemble optimization. In *Proceedings of COLING*.

Hyung Won Chung, Le Hou, Shayne Longpre, Barret Zoph, Yi Tay, William Fedus, Yunxuan Li, Xuezhi Wang, Mostafa Dehghani, Siddhartha Brahma, et al. 2024. Scaling instruction-finetuned language models. *Journal of Machine Learning Research*, 25:1–53.

Alexis Conneau, Kartikay Khandelwal, Naman Goyal, Vishrav Chaudhary, Guillaume Wenzek, Francisco Guzmán, Edouard Grave, Myle Ott, Luke Zettlemoyer, and Veselin Stoyanov. 2020. Unsupervised cross-lingual representation learning at scale. In *Proceedings of ACL*.

Elisa Corino, Carla Marello, Simona Colombo, et al. 2017. *Italiano di stranieri. I corpora VALICO e VINCA*, volume 6. Guerra.

Dbmdz. 2020. BERT-base italian cased model. `https://huggingface.co/dbmdz/bert-base-italian-cased`.

Iria del Río. 2020. Native language identification on l2 portuguese. In *Proceedings of PROPOR*.

Iria del Río, Marcos Zampieri, and Shervin Malmasi. 2018. A portuguese native language identification dataset. In *Proceedings of BEA*.

Jacob Devlin, Ming-Wei Chang, Kenton Lee, and Kristina Toutanova. 2019. BERT: Pre-training of deep bidirectional transformers for language understanding. In *Proceedings of NAACL*.

Rod Ellis. 2015. *Understanding second language acquisition 2nd edition*. Oxford university press.

Binyam Gebrekidan Gebre, Marcos Zampieri, Peter Wittenburg, and Tom Heskes. 2013. Improving native language identification with tf-idf weighting. In *Proceedings of BEA*.

Dhiman Goswami, Sharanya Thilagan, Kai North, Shervin Malmasi, and Marcos Zampieri. 2024. Native language identification in texts: A survey. In *Proceedings of NAACL*.

Cyril Goutte, Serge Léger, and Marine Carpuat. 2013. Feature space selection and combination for native language identification. In *Proceedings of BEA*.

Sylviane Granger, Estelle Dagneaux, and Fanny Meunier. 2009. The international corpus of learner english: Handbook and cd-rom, version 2. Presses Universitaires de Louvain, Louvain-la-Neuve, Belgium.

Aman Gupta. 2018. Team webarch at fire-2018 track on indian native language identification. In *FIRE*.

Radu Tudor Ionescu. 2015. A fast algorithm for local rank distance: Application to arabic native language identification. In *Proceedings of ICONIP*.

Shin'ichiro Ishikawa. 2011. A new horizon in learner corpus studies: The aim of the icnale projects. In *In G. Weir, S. Ishikawa, and K. Poonpon, editors, Cor56 pora and Language Technologies in Teaching, Learning and Research*. University of Strathclyde Publishing.

Scott Jarvis, Yves Bestgen, and Steve Pepper. 2013. Maximizing classification accuracy in native language identification. In *Proceedings of BEA*.

Scott Jarvis and Scott A Crossley. 2012. *Approaching Language Transfer Through Text Classification: Explorations in the Detectionbased Approach*. Multilingual Matters.

Albert Q Jiang, Alexandre Sablayrolles, Arthur Mensch, Chris Bamford, Devendra Singh Chaplot, Diego de las Casas, Florian Bressand, Gianna Lengyel, Guillaume Lample, Lucile Saulnier, et al. 2023. Mistral 7b. *arXiv preprint arXiv:2310.06825*.

Stephen Krashen. 1981. Second language acquisition. *Second Language Learning*.

G Radha Krishna, R Krishnan, and VK Mittal. 2019. An automated system for regional nativity identification of indian speakers from english speech. In *Proceedings of IEEE INDICON*.

Yinhan Liu, Myle Ott, Naman Goyal, Jingfei Du, Mandar Joshi, Danqi Chen, Omer Levy, Mike Lewis, Luke Zettlemoyer, and Veselin Stoyanov. 2019. Roberta: A robustly optimized BERT pretraining approach. *CoRR*, abs/1907.11692.

Ehsan Lotfi, Ilia Markov, and Walter Daelemans. 2020. A deep generative approach to native language identification. In *Proceedings of COLING*.

Roy C Major. 2007. Identifying a foreign accent in an unfamiliar language. *Studies in second language acquisition*.

Shervin Malmasi. 2016. *Native language identification: explorations and applications*. Ph.D. thesis, Macquarie University, Faculty of Science and Engineering, Department of CLT.

Shervin Malmasi, Iria del Río, and Marcos Zampieri. 2018. Portuguese native language identification. In *Proceedings of PROPOR*.

Shervin Malmasi and Mark Dras. 2014a. Arabic native language identification. In *Proceedings of EMNLP (ANLP)*.

Shervin Malmasi and Mark Dras. 2014b. Chinese native language identification. In *Proceedings of EACL*.

Shervin Malmasi and Mark Dras. 2014c. Finnish native language identification. In *Proceedings of ALTA*.

Shervin Malmasi and Mark Dras. 2017. Multilingual native language identification. *Natural Language Engineering*.

Shervin Malmasi, Mark Dras, and Irina Temnikova. 2015. Norwegian native language identification. In *Proceedings of RANLP*.

Shervin Malmasi, Keelan Evanini, Aoife Cahill, Joel Tetreault, Robert Pugh, Christopher Hamill, Diane Napolitano, and Yao Qian. 2017. A report on the 2017 native language identification shared task. In *Proceedings of BEA*.

Seifeddine Mechti, Nabil Khoufi, and Lamia Hadrich Belguith. 2020. Improving native language identification model with syntactic features: Case of arabic. In *SPring ISDA 2018*.

Shervin Minaee, Tomas Mikolov, Narjes Nikzad, Meysam Chenaghlu, Richard Socher, Xavier Amatriain, and Jianfeng Gao. 2024. Large language models: A survey. *arXiv preprint arXiv:2402.06196*.

Yee Man Ng and Ilia Markov. 2024. Leveraging open-source large language models for native language identification. In *Proceedings of VarDial*.

Marius Popescu and Radu Tudor Ionescu. 2013. The story of the characters, the dna and the native language. In *Proceedings of BEA*.

David Samuel, Andrey Kutuzov, Samia Touileb, Erik Velldal, Lilja Øvrelid, Egil Rønningstad, Elina Sigdel, and Anna Palatkina. 2023. NorBench – a benchmark for Norwegian language models. In *Proceedings of NoDaLiDa*.

KP Soman. 2018. Overview of the second shared task on indian native language identification (inli). In *CEUR workshop proceedings*.

Fábio Souza, Rodrigo Nogueira, and Roberto Lotufo. 2020. Bertimbau: pretrained bert models for brazilian portuguese. In *Proceedings of BRACIS*.

Kari Tenfjord, Paul Meurer, and Knut Hofland. 2006. The ask corpus–a language learner corpus of norwegian as a second language. In *Proceedings of LREC*.

Joel Tetreault, Daniel Blanchard, and Aoife Cahill. 2013. A report on the first native language identification shared task. In *Proceedings of BEA*.

Joel Tetreault, Daniel Blanchard, Aoife Cahill, and Martin Chodorow. 2012. Native tongues, lost and found: Resources and empirical evaluations in native language identification. In *Proceedings of COLING*.

Yulia Tsvetkov, Naama Twitto, Nathan Schneider, Noam Ordan, Manaal Faruqui, Victor Chahuneau, Shuly Wintner, and Chris Dyer. 2013. Identifying the l1 of non-native writers: the cmu-haifa system. In *Proceedings of BEA*.

Ludmila Tydlitátová. 2016. Native language identification of l2 speakers of czech. Bachelors thesis, Charles University.

Ahmet Yavuz Uluslu and Gerold Schneider. 2022. Scaling native language identification with transformer adapters. In *Procedings of ICNLSP*.

Ahmet Yavuz Uluslu and Gerold Schneider. 2023. Turkish native language identification. In *Proceedings of ICNLSP*.

Sze-Meng Jojo Wong and Mark Dras. 2011. Exploiting parse structures for native language identification. In *Proceedings of EMNLP*.

Sze-Meng Jojo Wong, Mark Dras, and Mark Johnson. 2012. Exploring adaptor grammars for native language identification. In *Proceedings of EMNLP*.

Wei Zhang and Alexandre Salle. 2023. Native language identification with large language models. *arXiv preprint arXiv:2312.07819*.

Generating Synthetic Free-text Medical Records with Low Re-identification Risk using Masked Language Modeling

Samuel Belkadi[1], **Libo Ren**[2], **Nicolo Micheletti**[3],
Lifeng Han[2,4*], **Goran Nenadic**[2]
[1] Department of Engineering, University of Cambridge, UK
[2] Department of Computer Science, The University of Manchester, UK
[3] Department of Computer Science and Technology, Tsinghua University, China
[3] LIACS & LUMC, Leiden University, Leiden, NL * *corresponding author*

Abstract

The abundance of medical records holds great promise for enhancing healthcare and advancing biomedical research. However, due to *privacy* constraints, access to such data is typically limited to internal use. Recent studies have attempted to overcome this challenge by generating synthetic data through Causal Language Modelling. Yet, this approach often fails to ensure patient anonymity and offers limited control over output diversity—unless additional computational cost is introduced. In response, we propose a method for generating synthetic free-text medical records based on *Masked Language Modelling*. Our approach retains key medical details while introducing variability in the generated texts and reducing the risk of patient re-identification. With a relatively lightweight architecture of approximately 120 million parameters, the system ensures low inference costs. Experimental results show that our method produces high-quality synthetic data, achieving a HIPAA-compliant PHI recall of 96% and a re-identification risk of only 3.5%. Furthermore, downstream evaluations reveal that models trained on the synthetic data perform comparably to those trained on real-world data. Our trained models are publicly available on Github as SynDeidMLM (at `https://github.com/SamySam0/SynDeidMLM`) (meaning **syn**thetic and **de-id**entified data generation using **MLM**).

1 Introduction

The widespread adoption of electronic medical record (EMR) systems has led to the accumulation of substantial volumes of patient data, offering considerable opportunities to improve healthcare delivery and biomedical research (Beam and Kohane, 2018; Shah et al., 2018). However, access to such data is heavily restricted due to privacy concerns, aiming to safeguard patients' personal information (Price and Cohen, 2019). One promising alternative is the use of synthetic data, which allows the generation of documents—such as discharge summaries—that retain medically relevant information while reducing privacy risks. This approach enables broader data sharing for purposes like healthcare system testing (Tucker et al., 2020), medical training (Li et al., 2024), and the development of artificial intelligence tools (Belkadi et al., 2023).

Much of the previous work on synthetic medical text generation has primarily relied on *Causal Language Modelling* (CLM), with comparatively limited attention paid to *Masked Language Modelling* (MLM). While CLM approaches have shown promise in replicating the statistical patterns of real-world clinical data, they present several challenges—specifically, ensuring privacy protection, managing diversity in generated texts, and mitigating the computational cost of generation.

Recent findings by Micheletti et al. (2024) demonstrate that Masked Language Modelling can perform on par with Causal Language Modelling across a wide range of synthetic generation tasks, while offering greater flexibility in controlling contextual information. Building on these insights, this paper introduces a system designed to generate synthetic English-language medical texts—such as discharge notes, admission records, and doctor-to-doctor communications—using Masked Language Modelling. The system integrates a cutting-edge de-identification tool capable of automatically detecting protected health information (Radhakrishnan et al., 2023), thereby removing the need for manual pre-processing. It also incorporates two named entity recognition (NER) models to help retain essential clinical information and strike a balance between diversity and fidelity in the generated output. Importantly, the system is based on an encoder-only, non-autoregressive architecture, significantly reducing both its size and inference cost. The code will be released for public access.

Proceedings of the 2025 Conference of the Nations of the Americas Chapter of the Association for Computational Linguistics: Human Language Technologies (Volume 4: Student Research Workshop), pages 200–206

2 Related Work

In their recent study, Yan et al. (2024) proposed a Generative Adversarial Network (GAN) to produce synthetic electronic health records. While effective in some respects, their method struggled to manage the similarity between synthetic and original data and failed to accurately capture temporal dependencies within medical histories. Building on similar techniques, Kasthurirathne et al. (2021) presented a system for generating synthetic medical records with a low risk of re-identification. Despite encouraging results, the authors noted that limited diversity in the generated samples reduced their usefulness for tasks like oversampling. They also assumed that synthetic generation alone sufficiently mitigates re-identification risk, signalling the continued need for explicit de-identification mechanisms. In one of the most recent contributions to synthetic medical data research, Falis et al. (2024) assessed GPT-3.5's ability to generate discharge summaries. Their findings revealed that GPT-3.5 often closely reproduced input concepts, thereby heightening the risk of re-identification. Additionally, the generated texts were often unnatural, omitting key medical details while introducing irrelevant or misleading information. Clinicians involved in the evaluation acknowledged the presence of correct content but highlighted weaknesses in narrative structure, variety, and supporting details. Another concern raised was the model's lack of data governance, as it is not maintained by the institution that owns the original data. Taken together, these studies highlight common challenges in synthetic medical text generation: persistent *privacy* concerns and limited *control* over output variability. In response, our work advocates for the use of Masked Language Modelling, which offers enhanced control over the content being generated while reducing privacy risks and maintaining lower computational costs.

3 System Design

The system architecture, illustrated in Figure 1, is designed to generate synthetic medical records—including discharge summaries, admission notes, and clinician correspondence—through a two-stage pipeline: a *Masker* and a *Mask-Filling System*. The Masker identifies which parts of the text should be hidden or retained, outputting a partially masked version of the original text. The Mask-Filling System then replaces the masked sections with context-aware content, producing one or more synthetic variants of the original record.

3.1 The Masker

The Masker operates in three sequential stages: I) **De-identification.** The initial step involves detecting Protected Health Information (PHI) using Philter (Norgeot et al., 2020), a rule-based tool that relies on regular expressions to extract six PHI categories: DATE, ID, NAME, CONTACT, AGE, and LOCATION. According to the authors, Philter achieves high recall scores—99.46% on the UCSF dataset and 99.92% on the i2b2 2014 dataset. To our knowledge, it is the first certified de-identification system that enables the release of clinical notes for nonhuman-subject research, exempt from further IRB approval during the time period outlined by Radhakrishnan et al.. II) **Medical Entity Recognition.** In the second stage, a medical named entity recognition (NER) model identifies essential clinical terms that should remain unmasked in the synthetic output. For this, we fine-tuned a pre-trained Stanza model[1] on the i2b2-2010 dataset to extract three categories of entities: PROBLEM, TEST, and TREATMENT. This model achieved an F1 score of 88.13% on the test set. The system is also adaptable—users can substitute the model to target other entity types (e.g. medication names or dosages), and control the degree of masking applied to each entity class. III) **Part-of-Speech Tagging.** The final phase involves part-of-speech (POS) tagging using Stanza's POS tagger. Based on user-specified ratios, a subset of the tagged tokens is randomly masked to influence the diversity of the synthetic output. For instance, a setting like NOUN: 0.7, VERB: 0.5 would randomly mask 70% of nouns and 50% of verbs, while leaving other word types untouched.

3.2 The Mask-Filling System

Once the Masker has produced masked letters, the Mask-Filling System reconstructs them into synthetic texts using a masked language model (MLM) and a replacement algorithm. I) **MLM Model.** The MLM is an encoder-based model that predicts context-sensitive replacements for masked tokens by generating a probability distribution over possible vocabulary items. In our system, we employ Bio_ClinicalBERT—a version of BioBERT (Lee et al., 2020) fine-tuned on clinical texts from

[1] stanfordnlp.github.io/stanza/available_biomed_models.html

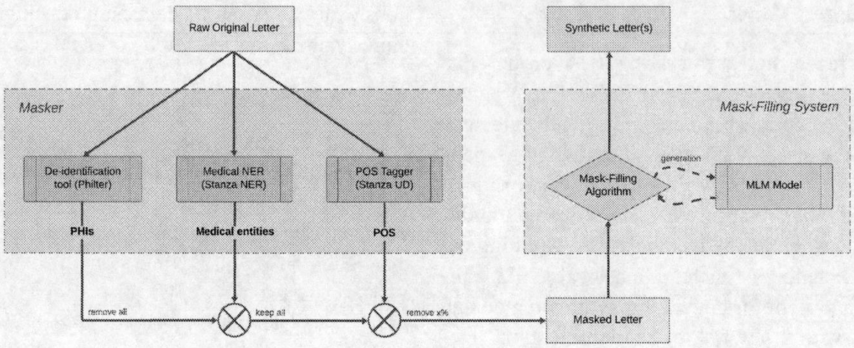

Figure 1: SYNDEIDMLM System Design: Masker and Mask-Filling two steps.

MIMIC III (Johnson et al., 2016). We further trained this model on a set of 790 clinical letters described in Section 4.1. While we did not compare it with alternative models, we encourage future research to explore different baselines. II) **Mask-Filling Algorithm.** This module prepares the masked input for the MLM model and chooses suitable replacements for each masked segment based on the model's predictions. We compare two strategies:

- *Simultaneous Chunk Filling*: In this approach, masked text is processed in chunks. Each chunk is passed through the MLM to generate probabilities for the masked elements. Replacements can be selected deterministically (using the highest probability term) or stochastically (by sampling from the distribution). While stochastic replacement enhances variation, it may also reduce fidelity by adding noise.

- *Iterative Mask Filling* (Kesgin and Amasyali, 2023): This method processes one masked entity at a time within a defined context window. As each masked token is resolved, it is replaced in the text, whereas upcoming masked items remain untouched until processed. This allows the model to focus on a specific context, improving generation quality and encouraging output diversity. Replacements, like in the previous approach, can be selected either deterministically or stochastically.

4 Experimental Setup

This section presents the dataset used to train and evaluate the MLM model, alongside the four system variants assessed in our experiments.

4.1 Datasets

The experiments are conducted using the i2b2 2014 shared task dataset for PHI de-identification (Stubbs and Uzuner, 2015; Stubbs et al., 2015), which includes 1,304 English clinical documents from 296 diabetic patients. These records comprise various note types such as discharge summaries, admission notes, and inter-physician communications. The dataset is pre-split into 790 training samples and 514 test samples. This resource offers a wide range of clinical scenarios and treatment contexts, making it well-suited for generating diverse synthetic outputs. All entries are annotated with HIPAA-compliant PHI labels. Furthermore, the dataset includes additional PHI sub-categories to reinforce privacy protection. The categories of annotations are Name, Profession, Location, Age, Contact, and IDs. Among these categories, only the following align with the official HIPAA-PHI definitions: NAME-PATIENT, LOCATION-STREET, LOCATION-CITY, LOCATION-ZIP, LOCATION-ORGANIZATION, AGE, DATE, CONTACT-PHONE, CONTACT-FAX, CONTACT-EMAIL, along with all sub-categories under ID.

4.2 Hyperparameters Tuning

The main parameters for system optimisation are the learning rate of the MLM model, the training batch size, the PHI's masking proportion, and the overall masking probability. We evaluate each instance using perplexity as it reflects the MLM model's confidence. We divided the data set into 80% and 20% for training and validation and retrained the model using the full data when the best parameter set is selected.

4.3 System Instances

We evaluated four system variants differing in masking ratios and mask-filling strategies:

- **System_S_0.5** and **System_S_0.7**: Both use Simultaneous Chunk Filling with stochastic sampling, mask all PHI, and retain all medical entities. They differ in lexical diversity, masking 50% and 70% of NOUNS, VERBS, and ADJECTIVES, respectively.
- **System_I_0.7** and **System_I_0.9**: These use Iterative Mask Filling with stochastic replacement, also masking all PHI while keeping medical entities. They apply 70% and 90% masking, respectively, for increased diversity.

The selected masking ratios are based on insights from Micheletti et al. (2024) but can be customised depending on the intended use case.

4.4 Evaluation Metrics

Our evaluation focuses on three main criteria: similarity to real data, utility, and privacy. **Lexical similarity** measures how well synthetic data reflects the structure and meaning of real text using ROUGE, BERTScore, and readability metrics (FRE[2], FKG[3], SMOG). It captures information retention, meaning preservation, and diversity, as well as how easy the text is to read. **Data utility** evaluates the effectiveness of synthetic data in training machine learning models. We assess this via a downstream NER task, comparing performance against models trained on real data (Belkadi et al., 2025; Micheletti et al., 2024). **Data privacy** is assessed by computing the F1 score for PHI removal (based on annotated HIPAA-PHI labels) and estimating re-identification risk.

5 Experiments and Results

5.1 Lexical Similarity Evaluation against References

The ROUGE and BERTScore results for the four system configurations are presented in Table 1. As expected, higher masking ratios tend to lower both ROUGE and BERTScore metrics, due to the increased noise introduced during generation. This confirms the trade-off between diversity and content fidelity, as previously discussed in Section 3.

Additionally, systems that utilise *iterative* mask filling consistently outperform those using simultaneous filling in terms of lexical *similarity* to the original text. For instance, with a masking ratio of 0.7, the iterative approach achieves ROUGE scores that are over 3 points higher and BERTScore improvements exceeding 0.3. This emphasises the benefit of iterative replacement, where each masked term is filled in using richer contextual information—either from unmasked or previously generated tokens—thereby reducing ambiguity. Moreover, even at a high masking ratio of 0.9, iterative systems exhibit a relatively small drop in BERTScore (0.04), whereas ROUGE scores decline more significantly (by 4 points). This indicates that although the surface wording may deviate more from the original, the core meaning is largely preserved.

These observations are further supported by findings in Table 2, where lexical variations between real and synthetic datasets are assessed through word overlap comparisons. Overall, all system configurations were capable of striking a balance between variation and content retention. The results illustrate a clear diversity–fidelity trade-off, which can be fine-tuned by adjusting the masking ratio and choice of mask-filling strategy, offering flexibility for different downstream tasks.

5.2 Readability Evaluation against References

As shown in Table 3, the synthetic medical letters generally exhibit higher readability scores compared to their original counterparts. This improvement is more pronounced at higher masking ratios, likely because the MLM model tends to substitute masked terms with simpler and more frequently used vocabulary. When comparing the different system configurations, there is no single system that consistently outperforms the others in terms of readability. This outcome is beneficial, as it suggests that users have the freedom to adjust the balance between fidelity and diversity without negatively impacting the readability of the generated

	RGE1	RGE2	RGE-L	BERTS
Sys_S_0.5	0.861	0.760	0.852	0.729
Sys_S_0.7	0.828	0.703	0.815	0.674
Sys_I_0.7	0.852	0.732	0.841	0.706
Sys_I_0.9	0.826	0.686	0.811	0.668

Table 1: Lexical similarities of the generated synthetic letters against references on the testing dataset.

[2]Flesch Reading Ease

[3]Flesch-Kincaid Grade

	Top 5	Top 20	Top 50	Top 100
System_S_0.5	3.848	15.593	38.420	78.670
System_S_0.7	3.601	14.607	35.971	73.695
System_I_0.7	3.712	15.095	37.233	76.093
System_I_0.9	3.537	14.551	35.510	72.298

Table 2: Average number of overlap between the top 5, 20, 50 and 100 words identified across the real and synthetic datasets, without stopwords. Additional results on lexical similarities.

	FRE	FKG	SMOG
System_S_0.5	64.024	7.647	10.823
System_S_0.7	65.091	7.466	10.696
System_I_0.7	63.792	7.707	10.878
System_I_0.9	64.294	7.636	10.832
References	61.597	8.06	11.067

Table 3: Readability scores of the generated synthetic letters against references on the testing dataset.

text.

5.3 Data Utility Evaluation

We investigate how effectively the synthetic data replicates key characteristics of real clinical text. To do so, we compare the performance of a medical NER model trained on synthetic data to that of a model trained on real data.

5.3.1 Downstream NER Task

For this task, the original test set is divided into new training and testing subsets. The real clinical letters are first passed through our system to generate synthetic equivalents. Both the real and synthetic texts are then processed using SciSpacy[4] (*en_ner_bc5cdr_md*), a named entity recognition model trained on the BC5CDR dataset, which achieves an F1 score of 0.84. This model identifies entities related to DISEASE and CHEMICAL terms. The extracted entities from the original and synthetic datasets are then used to create two distinct training sets. One SpaCy[5] model is trained using entities derived from the real data, while the other is trained on those extracted from the synthetic data. Both SpaCy models are then evaluated on the same test split. To study the effect of data *augmentation*, the experiment is repeated with twice as many synthetic letters generated per real letter. It is worth noting that while SciSpacy may introduce some errors during entity extraction, we assume these errors affect both the real and synthetic data consistently, preserving the fairness of

[4]https://allenai.github.io/scispacy/

[5]https://spacy.io/

		Precision	Recall	F1
	System_S_0.5	0.842	0.792	0.816
	System_S_0.7	0.851	0.797	0.823
x1	System_I_0.7	0.831	0.812	0.821
	System_I_0.9	0.846	0.810	0.827
	System_S_0.5	0.844	0.800	0.821
	System_S_0.7	0.850	0.805	0.828
x2	System_I_0.7	0.838	0.819	0.829
	System_I_0.9	0.855	0.819	**0.836**
	References	0.86	0.824	0.842

Table 4: Average Precision, Recall and F1 score for two labels (DISEASE and CHEMICAL) using Synthetic data $\times 1$, $\times 2$ and Real data, on the testing dataset.

the comparison.

5.3.2 Results of Downstream Task

The outcomes of the downstream evaluation are presented in Table 4. All system configurations performed *on par* with models trained using real data. Notably, systems with higher masking ratios achieved better F1 scores, likely due to the increased variability in the synthetic data, which may have provided SpaCy with a richer training set. In addition, when the volume of synthetic data was doubled, the F1 score rose to 0.836—just 0.006 below the performance of the model trained on authentic data.

5.4 Data Privacy Evaluation

To assess privacy preservation, we first measure the system's *de-identification* performance—specifically, how accurately the Masker detects all PHI instances in the test dataset. The Masker achieves a recall of 0.92 when considering all PHI categories, including additional sub-categories, and a recall of 0.96 when focusing solely on standard HIPAA-defined PHI types. Next, we assess the risk of *re-identification*, which refers to the likelihood that the MLM model inadvertently restores masked PHI entities. This step is crucial for safeguarding the privacy of individuals whose data contributed to model training. The results show that the model reintroduced PHI terms spanning more than two tokens at a very low rate of 0.035. In addition, we conducted a longest common substring analysis between original and synthetic texts for PHI segments. The overlap rates were minimal: 0.098 for substrings of 3 or more tokens, 0.020 for 5 or more, and just 0.009 for 7 or more. These findings demonstrate the system's strong performance in reliably removing HIPAA-sensitive information, while also maintaining a very low risk of re-identification.

6 Conclusion

In this work, we proposed a system using masked language models to generate synthetic clinical text, addressing challenges of data *scarcity* and *privacy*. The system includes a Masker (with de-identification, medical NER, and POS tagging) and a Mask-Filling module (supporting both simultaneous and iterative strategies). Key findings show that: **(1)** The system produces diverse yet clinically meaningful text, **(2)** Offers control over *diversity* and *fidelity* without reducing readability, **(3)** Performs well in downstream NER tasks—comparable to real data, **(4)** Ensures strong privacy protection (HIPAA-PHI recall of 0.96; re-ID risk of 0.035). The full system, SynDeidMLM, is available at `https://github.com/SamySam0/SynDeidMLM`.

Limitations and Future Work

Through close examination of the generated synthetic samples, we identified certain limitations—particularly with consistently reproducing temporal details and ensuring alignment with the original context. In some cases, maintaining *logical coherence* between related elements (e.g., referencing two names in the same scenario) proves difficult when the necessary context is outside the model's generation window. To address these issues, future work could incorporate a logic-based module for handling *temporal* data, which would enhance temporal consistency and further reduce re-identification risks. Another promising direction would be to supply the MLM model with the *type of entity* being replaced, which could increase the accuracy of PHI substitution and improve overall generation quality.

Regarding the masked language model itself, future research might explore the use of larger language models guided by prompt-based instructions to handle mask-filling. This strategy would specifically focus on the generation task, enabling a more in-depth comparison between Causal Language Models (CLMs) and Masked Language Models (MLMs) in terms of their ability to control fidelity and diversity in synthetic data. In such a setup, the Masker would remain unchanged, while the MLM and its mask-filling mechanism would be replaced by a CLM and a prompt-driven approach.

It is also important to acknowledge that our findings may have limited *generalisability*, as the experiments were conducted on a single dataset due to computational constraints. Future studies could expand the evaluation by testing the system on a wider variety of downstream tasks and datasets. For example, applying the system to specialised medical domains like radiology or oncology would be valuable. This would require replacing the current NER model with a more domain-specific one (e.g., *Stanza Radiology* or *Stanza Bionlp13cg*) to accurately extract relevant information. Such adaptation would likely necessitate re-evaluating masking strategies for both the NER component and the POS tagger to optimise performance.

We recognise that, at this stage, no alternative biomedical language models were assessed beyond Bio_ClinicalBERT. Nonetheless, future work should provide a more comprehensive rationale for selecting this model, including a comparative discussion of its strengths relative to other state-of-the-art options. A similar consideration applies to the use of Stanza for both NER and POS tagging tasks. In our readability evaluation, we reported that the synthetic letters appear easier to read than the originals, based solely on quantitative *evaluation metrics*. However, it is important to acknowledge the limitations of these metrics. Human evaluation will be necessary to more thoroughly assess the contextual appropriateness, narrative flow, and clinical usefulness of the generated content.

Acknowledgements

We thank the anonymous reviewers for valuable comments, which helped to make the paper better. LH and GN are grateful for the support from the grant "Assembling the Data Jigsaw: Powering Robust Research on the Causes, Determinants and Outcomes of MSK Disease", and the grant "Integrating hospital outpatient letters into the healthcare data space" (EP/V047949/1; funder: UKRI/EPSRC). LH is grateful for the 4D Picture EU project (`https://4dpicture.eu/`) on cancer patient journey support.

References

Andrew L Beam and Isaac S Kohane. 2018. Big data and machine learning in health care. *Jama*, 319(13):1317–1318.

Samuel Belkadi, Lifeng Han, Yuping Wu, and Goran Nenadic. 2023. Exploring the value of pre-trained language models for clinical named entity recognition. In *2023 IEEE International Conference on Big Data (BigData)*, pages 3660–3669. IEEE.

Samuel Belkadi, Nicolo Micheletti, Lifeng Han, Warren Del-Pinto, and Goran Nenadic. 2025. LT3: Generating medication prescriptions with conditional transformer. In *CL4Health 2025 Workshop at NAACL*.

Matúš Falis, Aryo Pradipta Gema, Hang Dong, Luke Daines, Siddharth Basetti, Michael Holder, Rose S Penfold, Alexandra Birch, and Beatrice Alex. 2024. Can gpt-3.5 generate and code discharge summaries? *arXiv preprint arXiv:2401.13512*.

Alistair EW Johnson, Tom J Pollard, Lu Shen, Li-wei H Lehman, Mengling Feng, Mohammad Ghassemi, Benjamin Moody, Peter Szolovits, Leo Anthony Celi, and Roger G Mark. 2016. Mimic-iii, a freely accessible critical care database. *Scientific data*, 3(1):1–9.

Suranga N Kasthurirathne, Gregory Dexter, and Shaun J Grannis. 2021. Generative adversarial networks for creating synthetic free-text medical data: a proposal for collaborative research and re-use of machine learning models. *AMIA Summits on Translational Science Proceedings*, 2021:335.

Himmet Toprak Kesgin and Mehmet Fatih Amasyali. 2023. Iterative mask filling: An effective text augmentation method using masked language modeling. In *International Conference on Advanced Engineering, Technology and Applications*, pages 450–463. Springer.

Jinhyuk Lee, Wonjin Yoon, Sungdong Kim, Donghyeon Kim, Sunkyu Kim, Chan Ho So, and Jaewoo Kang. 2020. Biobert: a pre-trained biomedical language representation model for biomedical text mining. *Bioinformatics*, 36(4):1234–1240.

Zihao Li, Samuel Belkadi, Nicolo Micheletti, Lifeng Han, Matthew Shardlow, and Goran Nenadic. 2024. Investigating Large Language Models and Control Mechanisms to Improve Text Readability of Biomedical Abstracts . In *2024 IEEE 12th International Conference on Healthcare Informatics (ICHI)*, pages 265–274, Los Alamitos, CA, USA. IEEE Computer Society.

Nicolo Micheletti, Samuel Belkadi, Lifeng Han, and Goran Nenadic. 2024. Exploration of masked and causal language modelling for text generation. *arXiv preprint arXiv:2405.12630*.

Beau Norgeot, Kathleen Muenzen, Thomas A Peterson, Xuancheng Fan, Benjamin S Glicksberg, Gundolf Schenk, Eugenia Rutenberg, Boris Oskotsky, Marina Sirota, Jinoos Yazdany, et al. 2020. Protected health information filter (philter): accurately and securely de-identifying free-text clinical notes. *NPJ digital medicine*, 3(1):57.

W Nicholson Price and I Glenn Cohen. 2019. Privacy in the age of medical big data. *Nature medicine*, 25(1):37–43.

Lakshmi Radhakrishnan, Gundolf Schenk, Kathleen Muenzen, Boris Oskotsky, Habibeh Ashouri Choshali, Thomas Plunkett, Sharat Israni, and Atul J Butte. 2023. A certified de-identification system for all clinical text documents for information extraction at scale. *JAMIA open*, 6(3):ooad045.

Nilay D Shah, Ewout W Steyerberg, and David M Kent. 2018. Big data and predictive analytics: recalibrating expectations. *Jama*, 320(1):27–28.

Amber Stubbs, Christopher Kotfila, and Özlem Uzuner. 2015. Automated systems for the de-identification of longitudinal clinical narratives: Overview of 2014 i2b2/uthealth shared task track 1. *Journal of biomedical informatics*, 58:S11–S19.

Amber Stubbs and Özlem Uzuner. 2015. Annotating longitudinal clinical narratives for de-identification: The 2014 i2b2/uthealth corpus. *Journal of biomedical informatics*, 58:S20–S29.

Allan Tucker, Zhenchen Wang, Ylenia Rotalinti, and Puja Myles. 2020. Generating high-fidelity synthetic patient data for assessing machine learning healthcare software. *NPJ digital medicine*, 3(1):1–13.

Chao Yan, Ziqi Zhang, Steve Nyemba, and Zhuohang Li. 2024. Generating synthetic electronic health record data using generative adversarial networks: Tutorial. *JMIR AI*, 3:e52615.

How many words does it take to understand a low-resource language?

Emily Chang
Department of Computer Science
University of Virginia
ec5ug@virginia.edu

Dr. Nada Basit
Department of Computer Science
University of Virginia
basit@virginia.edu

Abstract

When developing language technology, researchers have routinely turned to transfer learning to solve the data scarcity conundrum presented in low-resource languages. To our knowledge, this study is the first to evaluate the amount of documentation needed for transfer learning, specifically the smallest vocabulary size needed to create a sentence embedding space. In adopting widely spoken languages as a proxy for low-resource languages, our experiments show that the relationship between a sentence embedding's vocabulary size and performance is logarithmic with performance leveling at a vocabulary size of 25,000. It should be noted that this relationship cannot be replicated across all languages, and this level of documentation does not exist for many low-resource languages. We do observe, however, that performance accelerates at a vocabulary size of $\leq$ 1000, a quantity that is present in most low-resource language documentation. These results can aid researchers in understanding whether a low-resource language has enough documentation necessary to support the creation of a sentence embedding and language model.

1 Introduction

More than 43% of the languages spoken in the world are endangered (Zhang et al., 2022). Due to globalization and neocolonialism, language loss occurs at an accelerated rate (Zhang et al., 2022). Saving and revitalizing endangered languages has become very important for maintaining cultural diversity (Zhang et al., 2022). In times of crisis, these language technologies allow first responders to save lives. For example, the Low Resource Languages for Emergent Incidents (LORELEI) provides situational awareness based on information from any language and supports humanitarian assistance/disaster relief, peacekeeping, and infectious disease response (Strassel and Tracey, 2016).

Working with minimal data—as would be the case with endangered languages—makes it difficult to train natural language models from scratch. For these reasons, transfer learning is a potential method for language models to adapt to endangered languages (Alnajjar et al., 2023; Chen et al., 2019; Lee et al., 2021; Tran, 2020). We focus our research questions on cross-lingual transfer learning for low-resource languages to:

- **RQ 1**: What is the lower bound of documentation needed?
- **RQ 2**: When the target low-resource language is linguistically distant from the source high-resource language, does this lower bound of documentation change?

By establishing this lower-bound, we can better assess whether a low-resource language has enough documentation to support the creation of a sentence embedding space and language model.

2 Methodology

We analyze sentence embeddings as they are highly important in the creation of language models (Mao et al., 2024). In a survey of cross-lingual transfer learning learning methodologies, we found that Alnajjar et al. (2023)'s methodology to be the simplest. Alnajjar et al. (2023) draws on Finnish word embeddings to create embedding spaces and sentiment classifiers for endangered Uralic languages. The choice of Finnish as the source language is ideal as Finnish is part of the same language family as the endangered Uralic languages. We proceeded to modify the cross-lingual transfer methodology described in the paper.

When performing cross-lingual transfer learning, we select Dutch as the "high-resource" source language and English to train a Dutch sentiment classifier. To evaluate whether vocabulary size varies by proximity to the high-resource source language

Proceedings of the 2025 Conference of the Nations of the Americas Chapter of the Association for Computational Linguistics: Human Language Technologies (Volume 4: Student Research Workshop), pages 207–224

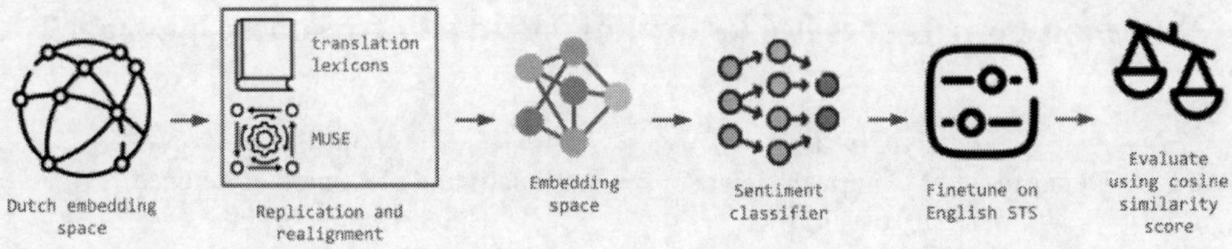

Figure 1: Overview of methodology. Using translation lexicons, the Dutch embedding space is replicated for each proxy language and aligned using MUSE. Sentiment classifiers are then built from the embedding spaces and finetuned on STS English examples. These classifiers are evaluated on their respective language in MTEB.

Dutch, we select four widely spoken languages as proxies for low-resource target languages: German, Turkish, Arabic, and Mandarin. We test Arabic and Mandarin separately to determine how replicable cross-lingual transfer is across different languages. Adopting high-resource languages as proxies allow us to experiment with varying degrees of language documentation, from the very small to the very large.

Our methodology is illustrated in Figure 1. We select a classic tokenizer that splits on whitespace and punctuation as an acknowledgment of the reality faced by many low-resource languages: a lack of data to train a more sophisticated tokenizer. With the help of translation lexicons, we replicate Dutch word embeddings for each proxy language before aligning all word embeddings. We then create sentence embeddings, each finetuned on English data as done in Alnajjar et al. (2023). We then evaluate these sentence embeddings by injecting sentence pairs into the sentence embedding space and comparing the model's cosine similarity score with the actual similarity score using the Spearman correlation (Spearman, 1904).

Language	Text
Dutch	Hij stierf dinsdag in Osaka.
German	Er verstarb am Dienstag in Osaka.
Turkish	Salı günü Osaka'da vefat etti.
Arabic	مات في أوساكا يوم الثلاثاء.
Mandarin	周二，他在大阪去世

Table 1: Languages analyzed in the study. Translations are provided for the phrase: "He died in Osaka on Tuesday" NLLB Team et al. (2024). Turkish uses a similar script similar to Dutch.

2.1 Evaluating the impact of genetic proximity using proxies

To account for genetic proximity, we adopt four high-resource languages as proxies for low-resource languages: German for its proximity to Dutch, Turkish because its typology is similar to Dutch but is in a different language family, and Arabic and Mandarin as their typologies are dissimilar to Dutch and are in a different language family (see Table 1 and Appendix A). Transfer learning is performed between two groups: (1) transfer of Dutch word embeddings to German, Turkish, and Arabic, and (2) transferring Dutch word embeddings to German, Turkish, and Mandarin, to see the relative performance of the languages most dissimilar to Dutch.

2.2 Tokenizing text

Word tokenizers facilitate the creation of organized representations of language, which is useful for language modeling (Dagan et al., 2024). The development of these tokenizers requires data (Dagan et al., 2024). For example, byte-pair encoding (BPE) tokenizers require training on text corpora to learn how to split words into frequently occurring subword units. While such tokenizers have proven successful for certain languages and have been used in state-of-the-art language models, their applicability to *low-resource* languages remains debated. Arnett and Bergen (2024) writes that differences in tokenizer performance can be attributed to disparities in dataset size. If a BPE tokenizer is exposed to limited data and does not segment words along morphological boundaries —a common occurrence in morphologically-rich languages —it may be difficult for the language model to efficiently learn the language (Arnett and Bergen, 2024). While less robust when compared to a BPE tokenizer, a classic tokenizer that splits on whitespace and punctuation is a nod to the reality of low-resource languages:

there may not exist sufficient data to train a well-performing tokenizer.

2.3 Using translation lexicons to generate word embeddings

To simulate our proxy languages under low-resource conditions, we adopt translation lexicons—dictionaries that translate from one language to another—provided by Facebook's Multilingual Unsupervised and Supervised Embeddings (MUSE) (Conneau et al., 2017) as the most common types of resource available for low-resource and endangered languages are translation lexicons and universal dependencies (Alnajjar et al., 2023). We chained together lexicons that translated from our proxy languages to English and English to Dutch. These translation lexicons allowed us to replicate the Dutch word embedding space and vocabulary as the proxy's. We forwent additional fine-tuning as performance remained unchanged (see Appendix B).

2.4 Alignment of word embeddings

We aligned the embedding spaces of English, Dutch, German, Turkish, Arabic, and Mandarin using the state-of-the-art supervised multilingual word embedding alignment technique developed in MUSE, resulting in cross-lingual word embeddings (Conneau et al., 2017). For example, the vector for "dog" in English embeddings points roughly in the same direction as the same word in all other languages. To confirm that realignment improves word translations, see subsection C.1.

2.5 Creating sentence embeddings

The procedure for creating sentence embeddings involves averaging the word embeddings of a given sentence and subsequently feeding them to two fully-connected feed-forward layers, thereby constructing a Deep Averaging Network (DAN) (Iyyer et al., 2015). The sentence embeddings are trained on the English subset of the Massive Text Embedding Benchmark (MTEB) Semantic Textual Similarity (STS) Benchmark (Muennighoff et al., 2023). While training the sentence embedding in its associated language may result in greater improvement in performance, such data may not always be present in a low-resource setting.

The resulting sentence embedding space was evaluated using its corresponding language subset in MTEB. We used the Spearman correlation score (Spearman, 1904) to compare the predicted cosine similarity scores with the actual similarity scores. In evaluating STS systems, researchers recommend using Spearman's rank correlation coefficient (Zesch, 2010). This metric assesses a monotonic relationship by ranking values (Zesch, 2010). Under the Spearman correlation, a model output does not need to match the ground truth; a model output that is *well-correlated* with the ground truth produces a high Spearman correlation, indicating that the sentence embedding can encode meaningful semantic information.

2.6 Creating a sentiment classifier

To assess the robustness of the transfer learning approach introduced by Alnajjar et al. (2023), we replicated Alnajjar et al. (2023)'s sentiment classifier for our proxy languages and compared its performance in our study to the results reported in Alnajjar et al. (2023). The model architecture is depicted in Figure 2.

To train the model, we used English samples from the Stanford Sentiment Treebank (Socher et al., 2013), Amazon Reviews Dataset (McAuley and Leskovec, 2013), and Yelp Dataset (Zhang et al., 2015), and their associated sentiment annotation (positive-negative). To evaluate the model on our target languages, XED (Öhman et al., 2020) —a multilabel sentiment classification dataset —was preprocessed into a binary classification dataset (see Appendix D).

3 Results

Under the methodology described in section 2, the quality of the translations improve as the vocabulary size of the proxy language grows (see subsection C.2). The relationship between vocabulary size and the performance of the sentence embedding is logarithmic. This is evident in the fact that the greatest increases in performance occur at smaller vocabulary sizes. Once the vocabulary size hits 25,000, we begin to see diminishing returns (see Figure 3 and Figure 4). The notable exception is Mandarin as increasing the vocabulary size consistently results in poor performance (see Figure 4). The poor performance in Mandarin can be attributed to its prediction of a constant or near-constant cosine similarity score (see Figure 11).

Interestingly, Turkish and Arabic—two of the languages that are considered linguistically different from the source language Dutch—outperformed German, the language

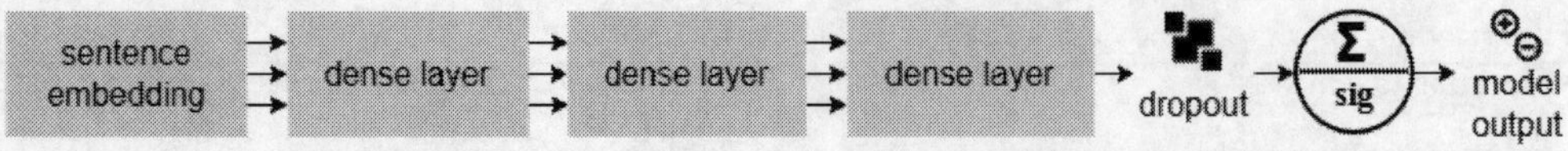

Figure 2: Architecture of sentiment classifier. To determine whether a sentence has a positive or negative connotation, the sentence is processed through a sentence embedding layer, followed by three dense layers, a dropout layer, and a sigmoid activation function.

that was deemed closest to the source language Dutch (see Figure 3). In Figure 4, this trend is replicated only in Turkish. It should be noted that the distributions of the model's predicted similarity scores do not mirror those of the actual similarity scores (see Appendix F).

Using the procedure discussed in subsection 2.6, we compare our results against Alnajjar et al. (2023) in Table 2.

Language	Label	Precision	Recall	F1-Score	Accuracy
Komi-Zyrian	neg	0.57	0.57	0.57	0.56
	pos	0.55	0.55	0.55	
Moksha	neg	0.63	0.65	0.64	0.63
	pos	0.64	0.62	0.63	
Erzya	neg	0.71	0.69	0.70	0.68
	pos	0.67	0.69	0.68	
Udmurt	neg	0.69	0.63	0.66	0.63
	pos	0.58	0.63	0.60	
German	neg	1.00	0.26	0.42	0.47
	pos	1.00	0.73	0.84	
Turkish	neg	1.00	0.46	0.63	0.50
	pos	1.00	0.56	0.72	
Arabic	neg	1.00	0.68	0.81	0.53
	pos	1.00	0.33	0.49	
Mandarin	neg	1.00	0.03	0.06	0.48
	pos	1.00	0.95	0.97	

Table 2: Proxy languages (in red) perform worse compared to the Uralic languages in Alnajjar et al. (2023) study (in black). While the sentiment classifiers in Alnajjar et al. (2023) achieve similar F1 scores for predicting both positive *and* negative labels, the sentiment classifiers for our proxy languages overfit to one of the labels. The classifiers achieve a high F1 score for predicting either positive *or* negative labels, but not both.

4 Discussion

4.1 Minimum tokens

Once a low-resource language's documented vocabulary size reaches 25,000, the performance of its sentence embedding plateaus. Without further finetuning the performance of the model will stagnate as evidenced in Figure 3 and Figure 4. While a vocabulary size of 25,000 exceeds existing documentation in low-resource translation lexicons, the **vocabulary size at which a sentence embedding space most improves ($\leq$ 1000) is accessible in most lexicons** (see Appendix G). This addresses our first research question (**RQ 1**).

4.2 Genetic proximity

Cross-lingual training between typologically-related languages has shown promising results in several NLP tasks especially in low-resource settings (Anastasopoulos and Neubig, 2019; McCarthy et al., 2019). Figure 3 and Figure 4 affirm this finding as German and Turkish—two target languages that share the typology of the source language —Dutch —benefit from cross-lingual transfer learning.

Genetic proximity appears to have little impact on the performance of a proxy language. Interestingly, German STS performance is inferior to that of Turkish's (see Figure 3 and Figure 4). This finding runs counter to Zhao et al. (2020) where researchers chose Lezgian and Tsez as target languages because they belong to the same language family as the source language. Moreover, Arabic—a language that is typologically dissimilar to the source language Dutch—performs the best out of all four languages. However, this trend is not replicated in Mandarin. As shown in Figure 5, naive whitespace tokenization alters the meaning of the sentence and may have negatively contributed to Mandarin's performance. This addresses our second research question (**RQ 2**).

5 Limitations and Future Work

5.1 Proxies

While we are interested in examining how well languages that are typologically dissimilar to the source language perform, the MTEB dataset only includes two such languages: Arabic and Mandarin. Consequently, our analysis was limited by the constraints of this evaluation dataset.

The data utilized in this study may not be fully representative of low-resource data. In reality, our proxy languages are high-resource languages and their associated datasets may contain a wider range

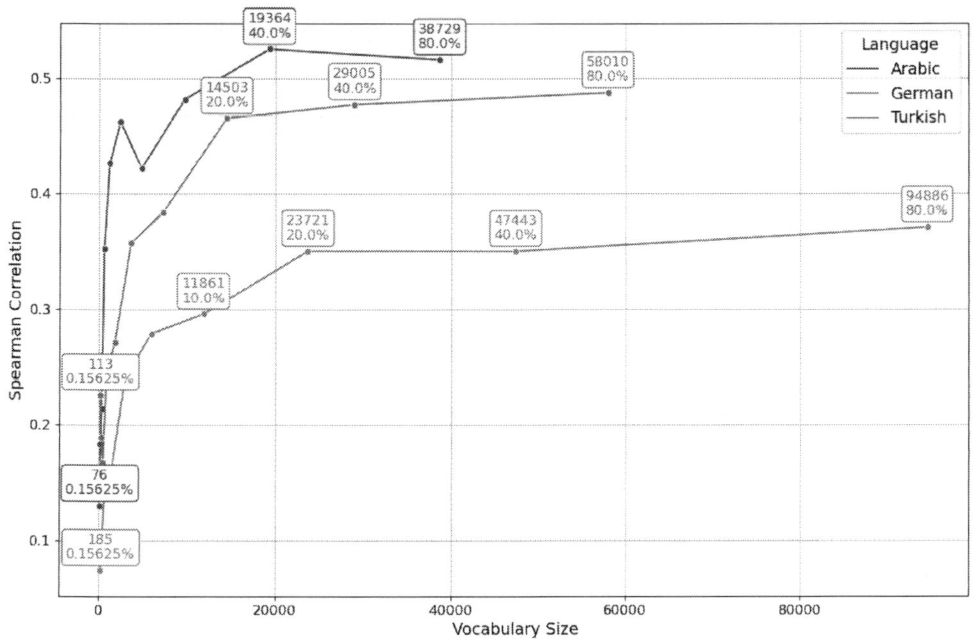

Figure 3: Transfer learning with German, Turkish, and Arabic as target languages. Performance achieves the greatest growth at vocabulary sizes of 371 (German), 906 (Turkish), and 151 (Arabic).

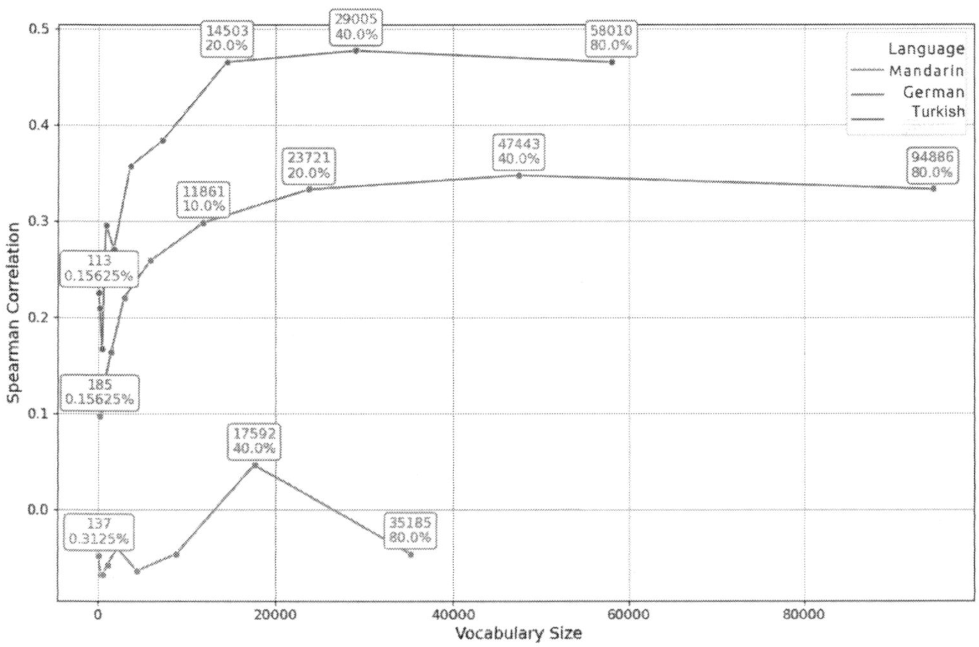

Figure 4: Transfer learning with German, Turkish, and Mandarin as target languages. Performance achieves the greatest growth at vocabulary sizes of 741 (German), 906 (Turkish), and 1100 (Mandarin).

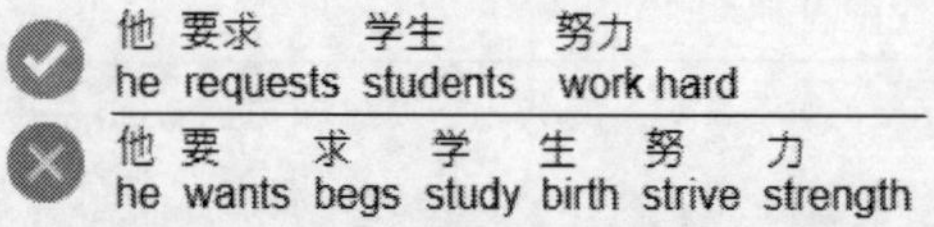

Figure 5: Correct tokenization of Mandarin Chinese (top) versus the study's whitespace tokenization (bottom). The semantic meaning of the sentence changes depending on the tokenization.

of contexts than those for actual low-resource languages (Marashian et al., 2025). Often, the only data available for low-resource languages are small amounts of religious texts (Marashian et al., 2025). Future work could verify findings by replicating the methodology for low-resource languages themselves where sufficient data is available.

5.2 Tokenization

The use of a classic tokenizer and the omission of a more sophisticated tokenizer excludes languages that lack explicit word boundaries. While German, Turkish, and Arabic can be tokenized using whitespace and punctuation, certain languages like Mandarin lack distinct spaces between words. Subword tokenization can better handle languages with non-standard word boundaries. To enhance this work, the study's methodology could be replicated with a subword tokenizer applied to a real-life low-resource language.

5.3 Methodology Utilized

Table 2 indicates the methodology adopted for this study overfits to the proxy languages; the study's sentiment classifiers lag well behind those of Alnajjar et al. (2023). Consequently, Alnajjar et al. (2023)'s methodology is unstable and cannot transfer knowledge across *all* languages. Multiple rounds of hyperparameter finetuning did not improve the model's performance (see Appendix E). One possible issue may stem from fine-tuning the sentiment classifier on English STS examples. Even with aligned word embeddings, the model may not possess enough cross-lingual knowledge to map knowledge gained from the English STS examples to the proxy language. The heavily skewed distributions in Figure 10 and Figure 11 suggest that insufficient knowledge is being captured in this step of fine-tuning. It is noted in Stevenson and Merlo (2022) that word embeddings are far from capturing human-like lexical abilities; a more effective vector representation of the language may be necessary to prevent under/over-fitting and pave the way for more efficient learning. Although there may exist other cross-lingual transfer methodologies that are more optimized than Alnajjar et al. (2023), we present one methodology that is simple and intuitive in design. While the languages we evaluated show enough linguistic variation and could generalize to other languages, we feel that such methodologies and results cannot transfer across *all* languages.

While sentiment classification is a foundational task in NLP, additional work could be done to explore how documentation requirements differ for tasks of varying complexity.

6 Conclusion

Genetic proximity between the source and target language may not have an impact on how well the target language performs on the STS task. We note that the performance of the target language plateaus at a vocabulary size of 25,000. This may be dependent on morphology as seen in the case of Mandarin. Based on data from PanLex, low-resource languages lack the level of documentation deemed necessary in this study but embedding spaces experience the greatest level of improvement when vocabularies are relatively small.

While word embeddings are useful in modeling language, they would not exist without a tokenizer. It can be argued that a tokenizer is just as an important area of research as word embeddings, if not more important; without a tokenizer, a model could not extract the relevant semantic features from text. Future research could investigate the minimum amount of data needed to develop this foundational tool in language processing.

Acknowledgments

I wanted to acknowledge the work and help of Caroline Gihlstorf and Jade Gregoire. Their feedback framed the study and laid the groundwork for the initial stages of research.

References

Khalid Alnajjar, Mika Hämäläinen, and Jack Rueter. 2023. Sentiment analysis using aligned word embeddings for Uralic languages. In *Proceedings of the Second Workshop on Resources and Representations for Under-Resourced Languages and Domains (RESOURCEFUL-2023)*, pages 19–24, Tórshavn, the Faroe Islands. Association for Computational Linguistics.

Antonios Anastasopoulos and Graham Neubig. 2019. Pushing the limits of low-resource morphological inflection. In *Proceedings of the 2019 Conference on Empirical Methods in Natural Language Processing and the 9th International Joint Conference on Natural Language Processing (EMNLP-IJCNLP)*, pages 984–996, Hong Kong, China. Association for Computational Linguistics.

Catherine Arnett and Benjamin K. Bergen. 2024. Why do language models perform worse for morphologically complex languages? *Preprint*, arXiv:2411.14198.

Vincent Beaufils and Johannes Tomin. 2020. Stochastic approach to worldwide language classification: the signals and the noise towards long-range exploration.

Xilun Chen, Ahmed Hassan Awadallah, Hany Hassan, Wei Wang, and Claire Cardie. 2019. Multi-source cross-lingual model transfer: Learning what to share. In *Proceedings of the 57th Annual Meeting of the Association for Computational Linguistics*, pages 3098–3112, Florence, Italy. Association for Computational Linguistics.

Alexis Conneau, Guillaume Lample, Marc'Aurelio Ranzato, Ludovic Denoyer, and Hervé Jégou. 2017. Word translation without parallel data. *CoRR*, abs/1710.04087.

Gautier Dagan, Gabriel Synnaeve, and Baptiste Rozière. 2024. Getting the most out of your tokenizer for pre-training and domain adaptation. *Preprint*, arXiv:2402.01035.

Mohit Iyyer, Varun Manjunatha, Jordan Boyd-Graber, and Hal Daumé III. 2015. Deep unordered composition rivals syntactic methods for text classification. In *Proceedings of the 53rd Annual Meeting of the Association for Computational Linguistics and the 7th International Joint Conference on Natural Language Processing (Volume 1: Long Papers)*, pages 1681–1691, Beijing, China. Association for Computational Linguistics.

David Kamholz, Jonathan Pool, and Susan Colowick. 2014. PanLex: Building a resource for panlingual lexical translation. In *Proceedings of the Ninth International Conference on Language Resources and Evaluation (LREC'14)*, pages 3145–3150, Reykjavik, Iceland. European Language Resources Association (ELRA).

Chanhee Lee, Kisu Yang, Taesun Whang, Chanjun Park, Andrew Matteson, and Heuiseok Lim. 2021. Exploring the data efficiency of cross-lingual post-training in pretrained language models. *Applied Sciences*, 11(5).

Zhuoyuan Mao, Chenhui Chu, and Sadao Kurohashi. 2024. Ems: Efficient and effective massively multilingual sentence embedding learning. *IEEE/ACM Transactions on Audio, Speech, and Language Processing*, 32:2841–2856.

Ali Marashian, Enora Rice, Luke Gessler, Alexis Palmer, and Katharina von der Wense. 2025. From priest to doctor: Domain adaptation for low-resource neural machine translation. *Preprint*, arXiv:2412.00966.

Julian McAuley and Jure Leskovec. 2013. Hidden factors and hidden topics: understanding rating dimensions with review text. In *Proceedings of the 7th ACM Conference on Recommender Systems*, RecSys '13, page 165–172, New York, NY, USA. Association for Computing Machinery.

Arya D. McCarthy, Ekaterina Vylomova, Shijie Wu, Chaitanya Malaviya, Lawrence Wolf-Sonkin, Garrett Nicolai, Christo Kirov, Miikka Silfverberg, Sabrina J. Mielke, Jeffrey Heinz, Ryan Cotterell, and Mans Hulden. 2019. The SIGMORPHON 2019 shared task: Morphological analysis in context and cross-lingual transfer for inflection. In *Proceedings of the 16th Workshop on Computational Research in Phonetics, Phonology, and Morphology*, pages 229–244, Florence, Italy. Association for Computational Linguistics.

Niklas Muennighoff, Nouamane Tazi, Loïc Magne, and Nils Reimers. 2023. Mteb: Massive text embedding benchmark. *Preprint*, arXiv:2210.07316.

NLLB Team, Marta R. Costa-jussà, James Cross, Onur Çelebi, Maha Elbayad, Kenneth Heafield, Kevin Heffernan, Elahe Kalbassi, Janice Lam, Daniel Licht, Jean Maillard, Anna Sun, Skyler Wang, Guillaume Wenzek, Al Youngblood, Bapi Akula, Loic Barrault, Gabriel Mejia Gonzalez, Prangthip Hansanti, John Hoffman, Semarley Jarrett, Kaushik Ram Sadagopan, Dirk Rowe, Shannon Spruit, Chau Tran, Pierre Andrews, Necip Fazil Ayan, Shruti Bhosale, Sergey Edunov, Angela Fan, Cynthia Gao, Vedanuj Goswami, Francisco Guzmán, Philipp Koehn, Alexandre Mourachko, Christophe Ropers, Safiyyah Saleem, Holger Schwenk, and Jeff Wang. 2024. Scaling neural machine translation to 200 languages. *Nature*, 630(8018):841–846.

Emily Öhman, Marc Pàmies, Kaisla Kajava, and Jörg Tiedemann. 2020. XED: A multilingual dataset for sentiment analysis and emotion detection. In *Proceedings of the 28th International Conference on Computational Linguistics*, pages 6542–6552, Barcelona, Spain (Online). International Committee on Computational Linguistics.

Richard Socher, Alex Perelygin, Jean Wu, Jason Chuang, Christopher D. Manning, Andrew Ng, and Christopher Potts. 2013. Recursive deep models for semantic compositionality over a sentiment treebank. In *Proceedings of the 2013 Conference on Empirical Methods in Natural Language Processing*, pages 1631–1642, Seattle, Washington, USA. Association for Computational Linguistics.

C. Spearman. 1904. The proof and measurement of association between two things. *The American Journal of Psychology*, 15(1):72–101.

Suzanne Stevenson and Paola Merlo. 2022. Beyond the benchmarks: Toward human-like lexical representations. *Frontiers in Artificial Intelligence*, 5.

Stephanie Strassel and Jennifer Tracey. 2016. LORELEI language packs: Data, tools, and resources for technology development in low resource languages. In *Proceedings of the Tenth International Conference on Language Resources and Evaluation (LREC'16)*, pages 3273–3280, Portorož, Slovenia. European Language Resources Association (ELRA).

Ke Tran. 2020. From english to foreign languages: Transferring pre-trained language models. *Preprint*, arXiv:2002.07306.

Torsten Zesch. 2010. *Study of Semantic Relatedness of Words Using Collaboratively Constructed Semantic Resources*. Ph.D. thesis, Technische Universität Darmstadt, Darmstadt, Germany.

Shiyue Zhang, Ben Frey, and Mohit Bansal. 2022. How can NLP help revitalize endangered languages? a case study and roadmap for the Cherokee language. In *Proceedings of the 60th Annual Meeting of the Association for Computational Linguistics (Volume 1: Long Papers)*, pages 1529–1541, Dublin, Ireland. Association for Computational Linguistics.

Xiang Zhang, Junbo Jake Zhao, and Yann LeCun. 2015. Character-level convolutional networks for text classification. *CoRR*, abs/1509.01626.

Xingyuan Zhao, Satoru Ozaki, Antonios Anastasopoulos, Graham Neubig, and Lori Levin. 2020. Automatic interlinear glossing for under-resourced languages leveraging translations. In *Proceedings of the 28th International Conference on Computational Linguistics*, pages 5397–5408, Barcelona, Spain (Online). International Committee on Computational Linguistics.

A Proximity to Dutch

See Table 3 for details on how distant our proxies were from the source language Dutch.

Language	Genetic Proximity to Dutch
German	13.5
Turkish	87.5
Arabic	82.8
Mandarin	83.8

Table 3: A genetic proximity between 1 and 30 indicates two highly related languages while a genetic proximity between 78 and 100 indicates two languages with no recognizable relationship (Beaufils and Tomin, 2020).

B Skipping additional finetuning

While Alnajjar et al. (2023) finetuned the word embeddings with books to expand the embedding's vocabulary, we discovered that this phase was unnecessary for our proxy languages. To evaluate the necessity of this phase, we compared the performance of (1) embedding spaces trained on translation lexicons and finetuned on English STS samples against (2) sentence embedding spaces trained on translation lexicons, *finetuned on Wikipedia articles from their respective languages*, and finetuned on English STS samples. Wikipedia was selected as a data source because its articles cover a wide range of domains. Embedding spaces that underwent this extra phase of finetuning on Wikipedia articles performed only marginally better than embedding spaces that skipped this phase (see Tables 4 and 5). Consequently, this extra phase of finetuning was skipped.

C Qualitative analysis of word embedding alignment

C.1 MUSE

To qualitatively assess how well MUSE alignment worked, we retrieved word embedding vectors that had the highest cosine similarity score with the English word "revolution." Tables 6, 7, and 8 depict how before alignment, the closest words to "revolution" stray from the original definition and take on a positive connotation (e.g. patriot) or negative tone (e.g. riots, uprising). Realignment under MUSE resulted in higher cosine similarity scores as well as words that were denotatively and/or connotatively similar to the word "revolution."

C.2 At varying lexicons sizes

For each proxy language, we examine words that have the highest cosine similarity score with the English word "revolution" across multiple vocabulary sizes. When aligned with small vocabulary sizes, Mandarin embedding spaces output words that are in a different language (see Table 12). At smaller vocabulary sizes ($\leq$ 200 words), words that are deemed most similar appear to be tangential to the concept of revolution. Certain terms such as "loyalisten" (German: "loyalists") and "japonlar" (Turkish: "Japanese") reflect potential bias (see Table 9 and 10). As vocabulary sizes grow, so do cosine similarity scores (see Tables 9, 10, 11, 12). Even at larger vocabulary sizes, many terms with a high cosine similarity score are ones that reflect a positive and/or negative connotation of revolution, such as "diktaturen" (German: "dictatorships") and "vatansever" (Turkish: "patriotism") (see Tables 9 and 10).

D Cleaning XED

XED is a multilabel classification dataset, annotating samples with labels such as anger, disgust, and anticipation. To convert the dataset into one for binary classification, we labeled samples as positive or negative based on specific rules, resulting in the positive-negative label distribution shown in Table 13.

- **A sample is positive** if it contains only positive labels (i.e. "anticipation", "joy", and "trust"). Samples that combined positive labels with a neutral label (i.e. "surprise") were still considered positive.
- **A sample is negative** if it contains only negative labels (i.e. "anger", "disgust", "fear", "sadness"). Samples that combined negative labels with a neutral label (i.e. "surprise") were also considered negative.

E Impacts of hyperparameter finetuning

Due to resource constraints and the computational load of the sentiment classifier, exhaustively exploring the hyperparameter space was intractable. We focused our efforts on tuning the number of neurons in the hidden layer as the low F1 scores in predicting certain labels indicate that the model was underfitting and potentially lacked sufficient complexity to effectively handle the sentiment analysis of sentences (see Table 2). Setting the dropout rate to 0.2,we fail to identify an optimal hidden layer neuron count as the model consistently predicts positive labels well at the expense of negative labels. This relationship is occasionally reversed: the model consistently predicts negative labels well at the expense of positive labels. Results are shown in Figure 6, Figure 7, Figure 8, and Figure 9.

F Distribution of Semantic Textual Similarity Scores

It is apparent that the distributions of the predicted cosine similarity scores do not mirror that of the actual cosine similarity scores (see Figure 10 and 11). Except for Mandarin, proxy languages show a left-skewed distribution in cosine similarity scores (see Figure 10 and 11). A higher cosine similarity score indicates greater similarity between sentences (Muennighoff et al., 2023), suggesting that the sentence embedding space is more likely to classify a pair of sentences as similar rather than dissimilar.

We normalized the actual similarity scores in Figure 10 and Figure 11 to allow for better comparison.

G Documentation Available in Low-Resource Languages

Table 14 indicates the number of word translation pairs available in PanLex (Kamholz et al., 2014). PanLex is a database that provides over 1.1 billion pairwise translations in about 9,000 language varieties, including 1,603 UNESCO-classified endangered and vulnerable languages. Using the methodology described in the paper, endangered languages in general do not possess 25,000 entries, the amount of data required to see a plateau in embedding performance. Notably, sentence embedding spaces experienced the greatest increase in performance when the vocabulary size was less than 1000, the average number of translations in a translation lexicon for an endangered language (see Table 14 and Figure 12).

H Comparison of proxy language sentence embedding spaces against MTEB models

Except for Mandarin, our best-performing sentence embedding spaces perform as well as the average model on the MTEB leaderboard (see Table 15). How to further improve these sentence embeddings is a matter of future research.

Language	Training and Finetuning Process	Spearman Correlation
German	translation dictionary, MUSE alignment	0.371
	translation dictionary, finetuning on Wikipedia articles, MUSE alignment	0.376
Turkish	translation dictionary, MUSE alignment	0.488
	translation dictionary, finetuning on Wikipedia articles, MUSE alignment	0.517
Arabic	translation dictionary, MUSE alignment	0.516
	translation dictionary, finetuning on Wikipedia articles, MUSE alignment	0.503

Table 4: Fine-tuning the word embedding space on Wikipedia articles resulted in marginal gains in performance for the German, Turkish, Arabic test group.

Language	Training and Finetuning Process	Spearman Correlation
German	translation dictionary, MUSE alignment	0.333
	translation dictionary, finetuning on Wikipedia articles, MUSE alignment	0.363
Turkish	translation dictionary, MUSE alignment	0.466
	translation dictionary, finetuning on Wikipedia articles, MUSE alignment	0.493
Mandarin	translation dictionary, MUSE alignment	-0.046
	translation dictionary, finetuning on Wikipedia articles, MUSE alignment	0.074

Table 5: Fine-tuning the word embedding space on Wikipedia articles resulted in marginal gains in performance for the German, Turkish, Mandarin test group.

Pre-MUSE			Post-MUSE		
Word	**Translation**	**Cosine Similarity**	**Word**	**Translation**	**Cosine Similarity**
muros	*not German*	0.1897	rebellion	rebellion	0.5144
mox	*not German*	0.1897	aufstand	revolt	0.5144
franken	franc	0.1910	radikalisierung	radicalization	0.5150
koadjutor	coadjutor	0.1917	aufstände	riots	0.5311
latein	Latin	0.1918	umwälzungen	upheavals	0.5371
palgrave	*not German*	0.1980	revolutionären	revolutionary	0.6200
neb	*not German*	0.1997	konterrevolution	counterrevolution	0.6209
emeritierung	emeritus	0.2100	revolutionäre	revolutionary	0.6590
emeritierter	emeritus	0.2100	revolutionär	revolutionary	0.6865
avalos	*not German*	0.2181	revolutionen	revolutions	0.6948

Table 6: German translations and cosine similarity scores of "revolution" before and after MUSE alignment. Quality of translation significantly improves following MUSE alignment.

Pre-MUSE			Post-MUSE		
Word	**Translation**	**Cosine Similarity**	**Word**	**Translation**	**Cosine Similarity**
bem	*not Turkish*	0.1850	revolutionibus	*not Turkish*	0.5010
galiçya	galicia	0.1863	diktatörlük	dictatorship	0.5081
gravis	gravis	0.1888	sosyalizm	socialism	0.5123
prism	*not Turkish*	0.1891	isyan	revel	0.5161
lennox	*not Turkish*	0.1905	ayaklanması	uprising	0.5161
gsc	*not Turkish*	0.1906	ayaklanmalar	riots	0.5292
frangı	franc	0.1917	devrimler	revolutions	0.5391
latin	*not Turkish*	0.1970	devrim	revolution	0.6237
palgrave	*not Turkish*	0.1980	devrimciler	revolutionaries	0.6611
neb	*not Turkish*	0.1997	devrimci	revolutionary	0.6611

Table 7: Turkish translations and cosine similarity scores of "revolution" before and after MUSE alignment. Quality of translation significantly improves following MUSE alignment.

Pre-MUSE			Post-MUSE		
Word	**Translation**	**Cosine Similarity**	**Word**	**Translation**	**Cosine Similarity**
回憶	recall	0.1800	推翻	overthrow	0.4902
大主教	archbishop	0.1803	愛國者	patriot	0.4991
退休	retire	0.1841	獨裁	dictatorship	0.5079
稜鏡	*not a phrase*	0.1891	專政	dictatorship	0.5079
pluribus	*not Mondarin*	0.1893	獨裁政權	dictatorship	0.5079
gsc	*not Mandarin*	0.1906	社會主義	socialism	0.5109
mox	*not Mandarin*	0.1910	起義	uprising	0.5115
拉丁文	Latin	0.1970	保皇黨	royalist	0.5148
教育	educate	0.1979	革命性	revolutionary	0.6875
palgrave	*not Mandarin*	0.1970	革命	revolution	0.6928

Table 8: Mandarin translations and cosine similarity scores of "revolution" before and after MUSE alignment. Quality of translation significantly improves following MUSE alignment.

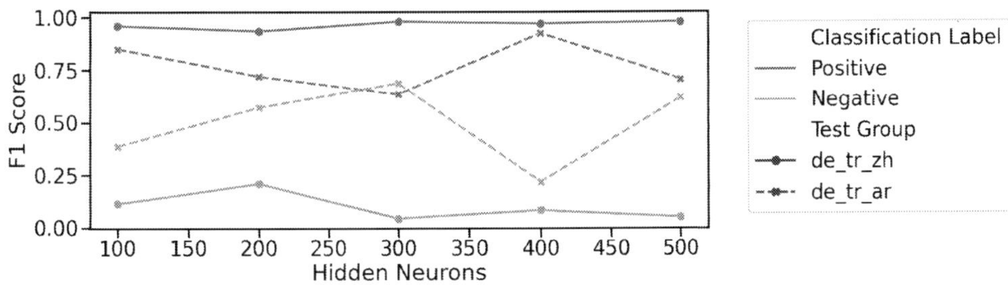

Figure 6: We evaluate the F1 scores of the German sentiment classifier on positive and negative labels across varying amounts of hidden layer neurons. The German classifier from the German, Turkish, and Mandarin test group (abbreviated as `de_tr_zh`) is depicted alongside that from the German, Turkish, and Arabic test group (abbreviated as `de_tr_ar`). Increasing the number of neurons causes a tradeoff in positive and negative label performance as shown in the `de_tr_zh` group. Moreover, increasing the number of neurons does not prevent the model from overfitting to positive labels or underfitting to negative labels as shown in the `de_tr_ar` group.

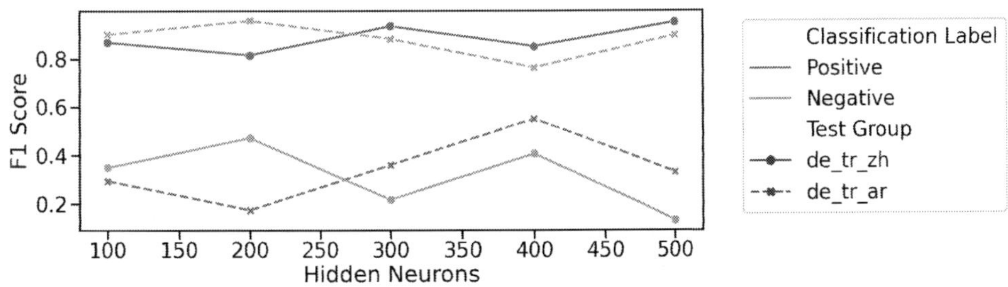

Figure 7: We evaluate the F1 scores of the Turkish sentiment classifier on positive and negative labels across varying amounts of hidden layer neurons. The Turkish classifier from the German, Turkish, and Mandarin test group (abbreviated as `de_tr_zh`) is depicted alongside that from the German, Turkish, and Arabic test group (abbreviated as `de_tr_ar`). In `de_tr_zh`, increasing the number of neurons does not prevent the Turkish sentiment classifier model from overfitting to positive labels and underfitting to negative labels. This is reversed in `de_tr_ar`; the Turkish model overfits to negative labels and underfits to positive labels.

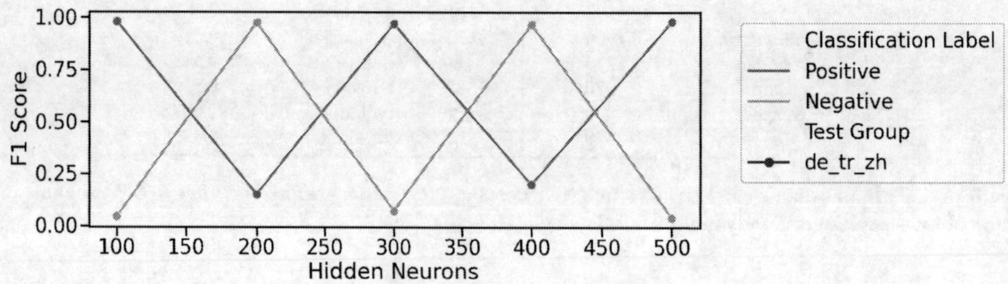

Figure 8: We evaluate the F1 scores of the Mandarin sentiment classifier on positive and negative labels across varying amounts of hidden layer neurons. Increasing the number of hidden neurons causes a tradeoff in positive and negative label performance.

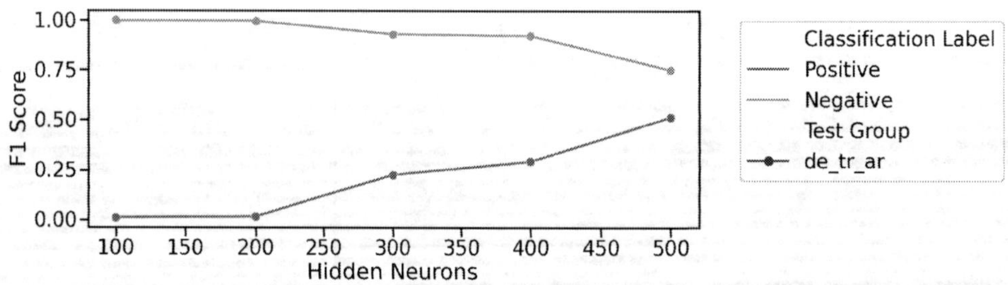

Figure 9: We evaluate the F1 scores of the Arabic sentiment classifier on positive and negative labels across varying amounts of hidden layer neurons. Increasing the number of hidden neurons seemingly causes a convergence in performance but the classifier's ability to correctly positive labels is sacrificed to correctly predict negative labels.

German **Turkish** **Arabic**

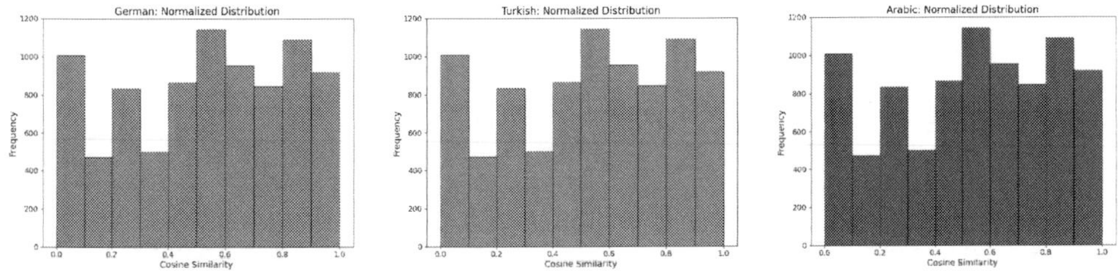

(a) Actual Cosine Similarity Distribution

(b) Actual Cosine Similarity Distribution

(c) Actual Cosine Similarity Distribution

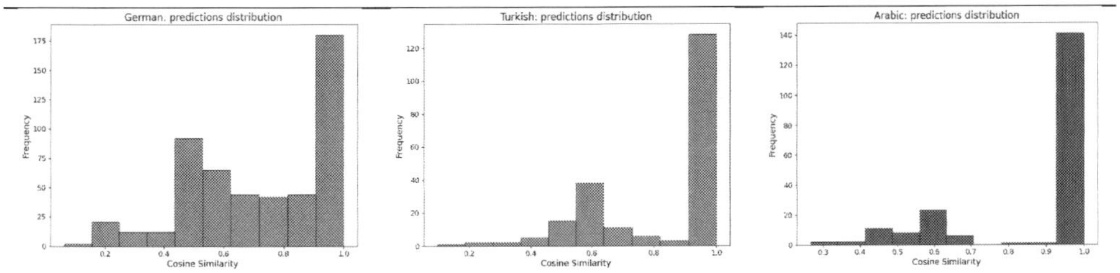

(d) Vocabulary size of 185

(e) Vocabulary size of 113

(f) Vocabulary size of 76

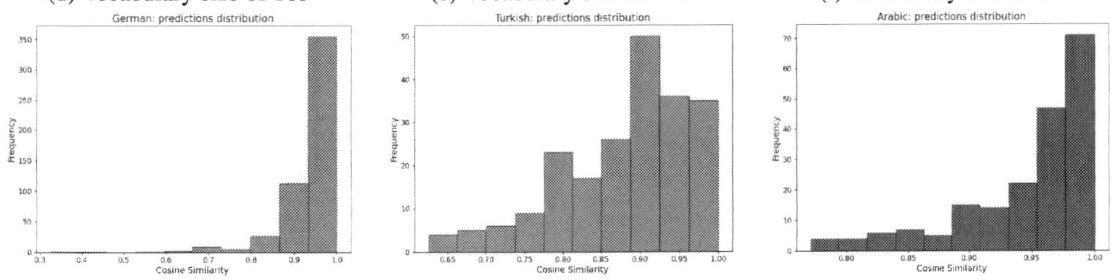

(g) Vocabulary size of 11,861

(h) Vocabulary size of 7,251

(i) Vocabulary size of 9,982

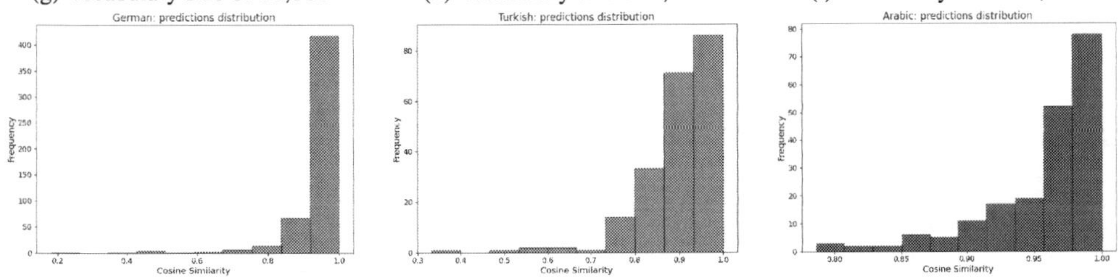

(j) Vocabulary size of 23,721

(k) Vocabulary size of 14,503

(l) Vocabulary size of 19,364

Figure 10: Distribution of cosine similarity scores across the MTEB evaluation German, Turkish, and Arabic datasets. As the vocabulary size increases, the distribution becomes more left-skewed.

German **Turkish** **Mandarin**

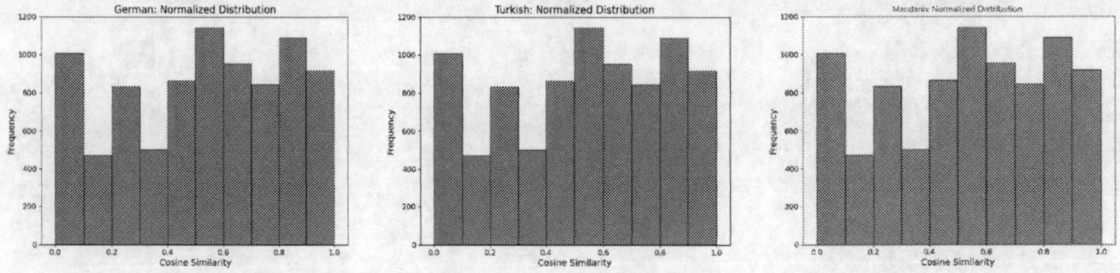

(a) Actual Cosine Similarity Distribution

(b) Actual Cosine Similarity Distribution

(c) Actual Cosine Similarity Distribution

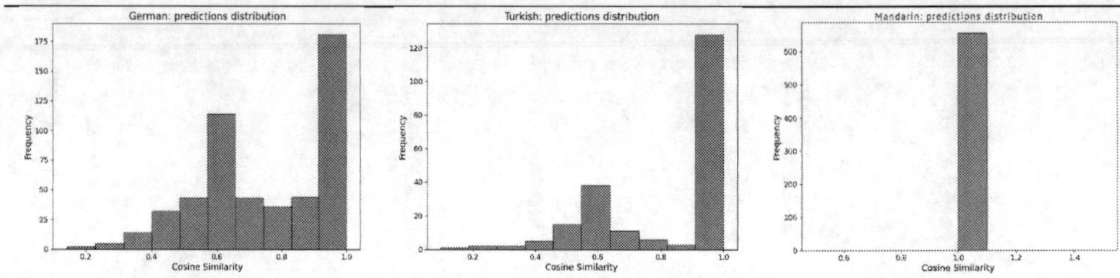

(d) Vocabulary size of 185

(e) Vocabulary size of 113

(f) Vocabulary size of 137

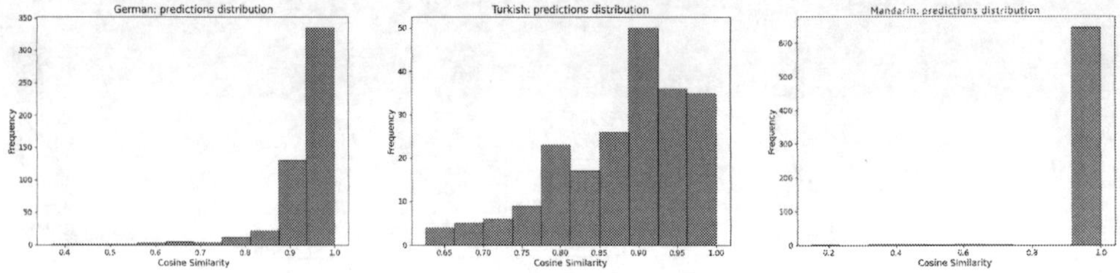

(g) Vocabulary size of 11,861

(h) Vocabulary size of 7,251

(i) Vocabulary size of 4,398

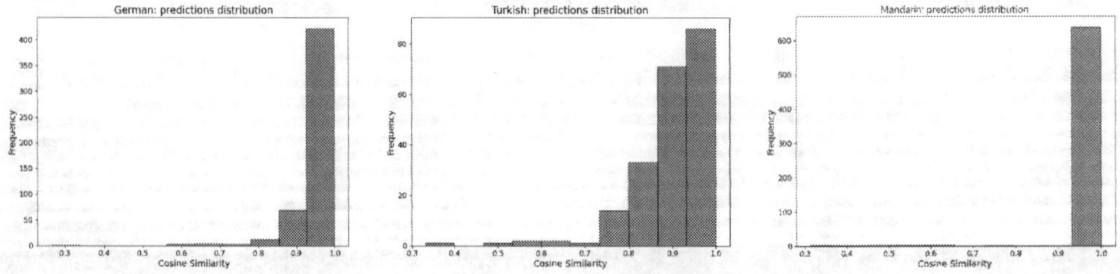

(j) Vocabulary size of 23,721

(k) Vocabulary size of 14,503

(l) Vocabulary size of 17,592

Figure 11: Distribution of cosine similarity scores for the MTEB evaluation German, Turkish, and Mandarin datasets. As the vocabulary size increases, the distribution becomes more left-skewed with the exception of Mandarin.

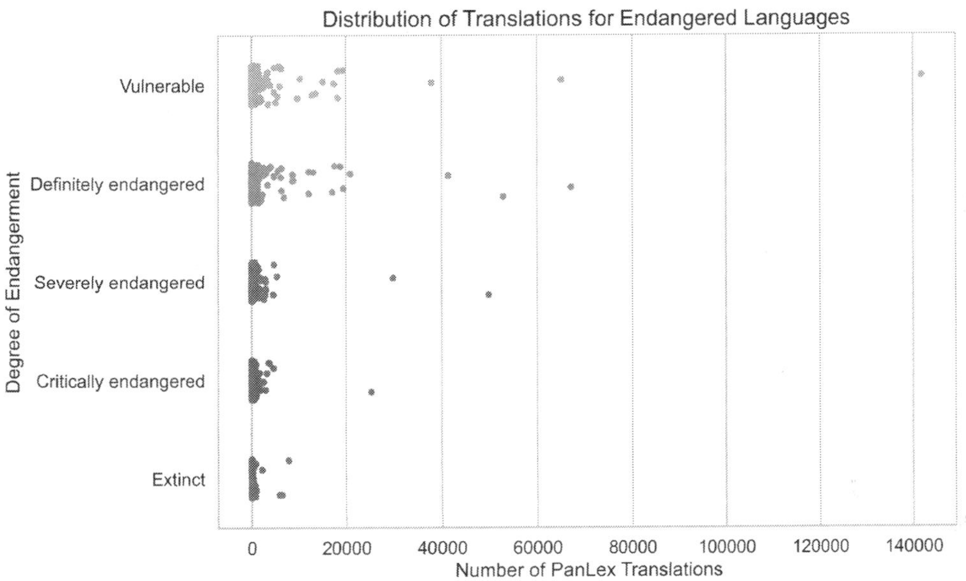

Figure 12: Distribution of PanLex translations for UNESCO-classified vulnerable and endangered languages. Most endangered languages have fewer than 20,000 translations.

Vocabulary size of 185		
Word	**Translation**	**Cosine Similarity**
verbiete	ban	0.2925
übergelaufen	defected	0.2986
stilllegung	decommissioning	0.3058
ausgleichszahlung	compensation	0.3131
besprechung	meeting	0.3206
überschreitung	exceedance	0.3213
allgemeinen	general	0.3235
passiert	happened	0.3322
loyalisten	loyalists	0.3407
umgestaltung	refactor	0.3612
Vocabulary size of 11,861		
Word	**Translation**	**Cosine Similarity**
demokratisierung	democratization	0.5395
zusammenbrechen	collapse	0.5429
absolutistischen	absolutist	0.5475
radikaler	more radical	0.5542
unterdrückt	suppressed	0.5601
unterdrückten	suppressed	0.5601
bevorstehende	upcoming	0.5727
feindschaft	enmity	0.5752
feindseligkeit	hostility	0.5752
revolutionären	revolutionary	0.6664
Vocabulary size of 23,721		
Word	**Translation**	**Cosine Similarity**
radikaler	more radical	0.5549
diktaturen	dictatorships	0.5596
unterdrückt	suppressed	0.5600
unterdrückten	suppressed	0.5600
feindseligkeit	suppressed	0.5740
feindschaft	enmity	0.5740
bevorstehende	upcoming	0.5748
unterdrückung	suppression	0.5854
verdrängung	displacement	0.5854
revolutionären	revolutionary	0.6645

Table 9: German translations and cosine similarity scores of "revolution" across varying dictionary sizes. Increasing the vocabulary size results in German translations that are semantically closer to "revolution."

Vocabulary size of 227		
Word	**Translation**	**Cosine Similarity**
ihtiyaç	need	0.3368
bazı	some	0.3381
japonlar	japanese	0.3422
saldırılar	attacks	0.3428
izdiham	confluence	0.3490
éluard	eluard	0.3596
hükümdarlık	reign	0.4241
danton	danton	0.4517
başla	start	0.4888
hürriyet	freedom	0.4929
Vocabulary size of 7,251		
Word	**Translation**	**Cosine Similarity**
muhalefet	opposition	0.5261
başarısızlık	failure	0.5275
üstünlüğü	superiority	0.5285
katılım	attendance	0.5317
getirildi	brought	0.5326
çöküş	collapse	0.5415
diriliş	resurrection	0.5435
düşmanlık	hostility	0.5734
vatansever	patriot	0.5926
devrim	revolution	0.6694
Vocabulary size of 14,503		
Word	**Translation**	**Cosine Similarity**
katılım	participation	0.5319
getirildi	brought	0.5321
çöküş	collapse	0.5416
diriliş	resurrection	0.5445
kapitalist	capitalist	0.5531
düşmanlık	hostility	0.5727
vatansever	patriotic	0.5913
vatanseverlik	patriotism	0.5933
devrim	revolution	0.6684
devrimci	revolutionary	0.6794

Table 10: Turkish translations and cosine similarity scores of "revolution" across varying dictionary sizes. Increasing the vocabulary size results in Turkish translations that are semantically closer to "revolution."

Vocabulary size of 76		
Word	**Translation**	**Cosine Similarity**
اخبار	need	0.2582
اجواء	atmosphere	0.2637
اعداء	enemies	0.2711
بصمت	silently	0.2897
السلالة	strain	0.2949
الحرائق	fires	0.3211
بريطاني	British	0.3326
الشرعية	legitimacy	0.3915
الفظائع	atrocities	0.4016
الاعتقاد	belief	0.4858
Vocabulary size of 9,982		
Word	**Translation**	**Cosine Similarity**
انهاء	end	0.5261
زمن	time	0.5275
الزمان	time	0.5285
وقت	time	0.5317
السخط	discontent	0.5326
القلاقل	unrest	0.5415
الديكتاتوريات	dictatorships	0.5435
فشل	failure	0.5734
التدخل	interference	0.5926
الدكتاتورية	dictatorship	0.6694
Vocabulary size of 19,364		
Word	**Translation**	**Cosine Similarity**
الديكتاتوريات	dictatorships	0.5262
فشل	failure	0.5262
سائد	prevalent	0.5269
التدخل	interference	0.5351
الدكتاتورية	dictatorship	0.5614
ناشئة	emerging	0.5748
العداء	hostility	0.5753
الاطاحة	overthrow	0.5833
القمع	suppression	0.5863
الثورات	revolutions	0.6672

Table 11: Arabic translations and cosine similarity scores of "revolution" across varying dictionary sizes. Increasing the vocabulary size results in Arabic translations that are semantically closer to "revolution."

Vocabulary size of 137		
Word	**Translation**	**Cosine Similarity**
北京	Beijing	0.2427
錯位	dislocation	0.2430
動態	dynamic	0.2463
革新	innovation	0.2473
amraam	*not Chinese*	0.2626
税	tax	0.2632
最多	maximum	0.2772
協作	collaboration	0.2779
永久	permanent	0.3895
然後	then	0.3965
Vocabulary size of 4,398		
Word	**Translation**	**Cosine Similarity**
束縛	binding	0.5042
奴隸制	slavery	0.5042
抵制	boycott	0.5070
演示	demo	0.5194
時間	time	0.5197
反對派	opposition	0.5240
混沌	chaos	0.5241
復蘇	recovery	0.5467
動蕩	turmoil	0.5567
敵意	hostility	0.5769
Vocabulary size of 17,592		
Word	**Translation**	**Cosine Similarity**
動亂	unrest	0.5526
獨裁政權	dictatorship	0.5629
受壓迫	oppressed	0.5636
敵意	hostility	0.5765
推翻	overturn	0.5807
愛國主義	patriotism	0.5874
抑制	inhibition	0.5884
政權	regime	0.5952
保皇黨	loyalist	0.6204
革命性	revolutionary	0.7352

Table 12: Mandarin translations and cosine similarity scores of "revolution" across varying dictionary sizes. Increasing the vocabulary size results in Mandarin translations that are semantically closer to "revolution."

Language	Positive Samples	Negative Samples
Arabic	1269	1735
German	2051	2614
Turkish	3570	4552
Mandarin	587	608

Table 13: Number of positive and negative samples in processed XED data. Ratio of positive to negative samples is 1:1.

Degree of endangerment	Average	Standard deviation
Vulnerable	1205.34	8063.48
Definitely endangered	1094.03	5183.69
Severely endangered	541.77	3359.48
Critically endangered	315.94	1542.20
Extinct	251.69	969.93

Table 14: The average number of translations found for UNESCO-classified vulnerable and endangered languages in PanLex. Existing documentation for endangered languages is generally low. The high standard deviation may be attributed to outliers (e.g. certain vulnerable languages may contain significantly more documentation than others in the category) as shown in Figure 12.

	German	Turkish	Arabic	Mandarin
best-performing sentence embedding	0.371	0.488	0.516	0.046
average MTEB score	0.391	0.466	0.439	0.588
minimum MTEB score	0.082	0.038	0.052	0.048
25th percentile MTEB score	0.266	0.370	0.304	0.600
50th percentile MTEB score	0.418	0.473	0.524	0.654
75th percentile MTEB score	0.506	0.582	0.571	0.668
maximum MTEB score	0.609	0.688	0.598	0.749

Table 15: Comparison of our models' Spearman correlation scores to MTEB models'. Data compiled from Muennighoff et al. (2023). Our models perform average (with the exception of Mandarin) compared to models in this leaderboard.

Linear Relational Decoding of Morphology in Language Models

Eric Xia
Brown University
eric_xia@brown.edu

Jugal Kalita
University of Colorado Colorado Springs
jkalita@uccs.edu

Abstract

A two-part affine approximation has been found to be a good approximation for transformer computations over certain subject-object relations. Adapting the Bigger Analogy Test Set, we show that the linear transformation $W\mathbf{s}$, where $\mathbf{s}$ is a middle layer representation of a subject token and W is derived from model derivatives, is also able to accurately reproduce final object states for many relations. This linear technique is able to achieve 90% faithfulness on morphological relations, and we show similar findings multi-lingually and across models. Our findings indicate that some conceptual relationships in language models, such as morphology, are readily interpretable from latent space, and are sparsely encoded by cross-layer linear transformations.

1 Introduction

Large language models display impressive capabilities for factual recall, which commonly involve relations between entities (Brown et al. 2020). Recent work has shown that affine transformations on subject representations can faithfully approximate model outputs for certain subject-object relations (Hernandez et al. 2023). Identifying transformer approximators is an important area of study, with applications in model training and editing.

The contributions of this paper are twofold. We reproduce and extend existing research. Specifically, we apply affine Linear Relational Embedding (LRE) method to novel diverse relational categories, including derivational and inflectional morphology, encyclopedic knowledge, and lexical semantics. By doing so, we confirm the efficacy of the affine technique. We show that relational approximation can be applied to adapted analogical datasets, and demonstrate relational approximation for a broad range of linguistic phenomena.

At the same time, this work makes a key contribution to research on relational representation in model latents. We show that for different relations, additive and multiplicative mechanisms play complementary roles in affine approximation. We find that an analogue to the original linear relational embedding developed by Paccanaro and Hinton (2001), using a single multiplicative operator, is effective within specific relations. In particular, linear approximation within contexts relating morphological forms reaches near-equivalent level of faithfulness to the affine LRE. We test faithfulness over eight different languages and find that this equivalence holds cross-typologically.

2 Related Work

Much work in machine learning has focused on learning concept representations with hierarchical structure. Relations between representations in concept spaces have been modeled successfully by both linear multiplicative and additive operations.

Multiplicative. Paccanaro and Hinton (2001) introduced the concept of the linear relational embedding for learning relational knowledge from triples (a, R, b). Concepts such as a and b are represented as n-length vectors, while relations such as R are represented as $n \times n$ matrices, akin to distributional models of compositional semantics proposed by Coecke et al. (2010).

Additive. Mikolov et al. (2013) used linear operations in word vector space derived from context-predictive neural nets, demonstrating a correspondence between directional binary relations (e.g. male-female, country-capital, verb tense) and the addition of embedding vectors. Later work found inflectional relations were better captured than derivational ones, and encyclopedic relations better than lexicographic ones. (Gladkova et al. 2016; Vylomova et al. 2016).

Proceedings of the 2025 Conference of the Nations of the Americas Chapter of the Association for Computational Linguistics: Human Language Technologies (Volume 4: Student Research Workshop), pages 225–235

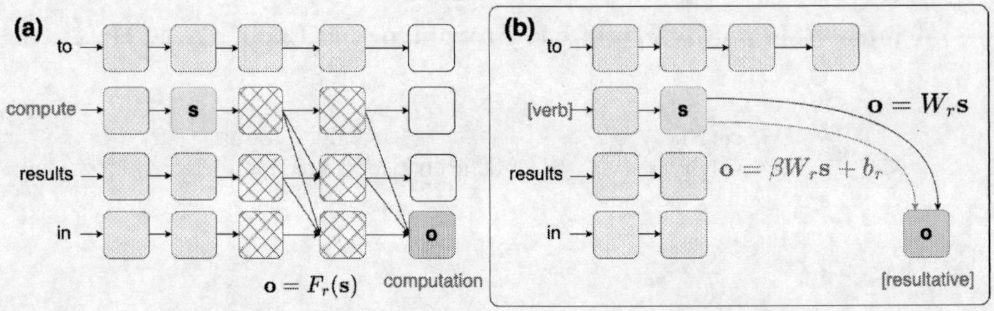

Figure 1: As seen in **(a)**, transformers resolve subject-object relations in a highly nonlinear fashion. As seen in **(b)**, both affine and linear approximators of the subject-object map $F_r(\mathbf{s})$ are demonstrated to be highly effective over relations such as morphology.

3 Background

3.1 Transformer Computation

In auto-regressive transformer language models, input text is converted to a sequence of tokens $t_1 \dots t_n$, which are subsequently embedded as $x_1 \dots x_n \in \mathbb{R}^d$ by an embedding matrix. They are then passed through L transformer layers, each composed of a self-attention layer and an multi-layer perceptron (MLP) layer. In GPT-J, the representation x_i^l of the ith token at layer l is obtained as:

$$x_i^l = x_i^{l-1} + a_i^l + m_i^l$$

where a_i^l is multi-headed Key-Value Query attention over x^{l-1}(Vaswani et al. 2017) and m_i^l is the ith output of the lth MLP sublayer. In this case, the output of the l-th MLP sublayer for the i-th representation depends on x_i^{l-1}, rather than $a_i^l + x_i^{l-1}$ (Wang and Komatsuzaki 2021). The final prediction t_{n+1} is then determined by the final hidden state x_n passed through a decoder head D, which consists of a linear layer and softmax to a token vocabulary: $t_{n+1} = \underset{t}{\operatorname{argmax}}\, D(x_n^L)_t$.

3.2 Relational Representation

Throughout this paper, we will focus on the subject-object relationship as expressed through a single fixed context. Following prior work (Meng et al. 2022b; Geva et al. 2023) that the last token state of a subject in middle layers are strongly casual on predictions (e.g. "Needle" in "The Space Needle"), we are interested in utilizing the gradient between the last token position of the subject s at an intermediate layer, and the object prediction state o.

4 Approach

4.1 Problem Statement

We first consider what it means for a context to express a relation. Many statements can be expressed in terms of a subject, relation, and object (*s,r,o*). For instance, the statement *Miles Davis plays the trumpet* expresses a relation F_r, connecting the subject s (*Miles Davis*) to the object o (*trumpet*): $F_r(s) = o$. We can then relate new subjects to objects: F_r(*Jimi Hendrix*) $=$ *guitar* and F_r(*Elton John*) $=$ *piano*. F_r is an inductive mechanism, from which statements relating subject and object pairs can be obtained. We are interested in how a language model implements this abstraction.

Affine LRE. As a starting point, we look at the affine linear relational embedding (LRE) method developed by Hernandez et al. (2023). The authors are able to approximate the transformer's relational function $F_r(s)$ with the affine approximator LRE(s), such that when applied to novel subjects, they reproduce LM object predictions.

The object retrieval function from a subject with a fixed relational context, $o = F_r(s)$, is modeled to be a first-order Taylor approximation of F_r about a number of subjects $s_1 \dots s_n$. For $i = 1 \dots n$:

$$\begin{aligned} F_r(s) &\approx F_r(s_i) + W_r(s - s_i) \\ &= F(s_i) + W_r s - W_r s_i \\ &= W_r s + b_r, \\ \text{where } b_r &= F_r(s_i) - W_r s_i \end{aligned}$$

In a relational context, a model may rely heavily on a singular subject state to produce the object state. Accordingly, the Jacobian matrix of derivatives between vector representations of the subject and object is hypothesized to serve as W_r. For a

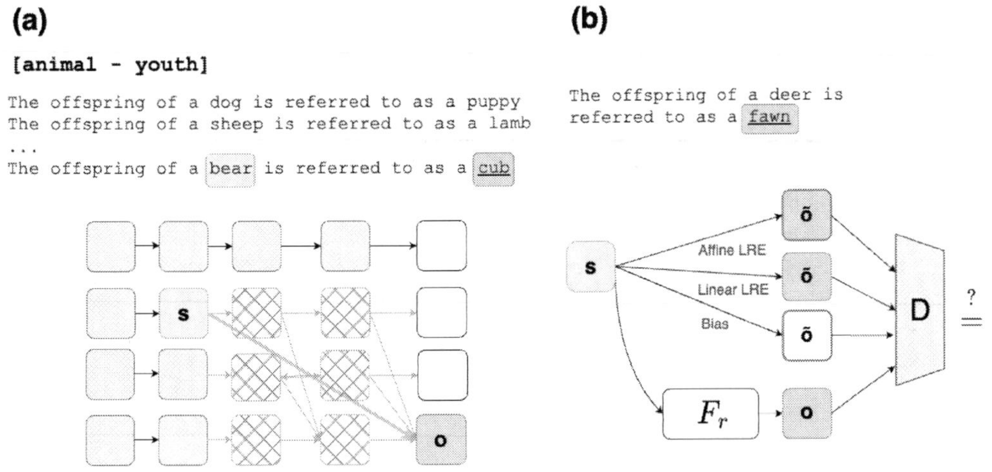

Figure 2: In **(a)**, we first assemble approximators from trained model Jacobians between middle-layer subject states and the final-layer object state. Then, in **(b)**, we evaluate approximated tokens against transformer computations.

fixed relation, they calculate the mean Jacobian and bias between n enriched subject states $\mathbf{s}_1 \dots \mathbf{s}_n$ and outputs $F_r(\mathbf{s}_1) \dots F_r(\mathbf{s}_n)$:

$$W_r = \mathbb{E}_{\mathbf{s}_i}\left[\left.\frac{\partial F_r}{\partial \mathbf{s}}\right|_{\mathbf{s}_i}\right] \qquad (d \times d \text{ matrix})$$

$$b_r = \mathbb{E}_{\mathbf{s}_i}\left[\left.F_r(\mathbf{s}) - \frac{\partial F_r}{\partial \mathbf{s}}\mathbf{s}\right|_{\mathbf{s}_i}\right] \qquad (d \text{ vector})$$

This yields a relational approximator capable of transforming a jth layer subject state $x_s^j = \mathbf{s}$ [1] into the final object hidden state $x_o^L = \mathbf{o}$ [2]:

$$\mathbf{o} \approx \text{LRE}(\mathbf{s}) = \beta W_r \mathbf{s} + b_r$$

For instance, $\mathbf{s}$ may be the hidden state of the 7th layer at the subject token, and $\mathbf{o}$ the hidden state of the 26th (last) layer at the object token, e.g. the next-token prediction state.

True Linear Encoding. The affine LRE diverges from the linear relational embedding introduced by Hinton (1986), in introducing a bias b_r and scaling term β. While linearity is assumed in Hernandez et al. (2023) by calculating W_r and b_r from $\mathbb{E}_{s_i}$ over $i = 1 \dots n$, using a Taylor approximation makes a weaker assumption, simply that the subject-object relation F_r is differentiable. With linearity, we would expect the following:

$$\mathbf{o} \approx F_r'(s_i)\mathbf{s}$$
$$= W_r \mathbf{s}$$

In this case, the linear approximation over $\mathbf{s}_1 \dots \mathbf{s}_n$ within the same relation would be the mean Jacobian. If this approximation generalizes to unseen objects, it would indicate the presence of a linear subject-object map.

4.2 Introducing New Relations

Analogy is traditionally seen as a special case of role-based relational reasoning (Sternberg and Rifkin 1979, Gentner 1983, Holyoak 2012), motivating the adaptation of analogical pairs to a relational setting. We choose to adapt the Bigger Analogy Test Set (BATS), originally introduced to explore linguistic regularities in word embeddings by Gladkova et al. (2016). The dataset comprises forty different categories, each with fifty pairs of words sharing a common relation. The categories span inflectional morphology, derivational morphology, encyclopedic knowledge, and lexical semantics.

4.3 Utilizing ICL

As seen in Figure 2, we adapt the relational pairs in BATS by introducing prompts which are compatible with each instance of the analogy.

[1]Following Meng et al. (2022a), both this paper and the affine LRE focus primarily on middle-layer states.

[2]Note the introduction of a β scaling parameter. The authors claim the affine LRE is limited by layer normalization: the $\mathbf{s}$ representation is normalized before contributing to $\mathbf{o}$, and $\mathbf{o}$ is normalized before token prediction by the LM head, resulting in a mismatch in the scale of the output approximation. We find that this conclusion is supported by empirical evidence from linear projections.

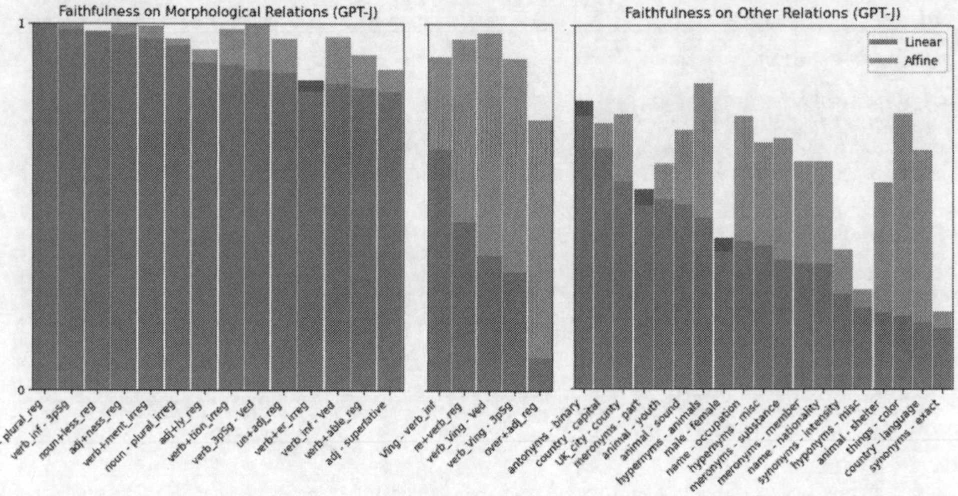

Figure 3: Comparing affine & linear LREs on GPT-J reveals many morphological relations are linearly approximable. With the exception of prefix and active form subjects, semantic and encyclopedic relations benefit more from the affine LRE than morphology. For subject layers 3-9, the best performing approximation is averaged ($n = 4$).

Following the procedure outlined in Hernandez (2023), we employ 8 in-context learning (ICL) examples for 8 different subject-object prompts for each relation. This allows us to obtain a Jacobian from the model computation which is most likely to exhibit the desired linear encoding.

We omit the subject-object pairs used in construction from the testing pool. We further restrict evaluation to the pairs for which the LM computation is successful in reproducing the object. [3]

4.4 Evaluating Operators

After passing through the activation function in the decoder, the approximated object tokens should faithfully replicate the true LM output.

Affine LRE. The original affine LRE is a two-step approximation involving both a weight term W_r and bias term b_r, which are applied to the subject state $\mathbf{s}$ to produce an approximated output state: $\tilde{\mathbf{o}} = \text{LRE}(\mathbf{s}) = \beta W_r \mathbf{s} + b_r$

Linear LRE. Our variants isolate the components of the LRE in order to inspect their contribution to the approximation. First, we define the linear LRE, a multiplicative operation. This is the subject hidden state $\mathbf{s}$ multiplied by the mean Jacobian for *other subject-object pairs* to derive a final object state: $\tilde{\mathbf{o}} = \text{Linear}(\mathbf{s}) = W_r \mathbf{s}$

Bias. Second, we define the Bias approximator, an additive operation. This approximator calculates $\tilde{\mathbf{o}}$ by adding b_r, the mean difference between $W_r \mathbf{s}$ and $\mathbf{o}$ for *other subject-object pairs*, to $\mathbf{s}$: $\tilde{\mathbf{o}} = \text{Bias}(\mathbf{s}) = \mathbf{s} + b_r$

Following Hernandez et al. (2023), we define *faithfulness* of an approximator by the top-one token match rate. For token t and decoder head D, we say an approximator is faithful if the top token approximation matches that of the LM: $\underset{t}{\text{argmax}}\, D(\mathbf{o})_t \stackrel{?}{=} \underset{t}{\text{argmax}}\, D(\tilde{\mathbf{o}})_t$

5 Results

5.1 The Linear LRE Faithfully Approximates Relations across Morphology

We first evaluate relational approximators for the GPT-J model (Wang and Komatsuzaki 2021). We build approximators for likely subject hidden states (layers 3-9) and the final object state (layer 27) through the process outlined above. We then evaluate the approximators four times for each relation, and average the best cross-layer approximation.[4] [5]

[3]For both GPT-J and Llama-7b, nearly all examples fit this criteria.

[4]There were two relations which were not tested on, **[adj+comparative]** and **[antonyms-gradable]**. This was due to preprocessing issues.

[5]For the LRE, we use $\beta = 7$, which was found to be optimal for BATS.

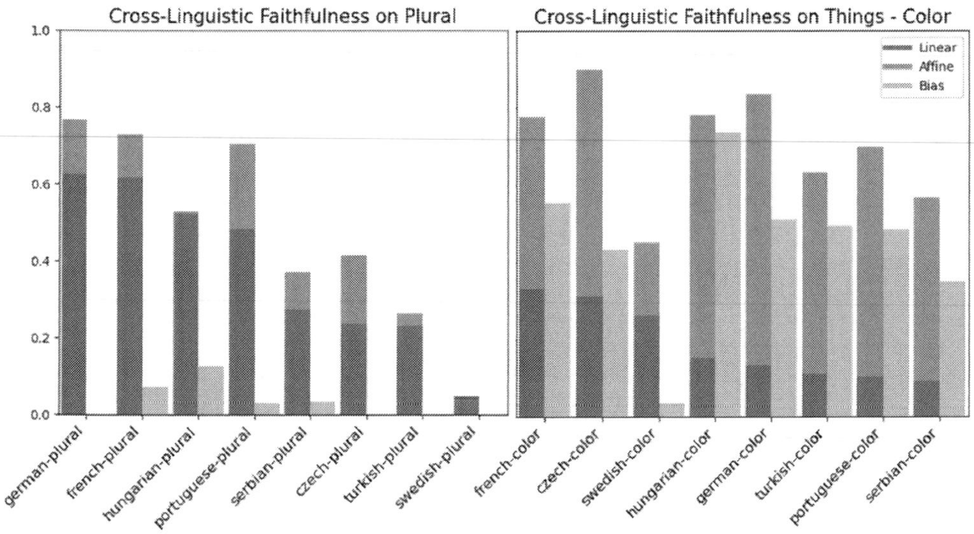

Figure 4: Evaluating languages present in Llama-7b reveal cross-typological linear encoding of morphology. Linear and affine LREs respectively score 56% and 68% on **[plural]** across German, French, Hungarian, and Portuguese. In contrast, on **[things - color]** relation the linear and affine techniques respectively score 19% and 70%. The Bias approximator scores 45%, suggesting the affine approximation for **[things - color]** is primarily additive.

As seen in Figure 3, the linear LRE achieves 90% faithfulness across 14 morphology relations, while the affine LRE achieves a faithfulness of 95%. In contrast, the linear LRE achieves 40% faithfulness over non-morphological relations, while the affine LRE achieves 61% faithfulness. This confirms the efficacy of the affine LRE found by Hernandez et al. (2023), while suggesting that some relations, e.g. morphology, may be encoded as truly linear.

To show that the Jacobian is not only sufficient but also necessary, in Appendix Figure 5 and Appendix Figure 6 we compare the LREs against two additive approximations, Bias and TRANSLATION. TRANSLATION adds the mean difference between the subject and object states to each subject state. In both cases, we find that an additive operator is unable to reproduce morphology.

5.2 Llama-7b Results

GPT-J utilizes parallel MLP and attention layers, unlike many other language models. Consequently, it is possible the observed linearity does not generalize to different architectures. We repeat the procedure for Llama-7b, which like most LLMs utilizes sequential attention and feedforward layers (Touvron et al. 2023). In the Appendix Figure 7, we display similar results to Figure 3; suggesting similar encoding mechanisms exist across models.

5.3 Cross-Linguistic Evidence

We have shown that morphological relations in English are largely linearly decodable. However, these results may be limited to fusional-analytic languages with fewer unique affixes. For Llama-7b, we test Czech, French, German, Hungarian, Portuguese, Serbian, Swedish, and Turkish, each comprising significant portions of the training dataset. Hungarian and Turkish are both highly agglutinative. We create templates for one morphological (**[plural]**) and non-morphological relation (**[things - color]**). We evaluate approximators as above.

As seen in Figure 4, affine and linear approximators achieve similar results on **[plural]**, while the additive operation performs well on **[things - color]**. These results indicate a multiplicative linear relational embedding for certain morphological relations, independent of linguistic typology. The high performance of the additive Bias operator on **[things - color]** provides evidence for complementary additive and multiplicative mechanisms.

6 Conclusion

In this work, we have adapted a large relational dataset for testing transformer approximation. We formulate the transformer version of the linear relational embedding found in Paccanaro and Hinton (2001) more precisely to be equivalent to a matrix-vector multiplication with the mean Jacobian. Surprisingly, we find this linear operation is able to model certain relations such as morphology nearly as well as the affine LRE. This suggests that certain conceptual relations surface linearly in the residual space of language models, and are sparsely encoded multiplicatively as opposed to additively.

7 Limitations

Our experiments were conducted exclusively on GPT-J and Llama-7b due to hardware constraints, which limited the scope of our evaluations. However, smaller models serve as a likely proxy for studying the interpretability of transformer-based language models due to identical architectures.

Throughout the work, we assume linear transformations observed are employed in token prediction through the same mechanism as in explicit relational contexts. Existing literature in activation patching and editing indicates that subject enrichment occurs independently from surrounding contexts (Geva et al. 2021), indicating that the relational embedding outlined here is consistent.

Unlike previous investigations of linear approximation, we did not investigate whether the faithfulness of the Jacobian approximation is associated with causality. Based on prior work which finds a consistent relationship between these variables (Hernandez et al. 2023), these two measures appear correlated.

Acknowledgments

The research done here was supported by the National Science Foundation under award number #XXX. Any opinion, finding, or conclusion in this study is that of the authors and does not necessarily reflect the views of the National Science Foundation.

References

Tom Brown, Benjamin Mann, Nick Ryder, Melanie Subbiah, Jared D Kaplan, Prafulla Dhariwal, Arvind Neelakantan, Pranav Shyam, Girish Sastry, Amanda Askell, et al. 2020. Language models are few-shot learners. *Advances in neural information processing systems*, 33:1877–1901.

Bob Coecke, Mehrnoosh Sadrzadeh, and Stephen Clark. 2010. Mathematical foundations for a compositional distributional model of meaning. *arXiv preprint arXiv:1003.4394*.

Dedre Gentner. 1983. Structure-mapping: A theoretical framework for analogy. *Cognitive science*, 7(2):155–170.

Mor Geva, Jasmijn Bastings, Katja Filippova, and Amir Globerson. 2023. Dissecting Recall of Factual Associations in Auto-Regressive Language Models. *arXiv preprint*. ArXiv:2304.14767 [cs].

Mor Geva, Roei Schuster, Jonathan Berant, and Omer Levy. 2021. Transformer feed-forward layers are key-value memories. In *Proceedings of the 2021 Conference on Empirical Methods in Natural Language Processing*, pages 5484–5495.

Anna Gladkova, Aleksandr Drozd, and Satoshi Matsuoka. 2016. Analogy-based detection of morphological and semantic relations with word embeddings: what works and what doesn't. In *Proceedings of the NAACL Student Research Workshop*, pages 8–15, San Diego, California. Association for Computational Linguistics.

Evan Hernandez, Arnab Sen Sharma, Tal Haklay, Kevin Meng, Martin Wattenberg, Jacob Andreas, Yonatan Belinkov, and David Bau. 2023. Linearity of relation decoding in transformer language models. *arXiv preprint arXiv:2308.09124*.

Geoffrey E Hinton. 1986. Learning distributed representations of concepts. In *Proceedings of the Eighth Annual Conference of the Cognitive Science Society*, volume 1, page 12. Amherst, MA.

Keith J Holyoak. 2012. Analogy and relational reasoning. *The Oxford handbook of thinking and reasoning*, pages 234–259.

Kevin Meng, David Bau, Alex Andonian, and Yonatan Belinkov. 2022a. Locating and editing factual associations in gpt. *Advances in Neural Information Processing Systems*, 35:17359–17372.

Kevin Meng, Arnab Sen Sharma, Alex J Andonian, Yonatan Belinkov, and David Bau. 2022b. Mass-editing memory in a transformer. In *The Eleventh International Conference on Learning Representations*.

Jack Merullo, Carsten Eickhoff, and Ellie Pavlick. 2023. Language models implement simple word2vec-style vector arithmetic. *arXiv preprint arXiv:2305.16130*.

Tomas Mikolov, Kai Chen, Greg Corrado, and Jeffrey Dean. 2013. Efficient estimation of word representations in vector space. *arXiv preprint arXiv:1301.3781*.

Alberto Paccanaro and Geoffrey E. Hinton. 2001. Learning distributed representations of concepts using linear relational embedding. *IEEE Transactions on Knowledge and Data Engineering*, 13(2):232–244.

Robert J Sternberg and Bathsheva Rifkin. 1979. The development of analogical reasoning processes. *Journal of experimental child psychology*, 27(2):195–232.

Hugo Touvron, Louis Martin, Kevin Stone, Peter Albert, Amjad Almahairi, Yasmine Babaei, Nikolay Bashlykov, Soumya Batra, Prajjwal Bhargava, Shruti Bhosale, et al. 2023. Llama 2: Open foundation and fine-tuned chat models. *arXiv preprint arXiv:2307.09288*.

Ashish Vaswani, Noam Shazeer, Niki Parmar, Jakob Uszkoreit, Llion Jones, Aidan N Gomez, Ł ukasz Kaiser, and Illia Polosukhin. 2017. Attention is All you Need. In *Advances in Neural Information Processing Systems*, volume 30. Curran Associates, Inc.

Ekaterina Vylomova, Laura Rimell, Trevor Cohn, and Timothy Baldwin. 2016. Take and took, gaggle and goose, book and read: Evaluating the utility of vector differences for lexical relation learning. In *Proceedings of the 54th Annual Meeting of the Association for Computational Linguistics (Volume 1: Long Papers)*, pages 1671–1682.

Ben Wang and Aran Komatsuzaki. 2021. GPT-J-6B: A 6 Billion Parameter Autoregressive Language Model. `https://github.com/kingoflolz/mesh-transformer-jax`.

A Reproducibility Statement

The approximation code is based on the LRE repository (Hernandez et al. 2023), and loads GPT-J and Llama-7b in half-precision. The code and dataset are available at {link}. Experiments were run remotely on a workstation with 24GB NVIDIA RTX 3090 GPUs using HuggingFace Transformers.

B Evidence of non-stemmed forms

As seen in Table 1, the linear LRE successfully replicates full forms for many derived object states. In Table 3, we can see consistent preferences for correct forms over stemmed forms on morphological relations. All examples shown are for GPT-J.

C Bias Results demonstrate W necessity

A comparison of linear and affine approximators against the bias approximator demonstrates that the bias term b_r alone cannot explain the relational encoding but contributes alongside the Jacobian W_r. This suggests that these operations play complementary roles in semantic and encyclopedic relations.

The TRANSLATION operator, inspired by Merullo et al. (2023) and vector arithmetic, is also additive and performs similarly to the Bias operator. Figure 6 demonstrates the additive TRANSLATION approximator against both the affine and linear LRE. Like the bias approximator, the TRANSLATION approximator succeeds when the gap between the Jacobian and LRE is large. This suggests that semantic information plays a crucial role in bridging some subject-object relations.

D Linear Projection

We find that linear projection to $\mathbb{R}^2$ can yield interpretable geometric representations. Specifically, we use a basis of the bias vector b and a random normalized vector, which has been orthogonalized with Gram-Schmidt to b, and compare approximated transformations against true object states. As seen in Figure 8, we find subspace distance corresponding heavily to faithfulness. Additionally, we validate that the β hyperparameter is necessary for recovering scale lost in layer normalization, as conjectured by Hernandez et al. (2023).

We project approximations $\mathbf{s}$, $\beta W\mathbf{s}$, $\beta W\mathbf{s} + b$, as well as a calculated hidden state for the correct object output $\mathbf{o}$. These projections suggest W is

Subject	**Jacobian Top-3**
society	societies, Soc, soc
child	children, children, Children
success	successes, success, Success
series	series, Series, Series
woman	women, women, Women
righteous	righteousness, righteous, ...
conscious	consciousness, conscious, ...
serious	seriousness, serious, serious
happy	happiness, happy, happy
mad	madness, mad, being
invest	investment, invest, investing
amuse	amusement, amuse, amusing
accomplish	accomplishment, accomplish, ...
displace	displacement, displ, dis
reimburse	reimbursement, reimburse, reimb
globalize	globalization, global, international
install	installation, install, Installation
continue	continuation, continu, contin
authorize	authorization, Authorization, ...
restore	restoration, restitution, re
manage	manager, managers, manager
teach	teacher, teachers, teach
compose	compos, composer, composing
borrow	borrower, lender, debtor
announce	announcer, announ, ann

Table 1: **[noun_plural]**, **[verb+er]**, **[verb+ment]**, **[adj+ness]**, **[verb+tion]** Selected examples of full subject tokens demonstrate that the linear Jacobian approximation captures irregular morphology effectively, reproducing both stemmed and full subject forms.

Relation	**# Unique**
un+adj	**7**
over+adj	**4**
re+verb	**15**
name - nationality	13
animal - shelter	18
synonyms - intensity	35
verb+able	47
noun - plural	47

Table 2: The number of unique start tokens for correct objects across selected BATS relations. Start tokens which occur frequently among objects indicate a non-injective subject-object map, making linear approximation a less suitable choice as an approximator.

Correct	**Stemmed**	**Incorrect**
42	0	0
23	11	9
7	35	6

Table 3: Correct, stemmed, and incorrect suffix counts for **[noun_plural]**, **[verb+tion]** and **[adj+ness]** from the top prediction of a fixed layer Jacobian approximation further suggests consistent linear encoding beyond stemmed forms.

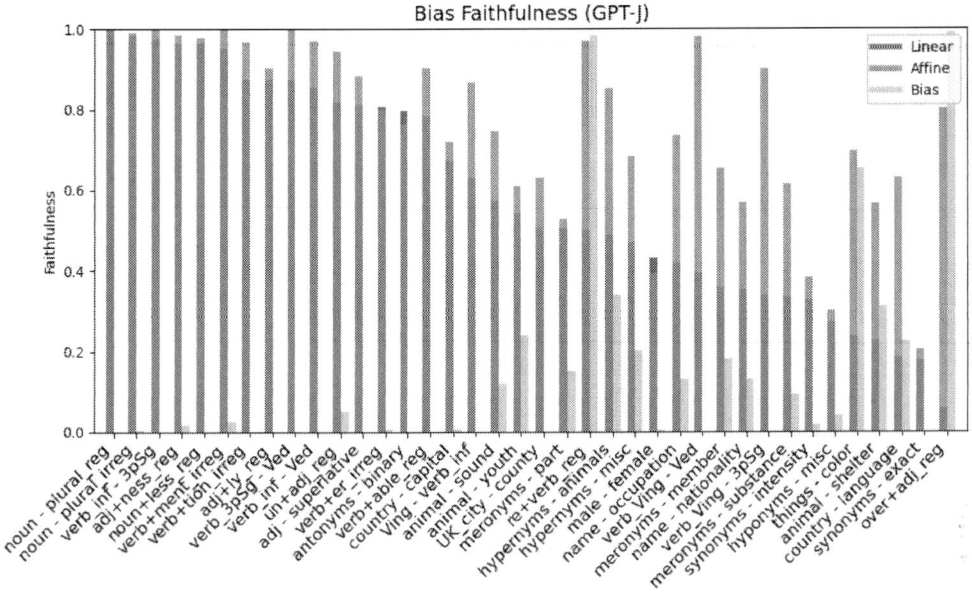

Figure 5: A comparison of the affine LRE against the Bias approximator demonstrates the necessity of the multiplicative (Jacobian) operator. Across semantic and encyclopedic relations, the additive Bias operator exhibits far better performance on morphology, providing evidence for complementary additive and multiplicative mechanisms.

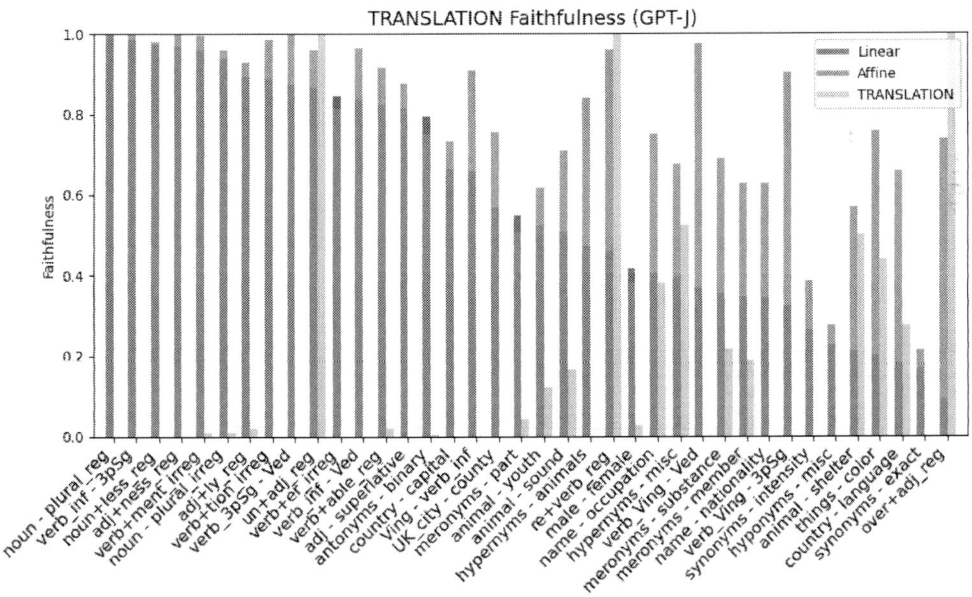

Figure 6: The TRANSLATION approximator $\tilde{\mathbf{o}} = \text{Bias}(\mathbf{s}) = \mathbf{s} + b_r$, with $b_r = \mathbb{E}(\mathbf{o} - \mathbf{s})$, performs well on semantic and encyclopedic relations, similar to the Bias approximator.

primarily responsible for transforming the underlying distribution to be geometrically similar to the output, while b contributes the majority of movement in vector space.

The term b_r could be compared to the vectors used by Mikolov and many others, and the concept vector subsequently formalized by Park. However, the bias vector and the concept vector are not truly analogous. The bias term describes an offset from the transformed subject to the object: $b_r = \mathbb{E}(o - W_r\mathbf{s})$, not $b_r = \mathbb{E}(o - \mathbf{s})$. In practice, we find that bias and concept vectors are close in cosine similarity, and likely serve similar roles.

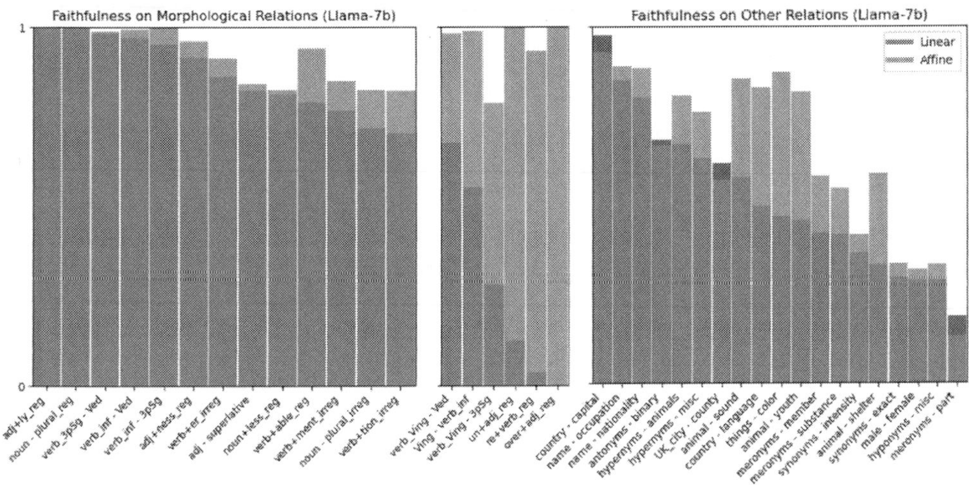

Figure 7: Llama-7b results support a generalization across models: many morphological relations are linearly approximable, while semantic and encyclopedic relations benefit greatly from the affine method. Out of a range of subject layers 4-16, the best performing approximation is averaged ($n = 4$).

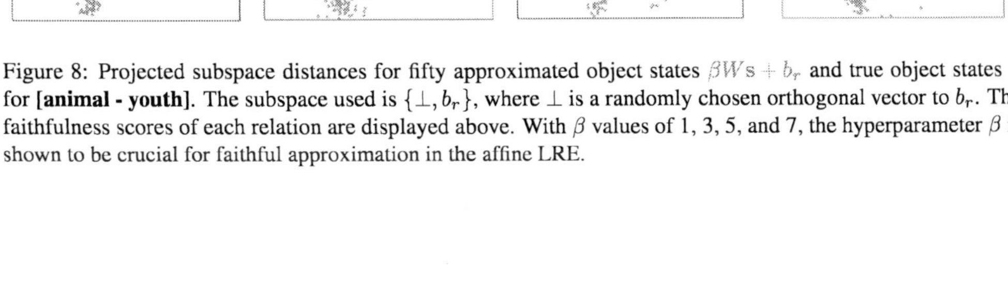

Figure 8: Projected subspace distances for fifty approximated object states $\beta W \mathrm{s} + b_r$ and true object states o for **[animal - youth]**. The subspace used is $\{\perp, b_r\}$, where $\perp$ is a randomly chosen orthogonal vector to b_r. The faithfulness scores of each relation are displayed above. With β values of 1, 3, 5, and 7, the hyperparameter β is shown to be crucial for faithful approximation in the affine LRE.

SPY: Enhancing Privacy with Synthetic PII Detection Dataset

Maksim Savkin[1,†] **Timur Ionov**[2,3,†] **Vasily Konovalov**[4,1]
[1]Moscow Institute of Physics and Technology
[2]MTS AI [3]ITMO University [4]AIRI
{savkin.mk, vasily.konovalov}@phystech.edu t.ionov@mts.ai

Abstract

We introduce the SPY dataset: a novel synthetic dataset designed for Personal Identifiable Information (PII) detection, underscoring the importance of safeguarding PII in modern data processing. Our approach innovates by using large language models (LLMs) to generate a dataset that emulates real-world PII scenarios. We evaluate the dataset's quality and position it as a reliable benchmark for PII detection.. Comparative analyses reveal that while PII detection and Named Entity Recognition (NER) share similarities, dedicated NER models exhibit limitations when applied to PII-specific contexts. This work contributes to the field by making the generation methodology and the generated dataset publicly accessible[1], thereby enabling further research and development in this field.

1 Introduction

In the expanding digital realm, the accumulation of personal data has reached unprecedented levels. Details encompassing our search queries, online activity, social connections, health records, and more are gathered and disseminated among advertisers, researchers, and government bodies, giving rise to complex privacy concerns about keeping personal information safe. What entities qualify as personally identifiable information? For example, a Social Security Number (SSN) is undoubtedly considered PII, but is a person's name considered PII? Narayanan and Shmatikov (2010) argues that PII is surprisingly difficult to define.

Historically, NER techniques have been employed for PII detection. However, when security is a primary concern, PII entities constitute a subset of NER entities. For instance, a person's name on a credit card is clearly PII, and revealing this information can indeed cause harm. Conversely, the name of the lead actress in the Titanic movie would likely not cause any harm upon disclosure. In this work, we define PII entities as those that can be used to identify, contact, or locate a specific individual and should not be disclosed to the public due to security concerns. The distinction between PII and NER entities is described in Table 1.

	PII vs NER
a)	Apple technical support for education customers: 1-800-800-2775.
	Satya Nadella is CEO of Microsoft Corp.
b)	Lucy Cechtelar lives at 426 Jordy Lodge Cartwrightshire, SC 88120-6700.

Table 1: Examples of **a)** NER entities; **b)** PII entities. All examples of personal information provided are generated using the Faker library (Faraglia, 2014).

If PII detection and NER are distinct, it implies that data-driven approaches for PII detection require their own specialized dataset. However, creating and sharing a dataset with actual PII entities online is not feasible due to privacy concerns. Consequently, there are two options: (1) use a dataset that contains real PII entities and substitute them with fake ones; (2) devise a methodology to generate a completely PII-focused dataset from scratch and then replace the placeholders of PII with fake entities generated by a tool such as Faker (Faraglia, 2014), see Section 3 for more details. The benefit of the former approach is that it maintains the data's characteristics. The drawback is in ensuring that all genuine PII entities have been accurately replaced.

In our work, we opt for the second approach. We used Faker to create artificial PII entities and Llama-3-70B (AI@Meta, 2024) to generate text where these fake entities could be seamlessly integrated.

The additional advantage of the fully generated approach lies in having complete control over the generation process. You can tailor it to your specific domain, including designated PII entities and

† These authors contributed equally to this work.
[1]https://github.com/LogicZMaksimka/SPY_Dataset

Proceedings of the 2025 Conference of the Nations of the Americas Chapter of the Association for Computational Linguistics: Human Language Technologies (Volume 4: Student Research Workshop), pages 236–246

their desired distribution or balance.

Our contributions can be summarized as follows.

- We present a methodology for developing the SPY dataset and compare it to other methodologies used for creating a synthetic PII datasets. Our approach does not require any external data and can be applied to any knowledge domain.

- We open-source the SPY dataset containing 4,491 medical consultations and 4,197 questions in the legal domain, which is specifically developed to highlight the contrast between an average task of named entity recognition and more fine-grained tasks of PII detection.

2 Related Work

Knowledge-based approaches for safeguarding PII like `regexp` achieve fair accuracy in identifying PII that have a strict and template-based format, but fall short when applied to unstructured text. This is where data-driven approaches, like Named Entity Recognition (NER), come into play. NER models offer greater flexibility in identifying PII in various contexts, particularly when dealing with unstructured data such as names or addresses, by learning from labeled datasets containing examples of PII instances (Johnson et al., 2020; Pilán et al., 2022; Li et al., 2023).

Detecting PII requires identifying entities that pose potential privacy risks, which may not always align with conventional NER categories. Existing PII detection tools and datasets often fail to distinguish between personal and non-personal entities within the same entity type, essentially performing as traditional NER systems. For example, Microsoft's **Presidio** (Microsoft, 2021), a popular tool for PII detection, combines NER models with regular expressions and pattern matching. However, this approach labels all entities of a given type (e.g., names) as PII, without differentiating between personal and non-personal entities. Similarly, **NER-PII** (Mazzarino et al., 2023), a pseudonymization tool for structured data, leverages Presidio and BERT (Devlin et al., 2019) for PII detection, but shares the same limitations.

One of the major challenges in PII detection is the scarcity of publicly available datasets due to privacy concerns. To address this, some approaches replace personal data in real texts with synthetic data, while others generate entirely synthetic texts. Below are some of the more popular datasets for PII detection:

The **BigCode**[2] PII dataset was created by manually annotation of The stack (Kocetkov et al., 2023) dataset. Specifically, it targets the identification of PII in programming contexts, making it less suitable for broader text-based PII scenarios.

The **AI4Privacy**[3] is a synthetic PII dataset created using proprietary algorithms. It spans six languages and eight jurisdictions, with 63 PII classes, making it one of the most comprehensive datasets available. However, its proprietary nature limits transparency, making it difficult to assess the representativeness of the data or adapt it to specific needs.

The **Kaggle PII Detection Competition** (Langdon et al., 2024) dataset contains around 22,000 student essays from a massive open online course. Unlike other PII datasets mentioned earlier, this one distinguishes between PII and non-PII entities, aligning more closely with the goal of this research. However, it has two significant limitations. First, all essays are written in response to a single assignment prompt, which limits the diversity of the data. Second, only 30% of the dataset is publicly available for training, with the remaining 70% reserved for testing, making it unsuitable for a comprehensive evaluation (see Figure 2 for detailed statistics). Although the dataset provides accurate PII annotations for seven entity types, these limitations in diversity and access make it less ideal for broader applications and thorough evaluations.

2.1 Synthetic NER Generation

Although research on PII datasets is limited due to privacy concerns, significant work has been done on generating synthetic NER datasets that share a similar format with PII data.

A notable approach is described by Tang et al. (2023), where a small set of human-labeled examples is used to guide LLMs in generating diverse synthetic datasets. This method encourages variability in sentence structures and linguistic patterns, ensuring that the synthetic data are not overly repetitive or predictable. A post-processing step is then employed to filter out low-quality or duplicate samples, ultimately improving the quality and diversity of the data.

[2] `https://hf.co/datasets/bigcode/bigcode-pii-dataset`

[3] `https://hf.co/datasets/ai4privacy/pii-masking-300k`

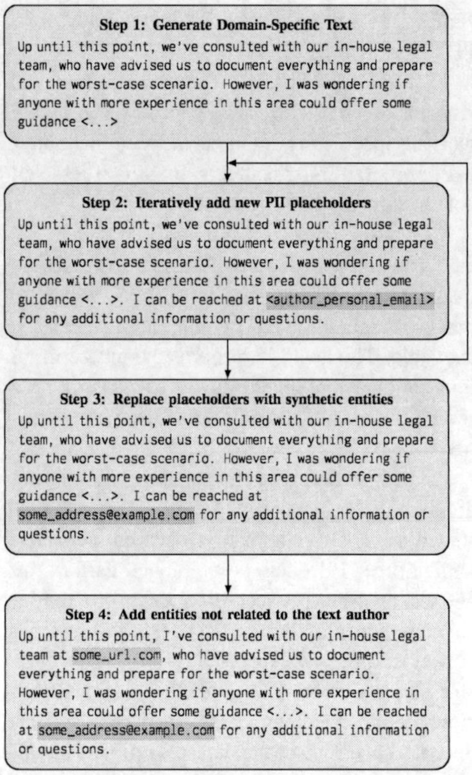

Figure 1: Multi-step prompting procedure. Red selection – author's personal data (PII); blue selection – NER entities not directly related to the text author. Prompts used in Steps 1–4 are shown in Figures 6,8,9 and 10, respectively.

Another promising technique involves automatic data annotation, where synthetic data is used to enrich an existing labeled dataset. Tools like **UniNER** (Zhou et al., 2024) and **NuNER** (Bogdanov et al., 2024) leverage GPT-3.5 to annotate large text corpora, such as The Pile (Gao et al., 2021) and C4 (Raffel et al., 2020). These models are pretrained on these annotated corpora to create versatile, general-purpose NER models, which can then be fine-tuned with a smaller amount of domain-specific data.

3 Data Construction

Although direct prompting of LLMs to annotate text data has proven effective for datasets rich in NER entities (Zhou et al., 2024; Bogdanov et al., 2024; Zaratiana et al., 2024), this approach is less effective in data-scarce environments. When only a small fraction of the dataset contains PII entities, LLM-based annotation becomes less efficient due to several challenges: (1) only a small portion of texts in the dataset will receive any annotations, (2) certain entity types will be underrepresented, and (3) the resulting annotations will be highly imbalanced across classes. For example, in the Kaggle competition dataset (Langdon et al., 2024), only 24% of all essays contain any personal data, and six of the seven entity types have fewer than 110 samples (see Figure 2), leading to class imbalance and limited representation. To address those constraints, we generate texts that contain placeholders for predetermined sets of personal entities. Then we replace these placeholders with PII entities generated by Faker - an open-source python library that generates realistic synthetic entities. It can produce a wide range of data types, including names, addresses, emails, dates, and more, supporting multiple locales and customization.

We chose two domains: (1) legal – informal questions in legal domain similar to r/LegalAdvice[4] and (2) medical – forms completed by patients for online medical consultations. Specifically, we select the following PII entity types: `name`, `email`, `phone number`, `personal url`, `personal identifier`, `username`, and `personal address`.

3.1 Prompting Pipeline

When designing a methodology for generating texts with personal data, it is important to clearly distinguish PII entities from other types of information. Any details about the text's author can be classified as PII, while information that can be referenced through links to web resources, papers, or articles is considered publicly available. Based on this distinction, we chose to prompt the LLM to generate only PII placeholders related to the text author. In contrast, all non-PII entities are unrelated to the author. These limitations helped ensure a clear separation between personal and publicly available information.

SPY prompting methodology was developed to meet the following criteria: (1) incorporate domain-specific details while naturally integrating PII entities, (2) include both personal and non-personal entities from predefined categories, and (3) maintain a clear distinction between personal and public data. To achieve this, we implemented a multi-stage prompting pipeline, as shown in Figure 1.

First, we used the Llama-3-70B model to generate texts in the *law* and *medical* domains, following

[4] https://www.reddit.com/r/legaladvice/

the prompt in Figure 6. Back when we conducted the main experiments, Llama-3-70B was one of the best 70B models available for instruction following. It performed well across the required data manipulations from the prompt, handling the diverse task requirements effectively. We did not opt for proprietary models due to budget constraints, which influenced our decision to use Llama-3-70B for this project. We did not opt for proprietary models due to budget constraints.

To enhance the diversity of the generated texts, we included details about the person's occupation and personality, which expanded the range of topics within each domain. The personalities were generated using the prompt shown in Figure 7.

When incorporating the author's personal information, we encountered difficulties embedding multiple PII entities at once. To address this, we adopted an iterative approach, prompting the model to refine each version of the text, progressively adding more entities as outlined in Figure 8. Although iterative text updates can be performed using CoD prompts (Adams et al., 2023), we found that Llama-3-70B struggled to apply multiple updates in a single generation due to the length of the initial texts. Furthermore, instead of directly inserting PII, we used placeholders (`<entity-type>`) during generation to minimize paraphrasing.

Before proceeding to the next stage, we replaced all placeholders with the corresponding synthetic entities to ensure consistency between the previously added PII and the new entities. The `Faker` library (Faraglia, 2014) was used to generate a diverse set of personal synthetic entities, located in six different countries.

After completion of this process, we obtained a dataset with personal information exclusively tied to the author of the text. In the final stage, we introduce non-PII entities that are not related to the author using the prompt in Figure 9.

4 Data Analysis

SPY's flexible pipeline for synthetic PII data generation demonstrates several key advantages:

Even Distribution of PII Entities: The pipeline ensures that PII entities are evenly distributed throughout the generated texts. This even distribution is visually represented in Figure 3 where the entities' positions are spread relatively uniformly across the texts, avoiding clustering in any specific section.

Entity	Legal Questions			Medical Consultations		
	pii 1	pii 2	final	pii 1	pii 2	final
Name	0.58	1.06 (+0.48)	0.91 (+0.33)	0.69	1.12 (+0.43)	0.99 (+0.3)
Email	1.03	1.15 (+0.12)	0.86 (-0.17)	1.01	1.12 (+0.11)	0.93 (-0.08)
Username	0.91	1.14 (+0.23)	1.30 (+0.39)	0.80	1.16 (+0.36)	1.33 (+0.53)
Phone	0.87	1.1 (+0.23)	0.75 (-0.12)	0.88	1.12 (+0.24)	0.89 (+0.01)
URL	1.07	1.34 (+0.27)	0.87 (-0.2)	1.03	1.32 (+0.29)	0.88 (-0.15)
Address	0.71	1.19 (+0.48)	0.87 (+0.16)	0.73	1.28 (+0.55)	1.06 (+0.33)
ID	0.39	0.98 (+0.59)	0.69 (+0.3)	0.53	1.05 (+0.52)	0.89 (+0.36)
avg.	0.79	1.14 (+0.35)	0.89 (+0.1)	0.81	1.17 (+0.36)	0.99 (+0.18)

Table 2: Frequency of entities calculated by dividing the total number of entities by the number of texts. Frequencies for each entity type are computed separately. *pii {k}* refers to the frequency of PII placeholders after k iterative updates using the prompt from Figure 8; *final* represents the frequency of PII entities after completing all stages of the pipeline from Figure 1.

Balanced Entity Counts: The number of entities by type is relatively balanced. For example, we observed that after running the pipeline, there were approximately 3,000–5,000 entities for every entity type, showing that the dataset maintains a fair balance across different types of PII entities. For more detailed statistics, see Figure 6.

Controlling PII Entity Density: The iterative update mechanism allows us to increase the number of PII entities in generated texts by repeating the update step multiple times. In Table 2 in column *pii 2* there is a steady increase in the frequency of entities, calculated as the total number of entities divided by the number of texts. This flexibility in entity injection enables the generation of more entity-rich texts. We opted against more than two updates to avoid compromising the natural flow of the text through excessive inclusion of personal information.

Controlling non-PII Entities: Another significant benefit of this pipeline is the ability to control the inclusion of non-PII entities, such as public names, organizations, or general locations. This degree of control would not be possible if real text data were simply marked up using a tool like ChatGPT, as that approach would not allow for the same precision in distinguishing between personal and non-personal data. However, a major limitation is that while generating non-PII entities, LLama-3-70B tends to drop some of the previously generated PII placeholders, as shown in Table 2 in column *final*.

The pipeline thus provides a robust solution for generating synthetic data with controlled distributions, balancing the number of entities while ensuring flexibility in both PII and non-PII management.

5 Experimental setup

5.1 Baselines

In the following, we outline several zero-shot baseline approaches we employ for PII detection.

Presidio (Microsoft, 2021) is a Microsoft SDK that provides a fast identification for PII entities by employing a combination of techniques including NER modules, regular expressions, and additional rule-based logic.

LLaMA-3-70B (AI@Meta, 2024) with zero-shot instruction to extract personal entities described in Figure 5. This model processes and identifies a wide range of personal information directly from text, demonstrating strong adaptability and generalization across different types of personal entities.

5.2 Our approach

Our supervised solution is based on `DeBERTaV3-base` encoder (He et al., 2023). Fine-tuned `DeBERTa` encoder-based models have exhibited their capabilities in identifying named entities (Tirskikh and Konovalov, 2023). Since we do not divide the data into training and test sets, we evaluated the model in a domain-transfer scenario. Specifically, we train the DeBERTa model on data from one domain and assess its performance in another. The training hyperparameters can be found in Appendix A.

5.3 Evaluation Metrics

For our evaluation, we use precision, recall, and F1 score, which are standard metrics to assess token classification tasks (Sang and Meulder, 2003).

Entity		Legal Questions			Medical Consultations		
		Llama-3	Presidio	DeBERTa	Llama-3	Presidio	DeBERTa
Name	P	64.7	17.9	**87.4**	73.0	17.1	**86.9**
	R	68.9	79.4	**93.2**	62.9	80.4	**88.7**
	F1	66.7	29.2	**90.2**	67.6	28.2	**87.8**
Email	P	91.8	33.7	**92.1**	92.7	37.6	**97.6**
	R	88.5	91.8	**99.1**	90.9	92.2	**99.5**
	F1	90.1	49.3	**95.5**	91.8	53.4	**98.5**
Username	P	66.1	-	**90.3**	68.8	-	**92.1**
	R	59.7	-	**98.0**	70.4	-	**95.4**
	F1	62.7	-	**94.0**	69.6	-	**93.8**
URL	P	84.5	7.9	**94.4**	83.6	6.9	**97.5**
	R	92.5	21.3	**99.0**	91.9	19.4	**98.9**
	F1	88.3	11.5	**96.7**	87.5	10.2	**98.2**
ID	P	91.9	20.6	**93.0**	91.7	26.1	**96.7**
	R	62.2	34.4	**96.6**	75.1	38.9	**98.3**
	F1	74.2	25.8	**94.8**	82.6	31.2	**97.5**
Phone	P	85.7	34.1	**87.5**	89.8	37.4	**93.3**
	R	92.8	68.1	**98.7**	90.0	65.5	**96.9**
	F1	89.1	45.4	**92.8**	89.9	47.6	**95.0**
Address	P	**93.7**	-	88.3	**96.2**	-	89.3
	R	81.3	-	**94.5**	90.4	-	**95.1**
	F1	87.1	-	**91.3**	**93.2**	-	92.1

Table 3: Performance metrics of models with various domain and entities, where P – Precision, R – recall, F1 – F-score. **Presidio** is a Microsoft SDK for fast PII detection using NER, regex, rule-based logic. **LLaMA-3** is LLaMA-3-70B zero-shot prompted LLM for PII task. **DeBERTa** is a model cross-validated on different domains of the SPY dataset. Blanks mean that entity class is not supported by the model.Presidio extracts addresses only at the geographical level, excluding street names and house numbers.

Legal Questions			Medical Consultations		
P	R	F1	P	R	F1
21.5	89.5	34.7	21.7	80.4	34.1

Table 4: UniNER evaluation results on the SPY dataset. Metrics are calculated specifically for `name` enity type, using prompts from the original UniNER paper (Zhou et al., 2024): *"What describes a person in the text?"*

6 Experimental results

First, we verify that SPY contains a substantial amount of non-PII entities. To do this, we evaluated UniNER (Zhou et al., 2024) on the `name` entity type using the prompt shown in Table 4. The results indicate that Recall is significantly higher than Precision, suggesting that UniNER identified additional non-PII names. This observation is also supported by the example provided in Table 4.

Following the pipeline presented, we generated two datasets from the legal and medical domains. Table 3 shows how different models perform PII detection on the SPY dataset. We can clearly see that Presidio has a much lower Precision than the Recall for all the categories, meaning that it misclassified a large portion of NER entities as PII entities. Another observation is that Llama-3-70B consistently outperforms Presidio, which can be attributed to its ability to differentiate between standard NER entities and PII entities.

DeBERTa validated on the SPY dataset in a domain-transfer setting is able to detect PII entities more precisely than zero-shot methods, getting a much higher precision with a smaller gap between recall. In general, encoder-based models have demonstrated their remarkable ability to transfer across tasks, domains, and languages (Karpov and Konovalov, 2023).

The encoder model specifically trained to detect

PII entities outperforms the general NER models, confirming the fact that the task of PII detection is not equivalent to NER. The distinction between them can be effectively learned by a supervised classification model.

7 Conclusions

In this study, we discuss the critical issue of PII detection, highlighting its importance in the realm of data privacy and security. We underscore the distinction between PII detection and NER, emphasizing that while related, PII detection carries unique nuances and requirements.

We highlight the disadvantages of existing datasets and PII tools and provide a robust methodology for creating diverse training datasets tailored for PII detection. Our approach is based on employing LLM to generate data and does not require human supervision. These advancements reinforce our commitment to safeguarding personal data, a significant area in today's digital landscape.

The generated dataset can be utilized to fine-tune the PII model independently or within the DeepPavlov framework (Savkin et al., 2024). To encourage research in the field, we make the SPY dataset freely available.

Limitations

While our research provides valuable insights, it is important to recognize its limitations. Specifically, our dataset was constructed with a narrow focus on certain domains and PII entities. Although this allowed us to develop a flexible methodology that is able to adapt to various domains, it also limits the dataset's generalizability.

Due to the lack of suitable manually annotated data, we were unable to fully assess the pipeline's transferability to real-world data.

Another significant limitation is that the generated PII entities only relate to the text's author. In many cases, personal information about individuals closely related to the author could also be classified as PII, but such cases are not covered in our dataset.

Taking all the aforementioned factors into account, the trained model and generated dataset should not be used in a real production system to detect PII entities, anonymize documents, or be utilized in any other manner, except for research purposes.

Ethics Statement

While SPY methodology enhances privacy-preserving technologies, we are aware that misuse of this dataset could lead to privacy violations, data manipulation, or exploitation of personal data in ways that harm individuals. To mitigate these risks, we have taken several precautions. First, our dataset is entirely synthetic, ensuring that no real-world PII is exposed or used in its creation. Second, all PII entities in the generated dataset are artificial.

We emphasize that the generated dataset and the methodology should be used only for research purposes.

We strongly discourage any use of our dataset that aims to undermine privacy protections or misuse the generated synthetic data for harmful purposes.

References

Griffin Adams, Alexander R. Fabbri, Faisal Ladhak, Eric Lehman, and Noémie Elhadad. 2023. From sparse to dense: GPT-4 summarization with chain of density prompting. *CoRR*, abs/2309.04269.

AI@Meta. 2024. Llama 3 model card.

Sergei Bogdanov, Alexandre Constantin, Timothée Bernard, Benoît Crabbé, and Etienne Bernard. 2024. Nuner: Entity recognition encoder pre-training via llm-annotated data. In *Proceedings of the 2024 Conference on Empirical Methods in Natural Language Processing, EMNLP 2024, Miami, FL, USA, November 12-16, 2024*, pages 11829–11841. Association for Computational Linguistics.

Jacob Devlin, Ming-Wei Chang, Kenton Lee, and Kristina Toutanova. 2019. BERT: pre-training of deep bidirectional transformers for language understanding. In *Proceedings of the 2019 Conference of the North American Chapter of the Association for Computational Linguistics: Human Language Technologies, NAACL-HLT 2019, Minneapolis, MN, USA, June 2-7, 2019, Volume 1 (Long and Short Papers)*, pages 4171–4186. Association for Computational Linguistics.

Daniele Faraglia. 2014. Faker. https://github.com/joke2k/faker.

Leo Gao, Stella Biderman, Sid Black, Laurence Golding, Travis Hoppe, Charles Foster, Jason Phang, Horace He, Anish Thite, Noa Nabeshima, Shawn Presser, and Connor Leahy. 2021. The pile: An 800gb dataset of diverse text for language modeling. *CoRR*, abs/2101.00027.

Pengcheng He, Jianfeng Gao, and Weizhu Chen. 2023. Debertav3: Improving deberta using electra-style pre-training with gradient-disentangled embedding sharing. In *The Eleventh International Conference on Learning Representations, ICLR 2023, Kigali, Rwanda, May 1-5, 2023*. OpenReview.net.

Alistair E. W. Johnson, Lucas Bulgarelli, and Tom J. Pollard. 2020. Deidentification of free-text medical records using pre-trained bidirectional transformers. In *ACM CHIL '20: ACM Conference on Health, Inference, and Learning, Toronto, Ontario, Canada, April 2-4, 2020 [delayed]*, pages 214–221. ACM.

Dmitry Karpov and Vasily Konovalov. 2023. Knowledge transfer between tasks and languages in the multi-task encoder-agnostic transformer-based models. In *Computational Linguistics and Intellectual Technologies*, volume 2023.

Denis Kocetkov, Raymond Li, Loubna Ben Allal, Jia Li, Chenghao Mou, Yacine Jernite, Margaret Mitchell, Carlos Muñoz Ferrandis, Sean Hughes, Thomas Wolf, Dzmitry Bahdanau, Leandro von Werra, and Harm de Vries. 2023. The stack: 3 TB of permissively licensed source code. *Trans. Mach. Learn. Res.*, 2023.

Holmes Langdon, Crossley Scott, Baffour Perpetual, King Jules, Burleigh Lauryn, Demkin Maggie, Holbrook Ryan, Reade Walter, and Howard Addison. 2024. The learning agency lab - pii data detection.

Raymond Li, Loubna Ben Allal, Yangtian Zi, Niklas Muennighoff, Denis Kocetkov, Chenghao Mou, Marc Marone, Christopher Akiki, Jia Li, Jenny Chim, Qian Liu, Evgenii Zheltonozhskii, Terry Yue Zhuo, Thomas Wang, Olivier Dehaene, Mishig Davaadorj, Joel Lamy-Poirier, João Monteiro, Oleh Shliazhko, Nicolas Gontier, Nicholas Meade, Armel Zebaze, Ming-Ho Yee, Logesh Kumar Umapathi, Jian Zhu, Benjamin Lipkin, Muhtasham Oblokulov, Zhiruo Wang, Rudra Murthy V, Jason T. Stillerman, Siva Sankalp Patel, Dmitry Abulkhanov, Marco Zocca, Manan Dey, Zhihan Zhang, Nour Fahmy, Urvashi Bhattacharyya, Wenhao Yu, Swayam Singh, Sasha Luccioni, Paulo Villegas, Maxim Kunakov, Fedor Zhdanov, Manuel Romero, Tony Lee, Nadav Timor, Jennifer Ding, Claire Schlesinger, Hailey Schoelkopf, Jan Ebert, Tri Dao, Mayank Mishra, Alex Gu, Jennifer Robinson, Carolyn Jane Anderson, Brendan Dolan-Gavitt, Danish Contractor, Siva Reddy, Daniel Fried, Dzmitry Bahdanau, Yacine Jernite, Carlos Muñoz Ferrandis, Sean Hughes, Thomas Wolf, Arjun Guha, Leandro von Werra, and Harm de Vries. 2023. Starcoder: may the source be with you! *Trans. Mach. Learn. Res.*, 2023.

Simona Mazzarino, Andrea Minieri, and Luca Gilli. 2023. NERPII: A python library to perform named entity recognition and generate personal identifiable information (short paper). In *Proceedings of the Seventh Workshop on Natural Language for Artificial Intelligence (NL4AI 2023) co-located with 22th International Conference of the Italian Association for Artificial Intelligence (AIxIA 2023), Rome, Italy, November 6th-7th, 2023*, volume 3551 of *CEUR Workshop Proceedings*. CEUR-WS.org.

Microsoft. 2021. Presidio. `https://microsoft.github.io/presidio/`.

Arvind Narayanan and Vitaly Shmatikov. 2010. Myths and fallacies of "personally identifiable information". *Commun. ACM*, 53(6):24–26.

Ildikó Pilán, Pierre Lison, Lilja Øvrelid, Anthi Papadopoulou, David Sánchez, and Montserrat Batet. 2022. The text anonymization benchmark (TAB): A dedicated corpus and evaluation framework for text anonymization. *Comput. Linguistics*, 48(4):1053–1101.

Colin Raffel, Noam Shazeer, Adam Roberts, Katherine Lee, Sharan Narang, Michael Matena, Yanqi Zhou, Wei Li, and Peter J. Liu. 2020. Exploring the limits of transfer learning with a unified text-to-text transformer. *J. Mach. Learn. Res.*, 21:140:1–140:67.

Erik F. Tjong Kim Sang and Fien De Meulder. 2003. Introduction to the conll-2003 shared task: Language-independent named entity recognition. In *Proceedings of the Seventh Conference on Natural Language Learning, CoNLL 2003, Held in cooperation with HLT-NAACL 2003, Edmonton, Canada, May 31 - June 1, 2003*, pages 142–147. ACL.

Maksim Savkin, Anastasia Voznyuk, Fedor Ignatov, Anna Korzanova, Dmitry Karpov, Alexander Popov, and Vasily Konovalov. 2024. DeepPavlov 1.0: Your gateway to advanced NLP models backed by transformers and transfer learning. In *Proceedings of the 2024 Conference on Empirical Methods in Natural Language Processing: System Demonstrations*, pages 465–474, Miami, Florida, USA. Association for Computational Linguistics.

Ruixiang Tang, Xiaotian Han, Xiaoqian Jiang, and Xia Hu. 2023. Does synthetic data generation of llms help clinical text mining? *CoRR*, abs/2303.04360.

Danil Tirskikh and Vasily Konovalov. 2023. Zero-shot NER via extractive question answering. In *Advances in Neural Computation, Machine Learning, and Cognitive Research VII*, pages 22–31, Cham. Springer Nature Switzerland.

Urchade Zaratiana, Nadi Tomeh, Pierre Holat, and Thierry Charnois. 2024. Gliner: Generalist model for named entity recognition using bidirectional transformer. In *Proceedings of the 2024 Conference of the North American Chapter of the Association for Computational Linguistics: Human Language Technologies (Volume 1: Long Papers), NAACL 2024, Mexico City, Mexico, June 16-21, 2024*, pages 5364–5376. Association for Computational Linguistics.

Wenxuan Zhou, Sheng Zhang, Yu Gu, Muhao Chen, and Hoifung Poon. 2024. Universalner: Targeted distillation from large language models for open named entity recognition. In *The Twelfth International Conference on Learning Representations, ICLR 2024, Vienna, Austria, May 7-11, 2024*. OpenReview.net.

A DeBERTa Hyperparameters

Hyperparameter	Value
Optimizer	AdamW
Adam β_1, β_2	0.9, 0.999
Adam ϵ	1e-6
Warm-up step	100
Context size	1,800
Learning rate (LR)	5e-6

Table 5: `DebertaV3-base` hyperparameters

B Data Analysis

Entity type	Domain	
	Legal questions	Medical Consultations
url	4,243	4,322
email	4,101	4,493
username	3,868	4,273
address	4,173	5,122
name	4,032	4,707
phone number	3,597	4,222
id_num	3,357	4,284

Table 6: Number of generated PII entities by type.

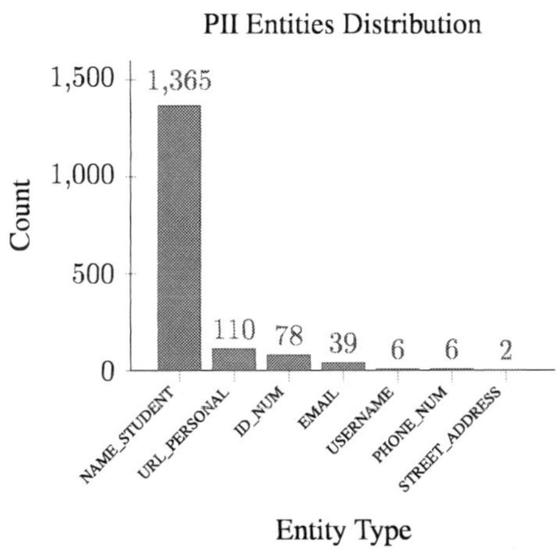

Figure 2: The distribution of entities present in the Kaggle PII dataset illustrates its highly imbalanced nature.

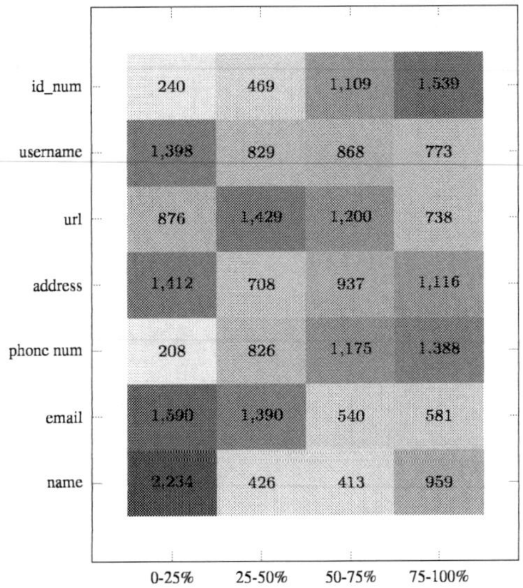

Figure 3: Heatmap showing the distribution of PII entity counts across relative position bins in the Legal Questions Domain of the SPY Dataset.

C UniNER "NAME" Class Prediction

> Hi all, I'm Nuria Batista, reaching out because I'm in a bit of a tricky situation and I'm hoping someone with legal expertise can offer some guidance. I'm a marketing coordinator at an advertising agency, and one of our clients is accusing us of breach of contract. My team and I have reviewed the contract thoroughly, and we're confident that we've met all of the requirements. However, the client is still pushing for a refund and is threatening to take legal action against me, specifically at the office of attorney Emily Brown, located at 123 Main St, San Francisco, CA 94105.

Figure 4: Name Nuria Batista is correctly classified as PII, while Emily Brown is misclassified due to the fact that UniNER doesn't differentiate between PII and non-PII.

D PII Dataset Generation Pipeline Prompts

Extract the following personal information entities from the provided text, ensuring that only personally identifiable information (PII) related to the author of the text is captured:

- **Person:** Names of the author. Do not include names of other people, famous authors, celebrities, or historical figures.
- **Email:** Personal email addresses of the author.
- **Phone:** Personal phone numbers of the author.
- **ID:** Personal identification numbers of the author (e.g., Social Security Number, passport number).
- **URL:** URLs that are personal to the author and lead to pages containing personal data (e.g., the author's personal blogs, social media profiles).
- **Username:** Personal usernames of the author for online platforms.
- **Address:** Personal home addresses of the author.

Text: "text"

Format your response in JSON as follows:
{{ "person": ["list of the author's personal names"],
"email": ["list of the author's personal emails"],
"phone": ["list of the author's personal phone numbers"],
"id": ["list of the author's personal IDs"],
"url": ["list of the author's personal URLs"],
"username": ["list of the author's personal usernames"],
"address": ["list of the author's personal addresses"]
}}

If there is no information for a particular category, return an empty list for that category.

Figure 5: LLaMA-3-70B prompt for extracting PII entities from text.

Step 1) Look through the personality of the text author and pretend to be that person.

occupation: ***<generated-occupation>***
personality: ***<generated-personality>***

Step 2) Use the following instructions to generate a text:

<domain-specific-instructions>

Requirements:
- At any circumstance do not include any personal information in generated text.

Respond only with generated text with no commentary. Here goes your text:

Figure 6: Prompt for generating texts, which do not contain any personal information. Placeholders "<generated-*>" and "<domain-specific-instructions>" are replaced with according descriptions.

Generate a biography of a fictional man named ***<generated-name-goes-here>***.

Occupation: any average job you can come up with
Personality: describe in 5 sentences

Present results in json format with fields "occupation": str, "personality": str

Figure 7: Prompt for biography generation. Placeholder "<generated-name-goes-here>" is replaced with random name.

Text: { }

Task: You are an author of the above Text. Your task is to add new placeholders in the Text from the list below. You will be penalized for mentioning any placeholders other than what is listed below!

Here is the list of placeholders representing your personal information:
<author_personal_name> - A full or partial name of the text author
<author_personal_email> - An author's email address
<author_personal_username> - An author's username on any website, social media etc.
<author_personal_phone_number> - A phone number associated with the author or his relatives
<author_personal_url> - A link to author's social media page or personal website
<author_personal_address> - A full or partial street address that is associated with the author, such as home address
<author_personal_identifier> - A number or sequence of characters that could be used to identify an author, such as a social security number or medical policy number

Requirements:
- Do NOT change existing placeholders
- Distribute placeholders evenly throughout your text, do not stack them all in one place
- New text must be more entity-dense than the previous one

Respond only with updated text with no commentary. Here goes an updated text:

Figure 8: Prompt for adding PII placeholders into the text.

Text: { }

Task: You are given a Text, which contains author's personal information. Your task is to add new entities, which are not related to the text author. Generate entities using the following classes: name, email, username, phone number, url, address, identifier.

Requirements:
- At any circumstance DO NOT change author's personal information in the above text
- Newly generated entities should not disclose the personal information of the author of the text

Respond only with updated text with no commentary. Here goes an updated text:

Figure 9: Prompt for adding entities with personal information that are not relatted to text author.

Extract the following personal information entities from the provided text, ensuring that only personally identifiable information (PII) related to the author of the text is captured:

- **Person:** Names of the author. Do not include names of other people, famous authors, celebrities, or historical figures.
- **Email:** Personal email addresses of the author.
- **Phone:** Personal phone numbers of the author.
- **ID:** Personal identification numbers of the author (e.g., Social Security Number, passport number).
- **URL:** URLs that are personal to the author and lead to pages containing personal data (e.g., the author's personal blogs, social media profiles).
- **Username:** Personal usernames of the author for online platforms.
- **Address:** Personal home addresses of the author.

Text: {text}

Format your response in JSON as follows:
{ "person": ["list of personal names"], "email": ["list of personal emails"], "phone": ["list of personal phone numbers"], "id": ["list of personal IDs"], "url": ["list of personal URLs"], "username": ["list of personal usernames"], "address": ["list of personal addresses"] }

If there is no information for a particular category, return an empty list for that category.

Figure 10: Prompt for extracting PII from text.

Tighter Clusters, Safer Code? Improving Vulnerability Detection with Enhanced Contrastive Loss

Pranav Kapparad[1] **Biju R Mohan**[1]
[1]National Institute of Technology Karnataka, Surathkal, India
pranavkapparad.211ai026@nitk.edu.in
biju@nitk.edu.in

Abstract

Distinguishing vulnerable code from non-vulnerable code is challenging due to high inter-class similarity. Supervised contrastive learning (SCL) improves embedding separation but struggles with intra-class clustering, especially when variations within the same class are subtle. We propose CLUSTER-ENHANCED SUPERVISED CONTRASTIVE LOSS (CESCL), an extension of SCL with a distance-based regularization term that tightens intra-class clustering while maintaining inter-class separation. Evaluating on CodeBERT and GraphCodeBERT with Binary Cross Entropy (BCE), BCE + SCL, and BCE + CESCL, our method improves F1 score by 1.76% on CodeBERT and 4.1% on GraphCodeBERT, demonstrating its effectiveness in code vulnerability detection and broader applicability to high-similarity classification tasks.

1 Introduction

Code vulnerability detection is a cornerstone of software security, particularly as the world undergoes rapid digitization. In domains like finance, healthcare, and government, software vulnerabilities exploited by malicious actors could have catastrophic consequences. The ability to detect such weaknesses efficiently is essential for safeguarding the trust that underpins modern technological systems. Beyond protecting sensitive data, robust vulnerability detection forms the backbone of a resilient digital society, ensuring confidence in the software solutions we rely on daily.

Recent years have witnessed a paradigm shift in this field with the rise of deep learning models, which have revolutionized how vulnerabilities are identified. These models far outperform traditional approaches such as static analysis tools and manual code reviews, which are labor-intensive, error-prone, and unable to keep pace with the accelerating rate of software development. Leveraging neural networks has enabled researchers to automate vulnerability detection, improving scalability and accuracy by identifying subtle patterns in code that signal potential flaws. Most deep learning models rely on loss functions such as binary cross-entropy to learn from labeled datasets of vulnerable and non-vulnerable code. However, despite these advancements, the field remains fraught with challenges.

One of the most significant bottlenecks in existing models is the high semantic and structural similarity between vulnerable and non-vulnerable code samples. This similarity often causes embeddings of the two classes to overlap in high-dimensional space, resulting in increased false positives and false negatives, thereby undermining the reliability of the models. To better quantify this challenge, we conducted a focused analysis of the embedding space. Using a simple, yet effective method, we computed the average cosine similarity between embeddings of samples with opposite labels across both code and general text datasets. The results, as seen in the figure below 1, revealed that code datasets exhibit significantly higher similarity across labels than general text data, underscoring the unique difficulty of separating vulnerable from non-vulnerable code. This inherent overlap in the embedding space presents a key challenge in ensuring accurate and reliable vulnerability detection.

Contrastive learning has emerged as a promising technique to address this challenge. By structuring the embedding space to maximize separation between samples with opposite labels and encouraging tighter clustering of samples within the same class, contrastive learning reduces overlap and enhances the discriminative power of embeddings. This is particularly critical in the context of code vulnerability detection, where subtle differences between classes demand a highly optimized embedding space.

However, existing contrastive learning methods,

Proceedings of the 2025 Conference of the Nations of the Americas Chapter of the Association for Computational Linguistics: Human Language Technologies (Volume 4: Student Research Workshop), pages 247–252
April 30 - May 1, 2025

such as Supervised Contrastive Loss (SCL), exhibit limitations in this domain. While SCL effectively prioritizes inter-class separation, it often fails to enforce sufficient intra-class cohesion. This can result in loosely clustered embeddings within each class, increasing the likelihood of misclassifications. Consequently, SCL struggles to handle the high similarity between vulnerable and non-vulnerable samples, limiting its effectiveness in real-world applications.

To overcome these limitations, we propose a novel loss function, Cluster Enhanced Supervised Contrastive Loss (CESCL). CESCL builds on the foundation of SCL by introducing additional regularization techniques aimed at simultaneously minimizing intra-class separation and penalizing high cosine similarity between embeddings of vulnerable and non-vulnerable code snippets. This dual objective ensures tighter clustering within the same class while amplifying the dissimilarity between different classes, resulting in a well-structured embedding space optimized for classification.

CESCL achieves this by incorporating penalties for misaligned embeddings and emphasizing the structural and semantic nuances that distinguish vulnerable from non-vulnerable code. By fostering tighter intra-class cohesion and greater inter-class separation, CESCL reduces embedding overlap, enabling models to better generalize across diverse and unseen code patterns. This results in lower false positive and false negative rates, addressing key reliability concerns in existing systems.

In summary, this research introduces CESCL as a targeted solution to the embedding challenges in code vulnerability detection. By addressing the shortcomings of existing loss functions, CESCL provides a more robust and generalizable embedding space, significantly improving classification accuracy. Our work also highlights the unique challenges of this domain through a quantitative analysis of embedding similarity, offering a new perspective on the limitations of current approaches.

As software vulnerabilities continue to rise alongside the pace of digitization, the need for reliable and efficient detection methods has become more urgent than ever. CESCL represents a step forward in building secure and trustworthy software systems, offering a foundation for future advancements in vulnerability detection. By bridging the gap between the limitations of SCL and the demands of real-world applications, this research provides both a theoretical and practical contribution to the field, paving the way for more secure digital ecosystems.

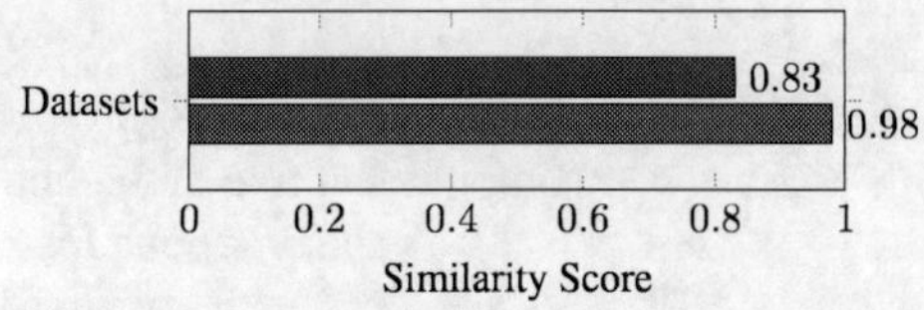

Figure 1: Cosine Similarity Between Opposite Labels. Text Data (Positive vs. Negative) is represented in blue, while Code Data (Vulnerable vs. Non-Vulnerable) is represented in red.

2 Related Work

Code vulnerability detection using deep learning has gained quite some attention in recent years, with various methods developed to address the challenges posed by detecting vulnerabilities within code (Grieco et al. (2016); Lin et al. (2017)). Early approaches Li et al. (2018), make use Long Bi Short-Term Memory (Bi-LSTM) networks to analyze code based on sequences of API calls, exhibiting the efficacy of deep learning models in capturing common patterns associated with vulnerbale code. SySeVR Li et al. (2021), built upon this approach by developing a deep learning framework for detecting vulnerabilities through sequence modeling of vulnerable function calls. While these methods provide useful insights, they often struggle with capturing the broader structural and semantic complexities of code, restricting their performance on more sophisticated code samples.

More recently, transformer-based models, which make use of attention mechanism, like CodeBERT Feng et al. (2020) and GraphCodeBERT Guo et al. (2020) have brought about major advancements. CodeBert is a pretrained model tailor made for both programming and natural languages, capturing both syntactic and semantic features from a large corpus of code. It has been adopted widely for vulnerability detection because of its ability to handle tasks like code summarization, generation, and classification. GraphCodeBERT extends CodeBert by incorporating data flow information within the model's architecture. This approach enhances the model's understanding of dependencies and control structures, allowing it to detect vulnerabilities that rely on intricate code flows, an area where traditional transformer models tend to disappoint. Such advancements highlight the potential of transformer based models in advancing the field of code vulnerability detection.

The Devign dataset Zhou et al. (2019) has been crucial in evaluating and benchmarking vulnerability detection models. Devign contains over 21,000 labeled C/C++ code snippets drawn from open-source projects, with each snippet classified as vulnerable or non-vulnerable. The dataset presents unique challenges due to the incorporation of a wide variety of vulnerabilities. The dataset also constitutes complex vulnerabilities making it hard for models to effectively generalise across samples. Devign also provides a rich structural context, including abstract syntax trees (ASTs) and control flow graphs (CFGs), which has proven useful for models designed to capture graph-based relationships in code, as demonstrated in Zhou et al. (2019) original work making use of graph neural networks.

Supervised Contrastive Learning (SCL), introduced by Khosla et al. (2020), is an emerging and powerful technique that focuses class separation by leveraging both positive and negative samples, making it immensely suitable for tasks where closely related samples are to be differentiated. In vulnerability detection, where samples of vulnerable and non vulnerable can appear notoriously similar, SCL has shown potential Du et al. (2022) by promoting embedding spaces that separate vulnerable and non-vulnerable samples.

Various regularization techniques have been applied to these losses to improve robustness in high-similarity domains such as the one tackled in this paper. For instance, Botev et al. (2022) explored regularizing for invariance to data augmentation, improving the ability of models to handle difficult samples.

In summary, this study builds on the strengths of transformer models like CodeBert and GraphCodeBERT, evaluates performance on the Devign dataset, and explores advanced contrastive learning techniques to enhance code vulnerability detection. By combining supervised contrastive learning with regularization strategies, we aim to improve the model's capability in embedding separation, thus enhancing overall classification performance.

3 Methodology

To ameliorate the effectiveness of code vulnerability detection, this study builds a classification model on top of the both CodeBERT and GraphCodeBERT models, with additional dropout and batch normalization layers. These layers reduce overfitting and ensure stable training by normalizing activations, contributing to more reliable model performance. The central novelty in this approach is the novel loss function, which integrates supervised contrastive learning with a distance-based regularization term to improve embedding separation between classes.

3.1 Dataset

For this research work, we make use of the Devign dataset, a benchmark dataset for code vulnerability detection in C/C++ programs. The Devign dataset constitutes over 21,000 code snippets, each labeled as either vulnerable or non-vulnerable, collected from real-world open-source projects, FFmpeg and qemu. Each code snippet is annotated with several features, including abstract syntax tree (AST) representations, control flow graphs (CFGs), and data flow information, which capture both structural and semantic information essential for identifying vulnerabilities. For this work, only the code function is made use of since the focus is on the embedding separation.

3.2 Model Architecture

The architecture begins with a pre-trained model, either CodeBERT or GraphCodeBERT, which is fine-tuned on domain-specific code datasets to generate meaningful code embeddings. On top of these embeddings, a classifier head consisting of fully connected layers is added. The classifier head takes as input a tensor of size 768 (the embedding output of CodeBERT or GraphCodeBERT), followed by a 128-dimensional layer, and finally an output layer of size 1. Dropout layers are interleaved within the classifier to reduce overfitting by randomly deactivating neurons during training, and batch normalization layers are employed to stabilize and accelerate the training process by standardizing layer inputs. The model output provides a binary classification, predicting whether a code snippet is vulnerable.

3.3 Loss Function Design

The novel contribution of this work is a custom loss function, cluster enhanced supervised contrastive loss (CESCL), that enhances embedding separation. This function combines the supervised contrastive loss (SCL loss) with a distance-based regularization term, which encourages tighter clustering within each class. The components of this loss function are as follows:

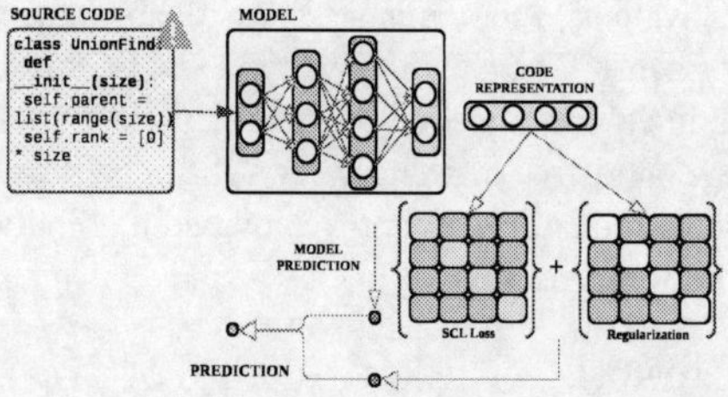

Figure 2: The framework of the proposed method.

Supervised Contrastive Loss (SCL): This loss maximizes agreement and similarity between embeddings of samples within the same class while pushing apart embeddings of different classes apart. Specifically, feature vectors are normalized, and a contrastive logits matrix is computed by dividing the dot product of normalized feature vectors by a temperature scaling factor.The novel contribution of this work is a custom loss function, cluster enhanced supervised contrastive loss (CESCL), that enhances embedding separation. This function combines the supervised contrastive loss (SCL loss) with a distance-based regularization term, which encourages tighter clustering within each class. The formula (Khosla et al., 2020) is as below

$$\mathcal{L}_{\text{SCL}} = -\frac{1}{N}\sum_{i=1}^{N}\frac{1}{|P(i)|}\sum_{p\in P(i)}\log\frac{\exp\left(\frac{\mathbf{z}_i\cdot\mathbf{z}_p}{\tau}\right)}{\sum_{a\in A(i)}\exp\left(\frac{\mathbf{z}_i\cdot\mathbf{z}_a}{\tau}\right)} \tag{1}$$

where:

- N is the batch size,
- $P(i)$ represents the set of positive samples for anchor i,
- $A(i)$ represents the set of all samples in the batch excluding i,
- $\mathbf{z}_i$ and $\mathbf{z}_p$ are the normalized feature vectors of the anchor and positive samples, respectively,
- τ is the temperature scaling factor, which helps control the distribution of the similarity scores.

While SCL effectively separates different classes, it does not explicitly enforce compactness within the same class, leading to loosely clustered embeddings. This is particularly problematic in high-similarity domains like vulnerability detection, where even minor variations can mislead classification.

Distance-Based Regularization Term: To further improve intra-class clustering, a regularization term is added that penalizes large distances between embeddings within the same class. This regularization term calculates the pairwise Euclidean distances between embeddings of the same class, averaging them over all possible pairs, and is scaled by a regularization factor.

The formula for the regularisation is as below

$$\mathcal{L}_{\text{reg}} = \frac{1}{n(n-1)}\sum_{i=1}^{n}\sum_{\substack{j=1\\ j\neq i}}^{n} 1_{[L(i)=L(j)]}\|\mathbf{z}_i - \mathbf{z}_j\|^2 \tag{2}$$

where:

- n is the total number of samples,
- $1_{[L(i)=L(j)]}$ is an indicator function, equal to 1 if samples i and j belong to the same class, and 0 otherwise,
- $\mathbf{z}_i$ and $\mathbf{z}_j$ are the feature vectors of samples i and j.

Cluster Enhanced Supervised Contrastive Loss is a combination of Supervised Contrastive Loss and the Distance Based Regularization Term (2). It is as below

$$\mathcal{L}_{\text{Cluster-Enhanced SCL}} = \mathcal{L}_{\text{SCL}} + \lambda_{\text{reg}}\cdot\mathcal{L}_{\text{reg}} \tag{3}$$

where λ_{reg} is a hyperparameter that scales the contribution of the regularization term.

3.4 Training

The model is trained using the combined loss function, which integrates the Binary Cross Entropy (BCE) loss with the Cluster-Enhanced Supervised Contrastive Loss. Specifically, the final loss is computed as:

$$\mathcal{L}_{\text{final}} = \mathcal{L}_{\text{BCE}} + \alpha\cdot\mathcal{L}_{\text{Cluster-Enhanced SCL}}, \tag{4}$$

where α is a balancing hyperparameter. The Cluster-Enhanced Supervised Contrastive Loss is defined as:

$$\mathcal{L}_{\text{Cluster-Enhanced SCL}} = \mathcal{L}_{\text{SCL}} + \lambda_{\text{reg}}\cdot\mathcal{L}_{\text{reg}} \tag{5}$$

where λ_{reg} is a hyperparameter that scales the contribution of the regularization term.

In our experiments, we set $\lambda_{\text{reg}} = 0.5$ and $\alpha = 0.2$ based on preliminary grid search evaluations.

4 Results and Analysis

In this study, three models were trained to assess the impact of different loss functions on code vulnerability detection. Each model uses the same architecture, a classifier built on top of a pre-trained CodeBERT or GraphCodeBERT model with dropout and batch normalization. The only difference between models being the loss function utilized during training:

- **Model 1:** Binary Cross Entropy (BCE) loss only.
- **Model 2:** BCE combined with Supervised Contrastive Loss (SCL).
- **Model 3:** BCE combined with Cluster Enhanced Supervised Contrastive Loss (CESCL).

To evaluate performance, F1 scores were calculated on the test set for each model. These scores provide a comparison between each model's precision and recall, informing how well the different loss functions contribute to the model's accuracy and embedding separation.

On top of this, the silhouette score was calculated as a measure of embedding separation. The silhouette score is a widely-used metric to evaluate clustering quality. It ranges from -1 to 1, where a value near 1 indicates that samples are well-separated and closely grouped within their respective clusters, and a value near -1 suggests significant overlap between clusters. In the context of our study, a higher silhouette score implies that code snippets belonging to the same class (vulnerable or non-vulnerable) are more similar to each other than to those in the opposing class, thereby indicating effective embedding separation.

Table 1: Performance Comparison of Models (F1 Score)

Model	F1 Score
CodeBERT	0.597
CodeBERT + SCL	0.614
CodeBERT + CESCL	0.625
GraphCodeBERT	0.594
GraphCodeBERT + SCL	0.607
GraphCodeBERT + CESCL	0.633

Table 2: Performance Comparison of Models (Silhouette Score)

Model	Silhouette Score
CodeBERT	0.052
CodeBERT + SCL	0.043
CodeBERT + CESCL	0.056
GraphCodeBERT	0.046
GraphCodeBERT + SCL	0.031
GraphCodeBERT + CESCL	0.050

5 Conclusion

In this work, we introduced Cluster-Enhanced Supervised Contrastive Loss (CESCL), a novel loss function designed to improve the embedding quality for code vulnerability detection. We evaluated the performance of CESCL in combination with both CodeBERT and GraphCodeBERT architectures, comparing it with the standard Binary Cross-Entropy (BCE) and BCE + Supervised Contrastive Learning (SCL) models.

The experimental results, as shown in Tables 1 and 2, demonstrate that CESCL consistently outperforms both BCE and BCE + SCL across the models tested. Notably, CodeBERT + CESCL achieved the highest F1 score of 0.625 among CodeBERT models and the best Silhouette score of 0.056, highlighting its ability to generate well-clustered and discriminative embeddings for vulnerability classification. Similarly, GraphCodeBERT + CESCL showed significant improvements, achieving a 4.1% increase in F1 score and a favorable Silhouette score of 0.050 compared to the other configurations.

It is worth noting that, although the incorporation of SCL in isolation sometimes led to a reduction in the silhouette score, the overall improvement in F1 score indicates that the CESCL framework effectively optimizes the embedding space for classification. This discrepancy suggests that while the silhouette score is a useful measure of clustering quality, it may not fully capture the nuances that contribute to enhanced detection performance in this context.

These results indicate that CESCL effectively improves intra-class compactness and inter-class separation, thereby enhancing the performance of the model in detecting vulnerabilities in code. Future work could explore further optimizations to the CESCL framework and test it on additional code-related tasks to fully realize its potential in improving the robustness and reliability of code classification models.

References

Aleksander Botev, Matthias Bauer, and Soham De. 2022. Regularising for invariance to data augmentation improves supervised learning. *arXiv preprint arXiv:2203.03304*.

Qianjin Du, Xiaohui Kuang, and Gang Zhao. 2022. Code vulnerability detection via nearest neighbor mechanism. In *Findings of the Association for Computational Linguistics: EMNLP 2022*, pages 6173–6178.

Zhangyin Feng, Daya Guo, Duyu Tang, Nan Duan, Xiaocheng Feng, Ming Gong, Linjun Shou, Bing Qin, Ting Liu, Daxin Jiang, et al. 2020. Codebert: A pre-trained model for programming and natural languages. *arXiv preprint arXiv:2002.08155*.

Gustavo Grieco, Guillermo Luis Grinblat, Lucas Uzal, Sanjay Rawat, Josselin Feist, and Laurent Mounier. 2016. Toward large-scale vulnerability discovery using machine learning. In *Proceedings of the sixth ACM conference on data and application security and privacy*, pages 85–96.

Daya Guo, Shuo Ren, Shuai Lu, Zhangyin Feng, Duyu Tang, Shujie Liu, Long Zhou, Nan Duan, Alexey Svyatkovskiy, Shengyu Fu, et al. 2020. Graphcodebert: Pre-training code representations with data flow. *arXiv preprint arXiv:2009.08366*.

Prannay Khosla, Piotr Teterwak, Chen Wang, Aaron Sarna, Yonglong Tian, Phillip Isola, Aaron Maschinot, Ce Liu, and Dilip Krishnan. 2020. Supervised contrastive learning. *Advances in neural information processing systems*, 33:18661–18673.

Zhen Li, Deqing Zou, Shouhuai Xu, Hai Jin, Yawei Zhu, and Zhaoxuan Chen. 2021. Sysevr: A framework for using deep learning to detect software vulnerabilities. *IEEE Transactions on Dependable and Secure Computing*, 19(4):2244–2258.

Zhen Li, Deqing Zou, Shouhuai Xu, Xinyu Ou, Hai Jin, Sujuan Wang, Zhijun Deng, and Yuyi Zhong. 2018. Vuldeepecker: A deep learning-based system for vulnerability detection. In *Proceedings 2018 Network and Distributed System Security Symposium*, NDSS 2018. Internet Society.

Guanjun Lin, Jun Zhang, Wei Luo, Lei Pan, and Yang Xiang. 2017. Poster: Vulnerability discovery with function representation learning from unlabeled projects. In *Proceedings of the 2017 ACM SIGSAC conference on computer and communications security*, pages 2539–2541.

Yaqin Zhou, Shangqing Liu, Jingkai Siow, Xiaoning Du, and Yang Liu. 2019. Devign: Effective vulnerability identification by learning comprehensive program semantics via graph neural networks. *Advances in neural information processing systems*, 32.

Text Extraction and Script Completion in Images of Arabic Script-Based Calligraphy: A Thesis Proposal

Dilara Zeynep Gürer and **Ümit Atlamaz** and **Şaziye Betül Özateş**
Boğaziçi University
{dilara.gurer@std., umit.atlamaz@, saziye.ozates@}bogazici.edu.tr

Abstract

Arabic calligraphy carries rich historical information and meaning. However, the complexity of its artistic elements and the absence of a consistent baseline make text extraction from such works highly challenging. In this paper, we provide an in-depth analysis of the unique obstacles in processing and interpreting these images, including the variability in calligraphic styles, the influence of artistic distortions, and the challenges posed by missing or damaged text elements. We explore potential solutions by leveraging state-of-the-art architectures and deep learning models, including visual language models, to improve text extraction and script completion.

1 Introduction

Arabic calligraphy initially emerged as a way to create a visually appealing script, evolving into a highly respected art form. This development was especially prominent during the Ottoman Empire, where calligraphy adorned buildings, mosque foundations, and a variety of other structures. From the reign of Mehmed II onwards, distinct schools of calligraphy began to emerge, gaining further momentum when Sheikh Hamdullah, the founder of the Ottoman calligraphy school, arrived in Istanbul during the rule of Bayezid II. Under Turkish craftsmen, Arabic calligraphy was refined and achieved its most perfect forms (Derman, 1997). This art has experienced significant development in several countries, including Iran, Egypt, Saudi Arabia, and Morocco. However, Istanbul is particularly notable for its diverse and well-established tradition in calligraphy, largely shaped by Ottoman influence. While most of these calligraphic works are in the Arabic language, calligraphy using Arabic letters also appears in other languages such as Urdu, Persian, and Ottoman Turkish. Arabic serves as the common language in these artworks, as it is central to Islamic texts, with many works featuring Quranic verses, Hadith, or prayers (duas) (Gündüz, 1988).

While the artistic dimension of calligraphy is often the main focus, these works also encode significant linguistic, cultural, and historical information. Calligraphy not only conveys Islamic thoughts and architectural aesthetics but also serves as a valuable record of historical and cultural contexts. However, the complexity of calligraphic styles—where sentences vary dramatically in layout and form—often makes them challenging to read, even for those fluent in Arabic. Traditional optical character recognition (OCR) techniques fall short in interpreting such intricate designs, as they are not suited for the overlapping, stylized, or highly curved forms that define calligraphy. Understanding and analyzing these works is crucial for preserving and studying historical and cultural heritage.

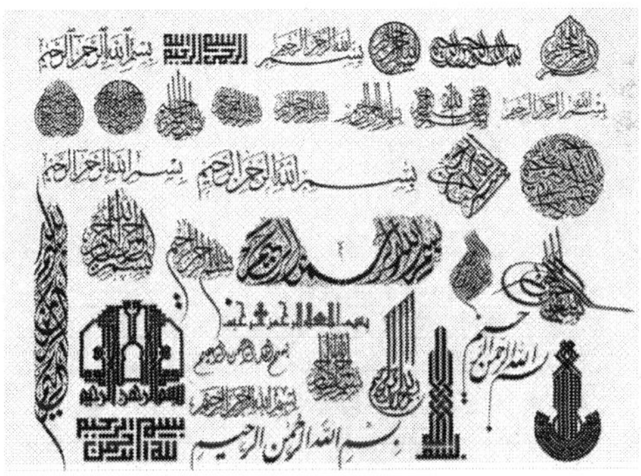

Figure 1: The phrase بِسْمِ اللّٰهِ الرَّحْمٰنِ الرَّحِيمِ (In the name of Allah, the Most Gracious, the Most Merciful) in different styles and with different letter combinations.

Figure 1 depicts the phrase بِسْمِ اللّٰهِ الرَّحْمٰنِ الرَّحِيمِ (In the name of Allah, the Most Gracious, the Most Merciful) in different styles and with different letter combinations. The phrase consists of five words with twelve distinct letters, but the calligraphic styles vary in

Proceedings of the 2025 Conference of the Nations of the Americas Chapter of the Association for Computational Linguistics: Human Language Technologies (Volume 4: Student Research Workshop), pages 253–259
April 30 - May 1, 2025 ©2025 Association for Computational Linguistics

how these letters are connected, arranged, and stylized through different ligatures and artistic compositions. As can be seen in the figure, same sentence in various calligraphic styles and arrangements is challenging to recognize—even identifying the beginning of the sentence can be difficult due to the non-standard layouts and artistic variations.

In this thesis proposal, we outline a specialized methodology designed to analyze and interpret documents and images featuring Arabic script-based calligraphy with high accuracy. This approach aims to bridge the gap between visual artistry and textual extraction, enabling both aesthetic appreciation and understanding of these culturally significant texts.

Thesis contributions will be as follows:

- A system for efficiently labeling datasets with limited annotated samples (scarce datasets), employing semi-supervised learning and transfer learning techniques. The system is designed to generalize well from small datasets and can be adapted to scale up when larger datasets become available.

- A rich dataset of real-world calligraphy images, annotated at the letter and word levels, encompassing diverse calligraphic styles to support tasks like style recognition, text extraction, and sentence reconstruction.

- An optimized pipeline for noise removal and artifact handling tailored for historical and architectural calligraphic content. This pipeline will incorporate deep learning techniques to enhance textual clarity, eliminate ornamental noise, and reconstruct missing portions of letters for improved accuracy.

- Implementation of advanced recognition techniques, leveraging architectures like Visual Question Answering (VQA) and Large Language Models (LLMs), designed to handle the artistic and structural intricacies of Arabic calligraphy while extracting textual content with contextual awareness.

2 Background

This research explores Arabic script-based calligraphy analysis, emphasizing its intricate and artistic nature. To develop a comprehensive approach, we reviewed related studies in Arabic script analysis, calligraphic works, and non Arabic calligraphy.

Arabic character recognition is challenging due to its cursive and context-sensitive script. Traditional methods like HOG with SVM achieved over 99% recognition on a dataset of 43,000 handwritten words (Jebril et al., 2018), while Random Forests, KNN, and MLP attained 100% accuracy on a dataset of 600 images across 28 classes (Boufenar et al., 2018). Though designed for handwriting, these approaches could aid in labeling calligraphy datasets.

Deep learning methods have further improved recognition. CNNs with LReLU achieved 99% accuracy by mitigating overfitting (Nayef et al., 2022), and foundation models like Qalam have advanced Arabic OCR and handwriting recognition capabilities (Bhatia et al., 2024). Qalam, combining a SwinV2 encoder and a RoBERTa decoder, excels in Arabic script recognition. Trained on over 4.5 million manuscript images and 60,000 synthetic pairs, it achieves a WER of 0.80% in handwriting recognition and 1.18% in OCR tasks. Its support for diacritics and high-resolution inputs addresses limitations of many OCR systems. However, while useful for initial insights, these methods are less suited to the artistic variability and baseline inconsistencies in Arabic calligraphy images.

Arabic calligraphy has been the focus of several research efforts, each contributing to the field with unique datasets, methodologies, and findings. The Calliar dataset (Alyafeai et al., 2022) is a comprehensive resource, featuring 2,500 sentences and over 40,000 strokes. It covers multiple levels—stroke, character, word, and sentence—and includes styles like Diwani, Thuluth, and Farisi, enabling tasks such as style classification, character recognition, and calligraphy generation.

The Salamah dataset (AlSalamah and King, 2018) contains 3,467 images across 32 categories of Arabic calligraphic letters, representing diverse styles. Kaoudja et al. (2021) developed feature descriptors tailored to specific calligraphy styles, achieving superior performance on a dataset of 1,685 images across nine styles compared to existing methods, including deep learning approaches. A complementary study (Gürer and Gökbay, 2024) analyzed two datasets for classification tasks, achieving F1 scores of 90% for style classification and 79% for letter classification using transfer learning techniques.

Efforts in content recognition remain limited despite valuable datasets and classification studies. A study (Alsalamah, 2020) on a dataset of 388 images achieved 75% accuracy in mapping calligraphic images to their corresponding quotations, highlighting the challenges in recognizing content from artistic calligraphy and underscoring the need for more advanced methodologies.

Generative Adversarial Networks (GANs) have been used to synthesize calligraphic styles like Nastaliq, blending traditional and contemporary elements (Sobhan et al., 2024). Similar methods in non-Arabic calligraphy, such as Chinese and Japanese scripts, have applied CNNs and transformers for style recognition and glyph generation (Wen and Sigüenza, 2020; Zhang et al., 2024; Aguilar, 2024; Wong et al., 2024; Kuwata et al., 2024).

While these methods offer valuable insights, their direct use for Arabic calligraphy content recognition is limited due to the unique features of Arabic script. However, the strategies in these studies can guide the development of tailored approaches for Arabic calligraphy.

3 Research Goals and Questions

The main goal of this thesis is to analyze Arabic calligraphy images to accurately extract the script contained within them.

Our main research question is:

RQ: What are the optimal methods for accurately extracting and reconstructing text from Arabic calligraphy images, considering the unique artistic and structural challenges?

We examine the challenges arising from the artistic elements and absence of consistent baselines, seeking methods to extract letters, phrases or complete sentences with high accuracy. To visually represent the methodology for tackling these challenges, Figure 2 illustrates the step-by-step process for analyzing and extracting text from Arabic calligraphy images.

We outline three objectives to answer our research question: (i) **Data Collection** - Gathering an extensive dataset of Arabic calligraphy images. (ii) **Text Extraction** - Developing methods to accurately extract textual data from images. (iii) **Script Completion** - Reconstructing incomplete scripts when necessary. In the following sections, we define sub-questions for these objectives.

3.1 Data Collection

A key challenge in this area is the lack of comprehensive datasets. While there is only one publicly available dataset (Alyafeai et al., 2022), obtain-

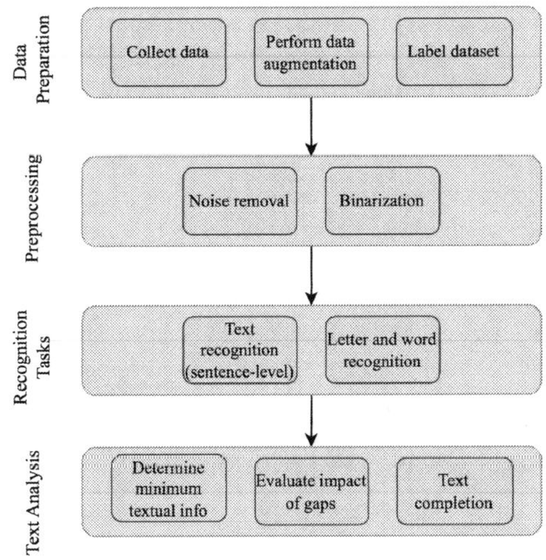

Figure 2: Flowchart of the proposed research.

ing accurate results will require more diverse, rich and versatile dataset. The existing dataset presents two main issues. First, all images are digitalized, meaning they do not represent the real-world images often encountered in historical or architectural contexts. As shown in Figure 3, these digitalized samples lack background noise, such as decorative elements or embellishments, which are often present in real-world calligraphy and can obscure or blend with the text. This results in clean images that do not fully capture the challenges of authentic calligraphy analysis.

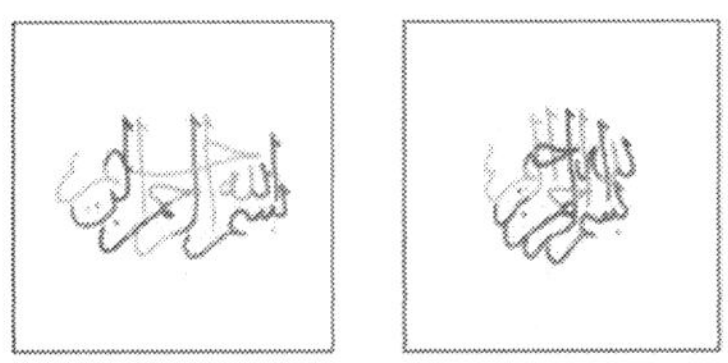

Figure 3: Examples from the existing dataset (Alyafeai et al., 2022).

Second, our analysis of the dataset revealed that each piece of content appears only a few times, with unique sentences and phrases that lack variations or alternative versions. For effective machine learning, however, the dataset needs multiple versions of each sentence or phrase to better train models in recognizing different stylistic forms of the same text. Although the orientations in the dataset vary, we also need examples with more diverse letter combinations, structural complexity, and realistic variations. Ultimately, a more representative dataset is essential for building an end-to-end architecture that can handle the nuances of Arabic calligraphy in various forms.

RQ1 How do we obtain authentic data for investigating the main research question? Istanbul's rich calligraphic heritage offers a unique advantage for data collection. We will gather images through on-site visits to historical sites, mosques, and architectural landmarks, supplemented by publicly shared photos from tourists and researchers. Since all these places are open to the public, taking photographs does not require special permissions. Additionally, we will meet with the owners of these photos to ensure proper context and information. To ensure diversity, our dataset will capture varied artistic styles and layouts. Image quality may vary due to factors such as different angles and lighting conditions, but this variability will benefit the model's training. The goal is for the model to be able to process and recognize calligraphy accurately, regardless of these variations, when it encounters new images during future data collection or use. Essentially, the model will be robust enough to perform well even if the conditions of the new images differ from the ones it was originally trained on.

Since most calligraphic works in Istanbul are in Arabic and Ottoman Turkish, our initial focus will be on these languages, which are central to Islamic calligraphy. This approach is particularly significant as Arabic serves as the lingua franca of the Islamic faith. Once a solid foundation is established, we will expand to Persian and Urdu for broader linguistic coverage. Additionally, we will source images from websites with proper permissions.

We have access to a comprehensive 136,000-page textual archive that explores the history, evolution, and artistic styles of Arabic calligraphy, along with its reading techniques, cultural significance, and traditional methodologies. This archive includes scholarly analyses, historical manuscripts, and instructional texts that provide deep insights into the art form. Before training our VQA model, we will fine-tune the language component—not the visual part—of a visual language model using text from these books. This will enhance the model's understanding of calligraphy's artistic and textual nuances.

RQ2 How should the collected data be labeled? The process will begin with the creation of an image-caption dataset, where each image will be paired with a caption describing the text within it. This dataset will be generated using digital tools such as web scraping techniques with BeautifulSoup or Selenium to gather digitized calligraphic images from web sites and manually collecting and labeling images from printed or physical sources. Once the image-caption dataset is established, the next step will involve labeling individual letters and words within the calligraphic images.

For this task, we will leverage an existing small dataset of online handwritten Arabic calligraphic letters and words. Although this small dataset is in the online handwriting format—where temporal stroke data is recorded—the dataset we will collect is in the offline handwriting format, derived from scanned or photographed calligraphic texts. To bridge this gap, we will use the online dataset to inform and guide the labeling process for offline data. By training the model on the online handwriting data first, it will gain a foundational understanding of Arabic calligraphic structures, which will then be applied to label offline handwritten datasets effectively. This alignment between the two formats will allow for a more robust and comprehensive training process.

Using semi-supervised learning techniques, the model will initially be trained on the small, labeled dataset. With pseudo-labeling, it will then generate labels for a larger set of unlabeled offline images. This hybrid approach will enable the model to learn both letter recognition and word recognition from the offline calligraphic images while leveraging the detailed structure of the online handwriting data. This process not only increases the dataset's size and diversity but also will enhance its applicability to real-world offline calligraphic texts.

RQ3 How to enrich the dataset to make it more comprehensive? To simulate the diverse artistic styles and orientations found in Arabic calligraphy, we plan to use data augmentation techniques such as rotation and scaling, allowing us to create variations within a structured dataset.

3.2 Text Extraction

To extract textual data, noise removal is essential as the first step. This leads us to a new sub-question:

RQ4 How can we effectively remove noise from the images? Identifying and removing unwanted elements, such as decorations, background patterns, and ornamental designs, is crucial for this sub-task. However, critical elements like diacritical marks in the text should not be treated as noise, as they are essential for accurate interpretation.

Template matching can be used to identify and remove consistent unwanted elements, such as decorative patterns, across images. Morphological operations, such as erosion and dilation, help eliminate small artifacts and background patterns while preserving the main calligraphic features. Additionally, Region of Interest (ROI) detection algorithms can focus on the text areas, removing surrounding noise and ensuring the calligraphy is the primary focus.

Figure 4: Example of an Arabic calligraphy artwork, from left to right: original artwork, region of interest highlighting the text, removal of unwanted noise and ornamental elements, and the final digitalized form retaining essential diacritical marks for accurate interpretation[1].

After addressing the challenges of noise removal, the next stage in text extraction involves exploring recognition and preprocessing methods that enable accurate analysis of calligraphic images. Consequently, we pose the following questions:

RQ5 Which recognition method is most effective for analyzing the text? Handling the overlap or extreme curvature of letters in Arabic calligraphy is complex and requires advanced segmentation. Arabic calligraphy often merges letters into intricate shapes, which traditional OCR systems may struggle to interpret. We plan to explore different recognition approaches, including character-level, word-level, and sentence-level recognition, to determine which method best captures the artistic variations in the text. To quantitatively evaluate the performance of these recognition methods, we will use several metrics. We will measure the accuracy of text extraction at different linguistic levels using Character Error Rate (CER) and Word Error Rate (WER). Additionally, we will assess the similarity between recognized text and ground truth using Levenshtein Distance.

For baseline comparisons, we will evaluate our approach against existing OCR systems, as well as modern handwriting recognition models such as transformer-based OCR architectures. Furthermore, we will compare our results to human-labeled transcriptions to establish an upper-bound accuracy for the recognition tasks. By incorporating both automated metrics and comparative benchmarks, we aim to identify the most effective recognition method that preserves the accuracy and readability of Arabic calligraphy text.

RQ6 Is preprocessing necessary? As discussed in the noise removal section, it may not be essential to eliminate decorative elements ("noise") entirely. To assess this, we will compare different methods by first testing the original images without noise preprocessing. We will also experiment with state-of-the-art visual question-answering models, using targeted prompts such as "focus on the text in the given image." To assess this, we plan to freeze the visual processing part of a multimodal model, such as BLIP-2 or LLaVA, and focus training on the language components using texts from books on Arabic calligraphy. This will align the model's understanding of the text with the linguistic and contextual nuances of calligraphy. This will allow us to improve the model's understanding of the textual and contextual features of calligraphy. After that, we will incorporate the image-text dataset for further fine-tuning. For this purpose, we will leverage advanced visual-language models such as BLIP-2 and LLaVA, which combine powerful image processing capabilities with language models, enabling them to interpret and understand intricate calligraphic text effectively.

3.3 Script Completion

The extracted data from the previous step may be incomplete due to segmentation failures or unreadable parts of phrases. Additionally, historical documents may be damaged, with some sections missing or too degraded to analyze directly. In such cases, further steps are required to reconstruct the content. We plan to utilize a large language model, trained on Islamic texts such as the Quran and Hadith, to complete sentences or phrases when extracted letters are incomplete.

We will employ several metrics to evaluate the performance of our script completion approach. Reconstruction accuracy will measure how accurately the model completes missing text based on context, compared to ground-truth transcriptions. CER and WER will also quantify the accuracy of the

[1]https://www.ketebe.org/eser/8111?ref=artworks

[2]https://tr.ucoin.net/coin/ottoman_empire-100-para-1808/?tid=83518

Figure 5: Example of images: left, an Ottoman coin with worn or incomplete calligraphic text; right, a wall with partially damaged calligraphic text, illustrating the challenges of dealing with incomplete or unreadable content in historical artifacts[2].

reconstructed text. Contextual accuracy will assess whether the completed sentences align with the linguistic and cultural context of Islamic texts. For baseline comparisons, we will evaluate our model against existing text completion and restoration techniques used for historical documents, including context-based generation models and traditional rule-based methods, to measure the improvement brought by our language model fine-tuned on Islamic texts.

RQ7 What is the minimum required information to understand the content of the images? We plan to analyze the impact of missing letters or words on sentence completion in Arabic scripts by testing different letter sets to reconstruct incomplete phrases or sentences. The goal is to evaluate the accuracy of the reconstructed text by comparing it to the expected phrase. This will involve using a trained model, such as Qalam, which leverages unique features of Arabic script, including its cursive and diacritic-rich structure. These models will be employed to predict and complete missing elements. The model will be assessed based on how well it fills gaps and ensures the reconstructed sentence or phrase is contextually and linguistically accurate. This approach will help improve extraction by reducing reliance on segmentation and allowing more robust handling of incomplete or damaged calligraphic text.

4 Conclusion

This proposal outlines steps to extract textual data from Arabic calligraphy images, addressing challenges from the language's unique features and the art's complexity. It focuses on reconstructing incomplete or damaged calligraphy using Arabic-specific language models to enhance recognition accuracy. The research aims to develop tools for Arabic calligraphy text recognition, benefiting areas such as historical document preservation and cultural heritage digitization. While primarily focused on text, it also acknowledges the importance of calligraphic styles and structures. It lays the groundwork for scalable, precise models capable of handling diverse calligraphic styles.

To respect the cultural and historical significance of Arabic calligraphy, the research will involve consultations with domain experts in art history and cultural heritage. This will ensure the accuracy and sensitivity of interpretations, while following best practices in digitization and preserving the integrity of these valuable artifacts.

References

Sergio Torres Aguilar. 2024. Handwritten text recognition for historical documents using visual language models and GANs. Hal-04716654v2.

Seetah Alsalamah. 2020. *Combining Image and Text Processing for the Computational Reading of Arabic Calligraphy*. Ph.D. thesis, The University of Manchester.

Seetah AlSalamah and Ross King. 2018. Towards the machine reading of Arabic calligraphy: A letters dataset and corresponding corpus of text. In *2018 IEEE 2nd International Workshop on Arabic and Derived Script Analysis and Recognition (ASAR)*, pages 19–23.

Z. Alyafeai, M. S. Al-Shaibani, M. Ghaleb, et al. 2022. Calliar: an online handwritten dataset for Arabic calligraphy. *Neural Computing and Applications*, 34:20701–20713.

Gagan Bhatia, El Moatez Billah Nagoudi, Fakhraddin Alwajih, and Muhammad Abdul-Mageed. 2024. Qalam: A multimodal LLM for Arabic optical character and handwriting recognition. In *Proceedings of The Second Arabic Natural Language Processing Conference*, pages 210–224, Bangkok, Thailand. Association for Computational Linguistics.

Chaouki Boufenar, Adlen Kerboua, and Mohamed Batouche. 2018. Investigation on deep learning for offline handwritten Arabic character recognition. *Cognitive Systems Research*, 50:180–195.

M. U. Derman. 1997. Hat. [Accessed: 28 November 2024].

H. Gündüz. 1988. Türk hat sanatında Şeyh Hamdullah ve Ahmed Karahisari ekolleri. Master's thesis, Mimar Sinan Fine Arts University.

Dilara Zeynep Gürer and İnci Zaim Gökbay. 2024. Arabic calligraphy images analysis with transfer learning. *Electrica*, 24(1):201–209.

N. A. Jebril, H. R. Al-Zoubi, and Q. Abu Al-Haija. 2018. Recognition of handwritten Arabic characters using histograms of oriented gradient (hog). *Pattern Recognition and Image Analysis*, 28:321–345.

Zineb Kaoudja, Mohammed Lamine Kherfi, and Belal Khaldi. 2021. A new computational method for Arabic calligraphy style representation and classification. *Applied Sciences*, 11(11).

Wakana Kuwata, Ryota Mibayashi, Masanori Tani, and Hiroaki Ohshima. 2024. Glyph generation for Japanese calligraphy based on encoding both content and style. In *2024 IEEE International Conference on Big Data and Smart Computing (BigComp)*, pages 207–214.

B. H. Nayef, S. N. H. S. Abdullah, R. Sulaiman, et al. 2022. Optimized leaky relu for handwritten Arabic character recognition using convolution neural networks. *Multimedia Tools and Applications*, 81:2065–2094.

Arshia Sobhan, Philippe Pasquier, and Adam Tindale. 2024. Unveiling new artistic dimensions in calligraphic Arabic script with generative adversarial networks. *Proc. ACM Comput. Graph. Interact. Tech.*, 7(4).

Yuanbo Wen and Juan Alberto Sigüenza. 2020. Chinese calligraphy: Character style recognition based on full-page document. In *Proceedings of the 2019 8th International Conference on Computing and Pattern Recognition*, ICCPR '19, page 390–394, New York, NY, USA. Association for Computing Machinery.

Adam Wong, Joseph So, and Zhi Ting Billy Ng. 2024. Developing a web application for Chinese calligraphy learners using convolutional neural network and scale invariant feature transform. *Computers and Education: Artificial Intelligence*, 6:100200.

Yuqing Zhang, Baoyi He, Yihan Chen, Hangqi Li, Han Yue, Shengyu Zhang, Huaiyong Dou, Junchi Yan, Zemin Liu, Yongquan Zhang, et al. 2024. Philogpt: A philology-oriented large language model for ancient Chinese manuscripts with dunhuang as case study. In *Proceedings of the 2024 Conference on Empirical Methods in Natural Language Processing*, pages 2784–2801.

Subasa - Adapting Language Models for Low-resourced Offensive Language Detection in Sinhala

Shanilka Haturusinghe♣, Tharindu Cyril Weerasooriya♢, Marcos Zampieri♠, Christopher M. Homan♢, S.R. Liyanage♣*

♣University of Kelaniya, Sri Lanka, ♢Rochester Institute of Technology, USA

♠George Mason University, USA

s.haturusinghe99@gmail.com, {tw3318,mazgla,cmhvcs}@rit.edu, sidath@kln.ac.lk

Abstract

This paper contains expressions that may offend the readers.

Accurate detection of offensive language is essential for a number of applications related to social media safety. There is a sharp contrast in performance in this task between low- and high-resource languages. In this paper, we adapt fine-tuning strategies that have not been previously explored for Sinhala in the downstream task of offensive language detection. Using this approach, we introduce four models: "Subasa-XLM-R", which incorporates an intermediate Pre-Finetuning step using Masked Rationale Prediction. Two variants of "Subasa-Llama" and "Subasa-Mistral", are fine-tuned versions of Llama (3.2) and Mistral (v0.3), respectively, with a task-specific strategy. We evaluate our models on the SOLD benchmark dataset for Sinhala offensive language detection. All our models outperform existing baselines. Subasa-XLM-R achieves the highest Macro F1 score (0.84) surpassing state-of-the-art large language models like GPT-4o when evaluated on the same SOLD benchmark dataset under zero-shot settings. The models and code are publicly available.[1]

1 Introduction

A major challenge in the field of NLP are the disparities between high- and low-resource languages. These impact foundational language models as well as downstream tasks such as offensive language detection (Weerasooriya et al., 2023a), an important task at the intersection of social media analysis and NLP.

As people increasingly spend a significant portion of their day on online platforms like social media, their exposure to offensive or abusive language has surged (Bertaglia et al., 2021). This trend is equally visible in Sri Lanka, where a substantial amount of social media content is generated in Sinhala. Studies show that an alarming amount of this content is hateful, and the severity of this issue is evident from several instances in recent years where the Sri Lankan government had to block social media platforms entirely to curb its spread, as it had fueled real-world unrest (Awais et al., 2020).

Sinhala (සිංහල) is an Indo-Aryan language spoken by over 17 million people in Sri Lanka and remains a low-resource language (De Silva, 2019). For offensive language detection specifically, systems for Sinhala lag behind those developed for resource-rich languages like English, Spanish, and Mandarin (Avetisyan and Broneske, 2023; Ranasinghe et al., 2024). To the best of our knowledge, fewer than five annotated offensive language datasets exist for Sinhala, demonstrating its status as a low-resource language (Ranasinghe et al., 2024).

While state-of-the-art large language models (LLM) like GPT-4o demonstrate strong performance in many languages, our evaluations suggest they struggle to reliably identify offensive language in Sinhala (results detailed in Section 4). At the time of submission, the Perspective API (Lees et al., 2022) which is utilized extensively in both academia and industry for the purpose of identifying offensive content does not provide support for Sinhala. Our work addresses these shortcomings by introducing *Subasa* ("සුබස"), which translates to *wholesome language*. In this paper, we present four variants of Subasa. These models improve the current state of offensive language detection for Sinhala by adapting fine-tuning strategies previously unexplored for Sinhala.

We address the following research questions:

RQ1: Can intermediate pre-finetuning tasks

*Shanilka Haturusinghe is the primary author. S.R. Liyanage is the Corresponding Author.

[1]Access code and models via
https://github.com/haturusinghe/subasa-llm and
https://github.com/haturusinghe/subasa-plm

Proceedings of the 2025 Conference of the Nations of the Americas Chapter of the Association for Computational Linguistics: Human Language Technologies (Volume 4: Student Research Workshop), pages 260–270
April 30 - May 1, 2025 ©2025 Association for Computational Linguistics

specifically masked rationale prediction (MRP)—effectively improve pre-trained language models (PLMs) for offensive language detection in Sinhala?

RQ2: Can task-specific fine-tuning strategies improve the effectiveness of LLMs for offensive language detection in Sinhala?

2 Related Work

Shared tasks like TRAC (Kumar et al., 2018) and HASOC (Chakravarthi et al., 2021) have established offensive language detection as an important NLP challenge, yet progress remains unevenly distributed across languages. Generally, building an effective model for offensive language detection is challenging due to the subjective nature of what constitutes offensive content, which can vary based according to individual beliefs (Weerasooriya et al., 2023b). Most research has focused on high-resource languages like English, French, German, and Spanish, benefiting from the availability of large datasets (Zampieri et al., 2022). In contrast, research on low-resource languages highlights the difficulties in detecting offensive language (Mozafari et al., 2022), with notable studies in Tamil (Balakrishnan et al., 2023), Arabic (Shannag et al., 2022), South African languages (Oriola and Kotzé, 2020) and also for Sinhala (Dias et al., 2018; Fernando et al., 2022; Munasinghe and Thayasivam, 2022).

Pretrained language models (PLM) have emerged as a powerful approach for a number of NLP tasks including offensive language detection. BERT variants have shown success when fine-tuned for this task across both high-resource languages like English (Jahan et al., 2021) and lower-resource contexts like Arabic (Althobaiti, 2022) and Sinhala (Rajapaksha et al., 2023). While intermediate task training has shown promise in enhancing PLM performance across various NLP tasks—from semantic parsing (Pruksachatkun et al., 2020) to natural language understanding (Aghajanyan et al., 2021)—its application to offensive language detection emerged only recently with the introduction of Masked Rationale Prediction (MRP) by Kim et al. (2022). Though MRP demonstrated significant improvements for English, its potential remains unexplored for low-resource languages. We are the first to adapt MRP to Sinhala, addressing the language's data scarcity.

LLMs are transformer-based models with billions of parameters trained on massive training corpora (Chowdhery et al., 2023). While LLMs perform well in high-resource languages like English, their effectiveness in low-resource languages is often limited, as highlighted in various studies (Ahuja et al., 2023). Adapting LLMs for low-resource languages is challenging because most are pre-trained primarily on English data. Approaches to address this include; (i) continuing training with non-English data, (ii) transferring knowledge via supervised fine-tuning, and (iii) extending the LLMs vocabulary to include non-English tokens (Toraman, 2024). For instance, Toraman (2024) demonstrated that fine-tuned LLMs can achieve strong performance even with limited data, as shown for Turkish. Jayakody and Dias (2024) evaluated the GPT-4o, Llama, and Mistral models for various tasks in the Sinhala language, revealing unsatisfactory results. Notably, offensive language detection was not attempted.

Prior work on offensive language detection has explored fine-tuning open-source LLMs like Llama and Mistral, primarily for high-resource languages like English (He et al., 2024; Christodoulou, 2024) and low-resource languages like Vietnamese (Truong et al., 2024). However, prior work has not explored open-source LLMs (e.g., Llama, Mistral) for Sinhala offensive language detection, despite their success in other low-resource languages like Vietnamese (Truong et al., 2024).

3 Method

3.1 Intermediate Pre-Finetuning Strategy

We adapt a two-stage fine-tuning strategy to optimize limited annotated data available for Sinhala. We train our models using the SOLD dataset (Ranasinghe et al., 2024) ($\mathcal{D}_{SOLD}$), which contains 7,500 training and 2,500 test samples. We split the training set into 9:1 (6,750 training, 750 validation) and reserve the test set for final evaluation. For more details on $\mathcal{D}_{SOLD}$, see Section 3.3.

Following Kim et al. (2022), we employ masked rationale prediction (MRP) as the intermediate task in the first stage of the fine-tuning strategy. For a sentence S, the embedded sentence can be represented as:

$$X^S = \left\{x_0^S, x_1^S, \ldots, x_{n-1}^S\right\} \in \mathbb{R}^{n\times d} \quad (1)$$

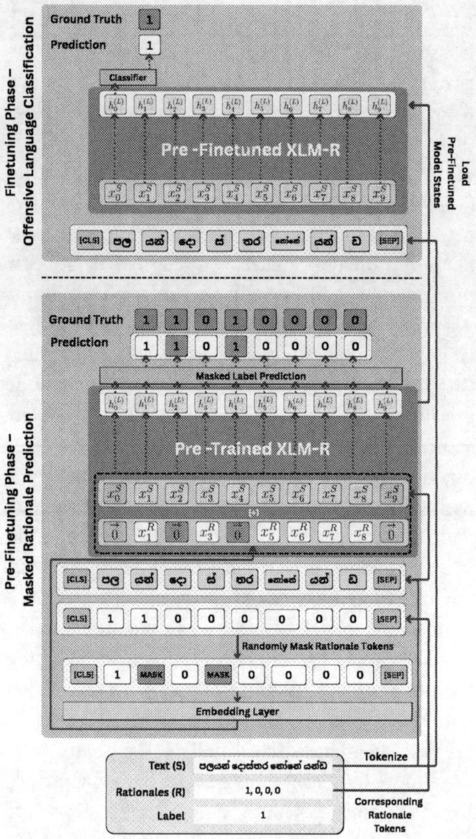

Figure 1: Two-stage fine-tuning strategy utilized to finetune a pre-trained `subasa-xlm-roberta-base` model.

where n is the sequence length and d is the embedding size. Similarly, the rationale labels R can be represented as:

$$X^R = \left\{x_0^R, x_1^R, \ldots, x_{n-1}^R\right\} \in \mathbb{R}^{n \times d} \tag{2}$$

Unlike XLM-R's masked language modeling (MLM), which masks tokens, MRP masks rationale labels to construct partially masked rationale embeddings $\tilde{X}^R$. We randomly select and replace 75% of non-special rationale labels with zero vectors $\vec{0}$. For example, if x_2^R and x_4^R are masked:

$$\tilde{X}^R = \left\{\vec{0}, x_1^R, \vec{0}, x_3^R, \vec{0}, \ldots, x_{n-2}^R, \vec{0}\right\} \tag{3}$$

where the first and last tokens (CLS/SEP) are also zeroed. The model predicts masked rationale labels by combining X^S with $\tilde{X}^R$:

$$H_{MRP}^{(0)} = X^S + \tilde{X}^R \tag{4}$$

$$H_{MRP}^{(l+1)} = \text{Transformer}\left(H_{MRP}^{(l)}\right) \tag{5}$$

$$\hat{X}^R = \text{MLP}\left(H_{MRP}^{(L)}\right) \tag{6}$$

Here, $H_{MRP}^{(l)}$ is the l-th transformer layer output, and $\hat{X}^R$ are predicted rationale labels.

Stage 1 - MRP: First we convert binary rationale labels (0/1 sequences) into padded tensors that align with the tokenized text length through rationale processing, ensuring dimensional compatibility with the input sequence. These processed rationales undergo embedding fusion, where token embeddings X^S (Equation 1) are combined with rationale embeddings X^R (Equation 2) via summation to form the initialized representation $H_{MRP}^{(0)}$ (Equation 6). The fused embeddings then enter a masking phase, where 75% (selected as a hyperparameter for our implementation) of non-special tokens in $\tilde{X}^R$ (Equation 3) are randomly masked. We mask 75% of non-special tokens-a value empirically validated through ablation (Table 6) as optimal for balancing noise and learning signal for our Sinhala setting.

Stage 2 - Offensive Language Detection: Using the model states from Stage 1, we fine-tune for binary classification and train on the full $\mathcal{D}_{SOLD}$ training set. During both stages, we add special tokens (@USER, <URL>) to the tokenizer to handle frequent artifacts in training data.

Hyper-parameter	Stage 1	Stage 2
Learning Rate	2×10^{-5}	2×10^{-5}
Batch Size	16	16
Epochs	5	5
Optimizer	RAdam	RAdam
Mask Ratio	0.75	-
Base Model	xlm-roberta-base	xlm-roberta-base

Table 1: hyper-parameters for intermediate pre-finetuning and task-specific fine-tuning

Figure 1 provides an overview of the two-stage strategy described above, while Table 1 lists the hyperparameters used during both stages of the Intermediate Pre-Finetuning Strategy.

To contextualize our results, we compare against three baselines: (1) a **1D CNN** adapted from English sentiment analysis (Kim, 2014), (2) a **2D CNN** previously used for Sinhala NLP

(Ranasinghe et al., 2019) (both using FastText (Bojanowski et al., 2017) embeddings), and (3) a vanilla fine-tuning of `xlm-roberta-base` on $\mathcal{D}_{SOLD}$. These represent traditional, domain-specific, and PLM-based approaches, respectively.

The performance of the models under the intermediate pre-finetuning strategy experiments is presented in Table 3.

3.1.1 Ablation Study Design

To validate the impact of our intermediate Pre-Finetuning strategy, we conducted three ablation experiments using `xlm-roberta-base`:

1. **Masking Ratio Variation**: We trained models with MRP mask ratios $\in \{0.25, 0.75, 0.9, 1.0\}$, keeping all other hyper-parameters fixed (Table 1).

2. **Intermediate Task Replacement**: We replaced MRP with standard masked language modeling (MLM), using mask probabilities $\in \{0.15, 0.5\}$ and finetuned on $\mathcal{D}_{SOLD}$.

3. **No Intermediate Task**: Direct fine-tuning on $\mathcal{D}_{SOLD}$ without MRP/MLM, starting from the default `xlm-roberta-base` model states. Results are summarized in Table 6, with full metrics in Appendix Table 8.

3.2 Task Specific Fine-tuning Strategy

We instruction-finetune Llama-3 and Mistral models using parameter-efficient fine-tuning (PEFT) with 4-bit quantization (QLoRA). Our prompt (see Appendix A for the full prompt template) is structured for classification (`OFF`/`NOT`) and offensive phrase extraction, encouraging localization of offensive content. We employ LoRA (Hu et al., 2021) (rank=16, α=16) targeting all linear projections, balancing efficiency and performance. Table 2 shows the list of hyper-parameters used during training for task specific fine-tuning.

Training Data: Using the prompt template (Appendix A) for each $\mathcal{D}_{SOLD}$ training sample, we populate the prompt with: The original Sinhala text in the '[TWEET]' field, The ground-truth label (`OFF`/`NOT`) in the '[LABEL]' field, and offensive phrases extracted from contiguous spans of rationale-annotated tokens in the '[PHRASES]' field. We validate the effectiveness of our fine-tuning strategy with the following baselines:

Aya101 (Üstün et al., 2024) (multilingual instruction-finetuned) and **GPT-4o** are evaluated using the same prompt in zero-shot mode with the same prompt template. The performance of the models following task specific fine-tuning are presented in Table 4.

Hyper-parameter	**Value**
Learning Rate	2×10^{-4}
Batch Size	16
Epochs	5
Optimizer	AdamW (8-bit)
Mask Ratio	0.75
Lora-R	16
Lora-Alpha	16
Lora-Dropout	0
Target Modules	{ "q_proj", "k_proj", "v_proj", "o_proj", "gate_proj", "up_proj", "down_proj" }
Max Sequence Length	2048
Per Device Train Batch Size	4
Gradient Accumulation Steps	4
Weight Decay	0.01

Table 2: hyper-parameters for task specific fine-tuning

3.3 Dataset

We utilize $\mathcal{D}_{SOLD}$ (Ranasinghe et al., 2024), the largest publicly available dataset for identifying offensive language in the Sinhala script. Among the limited number of Sinhala offensive language datasets, $\mathcal{D}_{SOLD}$ stands out as the only one providing rationale labels, where `1` indicates a token that serves as a rationale for the offensive label, and `0` denotes a non-rationale token. A rationale can be defined as a specific text segment that justifies the human annotators decision of the sentence-level labels.

$\mathcal{D}_{SOLD}$ consists of data collected from Twitter and only contains tweets written in the Sinhala script, excluding those in Roman script or mixed script. Sentence-level offensive labels were determined by majority voting among the three annotators. Offensive tokens were identified based on agreement between at least two out of the three annotators, establishing the ground truth for token-level annotations (Ranasinghe et al., 2024). Selected examples from $\mathcal{D}_{SOLD}$ are given in Appendix Table 7.

From the original dataset, a random split was performed, where 75% of the instances were assigned to the training set, and the remaining instances were assigned to the testing set. We split the training set again into 9:1 (6,750 training, 750 validation) and reserve the testing set for final evaluation. Appendix figure 2 describes the class distribution in the dataset.

Model	OFFENSIVE			NOT OFFENSIVE			Weighted			Macro
	P	R	F1	P	R	F1	P	R	F1	F1
1D CNN Model (Kim, 2014)	0.60	0.81	0.69	0.83	0.64	0.71	0.84	0.70	0.70	0.69
2D CNN Model based on Ranasinghe et al. (2019)	0.79	0.65	0.69	0.79	0.85	0.82	0.78	0.78	0.77	0.76
xlm-roberta-base-no-finetuning	0.00	0.00	0.00	0.59	1.00	0.74	0.35	0.59	0.44	0.37
xlm-roberta-base-vanilla-finetuned	0.77	0.82	0.79	0.87	0.83	0.85	0.83	0.82	0.82	0.82
Subasa-XLM-R	0.78	0.84	0.81	0.89	0.84	0.86	0.84	0.84	0.84	**0.84**

Table 3: Evaluation results of **Subasa-XLM-R** and other baselines on $\mathcal{D}_{SOLD}$. We report per class (OFFENSIVE, NOT OFFENSIVE) precision (P), recall (R), and F1, and their weighted averages. Macro-F1 is listed with the best result in bold.

Model	OFFENSIVE			NOT OFFENSIVE			Weighted			Macro
	P	R	F1	P	R	F1	P	R	F1	F1
Mistral-7b-instruct-v0.3	0.405	0.991	0.575	0.550	0.007	0.014	0.491	0.406	0.242	0.295
Meta-Llama-3.1-8B-Instruct	0.564	0.375	0.449	0.655	0.805	0.723	0.619	0.6315	0.612	0.586
Meta-Llama-3.2-3B-Instruct	1.000	0.000	0.000	0.594	1.000	0.745	0.758	0.594	0.443	0.373
Aya101 (Üstün et al., 2024)	0.864	0.422	0.567	0.707	0.954	0.812	0.771	0.738	0.713	0.690
GPT-4o-2024-05-13	0.622	0.584	0.748	0.928	0.938	0.717	0.799	0.734	0.730	0.733
Subasa-Mistral-7b-instruct-v0.3	0.917	0.611	0.734	0.783	0.962	0.863	0.838	0.820	0.811	0.799
Subasa-Llama-3.2-3B	0.822	0.698	0.755	0.813	0.896	0.853	0.816	0.816	0.813	0.804
Subasa-Llama-3.1-8B	0.837	0.738	0.785	0.834	0.902	0.867	0.836	0.836	0.834	**0.826**

Table 4: Evaluation results of **Subasa-Llama** and **Subasa-Mistral** and other baselines on $\mathcal{D}_{SOLD}$. We report per class (OFFENSIVE, NOT OFFENSIVE) precision (P), recall (R), and F1, and their weighted averages. Macro-F1 is listed with the best result in bold.

Example		GT	Our Models (Subasa)			Baselines					
Sinhala Text	Translation		Llama3.1	Mistral	XLM-R	GPT4o	Aya101	Mistral	Llama3.1	XLM-R-L	XLM-R-B
@USER පොහොට්ටුවේ උන්ගේ සැබෑ ස්වරූපය තමයි ඕක. අමු තිරිසන්නු	@USER That is the true nature of those in Pohottuwa. Real savages.	OFF	OFF	OFF	OFF	NOT	OFF	NOT	NOT	OFF	NOT
@USER ඒ දෙක පස්ස පැත්තෙ ගහගනිං	@USER stick those two up your ass.	OFF	OFF	NOT	NOT	NOT	NOT	NOT	NOT	NOT	NOT
"ඒ ගොනා වික්කා" කියලා කොහොමද ඉංග්‍රීසියෙන් කියන්නේ #askingforafriend	How do you say "I sold that bull" in English?	OFF	NOT	NOT	OFF	OFF	OFF	OFF	OFF	OFF	OFF

Table 5: Classification examples from $\mathcal{D}_{SOLD}$ showing model predictions. Original Sinhala text with translations, ground truth (GT), our Subasa models' predictions, and baseline comparisons. **OFF**: Offensive, **NOT**: Non-offensive.

4 Results and Discussion

Concerning **RQ1**, our Subasa-XLM-R model achieves a macro-F1 of 0.84 (Table 3), outperforming both CNN baselines and the vanilla fine-tuned XLM-R (0.82 macro-F1). This 2% improvement demonstrates that MRP effectively bridges the gap between pre-training and downstream task adaptation in Sinhala's low-resource setting. The class imbalance in $\mathcal{D}_{SOLD}$ (Appendix 2) was the reason behind the use of macro-F1 for performance comparison, which equally weights both classes despite the majority NOT OFFENSIVE examples.

Ablation Study insights show that MLM with 50% masking matches MRP's performance (0.83 vs 0.84 macro-F1). This suggests that in low-resource settings, *any* token-level intermediate task (MLM/MRP) can enhance downstream performance by reinforcing local context understand ing. While both MRP and MLM improve performance, their similar results warrant further study into task-specific intermediate objectives for low-resource languages.

Concerning **RQ2**, our results (Table 4) show significant gains across all LLM variants. The Subasa-Llama-3.1-8B model, derived from Meta-Llama-3.1-8B-Instruct, achieves the highest macro-F1 of 0.826, outperforming its base version (0.586 to 0.826). Similarly, Subasa-Llama-3.2-3B–adapted from Meta-Llama-3.2-3B-Instruct–achieves a macro-F1 of 0.804, more than doubling its base model's performance (0.373 to 0.804). The Subasa-Mistral-7B variant, built on Mistral-7B-Instruct-v0.3, also shows improvement compared to its base version (0.295 to 0.799). All our models surpass GPT-4o's zero-shot performance (0.733 macro-F1), with even the 3B Subasa-Llama model outperforming GPT-4o despite being a significantly smaller model. This highlights how task-specific fine-tuning with QLoRA enables open-source LLMs to specialize for low-resource languages.

When comparing results from Table 3 and Table 4, while Subasa-Llama-3.1-8B (0.826 macro-F1) leads among LLM variants, it slightly trails the smaller Subasa-XLM-R model (0.84 macro-F1). This counterintuitive result, where a 270M-parameter model outperforms an 8B-parameter LLM, suggests MRP's intermediate task provides a focused learning signal for offensive language detection, compensating for the XLM-R model's smaller size. Another factor is that the Subasa-Llama variants, despite their larger parameter count, inherit base models (Llama-3.1/3.2-Instruct) with minimal Sinhala pre-training data compared to XLM-R's multilingual foundation which contains the Sinhala language in its pre-training corpus.

Configuration	**Accuracy**	**Macro F1**
Intermediate Task = MRP		
Mask Ratio = 0.25	0.83	0.83
Mask Ratio = 0.5	0.82	0.82
Mask Ratio = 0.75	**0.84**	**0.84**
Mask Ratio = 1.00	0.83	0.83
Intermediate Task = MLM		
Mask Prob = 0.15	0.84	0.83
Mask Prob = 0.50	0.84	0.83
No Intermediate Task	0.82	0.82

Table 6: Ablation Study Results

5 Conclusion

This study addresses the challenge of offensive language detection in Sinhala, a low-resource language, by introducing four novel models: Subasa-XLM-R, Subasa-Llama (two variants), and Subasa-Mistral. To the best of our knowledge, our work is the first to adapt intermediate pre-finetuning and task-specific fine-tuning strategies for Sinhala, demonstrating significant advancements over existing baselines and state-of-the-art LLMs like GPT-4o. Below, we summarize our findings in relation to our initial research questions posed in Section 1:

***RQ1**: Can intermediate pre-finetuning tasks (e.g., masked rationale prediction) improve PLMs for offensive language detection in Sinhala?* Our results confirm that intermediate pre-finetuning with MRP enhances model performance, with Subasa-XLM-R achieving a macro-F1 of 0.84, surpassing vanilla fine-tuned XLM-R (0.82). Ablation studies reveal that token-level intermediate tasks—whether MRP or standard MLM—improve downstream task performance for Sinhala (a low resource setting). Notably, MLM with 50% masking nearly matches MRPs gains (0.83 vs. 0.84 macro-F1), suggesting that reinforcing local context understanding through intermediate tasks aids the performance of the downstream task for Sinhala.

***RQ2**: Can task-specific fine-tuning improve LLMs for offensive language detection in Sinhala?* Our results indicate that QLoRA enables open-source LLMs to specialize effectively for Sinhala and surpass GPT-4o's zero-shot performance. (e.g., Subasa-Llama-3.1-8B achieves a macro-F1 of 0.826, outperforming GPT-4o (0.733) and its base model (0.586).)

We publicly release all models and code to support Sinhala NLP research. Our results establish that strategic fine-tuning is beneficial for low-resource offensive language detection, with implications for other underrepresented languages.

Limitations

In our approach, we adopted `xlm-roberta-base` as the foundation for Subasa-XLM-R due to hardware and computational resource limitations. This choice precludes direct comparisons with larger variants such as `xlm-roberta-large`, which might exhibit different behaviors when subjected to our intermediate pre-finetuning strategy. Similarly, our experiments with Mistral and Llama 3 models were restricted to smaller variants, limiting insights into how larger variants of these LLMs might perform in our task-specific fine-tuning strategy.

Our approach to the task-specific fine-tuning strategy utilized a single prompt template in a zero-shot prompting setting during training for consistency. While this approach reduced variability in experiments, it limited insights into the sensitivity of results against alternative prompting strategies.

Acknowledgments

This work was supported by the Google Cloud Research Credits program (Award GCP19980904) and the OpenAI Researcher Access Program with API Credits. We would like to thank the anonymous reviewers for their valuable feedback and suggestions. Additionally, we thank Nate Raw for their insightful discussions.

References

Armen Aghajanyan, Anchit Gupta, Akshat Shrivastava, Xilun Chen, Luke Zettlemoyer, and Sonal Gupta. 2021. Muppet: Massive multi-task representations with pre-finetuning. In *Proceedings of the 2021 Conference on Empirical Methods in Natural Language Processing*.

Kabir Ahuja, Harshita Diddee, Rishav Hada, Millicent Ochieng, Krithika Ramesh, Prachi Jain, Akshay Nambi, Tanuja Ganu, Sameer Segal, Mohamed Ahmed, Kalika Bali, and Sunayana Sitaram. 2023. MEGA: Multilingual evaluation of generative AI. In *Proceedings of the 2023 Conference on Empirical Methods in Natural Language Processing*.

Maha Jarallah Althobaiti. 2022. BERT-based Approach to Arabic Hate Speech and Offensive Language Detection in Twitter: Exploiting Emojis and Sentiment Analysis. *International Journal of Advanced Computer Science and Applications*, 13(5).

Hayastan Avetisyan and David Broneske. 2023. Large language models and low-resource languages: An examination of armenian nlp. *Findings of the Association for Computational Linguistics: IJCNLP-AACL 2023 (Findings)*, pages 199–210.

Muhammad Awais, Farahat Ali, and Asma Kanwal. 2020. Individual-level factors and variation in exposure to online hate material: A cross-national comparison of four asian countries. *Journal of Media Studies*, 35(2).

Vimala Balakrishnan, Vithyatheri Govindan, and Kumanan N Govaichelvan. 2023. Tamil Offensive Language Detection: Supervised Versus Unsupervised Learning Approaches. *ACM Transactions on Asian and Low-Resource Language Information Processing*, 22(4):1–14.

Thales Bertaglia, Andreea Grigoriu, Michel Dumontier, and Gijs van Dijck. 2021. Abusive language on social media through the legal looking glass. In *Proceedings of the 5th Workshop on Online Abuse and Harms (WOAH 2021)*.

Piotr Bojanowski, Edouard Grave, Armand Joulin, and Tomas Mikolov. 2017. Enriching word vectors with subword information. *Transactions of the Association for Computational Linguistics*, 5:135–146.

Bharathi Raja Chakravarthi, Prasanna Kumar Kumaresan, Ratnasingam Sakuntharaj, Anand Kumar Madasamy, Sajeetha Thavareesan, Premjith B, Subalalitha Chinnaudayar Navaneethakrishnan, John P. McCrae, and Thomas Mandl. 2021. Overview of the HASOC-DravidianCodeMix Shared Task on Offensive Language Detection in Tamil and Malayalam. In *Working Notes of FIRE 2021 - Forum for Information Retrieval Evaluation*.

Aakanksha Chowdhery, Sharan Narang, Jacob Devlin, Maarten Bosma, Gaurav Mishra, Adam Roberts, Paul Barham, Hyung Won Chung, Charles Sutton, Sebastian Gehrmann, Parker Schuh, Kensen Shi, Sashank Tsvyashchenko, Joshua Maynez, Abhishek Rao, Parker Barnes, Yi Tay, Noam Shazeer, Vinodkumar Prabhakaran, Emily Reif, Nan Du, Ben Hutchinson, Reiner Pope, James Bradbury, Jacob Austin, Michael Isard, Guy Gur-Ari, Pengcheng Yin, Toju Duke, Anselm Levskaya, Sanjay Ghemawat, Sunipa Dev, Henryk Michalewski, Xavier Garcia, Vedant Misra, Kevin Robinson, Liam Fedus, Denny Zhou, Daphne Ippolito, David Luan, Hyeontaek Lim, Barret Zoph, Alexander Spiridonov, Ryan Sepassi, David Dohan, Shivani Agrawal, Mark Omernick, Andrew M. Dai, Thanumalayan Sankaranarayana Pillai, Marie Pellat, Aitor Lewkowycz, Erica Moreira, Rewon Child, Oleksandr Polozov, Katherine Lee, Zongwei Zhou, Xuezhi Wang, Brennan Saeta, Mark Diaz, Orhan Firat, Michele Catasta, Jason Wei, Kathy Meier-Hellstern, Douglas Eck, Jeff Dean, Slav Petrov, and Noah Fiedel. 2023. Palm: scaling language modeling with pathways. *J. Mach. Learn. Res.*, 24(1).

Christina Christodoulou. 2024. NLPDame at ClimateActivism 2024: Mistral sequence classification with PEFT for hate speech, targets and stance event detection. In *Proceedings of the 7th Workshop on Challenges and Applications of Automated Extraction of Socio-political Events from Text (CASE 2024)*.

Nisansa De Silva. 2019. Survey on publicly available sinhala natural language processing tools and research. *arXiv preprint arXiv:1906.02358*.

Dulan S Dias, Madhushi D Welikala, and Naomal GJ Dias. 2018. Identifying racist social media comments in sinhala language using text analytics models with machine learning. In *Proceedings of 18th International Conference on Advances in ICT for Emerging Regions (ICTer)*.

W.S.S. Fernando, Ruvan Weerasinghe, and E.R.A.D. Bandara. 2022. Sinhala hate speech detection in social media using machine learning and deep learning. In *Proceedings of 22nd International Conference on Advances in ICT for Emerging Regions (ICTer)*.

Jianfei He, Lilin Wang, Jiaying Wang, Zhenyu Liu, Hongbin Na, Zimu Wang, Wei Wang, and Qi Chen. 2024. Guardians of discourse: Evaluating llms on multilingual offensive language detection. *arXiv preprint arXiv:2410.15623*.

Edward J. Hu, Yelong Shen, Phillip Wallis, Zeyuan Allen-Zhu, Yuanzhi Li, Shean Wang, Lu Wang, and Weizhu Chen. 2021. Lora: Low-rank adaptation of large language models. *arXiv preprint*, arXiv:2106.09685.

M. S. Jahan, D. R. Beddiar, M. Oussalah, and N. Arhab. 2021. Hate and offensive language detection using bert for english subtask a. In *Proceedings of the FIRE 2021: Forum for Information Retrieval Evaluation*.

Ravindu Jayakody and Gihan Dias. 2024. Performance of recent large language models for a low-resourced language. In *Proceedings of the 2024 International Conference on Asian Language Processing (IALP)*.

Jiyun Kim, Byounghan Lee, and Kyung-Ah Sohn. 2022. Why is it hate speech? masked rationale prediction for explainable hate speech detection. In *Proceedings of the 29th International Conference on Computational Linguistics*.

Yoon Kim. 2014. Convolutional neural networks for sentence classification. In *Proceedings of the 2014 Conference on Empirical Methods in Natural Language Processing (EMNLP)*.

Ritesh Kumar, Guggilla Bhanodai, Rajendra Pamula, and Maheshwar Reddy Chennuru. 2018. TRAC-1 shared task on aggression identification: IIT(ISM)@COLING'18. In *Proceedings of the First Workshop on Trolling, Aggression and Cyberbullying (TRAC-2018)*.

Alyssa Lees, Vinh Q. Tran, Yi Tay, Jeffrey Sorensen, Jai Gupta, Donald Metzler, and Lucy Vasserman. 2022. A new generation of perspective api: Efficient multilingual character-level transformers. In *Proceedings of the 28th ACM SIGKDD Conference on Knowledge Discovery and Data Mining*.

Marzieh Mozafari, Reza Farahbakhsh, and Noel Crespi. 2022. Cross-Lingual Few-Shot Hate Speech and Offensive Language Detection Using Meta Learning. *IEEE Access*, 10:14880–14896.

Sidath Munasinghe and Uthayasanker Thayasivam. 2022. A deep learning ensemble hate speech detection approach for sinhala tweets. In *Proceedings of Moratuwa Engineering Research Conference (MERCon)*.

Oluwafemi Oriola and Eduan Kotzé. 2020. Evaluating Machine Learning Techniques for Detecting Offensive and Hate Speech in South African Tweets. *IEEE Access*, 8:21496–21509.

Yada Pruksachatkun, Jason Phang, Haokun Liu, Phu Mon Htut, Xiaoyi Zhang, Richard Yuanzhe Pang, Clara Vania, Katharina Kann, and Samuel R. Bowman. 2020. Intermediate-Task Transfer Learning with Pretrained Language Models: When and Why Does It Work? In *Proceedings of the 58th Annual Meeting of the Association for Computational Linguistics*.

Nirupama Rajapaksha, Supunmali Ahangama, and Shalinda Adikari. 2023. Fine-tuning xlm-r for the detection of sinhala hate speech content on twitter and youtube. In *Proceedings of 3rd International Conference on Advanced Research in Computing (ICARC)*.

Tharindu Ranasinghe, Isuri Anuradha, Damith Premasiri, Kanishka Silva, Hansi Hettiarachchi, Lasitha Uyangodage, and Marcos Zampieri. 2024. Sold: Sinhala offensive language dataset. *Language Resources and Evaluation*, pages 1–41.

Tharindu Ranasinghe, Marcos Zampieri, and Hansi Hettiarachchi. 2019. Brums at hasoc 2019: Deep learning models for multilingual hate speech and offensive language identification. In *FIRE (working notes)*, pages 199–207.

Fatima Shannag, Bassam Hammo, and Hossam Faris. 2022. The Design, Construction and Evaluation of Annotated Arabic Cyberbullying Corpus. *Education and Information Technologies*, 27(8):10977–11023.

Cagri Toraman. 2024. Adapting open-source generative large language models for low-resource languages: A case study for Turkish. In *Proceedings of the Fourth Workshop on Multilingual Representation Learning (MRL 2024)*.

Sang Truong, Duc Nguyen, Toan Nguyen, Dong Le, Nhi Truong, Tho Quan, and Sanmi Koyejo. 2024. Crossing linguistic horizons: Finetuning and comprehensive evaluation of Vietnamese large language models. In *Findings of the Association for Computational Linguistics: NAACL 2024*.

Ahmet Üstün, Viraat Aryabumi, Zheng Yong, Wei-Yin Ko, Daniel D'souza, Gbemileke Onilude, Neel Bhandari, Shivalika Singh, Hui-Lee Ooi, Amr Kayid, Freddie Vargus, Phil Blunsom, Shayne Longpre, Niklas Muennighoff, Marzieh Fadaee, Julia Kreutzer, and Sara Hooker. 2024. Aya model: An instruction finetuned open-access multilingual language model. In *Proceedings of the 62nd Annual Meeting of the Association for Computational Linguistics (Volume 1: Long Papers)*.

Tharindu Weerasooriya, Sujan Dutta, Tharindu Ranasinghe, Marcos Zampieri, Christopher Homan, and Ashiqur KhudaBukhsh. 2023a. Vicarious Offense and Noise Audit of Offensive Speech Classifiers: Unifying Human and Machine Disagreement on What is Offensive. In *Proceedings of the 2023 Conference on Empirical Methods in Natural Language Processing*.

Tharindu Cyril Weerasooriya, Sarah Luger, Saloni Poddar, Ashiqur KhudaBukhsh, and Christopher Homan. 2023b. Subjective Crowd Disagreements for Subjective Data: Uncovering Meaningful CrowdOpinion with Population-level Learning. In *Proceedings of the 61st Annual Meeting of the Association for Computational Linguistics (Volume 1: Long Papers)*.

Marcos Zampieri, Tharindu Ranasinghe, Mrinal Chaudhari, Saurabh Gaikwad, Prajwal Krishna, Mayuresh Nene, and Shrunali Paygude. 2022. Predicting the Type and Target of Offensive Social Media Posts in Marathi. *Social Network Analysis and Mining*, 12(1):77.

A Prompt Template

The full instruction template used for fine-tuning is shown below:

```
System: "You are an emotionally
    intelligent assistant who
    speaks Sinhala and English
    Languages. Your task is to
    determine whether each tweet
    is OFFENSIVE or NOT OFFENSIVE.
     For each tweet, provide a
    single word as your output:
    either \"OFF\" or \"NOT\". For
     offensive tweets, identify
    and list the specific
    offensive phrases without
    translation.\n"

User: "Please classify the
    following tweet as \"OFF\" or
    \"NOT\". If offensive, list
    the specific offensive phrases
    :\n\n'[TWEET]'"

Assistant: "[LABEL]\nPhrases: [
    PHRASES]"
```

Placeholders: - [TWEET]: Original Sinhala text from $\mathcal{D}_{SOLD}$. - [LABEL]: Ground-truth label (OFF or NOT). - [PHRASES]: Offensive phrases extracted from rationale annotations.

Tweet	Human Translation	Label	Rationales
@USER ඒ හිතන් ඉන්නේ @USER වගේම මටත් මෝඩ විමසම් කියලා .සැමක් mate.	@USER She thinks that I get aroused like her. Poor thing mate.	NOT	[]
@USER @USER නේ. ඇය ඉස්සර විචාරක කෙනෙක්?	@USER @USER Damn, isnt this the girl who used to be a news anchor	NOT	[]
@USER .. . එන්න ඔබේ ජන්ම දා උෟ * පරීක්ෂා කරනවා	@USER @USER Yo.. do you like to get your a** cracked open on your birth-day	OFF	[0, 0, 0, 0, 0, 0, 0, 0, 1, 0, 1, 0, 0, 0]

Table 7: Examples from $\mathcal{D}_{SOLD}$.

Configuration	OFFENSIVE			NOT OFFENSIVE			Weighted			Macro
	P	R	F1	P	R	F1	P	R	F1	F1
MRP (Ours)										
Mask Ratio = 0.25	0.79	0.82	0.80	0.87	0.85	0.86	0.84	0.84	0.84	0.83
Mask Ratio = 0.50	0.85	0.72	0.78	0.83	0.91	0.87	0.83	0.83	0.83	0.82
Mask Ratio = 0.75	0.79	0.85	0.82	0.89	0.84	0.87	0.85	0.85	0.85	**0.84**
Mask Ratio = 1.00	0.78	0.81	0.80	0.87	0.84	0.85	0.83	0.83	0.83	0.83
MLM Intermediate										
Mask Prob = 0.15	0.81	0.80	0.81	0.87	0.87	0.87	0.85	0.85	0.85	0.84
Mask Prob = 0.50	0.82	0.79	0.80	0.86	0.88	0.87	0.84	0.84	0.84	0.84
No Intermediate Task	0.77	0.82	0.80	0.87	0.83	0.85	0.83	0.83	0.83	0.82

Table 8: Complete ablation study results on XLM-R-Base with per-class metrics. All experiments used identical training data, validation splits, and hyperparameters (Table 1). We report Precision (P), Recall (R), and F1 for both classes, along with weighted averages and Macro-F1. Best MRP configuration (Mask Ratio = 0.75) shown in bold.

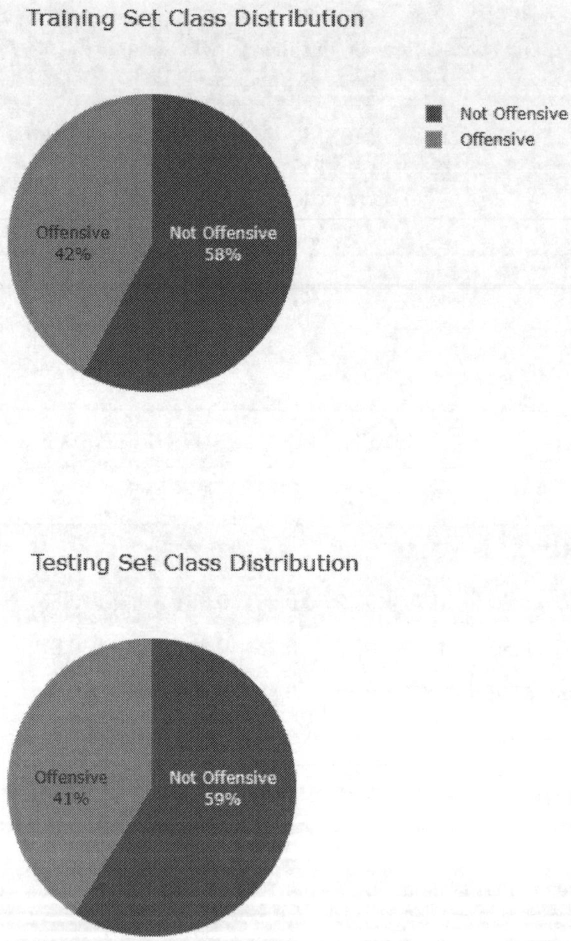

Figure 2: Class Distribution of Training and Testing Sets: The pie charts illustrate the distribution of 'NOT Offensive' and 'Offensive' instances in the training set (75% of the original dataset) and testing set (25% of the original dataset). $\mathcal{D}_{SOLD}$ contains 10,000 Sinhala tweets in total, and out of these 4191 are labeled as offensive and 5,809 labelled as non-offensive.

Integrating Symbolic Execution into the Fine-Tuning of Code-Generating LLMs

Marina Sakharova and **Abhinav Anand** and **Mira Mezini**
TU Darmstadt

Abstract

Code-generating Large Language Models (LLMs) have become essential tools in modern software development, enhancing productivity and accelerating development. This paper aims to investigate the fine-tuning of code-generating LLMs using Reinforcement Learning and Direct Preference Optimization, further improving their performance. To achieve this, we enhance the training data for the reward model with the help of symbolic execution techniques, ensuring more comprehensive and objective data. With symbolic execution, we create a custom dataset that better captures the nuances in code evaluation. Our reward models, fine-tuned on this dataset, demonstrate significant improvements over the baseline, CodeRL, in estimating the quality of generated code. Our code-generating LLMs, trained with the help of reward model feedback, achieve similar results compared to the CodeRL benchmark.

1 Introduction

Reinforcement Learning (RL) has become one of the most powerful LLM fine-tuning techniques (Ouyang et al., 2022). RL integrates feedback into the fine-tuning process, steering the training in the direction of human preferences. There are various approaches to applying RL to LLMs, but the general idea often consists of three steps:

1. Fine-tune a pre-trained LLM with supervised training, generate multiple answers for each given prompt and assign each answer a quality score.

2. Use the resulting *preference data* to train a reward model - an LLM that learns to produce a feedback score for a given code snippet.

3. Generate feedback with the trained reward model and use this feedback to fine-tune the text-generating LLM.

RL has found many applications, one of which being coding assistance (Le et al., 2022; Dou et al., 2024; Wang et al., 2022). According to Yu et al. (2024), code generation is particularly well-suited for RL because, unlike natural language tasks, the preference data can be created automatically and more objectively through the percentage of passed unit tests.

However, the quality of unit test feedback is highly dependent on the test data quality (Beller et al., 2015). When human developers design test cases, they may overlook a path in the Control Flow Graph (CFG) or cover one path multiple times (Huang, 2017). These errors may result in biased feedback and, thus, incorrect RL training data.

Our work aims to evaluate whether **symbolic execution** improves reward-based fine-tuning of code-generating models. To achieve this, we enhance the APPS dataset (Hendrycks et al., 2021), a real-world coding dataset, by augmenting it with automatically generated test cases created through symbolic execution. This technique executes code with symbolic values (King, 1976), restricted to specific ranges for each control flow graph (CFG) path, ensuring that every path is covered exactly once. Symbolic execution tools analyze the CFG and generate a sample input for every path, eliminating human biases in test case creation.

Using the augmented APPS dataset, we fine-tune the *CodeT5* model (Wang et al., 2021) with RL, comparing its performance to *CodeT5-finetuned-CodeRL* (Le et al., 2022), a *CodeT5* version fine-tuned with RL on the original APPS that achieved SOTA performance on the MBPP benchmark (Austin et al., 2021) at the time of its release.

Finally, we evaluate symbolic execution for Direct Preference Optimization (DPO), a supervised alternative to RL, where the model can be trained directly on a dataset of chosen-rejected code pairs, without the usage of a reward model (Rafailov et al., 2024). This addition allows us to evaluate the per-

Proceedings of the 2025 Conference of the Nations of the Americas Chapter of the Association for Computational Linguistics: Human Language Technologies (Volume 4: Student Research Workshop), pages 271–278

formance of symbolic execution under both explicit (RL) and implicit (DPO) reward settings.

2 Related work

There have been invented several frameworks for fine-tuning coding models with RL-based strategies. RLTF, Reinforcement Learning from Unit Test Feedback, utilizes unit test results as multi-granular feedback signals that penalize incorrect basic blocks (Liu et al., 2023). PPOCoder extends unit test feedback with syntactic and semantic matching scores between generated and ground truth code (Shojaee et al., 2023). Dou et al. (2024) introduce StepCoder, addressing the issue of not penalizing unexecuted code by decomposing generation problems into simple sub-tasks and masking out unreached code.

Several recent papers introduce systems that combine symbolic execution tools and LLMs during inference. Wang et al. (2024) propose an LLM agent that generates execution path constraints for Python code by iteratively calling a satisfiability solver. Zaharudin et al. (2024) combine LLMs with symbolic execution tools to identify code vulnerabilities, while Chen et al. (2024) apply both to secure medical software.

Although research has explored RL for fine-tuning code-generating models and integrated symbolic execution with LLM inference frameworks, little attention has been paid to combining these approaches. Specifically, the use of symbolic execution for fine-tuning code-generating models remains largely unexplored. This paper aims to bridge this gap.

3 Methodology

Our approach consists of two main steps: preference dataset creation and LLM fine-tuning. First, we use symbolic execution to generate test cases for APPS train tasks, produce code solutions, and rank them by performance. We then sample from the ranked codes to train *CodeT5-base* (Wang et al., 2021) as a reward model, which is subsequently used to optimize the code-generating LLM, *CodeT5-large-ntp-py* (Le et al., 2022).

3.1 APPS analysis

We apply symbolic execution tools on APPS (Hendrycks et al., 2021) - a dataset of coding problems scraped from open-source websites. APPS consists of 5000 train and 5000 test tasks of three difficulty levels, all in Python. For each task, there are several input-output pairs available for testing. We are especially interested in test cases for training data since we use them to train the reward model on code-feedback pairs. Figure 3 presents that 2012 out of 5000 tasks in the train set contain only one test case each. This distribution results in a percentage of passed tests being either 100% or 0%, leading to highly coarse and unrefined feedback. Moreover, APPS test cases were manually created by humans, which opens the possibility of overseeing an execution path (Huang, 2017). In order to extend the number of test cases and ensure the coverage of all CFG paths, we generate our custom inputs.

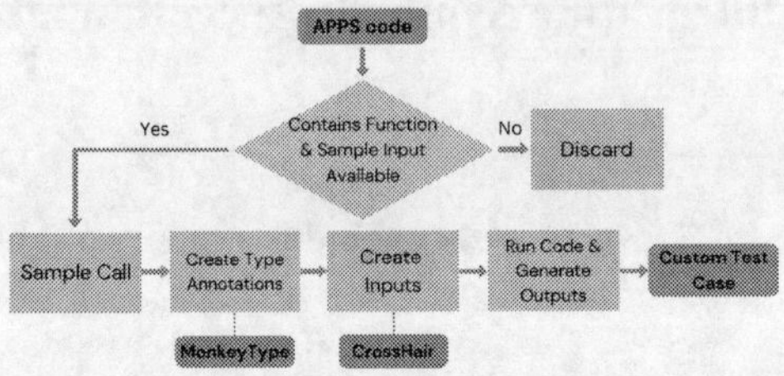

Figure 1: Test case generation pipeline.

3.2 Test case generation

Our input generation pipeline is presented in Figure 1. This pipeline employs CrossHair[1] - an example input generation tool for Python functions. With the help of a Satisfiability Modulo Theories solver, CrossHair explores all execution paths and finds examples and counterexamples of values.

To run correctly, CrossHair requires a Python function with annotated input types. Without type annotation, CrossHair outputs data of all possible types, including those irrelevant to the task. Since APPS functions lack default type hints, we use the MonkeyType annotation tool [2] to automatically infer and generate type annotations for ground truth functions based on sample input. We discard tasks that deviate from the structure of a single, standalone function and tasks that do not have any sample inputs. This filtering results in a dataset of 2402 tasks that are processed through the input generation pipeline and used for reward model training.

[1] https://github.com/pschanely/CrossHair
[2] https://github.com/Instagram/MonkeyType

3.4 DPO training

In DPO, we begin the first two steps of the RL pipeline: supervised warm-up, followed by code generation for training set tasks with the new model. For each task, we select one correct solution and uniformly sample one incorrect solution to create a dataset of chosen-rejected pairs. This dataset is used to train *CodeT5* with DPO trainer from the Huggingface TRL library [3].

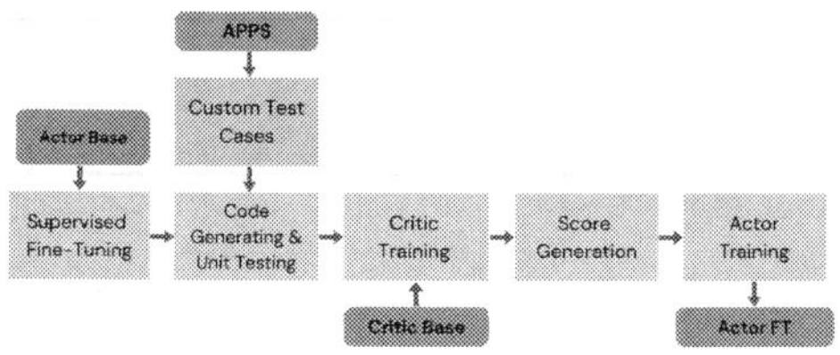

Figure 2: CodeRL training pipeline. Our pipeline extension is marked green.

3.3 Fine-tuning workflow

Our fine-tuning pipeline relies on CodeRL (Le et al., 2022) - a framework for RL-based LLM training. CodeRL implements an actor-critic architecture with the code-generating model as the actor and the reward model as the critic. We modify CodeRL to integrate custom test cases created with symbolic execution, as depicted in Figure 2.

The training begins with a supervised warm-up phase to expose the model to NL-To-Python generation examples. We employ the original APPS training set as training data for the warm-up. A validation set, created by sampling 50% of the original APPS test data, is used to optimize the number of warm-up epochs, with the remaining 50% reserved for intermediate and final testing.

After warm-up, the LLM generates 100 codes per task for the custom training set. These codes are tested against the corresponding custom input values. For each code, the tests return a category: Compile Error, Runtime Error, (at least one) Test Failed, or Test Passed. The resulting code-feedback pairs are used to supervisely train *CodeT5-base* as the critic model that classifies codes into four categories.

After training, the critic predicts test outcomes for each actor-generated code in the custom train set. These codes and predictions, along with ground truth solutions, are passed into the actor's training loop. Following CodeRL, we compute cross-entropy loss for ground truth data and RL loss for generated codes based on critic scores.

The final model is evaluated on 2,500 tasks from the APPS test set, excluding those in the validation set, and compared to the warm-up model and CodeRL baseline.

3.5 Metrics

For evaluating actor models, we use pass@k (Chen et al., 2021), the standard for measuring the performance of generated code. For each problem, if a model generates n code samples and c of them are correct, pass@$k(n, c, k)$ will measure the probability that at least one of the top k codes passes all unit tests. The mathematical definition of this metric is presented in 1.

$$pass@k := \mathop{\mathbb{E}}_{\text{Problems}} \left[1 - \frac{\binom{n-c}{k}}{\binom{n}{k}} \right] \qquad (1)$$

In this paper, we use a k of 5.

For the critic evaluation, we employ two metrics. First, we use accuracy, as the model is a classifier that predicts categorical labels. However, accuracy alone is not sufficient since it only reflects the percentage of correct predictions without considering the severity of misclassifications. The categories have an inherent order: If a code results in a compile error, it would be a less crucial mistake to predict a run-time error than code correctness. Thus, we also employ Mean Average Error, or MAE. We accordingly assign numbers from 0 to 3 to each category and calculate the absolute difference between the predicted and actual category values. This metric ensures that misclassifications involving more dissimilar categories (e.g., predicting "Test Passed" for code with a compile error) are penalized more heavily than those involving similar categories (e.g., predicting "Run-time Error" for a compile error).

4 Experiment details

4.1 Critics

We explore two training configurations to evaluate the impact of symbolic execution data:

- **CodeRL-SE-critic**: Fine-tunes the existing CodeRL critic model *CodeT5-finetuned-critic*

[3] https://huggingface.co/docs/trl/main/en/dpo_trainer

(Le et al., 2022), enhancing it with symbolic execution inputs.

- **CodeT5-SE-critic**: Trains a new critic model from scratch using *CodeT5-base* (Wang et al., 2021), the same base model used by CodeRL (Le et al., 2022), but with symbolic execution training data.

We train both models for one epoch using a learning rate of 2e-5. Both values are determined empirically.
Additionally, we evaluate the CodeRL critic model *CodeT5-finetuned-critic* since the paper (Le et al., 2022) does not provide any information about critic performance.

4.2 Actors

For actor training, we use *CodeT5-large-ntp-py* (Le et al., 2022), a version of *CodeT5* optimized for Python code generation tasks. We use this model because it was used as the base model for CodeRL model training. We perform two training experiments, each with one of our trained critic models, and evaluate these actors alongside the CodeRL actor. We train these models for one epoch with a learning rate of 2e-6. We determined these values empirically as well. Besides training our models, we run the inference on CodeRL actor and compare it with our results.

4.3 DPO

In DPO, *CodeT5-large-ntp-py* is trained for one epoch, with a learning rate of 2e-6 and a β of 0.1. β determines how close the DPO model remains to the supervise fine-tuned model, where a smaller β means a further deviation toward DPO loss (Rafailov et al., 2024).

5 Results

5.1 Enhancing APPS

Figure 3 compares the test case distributions of the original and custom symbolic execution train sets. The custom data displays a noticeable rightward skew, reflecting an increase in test case number per task. The mean number of test cases increases from 1 to 5, and the median from 5.16 to 7.22. This observation indicates that our approach succeeded in the quantitative enhancement of the training dataset by adding more test cases.

5.2 Critic models

The evaluation results for the critic models are presented in Table 1. Both of our models, *CodeRL-SE-critic* and *CodeT5-SE-critic*, demonstrate significant improvements over the baseline *CodeT5-finetuned-critic* used in CodeRL. Among these, *CodeRL-SE-critic*, a fine-tuned version of *CodeT5-finetuned-critic*, achieves the highest accuracy, surpassing the original model by 37.19%. Similarly, *CodeT5-SE-critic*, which uses *CodeT5-base* as its foundation, outperforms CodeRL by 11.33%. These findings show the effectiveness of training with the symbolic execution-enhanced dataset, which positively influences the reward model's performance.

Model	Accuracy	MAE
CodeRL-SE-critic	**0.4250**	**0.6617**
CodeT5-SE-critic	0.3449	0.8377
CodeT5-finetuned-critic	0.3098	0.9843

Table 1: Evaluation results for critic models, sorted by accuracy.

5.3 Actor models

The performance of *CodeT5-large-ntp-py* before and after the warm-up, the actor models, and the DPO model is shown in Table 2, divided into three difficulty levels, along with overall performance across all levels.
First, we can see the importance of a supervised warm-up before RL training: the results of the supervisely warmed-up model are significantly better than the base model - *CodeT5-large-ntp-py*. This results in the warmed-up model being a solid base model for further fine-tuning. Moreover, we can see that all fine-tuned models, regardless of the technique and dataset used, outperform supervisely warmed-up *CodeT5-large-ntp-py*. Thus, all our settings have the potential to improve LLM coding performance.
Nonetheless, our best actor model, *RL with CodeRL-SE-critic*, achieves only a slight improvement over the CodeRL baseline *CodeT5-finetuned-CodeRL*, with an overall performance gain of 0.14, measured in absolute difference. It outperforms the baseline for more complex tasks but loses for the simplest category. In contrast, our second actor, *RL with CodeT5-SE-critic*, demonstrates inferior performance compared to CodeRL. Several factors could contribute to these results. In RL, if

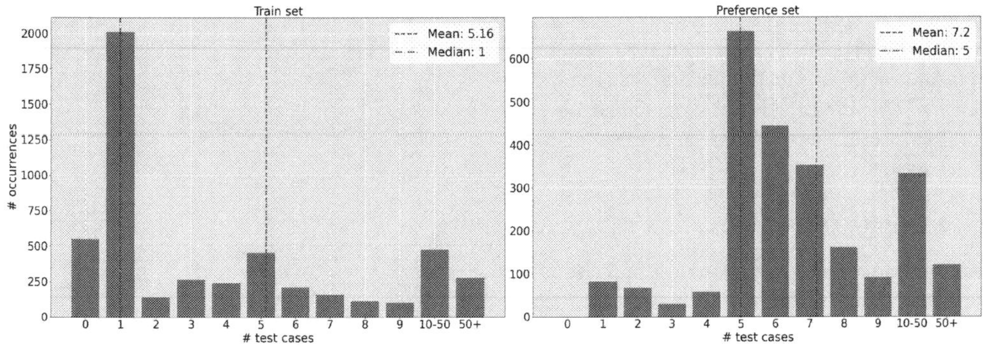

Figure 3: The distribution of test case number in the original train set (left) and the modified train set (right).

Training method	Introductory	Interview	Competition	Total
RL with *CodeRL-SE-critic*	9.42	**3.52**	**1.91**	**4.37**
RL (*CodeT5-finetuned-CodeRL*)	**10.11**	3.09	1.90	4.23
DPO	8.35	3.08	1.53	3.81
RL with *CodeT5-SE-critic*	8.09	2.53	1.66	3.44
Supervised warm-up	7.91	2.71	0.67	3.33
None (*CodeT5-large-ntp-py*)	0.00	0.00	0.00	0.00

Table 2: Pass@5 results for actor models, sorted by overall performance.

the training and evaluation distributions differ, the actor may learn to perform poorly even if the reward model scores are correct (Casper et al., 2023). Furthermore, RL training involves numerous hyperparameters that are challenging to optimize (Eimer et al., 2023), and suboptimal hyperparameter tuning may have negatively impacted the model's performance.

Similarly, our DPO model also underperforms relative to CodeRL. According to Xu et al. (2024), DPO models might assign disproportionately high probabilities to out-of-distribution data due to the absence of an explicit KL-divergence term. This phenomenon may explain the poor performance of DPO.

While our best actor model demonstrates a slight advantage over CodeRL, the overall improvements for the actor models are notably less pronounced than those observed in the critic models. This finding challenges the intuitive expectation that a stronger reward model would lead to a more effective policy. The results raise an important question for future research: if improvements in the critic do not directly translate to better actor performance, to what extent does critic quality contribute to actor optimization compared to other factors, such as hyperparameter selection?

6 Conclusion

In this study, we investigated the intersection of fine-tuning for code-generating models and symbolic execution. By enhancing the APPS dataset with symbolic execution inputs, we ensured a solid coverage of paths within the Control Flow Graph. Using this enriched dataset, we trained two critic models that significantly outperformed the baseline - the CodeRL critic. These results indicate the high potential of using symbolic execution tools to generate training data for reward models. The enhanced coverage provided by symbolic execution enabled the reward models to access more informative and accurate training data, thereby improving their ability to evaluate a code's performance.

At the same time, while actor and DPO models outperformed their base models, they gained only a slight advantage over the CodeRL actor. Although our critic models predict more precise feedback, the actors stay on a similar level to CodeRL.

We believe that the intersection of Reinforcement Learning and symbolic execution holds significant potential for advancing code-generating models. Future work could investigate the relationship between critic performance and actor effectiveness, optimize hyperparameter configurations for actor training, and explore datasets with further programming languages or other fine-tuning tasks to achieve similar gains for actor models. With further research, we suggest that symbolic execution combined with Reinforcement Learning will enable the development of more accurate and robust coding assistants.

7 Acknowledgements

I am grateful to the Zuse School ELIZA for their support throughout my academic journey. Their valuable networking opportunities have significantly contributed to my professional and personal growth.

References

Jacob Austin, Augustus Odena, Maxwell Nye, Maarten Bosma, Henryk Michalewski, David Dohan, Ellen Jiang, Carrie Cai, Michael Terry, Quoc Le, and Charles Sutton. 2021. Program Synthesis with Large Language Models. *Preprint*, arXiv:2108.07732.

Moritz Beller, Georgios Gousios, Annibale Panichella, and Andy Zaidman. 2015. When, how, and why developers (do not) test in their IDEs. In *Proceedings of the 2015 10th Joint Meeting on Foundations of Software Engineering*, pages 179–190, Bergamo Italy. ACM.

Stephen Casper, Xander Davies, Claudia Shi, Thomas Krendl Gilbert, Jérémy Scheurer, Javier Rando, Rachel Freedman, Tomasz Korbak, David Lindner, Pedro Freire, Tony Wang, Samuel Marks, Charbel-Raphaël Segerie, Micah Carroll, Andi Peng, Phillip Christoffersen, Mehul Damani, Stewart Slocum, Usman Anwar, Anand Siththaranjan, Max Nadeau, Eric J. Michaud, Jacob Pfau, Dmitrii Krasheninnikov, Xin Chen, Lauro Langosco, Peter Hase, Erdem Bıyık, Anca Dragan, David Krueger, Dorsa Sadigh, and Dylan Hadfield-Menell. 2023. Open Problems and Fundamental Limitations of Reinforcement Learning from Human Feedback. *Preprint*, arXiv:2307.15217.

Jingxue Chen, Liangjun Deng, Yao Qiu, Pengbiao Zhao, Hang Lei, Jingcheng Song, and Xiaopei Wang. 2024. Llm-Based Automated Modeling in Symbolic Execution for Securing Medical Software. *Preprint*, Social Science Research Network:4938953.

Mark Chen, Jerry Tworek, Heewoo Jun, Qiming Yuan, Henrique Ponde de Oliveira Pinto, Jared Kaplan, Harri Edwards, Yuri Burda, Nicholas Joseph, Greg Brockman, Alex Ray, Raul Puri, Gretchen Krueger, Michael Petrov, Heidy Khlaaf, Girish Sastry, Pamela Mishkin, Brooke Chan, Scott Gray, Nick Ryder, Mikhail Pavlov, Alethea Power, Lukasz Kaiser, Mohammad Bavarian, Clemens Winter, Philippe Tillet, Felipe Petroski Such, Dave Cummings, Matthias Plappert, Fotios Chantzis, Elizabeth Barnes, Ariel Herbert-Voss, William Hebgen Guss, Alex Nichol, Alex Paino, Nikolas Tezak, Jie Tang, Igor Babuschkin, Suchir Balaji, Shantanu Jain, William Saunders, Christopher Hesse, Andrew N. Carr, Jan Leike, Josh Achiam, Vedant Misra, Evan Morikawa, Alec Radford, Matthew Knight, Miles Brundage, Mira Murati, Katie Mayer, Peter Welinder, Bob McGrew, Dario Amodei, Sam McCandlish, Ilya Sutskever, and Wojciech Zaremba. 2021. Evaluating Large Language Models Trained on Code. *Preprint*, arXiv:2107.03374.

Shihan Dou, Yan Liu, Haoxiang Jia, Limao Xiong, Enyu Zhou, Wei Shen, Junjie Shan, Caishuang Huang, Xiao Wang, Xiaoran Fan, Zhiheng Xi, Yuhao Zhou, Tao Ji, Rui Zheng, Qi Zhang, Xuanjing Huang, and Tao Gui. 2024. StepCoder: Improve Code Generation with Reinforcement Learning from Compiler Feedback. *Preprint*, arXiv:2402.01391.

Theresa Eimer, Marius Lindauer, and Roberta Raileanu. 2023. Hyperparameters in Reinforcement Learning and How To Tune Them.

Dan Hendrycks, Steven Basart, Saurav Kadavath, Mantas Mazeika, Akul Arora, Ethan Guo, Collin Burns, Samir Puranik, Horace He, Dawn Song, and Jacob Steinhardt. 2021. Measuring Coding Challenge Competence With APPS. *Preprint*, arXiv:2105.09938.

Fuqun Huang. 2017. Human Error Analysis in Software Engineering. In *Theory and Application on Cognitive Factors and Risk Management - New Trends and Procedures*. IntechOpen.

James C. King. 1976. Symbolic execution and program testing. *Commun. ACM*, 19(7):385–394.

Hung Le, Yue Wang, Akhilesh Deepak Gotmare, Silvio Savarese, and Steven C. H. Hoi. 2022. CodeRL: Mastering Code Generation through Pretrained Models and Deep Reinforcement Learning. *Preprint*, arXiv:2207.01780.

Jiate Liu, Yiqin Zhu, Kaiwen Xiao, Qiang Fu, Xiao Han, Wei Yang, and Deheng Ye. 2023. RLTF: Reinforcement Learning from Unit Test Feedback. *Preprint*, arXiv:2307.04349.

Long Ouyang, Jeff Wu, Xu Jiang, Diogo Almeida, Carroll L. Wainwright, Pamela Mishkin, Chong Zhang, Sandhini Agarwal, Katarina Slama, Alex Ray, John Schulman, Jacob Hilton, Fraser Kelton, Luke Miller, Maddie Simens, Amanda Askell, Peter Welinder, Paul Christiano, Jan Leike, and Ryan Lowe. 2022. Training language models to follow instructions with human feedback. *Preprint*, arXiv:2203.02155.

Rafael Rafailov, Archit Sharma, Eric Mitchell, Stefano Ermon, Christopher D. Manning, and Chelsea Finn. 2024. Direct Preference Optimization: Your Language Model is Secretly a Reward Model. *Preprint*, arXiv:2305.18290.

Parshin Shojaee, Aneesh Jain, Sindhu Tipirneni, and Chandan K. Reddy. 2023. Execution-based Code Generation using Deep Reinforcement Learning. *Preprint*, arXiv:2301.13816.

Wenhan Wang, Kaibo Liu, An Ran Chen, Ge Li, Zhi Jin, Gang Huang, and Lei Ma. 2024. Python Symbolic Execution with LLM-powered Code Generation. *Preprint*, arXiv:2409.09271.

Xin Wang, Yasheng Wang, Yao Wan, Fei Mi, Yitong Li, Pingyi Zhou, Jin Liu, Hao Wu, Xin Jiang, and Qun Liu. 2022. Compilable Neural Code Generation with Compiler Feedback. *Preprint*, arXiv:2203.05132.

Yue Wang, Weishi Wang, Shafiq Joty, and Steven C. H. Hoi. 2021. CodeT5: Identifier-aware Unified Pre-trained Encoder-Decoder Models for Code Understanding and Generation. *Preprint*, arXiv:2109.00859.

Shusheng Xu, Wei Fu, Jiaxuan Gao, Wenjie Ye, Weilin Liu, Zhiyu Mei, Guangju Wang, Chao Yu, and Yi Wu. 2024. Is DPO Superior to PPO for LLM Alignment? A Comprehensive Study. *Preprint*, arXiv:2404.10719.

Zishun Yu, Yunzhe Tao, Liyu Chen, Tao Sun, and Hongxia Yang. 2024. $\mathcal{B}$-Coder: Value-Based Deep Reinforcement Learning for Program Synthesis. *Preprint*, arXiv:2310.03173.

Muhammad Nabel Zaharudin, Muhammad Haziq Zuhaimi, and Faysal Hossain Shezan. 2024. Poster: Enhancing Symbolic Execution with LLMs for Vulnerability Detection.

Through the Looking Glass: Common Sense Consistency Evaluation of Weird Images

Elisei Rykov[1] **Kseniia Petrushina**[1,4] **Kseniia Titova**[1,3]
Anton Razzhigaev[2] **Alexander Panchenko**[1,2] **Vasily Konovalov**[2,4]
[1]Skoltech [2]AIRI [3]MTS AI
[4]Moscow Institute of Physics and Technology
{Elisei.Rykov, Kseniia.Petrushina, A.Panchenko}@skol.tech

Abstract

Measuring how real images look is a complex task in artificial intelligence research. For example, an image of a boy with a vacuum cleaner in a desert violates common sense. We introduce a novel method, which we call Through the Looking Glass (TLG), to assess image common sense consistency using Large Vision-Language Models (LVLMs) and Transformer-based encoder. By leveraging LVLMs to extract atomic facts from these images, we obtain a mix of accurate facts. We proceed by fine-tuning a compact attention-pooling classifier over encoded atomic facts. Our TLG has achieved a new state-of-the-art performance on the WHOOPS! and WEIRD datasets while leveraging a compact fine-tuning component.[1]

1 Introduction

People quickly notice something unusual in images that defy common sense, like Einstein holding a smartphone. We find it odd even though each part seems normal. Our brain's ability to understand normality goes beyond just identifying objects (Zellers et al., 2019). It involves connecting visual cues with everyday knowledge.

In this work, we propose a visual commonsense model that utilizes the observation that LVLMs may generate contradictory facts when confronted with images defying common sense (Liu et al., 2024b). By leveraging LVLMs to extract atomic facts from these images, we obtain a mix of accurate facts and erroneous hallucinations. Then we fine-tune a compact attention-pooling model over encoded atomic facts.

Our results indicate that using the classifier for basic facts can efficiently spot strange images. Surprisingly, this method outperforms existing more complex techniques.

In addition, we introduce a synthesized WEIRD dataset, a dataset of 824 samples of normal and strange images. Using this dataset, we further confirmed the performance of our model.

Our contributions are as follows:

- We present a *new method* called TLG that achieved state-of-the-art performance on the existing dataset of normal and strange images WHOOPS!.
- We present a *new dataset* dubbed WEIRD which is more challenging and nearly four times larger than WHOOPS!.

2 Related Work

Recently, commonsense reasoning has attracted substantial interest from the research community, spanning disciplines within NLP and CV, with numerous tasks being introduced.

Guetta et al. (2023) introduced the WHOOPS! benchmark, comprised of purposefully commonsense-defying images created by designers using publicly available image generation tools like Midjourney. They used a supervised approach based on BLIP-2 Flan-T5 (Li et al., 2023a) on multiple scales. The proposed fine-tuned model managed to outperform a random baseline, but still falls significantly short of human performance.

LLMs are capable of producing highly fluent responses to a wide range of user prompts, but they are notorious for hallucinating and making non-factual statements. Manakul et al. (2023b) proposed SelfCheckGPT, a straightforward sampling-based method that enables fact-checking of black-box models with zero resources.

To assess consistency among multiple sampled responses, SelfCheckGPT utilizes several techniques, including BERTScore, an automatic multiple-choice question answering generation (MQAG) framework (Manakul et al., 2023a), and

[1]`https://github.com/s-nlp/through-the-looking-glass`

Proceedings of the 2025 Conference of the Nations of the Americas Chapter of the Association for Computational Linguistics: Human Language Technologies (Volume 4: Student Research Workshop), pages 279–293

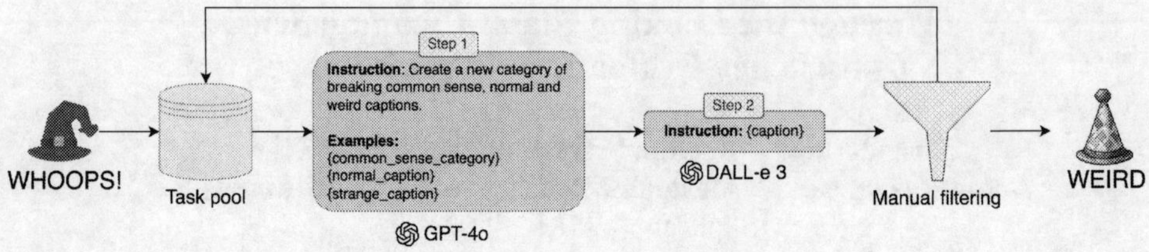

Figure 1: WEIRD dataset generation process. First, we formed a task pool for the few-shot generation of new samples from the WHOOPS! benchmark. Next, we randomly sampled few-shots from the task pool and asked GPT-4o to generate new samples. The samples were then visualized using Dall-E 3 and manually filtered. Good samples were added to the task pool for the next few-shot sampling.

NLI contradiction scores to detect hallucinations in the generated responses. However, the most effective method found was prompting the LLM to verify if the generations are supported by the context or not.

Regarding multi-modal case, Jing et al. (2023) proposed FAITHSCORE, a reference-free and fine-grained evaluation metric that measures the faithfulness of the generated free-form answers from large vision-language models. The FAITHSCORE uses multistep approach: (1) identify the descriptive content, (2) extract corresponding atomic facts from the identified sentences, and (3) the faithfulness of all atomic facts is verified according to the input image by applying Visual Entailment Model (VEM), which is able to predict whether the image semantically entails the text. Analogously, NLI has been used in textual mode to verify premises and hypotheses and subsequently to detect hallucinations (Maksimov et al., 2024).

Rykov et al. (2025) proposed an approach, in which LVLM is used to first generate atomic facts from images, resulting in a combination of accurate facts and erroneous hallucinations. The next step involves calculating pairwise entailment scores among these facts and aggregating these values to produce a single reality score.

Our approach is similar to the preceding methods, as we also utilize LVLMs to extract atomic facts from the image. We then train a supervised model to learn the relationships between the derived facts. If the classifier identifies a high contradiction among atomic facts, it indicates that one of the generated atomic facts is likely a hallucination. This often occurs when the LVLMs encounter an unusual image (Liu et al., 2024b), leading to such inconsistencies in most cases.

	WHOOPS!	WEIRD
# of samples	204	824
# of categories	26	12
# of sub-categories	—	181
Human baseline	92%	82.22%

Table 1: Comparison details between WHOOPS! and WEIRD. WEIRD contains 4 times more samples than WHOOPS!. In addition, WEIRD contains 181 different generated commonsense-breaking categories, which have been grouped into 12 global categories.

3 Dataset

This section describes the datasets we used to evaluate our methodology.

3.1 WHOOPS!

To evaluate our methods, we employ the WHOOPS![2] benchmark, focusing on a subset comprising 102 pairs of weird and normal images. Performance is measured by binary accuracy within this paired dataset, where a random guess would yield 50% accuracy. To assess human performance, three annotators were enlisted to categorize each image as weird or normal, relying on a majority vote for the final determination. Impressively,the human baseline reached 92%, indicating that despite subjectivity, there is a clear consensus on what constitutes weirdness within the specific context of the WHOOPS! benchmark.

3.2 WEIRD

Due to the fact that the WHOOPS! benchmark is relatively small, we generated a larger benchmark for quantifying image realism to validate our methodology – WEIRD[3].

[2]**W**eird and **H**eterogene**O**us **O**bjects, **P**henomena, and **S**ituations

[3]**W**eird **E**xamples of **I**mages with **R**eal-life **D**iscrepancies

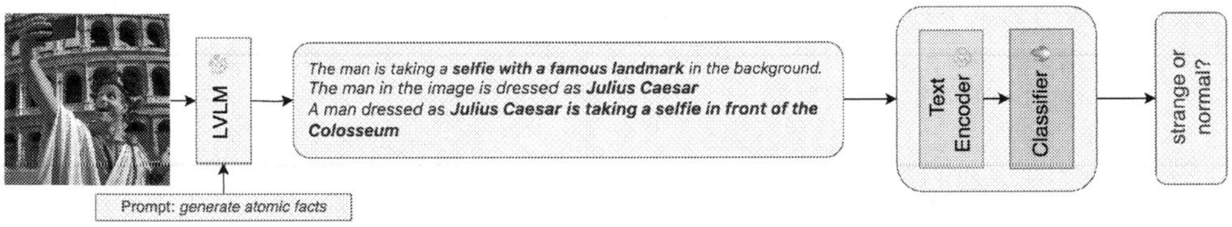

Figure 2: The proposed approach TLG for image commonsense consistency evaluation. Using the LVLM-generated atomic facts about the image, we train a classifier using hidden states from the textual encoder.

The detailed process of WEIRD dataset creation is shown in Figure 1. Like the Self-Instruct (Wang et al., 2023) dataset, WEIRD was generated in an iterative, semi-automatic manner using LLM. Specifically, we used WHOOPS! as an initial task pool with few-shot samples. In each iteration, we randomly sampled 5 pairs of normal and weird situations, along with the commonsense-breaking category. Each few-shot sample contains the breaking commonsense category, a caption of the normal image, and a caption of a strange image. The randomly sampled few-shots were passed to GPT-4o to generate a new category and captions. See the exact prompt used for generation in Appendix I. In the next step, these textual captions were used to generate images with Dall-E 3.

In each iteration, we generated 50 pairs of normal and strange images, resulting in 100 samples after each iteration. We also manually filtered out bad samples. We considered bad samples to be those with inconsistencies between image and caption, or with textual noisy captions. For example, there were many inconsistencies in the captions that mention celebrities. It turned out that Dall-E 3 struggled with the generation of celebrity faces, while some strange captions were based on putting certain celebrities in inappropriate conditions.

In total, we generated 2,000 unique samples of commonsense-breaking situations before the filtering stage. After filtering, only 824 samples remained. To evaluate human performance on WEIRD, we additionally annotated the dataset on the Yandex Tasks[4] crowd-source platform. Each example was annotated by five annotators with overlapping assignments. In order to introduce crowd sources to the task, we added 10 training samples. As a result of the annotation process, Krippendorff's alpha coefficient of consistency was 0.69 with a human accuracy of 82.22%. WHOOPS! and WEIRD comparison details can be seen in Table 1.

[4]https://tasks.yandex.com

4 Visual Commonsense Evaluation Method using Atomic Fact Extraction

The idea of our method dubbed TLG (Through the Looking Glass) is inspired by FactScore (Min et al., 2023): we adopt the principle of atomic facts generation for trustworthiness verification for the image modality. Namely, the common sense evaluation method is based on the classification of atomic facts generated by LVLMs using textual encoders. The approach is depicted in Figure 2.

We use LVLMs to collect different atomic facts that describe different aspects of the scene in the image. To sample as many different facts as possible, we use the Diverse Beam Search (Vijayakumar et al., 2016). So, given an image I and an LVLM, we sample N facts $F = \{f_1, f_2, \dots, f_N\}$, where $F = \text{LVLM}(I)$.

Next, we use a frozen textual encoder to extract representations H of the generated atomic facts. Each fact representation is computed as

$$H_i = \text{Encoder}(f_i) \in \mathbb{R}^{N \times T \times d}, \quad (1)$$

where T – number of tokens, d – embeddings dimensionality.

Since each encoder output H is a set of hidden representations for each token and fact, we perform average pooling to extract a single representation V for each fact. Thus, using the attention masks m obtained by the encoder tokenizer and the hidden representations H, we compute a single fact representation by averaging the vectors of its tokens

$$V_i = \frac{\sum_{j=1}^{T} m_{ij} H_{ij}}{\sum_{j=1}^{T} m_{ij} + \varepsilon}. \quad (2)$$

Furthermore, we train an attention-based pooling classifier using individual representations V. This classifier maps each representation to a single value. Then, we convert a set of attention values into probabilities using the softmax function:

$$A = \text{softmax}(W_a V + b_a) \in \mathbb{R}^N. \quad (3)$$

Later, these scores are used to perform a weighted averaging of the set of representations for each fact into a single representation:

$$v_{\text{weighted}} = \frac{\sum_{i=1}^{N} A_i V_i}{\sum_{i=1}^{N} A_i} \in \mathbb{R}^d. \quad (4)$$

Finally, we classify the final representation by mapping it to a single common sense violation probability:

$$\text{prob} = \sigma(W_c v_{\text{weighted}} + b_c) \in [0, 1]. \quad (5)$$

5 Experimental Setup

To run the experiments, we strictly follow the evaluation setup suggested in WHOOPS! (Guetta et al., 2023). Thus, we evaluate several models using 5-fold cross-validation in a supervised configuration. See the detailed list of checkpoints used for the main approach and baselines in Appendix E.

For fact generation, we set `num_beams` and `num_beam_groups` to 5, and the `diversity_penalty` to 1.0. Regarding penalty, we find this value to be optimal for adding diversity and preserving the model's ability to follow instructions. For LVLMs, with various backbone architectures, we utilized the following prompt for fact generation: *"Provide a brief, one-sentence descriptive fact about this image"*. To generate atomic facts, we used different LVLMs with different sizes (from 0.5B to 13B) of the LLaVA architecture. Given the generated atomic facts, we encode them using several DeBERTa-v3-large-based encoders.

We also consider the following baselines:

LVLM with the prompt, which was found to be effective in detecting weird images (Liu et al., 2024a): *"<image> Is this unusual? Please explain briefly with a short sentence."*

Linear Probing resemble our approach in that it requires a small learnable component. This baseline involves learning a logistic regression classifier on the hidden representation of LLaVAs at each layer. We consider two setups: (a) using the <image> as the sole input (**Image only**), and (b) using <image> the with a prompt *"Provide a short, one-sentence descriptive fact about this image"* (**+Prompt**), which was used to generate atomic facts.

CLIP-based models were evaluated by passing images and measuring the distance from the `strange` and `normal` classes in a zero-shot setting. In addition, we fine-tuned CLIP in a cross-validation setting. More details on the hyperparameters and detailed baseline results can be found in the Appendix C.

LLM zero-shot baselines were represented by Gemma-2-9B-Instruct and Qwen2.5-7B-Instruct. As input, we passed generated atomic facts about the image and asked the model to determine whether the facts were strange or not using the following prompt: *"Your task is to classify a series of facts as normal or strange. The set of facts is strange if some of the facts contradict common sense. Answer using 'normal' or 'strange'. Do not write anything else"*.

Furthermore, we used two fine-tuned baselines based on BLIP2 (Li et al., 2023b): BLIP2 FlanT5-XL and BLIP2 FlanT5-XXL that were reported in Guetta et al. (2023).

Moreover, we conducted experiments on knowledge transfer between WEIRD and WHOOPS! for fine-tunable methods to explore the generalization ability to another dataset.

6 Results

The results of our experiments on both WHOOPS! and WEIRD datasets are presented in Table 2. The proprietary GPT-4o model has been included as a baseline to illustrate the complexity of benchmarks for proprietary systems and to demonstrate the performance gap between human-generated and proprietary systems. It is not directly comparable to other open-source methods. The results of the linear probing baselines can be found in the Appendix B. For the TLG method and LLM-based baselines, we used facts produced by LLaVA 1.6 Mistral 7B; see the Appendix F for more details. The total number of parameters is calculated as the sum of all parameters in the method. As LLMs and text encoders use pre-generated atomic facts, we report their parameters together with the LVLMs parameters. See also Appendix D for more details of the generated facts.

TLG achieves an accuracy of 73.54% on WHOOPS! and 87.57% on WEIRD, demonstrating the state-of-the-art performance both datasets.

BLIP2 FlanT5 vs. TLG Next, we compare our best-performing approach to the baselines from Guetta et al. (2023). TLG outperforms the

Method	# Total	Mode	WHOOPS!	WEIRD
Humans	–	–	92.00	82.22
BLIP2 FlanT5-XL	3.94B	fine-tuned	60.00	71.47
BLIP2 FlanT5-XXL	12.4B		73.00	72.31
BLIP2 FlanT5-XXL	12.4B	zero-shot	50.00	63.84
nanoLLaVA Qwen1.5 0.5B	1.05B		66.66	70.90
LLaVA 1.6 Mistral 7B	7.57B		56.86	61.18
LLaVA 1.6 Vicuna 7B	7.06B		65.68	76.54
LLaVA 1.6 Vicuna 13B	13.4B		56.37	58.36
InstructBLIP Vicuna 7B	7B		61.27	69.41
InstructBLIP Vicuna 13B	13B		62.24	66.58
Qwen2.5 7B Instruct	15.18B	zero-shot	67.65	66.46
Gemma2-9B	16.57B		73.04	82.92
LP - LLaVA	13B	fine-tuned	73.50	85.26
CLIP	0.65B	–	60.78	81.57
TLG (Ours)	8B	fine-tuned	**73.54**	**87.57**
GPT-4o	–	zero-shot	79.90	81.64

Table 2: The results of different approaches on WHOOPS! and WEIRD datasets. Both benchmarks are balanced and accuracy is the evaluation metric. Fine-tuned methods are displayed at the top, while zero-shot methods are presented in the middle. The best linear probing results for all configurations along with our method are displayed at the bottom.

original fine-tuned approach (BLIP2-FLAN-T5-XXL). This suggests that the task of detecting anomalous images should be tackled by fine-tuning a compact classifier on either textual representations or images, rather than adapting an entire LVLM for this purpose.

Linear Probing and CLIP vs. TLG The results of our baselines, which were conducted using Linear Probing and CLIP, are detailed in the Appendices B, C. For the LLaVA models, hidden states of the Vicuna 13B achieved the second-best accuracy on both datasets, with 73.50% on WHOOPS! with prompt and 85.26% on WEIRD in image-only mode. Since WHOOPS! is a smaller dataset, evaluating methods with cross-validation results in high variance, making the ranking of methods less stable. However, the strong performance on WEIRD supports the effectiveness of this approach.

As for the CLIP baseline, OpenAI/CLIP excelled with an accuracy of 60.78% in zero-shot mode for WHOOPS!. On the other hand, on the WEIRD dataset, SigLIP outperformed other models, achieving an accuracy of 81.57% in fine-tuning mode.

LLM Qwen2.5-7B-Instruct achieved a relatively high score of 67.65% on WHOOPS! and 66.46% on WEIRD. However, it falls behind Gemma2-9B-Instruct with a score of 73.04% on WHOOPS! and 82.92% on WEIRD. Although LLMs show strong performance, they require more computing resources than TLG.

GPT-4o performance illustrates the complexity of the benchmarks for proprietary systems and demonstrates the performance gap between human-generated content and proprietary systems (it should not be directly compared with other open-source methods). The results are rather surprising; GPT-4o outperforms all the methods mentioned here on the WHOOPS! dataset (Guetta et al., 2023). However, it lags significantly behind all the considered baselines and our method on the newly generated WEIRD dataset.

Method	#	Accuracy
WEIRD→WHOOPS!		
BLIP-XL	4B	70.59
BLIP-XXL	12B	72.06
LP (+Prompt)	13B	72.06
LP (Image only)	13B	**75.00**
TLG (Ours)	8B	74.02
WHOOPS!→WEIRD		
BLIP-XL	4B	72.11
BLIP-XXL	12B	75.06
LP (+Prompt)	13B	74.69
LP (Image only)	13B	79.61
TLG (Ours)	8B	**83.05**

Table 3: Knowledge transfer between datasets. WEIRD→WHOOPS! means that the approach has been fine-tuned on the WEIRD dataset and tested on the WHOOPS! dataset.

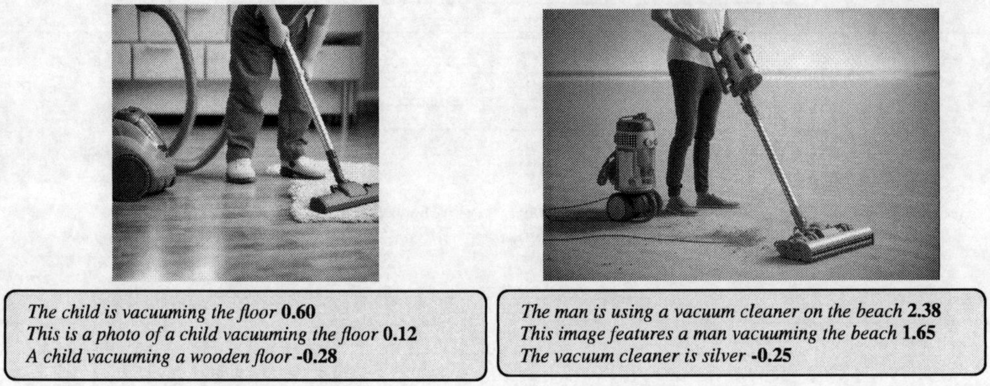

Figure 3: A pair of images from WHOOPS! with corresponding generated atomic facts. The normal image is on the left, and the unusual image is on the right.

Knowledge Transfer To measure the knowledge transfer ability, we fine-tuned a model on one dataset and tested it on another. The results are shown in Table 3.

For WHOOPS!, the linear probing baseline with image-only input on 13B Vicuna backbone with WEIRD calibration outperforms other approaches with an accuracy of 75%. However, the TLG approach with *deberta-v3-large-tasksource-nli* is a second best method with an accuracy of 74.02%. As for WEIRD, TLG trained on WHOOPS! is the best performing approach - 83.05%. Linear probing in image-only mode on 13B Vicuna with a score of 79.61% accuracy. Unlike the previous setting with WEIRD training and WHOOPS! testing, there is a large gap between the best performing approach and the second. This probably indicates that our approach is robust to a small training set, while linear probing requires a larger amount of data for calibration.

TLG Attention Scores Analysis Since TLG is based on a learning classifier that includes part of assigning an attention weight to each fact, we interpreted the meaning of these scores. The example of the score distribution for images is shown in Figure 3. In fact, TLG assigns higher attention weights to facts that violate common sense. In this example, the fact *"The vacuum cleaner is silver and purple"* has a lower score than the more inconsistent fact *"The man is using a vacuum cleaner on the beach"*. As a result, TLG gives higher scores to more strange facts, meaning that TLG could also be used as a pure text reality ranker, rating the realism of text facts.

7 Conclusion

In this work, we propose a straightforward yet effective approach to visual common sense recognition. Our method exploits an imperfection in LVLMs, causing them to generate hallucinations when presented with unrealistic or strange images. The method entails transitioning to a text modality and addressing the problem from this perspective. Our three-step process involves generating atomic facts, encoding atomic facts with Transformer-based text encoder, and training classifier based on attention-pooling to detect strange images.

Despite the shift in modality, our approach outperforms previous baselines and other supervised methods applied in the image domain, including CLIP-based image encoders and linear probing of LVLMs.

In addition, we developed a methodology to synthesize strange images. Using this methodology, we created WEIRD, a dataset consisting of 824 images that include both strange and normal visuals, which we have made openly available. Surprisingly, our TLG method outperformed the proprietary GPT-4o on our newly generated WEIRD benchmark.

Limitations

First, we acknowledge that we did not consider all possible open LVLMs that became available recently, such as Qwen2.5-VL. Also, among the proprietary systems, we only evaluated GPT-4o. However, we believe that our choice of both proprietary and open models was representative of the state-of-the-art.

Second, although we tested several prompts for zero-shot baselines and selected the best one, more prompt engineering work could lead to better performance.

Ethics Statement

We have carefully curated the generated WEIRD dataset, and we have not encountered any inappropriate or offensive content within it.

References

Jinze Bai, Shuai Bai, Yunfei Chu, Zeyu Cui, Kai Dang, Xiaodong Deng, Yang Fan, Wenbin Ge, Yu Han, Fei Huang, Binyuan Hui, Luo Ji, Mei Li, Junyang Lin, Runji Lin, Dayiheng Liu, Gao Liu, Chengqiang Lu, Keming Lu, Jianxin Ma, Rui Men, Xingzhang Ren, Xuancheng Ren, Chuanqi Tan, Sinan Tan, Jianhong Tu, Peng Wang, Shijie Wang, Wei Wang, Shengguang Wu, Benfeng Xu, Jin Xu, An Yang, Hao Yang, Jian Yang, Shusheng Yang, Yang Yao, Bowen Yu, Hongyi Yuan, Zheng Yuan, Jianwei Zhang, Xingxuan Zhang, Yichang Zhang, Zhenru Zhang, Chang Zhou, Jingren Zhou, Xiaohuan Zhou, and Tianhang Zhu. 2023. Qwen technical report. *CoRR*, abs/2309.16609.

Samuel R. Bowman, Gabor Angeli, Christopher Potts, and Christopher D. Manning. 2015. A large annotated corpus for learning natural language inference. In *Proceedings of the 2015 Conference on Empirical Methods in Natural Language Processing, EMNLP 2015, Lisbon, Portugal, September 17-21, 2015*, pages 632–642. The Association for Computational Linguistics.

Wei-Lin Chiang, Zhuohan Li, Zi Lin, Ying Sheng, Zhanghao Wu, Hao Zhang, Lianmin Zheng, Siyuan Zhuang, Yonghao Zhuang, Joseph E. Gonzalez, Ion Stoica, and Eric P. Xing. 2023. Vicuna: An open-source chatbot impressing gpt-4 with 90%* chatgpt quality.

Nitzan Bitton Guetta, Yonatan Bitton, Jack Hessel, Ludwig Schmidt, Yuval Elovici, Gabriel Stanovsky, and Roy Schwartz. 2023. Breaking common sense: Whoops! A vision-and-language benchmark of synthetic and compositional images. In *IEEE/CVF International Conference on Computer Vision, ICCV 2023, Paris, France, October 1-6, 2023*, pages 2616–2627. IEEE.

Albert Q. Jiang, Alexandre Sablayrolles, Arthur Mensch, Chris Bamford, Devendra Singh Chaplot, Diego de Las Casas, Florian Bressand, Gianna Lengyel, Guillaume Lample, Lucile Saulnier, Lélio Renard Lavaud, Marie-Anne Lachaux, Pierre Stock, Teven Le Scao, Thibaut Lavril, Thomas Wang, Timothée Lacroix, and William El Sayed. 2023. Mistral 7b. *CoRR*, abs/2310.06825.

Liqiang Jing, Ruosen Li, Yunmo Chen, Mengzhao Jia, and Xinya Du. 2023. FAITHSCORE: evaluating hallucinations in large vision-language models. *CoRR*, abs/2311.01477.

Junnan Li, Dongxu Li, Silvio Savarese, and Steven C. H. Hoi. 2023a. BLIP-2: bootstrapping language-image pre-training with frozen image encoders and large language models. In *International Conference on Machine Learning, ICML 2023, 23-29 July 2023, Honolulu, Hawaii, USA*, volume 202 of *Proceedings of Machine Learning Research*, pages 19730–19742. PMLR.

Junnan Li, Dongxu Li, Silvio Savarese, and Steven C. H. Hoi. 2023b. BLIP-2: bootstrapping language-image pre-training with frozen image encoders and large language models. In *International Conference on Machine Learning, ICML 2023, 23-29 July 2023, Honolulu, Hawaii, USA*, volume 202 of *Proceedings of Machine Learning Research*, pages 19730–19742. PMLR.

Chin-Yew Lin. 2004. ROUGE: A package for automatic evaluation of summaries. In *Text Summarization Branches Out*, pages 74–81, Barcelona, Spain. Association for Computational Linguistics.

Haotian Liu, Chunyuan Li, Yuheng Li, and Yong Jae Lee. 2024a. Improved baselines with visual instruction tuning. In *IEEE/CVF Conference on Computer Vision and Pattern Recognition, CVPR 2024, Seattle, WA, USA, June 16-22, 2024*, pages 26286–26296. IEEE.

Jiazhen Liu, Yuhan Fu, Ruobing Xie, Runquan Xie, Xingwu Sun, Fengzong Lian, Zhanhui Kang, and Xirong Li. 2024b. Phd: A prompted visual hallucination evaluation dataset. *CoRR*, abs/2403.11116.

Ivan Maksimov, Vasily Konovalov, and Andrei Glinskii. 2024. DeepPavlov at SemEval-2024 task 6: Detection of hallucinations and overgeneration mistakes with an ensemble of transformer-based models. In *Proceedings of the 18th International Workshop on Semantic Evaluation (SemEval-2024)*, pages 274–278, Mexico City, Mexico. Association for Computational Linguistics.

Potsawee Manakul, Adian Liusie, and Mark J. F. Gales. 2023a. MQAG: multiple-choice question answering and generation for assessing information consistency in summarization. In *Proceedings of the 13th International Joint Conference on Natural Language Processing and the 3rd Conference of the Asia-Pacific Chapter of the Association for Computational Linguistics, IJCNLP 2023 -Volume 1: Long Papers, Nusa Dua, Bali, November 1 - 4, 2023*, pages 39–53. Association for Computational Linguistics.

Potsawee Manakul, Adian Liusie, and Mark J. F. Gales. 2023b. Selfcheckgpt: Zero-resource black-box hallucination detection for generative large language models. In *Proceedings of the 2023 Conference on Empirical Methods in Natural Language Processing, EMNLP 2023, Singapore, December 6-10, 2023*, pages 9004–9017. Association for Computational Linguistics.

Sewon Min, Kalpesh Krishna, Xinxi Lyu, Mike Lewis, Wen-tau Yih, Pang Koh, Mohit Iyyer, Luke Zettlemoyer, and Hannaneh Hajishirzi. 2023. FActScore: Fine-grained atomic evaluation of factual precision in long form text generation. In *Proceedings of the 2023 Conference on Empirical Methods in Natural Language Processing*, pages 12076–12100, Singapore. Association for Computational Linguistics.

Alec Radford, Jong Wook Kim, Chris Hallacy, Aditya Ramesh, Gabriel Goh, Sandhini Agarwal, Girish Sastry, Amanda Askell, Pamela Mishkin, Jack Clark, Gretchen Krueger, and Ilya Sutskever. 2021. Learning transferable visual models from natural language supervision. In *Proceedings of the 38th International Conference on Machine Learning, ICML 2021, 18-24 July 2021, Virtual Event*, volume 139 of *Proceedings of Machine Learning Research*, pages 8748–8763. PMLR.

Nils Reimers and Iryna Gurevych. 2019. Sentence-bert: Sentence embeddings using siamese bert-networks. In *Proceedings of the 2019 Conference on Empirical Methods in Natural Language Processing and the 9th International Joint Conference on Natural Language Processing, EMNLP-IJCNLP 2019, Hong Kong, China, November 3-7, 2019*, pages 3980–3990. Association for Computational Linguistics.

Elisei Rykov, Kseniia Petrushina, Kseniia Titova, Alexander Panchenko, and Vasily Konovalov. 2025. Don't fight hallucinations, use them: Estimating image realism using nli over atomic facts. *Preprint*, arXiv:2503.15948.

Christoph Schuhmann, Romain Beaumont, Richard Vencu, Cade Gordon, Ross Wightman, Mehdi Cherti, Theo Coombes, Aarush Katta, Clayton Mullis, Mitchell Wortsman, Patrick Schramowski, Srivatsa Kundurthy, Katherine Crowson, Ludwig Schmidt, Robert Kaczmarczyk, and Jenia Jitsev. 2022. LAION-5B: an open large-scale dataset for training next generation image-text models. In *Advances in Neural Information Processing Systems 35: Annual Conference on Neural Information Processing Systems 2022, NeurIPS 2022, New Orleans, LA, USA, November 28 - December 9, 2022*.

Damien Sileo. 2024. tasksource: A large collection of NLP tasks with a structured dataset preprocessing framework. In *Proceedings of the 2024 Joint International Conference on Computational Linguistics, Language Resources and Evaluation (LREC-COLING 2024)*, pages 15655–15684, Torino, Italia. ELRA and ICCL.

Gemma Team. 2024. Gemma.

Ashwin K. Vijayakumar, Michael Cogswell, Ramprasaath R. Selvaraju, Qing Sun, Stefan Lee, David J. Crandall, and Dhruv Batra. 2016. Diverse beam search: Decoding diverse solutions from neural sequence models. *CoRR*, abs/1610.02424.

Yizhong Wang, Yeganeh Kordi, Swaroop Mishra, Alisa Liu, Noah A. Smith, Daniel Khashabi, and Hannaneh Hajishirzi. 2023. Self-instruct: Aligning language models with self-generated instructions. In *Proceedings of the 61st Annual Meeting of the Association for Computational Linguistics (Volume 1: Long Papers)*, pages 13484–13508, Toronto, Canada. Association for Computational Linguistics.

Adina Williams, Nikita Nangia, and Samuel Bowman. 2018. A broad-coverage challenge corpus for sentence understanding through inference. In *Proceedings of the 2018 Conference of the North American Chapter of the Association for Computational Linguistics: Human Language Technologies, Volume 1 (Long Papers)*, pages 1112–1122. Association for Computational Linguistics.

An Yang, Baosong Yang, Beichen Zhang, Binyuan Hui, Bo Zheng, Bowen Yu, Chengyuan Li, Dayiheng Liu, Fei Huang, Haoran Wei, Huan Lin, Jian Yang, Jianhong Tu, Jianwei Zhang, Jianxin Yang, Jiaxi Yang, Jingren Zhou, Junyang Lin, Kai Dang, Keming Lu, Keqin Bao, Kexin Yang, Le Yu, Mei Li, Mingfeng Xue, Pei Zhang, Qin Zhu, Rui Men, Runji Lin, Tianhao Li, Tingyu Xia, Xingzhang Ren, Xuancheng Ren, Yang Fan, Yang Su, Yichang Zhang, Yu Wan, Yuqiong Liu, Zeyu Cui, Zhenru Zhang, and Zihan Qiu. 2024. Qwen2.5 technical report. *CoRR*, abs/2412.15115.

Rowan Zellers, Yonatan Bisk, Ali Farhadi, and Yejin Choi. 2019. From recognition to cognition: Visual commonsense reasoning. In *IEEE Conference on Computer Vision and Pattern Recognition, CVPR 2019, Long Beach, CA, USA, June 16-20, 2019*, pages 6720–6731. Computer Vision Foundation / IEEE.

Xiaohua Zhai, Basil Mustafa, Alexander Kolesnikov, and Lucas Beyer. 2023. Sigmoid loss for language image pre-training. In *IEEE/CVF International Conference on Computer Vision, ICCV 2023, Paris, France, October 1-6, 2023*, pages 11941–11952. IEEE.

A Performance on WEIRD with Standard Deviation

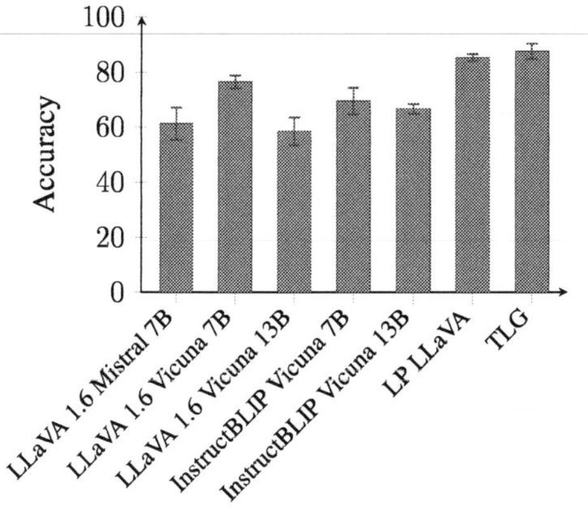

Figure 4: Accuracy with standard deviation for different setups

B Linear Probing Baseline

We collect hidden states by passing the image with corresponding to the setup (**Image only**, **+Prompt**) prompt through LLaVA decoder. The results are presented in Table 4.

We trained a logistic regression with L2 regularization, with a maximum of 100 iterations and a tolerance of 0.1 on standardized hidden states.

Model	Image only	+Prompt
WHOOPS!		
LLaVA 1.6 Mistral 7B	67.63	67.13
LLaVA 1.6 Vicuna 7B	73.01	72.02
LLaVA 1.6 Vicuna 13B	69.06	**73.50**
WEIRD		
LLaVA 1.6 Mistral 7B	78.13	81.82
LLaVA 1.6 Vicuna 7B	84.65	83.91
LLaVA 1.6 Vicuna 13B	**85.26**	84.02

Table 4: Linear probing baseline results on WHOOPS! and WEIRD.

C CLIP Baseline

We fine-tuned the model for 5 epochs with batch size 1 using AdamW optimizer with learning rate 1e-3. Other hyperparameters are the same as in the HuggingFace trainer.

The detailed results for WHOOPS! and WEIRD are given in Table 5. An interesting result is that SigLIP is more accurate than the standard CLIP-based models of OpenAI and LAION.

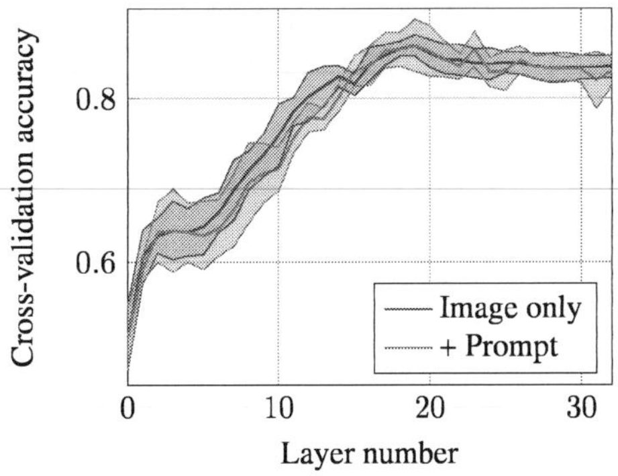

Figure 5: Cross-validation accuracy depending on the LLaVA 1.6 Vicuna 13B index layer for linear probing on the WEIRD dataset. Layers containing the most relevant information are in the middle of the decoder.

Model	#	zero-shot	fine-tuned
WHOOPS!			
OpenAI/CLIP	0.15B	**60.78**	56.86
Google/SigLIP	0.88B	50.49	73.01
LAION/CLIP	0.43B	53.92	54.39
WEIRD			
OpenAI/CLIP	0.15B	56.15	65.65
Google/SigLIP	0.88B	48.87	**81.57**
LAION/CLIP	0.43B	57.34	74.86

Table 5: CLIP results on WHOOPS! and WEIRD.

D Analysis of the Generated Facts

Category	Keywords
common	*common* *usual* *normal* *natural* *real*
weird	*unusual* *strange* *playful* *creative* *unreal* *weird*
real (as not generated)	*real* *realistic* *photo*
digital	*digital* *generated* *3D* *fantastic* *rendering* *artistic*

Table 6: List of keywords with corresponding categories to analyze generated atomic facts.

LLaVA Backbone	Type	Length	ROUGE	Cosine Similarity	Marker words			
					common	weird	real	digital
WHOOPS!								
Mistral-7B	normal	61.80	45.46	79.65	9	1	33	37
	strange	64.34	46.28	79.57	5	12	19	68
Qwen-0.5B	normal	140.15	45.02	83.19	55	4	20	8
	strange	144.01	45.07	83.36	46	26	17	17
Vicuna-7B	normal	99.57	64.71	88.27	8	0	54	42
	strange	103.63	63.75	87.88	5	4	25	66
Vicuna-13B	normal	86.69	64.24	88.24	8	0	21	37
	strange	92.88	64.64	88.13	4	8	15	58
WEIRD								
Mistral-7B	normal	72.94	52.43	72.94	24	1	95	201
	strange	77.81	51.37	77.81	31	57	79	270
Qwen-0.5B	normal	129.17	54.67	68.46	170	24	35	36
	strange	131.84	54.70	68.40	184	130	24	69
Vicuna-7B	normal	74.39	60.09	68.41	6	1	146	213
	strange	79.35	60.32	68.55	3	16	130	262
Vicuna-13B	normal	67.13	58.04	69.36	10	0	108	242
	strange	69.82	59.08	69.46	3	19	106	291

Table 7: Metrics for generated atomic facts on the WHOOPS! and WEIRD datasets are computed separately for each of the four models, assessing them on both normal and strange images. ROUGE and Cosine Similarity metrics evaluate the similarity of facts derived from a single image, while marker words denote the presence of at least one characteristic marker term in the group of facts. From these results, we can conclude that the facts generated by *llava-v1.6-mistral-7b* are of the finest quality in atomicity — they are the briefest and exhibit the greatest semantic independence.

We measured Cosine Similarity of the generated facts by using *all-MiniLM-L6-v2*[5] embedder. We also calculated ROUGE (Lin, 2004) metric for lexical similarity. We calculate the metric values pair-wise for each unique pair of facts and then averaging the results. There is no significant difference in lexical/semantic similarity (as measured by ROUGE and Cosine Similarity) between strange and normal images within the same LLaVA. However, a significant difference can be observed when comparing similarity between different LLaVAs. In Table 7 we provide metrics on generated atomic facts. We noticed that there are several groups of different marker words that all LVLMs tend to generate. Table 6 shows the exact list of marker words for each observed group.

nanoLLaVA 1.5B generates significantly different facts from all other LLaVA models in terms of used vocabulary. By analyzing occurring marker words, it becomes evident that nanoLLaVA-1.5 more frequently employs words from the `common` and `weird` sets, indicating a greater tendency to comment on the plausibility of images and use evaluative terms. Conversely, it uses words from the `real` and `digital` sets less often. The facts of nanoLLaVA-1.5 are significantly longer than others.

LLaVA 1.6 Mistral 7B vs LLaVA 1.6 Vicuna 7B The difference between facts generated by these two is quite noticeable. The Mistral-based LLaVA generates the shorter responses, and judging by the ROUGE metric, these responses are less similar to each other. In terms of the atomicity of the generated facts, the facts produced by Mistral can be considered more qualitative. However, the presence of digital markers can be misleading for the model.

LLaVA 1.6 Vicuna 7B vs 13B The metrics of both Vicuna-based models are similar; however, the generations from 13B are shorter on average. We also notice that the facts generated for strange images are generally longer than those for truthful ones.

[5]https://hf.co/sentence-transformers/all-MiniLM-L6-v2

E Checkpoints

For generating atomic facts we leverage the following LVLMs:

- llava-v1.6-mistral-7b-hf: a 7B LVLM with based on a Mistral (Jiang et al., 2023);
- nanoLLaVA-1.5: a 2B LVLM based on a Qwen1.5-0.5B (Bai et al., 2023);
- llava-v1.6-vicuna-7b-hf: a 7B LVLM based on a Vicuna (Chiang et al., 2023);
- llava-v1.6-vicuna-13b-hf: a 13B LVLM based on a Vicuna.

The following encoders were used for our main approach:

- deberta-v3-large: an original DeBERTa without fine-tuning;
- nli-deberta-v3-large: DeBERTa fine-tuned by Sentence Transformer (Reimers and Gurevych, 2019) on NLI datasets. Specifically, the model was fine-tuned on the SNLI (Bowman et al., 2015) and MultiNLI (Williams et al., 2018) datasets.
- deberta-v3-large-tasksource-nli: a multi-task text encoder based on DeBERTa-v3-large fine-tuned on 600 `tasksource` tasks, outperforming every publicly available text encoder of comparable size in an external evaluation (Sileo, 2024).

As for the CLIP-based baseline, the following models were utilized:

- clip-vit-base-patch32: a pre-trained CLIP model published by OpenAI with 0.15B parameters (Radford et al., 2021).
- siglip-so400m-patch14-384: a novel image encoder with 0.88B parameters trained by Google. This encoder inherits the CLIP architecture but features a better loss function (Zhai et al., 2023).
- CLIP-ViT-L-14-laion2B-s32B-b82K: a pre-trained CLIP encoder with 0.43B parameters, trained on the LAION-2B dataset (Schuhmann et al., 2022).

For the LLM zero-shot baseline, these LLMs were used:

- Qwen2.5-7B-Instruct: a 7B instruction-tuned LLM trained by Qwen (Yang et al., 2024).
- Gemma-2-9b-it: a 9B instruction-tuned LLM trained by Google (Team, 2024).

F TLG Evaluation Details

Detailed results of TLG evaluation are given in Table 8. A distinct pattern emerges: DeBERTa models fine-tuned on the `tasksource` collection outperform methods that rely on alternative text encoders, largely due to their enhanced encoding capabilities. This superiority can be attributed to extensive fine-tuning on a diverse range of knowledge-intensive tasks sourced from the `tasksource` repository. Using `tasksource` DeBERTa, the best performance was achieved with Mistral-7B backbone, while the poorest performance was observed with the smallest Qwen-0.5B model, and Vicuna fell in the middle.

The results, averaged over five folds, for the evaluated text encoders paired with various LLaVAs on both benchmarks are presented in Table 8. The highest performance for both benchmarks was achieved by generating facts using LLaVA 1.6 Mistral 7B in conjunction with *deberta-v3-large-tasksource-nli* as the text encoder. Thus, we used facts produced by LLaVA 1.6 Mistral 7B in our other approaches and baselines.

Text Encoder	**LLaVA Backbone**			
	Mistral-7B	Vicuna-7B	Vicuna-13B	Qwen-0.5B
	WEIRD Cross-Validation			
deberta-v3-large-tasksource-nli	**87.57**	80.51	81.37	77.11
nli-deberta-v3-large	77.97	74.00	77.11	74.57
deberta-v3-large	59.92	63.86	63.59	63.29
	WHOOPS! Cross-Validation			
deberta-v3-large-tasksource-nli	**73.54**	69.15	64.72	64.68
nli-deberta-v3-large	64.60	63.61	66.59	65.15
deberta-v3-large	49.49	50.48	47.57	53.93

Table 8: The results of our approach with various LVLMs and text encoders for both benchmarks, WHOOPS! and WEIRD, are presented. Accuracy, averaged over five folds, serves as the performance metric. For both benchmarks, LLaVa 1.6 Mistral-7B paired with *deberta-v3-large-tasksource-nli* demonstrates the best outcome. A clear trend emerges: tasksource DeBERTa outperforms all others, partly due to its superior encoding capabilities. This trend is clearer for the WEIRD dataset due to its larger size.

G Examples of Strange Images From WEIRD

H Examples of Normal Images From WEIRD

I Prompt for WEIRD Samples Generation Using GPT-4o

```
Your task is to generate a new COMMONSENSE_CATEGORY, EXPLANATION, NORMAL_CAPTION, STRANGE_CAPTION using
the presented ones from the EXAMPLES.
COMMONSENSE_CATEGORY is the category of common sense disturbance, so follow this information when
creating your own captions, as they must disturb common sense in the same category.
Use presented COMMONSENSE_CATEGORIES only as an example, because you task is to generate a new one.
After generating a new COMMONSENSE_CATEGORY, generate 1 new pair based on this category.
Each pair should start with EXPLANATION. EXPLANATION is a description of an inconsistent situation.
You should create EXPLANATION first.
Next, based on EXPLANATION, generate NORMAL_CAPTION and a STRANGE_CAPTION.
NORMAL_CAPTION describes an image that is suitable for common sense, it does not contradict facts about
the world, etc.
On the other hand, STRANGE_CAPTION contradicts common sense. Also, captions can represent past time,
so a caption about something that happened a long time ago is not strange.
Do not generate something that is too hard to understand or imagine.
Make the captions as specific and descriptive as possible. Describe all the details.
Generate only 1 pair of EXPLANATION, NORMAL_CAPTION and a STRANGE_CAPTION.

EXAMPLES:

COMMONSENSE_CATEGORY: Tool Misapplication
EXPLANATION: A whisk is a kitchen tool specifically designed for mixing ingredients together smoothly
or incorporating air into a mixture, such as when making whipped cream or beating eggs. Its structure,
consisting of multiple loops of wire, is not intended for hammering nails into wood. Using a whisk to
hammer nails is not only ineffective but is likely to damage the whisk and offer no benefit, as its
delicate wires are neither strong nor solid enough to drive nails.
NORMAL_CAPTION: A whisk being used to beat eggs in a bowl
STRANGE_CAPTION: A whisk being used to hammer nails into a wooden plank

COMMONSENSE_CATEGORY: Impossible interaction
EXPLANATION: Cats are known for their playful and curious nature, but they do not have the physical
ability to solve complex math problems, as they lack the understanding and cognitive functions necessary
for such tasks.
NORMAL_CAPTION: a cat playing with a ball of yarn on the floor
STRANGE_CAPTION: A cat solving a complex math equation on a blackboard.

COMMONSENSE_CATEGORY: Untypical behavior
EXPLANATION: Octopuses are sea creatures that live underwater and are adapted to life in the ocean.
However, seeing an octopus wearing clothes, something made specifically for humans to provide warmth
and protection, is highly unusual and outside the realms of normal behavior or biological needs.
NORMAL_CAPTION: An octopus swimming in the ocean.
STRANGE_CAPTION: An octopus wearing a suit and tie.

COMMONSENSE_CATEGORY: Inappropriate Object Utility
EXPLANATION: Hairdryers are designed to dry hair by blowing warm air. Using a hairdryer to open a locked
door is incorrect and impractical, as hairdryers do not have the functionality or mechanism to open
locks.
NORMAL_CAPTION: A person drying their hair with a hairdryer in front of a mirror.
STRANGE_CAPTION: A person using a hairdryer to open a locked door.
```

Figure 6: Example of prompt used for synthetic samples generation for WEIRD benchmark. In total, 5 random categories from the task pool were taken on each step of generation. The model is expected to generate a new common sense category, a new explanation and a pair of caption. Further, captions are used for image generation.

ColorFoil: Investigating Color Blindness in Large Vision and Language Models

Ahnaf Mozib Samin[†◇*] **M Firoz Ahmed**[△] **Md. Mushtaq Shahriyar Rafee**[§]
[†]Queen's University, Kingston, Canada
[◇]University of Malta, Msida, Malta
[△]Shahjalal University of Science and Technology, Sylhet, Bangladesh
[§]Metropolitan University, Sylhet, Bangladesh
ahnaf.samin@queensu.ca[†], mfiroz.sust@gmail.com[△], rafee@metrouni.edu.bd[§]

Abstract

With the utilization of Transformer architecture, large Vision and Language (V&L) models have shown promising performance in even zero-shot settings. Several studies, however, indicate a lack of robustness of the models when dealing with complex linguistics and visual attributes. In this work, we introduce a novel V&L benchmark - ColorFoil, by creating color-related foils to assess the models' perception ability to detect colors like red, white, green, etc. We evaluate seven state-of-the-art V&L models including CLIP, ViLT, GroupViT, and BridgeTower, etc. in a zero-shot setting and present intriguing findings from the V&L models. The experimental evaluation indicates that ViLT and BridgeTower demonstrate much better color perception capabilities compared to CLIP and its variants and GroupViT. Moreover, CLIP-based models and GroupViT struggle to distinguish colors that are visually distinct to humans with normal color perception ability.

1 Introduction

Vision and language models (V&L) have exhibited improved performance for many V&L tasks in recent years (Lu et al., 2019; Su et al., 2019; Chen et al., 2020; Li et al., 2020; Radford et al., 2021; Dou et al., 2022). Thus, the current paradigm has now been shifting towards zero-shot learning, where models are evaluated without fine-tuning for specific tasks (Radford et al., 2021). Large-scale V&L models, in particular, show promise for task-independent zero-shot evaluation (Radford et al., 2021).

Several studies have been conducted to perform comprehensive evaluations of V&L models on a variety of tasks to identify their strengths and weaknesses (Agrawal et al., 2016; Jabri et al., 2016; Goyal et al., 2017; Shekhar et al., 2017; Agarwal et al., 2020). For instance, the VALSE evaluation benchmark has been proposed to assess the state-of-art V&L models for challenging linguistic constructs (Parcalabescu et al., 2021a). Therefore, five distinct tasks, including existence, plurality, counting, relations, actions, and coreference, have been introduced. In this benchmark, foils are generated from the existing V&L datasets for each of the tasks. A foil is referred to as a distractor or slightly incorrect example that is passed along with the correct example to the V&L model to assess the model's ability to correctly distinguish them (Shekhar et al., 2017; Parcalabescu et al., 2021a). Although the existing V&L benchmarks like VALSE help the community to test the capabilities of V&L models, there is still much work to be done to evaluate the robustness and generalizability of the models on numerous other tasks. It remains unknown how well the large V&L models can perceive colors from the visual content.

Color perception requires a human-like understanding of visual content. Thus, by evaluating the V&L models on color attributes, we can determine how closely the large V&L models perceive colors to humans. A V&L model can be biased towards detecting particular colors and perform poorly with others. Therefore, it is essential to investigate it in order to improve the explainability and interpretability of the models. By assessing the V&L models with their color-perception ability, we can ensure robustness in real-life applications.

In this study, we aim to shed light on the following research question: how well can the state-of-the-art large-scale V&L models perceive color-related attributes, such as red, green, yellow, etc.? Our contributions are mainly twofold:

- We introduce a novel V&L benchmark **ColorFoil** by creating foils from the MS COCO and Flickr30k datasets (Lin et al., 2014; Plummer et al., 2015) to investigate how well the

*Work performed while at University of Malta.

Proceedings of the 2025 Conference of the Nations of the Americas Chapter of the Association for Computational Linguistics: Human Language Technologies (Volume 4: Student Research Workshop), pages 294–300
April 30 - May 1, 2025 ©2025 Association for Computational Linguistics

models perceive and identify the color-related attributes.

- We perform a comparison between seven of the state-of-the-art V&L models including CLIP (Radford et al., 2021), ViLT (Kim et al., 2021), ViT (Dosovitskiy et al., 2020) and BridgeTower(Xu et al., 2022b) using our benchmark.

The outline of this paper is as follows. We provide a background study in Section 2. In Section 3, we describe the process of constructing ColorFoil from the MS COCO dataset. Experiments and results are discussed in Section 4. In Section 5, we discuss the limitations of our work. Ethical considerations are provided in 5. A conclusion and future scope is presented in Section 5.

2 Background

V&L Models The current state-of-art models are first pre-trained in a self-supervised way with a multi-task learning objective. The learning objectives can be predicting the masked texts or masked region in the images, determining whether or not the image and text corresponds, etc. The text and image input features can be concatenated together and passed to a Transformer encoder. This approach is known as single stream. Alternatively, the text and image inputs can be separately encoded to two different Transformers and then additional layers to merge them into multi-modal features.

CLIP Contrastive Language-Image Pre-training (CLIP) is a V&L model that is pre-trained with 400M image-text pairs with a contrastive objective (Radford et al., 2021). The model jointly trains a text encoder and an image encoder to maximize the cosine similarity of the image-text embeddings of real pairing while minimizing the cosine similarity of the embeddings of the incorrect pairings within a multi-modal embedding space. Each of the encoders are based on transformers. CLIP demonstrates the ability to perform zero-shot visual classification, object detection, and image generation tasks.

ViLT Vision-and-Language Transformer (ViLT) is pre-trained using a Transformer with more than 4M images with two objectives such as image text matching and masked language modeling (Kim et al., 2021). The text embedding and the image features are concatenated into a sequence and then fed into the transformer. Thus, ViLT is a single stream model. ViLT achieves competitive or better performance than other V&L models on downstream tasks while being 10 times faster due to simpler processing of visual inputs.

BridgeTower There is a visual encoder, a textual encoder and a cross-modal encoder with multiple lightweight bridge layers in the BridgeTower architecture (Xu et al., 2022b). The top layers of the unimodal encoders and each layer of the cross-modal encoder are connected with the bridge layers, thus enabling extensive interactions at each layer of the cross-modal encoder. Each of visual, textual and cross-modal encoders is transformer-based encoders. The model is pre-trained with 4M images with two common objectives: masked language modeling and image text matching. The model is found to outperform in all downstream V&L tasks with negligible additional computational cost.

ViT A Vision Transformer (ViT) is designed for image classification tasks, adapting the Transformer architecture from natural language processing (Dosovitskiy et al., 2020). It divides an image into fixed-size patches, linearly embeds each patch, and treats these embeddings as sequences akin to word tokens in text. Using self-attention mechanisms, the ViT captures global image context more effectively than convolutional networks, allowing for superior performance on large-scale image datasets. ViTs leverage transfer learning and pretraining for enhanced accuracy and efficiency.

GroupViT (Group Vision Transformer) is a variant of the Vision Transformer designed to improve efficiency and scalability in image classification tasks (Xu et al., 2022a). It enhances the standard ViT by introducing a group-wise processing mechanism, where the input image is divided into smaller groups of patches. Each group is processed independently through parallel self-attention layers, reducing computational complexity. The results from these groups are then aggregated to form a cohesive representation. GroupViT aims to retain the global context modeling capabilities of ViTs while optimizing resource usage, making it more suitable for large-scale and real-time applications.

Related Work Several V&L tasks include visual question answering (Goyal et al., 2017), visual reasoning (Suhr et al., 2018), image retrieval (Plummer et al., 2015), etc. Foiling is an approach that slightly edits the original captions to evaluate the robustness of the V&L models (Shekhar et al., 2017). Similar to our work, Shekhar et al. (2017) foiled the MS COCO dataset, and constructed the

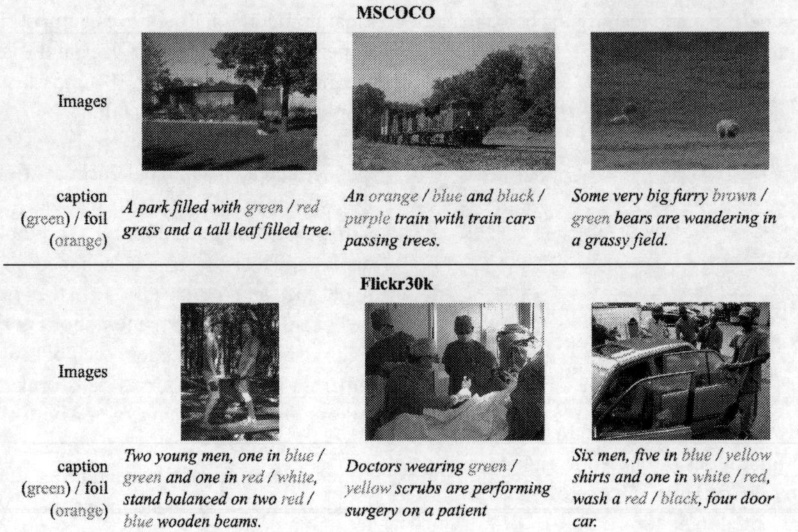

Figure 1: Examples from the ColorFoil benchmark where color-related attributes in the original captions have been modified to different colors.

FOIL-COCO dataset. However, their work did not focus on the perception of colors of the V&L models. Following the work of Shekhar et al. (2017), several studies have been performed that evaluated the V&L models (Shekhar et al., 2019; Gokhale et al., 2020; Bitton et al., 2021; Parcalabescu et al., 2021b; Rosenberg et al., 2021).

3 Construction of the ColorFoil Benchmark

The ColorFoil benchmark is automatically derived from the MS COCO (Microsoft Common Objects in Context) and Flickr30k dataset, which serves as a resource for studying image understanding, object recognition, image captioning, and visual question-answering tasks (Lin et al., 2014; Plummer et al., 2015). In the MS COCO dataset, textual annotations are provided solely for the train and validation (val) sets. To construct the ColorFoil, we obtain the images and annotations from the 2017 MS COCO validation set, resulting in a total of 5,000 image-text pairs. Among these instances, each of 2,511 pairs includes at least one word related to color. For Flickr30k dataset, we use the standard val and test sets to prepare the ColorFoil benchmark.

Our aim is to foil only the color name from the textual input, leaving the original image and the rest of the text input as it is. For example, given a caption like *A **blue** bus driving down a street past a park.* We foil the color-related word, resulting in a modified sentence like - *A **brown** bus driving down a street past a park.* If there are multiple color attributes in a caption, we foil all of them.

We utilize the **webcolors 1.3** python package to determine whether a substring within a caption corresponds to a color (Webcolors, 2023). This package encompasses a total of 147 colors. Our filtering process involves excluding captions that lack color names and selecting solely those containing at least one color name.

When replacing the original color name with a foiled alternative, we consider the most widely used colors. The chosen target colors for foiling consist of "blue", "black", "red", "pink", "yellow", "grey", "orange", "white", "green", and "brown." So, rather than utilizing the complete list of 147 colors from the **webcolors** package, we opt for a narrower selection of common colors for foiling. This decision is based on the fact that numerous colors in the package have limited practical usage (e.g. medium blue, mint cream, etc.). The target color for foiling is selected randomly from the 10 common colors. If the original color in the caption is one of the common colors, we randomly select any other common color for foiling except for the one found in the caption.

After excluding four instances of two-dimensional grayscale images due to compatibility issues with certain models, our resulting dataset

Models	1 Foil				2 Foils				4 Foils			
	MSCOCO		**Flickr30k**		**MSCOCO**		**Flickr30k**		**MSCOCO**		**Flickr30k**	
	Acc.	F1	Acc.	F1	Acc.	F1	Acc.	F1	Acc.	F1	Acc.	F1
ALIGN	86.03	93.32	87.70	93.45	79.47	88.75	81.43	89.76	71.03	83.06	74.57	85.43
AltCLIP	84.89	91.82	82.69	90.52	77.29	87.19	73.68	84.84	69.08	81.71	64.39	78.34
BridgeTower	97.31	98.63	96.83	98.32	95.71	97.81	94.46	97.15	92.61	96.16	90.81	95.18
CLIP	84.42	91.55	85.24	92.07	76.19	86.49	76.26	86.53	67.37	80.50	68.33	81.18
CLIPSeg	83.05	91.09	82.01	90.12	74.00	85.42	72.97	84.37	64.56	78.45	63.07	77.35
GroupViT	82.73	91.67	81.64	89.89	73.10	83.98	71.77	83.57	63.80	77.89	62.12	76.63
ViLT	95.69	97.79	94.29	97.06	92.83	96.28	91.85	95.35	88.74	94.04	87.38	93.27

Table 1: **Experiment results.** We evaluate seven of the state-of-the-art V&L models on the MS COCO and Flickr30k subsets from ColorFoil. Accuracy (%) and F1-scores (%) are reported. We conduct three experiments in which the models are presented different number of foils (modified caption) along with the original caption. The V&L models tend to struggle in challenging conditions with more foils. BridgeTower and ViLT outperform other V&L models including CLIP and its variants and GroupViT by a large margin.

comprises 2,507 pairs of RGB images along with their captions and foils from MSCOCO and 2500 pairs of RGB image-caption pairs from Flickr30k. To ensure data integrity, we conduct manual validation on a significant number of image-text pairs randomly selected from the benchmark and find no anomalies. Examples of original captions and corresponding foils are illustrated in Figure 1.

4 Experiments

Experimental Setup: We pass the original caption, foil as well as the corresponding image to a V&L model. The model provides the logits for each of the caption and foil corresponding to the image. We take the softmax of the logits. Our hypothesis is that a model with a well-perceivable ability to distinguish colors is supposed to provide a higher probability for the original caption and a lower probability for the foil.

We evaluate all the models in a zero-shot setting. We utilize the HuggingFace transformer library to load the models (Wolf et al., 2019). These models are chosen due to the fact that they represent different architectural variants. CLIP has a text encoder and an image encoder, which are jointly trained with a contrastive loss. ViLT is a single-stream model. BridgeTower contains multiple bridge layers that connect the uni-modal encoders with the cross-modal encoder.

The evaluation metric employed in our study is accuracy and F1-score, which are widely used in similar contexts. To elaborate, if the model accurately identifies the foil in comparison to the original caption, the accuracy of that particular example is incremented.

Results: Table 1 shows the performance of different V&L models evaluated on the ColorFoil. All the models achieve much higher accuracy compared to a baseline random classifier with a 50% accuracy. CLIP obtains 83.1% accuracy while ViLT and BridgeTower get substantially higher accuracy of 95.6% and 97.2%, respectively on the 1-Foil experiment. It is worthwhile to mention that CLIP is pre-trained with 400M images, although this model is outperformed by both ViLT and BridgeTower pre-trained with only 4M images. BridgeTower architecture, which contains multiple bridges to make connections between the uni-modal encoders and the cross-modal encoder, achieves the highest accuracy.

The relatively poor performance of CLIP is also evident in its variants, including AltCLIP (Chen et al., 2023) and CLIPSeg (Lüddecke and Ecker, 2022). While the ALIGN model outperforms CLIP, it still lags behind BridgeTower and ViLT. GroupViT, similar to CLIP, struggles to achieve high performance. This performance trend is consistent across both MSCOCO and Flickr30k datasets, reinforcing our observations. When presented with more foils alongside the original caption, the models exhibit performance degradation. Nonetheless, BridgeTower and ViLT maintain strong performance even under these challenging conditions with more foils.

We present several examples for which the CLIP model incorrectly assigns higher probabilities to the foils (See Figure 2). These examples demonstrate that the CLIP model is unable to distin-

Images			
Captions	*A surfer is riding a wave in light blue water.*	*A man in black jersey pitching in baseball game.*	*A red traffic light at night next to a Christmas Tree.*
CLIP Predictions	*A surfer is riding a wave in light brown water.*	*A man in red jersey pitching in baseball game.*	*A white traffic light at night next to a Christmas Tree.*

Figure 2: Examples for which the CLIP model wrongly choose the foils instead of the captions.

guish between blue-brown, black-red, and red-white pairs, despite the fact that they are visually distinct to most humans.

5 Conclusion and Future Work

In this work, we introduce a novel benchmark, ColorFoil, derived from the MS COCO and Flickr30k datasets, to assess the perception ability of the cutting-edge V&L models to detect colors. To this end, we foil the colors from the original captions and feed both caption and foil along with the corresponding image to the model to observe whether it can provide a higher probability for the caption or not. Seven state-of-the-art V&L models, including CLIP, ViLT, ViT, and BridgeTower, have been benchmarked using the ColorFoil. While all models outperform a random classifier, ViLT and BridgeTower are much more capable to perceive colors compared to CLIP and ViT. This intriguing finding is seen using both MS COCO and Flickr30k datasets, which strengthens our analysis.

As part of our future work, we would like to evaluate the robustness of V&L models on additional tasks by constructing foils that swap gender (man -> woman), size (small -> large), emotions (smiling -> crying), and sentence negation (playing football -> not playing football), etc.

Limitations

We consider the 10 most common colors for our foils. However, our choice of common colors is subjective and there might be other frequently used colors that are not present in our foils.

Ethical Considerations

Training V&L models using images and corresponding texts that may contain gender bias, private data, or harmful content presents challenges in manual detection. To address this, we utilize the widely recognized MS COCO and Flickr30k datasets to create the ColorFoil benchmark, as it provides a reliable foundation (Lin et al., 2014; Plummer et al., 2015).

Ensuring reproducibility is a crucial aspect of scientific research. To foster open research practices, we will make our code publicly accessible, allowing others to reproduce and verify our findings.

Acknowledgments

Work supported by the Language and Communication Technologies program of the Erasmus+ project of the European Commission.

References

Vedika Agarwal, Rakshith Shetty, and Mario Fritz. 2020. Towards causal vqa: Revealing and reducing spurious correlations by invariant and covariant semantic editing. In *Proceedings of the IEEE/CVF Conference on Computer Vision and Pattern Recognition*, pages 9690–9698.

Aishwarya Agrawal, Dhruv Batra, and Devi Parikh. 2016. Analyzing the behavior of visual question answering models. *arXiv preprint arXiv:1606.07356*.

Yonatan Bitton, Gabriel Stanovsky, Roy Schwartz, and Michael Elhadad. 2021. Automatic generation of contrast sets from scene graphs: Probing the compositional consistency of gqa. *arXiv preprint arXiv:2103.09591*.

Yen-Chun Chen, Linjie Li, Licheng Yu, Ahmed El Kholy, Faisal Ahmed, Zhe Gan, Yu Cheng, and Jingjing Liu. 2020. Uniter: Universal image-text representation learning. In *Computer Vision–ECCV 2020: 16th European Conference, Glasgow, UK, August 23–28, 2020, Proceedings, Part XXX*, pages 104–120. Springer.

Zhongzhi Chen, Guang Liu, Bo-Wen Zhang, Qinghong Yang, and Ledell Wu. 2023. Altclip: Altering the language encoder in clip for extended language capabilities. In *Findings of the Association for Computational Linguistics: ACL 2023*, pages 8666–8682.

Alexey Dosovitskiy, Lucas Beyer, Alexander Kolesnikov, Dirk Weissenborn, Xiaohua Zhai, Thomas Unterthiner, Mostafa Dehghani, Matthias Minderer, Georg Heigold, Sylvain Gelly, et al. 2020. An image is worth 16x16 words: Transformers for image recognition at scale. In *International Conference on Learning Representations*.

Zi-Yi Dou, Yichong Xu, Zhe Gan, Jianfeng Wang, Shuohang Wang, Lijuan Wang, Chenguang Zhu, Pengchuan Zhang, Lu Yuan, Nanyun Peng, et al. 2022. An empirical study of training end-to-end vision-and-language transformers. In *Proceedings of the IEEE/CVF Conference on Computer Vision and Pattern Recognition*, pages 18166–18176.

Tejas Gokhale, Pratyay Banerjee, Chitta Baral, and Yezhou Yang. 2020. Mutant: A training paradigm for out-of-distribution generalization in visual question answering. *arXiv preprint arXiv:2009.08566*.

Yash Goyal, Tejas Khot, Douglas Summers-Stay, Dhruv Batra, and Devi Parikh. 2017. Making the v in vqa matter: Elevating the role of image understanding in visual question answering. In *Proceedings of the IEEE conference on computer vision and pattern recognition*, pages 6904–6913.

Allan Jabri, Armand Joulin, and Laurens Van Der Maaten. 2016. Revisiting visual question answering baselines. In *Computer Vision–ECCV 2016: 14th European Conference, Amsterdam, The Netherlands, October 11-14, 2016, Proceedings, Part VIII 14*, pages 727–739. Springer.

Wonjae Kim, Bokyung Son, and Ildoo Kim. 2021. Vilt: Vision-and-language transformer without convolution or region supervision. In *International Conference on Machine Learning*, pages 5583–5594. PMLR.

Gen Li, Nan Duan, Yuejian Fang, Ming Gong, and Daxin Jiang. 2020. Unicoder-vl: A universal encoder for vision and language by cross-modal pre-training. In *Proceedings of the AAAI Conference on Artificial Intelligence*, volume 34, pages 11336–11344.

Tsung-Yi Lin, Michael Maire, Serge Belongie, James Hays, Pietro Perona, Deva Ramanan, Piotr Dollár, and C Lawrence Zitnick. 2014. Microsoft coco: Common objects in context. In *Computer Vision–ECCV 2014: 13th European Conference, Zurich, Switzerland, September 6-12, 2014, Proceedings, Part V 13*, pages 740–755. Springer.

Jiasen Lu, Dhruv Batra, Devi Parikh, and Stefan Lee. 2019. Vilbert: Pretraining task-agnostic visiolinguistic representations for vision-and-language tasks. *Advances in neural information processing systems*, 32.

Timo Lüddecke and Alexander Ecker. 2022. Image segmentation using text and image prompts. In *Proceedings of the IEEE/CVF conference on computer vision and pattern recognition*, pages 7086–7096.

Letitia Parcalabescu, Michele Cafagna, Lilitta Muradjan, Anette Frank, Iacer Calixto, and Albert Gatt. 2021a. Valse: A task-independent benchmark for vision and language models centered on linguistic phenomena. *arXiv preprint arXiv:2112.07566*.

Letitia Parcalabescu, Albert Gatt, Anette Frank, and Iacer Calixto. 2021b. Seeing past words: Testing the cross-modal capabilities of pretrained V&L models on counting tasks. In *Proceedings of the 1st Workshop on Multimodal Semantic Representations (MMSR)*, pages 32–44, Groningen, Netherlands (Online). Association for Computational Linguistics.

Bryan A Plummer, Liwei Wang, Chris M Cervantes, Juan C Caicedo, Julia Hockenmaier, and Svetlana Lazebnik. 2015. Flickr30k entities: Collecting region-to-phrase correspondences for richer image-to-sentence models. In *Proceedings of the IEEE international conference on computer vision*, pages 2641–2649.

Alec Radford, Jong Wook Kim, Chris Hallacy, Aditya Ramesh, Gabriel Goh, Sandhini Agarwal, Girish Sastry, Amanda Askell, Pamela Mishkin, Jack Clark, et al. 2021. Learning transferable visual models from natural language supervision. In *International conference on machine learning*, pages 8748–8763. PMLR.

Daniel Rosenberg, Itai Gat, Amir Feder, and Roi Reichart. 2021. Are vqa systems rad? measuring robustness to augmented data with focused interventions. *arXiv preprint arXiv:2106.04484*.

Ravi Shekhar, Sandro Pezzelle, Yauhen Klimovich, Aurélie Herbelot, Moin Nabi, Enver Sangineto, and Raffaella Bernardi. 2017. Foil it! find one mismatch between image and language caption. *arXiv preprint arXiv:1705.01359*.

Ravi Shekhar, Ece Takmaz, Raquel Fernández, and Raffaella Bernardi. 2019. Evaluating the representational hub of language and vision models. *arXiv preprint arXiv:1904.06038*.

Weijie Su, Xizhou Zhu, Yue Cao, Bin Li, Lewei Lu, Furu Wei, and Jifeng Dai. 2019. Vl-bert: Pre-training of generic visual-linguistic representations. *arXiv preprint arXiv:1908.08530*.

Alane Suhr, Stephanie Zhou, Ally Zhang, Iris Zhang, Huajun Bai, and Yoav Artzi. 2018. A corpus for reasoning about natural language grounded in photographs. *arXiv preprint arXiv:1811.00491*.

Webcolors. 2023. Python package index - webcolors 1.3.

Thomas Wolf, Lysandre Debut, Victor Sanh, Julien Chaumond, Clement Delangue, Anthony Moi, Pierric Cistac, Tim Rault, Rémi Louf, Morgan Funtowicz, et al. 2019. Huggingface's transformers: State-of-the-art natural language processing. *arXiv preprint arXiv:1910.03771*.

Jiarui Xu, Shalini De Mello, Sifei Liu, Wonmin Byeon, Thomas Breuel, Jan Kautz, and Xiaolong Wang. 2022a. Groupvit: Semantic segmentation emerges from text supervision. In *Proceedings of the IEEE/CVF Conference on Computer Vision and Pattern Recognition*, pages 18134–18144.

Xiao Xu, Chenfei Wu, Shachar Rosenman, Vasudev Lal, and Nan Duan. 2022b. Bridge-tower: Building bridges between encoders in vision-language representation learning. *arXiv preprint arXiv:2206.08657*.

Towards Practical and Knowledgeable LLMs for a Multilingual World: A Thesis Proposal

Bryan Li
University of Pennsylvania
Philadelphia, PA, USA
bryanli@seas.upenn.edu

Abstract

The frontier of large language model (LLM) development has largely been substantiated by knowledge-intensive tasks specified in English. In this proposed thesis, I argue for the key role that multilinguality occupies in the development of *practical* and *knowledgeable* LLMs.

First, I consider practical methods to improve LLM's performance on standard natural language processing (NLP) tasks by leveraging their existing multilingual knowledge. Then, I investigate the underlying multilingual knowledge of LLMs with two benchmarks: on complex reasoning, and on territorial disputes. These benchmarks reveal LLMs' inconsistent performance across languages. I then design efficient techniques, both at inference-time and training-time, to address these discrepancies. Finally, I extend the territorial disputes benchmark to retrieval-augmented generation (RAG) setting, comparing the effects of different retrieval settings on cross-lingual robustness. My proposal shows that informed use of multilinguality enhances LLMs' capabilities, and our understanding thereof.

1 Introduction

The vast diversity of languages is both a contemporary and historical reality, with more than 7000 languages spoken throughout the world today (Eberhard et al., 2015). Each language is strikingly different at a surface level, with its own vocabulary, syntax, grammar. However, to quote Akmajian et al. (2017), "all known languages are at a similar level of complexity and detail." All languages build meaning in recursive units, from words, to sentences, to discourses. And anything can be expressed as validly in one language as in another.

Thus, multilinguality serves as a dual lens into human intelligence. First, any human possesses the capacity to, with enough practice and exposure, acquire fluency in any one or more language. Second, any language can be used to enable communication in a society. That is, multilinguality demonstrates how *knowledgeable* individual humans are and serves a *practical* purpose for societies.

If multilinguality comes so naturally to humans, then in our quest to develop machines that possess artificial intelligence (AI) capabilities, then it is also natural that these machines should be able to think in different languages. Developers of an advanced AI chatbot would like to adapt their system for different linguistic communities. And users within them would like to access information about current events in their language and preferences.

Indeed, many of the major advancements in NLP have been substantiated by multilingual concerns. Of particular note is machine translation (MT), the task of translating text from one language to another language. MT is a well-defined task with clear use-cases and a lot of data. Key to neural language models, has been the introduction of the attention mechanism (Bahdanau et al., 2015), and the Transformer model (Vaswani et al., 2017); these were first developed with MT as an illustrative task, before researchers soon found that the strong language representations learned here lead to effective models for all NLP tasks. This has led to our current era of large language models (LLMs), which are large in both their size – over 1 billion parameters – and their datasets – over 1 trillion tokens.

Despite this, there has been a widespread public sentiment that the current brisk pace of NLP development is leaving behind most of the world's languages, and the people that speak them. From the New York Times (Ruberg, 2024) to the World Economic Forum (Chhabria, 2024), articles abound about the phenomenon of the 'linguistic gap.'

How do we feel about the state of multilinguality in our field of NLP? Certainly, multilinguality has been and remains a primary area of research. Taking inventory of conferences run by the Association for Computational Linguistics from 2020-2025, we

Proceedings of the 2025 Conference of the Nations of the Americas Chapter of the Association for Computational Linguistics: Human Language Technologies (Volume 4: Student Research Workshop), pages 301–310

see that of the 16 conferences that have *Theme Tracks* of special interest, 4 directly concern multilinguality[1] – not to mention workshops and other events. Still, sentiment on the state of multilinguality among NLP researchers remains mixed.

We can thus say that *multilinguality has become a primary but parallel concern*. The frontier of LLM development has largely been substantiated by knowledge-intensive tasks specified in English. Only in parallel are multilingual efforts. One approach to building frontier LLMs is to start by training an English model, then adding multilingual support later. Such is the case with the open-weight LLMs Llama-3 (Dubey et al., 2024), Mistral (Jiang et al., 2023), and Gemma (Team, 2024), and their multilingual follow-ups Llama 3.1, Mistral 2, and Gemma 2. A second approach is to pursue LLM development where multilinguality is considered from the ground up, such as Aya (Üstün et al., 2024) and Bloom (Le Scao et al., 2022). These work well but have been largely relegated to non-English or multilingual use cases. This is because of the popular view is that supporting more languages decreases LLM ability in any one of them. In this proposal, I will show that this need not be the case.

Thesis Statement Multilinguality does and should continue to occupy a key role in the development of *practical* and *knowledgeable* LLMs. Informed use of multilinguality enhances these capabilities of LLMs, and our understanding thereof.

In this proposed thesis, I first consider *practical* methods for several standard NLP tasks, improving performance by leveraging the innate multilingual knowledge of LLMs. Next, I study how multilinguality can be used to make LLMs that are more *knowledgeable*. I introduce two benchmarks, on complex reasoning, and on geopolitical knowledge. These calls into question the consistency of LLMs' knowledge representations across languages. I then introduce informed and efficient techniques that again leverage multilinguality to boost performance across all languages.

2 Practical Applications of LLMs

I consider two characteristics of *practicality*: *real-world utility* concerns performing useful tasks, and *ease of development* concerns being easy to use and easy to extend. These are precisely why LLMs have become popular – users can converse with them in natural language, and developers can easily access their internal knowledge, and extend their functionality through techniques such as finetuning and prompting. The section covers two papers studying both characteristics.

Training Data	**cross-l (6 pairs)**	**mono-l (3 pairs)**	**Avg (9 pairs)**
SQuAD	61.9	73.3	65.7
+ Riabi et al. (2021)	69.4	72.7	70.5
+ PAXQA$_{\text{human}}$ GT	69.5	73.6	70.8
+ PAXQA$_{\text{human}}$ lex cons	**70.7**	**74.3**	**71.9**
+ PAXQA$_{\text{auto}}$ lex cons	69.4	73.9	70.9

Table 1: F1 scores on MLQA test set (Lewis et al., 2020a), for all 9 pairs involving {ar, zh, en}. The base model is XLM-RoBERTa (Conneau et al., 2020); all models are fine-tuned on SQuAD (Rajpurkar et al., 2016); the rows with + additionally use on generated Q&A pairs from their respective methods.

2.1 Cross-lingual Question Answering

QA is an intuitive way to interact with a system. It can empower information access in a cross-lingual setting, where a user may want to ask a question in their native language, but wish to access information stored in another language. We are thus motivated to develop a system that can perform cross-lingual QA. But where do we get the data to train such a system? Prior studies trained systems to perform synthetic data generation, requiring the existence of some labeled Q&A data.

I instead propose a training-free generation method which leverages indirect supervision from existing parallel corpora (Li and Callison-Burch, 2023). Our method termed PAXQA (Projecting annotations for cross-lingual (x) QA) decomposes cross-lingual QA into two stages, as illustrated in Appendix Figure 6. First, a question generation (QG) model is applied to the English side of the corpora. Second, we word alignment-informed translation is applied to the translate both questions and answers. Answers can be directly projected across the alignments. To better translate questions, I utilize lexically-constrained MT, in which constrained entities are extracted from the parallel bitexts. We show the quality of our generations by finetuning models to perform QA. As shown in Table 1, using PAXQA achieves the best results; furthermore, our method is also robust to alignment noise, given the small drop (-1.0 F1) using

[1]These are "Language Diversity: from Low-Resource to Endangered Languages" (ACL 2022), "Large Language Models and Regional/Low-Resource Languages" (AACL 2023), "Languages of Latin America" (NAACL 2024), "NLP in a Multicultural World" (NAACL 2025).

Domain Knowledge?		Gemma-2 27B IT					
		Law		Med.		Koran	
zero-shot		84.8		85.2		75.1	
retrieved	terms	85.9*	↑1.1	87.8*	↑2.6	74.6	↓0.5
	demos	88.6*	↑3.8	89.9*	↑4.7	76.7*	↑1.6
generated	terms	85.2	↑0.4	87.1*	↑1.9	75.7*	↑0.6
	demos	86.0*	↑1.2	88.1*	↑2.9	76.1*	↑1.0

Table 2: Results for domain-adapted MT, comparing the zero-shot baseline with 4 settings for prompting with knowledge, reported on the COMET22 metric (Rei et al., 2022) and the Gemma-2 27B model (Team, 2024).

automated word alignments.

2.2 Domain-Adapted MT

How can we improve MT in specialist domains such as law or medicine? These domains pose the challenges of specialized terminologies and styles, which may not have been seen at training-time. With LLMs comes the promise of inference-time adaptation through prompting. Prior work has found some success by retrieving domain knowledge from external resources, then including it in the prompt (Agrawal et al., 2023; Moslem et al., 2023). Recent efforts have further shown that this knowledge can be instead generated from an LLM's own parametric memory, and this intermediate step followed by the translation step can be effective for general-domain MT (Briakou et al., 2024; He et al., 2024).

I thus perform an analytical study into approaches for domain-adapted MT with LLMs (Li et al., 2025b). A careful prompting setup compares MT under four settings – two knowledge *strategies* and knowledge *sources*, as illustrated in Appendix Figure 7. The *strategies* are demonstrations of translation pairs, and bilingual terminologies of key terms. The *sources* are external retrieval, and internal generation from an LLM's own knowledge.

The results are shown in Table 2, and our findings are threefold. First, demonstrations outperform terminology, and that this effect is magnified for larger LLMs over smaller ones. Second, retrieval outperforms generation as expected. This leads to the third finding, that generation is an efficient way to boost MT performance, especially weaker ones. Notably, for a smaller LLM, translating with demonstrations generated from its own parametric memory matches zero-shot MT with a much larger LLM, Gemini. Our further analyses suggest that a) few-shot exemplars are especially effective due to their assistance with translation style, rather than terminology; and b) domain-specificity is key, and can equally derive from generated demos, or static retrieved demos.

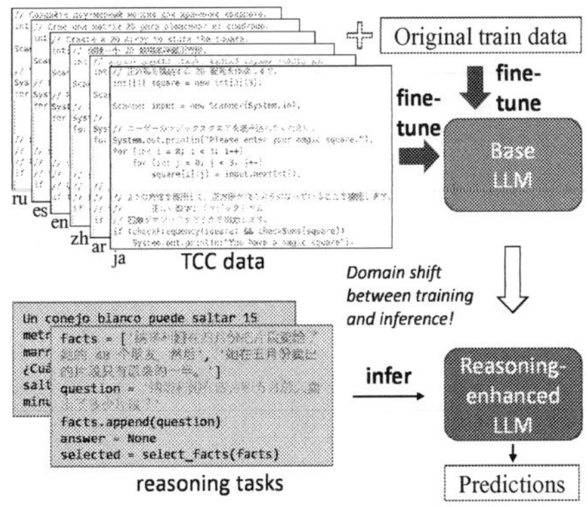

Figure 1: An overview of the methods used to improve multilingual structured reasoning. Top: during training, I create a multilingually commented code dataset, and use it in a finetuning setup. Bottom: during inference, I apply several prompting formats, finding most success with our code prompts format.

3 Evaluations of LLMs' Knowledge

I consider three characteristics of *knowledgeability*: *factuality* concerns utilization of factual information, *complex reasoning* concerns using logic and analytical abilities, and *consistency* concerns giving similar responses to similar queries.

I thus introduce two benchmarks which by design evaluate factuality and complex reasoning. These benchmarks highlight the issues LLMs have with consistent responses across languages, by eliciting responses for the same underlying queries, but specified in different languages.[2]

3.1 Consistency of Complex Reasoning

While a human learns a new language one at a time, a multilingual LLM can learn multiple languages at once in its pretraining stage by simply including multilingual data and following the standard self-supervised LM objective. On one hand, this imbues an LLM to super-human polyglot abilities – mT5 and Aya, for example, support over 100+ languages (Xue et al., 2021; Üstün et al., 2024). On the other hand, for each language, the performance is *inconsistently* distributed, dropping steeply from English, to lower-resource languages.

[2]Note that my focus on tasks where responses should be consistent cross-lingually. This contrasts with the more-studied tasks of cultural concerns, wherein the language used can indicate a user's preferences, and thus the responses should accordingly vary cross-lingually.

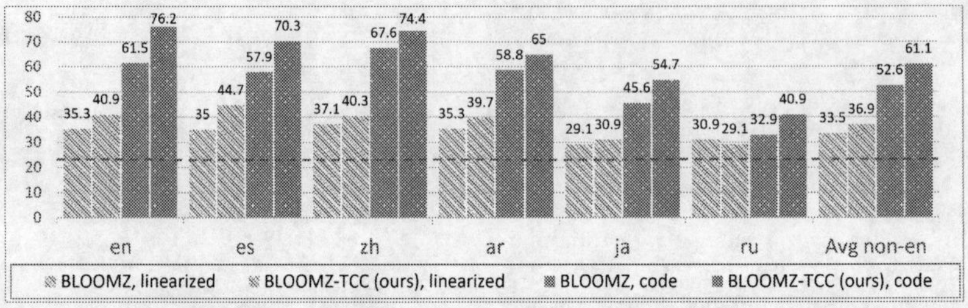

Figure 2: Results on xSTREET for the ARC subtask of scientific reasoning, with BLOOMZ-based models. The random baseline is 25%. 'Avg' bars are across the 5 non-English languages.

I thus introduce xSTREET, a multilingual structured reasoning and explanation dataset that covers four tasks across six diverse languages (Li et al., 2024a). xSTREET exposes a gap in base LLM performance between English and non-English reasoning tasks. To remedy the gap, I propose two methods, as illustrated in Figure 1. which follow from the insight that LLMs trained on code are better reasoners. For training-time, I augment a code dataset with multilingual comments using MT, while keeping program code as-is. Parameter-efficient finetuning of a base LLM is then applied on the dataset. This leads to a model with improved complex reasoning performance, while maintaining performance on other language benchmarks. For inference-time, I bridge the gap between training and inference by employing a prompt structure that incorporates step-by-step code primitives to derive new facts and find a solution.

Our code and multilinguality-informed methods are individually effective and can be used in tandem to achieve the best performance (Table 2 and Appendix Table 8). Notably, despite adding only non-English data, the largest gains occur for English, suggesting that the model leverages multilingual formulations of a problem, then generalizes reasoning improvements across languages. Our findings further underscore the role of code for enhancing LLM's reasoning capabilities.

3.2 Consistency of Geopolitical Knowledge

Information in the real world comes from various sources, mediums, and perspectives. It is very natural that information can be conflicting, yet a human encountering all of this has little issue synthesizing it together into a consistent set of personal beliefs; this holds across the languages they speak. Yet given the discrete nature of LLM's pretraining on texts from different languages, how consistent can LLMs be in their responses on factual queries?

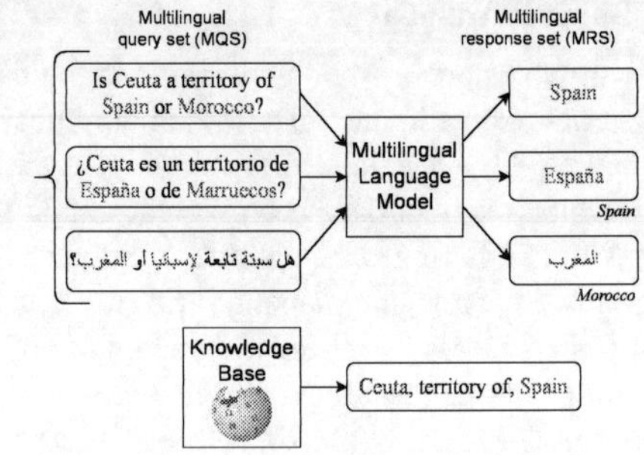

Figure 3: Illustration of a disputed territory task, which considers a single territory with queries presented in different languages. The KB says "Ceuta" belongs to "Spain". The LLM responds inconsistently: in Spanish and English "Spain", while in Arabic "Morocco", demonstrating geopolitical bias.

To answer this question, I introduce BORDERLINES, a dataset of territorial disputes which covers 251 territories, each associated with a set of queries in the languages of each claimant country (Li et al., 2024b). The dataset has 720 queries in 49 languages. Figure 3 provides an illustration of the task. In this context, I study the phenomenon of *geopolitical bias*, which is the tendency to report geopolitical knowledge differently depending on the language of interaction. I then propose a suite of evaluation metrics to quantify differences in responses across languages. These metrics, as detailed in Appendix B, are based on a simple accuracy metric termed *Concurrence Score* (CS).

I benchmark several LLMs on BORDERLINES, as shown in Table 3, and arrive at several findings. I find that instruction-tuned models are less knowledgeable about these disputes than their base LLM counterparts. I also find that the most knowledgeable LLMs in English tend to be more geopolitically biased. I further find that models are less consistent with responses for territories with un

	Model	Strategy	KB CS ↑	Con CS ↑	Non CS ↑	ΔCS ↓	Cst CS (unk) ↑	Cst CS (all) ↑
	RANDOM	—	43.5	43.5	43.5	0	43.5	43.5
1	BLOOM_{560M}	—	**60.5**	66.7	29.9	123.3	**57.3**	49.5
2	$\text{BLOOM}_{7.1B}$	—	57.4	**71.9**	**39.2**	**83.2**	50.4	**55.1**
3	BLOOMZ_{560M}	—	46.9	65.4	36.1	81.0	48.0	51.1
4	$\text{BLOOMZ}_{7.1B}$	—	45.1	57.5	43.8	31.5	39.2	53.6
6	GPT-3_{DV}	—	**60.5**	**60.0**	**51.3**	**17.0**	**63.1**	**63.3**
7	GPT-4	Vanilla	79.5	76.9	63.2	21.6	65.6	70.8
8	GPT-4	UN Peacekeeper	**80.1**	74.6	**67.7**	**10.2**	56.3	72.3
9	GPT-4	Nationalist	–	**80.6**	60.3	33.8	52.8	63.7
10	GPT-4	Demographic reasoning	70.8	74.8	61.6	21.5	**70.5**	**76.3**

Table 3: Results on BORDERLINES for different models. We report the first 4 CS metrics for only the subset of territories with defined controllers. Greyed rows are for instruction tuned models.

known controllers vs. known ones.

Finally, I explore several prompt modification strategies, aiming to either amplify or mitigate geopolitical bias. This highlights how brittle LLM's knowledge is to cues from the interaction context. I explore 4 prompting strategies: a *vanilla* baseline; a *nationalist* persona, a *UN peacekeeper* persona; and a *demographic reasoning* approach, which asks the model to reason by considering the religion and language of the territory, as well as each claimant country.

As the status of each individual disputed territory is complex, let us consider a notable case study. Taiwan is an island in East Asia with a population of 23.9 million. It is controlled by the Republic of China (ROC), but also claimed by the People's Republic of China (PRC). For *vanilla* and *demographic reasoning*, querying in Traditional Chinese (zht, used in ROC) and Simplified Chinese (zhs, used in PRC) both return 'ROC'. Adopting *nationalist* and *UN* prompts results in differing responses: PRC in zhs, and ROC in zht.

3.3 Robustness of Multilingual Retrieval Augmented Generation

Despite the impressive knowledgeability of LLMs, a major limitation is that their knowledge is frozen in time to their training data. The paradigm of *retrieval augmented generation* (RAG) was developed to address these issues, by grounding LLM responses in relevant passages retrieved from an external datastore (Lewis et al., 2020b). The external datastore can be updated with new information, or swapped out entirely for different needs. In the multilingual setting, RAG can empower LLMs to access information which is inequitably distributed across languages, thereby improving responses (Asai et al., 2022).

While several recent studies have investigated RAG in small-scale multilingual settings, they consider artificially construed scenarios and documents (Sharma et al., 2024; Wu et al., 2024). Also related is the field of open-retrieval multilingual QA (Clark et al., 2020); however these focus on simple fact-seeking questions where right answers are easily memorized by LLMs.

Our previously introduced BORDERLINES benchmark on territorial disputes provides an fact-seeking yet culturally-sensitive setting, which can serve as a challenge to the RAG setting. Given documents from different languages may espouse different viewpoints, many questions arise: How does the linguistic composition of the set of documents impact responses? Does sourcing information from different languages increase or decrease consistency? And is presenting conflicting information to LLM's base preferences better expressed in certain languages?

In this work, I introduce BORDIRLINES, a benchmark consisting of 720 territorial dispute queries paired with 14k Wikipedia documents across 49 languages (Li et al., 2025a). To evaluate LLMs' *cross-lingual robustness* for this task, I formalize several modes for multilingual retrieval, as depicted in Figure 4, each of which reflects a real-world information access need.

I use BORDIRLINES and the IR modes to systematically evaluate the *cross-lingual robustness* of various LLMs. The main results are shown in Figure 5. As expected, *factuality* generally increases when using RAG compared to the `no_ir` baseline. As for *consistency*, we find that `qlang` has mixed effects, depending on the model – negative for GPT, positive for Command-R. Meanwhile,

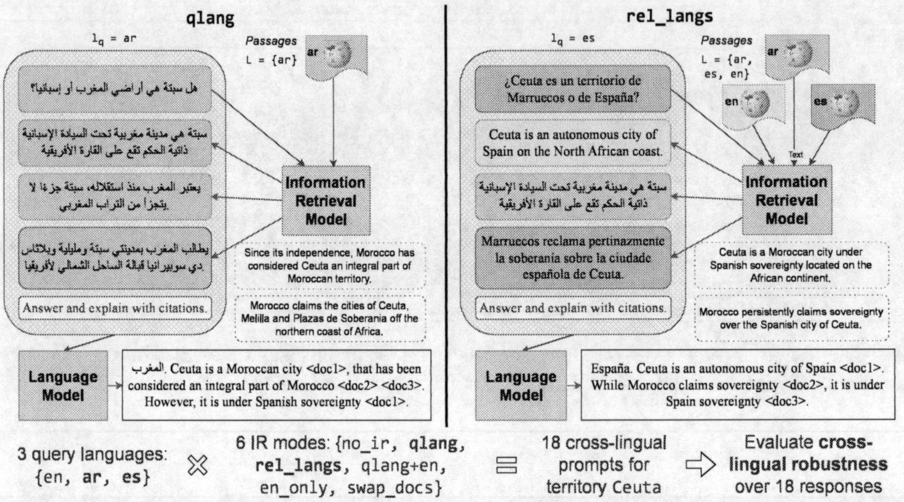

Figure 4: Illustration of 2 cross-lingual RAG prompts from the BORDIRLINES benchmark, on the disputed territory "Ceuta". Observe the differences in the retrieved documents from the cross-lingual IR system, as well as the differences in answers and explanations. For a given territory, we create several prompts by varying the languages and the IR modes (18 here). Our evaluation of *cross-lingual robustness* is over the set of responses.

`rel_langs` has a positive effect, with a huge boost for Command-R. On *geopolitical bias*, I find reliable decreases when using RAG. Moreover, we observe that different LLM display different sensitivities to RAG, with Llama least affected and Command-R most.

Further experiments analyze all facets of the cross-lingual RAG setting. Considering the citations given by RAG responses, low-resource languages demonstrate much wider variability in citation rates than high-resource languages. Considering IR, there is a preference towards retrieving query-language documents. Considering the contents of documents, LLMs can selectively interpret the same documents to fit their own viewpoints.

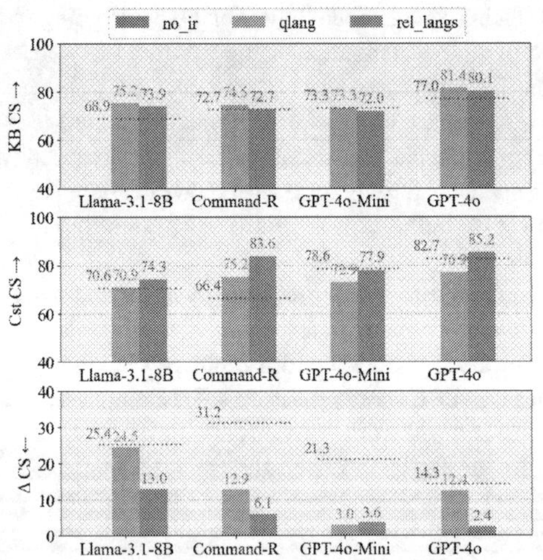

Figure 5: Results for the concurrence score (CS) metrics, which measure attributes of cross-lingual robustness: KB CS for *factuality*, Cst CS for *consistency*, and Δ CS for *geopolitical bias*. Within each subplot, we display the results for the `no_ir` baseline compared to 2 RAG settings: `qlang`, with in-language documents, and `rel_langs` with all relevant language documents.

Acknowledgements

Reflecting on my PhD studies up until now, I have many people to thank: my doctoral adviser, Prof. Chris Callison-Burch, the PennNLP community, my many research collaborators, my friends, and my family. And looking a bit ahead, I am thankful for my thesis committee members Prof. Lyle Ungar, Prof. Duncan Watts, Prof. Dan Roth, Dr. Mohammad Sadegh Rasooli, and Dr. Colin Cherry.

References

Sweta Agrawal, Chunting Zhou, Mike Lewis, Luke Zettlemoyer, and Marjan Ghazvininejad. 2023. In-context examples selection for machine translation.

In *Findings of the Association for Computational Linguistics: ACL 2023*, pages 8857–8873.

Adrian Akmajian, Ann K Farmer, Lee Bickmore, Richard A Demers, and Robert M Harnish. 2017. What is linguistics? In *Linguistics: An introduction to language and communication*, chapter 1, pages 5–9. MIT Press.

Akari Asai, Shayne Longpre, Jungo Kasai, Chia-Hsuan Lee, Rui Zhang, Junjie Hu, Ikuya Yamada, Jonathan H Clark, and Eunsol Choi. 2022. Mia 2022 shared task: Evaluating cross-lingual open-retrieval question answering for 16 diverse languages. In *Proceedings of the Workshop on Multilingual Information Access (MIA)*, pages 108–120.

Dzmitry Bahdanau, Kyung Hyun Cho, and Yoshua Bengio. 2015. Neural machine translation by jointly learning to align and translate. In *3rd International Conference on Learning Representations, ICLR 2015*.

Eleftheria Briakou, Jiaming Luo, Colin Cherry, and Markus Freitag. 2024. Translating step-by-step: Decomposing the translation process for improved translation quality of long-form texts. In *Proceedings of the Ninth Conference on Machine Translation*, pages 1301–1317.

Pooja Chhabria. 2024. The "missed opportunity" with ai's linguistic diversity gap. *World Economic Forum*.

Jonathan H. Clark, Eunsol Choi, Michael Collins, Dan Garrette, Tom Kwiatkowski, Vitaly Nikolaev, and Jennimaria Palomaki. 2020. Tydi qa: A benchmark for information-seeking question answering in typologically diverse languages. *Transactions of the Association for Computational Linguistics*, 8:454–470.

Alexis Conneau, Kartikay Khandelwal, Naman Goyal, Vishrav Chaudhary, Guillaume Wenzek, Francisco Guzmán, Édouard Grave, Myle Ott, Luke Zettlemoyer, and Veselin Stoyanov. 2020. Unsupervised cross-lingual representation learning at scale. In *Proceedings of the 58th Annual Meeting of the Association for Computational Linguistics*, pages 8440–8451.

Abhimanyu Dubey, Abhinav Jauhri, Abhinav Pandey, Abhishek Kadian, Ahmad Al-Dahle, Aiesha Letman, Akhil Mathur, Alan Schelten, Amy Yang, Angela Fan, et al. 2024. The llama 3 herd of models. *arXiv preprint arXiv:2407.21783*.

David M Eberhard, Gary Francis Simons, and Charles D Fenning. 2015. Ethnologue: Languages of the world.

Zhiwei He, Tian Liang, Wenxiang Jiao, Zhuosheng Zhang, Yujiu Yang, Rui Wang, Zhaopeng Tu, Shuming Shi, and Xing Wang. 2024. Exploring human-like translation strategy with large language models. *Transactions of the Association for Computational Linguistics*, 12:229–246.

Albert Q. Jiang, Alexandre Sablayrolles, Arthur Mensch, Chris Bamford, Devendra Singh Chaplot, Diego de las Casas, Florian Bressand, Gianna Lengyel, Guillaume Lample, Lucile Saulnier, Lélio Renard Lavaud, Marie-Anne Lachaux, Pierre Stock, Teven Le Scao, Thibaut Lavril, Thomas Wang, Timothée Lacroix, and William El Sayed. 2023. Mistral 7b. *Preprint*, arXiv:2310.06825.

Teven Le Scao, Angela Fan, Christopher Akiki, Ellie Pavlick, Suzana Ilić, Daniel Hesslow, Roman Castagné, Alexandra Sasha Luccioni, François Yvon, Matthias Gallé, et al. 2022. Bloom: A 176b-parameter open-access multilingual language model. *arXiv preprint arXiv:2211.05100*.

Patrick Lewis, Barlas Oguz, Ruty Rinott, Sebastian Riedel, and Holger Schwenk. 2020a. Mlqa: Evaluating cross-lingual extractive question answering. In *Proceedings of the 58th Annual Meeting of the Association for Computational Linguistics*, pages 7315–7330.

Patrick Lewis, Ethan Perez, Aleksandra Piktus, Fabio Petroni, Vladimir Karpukhin, Naman Goyal, Heinrich Küttler, Mike Lewis, Wen-tau Yih, Tim Rocktäschel, et al. 2020b. Retrieval-augmented generation for knowledge-intensive nlp tasks. *Advances in Neural Information Processing Systems*, 33:9459–9474.

Bryan Li, Tamer Alkhouli, Daniele Bonadiman, Nikolaos Pappas, and Saab Mansour. 2024a. Eliciting better multilingual structured reasoning from llms through code. *62nd Annual Meeting of the Association for Computational Linguistics (ACL)*.

Bryan Li and Chris Callison-Burch. 2023. PAXQA: Generating cross-lingual question answering examples at training scale. *Findings of the Association for Computational Linguistics: EMNLP 2023*.

Bryan Li, Samar Haider, and Chris Callison-Burch. 2024b. This land is {Your, My} land: Evaluating geopolitical biases in language models through territorial disputes. *2024 Annual Conference of the North American Chapter of the Association for Computational Linguistics (NAACL)*.

Bryan Li, Fiona Luo, Samar Haider, Adwait Agashe, Miranda Miao, Shriya Ramakrishnan, Tammy Li, Vickie Liu, Yuan Yuan, and Chris Callison-Burch. 2025a. Multilingual retrieval augmented generation for culturally-sensitive tasks: A benchmark for cross-lingual robustness.

Bryan Li, Jiaming Luo, Eleftheria Briakou, and Colin Cherry. 2025b. Leveraging domain knowledge for llm translation: The cases of retrieval vs. generation. *in review at ACL Rolling Review, February 2025*.

Yasmin Moslem, Rejwanul Haque, John D Kelleher, and Andy Way. 2023. Adaptive machine translation with large language models. In *24th Annual Conference of the European Association for Machine Translation*, page 227.

Pranav Rajpurkar, Jian Zhang, Konstantin Lopyrev, and Percy Liang. 2016. Squad: 100,000+ questions for machine comprehension of text. In *Proceedings of the 2016 Conference on Empirical Methods in Natural Language Processing*, pages 2383–2392.

Ricardo Rei, José GC De Souza, Duarte Alves, Chrysoula Zerva, Ana C Farinha, Taisiya Glushkova, Alon Lavie, Luisa Coheur, and André FT Martins. 2022. Comet-22: Unbabel-ist 2022 submission for the metrics shared task. In *Proceedings of the Seventh Conference on Machine Translation (WMT)*, pages 578–585.

Arij Riabi, Thomas Scialom, Rachel Keraron, Benoît Sagot, Djamé Seddah, and Jacopo Staiano. 2021. Synthetic data augmentation for zero-shot cross-lingual question answering. In *Proceedings of the 2021 Conference on Empirical Methods in Natural Language Processing*, pages 7016–7030.

Sara Ruberg. 2024. When a.i. fails the language test, who is left out of the conversation? *The New York Times*.

Nikhil Sharma, Kenton Murray, and Ziang Xiao. 2024. Faux polyglot: A study on information disparity in multilingual large language models. *arXiv preprint arXiv:2407.05502*.

Gemma Team. 2024. Gemma: Open models based on gemini research and technology. *Preprint*, arXiv:2403.08295.

Ahmet Üstün, Viraat Aryabumi, Zheng Yong, Wei-Yin Ko, Daniel D'souza, Gbemileke Onilude, Neel Bhandari, Shivalika Singh, Hui-Lee Ooi, Amr Kayid, Freddie Vargus, Phil Blunsom, Shayne Longpre, Niklas Muennighoff, Marzieh Fadaee, Julia Kreutzer, and Sara Hooker. 2024. Aya model: An instruction finetuned open-access multilingual language model. In *Proceedings of the 62nd Annual Meeting of the Association for Computational Linguistics (Volume 1: Long Papers)*, pages 15894–15939, Bangkok, Thailand. Association for Computational Linguistics.

Ashish Vaswani, Noam M. Shazeer, Niki Parmar, Jakob Uszkoreit, Llion Jones, Aidan N. Gomez, Lukasz Kaiser, and Illia Polosukhin. 2017. Attention is all you need. In *Neural Information Processing Systems*.

Suhang Wu, Jialong Tang, Baosong Yang, Ante Wang, Kaidi Jia, Jiawei Yu, Junfeng Yao, and Jinsong Su. 2024. Not all languages are equal: Insights into multilingual retrieval-augmented generation. *arXiv preprint arXiv:2410.21970*.

Linting Xue, Noah Constant, Adam Roberts, Mihir Kale, Rami Al-Rfou, Aditya Siddhant, Aditya Barua, and Colin Raffel. 2021. mT5: A massively multilingual pre-trained text-to-text transformer. In *Proceedings of the 2021 Conference of the North American Chapter of the Association for Computational Linguistics: Human Language Technologies*, pages 483–498, Online. Association for Computational Linguistics.

A Supplementary Figures and Tables

Figure 6 depicts the PAXQA pipeline. Figure 7 depicts the prompting setup for domain-adapted MT. Figure 8 presents the results of GPT-3 on the xSTREET benchmark.

B Details on Metrics for BORDERLINES

Figure 9 illustrates the comparisons made for each CS metric, and Table 4 shows the formulas.

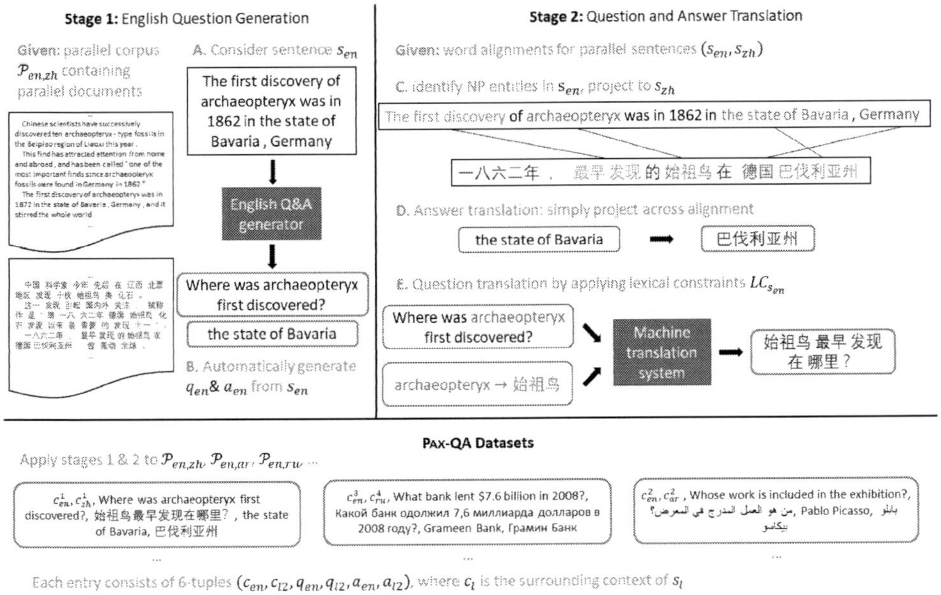

Figure 6: The PAXQA method generates a cross-lingual question-answering (QA) dataset given a word-aligned and parallel corpus. The two stages are English question generation (left), and Q&A translation (right). We run the pipeline on {ar-en}, {zh-en}, and {ru-en} datasets (bottom), resulting in 662K cross-lingual QA examples.

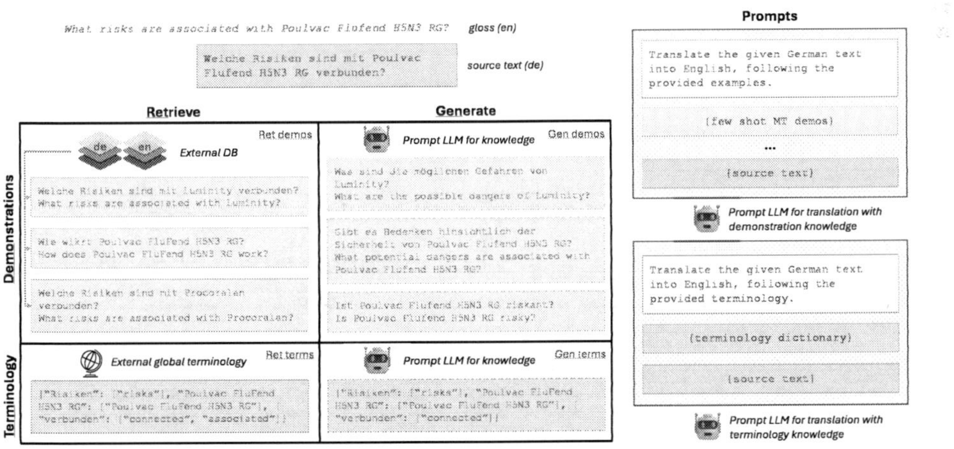

Figure 7: Illustration of the main MT settings, for an example source text in German. Left: we compare the knowledge *strategies* (rows) and the knowledge *sources* (columns). Right: the prompt templates used.

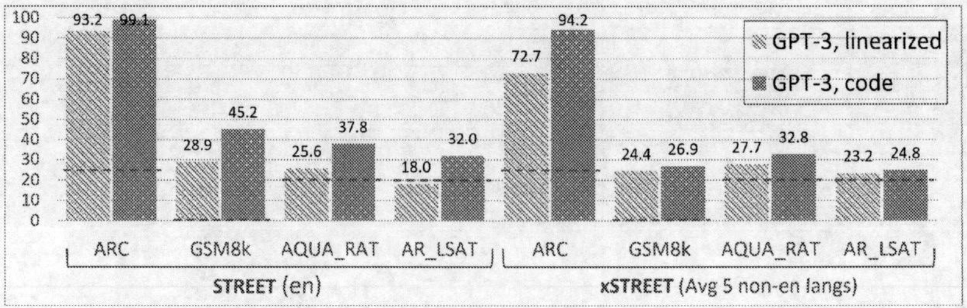

Figure 8: Results on GSM8k, AQUA_RAT, AR_LSAT tasks of STREET (left) and xSTREET (right), with GPT-3 (`text-davinci-003`). xSTREET results are averaged over 5 languages.

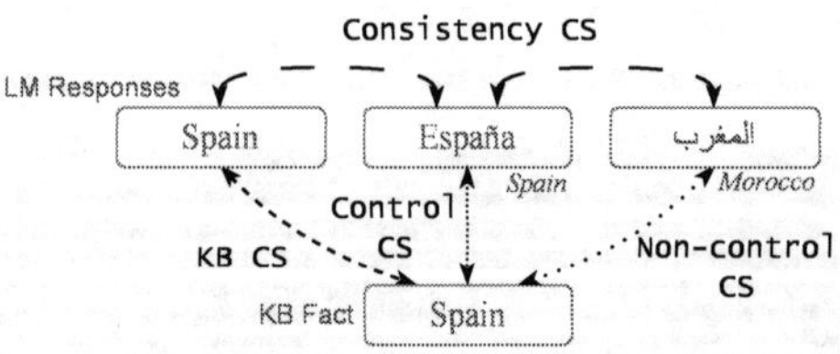

Figure 9: Illustration of comparisons made for the CS metrics. KB CS, Control CS, and Non-control CS all compare between the KB country and a response, while Consistency CS compares between responses.

$$\text{CS}(c_i, c_j) = 100 * \begin{cases} 1 \text{ if } c_i = c_j, \\ 0 \text{ otherwise} \end{cases}$$

$$\text{Con CS}(t) = \text{CS}(c_{KB}, c_i)$$

$$\text{Non CS}(t) = \frac{1}{n} \sum_{c \in C^{\text{non}}} \text{CS}(c_{KB}, c)$$

$$\Delta\, \text{CS}(t) = \frac{\text{Con CS} - \text{Non CS}}{\text{Non CS}}$$

$$\text{Cst CS}(t) = \frac{1}{n(n-1)} \sum_{i=1}^{n} \sum_{j=1, j \neq i}^{n} \text{CS}(c_i, c_j)$$

Table 4: Formulas for concurrence score (CS) metrics. We denote all claimants of a territory t as $C = c_1, ..., c_n$, a controller as c_{con}, the set of non-controllers as C^{non}.

MDC^3: A Novel Multimodal Dataset for Commercial Content Classification in Bengali

Anik Mahmud Shanto[1], **MST. Sanjida Jamal Priya**[1]
Fahim Shakil Tamim[1,2] and **Mohammed Moshiul Hoque**[1]
[1] Chittagong University of Engineering & Technology, Chittagong-4349, Bangladesh
[2] International University of Business Agriculture and Technology, Dhaka, Bangladesh
{u1904049, u1904057}@student.cuet.ac.bd,
fstamim9@gmail.com, moshiul_240@cuet.ac.bd

Abstract

Identifying commercial posts in resource-constrained languages among diverse and unstructured content remains a significant challenge for automatic text classification tasks. To address this, this work introduces a novel dataset named **MDC**^{3} (Multimodal Dataset for Commercial Content Classification), comprising 5,007 annotated Bengali social media posts classified as commercial and noncommercial. A comprehensive annotation guideline accompanies the dataset to aid future creation in resource-constrained languages. Furthermore, we performed extensive experiments on MDC^3 considering both unimodal and multimodal domains. Specifically, the late fusion of textual (mBERT) and visual (ViT) models (i.e., **ViT+mBERT**) achieves the highest F1 score of 90.91, significantly surpassing other baselines.

1 Introduction

Social media platforms are crucial for communication, enabling individuals and businesses to share diverse content. Commercial posts influence consumer behavior and brand perception, making their identification essential for transparency, consumer protection, and regulatory compliance (McQuarrie and Munson, 2014; Boerman and van Reijmersdal, 2016a). However, native advertising and influencer marketing blur the lines between ads and personal content, complicating detection (Boerman and van Reijmersdal, 2016b; Chia, 2012).

Detecting commercial posts is vital for targeted advertising, brand monitoring, and consumer behavior analysis. While most research focuses on English, Bengali social media lacks annotated datasets and faces challenges from multimodal content and cultural nuances. To address this, we introduce **MDC**^{3}, a dataset for classifying Bengali social media posts as commercial or non-commercial. Various unimodal and multimodal baselines are explored based on **MDC**^{3}.

Key contributions:

- Introduced **MDC**^{3}, a multimodal dataset with 5,007 labeled samples.
- Evaluated unimodal and multimodal baselines for Bengali commercial content classification.

2 Related Work

Social media's growing influence has made user-generated and influencer-created content pivotal in shaping consumer behavior (Gamage and Ashill, 2023). Influencers act as trusted figures but often blur the lines between personal and commercial content, complicating automatic detection (Vanninen et al., 2023; Weismueller et al., 2022; Ahammad et al., 2024). Subtle advertising strategies, such as conversational language and self-focused visuals, enhance audience engagement but hinder content classification (Hidarto and Andrieza, 2022; Kim et al., 2020). Multimodal approaches have shown promise in addressing these challenges. Vedula et al. (2017) leveraged text, audio, and video embeddings for ad effectiveness prediction, while Villegas et al. (2023) introduced datasets combining textual and visual modalities for better ad detection. These studies highlight the advantages of multimodal models over unimodal counterparts.

Beyond influencer marketing, multimodal research spans diverse applications, including

Proceedings of the 2025 Conference of the Nations of the Americas Chapter of the Association for Computational Linguistics: Human Language Technologies (Volume 4: Student Research Workshop), pages 311–320

trend detection (Pandit et al., 2019), COVID-19 impact analysis (Unal et al., 2022), and gender-based communication studies (Hidarto and Andrieza, 2022). However, resource-constrained languages like Bengali remain underexplored, with most models trained on English-centric datasets, limiting their applicability to non-English contexts. This study addresses this gap by introducing a Bengali dataset for commercial content classification and proposing a multimodal approach that combines textual and visual features to enhance classification accuracy.

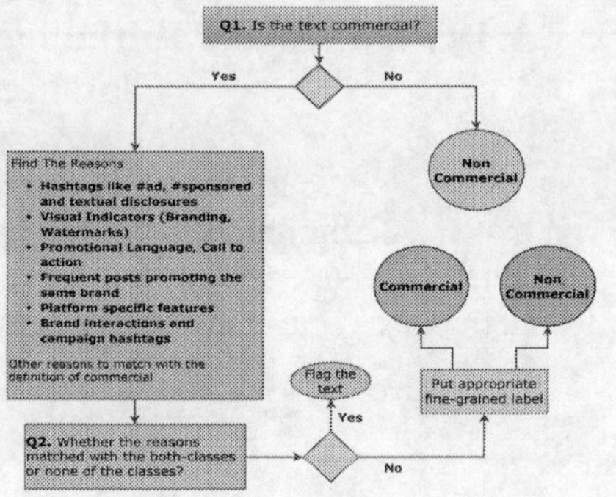

Figure 1: Data Annotation Process

3 Developement of MDC^3

As per our investigation's outcome, no benchmark dataset is explicitly available for detecting influencer commercial content in Bengali. Therefore, this work presents a benchmark dataset, **MDC**^{3} (Multimodal Commercial Content Classification Dataset), from Bengali social media posts comprising Facebook and Instagram posts categorized into two classes, *commercial* and *non-commercial*. The definitions of each class within the dataset are provided below, as described by (Villegas et al., 2023).

- **Commercial (Com):** Commercial posts promote or endorse a brand or its products or services, a free product or service, or any other incentive.
- **Non-commercial (NCom):** Non-commercial posts refer to organic content such as personal ideas, comments, and life updates that do not aim to be monetized.

3.1 Data Collection and Annotation

From April to November 2024, we collected 5,007 multimodal influencer posts from Facebook (66.2%) and Instagram (33.8%), including 2,750 commercial and 2,257 non-commercial entries. These were sourced from Bangladeshi influencers and commercial pages. The dataset prioritizes authenticity by including only Bengali content with authentic or captured visuals. To ensure ethical standards, all data were sourced from publicly accessible domains, excluding entries without multimodal elements, unclear visuals, cartoons, or insufficient text.

Three experienced annotators annotated the dataset following clear guidelines on labeling (Figure 1), tool use, and quality standards. Annotators received training to ensure adherence to criteria for commercial and non-commercial content. The process was independent and there were regular meetings to resolve ambiguities and reach consensus. A senior professor with 10+ years of experience evaluated inter-annotator agreement using majority voting (Algorithm 1), ensuring the dataset's reliability. Appendix A describes the details of the majority voting algorithm.

We applied inter-annotator agreement standards (i.e., Cohen's kappa coefficient (Cohen, 1960), to measure the quality of the annotations. On the kappa scale, we achieved 0.86 implies an almost ideal agreement.

3.2 Statistics

We have stratified the dataset into three sets: train (60%), validation (20%), and test (20%). Table 1 demonstrates the statistics of the dataset.

Figure 2 illustrates samples of the dataset. The dataset is available on online: https://github.com/anik5099/Multimodal-Commercial-Content-Classification-Binary

4 Methodology

This section describes the baseline models for classifying commercial content, which in-

Split	Com	NCom	T_W	U_W
Train	1631	1372	57292	6930
Val	546	456	17843	4291
Test	573	429	20086	4454
Total	2740	2257	95221	15675

Table 1: Class distribution in train, validation, and test sets. The acronyms T_W, U_W denotes total words and unique words, respectively

Figure 2: Dataset samples.

clude unimodal (visual or textual) and multimodal (visual and textual) models. Figure 3 depicts the abstract process of commercial content classification employing textual and visual modalities. For this classification task, image and textual modalities have been trained separately. Then the unimodal models have been fused to produce multimodal classification. **Experimental Settings** is explained in Appendix 5.

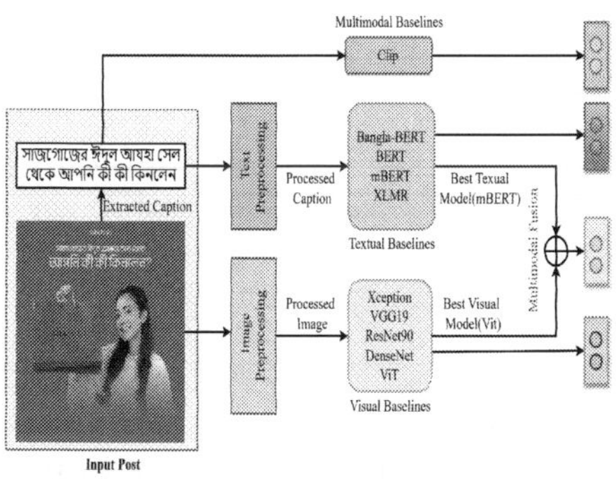

Figure 3: Abstract process of multimodal content classification

4.1 Data Preprocessing

For the multimodal commercial content classification task, separate pipelines have been applied to prepare text and image data. Captions have been cleaned, tokenized, and converted into input IDs and attention masks using a subword tokenizer for text data. Sequences have been padded or truncated to a fixed length. Images have been resized to 224×224, and normalized. Processed images have been converted to tensors. The dataset labels have been encoded (1 for commercial and '0' for non-commercial). The dataset has been split into 60-20-20 for training, validation and test set.

4.2 Unimodal Baselines

This work explores several unimodal (visual or textual) and multimodal (visual and textual) baselines to classify the commercial content in Bengali. The **Hyperparameter Settings** for unimodal and multimodal models have been described in section B.

4.2.1 Visual Modality

We fine-tuned prominent convolutional neural network (CNN) architectures to classify visual data. The input images were resized to $224 \times 224 \times 3$ and preprocessed using standard normalization techniques. Specifically, we employed the following CNN models:

- **Xception** (Chollet, 2017): A depthwise separable convolutional network optimized for computational efficiency.
- **VGG19** (Simonyan and Zisserman, 2015): Known for its more profound architecture, this model emphasizes hierarchical feature extraction.
- **ResNet50** (He et al., 2015): A residual network addressing vanishing gradient issues through skip connections.
- **DenseNet** (Huang et al., 2018): A densely connected architecture designed to enhance feature reuse across layers.
- **ViT** (Dosovitskiy et al., 2021): Vision Transformer (ViT) uses self-attention to

process image patches as sequences, achieving competitive performance in image recognition tasks compared to traditional CNNs.

The top layers of each model were replaced with a dense layer of 32 neurons and a sigmoid layer for binary classification. These architectures were fine-tuned on our dataset using transfer learning techniques.

4.2.2 Textual Modality

Transformer-based models have been proven superior in many text classification tasks (Shanto et al., 2024; Chowdhury et al., 2024; Tamim et al., 2023a,b). Therefore, for text classification, we utilized transformer-based architectures, fine-tuned for our specific task:

- **BERT** (Devlin et al., 2019): A bidirectional transformer pre-trained on large-scale English text corpora.
- **mBERT** (Devlin et al., 2019): A multilingual version of BERT designed for cross-lingual tasks.
- **Bangla-BERT** (Bhattacharjee et al., 2022): A language-specific transformer model pre-trained on Bangla text.
- **XLM-Roberta** (Conneau et al., 2020): A cross-lingual transformer optimized for multilingual tasks.

Each model processed tokenized text sequences and generated contextual embeddings of size 768. These embeddings were passed through a dense layer with 32 neurons, followed by a sigmoid layer for classification.

4.3 Multimodal Baselines

This work exploited several multimodal techniques to analyze the multimodal data (visual and textual). A dense layer with 768 neurons was applied separately to the visual and textual modalities for model construction. The outputs from these layers were then concatenated to create a combined representation of visual and textual features. This combined feature was further processed through another dense layer of 768 neurons, followed by a softmax layer to classify posts into commercial or non-commercial categories. We have used the late fusion technique for measuring baselines because late fusion is more interpretable and allows each modality to leverage its unique characteristics. Besides, Contrastive Language-Image Pretraining (CLIP) (Radford et al., 2021) was employed to align visual and textual data, leveraging contrastive learning techniques (Chen et al., 2020).

The late fusion process can be mathematically expressed as follows:

$$\mathbf{z}_{\text{combined}} = \text{Concat}\left(\mathbf{z}_{\text{visual}}, \mathbf{z}_{\text{text}}\right) \quad (1)$$

Here, the visual and textual features are extracted as:

$$\mathbf{z}_{\text{visual}} = \sigma(\mathbf{W}_{\text{visual}}\mathbf{x}_{\text{visual}} + \mathbf{b}_{\text{visual}}) \quad (2)$$

$$\mathbf{z}_{\text{text}} = \sigma(\mathbf{W}_{\text{text}}\mathbf{x}_{\text{text}} + \mathbf{b}_{\text{text}}) \quad (3)$$

where σ is the activation function (Softmax), $\mathbf{W}_{\text{visual}}$ and $\mathbf{W}_{\text{text}}$ are the weights, and $\mathbf{b}_{\text{visual}}$ and $\mathbf{b}_{\text{text}}$ are the biases for the respective modalities. Concat denotes the concatenation operation.

The concatenated feature vector $\mathbf{z}_{\text{combined}}$ is passed through a dense layer followed by a softmax layer for classification:

$$\mathbf{y}_{\text{pred}} = \text{Softmax}(\mathbf{W}_{\text{class}}\mathbf{z}_{\text{combined}} + \mathbf{b}_{\text{class}}) \quad (4)$$

Here, $\mathbf{W}_{\text{class}}$ and $\mathbf{b}_{\text{class}}$ represent the weights and biases of the classification layer, respectively. The Softmax function maps the output to probabilities for the two categories (commercial and non-commercial).

This formulation effectively integrates features from both modalities, showcasing the power of late fusion for joint multimodal learning.

5 Experimental Setup

This section describes the summary of the experimental setup while training and evaluating our model on the dataset. The simulation was run on a personal computer with an NVIDIA GeForce GTX 2060 GPU and an Intel Core i7-9700 CPU running at 3.00 GHz. Additionally, a Kaggle Notebook with a P100 GPU was uti-

App	A(%)	P(%)	R(%)	F1(%)
Visual Only				
Xception	64.17 ± 0.87	65.78	62.67	63.59 ± 0.77
VGG19	73.65 ± 0.49	69.70	69.66	73.53 ± 0.36
VGG16	74.18 ± 0.60	73.18	70.66	74.23 ± 0.58
ResNet	79.14 ± 0.21	73.86	68.66	79.11 ± 0.16
DenseNet	67.84 ± 0.54	63.03	63.07	67.90 ± 0.43
ViT	**81.70** ±0.013	**82.85**	**81.94**	**81.71** ±0.011
Textual Only				
B-BERT	84.56 ± 0.01	83.60	82.91	83.21 ± 0.03
BERT	81.18 ± 0.04	83.12	79.44	81.14 ± 0.01
mBERT	**86.83** ± 0.003	**91.10**	**84.27**	**87.43** ± .006
XLM-R	74.25 ± 0.27	74.08	94.44	81.95 ± 0.09
Multimodal				
CLIP	77.94 ± 0.01	77.88	77.94	77.75 ± 0.00
ViT+mBERT	**90.92** ± 0.001	**90.91**	**90.92**	**90.91** ± .001

Table 2: Performance comparison of unimodal and multimodal models on the test set. The symbols A, P, R, and F1 denote accuracy, precision, recall, and F1-score, respectively. The standard deviation (±) with three random seeds is reported.

lized to ensure sufficient processing capability.

5.1 Results

Table 2 provides an overview of the performance of various unimodal and multimodal models. Among the visual-only models, ViT emerges as the top performer with an F1 score of 82.03, surpassing other models like ResNet and Xception. On the textual side, m-BERT outshines all other unimodal models, achieving a remarkable F1 score of 87.43. However, the proposed model **ViT+mBERT** demonstrates the most significant advancement, achieving an F1 score of **90.92**, marking an improvement of several percentage points over the best baseline model. This result underscores the proposed approach's superior effectiveness in leveraging visual and textual modalities. The CLIP model showed inferior performance (F1 score of 77.75%) due to the domain gap in pretraining, limited fine-tuning, lack of modality-specific processing, and insufficient task-specific adaptation.

6 Error Analysis

In our study on the classification of multimodal commercial content from social media, we performed an extensive error analysis to identify the strengths and weaknesses of our proposed model. The analysis was conducted quantitatively and qualitatively to understand the model's performance comprehensively.

Quantitative Analysis: During the evaluation, we conducted a detailed quantitative analysis using confusion matrices to assess the model's performance.

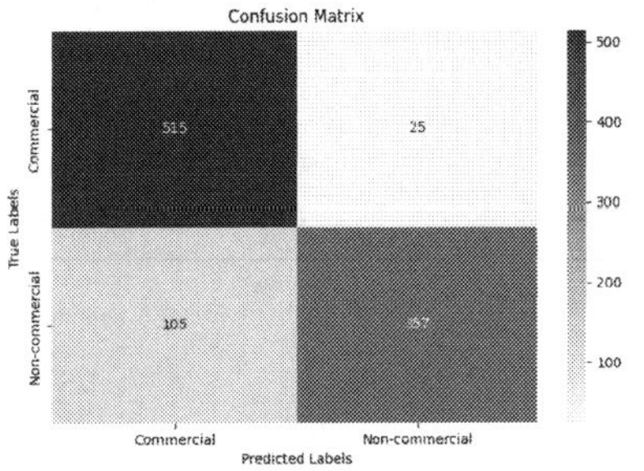

(a) Best textual model

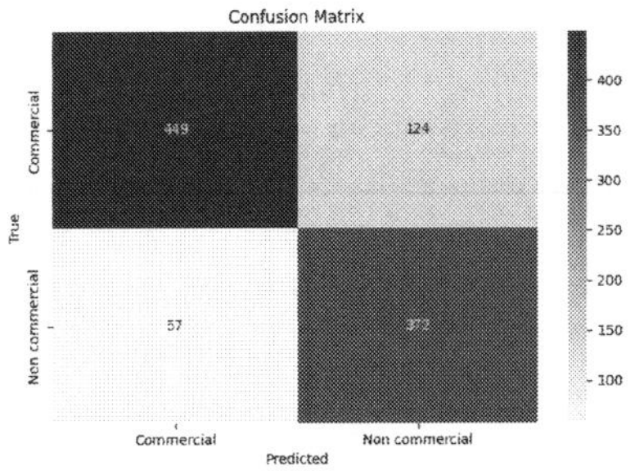

(b) Best visual model

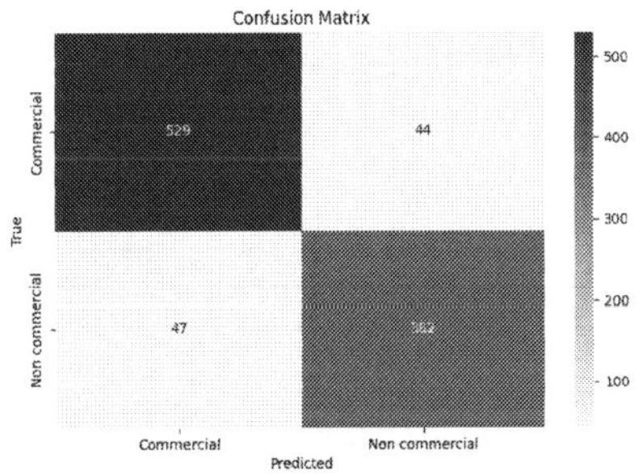

(c) Proposed model

Figure 4: Confusion matrices of employed models

The confusion matrices are shown in Figure 4 states that the proposed multimodal model **ViT+mBERT**, which integrates both text and visual data, achieved an accuracy of 90.92%. This represents a significant improvement over unimodal models that rely solely on visual or textual data, demonstrating the model's effectiveness in accurately classifying commercial content on social media platforms. The analysis revealed specific challenges, particularly with subtle commercial content. Posts that casually mentioned products without explicit promotional intent were occasionally misclassified as non-commercial despite the presence of brand-related keywords. For instance, these errors occurred in 7.68% of the cases. Conversely, non-commercial posts that included neutral or critical discussions of products were sometimes wrongly categorized as commercial, likely due to an overreliance on product-related keywords. This misclassification was observed in 10.95% of the cases. Moreover, the complexity of multimodal data led to further misclassification issues. Specifically, posts with ambiguous text and neutral visuals were prone to errors, which occurred 15.87% of the time. This underscores the need for more sophisticated textual and visual data integration to improve classification accuracy and reduce errors. Table 3 shows the error rate of both unimodal and multimodal models. The detailed **Qualitative Analysis** is explained in Appendix C.

Approach	% of Error
Visual Only	
Xception	35.83
VGG19	26.35
VGG16	25.82
ResNet	20.86
DenseNet	32.16
ViT	**18.30**
Textual Only	
BERT	18.82
XLM-R	25.75
B-BERT	15.44
m-BERT	13.17
Multimodal	
CLIP	22.25
ViT+mBERT	**9.09**

Table 3: Error rate of employed models

7 Conclusion

This paper proposed a multimodal framework for detecting commercial content in Bengali social media posts, evaluated on the newly developed **MDC**^{3} dataset with 5,007 posts labeled as commercial and non-commercial. The study utilized models such as mBERT for textual features and ViT for visual features. Results show that multimodal approaches significantly outperform unimodal methods, with ViT+mBERT achieving the best performance. Error analysis identified challenges in detecting subtle advertising styles. Future work will expand the dataset, incorporate diverse domains, and explore advanced fusion techniques to improve model robustness and performance. Moreover, explainability analysis will also be included to improve the model's clarity.

Limitations

The proposed methodology utilized a late fusion, which possesses several limitations. The class imbalance within the dataset may lead to biased predictions toward the more prevalent class, thereby compromising the model's performance. The explainability of how the model mitigates bias is not explained in the paper. The dynamic nature of social media content may hinder the model's ability to generalize to novel content types not sufficiently represented in the training data. While the late fusion technique effectively merges visual and textual features, it may not fully capture the intricate interdependencies between these modalities, thus limiting the model's capacity to generate optimal predictions.

References

Tanzin Ahammad, Zaima Sartaj Taheri, and Fahim Shakil Tamim. 2024. Sentiment classification of multi-modal memes using deep learning and transformer techniques. In *2024 IEEE International Conference on Computing, Applications and Systems (COMPAS)*, pages 1–6.

Nadir On The Go Bangla. 2024. [Online; accessed 24-August-2024]. [link].

Abhik Bhattacharjee, Tahmid Hasan, Wasi Uddin Ahmad, Kazi Samin, Md Saiful Islam, Anindya Iqbal, M. Sohel Rahman, and Rifat Shahriyar. 2022. Banglabert: Language model pretraining and benchmarks for low-resource language understanding evaluation in bangla. *Preprint*, arXiv:2101.00204.

S. C. Boerman and E. A. van Reijmersdal. 2016a. The effects of disclosure of sponsored content on social media influencers' credibility and engagement. *Journal of Advertising*, 45(4):466–475.

Sophie C. Boerman and Eva A. van Reijmersdal. 2016b. The effects of the standardized disclosure for online sponsored content: A systematic review. *Journal of Advertising*, 45(4):458–472.

Ting Chen, Simon Kornblith, Mohammad Norouzi, and Geoffrey Hinton. 2020. A simple framework for contrastive learning of visual representations. *Preprint*, arXiv:2002.05709.

Aleena Chia. 2012. Welcome to me-mart: The politics of user-generated content in personal blogs. *American Behavioral Scientist*, 56(4):421–438.

François Chollet. 2017. Xception: Deep learning with depthwise separable convolutions. *Preprint*, arXiv:1610.02357.

Rafsan The Chotovai. 2024. [Online; accessed 2-January-2025]. [link].

Md. Sajid Alam Chowdhury, Mostak Chowdhury, Anik Shanto, Hasan Murad, and Udoy Das. 2024. Fired_from_NLP at AraFinNLP 2024: Dual-phase-BERT - a fine-tuned transformer-based model for multi-dialect intent detection in the financial domain for the Arabic language. In *Proceedings of The Second Arabic Natural Language Processing Conference*, pages 410–414, Bangkok, Thailand. Association for Computational Linguistics.

Jacob Cohen. 1960. A coefficient of agreement for nominal scales. *Educational and Psychological Measurement*, 20(1):37–46.

Alexis Conneau, Kartikay Khandelwal, Naman Goyal, Vishrav Chaudhary, Guillaume Wenzek, Francisco Guzmán, Edouard Grave, Myle Ott, Luke Zettlemoyer, and Veselin Stoyanov. 2020. Unsupervised cross-lingual representation learning at scale. *Preprint*, arXiv:1911.02116.

Jacob Devlin, Ming-Wei Chang, Kenton Lee, and Kristina Toutanova. 2019. Bert: Pre-training of deep bidirectional transformers for language understanding. *Preprint*, arXiv:1810.04805.

Alexey Dosovitskiy, Lucas Beyer, Alexander Kolesnikov, Dirk Weissenborn, Xiaohua Zhai, Thomas Unterthiner, Mostafa Dehghani, Matthias Minderer, Georg Heigold, Sylvain Gelly, Jakob Uszkoreit, and Neil Houlsby. 2021. An image is worth 16x16 words: Transformers for image recognition at scale. *Preprint*, arXiv:2010.11929.

Neha Fun Fitness. 2024. [Online; accessed 24-September-2024]. [link].

Thilini Chathurika Gamage and Nicholas Jeremy Ashill. 2023. # sponsored-influencer marketing: effects of the commercial orientation of influencer-created content on followers' willingness to search for information. *Journal of Product & Brand Management*, 32(2):316–329.

Kaiming He, Xiangyu Zhang, Shaoqing Ren, and Jian Sun. 2015. Deep residual learning for image recognition. *Preprint*, arXiv:1512.03385.

Anderson Hidarto and Aryani Andrieza. 2022. Gender differences in influencer advertisements on instagram: A multimodal perspective. *Journal of Language and Literature*, 22(1):220–237.

Gao Huang, Zhuang Liu, Laurens van der Maaten, and Kilian Q. Weinberger. 2018. Densely connected convolutional networks. *Preprint*, arXiv:1608.06993.

Seungbae Kim, Jyun-Yu Jiang, Masaki Nakada, Jinyoung Han, and Wei Wang. 2020. Multimodal post attentive profiling for influencer marketing. In *Proceedings of The Web Conference 2020*, pages 2878–2884.

E. F. McQuarrie and J. M. Munson. 2014. Fusing advertising and entertainment: A review of the literature. *Journal of Advertising Research*, 54(3):234–249.

Sushain Pandit, Fang Wang, Vijay Ekambaram, and Sarbajit K Rakshit. 2019. Trend identification and modification recommendations based on influencer media content analysis. US Patent App. 16/449,419.

Alec Radford, Jong Wook Kim, Chris Hallacy, Aditya Ramesh, Gabriel Goh, Sandhini Agarwal, Girish Sastry, Amanda Askell, Pamela Mishkin, Jack Clark, Gretchen Krueger, and Ilya Sutskever. 2021. Learning transferable visual models from natural language supervision. *Preprint*, arXiv:2103.00020.

Shajgoj. 2024. [Online; accessed 24-October-2024]. [link].

Anik Shanto, Md. Sajid Alam Chowdhury, Mostak Chowdhury, Udoy Das, and Hasan Murad. 2024. Fired_from_NLP at SemEval-2024 task 1: Towards developing semantic textual relatedness predictor - a transformer-based approach. In *Proceedings of the 18th International Workshop on Semantic Evaluation (SemEval-2024)*, pages 859–864, Mexico City, Mexico. Association for Computational Linguistics.

Shorodindu. 2024. [Online; accessed 1-January-2025]. [link].

Karen Simonyan and Andrew Zisserman. 2015. Very deep convolutional networks for large-scale image recognition. *Preprint*, arXiv:1409.1556.

Fahim Shakil Tamim, Sourav Saha, Avishek Das, and Mohammed Moshiul Hoque. 2023a. Detecting violence inciting texts based on pre-trained transformers. In *2023 26th International Conference on Computer and Information Technology (ICCIT)*, pages 1–6.

Fahim Shakil Tamim, Zaima Sartaj Taheri, and Mohammed Moshiul Hoque. 2023b. Detecting signs of depression from social media texts using generalized autoregressive pretraining transformer model. In *2023 26th International Conference on Computer and Information Technology (ICCIT)*, pages 1–6.

Mesut Erhan Unal, Adriana Kovashka, Wen-Ting Chung, and Yu-Ru Lin. 2022. Visual persuasion in covid-19 social media content: A multi-modal characterization. In *Companion Proceedings of the Web Conference 2022*, pages 694–704.

Heini Vanninen, Joel Mero, and Eveliina Kantamaa. 2023. Social media influencers as mediators of commercial messages. *Journal of Internet Commerce*, 22(sup1):S4–S27.

N Vedula, W Sun, H Lee, H Gupta, M Ogihara, J Johnson, G Ren, and S Parthasarathy. 2017. Multimodal content analysis for effective advertisements on youtube. arxiv.

Danae Sánchez Villegas, Catalina Goanta, and Nikolaos Aletras. 2023. A multimodal analysis of influencer content on twitter. *Preprint*, arXiv:2309.03064.

Jason Weismueller, Richard L Gruner, and Paul Harrigan. 2022. Consumer engagement in influencer marketing video campaigns: An abstract. In *Academy of Marketing Science Annual Conference*, pages 71–72. Springer.

A Annotation with Majority Voting

Algorithm 1 determines whether influencer posts on social media are commercial or non-commercial using majority voting from three annotators.

Algorithm 1 Majority Voting with 3 Annotators

Require: A set of posts $P = \{p_1, p_2, \ldots, p_n\}$. Each post p_i has three labels L_1, L_2, L_3 given by three annotators.

Ensure: Final labels for each post indicate "Commercial" (C) or "Non-Commercial" (NC).

function MajorityVoting($annotations$)
    $final\_labels \leftarrow []$
    for all $annotation \in annotations$ **do**
        $C, NC \leftarrow 0, 0$
        for all $label \in annotation$ **do**
            if $label ==' C'$ **then** $C \leftarrow C + 1$
            else if $label ==' NC'$ **then** $NC \leftarrow NC + 1$
        end for
        if $C \geq 2$ **then** $final\_labels$.append($'Commercial'$)
        else $final\_labels$.append($'Non-Commercial'$)
    end for
    return $final\_labels$
end function

B Hyperparameter Configuration

Different hyperparameters are tuned for visual and textual models. The best multimodal model's hyperparameters are also tuned based on the training dataset.

Textual Models: The textual models leverage transformer-based architectures like Bangla-BERT and m-BERT, requiring specific configurations to handle tokenized text effectively. The hyperparameters were fine-tuned to ensure optimal training for the text modality. Table 4 gives a brief overview of the parameter setups we have used in the model.

Parameter	Value
Learning Rate	5×10^{-5}
Optimizer	AdamW
Batch Size	16
Number of Epochs	8
Loss Function	CrossEntropyLoss
Maximum Sequence Length	128
Warmup Steps	500
Weight Decay	1×10^{-2}

Table 4: Hyperparameter configurations for textual models

Visual Models: For visual models, the configurations were adapted to focus on efficient processing of high-dimensional image data. Specific adjustments were made to cater to the requirements of convolutional networks. Table 5 gives a brief overview of the parameter setups we have used in the model.

Parameter	Value
Learning Rate	1×10^{-4}
Optimizer	SGD
Batch Size	64
Number of Epochs	20
Loss Function	BinaryCrossEntropyLoss
Image Size	224×224
Weight Decay	5×10^{-4}
Momentum	0.9

Table 5: Hyperparameter configurations for visual models

Multimodal Models: The multimodal models were designed to effectively integrate visual and textual features, leveraging their complementary nature for improved classification performance. The hyperparameters were carefully chosen to balance the unique requirements of each modality while optimizing the late fusion process. Table 6 gives a brief overview of the parameter setups we have used in the model.

C Qualitative Analysis

The qualitative analysis revealed that the model effectively identifies straightforward commercial content by integrating textual and visual cues, accurately classifying posts with explicit promotional language and product images. However, it struggles with subtle commercial content and ambiguous multimodal posts.

Parameter	Value
Learning Rate	2×10^{-5}
Optimizer	AdamW
Batch Size	32
Number of Epochs	10
Loss Function	BinaryCrossEntropyLoss
Fusion Method	Late Fusion (Concatenation)
Visual Feature Dimension	512
Textual Feature Dimension	768
Combined Feature Dimension	768
Dropout Rate	0.3
Weight Decay	1×10^{-3}

Table 6: Hyperparameter configurations for multimodal models

দাদাদের ৩৫০+ রান হলেই একটি পিৎজার সাথে আরেকটি ফ্রি
(If Dadas score 350+ runs, Buy one pizza, get one free)

(a)
Textual: Com (✓)
Visual: Non-Com (✗)
ViT+mBERT: Com (✓)

দেশাল ঈদ কালেকশন
(Deshal Eid Collection)

(b)
Actual: Com
Predicted: Non-Com

Figure 5: Example (a) illustrates a picture where the proposed method produces better predictions, and example (b) illustrates a wrongly classified sample. The symbols (✓) and (✗) indicate the correct and incorrect prediction.

For example, posts with brand mentions or subtle product placements and those with abstract images and vague text were often misclassified. These findings highlight the need for improved semantic understanding and differentiation between neutral and promotional content. Figure 5 depicts the label of data samples predicted by the proposed model.

D Social Media Profiles and Activity

The developed dataset is dedicated to multi-modal commercial content classification tasks. For developing the dataset, we have collected data samples from many social media pages. Table 7 shows some data sources from where data have been collected.

Name	Type	Affiliation	Popularity
Shajgoj (Shajgoj, 2024)	FP/IG	Beauty	2.1M
Nadir On The Go Bangla (Bangla, 2024)	FP	Travel	2.8M
Neha Fun & Fitness (Fitness, 2024)	FP/IG	Fitness	1.9M
Rafsan The Choto-vai (Chotovai, 2024)	FP/IG	Food	4.3M
Shorodindu (Shorodindu, 2024)	FP	Lifestyle	620k

Table 7: Social media profiles and activity

DateLogicQA: Benchmarking Temporal Biases in Large Language Models

Gagan Bhatia [ϕ], **MingZe Tang** [ϕ], **Cristina Mahanta** [ϕ], **Madiha Kazi** [ϕ]
University of Aberdeen
{g.bhatia.24,m.tang.24,c.mahanta.24,m.kazi.24}@abdn.ac.uk

Abstract

We introduce **DateLogicQA**, a human curated benchmark of *190* questions specifically designed to understand temporal bias in Large Language Models (LLMs). Covering seven date formats across past, present, and future contexts, DateLogicQA examines four reasoning types: commonsense, factual, conceptual, and numerical. Through human-led evaluations of 12 state-of-the-art LLMs, we identify Representation-Level Bias, arising from suboptimal embeddings that distort date semantics, and Logical-Level Bias, manifesting when correct date tokens yield flawed temporal reasoning. Our findings underscore persistent challenges in handling various date formats and temporal contexts, revealing the need for more robust pretraining data, targeted post-training methods, and precise tokenization strategies. By illuminating these biases, we provide actionable insights to guide the development of LLMs for accurate temporal reasoning across diverse real-world applications.

1 Introduction

Accurate temporal reasoning is essential for real-world applications like event planning and historical questions. However, biases in Large Language Models (LLMs) can lead to misinterpretations or errors in date-related tasks. Understanding these biases is essential for precisely handling numerical structures and contextual meanings, making temporal reasoning ideal for identifying and analysing biases in tokenization, representation, and logical reasoning.

A significant source of these biases originates from the tokenization process. While tokenizers divide the text into subword units, inconsistencies in tokenizing dates can disrupt reasoning tasks. This can lead to two types of biases: Representation-Level Bias, caused by inconsistencies in embeddings affecting semantic structures of dates, and Logical-Level Bias, where correct tokens do not yield accurate outputs due to misaligned internal processing. Together, these biases highlight the challenges LLMs face in preserving the integrity and interpretability of temporal data across diverse formats and contexts.

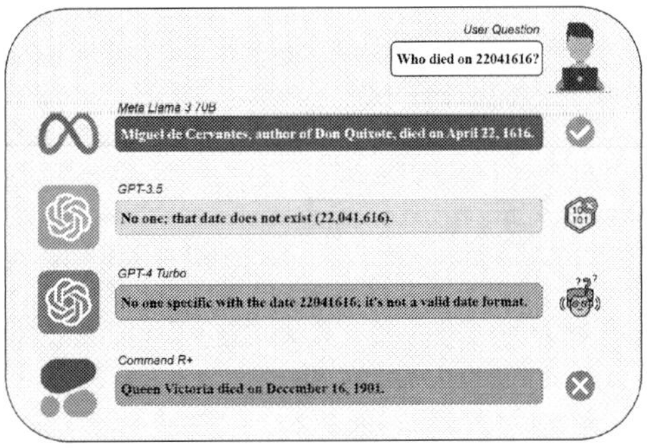

Figure 1: Examples of temporal biases in LLMs. **Incorrect** Response, **Faulty Date** but accurate reasoning indicating representation level temporal bias, **Faulty reasoning** but accurate date indicating logical level temporal bias, **Correct** response

This paper makes two significant contributions to understanding temporal biases in LLMs. **(1)** We introduce **DateLogicQA**, a dataset of 190 curated questions for evaluating temporal reasoning across various date formats, contexts (past, present, future), and reasoning types (commonsense, factual, conceptual, numerical). **(2)** We conduct human evaluations of model responses to analyse tokenization accuracy and reasoning quality, providing insights beyond automated metrics.

We have organised the paper as follows: Section 2 reviews related works, summarising the impact of tokenization on LLM performance and past temporal reasoning approaches. Section 3 details the creation of the DateLogicQA dataset, including its design principles and examples. Section 4 outlines methods for temporal reasoning, and biases. Section 5 presents experiment results, followed by a

Proceedings of the 2025 Conference of the Nations of the Americas Chapter of the Association for Computational Linguistics: Human Language Technologies (Volume 4: Student Research Workshop), pages 321–332
April 30 - May 1, 2025 ©2025 Association for Computational Linguistics

discussion of findings and bias mitigation in Section 6. Lastly, Section 7 summarises our contributions.

2 Related Works

Impact of Tokenization on Language Models Tokenization significantly affects the efficiency and reasoning abilities of large language models (LLMs). Research by Gu et al. (2024) and Goldman et al. (2024) highlights that tokenizers with higher compression rates enhance representation efficiency, particularly in smaller models. However, Schmidt et al. (2024) argue that effective tokenization also depends on pre-tokenization and vocabulary design. Studies like Ahia et al. (2023) show that poorly tokenized languages face performance and fairness issues. Furthermore, choices in tokenization impact reasoning; Zhang et al. (2024) and Singh and Strouse (2024) indicate that numerical tokenization can lead to errors in arithmetic and counting tasks. Rajaraman et al. (2024), Alberts et al. (2024), Minixhofer et al. (2024), and Gastaldi et al. (2024) show how well-designed tokenizers improve sequence pattern modelling and numerical reasoning through advanced embedding methods. Our study extends this work by examining tokenization's role in handling diverse date formats for temporal reasoning.

Temporal Reasoning in LLMs Temporal reasoning poses challenges for LLMs due to inherent biases. Zhu et al. (2024) discussed "nostalgia bias" (favouring outdated knowledge) and "neophilia bias" (speculative future predictions), while Tan et al. (2023b) observed inconsistent generalisation across different time periods. Structured approaches like temporal graphs (Xiong et al., 2024a) and synthetic datasets (Fatemi et al., 2024) enhance performance by explicitly encoding temporal relationships. Additionally, tokenization critically affects temporal reasoning; Zhao et al. (2024) found that temporal misalignment hampers accuracy, and Kishore and He (2024) identified inductive biases in models like GPT-3.5 and GPT-4. Su et al. (2024a) propose task-agnostic approaches to enhance temporal reasoning, while Gastaldi et al. (2024) and Rajaraman et al. (2024) link tokenization to reasoning performance. By analysing how tokenization strategies affect temporal reasoning, especially for date formats, our work fills a gap in understanding the interplay between tokenization and temporal task performance.

3 DateLogicQA

We introduce **DateLogicQA**, a dataset designed to explore how LLMs handle dates in various formats and contexts to tokenize, interpret, and reason with them. It consists of 190 questions divided into four categories: *commonsense*, *factual*, *conceptual*, and *numerical*. Each category features one of seven date formats across three temporal contexts: *past*, *present*, and *future*. This systematic variation allows for an in-depth analysis of LLMs' performance with temporal information.

Objective and Purpose The dataset aims to assess LLMs' tokenization and understanding of dates, as errors can lead to interpretative biases. By embedding dates within questions, we evaluate context-rich date interpretation, simulate real-world scenarios where dates carry contextual significance, and test LLMs' ability to extract and interpret date information accurately.

Concepts	Example
Numerical	What is the time 7 years and 9 months after 27101446?
Factual	Which of the people died on 23041616? A) Shah Jahan B) Miguel de Cervantes C) Princess Diana D) William Shakespeare
Conceptual	The first iPhone was released on 29062007. How many years has it been since its release?
Commonsense	John was born on 15-03-1985. He graduated from college on 01-05-2007. Was John older than 18 when he graduated?

Table 1: Dataset samples illustrating different temporal reasoning concepts.

Date Format	Example
DDMMYYYY	23041616
MMDDYYYY	04231616
DDMonYYYY	23April1616
DD-MM-YY	23-04-16
YYYY, Mon DD	1616, April 23
DD/YYYY (Julian calendar)	113/1616
YYYY/DD (Julian calendar)	1616/113

Table 2: Dataset samples illustrating different date formats used.

This approach comprehensively examines various temporal notations, including uncommon formats like Julian calendar representations.

Temporal Distribution DateLogicQA spans a broad temporal range, featuring dates from his

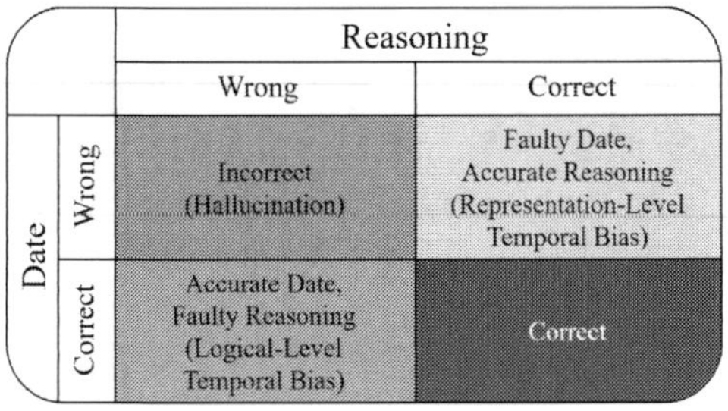

Figure 2: Human evaluation rubric

torical periods (e.g., the 1600s), modern contexts (e.g., the 2000s), and hypothetical futures (e.g., the 2100s). For clarity, we categorised dates into *past*, *present*, and *future*, with some questions covering multiple dates to assess LLMs' ability to manage temporal relationships across contexts.

Rationale for Design The dataset prioritises models' ability to interpret dates within broader narratives rather than as isolated data points. Its smaller size allows for careful curation of high-quality, linguistically diverse questions, focusing on specific nuances of temporal reasoning. This enables detailed analysis of model behaviour and understanding of temporal biases.

4 Methodology

4.1 Human-Led Temporal Bias Assessment

Understanding temporal contexts is crucial for analysing events over time. This includes grasping temporal references like *"How many years has it been since..."* (Past) and *"What will the contract's last day be..."* (Future), along with the maintenance of logical chronological order and adaptation to changes in context. For large language models, this capability is vital for tasks such as historical inquiries, time-sensitive query handling and predictions about future events. Assessing biases in temporal reasoning is essential for accuracy across various applications. We utilized the dataset referenced in Section 3.

We conduct a human evaluation to assess the temporal bias of LLMs as automated methods may exhibit inherent biases that affect results, ultimately undermining the evaluation's purpose. This methodology provides a more reliable analysis, identifying outliers that respond accurately without fully comprehending temporal aspects. Instead, it relies on contextual clues or learned patterns acquired during training or through retrieval-augmented generation.

Model responses are categorised based on colours in Figure 2, representing levels of temporal understanding. **Dark Orange** (■) denotes incorrect answers or temporal hallucinations from failure to tokenize dates or grasp context. **Light Orange** (■) reflects Representation-Level Temporal Bias, where the model tokenizes dates inaccurately but reaches the correct answer through logical reasoning. This suggests that some internal reasoning within the model compensates for misunderstanding the date format. **Light Teal** (■) signifies Logical-Level Temporal Bias, where the model tokenizes correctly but misapplies logic due to misattributing events or calculation errors. Finally, **Dark Teal** (■) denotes correct answers, indicating successful tokenization and logical reasoning. This illustrates a complete understanding of the question.

5 Results

5.1 Temporal Reasoning Analysis

Temporal reasoning, including processing and drawing inferences from historical and future dates, is one of the most challenging tasks for large language models. The current study investigates whether there are any differences in LLM performance when reasoning with historical dates, such as "July 20, 1969", and future dates, such as "January 1, 2050". To this end, we present the testing of 12 state-of-the-art LLMs using a question-answer dataset encompassing different date formats and various temporal contexts. This paper examines their skills in tokenization, comprehension, and inference on dates. We classify the answers into four categories based on their accuracy and treatment of the dates and logical structure involved, thereby providing a systematic evaluation framework.

In order to ensure that the assessment is robust, four human annotators, each with at least four years of experience in computer science, evaluated the responses across the four categories. The labelling achieved a high inter-annotator agreement with a Cohen's kappa (K) score of 0.80, confirming the reliability of the evaluation framework. These results evidence two critical areas where LLMs shine and their struggles, giving further information about their strengths and limitations concerning temporal reasoning.

Performance of Selected LLMs The evaluation of 12 language models, accessed through Hugging

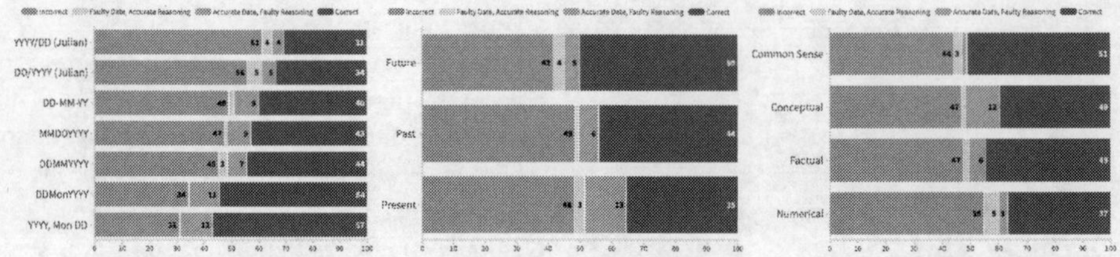

(a) Date Format visualisation (b) Time period visualisation (c) Question Type visualisation

Figure 3: Results Visualisations

Type of Q	Question	Answer	Date Format	Llama3-70B	Qwen2.5-72B	GPT-4o	GPT-4-turbo	CMDR+
Factual	Which of the following famous people died on 23041616? Answer only with A, B, C, or D: A) Shah Jahan B) Miguel de Cervantes C) Princess Diana D) William Shakespeare	William Shakespeare **OR** Miguel de Cervantes	DDMMYYYY	B) Miguel de Cervantes and D) William Shakespeare	B, D	B) Miguel de Cervantes	D)William Shakespeare	A
Conceptual	The Eiffel Tower was built between 028/1887 to 090/1889. How long did it take to build the Eiffel Tower?	2 years, 2 months, and 3 days	DD/YYYY (Julian)	The Eiffel Tower took 2 years and 1 month to build.	2 years, 10 months, 2 days.	2 years and 1 month.	It took 2 years and 2 months to build.	Construction of the Eiffel Tower took about two years and two months.
Common Sense	A new electric car model is set to be released on 273/2040. Pre-orders open 6 months earlier. On what date can customers start preordering?	On March 30, 2040	DD/YYYY (Julian)	273/2040 - 6 months = 93/2039. Customers can start preordering on this date.	Pre-orders open on 273/2039.	Customers can start pre-ordering on March 273/2039.	Customers can start preordering on March 273, 2040.	The pre-order date is July 273, 2039.
Numerical	What is the time 7 years and 9 months after 10271446?	July 27, 1454	MMDDYYYY	October 27, 2040.	10271446 + 7 years 9 months = 10353406	October 2023 plus 7 years and 9 months is July 2031.	Time: 10429846 (Unix timestamp format)	10279141

Table 3: Model Performance on DateLogicQA

Face and OpenAI APIs, provided a comprehensive overview of their performance on temporal reasoning tasks. Small models like Llama-3.2-3B (Dubey et al., 2024) and Phi-3.5-mini (Abdin et al., 2024) gave bad performances, with 58% and 66% incorrect answers, respectively. Due to their restricted processing and resources, these models performed poorly in tokenization and reasoning. Mid-sized models, including Mistral-7B (Jiang et al., 2023), Llama-3-8B (Dubey et al., 2024), and Llama-2-7B (Touvron et al., 2023), demonstrated a more moderate improvement. They had trouble with complex reasoning problems, although they were able to improve their tokenization accuracy. Larger models, including Llama-3-70B (Dubey et al., 2024), Qwen2.5-72B (Yang et al., 2024), and Command R+ (Cohere, 2024), were more robust in their performance, especially in date interpretation and logical reasoning. However, there were inconsistencies in specific formats. Proprietary models, including GPT-3.5 (Brown et al., 2020), GPT-4-turbo (OpenAI et al., 2023), GPT-4o, and GPT-4o-mini (OpenAI et al., 2024) outperformed all the rest, with GPT-4-turbo leading on correct responses with 63% and the lowest rate of incorrect answers at 16%. These results emphasise that model size, architecture, and diversity of pretraining data all bear on performance related to temporal reasoning tasks.

Performance Based on Date Formats The format of the date had a significant impact on model performance. Models performed best for formats that included clear separators and natural language cues, such as "YYYY, Mon DD" with 57% correct and "DDMonYYYY" with 54% correct. The poorest performance was from formats like "YYYY/DD (Julian)" and "DD/YYYY (Julian)", with only 31%

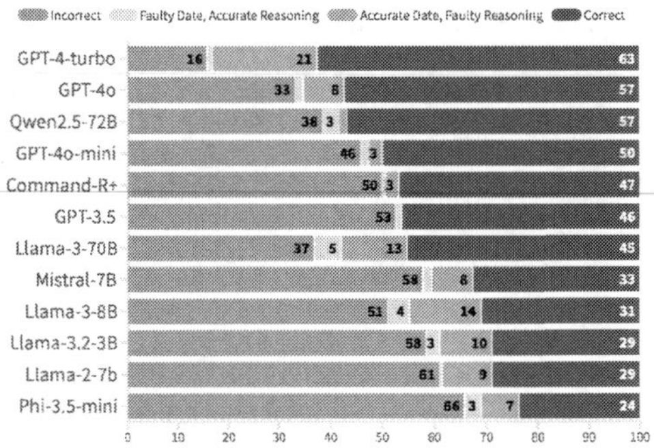

Figure 4: Each bar is segmented into four colors representing the quality of responses: ▩ **Incorrect** Response, ▩ **Faulty Date** but accurate reasoning indicating representation level temporal bias, ▩ **Faulty reasoning** but accurate date indicating logical level temporal bias, ■ **Correct** response

and 34% correct, respectively, since the representation is less common and more complex in tokenization. This trend indicates format standardisation's apparent relevance in improving date processing efficiency in LLMs.

Performance Across Temporal Contexts Temporal context also mattered a lot. Models were better with future dates, 50% correct, compared to historical dates, 44%, and present dates, 35%. This runs contrary to the expectations and may point to the fact that future-oriented reasoning tasks tap into the generative and predictive capabilities of the models. Historical and present contexts, which often require exact recall or conformity to training data, proved more difficult due to inconsistencies in the coverage of pretraining corpora.

Performance by Question Type Question type further modified results, with commonsense reasoning questions reaching the highest percentage of correctness: 51%. These questions depended less on explicit tokenization and more on logical inference, which LLMs did comparatively well. Factual questions were at 45%, while conceptual questions reached slightly lower performances of 40%. Numerical reasoning questions were the hardest; only 37% were correct since these often included some calculation or logical deduction that exposed the weaknesses in the models' reasoning capability.

6 Discussion

This study highlights the need for targeted strategies to address temporal biases in large language models (LLMs). A key step is to enhance pretraining datasets to ensure temporal diversity, incorporating historical, contemporary, and futuristic contexts. While resources like Redpajama (Weber et al., 2024) and Dolma (Soldaini et al., 2024) are open source, researchers should develop data focused on temporal reasoning with varied formats and cultural contexts.

Post-training methods, such as Direct Preference Optimization (DPO) (Rafailov et al., 2024), offer a promising avenue for fine-tuning models using curated datasets specifically designed to improve their logical temporal reasoning capabilities (Su et al., 2024b; Tan et al., 2023a). These approaches can help align the models' outputs with human-preferred logical reasoning patterns, addressing specific shortcomings in temporal tasks. Additionally, Retrieval-Augmented Generation (RAG) (Liu et al., 2024) enhances LLMs by integrating external knowledge dynamically during inference, allowing the models to access up-to-date or context-specific temporal information beyond their static training data. Moreover, prompting techniques such as Chain of Thought (CoT) prompting (Wei et al., 2023) enable models to break down complex temporal reasoning tasks into incremental steps, improving interpretability and logical coherence (Liu et al., 2024; Xiong et al., 2024b).

However, while these post-training methods significantly mitigate biases in temporal reasoning and improve model performance, they are not sufficient to completely eliminate inherent biases. Factors such as the limitations of pre-trained embeddings, the static nature of foundational knowledge, and the variability in task-specific datasets mean that biases are likely to persist at some level. Thus, post-training approaches should be viewed as an important step toward reducing biases.

7 Conclusion

Our paper addresses the challenges of temporal biases in large language models (LLMs) and proposes a structured approach to analyse their performance with temporal data. We introduced the DateLogicQA dataset and the Semantic Integrity Metric to evaluate the impact of diverse date formats and contexts on tokenization and reasoning. Our findings highlighted representation-level biases, where temporal contexts are inconsistently encoded, and logical-level biases, evident in varying outputs for similar prompts. We suggest mitigation strategies, such as temporally balanced pretraining datasets, post training and prompting methods.

Limitations

Future Scalability. The manual human evaluation approach for temporal reasoning performance analysis was time-consuming and challenging for future scalability. Furthermore, the evaluation technique requires high consensus among evaluators, especially when team size expands. Maintaining the evaluation quality in a larger team is also particularly difficult, and it might require more effort to cross-validate the results.

Ethical Considerations

AI usage. It's pertinent to acknowledge the role of AI tools such as ChatGPT in our project. Specifically, Grammarly was utilized minimally and primarily for grammar corrections in our documents. This use was strictly confined to enhancing linguistic accuracy and improving the readability of our written materials. It's important to clarify that the core research, analysis, and development were conducted independently by our team.

Human Annotation. The human annotators involved in this project are professionals with expertise in computer science. No sensitive or personally identifiable data was used in the annotation process, adhering to ethical guidelines and data privacy standards. The human annotators are co authors on this paper.

References

Marah Abdin, Jyoti Aneja, Hany Awadalla, Ahmed Awadallah, Ammar Ahmad Awan, Nguyen Bach, Amit Bahree, Arash Bakhtiari, Jianmin Bao, Harkirat Behl, Alon Benhaim, Misha Bilenko, Johan Bjorck, Sébastien Bubeck, Martin Cai, Qin Cai, Vishrav Chaudhary, Dong Chen, Dongdong Chen, Weizhu Chen, Yen-Chun Chen, Yi-Ling Chen, Hao Cheng, Parul Chopra, Xiyang Dai, Matthew Dixon, Ronen Eldan, Victor Fragoso, Jianfeng Gao, Mei Gao, Min Gao, Amit Garg, Allie Del Giorno, Abhishek Goswami, Suriya Gunasekar, Emman Haider, Junheng Hao, Russell J. Hewett, Wenxiang Hu, Jamie Huynh, Dan Iter, Sam Ade Jacobs, Mojan Javaheripi, Xin Jin, Nikos Karampatziakis, Piero Kauffmann, Mahoud Khademi, Dongwoo Kim, Young Jin Kim, Lev Kurilenko, James R. Lee, Yin Tat Lee, Yuanzhi Li, Yunsheng Li, Chen Liang, Lars Liden, Xihui Lin, Zeqi Lin, Ce Liu, Liyuan Liu, Mengchen Liu, Weishung Liu, Xiaodong Liu, Chong Luo, Piyush Madan, Ali Mahmoudzadeh, David Majercak, Matt Mazzola, Caio César Teodoro Mendes, Arindam Mitra, Hardik Modi, Anh Nguyen, Brandon Norick, Barun Patra, Daniel Perez-Becker, Thomas Portet, Reid Pryzant, Heyang Qin, Marko Radmilac, Liliang Ren, Gustavo de Rosa, Corby Rosset, Sambudha Roy, Olatunji Ruwase, Olli Saarikivi, Amin Saied, Adil Salim, Michael Santacroce, Shital Shah, Ning Shang, Hiteshi Sharma, Yelong Shen, Swadheen Shukla, Xia Song, Masahiro Tanaka, Andrea Tupini, Praneetha Vaddamanu, Chunyu Wang, Guanhua Wang, Lijuan Wang, Shuohang Wang, Xin Wang, Yu Wang, Rachel Ward, Wen Wen, Philipp Witte, Haiping Wu, Xiaoxia Wu, Michael Wyatt, Bin Xiao, Can Xu, Jiahang Xu, Weijian Xu, Jilong Xue, Sonali Yadav, Fan Yang, Jianwei Yang, Yifan Yang, Ziyi Yang, Donghan Yu, Lu Yuan, Chenruidong Zhang, Cyril Zhang, Jianwen Zhang, Li Lyna Zhang, Yi Zhang, Yue Zhang, Yunan Zhang, and Xiren Zhou. 2024. Phi-3 technical report: A highly capable language model locally on your phone.

Orevaoghene Ahia, Sachin Kumar, Hila Gonen, Jungo Kasai, David R. Mortensen, Noah A. Smith, and Yulia Tsvetkov. 2023. Do all languages cost the same? tokenization in the era of commercial language models.

Marvin Alberts, Gianmarco Gabrieli, and Irina Espejo Morales. 2024. Interleaving text and number embeddings to solve mathemathics problems.

Tom B. Brown, Benjamin Mann, Nick Ryder, Melanie Subbiah, Jared Kaplan, Prafulla Dhariwal, Arvind Neelakantan, Pranav Shyam, Girish Sastry, Amanda Askell, Sandhini Agarwal, Ariel Herbert-Voss, Gretchen Krueger, Tom Henighan, Rewon Child, Aditya Ramesh, Daniel M. Ziegler, Jeffrey Wu, Clemens Winter, Christopher Hesse, Mark Chen, Eric Sigler, Mateusz Litwin, Scott Gray, Benjamin Chess, Jack Clark, Christopher Berner, Sam McCandlish, Alec Radford, Ilya Sutskever, and Dario Amodei. 2020. Language models are few-shot learners.

Cohere. 2024. Command r+ model documentation. Comprehensive documentation and model details for the Command R+ model.

Abhimanyu Dubey, Abhinav Jauhri, Abhinav Pandey, Abhishek Kadian, Ahmad Al-Dahle, Aiesha Letman, Akhil Mathur, Alan Schelten, Amy Yang, Angela Fan, Anirudh Goyal, Anthony Hartshorn, Aobo Yang, Archi Mitra, Archie Sravankumar, Artem Korenev, Arthur Hinsvark, Arun Rao, Aston Zhang, Aurelien Rodriguez, Austen Gregerson, Ava Spataru, Baptiste Roziere, Bethany Biron, Binh Tang, Bobbie Chern, Charlotte Caucheteux, Chaya Nayak, Chloe Bi, Chris Marra, Chris McConnell, Christian Keller, Christophe Touret, Chunyang Wu, Corinne Wong, Cristian Canton Ferrer, Cyrus Nikolaidis, Damien Allonsius, Daniel Song, Danielle Pintz, Danny Livshits, David Esiobu, Dhruv Choudhary, Dhruv Mahajan, Diego Garcia-Olano, Diego Perino, Dieuwke Hupkes, Egor Lakomkin, Ehab AlBadawy, Elina Lobanova, Emily Dinan, Eric Michael Smith, Filip Radenovic,

Frank Zhang, Gabriel Synnaeve, Gabrielle Lee, Georgia Lewis Anderson, Graeme Nail, Gregoire Mialon, Guan Pang, Guillem Cucurell, Hailey Nguyen, Hannah Korevaar, Hu Xu, Hugo Touvron, Iliyan Zarov, Imanol Arrieta Ibarra, Isabel Kloumann, Ishan Misra, Ivan Evtimov, Jade Copet, Jaewon Lee, Jan Geffert, Jana Vranes, Jason Park, Jay Mahadeokar, Jeet Shah, Jelmer van der Linde, Jennifer Billock, Jenny Hong, Jenya Lee, Jeremy Fu, Jianfeng Chi, Jianyu Huang, Jiawen Liu, Jie Wang, Jiecao Yu, Joanna Bitton, Joe Spisak, Jongsoo Park, Joseph Rocca, Joshua Johnstun, Joshua Saxe, Junteng Jia, Kalyan Vasuden Alwala, Kartikeya Upasani, Kate Plawiak, Ke Li, Kenneth Heafield, Kevin Stone, Khalid El-Arini, Krithika Iyer, Kshitiz Malik, Kuenley Chiu, Kunal Bhalla, Lauren Rantala-Yeary, Laurens van der Maaten, Lawrence Chen, Liang Tan, Liz Jenkins, Louis Martin, Lovish Madaan, Lubo Malo, Lukas Blecher, Lukas Landzaat, Luke de Oliveira, Madeline Muzzi, Mahesh Pasupuleti, Mannat Singh, Manohar Paluri, Marcin Kardas, Mathew Oldham, Mathieu Rita, Maya Pavlova, Melanie Kambadur, Mike Lewis, Min Si, Mitesh Kumar Singh, Mona Hassan, Naman Goyal, Narjes Torabi, Nikolay Bashlykov, Nikolay Bogoychev, Niladri Chatterji, Olivier Duchenne, Onur Çelebi, Patrick Alrassy, Pengchuan Zhang, Pengwei Li, Petar Vasic, Peter Weng, Prajjwal Bhargava, Pratik Dubal, Praveen Krishnan, Punit Singh Koura, Puxin Xu, Qing He, Qingxiao Dong, Ragavan Srinivasan, Raj Ganapathy, Ramon Calderer, Ricardo Silveira Cabral, Robert Stojnic, Roberta Raileanu, Rohit Girdhar, Rohit Patel, Romain Sauvestre, Ronnie Polidoro, Roshan Sumbaly, Ross Taylor, Ruan Silva, Rui Hou, Rui Wang, Saghar Hosseini, Sahana Chennabasappa, Sanjay Singh, Sean Bell, Seohyun Sonia Kim, Sergey Edunov, Shaoliang Nie, Sharan Narang, Sharath Raparthy, Sheng Shen, Shengye Wan, Shruti Bhosale, Shun Zhang, Simon Vandenhende, Soumya Batra, Spencer Whitman, Sten Sootla, Stephane Collot, Suchin Gururangan, Sydney Borodinsky, Tamar Herman, Tara Fowler, Tarek Sheasha, Thomas Georgiou, Thomas Scialom, Tobias Speckbacher, Todor Mihaylov, Tong Xiao, Ujjwal Karn, Vedanuj Goswami, Vibhor Gupta, Vignesh Ramanathan, Viktor Kerkez, Vincent Gonguet, Virginie Do, Vish Vogeti, Vladan Petrovic, Weiwei Chu, Wenhan Xiong, Wenyin Fu, Whitney Meers, Xavier Martinet, Xiaodong Wang, Xiaoqing Ellen Tan, Xinfeng Xie, Xuchao Jia, Xuewei Wang, Yaelle Goldschlag, Yashesh Gaur, Yasmine Babaei, Yi Wen, Yiwen Song, Yuchen Zhang, Yue Li, Yuning Mao, Zacharie Delpierre Coudert, Zheng Yan, Zhengxing Chen, Zoe Papakipos, Aaditya Singh, Aaron Grattafiori, Abha Jain, Adam Kelsey, Adam Shajnfeld, Adithya Gangidi, Adolfo Victoria, Ahuva Goldstand, Ajay Menon, Ajay Sharma, Alex Boesenberg, Alex Vaughan, Alexei Baevski, Allie Feinstein, Amanda Kallet, Amit Sangani, Anam Yunus, Andrei Lupu, Andres Alvarado, Andrew Caples, Andrew Gu, Andrew Ho, Andrew Poulton, Andrew Ryan, Ankit Ramchandani, Annie Franco, Aparajita Saraf, Arkabandhu Chowdhury, Ashley Gabriel, Ashwin Bharambe, Assaf Eisenman, Azadeh Yazdan, Beau James, Ben Maurer, Benjamin Leonhardi, Bernie Huang, Beth Loyd, Beto De Paola, Bhargavi Paranjape, Bing Liu, Bo Wu, Boyu Ni, Braden Hancock, Bram Wasti, Brandon Spence, Brani Stojkovic, Brian Gamido, Britt Montalvo, Carl Parker, Carly Burton, Catalina Mejia, Changhan Wang, Changkyu Kim, Chao Zhou, Chester Hu, Ching-Hsiang Chu, Chris Cai, Chris Tindal, Christoph Feichtenhofer, Damon Civin, Dana Beaty, Daniel Kreymer, Daniel Li, Danny Wyatt, David Adkins, David Xu, Davide Testuggine, Delia David, Devi Parikh, Diana Liskovich, Didem Foss, Dingkang Wang, Duc Le, Dustin Holland, Edward Dowling, Eissa Jamil, Elaine Montgomery, Eleonora Presani, Emily Hahn, Emily Wood, Erik Brinkman, Esteban Arcaute, Evan Dunbar, Evan Smothers, Fei Sun, Felix Kreuk, Feng Tian, Firat Ozgenel, Francesco Caggioni, Francisco Guzmán, Frank Kanayet, Frank Seide, Gabriela Medina Florez, Gabriella Schwarz, Gada Badeer, Georgia Swee, Gil Halpern, Govind Thattai, Grant Herman, Grigory Sizov, Guangyi, Zhang, Guna Lakshminarayanan, Hamid Shojanazeri, Han Zou, Hannah Wang, Hanwen Zha, Haroun Habeeb, Harrison Rudolph, Helen Suk, Henry Aspegren, Hunter Goldman, Ibrahim Damlaj, Igor Molybog, Igor Tufanov, Irina-Elena Veliche, Itai Gat, Jake Weissman, James Geboski, James Kohli, Japhet Asher, Jean-Baptiste Gaya, Jeff Marcus, Jeff Tang, Jennifer Chan, Jenny Zhen, Jeremy Reizenstein, Jeremy Teboul, Jessica Zhong, Jian Jin, Jingyi Yang, Joe Cummings, Jon Carvill, Jon Shepard, Jonathan McPhie, Jonathan Torres, Josh Ginsburg, Junjie Wang, Kai Wu, Kam Hou U, Karan Saxena, Karthik Prasad, Kartikay Khandelwal, Katayoun Zand, Kathy Matosich, Kaushik Veeraraghavan, Kelly Michelena, Keqian Li, Kun Huang, Kunal Chawla, Kushal Lakhotia, Kyle Huang, Lailin Chen, Lakshya Garg, Lavender A, Leandro Silva, Lee Bell, Lei Zhang, Liangpeng Guo, Licheng Yu, Liron Moshkovich, Luca Wehrstedt, Madian Khabsa, Manav Avalani, Manish Bhatt, Maria Tsimpoukelli, Martynas Mankus, Matan Hasson, Matthew Lennie, Matthias Reso, Maxim Groshev, Maxim Naumov, Maya Lathi, Meghan Keneally, Michael L. Seltzer, Michal Valko, Michelle Restrepo, Mihir Patel, Mik Vyatskov, Mikayel Samvelyan, Mike Clark, Mike Macey, Mike Wang, Miquel Jubert Hermoso, Mo Metanat, Mohammad Rastegari, Munish Bansal, Nandhini Santhanam, Natascha Parks, Natasha White, Navyata Bawa, Nayan Singhal, Nick Egebo, Nicolas Usunier, Nikolay Pavlovich Laptev, Ning Dong, Ning Zhang, Norman Cheng, Oleg Chernoguz, Olivia Hart, Omkar Salpekar, Ozlem Kalinli, Parkin Kent, Parth Parekh, Paul Saab, Pavan Balaji, Pedro Rittner, Philip Bontrager, Pierre Roux, Piotr Dollar, Polina Zvyagina, Prashant Ratanchandani, Pritish Yuvraj, Qian Liang, Rachad Alao, Rachel Rodriguez, Rafi Ayub, Raghotham Murthy, Raghu Nayani, Rahul Mitra, Raymond Li, Rebekkah Hogan, Robin Battey, Rocky Wang, Rohan Maheswari, Russ Howes, Ruty Rinott, Sai Jayesh Bondu, Samyak Datta, Sara Chugh, Sara Hunt, Sargun Dhillon, Sasha Sidorov, Satadru Pan, Saurabh Verma, Seiji Yamamoto, Sharadh Ramaswamy, Shaun Lindsay, Shaun Lindsay, Sheng Feng, Shenghao Lin, Shengxin Cindy Zha, Shiva Shankar, Shuqiang

Zhang, Shuqiang Zhang, Sinong Wang, Sneha Agarwal, Soji Sajuyigbe, Soumith Chintala, Stephanie Max, Stephen Chen, Steve Kehoe, Steve Satterfield, Sudarshan Govindaprasad, Sumit Gupta, Sungmin Cho, Sunny Virk, Suraj Subramanian, Sy Choudhury, Sydney Goldman, Tal Remez, Tamar Glaser, Tamara Best, Thilo Kohler, Thomas Robinson, Tianhe Li, Tianjun Zhang, Tim Matthews, Timothy Chou, Tzook Shaked, Varun Vontimitta, Victoria Ajayi, Victoria Montanez, Vijai Mohan, Vinay Satish Kumar, Vishal Mangla, Vítor Albiero, Vlad Ionescu, Vlad Poenaru, Vlad Tiberiu Mihailescu, Vladimir Ivanov, Wei Li, Wenchen Wang, Wenwen Jiang, Wes Bouaziz, Will Constable, Xiaocheng Tang, Xiaofang Wang, Xiaojian Wu, Xiaolan Wang, Xide Xia, Xilun Wu, Xinbo Gao, Yanjun Chen, Ye Hu, Ye Jia, Ye Qi, Yenda Li, Yilin Zhang, Ying Zhang, Yossi Adi, Youngjin Nam, Yu, Wang, Yuchen Hao, Yundi Qian, Yuzi He, Zach Rait, Zachary DeVito, Zef Rosnbrick, Zhaoduo Wen, Zhenyu Yang, and Zhiwei Zhao. 2024. The llama 3 herd of models.

Bahare Fatemi, Mehran Kazemi, Anton Tsitsulin, Karishma Malkan, Jinyeong Yim, John Palowitch, Sungyong Seo, Jonathan Halcrow, and Bryan Perozzi. 2024. Test of time: A benchmark for evaluating llms on temporal reasoning.

Juan Luis Gastaldi, John Terilla, Luca Malagutti, Brian DuSell, Tim Vieira, and Ryan Cotterell. 2024. The foundations of tokenization: Statistical and computational concerns.

Omer Goldman, Avi Caciularu, Matan Eyal, Kris Cao, Idan Szpektor, and Reut Tsarfaty. 2024. Unpacking tokenization: Evaluating text compression and its correlation with model performance.

Shuhao Gu, Mengdi Zhao, Bowen Zhang, Liangdong Wang, Jijie Li, and Guang Liu. 2024. Retok: Replacing tokenizer to enhance representation efficiency in large language model.

Albert Q. Jiang, Alexandre Sablayrolles, Arthur Mensch, Chris Bamford, Devendra Singh Chaplot, Diego de las Casas, Florian Bressand, Gianna Lengyel, Guillaume Lample, Lucile Saulnier, Lélio Renard Lavaud, Marie-Anne Lachaux, Pierre Stock, Teven Le Scao, Thibaut Lavril, Thomas Wang, Timothée Lacroix, and William El Sayed. 2023. Mistral 7b.

Sindhu Kishore and Hangfeng He. 2024. Unveiling divergent inductive biases of llms on temporal data.

Jingyu Liu, Jiaen Lin, and Yong Liu. 2024. How much can rag help the reasoning of llm?

Benjamin Minixhofer, Edoardo Maria Ponti, and Ivan Vulić. 2024. Zero-shot tokenizer transfer.

OpenAI, :, Aaron Hurst, Adam Lerer, Adam P. Goucher, Adam Perelman, Aditya Ramesh, Aidan Clark, AJ Ostrow, Akila Welihinda, Alan Hayes, Alec Radford, Aleksander Mądry, Alex Baker-Whitcomb, Alex Beutel, Alex Borzunov, Alex Carney, Alex Chow, Alex Kirillov, Alex Nichol, Alex Paino, Alex Renzin, Alex Tachard Passos, Alexander Kirillov, Alexi Christakis, Alexis Conneau, Ali Kamali, Allan Jabri, Allison Moyer, Allison Tam, Amadou Crookes, Amin Tootoochian, Amin Tootoonchian, Ananya Kumar, Andrea Vallone, Andrej Karpathy, Andrew Braunstein, Andrew Cann, Andrew Codispoti, Andrew Galu, Andrew Kondrich, Andrew Tulloch, Andrey Mishchenko, Angela Baek, Angela Jiang, Antoine Pelisse, Antonia Woodford, Anuj Gosalia, Arka Dhar, Ashley Pantuliano, Avi Nayak, Avital Oliver, Barret Zoph, Behrooz Ghorbani, Ben Leimberger, Ben Rossen, Ben Sokolowsky, Ben Wang, Benjamin Zweig, Beth Hoover, Blake Samic, Bob McGrew, Bobby Spero, Bogo Giertler, Bowen Cheng, Brad Lightcap, Brandon Walkin, Brendan Quinn, Brian Guarraci, Brian Hsu, Bright Kellogg, Brydon Eastman, Camillo Lugaresi, Carroll Wainwright, Cary Bassin, Cary Hudson, Casey Chu, Chad Nelson, Chak Li, Chan Jun Shern, Channing Conger, Charlotte Barette, Chelsea Voss, Chen Ding, Cheng Lu, Chong Zhang, Chris Beaumont, Chris Hallacy, Chris Koch, Christian Gibson, Christina Kim, Christine Choi, Christine McLeavey, Christopher Hesse, Claudia Fischer, Clemens Winter, Coley Czarnecki, Colin Jarvis, Colin Wei, Constantin Koumouzelis, Dane Sherburn, Daniel Kappler, Daniel Levin, Daniel Levy, David Carr, David Farhi, David Mely, David Robinson, David Sasaki, Denny Jin, Dev Valladares, Dimitris Tsipras, Doug Li, Duc Phong Nguyen, Duncan Findlay, Edede Oiwoh, Edmund Wong, Ehsan Asdar, Elizabeth Proehl, Elizabeth Yang, Eric Antonow, Eric Kramer, Eric Peterson, Eric Sigler, Eric Wallace, Eugene Brevdo, Evan Mays, Farzad Khorasani, Felipe Petroski Such, Filippo Raso, Francis Zhang, Fred von Lohmann, Freddie Sulit, Gabriel Goh, Gene Oden, Geoff Salmon, Giulio Starace, Greg Brockman, Hadi Salman, Haiming Bao, Haitang Hu, Hannah Wong, Haoyu Wang, Heather Schmidt, Heather Whitney, Heewoo Jun, Hendrik Kirchner, Henrique Ponde de Oliveira Pinto, Hongyu Ren, Huiwen Chang, Hyung Won Chung, Ian Kivlichan, Ian O'Connell, Ian O'Connell, Ian Osband, Ian Silber, Ian Sohl, Ibrahim Okuyucu, Ikai Lan, Ilya Kostrikov, Ilya Sutskever, Ingmar Kanitscheider, Ishaan Gulrajani, Jacob Coxon, Jacob Menick, Jakub Pachocki, James Aung, James Betker, James Crooks, James Lennon, Jamie Kiros, Jan Leike, Jane Park, Jason Kwon, Jason Phang, Jason Teplitz, Jason Wei, Jason Wolfe, Jay Chen, Jeff Harris, Jenia Varavva, Jessica Gan Lee, Jessica Shieh, Ji Lin, Jiahui Yu, Jiayi Weng, Jie Tang, Jieqi Yu, Joanne Jang, Joaquin Quinonero Candela, Joe Beutler, Joe Landers, Joel Parish, Johannes Heidecke, John Schulman, Jonathan Lachman, Jonathan McKay, Jonathan Uesato, Jonathan Ward, Jong Wook Kim, Joost Huizinga, Jordan Sitkin, Jos Kraaijeveld, Josh Gross, Josh Kaplan, Josh Snyder, Joshua Achiam, Joy Jiao, Joyce Lee, Juntang Zhuang, Justyn Harriman, Kai Fricke, Kai Hayashi, Karan Singhal, Katy Shi, Kavin Karthik, Kayla Wood, Kendra Rimbach, Kenny Hsu, Kenny Nguyen, Keren Gu-Lemberg, Kevin Button, Kevin Liu, Kiel Howe, Krithika Muthukumar, Kyle Luther, Lama Ahmad, Larry Kai, Lauren Itow, Lauren Workman, Leher Pathak, Leo Chen, Li Jing, Lia

Guy, Liam Fedus, Liang Zhou, Lien Mamitsuka, Lilian Weng, Lindsay McCallum, Lindsey Held, Long Ouyang, Louis Feuvrier, Lu Zhang, Lukas Kondraciuk, Lukasz Kaiser, Luke Hewitt, Luke Metz, Lyric Doshi, Mada Aflak, Maddie Simens, Madelaine Boyd, Madeleine Thompson, Marat Dukhan, Mark Chen, Mark Gray, Mark Hudnall, Marvin Zhang, Marwan Aljubeh, Mateusz Litwin, Matthew Zeng, Max Johnson, Maya Shetty, Mayank Gupta, Meghan Shah, Mehmet Yatbaz, Meng Jia Yang, Mengchao Zhong, Mia Glaese, Mianna Chen, Michael Janner, Michael Lampe, Michael Petrov, Michael Wu, Michele Wang, Michelle Fradin, Michelle Pokrass, Miguel Castro, Miguel Oom Temudo de Castro, Mikhail Pavlov, Miles Brundage, Miles Wang, Minal Khan, Mira Murati, Mo Bavarian, Molly Lin, Murat Yesildal, Nacho Soto, Natalia Gimelshein, Natalie Cone, Natalie Staudacher, Natalie Summers, Natan LaFontaine, Neil Chowdhury, Nick Ryder, Nick Stathas, Nick Turley, Nik Tezak, Niko Felix, Nithanth Kudige, Nitish Keskar, Noah Deutsch, Noel Bundick, Nora Puckett, Ofir Nachum, Ola Okelola, Oleg Boiko, Oleg Murk, Oliver Jaffe, Olivia Watkins, Olivier Godement, Owen Campbell-Moore, Patrick Chao, Paul McMillan, Pavel Belov, Peng Su, Peter Bak, Peter Bakkum, Peter Deng, Peter Dolan, Peter Hoeschele, Peter Welinder, Phil Tillet, Philip Pronin, Philippe Tillet, Prafulla Dhariwal, Qiming Yuan, Rachel Dias, Rachel Lim, Rahul Arora, Rajan Troll, Randall Lin, Rapha Gontijo Lopes, Raul Puri, Reah Miyara, Reimar Leike, Renaud Gaubert, Reza Zamani, Ricky Wang, Rob Donnelly, Rob Honsby, Rocky Smith, Rohan Sahai, Rohit Ramchandani, Romain Huet, Rory Carmichael, Rowan Zellers, Roy Chen, Ruby Chen, Ruslan Nigmatullin, Ryan Cheu, Saachi Jain, Sam Altman, Sam Schoenholz, Sam Toizer, Samuel Miserendino, Sandhini Agarwal, Sara Culver, Scott Ethersmith, Scott Gray, Sean Grove, Sean Metzger, Shamez Hermani, Shantanu Jain, Shengjia Zhao, Sherwin Wu, Shino Jomoto, Shirong Wu, Shuaiqi, Xia, Sonia Phene, Spencer Papay, Srinivas Narayanan, Steve Coffey, Steve Lee, Stewart Hall, Suchir Balaji, Tal Broda, Tal Stramer, Tao Xu, Tarun Gogineni, Taya Christianson, Ted Sanders, Tejal Patwardhan, Thomas Cunninghman, Thomas Degry, Thomas Dimson, Thomas Raoux, Thomas Shadwell, Tianhao Zheng, Todd Underwood, Todor Markov, Toki Sherbakov, Tom Rubin, Tom Stasi, Tomer Kaftan, Tristan Heywood, Troy Peterson, Tyce Walters, Tyna Eloundou, Valerie Qi, Veit Moeller, Vinnie Monaco, Vishal Kuo, Vlad Fomenko, Wayne Chang, Weiyi Zheng, Wenda Zhou, Wesam Manassra, Will Sheu, Wojciech Zaremba, Yash Patil, Yilei Qian, Yongjik Kim, Youlong Cheng, Yu Zhang, Yuchen He, Yuchen Zhang, Yujia Jin, Yunxing Dai, and Yury Malkov. 2024. Gpt-4o system card.

OpenAI, Josh Achiam, Steven Adler, Sandhini Agarwal, Lama Ahmad, Ilge Akkaya, Florencia Leoni Aleman, Diogo Almeida, Janko Altenschmidt, Sam Altman, Shyamal Anadkat, Red Avila, Igor Babuschkin, Suchir Balaji, Valerie Balcom, Paul Baltescu, Haiming Bao, Mohammad Bavarian, Jeff Belgum, Irwan Bello, Jake Berdine, Gabriel Bernadett-Shapiro, Christopher Berner, Lenny Bogdonoff, Oleg Boiko, Madelaine Boyd, Anna-Luisa Brakman, Greg Brockman, Tim Brooks, Miles Brundage, Kevin Button, Trevor Cai, Rosie Campbell, Andrew Cann, Brittany Carey, Chelsea Carlson, Rory Carmichael, Brooke Chan, Che Chang, Fotis Chantzis, Derek Chen, Sully Chen, Ruby Chen, Jason Chen, Mark Chen, Ben Chess, Chester Cho, Casey Chu, Hyung Won Chung, Dave Cummings, Jeremiah Currier, Yunxing Dai, Cory Decareaux, Thomas Degry, Noah Deutsch, Damien Deville, Arka Dhar, David Dohan, Steve Dowling, Sheila Dunning, Adrien Ecoffet, Atty Eleti, Tyna Eloundou, David Farhi, Liam Fedus, Niko Felix, Simón Posada Fishman, Juston Forte, Isabella Fulford, Leo Gao, Elie Georges, Christian Gibson, Vik Goel, Tarun Gogineni, Gabriel Goh, Rapha Gontijo-Lopes, Jonathan Gordon, Morgan Grafstein, Scott Gray, Ryan Greene, Joshua Gross, Shixiang Shane Gu, Yufei Guo, Chris Hallacy, Jesse Han, Jeff Harris, Yuchen He, Mike Heaton, Johannes Heidecke, Chris Hesse, Alan Hickey, Wade Hickey, Peter Hoeschele, Brandon Houghton, Kenny Hsu, Shengli Hu, Xin Hu, Joost Huizinga, Shantanu Jain, Shawn Jain, Joanne Jang, Angela Jiang, Roger Jiang, Haozhun Jin, Denny Jin, Shino Jomoto, Billie Jonn, Heewoo Jun, Tomer Kaftan, Łukasz Kaiser, Ali Kamali, Ingmar Kanitscheider, Nitish Shirish Keskar, Tabarak Khan, Logan Kilpatrick, Jong Wook Kim, Christina Kim, Yongjik Kim, Jan Hendrik Kirchner, Jamie Kiros, Matt Knight, Daniel Kokotajlo, Łukasz Kondraciuk, Andrew Kondrich, Aris Konstantinidis, Kyle Kosic, Gretchen Krueger, Vishal Kuo, Michael Lampe, Ikai Lan, Teddy Lee, Jan Leike, Jade Leung, Daniel Levy, Chak Ming Li, Rachel Lim, Molly Lin, Stephanie Lin, Mateusz Litwin, Theresa Lopez, Ryan Lowe, Patricia Lue, Anna Makanju, Kim Malfacini, Sam Manning, Todor Markov, Yaniv Markovski, Bianca Martin, Katie Mayer, Andrew Mayne, Bob McGrew, Scott Mayer McKinney, Christine McLeavey, Paul McMillan, Jake McNeil, David Medina, Aalok Mehta, Jacob Menick, Luke Metz, Andrey Mishchenko, Pamela Mishkin, Vinnie Monaco, Evan Morikawa, Daniel Mossing, Tong Mu, Mira Murati, Oleg Murk, David Mély, Ashvin Nair, Reiichiro Nakano, Rajeev Nayak, Arvind Neelakantan, Richard Ngo, Hyeonwoo Noh, Long Ouyang, Cullen O'Keefe, Jakub Pachocki, Alex Paino, Joe Palermo, Ashley Pantuliano, Giambattista Parascandolo, Joel Parish, Emy Parparita, Alex Passos, Mikhail Pavlov, Andrew Peng, Adam Perelman, Filipe de Avila Belbute Peres, Michael Petrov, Henrique Ponde de Oliveira Pinto, Michael, Pokorny, Michelle Pokrass, Vitchyr H. Pong, Tolly Powell, Alethea Power, Boris Power, Elizabeth Proehl, Raul Puri, Alec Radford, Jack Rae, Aditya Ramesh, Cameron Raymond, Francis Real, Kendra Rimbach, Carl Ross, Bob Rotsted, Henri Roussez, Nick Ryder, Mario Saltarelli, Ted Sanders, Shibani Santurkar, Girish Sastry, Heather Schmidt, David Schnurr, John Schulman, Daniel Selsam, Kyla Sheppard, Toki Sherbakov, Jessica Shieh, Sarah Shoker, Pranav Shyam, Szymon Sidor, Eric Sigler, Maddie Simens, Jordan Sitkin, Katarina Slama, Ian Sohl, Benjamin Sokolowsky, Yang Song, Natalie Staudacher, Felipe Petroski Such, Natalie Summers, Ilya Sutskever, Jie Tang, Nikolas Tezak, Madeleine B. Thompson, Phil Tillet, Amin Tootoonchian, Elizabeth Tseng, Preston Tuggle, Nick Turley, Jerry Tworek, Juan Felipe Cerón Uribe, Andrea Vallone, Arun Vijayvergiya, Chelsea Voss, Carroll Wainwright, Justin Jay Wang, Alvin Wang, Ben Wang, Jonathan Ward, Jason Wei, CJ Weinmann, Akila Welihinda, Peter Welinder, Jiayi Weng, Lilian Weng, Matt Wiethoff, Dave Willner, Clemens Winter, Samuel Wolrich, Hannah Wong, Lauren Workman, Sherwin Wu, Jeff Wu, Michael Wu, Kai Xiao, Tao Xu, Sarah Yoo, Kevin Yu, Qiming Yuan, Wojciech Zaremba, Rowan Zellers, Chong Zhang, Marvin Zhang, Shengjia Zhao, Tianhao Zheng, Juntang Zhuang, William Zhuk, and Barret Zoph. 2023. Gpt-4 technical report.

Rafael Rafailov, Archit Sharma, Eric Mitchell, Stefano Ermon, Christopher D. Manning, and Chelsea Finn. 2024. Direct preference optimization: Your language model is secretly a reward model.

Nived Rajaraman, Jiantao Jiao, and Kannan Ramchandran. 2024. Toward a theory of tokenization in llms.

Craig W. Schmidt, Varshini Reddy, Haoran Zhang, Alec Alameddine, Omri Uzan, Yuval Pinter, and Chris Tanner. 2024. Tokenization is more than compression.

Aaditya K. Singh and DJ Strouse. 2024. Tokenization counts: the impact of tokenization on arithmetic in frontier llms.

Luca Soldaini, Rodney Kinney, Akshita Bhagia, Dustin Schwenk, David Atkinson, Russell Authur, Ben Bogin, Khyathi Chandu, Jennifer Dumas, Yanai Elazar, Valentin Hofmann, Ananya Harsh Jha, Sachin Kumar, Li Lucy, Xinxi Lyu, Nathan Lambert, Ian Magnusson, Jacob Morrison, Niklas Muennighoff, Aakanksha Naik, Crystal Nam, Matthew E. Peters, Abhilasha Ravichander, Kyle Richardson, Zejiang Shen, Emma Strubell, Nishant Subramani, Oyvind Tafjord, Pete Walsh, Luke Zettlemoyer, Noah A. Smith, Hannaneh Hajishirzi, Iz Beltagy, Dirk Groeneveld, Jesse Dodge, and Kyle Lo. 2024. Dolma: an open corpus of three trillion tokens for language model pretraining research.

Zhaochen Su, Jun Zhang, Tong Zhu, Xiaoye Qu, Juntao Li, Min Zhang, and Yu Cheng. 2024a. Timo: Towards better temporal reasoning for language models.

Zhaochen Su, Jun Zhang, Tong Zhu, Xiaoye Qu, Juntao Li, Min Zhang, and Yu Cheng. 2024b. Timo: Towards better temporal reasoning for language models.

Qingyu Tan, Hwee Tou Ng, and Lidong Bing. 2023a. Towards benchmarking and improving the temporal reasoning capability of large language models.

Qingyu Tan, Hwee Tou Ng, and Lidong Bing. 2023b. Towards robust temporal reasoning of large language models via a multi-hop qa dataset and pseudo-instruction tuning.

Hugo Touvron, Louis Martin, Kevin Stone, Peter Albert, Amjad Almahairi, Yasmine Babaei, Nikolay Bashlykov, Soumya Batra, Prajjwal Bhargava, Shruti Bhosale, Dan Bikel, Lukas Blecher, Cristian Canton Ferrer, Moya Chen, Guillem Cucurull, David Esiobu, Jude Fernandes, Jeremy Fu, Wenyin Fu, Brian Fuller, Cynthia Gao, Vedanuj Goswami, Naman Goyal, Anthony Hartshorn, Saghar Hosseini, Rui Hou, Hakan Inan, Marcin Kardas, Viktor Kerkez, Madian Khabsa, Isabel Kloumann, Artem Korenev, Punit Singh Koura, Marie-Anne Lachaux, Thibaut Lavril, Jenya Lee, Diana Liskovich, Yinghai Lu, Yuning Mao, Xavier Martinet, Todor Mihaylov, Pushkar Mishra, Igor Molybog, Yixin Nie, Andrew Poulton, Jeremy Reizenstein, Rashi Rungta, Kalyan Saladi, Alan Schelten, Ruan Silva, Eric Michael Smith, Ranjan Subramanian, Xiaoqing Ellen Tan, Binh Tang, Ross Taylor, Adina Williams, Jian Xiang Kuan, Puxin Xu, Zheng Yan, Iliyan Zarov, Yuchen Zhang, Angela Fan, Melanie Kambadur, Sharan Narang, Aurelien Rodriguez, Robert Stojnic, Sergey Edunov, and Thomas Scialom. 2023. Llama 2: Open foundation and fine-tuned chat models.

Maurice Weber, Daniel Fu, Quentin Anthony, Yonatan Oren, Shane Adams, Anton Alexandrov, Xiaozhong Lyu, Huu Nguyen, Xiaozhe Yao, Virginia Adams, Ben Athiwaratkun, Rahul Chalamala, Kezhen Chen, Max Ryabinin, Tri Dao, Percy Liang, Christopher Ré, Irina Rish, and Ce Zhang. 2024. Redpajama: an open dataset for training large language models.

Jason Wei, Xuezhi Wang, Dale Schuurmans, Maarten Bosma, Brian Ichter, Fei Xia, Ed Chi, Quoc Le, and Denny Zhou. 2023. Chain-of-thought prompting elicits reasoning in large language models.

Siheng Xiong, Ali Payani, Ramana Kompella, and Faramarz Fekri. 2024a. Large language models can learn temporal reasoning.

Siheng Xiong, Ali Payani, Ramana Kompella, and Faramarz Fekri. 2024b. Large language models can learn temporal reasoning.

An Yang, Baosong Yang, Binyuan Hui, Bo Zheng, Bowen Yu, Chang Zhou, Chengpeng Li, Chengyuan Li, Dayiheng Liu, Fei Huang, Guanting Dong, Haoran Wei, Huan Lin, Jialong Tang, Jialin Wang, Jian Yang, Jianhong Tu, Jianwei Zhang, Jianxin Ma, Jianxin Yang, Jin Xu, Jingren Zhou, Jinze Bai, Jinzheng He, Junyang Lin, Kai Dang, Keming Lu, Keqin Chen, Kexin Yang, Mei Li, Mingfeng Xue, Na Ni, Pei Zhang, Peng Wang, Ru Peng, Rui Men, Ruize Gao, Runji Lin, Shijie Wang, Shuai Bai, Sinan Tan, Tianhang Zhu, Tianhao Li, Tianyu Liu, Wenbin Ge, Xiaodong Deng, Xiaohuan Zhou, Xingzhang Ren, Xinyu Zhang, Xipin Wei, Xuancheng Ren, Xuejing Liu, Yang Fan, Yang Yao, Yichang Zhang, Yu Wan, Yunfei Chu, Yuqiong Liu, Zeyu Cui, Zhenru Zhang, Zhifang Guo, and Zhihao Fan. 2024. Qwen2 technical report.

Xiang Zhang, Juntai Cao, and Chenyu You. 2024. Counting ability of large language models and impact of tokenization.

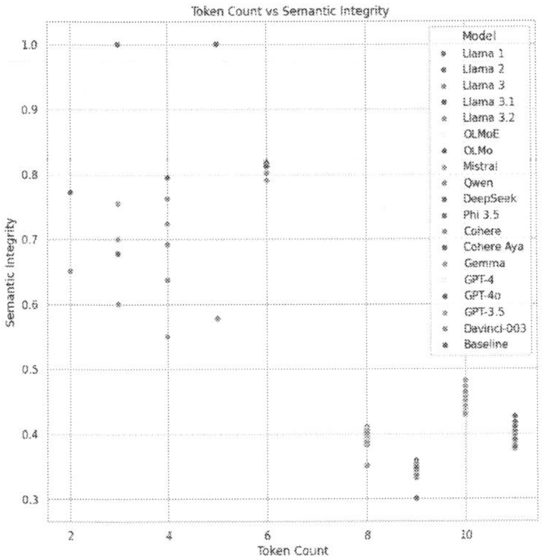

Figure 5: Correlation plot between semantic integrity score against token count

Bowen Zhao, Zander Brumbaugh, Yizhong Wang, Hannaneh Hajishirzi, and Noah A. Smith. 2024. Set the clock: Temporal alignment of pretrained language models.

Chenghao Zhu, Nuo Chen, Yufei Gao, Yunyi Zhang, Prayag Tiwari, and Benyou Wang. 2024. Is your llm outdated? evaluating llms at temporal generalization.

A Appendix

Format	Model	Date	Year	Time Period	Century	TC	Tokenized Output	SI	SC	PS
MMDDYYYY	Baseline	10271606	1606	Historical (Pre-2000)	17th Century	3	10 27 1606	1.00	false	true
MMDDYYYY	OLMoE	10271606	1606	Historical (Pre-2000)	17th Century	4	10 27 16 06	0.66	true	true
MMDDYYYY	OLMo	10271606	1606	Historical (Pre-2000)	17th Century	4	10 27 16 06	0.66	true	true
MMDDYYYY	Llama 3	10271606	1606	Historical (Pre-2000)	17th Century	3	102 716 06	0.60	true	true
MMDDYYYY	Llama 3.1	10271606	1606	Historical (Pre-2000)	17th Century	3	102 716 06	0.60	true	true
MMDDYYYY	Llama 3.2	10271606	1606	Historical (Pre-2000)	17th Century	3	102 716 06	0.60	true	true
MMDDYYYY	Davinci-003	10271606	1606	Historical (Pre-2000)	17th Century	3	1027 16 06	0.60	true	true
MMDDYYYY	GPT-3.5	10271606	1606	Historical (Pre-2000)	17th Century	3	102 716 06	0.60	true	true
MMDDYYYY	GPT-4o	10271606	1606	Historical (Pre-2000)	17th Century	3	102 716 06	0.60	true	true
MMDDYYYY	GPT-4	10271606	1606	Historical (Pre-2000)	17th Century	3	102 716 06	0.60	true	true
MMDDYYYY	Cohere Aya	10271606	1606	Historical (Pre-2000)	17th Century	8	1 0 2 7 1 6 0 6	0.45	true	true
MMDDYYYY	Gemma	10271606	1606	Historical (Pre-2000)	17th Century	8	1 0 2 7 1 6 0 6	0.45	true	true
MMDDYYYY	DeepSeek	10271606	1606	Historical (Pre-2000)	17th Century	8	1 0 2 7 1 6 0 6	0.45	true	true
MMDDYYYY	Cohere	10271606	1606	Historical (Pre-2000)	17th Century	8	1 0 2 7 1 6 0 6	0.45	true	true
MMDDYYYY	Qwen	10271606	1606	Historical (Pre-2000)	17th Century	8	1 0 2 7 1 6 0 6	0.45	true	true
MMDDYYYY	Phi 3.5	10271606	1606	Historical (Pre-2000)	17th Century	9	_ 1 0 2 7 1 6 0 6	0.40	true	true
MMDDYYYY	Llama 2	10271606	1606	Historical (Pre-2000)	17th Century	9	_ 1 0 2 7 1 6 0 6	0.40	true	true
MMDDYYYY	Mistral	10271606	1606	Historical (Pre-2000)	17th Century	9	_ 1 0 2 7 1 6 0 6	0.40	true	true
MMDDYYYY	Llama 1	10271606	1606	Historical (Pre-2000)	17th Century	9	_ 1 0 2 7 1 6 0 6	0.40	true	true

Table 4: Generated by Spread-LaTeX

AMR-RE: Abstract Meaning Representations for Retrieval-Based In-Context Learning in Relation Extraction

Peitao Han[1], Lis Kanashiro Pereira[2], Fei Cheng[3], Wan Jou She[4], Eiji Aramaki[1]
[1] Nara Institute of Science and Technology, Japan
[2] National Institute of Information and Communications Technology (NICT), Japan
[3] Kyoto University, Japan
[4] Kyoto Institute of Technology, Japan
han.peitao.hr3@is.naist.jp, liskanashiro@nict.go.jp, feicheng@i.kyoto-u.ac.jp
wjs2004@kit.ac.jp, aramaki@is.naist.jp

Abstract

Existing in-context learning (ICL) methods for relation extraction (RE) often prioritize language similarity over structural similarity, which may result in overlooking entity relationships. We propose an AMR-enhanced retrieval-based ICL method for RE to address this issue. Our model retrieves in-context examples based on semantic structure similarity between task inputs and training samples. We conducted experiments in the *Supervised* setting on four standard English RE datasets. The results show that our method achieves state-of-the-art performance on three datasets and competitive results on the fourth. Furthermore, our method outperforms baselines by a large margin across all datasets in the more demanding *Unsupervised* setting.

1 Introduction

Large language models (LLMs) exhibit strong in-context learning (ICL) abilities across various NLP tasks simply by being given a few examples of the task. However, the quality of few-shot demonstrations can substantially impact the performance of ICL, and tasks requiring high precision, such as relation extraction, remain challenging.

Relation extraction (RE) is a task to identify a predefined semantic relation between entity pairs mentioned in the context. Relations between entity pairs are often implicitly expressed, which can lead to suboptimal ICL performance. Existing ICL methods for RE often overlook the semantic associations between entity pairs, relying primarily on entity mentions or overall sentence semantics for representation (Han et al., 2023; Wan et al., 2023; Li et al., 2024; Ma et al., 2023; Sun et al., 2023).

Abstract Meaning Representation (AMR) (Banarescu et al., 2013) provides a detailed semantic graph structure that represents semantics through nodes and edges, where nodes correspond to semantic elements such as events, entities and arguments, and edges indicate the relationships between them. AMR graphs offer precise descriptions of entities by incorporating their arguments and semantic roles, making them well suited for the RE task (Hu et al., 2023; Zhang and Ji, 2021; Gururaja et al., 2023).

As shown in Figure 1, the input sentence, "... get great joy from eating ...", is parsed into a semantic graph, where the node "source" connects to two entity nodes ("joy" and "eat-01"). This structure explicitly represents the Cause-Effect relation between these two arguments, illustrating how semantic graphs can capture underlying relational meanings beyond surface text.

To bridge the contextual gap caused by missing semantic structure, we propose ***AMR-RE***, an AMR-enhanced retrieval-based ICL method that leverages AMR graphs to select in-context examples based on semantic structure similarity. Evaluations on four English RE datasets show that our method surpasses state-of-the-art methods on three datasets with the *Supervised* AMR-based retriever (Section 4.1). To comprehensively assess our approach, we further evaluate AMR-RE in the more challenging *Unsupervised* setting. Our simple yet effective architecture (Section 4.2) consistently achieves higher F1 scores compared to sentence embedding-based ICL baselines.

2 Preliminaries

2.1 Task Definition

Given a set of pre-defined relation classes $\mathbb{R}$, relation extraction aims to predict the relation $y \in \mathbb{R}$ between the given pair of subject and object entities (e_{sub}, e_{obj}) within the input context $\mathbf{C}$, or if there is no pre-defined relation between them, predict $y =$ NULL. We formalize RE as a language generation task, and introduce the prompt construction in the next section.

Proceedings of the 2025 Conference of the Nations of the Americas Chapter of the Association for Computational Linguistics: Human Language Technologies (Volume 4: Student Research Workshop), pages 333–342

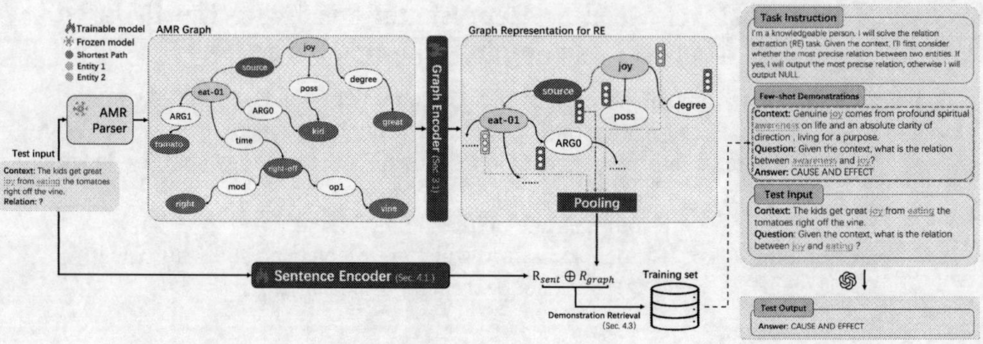

Figure 1: **An overview of our proposed method in the *Supervised* Setting (Section 3, Section 4.1).** Given a test input, we first adopt our AMR-enhanced demonstration retrieval method to select proper demonstrations from the training set. Subsequently, all retrieved demonstrations are included in the prompt construction.

2.2 Prompt Construction

We construct a prompt for each test example. Each prompt consists of three components:

Instructions: We provide a precise description of the RE task and a set of pre-defined relation classes $\mathbb{R}$. The model is required to output the relation corresponding to these predefined classes; if the relation does not belong to any of these classes, the model will output NULL.

ICL Demonstrations: Given one test example, we search k-Nearest Neighbor (kNN) demonstrations via two different frameworks: *Supervised* (Section 4.1) and *Unsupervised* (Section 4.2). All demonstrations are included in the prompt.

Test Input: We provide the test input in the same format as the ICL Demonstrations, and the LLM is expected to output the relation.

3 The AMR-RE Model

This section gives an overview of our ***AMR-RE*** method (Figure 1). Given an input text, AMR-RE first generates its AMR graph using an off-the-shelf AMR parser. A self-supervised graph model then encodes this graph to obtain the graph embeddings. These embeddings are then used to retrieve kNN examples from the training set for ICL (Wan et al., 2023).

Our method leverages the shortest path between two entities for retrieving RE demonstrations, as it aligns with the core objective (supplying semantic structure) of the RE task.

3.1 AMR Graph Encoding

AMR Graph Construction: To generate the AMR graph from the input text, we adopt an off-the-shelf AMR parser[1]. We parse the input sentence into an AMR graph $G = \{V, E, R\}$, where V, E, R are the sets of nodes, edges, and relation types, respectively. In G, the edge labeled $(u, r, v) \in E$, where $u, v \in V$ and $r \in R$, means that there is an edge labeled r from node u to node v.

Self-supervised Graph Encoder: After constructing the AMR graph from the input text, we use a graph encoder to produce the graph embeddings. Shou and Lin (2023) employ a self-supervised approach to train an AMR graph-based neural network; this model assesses the AMR similarity through the encoded representations, hereafter referred to as the *SS-GNN* model. We adapt *SS-GNN* for the RE task by optimizing it on our proposed graph RE representations. Notably, this training framework only depends on the corpus without annotated relation labels. This method explicitly optimizes representations by assessing the similarity between two AMR graphs via a contrastive loss. Training details are added in Appendix A. Given an AMR graph $G = [(u_1, r_1, v_1), \cdots, (u_n, r_n, v_n)]$, G is linearized by a depth-first traversal algorithm $G = [u_1, r_1, v_1, \cdots, u_n, r_n, v_n; \mathcal{A}]$, where $\mathcal{A}$ is the adjacency matrix. G will be fed to SS-GNN to obtain the node representations $H_{node} = \{h^{u_1}_{node}, h^{r_1}_{node}, \cdots, h^{v_n}_{node}\}$ where h^{a}_{node} denotes as the node representation of node a.

$$H_{node} = \text{SS-GNN}([u_1, r_1, v_1, \cdots, v_n]; \mathcal{A}) \quad (1)$$

3.2 Graph Representation for RE

The *SS-GNN* model originally employs mean pooling of all nodes in the AMR graph as the graph representation, which is also used for self-supervised

[1]https://github.com/IBM/transition-amr-parser

training. While this approach has demonstrated significant advancements in overall AMR similarity assessment, it is not optimized for identifying relationships between two specific entities. To address this limitation, we construct graph RE representations specifically designed for RE, focusing on capturing the structural and semantic information of entities and their relationships.

Inspired by previous works, the shortest path between two entities in the semantic structure (Hu et al., 2023) or the syntactic structure (Cheng and Miyao, 2017) often contains crucial information needed to determine relations. Based on these insights, we focus on leveraging the shortest AMR path (SAP) as the most informative subgraph for retrieving the relevant RE demonstrations.

To investigate the optimal way of representing a relation with AMR graph representations for the RE task, we establish fine-grained setups for the graph RE representation R_{graph}. Typically, the shortest path between the entity pair (e_{obj}, e_{sub}) can be denoted as $V_{path} = \{e_{obj}, p_1, p_2, \cdots, p_n, e_{sub}\}$ where $V_{path} \in V$, and p_i represents intermediate nodes on the shortest AMR path (SAP). We investigated two different pooling strategies and two path modeling strategies.

Pooling Strategy: To analyze the impact of the pooling strategy on R_{graph}, we adopt two pooling methods:

(1) *Mean Pooling*: We use the average of all node representations from the shortest path for retrieval, formally $R_{graph} = \frac{1}{|V_{path}|} \sum_{v_i \in V_{path}} h_{node}^{v_i}$.

(2) *Concatenation*: The node representations of the entity pair, $h_{node}^{e_{obj}}$ and $h_{node}^{e_{sub}}$, are concatenated with the mean pooling of the nodes along the shortest AMR path to form the final graph representation, formally $R_{graph} = h_{node}^{e_{obj}} \oplus h_{node}^{e_{sub}} \oplus h_P$, where $h_P = \frac{1}{n} \sum_{i=1}^{n} h_{node}^{p_i}$.

Path Modeling: We use two distinct methods to explore how to effectively leverage information from the shortest path:

(1) *SAP*: This approach strictly isolates all the information from the components not in the shortest path between entity nodes, and only the shortest AMR path is fed to *SS-GNN*, which encodes the node representations along the path. The final graph RE representation R_{graph} is constructed by pooling the node representations within the path.

(2) *SAP+CTX*: We use the whole AMR graph as the input for *SS-GNN*. In this setup, the node representations benefit from bidirectional attention and the GNN adapter, allowing them to integrate contextual information from neighbor nodes. The pooling of the node representations within the shortest AMR path is then formed as the graph RE representation.

By combining the pooling and path modeling strategies, we obtained four distinct configurations, with detailed results provided in Table 5.

4 AMR-Based Demonstration Retrieval

In this section, we introduce two settings for incorporating AMR graph information to retrieve ICL demonstrations. First, we present the *Supervised* setting, where AMR-RE benefits from both graph and sentence RE representations (Section 4.1). To further evaluate the effectiveness of our method, we assess AMR-RE under the more challenging *Unsupervised* setting (Section 4.2). AMR-RE retrieves in-context examples by kNN retrieval from the training set using the relation representation R_{rel} (Section 4.3).

4.1 *Supervised* Setting

In the *Supervised* setting, we integrate both sentence-level and structural information to achieve optimal performance and explore the potential interactions between these two types of representations.

Sentence RE Representations: We use PURE (Zhong and Chen, 2021), an entity marker-based RE model. For example, given the input sentence "And we will see you then", the subject entity "we" and object entity "you", the sentence becomes: "[CLS] And [SUB_ORG] we [/SUB_ORG] will see [OBJ_PER] you [/OBJ_PER] then [SEP]". The final hidden representations of the BERT encoder are denoted as $H_{sent} = \{h_{sent}^1, \cdots, h_{sent}^m\}$ where h_{sent}^i denotes the i-th hidden representation. Let s_{obj} and s_{sub} be the indices of the beginning of the entity markers [SUB_ORG] and [OBJ_PER]. We define the sentence representation as $R_{sent} = h_{sent}^{s_{obj}} \oplus h_{sent}^{s_{sub}}$, where $\oplus$ denotes the concatenation of representations along the first dimension.

Graph RE Representations: We obtain graph RE representations R_{graph} from the SS-GNN as we introduced in Section 3.1.

We use the concatenation of AMR graph embeddings R_{graph} from SS-GNN and sentence embeddings R_{sent} from PURE, formally $R_{rel} = R_{graph} \oplus R_{sent}$. SS-GNN and PURE are fine-tuned on RE datasets by predicting the relation probability from R_{rel} through a feedforward network. Notably, SS-GNN is first self-supervised trained, then subsequently fine-tuned on RE task.

4.2 *Unsupervised* Setting

We further evaluate our approach in the more challenging *Unsupervised* setting for comprehensively analyzing the effectiveness of AMR graph. In this setting, AMR-RE retrieves examples using only graph RE representations R_{graph}, which means $R_{rel} = R_{graph}$. Note that SS-GNN is only self-supervised on the corpus without annotated relation labels in *Unsupervised* setting. We compare our model with Sentence RE Representations-based baselines.

4.3 Demonstration Retrieval

The relation representation R_{rel} is used to perform kNN retrieval, where the top-k most similar demonstrations are selected and included in the prompt. To efficiently implement kNN demonstration retrieval, we adopt FAISS (Johnson et al., 2019) library for efficient search.

5 Experiments

Backbone LLM: We use OpenAI's GPT-4 as the LLM model in AMR-RE and in all baselines, and we set the number of demonstrations to $k = 10$ in the main results. For a fair comparison, all results are reproduced by ourselves. Baselines such as Wan et al. (2023) originally used GPT-3.5 (text-davinci-003), however, this model is not available through the OpenAI API anymore. In addition, GPT-4 has been shown to outperform its previous versions in several NLP tasks and was the SOTA backbone for ICL at the time. Our method can be easily applied to other backbones as well, however, models such as Llama currently cannot match GPT-4's performance in ICL (Chatterjee et al., 2024).

Evaluation Datasets: We evaluate our model on four English RE datasets. Two general domain RE datasets: SemEval 2010 Task 8 (Hendrickx et al., 2010) and ACE05[2], one temporal RE dataset: TimeBank-Dense (Cassidy et al., 2014), and one scientific domain dataset: SciERC (Luan et al., 2018). Due to the high cost of the OpenAI API, following Wan et al. (2023), we sample a subset of ACE05 dataset (due to its large size) for our experiments. Details of each dataset are provided in Appendix B. We adopt Micro-F1 as evaluation metrics. The hyperparameter settings are provided in the Appendix C.

[2]https://catalog.ldc.upenn.edu/LDC2006T06

6 Main Results

6.1 Results in the *Supervised* Setting

Baselines in *Supervised* Setting: To analyze the effectiveness of the AMR graph, we select two baseline methods for comparison with AMR-RE.

(1) *Supervised* RE Baseline w/o ICL: We implement *PURE* (Zhong and Chen, 2021) as a directly comparable baseline to show the impact of ICL.

(2) Baseline with *Supervised* Retrievers: We implement *GPT-RE_FT* (Wan et al., 2023) as the baseline with a *Supervised* retriever. GPT-RE_FT employs representations encoded by PURE (Zhong and Chen, 2021).

Results: Table 1 shows our results. Overall, AMR-RE outperforms the baselines in the *Supervised* setting. This indicates that the more explicit representation of AMR graphs enhances the quality of the retrieved demonstrations. In the *Supervised* setting, AMR-RE achieves SOTA performance on the SemEval, SciERC and TB-Dense datasets while delivering competitive results on the ACE05 dataset. The results indicate that the fine-tuned structure representation benefits from both structural and semantic information. However, ACE05 contains a large proportion of the samples annotated as NULL relation, which introduces significant noise. This can mislead the model during both retriever training and ICL inference, resulting in decreased performance compared to the fully-supervised baseline, PURE.

6.2 Results in the *Unsupervised* Setting

Baselines in *Unsupervised* Setting: We select three baselines that are comparable to AMR-RE in *Unsupervised* setting. The details of each baseline are introduced below:

(1) *GPT-Random:* we randomly select few-shot ICL demonstrations with additional constraints to ensure a more uniform label distribution;

(2) *GPT-Sent:* we follow Gutierrez et al. (2022) to retrieve kNN demonstrations with SimCSE (Gao et al., 2021), which is a widely used sentence embedding model;

(3) *GPT-RE_Entity+:* we adopt the entity-prompted sentence embedding proposed by Wan et al. (2023) that incorporates both the entity pair and contextual information for retrieval.

Method	Retriever	SemEval (Δ%)	TB-DENSE (Δ%)	SciERC (Δ%)	ACE05 (Δ%)	Avg
			Supervised Setting			
PURE	-	90.77	66.70	67.08	**68.62**	73.57
GPT-RE_FT	*PURE*	91.46	67.58	67.32	68.59	73.74
AMR-RE (Ours)	*SS-GNN+PURE*	**<u>91.97</u> (↑ 0.6)**	**71.54 (↑ 5.9)**	**68.10* (↑ 1.1)**	67.94* (↓ 0.9)	**74.89**
			Unsupervised Setting			
GPT-Random	-	67.83	22.03	16.48	9.73	29.02
GPT-Sent	SimCSE	77.64	28.73	21.60	10.04	34.50
GPT-RE_Entity+	SimCSE	80.25	31.19	26.15	13.10	37.67
AMR-RE (Ours)	*SS-GNN*	**<u>84.68</u> (↑ 5.5)**	**38.17 (↑ 22.4)**	**27.89* (↑ 6.7)**	**15.04* (↑ 14.8)**	**41.45**

Table 1: **Main results.** We set the number of demonstrations to $k = 10$. For AMR-RE, we only report the best results from the four distinct configurations obtained by combining the pooling and path modeling strategies, explained in Section 3.1 (see Table 5 for detailed results). Underlined results refer to the *SAP* graph RE representation, otherwise, *SAP+CTX* is applied. The Δ% indicates the corresponding differences in percentage when compared to GPT-RE_FT and GPT-RE_Entity+ in *Supervised* and *Unsupervised* settings respectively. The Avg column shows the average score for all datasets. The highest results are in **bold**. $*$ denotes that this result is implemented by concatenation pooling, otherwise, mean pooling is used.

Method	SemEval (Δ%)	SciERC (Δ%)
	Supervised Setting	
AMR-RE	**91.97**	**68.10**
w/o self-sup	90.82 (↓ 1.3)	67.04 (↓ 1.6)
w/o R_{sent}	89.71 (↓ 2.5)	67.19 (↓ 1.3)
w/o R_{graph}	91.46 (↓ 0.6)	67.32 (↓ 1.2)
	Unsupervised Setting	
AMR-RE	**84.68**	**27.56**
w/o self-sup	81.67 (↓ 3.6)	26.01 (↓ 5.6)

Table 2: **Ablation study.** For the full model, we show the best configuration results from Table 1. *w/o self-sup* indicates that the retriever is not self-supervised on the target dataset. The Δ% is the percentage of corresponding difference.

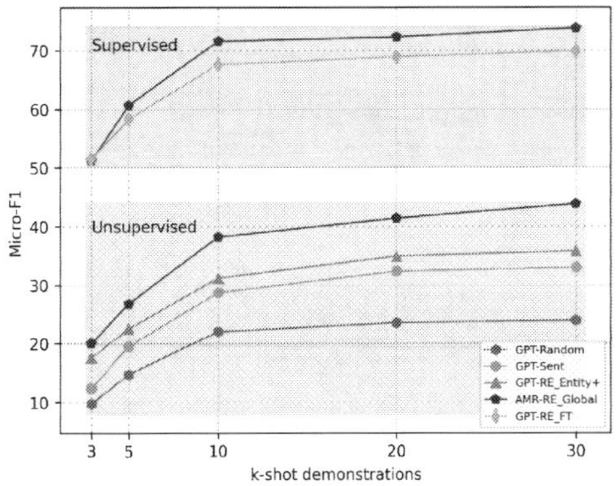

Figure 2: Performance for the different number of few-shot examples on TB-Dense.

Results: Table 1 shows our results in the *Unsupervised* setting. AMR-RE consistently outperforms the baselines on all four datasets. These findings underscore the efficacy of AMR-enhanced graph RE representations in effectively capturing relational information. In particular, by focusing on the shortest AMR path, AMR-RE highlights core entities and the semantic relations between them, thereby reducing noise and providing clearer relational cues compared to conventional sentence-embedding-based approaches.

7 Ablation Study

Table 2 illustrates the impact of self-supervision on the graph encoder and the roles of sentence and graph RE representations in the relation representations. The results show that self-supervision enhances performance, with graph (R_{graph}) and sentence (R_{sent}) representations both being crucial in the *Supervised* setting. We also investigated the impact of the number of demonstrations on performance. Figure 2 shows that AMR-RE consistently outperforms the baselines across all k-shots, demonstrating the effectiveness of incorporating AMR graphs for retrieval.

8 Case Study

To demonstrate how semantic structure similarity enables the retrieval of highly relevant demonstrations and surpasses sentence-based baselines on RE ICL, we present two representative case studies in the *Unsupervised* Setting. Figure 3 illustrates that our proposed AMR enhanced retrieval method effectively captures both the similarity of event structure and the semantics of the entities. This shows that demonstrations with high semantic structure similarity serve as more suitable and informative RE demonstrations for ICL. Figure 4 highlights the effectiveness of **AMR-RE**. Our proposed method successfully retrieves few-shot RE demonstrations with semantically equivalent entities (e.g., "proto-

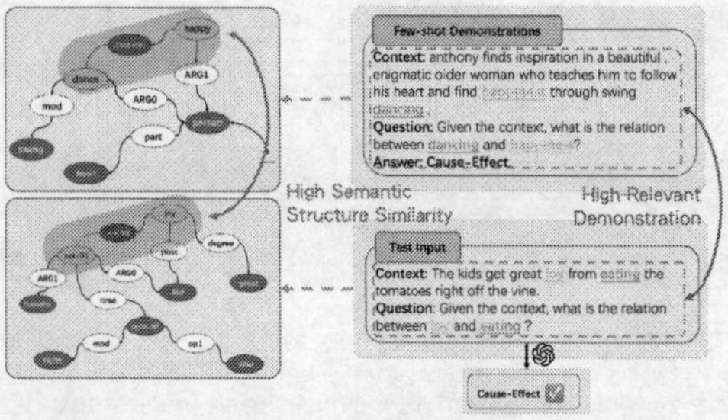

Figure 3: A case study of semantic structure similarity. The demonstration with similar semantic structure enables the LLM to correctly generate the gold label, "Cause-Effect".

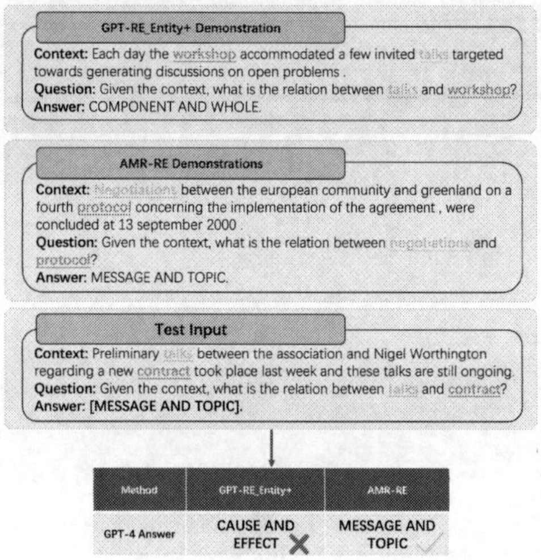

Figure 4: A case study of **AMR-RE** retrieved demonstration quality. MESSAGE AND TOPIC is the gold label.

col"–"contract", "negotiations"–"talks"), while also capturing implicit relational connections. It demonstrates AMR-RE's ability to align both explicit and implicit semantic information for improved relation extraction. In contrast, the sentence-based retrieval method fails to model such information.

9 Conclusions

We proposed ***AMR-RE***, an AMR-enhanced retrieval-based ICL method that uses AMR graphs to select demonstrations based on semantic structure similarity. Evaluations on four English RE datasets show that AMR-RE outperforms the baselines. This underscores the effectiveness of combining graph learning with LLMs for relation extraction. Our experiments further demonstrate that AMR graph information can lead to more accurate and robust relation extraction, even in *Unsupervised* settings.

10 Limitations

We focused our work on: 1) demonstrating the effectiveness of graph similarity in retrieval-based ICL on the RE task. However, our work can be generalized beyond RE, as AMR is a universal semantic analysis tool applicable to other tasks, and ICL is also not restricted to RE; 2) evaluating our method on English RE datasets, mainly because AMR parsers only offer promising performance in English (Cai et al., 2021). There are other semantic tools, such as multilingual dependency parser (Üstün et al., 2020), for constructing graphs that extend beyond English.

References

Laura Banarescu, Claire Bonial, Shu Cai, Madalina Georgescu, Kira Griffitt, Ulf Hermjakob, Kevin Knight, Philipp Koehn, Martha Palmer, and Nathan Schneider. 2013. Abstract meaning representation for sembanking. In *Proceedings of the 7th linguistic annotation workshop and interoperability with discourse*, pages 178–186.

Iz Beltagy, Kyle Lo, and Arman Cohan. 2019. SciBERT: A pretrained language model for scientific text. In *Proceedings of the 2019 Conference on Empirical Methods in Natural Language Processing and the 9th International Joint Conference on Natural Language Processing (EMNLP-IJCNLP)*, pages 3615–3620, Hong Kong, China. Association for Computational Linguistics.

Deng Cai, Xin Li, Jackie Chun-Sing Ho, Lidong Bing, and Wai Lam. 2021. Multilingual AMR parsing with noisy knowledge distillation. In *Findings of the Association for Computational Linguistics: EMNLP 2021*, pages 2778–2789, Punta Cana, Dominican Republic. Association for Computational Linguistics.

Taylor Cassidy, Bill McDowell, Nathanael Chambers, and Steven Bethard. 2014. An annotation framework for dense event ordering. In *Proceedings of the 52nd Annual Meeting of the Association for Computational Linguistics (Volume 2: Short Papers)*, pages 501–506, Baltimore, Maryland. Association for Computational Linguistics.

Anwoy Chatterjee, Eshaan Tanwar, Subhabrata Dutta, and Tanmoy Chakraborty. 2024. Language models can exploit cross-task in-context learning for data-scarce novel tasks. In *Proceedings of the 62nd Annual Meeting of the Association for Computational Linguistics (Volume 1: Long Papers)*, pages 11568–11587, Bangkok, Thailand. Association for Computational Linguistics.

Fei Cheng and Yusuke Miyao. 2017. Classifying temporal relations by bidirectional LSTM over dependency paths. In *Proceedings of the 55th Annual Meeting of the Association for Computational Linguistics (Volume 2: Short Papers)*, pages 1–6, Vancouver, Canada. Association for Computational Linguistics.

Jacob Devlin, Ming-Wei Chang, Kenton Lee, and Kristina Toutanova. 2019. BERT: Pre-training of deep bidirectional transformers for language understanding. In *Proceedings of the 2019 Conference of the North American Chapter of the Association for Computational Linguistics: Human Language Technologies, Volume 1 (Long and Short Papers)*, pages 4171–4186, Minneapolis, Minnesota. Association for Computational Linguistics.

Tianyu Gao, Xingcheng Yao, and Danqi Chen. 2021. SimCSE: Simple contrastive learning of sentence embeddings. In *Proceedings of the 2021 Conference on Empirical Methods in Natural Language Processing*, pages 6894–6910, Online and Punta Cana, Dominican Republic. Association for Computational Linguistics.

Sireesh Gururaja, Ritam Dutt, Tinglong Liao, and Carolyn Rosé. 2023. Linguistic representations for fewer-shot relation extraction across domains. In *Proceedings of the 61st Annual Meeting of the Association for Computational Linguistics (Volume 1: Long Papers)*, pages 7502–7514, Toronto, Canada. Association for Computational Linguistics.

Bernal Gutierrez, Nikolas McNeal, Clayton Washington, You Chen, Lang Li, Huan Sun, and Yu Su. 2022. Thinking about GPT-3 in-context learning for biomedical IE? think again. In *Findings of the Association for Computational Linguistics: EMNLP 2022*, pages 4497–4512, Abu Dhabi, United Arab Emirates. Association for Computational Linguistics.

Ridong Han, Tao Peng, Chaohao Yang, Benyou Wang, Lu Liu, and Xiang Wan. 2023. Is information extraction solved by chatgpt? an analysis of performance, evaluation criteria, robustness and errors. *arXiv preprint arXiv:2305.14450*.

Iris Hendrickx, Su Nam Kim, Zornitsa Kozareva, Preslav Nakov, Diarmuid Ó Séaghdha, Sebastian Padó, Marco Pennacchiotti, Lorenza Romano, and Stan Szpakowicz. 2010. SemEval-2010 task 8: Multi-way classification of semantic relations between pairs of nominals. In *Proceedings of the 5th International Workshop on Semantic Evaluation*, pages 33–38, Uppsala, Sweden. Association for Computational Linguistics.

Zhilei Hu, Zixuan Li, Xiaolong Jin, Long Bai, Saiping Guan, Jiafeng Guo, and Xueqi Cheng. 2023. Semantic structure enhanced event causality identification. In *Proceedings of the 61st Annual Meeting of the Association for Computational Linguistics (Volume 1: Long Papers)*, pages 10901–10913, Toronto, Canada. Association for Computational Linguistics.

Jeff Johnson, Matthijs Douze, and Hervé Jégou. 2019. Billion-scale similarity search with gpus. *IEEE Transactions on Big Data*, 7(3):535–547.

Guozheng Li, Peng Wang, Wenjun Ke, Yikai Guo, Ke Ji, Ziyu Shang, Jiajun Liu, and Zijie Xu. 2024. Recall, retrieve and reason: Towards better in-context relation extraction. In *Proceedings of the Thirty-Third International Joint Conference on Artificial Intelligence, IJCAI-24*, pages 6368–6376. International Joint Conferences on Artificial Intelligence Organization. Main Track.

Yi Luan, Luheng He, Mari Ostendorf, and Hannaneh Hajishirzi. 2018. Multi-task identification of entities, relations, and coreference for scientific knowledge graph construction. In *Proceedings of the 2018 Conference on Empirical Methods in Natural Language Processing*, pages 3219–3232, Brussels, Belgium. Association for Computational Linguistics.

Xilai Ma, Jing Li, and Min Zhang. 2023. Chain of thought with explicit evidence reasoning for few-shot relation extraction. In *Findings of the Association for Computational Linguistics: EMNLP 2023*, pages 2334–2352, Singapore. Association for Computational Linguistics.

James Pustejovsky, Patrick Hanks, Roser Sauri, Andrew See, Robert Gaizauskas, Andrea Setzer, Dragomir Radev, Beth Sundheim, David Day, Lisa Ferro, et al. 2003. The timebank corpus. In *Corpus linguistics*, volume 2003, page 40. Lancaster, UK.

Ziyi Shou and Fangzhen Lin. 2023. Evaluate AMR graph similarity via self-supervised learning. In *Proceedings of the 61st Annual Meeting of the Association for Computational Linguistics (Volume 1: Long Papers)*, pages 16112–16123, Toronto, Canada. Association for Computational Linguistics.

Xiaofei Sun, Linfeng Dong, Xiaoya Li, Zhen Wan, Shuhe Wang, Tianwei Zhang, Jiwei Li, Fei Cheng, Lingjuan Lyu, Fei Wu, et al. 2023. Pushing the limits of chatgpt on nlp tasks. *arXiv preprint arXiv:2306.09719*.

Ahmet Üstün, Arianna Bisazza, Gosse Bouma, and Gertjan van Noord. 2020. UDapter: Language adaptation for truly Universal Dependency parsing. In *Proceedings of the 2020 Conference on Empirical Methods in Natural Language Processing (EMNLP)*, pages 2302–2315, Online. Association for Computational Linguistics.

Naushad UzZaman, Hector Llorens, Leon Derczynski, James Allen, Marc Verhagen, and James Pustejovsky. 2013. SemEval-2013 task 1: TempEval-3: Evaluating time expressions, events, and temporal relations. In *Second Joint Conference on Lexical and Computational Semantics (*SEM), Volume 2: Proceedings of the Seventh International Workshop on Semantic Evaluation (SemEval 2013)*, pages 1–9, Atlanta, Georgia, USA. Association for Computational Linguistics.

Zhen Wan, Fei Cheng, Zhuoyuan Mao, Qianying Liu, Haiyue Song, Jiwei Li, and Sadao Kurohashi. 2023. GPT-RE: In-context learning for relation extraction using large language models. In *Proceedings of the 2023 Conference on Empirical Methods in Natural Language Processing*, pages 3534–3547, Singapore. Association for Computational Linguistics.

Xiaozhi Wang, Yulin Chen, Ning Ding, Hao Peng, Zimu Wang, Yankai Lin, Xu Han, Lei Hou, Juanzi Li, Zhiyuan Liu, Peng Li, and Jie Zhou. 2022. MAVEN-ERE: A unified large-scale dataset for event coreference, temporal, causal, and subevent relation extraction. In *Proceedings of the 2022 Conference on Empirical Methods in Natural Language Processing*, pages 926–941, Abu Dhabi, United Arab Emirates. Association for Computational Linguistics.

Zixuan Zhang and Heng Ji. 2021. Abstract Meaning Representation guided graph encoding and decoding for joint information extraction. In *Proceedings of the 2021 Conference of the North American Chapter of the Association for Computational Linguistics: Human Language Technologies*, pages 39–49, Online. Association for Computational Linguistics.

Zexuan Zhong and Danqi Chen. 2021. A frustratingly easy approach for entity and relation extraction. In *Proceedings of the 2021 Conference of the North American Chapter of the Association for Computational Linguistics: Human Language Technologies*, pages 50–61, Online. Association for Computational Linguistics.

A Self-supervised Training for AMR Graph Encoding

SS-GNN (Shou and Lin, 2023) adopts a self-supervised approach, Contrastive Tension (CT) to optimize the representation of an AMR graph. The main assumption is that AMR graphs with adjacent distributions have similar meanings. In our work, we adapt this approach to our novel AMR graph representation.

Two independent transformer-based encoders that also incorporate graph neural networks are identically initalized. The training objective is to maximize the dot product between positive pairs (G_p, G_p^+) while minimizing the dot product between negative pairs (G_p, G_p^-). For each randomly selected AMR graph G_p, we use $G_p^+ = G_p$ to create a positive pair. Then, we construct negative instances by pairing G_p with K randomly sampled different graphs. The $K+1$ instances are included in the same batch. The training contrastive loss $\mathcal{L}$ is binary cross-entropy between similarity scores and labels.

$$\mathcal{L} = \begin{cases} -\log\sigma(h_{graph} \cdot h^{+}_{graph}) \\ -\log\sigma(1 - h_{graph} \cdot h^{-}_{graph}) \end{cases} \quad (2)$$

Hyperparameter	Value
Engine Name	GPT-4-0314
Temperature	0
Top_P	1
Frequency_penalty	0
Presence_penalty	0
Best_of	1

Table 3: GPT-4 hyperparameters.

where σ refers to the Logistic function; h_{graph} is the graph representation. The model is then updated to compute the similarity between the two graphs.

B Evaluation Datasets

In this section, we describe the evaluation datasets used in our experiments. Table 4 shows the statistics for each dataset.

SemEval 2010 Task 8 (Hendrickx et al., 2010): This data set focuses on the semantic relations between pairs of nominals. It was annotated from general domain resources. The task is to classify the semantic relations into one of nine directed relation types: Cause-Effect, Instrument-Agency, Product-Producer, Content-Container, Entity-Origin, Entity-Destination, Component-Whole, Member-Collection, Message-Topic, and Other (to indicate that there is no relation between the pair of nominals). An example of a sentence with an event pair that holds the Cause-Effect relation is shown below:

> The **(e1:discomfort)** from the **(e2:injury)** was now precluding him from his occupation which involved prolonged procedures in the standing position.

ACE05: This dataset contains entities, relations, and events annotated from resources from domains including newswire, broadcast news, broadcast conversation, weblog, discussion forums, and conversational telephone speech. It requires identifying semantic relations into the following six types: artifact, general-affiliation, organization-affiliation, part-whole, person-social, physical. The following example contains an entity pair with the part-whole relation:

> Witnesses say they heard blasts around a presidential complex in the **(e1:center)** of the **(e2:city)**.

Dataset	# Relation	# Train	# Dev	# Test (# Subset)
SemEval	9	6,507	1,493	2,717 (2,717)
TB-Dense	6	7,553	898	2,299 (2,299)
SciERC	7	16,872	2,033	4,088 (4,088)
ACE05	6	121,368	27,597	24,420 (2,442)

Table 4: Statistics of the evaluation datasets. # Subset denotes the number of instances sampled from the original test set, due to the high cost of the OpenAI API.

TB-Dense (Cassidy et al., 2014): TB-Dense is a public benchmark for temporal relation extraction (TRE). It was annotated from TimeBank (Pustejovsky et al., 2003) and TempEval (UzZaman et al., 2013). We use a preprocessed version from (Wang et al., 2022) for experiments. TB-Dense annotates temporal relations for event pairs within adjacent sentences. To handle this, we separately parse the two sentences into AMR graphs and then connect the two graphs through a shared root node following (Cheng and Miyao, 2017). Given a passage and two event points, the task is to classify the relations between events into one of six types: BEFORE, AFTER, SIMULTANEOUS, VAGUE, IS_INCLUDED, and INCLUDES. An example with two events, e1 and e2 (in bold) that hold the SIMULTANEOUS relation is shown below:

> Nobody **(e1:hurried)** her up. No one **(e2:held)** her back.

SciERC (Luan et al., 2018): This dataset includes annotations for scientific entities and their relations annotated from 500 scientific abstracts taken from Artificial Intelligence conferences and workshops proceedings. The relation types are: *used-for*, *feature-of*, *hyponym-of*, *part-of*, *compare*, *conjunction* and *corefence*. Following example contains the *feature-of* relation between two entities:

> They improve the reconstruction results and enforce their consistency with a **(e1:priori knowledge)** about **(e2:object shape)**.

C Hyperparameters

GPT-4: We used GPT-4 by the OpenAI API [3] during the experiments. The hyperparameters used can be found in Table 3, we report the result of the single run for all experiments.

Unsupervised Sentence Embedding Model: We use the sentence embedding method SimCSE in our experiments. We use the *sup-simcse-bert-base-uncased* model as the base encoder.

Graph Encoder (SS-GNN): During training, we set the positive ratio to 4/16, meaning each batch of 16 contains 4 positive graph pairs and 12 negative pairs. Specifically, we sampled 4 graphs and generated one positive pair and three negative pairs for each graph. The transformer parameters were initialized using the uncased BERT base model (Devlin et al., 2019), while the graph adapter parameters were initialized randomly. Hyperparameters were set as follows: 1 epoch, learning rate as 1e-5, dropout rate as 0.1, and graph adapter size as 128. We experimented with sequence length of 128 for SemEval and 256 for the other three datasets. The training was done using NVIDIA Quadro RTX 8000.

Supervised RE Model (PURE): To maintain consistency across datasets, we use a single-sentence setup for Semeval, as it is a sentence-level relation extraction dataset. For pre-trained language models (PLMs), we follow PURE by using scibert-scivocab-uncased (Beltagy et al., 2019) as the base encoder for SciERC and bert-base-uncased (Devlin et al., 2019) for the other three datasets. We also adhere to the hyperparameters specified in their paper.

D Results of All AMR-RE configurations

Table 5 shows the results for all the configurations in our experiments.

[3] `https://platform.openai.com/docs/api-reference/introduction`

Setting	Path	Pooling	SemEval	TB-DENSE	SciERC	ACE05	Avg
Supervised	SAP+CTX	*Mean*	90.84	**71.54**	67.92	67.37	74.22
		Concatenation	90.03	70.56	**68.10**	**67.94**	74.36
	SAP	*Mean*	**91.97**	68.23	67.81	66.80	73.70
		Concatenation	91.70	67.89	68.04	67.21	73.71
Unsupervised	SAP+CTX	*Mean*	81.40	**38.17**	27.64	14.82	40.51
		Concatenation	79.48	37.78	**27.89**	**15.04**	40.05
	SAP	*Mean*	**84.68**	35.64	27.56	14.65	40.63
		Concatenation	83.51	33.75	27.61	14.69	39.89

Table 5: **AMR-RE results with all configurations.** The results in **bold** are reported in the main results.

Linguistic Analysis of Veteran Job Interviews to Assess Effectiveness in Translating Military Expertise to the Civilian Workforce

Caroline J. Wendt[1], Ehsanul Haque Nirjhar[2], Theodora Chaspari[1]
[1] University of Colorado Boulder, [2] Texas A&M University
{caroline.wendt, theodora.chaspari}@colorado.edu
nirjhar71@tamu.edu

Abstract

The ways in which natural language processing (NLP) can inform how veterans can improve effectiveness in translating military experience to workforce utility is underexplored. We design NLP experiments to evaluate the degree of explanation in veteran job interview responses as a proxy for perceived hireability. We examine linguistic and psycholinguistic features, context, and participant variability to investigate the mechanics of effective communication in employee selection. Results yield good performance when distinguishing between varying degrees of explanation in responses using LIWC features, indicating robustness of linguistic feature integration. Classifying Over- and Under-explained responses reflects challenges of class imbalance and the limitations of tested NLP methods for detecting subtleties in overly verbose or concise communication. Our findings have immediate applications for assistive technologies in job interview settings, and broader implications for enhancing automated communication assessment tools and refining strategies for training and interventions in communication-heavy fields.

1 Introduction

The complexity of verbal communication is a fundamental factor in various realms, including psychology, education, and human-computer interaction (HCI). The degree to which individuals explain themselves reveals insights into their cognitive processes, social interactions, and personality traits. These factors both explicitly and implicitly define the ways in which speakers are perceived, and are thus essential for assessing candidates in structured job interviews (Levashina et al., 2014). The qualifications, background, and training of the majority of military veterans are notably different from job candidates in the general population. Many companies acknowledge that hiring veterans is beneficial, as veterans often posses desirable workforce qualities that arise from their unique experiences, such as strong work ethics, leadership skills, adaptability, team orientation, and professionalism (Sakib et al., 2024). Yet, veterans commonly experience persistent employment challenges post-service due to organizational and societal barriers such as lack of transition support, stressful experiences, and perceived discrimination, as well as personal barriers like incongruence between military and civilian culture (Keeling et al., 2018; Nirjhar et al., 2022). Veterans demonstrate distinct verbal communication gaps in explaining their military experience, references, jargon, and specialized skills relative to the workplace (Mael et al., 2022; Roy et al., 2020; Sakib et al., 2024). Industry interviewers are often unaware of these factors (Mael et al., 2022), further exacerbating the problem with negative stereotypes, stigma, and exclusion (McAllister et al., 2015).

Artificial intelligence (AI) enhances a range of individualized assistive tools to address visual, auditory, cognitive, and physical needs (Zdravkova, 2022). Automated natural language processing (NLP) and understanding can help specific populations communicate and interact with surroundings more effectively and efficiently. One immediate application is intelligent interview training, which provides a suitable environment for individuals to practice and refine relevant verbal and nonverbal behaviors. Such training can help participants adapt to cognitively demanding and socially challenging interview situations (Hemamou et al., 2019a). Given that employment interviews are an immediate obstacle in the hiring process, AI-powered interview training, augmented with NLP, has potential to identify linguistic and communicative behaviors that may hinder candidates' performance, then suggest precise modifications to improve their communication skills (Marienko et al., 2020).

Previous research in intervention technologies for interview training primarily seeks to investigate and improve social skills and positive personality

Proceedings of the 2025 Conference of the Nations of the Americas Chapter of the Association for Computational Linguistics: Human Language Technologies (Volume 4: Student Research Workshop), pages 343–355

signals. Various games, systems, and virtual reality platforms have been developed to help users improve interview performance and stress levels through simulated interactions, providing feedback on behavioral and emotional cues (Anderson et al., 2013; Gebhard et al., 2018; Hoque et al., 2013; Hartholt et al., 2019). Other work has used multimodal data from asynchronous job interviews, analyzing linguistic, acoustic, and visual signals to predict personality traits, hireability, and communication skills, with factors such as word choice, personal pronoun use, and speech fluency shown to significantly impact interview outcomes (Chen et al., 2017; Hemamou et al., 2019a,b; Nguyen and Gatica-Perez, 2016; Muralidhar et al., 2016; Naim et al., 2016).

Departing from prior studies, we present foundational knowledge to improve interview training with several key contributions to enhance the development of intervention technologies that use NLP. While some related studies have contributed to adaptive solutions for specific populations (Hartholt et al., 2019; Marienko et al., 2020), we focus on military veterans, a population encountering distinct difficulties in job interviews. Rather than investigating global characteristics of interviewees, such as personality and overall interview outcomes (Anderson et al., 2013; Gebhard et al., 2018; Hoque et al., 2013; Hartholt et al., 2019), this research provides detailed analysis of turn-level linguistic behaviors that influence verbal communication patterns. We examine dynamic and complex synchronous (instead of static, asynchronous) interactions between interviewers and interviewees. We not only consider interview responses (Verrap et al., 2022), but also account for the content of interview questions, context, turn-taking behaviors, and individualized interviewee variability.

2 Methods

2.1 Data

The data are from a concluded mock job interview study between experienced industry professionals and military veterans in transition to civilian life post-service (Verrap et al., 2022). Interviews were conducted in a hybrid format, where veterans voluntarily participated in the lab, while interviewers joined virtually via Zoom. In total, 38 veterans representing all branches of the military completed the study. The demographic information of participants and interviewers is summarized in Table 1. Participants each received a customized job description created based on their individual qualifications. Participants were thus instructed to act as if they were applying to and interviewing for their unique jobs, and interviewers conducted the calls as they would in their professional roles. Transcript data from the audio and video recordings were automatically generated with Zoom's speech recognition tool, then manually corrected for errors. Response data from the cases in which interviewers asked follow-up questions were aggregated as part of the original question's response.

Three undergraduate psychology students with experience in behavioral coding annotated the interview data (Chorney et al., 2015). The degree of explanation in responses is categorized into four target classes:

- **Under-explained**: Brief and do not fully answer the question, often end abruptly
- **Succinct**: Concise and complete
- **Comprehensive**: Detailed and fully answer the question
- **Over-explained**: Long with excessive detail that can affect coherence

The length (word count) and duration (time in seconds) of responses are correlated ($r(284) = 0.97, p < 0.001$) and tend to increase across these categories. Annotator agreement for the degree of explanation is moderate with Krippendorff's $\alpha = 0.677$, when all samples are included and after adjudication (Krippendorff, 2011). Final labels corresponding to each response were determined by majority voting. Figure 1 shows the imbalanced distribution of the classes at the extremes, with "Under-explained" and "Over-explained" as the minority classes, which are of particular interest due to their negative impact on interview performance and overall perceived hireability.

2.2 Experiments

Rather than pursuing a traditional four-way classification task, we calibrate our experimental approach to the imbalanced nature of the dataset by defining two distinct binary classification problems where we distinguish between (1) Comprehensive and Over-explained responses and (2) Under-explained and Succinct responses. In each of these classification problems, we experiment with NLP feature extraction and selection techniques and optimize performance over various text inputs, representation methods, and linguistic features to gain insight

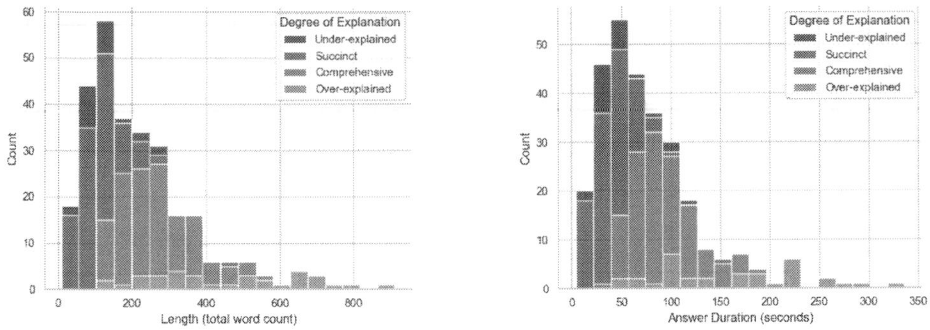

Figure 1: Histograms of total word count and duration of responses per class of degree of explanation. These figures show the dataset's class imbalance, where classes at the extremes are underrepresented.

into what differentiates the level of explanation in veteran responses.

2.3 Features

We use the Linguistic Inquiry and Word Count (LIWC) method to extract a feature set for each input (Boyd et al., 2022). LIWC features are 117 in total and provide a structured and interpretable way to quantify the content of the text by capturing critical aspects of language use, enabling the analysis of linguistic patterns and their relationship to different psychological or social outcomes, which is relevant in the context of job interviews. In our text analysis, for instance, we observe that for LIWC features which capture cognitive processes and perception, Comprehensive responses more frequently contain "causation" language ($t(76.16) = 2.29, p = 0.02$), whereas Over-explained responses more frequently contain "focuspast" language ($t(53.66) = -2.30, p = 0.03$). Causation words (e.g., how, because, make, why) explain why something happened, connecting events or ideas through cause-and-effect relationships, such as when the veteran elaborates on their explanations or justifies their points. Over-explained responses, however, often involve recounting stories or providing excessive context; speakers frequently describe past events, actions, or experiences to justify or elaborate on their point. By contrast, Under-explained responses have a higher frequency of words in the LIWC "tentative" category ($t(52.09) = -2.30, p = 0.03$). These words (e.g., might, could, maybe, not sure) express hesitation and uncertainty, like when the speaker deliberately hedges their statements to avoid being challenged or questioned further, or takes a cautious approach to statements due to low confidence in knowledge or ability to articulate their point or lack of clarity in the question. Political or socially strategic language occurs more frequently in Succinct responses ($t(28.79) = 2.42, p = 0.02$), reflecting topics of governance, politeness markers, and harmonious language. Succinct responses aim to convey necessary information clearly and directly without overloading the interviewer. In doing so, Succinct responses often use language to ensure the response is well-received due to awareness of the interviewer's expectations, while avoiding unnecessary details or uncertain language, and instead focusing on clear and positive expressions.

To capture the syntactic structure of the text and to further analyze patterns in participants' language use, we experiment with 48 part-of-speech (POS) features (Honnibal et al., 2020). For example, we observe that Comprehensive responses tend to include more wh-pronouns (WP) (e.g., (who, what, when, where, why, how) compared to Over-explained responses ($t(84.40) = 2.86, p = 0.01$). Comprehensive responses aim to address key details, provide clarity, and cover the full context of a topic such that this language is often leveraged to introduce or elaborate on specific aspects, answering questions directly and fully. Yet, Over-explained responses tend to contain more personal pronouns (PRP) ($t(57.46) = -2.20, p = 0.03$). A potential reason for this might be that over-explaining often involves recounting personal stories or providing excessive background information, leading to a higher frequency of self-references. Frequent use of personal pronouns tends to overly center the narrative on personal experiences and viewpoints, reflected in Over-explained responses that tend to emphasize the speaker's experiences, actions, and opinions. Succinct responses tend to use more coordinating conjunctions (CC, e.g., and, but, or) because they aim to compactly connect ideas, actions, or clauses within a limited scope ($t(34.15) = 2.12, p = 0.04$). In contrast, Under-explained responses often omit details and connections, resulting in fewer opportunities for conjunctions to bridge ideas effectively. See Table 2 and Table 3.

We reduce each set to the most informative psychological and linguistic data in the text by retaining only the features that are statistically relevant to each classification task. We conduct t-tests to select the POS and LIWC features that significantly differ between classes, where features are considered statistically important for distinguishing between the classes at the 5% significance level.

We additionally experiment with normalized military jargon term counts as a feature for analyzing response texts. Jargon term counts refer to the raw frequency of predefined military-specific phrases (e.g., mission, operation, sergeant) appearing in the text, providing a direct measure of the use of military language (Figure 2). Normalized counts, calculated as the proportion of military terms relative to the total word count of the turn, account for text length, enabling fair relative comparisons of the use of military jargon across responses of varying lengths. These features are explored to test if higher counts may indicate a speaker's familiarity with or connection to military culture, and thus help distinguish between responses.

For text representation, we assess Bag-of-Words (BoW), Term Frequency-Inverse Document Frequency (TF-IDF) vectorizers, and Bidirectional Encoder Representations from Transformers (BERT) embeddings (Salton et al., 1975; Devlin et al., 2019). The vocabulary sizes after standard NLP preprocessing for the question and response transcript corpora are 1,578 and 3,593, respectively. On average, the dimensions of the BoW and TF-IDF vectors are 3058.32 (range: 1977 – 4056). The BERT embedding dimensionality is 768 across representations.

2.4 Models

Our modeling approach leverages advanced preprocessing, feature extraction, and a robust classification algorithm within a participant-independent evaluation framework. The experimental approach

Figure 2: Word cloud illustrating the frequency of various military jargon terms in the response dataset, where larger font size indicates more frequent.

utilizes machine learning pipelines to preprocess text and extract features for two binary classification tasks (i.e., Under-explained vs. Succinct, and Comprehensive vs. Over-explained). We examine each text representation (i.e., BoW, TF-IDF, BERT) alone for a baseline and in combination with the considered features (i.e., LIWC, POS tags, normalized jargon). These are extracted based on the interviewee's response only, as well as based on the interviewer's question and the interviewee's response.

To control for participant-level variation and maximize the training data available for model fitting, Leave-One-Participant-Out (LOPO) cross-validation is used to evaluate the model. LOPO emulates real-world scenarios where generalization to unseen participants is critical (Figure 3). To further control variability and assess the performance of the features of interest, we use the Extreme Gradient Boosting (XGBoost) classifier across all experiments, configured with the multi-class log loss evaluation metric, 100 trees with a depth of 6, and minimal regularization. We use XGBoost due to its ability to capture complex feature interactions, handle class imbalance, regularize against overfitting, and efficiently scale to diverse, high-dimensional data types such as BERT embeddings and LIWC features. Compared to preliminary experiments with various classifiers (Multinomial Naïve Bayes, Logistic Regression, Linear SVC, Decision Trees, and Random Forests), we find that XGBoost demonstrates both predictive power and robustness within the LOPO evaluation framework.

3 Results

Table 4 and Table 5 provide an evaluation of multiple text classification experiments, comparing the effectiveness of different input configurations, text

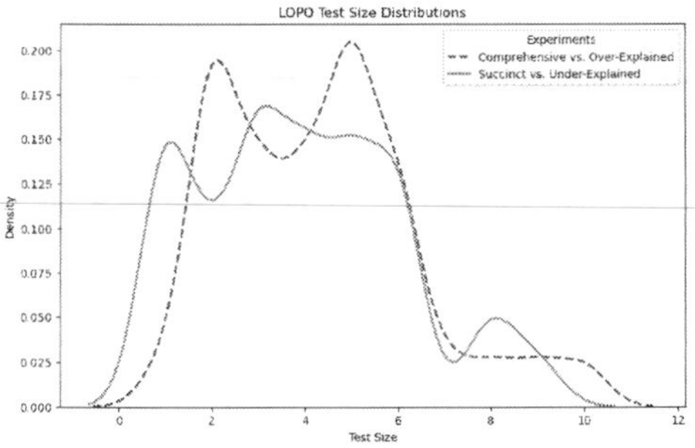

Figure 3: A comparison of the distributions of test sizes between the major experimental categories. The smooth curves represent kernel density estimates, highlighting differences in the spread and concentration of test sizes across experiment types under LOPO cross-validation, where the number of observations associated with each participant varies.

representations, and feature sets. Figure 4 provides an overview of feature performance for the best model results for each feature category across experiments with different inputs. Key insights are summarized below.

In terms of a comparison across features, LIWC features consistently outperform others. Across all setups, the use of LIWC features leads to the best or same overall performance. Over-explained or Under-explained performance (i.e., Class1 F1) also benefit notably from LIWC, suggesting its utility in handling minority or challenging classes. The baseline model, which does not utilize additional features, consistently underperforms compared to models that incorporate LIWC, but tends to perform comparably to other feature sets. Notable gaps are observed in Class1 F1, where the baseline scores range from 0.00 to 0.50, indicating poor detection of the Over-explained and Under-explained responses. However, for the case of distinguishing Under-explained responses, the baseline often performs no worse than more complex models. Models leveraging POS and normalized jargon count features, generally perform similarly to the baseline, with slight improvements in macro F1 and weighted F1 in some cases. For instance, normalized jargon count marginally improves performance over POS in certain cases, but still trails behind the LIWC model performance. Models using both question and response inputs outperform those using only responses in some configurations. Adding question context tends to not improve results significantly for longer responses, but does show some lift when distinguishing between shorter classes, particularly when identifying Under-explained responses. This highlights the importance of leveraging the full conversational context for classification tasks with limited information. For text representation methods, we observe BERT-based representations do not show a clear advantage for these tasks, possibly due to limited feature integration or insufficient fine-tuning. Simpler BoW and TF-IDF representations yield comparable results, but benefit significantly from feature augmentation like LIWC. Performance trends across classes indicate that performance for Succinct and Comprehensive classes, which represent the majority classes, remain high across all setups, with F1 scores consistently above 0.84. This suggests that models can reliably identify less extreme responses regardless of the features used. Over-explained and Under-explained classes remain challenging, with low F1 scores, particularly in baseline and non-LIWC models. This highlights the class imbalance or inherent difficulty in detecting these classes. LIWC consistently improves Over-Explained and Under-Explained F1 scores, e.g., achieving up to 0.50 in classification of Over-explained and 0.21 in Under-explained responses.

4 Limitations and Future Work

A limitation of this study lies in the small data sample. Although difficult to obtain given the interpersonal nature of our dataset, further analyses would benefit from a larger, balanced, and more comprehensively diverse population to improve performance, robustness, and generalizability of algorithms for assistive systems. Increasingly complex data, features, and models, would present greater computational expense. More advanced classification strategies to capture the linguistic subtleties between Comprehensive and Over-explained responses or Succinct and Under-explained responses may possibly require additional data with higher annotator agreement or data augmentation, as well as careful tuning of vectorizers, classifiers, and class weights. Future work could explore advanced integration of LIWC with deep learning approaches, combined feature sets, or fine-tuning BERT embeddings with domain-specific linguistic features to enhance performance. It would be constructive to also investigate the ways in which other linguistic (e.g., reference to military), physical (e.g., body language, posture), and speech (e.g., volume,

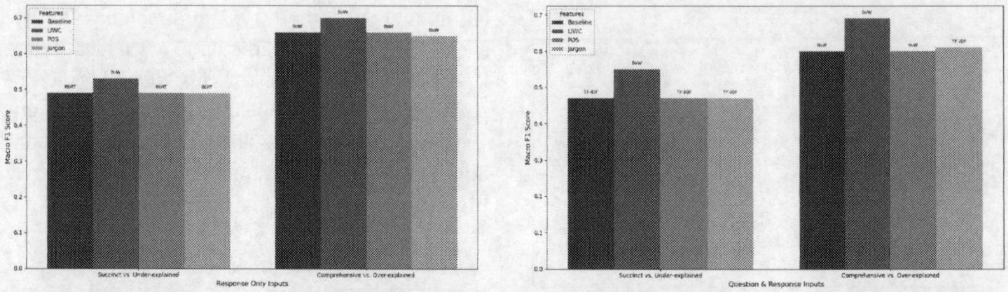

Figure 4: A comparison of feature performance for the best results for each feature category across experiments with response inputs (left) and question and response inputs (right). Bars are colored by feature type and labels above each bar indicate the respective text representation method associated with the best given model. The experiments demonstrate the efficacy of LIWC features for text classification tasks involving nuanced categories like explanation levels. LIWC consistently outperforms baseline and alternative feature sets across all metrics, particularly for the challenging Over- and Under-explained and categories. Combining question and response inputs further boosts model performance, while feature integration remains critical for improving representation-based models like TF-IDF and BERT.

intonation) factors influence the degree of explanation. Future related work should explore these variables in both binary and four-way classification settings. Methods employed and results obtained in our work provide a basis for developing technologies that offer personalized, granular interview feedback in real time. As such, a promising direction for future investigation may involve leveraging large language models and chain-of-thought prompting (Wei et al., 2022) to design interactive interview training interfaces. Specialized applications of further research to narrow communication gaps may extend beyond job interviews to areas like educational assessments and automated dialogue systems. In addition to military veterans, upcoming studies in this space should aim to make interactions more constructive and meaningful for other sensitive groups, such as formerly incarcerated individuals, non-Native speakers, and older adults seeking to re-enter the workforce, by tailoring systems to their unique needs.

5 Conclusion

We use NLP to inform the development of personalized training methods and assistive technologies to aid military veterans in their transition to the civilian workforce. This study integrates advanced linguistic features with robust text representation strategies and participant-dependent cross-validation to detect the degree of explanation in veteran job interview responses. We incorporate LIWC features, which analyze the psychological and cognitive dimensions of text, and POS tagging, which provides syntactic insights, into the text classification pipeline. These features are combined with traditional BoW and TF-IDF vectorization and BERT embedding methods to create a comprehensive feature set that can capture both surface-level and deep linguistic patterns. We advance prior studies by looking beyond the ways in which personal, social, and behavioral impressions and physical characteristics impact interview outcomes (Anderson et al., 2013; Gebhard et al., 2018; Hoque et al., 2013; Hartholt et al., 2019). We also extend existing work by not only considering interview responses, but also accounting for the content of the interview question to understand contextual and turn-taking aspects of conversational communication (Verrap et al., 2022). Classification results from our binary classification experiments reveal that while tested models can generally distinguish between responses with moderate accuracy, correctly identifying certain subclasses within these categories is more challenging, particularly for Under-explained responses. The choice of input features as well as text representation methods significantly impact performance, with LIWC features generally leading to better overall results. This research will contribute to the eventual development of intelligent training technologies that provide personalized learning and reintegration support through mechanisms such as real-time automatic feedback to optimize veterans' job interview outcomes and improve the workforce.

Ethics Statement

Data collection was approved by the institutional review board of the authors' university. All authors strove to maintain highest standards of professional conduct and ethical practice when conducting this work via respecting and maintaining the privacy of participants and security of the data, and disclosing all pertinent system capabilities and limitations.

Acknowledgments

The authors acknowledge the support of the National Science Foundation (#1956021) for this work.

References

Keith Anderson, Elisabeth André, Tobias Baur, Sara Bernardini, Mathieu Chollet, Evi Chryssafidou, Ionut Damian, Cathy Ennis, Arjan Egges, Patrick Gebhard, et al. 2013. The tardis framework: intelligent virtual agents for social coaching in job interviews. In *International conference on advances in computer entertainment technology*, pages 476–491. Springer.

Ryan L Boyd, Ashwini Ashokkumar, Sarah Seraj, and James W Pennebaker. 2022. The development and psychometric properties of liwc-22. *Austin, TX: University of Texas at Austin*, 10.

Lei Chen, Ru Zhao, Chee Wee Leong, Blair Lehman, Gary Feng, and Mohammed Ehsan Hoque. 2017. Automated video interview judgment on a large-sized corpus collected online. In *2017 Seventh International Conference on Affective Computing and Intelligent Interaction (ACII)*, pages 504–509. IEEE.

Jill MacLaren Chorney, C Meghan McMurtry, Christine T Chambers, and Roger Bakeman. 2015. Developing and modifying behavioral coding schemes in pediatric psychology: a practical guide. *Journal of pediatric psychology*, 40(1):154–164.

Jacob Devlin, Ming-Wei Chang, Kenton Lee, and Kristina Toutanova. 2019. BERT: Pre-training of deep bidirectional transformers for language understanding. In *Proceedings of the 2019 Conference of the North American Chapter of the Association for Computational Linguistics: Human Language Technologies, Volume 1 (Long and Short Papers)*, pages 4171–4186, Minneapolis, Minnesota. Association for Computational Linguistics.

Patrick Gebhard, Tanja Schneeberger, Elisabeth André, Tobias Baur, Ionut Damian, Gregor Mehlmann, Cornelius König, and Markus Langer. 2018. Serious games for training social skills in job interviews. *IEEE Transactions on Games*, 11(4):340–351.

Arno Hartholt, Sharon Mozgai, and Albert" Skip" Rizzo. 2019. Virtual job interviewing practice for high-anxiety populations. In *Proceedings of the 19th ACM international conference on intelligent virtual agents*, pages 238–240.

Léo Hemamou, Ghazi Felhi, Jean-Claude Martin, and Chloé Clavel. 2019a. Slices of attention in asynchronous video job interviews. In *2019 8th International Conference on Affective Computing and Intelligent Interaction (ACII)*, pages 1–7. IEEE.

Léo Hemamou, Ghazi Felhi, Vincent Vandenbussche, Jean-Claude Martin, and Chloé Clavel. 2019b. Hirenet: A hierarchical attention model for the automatic analysis of asynchronous video job interviews. In *Proceedings of the AAAI conference on artificial intelligence*, volume 33, pages 573–581.

Matthew Honnibal, Ines Montani, Sofie Van Landeghem, and Adriane Boyd. 2020. spaCy: Industrial-strength Natural Language Processing in Python.

Mohammed Hoque, Matthieu Courgeon, Jean-Claude Martin, Bilge Mutlu, and Rosalind W Picard. 2013. Mach: My automated conversation coach. In *Proceedings of the 2013 ACM international joint conference on Pervasive and ubiquitous computing*, pages 697–706.

Mary Keeling, Sara Kintzle, and Carl A Castro. 2018. Exploring us veterans' post-service employment experiences. *Military Psychology*, 30(1):63–69.

Klaus Krippendorff. 2011. Computing krippendorff's alpha-reliability.

Julia Levashina, Christopher J Hartwell, Frederick P Morgeson, and Michael A Campion. 2014. The structured employment interview: Narrative and quantitative review of the research literature. *Personnel Psychology*, 67(1):241–293.

Fred Mael, Will Wyatt, and Uma Janardana Iyer. 2022. Veterans to workplace: Keys to successful transition. *Military Psychology*, 34(5):516–529.

Maiia Marienko, Yulia Nosenko, and Mariya Shyshkina. 2020. Personalization of learning using adaptive technologies and augmented reality. *arXiv preprint arXiv:2011.05802*.

Charn P McAllister, Jeremy D Mackey, Kaylee J Hackney, and Pamela L Perrewé. 2015. From combat to khakis: An exploratory examination of job stress with veterans. *Military Psychology*, 27(2):93–107.

Skanda Muralidhar, Laurent Son Nguyen, Denise Frauendorfer, Jean-Marc Odobez, Marianne Schmid Mast, and Daniel Gatica-Perez. 2016. Training on the job: Behavioral analysis of job interviews in hospitality. In *Proceedings of the 18th acm international conference on multimodal interaction*, pages 84–91.

Iftekhar Naim, Md Iftekhar Tanveer, Daniel Gildea, and Mohammed Ehsan Hoque. 2016. Automated analysis and prediction of job interview performance. *IEEE Transactions on Affective Computing*, 9(2):191–204.

Laurent Son Nguyen and Daniel Gatica-Perez. 2016. Hirability in the wild: Analysis of online conversational video resumes. *IEEE Transactions on Multimedia*, 18(7):1422–1437.

Ehsanul Haque Nirjhar, Md Nazmus Sakib, Ellen Hagen, Neha Rani, Sharon Lynn Chu, Winfred Arthur, Amir H Behzadan, and Theodora Chaspari. 2022. Investigating the interplay between self-reported and bio-behavioral measures of stress: A pilot study of civilian job interviews with military veterans. In *2022 10th International Conference on Affective Computing and Intelligent Interaction (ACII)*, pages 1–8. IEEE.

Deborah Roy, Jana Ross, and Cherie Armour. 2020. Making the transition: How finding a good job is a risky business for military veterans in northern ireland. *Military Psychology*, 32(5):428–441.

Md Nazmus Sakib, Ellen Hagen, Nidhal Mazza, Neha Rani, Ehsanul Haque Nirjhar, Sharon L Chu, Theodora Chaspari, Amir H Behzadan, and Winfred Arthur Jr. 2024. Capitalizing on strengths and minimizing weaknesses of veterans in civilian employment interviews: Perceptions of interviewers and veteran interviewees. *Military Psychology*, pages 1–13.

Gerard Salton, Anita Wong, and Chung-Shu Yang. 1975. A vector space model for automatic indexing. *Communications of the ACM*, 18(11):613–620.

Raghu Verrap, Ehsanul Nirjhar, Ani Nenkova, and Theodora Chaspari. 2022. "am i answering my job interview questions right?": A nlp approach to predict degree of explanation in job interview responses. In *Proceedings of the Second Workshop on NLP for Positive Impact (NLP4PI)*, pages 122–129.

Jason Wei, Xuezhi Wang, Dale Schuurmans, Maarten Bosma, Fei Xia, Ed Chi, Quoc V Le, Denny Zhou, et al. 2022. Chain-of-thought prompting elicits reasoning in large language models. *Advances in neural information processing systems*, 35:24824–24837.

Katerina Zdravkova. 2022. The potential of artificial intelligence for assistive technology in education. In *Handbook on Intelligent Techniques in the Educational Process: Vol 1 Recent Advances and Case Studies*, pages 61–85. Springer.

A Appendix

Population	Demographic Feature	Value
Interviewers	N	11
	Mean age in years (SD)	44.91 (11.67)
	Male:Female	8:3
	Ethnicity (W, BAA, M)	9, 1, 1
Interviewees (Military Veterans)	N completed (total)	38 (41)
	Mean age in years (SD)	40.3 (12.3)
	Male:Female	37:4
	Ethnicity (W, HL, NHPI, A, M, O)	24, 13, 1, 1, 1, 1
	Employed (full, part, not)	25, 4, 12
	Mean years of service (SD)	12.7 (9.1)
	Mean years since end of service (SD)	8.8 (10.6)
	Attended transition assistance	27

Table 1: A summary of the demographic information for the full dataset. The ethnicities represented in the data are abbreviated as follows: White (W), Hispanic or Latino (HL), Black or African American (BAA), Native Hawaiian or Other Pacific Islander (NHPI), Asian (A), Two or More Races (M), and Other (O).

Experiment	Input	Feature	Description	Mean (SD) Class0	Mean (SD) Class1	t-test Result
		WC	total number of words in the text	262.96 (97.73)	458.56 (206.04)	t(37.23)=-5.37, p<0.01
		BigWords	percentage of words longer than six letters	15.43 (4.64)	12.81 (2.93)	t(84.04)=4.00, p<0.01
		number	percentage of numerical terms (e.g., one, two, 100)	1.17 (1.16)	1.81 (1.29)	t(49.14)=-2.64, p=0.01
		prep	percentage of prepositions (e.g., in, on, about)	13.84 (3.10)	12.72 (2.15)	t(74.65)=2.43, p=0.02
		negate	percentage of negation words (e.g., not, never, no)	1.01 (0.87)	1.51 (1.01)	t(47.54)=-2.59, p=0.01
		Drives	percentage of words related to motivation and needs	5.98 (2.88)	4.93 (2.12)	t(70.53)=2.33, p=0.02
Comprehensive (0)		achieve	percentage of words related to achievement or success	2.05 (1.20)	1.38 (1.00)	t(62.55)=3.35, p<0.01
vs.	response	Cognition	percentage of words related to thinking and reasoning	14.02 (4.21)	12.54 (3.54)	t(61.50)=2.06, p=0.04
Over-explained (1)		cogproc	percentage of words related to cognitive processes	12.88 (4.06)	11.10 (3.53)	t(59.55)=2.52, p=0.01
		cause	percentage of words indicating cause and effect	1.82 (1.24)	1.40 (0.85)	t(76.16)=2.29, p=0.02
		tentat	percentage of words expressing uncertainty	3.13 (2.42)	2.22 (1.30)	t(101.24)=2.90, p<0.01
		socbehav	percentage of words related to social actions and interactions	2.90 (1.65)	2.0 (1.08)	t(80.11)=2.95, p<0.01
		work	percentage of words related to working	3.94 (2.45)	2.92 (1.81)	t(70.45)=2.69, p<0.01
		auditory	percentage of words related to hearing or sound	0.22 (0.43)	0.08 (0.20)	t(117.74)=2.80, p<0.01
		focuspast	percentage of words referencing past events	4.30 (2.85)	5.55 (2.80)	t(53.66)=-2.30, p=0.03
		OtherP	percentage of punctuation not categorized as periods, commas, or question marks	2.15 (3.17)	1.09 (2.23)	t(74.41)=2.20, p=0.03
	question	Analytic	a measure of logical and structured thinking based on word patterns	24.18 (23.71)	16.60 (17.91)	t(68.65)=2.02, p=0.04
		conj	percentage of conjunctions (e.g., and, but, or)	7.74 (4.01)	9.54 (4.51)	t(48.48)=-2.11, p=0.04
		tentat	see above	2.34 (1.75)	3.40 (2.92)	*t(52.09)=-2.30, p=0.03*
		polite	percentage of words indicating politeness	0.02 (0.08)	0.11 (0.47)	t(125.79)=-1.98 p=0.04
		politic	percentage of words related to political topics	0.78 (0.95)	0.27 (0.78)	t(28.79)=2.42, p=0.02
	response	health	percentage of words related to health and well-being	0.04 (0.19)	0.22 (0.54)	t(103.24)=-2.80, p<0.01
		illness	percentage of words related to illness or medical conditions	0 (0)	0.06 (0.32)	t(106)=-2.13, p=0.04
		food	percentage of words related to food and eating	0 (0)	0.09 (0.36)	t(106)=-2.55, p=0.01
		auditory	see above	0.02 (0.08)	0.10 (0.38)	t(127.58)=-1.99, p=0.04
		OtherP	see above	1.12 (2.14)	2.61 (3.99)	t(60.39)=-2.53, p=0.01
		Authentic	a measure of personal authenticity based on word usage	25.01 (30.61)	43.07 (34.7)	t(29.02)=-2.37, p=0.02
Succinct (0)		Tone	a calculated score reflecting positive or negative tone	83.20 (23.94)	69.84 (27.44)	t(28.45)=2.07, p=0.04
vs.		we	percentage of first-person plural pronouns (e.g., we, us, our)	0.43 (1.21)	1.06 (1.89)	t(48.67)=-2.03, p=0.04
Under-explained (1)		quantity	percentage of words indicating quantity or amount	5.04 (3.73)	3.15 (3.61)	t(31.46)=2.22, p=0.03
		insight	percentage of words reflecting understanding or awareness	2.69 (3.22)	4.61 (4.78)	t(45.67)=-2.36, p=0.02
		tentat	see above	2.76 (2.94)	4.37 (4.74)	t(50.21)=-2.09, p=0.04
		emo_neg	percentage of words expressing negative emotions	0 (0)	0.20 (1.02)	t(106)=-2.04, p=0.04
	question	tech	percentage of words related to technology	0.03 (0.14)	0.27 (0.83)	t(125.92)=-2.76, p<0.01
		want	percentage of words expressing desire	0.04 (0.18)	0.22 (0.70)	t(123.56)=-2.38, p=0.02
		Perception	percentage of words related to perception (e.g., look, feel).	3.63 (3.54)	6.52 (4.72)	t(40.71)=-3.33, p<0.01
		attention	percentage of words indicating focus or attention	0.14 (0.46)	0.51 (1.14)	t(87.60)=-2.56, p=0.01
		motion	percentage of words related to movement	0.60 (0.91)	1.14 (1.68)	t(59.33)=-2.19, p=0.03
		space	percentage of words related to space and location	2.36 (2.92)	3.93 (3.34)	t(35.50)=-2.28, p=0.03
		time	percentage of words related to time	1.32 (1.88)	2.75 (3.24)	t(54.65)=-2.85, p<0.01
		OtherP	see above	1.71 (3.16)	3.37 (4.83)	t(47.15)=-2.06, p=0.04

Table 2: Significant LIWC feature t-test results for the various experiments. We use an independent samples t-test. The t-statistic indicates how much the means of the two groups differ relative to the variation in the sample data. We consider $p < 0.05$ to be statistically significant, meaning there is strong evidence against the null hypothesis of no difference between the groups, such that the observed difference in means is unlikely to have occurred by random chance. Here, we do not assume equal variance, utilizing Welch's t-test. As an interpretation example, suppose we are comparing the LIWC scores for the word count feature, where Class0 indicates Comprehensive responses and Class1 indicates Over-explained responses. A negative t-statistic would imply that the average word count of Comprehensive responses is lower than that of Over-explained responses. The small p-value in this case supports the conclusion that the long responses statistically tend to have more words compared to the short responses.

Experiment	Input	Feature	Description	Mean (SD) Class0	Mean (SD) Class1	t-test Result
Comprehensive (0) vs. Over-explained (1)	response	PRP	personal pronoun (e.g., I, you, he, she, it, we, they)	0.11 (0.03)	0.13 (0.03)	t(57.46)=-2.20, p=0.03
		VBZ	verb, 3rd person singular present (e.g., runs, talks, is)	0.03 (0.02)	0.03 (0.01)	t(68.74)=2.01, p=0.04
		CD	cardinal number (e.g., one, two, 3, 100)	0.01 (0.01)	0.02 (0.01)	t(45.77)=-2.20, p=0.03
		VBD	verb, past tense (e.g., ran, talked, was)	0.03 (0.03)	0.05 (0.03)	t(55.14)=-2.50, p=0.02
		VBG	verb, gerund or present participle (e.g., running, talking)	0.03 (0.01)	0.02 (0.01)	t(61.51)=2.17, p=0.03
		HYPH	hyphen	<0.01 (0.01)	<0.01 (<0.01)	t(88.35)=2.43, p=0.02
		WP	wh-pronoun (e.g., who, what, whom, which)	0.01 (0.01)	0.01 (<0.01)	t(84.40)=2.86, p=0.01
	question	RB	adverb (e.g., quickly, silently, very, too)	0.06 (0.04)	0.08 (0.04)	t(52.47)=-2.22, p=0.03
Succinct (0) vs. Under-explained (1)	response	CC	coordinating conjunction (e.g., and, or, but, yet)	0.05 (0.02)	0.04 (0.02)	t(34.15)=2.12, p=0.04
	question	VBP	verb, non-3rd person singular present (e.g., run, talk, are)	0.05 (0.03)	0.07 (0.04)	t(40.61)=-3.54, p<0.01
		NNS	plural noun (e.g., dogs, cars, ideas)	0.01 (0.01)	0.03 (0.03)	t(61.75)=-3.76, p<0.01
		POS	possessive ending ('s)	0 (0)	<0.01 (<0.01)	t(106)=-2.06, p=0.04

Table 3: Significant POS feature t-test results for the various experiments. We use an independent samples t-test. The t-statistic indicates how much the means of the two groups differ relative to the variation in the sample data. We consider $p < 0.05$ to be statistically significant, meaning there is strong evidence against the null hypothesis of no difference between the groups, such that the observed difference in means is unlikely to have occurred by random chance. Here, we do not assume equal variance, utilizing Welch's t-test. See the interpretation example in Table 4.

Experiment	Input	Text Representation	Features	Class0 F1	Class1 F1	Macro F1	Weighted F1
Comprehensive (0) vs. Over-explained (1)	response	BoW	none (baseline)	0.87	0.44	0.66	0.78
			LIWC	**0.88**	**0.48**	**0.68**	**0.79**
			POS	0.87	0.44	0.66	0.78
			jargon count	0.86	0.43	0.64	0.77
			normalized jargon count	0.86	0.44	0.65	0.77
		TF-IDF	none (baseline)	0.86	0.18	0.52	0.71
			LIWC	**0.89**	**0.41**	**0.65**	**0.78**
			POS	0.86	0.18	0.52	0.71
			jargon count	0.86	0.22	0.54	0.72
			normalized jargon count	0.87	0.26	0.56	0.73
		BERT	none (baseline)	0.86	0.09	0.47	0.69
			LIWC	**0.90**	**0.45**	**0.67**	**0.80**
			POS	0.86	0.09	0.47	0.69
			jargon count	0.86	0.09	0.47	0.69
			normalized jargon count	0.86	0.09	0.47	0.69
	question & response	BoW	none (baseline)	0.85	0.35	0.60	0.75
			LIWC	**0.90**	**0.54**	**0.72**	**0.82**
			POS	0.85	0.35	0.60	0.75
			jargon count	0.86	0.38	0.62	0.75
			normalized jargon count	0.84	0.35	0.59	0.73
		TF-IDF	none (baseline)	0.87	0.26	0.56	0.73
			LIWC	**0.89**	**0.48**	**0.69**	**0.80**
			POS	0.87	0.26	0.56	0.73
			jargon count	0.87	0.26	0.56	0.73
			normalized jargon count	0.88	0.33	0.61	0.76
		BERT	none (baseline)	0.86	0.05	0.45	0.68
			LIWC	**0.88**	**0.28**	**0.58**	**0.75**
			POS	0.86	0.05	0.45	0.68
			jargon count	0.86	0.05	0.45	0.68
			normalized jargon count	0.86	0.05	0.45	0.68

Table 4: Classification results for the Comprehensive vs. Over-explained experiments with specified text representation methods and features. "Class0" or "Class1" refers to the class listed first or second in the "Experiment." Bold text indicates the best model performance for each experiment.

Experiment	Input	Text Representation	Features	Class0 F1	Class1 F1	Macro F1	Weighted F1
Succinct (0) vs. Under-explained (1)	response	BoW	none (baseline)	0.87	0.06	0.47	0.73
			LIWC	**0.89**	**0.19**	**0.54**	**0.76**
			POS	0.87	0.06	0.47	0.73
			jargon count	0.87	0.06	0.47	0.73
			normalized jargon count	0.87	0.06	0.47	0.73
		TF-IDF	**none (baseline)**	**0.89**	**0.00**	**0.44**	**0.73**
			LIWC	0.88	0.00	0.44	0.72
			POS	0.89	0.00	0.44	0.73
			jargon count	0.89	0.00	0.44	0.73
			normalized jargon count	0.89	0.00	0.44	0.73
		BERT	**none (baseline)**	**0.90**	**0.08**	**0.49**	**0.75**
			LIWC	0.90	0.08	0.49	0.75
			POS	0.90	0.08	0.49	0.75
			jargon count	0.90	0.08	0.49	0.75
			normalized jargon count	0.90	0.08	0.49	0.75
	question & response	BoW	none (baseline)	0.89	0.00	0.44	0.73
			LIWC	**0.90**	**0.26**	**0.58**	**0.79**
			POS	0.89	0.00	0.44	0.73
			jargon count	0.89	0.00	0.44	0.73
			normalized jargon count	0.89	0.00	0.44	0.73
		TF-IDF	none (baseline)	0.88	0.07	0.47	0.73
			LIWC	**0.89**	**0.14**	**0.51**	**0.76**
			POS	0.88	0.07	0.47	0.73
			jargon count	0.88	0.07	0.47	0.73
			normalized jargon count	0.88	0.07	0.47	0.73
		BERT	none (baseline)	0.90	0.00	0.45	0.74
			LIWC	**0.89**	**0.07**	**0.48**	**0.75**
			POS	0.90	0.00	0.45	0.74
			jargon count	0.90	0.00	0.45	0.74
			normalized jargon count	0.90	0.00	0.45	0.74

Table 5: Classification results for the Succinct vs. Under-explained experiments with specified text representation methods and features. "Class0" or "Class1" refers to the class listed first or second in the "Experiment." Bold text indicates the best model performance for each experiment.

MetaMeme: A Dataset for Meme Template and Meta-Category Classification

Benjamin Lambright* and **Jordan Youner*** and **Constantine Lignos****
Michtom School of Computer Science
Brandeis University
bwlambright@gmail.com, jordan.youner@gmail.com, lignos@brandeis.edu

Abstract

This paper introduces a new dataset for classifying memes by their template and communicative intent. It includes a broad selection of meme templates and examples scraped from Imgflip and a smaller hand-annotated set of memes scraped from Reddit. The Reddit memes have been annotated for meta-category using a novel annotation scheme that classifies memes by the structure of the perspective they are being used to communicate. YOLOv11 and ChatGPT 4o are used to provide baseline modeling results. We find that YOLO struggles with template classification on real-world data, but outperforms ChatGPT in classifying meta-categories.

1 Introduction and Related Work

The majority of the previous research on the automatic classification of memes revolves around specific domains like the detection of politics or hate speech or classifying memes by humor "type" (Courtois and Frissen, 2023). Little work addresses task of identifying which *template*—not necessary a single literal image, but a recognizable reference format for the meme—a meme falls into, but Courtois and Frissen offer one of the most promising recent attempts to do so. Their work uses two datasets: a dataset of randomly selected memes and hand-annotated templates from one of the most widely used meme documentation websites, KnowYourMeme, and a dataset of memes paired with their templates scraped from the aggregator website 9gag. Their method for template identification involved CNNs for detecting features common across examples, calculating accuracy with a geometric mean given that parts of their datasets had templates not seen in training.

Along similar lines, Gleason et al. (2019) attempt simple meme template detection. They use a combination of the the Multi-Scale Structural Similarity (MS-SSIM) index and a color histogram between the input and template image (Wang et al., 2003) to match memes to their templates. Even with their small dataset of 385 memes and 137 templates, they achieved an accuracy of 92.25%.

This paper offers a similar methodology for obtaining the dataset to Courtois and Frissen (2023), but with a larger and more varied set of templates. While Gleason et al. (2019) provides promising results for a small dataset, we expect our template identification task to be much more difficult, with over 2,000 template classes compared to their 137. Additionally, Gleason et al. (2019) likely reached near-ceiling performance because all of their memes were generated using the exact same source images for templates, but the reality of meme usage across the internet is that there is more room for variation, as they are often not made using generators with consistent template images.

Along with examples from Imgflip (a meme generator website), we also include memes sourced from Reddit. In total, our dataset covers 2,059 meme templates with a collection of 274,748 examples scraped from Imgflip and a collection of 242 hand-annotated memes from Reddit. With the inclusion of social media-obtained memes, we expose our model to examples of a given template that are likely much more diverse than those found exclusively on generator websites, which gives a better window into performance on real-world data.

To support the annotation of the Reddit memes, we introduce an ontology of *meta-categories* meant to explore the communicative intent behind memes. Recent work has used LLMs and VL (vision language) models to identify the metaphors represented by a given meme, as well as explaining the entire joke itself (Hwang and Shwartz, 2023). As an alternative to this, we explore a structure-based approach with the assumption that an understanding of the desired intent in using a meme can be

*Equal contribution. **Corresponding author.

Proceedings of the 2025 Conference of the Nations of the Americas Chapter of the Association for Computational Linguistics: Human Language Technologies (Volume 4: Student Research Workshop), pages 356–367
April 30 - May 1, 2025

identified without requiring any context. Between the meta-category classification task and the more traditional meme template classification task, this dataset contributions a novel resource for the study of meme creation and usage.[1]

2 Dataset

2.1 Data Sources

2.1.1 Imgflip

The large amount of unannotated data that we collect for the purpose of identifying meme templates was collected from imgflip by modifying an open-source codebase.[2] Imgflip was the best website for this dataset for two reasons: it is easy to scrape memes and their corresponding templates, and the website documents thousands of templates.

Our dataset contains 1,992 template classes from the "Top *All Time*" page from imgflip. While there were initially more classes, we found that some of the templates on imgflip were duplicates. In order to handle this, we used an image hashing algorithm to remove duplicates. Some template duplicates were also removed manually, if image hashing could not identify them.

All additional template classes come from our Reddit data. In order to ensure that our model has trained on all templates represented in the Reddit data, we scraped 67 additional templates from Imgflip that appeared in the Reddit data but were not in the original top 2,000 classes. In total, this dataset includes 274,748 meme examples from 2,059 templates.

The dataset is organized in two ways. For image classification tasks, each template is a directory that includes all the image files for the template class. The dataset also includes a json file of all the metadata for each example meme, including the image url, post url, captioning for the meme, and other metadata.

Meta-category	Count
Reaction	100
Exploitable	89
Image Macro	7
Duality	30
Escalating Progression	9
None	7

Table 1: Counts of the various meta-categories in our annotated Reddit data, including examples that were annotated as having no meta-category.

Figure 1: An example of a meme template. "Drake-posting" or "Drake Hotline Bling" is a meme whose template involves two frames of Drake from the *Hotline Bling* music video that are set up to rate something as bad and something else as good. The user of the template then fills in the whitespace with two images or pieces of text to pair with the Drake ones.

2.1.2 Reddit

In order to have data that reflects more real-world usage than output from meme generator websites, we also scraped images from Reddit's r/memes community (subreddit).[3] We scraped the following from Reddit: 100 memes from the top of all time, 100 from the top of the month scraped on November 13th 2024, and 50 from the top of the month scraped on December 13th 2024. For each example, the annotators identified the corresponding imgflip template (if one could be found) and selected the meta-category that best fits the meme. In total, there were 242 annotated examples,[4] 74 of which did not have a template and 20 that had an identifiable template, but that template was not documented on imgflip.

[1]Our dataset and the code used in this paper are available in this repository: https://github.com/BenLambright/Meme-template-classification.

[2]https://github.com/schesa/ImgFlip575K_Dataset/tree/master

[3]https://www.reddit.com/r/memes

2.2 Task Definitions

2.2.1 Meme Template Classification

The primary task of this dataset is to identify the template a meme is built from. A meme template is a recognizable joke format that the user fills in the details of when they create a meme. Figure 1 gives an example template. The task involves mapping a human-created meme to the template that was used when creating it.

2.2.2 Meta-category Classification

In order to facilitate capturing the semantic and pragmatic content of memes, we developed an ontology of meta-category categories which define formats and structures that are common across templates. This can potentially augment meme template detection and offer a way to group memes of unseen templates. This set of categories is in part derived from the ontology presented by knowyourmeme.com. Consequently, an alternative task for this dataset is to classify these general categories of memes in order to classify their sentiment.

2.3 Annotation Ontology and Results

The annotators for this project are two male graduate students at Brandeis University between 20-30 years old, receiving course credit for their annotation work. They were asked to annotate 250 images scraped from Reddit and the top 100 most popular template images from Imgflip. The former were annotated for both templates and meta-categories, while the latter were only annotated for the most common meta-category that meme template would have. For the Reddit dataset, the template annotations were almost always consistent between the two annotators. In the few cases they were not, the annotators discussed the difference and performed adjudication jointly.

These meta-categories are derived from some of the higher-level categories presented in the KnowYourMeme ontology. While the website contains hundreds of categories, the ones we chose to use more as they were presented on the website (image macro, exploitable, reaction) are comparably more general and high-level. For duality and escalating progression, we came across the Drakeposting category, which describes memes that resemble the duality/escalating progression structure, and decided to create two distinct categories that capture similar structural information but mainly differ in terms of semantic content (and enable categorization of such memes without referring to a specific example template). With these selections, we feel that we were able to encompass nearly all memes and enable capturing of some semantic information.

The inter-annotator agreement for our meta-categories was consistently around 70%. This section provides a description of our ontology and a summary of the annotation approach. The full guidelines along with examples of all meta-categories and the guidance for annotation edge cases can be found in the Appendix. Counts for each meta-category annotated are given in Table 1.

Image Macro Image macros can be thought of as memes for which the setup of the joke is given by the image, and the text fills in the details and punchline. For our purposes, we consider image macros as consisting of a single image. The most typical presentation of these memes involves a picture of some kind of entity, often an animal or person, with white text in impact font on the top and bottom of the image.

Reaction Image Reaction images are, in a sense, an inversion of image macros. Instead of the image setting up the joke and the text filling in the punchline, the joke is set up by a text caption that is almost always above or below the image content. The punchline is the image. The images in these memes are usually of people emoting or reacting in some fashion, and the humor often derives in part from the fact that the text caption completely recontextualizes the image from its origin.

Exploitable An exploitable is a meme in which an existing image such as a comic, or still frame(s) from a movie is augmented by adding or replacing text or characters to tell a joke. The idea is that there is some extant structure inside the original image that is "exploited" using additional text or images.

Duality A meme exhibiting duality is one that compares two (or more) situations or contexts that are related across some dimension in opposition to each other. The typical components of a duality meme are a set of discrete contexts and a set of images that visualize the relationship between the contexts. A common format is a "4-panel" layout

[4] Some images were removed due to broken links, deleted posts, or offensive subject matter.

in which a pair of contexts and images are stacked vertically.

Escalating Progression Escalating progression memes are those that express a reaction to points sampled along a continuum of context. Unlike in duality where the situations are connected in terms of directly opposing each other (bad vs. good), with escalating progression there is an intensification between each state along an axis (good, better, best). Typically these memes have at least 3 sets of image-context pairs, but it is not required as long as there is an obvious sense of continuum between the contexts.

None While the previous categories are designed to cover as much of the semantic-pragmatic space of memes as is feasible, there are examples that do not align well with any of them. Annotators were always encouraged to mark a category, but it was permissible to label the meta-category as "none" if they felt strongly that none of them fit. There exist other "genres" of memes such as surreal, "deep-fried" or anti-memes which are not addressed by the ontology because they exist in small niches. One could realistically add several more categories to this ontology, but the point of this ontology is for it to be small and representative of most existing memes.

3 Experiments

3.1 Experiment Design

For template classification, we divided our dataset into the images annotated from Reddit and the images scraped from imgflip. From these, we further split the imgflip data into train, dev, and test sets using a 90-5-5 split. We treated the Reddit data as a unique test set, because this would allow us to test on data which the model mostly likely has never seen before, unlike the test set of the imgflip data, which was normally the same images with different text overlayed on it.

Along with classifying the specific templates for each image, we also classified meta-categories (image macro, reaction image, exploitable, duality, escalating progression, and none). In order to do this, we train on two different datasets to see which can best identify the meta-categories. For the imgflip data, each template is annotated with a meta-category and the label is transferred to all images that were generated using that template. For the Reddit data, each image has its meta-category hand-annotated since the template used to generate is not given automatically through the scraping process (unlike the imgflip data).

Task/Dataset	Accuracy
Imgflip Data Template	99.8
Reddit Data Template	40.5
Imgflip Data Meta-category	51.5
Reddit Data Meta-category	68.8

Table 2: Accuracies for the YOLO model on the classification tasks: template identification and meta-category identification.

The imgflip data was split into train, validation, and test portions using a 90-5-5 split. For the Reddit data, we used an 85-15 train-test split.

3.2 Models

We use two different models to provide baseline results for our dataset: YOLOv11's image classification model and ChatGPT 4o.

3.2.1 YOLOv11

We chose to use YOLOv11 because YOLO has consistently strong performance on image classification tasks (Khanam and Hussain, 2024) and focuses on data examples beyond ImageNet. We fine-tuned the model on scraped data from imgflip. After fine-tuning the model with optimized hyperparameters,[5] we evaluated the model on a test set from imgflip and Reddit. By evaluating these two test sets separately, we are able to see how the model predicts images that are the same as the training data with different text (imgflip), versus images that are conceptually similar, but often vary significantly from the training data (Reddit).

As shown in Table 2, while the template classification YOLO model reaches near-100% accuracy when testing on the imgflip test data, it struggles with the Reddit data. This is because the memes posted on Reddit do not always use the same images that define the template on imgflip, especially in the cases where they were not directly generated from an imgflip template. As a result, these "in the wild" examples [6] are much harder for the YOLO model to identify. The imgflip meme template classification task is very simple because it is

[5]Values: patience=2, image size=640, optimizer="AdamW", learning rate=0.01, momentum=0.937, weight decay=0.0005.

[6]See the appendix for examples.

almost always the same image with different text overlayed on it.

As for the Reddit template identification, 40.5% accuracy indicates that the model is still able to identify the template some of the time. There are 2,059 meme templates for the classifier to select from, so this indicates some level of understanding, even if it does not match the performance of other models trained on fewer classes in prior work (Gleason et al., 2019).

In terms of meta-category classification, YOLO performed reasonably when trained and tested on imgflip data (51.5%), and even better when tested on the Reddit data (68.8%), where a random selection of classes would ne expected to produce 16.7% accuracy.

However, Table 3 indicates that there was a significant amount of overfitting due to dataset imbalance. The less common classes (none, image macro, duality, and escalating progression) were classified correctly significantly less frequently than the common classes of exploitable and reaction Image. Reaction images were correctly classified 82% of the time, and exploitables 89.5% of the time, indicating that at least as a binary classification task these two classes can be correctly understood by the model.

These results indicate that the YOLO model is learning some sort of structural information that allows it to predict at least the most common meta-categories with reasonable accuracy. Furthermore, the fact that the Reddit dataset had a much larger number of templates relative to the number of examples of each may have pushed the model away from relying on direct relationships between templates and meta-categories.

3.3 ChatGPT 4o

In addition to testing our data using the YOLOv11 model, we also used ChatGPT's 4o API. Because of the complexity of identifying the semantic structure of memes, we posited that an LLM might be well suited for the task. In all of these experiments, we always started with the exact same initial and final prompt, which can be found in the Appendix. Additionally, we kept the prompting parameters, temperature and top P, at their default values: 1.00 and 1.00.

We performed three different few-shot experiments with this model: text-based few-shot prompting, image-based few-shot prompting, and a combination of both. In our first experiment, the prompt describes each of the meta-category categories in a few sentences as text, based on the annotation guidelines. In the second experiment, we prompt with an image example for each meta-category category and explain why that image is an example of the meta-category. In the third experiment, we give the prompts from both the first and second experiments together. All of these prompts are recorded in the Appendix. Because this model is nondeterministic, we ran these experiments three times and calculated the mean score and standard error of the mean.

As shown in Tables 4 and 5, ChatGPT performed significantly better on the Reddit data than the imgflip data, but the specific prompt style used did not have much impact. Given that these two datasets were annotated by the same annotators with the same guidelines, this suggests that the memes in the Reddit dataset were easier for the model to interpret. Having both text and image examples in the prompt likely caused the model to have too much information to properly process it all, but providing text or image prompts provided the same mean score.[7]

While it be reasonable to expect that ChatGPT would be better at reasoning how to classify meta-categories if it necessitates understanding the semantics of the meme, ChatGPT was still not very successful at identifying the meta-categories. Importantly, the model did not always guess the same category, it simply chose a different wrong category most of the time. This suggests that this was still a difficult task for the model, even if the prompts could be improved, and the model was not overfitting.

4 Future Work and Conclusion

While the ChatGPT results were disappointing, the consistency of the poor results could suggest that the model might need something more complex than just prompts. For example, using chain-of-thought or reinforcement learning might help the model improve perform performance by allowing it to reason more. For the same reason, ChatGPT's o1 pro model, which now has vision capabilities, might show stronger results as well (Noda et al., 2025). As for the YOLO models, it suggests that the meta-category ontology can be predicted, with reasonable accuracy, using a pure computer vision

[7]The individual scores for text and image prompts generally varied between 40% and 43%; they never produced exactly the same result.

	Predicted					
Actual	None	Exploitable	Image Macro	Duality	Escalating Progression	Reaction
None	0	2	0	0	0	1
Exploitable	0	76	2	0	0	7
Image Macro	0	2	1	0	0	6
Duality	0	18	0	4	0	7
Escalating Progression	0	5	0	1	0	5
Reaction	0	17	1	0	0	82

Table 3: Confusion Matrix for the predictions from the YOLO model on the Reddit data meta-category identification task

Task	Accuracy
Imgflip Data Meta-category	$29.6_{\pm 1.8}$
Reddit Data Meta-category	$47.7_{\pm 0.2}$

Table 4: Mean accuracies and standard errors for ChatGPT meta-category classification with image prompts on different datasets.

Prompt Content	Mean Score
Text	$42.2_{\pm 1.1}$
Image	$42.2_{\pm 0.6}$
Both	$37.8_{\pm 1.6}$

Table 5: Mean accuracies and standard errors for ChatGPT meta-category classification across all test sets using different prompting strategies.

approach. This could help classify the semantic meaning of a meme without requiring the context of an entire joke.

Knowing that annotators considered the text when annotating memes, it would likely also be helpful for the text to be included in the pipeline for meta-category classification. It would be easy to prompt for this with ChatGPT, asking to include this information in its final inference.

The best way to improve the performance of both tasks is likely to be getting more data. Scraping from more sources than imgflip and Reddit would provide a more diverse dataset, as well as being able to handle more meme formats, like GIFs.

The Reddit dataset was also very small due to the limited amount of annotator time available, and more data would likely have improved the performance of our models. On a similar note, in the imgflip dataset, there were meme templates that were extremely similar to each other, as discussed further in the Appendix. While we removed exact duplicates in data preprocessing, there are likely still meme template classes that could be combined, and would likely improve the performance of the YOLO model on meme template classification.

5 Limitations

Some templates that are functionally duplicates (such as two examples of "Drakeposting" using slightly different stills from the video) may not have been discarded from our image hashing algorithm, potentially causing a dip in accuracy. We recommend using a deep learning model to identify these near-duplicate templates in the future. Also, the total amount of annotated Reddit data is very small, making both learning and inference more difficult. A larger group of annotators combine with a more varied set of data would allow for greater exploration of the machine-learnability of meta-categories, and would also enable further refinement of the ontology. This dataset was even smaller when testing on specifically the meme template classification task, because 74 memes could not be included because the annotators marked them as not having a template.

6 Ethical Considerations and Broader Impact

The authors would like to state that while they made efforts to comb through the data and remove memes with questionable or offensive content, they cannot guarantee that every example in this dataset is free from such content, and furthermore would like to state that they do not endorse anything that may be expressed by memes included in this dataset. Beyond the nature of the memes' content, it is also important to consider that the sources of the scraped memes (imgflip and the r/memes subReddit) may limit perspectives in terms of their respective userbases, and future work should endeavor to capture memes from a wider variety of creators.

References

Cedric Courtois and Thomas Frissen. 2023. Computer vision and internet meme genealogy: An evaluation of image feature matching as a technique for pattern detection. *Communication Methods and Measures*, 17(1):17–39.

Cole Gleason, Amy Pavel, Xingyu Liu, Patrick Carrington, Lydia B. Chilton, and Jeffrey P. Bigham. 2019. Making memes accessible. In *Proceedings of the 21st International ACM SIGACCESS Conference on Computers and Accessibility*, ASSETS '19, page 367–376, New York, NY, USA. Association for Computing Machinery.

EunJeong Hwang and Vered Shwartz. 2023. MemeCap: A dataset for captioning and interpreting memes. In *Proceedings of the 2023 Conference on Empirical Methods in Natural Language Processing*, pages 1433–1445, Singapore. Association for Computational Linguistics.

Rahima Khanam and Muhammad Hussain. 2024. YOLOv11: An Overview of the Key Architectural Enhancements. *Preprint*, arXiv:2410.17725.

Ryunosuke Noda, Chiaki Yuasa, Fumiya Kitano, Daisuke Ichikawa, and Yugo Shibagaki. 2025. Performance of o1 pro and GPT-4 in Self-Assessment Questions for Nephrology Board Renewal. *medRxiv*.

Z. Wang, E.P. Simoncelli, and A.C. Bovik. 2003. Multiscale structural similarity for image quality assessment. In *The Thrity-Seventh Asilomar Conference on Signals, Systems & Computers, 2003*, volume 2, pages 1398–1402 Vol.2.

A Annotation Guidelines

For each annotation in the project, perform the following steps:

1. Transcribe the text in the meme. Each section of text (either split up as labels, lines of dialogue, or other obvious spacing) should be typed into the box followed by the enter key.

2. Attempt to identify the meme template. If it is immediately recognized, find the corresponding link to the **template** (i.e imgflip.com/memetemplate/... and not imgflip.com/memegenerator/...) if one exists. Otherwise if it is unrecognized, query search engines with a description of the image and the word "meme." If all else fails, obtain the link to the source image (through Label Studio) and input it into Google's search by image feature to obtain a name or description that would lead one to an associated imgflip template. Note that in the case of multiple templates in an image, one should choose a single template that is ideally the most prominently featured and most easily recognizable in the image. If there are no recognizable templates in the image, leave the link section blank.

3. Choose one of the associated meta-categories according to the ontology. While it is possible to leave this selection blank, it is generally recommended to avoid this unless one feels very strongly that none of the associated meta-categories fit at all.

A.1 Image Macro Example

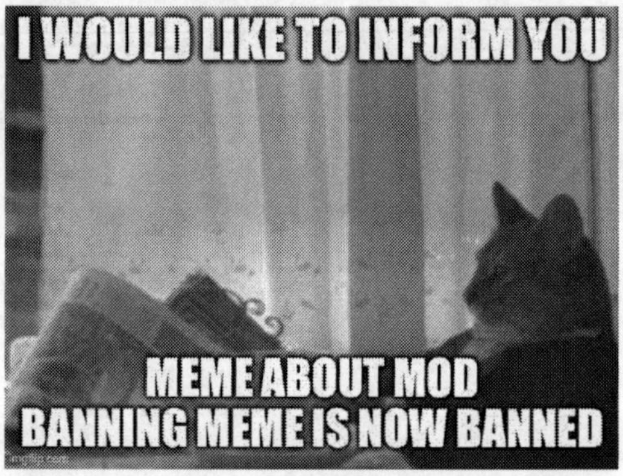

This example involves an image of a cat in a suit sitting at a table as if it were looking up from reading the newspaper with a shocked expression. With the image as the context, the caption continues the (presumably meta) joke by delivering an announcement about banned meme posts.

A.2 Reaction Image Example

In this example, the joke is derived from the situation set up in the caption "when you donate 1$ to a streamer" and the punchline in the reaction image of Walter White from *Breaking Bad* saying "Now say my name."

A.3 Exploitable Example

This example is using a scene from the cartoon *Scooby Doo, Where Are You!* in which the character Fred is revealing the identity of the villain. The masked villain is labeled as "Being able to cook," and then once unmasked, labeled as "Just following the recipe."

A.4 Duality Example

This example shows the duality between two situations in a video game. The first one is where the player of a game is able to heal their character several times, and the second is where the boss heals a single time. The images of Mordecai from the cartoon *Regular Show* express a neutral-positive reaction to the first situation and a disgusted reaction to the second.

A.5 Escalating Progression Example

The example shown here demonstrates the escalating progression of deciding when to purchase and play a video game. The first context, "pre-order a game" is the neutral ("good") state, associated with the normal image of Winnie the Pooh. The second, "buy the game when it releases," is the next step up ("better"), and the corresponding image is Pooh in fancy dress. The final context, "wait almost a decade so you can get it for free," is the "best" decision, and as a result the corresponding Pooh is dressed in even fancier clothing to communicate this.

A.6 "None" meta-category Example

This example is not much more than a picture with a caption. There does not appear to be any larger structural relationship between the text and image beyond that.

B Differences Between Imgflip and Reddit Memes

Often, memes that are obtained from sources other than generator websites (i.e "in the wild") look very different from the prototypical template image from which the meme is derived. As an illustrative example, consider the "Sad Hulk" meme. The template image is that of two frames of the Incredible Hulk with tears in his eyes. Typically, examples of this meme will use the exact same image of the Hulk, only having the text changed.

This is the same image as that which is found on the Crying Hulk template on imgflip. However, there are other examples that are clearly referencing the same template without using the exact same picture.

Template	Confidence
odd1sout-vs-computer-chess	0.09
Running-Away-Balloon	0.09
hello-human-resources	0.05
Apu-takes-bullet	0.04
how-i-sleep-homer-simpson	0.04
American-Chopper-Argument	0.10
thanos-what-did-it-cost	0.06
Squidward	0.04
Hide-the-Pain-Harold	0.04
Out-of-line-but-hes-right	0.04

Table 6: Top 5 template labels by confidence from the YOLO model for the Incredible Krunk (top) and Hulk Hogan (bottom) examples.

While both of these examples are using very different images from the template, they are still clearly derived from the original in terms of the joke being made (especially since the first picture is a parody of the Hulk and the second is a picture of Hulk Hogan). Given how different these images are compared to any output from the Crying Hulk meme generator, it stands to reason that these would be especially difficult for a simple CV model to determine that they should be classified as the same template. Accordingly, our YOLO model did not put Crying Hulk in the top 5 for either example.

C Meta-category Edge Cases

Sometimes it is not clear which meta-category label is appropriate for a given meme. This section provides some examples encountered by the annotators along with discussion of the relevant labels to hopefully elucidate what the ontology is trying to capture.

C.1 Image Macro vs. Reaction

This meme structurally resembles a reaction (the text on top separate from the image) but the actual relationship between the text and image is that of an image macro because the joke is a play on a well-known phrase from the character pictured.

C.2 Reaction vs. Exploitable

Even though the image is from an established piece of media (the Thriller music video), the structure in this meme comes from outside the scene. The image essentially functions as a reaction to the setup in the text.

C.3 Exploitable vs. Reaction

While the image on the bottom of the meme is often deployed as a reaction, in this case the structure of the meme is derived from multiple frames of the actual scene, so it is an exploitable.

C.4 Duality vs. Exploitable

Even though the source for the images in this meme is the TV show Tom and Jerry, it is not considered an exploitable because the two frames are from entirely different parts of the TV show, and the structure of the meme is as a result not derived from the scene. The duality comes from the comparison between the two image-caption pairs.

C.5 Duality vs. Escalating progression

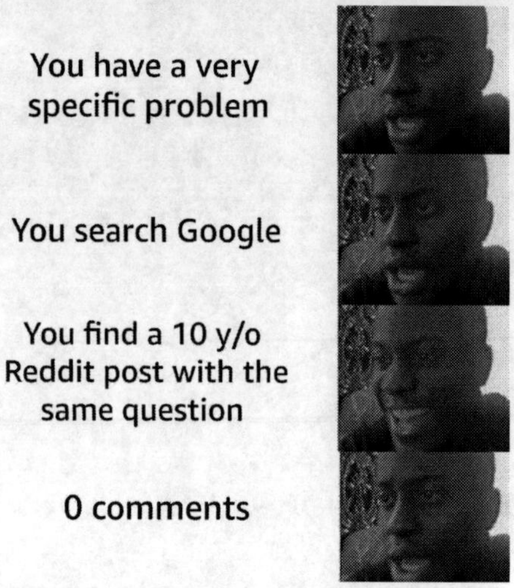

The images in this meme communicate two opposing emotional states occurring across the various stages described by the captions. Rather than being a continuum, they express discrete negative and positive emotions. As a result, despite having more than two parts, this meme is an example of duality and not escalating progression.

D ChatGPT 4o API Prompts

Initial prompt: "You will be given a list of example images for image macro, reaction, escalating progression, duality, and exploitable memes, and afterwards you will have to classify them"

Final prompt: "Given the descriptions of memes from before, how would you describe the following meme? Select a response for the following list and only use the words from this list: image macro, reaction, escalating progression, duality, or exploitable. Only output the template class you decided."

D.1 Experiment 1: Text Prompts

Image Macros: "Image macros can be thought of as memes for which the setup of the joke is given by the image, and the text fills in the details and punchline. For our purposes, we consider image macros as consisting of a single image. The most typical presentation of these memes involves a picture of some kind of entity (often an animal or person) with white text in impact font on the top and bottom of the image."

Reaction Images: "Reaction images are in a sense an inversion of image macros. Instead of the image setting up the joke and the text filling in the punchline, the joke is set up by a text caption (almost always separated from the image portion) and then the punchline is the image. The images in these memes are usually of people emoting or reacting in some fashion, and the humor often derives in part from the fact that the text caption completely recontextualizes the image from its origin."

Escalating Progression: "Escalating progression memes are those that express a reaction to points sampled along a continuum of context. Unlike in duality where the situations are related in terms of opposing each other (e.g good thing vs. bad thing), with escalating progression there is an intensification between each state (e.g good thing vs. better thing vs. best thing). Typically, these memes have at least 3 sets of image-context pairs, but it is not required as long as there is an obvious sense of continuity between the contexts. It does not have to be 3+ images, like it can still be one, the difference is that it represents something escalating, rather than a good or bad. It has a continuum moving in a consistent and intensifyingly humorous direction."

Duality: "A meme exhibiting duality is one that compares two (or more) situations or contexts that are related across some dimension, usually in opposition to each other. The typical components of a duality meme are a set of discrete contexts and a set of images (most often variations on the same image) that visualize the relationship between the contexts. A common format is a '4-panel' layout in which two pairs of contexts and images are stacked vertically."

Exploitable: "An exploitable is a meme in which an existing image (such as a comic, or one or more scenes from a movie) of some sort is augmented by adding and/or replacing some set of things (like dialogue, characters, labels etc.) to tell a joke. The idea is that there is some extant structure inside an image that is 'exploited' using text or additional pictures within the bounds of the original image (unlike a caption in a reaction image, which is typically outside it)."

D.2 Experiment 2: Image Prompts

Image Macros: "Here is an example of an image macro, where you have the classic text on top and below, where the entire joke could be understood without the image:"

url: "https://imgflip.com/i/3yhgyo"

Reaction Images: "Here is an example of a reaction, where the monkey looks awkwardly in reaction to the text which follows a 'me-when' style:"

url: "https://i.imgflip.com/4zv2v9.jpg"

Escalating Progression: "Here is an example of an escalating progression, where the brain gets bigger and bigger as the text describes something smarter and smarter:"

url: "https://i.imgflip.com/4iyi3q.jpg"

Duality: "Here is an example of an duality, where drake at first thinks it's bad, but then thinks it's good:"

url: "https://i.imgflip.com/4izfsm.jpg"

Exploitable: "Here is an example of an exploitable, where the text is overlayed over all of the people, representing who they are in the context of the joke:"

url: "https://i.imgflip.com/3fys88.jpg"

Representing and Clustering Errors in Offensive Language Detection

Jood Otey
Oakland University
joodotey@oakland.edu

Laura Biester
Middlebury College
lbiester@middlebury.edu

Steven R. Wilson
University of Michigan-Flint
steverw@umich.edu

Abstract

WARNING: paper contains offensive content. Content moderation is essential in preventing the spread of harmful content on the Internet. However, there are instances where moderation fails and it is important to understand when and why that happens. Workflows that aim to uncover a system's weakness typically use clustering of the data points' embeddings to group errors together. In this paper, we evaluate the K-Means clustering of four text representations for the task of offensive language detection in English and Levantine Arabic. We find Sentence-BERT (SBERT) embeddings give the most human-interpretable clustering for English errors and the grouping is mainly based on the targeted group in the text. Meanwhile, SBERT embeddings of Large Language Model (LLM)-generated linguistic features give the most interpretable clustering for Arabic errors.[1]

1 Introduction

Content moderation systems are used to mitigate the spread of offensive content online. These systems are usually successful at flagging offensive language, but may also incorrectly remove non-offensive content, and this incorrectly flagged non-offensive content is disproportionately shared by people who identify with a marginalized group. Previous works have shown bias in hate speech detection systems when it comes to text written in African American English (Xia et al., 2020; Sap et al., 2019; Harris et al., 2022). Moreover, moderation systems struggle to classify implicit offensive language. Mendelsohn et al. (2023) tested dog whistle detection on the Perspective API[2] and found that it assigned lower ratings to examples that used dog whistles (subtle, potentially harmful messages intended to only be understood by certain groups) instead of slurs.

In order to work toward correcting these types of issues, offensive language detection models must be examined more closely to understand how and why they are making mistakes. Evaluation metrics like F1-score and accuracy provide a compact and high-level means of scoring models, but are not enough to fully understand a model's behavior. To uncover where a model underperforms, researchers have recently shifted to automating aspects of the error analysis process and providing a systematic approach to analyzing a model's performance. These approaches are presented as error analysis tools (Rajani et al., 2022; McMillan-Major et al., 2022; R Menon and Srivastava, 2024; Gauthier-melancon et al., 2022; Tenney et al., 2020; Grace et al., 2023; Yuan et al., 2022; Wu et al., 2019) or Slice Detection Models (SDMs) (Hua et al., 2023; d'Eon et al., 2022; Sohoni et al., 2020; Eyuboglu et al., 2022). Error analysis tools provide a user-interface that allows practitioners to closely examine their systems and SDMs partition the data to "slices", aiming to identify those partitions on which the model underperforms, without the need for explicitly labeled subgroups.

These tools and models typically involve grouping the data points according to some human-understandable concept (e.g., gender, race). Clustering textual data requires them to be converted to a vector representation, like contextual embeddings, which gained popularity with the rise of pre-trained language models. SDMs and error analysis tools frequently use contextual embeddings when developing their frameworks (Rajani et al., 2022; McMillan-Major et al., 2022; R Menon and Srivastava, 2024; Hua et al., 2023; d'Eon et al., 2022; Sohoni et al., 2020; Eyuboglu et al., 2022).

Embeddings of text from neural networks encode information that can go beyond the label and these interpretable features or subclasses are not

[1] We publicly release all the code, models, and data needed to reproduce our results https://github.com/wetey/cluster-errors

[2] https://perspectiveapi.com/

Proceedings of the 2025 Conference of the Nations of the Americas Chapter of the Association for Computational Linguistics: Human Language Technologies (Volume 4: Student Research Workshop), pages 368–380

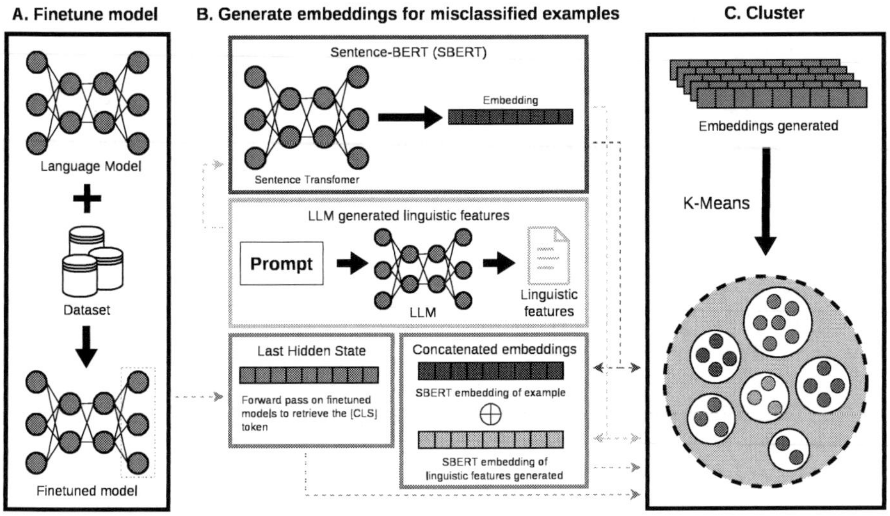

Figure 1: Overview of the methodology followed in the paper. **A.** Two Pretrained language models are finetuned on offensive language datasets (one on English and one on Arabic). **B.** We take the misclassified examples and generate embeddings to then cluster. We experiment with four types of embeddings: **(1)** **Last Hidden State (LHS)** are generated by extracting the [CLS] token from the last layer of the finetuned models. **(2)** **Sentence-BERT (SBERT)** are generated by running a sentence transformer model trained to generate semantically meaningful sentence embeddings. **(3)** **Linguistic features** are generated by prompting an LLM to generate linguistic features for the example, then the generated features are encoded using the same models as in embedding type **2**. **(4)** **Concatenated embeddings** are generated by concatenating the embeddings from **2** and **3**. **C.** The final step is running K-Means clustering on the generated embeddings.

always available with the dataset (Sohoni et al., 2022). In this work, we experiment with four types of embeddings of texts that were erroneously classified by offensive language detection models. Figure 1 summarizes the process used in this paper. We evaluate the embedding approaches to determine which leads to the most interpretable clustering and analyze what information about the underlying instances is represented by the embeddings. We find that for English, the two methods of clustering text using Sentence-BERT (SBERT) embeddings (Reimers and Gurevych, 2019) and concatenating those embeddings to embeddings of additional LLM-generated linguistic features yield the most human-interpretable clusters. Moreover, the clusters are primarily based on the group that was the target of the offensive language in the text. For Arabic, we find that clustering text using LLM-generated linguistic features yields the most human-interpretable clustering.

2 Background

Ad-hoc approaches to understand model performance for NLP classification tasks involve manually grouping the errors and giving each group/cluster a label. The process of having humans provide the label is laborious and subjective, leading to results that are often not reproducible (Wu et al., 2019).

Recent works that propose systematic error analysis frameworks for NLP classification tasks use clustering algorithms like K-Means and hierarchical clustering to group misclassified instances in an attempt to understand where the model underperforms (Rajani et al., 2022; McMillan-Major et al., 2022; R Menon and Srivastava, 2024). Similarly, popular Slice Detection Models (SDM)s are based on Gaussian Mixture Models (a generalized version of K-Means clustering) (Hua et al., 2023; d'Eon et al., 2022; Sohoni et al., 2020; Eyuboglu et al., 2022).

A popular vector representation used to cluster the textual data points is the last hidden layer of deep learning models, because it contains the learned representation of the entire sequence of tokens. When using pre-trained language models based on the transformer architecture like BERT (Devlin et al., 2019) and RoBERTa (Liu et al., 2019) the final representation of their [CLS] token is commonly used. These vector representations are used for understanding model performance in error analysis tools and SDMs for NLP classification tasks (Rajani et al., 2022; d'Eon et al., 2022; Hua et al., 2023). Other works such as McMillan-Major et al. (2022) use Sentence-BERT (SBERT) embeddings as the representation of the data points. SBERT embeddings (Reimers and Gurevych, 2019) use Siamese network structures (Bromley et al., 1993) to build a sequence-level text representation, which shows improvements over previous state-of-the-art sentence embedding methods on Semantic Textual Similarity tasks.

Prior works focused on quantitative evaluation of groups of embeddings with limited evaluation of how the choice of embedding approach might impact the final result (Rajani et al., 2022; McMillan-Major et al., 2022; R Menon and Srivastava, 2024). In this work we leverage two embedding types that have been commonly used to perform error analysis, last hidden state embeddings and SBERT embeddings, to build representations of the misclassified examples. Moreover, we propose a new method of representing errors which uses LLMs to generate linguistic features present in the errors. We evaluate the interpretability of the clusterings and provide insights into the type information the embeddings hold.

3 Data and Models

3.1 Datasets

The English dataset we use is the Measuring Hate Speech (MHS) dataset (Kennedy et al., 2020). The dataset originally contained 135,556 total annotations of 39,565 texts (~ 3.42 annotations per text), including statements about 7 target groups (gender, religion, sexuality, origin, race, age, and disability). The dataset is sourced from Twitter (40%), Reddit (40%), and YouTube comments (20%) and was annotated by 10,000 Amazon Mechanical Turk workers. We converted the continuous hatespeech scores to categorical labels using the ranges suggested by the authors:[3] examples with hate speech scores that are lower than -1 are considered `supportive`, between -1 and 0.5 are `neutral`, and scores greater than 0.5 are `hatespeech`. We remove duplicate examples along with those that received fewer than three total annotations, and we drop the neutral class. After these steps, we were left with 12,289 examples with 7497 examples labeled as `supportive` and 4792 labeled as `hatespeech`. We use 85% of the dataset for fine-tuning and 15% for testing.

The Arabic dataset we use is the Levantine Hate Speech and ABusive (L-HSAB) dataset (Mulki et al., 2019). The examples are in Levantine Arabic and the original dataset has 5,846 instances, which were all sourced from Twitter and annotated by three native Levantine Arabic speakers. After removing duplicates we were left with 5,754 examples. The dataset has three labels: `normal` (3576 examples), `abusive` (1713 examples), and `hate` (465). We use 85% of the dataset for fine-tuning and 15% for testing.

3.2 Classification Models

We finetune DistilBERT base uncased (Sanh et al., 2020) on the English dataset using an NVIDIA RTX A6000 GPU with a learning rate of $1e-05$ for 5 epochs. The model achieved an accuracy of 89.3%.

Since we are working with dialectal Arabic rather than Modern Standard Arabic (MSA), we finetuned MARBERT (Abdul-Mageed et al., 2021), a language model pre-trained on dialectal Arabic. We used the same hardware and hyperparameters as stated previously. The model achieved an accuracy of 87.9%.

We perform a forward pass on the models to obtain the predictions on the test set and the last hidden state embeddings from the classifiers. The finetuning and inference took less than an hour for both English and Arabic. To better understand where the models underperform, we focus on the misclassified examples (196 English examples and 106 Arabic examples).

4 Clustering Errors

4.1 Text Embeddings

We use KMeans++ from SKlearn[4] to cluster the errors. To determine the optimal number of clusters, we plot the inertia against the number of clusters and identify the elbow. We experiment with four types of vector representations for the errors.

The first representation is the **last hidden state** (LHS) from the classifiers we finetuned.

[3]The ranges are listed on the HuggingFace Dataset card: https://huggingface.co/datasets/ucberkeley-dlab/measuring-hate-speech

[4]https://scikit-learn.org/stable/modules/generated/sklearn.cluster.KMeans.html

The second representation uses **SBERT embeddings** (Reimers and Gurevych, 2019). We use the `all-distilroberta-v1` model for English and the `distiluse-base-multilingual-cased-v1` model for Arabic. These models effectively balance size, speed, and performance.

The third representation is built by prompting an LLM to extract **linguistic features** (using zero-shot prompting) and uses the same SBERT models mentioned above to convert the features to a vector representation. The linguistic features add more information that is not explicitly mentioned in the text, which we hypothesize will help bring errors with similar hidden features together. We use Mixtral 8x7b (Jiang et al., 2024) to extract features of the English errors ($temperature = 0.90$). To extract features of the Arabic errors, we use the Command-R[5] model ($temperature = 0.80$). We opt to use open-weight, freely accessible LLMs without automated guardrails that prevent generation of offensive content.

We use a 4-bit quantized version of Mixtral 8x7b because the full model is too large to run on the available hardware. It took approximately 1.5 hours to generate all the features. For Command-R we use Cohere's trial API.[6] Figure 2 displays an example of linguistic features generated by Mixtral 8x7b and Command-R as well as the prompts used (for the full linguistic features generated see Table 4).

The last representation we experiment with is **concatenating** the SBERT and linguistic feature embeddings. We use the same embeddings generated from the second and third representations. This approach includes a representation of the actual errors as well as the extra information the linguistic features provide.

4.2 Evaluation

Our method for evaluating the clustering is inspired by prior work on topic model evaluation (Chang et al., 2009). In that work, the five most probable words from a given topic t are presented to the annotator, in addition to an "intruder", which is a word with low probability for topic t, but high probability for a different topic. The words are shuffled, and the annotator is tasked with identifying the intruder. If the intruder is correctly identified, it implies that the topic is semantically coherent.

[5]`https://cohere.com/command`

[6]`https://docs.cohere.com/reference/about`

Representation	Number of Clusters	
	English	Arabic
LHS	8	7
SBERT	20	7
Features	16	7
Concatenated	21	9

Table 1: Number of clusters chosen for each representation-language pair using the elbow method.

In our work, annotators were shown questions that included four examples from a cluster and an "intruder" example that did not belong to the cluster and were asked to identify the intruder. To generate these questions, we randomly pick four examples from a cluster without replacement and then pick a random intruder from a different randomly selected cluster. Once an intruder is picked it is removed from the list of potential intruders to be used in future questions. We generate questions for all the text representations we described previously for both English and Arabic.

We recruited fluent speakers of English (2 Males, 9 Females, and 2 Non-binary; 8 ages 18-24 and 5 ages 25-34) and Levantine Arabic (3 Males and 4 Females; 2 ages 55-64, 2 ages 45-64, 1 age 34-44, and 2 ages 18-24) to annotate. We did not provide the annotators any additional details about the task beyond what was written in the questions. Every question was annotated three times in order to avoid ties. Before beginning the annotation process, the annotators were warned about potentially offensive content and informed that they were free to stop annotating at any point. Figure 3 and Figure 4 show an example of a question for evaluating the English and Arabic clustering respectively.

5 Results

5.1 Qualitative Analysis of Clusters

Table 1 shows the number of clusters we used for each vector representation for Arabic and English.

In the case of LHS clustering, we notice that the partitions are based on the (incorrectly) predicted label for both English and Arabic. Table 3 summarizes the percentage of data points with a predicted label that matches the primary label found in their cluster. We see that 96.59% of English and 91.43% of Arabic data points have a label that matches the majority predicted label in their cluster (per-cluster predicted label distributions can be found in Figure 5 and Figure 6). The reason for this outcome is

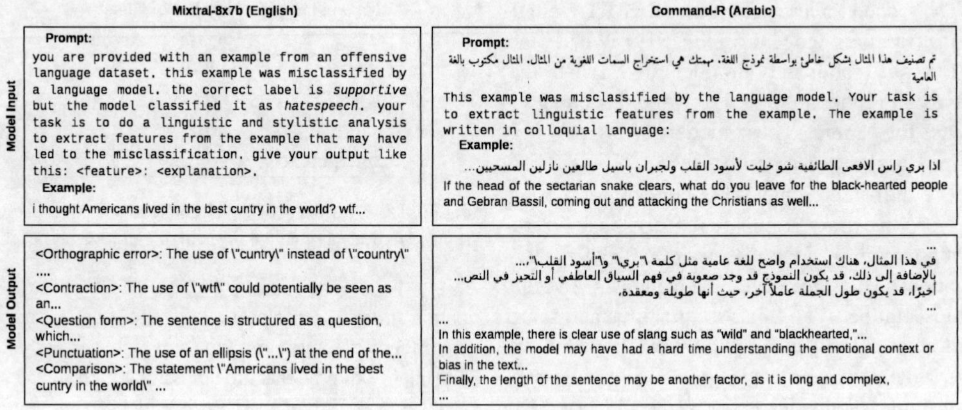

Figure 2: Example of LLM generated linguistic features.

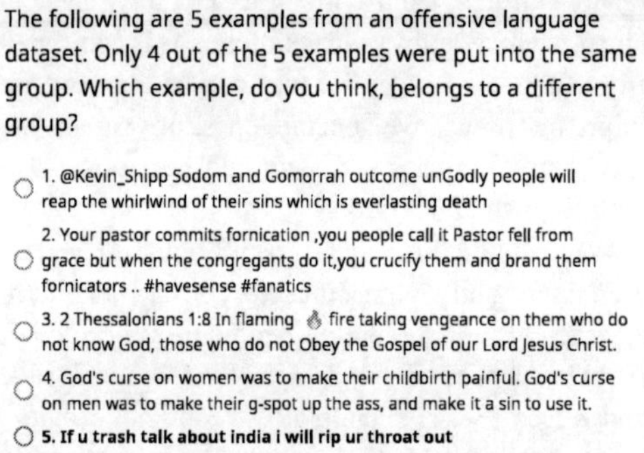

Figure 3: Example of an English clustering evaluation question, with the intruder highlighted in bold. Choices 1-4 are about religion and the last choice (the intruder) is targeting a specific origin.

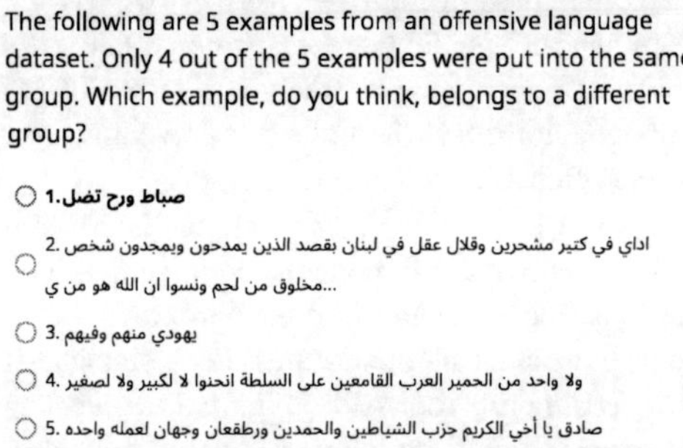

Figure 4: Example of an Arabic clustering evaluation question, with the intruder highlighted in bold. All the choices aside from the intruder mention a certain demographic. The first choice (the intruder) does not mention a specific demographic, the second is about Lebanese people, the third is referring to Jews, the forth is targeting Arabs, and the last choice mentions sects in Islam.

intuitive: since the LHS embeddings are extracted from the finetuned classifier, we expected a representation of the label to be embedded in the vector. Moreover, we notice SBERT clustering of the English errors is based on the target group, which we are able to verify because the target groups are annotated in the dataset (refer to Figure 7 for the target group distributions). We do not notice any pattern in the Arabic SBERT clustering. Moreover, for both languages, the clusterings of LLM generated linguistic features are not based on the target group or predicted label.

5.2 Human interpretability of clusters

We use accuracy to evaluate the clustering and define it as the percentage of questions where the majority of the annotators select the correct choice. Table 2 shows the results of the human evaluation on the clustering task. Humans achieved above baseline accuracy for all the text representations for English. The best performance was on SBERT and the concatenated embeddings, for which both approaches have human accuracy of 67.65%. We expected annotators to perform the best with SBERT embeddings because the clustering was primarily based on the targeted group in the text, which is often easier to identify based on keywords in the text. We find that using only the linguistic features did not improve the evaluators' performance.

Annotators were able to correctly identify the intruder only 27.78% of the time with LHS embeddings; this is particularly meaningful as LHS embeddings have been used in prior work on error analysis, such as the SEAL system (Rajani et al.,

Representation	Accuracy	
	English	Arabic
Baseline	20%	20%
LHS	27.8%	15.8%
SBERT	**67.6%**	12.5%
Features	34.3%	**31.6%**
Concatenated	**67.6%**	17.6%

Table 2: Evaluation results of clustering task.

Representation	% with majority label	
	English	Arabic
LHS	**96.59%**	**91.43%**
SBERT	65.76%	53.81%
Features	68.37%	50.51%
Concatenated	64.82%	51.61%

Table 3: Percentage of data points with a label that matches the majority label of their cluster.

2022). Lastly, the evaluators had an accuracy of 34.39% when choosing the intruder for the linguistic features clustering. We computed agreement using Cohen's Kappa (Cohen, 1960), and average scores ranged from 0.176-0.538 (detailed agreement results can be found in Table 5).

We use the same method to evaluate the Arabic clusters. Out of the four text representation approaches tested, only clustering the features yielded performance above the baseline (20%), with evaluators correctly identifying the intruder 31.58% of the time. A possible explanation for the improved performance is that the linguistic features are in MSA which is what the SBERT model is trained on.

The clusters of Arabic SBERT embeddings were the least human interpretable with accuracy of 12.5%, which indicates that SBERT embeddings using `distiluse-base-multilingual-cased-v1` may not yield meaningful embeddings for this task. There is a slight increase in performance with LHS embeddings, where evaluators had an accuracy of 15.79%. Lastly, the addition of the linguistic features slightly improved the clustering interpretability over only clustering SBERT embeddings. The accuracy of identifying the intruder with the concatenated embeddings was 17.65%. Average agreement Kappa score ranged from 0.130-0.314 (detailed agreement results can be found in Table 5).

6 Conclusion

Contextual embeddings are frequently used as a vector representation of textual data when performing error analysis. In this work, we evaluate four types of text representations of erroneously classified text in the context of offensive language in English and Arabic. We find that SBERT clustering provides the most human-interpretable clustering of English text, with each cluster focusing mainly on one target group. For Arabic we find that the SBERT embeddings of LLM generated features give the most interpretable clustering and the only approach to have above baseline performance. We notice the clustering of LHS in both English and Arabic is based on the predicted label. This paper builds on a growing area of research in error analysis for offensive language detection and provides insights into what information about the errors is encoded in their representation. Future work should explore other clustering algorithms and the effects of them on the interpretability and usefulness for error analysis, as well as automatic methods to generate informative labels about the clusters.

Limitations

We found that a major limitation when it came to working with Arabic was the lack of language models pre-trained on dialectal Arabic. The SBERT model we used as well as the LLM are only trained on Modern Standard Arabic (MSA). Dialectal Arabic is very different from MSA in the way words are spelled, the way that sentences are structured, and has a different lexicon. In addition, we experiment on one dataset and one model per language. The examples in the datasets are not representative of all the types of offensive language for English or Levantine Arabic. Moreover, human interpretability is only one way to measure a clustering's quality, future work should explore other ways to evaluate the choice of embedding for error analysis.

Ethical Considerations

This work aims to add to the ongoing research on error analysis for NLP and offensive language detection. We adhere to the intended usage guidelines of the models and datasets set by the developers of the models and datasets. In addition, annotators were warned about potentially being subject to offensive content and were informed they could stop annotating at any point. No information that could potentially expose the identity of the annotator was collected and they could opt out all of the demographic questions if they wished.

7 Acknowledgments

We thank the reviewers for their feedback, and all the annotators, without whom this work would not have been possible. We also thank Dr. Alycen Wiacek and Dr. Lanyu Xu at Oakland University, who served as thesis committee members, for their feedback and questions that helped polish this work.

References

Muhammad Abdul-Mageed, AbdelRahim Elmadany, and El Moatez Billah Nagoudi. 2021. ARBERT & MARBERT: Deep bidirectional transformers for Arabic. In *Proceedings of the 59th Annual Meeting of the Association for Computational Linguistics and the 11th International Joint Conference on Natural Language Processing (Volume 1: Long Papers)*, pages 7088–7105, Online. Association for Computational Linguistics.

Jane Bromley, Isabelle Guyon, Yann LeCun, Eduard Säckinger, and Roopak Shah. 1993. Signature verification using a "siamese" time delay neural network. In *Advances in Neural Information Processing Systems*, volume 6. Morgan-Kaufmann.

Jonathan Chang, Sean Gerrish, Chong Wang, Jordan Boyd-graber, and David Blei. 2009. Reading tea leaves: How humans interpret topic models. In *Advances in Neural Information Processing Systems*, volume 22. Curran Associates, Inc.

Jacob Cohen. 1960. A coefficient of agreement for nominal scales. *Educational and Psychological Measurement*, 20(1):37–46.

Greg d'Eon, Jason d'Eon, James R. Wright, and Kevin Leyton-Brown. 2022. The spotlight: A general method for discovering systematic errors in deep learning models. In *Proceedings of the 2022 ACM Conference on Fairness, Accountability, and Transparency*, FAccT '22, page 1962–1981, New York, NY, USA. Association for Computing Machinery.

Jacob Devlin, Ming-Wei Chang, Kenton Lee, and Kristina Toutanova. 2019. BERT: Pre-training of deep bidirectional transformers for language understanding. In *Proceedings of the 2019 Conference of the North American Chapter of the Association for Computational Linguistics: Human Language Technologies, Volume 1 (Long and Short Papers)*, pages 4171–4186, Minneapolis, Minnesota. Association for Computational Linguistics.

Sabri Eyuboglu, Maya Varma, Khaled Saab, Jean-Benoit Delbrouck, Christopher Lee-Messer, Jared Dunnmon, James Zou, and Christopher Ré. 2022. Domino: Discovering systematic errors with cross-modal embeddings. *Preprint*, arXiv:2203.14960.

Gabrielle Gauthier-melancon, Orlando Marquez Ayala, Lindsay Brin, Chris Tyler, Frederic Branchaud-charron, Joseph Marinier, Karine Grande, and Di Le. 2022. Azimuth: Systematic error analysis for text classification. In *Proceedings of the 2022 Conference on Empirical Methods in Natural Language Processing: System Demonstrations*, pages 298–310, Abu Dhabi, UAE. Association for Computational Linguistics.

Marie Grace, Jay Seabrum, Dananjay Srinivas, and Alexis Palmer. 2023. OLEA: Tool and infrastructure for offensive language error analysis in English. In *Proceedings of the 17th Conference of the European Chapter of the Association for Computational Linguistics: System Demonstrations*, pages 209–218, Dubrovnik, Croatia. Association for Computational Linguistics.

Camille Harris, Matan Halevy, Ayanna Howard, Amy Bruckman, and Diyi Yang. 2022. Exploring the role of grammar and word choice in bias toward african american english (aae) in hate speech classification. In *Proceedings of the 2022 ACM Conference on Fairness, Accountability, and Transparency*, FAccT '22, page 789–798, New York, NY, USA. Association for Computing Machinery.

Wenyue Hua, Lifeng Jin, Linfeng Song, Haitao Mi, Yongfeng Zhang, and Dong Yu. 2023. Discover, explain, improve: An automatic slice detection benchmark for natural language processing. *Transactions of the Association for Computational Linguistics*, 11:1537–1552.

Albert Q. Jiang, Alexandre Sablayrolles, Antoine Roux, Arthur Mensch, Blanche Savary, Chris Bamford, Devendra Singh Chaplot, Diego de las Casas, Emma Bou Hanna, Florian Bressand, Gianna Lengyel, Guillaume Bour, Guillaume Lample, Lélio Renard Lavaud, Lucile Saulnier, Marie-Anne Lachaux, Pierre Stock, Sandeep Subramanian, Sophia Yang, Szymon Antoniak, Teven Le Scao, Théophile Gervet, Thibaut Lavril, Thomas Wang, Timothée Lacroix, and William El Sayed. 2024. Mixtral of experts. *Preprint*, arxiv:2401.04088 [cs].

Chris J. Kennedy, Geoff Bacon, Alexander Sahn, and Claudia von Vacano. 2020. Constructing interval variables via faceted rasch measurement and multitask deep learning: a hate speech application. *Preprint*, arxiv:2009.10277 [cs].

Yinhan Liu, Myle Ott, Naman Goyal, Jingfei Du, Mandar Joshi, Danqi Chen, Omer Levy, Mike Lewis, Luke Zettlemoyer, and Veselin Stoyanov. 2019. RoBERTa: A robustly optimized BERT pretraining approach. *Preprint*, arxiv:1907.11692 [cs].

Angelina McMillan-Major, Amandalynne Paullada, and Yacine Jernite. 2022. An interactive exploratory tool for the task of hate speech detection. In *Proceedings of the Second Workshop on Bridging Human–Computer Interaction and Natural Language Processing*, pages 11–20, Seattle, Washington. Association for Computational Linguistics.

Julia Mendelsohn, Ronan Le Bras, Yejin Choi, and Maarten Sap. 2023. From dogwhistles to bullhorns: Unveiling coded rhetoric with language models. In *Proceedings of the 61st Annual Meeting of the Association for Computational Linguistics (Volume 1: Long Papers)*, pages 15162–15180, Toronto, Canada. Association for Computational Linguistics.

Hala Mulki, Hatem Haddad, Chedi Bechikh Ali, and Halima Alshabani. 2019. L-HSAB: A Levantine Twitter dataset for hate speech and abusive language. In *Proceedings of the Third Workshop on Abusive Language Online*, pages 111–118, Florence, Italy. Association for Computational Linguistics.

Rakesh R Menon and Shashank Srivastava. 2024. DISCERN: Decoding systematic errors in natural language for text classifiers. In *Proceedings of the 2024 Conference on Empirical Methods in Natural Language Processing*, pages 19565–19583, Miami, Florida, USA. Association for Computational Linguistics.

Nazneen Rajani, Weixin Liang, Lingjiao Chen, Margaret Mitchell, and James Zou. 2022. SEAL: Interactive tool for systematic error analysis and labeling. In *Proceedings of the 2022 Conference on Empirical Methods in Natural Language Processing: System Demonstrations*, pages 359–370, Abu Dhabi, UAE. Association for Computational Linguistics.

Nils Reimers and Iryna Gurevych. 2019. Sentence-BERT: Sentence embeddings using Siamese BERT-networks. In *Proceedings of the 2019 Conference on Empirical Methods in Natural Language Processing and the 9th International Joint Conference on Natural Language Processing (EMNLP-IJCNLP)*, pages 3982–3992, Hong Kong, China. Association for Computational Linguistics.

Victor Sanh, Lysandre Debut, Julien Chaumond, and Thomas Wolf. 2020. DistilBERT, a distilled version of BERT: smaller, faster, cheaper and lighter. *Preprint*, arxiv:1910.01108 [cs].

Maarten Sap, Dallas Card, Saadia Gabriel, Yejin Choi, and Noah A. Smith. 2019. The risk of racial bias in hate speech detection. In *Proceedings of the 57th Annual Meeting of the Association for Computational Linguistics*, pages 1668–1678, Florence, Italy. Association for Computational Linguistics.

Nimit Sohoni, Jared Dunnmon, Geoffrey Angus, Albert Gu, and Christopher Ré. 2020. No subclass left behind: Fine-grained robustness in coarse-grained classification problems. In *Advances in Neural Information Processing Systems*, volume 33, pages 19339–19352. Curran Associates, Inc.

Nimit S. Sohoni, Jared A. Dunnmon, Geoffrey Angus, Albert Gu, and Christopher Ré. 2022. No subclass left behind: Fine-grained robustness in coarse-grained classification problems. *Preprint*, arXiv:2011.12945.

Ian Tenney, James Wexler, Jasmijn Bastings, Tolga Bolukbasi, Andy Coenen, Sebastian Gehrmann, Ellen Jiang, Mahima Pushkarna, Carey Radebaugh, Emily Reif, and Ann Yuan. 2020. The language interpretability tool: Extensible, interactive visualizations and analysis for NLP models. In *Proceedings of the 2020 Conference on Empirical Methods in Natural Language Processing: System Demonstrations*, pages 107–118, Online. Association for Computational Linguistics.

Tongshuang Wu, Marco Tulio Ribeiro, Jeffrey Heer, and Daniel Weld. 2019. Errudite: Scalable, reproducible, and testable error analysis. In *Proceedings of the 57th Annual Meeting of the Association for Computational Linguistics*, pages 747–763, Florence, Italy. Association for Computational Linguistics.

Mengzhou Xia, Anjalie Field, and Yulia Tsvetkov. 2020. Demoting racial bias in hate speech detection. In *Proceedings of the Eighth International Workshop on Natural Language Processing for Social Media*, pages 7–14, Online. Association for Computational Linguistics.

Jun Yuan, Jesse Vig, and Nazneen Rajani. 2022. isea: An interactive pipeline for semantic error analysis of nlp models. IUI '22, page 878–888, New York, NY, USA. Association for Computing Machinery.

A Linguistic features example

Table 4 shows an example of LLM generated features. The English features were generated by Mixtral-7x8b and the Arabic features were generated by Command-R.

B Predicted label distributions

Figure 5 and Figure 6 show the predicted label distribution for each cluster. The LHS clustering for Arabic (see Figure 6) and English (see Figure 6) is primarily based on the predicted label. We do not observe a similar distribution in the other clusterings, every cluster has examples from every label.

C Target group distributions

Figures 7a to 7d show the percentage of each target group per cluster. It is important to note that some examples may belong to multiple target groups, hence the total percentage for some of the clusters is more than 1. In addition, no misclassified examples belonged to the `disability` target group, hence it is not included in the figures.

We observe in the LHS clustering (see Figure 7a) every cluster has examples from almost every target group, whereas the distribution for SBERT clustering (see Figure 7b) shows there is a majority target group per cluster. Figure 7c and Figure 7d shows the target group distribution for linguistic features clustering and concatenated embeddings clustering respectively. Their distribution is more similar to the SBERT distribution.

D Annotator agreement on clustering task

Table 5 shows the average Cohen's Kappa score (annotator agreement) for the human evaluation of the clustering.

Example	LLM generated features
i thought Americans lived in the best cuntry in the world? wtf...	*<Orthographic error>: The use of "cuntry" instead of "country" may have confused the model, as it is a non-standard spelling that could be indicative of a variety of different tones or emotions, including hate speech.* *<Contraction>: The use of "wtf" could potentially be seen as an informal and colloquial expression, which might be associated with a more supportive tone rather than a hateful one.* *<Question form>: The sentence is structured as a question, which might be interpreted as seeking information or clarification rather than expressing hate speech.* *<Punctuation>: The use of an ellipsis ("...") at the end of the sentence could indicate a sense of uncertainty or confusion, which is more in line with a supportive tone.* *<Comparison>: The statement "Americans lived in the best cuntry in the world" could be seen as a positive comparison or boast, rather than a derogatory statement towards any particular group of people.* *Overall, the combination of these features might have led the model to misclassify the sentence as hate speech, when in fact it is more likely to be supportive in tone.*
اذا بري راس الافعى الطائفية شو خليت لأسود القلب ولجبران باسيل طالعين نازلين المسحيين If the head of the sectarian snake clears, what do you leave for the black-hearted people and Gebran Bassil, coming out and attacking the Christians as well...	يبدو أن النص يحتوي على لغة عامية وشتائم، وقد يكون محتواه عاطفياً للغاية، مع وجود إشارات إلى الطائفية والتحيز الديني. هذه السمات قد تجعل من الصعب على النموذج اللغوي تصنيف النص بشكل صحيح، حيث يمكن أن تكون العاطفة واللغة العامية تحديات صعبة للنماذج اللغوية لتفسيرها والتعامل معها. بالإضافة إلى ذلك، قد يكون المحتوى الطائفي أو التحيز الديني حساساً للغاية ويمكن أن يؤثر أيضاً على قدرة النموذج على فهم السياق والتصنيف بدقة *The text appears to contain slang and expletives, and its content may be highly emotional, with references to sectarianism and religious bias. These features may make it difficult for a linguistic model to classify text correctly, as emotion and slang can be difficult challenges for linguistic models to interpret and deal with. In addition, sectarian content or religious bias may be very sensitive and can also affect the model's ability to accurately understand context and classification.*

Table 4: Example of linguistic features generated using LLMs.

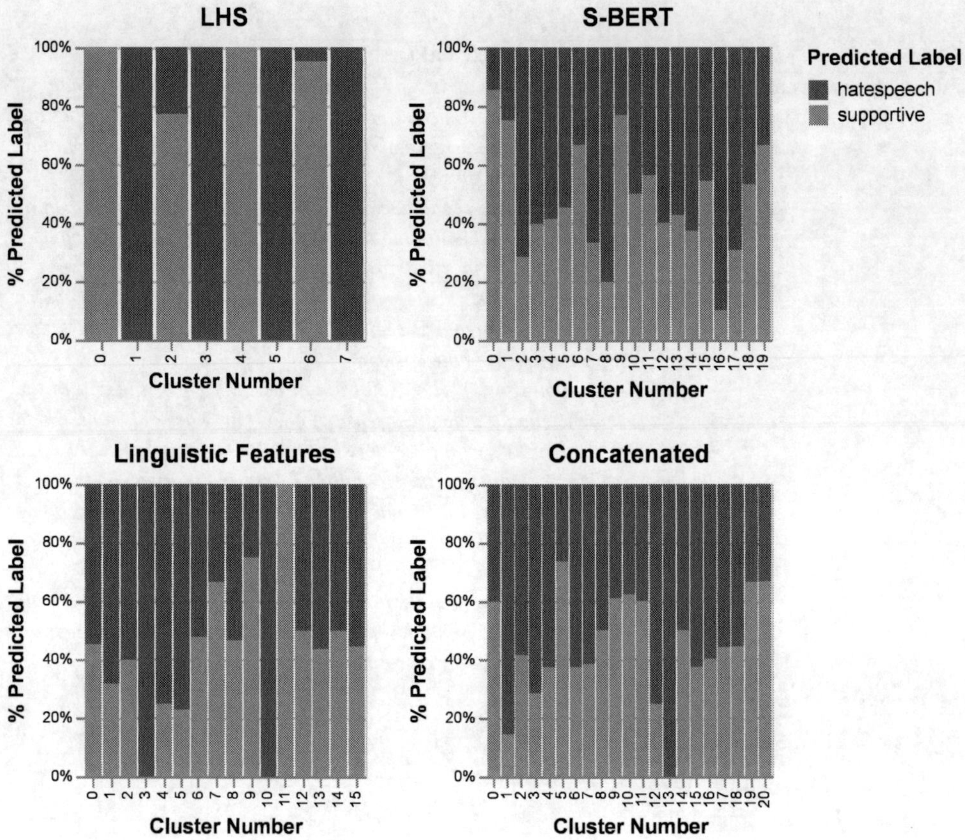

Figure 5: Predicted label distribution for English clusters.

Survey	Average Kappa
English LHS	0.176
English SBERT	0.484
English linguistic features	0.232
English concatenated embeddings	0.538
Arabic LHS	0.199
Arabic SBERT	0.130
Arabic linguistic features	0.231
Arabic concatenated embeddings	0.314

Table 5: Cohen's Kappa score between annotators on error intrusion task for evaluating the clustering.

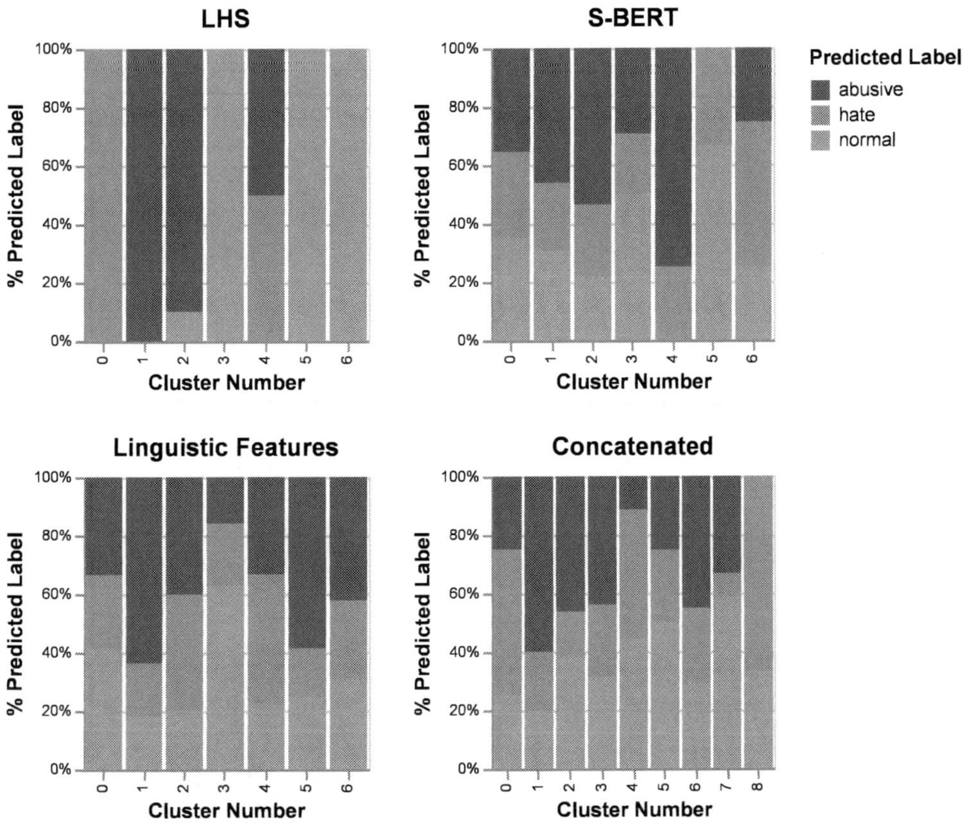

Figure 6: Predicted label distribution for Arabic clusters.

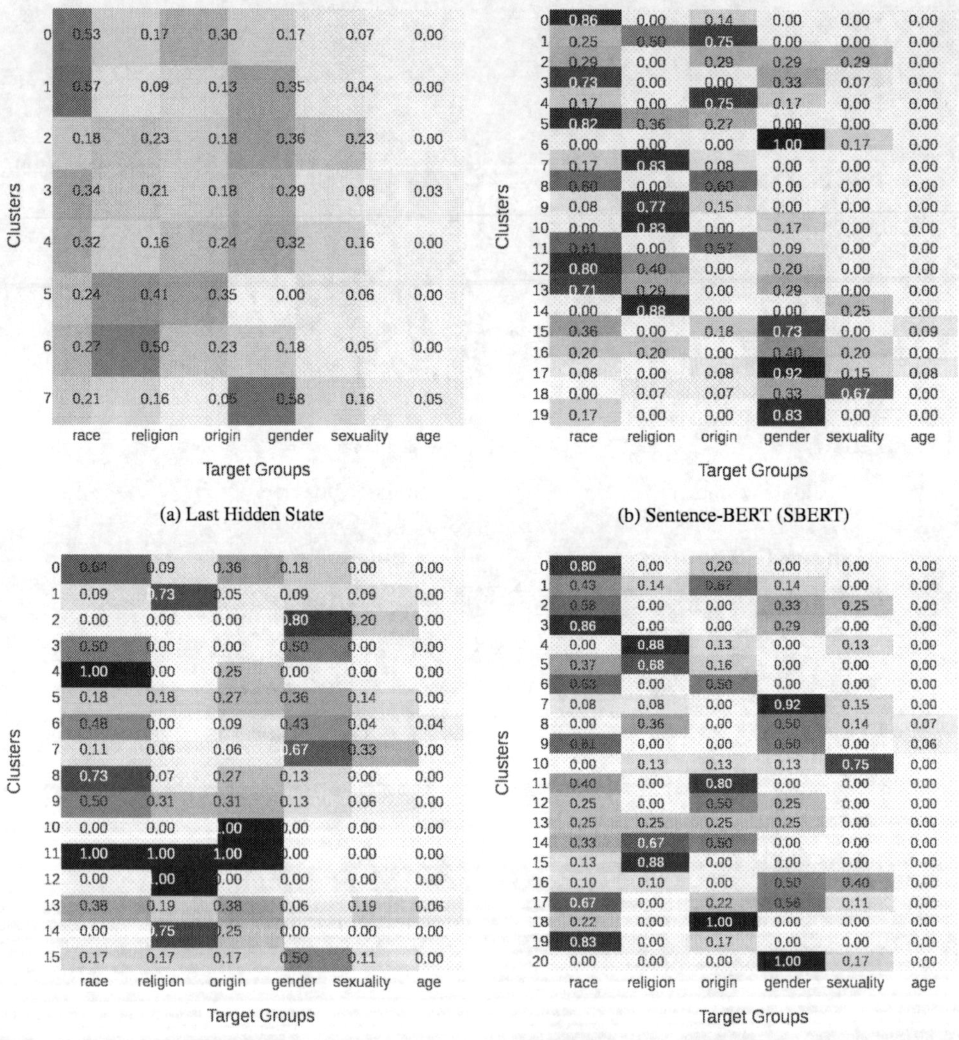

(a) Last Hidden State

(b) Sentence-BERT (SBERT)

(c) Linguistic features

(d) Concatenated (SBERT and Linguistic features)

Figure 7: Target group distribution for each embedding representation.

ELIOT: Zero-Shot Video-Text Retrieval through Relevance-Boosted Captioning and Structural Information Extraction

Xuye Liu
University of Waterloo
xuye.liu@uwaterloo.ca

Yimu Wang
University of Waterloo
yimu.wang@uwaterloo.ca

Jian Zhao
University of Waterloo
jianzhao@uwaterloo.ca

Abstract

Recent advances in video-text retrieval (VTR) have largely relied on supervised learning and fine-tuning. In this paper, we introduce ELIOT, a novel zero-shot VTR framework that leverages off-the-shelf video captioners, large language models (LLMs), and text retrieval methods—entirely **without** additional training or annotated data. Due to the limited power of captioning methods, the captions often miss important content in the video, resulting in unsatisfactory retrieval performance. To translate more information into video captions, we first generates initial captions for videos, then enhances them using a relevance-boosted captioning strategy powered by LLMs, enriching video descriptions with salient details. To further emphasize key content, we propose structural information extraction, organizing visual elements such as objects, events, and attributes into structured templates, further boosting the retrieval performance. Benefiting from the enriched captions and structuralized information, extensive experiments on several video-text retrieval benchmarks demonstrate the superiority of ELIOT over existing fine-tuned and pretraining methods without any data. They also show that the enriched captions capture key details from the video with minimal noise. Code and data will be released to facilitate future research.

1 Introduction

Video-text retrieval (VTR) (Luo et al., 2022; Gao et al., 2021; Ma et al., 2022; Liu et al., 2022a; Zhao et al., 2022; Gorti et al., 2022; Fang et al., 2022) aims to retrieve the corresponding video or text given the query in another modality. Recent years have witnessed the rapid development of VTR with the support from powerful pretraining models (Luo et al., 2022; Gao et al., 2021; Ma et al., 2022; Liu et al., 2022a), improved retrieval methods (Bertasius et al., 2021; Dong et al., 2019; Jin et al., 2021), and video-language datasets construction (Xu et al., 2016). However, it remains challenging to precisely match video and language due to the raw data being in heterogeneous spaces and the use of modality-specific encoders.

The most popular paradigm in VTR (Luo et al., 2022; Ma et al., 2022; Liu et al., 2022b) firstly learns a joint feature space across modalities and then compares representations in this space. However, with the discrepancy between different modalities and the design of modality-independent encoders, it is challenging to directly match representations of different modalities generated from different encoders (Liang et al., 2022). On the other side, pioneering works (Wang et al., 2021, 2022e) convert images into captions for better presentation learning on image-language tasks, demonstrating that captioners can mitigate modality discrepancy.

In this work, we propose ELIOT, a zero-shot generative video-to-text retrieval framework. ELIOT transforms raw videos into enriched generative identifiers by employing a distillation-enhanced generative approach. Drawing from recent advancements in identifier generation (e.g., titles, substrings, multiview representations) and inspired by distillation-enhanced generative retrieval (DGR), our method incorporates the structural benefits of multiview generative identifiers while addressing the challenges of modality alignment. Key to our approach is a novel relevance-boosted captioning mechanism that generates comprehensive textual descriptions for videos. This process ensures that important details such as objects, events, and attributes are captured. To refine these captions, we employ a distilled generative identifier extraction method, replacing traditional structural extraction with a generative paradigm that encodes semantic and contextual cues from videos into identifier representations. By distilling fine-grained ranking knowledge from a teacher model into the generative process, ELIOT enhances the quality of

Proceedings of the 2025 Conference of the Nations of the Americas Chapter of the Association for Computational Linguistics: Human Language Technologies (Volume 4: Student Research Workshop), pages 381–391

identifiers without additional training.

Finally, to evaluate the effectiveness of our proposed zero-shot ELIOT, we conducted experiments on three representative video-text benchmarks (Chen and Dolan, 2011; Fabian Caba Heilbron and Niebles, 2015; Xu et al., 2016). Results show that ELIOT outperforms previous methods, including fine-tuning methods and few-shot methods benefiting from relevance-boosted captioning and structural information extraction.

In summary, our contributions are as follows:

- We propose a real zero-shot video-text retrieval method without requiring any training procedure or human-annotated data, only using the off-the-shelf captioning method, large language models, and text retrieval methods.

- Our proposed ELIOT achieves SOTA performance on several metrics across three VTR benchmarks.

- Detailed analysis reveals the importance of relevance-boosted captioning and vision memory mechanisms. We will open-source the code and data to facilitate future research.

2 Related Work

Video-text retrieval, which involves cross-modal alignment and abstract understanding of temporal images (videos), has been a popular and fundamental task of language-grounding problems (Wang et al., 2020a,b, 2021; Yu et al., 2023). Most of the existing video-text retrieval frameworks (Yu et al., 2017; Dong et al., 2019; Zhu and Yang, 2020; Miech et al., 2020; Gabeur et al., 2020; Dzabraev et al., 2021; Croitoru et al., 2021) focus on learning powerful representations for video and text and extracting separated representations. For example, in Dong et al. (2019), videos and texts are encoded using convolutional neural networks and a bi-GRU (Schuster and Paliwal, 1997) while mean pooling is employed to obtain multi-level representations. MMT (Gabeur et al., 2020) uses a cross-modal encoder to aggregate features extracted by temporal images, audio, and speech for encoding videos. Following that, MDMMT (Dzabraev et al., 2021) further utilizes knowledge learned from multi-domain datasets to improve performance empirically. Further, MIL-NCE (Miech et al., 2020) adopts Multiple Instance Learning and Noise Contrastive Estimation, addressing the problem of visually misaligned narrations from uncurated videos.

Recently, with the success of self-supervised pretraining methods (Devlin et al., 2019; Radford et al., 2019; Brown et al., 2020), vision-language pretraining (Li et al., 2020b; Gan et al., 2020; Singh et al., 2022) on large-scale unlabeled cross-modal data has shown promising performance in various tasks, *e.g.*, image retrieval (Radford et al., 2021), image captioning (Chan et al., 2023), and video retrieval (Luo et al., 2022; Wang and Shi, 2023a). Recent works (Lei et al., 2021; Cheng et al., 2021; Gao et al., 2021; Ma et al., 2022; Park et al., 2022a; Wang et al., 2022b,d; Zhao et al., 2022; Gorti et al., 2022) have attempted to pretrain or fine-tune video-text retrieval models in an end-to-end manner. CLIPBERT (Lei et al., 2021; Bain et al., 2021), as a pioneer, proposes to sparsely sample video clips for end-to-end training to obtain clip-level predictions and then summarize them. Frozen in time (Bain et al., 2021) uses end-to-end training on both image-text and video-text pairs data by uniformly sampling video frames. CLIP4Clip (Luo et al., 2022) finetunes models and investigates three similarity calculation approaches for video-sentence contrastive learning on CLIP (Radford et al., 2021). Further, TS2-Net (Liu et al., 2022b) proposes a novel token shift and selection transformer architecture that adjusts the token sequence and selects informative tokens in both temporal and spatial dimensions from input video samples. While the mainstream of VTR models (Xue et al., 2023; Wu et al., 2023) focuses on fine-tuning powerful image-text pre-trained models, on the other side, as a pioneer, (Tiong et al., 2022; Wang et al., 2022e) propose to use large language models (LLMs) for zero-shot video question answering.

Zero-shot cross-modal retrieval. With the huge success of pretrained visual-language model (Radford et al., 2021; Luo et al., 2022), zero-shot cross-modal retrieval has attracted more and more research interest recently. Due to the powerful representation learning ability in image and text domains, CLIP (Radford et al., 2021) achieves satisfying zero-shot retrieval performance on several representative image-text retrieval benchmarks (Huiskes and Lew, 2008; Lin et al., 2014). Inspired by this achievement, Liu et al. (2023a,b); Chen et al. (2023c); Liu et al. (2024); Guo et al. (2024) boost the performance of zero-shot image-text retrieval by better representation learning meth-

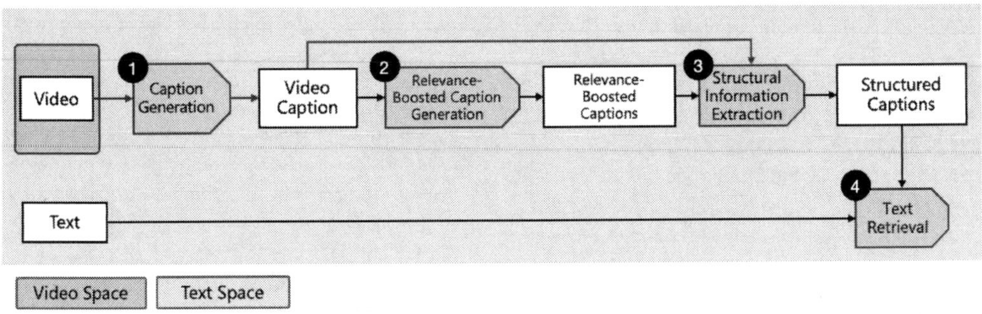

Figure 1: The illustration of our proposed ELIOT. ELIOT includes four steps. First, we generate video captions for video using off-the-shelf video captioning methods. Second, to enrich the captions, we propose the relevance-boosted caption-generation method using LLMs. Third, to emphasize the important information in the captions, we propose a novel structural information extraction. Finally, after obtaining structured video captions, we employ off-the-shelf text retrieval methods to perform zero-shot video-text retrieval.

ods. On the other side, benefiting from large-scale video-text benchmarks (Xu et al., 2016; Chen and Dolan, 2011; Fabian Caba Heilbron and Niebles, 2015), video-language pre-trained models (Wang et al., 2022c; Chen et al., 2023a; Xu et al., 2023; Chen et al., 2023c; Li et al., 2023a; Liu et al., 2023c; Zhu et al., 2024) also achieve satisfying zero-shot video-text retrieval results.

In this paper, inspired by these pioneering works, to explore zero-shot video-text retrieval, we step forward and propose a simple but effective zero-shot video-text retrieval method, ELIOT, by utilizing off-the-shelf captioning, large language models, and text retrieval methods.

3 ELIOT - Zero-Shot Video Text Retrieval

In this section, we present the details of our proposed method, ELIOT. Specifically, we first generate captions for videos using video caption generation methods. Then, to cover most of the details in videos, with our proposed **relevance-boosted caption generation**, we obtain a detailed caption containing almost all the details. Finally, we propose the **structural information extraction** to emphasize important information in the captions for better video-text retrieval performance. **The whole procedure and figure are summarized in Figure 1.**

3.1 Step 1 - Video Caption Generation

Video captioning with off-the-shelf captioners. Specifically, we employ Tewel et al. (2021, 2022) to generate video captions and then use GPT-2 (Radford et al., 2019) to enrich sentences using the prompts, *i.e.*, "Video presents".

3.2 Step 2 - Relevance-Boosted Caption Generation

We notice that the generated captions always miss some important information, leading to unsatisfying retrieval performance. A simple solution to this problem is to fine-tune the captioning models, which will improve their caption-generation abilities. However, this approach needs a huge amount of annotated video-caption data and expensive computation resources, and the fine-tuned models are always not able to be transferred to other benchmarks(Tang et al., 2021). To this end, we propose the **relevance-boosted caption generation**, which is training-free and generates detailed captions that contain almost every detail of the video.

Specifically, we use large language models (LLMs) (Brown et al., 2020; Touvron et al., 2023) to conduct the relevance-boosted generation using the following prompt template.

```
The following is a caption from a
video: [" + <Video Caption> + "].
Based on this caption, generate two
paraphrased captions capturing the
key information and main themes,
each of which should be in one
sentence with up to twenty words.
Meanwhile, please be creative, you
can have some imagination and add
the necessary details. Generated
sentences should be in the number
list. Also please generate text
without any comment.
```

Our proposed method generates multiple captions (*e.g.*, 1, 2, and 3). However, some of these captions might introduce noise or lack strong relevance to the video's content. To mitigate potential negative impacts, we apply a filtering method to assess the semantic similarity between relevance-boosted captions and the original video caption by leveraging a pre-trained text encoder (Reimers and Gurevych, 2019). Specifically, each video in our dataset has two generated captions associated with it. For the retrieval process, we concatenate these captions for each video and then perform the ranking.

3.3 Step 3 - Structural Information Extraction

To understand which kind of information is essential to VTR, we analyze the contextual text of video captions by breaking down the video captions into four different visual tokens using NLTK (Bird et al., 2009), *i.e.*, phrase, object, event, and attribute. Finally, we structure the information into the following structure,

```
<Caption> <Phrases> <Attributes> <
Events> <Objects>
```

3.4 Step 4 - Video (Video Caption)-Text Retrieval

Finally, after obtaining structured video caption data, we are ready to perform the retrieval step. Specifically, we compute the similarity score at the video level between text and video caption using off-the-shelf retrieval methods, *i.e.*, BM25 (Robertson and Walker, 1994) and Sentence transformers (Reimers and Gurevych, 2019).

4 Experiments

4.1 Benchmarks

- **MSR-VTT** (Xu et al., 2016) contains 10,000 videos with length varying from 10 to 32 seconds, each paired with about 20 human-labeled captions. Following the evaluation protocol from previous works (Yu et al., 2018; Miech et al., 2019), we use the training-9k / test 1k-A splits for training and testing respectively.

- **MSVD** (Chen and Dolan, 2011) contains 1,970 videos with a split of 1200, 100, and 670 as the train, validation, and test set, respectively. The duration of videos varies from 1 to 62 seconds. Each video is paired with 40 English captions.

- **ActivityNet** (Fabian Caba Heilbron and Niebles, 2015) is consisted of 20,000 Youtube videos with 100,000 densely annotated descriptions. For a fair comparison, following the previous setting (Luo et al., 2022; Gabeur et al., 2020), we concatenate all captions together as a paragraph to perform a video-paragraph retrieval task by concatenating all the descriptions of a video. Performances are reported on the "val1" split of the ActivityNet.

4.2 Baselines

To show the empirical efficiency of our ELIOT, we compare it with fine-tuned models (LiteVL (Chen et al., 2022), NCL (Park et al., 2022b), TABLE (Chen et al., 2023b), VOP (Huang et al., 2023), X-CLIP (Ma et al., 2022), DiscreteCodebook (Liu et al., 2022a), TS2-Net (Liu et al., 2022b), VCM (Cao et al., 2022), HiSE (Wang et al., 2022b), CenterCLIP (Zhao et al., 2022), X-Pool (Gorti et al., 2022), S3MA (Wang and Shi, 2023b)), and MV-Apapter (Jin et al., 2024), pre-trained methods (VLM (Xu et al., 2021a), HERO (Li et al., 2020a), VideoCLIP (Xu et al., 2021b), EvO (Shvetsova et al., 2022), OA-Trans (Wang et al., 2022a), RaP (Wu et al., 2022), OmniVL (Wang et al., 2022c), mPLUG-2 (Xu et al., 2023), InternVL (Chen et al., 2023c), LangaugeBind (Zhu et al., 2024), UCOFIA (Wang et al., 2023b), ProST (Li et al., 2023b), and UATVR (Fang et al., 2023),), and a few-shot method, *i.e.*, VidIL (Wang et al., 2022e).

4.3 Evaluation metric.

To evaluate the retrieval performance of our proposed model, we use recall at Rank K (R@K, higher is better), median rank (MdR, lower is better), and mean rank (MnR, lower is better) as retrieval metrics, which are widely used in previous retrieval works (Radford et al., 2021; Luo et al., 2022; Ma et al., 2022).

Implementation details and related model details are defferd to Appendix A.

4.4 Quantitative Results

In this part, we present the qualitative results of ELIOT on three VTR benchmarks.

MSR-VTT. We found that the contextual video text obtained directly through video captioning methods generally have mediocre performance (R@1:

Methods	Venue	Text-to-Video Retrieval R@1↑	R@5↑	R@10↑	MdR↓	MnR↓
Training-based						
LiteVL-S	EMNLP'2022	46.7	71.8	81.7	2.0	-
X-Pool	CVPR'2022	46.9	72.8	82.2	2.0	14.3
CenterCLIP	SIGIR'2022	44.2	71.6	82.1	2.0	15.1
TS2-Net	ECCV'2022	47.0	74.5	83.8	2.0	13.0
X-CLIP	ACM MM'2022	46.1	74.3	83.1	2.0	13.2
NCL	EMNLP'2022	43.9	71.2	81.5	2.0	15.5
TABLE	AAAI'2023	47.1	74.3	82.9	2.0	13.4
VOP	CVPR'2023	44.6	69.9	80.3	2.0	16.3
DiscreteCodebook	ACL'2022	43.4	72.3	81.2	-	14.8
VCM	AAAI'2022	43.8	71.0	-	2.0	14.3
CenterCLIP	SIGIR'2022	48.4	73.8	82.0	2.0	13.8
HiSE	ACM MM'2022	45.0	72.7	81.3	2.0	-
TS2-Net	ECCV'2022	49.4	75.6	85.3	2.0	13.5
S3MA	EMNLP'2023	53.1	78.2	86.2	1.0	10.5
UCOFIA	ICCV'2023	49.4	72.1	-	-	12.9
ProST	ICCV'2023	49.5	75.0	84.0	2.0	11.7
UATVR	ICCV'2023	49.8	76.1	85.5	2.0	12.9
MV-Adapter	CVPR'2024	46.2	73.2	82.7	-	-
Zero-Shot (Pretrained Models)						
VLM	ACL'2021	28.1	55.5	67.4	4.0	-
HERO	EMNLP'2021	16.8	43.3	57.7	-	-
VideoCLIP	EMNLP'2021	30.9	55.4	66.8	-	-
EvO	CVPR'2022	23.7	52.1	63.7	4.0	-
OA-Trans	CVPR'2022	35.8	63.4	76.5	3.0	-
RaP	EMNLP'2022	40.9	67.2	76.9	2.0	-
OmniVL	NeurIPS'2022	34.6	58.4	66.6	-	-
mPLUG-2	ICML'2023	48.3	75.0	83.2	-	-
InternVL	arXiv'2023	42.4	65.9	75.4	-	-
LanguageBind	ICLR'2024	42.6	65.4	75.5	-	-
Few-Shot						
VidIL	NeurIPS'2022	40.8	65.2	-	-	-
Zero-Shot						
ELIOT w/o paraphrase and visual tokens		20.3	40.9	51.7	9.0	60.3
ELIOT w/o visual tokens		54.0	73.9	80.2	1.0	24.5
ELIOT		**58.2**	**75.8**	**83.5**	1.0	**18.9**

Table 1: Text-to-Video retrieval results on MSR-VTT. The best results are marked in **bold**. The second best results are underlined.

Methods	Venue	Text-to-Video Retrieval R@1↑	R@5↑	R@10↑	MnR↓
MSVD					
RaP	EMNLP'22	35.9	64.3	73.7	-
LanguageBind	ICLR'24	52.2	79.4	87.3	-
ELIOT		**57.2**	**80.0**	**88.2**	15.6
ActivityNet					
LanguageBind	ICLR'24	35.1	63.4	76.6	-
ELIOT		**59.0**	**71.4**	**77.0**	387.4

Table 2: Text-to-Video retrieval results on MSVD and ActivityNet. The best results are marked in **bold**.

20.3) compared to other baseline Text-Video Retrieval method. We boosted each sentence and expanded it into two sentences. From the results presented in Table 1, it can be seen that this approach outperforms the second-best method by 9.9. This indicates the significant impact of relevance boosting and expanding captions on enhancing the performance of Text-Video Retrieval systems. Compared to DiscreteCodebook (Liu et al., 2022a), which aligns modalities in an unsupervised manner, ELIOT outperforms DiscreteCodebook on every metric. Meanwhile, ELIOT also outperforms VidIL (Wang et al., 2022e), which uses few-shot prompting, demonstrating the usability of integrating zero-shot LLM on text-to-video retrieval. This suggests that leveraging zero-shot on LLMs is a promising approach to enhance text-to-video retrieval performance.

Caption	Phrase	Object	Event	Attribute	Text-to-Video Retrieval R@1↑	R@5↑	R@10↑	MdR↓	MnR↓
✓					54.0	73.9	80.2	1.0	24.5
✓	✓				57.4	76.2	83.0	1.0	19.3
✓		✓			56.9	**77.5**	83.8	1.0	18.6
✓			✓		54.2	73.2	79.6	1.0	24.9
✓				✓	55.0	74.2	80.2	1.0	24.1
✓	✓	✓			57.4	76.2	83.5	1.0	18.7
✓	✓		✓		57.3	76.3	82.6	1.0	19.8
✓	✓			✓	57.6	76.3	83.5	1.0	19.1
✓		✓	✓		56.9	76.6	83.2	1.0	19.3
✓		✓		✓	57.6	77.4	83.8	1.0	**18.2**
✓			✓	✓	54.0	73.3	79.6	1.0	24.9
✓	✓	✓	✓		58.0	75.9	83.7	1.0	19.3
✓	✓	✓		✓	57.8	76.3	**84.1**	1.0	18.3
✓	✓		✓	✓	57.8	76.0	82.5	1.0	19.5
✓		✓	✓	✓	57.3	76.7	83.2	1.0	18.9
✓	✓	✓	✓	✓	**58.2**	75.8	83.5	1.0	18.9

Table 3: Retrieval performance with different combinations of four visual tokens (Phrase, Object, Event, Attribute) on MSR-VTT using ELIOT. Best in **Bold**.

Order List	Text-to-Video Retrieval R@1↑	R@5↑	R@10↑	MdR↓	MnR↓
Order List 1	**58.2**	75.8	**83.5**	1.0	18.9
Order List 2	57.9	**75.9**	83.4	1.0	**18.7**
Order List 3	58.0	75.7	83.2	1.0	19.1

Table 4: Retrieval performance with different order of four visual tokens (Phrase, Object, Event, Attribute) on MSR-VTT using ELIOT. Best in **Bold**.

MSVD and ActivityNet. The results on MSVD and ActicityNet are shown in Table 2. ELIOT achieves the best R@1 on text-to-video retrieval on two datasets compared to the previous methods.

4.5 Ablation Studies

In this part, we present a series of ablation experiments on MSR-VTT to better understand the effectiveness of different components of ELIOT, using LLaMA2-7b-chat-hf and BM25.

Impact of combination of structural information (visual tokens). To choose the best combination method for the extracted visual tokens (phrases, attributes, objects, and events), we conduct experiments using different arrangements of these visual tokens, as shown in Table 3. By reducing the inclusion of visual tokens, the retrieval performance of ELIOT decreases, thereby proving the usefulness of integrating these four visual tokens together.

The order of different structural information. Another important factor to consider is the order of these visual tokens. To this end, we systematically evaluate which specific order of <phrase>, <object>, <attribute>, and <event> maximizes the efficiency and accuracy of the retrieval process. The results are shown in Table 4. We discover that among various arrangements, the model performs best when either phrases or objects are placed at the end of the sequence. This superior performance might be due to the detailed and specific information that phrases and objects offer, enhancing the model's ability to accurately match and retrieve relevant video content.

5 Conclusion

In this paper, we present an innovative zero-shot framework, ELIOT, which revolutionizes video-text retrieval by capitalizing on existing captioning methods, large language models (LLMs), and text retrieval techniques. By sidestepping the need for model training or fine-tuning, our framework offers a streamlined approach to retrieval. To overcome the shortcomings of traditional captioning methods, we propose a groundbreaking relevance-boosted caption generation technique that incorporates LLMs' generated information into video captions. Moreover, our introduction of structural information extraction further enhances retrieval performance by highlighting key visual tokens. Through extensive experimentation across diverse benchmarks, we demonstrate the superior efficacy of ELIOT compared to conventional fine-tuned and pretraining methods, even in the absence of training data.

Limitations

In the future, it would be interesting to explore more detailed methods for zero-shot video-text retrieval, such as incorporating the audio modality and corresponding off-the-shelf foundation models. Moreover, as a pioneering work, our work mainly focuses on establishing the paradigm. It would be great if we could explore more text retrieval methods, video captioning methods, and LLMs for relevance-boosted caption generation.

References

Max Bain, Arsha Nagrani, Gül Varol, and Andrew Zisserman. 2021. Frozen in time: A joint video and image encoder for end-to-end retrieval. In *2021 IEEE/CVF International Conference on Computer Vision, ICCV 2021, Montreal, QC, Canada, October 10-17, 2021*, pages 1708–1718. IEEE.

Gedas Bertasius, Heng Wang, and Lorenzo Torresani. 2021. Is space-time attention all you need for video understanding? In *Proceedings of the 38th International Conference on Machine Learning, ICML 2021, 18-24 July 2021, Virtual Event*, volume 139 of *Proceedings of Machine Learning Research*, pages 813–824. PMLR.

Steven Bird, Ewan Klein, and Edward Loper. 2009. *Natural language processing with Python: analyzing text with the natural language toolkit.* " O'Reilly Media, Inc.".

Tom B. Brown, Benjamin Mann, Nick Ryder, Melanie Subbiah, Jared Kaplan, Prafulla Dhariwal, Arvind Neelakantan, Pranav Shyam, Girish Sastry, Amanda Askell, Sandhini Agarwal, Ariel Herbert-Voss, Gretchen Krueger, Tom Henighan, Rewon Child, Aditya Ramesh, Daniel M. Ziegler, Jeffrey Wu, Clemens Winter, and 12 others. 2020. Language models are few-shot learners. In *Advances in Neural Information Processing Systems 33: Annual Conference on Neural Information Processing Systems 2020, NeurIPS 2020, December 6-12, 2020, virtual.*

Shuqiang Cao, Bairui Wang, Wei Zhang, and Lin Ma. 2022. Visual consensus modeling for video-text retrieval. In *Thirty-Sixth AAAI Conference on Artificial Intelligence, AAAI 2022, Thirty-Fourth Conference on Innovative Applications of Artificial Intelligence, IAAI 2022, The Twelveth Symposium on Educational Advances in Artificial Intelligence, EAAI 2022 Virtual Event, February 22 - March 1, 2022*, pages 167–175. AAAI Press.

David M. Chan, Austin Myers, Sudheendra Vijayanarasimhan, David A. Ross, and John Canny. 2023. IC^3: Image Captioning by Committee Consensus. *arXiv preprint.* ArXiv:2302.01328 [cs].

David Chen and William Dolan. 2011. Collecting highly parallel data for paraphrase evaluation. In *Proceedings of the 49th Annual Meeting of the Association for Computational Linguistics: Human Language Technologies*, pages 190–200, Portland, Oregon, USA. Association for Computational Linguistics.

Dongsheng Chen, Chaofan Tao, Lu Hou, Lifeng Shang, Xin Jiang, and Qun Liu. 2022. LiteVL: Efficient video-language learning with enhanced spatial-temporal modeling. In *Proceedings of the 2022 Conference on Empirical Methods in Natural Language Processing*, pages 7985–7997, Abu Dhabi, United Arab Emirates. Association for Computational Linguistics.

Sihan Chen, Handong Li, Qunbo Wang, Zijia Zhao, Mingzhen Sun, Xinxin Zhu, and Jing Liu. 2023a. VAST: A vision-audio-subtitle-text omni-modality foundation model and dataset. In *Thirty-seventh Conference on Neural Information Processing Systems*.

Yizhen Chen, Jie Wang, Lijian Lin, Zhongang Qi, Jin Ma, and Ying Shan. 2023b. Tagging before Alignment: Integrating Multi-Modal Tags for Video-Text Retrieval. In *AAAI Conference on Artificial Intelligence*. arXiv. ArXiv:2301.12644 [cs].

Zhe Chen, Jiannan Wu, Wenhai Wang, Weijie Su, Guo Chen, Sen Xing, Muyan Zhong, Qinglong Zhang, Xizhou Zhu, Lewei Lu, Bin Li, Ping Luo, Tong Lu, Yu Qiao, and Jifeng Dai. 2023c. Internvl: Scaling up vision foundation models and aligning for generic visual-linguistic tasks. *arXiv preprint arXiv:2312.14238*.

Xing Cheng, Hezheng Lin, Xiangyu Wu, Fan Yang, and Dong Shen. 2021. Improving video-text retrieval by multi-stream corpus alignment and dual softmax loss. *CoRR*, abs/2109.04290.

Ioana Croitoru, Simion-Vlad Bogolin, Marius Leordeanu, Hailin Jin, Andrew Zisserman, Samuel Albanie, and Yang Liu. 2021. Teachtext: Crossmodal generalized distillation for text-video retrieval. In *2021 IEEE/CVF International Conference on Computer Vision, ICCV 2021, Montreal, QC, Canada, October 10-17, 2021*, pages 11563–11573. IEEE.

Jacob Devlin, Ming-Wei Chang, Kenton Lee, and Kristina Toutanova. 2019. BERT: Pre-training of deep bidirectional transformers for language understanding. In *Proceedings of the 2019 Conference of the North American Chapter of the Association for Computational Linguistics: Human Language Technologies, Volume 1 (Long and Short Papers)*, pages 4171–4186, Minneapolis, Minnesota. Association for Computational Linguistics.

Jianfeng Dong, Xirong Li, Chaoxi Xu, Shouling Ji, Yuan He, Gang Yang, and Xun Wang. 2019. Dual encoding for zero-example video retrieval. In *IEEE Conference on Computer Vision and Pattern Recognition, CVPR 2019, Long Beach, CA, USA, June 16-20, 2019*, pages 9346–9355. Computer Vision Foundation / IEEE.

Maksim Dzabraev, Maksim Kalashnikov, Stepan Komkov, and Aleksandr Petiushko. 2021. MDMMT: multidomain multimodal transformer for video retrieval. In *IEEE Conference on Computer Vision and Pattern Recognition Workshops, CVPR Workshops 2021, virtual, June 19-25, 2021*, pages 3354–3363. Computer Vision Foundation / IEEE.

Bernard Ghanem Fabian Caba Heilbron, Victor Escorcia and Juan Carlos Niebles. 2015. Activitynet: A large-scale video benchmark for human activity understanding. In *Proceedings of the IEEE Conference on Computer Vision and Pattern Recognition*, pages 961–970.

Bo Fang, Wenhao Wu, Chang Liu, Yu Zhou, Yuxin Song, Weiping Wang, Xiangbo Shu, Xiangyang Ji, and Jingdong Wang. 2023. Uatvr: Uncertainty-adaptive text-video retrieval. *Preprint*, arXiv:2301.06309.

Xiang Fang, Daizong Liu, Pan Zhou, and Yuchong Hu. 2022. Multi-modal cross-domain alignment network for video moment retrieval. *IEEE Transactions on Multimedia*.

Valentin Gabeur, Chen Sun, Karteek Alahari, and Cordelia Schmid. 2020. Multi-modal transformer for video retrieval. In *Computer Vision - ECCV 2020 - 16th European Conference, Glasgow, UK, August 23-28, 2020, Proceedings, Part IV*, volume 12349 of *Lecture Notes in Computer Science*, pages 214–229. Springer.

Zhe Gan, Yen-Chun Chen, Linjie Li, Chen Zhu, Yu Cheng, and Jingjing Liu. 2020. Large-scale adversarial training for vision-and-language representation learning. In *Advances in Neural Information Processing Systems 33: Annual Conference on Neural Information Processing Systems 2020, NeurIPS 2020, December 6-12, 2020, virtual*.

Zijian Gao, Jingyu Liu, Sheng Chen, Dedan Chang, Hao Zhang, and Jinwei Yuan. 2021. CLIP2TV: an empirical study on transformer-based methods for video-text retrieval. *CoRR*, abs/2111.05610.

Satya Krishna Gorti, Noël Vouitsis, Junwei Ma, Keyvan Golestan, Maksims Volkovs, Animesh Garg, and Guangwei Yu. 2022. X-pool: Cross-modal language-video attention for text-video retrieval. In *IEEE/CVF Conference on Computer Vision and Pattern Recognition, CVPR 2022, New Orleans, LA, USA, June 18-24, 2022*, pages 4996–5005. IEEE.

Qingpei Guo, Furong Xu, Hanxiao Zhang, Wang Ren, Ziping Ma, Lin Ju, Jian Wang, Jingdong Chen, and Ming Yang. 2024. M2-encoder: Advancing bilingual image-text understanding by large-scale efficient pre-training. *Preprint*, arXiv:2401.15896.

Siteng Huang, Biao Gong, Yulin Pan, Jianwen Jiang, Yiliang Lv, Yuyuan Li, and Donglin Wang. 2023. VoP: Text-Video Co-Operative Prompt Tuning for Cross-Modal Retrieval. In *Proceedings of the IEEE/CVF Conference on Computer Vision and Pattern Recognition*, pages 6565–6574.

Mark J. Huiskes and Michael S. Lew. 2008. The MIR Flickr Retrieval Evaluation. In *Proceedings of the 1st ACM International Conference on Multimedia Information Retrieval*, MIR '08, pages 39–43, New York, NY, USA. Association for Computing Machinery. Event-place: Vancouver, British Columbia, Canada.

Weike Jin, Zhou Zhao, Pengcheng Zhang, Jieming Zhu, Xiuqiang He, and Yueting Zhuang. 2021. Hierarchical cross-modal graph consistency learning for video-text retrieval. In *SIGIR '21: The 44th International ACM SIGIR Conference on Research and Development in Information Retrieval, Virtual Event, Canada, July 11-15, 2021*, pages 1114–1124. ACM.

Xiaojie Jin, Bowen Zhang, Weibo Gong, Kai Xu, XueQing Deng, Peng Wang, Zhao Zhang, Xiaohui Shen, and Jiashi Feng. 2024. Mv-adapter: Multimodal video transfer learning for video text retrieval. *Preprint*, arXiv:2301.07868.

Jie Lei, Linjie Li, Luowei Zhou, Zhe Gan, Tamara L. Berg, Mohit Bansal, and Jingjing Liu. 2021. Less is more: Clipbert for video-and-language learning via sparse sampling. In *IEEE Conference on Computer Vision and Pattern Recognition, CVPR 2021, virtual, June 19-25, 2021*, pages 7331–7341. Computer Vision Foundation / IEEE.

Kunchang Li, Yali Wang, Yizhuo Li, Yi Wang, Yinan He, Limin Wang, and Yu Qiao. 2023a. Unmasked teacher: Towards training-efficient video foundation models. In *Proceedings of the IEEE/CVF International Conference on Computer Vision (ICCV)*, pages 19948–19960.

Linjie Li, Yen-Chun Chen, Yu Cheng, Zhe Gan, Licheng Yu, and Jingjing Liu. 2020a. HERO: Hierarchical encoder for Video+Language omni-representation pre-training. In *Proceedings of the 2020 Conference on Empirical Methods in Natural Language Processing (EMNLP)*, pages 2046–2065, Online. Association for Computational Linguistics.

Pandeng Li, Chen-Wei Xie, Liming Zhao, Hongtao Xie, Jiannan Ge, Yun Zheng, Deli Zhao, and Yongdong Zhang. 2023b. Progressive spatio-temporal prototype matching for text-video retrieval. In *2023 IEEE/CVF International Conference on Computer Vision (ICCV)*, pages 4077–4087.

Xiujun Li, Xi Yin, Chunyuan Li, Pengchuan Zhang, Xiaowei Hu, Lei Zhang, Lijuan Wang, Houdong Hu, Li Dong, Furu Wei, Yejin Choi, and Jianfeng Gao. 2020b. Oscar: Object-semantics aligned pretraining for vision-language tasks. In *Computer Vision - ECCV 2020 - 16th European Conference, Glasgow, UK, August 23-28, 2020, Proceedings, Part XXX*, volume 12375 of *Lecture Notes in Computer Science*, pages 121–137. Springer.

Weixin Liang, Yuhui Zhang, Yongchan Kwon, Serena Yeung, and James Zou. 2022. Mind the gap: Understanding the modality gap in multi-modal contrastive representation learning. In *Advances in neural information processing systems*.

Tsung-Yi Lin, Michael Maire, Serge Belongie, James Hays, Pietro Perona, Deva Ramanan, Piotr Dollár, and C. Lawrence Zitnick. 2014. Microsoft COCO: Common Objects in Context. In *Computer Vision – ECCV 2014*, pages 740–755, Cham. Springer International Publishing.

Alexander Liu, SouYoung Jin, Cheng-I Lai, Andrew Rouditchenko, Aude Oliva, and James Glass. 2022a. Cross-modal discrete representation learning. In *Proceedings of the 60th Annual Meeting of the Association for Computational Linguistics (Volume 1: Long Papers)*, pages 3013–3035, Dublin, Ireland. Association for Computational Linguistics.

Haotian Liu, Chunyuan Li, Yuheng Li, and Yong Jae Lee. 2023a. Improved baselines with visual instruction tuning.

Haotian Liu, Chunyuan Li, Yuheng Li, Bo Li, Yuanhan Zhang, Sheng Shen, and Yong Jae Lee. 2024. Llavanext: Improved reasoning, ocr, and world knowledge.

Haotian Liu, Chunyuan Li, Qingyang Wu, and Yong Jae Lee. 2023b. Visual instruction tuning.

Ruyang Liu, Chen Li, Yixiao Ge, Ying Shan, Thomas H Li, and Ge Li. 2023c. One for all: Video conversation is feasible without video instruction tuning. *arXiv preprint arXiv:2309.15785*.

Xuye Liu, Dakuo Wang, April Wang, Yufang Hou, and Lingfei Wu. 2021. Haconvgnn: Hierarchical attention based convolutional graph neural network for code documentation generation in jupyter notebooks. *arXiv preprint arXiv:2104.01002*.

Yuqi Liu, Pengfei Xiong, Luhui Xu, Shengming Cao, and Qin Jin. 2022b. Ts2-net: Token shift and selection transformer for text-video retrieval. In *Computer Vision - ECCV 2022 - 17th European Conference, Tel Aviv, Israel, October 23-27, 2022, Proceedings, Part XIV*, volume 13674 of *Lecture Notes in Computer Science*, pages 319–335. Springer.

Huaishao Luo, Lei Ji, Ming Zhong, Yang Chen, Wen Lei, Nan Duan, and Tianrui Li. 2022. Clip4clip: An empirical study of CLIP for end to end video clip retrieval and captioning. *Neurocomputing*, 508:293–304.

Yiwei Ma, Guohai Xu, Xiaoshuai Sun, Ming Yan, Ji Zhang, and Rongrong Ji. 2022. X-CLIP: End-to-end multi-grained contrastive learning for video-text retrieval. In *ACM international conference on multimedia*, MM '22, pages 638–647, New York, NY, USA. Association for Computing Machinery. Number of pages: 10 Place: Lisboa, Portugal.

Antoine Miech, Jean-Baptiste Alayrac, Lucas Smaira, Ivan Laptev, Josef Sivic, and Andrew Zisserman. 2020. End-to-end learning of visual representations from uncurated instructional videos. In *2020 IEEE/CVF Conference on Computer Vision and Pattern Recognition, CVPR 2020, Seattle, WA, USA, June 13-19, 2020*, pages 9876–9886. Computer Vision Foundation / IEEE.

Antoine Miech, Dimitri Zhukov, Jean-Baptiste Alayrac, Makarand Tapaswi, Ivan Laptev, and Josef Sivic. 2019. Howto100m: Learning a text-video embedding by watching hundred million narrated video clips. In *2019 IEEE/CVF International Conference on Computer Vision, ICCV 2019, Seoul, Korea (South), October 27 - November 2, 2019*, pages 2630–2640. IEEE.

Jae Sung Park, Sheng Shen, Ali Farhadi, Trevor Darrell, Yejin Choi, and Anna Rohrbach. 2022a. Exposing the limits of video-text models through contrast sets. In *Proceedings of the 2022 Conference of the North American Chapter of the Association for Computational Linguistics: Human Language Technologies*, pages 3574–3586, Seattle, United States. Association for Computational Linguistics.

Yookoon Park, Mahmoud Azab, Seungwhan Moon, Bo Xiong, Florian Metze, Gourab Kundu, and Kirmani Ahmed. 2022b. Normalized contrastive learning for text-video retrieval. In *Proceedings of the*

2022 Conference on Empirical Methods in Natural Language Processing, pages 248–260, Abu Dhabi, United Arab Emirates. Association for Computational Linguistics.

Alec Radford, Jong Wook Kim, Chris Hallacy, Aditya Ramesh, Gabriel Goh, Sandhini Agarwal, Girish Sastry, Amanda Askell, Pamela Mishkin, Jack Clark, Gretchen Krueger, and Ilya Sutskever. 2021. Learning transferable visual models from natural language supervision. In *Proceedings of the 38th International Conference on Machine Learning, ICML 2021, 18-24 July 2021, Virtual Event*, volume 139 of *Proceedings of Machine Learning Research*, pages 8748–8763. PMLR.

Alec Radford, Jeffrey Wu, Rewon Child, David Luan, Dario Amodei, Ilya Sutskever, and 1 others. 2019. Language models are unsupervised multitask learners. *OpenAI blog*, 1(8):9.

Nils Reimers and Iryna Gurevych. 2019. Sentence-bert: Sentence embeddings using siamese bert-networks. *arXiv preprint arXiv:1908.10084*.

Stephen E Robertson and Steve Walker. 1994. Some simple effective approximations to the 2-poisson model for probabilistic weighted retrieval. In *SIGIR'94: Proceedings of the Seventeenth Annual International ACM-SIGIR Conference on Research and Development in Information Retrieval, organised by Dublin City University*, pages 232–241. Springer.

Mike Schuster and Kuldip K. Paliwal. 1997. Bidirectional recurrent neural networks. *IEEE Trans. Signal Process.*, 45(11):2673–2681.

Nina Shvetsova, Brian Chen, Andrew Rouditchenko, Samuel Thomas, Brian Kingsbury, Rogerio Feris, David Harwath, James Glass, and Hilde Kuehne. 2022. Everything at Once – Multi-modal Fusion Transformer for Video Retrieval. In *2022 IEEE/CVF Conference on Computer Vision and Pattern Recognition (CVPR)*, pages 19988–19997, New Orleans, LA, USA. IEEE.

Amanpreet Singh, Ronghang Hu, Vedanuj Goswami, Guillaume Couairon, Wojciech Galuba, Marcus Rohrbach, and Douwe Kiela. 2022. FLAVA: A foundational language and vision alignment model. In *IEEE/CVF Conference on Computer Vision and Pattern Recognition, CVPR 2022, New Orleans, LA, USA, June 18-24, 2022*, pages 15617–15629. IEEE.

Mingkang Tang, Zhanyu Wang, Zhenhua Liu, Fengyun Rao, Dian Li, and Xiu Li. 2021. Clip4caption: Clip for video caption. In *Proceedings of the 29th ACM International Conference on Multimedia*, pages 4858–4862.

Yoad Tewel, Yoav Shalev, Roy Nadler, Idan Schwartz, and Lior Wolf. 2022. Zero-shot video captioning with evolving pseudo-tokens. *arXiv preprint arXiv:2207.11100*.

Yoad Tewel, Yoav Shalev, Idan Schwartz, and Lior Wolf. 2021. Zero-shot image-to-text generation for visual-semantic arithmetic. *arXiv preprint arXiv:2111.14447*, 1(3):6.

Anthony Meng Huat Tiong, Junnan Li, Boyang Li, Silvio Savarese, and Steven C.H. Hoi. 2022. Plug-and-play VQA: Zero-shot VQA by conjoining large pretrained models with zero training. In *Findings of the Association for Computational Linguistics: EMNLP 2022*, pages 951–967, Abu Dhabi, United Arab Emirates. Association for Computational Linguistics.

Hugo Touvron, Louis Martin, Kevin Stone, Peter Albert, Amjad Almahairi, Yasmine Babaei, Nikolay Bashlykov, Soumya Batra, Prajjwal Bhargava, Shruti Bhosale, Dan Bikel, Lukas Blecher, Cristian Canton Ferrer, Moya Chen, Guillem Cucurull, David Esiobu, Jude Fernandes, Jeremy Fu, Wenyin Fu, and 49 others. 2023. Llama 2: Open foundation and fine-tuned chat models. *Preprint*, arXiv:2307.09288.

Alex Jinpeng Wang, Yixiao Ge, Guanyu Cai, Rui Yan, Xudong Lin, Ying Shan, Xiaohu Qie, and Mike Zheng Shou. 2022a. Object-aware Video-language Pre-training for Retrieval. In *2022 IEEE/CVF Conference on Computer Vision and Pattern Recognition (CVPR)*, pages 3303–3312, New Orleans, LA, USA. IEEE.

Dakuo Wang, Lingfei Wu, Xuye Liu, Yi Wang, Chuang Gan, Jing Xu, Xue Ying Zhang, Jun Wang, and Jing James Xu. 2024. Learning-based automated machine learning code annotation with graph neural network. US Patent 11,928,156.

Fengjie Wang, Xuye Liu, Oujing Liu, Ali Neshati, Tengfei Ma, Min Zhu, and Jian Zhao. 2023a. Slide4n: Creating presentation slides from computational notebooks with human-ai collaboration. In *Proceedings of the 2023 CHI Conference on Human Factors in Computing Systems*, pages 1–18.

Haoran Wang, Di Xu, Dongliang He, Fu Li, Zhong Ji, Jungong Han, and Errui Ding. 2022b. Boosting video-text retrieval with explicit high-level semantics. In *MM '22: The 30th ACM International Conference on Multimedia, Lisboa, Portugal, October 10 - 14, 2022*, pages 4887–4898. ACM.

Junke Wang, Dongdong Chen, Zuxuan Wu, Chong Luo, Luowei Zhou, Yucheng Zhao, Yujia Xie, Ce Liu, Yu-Gang Jiang, and Lu Yuan. 2022c. Omnivl: One foundation model for image-language and video-language tasks. In *Advances in Neural Information Processing Systems*, volume 35, pages 5696–5710. Curran Associates, Inc.

Xiaohan Wang, Linchao Zhu, Zhedong Zheng, Mingliang Xu, and Yi Yang. 2022d. Align and tell: Boosting text-video retrieval with local alignment and fine-grained supervision. *IEEE Transactions on Multimedia*, pages 1–11.

Yimu Wang, Shiyin Lu, and Lijun Zhang. 2020a. Searching privately by imperceptible lying: A novel private hashing method with differential privacy. In *Proceedings of the 28th ACM International Conference on Multimedia*, page 2700–2709.

Yimu Wang and Peng Shi. 2023a. Video-Text Retrieval by Supervised Multi-Space Multi-Grained Alignment. *arXiv preprint*. ArXiv:2302.09473 [cs].

Yimu Wang and Peng Shi. 2023b. Video-text retrieval by supervised sparse multi-grained learning. In *Findings of the Association for Computational Linguistics: EMNLP 2023*, pages 633–649, Singapore. Association for Computational Linguistics.

Yimu Wang, Xiu-Shen Wei, Bo Xue, and Lijun Zhang. 2020b. Piecewise hashing: A deep hashing method for large-scale fine-grained search. In *Pattern Recognition and Computer Vision - Third Chinese Conference, PRCV 2020, Nanjing, China, October 16-18, 2020, Proceedings, Part II*, pages 432–444.

Yimu Wang, Bo Xue, Quan Cheng, Yuhui Chen, and Lijun Zhang. 2021. Deep unified cross-modality hashing by pairwise data alignment. In *Proceedings of the Thirtieth International Joint Conference on Artificial Intelligence, IJCAI-21*, pages 1129–1135.

Zhenhailong Wang, Manling Li, Ruochen Xu, Luowei Zhou, Jie Lei, Xudong Lin, Shuohang Wang, Ziyi Yang, Chenguang Zhu, Derek Hoiem, Shih-Fu Chang, Mohit Bansal, and Heng Ji. 2022e. Language models with image descriptors are strong few-shot video-language learners. In *Advances in Neural Information Processing Systems 35: Annual Conference on Neural Information Processing Systems 2022, NeurIPS 2022, New Orleans, LA, USA, November 28 - December 9, 2022*.

Ziyang Wang, Yi-Lin Sung, Feng Cheng, Gedas Bertasius, and Mohit Bansal. 2023b. Unified coarse-to-fine alignment for video-text retrieval. *Preprint*, arXiv:2309.10091.

Wenhao Wu, Haipeng Luo, Bo Fang, Jingdong Wang, and Wanli Ouyang. 2023. Cap4Video: What Can Auxiliary Captions Do for Text-Video Retrieval? In *Proceedings of the IEEE/CVF Conference on Computer Vision and Pattern Recognition*, pages 10704–10713.

Xing Wu, Chaochen Gao, Zijia Lin, Zhongyuan Wang, Jizhong Han, and Songlin Hu. 2022. RaP: Redundancy-aware video-language pre-training for text-video retrieval. In *Findings of the Association for Computational Linguistics: EMNLP 2022*, pages 3036–3047, Abu Dhabi, United Arab Emirates. Association for Computational Linguistics.

Haiyang Xu, Qinghao Ye, Ming Yan, Yaya Shi, Jiabo Ye, Yuanhong Xu, Chenliang Li, Bin Bi, Qi Qian, Wei Wang, Guohai Xu, Ji Zhang, Songfang Huang, Fei Huang, and Jingren Zhou. 2023. mplug-2: A modularized multi-modal foundation model across text, image and video. *ArXiv*, abs/2302.00402.

Hu Xu, Gargi Ghosh, Po-Yao Huang, Prahal Arora, Masoumeh Aminzadeh, Christoph Feichtenhofer, Florian Metze, and Luke Zettlemoyer. 2021a. VLM: Task-agnostic video-language model pre-training for video understanding. In *Findings of the Association for Computational Linguistics: ACL-IJCNLP 2021*, pages 4227–4239, Online. Association for Computational Linguistics.

Hu Xu, Gargi Ghosh, Po-Yao Huang, Dmytro Okhonko, Armen Aghajanyan, Florian Metze, Luke Zettlemoyer, and Christoph Feichtenhofer. 2021b. VideoCLIP: Contrastive pre-training for zero-shot video-text understanding. In *Proceedings of the 2021 Conference on Empirical Methods in Natural Language Processing*, pages 6787–6800, Online and Punta Cana, Dominican Republic. Association for Computational Linguistics.

Jun Xu, Tao Mei, Ting Yao, and Yong Rui. 2016. MSR-VTT: A Large Video Description Dataset for Bridging Video and Language. In *2016 IEEE Conference on Computer Vision and Pattern Recognition (CVPR)*, pages 5288–5296, Las Vegas, NV, USA. IEEE.

Hongwei Xue, Yuchong Sun, Bei Liu, Jianlong Fu, Ruihua Song, Houqiang Li, and Jiebo Luo. 2023. CLIP-ViP: Adapting Pre-trained Image-Text Model to Video-Language Alignment. In *The Eleventh International Conference on Learning Representations*.

Qiying Yu, Yang Liu, Yimu Wang, Ke Xu, and Jingjing Liu. 2023. Multimodal federated learning via contrastive representation ensemble. In *The Eleventh International Conference on Learning Representations*.

Youngjae Yu, Jongseok Kim, and Gunhee Kim. 2018. A joint sequence fusion model for video question answering and retrieval. In *Computer Vision - ECCV 2018 - 15th European Conference, Munich, Germany, September 8-14, 2018, Proceedings, Part VII*, volume 11211 of *Lecture Notes in Computer Science*, pages 487–503. Springer.

Youngjae Yu, Hyungjin Ko, Jongwook Choi, and Gunhee Kim. 2017. End-to-end concept word detection for video captioning, retrieval, and question answering. In *2017 IEEE Conference on Computer Vision and Pattern Recognition, CVPR 2017, Honolulu, HI, USA, July 21-26, 2017*, pages 3261–3269. IEEE Computer Society.

Shuai Zhao, Linchao Zhu, Xiaohan Wang, and Yi Yang. 2022. Centerclip: Token clustering for efficient text-video retrieval. In *Proceedings of the 45th International ACM SIGIR Conference on Research and Development in Information Retrieval*, SIGIR '22, page 970–981, New York, NY, USA. Association for Computing Machinery.

Bin Zhu, Bin Lin, Munan Ning, Yang Yan, Jiaxi Cui, WANG HongFa, Yatian Pang, Wenhao Jiang, Junwu Zhang, Zongwei Li, Cai Wan Zhang, Zhifeng Li, Wei Liu, and Li Yuan. 2024. Languagebind: Extending video-language pretraining to n-modality by language-based semantic alignment. In *The Twelfth International Conference on Learning Representations*.

Linchao Zhu and Yi Yang. 2020. Actbert: Learning global-local video-text representations. In *2020 IEEE/CVF Conference on Computer Vision and Pattern Recognition, CVPR 2020, Seattle, WA, USA, June 13-19, 2020*, pages 8743–8752. Computer Vision Foundation / IEEE.

A Implementation Details

For video caption generation, we use Tewel et al. (2021, 2022) to generate video captions and GPT-2 (Radford et al., 2019) to enrich sentences. For relevance-boosted caption generation, we employ LLaMA2-7b-chat-hf (Touvron et al., 2023) and get two boosted captions. For structural information extraction, we use NLTK (Bird et al., 2009). For text retrieval, we use BM25 (Robertson and Walker, 1994).

We use **GPT2** (Radford et al., 2019) for sentence enrichment during video caption generation. GPT-2 (Radford et al., 2019), developed by OpenAI, is a large-scale transformer-based language model renowned for its ability to generate coherent and contextually relevant text. With 1.5 billion parameters, GPT-2 can be fine-tuned for a variety of natural language processing tasks, such as text generation, summarization, and captioning. In our task, we enrich image captions with GPT-2 with one NVIDIA A100 GPU using around 20 hours.

We use Llama (Touvron et al., 2023)(version: Llama-2-7b-chat-hf) to conduct the relevance-boosted caption generation task, inspired by (Liu et al., 2021; Wang et al., 2023a, 2024). **Llama** (Touvron et al., 2023) is an advanced language model with approximately 65 billion parameters. Its default backend is designed for efficiency and scalability. The computational budget for LlaMA in our task is approximately 23 hours with one NVIDIA A100 GPU. Its ability to understand context, generate coherent and contextually relevant responses, and perform a wide range of language-related tasks is significantly enhanced. LlaMA is a powerful and accessible tool, widely used in various applications. Therefore, it is included as an advanced baseline.

Can Large Language Models Advance Crosswalks? The Case of Danish Occupation Codes

Bolei Ma[♣,♡] Cynthia A. Huang[♠] Anna-Carolina Haensch[♣,◊]

[♣]LMU Munich [♡]Munich Center for Machine Learning
[♠]Monash University [◊]University of Maryland, College Park

{bolei.ma, c.haensch}@lmu.de, cynthia.huang@monash.edu

Abstract

Crosswalks, which map one classification system to another, are critical tools for harmonizing data across time, countries, or frameworks. However, constructing crosswalks is labor-intensive and often requires domain expertise. This paper investigates the potential of Large Language Models (LLMs) to assist in creating crosswalks, focusing on two Danish occupational classification systems from different time periods as a case study. We propose a two-stage, prompt-based framework for this task, where LLMs perform similarity assessments between classification codes and identify final mappings through a guided decision process. Using four instruction-tuned LLMs and comparing them against an embedding-based baseline, we evaluate the performance of different models in crosswalks. Our results highlight the strengths of LLMs in crosswalk creation compared to the embedding-based baseline, showing the effectiveness of the interactive prompt-based framework for conducting crosswalks by LLMs. Furthermore, we analyze the impact of model combinations across two interactive rounds, highlighting the importance of model selection and consistency. This work contributes to the growing field of NLP applications for domain-specific knowledge mapping and demonstrates the potential of LLMs in advancing crosswalk methodologies.

1 Introduction

Crosswalks are structured mappings that connect one classification system to another, enabling data to be compared or integrated across different contexts. These mappings are essential in numerous domains, from harmonizing occupational codes across time or countries (Rémen et al., 2018) to aligning taxonomies in biology (Cheng et al., 2017) or mapping educational milestones between frameworks (Subramaniam et al., 2013). While the contexts vary, the underlying challenge remains the same: translating between systems that often reflect different conceptual frameworks, levels of granularity, or terminologies.

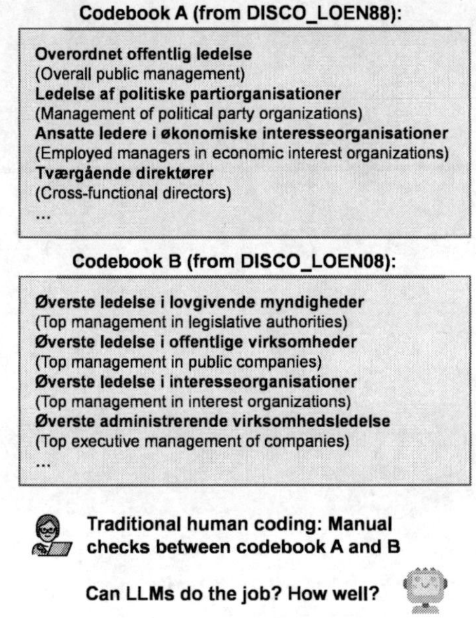

Figure 1: An example of crosswalks between two codebooks from the Danish occupation data. Translations are in commas. Traditionally, crosswalks are created manually by humans. Can LLMs assist in this process?

In the context of occupational classifications, for instance, crosswalks allow researchers to analyze labor market trends across time or national boundaries despite differences in coding systems. Figure 1 gives an example of crosswalks based on Danish occupation data. However, creating these mappings is a complex and labor-intensive process (Rémen et al., 2018). Large Language Models (LLMs) offer a promising avenue for addressing this challenge. Yet, their use in creating crosswalks raises essential questions: How can LLMs reliably infer mappings

Proceedings of the 2025 Conference of the Nations of the Americas Chapter of the Association for Computational Linguistics: Human Language Technologies (Volume 4: Student Research Workshop), pages 392–399
April 30 - May 1, 2025 ©2025 Association for Computational Linguistics

between systems with limited contextual overlap? What are the best strategies for prompting LLMs to elicit meaningful, interpretable outputs? And how do we ensure that the outputs of LLMs align with domain-specific requirements while remaining accessible to human users?

This paper explores the potential of LLMs to assist in creating crosswalks, using Danish occupational classifications from two different time points as a case study (Statistics Denmark, 2025b,a). Our aim is not to fully automate crosswalk creation but to develop an assisted workflow that combines the efficiency of LLMs with the judgment of human experts. Using a curated two-round judgment framework, we compare the performance of different LLMs to evaluate their strengths and limitations in supporting this task. Our empirical findings indicate that, despite certain limitations, the interactive LLM-based crosswalking process outperforms an embedding-based baseline. Through this work, we contribute to the growing field of NLP applications in social science research, showing how LLMs can be effectively integrated into complex domain-specific knowledge-mapping tasks.

2 Background

Much of the work at the intersection of NLP and Computational Social Science (CSS) focuses on labeling texts from social science domains to systematically analyze patterns, opinions, or topics (Chae and Davidson, 2023; Ziems et al., 2024). Occupational coding, a critical task in labor market research and social science, is an excellent use case to explore if and how large language models can enhance methodological approaches in these fields (Liu et al., 2022; Safikhani et al., 2023; Laughlin et al., 2024; Kononykhina et al., 2025).

Occupational codes are standardized labels assigned to jobs based on their duties, responsibilities, and required skills. However, occupational coding is a particularly complicated task because job descriptions can be context-dependent, and often ambiguous (Schierholz and Schonlau, 2020). Adding to this complexity, different countries and time periods often use distinct occupational classification schemes, each tailored to specific economic, social, or policy contexts. For instance, the International Standard Classification of Occupations (ILO, 2025) may differ significantly from national systems like the U.S. Standard Occupational Classification (BLS, 2025), necessitating the development of crosswalks to translate codes from one system to another. Crosswalks like the one by (Rémen et al., 2018) establish equivalencies between two occupational classification schemes allowing data coded in one system or country (US vs. Canada) to be translated into another. This process is essential for enabling international comparisons, historical analyses, and the integration of datasets that rely on different coding standards.

These crosswalks are typically created manually by domain experts who possess deep knowledge of the classification schemes in question. For example, Humlum (2021) developed a detailed crosswalk for Denmark's DISCO classifications. While such manually created crosswalks are highly accurate and tailored to specific needs, they are also exceptionally time-intensive and resource-intensive to produce, as they require establishing mappings between several hundred codes in each classification scheme. Therefore, there is growing interest in exploring whether LLMs can assist in the creation of crosswalks. Similar efforts have been made in other domains, such as healthcare and biomedical research, where tools like MapperGPT use large language models to refine and align entity mappings (Matentzoglu et al., 2023).

3 Method

We propose a two-round prompt-based framework to conduct the crosswalks for the occupation codes. The basic idea of the crosswalk is to find the possible matching code from codebook B for every code in codebook A. Figure 2 illustrates the basic workflow of our framework. The first round is about prompting the models to do similarity checks with certain degrees across all codes in both codebooks. Based on the results from the first round, the second round is about selecting the final candidate matching code from another codebook. This search is done for every code in one of the codebooks. The workflow is detailed as follows:

Round 1: Similarity Check across Codes. We begin with two codebooks (A and B) to work on, where codebook A contains a codeset of unique code names (Code A 1, Code A 2, ...), and codebook B contains a codeset of unique code names (Code B 1, Code B 2, ...). The task of the crosswalk is to map the codes from A to the codes from B. Therefore, in the initial step, we construct code pairs for each code from codebook A to every code from codebook B.

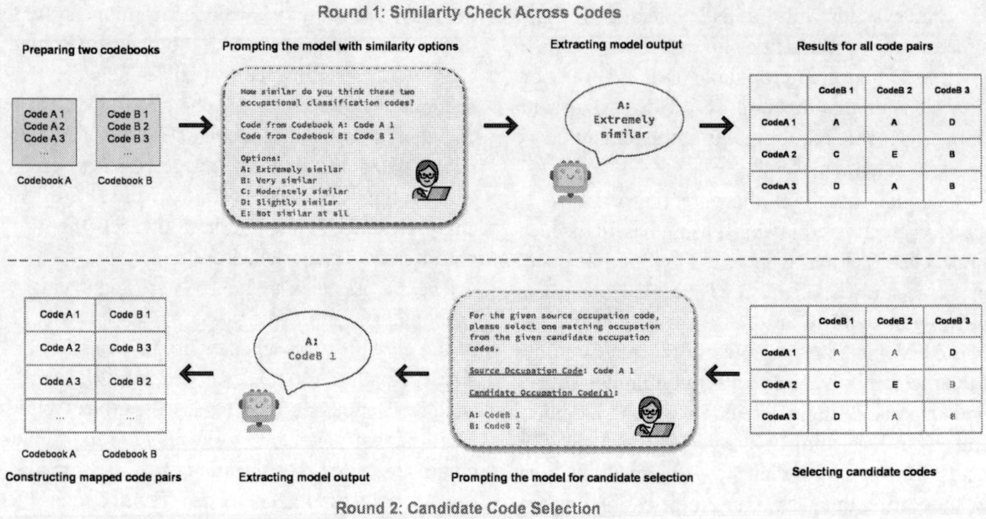

Figure 2: Our two-round prompt-based framework to conduct the crosswalks for the occupation codes using zero-shot LLM prompting.

For each code pair, we prompt the LLM with a question asking for the similarity and options indicating different similarity polarities at 5 scales (from A to E indicating extremely similar towards not similar at all). This scale is commonly used for survey questionnaires, due to its structured design, which presents respondents with predefined answer options, reducing ambiguity and ensuring consistency in responses; as well as its format, which facilitates faster decision-making by guiding participants through a clear set of choices, minimizing cognitive load and improving response accuracy (Likert, 1932; Groves, 2011). This setup has also been recently increasingly introduced in LLM evaluation, to assess the opinions, knowledge, and behaviors embedded in LLM models (e.g., Hendrycks et al., 2021b,a; Huang et al., 2023; Santurkar et al., 2023; Sravanthi et al., 2024; Ma et al., 2024, 2025).

The response of the LLM is then extracted using a string matching method using RegEx to map the responses to the 5 scale points. After all code pairs have been evaluated, we save the results in a table representing the similarities between the codes in matrix format.

Round 2: Candidate Code Selection. With the similarity results for all code pairs collected from the first round, the task of the second round is to find one final code partner for each code of codebook A. As the results from the first round are distributed across the five scale points A-E, we select the potential code matches by taking the codes rated with "A. Extremely similar" or "B. Very similar" to be the candidates for final selection. In case there are no A or B results, we consider that this source code does not have a matching code in codebook B.

We then prompt the LLM with the source code from codebook A and the candidate codes from codebook B (i.e., those that have a similarity result of "Extremely similar" or "Very similar"). We ask the LLM to select the code from the candidate codes B that matches A best, and extract the model output. In the end, we construct the final codebook for the mapped code pairs.

4 Experimental Setups

Data - The Danish Occupation Codes. We use the 6-digit, level 5 granularity of DISCO-LOEN[1] 88 and 08 from Statistics Denmark as codebook A and B respectively to test our framework. It is standard practice for crosswalks to be produced at the most granular level of a hierarchical code system to utilize the specificity of description. Mapping code pairs at lower levels of granularities can be aggregated to produce associations between codes in higher-level granularities (e.g. level 5 to level 4), but the reverse is not true.

[1] https://www.dst.dk/da/Statistik/dokumentation/nomenklaturer/disco-loen

Round 1

```
How similar do you think these two occupational classification codes are in terms of tasks,
skills, and responsibilities? Please respond with only the option letter out of "A", "B", "C",
"D", or "E".
Code1: {code1}
Code2: {code2}
Options:
A Extremely similar
B Very similar
C Moderately similar
D Slightly similar
E Not similar at all
```

Round 2

```
Below are a source occupation title (Occupation 1) and a number of potential matching occupation
titles (Occupation 2).
For the given source occupation title, please select one matching occupation from the given
Occupation 2 options.
Please select only one occupation option from Occupation 2, corresponding to the most similar
matching occupation based on tasks, skills, and responsibilities.
Please only return the option letter of the selected match (A, B, C, ...) and don't say any
other extra thing.
Source Occupation Title (Occupation 1): {code1}
Potential Matching Occupation Title(s) (Occupation 2): {options}
```

Figure 3: Prompts for the 2 rounds.

Ground-Truth Data. There are existing attempts at generating crosswalks between them for comparison. This includes a partial Many-to-1 crosswalk published by Statistics Denmark. The latter contains 332 code pairs linking DISCO-LOEN88 codes to 332 DISCO-LOEN08 code deemed equivalent by Statistics Denmark. Notably, as shown in Table 1, this crosswalk does not provide correspondences for all 570 and 559 level 5 codes in each codebook, leaving researchers to develop their own correspondences for the remaining codes, as conducted by Humlum (2021).

	Version 88	Version 08	Mapped Code Pairs
Count	570	559	332

Table 1: Summary of counts of the unique occupation codes in the codebooks and in the code mapping. Version 88 denotes the DISCO-LOEN88 codes and version 08 the DISCO-LOEN08 codes.

We use the partial Statistics Denmark crosswalk as ground truth mapping code pairs to evaluate the performance of our framework. Under our framework, every pairwise combination of codes from codebook A and B are potential mapping code pairs.

Models. We choose four instruction-tuned open-weight LLMs for conducting the experiments: Llama-3.1 8B (AI@Meta, 2024), Mistral 7B (Jiang et al., 2023), Gemma-2 9B (Team, 2024a), Qwen-2.5 7B (Team, 2024b).

Prompt Design. We design the prompt based on similar instructions and options given to the human participants in real surveys. The prompts used for the two rounds are presented in Figure 3.

Baseline. We compare our LLM-based framework to the approach using embeddings to find the most similar code for the given code, as applied in Liu et al. (2022) and Kononykhina et al. (2025). Since the data is in Danish, we use the multilingual version of the sentence transformers (Reimers and Gurevych, 2020). Specifically, we use the model for paraphrasing (`paraphrase-multilingual-MiniLM-L12-v2`). The basic workflow is this: For each code in the source code, it calculates the cosine similarity of the embeddings of the source code and every target code; the target code with the highest similarity score to the source code is then selected as the mapped code for the target code.

Evaluation Metrics. We use the weighted F1 score to evaluate the model performance of our approach compared to the baseline. Further, as we apply different LLMs in our framework, we are also interested in how those models agree with each other while doing the crosswalks. Therefore, in further analysis, we calculate the inter-annotator agreement metric Cohen's Kappa (κ) to investigate the agreement between different LLMs.

5 Results

Main Results. Table 2 presents the main results of our framework applied to four LLMs and the embedding model baseline. Among the models evaluated, Qwen2.5 achieved the highest F1 score of 70.01%, indicating its strong ability to identify correct crosswalk mappings. This suggests that Qwen2.5 is particularly effective at capturing the semantic relationships between occupational codes in the Danish context. Gemma2 and Llama3.1 also demonstrated solid performance, with F1 scores of 67.35% and 61.25%, respectively, reflecting their capability for the task.

	Baseline	Gemma2	Llama3.1	Mistral	Qwen2.5
F1	57.12	67.35	61.25	40.58	70.01

Table 2: Main results of model performance in F1 (%) compared to the baseline.

Mistral, however, achieved an F1 score of only 40.58%, showing limited effectiveness in this specific application. This result may reflect differences in the architecture or training data of the model, which could make it less suited for nuanced crosswalk mapping tasks in Danish. The multilingual embedding model baseline attained an F1 score of 57.12%, performing better than Mistral but falling short of the other three instruction-tuned LLMs. These results highlight the advantages of instruction-tuned models for complex semantic tasks compared to traditional embedding-based methods.

Agreement Analysis. We next analyze the agreement between the four LLMs based on their final outputs. Figure 4 presents the heatmap of Cohen's Kappa scores, which measure the level of agreement between each model pair. Overall, the models exhibit relatively low agreement, with all Kappa scores falling below 60%. The Qwen2.5 model shows the highest agreement with the other models, which can be attributed to its better performance, as indicated by the results in Table 2. In contrast, the Mistral model shows more variability in their outputs, which is reflected in their lower Kappa scores.

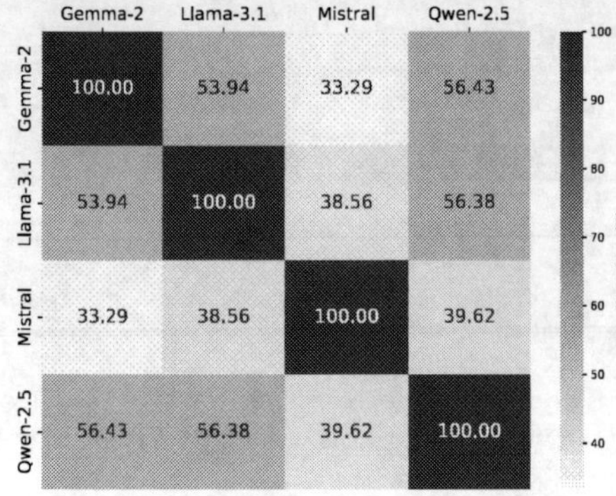

Figure 4: Kappa scores between models.

The Effect of Different Models in Two Rounds. Our framework operates in two rounds, where the results presented earlier assume that the same LLM is queried in both rounds. However, since the models are used independently in each round, we now investigate whether varying the models between rounds affects overall performance. Specifically, we explore whether swapping models leads to any significant changes in the results. The results, as shown in Figure 5, present the performance of different model combinations.

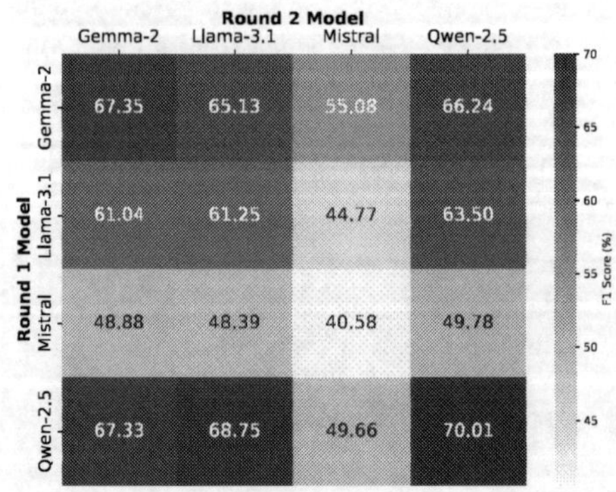

Figure 5: F1 results for experiments with different models in two rounds. X-axis: Round 1 models, Y-axis: Round 2 models.

Overall, the diagonal values in the table represent scenarios where the same model is used in both rounds, corresponding to the main results. These values generally indicate the highest or near-highest performance across rows and columns, suggesting that maintaining model consistency benefits performance. An exception is observed with Mistral, where using the same model in both rounds results in the worst performance. This reinforces Mistral's overall weaker effectiveness in the task, indicating that its predictions do not improve even when it has access to its own prior outputs.

Among the evaluated models, Qwen2.5 consistently outperforms others across different pairings, highlighting its robustness in identifying correct crosswalk mappings. Its closest competitor, Gemma2, also shows strong performance, particularly when paired with itself or with Qwen2.5. In contrast, Llama3.1 exhibits moderate performance, benefiting from combinations with stronger models but falling short of top-tier results.

These findings suggest that performance is optimized when stronger models like Qwen2.5 and Gemma2 are used consistently. Swapping models, especially involving Mistral, tends to reduce effectiveness, highlighting the importance of model selection.

6 Discussion & Conclusion

The results of this study demonstrate the potential of LLMs to assist in creating crosswalks for occupational classifications. Our findings highlight the advantages of instruction-tuned LLMs in handling semantic complexity and improving efficiency compared to traditional embedding-based approaches. Models like Qwen2.5 showed strong performance in aligning Danish occupational codes, emphasizing the value of instruction tuning and contextual understanding in these tasks.

However, the relatively low inter-model agreement underscores the variability in outputs across different LLMs, pointing to the importance of model selection and parameter tuning. This variability also highlights the need for integrating human expertise into the workflow to validate and refine LLM-generated mappings. The interactive, prompt-based framework we proposed aligns with the concept of human-in-the-loop workflows, where LLMs augment rather than replace expert judgment.

Additionally, our findings highlight the advantages of maintaining model consistency across rounds, especially for strong models like Qwen2.5. Swapping models, particularly when involving weaker ones like Mistral, leads to diminished results, emphasizing the need for robust and consistent modeling strategies.

Our findings also resonate with similar efforts in other domains, such as MapperGPT, which refines entity mappings in fields like healthcare and biomedical research (Matentzoglu et al., 2023). These parallels reinforce the versatility of LLMs in supporting knowledge-mapping tasks across diverse contexts, though domain-specific adaptations remain critical for success. Future work could explore how our two-step prompting framework can be extended beyond occupational classifications to other classification mapping tasks in fields such as finance, education, and public administration, where structured yet flexible mappings are essential for accurate data integration and interoperability.

7 Limitations

Despite the promising results, this study has several limitations. First, the reliance on Danish occupational codes limits the generalizability of our findings to other languages and classification systems. Future studies should investigate the performance of LLMs on crosswalks involving additional languages and classification schemes, such as ISCO and SOC.

Second, the use of multiple-choice questions to evaluate LLMs may introduce biases inherent to this format, such as response tendencies (Li et al., 2024; Pezeshkpour and Hruschka, 2024; Wang et al., 2024). Further exploration of alternative evaluation frameworks, such as open-ended prompting or pairwise ranking, could provide more robust insights into LLM performance.

8 Ethical Considerations

The use of LLMs for creating crosswalks must consider potential biases (e.g., regarding gender) in the models, which could lead to inaccurate or inequitable mappings, especially for underrepresented groups (Touileb et al., 2023; Nghiem et al., 2024; Sancheti et al., 2024). Ensuring human oversight is crucial to validate and refine LLM outputs, preventing the propagation of errors that may impact labor market analyses or policy decisions.

References

AI@Meta. 2024. Llama 3.1 model card.

U.S. Bureau of Labor Statistics BLS. 2025. Standard occupational classification (soc). Accessed: 2025-01-25.

Youngjin Chae and Thomas Davidson. 2023. Large language models for text classification: From zero-shot learning to fine-tuning. Open Science Foundation.

Yi-Yun Cheng, Nico Franz, Jodi Schneider, Shizhuo Yu, Thomas Rodenhausen, and Bertram Ludäscher. 2017. Agreeing to disagree: Reconciling conflicting taxonomic views using a logic-based approach. *Proceedings of the Association for Information Science and Technology*, 54(1):46–56.

Robert M. Groves. 2011. Three eras of survey research. *Public Opinion Quarterly*, 75(5):861–871.

Dan Hendrycks, Collin Burns, Steven Basart, Andrew Critch, Jerry Li, Dawn Song, and Jacob Steinhardt. 2021a. Aligning ai with shared human values. *Proceedings of the International Conference on Learning Representations (ICLR)*.

Dan Hendrycks, Collin Burns, Steven Basart, Andy Zou, Mantas Mazeika, Dawn Song, and Jacob Steinhardt. 2021b. Measuring massive multitask language understanding. *Proceedings of the International Conference on Learning Representations (ICLR)*.

Yuzhen Huang, Yuzhuo Bai, Zhihao Zhu, Junlei Zhang, Jinghan Zhang, Tangjun Su, Junteng Liu, Chuancheng Lv, Yikai Zhang, jiayi lei, Yao Fu, Maosong Sun, and Junxian He. 2023. C-eval: A multi-level multi-discipline chinese evaluation suite for foundation models. In *Thirty-seventh Conference on Neural Information Processing Systems Datasets and Benchmarks Track*.

Anders Humlum. 2021. Crosswalks between (d)isco88 and (d)isco08 occupational codes.

International Labour Organization ILO. 2025. Classification of occupations: Concepts and definitions. Accessed: 2025-01-25.

Albert Q. Jiang, Alexandre Sablayrolles, Arthur Mensch, Chris Bamford, Devendra Singh Chaplot, Diego de las Casas, Florian Bressand, Gianna Lengyel, Guillaume Lample, Lucile Saulnier, Lélio Renard Lavaud, Marie-Anne Lachaux, Pierre Stock, Teven Le Scao, Thibaut Lavril, Thomas Wang, Timothée Lacroix, and William El Sayed. 2023. Mistral 7b. *Preprint*, arXiv:2310.06825.

Olga Kononykhina, Malte Schierholz, and Frauke Kreuter. 2025. Can large language models advance occupational coding? evidence and methodological insights. Unpublished Manuscript.

Lynda Laughlin, Xi Song, Megan Wisniewski, and Jiahui Xu. 2024. From job descriptions to occupations: Using neural language models to code job data.

Wangyue Li, Liangzhi Li, Tong Xiang, Xiao Liu, Wei Deng, and Noa Garcia. 2024. Can multiple-choice questions really be useful in detecting the abilities of LLMs? In *Proceedings of the 2024 Joint International Conference on Computational Linguistics, Language Resources and Evaluation (LREC-COLING 2024)*, pages 2819–2834, Torino, Italia. ELRA and ICCL.

Rensis Likert. 1932. A technique for the measurement of attitudes. *Archives of psychology*.

Junhua Liu, Yung Chuen Ng, Zitong Gui, Trisha Singhal, Lucienne T. M. Blessing, Kristin L. Wood, and Kwan Hui Lim. 2022. Title2vec: A contextual job title embedding for occupational named entity recognition and other applications. *Journal of Big Data*, 9:99.

Bolei Ma, Yuting Li, Wei Zhou, Ziwei Gong, Yang Janet Liu, Katja Jasinskaja, Annemarie Friedrich, Julia Hirschberg, Frauke Kreuter, and Barbara Plank. 2025. Pragmatics in the era of large language models: A survey on datasets, evaluation, opportunities and challenges. *Preprint*, arXiv:2502.12378.

Bolei Ma, Xinpeng Wang, Tiancheng Hu, Anna-Carolina Haensch, Michael A. Hedderich, Barbara Plank, and Frauke Kreuter. 2024. The potential and challenges of evaluating attitudes, opinions, and values in large language models. In *Findings of the Association for Computational Linguistics: EMNLP 2024*, pages 8783–8805, Miami, Florida, USA. Association for Computational Linguistics.

Nicolas A. Matentzoglu, John Harry Caufield, Harshad B. Hegde, Justin T. Reese, Sierra A T Moxon, Hyeongsik Kim, Nomi L. Harris, Melissa A. Haendel, Christopher J. Mungall, and Robert Bosch. 2023. Mappergpt: Large language models for linking and mapping entities. *ArXiv*, abs/2310.03666.

Huy Nghiem, John Prindle, Jieyu Zhao, and Hal Daumé Iii. 2024. "you gotta be a doctor, lin" : An investigation of name-based bias of large language models in employment recommendations. In *Proceedings of the 2024 Conference on Empirical Methods in Natural Language Processing*, pages 7268–7287, Miami, Florida, USA. Association for Computational Linguistics.

Pouya Pezeshkpour and Estevam Hruschka. 2024. Large language models sensitivity to the order of options in multiple-choice questions. In *Findings of the Association for Computational Linguistics: NAACL 2024*, pages 2006–2017, Mexico City, Mexico. Association for Computational Linguistics.

Nils Reimers and Iryna Gurevych. 2020. Making monolingual sentence embeddings multilingual using knowledge distillation. In *Proceedings of the 2020 Conference on Empirical Methods in Natural Language Processing (EMNLP)*, pages 4512–4525, Online. Association for Computational Linguistics.

Thomas Rémen, Lesley Richardson, Corinne Pilorget, Gilles Palmer, Jack Siemiatycki, and Jérôme Lavoué. 2018. Development of a coding and crosswalk tool for occupations and industries. *Annals of work exposures and health*, 62(7):796–807.

Parisa Safikhani, Hayastan Avetisyan, Dennis Föste-Eggers, and David Broneske. 2023. Automated occupation coding with hierarchical features: A data-centric approach to classification with pre-trained language models. *Discover Artificial Intelligence*, 3:6.

Abhilasha Sancheti, Haozhe An, and Rachel Rudinger. 2024. On the influence of gender and race in romantic relationship prediction from large language models. In *Proceedings of the 2024 Conference on Empirical Methods in Natural Language Processing*, pages 479–494, Miami, Florida, USA. Association for Computational Linguistics.

Shibani Santurkar, Esin Durmus, Faisal Ladhak, Cinoo Lee, Percy Liang, and Tatsunori Hashimoto. 2023. Whose opinions do language models reflect? In *Proceedings of the 40th International Conference on Machine Learning*, ICML'23. JMLR.org.

Malte Schierholz and Matthias Schonlau. 2020. Machine learning for occupation coding—a comparison study. *Journal of Survey Statistics and Methodology*, 9(5):1013–1034.

Settaluri Sravanthi, Meet Doshi, Pavan Tankala, Rudra Murthy, Raj Dabre, and Pushpak Bhattacharyya. 2024. PUB: A pragmatics understanding benchmark for assessing LLMs' pragmatics capabilities. In *Findings of the Association for Computational Linguistics: ACL 2024*, pages 12075–12097, Bangkok, Thailand. Association for Computational Linguistics.

Statistics Denmark. 2025a. DISCO-08 Classification - Statistics Denmark. https://www.dst.dk/en/Statistik/dokumentation/nomenklaturer/disco-loen. Accessed: 2025-01-24.

Statistics Denmark. 2025b. DISCO Classification - Statistics Denmark. https://www.dst.dk/en/Statistik/dokumentation/nomenklaturer/disco?id=ec4f3246-ea1a-4e8b-b229-f03c0dc680c6. Accessed: 2025-01-24.

Mega Subramaniam, June Ahn, Amanda Waugh, Natalie Greene Taylor, Allison Druin, Kenneth R Fleischmann, and Greg Walsh. 2013. Crosswalk between the" framework for k-12 science education" and" standards for the 21st-century learner": School librarians as the crucial link. *School Library Research*, 16.

Gemma Team. 2024a. Gemma 2: Improving open language models at a practical size. *Preprint*, arXiv:2403.05530.

Qwen Team. 2024b. Qwen2.5: A party of foundation models.

Samia Touileb, Lilja Øvrelid, and Erik Velldal. 2023. Measuring normative and descriptive biases in language models using census data. In *Proceedings of the 17th Conference of the European Chapter of the Association for Computational Linguistics*, pages 2242–2248, Dubrovnik, Croatia. Association for Computational Linguistics.

Xinpeng Wang, Bolei Ma, Chengzhi Hu, Leon Weber-Genzel, Paul Röttger, Frauke Kreuter, Dirk Hovy, and Barbara Plank. 2024. "my answer is C": First-token probabilities do not match text answers in instruction-tuned language models. In *Findings of the Association for Computational Linguistics: ACL 2024*, pages 7407–7416, Bangkok, Thailand. Association for Computational Linguistics.

Caleb Ziems, William Held, Omar Shaikh, Jiaao Chen, Zhehao Zhang, and Diyi Yang. 2024. Can large language models transform computational social science? *Computational Linguistics*, 50(1):237–291.

Paraphrase-based Contrastive Learning for Sentence Pair Modeling

Seiji Sugiyama Risa Kondo Tomoyuki Kajiwara Takashi Ninomiya
Graduate School of Science and Engineering, Ehime University, Japan
sugiyama@ai.cs.ehime-u.ac.jp kondo@ai.cs.ehime-u.ac.jp
kajiwara@cs.ehime-u.ac.jp ninomiya.takashi.mk@ehime-u.ac.jp

Abstract

To improve the performance of sentence pair modeling tasks, we propose an additional pre-training method, also known as transfer fine-tuning, for pre-trained masked language models. Pre-training for masked language modeling is not necessarily designed to bring semantically similar sentences closer together in the embedding space. Our proposed method aims to improve the performance of sentence pair modeling by applying contrastive learning to pre-trained masked language models, in which sentence embeddings of paraphrase pairs are made similar to each other. While natural language inference corpora, which are standard in previous studies on contrastive learning, are not available on a large-scale for non-English languages, our method can construct a training corpus for contrastive learning from a raw corpus and a paraphrase dictionary at a low cost. Experimental results on four sentence pair modeling tasks revealed the effectiveness of our method in both English and Japanese.

1 Introduction

Sentence pair modeling (Lan and Xu, 2018), which estimates the relationship between two texts, is an important technique for various natural language processing tasks, from semantic textual similarity estimation (Cer et al., 2017) and recognizing textual entailment (Bowman et al., 2015) to information retrieval (Wang et al., 2024) and question answering (Zhang et al., 2023). For sentence pair modeling tasks, surface matching such as bag-of-words and word embeddings such as word2vec (Mikolov et al., 2013) have traditionally been used, followed by task-specific neural networks (He and Lin, 2016; Chen et al., 2017), and recently fine-tuning pre-trained masked language models such as BERT (Devlin et al., 2019) has become the de facto standard. However, training in masked language modeling does not necessarily bring semantically similar sentences closer together in the embedding space (Li et al., 2020). Therefore, to maximize the effectiveness of fine-tuning for sentence pair modeling tasks, it is useful to follow the pre-training of masked language modeling with additional pre-training to estimate the semantic relationships between texts, also known as transfer fine-tuning (Arase and Tsujii, 2019).

One such method recently been attracting attention is contrastive learning. Contrastive learning for sentence embeddings, like SimCSE (Gao et al., 2021; Chuang et al., 2022; Liu et al., 2023), uses annotated corpora of natural language inference (NLI) to bring embeddings of entailing and entailed sentences closer together and to separate embeddings of contradictory sentence pairs. However, while NLI corpora with hundreds of thousands of sentence pairs, such as Stanford NLI (SNLI) (Bowman et al., 2015) and Multi-Genre NLI (MNLI) (Williams et al., 2018), are available for English, there are no large-scale NLI corpora for other languages, making it difficult to obtain high-quality sentence embeddings by contrastive learning for languages other than English.

To improve the performance of sentence pair modeling in various languages, we propose a method of contrastive learning that does not rely on the NLI corpus. Our method uses a raw corpus and a paraphrase dictionary to automatically generate a large-scale training corpus for contrastive learning at a low cost. Since paraphrase dictionaries are available in many languages,[1] this method is widely applicable.

Experimental results in English and Japanese revealed that the proposed method could improve the performance of the masked language models in four types of sentence pair modeling tasks (product retrieval, similarity estimation, recognizing textual entailment, and paraphrase identifi-

[1]For example, the Multilingual PPDB (Ganitkevitch and Callison-Burch, 2014) collects millions to hundreds of millions of paraphrase pairs in 23 languages.

Proceedings of the 2025 Conference of the Nations of the Americas Chapter of the Association for Computational Linguistics: Human Language Technologies (Volume 4: Student Research Workshop), pages 400–407
April 30 - May 1, 2025

(1) Dictionary-based paraphrase

Input sentence
The store offers a wide range of merchandise and accessories.

Paraphrase dictionary		
src	dst	p(dst|src)
offers a wide	provides a wide	0.13
offers a wide	offers a broad	0.13
merchandise and	of goods and	0.18
merchandise and	goods and	0.57

(2) Filtering candidates by perplexity

Paraphrase candidates	Perplexity↓
The store provides a wide range ...	23.6
The store offers a broad range ...	30.2
... range of of goods and accessories.	33.5
... range of goods and accessories.	21.4

(3) Contrastive learning

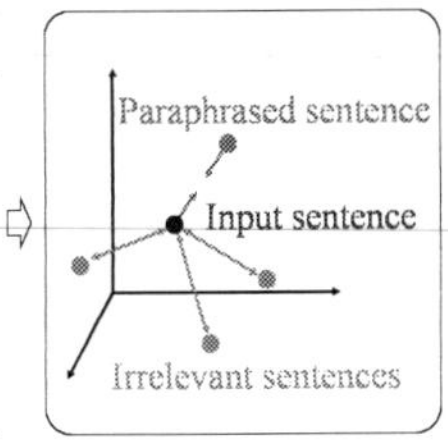

Figure 1: Overview of our paraphrase-based contrastive learning.

cation). Regarding the average performance of all tasks, the proposed method achieved the best performance for both English and Japanese compared to existing methods that learn paraphrases but do not use contrastive learning (Arase and Tsujii, 2019), contrastive learning with raw corpus or NLI corpus (Gao et al., 2021), and state-of-the-art RankCSE (Liu et al., 2023).

2 Related Work

2.1 Contrastive Learning

Contrastive learning is a method that brings semantically close data closer together in vector space and separates semantically distant data apart in vector space. Methods for acquiring sentence embeddings by applying contrastive learning to pre-trained masked language models have been actively studied in recent years (Gao et al., 2021; Chuang et al., 2022; Liu et al., 2023).

Previous studies of sentence embedding based on contrastive learning have relied on the NLI corpus (Bowman et al., 2015), in which sentence pairs are labeled with semantic relations of entailment, contradiction, and neutral, for training. However, annotating such corpora in non-English languages at high-quality and on a large-scale is expensive, so this study proposes a lower-cost alternative.

2.2 Paraphrasing for Additional Training

Paraphrasing is the task of generating text that is semantically equivalent to the input text. This technique can be applied to pre-editing (Mehta et al., 2020; Miyata and Fujita, 2021) and data augmentation (Effendi et al., 2018; Okur et al., 2022) to improve the performance of various natural language processing applications.

One such promising application of paraphrasing is additional training of pre-trained models. Pre-trained encoders can be additionally trained on the paraphrase identification task to increase the fine-tuning performance of similarity estimation and recognizing textual entailment (Arase and Tsujii, 2019). Similarly, pre-trained encoder-decoder models can be additionally trained on the paraphrase generation task to enhance the fine-tuning performance of style transfer and text simplification (Kajiwara et al., 2020). This study combines paraphrasing and contrastive learning to further improve additional training for pre-trained encoders.

3 Proposed Method

We improve the performance of sentence pair modeling with masked language models by contrastive learning that does not rely on the NLI corpus. As shown in the following steps, we boost the effectiveness of fine-tuning by conducting additional training between pre-training and fine-tuning.

1. Pre-training: masked language modeling
2. Our contrastive learning
3. Fine-tuning: supervised learning on the target task of sentence pair modeling

As shown in Figure 1, our contrastive learning uses paraphrase sentence pairs instead of entailment pairs in the NLI corpus. (1) Paraphrase an input sentence from the raw corpus based on the dictionary, (2) Select the most fluent paraphrase among the candidates, and (3) Conduct contrastive learning, which brings embeddings of the input sentence and the paraphrased sentence closer together and separates embeddings of the input sentence from the rest of the sentences in the batch.

3.1 Paraphrase-based Contrastive Learning

Although the proposed method employs the same contrastive learning loss as SimCSE (Gao et al., 2021), we use paraphrase sentence pairs (described in § 3.2) instead of entailment sentence pairs as positive instances for contrastive learning, and other

	Train	Dev	Test
Shopping Queries	1,254,438	138,625	425,762
STS-B	5,749	1,500	1,379
SICK	4,439	495	4,906
SNLI	549,367	9,842	9,824
PAWS	49,401	8,000	8,000

Table 1: Number of sentence pairs for English datasets.

	Train	Dev	Test
Shopping Queries	294,874	32,272	118,907
JSTS	11,205	1,246	1,457
JSICK	4,500	500	4,927
JNLI	18,065	2,008	2,434
PAWS-X	49,401	2,000	2,000

Table 2: Number of sentence pairs for Japanese datasets.

sentences in the batch instead of contradictory sentence pairs as negative instances. Since this study assumes no semantic relationship between sentences in a batch, the other sentences x_j in the batch work as negative instances that are semantically unrelated to the input sentence x_i. The paraphrase of the input sentence is x_i^+ and embeddings of the paraphrase pair are $\mathbf{h}_i$ and $\mathbf{h}_i^+$, respectively, and we train to minimize the loss function in Equation (1):

$$\ell_i = -\log \frac{e^{\mathrm{sim}(\mathbf{h}_i,\mathbf{h}_i^+)/\tau}}{\sum_{j=1}^{N} e^{\mathrm{sim}(\mathbf{h}_i,\mathbf{h}_j^+)/\tau}}, \qquad (1)$$

where N is the batch size, τ is the temperature parameter and $\mathrm{sim}(\cdot)$ is the cosine similarity between sentence embeddings.

3.2 Generating Paraphrase Sentence Pairs

We automatically generate paraphrase sentence pairs to be used as positive instances for contrastive learning, from a raw corpus and a paraphrase dictionary.[2] Our paraphrase dictionary consists of three pairs of source phrase s, target phrase d, and paraphrase probability $p(d|s)$. In this study, we employ only paraphrase pairs $\{(s,d) \mid p(d|s) \geq \theta\}$ that have a paraphrase probability above a threshold θ. The paraphrase dictionary is applied to the input sentence from the raw corpus $x_i \in \mathcal{D}$, substituting phrases s into d to generate paraphrase candidates.

Here, as shown in Figure 1 (2), paraphrase candidates may include ungrammatical expressions. To avoid the negative effects from such ungrammatical sentences, we select the most fluent candidate with minimum perplexity to use as positive instances for contrastive learning.

[2]For paraphrase generation, we can also employ methods based on machine translation (Hu et al., 2019; Kajiwara et al., 2020) or large language models (Witteveen and Andrews, 2019). Comparison with them is left for our future work. In this study, we employ a dictionary-based paraphrase method that is computationally inexpensive and highly interpretable.

4 Experiments

We evaluated the effectiveness of the proposed method for four types of sentence pair modeling tasks in both English and Japanese.

4.1 Tasks

Our evaluation tasks are product retrieval, similarity estimation, recognizing textual entailment (RTE), and paraphrase identification. Statistics for each dataset are shown in Tables 1 and 2.

Retrieval Product retrieval is a four-class classification task of the relationships between product titles and their search queries, and we employed both English and Japanese versions of the Shopping Queries dataset[3] (Reddy et al., 2022).

Similarity Similarity estimation is a regression task that estimates the semantic similarity between two sentences, and we employed datasets of STS-B[4] (Cer et al., 2017) and SICK[5] (Marelli et al., 2014) for English and JSTS[6] (Kurihara et al., 2022) and JSICK[7] (Yanaka and Mineshima, 2022) for Japanese.

RTE RTE is a three-class classification task of semantic relationships between two sentences, and we employed datasets of SNLI[8] (Bowman et al., 2015) and SICK for English and JNLI[6] (Kurihara et al., 2022) and JSICK for Japanese.

Paraphrase Paraphrase identification is a two-class classification task of synonymity between two sentences, and we employed datasets of PAWS[9] (Zhang et al., 2019) for English and PAWS-X[9] (Yang et al., 2019) for Japanese.

[3]https://github.com/amazon-science/esci-data

[4]http://ixa2.si.ehu.es/stswiki/index.php/STSbenchmark

[5]https://zenodo.org/records/2787612

[6]https://github.com/yahoojapan/JGLUE

[7]https://github.com/verypluming/JSICK

[8]https://nlp.stanford.edu/projects/snli/

[9]https://github.com/google-research-datasets/paws

For evaluation metrics, we used the micro-f1 score for the retrieval tasks, Spearman's rank correlation coefficient for the similarity tasks, and the macro-f1 score for both the RTE and the paraphrase tasks.

4.2 Implementation Details

We fine-tuned English BERT[10] (Devlin et al., 2019) and Japanese RoBERTa[11] (Liu et al., 2019) on the sentence pair modeling tasks in Section 4.1. We want to evaluate whether the performance of each task can be improved by applying additional training of the proposed method or comparative methods before fine-tuning.

Pre-processing We used Wikipedia text from Wiki-40B[12] (Guo et al., 2020) for our contrastive learning. As pre-processing, we applied sentence segmentation and word segmentation with Moses[13] (Koehn et al., 2007) for English, and sentence segmentation with ja_sentence_segmenter[14] and word segmentation with MeCab (IPAdic)[15] (Kudo et al., 2004) for Japanese. In addition, language identification by langdetect[16] was performed, and only sentences with a confidence level of 99% or higher were used in each corpus for English and Japanese. Finally, we excluded both short sentences of 5 words or less and long sentences of 50 words or more.

Paraphrase For paraphrase dictionary, we used PPDB 2.0[17] (Pavlick et al., 2015) for English and EhiMerPPDB[18] for Japanese. These dictionaries cover phrases of up to six words in English and seven words in Japanese. To filter paraphrase candidates, perplexity was calculated with English[19] or Japanese[20] models of GPT-2 (Radford et al., 2019).

Hyperparameters The learning rate was set to 5×10^{-5}, temperature to $\tau = 0.05$, batch size to 64 sentence pairs, and Adam (Kingma and Ba, 2015) was used as our optimization method, and training was terminated when the loss on the Dev set did not improve for 3 consecutive epochs. In addition, we selected the threshold for paraphrase probability $\theta \in \{0.1, 0.2, 0.3, 0.4, 0.5\}$ and the number of sentences for additional training $|\mathcal{D}| \in \{10k, 20k, 40k, 80k, 160k\}$ to maximize metrics on the Dev set among these combinations.

4.3 Comparative Methods

To evaluate the effectiveness of paraphrase-based contrastive learning, we compare the proposed method to existing methods that employ paraphrase but not contrastive learning (Transfer Fine-Tuning) (Arase and Tsujii, 2019), contrastive learning without paraphrase (both unsupervised and supervised SimCSE (Gao et al., 2021) and state-of-the-art RankCSE (Liu et al., 2023)), and fine-tuning without additional training.

Transfer Fine-Tuning (Arase and Tsujii, 2019) is a method for additional training to identify phrasal paraphrases on approximately 30 million paraphrase pairs. Since we use the official trained model[21] in English, it is compared only in English experiments. Unsupervised SimCSE (Gao et al., 2021) is dropout-based contrastive learning with raw corpora, and we replicate it with Wikipedia in the same settings as in § 4.2. Supervised SimCSE (Gao et al., 2021) is contrastive learning with NLI corpora, and we replicate it with SNLI (Bowman et al., 2015) and MNLI (Williams et al., 2018) for English, and with JSNLI,[22] a Japanese translation of SNLI, for Japanese. RankCSE (Liu et al., 2023) is a state-of-the-art contrastive learning that incorporates ranking consistency and ranking distillation, and we replicate it using the English[23] or Japanese[24] SimCSE as a teacher model. The hyperparameters of SimCSE and RankCSE are the same as those of the proposed method in § 4.2.[25]

4.4 Results

Experimental results are shown in Table 3. Our method achieved performance better than the base-

[10] https://huggingface.co/google-bert/bert-base-uncased

[11] https://huggingface.co/rinna/japanese-roberta-base

[12] https://www.tensorflow.org/datasets/catalog/wiki40b

[13] https://github.com/moses-smt/mosesdecoder/

[14] https://github.com/wwwcojp/ja_sentence_segmenter

[15] https://taku910.github.io/mecab/

[16] https://pypi.org/project/langdetect/

[17] http://paraphrase.org/#/download

[18] https://github.com/EhimeNLP/EhiMerPPDB

[19] https://huggingface.co/openai-community/gpt2

[20] https://huggingface.co/rinna/japanese-gpt2-medium

[21] https://github.com/yukiar/TransferFT

[22] https://nlp.ist.i.kyoto-u.ac.jp/?%E6%97%A5%E6%9C%AC%E8%AA%9ESNLI%28JSNLI%29%E3%83%87%E3%83%BC%E3%82%BF%E3%82%BB%E3%83%83%E3%83%88

[23] https://huggingface.co/princeton-nlp/unsup-simcse-bert-base-uncased

[24] https://huggingface.co/cl-nagoya/unsup-simcse-ja-base

[25] Since JSNLI has less than $160k$ sentence pairs, we set the maximum number for additional training to $140k$ pairs.

English	Retrieval Shopping Queries	Similarity STS-B	 SICK	RTE SNLI	 SICK	Paraphrase PAWS	Avg.
w/o Additional Training	0.654	0.824	0.815	**0.904**	0.858	0.913	0.828
Transfer Fine-Tuning	0.652	0.854	0.821	0.902	0.860	0.901	0.832
Unsupervised SimCSE	**0.655**	0.830	0.806	**0.904**	**0.868**	**0.918**	0.830
RankCSE	0.652	**0.858**	0.821	0.903	0.854	0.912	0.833
Supervised SimCSE	**0.655**	0.857	0.824	0.901	0.865	0.913	0.836
Ours	**0.655**	0.841	**0.842**	**0.904**	0.866	**0.918**	**0.838**
Japanese	**Retrieval Shopping Queries**	**Similarity JSTS**	** JSICK**	**RTE JNLI**	** JSICK**	**Paraphrase PAWS-X**	**Avg.**
w/o Additional Training	0.576	0.859	0.890	0.785	0.839	0.793	0.790
Unsupervised SimCSE	**0.587**	**0.861**	0.886	0.781	0.837	0.790	0.790
RankCSE	0.574	0.855	0.893	0.829	0.838	0.779	0.795
Supervised SimCSE	0.576	0.825	0.886	**0.843**	0.843	**0.800**	0.796
Ours	**0.587**	**0.861**	**0.896**	0.828	**0.856**	0.791	**0.803**

Table 3: Evaluation of four sentence pair modeling tasks. Retrieval is a product retrieval task and reports Micro-F1. Similarity is a semantic textual similarity estimation task and reports Spearman correlation. RTE and Paraphrase are tasks of recognizing textual entailment and paraphrase identification, respectively, and report Macro-F1.

line w/o additional training on all tasks in English, and better than the baseline on all tasks except the paraphrase identification task in Japanese. Here, PAWS-X focuses on word reordering, which may be incompatible with our paraphrase, which does not reorder but only substitutes phrases. Nevertheless, our method is effective for many other tasks.

Compared to the existing methods, our method achieved the best average performance in both English and Japanese. Our method has the advantage of achieving higher performance at a lower cost than traditional contrastive learning because it does not require expensive annotation like NLI corpora.

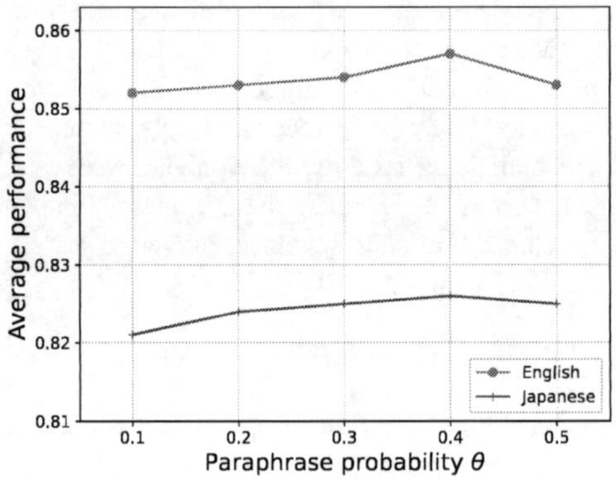

Figure 2: Relationship between paraphrase probability and average performance of sentence pair modeling. The larger the probability, the higher quality and smaller quantity of paraphrases we use in our training.

4.5 Analysis: Paraphrase Quality

The quality and quantity of paraphrases may affect the performance of our contrast learning. There is a trade-off between quality and quantity of paraphrases, which can be controlled using the paraphrase probabilities listed in the dictionary. In other words, if only paraphrases with high probability are targeted, a high quality and small quantity of paraphrases will be used.

The average performance of the sentence pair modeling tasks on the Dev set for each paraphrase probability threshold is shown in Figure 2. We found that the best performance was achieved by using only paraphrases with a probability of 0.4 or higher in both English and Japanese.

5 Summary and Future Work

In this study, we proposed paraphrase-based contrastive learning to improve the performance of sentence pair modeling. Our method can achieve high performance from automatically generated corpora, even though it is freed from the expensive annotation of NLI corpora that traditional contrastive learning relies on. Experimental results reveal performance improvements in a wide range of tasks, including product retrieval, similarity estimation, recognizing textual entailment, and paraphrase identification, in both English and Japanese.

Our future work includes both further improvement of positive instances and negative instances. Especially for positive instances, paraphrase generation could be based on machine translation or large language models.

Limitations

Language Dependency: While our method does not require expensive annotation like the NLI corpus, it relies on a raw corpus and a paraphrase dictionary. Even though paraphrase dictionaries already exist for many languages, they vary in size and quality. Since our experiments are conducted in two languages, English and Japanese, we cannot necessarily guarantee the effectiveness of the proposed method in other languages.

Training Time: We added a new training step between pre-training and fine-tuning of masked language models. This requires about 30 minutes of additional training time when running on a single NVIDIA RTX A6000 GPU with 48 GB memory.

Acknowledgments

The authors wish to thank Mercari Inc. and the Mercari R4D team for funding this research.

References

Yuki Arase and Jun'ichi Tsujii. 2019. Transfer Fine-Tuning: A BERT Case Study. In *Proceedings of the 2019 Conference on Empirical Methods in Natural Language Processing and the 9th International Joint Conference on Natural Language Processing*, pages 5393–5404.

Samuel R. Bowman, Gabor Angeli, Christopher Potts, and Christopher D. Manning. 2015. A Large Annotated Corpus for Learning Natural Language Inference. In *Proceedings of the 2015 Conference on Empirical Methods in Natural Language Processing*, pages 632–642.

Daniel Cer, Mona Diab, Eneko Agirre, Iñigo Lopez-Gazpio, and Lucia Specia. 2017. SemEval-2017 Task 1: Semantic Textual Similarity Multilingual and Crosslingual Focused Evaluation. In *Proceedings of the 11th International Workshop on Semantic Evaluation*, pages 1–14.

Qian Chen, Xiaodan Zhu, Zhen-Hua Ling, Si Wei, Hui Jiang, and Diana Inkpen. 2017. Enhanced LSTM for Natural Language Inference. In *Proceedings of the 55th Annual Meeting of the Association for Computational Linguistics*, pages 1657–1668.

Yung-Sung Chuang, Rumen Dangovski, Hongyin Luo, Yang Zhang, Shiyu Chang, Marin Soljacic, Shang-Wen Li, Scott Yih, Yoon Kim, and James Glass. 2022. DiffCSE: Difference-based Contrastive Learning for Sentence Embeddings. In *Proceedings of the 2022 Conference of the North American Chapter of the Association for Computational Linguistics: Human Language Technologies*, pages 4207–4218.

Jacob Devlin, Ming-Wei Chang, Kenton Lee, and Kristina Toutanova. 2019. BERT: Pre-training of Deep Bidirectional Transformers for Language Understanding. In *Proceedings of the 2019 Conference of the North American Chapter of the Association for Computational Linguistics: Human Language Technologies*, pages 4171–4186.

Johanes Effendi, Sakriani Sakti, Katsuhito Sudoh, and Satoshi Nakamura. 2018. Multi-paraphrase Augmentation to Leverage Neural Caption Translation. In *Proceedings of the 15th International Conference on Spoken Language Translation*, pages 181–188.

Juri Ganitkevitch and Chris Callison-Burch. 2014. The Multilingual Paraphrase Database. In *Proceedings of the Ninth International Conference on Language Resources and Evaluation*, pages 4276–4283.

Tianyu Gao, Xingcheng Yao, and Danqi Chen. 2021. SimCSE: Simple Contrastive Learning of Sentence Embeddings. In *Proceedings of the 2021 Conference on Empirical Methods in Natural Language Processing*, pages 6894–6910.

Mandy Guo, Zihang Dai, Denny Vrandečić, and Rami Al-Rfou. 2020. Wiki-40B: Multilingual Language Model Dataset. In *Proceedings of the Twelfth Language Resources and Evaluation Conference*, pages 2440–2452.

Hua He and Jimmy Lin. 2016. Pairwise Word Interaction Modeling with Deep Neural Networks for Semantic Similarity Measurement. In *Proceedings of the 2016 Conference of the North American Chapter of the Association for Computational Linguistics: Human Language Technologies*, pages 937–948.

J. Edward Hu, Rachel Rudinger, Matt Post, and Benjamin Van Durme. 2019. PARABANK: Monolingual Bitext Generation and Sentential Paraphrasing via Lexically-constrained Neural Machine Translation. In *Proceedings of the AAAI Conference on Artificial Intelligence*, pages 6521–6528.

Tomoyuki Kajiwara, Biwa Miura, and Yuki Arase. 2020. Monolingual Transfer Learning via Bilingual Translators for Style-sensitive Paraphrase Generation. In *Proceedings of the AAAI Conference on Artificial Intelligence*, pages 8042–8049.

Diederik P. Kingma and Jimmy Lei Ba. 2015. Adam: A Method for Stochastic Optimization. In *Proceedings of the 3rd International Conference for Learning Representations*.

Philipp Koehn, Hieu Hoang, Alexandra Birch, Chris Callison-Burch, Marcello Federico, Nicola Bertoldi, Brooke Cowan, Wade Shen, Christine Moran, Richard Zens, Chris Dyer, Ondřej Bojar, Alexandra Constantin, and Evan Herbst. 2007. Moses: Open Source Toolkit for Statistical Machine Translation. In *Proceedings of the 45th Annual Meeting of the Association for Computational Linguistics Companion Volume Proceedings of the Demo and Poster Sessions*, pages 177–180.

Taku Kudo, Kaoru Yamamoto, and Yuji Matsumoto. 2004. Applying Conditional Random Fields to Japanese Morphological Analysis. In *Proceedings of the 2004 Conference on Empirical Methods in Natural Language Processing*, pages 230–237.

Kentaro Kurihara, Daisuke Kawahara, and Tomohide Shibata. 2022. JGLUE: Japanese General Language Understanding Evaluation. In *Proceedings of the Thirteenth Language Resources and Evaluation Conference*, pages 2957–2966.

Wuwei Lan and Wei Xu. 2018. Neural Network Models for Paraphrase Identification, Semantic Textual Similarity, Natural Language Inference, and Question Answering. In *Proceedings of the 27th International Conference on Computational Linguistics*, pages 3890–3902.

Bohan Li, Hao Zhou, Junxian He, Mingxuan Wang, Yiming Yang, and Lei Li. 2020. On the Sentence Embeddings from Pre-trained Language Models. In *Proceedings of the 2020 Conference on Empirical Methods in Natural Language Processing*, pages 9119–9130.

Jiduan Liu, Jiahao Liu, Qifan Wang, Jingang Wang, Wei Wu, Yunsen Xian, Dongyan Zhao, Kai Chen, and Rui Yan. 2023. RankCSE: Unsupervised Sentence Representations Learning via Learning to Rank. In *Proceedings of the 61st Annual Meeting of the Association for Computational Linguistics*, pages 13785–13802.

Yinhan Liu, Myle Ott, Naman Goyal, Jingfei Du, Mandar Joshi, Danqi Chen, Omer Levy, Mike Lewis, Luke Zettlemoyer, and Veselin Stoyanov. 2019. RoBERTa: A Robustly Optimized BERT Pretraining Approach. *arXiv:1907.11692*.

Marco Marelli, Stefano Menini, Marco Baroni, Luisa Bentivogli, Raffaella Bernardi, and Roberto Zamparelli. 2014. A SICK Cure for the Evaluation of Compositional Distributional Semantic Models. In *Proceedings of the Ninth International Conference on Language Resources and Evaluation*, pages 216–223.

Sneha Mehta, Bahareh Azarnoush, Boris Chen, Avneesh Saluja, Vinith Misra, Ballav Bihani, and Ritwik Kumar. 2020. Simplify-then-Translate: Automatic Preprocessing for Black-Box Machine Translation. In *Proceedings of the Thirty-Fourth AAAI Conference on Artificial Intelligence*, pages 8488–8495.

Tomas Mikolov, Kai Chen, Greg Corrado, and Jeffrey Dean. 2013. Efficient Estimation of Word Representations in Vector Space. *arXiv:1301.3781*.

Rei Miyata and Atsushi Fujita. 2021. Understanding Pre-Editing for Black-Box Neural Machine Translation. In *Proceedings of the 16th Conference of the European Chapter of the Association for Computational Linguistics*, pages 1539–1550.

Eda Okur, Saurav Sahay, and Lama Nachman. 2022. Data Augmentation with Paraphrase Generation and Entity Extraction for Multimodal Dialogue System. In *Proceedings of the Thirteenth Language Resources and Evaluation Conference*, pages 4114–4125.

Ellie Pavlick, Pushpendre Rastogi, Juri Ganitkevitch, Benjamin Van Durme, and Chris Callison-Burch. 2015. PPDB 2.0: Better Paraphrase Ranking, Fine-grained Entailment Relations, Word Embeddings, and Style Classification. In *Proceedings of the 53rd Annual Meeting of the Association for Computational Linguistics and the 7th International Joint Conference on Natural Language Processing*, pages 425–430.

Alec Radford, Jeff Wu, Rewon Child, David Luan, Dario Amodei, and Ilya Sutskever. 2019. Language Models Are Unsupervised Multitask Learners.

Chandan K. Reddy, Lluís Màrquez, Fran Valero, Nikhil Rao, Hugo Zaragoza, Sambaran Bandyopadhyay, Arnab Biswas, Anlu Xing, and Karthik Subbian. 2022. Shopping Queries Dataset: A Large-Scale ESCI Benchmark for Improving Product Search. *arXiv:2206.06588*.

Jiajia Wang, Jimmy Xiangji Huang, Xinhui Tu, Junmei Wang, Angela Jennifer Huang, Md Tahmid Rahman Laskar, and Amran Bhuiyan. 2024. Utilizing BERT for Information Retrieval: Survey, Applications, Resources, and Challenges. *ACM Computing Surveys*, 56(7):1–33.

Adina Williams, Nikita Nangia, and Samuel Bowman. 2018. A Broad-Coverage Challenge Corpus for Sentence Understanding through Inference. In *Proceedings of the 2018 Conference of the North American Chapter of the Association for Computational Linguistics: Human Language Technologies*, pages 1112–1122.

Sam Witteveen and Martin Andrews. 2019. Paraphrasing with Large Language Models. In *Proceedings of the 3rd Workshop on Neural Generation and Translation*, pages 215–220.

Hitomi Yanaka and Koji Mineshima. 2022. Compositional Evaluation on Japanese Textual Entailment and Similarity. *Transactions of the Association for Computational Linguistics*, 10:1266–1284.

Yinfei Yang, Yuan Zhang, Chris Tar, and Jason Baldridge. 2019. PAWS-X: A Cross-lingual Adversarial Dataset for Paraphrase Identification. In *Proceedings of the 2019 Conference on Empirical*

Methods in Natural Language Processing and the 9th International Joint Conference on Natural Language Processing, pages 3687–3692.

Qin Zhang, Shangsi Chen, Dongkuan Xu, Qingqing Cao, Xiaojun Chen, Trevor Cohn, and Meng Fang. 2023. A Survey for Efficient Open Domain Question Answering. In *Proceedings of the 61st Annual Meeting of the Association for Computational Linguistics*, pages 14447–14465.

Yuan Zhang, Jason Baldridge, and Luheng He. 2019. PAWS: Paraphrase Adversaries from Word Scrambling. In *Proceedings of the 2019 Conference of the North American Chapter of the Association for Computational Linguistics: Human Language Technologies*, pages 1298–1308.

Do Video Language Models really understand the video contexts?

Jeongwan Shin*
Kyungpook National University
jwshin@knu.ac.kr

Jinhyeong Lim*
AI Center,
HD Korea Shipbuilding
Offshore Engineering
jinhyeong.lim@hd.com

Hyeyoung Park†
Kyungpook National University
hypark@knu.ac.kr

Abstract

This paper examines how well visual language models (VLMs) understand video question answering (VideoQA) tasks and generate responses accordingly. Recently, VLMs based on Large Language Models (LLMs) have shown remarkable performance, but the processes of understanding and reasoning in VLMs remain under-explored. To tackle this challenge, we propose **V**ideo **U**nderstanding and **R**esponse **C**onsistency **A**ssessment, **VURCA**, a framework that incorporates a fine-grained question generation and answering process to measure how well the responses generated by VLMs align with what the model understands. In addition, we introduce an extended benchmark dataset, FgNExT-QA, which builds upon NExT-QA by incorporating more fine-grained VideoQA tasks. FgNExT-QA is designed to evaluate fine-grained understanding in video question answering. Through experiments, we found that despite the strong overall QA performance of VLMs, their understanding of both the video content and the question remains limited. In particular, they exhibit poor video comprehension in fine-grained VideoQA tasks.

1 Introduction

Video Question Answering (VideoQA) (Fei et al., 2024; Min et al., 2024) serves as a critical benchmark for evaluating the capabilities of foundational Visual Language Models (VLMs) (Zhang et al., 2023; Liu et al., 2024), particularly those trained on large-scale multi-modal datasets (Ye et al., 2023). Despite recent advancements in VideoQA performance, several fundamental concerns remain under-explored. A key question is whether these models accurately comprehend video and question to enable robust multi-modal reasoning, or if they merely mimic learned patterns from the training dataset (Xiao et al., 2024). Responses based on incomplete understanding can lead to significant issues in real-world applications, emphasizing the need for efforts to evaluate and address these limitations.

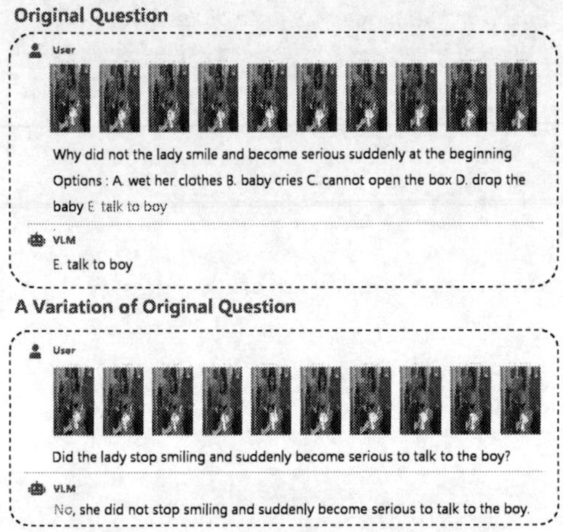

Figure 1: Example responses generated by VLMs(LLaVA-OneVision) on the NExT-QA dataset.

Figure 1 illustrates that VLMs often struggle to answer a variation of the original question, which are derived from the original question and its corresponding ground truth answer, even though VLMs generate correct answer. This observation demonstrates that VLMs can choose correct answer even without a precise understanding. If the answer is chosen based on accurate understanding, it should generate a consistent response to the variation. From the observation, VLMs for VideoQA still fall short in accurately understanding video contents and remain under-resourced in terms of the evaluation metrics and datasets required to assess trained models effectively. Existing research has primarily explored the estimation of consistency between generated textual outputs and image inputs in VLMs (Khan and Fu, 2024; Geng et al., 2024). However, we aim to evaluate the under-

* Equal contribution.
† Corresponding author.

Proceedings of the 2025 Conference of the Nations of the Americas Chapter of the Association for Computational Linguistics: Human Language Technologies (Volume 4: Student Research Workshop), pages 408–417
April 30 - May 1, 2025

standing of video content by VLMs. This marks a novel attempt to measure the consistency between responses and understanding in the domain of VideoQA.

As a novel approach, we propose the **V**ideo **U**nderstanding and **R**esponse **C**onsistency **A**ssessment, **VURCA**, a framework designed to investigate the understanding of VLMs through the process of generating fine-grained verification questions, integrating answer of the VideoQA, evaluating the consistency between fine-grained answers and initial response. First, VLMs generate an initial response by taking a video and original question as input. Based on the initial response and the original question, fine-grained verification questions are generated using an LLM. If VLM's answer is generated under through understanding on Video context, it should consistently generate responses to the variation of original questions that are semantically equivalent to the initial response. To investigate this, we input the fine-grained verification questions along with the video into the VLMs again to derive verification responses. Then, the verification responses are aggregated to quantitatively evaluate the VLM's understanding.

Moreover, our approach also enables the automatic expansion of VideoQA datasets, which are costly and time-intensive to construct. By extending the NExT-QA dataset, we construct FgNExT-QA, a fine-grained question-answering dataset with binary gold answer labels. FgNExT-QA allows us to verify that VLMs specifically understand the questions and can determine the correct answers. It can also be used as an independent benchmark for VideoQA performance evaluation.

In the experiments, we conduct a comprehensive analysis of how well state-of-the-art VLMs understand and response correct answers in VideoQA. Despite achieving high accuracy on VideoQA, VLMs exhibit inconsistencies when responding to semantically identical but rephrased questions. This observation highlights the challenges VLMs still face in aligning visual evidence with linguistic semantics, revealing areas that require further improvement. To encapsulate our contributions: 1) Introducing VURCA framework: We propose a novel framework for evaluating the alignment between video understanding and responses generated by VLMs; 2) Fine-Grained VideoQA dataset generated automatically: We present a fine-grained VideoQA dataset generated automatically, containing binary gold answer labels to systematically assess VLM understanding and response consistency; 3) Comprehensive Analysis of VLM Performance: Through experiments on various VLMs, we analyze their current challenges and interpret these issues in terms of understanding and response alignment.

2 Related Work

In videoQA tasks, a primary objective is to ensure that the model accurately comprehends video data and generates appropriate responses. Previous research has focused on building models for video action and dynamics recognition (Lei et al., 2018; Bertasius et al., 2021). However, most of these efforts fall under the category of simple perceptual-level understanding, such as handling straightforward video (Zolfaghari et al., 2018; Lin et al., 2019). Recent advancements in Transformer-based language models (Vaswani et al., 2017; Brown et al., 2020) have been accompanied by substantial progress in visual-language models (VLMs), leading to significant improvements in video question answering performance. Ko et al. (2023) integrated visual encoders and LLaMA-Adapter (Zhang et al., 2024) into LLMs to enable video understanding, training the model to process both textual and visual inputs effectively. Min et al. (2024) and Wang et al. (2024) demonstrated remarkable performance improvements by first generating image captions using a VLM, selecting frames directly relevant to the question from the video, and then integrating these captions with the reasoning process of an LLM, such as ChatGPT (OpenAI, 2024). (Fei et al., 2024) extended this approach by applying Chain-of-Thought (CoT) (Wei et al., 2024) reasoning capabilities from LLMs to VLMs. Recently, Xiao et al. (2024) critically questioned the degree to which the answers generated by such techniques are truly grounded in the relevant visual content. However, research verifying the alignment between understanding and response in VLMs has yet to be extensively explored.

3 Fine-Grained NExT-QA benchmark

Data Source. We introduce an extended benchmark dataset, FgNExT-QA, which builds upon NExT-QA (Xiao et al., 2021) to better align with fine-grained VideoQA tasks. Most existing VideoQA datasets (Yu et al., 2019; Mangalam et al., 2023) either consist of trimmed, short videos or lack closed-ended answers, making them unsuit-

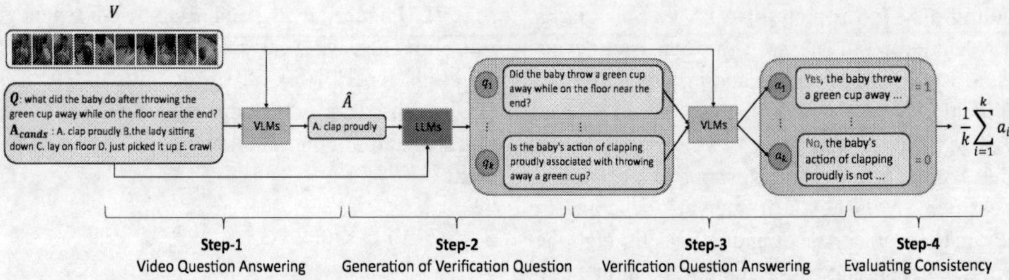

Figure 2: An overview of the proposed framework.

able for our purpose. In contrast, we chose the closed-ended VideoQA subset of NExT-QA, which provides five possible answer choices for each question, with one correct answer. NExT-QA comprises 1,000 videos and includes a total of 8.56k existing question-video pairs. For each question-option pair, we generated five variations. As a result, we created 42.82k newly generated binary-answerable questions. Furthermore, we include a comprehensive discussion of the core limitations inherited from NExT-QA in Appendix. D

Fine-grained Question Generation. To facilitate fine-grained question generation, we adopt open-source LLMs. First, a question and a option are input into the LLMs, along with few-shot examples, to generate fine-grained questions. Detailed prompts and examples are provided in Appendix A. For each question-option pair, up to five questions are generated. Empirically, we observed that generating more than five questions often results in duplicate questions. The generated questions are closed-ended questions (Xiao et al., 2021; Mangalam et al., 2023) that can be answered with "Yes" or "No," which facilitates verifying consistency with the original answer. However, due to the sampling characteristics of LLMs, unintended types of questions are occasionally generated, and such questions are excluded from the results. Detailed statistics on the generated questions are provided in Appendix B.

4 Video Understanding and Response Consistency Assessment

To investigate the understanding of VLMs, we present VURCA, a framework designed to quantify the consistency between video understanding and responses by integrating VideoQA with fine-granined questions generation. As illustrated in Figure 2, the process of the proposed framework consists of four main steps: video question answering, generation of verification question, verification question answering and evaluating consistency

Step-1: Video Question Answering

In the first step of our framework, we instruct the VLMs to respond to the closed-set VideoQA task. Specifically, a video V, the original question Q, and a set of candidate options $\mathbf{A}_{\text{cands}} = \{A_1, A_2, \ldots, A_5\}$, are used as inputs for VLMs to generate an initial response $\hat{A}$, which is represented as:

$$\text{VLM}(V, Q, \mathbf{A}_{\text{cands}}) \mapsto \hat{A}.$$

The VLMs utilize their multimodal abilities to derive $\hat{A}$ through an integration of visual and textual reasoning. However, the processes underlying visual and textual reasoning remain a black box and cannot be directly observed.

Step-2:Generation of Verification Question

In this step, we generate fine-grained verification questions to investigate the understanding demonstrated by VLMs in their responses. Q and $\hat{A}$ are input into the LLM, generating a set of fine-grained questions $\mathbf{q}_{\text{fg}}$:

$$\text{LLM}(\mathcal{E}_{\text{few-shot}}, Q, \hat{A}) \mapsto \mathbf{q}_{\text{fg}}.$$

Using a few-shot example set $\mathcal{E}_{\text{few-shot}} = \{(Q^1, \hat{A}^1, \mathbf{q}^1_{\text{fg}}), (Q^2, \hat{A}^2, \mathbf{q}^2_{\text{fg}}), \ldots, (Q^n, \hat{A}^n, \mathbf{q}^n_{\text{fg}})\}$, where n represents the number of examples provided to LLMs, we generated fine-grained questions $\mathbf{q}_{\text{fg}} = \{q_i\}_{i=1}^{k}$, where k is the number of questions. Each q_i is generated as a closed-ended question form with a "Yes" or "No" response.

Step-3:Verification Question Answering

Each fine-grained question q_i in $\mathbf{q}_{\text{fg}}$ is individually input into the VLMs along with V to generate a binary verification response a_i. This process can be expressed as follows:

$$\text{VLM}(V, q_i) \mapsto a_i \in \{1, 0\}.$$

Note that we encode the verification responses of VLMs as binary numbers: 1 for "Yes" and 0 for "No". These binary responses ensure a simple, objective, and accurate evaluation, minimizing ambiguity and streamlining the verification process.

Step-4:Evaluating Consistency

Finally, $\{a_i\}_{i=1}^{k}$ are aggregated to compute a consistency score for VLM's understanding for given Q. The consistency score is calculated as the ratio of the number of "Yes" responses to the number of the fine-grained questions. "Yes" responses indicate that the model demonstrates the same understanding for rephrased questions based on $\hat{A}$. Formally, the consistency score S_{cons} is defined as:

$$S_{\text{cons}} = \frac{1}{k}\sum_{i=1}^{k} a_i.$$

By evaluating the consistency for all the questions in VideoQA datasets, proposed framework provides an objective score to reflect its interpretative reliability.

5 Experiments

5.1 Overview

Our study aims to address three key research questions to evaluate and comprehensively analyze video comprehension and response consistency in VLMs. **Q1:** To what extent do VLMs exhibit consistent comprehension with the initial responses? Specifically, how does the comprehension manifest in cases where the response is correct versus when the response is incorrect? **Q2:** What is VLMs' level of understanding of other options not selected in the initial response? **Q3:** Do VLMs perform well even on fine-grained questions? To investigate these questions, we conduct the proposed framework to obtain S_{cons} and then perform additional comparative analyses to answer the key questions.

5.2 Experimental Settings

Our experiments, based on the close-ended videoQA tasks of the NExT-QA benchmark, were conducted using the proposed framework with state-of-the-art VLMs, including Llava-OneVision 0.5b, Llava-OneVision 7b, and Llava-Video 7b. For all VLMs, we uniformly sample 32 frames from the videos and input them, along with the corresponding questions and options, into the models. The generation of fine-grained questions, which is a part of the proposed framework, is carried out using the microsoft/Phi-3.5-mini-instruct (Abdin et al., 2024) LLM model. We implemented greedy search decoding by selecting the highest-probability token at each step in a fully deterministic manner. To this end, we set the temperature to 0 and disabled sampling-based parameters such as top-k and top-p.

Model	NExT-QA	Consistency Score		
	Acc	$S_{\text{cons}}^{\text{Total}}$	$S_{\text{cons}}^{\hat{A}=A^*}$	$S_{\text{cons}}^{\hat{A}\neq A^*}$
Llava-ov 0.5b	0.572	0.903	0.918	0.884
Llava-ov 7b	0.794	0.924	0.935	0.881
Llava-video 7b	0.832	0.924	0.936	0.878

Table 1: Evaluation of VLMs understanding of the initial responses.

5.3 Result and Analysis

5.3.1 Q1: Understanding of the Initial Responses

In this experiment, we investigate understanding exhibited by VLMs in the initial responses. To conduct this, we calculate $S_{\text{cons}}^{\text{Total}}$ which is the average S_{cons} over 8,564 question-video pairs in the test data of the NExT-QA benchmark using state-of-the-art VLMs. Additionally, we analyze the differences in S_{cons} between cases where the initial response $\hat{A}$ was correct ($\hat{A} = A^*$) and those where $\hat{A}$ was incorrect ($\hat{A} \neq A^*$), where A^* denotes the gold answer in $\mathbf{A}_{\text{cands}}$. The results are summarized in Table 1.

All VLMs show scores above 0.9 for $S_{\text{cons}}^{\text{Total}}$, indicating that the models provided a high consistent responses. Furthermore, each model showed a higher $S_{\text{cons}}^{\hat{A}=A^*}$ score when generating correct answers, while exhibiting a lower $S_{\text{cons}}^{\hat{A}\neq A^*}$ when VLMs fail to generate correct answers. These results suggest that when VLMs generate initial responses based on uncertain understanding of the video content, VLMs generate inconsistent response to fine-grained verification questions. This behavior becomes more pronounced as model size increases. $S_{\text{cons}}^{\hat{A}\neq A^*}$ score shows the largest gap of 0.057 in the 7B model, indicating that as the size and performance of VLMs increase, the consistency between the fine-grained verification answer and the initial response decreases when generating incorrect answers.

Model	$S_{\text{cons}}^{\text{Total}}$	S_{cons}^{-}
Llava-ov 0.5b	0.903	0.241
Llava-ov 7b	0.924	0.425
Llava-video 7b	0.924	0.437

Table 2: Comparison of VLMs overall consistency score $S_{\text{cons}}^{\text{Total}}$ and negative consistency score S_{cons}^{-}.

Model	NExT-QA	Fine-grained QA		
	Acc	**Acc**$^{+}$	**Acc**$^{-}$	**Acc**^{Total}
Llava-ov 0.5b	0.572	0.895	0.242	0.373
Llava-ov 7b	0.794	0.916	0.435	0.529
Llava-video 7b	0.832	0.921	0.444	0.537

Table 3: Evaluation of VLMs performance on fine-grained questions for all options.

5.3.2 Q2: Evaluation of understanding to unselected options

In this experiment, we generate additional fine-grained questions based on randomly selected options different from $\hat{A}$ to investigate whether the VLM can generate negative responses for the options excluding $\hat{A}$. Specifically, the VLMs understanding about the original question is considered higher when it generates more "No" responses for the fine-grained questions that conflict with its initial response. To quantify this, the negative consistency score S_{cons}^{-} is defined as:

$$S_{\text{cons}}^{-} = \frac{1}{k}\sum_{i=1}^{k}(1 - a_i).$$

As shown in Table 2, S_{cons}^{-} is significantly lower than the $S_{\text{cons}}^{\text{Total}}$ across all VLMs. A low S_{cons}^{-} indicates that VLMs fail to demonstrate a clear understanding of why unchosen options were excluded. In other words, the results suggest that VLMs do not accurately understand the video content well enough to make a clear and justified choice among the options. In particular, for the 0.5b model, S_{cons}^{-} was 0.662 lower than the corresponding S_{cons}. For the 7b models, the differences were 0.499 and 0.487. These results indicate that scaling the model size leads to increased consistency score in its responses, reflecting enhanced certainty in its comprehension and decision-making processes.

5.3.3 Q3: Evaluation of Fine-Grained Question Responses

For the final experiment, we generated fine-grained questions for all options, covering both the gold answer and the other options and evaluated the accuracy **Acc**^{Total}. We also measured separately the accuracy on questions for the gold answers (**Acc**$^{+}$) and the accuracy on questions for other options (**Acc**$^{-}$). The results, compared to those of the original questions in NExT-QA, are summarized in Table 3.

The 0.5b and 7b models showed a 0.253 difference in **Acc**$^{+}$, but a significantly larger performance gap of 0.201 in **Acc**$^{-}$, demonstrating superior performance by the larger model. Despite this improvement, the 7B model still exhibits insufficient performance. These results highlight that video comprehension is not only about accurately identifying the correct answer but also about understanding objects or actions that are irrelevant or unsuitable for the VideoQA task. Furthermore, even though Llava models with 7B parameters achieve around 80% performance on the NExT-QA dataset, they exhibit low performance in **Acc**$^{-}$. The results also suggest that relying solely on accuracy in multiple-choice VideoQA is not sufficient to evaluate the understanding of VLMs, emphasizing the need for further advancements to address the current limitations of VLMs.

6 Conclusion

This paper explores how visual language models understand VideoQA tasks and generate appropriate responses. However, evaluating whether these models truly understand both video and language inputs remains a challenging task. To address the challenge of evaluating VLMs comprehension, we propose VURCA, a framework to assess the alignment between the initial responses and VLMs understanding. VURCA achieves this by generating verification questions and comparing the subsequent responses with its initial answers. Additionally, we introduce FgNeXT-QA, a benchmark dataset designed for fine-grained VideoQA tasks, which offers more fine-grained assessment scenarios. Our experimental results indicate that despite their impressive performance in QA tasks, VLMs often fail to adequately understand video content and the corresponding questions. These results provide valuable insights for the development of advanced evaluation frameworks, the design of more robust model architectures, and the refinement of training methodologies. Future research should aim to enhance the reasoning capabilities of VLMs through improved pre-training strategies that integrate a more comprehensive understanding of video content and question semantics.

7 Limitation

While our proposed framework and dataset extension provide valuable insights into fine-grained VideoQA evaluation, several limitations remain. The generation of verification questions in FgNExT-QA relies on large language models (LLMs), which may introduce noise or bias in the reformulated binary questions. This could potentially affect the reliability and objectivity of the evaluation process. Therefore, we guided the model through few-shot examples to generate questions that can be answered with a simple "yes" or "no" which significantly reduced errors. However, since the model also tended to generate questions starting with The Five Ws (what, where, who, when, why, how), we excluded those from our final set. A detailed discussion of these inherited issues is provided in Appendix B.

Moreover, our research specifically focuses on the VideoQA task, which is important but may limit its applicability to broader multimodal or general video understanding research. Therefore, as a next step, we plan to expand our work to tackle more challenging benchmarks such as VideoMME and explore tasks like description generation and open-ended question answering.

8 Acknowledgement

This work was supported by Institute of Information & communications Technology Planning & Evaluation (IITP) grant funded by the Korea government(MSIT) (No.RS-2021-II212068, Artificial Intelligence Innovation Hub). We would like to thank YoungOk Kim, Chunhwan Jung, and Yubin Ock for their support to this project. This research was supported by the AI Center at HD Korea Shipbuilding & Offshore Engineering.

References

Marah Abdin, Jyoti Aneja, Hany Awadalla, and Ahmed Awadallah et al. 2024. Phi-3 technical report: A highly capable language model locally on your phone. *Preprint*, arXiv:2404.14219.

Gedas Bertasius, Heng Wang, and Lorenzo Torresani. 2021. Is space-time attention all you need for video understanding? In *Proceedings of the 38th International Conference on Machine Learning*, volume 139 of *Proceedings of Machine Learning Research*, pages 813–824. PMLR.

Tom Brown, Benjamin Mann, Nick Ryder, Melanie Subbiah, Jared D Kaplan, and Dhariwal et al. 2020. Language models are few-shot learners. In *Advances in Neural Information Processing Systems*, volume 33, pages 1877–1901. Curran Associates, Inc.

Hao Fei, Shengqiong Wu, Wei Ji, Hanwang Zhang, Meishan Zhang, Mong-Li Lee, and Wynne Hsu. 2024. Video-of-thought: Step-by-step video reasoning from perception to cognition. In *Forty-first International Conference on Machine Learning*.

Jiahui Geng, Fengyu Cai, Yuxia Wang, Heinz Koeppl, Preslav Nakov, and Iryna Gurevych. 2024. A survey of confidence estimation and calibration in large language models. In *Proceedings of the 2024 Conference of the North American Chapter of the Association for Computational Linguistics: Human Language Technologies (Volume 1: Long Papers)*, pages 6577–6595, Mexico City, Mexico. Association for Computational Linguistics.

Zaid Khan and Yun Fu. 2024. Consistency and uncertainty: Identifying unreliable responses from black-box vision-language models for selective visual question answering. In *Proceedings of the IEEE/CVF Conference on Computer Vision and Pattern Recognition (CVPR)*, pages 10854–10863.

Dohwan Ko, Ji Lee, Woo-Young Kang, Byungseok Roh, and Hyunwoo Kim. 2023. Large language models are temporal and causal reasoners for video question answering. In *Proceedings of the 2023 Conference on Empirical Methods in Natural Language Processing*, pages 4300–4316, Singapore. Association for Computational Linguistics.

Jie Lei, Licheng Yu, Mohit Bansal, and Tamara Berg. 2018. TVQA: Localized, compositional video question answering. In *Proceedings of the 2018 Conference on Empirical Methods in Natural Language Processing*, pages 1369–1379, Brussels, Belgium. Association for Computational Linguistics.

Ji Lin, Chuang Gan, and Song Han. 2019. Tsm: Temporal shift module for efficient video understanding. In *2019 IEEE/CVF International Conference on Computer Vision (ICCV)*, pages 7082–7092.

Haotian Liu, Chunyuan Li, Yuheng Li, and Yong Jae Lee. 2024. Improved baselines with visual instruction tuning. In *Proceedings of the IEEE/CVF Conference on Computer Vision and Pattern Recognition (CVPR)*, pages 26296–26306.

Karttikeya Mangalam, Raiymbek Akshulakov, and Jitendra Malik. 2023. Egoschema: A diagnostic benchmark for very long-form video language understanding. In *Thirty-seventh Conference on Neural Information Processing Systems Datasets and Benchmarks Track*.

Juhong Min, Shyamal Buch, Arsha Nagrani, Minsu Cho, and Cordelia Schmid. 2024. Morevqa: Exploring modular reasoning models for video question answering. In *Proceedings of the IEEE Conference on Computer Vision and Pattern Recognition (CVPR)*.

OpenAI. 2024. Gpt-4 technical report. *Preprint*, arXiv:2303.08774.

Ashish Vaswani, Noam Shazeer, Niki Parmar, Jakob Uszkoreit, Llion Jones, Aidan N Gomez, Ł ukasz Kaiser, and Illia Polosukhin. 2017. Attention is all you need. In *Advances in Neural Information Processing Systems*, volume 30. Curran Associates, Inc.

Ziyang Wang, Shoubin Yu, Elias Stengel-Eskin, Jaehong Yoon, Feng Cheng, Gedas Bertasius, and Mohit Bansal. 2024. Videotree: Adaptive tree-based video representation for LLM reasoning on long videos.

Jason Wei, Xuezhi Wang, Dale Schuurmans, Maarten Bosma, Brian Ichter, Fei Xia, Ed H. Chi, Quoc V. Le, and Denny Zhou. 2024. Chain-of-thought prompting elicits reasoning in large language models. In *Proceedings of the 36th International Conference on Neural Information Processing Systems*, NIPS '22, Red Hook, NY, USA. Curran Associates Inc.

Junbin Xiao, Xindi Shang, Angela Yao, and Tat-Seng Chua. 2021. Next-qa: Next phase of question-answering to explaining temporal actions. In *Proceedings of the IEEE/CVF Conference on Computer Vision and Pattern Recognition (CVPR)*, pages 9777–9786.

Junbin Xiao, Angela Yao, Yicong Li, and Tat-Seng Chua. 2024. Can i trust your answer? visually grounded video question answering. In *Proceedings of the IEEE/CVF Conference on Computer Vision and Pattern Recognition (CVPR)*, pages 13204–13214.

Qinghao Ye, Guohai Xu, Ming Yan, Haiyang Xu, Qi Qian, Ji Zhang, and Fei Huang. 2023. Hitea: Hierarchical temporal-aware video-language pre-training. In *Proceedings of the IEEE/CVF International Conference on Computer Vision (ICCV)*, pages 15405–15416.

Zhou Yu, Dejing Xu, Jun Yu, Ting Yu, Zhou Zhao, Yueting Zhuang, and Dacheng Tao. 2019. Activitynet-qa: A dataset for understanding complex web videos via question answering. 33:9127–9134.

Hang Zhang, Xin Li, and Lidong Bing. 2023. Video-LLaMA: An instruction-tuned audio-visual language model for video understanding. In *Proceedings of the 2023 Conference on Empirical Methods in Natural Language Processing: System Demonstrations*, pages 543–553, Singapore. Association for Computational Linguistics.

Renrui Zhang, Jiaming Han, Chris Liu, Aojun Zhou, Pan Lu, Yu Qiao, Hongsheng Li, and Peng Gao. 2024. LLaMA-adapter: Efficient fine-tuning of large language models with zero-initialized attention. In *The Twelfth International Conference on Learning Representations*.

Mohammadreza Zolfaghari, Kamaljeet Singh, and Thomas Brox. 2018. Eco: Efficient convolutional network for online video understanding. In *Computer Vision – ECCV 2018: 15th European Conference, Munich, Germany, September 8-14, 2018, Proceedings, Part II*, page 713–730, Berlin, Heidelberg. Springer-Verlag.

A Prompt Example

This section introduces the prompts used for VLMs and LLMs. Table 4 shows the prompts used in VideoQA. By providing a simple task description along with the video, video question, and answer options, the VLMs generate the system output, which is the final answer. In this paper, NExT-QA data was used, where there are a total of five options, A to E. The final answer is to select one of them. Table 5 presents the prompt for fine-grained question generation. It begins with a simple task instruction, followed by a few-shot example to produce the desired context as output. The few-shot example consists of a question, an answer, and five atomic questions. After the few-shot example, the target question and answer are provided to the LLMs, which then generate the corresponding atomic questions. Table 6 shows the prompt for generating verification responses using atomic questions as input. Similar to Table 4, this prompt excludes the answer options and instead focuses solely on inputting the atomic question to guide the output generation.

B FgNExT-QA statistics

We generated five atomic questions for each of the 8.56k question-video pairs in NExT-QA, with 5 answer options per pair, resulting in 21.41k atomic questions. Due to the characteristics of the LLM, we excluded potential questions that could be generated starting with The Five Ws (what, where, who, when, why, how). These excluded questions accounted for approximately 0.78% of the total. After this filtering process, 21.24k questions were retained for the experiments.

C Qualitative Example from FgNExT-QA

In this section, we perform a qualitative analysis based on actual output examples. Figure 3 illustrates a case where the VLM correctly identified the answer. For the fine-grained questions, the VLM responded with "Yes" to all questions generated for the correct option, while it generated responses including "No" for fine-grained questions generated for other options. In contrast, Figure 4 shows a case where the VLM generated a response different from the target. In this case, the VLM demonstrated a slightly higher proportion of "Yes" responses for the answer it generated. This suggests that the model tends to provide answers consistent with its earlier response, even in fine-grained questions. The similar distribution of responses across diverse questions indicates a lack of understanding and confidence in its answers.

D Inheriting Limitations from NExT-QA

Although FgNExT-QA reformulates the original NExT-QA into binary QA format by decomposing multiple-choice questions into individual question-option pairs, it inherits limitations from NExT-QA, as it is built upon the same question-answer pairs and video contexts. For example, NExT-QA has been shown to contain biases in its answer distribution, and some questions may rely more on textual commonsense knowledge rather than visual evidence from the video. These aspects can limit the effectiveness of evaluating true video-text understanding. While converting to a binary QA format allows for more granular evaluation of model understanding for each candidate option, the quality of distractor options in NExT-QA still affects the difficulty level and diagnostic power of the dataset.

As a result, although FgNExT-QA enhances the evaluation granularity by shifting to binary QA, its reliance on NExT-QA's original structure and content means that certain dataset-level limitations—such as superficial distractors or a lack of visually grounded reasoning—may still affect the robustness and generalizability of model performance.

System
You are a helpful assistant.
User
<video> {input question} A. {option} B. {option} C. {option} D. {option} E. {option}
System
assistant:

Table 4: Examples of instructions used in the video question answering.

User
After reviewing the questions and answers, generate atomic questions to clarify and verify your responses, ensuring that the questions can be answered with a simple 'yes' or 'no'. Question:how does the girl show her excitment over the toy? Answer:By turning it around repeatedly Atomic Questions: -Can it be said that the girl is excited about the toy, as shown by her turning it around repeatedly? -Is the girl turning the toy around repeatedly to show her excitement? -Can the girl's excitement be inferred from her action of turning the toy around repeatedly? -Is the toy the reason for the girl's excitement, as evidenced by her turning it around repeatedly? -Does the girl's action of turning the toy around repeatedly suggest she is excited? *<Few shot examples>* Question:{input question} Answer:{input answer}
System
Atomic Questions:

Table 5: Examples of instructions and few-shot examples used in the fine-grained question generation.

System
You are a helpful assistant.
User
<video> {input atomic question}
System
assistant:

Table 6: Examples of instructions used in the fine-grained question answering.

- **Video** :

- **Question** : where is this place?
- **Options** : A. restaurant B. theatre C. farm D. kitchen E. living room
- **Target** : E. living room
- **VLM Answer** : E. living room

- **Fine-grained questions andanswers**:
  - C. farm
    - Is this place located on a farm? No.
    - Can it be inferred that the location of this place is a farm? No, it cannot be inferred that the location is a farm.
    - Is the farm the setting for this place? No, the setting is a toy train set.
    - Does this place belong to or take place on a farm? No, the place is a cozy living room.
    - Is 'farm' the correct term to describe where this place is situated? No, 'farm' is not the correct term; it should be 'home'.
  - E. living room
    - Is the place being referred to as a living room? Yes
    - Can it be said that the location in question is a living room? Yes
    - Is the place described as a living room? Yes
    - Does this place have the designation of a living room? Yes
    - Is 'living room' an accurate description for this location? Yes

Figure 3: Example of a correct prediction by the VLM.

- **Video** :

- **Question** : why did the woman in red sitting down lean forward in the middle?
- **Options** : A. stabilize her B. service staff C. for support to writeD. observe the childrenE. laughing
- **Target** : E. laughing
- **VLM Answer** : A. stabilize her

- **Fine-grained questions andanswers**:
  - A. stabilize her
    - Is the woman in red leaning forward to stabilize herself while sitting down in the middle? No, the woman in red is standing with her arms crossed.
    - Does the woman in red sit down and then lean forward for stabilization purposes? No, the woman in red stands with her arms crossed and leans forward for stabilization purposes.
    - Is the action of leaning forward by the woman in red observed for stabilization reasons? Yes, the action of leaning forward by the woman in red is observed for stabilization reasons.
    - Does the woman in red use her body position (leaning forward) to achieve stability while sitting down in the middle?Yes, the woman in red uses her body position (leaning forward) to achieve stability while sitting down in the middle.
    - Can it be inferred that the woman's leaning forward is a method of stabilizing herself while seated at this location?Yes, it can be inferred that the woman's leaning forward is a method of stabilizing herself while seated at this location.
  - E. laughing
    - Is the woman in red leaning forward because she is laughing? No, the woman in red is leaning forward with her arms crossed.
    - Did the woman in red sit down and then lean forward due to laughter? No, the woman in red leaned forward due to laughter before sitting down.
    - Can it be inferred that the woman's laughter caused her to lean forward while sitting down in the middle ? Yes, it can be inferred that the woman's laughter caused her to lean forward while sitting down in the middle.
    - Is laughing a reason for the woman in red to lean forward while seated in the middle? Yes, laughing is a reason for the woman in red to lean forward while seated in the middle.
    - Does the act of laughing explain why the woman in red leans forward while sitting down in the middle? No, the act of laughing does not explain why the woman in red leans forward while sitting down in the middle.

Figure 4: Example of an incorrect prediction by the VLM.

Evaluating Text Style Transfer Evaluation: Are There Any Reliable Metrics?

Sourabrata Mukherjee[1], **Atul Kr. Ojha**[2], **John P. McCrae**[2], **Ondřej Dušek**[1]
[1]Charles University, Faculty of Mathematics and Physics, Prague, Czechia
[2]Insight Research Ireland Centre for Data Analytics, DSI, University of Galway, Ireland
`{mukherjee,odusek}@ufal.mff.cuni.cz`
`{atulkumar.ojha,john.mccrae}@insight-centre.org`

Abstract

Text style transfer (TST) is the task of transforming a text to reflect a particular style while preserving its original content. Evaluating TST outputs is a multidimensional challenge, requiring the assessment of style transfer accuracy, content preservation, and naturalness. Using human evaluation is ideal but costly, as is common in other natural language processing (NLP) tasks; however, automatic metrics for TST have not received as much attention as metrics for, e.g., machine translation or summarization. In this paper, we examine both set of existing and novel metrics from broader NLP tasks for TST evaluation, focusing on two popular subtasks—sentiment transfer and detoxification—in a multilingual context comprising English, Hindi, and Bengali. By conducting meta-evaluation through correlation with human judgments, we demonstrate the effectiveness of these metrics when used individually and in ensembles. Additionally, we investigate the potential of large language models (LLMs) as tools for TST evaluation. Our findings highlight newly applied advanced NLP metrics and LLM-based evaluations provide better insights than existing TST metrics. Our oracle ensemble approaches show even more potential.

1 Introduction

Text style transfer (TST) refers to the task of modifying a given text to reflect a specific style while preserving its original content (Hu et al., 2022). Previous work in this domain has explored altering various stylistic dimensions, such as sentiment (Prabhumoye et al., 2018), romantic tone (Li et al., 2018), politeness (Madaan et al., 2020), or political slant (Prabhumoye et al., 2018). Different modeling approaches have been proposed for TST, including methods that manipulate latent representations of text (Zhao et al., 2018; Prabhumoye et al., 2018) and techniques that identify and replace style-related lexicons directly (Li et al., 2018; Fu et al., 2019). Despite the growing interest in TST, reliably assessing the performance of TST models continues to be a bottleneck (Hu et al., 2022). While human evaluation is often regarded as the standard for capturing subtle cues in style, it is expensive, time-intensive, and difficult to reproduce at scale (Briakou et al., 2021b). Consequently, automated metrics have become a proxy for human judgment, but there is a notable lack of standardization and consensus on which metrics best capture style transfer accuracy, content preservation, and overall naturalness (Mir et al., 2019a; Briakou et al., 2021a). In addition, large language models (LLMs) could serve as alternatives to traditional human evaluation and automated metrics for TST evaluation (Ostheimer et al., 2024). However, the rapid evolution of LLMs, particularly for closed-source models, raises concerns about reproducibility (Gao et al., 2024; Chen et al., 2024).

We address this gap by examining existing and novel metrics for two popular TST subtasks: *sentiment transfer* (Prabhumoye et al., 2018) and *detoxification* (Dementieva et al., 2022). Our experiments span a multilingual setting, covering English, Hindi, and Bengali, to investigate the utility of these metrics across diverse linguistic contexts. We then conduct a meta-evaluation of the proposed metrics by measuring their correlation with human judgments. To further explore the potential of automated metrics, we also combine them in ensembles, experimentally creating hybrid scores. Additionally, we investigate the applicability of large language models (LLMs) as an alternative evaluation tool. Our results show that existing metrics newly applied to TST, hybrid approaches, and LLMs can improve correlation with human evaluations, offering a more robust and comprehensive assessment of TST outputs. Our experimental code and resources are released on GitHub.[1]

[1]`https://github.com/souro/tst_evaluation`

Proceedings of the 2025 Conference of the Nations of the Americas Chapter of the Association for Computational Linguistics: Human Language Technologies (Volume 4: Student Research Workshop), pages 418–434

2 Related Work

TST tasks are traditionally evaluated using three key dimensions: *style transfer accuracy*, *content preservation*, and *fluency* (Mukherjee and Dušek, 2024; Hu et al., 2022; Jin et al., 2022). Prior work underscores the challenge of jointly capturing subtle stylistic nuances and preserving semantic content (Briakou et al., 2021b; Tikhonov et al., 2019).

Style Transfer Accuracy A common approach is to train a dedicated classifier to check whether the transformed text reflects the intended style (Prabhumoye et al., 2018; Shen et al., 2017). Alternatively, unsupervised methods rely on distributional shifts in style-related features (Yang et al., 2018; Tikhonov et al., 2019).

Content Preservation Metrics such as *BLEU* (Papineni et al., 2002) and embedding-based similarity (Rahutomo et al., 2012; Reimers and Gurevych, 2019) often serve as proxies for semantic fidelity. However, they may overlook nuances introduced by stylistic transformations in both single-language and multilingual contexts (Yamshchikov et al., 2021; Briakou et al., 2021a), and recent studies highlight the shortcomings of traditional similarity measures when evaluating paraphrase-like modifications (Yamshchikov et al., 2021; Briakou et al., 2021b).

Fluency *Fluency* is typically estimated using perplexity from a pre-trained language model such as *GPT-2* (Radford et al., 2019). Nonetheless, perplexity may fail to capture context-specific grammatical coherence, especially if the style domain diverges from the model's training data (Tikhonov et al., 2019; Briakou et al., 2021b), and can yield inconsistent performance across languages (Briakou et al., 2021a).

3 Metrics Compared

We follow the criteria of transfer accuracy, content preservation, and fluency described in Section 2, and we conduct evaluations in two scenarios: (1) *reference-based*, where metrics are computed against a reference text (when available), and (2) *reference-free*, where metrics directly compare the generated text against the source text (measuring similarity or distance from the original), without requiring a reference.

Previously Used TST Metrics For style transfer accuracy, we include *Sentence Accuracy* based on a fine-tuned *XLM-RoBERTa-base* (Conneau et al., 2020) classifier (Prabhumoye et al., 2018), and *WMD* (Kusner et al., 2015; Wei et al., 2023; Mir et al., 2019b). For content preservation: *BLEU* (Papineni et al., 2002; Tikhonov et al., 2019), *Cosine Similarity* (Rahutomo et al., 2012; Reimers and Gurevych, 2019), ***Masked BLEU and Masked Cosine Similarity*** (Mukherjee et al., 2022), *ROUGE-2* and *ROUGE-L* (Lin and Hovy, 2003; Lin, 2004; Lin and Och, 2004; Yamshchikov et al., 2021). For fluency, we use *Perplexity* of *GPT-2* (Radford et al., 2019; Briakou et al., 2021c) and *MGPT* (Shliazhko et al., 2024).

Newly Applied Text Metrics We expand the TST evaluation by incorporating additional metrics from related NLP tasks, categorizing them into trainable and non-trainable metrics as well as word-overlap-based and embedding-based measures.

For style transfer accuracy, we utilize non-trainable statistical measures such as *Earth Mover's Distance (EMD)* (Rubner et al., 2000), *KL Divergence* (Kullback, 1997), *Cosine Similarity* (Rahutomo et al., 2012), and *Jensen-Shannon Divergence* (Lin, 1991), which quantify the distributional shift between source and generated text. Additionally, we incorporate a trainable *Classifier Confidence* score, derived from the Sentence Accuracy classifier described earlier.

For content preservation, we include both word-overlap-based and embedding-based metrics. The word-overlap-based metrics include *PINC* (Chen and Dolan, 2011), which measures the proportion of n-grams in the generated text that do not appear in the source text (higher values indicate greater lexical divergence), *METEOR* (Banerjee and Lavie, 2005), which accounts for synonymy and stemming, and *Translation Edit Rate (TER)* (Snover et al., 2006), which evaluates the number of edits required to transform the generated text into the reference. Embedding-based measures include *Word Mover's Distance (WMD)* (Kusner et al., 2015; Wei et al., 2023), *BERTScore* (Zhang et al., 2020), *S^3BERT* (Opitz and Frank, 2022), and *BLEURT* (Sellam et al., 2020), all of which assess content similarity based on contextualized vector representations. Additionally, we introduce *Tree Edit Distance (TED)* (Zhang and Shasha, 1989), which measures structural similarity by computing the minimum number of tree edit operations (insertion, deletion, substitution) required to transform one syntactic tree into another. This metric is particularly useful in evaluating syntactic shifts in generated text.

For fluency evaluation, we employ language model perplexity, using *Finetuned GPT-2* and *Finetuned MGPT* trained on target styles (see finetuning details in Appendix C). Lower perplexity scores indicate higher fluency, as they reflect the model's confidence in the generated text.

Novel Metrics We analyze the structural similarity between the source/reference and the system-generated outputs by parsing them into abstract meaning representation (AMR) (Banarescu et al., 2013) and syntactic dependency trees (Straka and Straková, 2017). AMR provides a semantic abstraction of sentences by capturing their core meaning as directed graphs, while syntactic dependencies represent the grammatical relationships between words in tree form. To measure structural similarity, we first convert syntactic dependency trees into AMR-style structure trees, ensuring both syntactic and semantic representations are in a comparable graph format. We then compute Smatch similarity (Cai and Knight, 2013) for both AMR graphs and the syntactic trees translated to AMR-style trees. Smatch (a graph-matching metric) computes the F-score between AMR graphs by aligning their nodes and edges optimally, regardless of differences in variable naming or graph representation. A higher Smatch score, i.e., a higher AMR graph and syntactic tree similarity, indicates greater preservation of meaning and syntactic structure in the transformed text.

LLM Prompting Following Ostheimer et al. (2024) and Mukherjee et al. (2024b), we use LLMs as TST evaluators and extend their methods to newer LLMs, more TST tasks, and additional languages. We used GPT-4 (Achiam et al., 2023) and Llama-3.1 8B (Dubey et al., 2024) to assess the TST tasks. We employed a Likert-scale-based approach to evaluate style transfer accuracy, content preservation, and fluency. To facilitate direct comparison with *Sentence Accuracy*, we also conducted a binary evaluation for style transfer accuracy (*GPT4-bin-acc, Llama-bin-acc*). Detailed prompt instructions are provided in Appendix D.

Hybrid We propose two ensemble-based oracle metrics – *Hybrid-Simulation* and *Hybrid-Learned* – to show the potential of integrating multiple evaluation metrics.[2] In *Hybrid-Simulation*, we first select the top three metrics (based on correlation with human judgments) for each task and language from Tables 1 and 2. We then conduct a simulation to determine the selected metrics' relative weights by tuning them on human-labeled target data and compute their geometric average to form the final ensemble score. In *Hybrid-Learned*, we train a random forest regressor (Liaw, 2002) using all available metrics as features and human ratings as the target labels. The model assigns importance scores to each metric, and we select the top three metrics with the highest normalized importance scores. Their geometric average, weighted by these importance scores, is used to generate the ensemble result. For details on the selected metrics and their respective weights, see Tables 5 and 6 in Appendix A.

Overall Score Following Loakman et al. (2023) and Yang and Jin (2023), we adopt the geometric mean of style transfer accuracy, content preservation, and fluency as a single aggregated score for comparison. We again aim to show the potential of this approach by producing oracle metrics. Based on the Pearson correlation results from our experiments (Tables 1, 2 and, 3), we first select the best-performing metrics for these three dimensions from previously used methods (*Existing*). We also do the same selection using newly proposed methods (excluding hybrid approaches), creating the $Ours_1$ score. We then extend $Ours_1$ by incorporating the top-performing metrics from our proposed approaches, including hybrids, to construct $Ours_2$. In addition to geometric mean scores, we directly prompt *GPT-4* and *Llama* for this task. Table 7 in Appendix A detail the metrics selected for each language and task.

4 Experiment Setup

Evaluation Data: Tasks, Languages and Model Outputs We evaluate our methods on the outputs of TST models and human annotations provided by Mukherjee et al. (2024b). This comprises two TST tasks – sentiment transfer (positive to negative statements and vice versa), where data is available for English, Hindi and Bengali, and detoxification (toxic to clean text), with English and Hindi data. Model outputs for all tasks were produced by GPT-3.5 (OpenAI, 2023), LLaMA-2-7B-Chat (Touvron et al., 2023) and Mistral-7B-Instruct (Jiang et al., 2023), as well as previous finetuned BART models by Mukherjee et al. (2024a, 2023).

Meta-Evaluation Approach We follow common practice for meta-evaluation (Kilickaya et al.,

[2]These metrics are considered "oracle", since the approach learns optimal weights based on the target data.

2017; Zhang et al., 2020; Liu et al., 2023) and compute all metrics' correlation with human judgment using Pearson (PC), Spearman (SC), and Kendall's Tau (KC) Correlations (Schober et al., 2018; Puka, 2011).

5 Results Analysis

Since we found that reference-based metrics generally underperform their reference-free variants, we focus on the reference-free setting in the analysis. We include reference-based results in Appendix B.

5.1 Style Transfer Accuracy

The results for style transfer accuracy in the reference-free setting are shown in Table 1.

Previously Used: *Sentence Accuracy* generally achieves moderate to good correlation with human judgments, suggesting that direct style classification accuracy can be a reliable indicator of style transfer quality. Meanwhile, *EMD* demonstrates a moderate degree of alignment, implying that capturing distributional shifts of stylistic cues correlates moderately with human perceptions.

Newly Applied: *Classifier Confidence*, *Cosine Similarity*, *KL Divergence*, and *Jensen-Shannon Divergence* generally exhibit stronger alignment with human judgments compared to existing metrics, highlighting the effectiveness of distributional measures for style intensity comparisons.

LLMs: *GPT-4* exhibits consistently high correlations, whereas *Llama* performs notably worse, although a binarized version (*Llama-bin-acc*) shows some moderate improvements.

Hybrid: *Hybrid-Simulation* demonstrates strong alignment with human ratings by combining multiple signals into a single score, while *Hybrid-Learned* performs comparably, though it may fall marginally below its simulation-based counterpart in certain cases.

Direct classification metrics reliably capture style accuracy, while distribution-based and LLM-based evaluations enhance overall alignment with human judgments, especially when integrated in hybrid frameworks. In English tasks, approaches like GPT-4 and hybrid methods achieve particularly high correlations, whereas in Hindi and Bengali, top metrics (e.g., KL, JS Divergence, and hybrid approaches) remain strong but show more pronounced performance gaps, potentially due to greater linguistic complexity.

5.2 Content Preservation

We present the meta-evaluation of content preservation metrics in a reference-free setting in Table 2.

Previously Used: *BLEU* generally shows low alignment with human judgments, while *Cosine Similarity* exhibits better performance in several tasks. *Masked BLEU* and *Masked Cosine Similarity* offer slight improvements over their unmasked counterparts, yet they still lag behind more recent methods. *ROUGE-2* and *ROUGE-L* provide moderate correlations but do not consistently outperform newer metrics.

Newly Applied: *BLEURT* remains consistently reliable, while *BERTScore* also proves robust across various styles and languages. *TER* and *TED* offer competitive results, particularly for certain language-specific tasks. In contrast, PINC shows weak correlations, indicating its limited effectiveness in capturing content preservation.

Novel: *Smatch (Dependency Trees)* and *Smatch (AMR)* outperform or at least match the performance of traditional metrics, though they generally fall behind the newly introduced text-based methods and LLM-driven approaches on average.

LLMs: *GPT-4* achieves higher correlations than traditional metrics across different styles and languages, demonstrating its strong ability to capture human-like judgments of text transformations. In contrast, *Llama* tends to underperform, indicating considerable variability in how well different LLMs reflect stylistic and content-based shifts.

Hybrid: *Hybrid-Simulation* achieves robust alignment with human ratings by unifying multiple signals into a single score, whereas *Hybrid-Learned* shows comparable performance, albeit slightly trailing the simulation-based approach in some scenarios.

5.3 Fluency

Table 3 presents fluency evaluation results. *GPT-2 Perplexity* displays limited correlations with human judgments, while *Finetuned GPT-2 Perplexity* yields only marginal gains. *MGPT Perplexity* and *Finetuned MGPT Perplexity* provide moderate improvements under fine-tuning, underscoring the importance of multilingual modeling and style-specific training for better alignment with human fluency assessments. *GPT-4* demonstrates relatively strong correlations with human assessments of fluency for sentiment-related tasks, suggesting it captures fluidity and coherence more effectively

Metrics	Sentiment Transfer English PC	SC	KC	Hindi PC	SC	KC	Bengali PC	SC	KC	Detoxification English PC	SC	KC	Hindi PC	SC	KC
Previously used & LLMs															
Sentence Accuracy	**0.51**	**0.49**	**0.48**	**0.61**	**0.61**	**0.59**	**0.57**	**0.57**	**0.54**	**0.36**	**0.36**	**0.35**	0.38	0.37	0.36
EMD	0.27	0.24	0.20	0.36	0.43	0.34	0.50	0.52	0.40	0.29	0.21	0.17	**0.47**	**0.53**	**0.43**
GPT4	**0.92**	**0.81**	**0.79**	**0.87**	**0.84**	0.79	**0.82**	**0.83**	**0.77**	**0.74**	**0.72**	**0.65**	**0.74**	**0.74**	**0.68**
GPT4-bin-acc	0.89	0.78	0.77	0.84	0.83	**0.80**	0.77	0.78	0.74	0.61	0.61	0.59	0.60	0.61	0.59
Llama	0.16	0.17	0.15	-0.11	-0.10	-0.09	-0.17	-0.15	-0.13	0.20	0.18	0.17	0.20	0.16	0.15
Llama-bin-acc	0.49	0.44	0.43	0.50	0.51	0.49	0.31	0.31	0.30	0.24	0.24	0.23	0.27	0.27	0.27
Newly applied & Novel															
Classifier Confidence	0.51	**0.43**	**0.35**	0.66	0.57	0.46	0.59	0.52	0.40	0.39	0.32	0.25	0.41	0.38	0.30
KL Divergence	0.59	0.31	0.24	0.66	0.66	0.54	**0.62**	0.62	0.50	**0.46**	0.46	0.36	0.51	**0.60**	0.49
Cosine Similarity	-0.55	-0.44	-0.36	-0.66	-0.67	-0.54	-0.53	-0.59	-0.46	-0.43	-0.40	-0.32	-0.48	-0.58	-0.47
Jensen-Shannon Divergence	**0.67**	0.40	0.32	**0.69**	**0.67**	**0.55**	**0.62**	**0.64**	**0.51**	0.41	**0.50**	**0.39**	**0.53**	**0.60**	**0.50**
Hybrid-Simulation	**0.69**	**0.40**	**0.32**	**0.71**	**0.67**	**0.54**	**0.62**	**0.64**	**0.51**	**0.44**	**0.47**	**0.37**	0.53	0.61	0.49
Hybrid-Learned	0.67	0.37	0.30	0.70	0.63	0.50	0.61	0.62	0.49	0.43	0.47	0.37	**0.55**	**0.62**	**0.50**

Table 1: Style transfer quality (reference-free). Pearson (PC), Spearman (SC) and Kendall's Tau (KC) correlations.

Metrics	Sentiment Transfer English PC	SC	KC	Hindi PC	SC	KC	Bengali PC	SC	KC	Detoxification English PC	SC	KC	Hindi PC	SC	KC
Previously used & LLMs															
BLEU	0.24	0.22	0.18	0.24	0.19	0.15	0.32	0.31	0.25	0.14	0.13	0.11	0.45	0.37	0.31
Cosine Similarity	**0.54**	**0.27**	**0.22**	**0.33**	**0.24**	**0.20**	**0.43**	**0.40**	**0.32**	**0.28**	**0.19**	**0.15**	**0.59**	**0.45**	**0.38**
Masked BLEU	0.21	0.21	0.17	0.15	0.12	0.10	0.23	0.24	0.19	0.15	0.15	0.12	0.45	0.39	0.32
Masked Cosine Similarity	0.36	0.17	0.14	0.19	0.13	0.11	0.28	0.29	0.23	0.23	0.15	0.12	0.56	**0.45**	0.37
METEOR	0.38	0.25	0.21	0.20	0.18	0.14	0.33	0.27	0.22	0.16	0.10	0.08	0.54	0.34	0.28
ROUGE-2	0.24	0.19	0.16	0.19	0.20	0.16	0.28	0.30	0.24	0.17	0.11	0.09	0.41	0.37	0.31
ROUGE-L	0.39	0.25	0.21	0.26	0.23	0.19	0.28	0.32	0.25	0.22	0.12	0.10	0.46	0.39	0.33
GPT4	**0.42**	**0.36**	**0.35**	**0.39**	**0.41**	**0.39**	**0.51**	**0.54**	**0.48**	**0.46**	**0.31**	**0.30**	**0.46**	**0.42**	**0.40**
Llama	0.24	0.26	0.24	0.32	0.28	0.26	0.32	0.38	0.35	0.25	0.11	0.10	0.28	0.16	0.16
Newly applied & Novel															
PINC	-0.18	-0.17	-0.15	-0.16	-0.12	-0.10	-0.27	-0.28	-0.23	-0.12	-0.12	-0.10	-0.41	-0.36	-0.30
WMD	0.35	0.28	0.23	0.27	0.24	0.20	0.34	0.35	0.28	0.15	0.14	0.11	0.41	0.38	0.32
BERTScore	**0.50**	**0.31**	**0.26**	**0.45**	0.33	0.27	0.49	0.44	0.36	0.21	0.19	0.15	**0.62**	0.38	0.31
Smatch (Dependency Trees)	0.25	0.24	0.20	0.18	0.20	0.17	0.26	0.30	0.25	0.16	0.15	0.12	0.34	0.31	0.26
Smatch (AMR)	0.38	0.25	0.20	0.22	0.20	0.17	0.32	0.32	0.26	0.19	0.13	0.11	0.37	0.34	0.28
S3BERT	0.46	0.23	0.19	0.30	0.18	0.14	0.30	0.30	0.24	0.22	0.20	0.16	0.49	0.38	0.31
BLEURT	0.47	0.30	0.25	0.41	**0.35**	**0.29**	**0.56**	**0.53**	**0.42**	0.18	0.17	0.14	**0.62**	**0.43**	**0.35**
TER	0.42	0.26	0.22	**0.45**	0.28	0.24	0.34	0.33	0.27	0.21	0.17	0.14	0.58	0.37	0.31
TED	0.43	0.24	0.22	0.42	0.29	0.25	0.20	0.28	0.24	**0.48**	**0.21**	**0.18**	0.48	0.36	0.30
Hybrid-Simulation	**0.57**	**0.32**	**0.26**	**0.48**	0.33	0.27	**0.57**	**0.53**	**0.43**	**0.28**	**0.19**	**0.15**	**0.68**	**0.43**	**0.35**
Hybrid-Learned	0.56	**0.32**	**0.26**	0.47	**0.35**	**0.29**	0.56	**0.53**	**0.43**	0.19	0.15	0.12	0.64	0.38	0.31

Table 2: Content preservation (reference-free). Pearson (PC), Spearman (SC) and Kendall's Tau (KC) correlations.

Metrics	Sentiment Transfer English PC	SC	KC	Hindi PC	SC	KC	Bengali PC	SC	KC	Detoxification English PC	SC	KC	Hindi PC	SC	KC
Previously used & LLMs															
Perplexity (GPT-2)	**0.13**	0.13	0.11	-0.11	-0.10	-0.08	-0.11	-0.07	-0.05	**0.06**	**0.00**	**0.00**	**0.17**	-0.13	-0.11
Perplexity (MGPT)	0.08	**0.19**	**0.15**	**0.00**	**0.07**	**0.05**	**0.16**	**0.19**	**0.15**	0.05	**0.00**	**0.00**	0.11	**0.03**	**0.03**
GPT4	**0.43**	**0.40**	**0.37**	**0.39**	**0.39**	**0.35**	**0.37**	**0.40**	**0.36**	**0.16**	**0.13**	**0.12**	**0.17**	**0.17**	**0.16**
Llama	0.17	0.18	0.17	0.15	0.17	0.15	0.08	0.06	0.06	**0.16**	**0.13**	**0.12**	-0.01	-0.02	-0.01
Newly applied															
Perplexity (Finetuned GPT-2)	**0.14**	**0.16**	**0.13**	0.08	0.14	0.11	0.02	0.05	0.04	**0.14**	0.00	0.00	0.11	-0.06	-0.05
Perplexity (Finetuned MGPT)	0.04	0.08	0.07	**0.17**	**0.15**	**0.12**	**0.23**	**0.21**	**0.16**	0.00	**0.03**	**0.03**	**0.23**	**0.04**	**0.03**

Table 3: Fluency (reference-free). Pearson (PC), Spearman (SC) and Kendall's Tau (KC) correlations.

when the stylistic shift involves changing sentiment. However, for detoxification tasks, its alignment with human judgments diminishes, indicating that removing toxicity poses different challenges for GPT-4. In contrast, *Llama* exhibits generally weaker correlations and struggles in various settings, implying that its evaluations of fluency do not consistently match human perceptions.

Language-wise, English generally shows better correlations and less variability across models over

	Sentiment Transfer									Detoxification					
	English			Hindi			Bengali			English			Hindi		
Metrics	PC	SC	KC	PC	SC	KC	PC	SC	KC	PC	SC	KC	PC	SC	KC
Existing	0.32	0.02	0.02	0.11	-0.02	-0.01	0.25	0.18	0.13	-0.04	-0.18	-0.14	0.07	-0.19	-0.14
GPT4	**0.73**	**0.62**	**0.54**	**0.78**	**0.75**	**0.61**	**0.78**	**0.77**	**0.63**	**0.65**	**0.62**	**0.51**	0.62	**0.59**	**0.46**
Llama	0.08	0.16	0.13	0.02	0.01	0.01	0.01	0.01	0.00	0.18	0.14	0.11	0.27	0.23	0.19
$Ours_1$	0.57	0.33	0.26	0.59	0.54	0.43	0.54	0.57	0.42	0.38	0.44	0.34	0.47	0.43	0.32
$Ours_2$	0.68	0.40	0.31	0.72	0.68	0.53	0.59	0.59	0.42	0.41	0.38	0.29	**0.63**	0.57	0.43

Table 4: Overall results (reference-free). Pearson (PC), Spearman (SC) and Kendall's Tau (KC) correlations.

Hindi and Bengali results.

5.4 Overall Score

Table 4 shows results for the different versions of the overall score aggregating style transfer accuracy, content preservation, and fluency.

Previously Used: Aggregating traditional metrics in the *Existing* metric often yields near-zero or negative correlations across various languages and tasks, indicating that simply merging these measures fails to capture the overall quality.

LLMs: In contrast, *GPT-4* consistently aligns well with human assessments of overall quality in both Sentiment Transfer and Detoxification. *Llama*, however, shows weaker correlations, indicating that not all LLMs possess the same evaluative capabilities.

Newly Applied & Hybrid: Our approaches (*$Ours_1$* and *$Ours_2$*) provide noticeable improvements over existing methods. Although they do not surpass GPT-4, they clearly outperform many traditional and alternative measures.

6 Conclusion

We presented a comprehensive evaluation of existing and newly proposed metrics for two TST subtasks—*Sentiment Transfer* and *Text Detoxification*—in English, Hindi, and Bengali. Our findings demonstrate that traditional word-overlap-based metrics like BLEU and ROUGE often show limited correlation with human judgments, whereas our proposed experimental metrics and prompted LLM-based evaluations provide significantly stronger alignment. Moreover, our oracle hybrid ensemble and combined approaches show an even greater potential of merging multiple metrics.

Limitations

Our study is limited to two specific tasks and three languages, leaving open the question of how well these metrics generalize to other styles, languages, and domains as future work. Additionally, while oracle ensemble metrics provide valuable insights, further research is needed to develop fully generalizable evaluation methods that do not rely on target-specific tuning.

Acknowledgments

This research was funded by the European Union (ERC, NG-NLG, 101039303) and Charles University project SVV 260 698. We acknowledge the use of resources provided by the LINDAT/CLARIAH-CZ Research Infrastructure (Czech Ministry of Education, Youth, and Sports project No. LM2018101). We also acknowledge Panlingua Language Processing LLP for collaborating on this research project.

Atul Kr. Ojha and John P. McCrae would like to acknowledge the support of the Research Ireland as part of Grant Number SFI/12/RC/2289_P2 Insight_2, Insight Research Ireland Centre for Data Analytics.

References

Josh Achiam, Steven Adler, Sandhini Agarwal, Lama Ahmad, Ilge Akkaya, Florencia Leoni Aleman, Diogo Almeida, Janko Altenschmidt, Sam Altman, Shyamal Anadkat, et al. 2023. GPT-4 technical report. *arXiv preprint arXiv:2303.08774*.

Laura Banarescu, Claire Bonial, Shu Cai, Madalina Georgescu, Kira Griffitt, Ulf Hermjakob, Kevin Knight, Philipp Koehn, Martha Palmer, and Nathan Schneider. 2013. Abstract Meaning Representation for sembanking. In *Proceedings of the 7th Linguistic Annotation Workshop and Interoperability with Discourse*, pages 178–186, Sofia, Bulgaria. Association for Computational Linguistics.

Satanjeev Banerjee and Alon Lavie. 2005. METEOR: An automatic metric for MT evaluation with improved correlation with human judgments. In *Proceedings of the ACL Workshop on Intrinsic and Extrinsic Evaluation Measures for Machine Translation and/or Summarization*, pages 65–72, Ann Arbor, Michigan. Association for Computational Linguistics.

Eleftheria Briakou, Sweta Agrawal, Joel Tetreault, and Marine Carpuat. 2021a. Evaluating the evaluation metrics for style transfer: A case study in multilingual formality transfer. In *Proceedings of the 2021 Conference on Empirical Methods in Natural Language Processing*, pages 1321–1336, Online and Punta Cana, Dominican Republic. Association for Computational Linguistics.

Eleftheria Briakou, Sweta Agrawal, Ke Zhang, Joel Tetreault, and Marine Carpuat. 2021b. A review of human evaluation for style transfer. In *Proceedings of the 1st Workshop on Natural Language Generation, Evaluation, and Metrics (GEM 2021)*, pages 58–67, Online. Association for Computational Linguistics.

Eleftheria Briakou, Sweta Agrawal, Ke Zhang, Joel Tetreault, and Marine Carpuat. 2021c. A review of human evaluation for style transfer. *arXiv preprint arXiv:2106.04747*.

Shu Cai and Kevin Knight. 2013. Smatch: an evaluation metric for semantic feature structures. In *Proceedings of the 51st Annual Meeting of the Association for Computational Linguistics (Volume 2: Short Papers)*, pages 748–752, Sofia, Bulgaria. Association for Computational Linguistics.

David Chen and William Dolan. 2011. Collecting highly parallel data for paraphrase evaluation. In *Proceedings of the 49th Annual Meeting of the Association for Computational Linguistics: Human Language Technologies*, pages 190–200, Portland, Oregon, USA. Association for Computational Linguistics.

Lingjiao Chen, Matei Zaharia, and James Zou. 2024. How Is ChatGPT's Behavior Changing Over Time? *Harvard Data Science Review*, 6(2).

Alexis Conneau, Kartikay Khandelwal, Naman Goyal, Vishrav Chaudhary, Guillaume Wenzek, Francisco Guzmán, Edouard Grave, Myle Ott, Luke Zettlemoyer, and Veselin Stoyanov. 2020. Unsupervised cross-lingual representation learning at scale. In *Proceedings of the 58th Annual Meeting of the Association for Computational Linguistics*, pages 8440–8451, Online. Association for Computational Linguistics.

Daryna Dementieva, Varvara Logacheva, Irina Nikishina, Alena Fenogenova, David Dale, Irina Krotova, Nikita Semenov, Tatiana Shavrina, and Alexander Panchenko. 2022. Russe-2022: Findings of the first russian detoxification shared task based on parallel corpora. *Komp'juternaja Lingvistika i Intellektual'nye Tehnologii*, 2022(21):114 – 131.

Abhimanyu Dubey, Abhinav Jauhri, Abhinav Pandey, Abhishek Kadian, Ahmad Al-Dahle, Aiesha Letman, Akhil Mathur, Alan Schelten, Amy Yang, Angela Fan, et al. 2024. The Llama 3 herd of models. *arXiv preprint arXiv:2407.21783*.

Yao Fu, Hao Zhou, Jiaze Chen, and Lei Li. 2019. Rethinking text attribute transfer: A lexical analysis. In *Proceedings of the 12th International Conference on Natural Language Generation*, pages 24–33, Tokyo, Japan. Association for Computational Linguistics.

Mingqi Gao, Xinyu Hu, Jie Ruan, Xiao Pu, and Xiaojun Wan. 2024. LLM-based NLG evaluation: Current status and challenges. *arXiv preprint arXiv:2402.01383*.

Zhiqiang Hu, Roy Ka-Wei Lee, Charu C. Aggarwal, and Aston Zhang. 2022. Text style transfer: A review and experimental evaluation. *SIGKDD Explor.*, 24(1):14–45.

Albert Q. Jiang, Alexandre Sablayrolles, Arthur Mensch, Chris Bamford, Devendra Singh Chaplot, Diego de las Casas, Florian Bressand, Gianna Lengyel, Guillaume Lample, Lucile Saulnier, Lélio Renard Lavaud, Marie-Anne Lachaux, Pierre Stock, Teven Le Scao, Thibaut Lavril, Thomas Wang, Timothée Lacroix, and William El Sayed. 2023. Mistral 7B. *arXiv preprint arXiv:2310.06825*.

Di Jin, Zhijing Jin, Zhiting Hu, Olga Vechtomova, and Rada Mihalcea. 2022. Deep learning for text style transfer: A survey. *Comput. Linguistics*, 48(1):155–205.

Mert Kilickaya, Aykut Erdem, Nazli Ikizler-Cinbis, and Erkut Erdem. 2017. Re-evaluating automatic metrics for image captioning. In *Proceedings of the 15th Conference of the European Chapter of the Association for Computational Linguistics: Volume 1, Long Papers*, pages 199–209, Valencia, Spain. Association for Computational Linguistics.

Solomon Kullback. 1997. *Information theory and statistics*. Courier Corporation.

Matt J. Kusner, Yu Sun, Nicholas I. Kolkin, and Kilian Q. Weinberger. 2015. From word embeddings to document distances. In *Proceedings of the 32nd International Conference on International Conference on Machine Learning - Volume 37*, ICML'15, page 957–966. JMLR.org.

Juncen Li, Robin Jia, He He, and Percy Liang. 2018. Delete, retrieve, generate: a simple approach to sentiment and style transfer. In *Proceedings of the 2018 Conference of the North American Chapter of the Association for Computational Linguistics: Human Language Technologies, Volume 1 (Long Papers)*, pages 1865–1874, New Orleans, Louisiana. Association for Computational Linguistics.

A Liaw. 2002. Classification and regression by randomforest. *R news*.

Chin-Yew Lin. 2004. ROUGE: A package for automatic evaluation of summaries. In *Text Summarization Branches Out*, pages 74–81, Barcelona, Spain. Association for Computational Linguistics.

Chin-Yew Lin and Eduard Hovy. 2003. Automatic evaluation of summaries using n-gram co-occurrence statistics. In *Proceedings of the 2003 Human Language Technology Conference of the North American Chapter of the Association for Computational Linguistics*, pages 150–157.

Chin-Yew Lin and Franz Josef Och. 2004. Automatic evaluation of machine translation quality using longest common subsequence and skip-bigram statistics. In *Proceedings of the 42nd Annual Meeting of the Association for Computational Linguistics (ACL-04)*, pages 605–612, Barcelona, Spain.

Jianhua Lin. 1991. Divergence measures based on the shannon entropy. *IEEE Transactions on Information theory*, 37(1):145–151.

Yang Liu, Dan Iter, Yichong Xu, Shuohang Wang, Ruochen Xu, and Chenguang Zhu. 2023. G-eval: NLG evaluation using gpt-4 with better human alignment. In *Proceedings of the 2023 Conference on Empirical Methods in Natural Language Processing*, pages 2511–2522, Singapore. Association for Computational Linguistics.

Tyler Loakman, Chen Tang, and Chenghua Lin. 2023. TwistList: Resources and baselines for tongue twister generation. In *Proceedings of the 61st Annual Meeting of the Association for Computational Linguistics (Volume 2: Short Papers)*, pages 579–589, Toronto, Canada. Association for Computational Linguistics.

Aman Madaan, Amrith Setlur, Tanmay Parekh, Barnabas Poczos, Graham Neubig, Yiming Yang, Ruslan Salakhutdinov, Alan W Black, and Shrimai Prabhumoye. 2020. Politeness transfer: A tag and generate approach. In *Proceedings of the 58th Annual Meeting of the Association for Computational Linguistics*, pages 1869–1881, Online. Association for Computational Linguistics.

Remi Mir, Bjarke Felbo, Nick Obradovich, and Iyad Rahwan. 2019a. Evaluating style transfer for text. In *Proceedings of the 2019 Conference of the North American Chapter ofthe Association for Computational Linguistics: Human Language Technologies,NAACL-HLT 2019, Minneapolis, MN, USA, June 2-7, 2019, Volume 1 (Longand Short Papers)*, pages 495–504. Association for Computational Linguistics.

Remi Mir, Bjarke Felbo, Nick Obradovich, and Iyad Rahwan. 2019b. Evaluating style transfer for text. In *Proceedings of the 2019 Conference of the North American Chapter of the Association for Computational Linguistics: Human Language Technologies, Volume 1 (Long and Short Papers)*, pages 495–504, Minneapolis, Minnesota. Association for Computational Linguistics.

Sourabrata Mukherjee, Akanksha Bansal, Atul Kr. Ojha, John P. McCrae, and Ondrej Dusek. 2023. Text detoxification as style transfer in English and Hindi. In *Proceedings of the 20th International Conference on Natural Language Processing (ICON)*, pages 133–144, Goa University, Goa, India. NLP Association of India (NLPAI).

Sourabrata Mukherjee and Ondrej Dušek. 2024. Text style transfer: An introductory overview. *arXiv preprint arXiv:2407.14822*.

Sourabrata Mukherjee, Zdenek Kasner, and Ondrej Dusek. 2022. Balancing the style-content trade-off in sentiment transfer using polarity-aware denoising. In *Text, Speech, and Dialogue - 25th International Conference, TSD 2022, Brno, Czech Republic, September 6-9, 2022, Proceedings*, volume 13502 of *Lecture Notes in Computer Science*, pages 172–186. Springer.

Sourabrata Mukherjee, Atul Kr. Ojha, Akanksha Bansal, Deepak Alok, John P. McCrae, and Ondrej Dusek. 2024a. Multilingual text style transfer: Datasets & models for Indian languages. In *Proceedings of the 17th International Natural Language Generation Conference*, pages 494–522, Tokyo, Japan. Association for Computational Linguistics.

Sourabrata Mukherjee, Atul Kr. Ojha, and Ondrej Dusek. 2024b. Are large language models actually good at text style transfer? In *Proceedings of the 17th International Natural Language Generation Conference*, pages 523–539, Tokyo, Japan. Association for Computational Linguistics.

OpenAI. 2023. Introducing ChatGPT. `https://openai.com/blog/chatgpt`. Accessed on January 9, 2024.

Juri Opitz and Anette Frank. 2022. SBERT studies meaning representations: Decomposing sentence embeddings into explainable semantic features. In *Proceedings of the 2nd Conference of the Asia-Pacific Chapter of the Association for Computational Linguistics and the 12th International Joint Conference on Natural Language Processing (Volume 1: Long Papers)*, pages 625–638, Online only. Association for Computational Linguistics.

Phil Sidney Ostheimer, Mayank Kumar Nagda, Marius Kloft, and Sophie Fellenz. 2024. Text style transfer evaluation using large language models. In *Proceedings of the 2024 Joint International Conference on Computational Linguistics, Language Resources and Evaluation (LREC-COLING 2024)*, pages 15802–15822, Torino, Italia. ELRA and ICCL.

Kishore Papineni, Salim Roukos, Todd Ward, and Wei-Jing Zhu. 2002. Bleu: a method for automatic evaluation of machine translation. In *Proceedings of the 40th Annual Meeting of the Association for Computational Linguistics*, pages 311–318, Philadelphia, Pennsylvania, USA. Association for Computational Linguistics.

Shrimai Prabhumoye, Yulia Tsvetkov, Ruslan Salakhutdinov, and Alan W Black. 2018. Style transfer through back-translation. In *Proceedings of the 56th Annual Meeting of the Association for Computational*

Linguistics (Volume 1: Long Papers), pages 866–876, Melbourne, Australia. Association for Computational Linguistics.

Llukan Puka. 2011. Kendall's tau. In *International Encyclopedia of Statistical Science*, pages 713–715, Berlin, Heidelberg. Springer Berlin Heidelberg.

Alec Radford, Jeff Wu, Rewon Child, David Luan, Dario Amodei, and Ilya Sutskever. 2019. Language models are unsupervised multitask learners. *OpenAI blog*.

Faisal Rahutomo, Teruaki Kitasuka, and Masayoshi Aritsugi. 2012. Semantic cosine similarity. In *The 7th international student conference on advanced science and technology ICAST*, volume 4, page 1.

Nils Reimers and Iryna Gurevych. 2019. Sentence-BERT: Sentence embeddings using Siamese BERT-networks. In *Proceedings of the 2019 Conference on Empirical Methods in Natural Language Processing and the 9th International Joint Conference on Natural Language Processing (EMNLP-IJCNLP)*, pages 3982–3992, Hong Kong, China. Association for Computational Linguistics.

Yossi Rubner, Carlo Tomasi, and Leonidas J Guibas. 2000. The earth mover's distance as a metric for image retrieval. *International journal of computer vision*, 40:99–121.

Patrick Schober, Christa Boer, and Lothar A Schwarte. 2018. Correlation coefficients: appropriate use and interpretation. *Anesthesia & analgesia*, 126:1763–1768.

Thibault Sellam, Dipanjan Das, and Ankur Parikh. 2020. BLEURT: Learning robust metrics for text generation. In *Proceedings of the 58th Annual Meeting of the Association for Computational Linguistics*, pages 7881–7892, Online. Association for Computational Linguistics.

Tianxiao Shen, Tao Lei, Regina Barzilay, and Tommi S. Jaakkola. 2017. Style Transfer from Non-Parallel Text by Cross-Alignment. In *Proc. NeurIPS*, pages 6830–6841.

Oleh Shliazhko, Alena Fenogenova, Maria Tikhonova, Anastasia Kozlova, Vladislav Mikhailov, and Tatiana Shavrina. 2024. mGPT: Few-shot learners go multilingual. *Transactions of the Association for Computational Linguistics*, 12:58–79.

Matthew Snover, Bonnie Dorr, Rich Schwartz, Linnea Micciulla, and John Makhoul. 2006. A study of translation edit rate with targeted human annotation. In *Proceedings of the 7th Conference of the Association for Machine Translation in the Americas: Technical Papers*, pages 223–231, Cambridge, Massachusetts, USA. Association for Machine Translation in the Americas.

Milan Straka and Jana Straková. 2017. Tokenizing, POS tagging, lemmatizing and parsing UD 2.0 with UDPipe. In *Proceedings of the CoNLL 2017 Shared Task: Multilingual Parsing from Raw Text to Universal Dependencies*, pages 88–99, Vancouver, Canada. Association for Computational Linguistics.

Alexey Tikhonov, Viacheslav Shibaev, Aleksander Nagaev, Aigul Nugmanova, and Ivan P. Yamshchikov. 2019. Style transfer for texts: Retrain, report errors, compare with rewrites. In *Proceedings of the 2019 Conference on Empirical Methods in NaturalLanguage Processing and the 9th International Joint Conference onNatural Language Processing, EMNLP-IJCNLP 2019, Hong Kong, China,November 3-7, 2019*, pages 3934–3943. Association for Computational Linguistics.

Hugo Touvron, Louis Martin, Kevin Stone, Peter Albert, Amjad Almahairi, Yasmine Babaei, Nikolay Bashlykov, Soumya Batra, Prajjwal Bhargava, Shruti Bhosale, Dan Bikel, et al. 2023. Llama 2: Open Foundation and Fine-tuned Chat Models. *arXiv preprint arXiv:2307.09288*.

Chengwei Wei, Bin Wang, and C.-C. Jay Kuo. 2023. Synwmd: Syntax-aware word mover's distance for sentence similarity evaluation. *Pattern Recognition Letters*, 170:48–55.

Ivan P. Yamshchikov, Viacheslav Shibaev, Nikolay Khlebnikov, and Alexey Tikhonov. 2021. Style-transfer and paraphrase: Looking for a sensible semantic similarity metric. *Proceedings of the AAAI Conference on Artificial Intelligence*, 35(16):14213–14220.

Dingyi Yang and Qin Jin. 2023. Attractive storyteller: Stylized visual storytelling with unpaired text. In *Proceedings of the 61st Annual Meeting of the Association for Computational Linguistics (Volume 1: Long Papers)*, pages 11053–11066, Toronto, Canada. Association for Computational Linguistics.

Zichao Yang, Zhiting Hu, Chris Dyer, Eric P. Xing, and Taylor Berg-Kirkpatrick. 2018. Unsupervised text style transfer using language models as discriminators. In *Advances in Neural Information Processing Systems 31: Annual Conferenceon Neural Information Processing Systems 2018, NeurIPS 2018, December3-8, 2018, Montréal, Canada*, pages 7298–7309.

Kaizhong Zhang and Dennis Shasha. 1989. Simple fast algorithms for the editing distance between trees and related problems. *SIAM Journal on Computing*, 18(6):1245–1262.

Tianyi Zhang, Varsha Kishore, Felix Wu, Kilian Q. Weinberger, and Yoav Artzi. 2020. BERTScore: Evaluating text generation with BERT. In *International Conference on Learning Representations*.

Junbo Jake Zhao, Yoon Kim, Kelly Zhang, Alexander M. Rush, and Yann LeCun. 2018. Adversarially regularized autoencoders. In *Proceedings of the*

35th International Conference on Machine Learning, ICML 2018, volume 80 of *Proceedings of Machine Learning Research*, pages 5897–5906, Stockholm, Sweden.

A Hybrid Approaches and Overall Score - Additional Details

In this section, we introduce our hybrid approaches by presenting both the selected metrics and their associated simulated weights, as well as the learned normalized feature importance. Further details on these weights, selected metrics, and feature scores can be found in Tables 5 and 6 respectively. Table 7 summarizes the selected metrics for each language and task, enabling single overall scores computation.

	Sentiment Transfer						Detoxification			
	Simulation			Learned			Simulation		Learned	
Metrics	English	Hindi	Bengali	English	Hindi	Bengali	English	Hindi	English	Hindi
BERTScore	0.20	0.40	0.40	-	0.36	0.14	-	-	-	0.30
BERTScore_IDF	-	-	-	0.27	0.35	-	-	-	-	0.11
BLEURT	0.30	0.20	0.50	0.43	0.29	0.65	-	0.40	-	-
BLEU	-	-	-	-	-	-	-	-	0.34	-
Masked BLEU	-	-	-	-	-	-	-	-	0.25	-
COSINE	0.50	-	0.10	0.30	-	0.21	0.20	0.30	-	-
TER	-	0.40	-	-	-	-	0.10	0.30	-	0.59
TED	-	-	-	-	-	-	0.70	-	0.40	-

	Sentiment Transfer						Detoxification			
	Simulation			Learned			Simulation		Learned	
Metrics	English	Hindi	Bengali	English	Hindi	Bengali	English	Hindi	English	Hindi
EMD	-	-	-	-	0.33	0.24	-	-	-	-
JS	0.60	0.40	0.40	0.38	0.46	0.35	0.30	0.30	0.42	0.45
KL	0.15	0.20	0.30	0.38	-	0.41	0.50	0.50	0.27	0.22
Style_Classifier_Confidence	0.25	0.40	0.30	0.24	0.21	-	0.20	0.20	0.31	0.33

Table 5: Hybrid Simulation - selected metrics and its weights.

	Sentiment Transfer (CS)			Detoxification	
Metrics	English	Hindi	Bengali	English	Hindi
BLEURT	0.16	0.13	0.37	0.05	0.04
COSINE	0.11	0.08	0.12	0.08	0.04
BERTScore_IDF	0.10	0.16	0.03	0.05	0.19
BERTScore	0.09	0.17	0.08	0.05	0.07
S3BERT	0.07	0.08	0.04	0.05	0.02
WMD	0.07	0.03	0.03	0.04	0.01
AMR_SMATCH	0.06	0.02	0.02	0.05	0.02
BLEU	0.06	0.03	0.07	0.12	0.03
ROUGE-L	0.06	0.02	0.03	0.07	0.05
Masked Cosine Similarity	0.06	0.02	0.02	0.06	0.04
Masked BLEU	0.05	0.04	0.03	0.09	0.02
METEOR	0.03	0.04	0.04	0.05	0.02
TED	0.02	0.04	0.02	0.14	0.02
SMATCH	0.02	0.02	0.02	0.02	0.03
TER	0.02	0.16	0.04	0.03	0.38
ROUGE-2	0.01	0.02	0.03	0.04	0.01
PINC	0.01	0.01	0.01	0.02	0.01
	Sentiment Transfer (SA)			**Detoxification**	
Metrics	**English**	**Hindi**	**Bengali**	**English**	**Hindi**
KL	0.34	0.17	0.33	0.21	0.18
JS	0.33	0.38	0.29	0.33	0.37
Style_Classifier_Confidence	0.21	0.17	0.18	0.25	0.26
EMD	0.11	0.27	0.20	0.21	0.18
Sentence_Accuracy	0.01	0.00	0.00	0.00	0.01

Table 6: Hybrid-Learned - metrics and its learned feature importance scores (normalized).

B Additional Results (reference-based)

In addition to the reference-free evaluations shown in Tables 1 and 2, the corresponding reference-based results are provided in Tables 8 and 9, respectively.

Task	Languages	Approach	BERTScore	BLEURT	Cosine Similarity	Hybrid_Learned_CP	Hybrid_Simulation_CP	Hybrid_Simulation_ST	JS	KL	Perplexity (MGPT)	MGPT_FT_PPL	Perplexity (GPT-2)	GPT2_FT_PPL	Sentence Accuracy	TED	TER
Sentiment Transfer	English	Existing	✗	✗	✓	✗	✗	✗	✗	✗	✗	✗	✓	✗	✓	✗	✗
		$Ours_1$	✓	✗	✗	✗	✗	✗	✓	✗	✗	✗	✗	✓	✗	✗	✗
		$Ours_2$	✗	✗	✗	✗	✓	✓	✗	✗	✗	✗	✗	✓	✗	✗	✗
	Hindi	Existing	✗	✗	✓	✗	✗	✗	✗	✗	✓	✗	✗	✗	✓	✗	✗
		$Ours_1$	✗	✗	✗	✗	✗	✗	✓	✗	✗	✓	✗	✗	✗	✗	✓
		$Ours_2$	✗	✗	✗	✗	✓	✓	✗	✗	✗	✓	✗	✗	✗	✗	✗
	Bengali	Existing	✗	✗	✓	✗	✗	✗	✗	✗	✓	✗	✗	✗	✓	✗	✗
		$Ours_1$	✗	✓	✗	✗	✗	✗	✓	✗	✗	✓	✗	✗	✗	✗	✗
		$Ours_2$	✗	✗	✗	✗	✓	✓	✗	✗	✗	✓	✗	✗	✗	✗	✗
Detoxification	English	Existing	✗	✗	✓	✗	✗	✗	✗	✗	✗	✗	✓	✗	✓	✗	✗
		$Ours_1$	✗	✗	✗	✗	✗	✗	✗	✓	✗	✗	✗	✓	✗	✓	✗
		$Ours_2$	✗	✗	✗	✗	✓	✓	✗	✗	✗	✗	✗	✓	✗	✗	✗
	Hindi	Existing	✗	✗	✓	✗	✗	✗	✗	✗	✓	✗	✗	✗	✓	✗	✗
		$Ours_1$	✗	✓	✗	✗	✗	✗	✓	✗	✗	✓	✗	✗	✗	✗	✗
		$Ours_2$	✗	✗	✗	✓	✗	✓	✗	✗	✗	✓	✗	✗	✗	✗	✗

Table 7: Overall Scores – language and task-wise selected metrics.

	Sentiment Transfer (reference-based)									Detoxification (reference-based)					
	English			Hindi			Bengali			English			Hindi		
Metrics	**PC**	**SC**	**KC**	**PC**	**SC**	**KC**	**PC**	**SC**	**KC**	**PC**	**SC**	**KC**	**PC**	**SC**	**KC**
EMD	-0.22	-0.27	-0.22	-0.28	-0.33	-0.26	-0.33	-0.37	-0.29	-0.28	-0.23	-0.18	-0.31	-0.28	-0.22
KL_DIS	-0.30	-0.36	-0.29	-0.62	-0.58	-0.46	-0.46	-0.48	-0.38	-0.34	-0.30	-0.24	-0.36	-0.28	-0.23
Cosine Similarity	**0.32**	**0.32**	**0.26**	**0.59**	**0.60**	**0.49**	**0.34**	**0.45**	**0.35**	**0.28**	**0.32**	**0.25**	**0.30**	**0.32**	**0.26**
JS_SIM	-0.29	-0.36	-0.29	-0.62	-0.58	-0.46	-0.46	-0.47	-0.37	-0.28	-0.29	-0.23	-0.35	-0.28	-0.23

Table 8: Automatic metrics results reference-based: style transfer. Pearson Correlation: PC, Spearman Correlation: SC Kendall Tau Correlation: KC

	Sentiment Transfer (reference-based)									Detoxification (reference-based)					
	English			Hindi			Bengali			English			Hindi		
Metrics	**PC**	**SC**	**KC**	**PC**	**SC**	**KC**	**PC**	**SC**	**KC**	**PC**	**SC**	**KC**	**PC**	**SC**	**KC**
Previously used & LLMs															
BLEU	0.18	0.22	0.18	0.17	0.16	0.13	0.19	0.20	0.16	0.10	0.10	0.08	0.18	0.18	0.14
Cosine Similarity	**0.39**	**0.26**	**0.22**	**0.20**	**0.24**	**0.19**	**0.31**	**0.32**	**0.25**	**0.18**	**0.13**	**0.10**	**0.30**	**0.25**	**0.20**
Masked BLEU	0.13	0.19	0.15	0.16	0.16	0.13	0.18	0.17	0.13	0.11	0.11	0.09	0.16	0.15	0.12
Masked Cosine Similarity	0.25	0.21	0.17	0.15	0.16	0.13	0.24	0.28	0.22	0.17	**0.13**	**0.10**	0.24	0.22	0.18
METEOR	0.31	0.22	0.18	0.12	0.13	0.10	0.16	0.18	0.14	0.11	0.09	0.08	0.23	0.17	0.14
ROUGE-2	0.22	0.21	0.17	0.17	0.18	0.15	0.23	0.23	0.18	0.11	0.09	0.07	0.24	0.24	0.20
ROUGE-L	0.31	0.24	0.20	0.19	0.19	0.16	0.21	0.23	0.18	0.13	0.09	0.07	0.23	0.24	0.19
Newly applied & Novel															
PINC	-0.12	-0.14	-0.12	-0.13	-0.12	-0.10	-0.17	-0.18	-0.16	-0.09	-0.07	-0.06	-0.17	-0.15	-0.13
WMD	0.25	0.26	0.21	0.21	0.22	0.18	0.25	0.27	0.21	0.11	0.08	0.07	0.19	0.19	0.15
BERTScore	0.34	**0.27**	**0.22**	0.25	0.25	0.20	0.24	0.25	0.20	0.18	0.16	**0.13**	0.32	0.19	0.15
UDPIPE_SMATCH	0.16	0.20	0.16	0.19	0.19	0.16	0.18	0.18	0.14	0.16	0.15	0.12	0.15	0.14	0.12
AMR_SMATCH	0.28	**0.27**	0.22	0.22	0.20	0.17	0.25	0.24	0.19	0.12	0.09	0.07	0.18	0.17	0.14
S3BERT	**0.41**	0.26	0.21	0.28	0.22	0.18	0.23	0.26	0.21	0.13	0.13	0.11	0.26	0.20	0.16
BLEURT	0.31	0.25	0.20	0.31	**0.31**	**0.25**	**0.42**	**0.41**	**0.32**	0.15	**0.17**	**0.13**	**0.35**	**0.23**	**0.19**
TER	0.35	0.23	0.19	**0.39**	0.26	0.21	0.22	0.21	0.17	**0.24**	0.10	0.09	0.23	0.14	0.12
TED	-0.29	-0.23	-0.20	-0.35	-0.26	-0.22	-0.17	-0.15	-0.13	-0.40	-0.16	-0.13	-0.32	-0.20	-0.17

Table 9: Automatic metrics results reference-based: content preservation. Pearson Correlation: PC, Spearman Correlation: SC Kendall Tau Correlation: KC

C GPT-2 and MGPT Finetune Details

We fine-tune both *GPT-2*[3] and *mGPT*[4] using the same hyperparameter configuration obtained through few random optimization experiments. Specifically, we set the maximum token length to 512 and use the target-style training data from (Mukherjee et al., 2024b) for fine-tuning. Each model is trained for 10 epochs with a batch size of 2, a learning rate of 1×10^{-5}, and a weight decay of 0.01.

D Prompt Details

This section provides a collection of example prompts (in English) for the evaluation of Text Sentiment Transfer task (prompt details in Tables 10, 11, 12 and 13)

[3]https://huggingface.co/openai-community/gpt2

[4]https://huggingface.co/ai-forever/mGPT

Prompt	
	Sentiment transfer task: transfer the sentiment of a sentence (from positive to negative or negative to positive) while keeping the rest of the sentiment-independent content unchanged. Please rate the sentiment transfer accuracy of the negative to positive sentiment transfer task between the following English source sentence S1 and the sentiment-transferred sentence S2. Use a scale of 1 to 5, where 1 indicates that the sentiment in S1 is completely identical to the sentiment in S2, and 5 indicates that the sentiment has been completely transferred to the target sentiment in S2. S1: so he can charge a bloody fortune for them. S2: so he can charge a fair amount of money for them. Sentiment transfer accuracy rating (on a scale of 1 to 5) =

Table 10: A Sample prompt for Sentiment Transfer Accuracy evaluation in Sentiment Transfer in English. It contains task definition, instruction, **and** input.

Prompt	
	Sentiment transfer task: transfer the sentiment of a sentence (from positive to negative or negative to positive) while keeping the rest of the sentiment-independent content unchanged. Please act as a binary classifier to evaluate the sentiment transfer accuracy of the positive to negative sentiment transfer task in English. Determine whether the target sentiment has been successfully transferred to the generated sentence (S2) from the source sentence (S1).If the target sentiment has been successfully transferred to S2, output '1'. If the target sentiment has not been successfully transferred to S2, output '0'. S1: so he can charge a bloody fortune for them. S2: so he can charge a fair amount of money for them. Sentiment transfer accuracy classification (0 or 1) =

Table 11: A Sample prompt for Sentiment Transfer Accuracy (binary) evaluation in Sentiment Transfer in English. It contains task definition, instruction, **and** input.

Prompt	
	Sentiment transfer task: transfer the sentiment of a sentence (from positive to negative or negative to positive) while keeping the rest of the content unchanged. Please rate the content preservation between the following English source sentence S1 and the sentiment-transferred sentence S2 for the negative to positive sentiment transfer task on a scale of 1 to 5, where 1 indicates very low content preservation and 5 indicates very high content preservation. To determine the content preservation between these two sentences, consider only the information conveyed by the sentences and ignore any differences in sentiment due to the negative to positive sentiment transfer. S1: so he can charge a bloody fortune for them. S2: so he can charge a fair amount of money for them. Content Preservation rating (on a scale of 1 to 5) =

Table 12: A sample prompt for Content Preservation evaluation in Sentiment Transfer in English. It contains task definition, instruction, **and** input.

Prompt	
	Please rate the fluency of the following English sentence S on a scale of 1 to 5, where 1 represents poor fluency, and 5 represents excellent fluency. S: so he can charge a fair amount of money for them. Fluency rating (on a scale of 1 to 5) =

Table 13: A same prompt for Fluency evaluation in Sentiment Transfer in English. It contains instruction, **and** input.

E Additional Statistics

In this section, we provide additional statistics for the Text Sentiment Transfer task in English, focusing on reference-free evaluation metrics. Specifically, we present heatmaps illustrating the correlations between each pair of metrics for style transfer accuracy, content preservation, and fluency in Figures 4, 5, and 6, respectively. We also show the distribution of each metric's values in Figures 1, 2, and 3 for style transfer accuracy, content preservation, and fluency, thereby offering a more comprehensive view of their behavior.

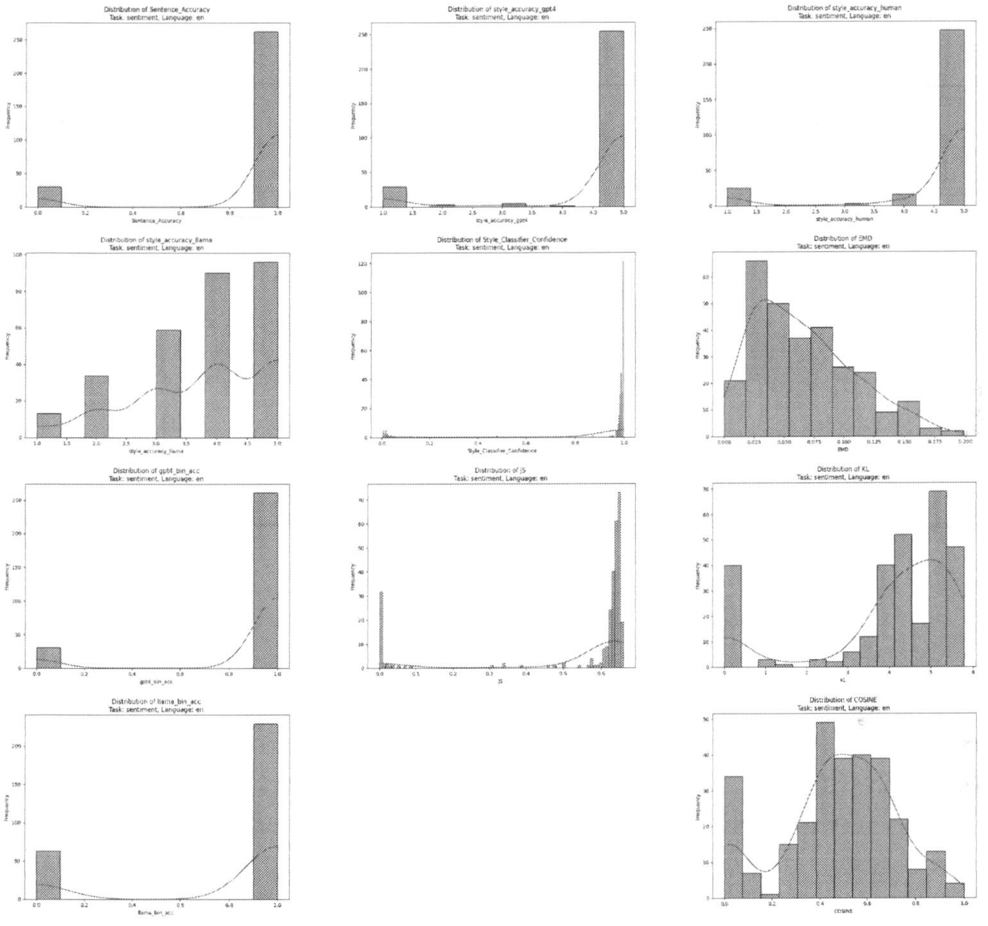

Figure 1: Style Transfer Accuracy - metrics' value distribution.

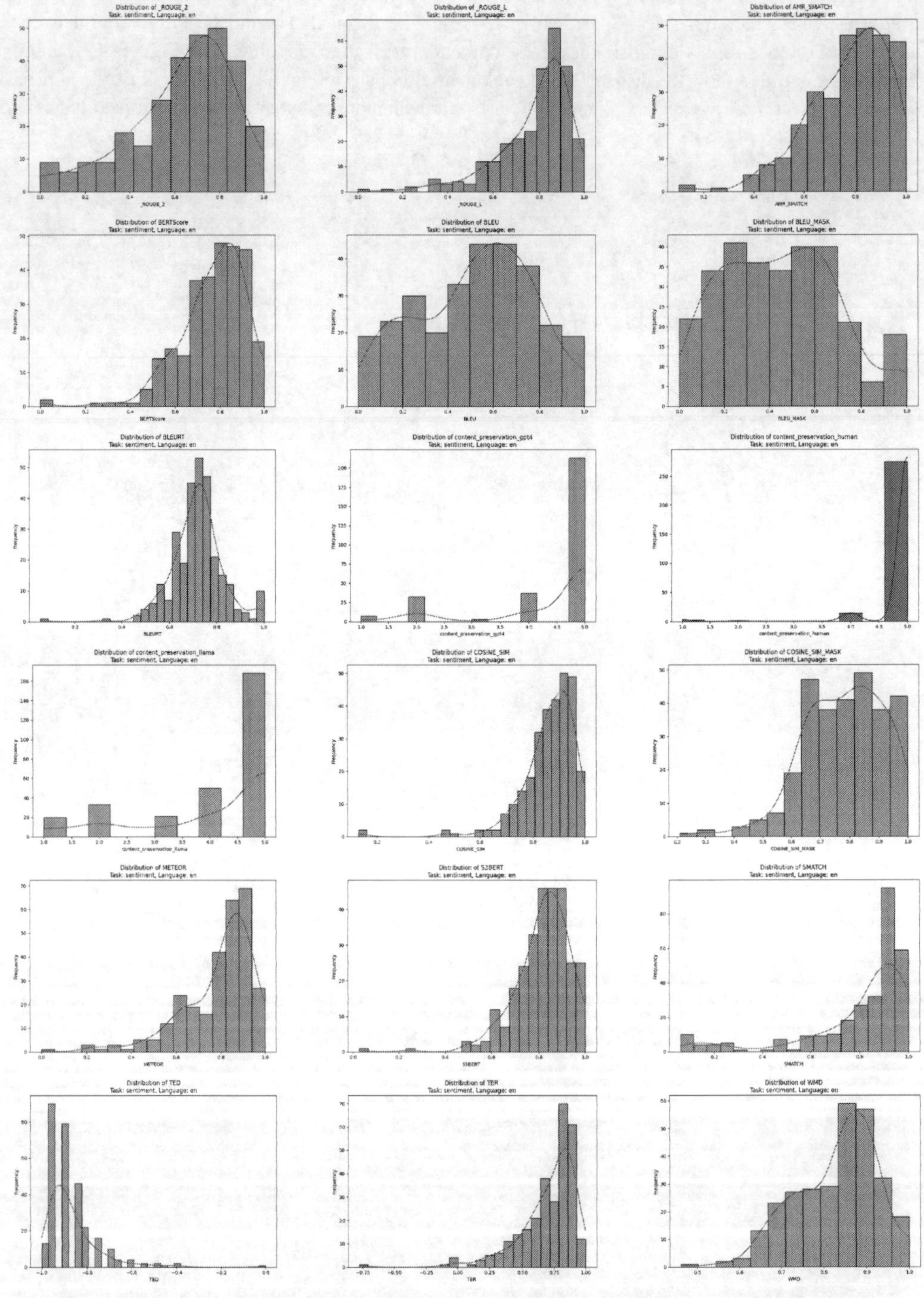

Figure 2: Content Preservation- - metrics' value distribution.

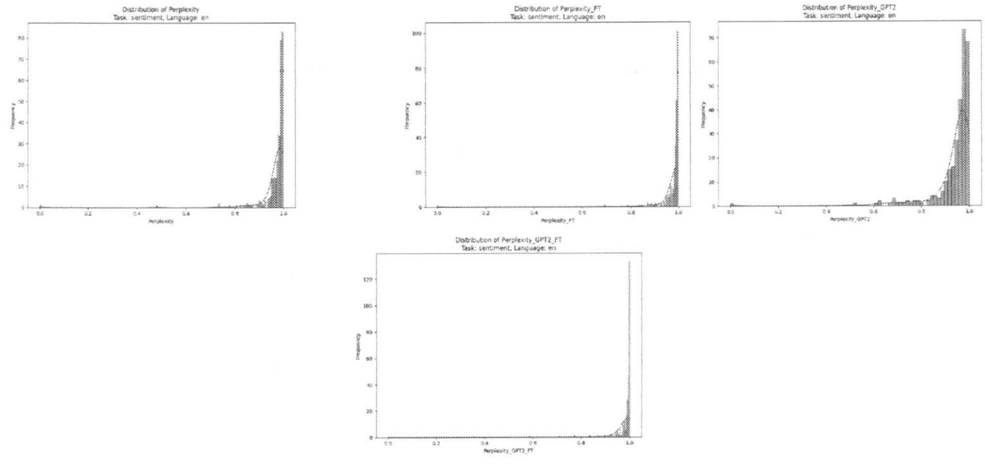

Figure 3: Fluency - metrics' value distribution.

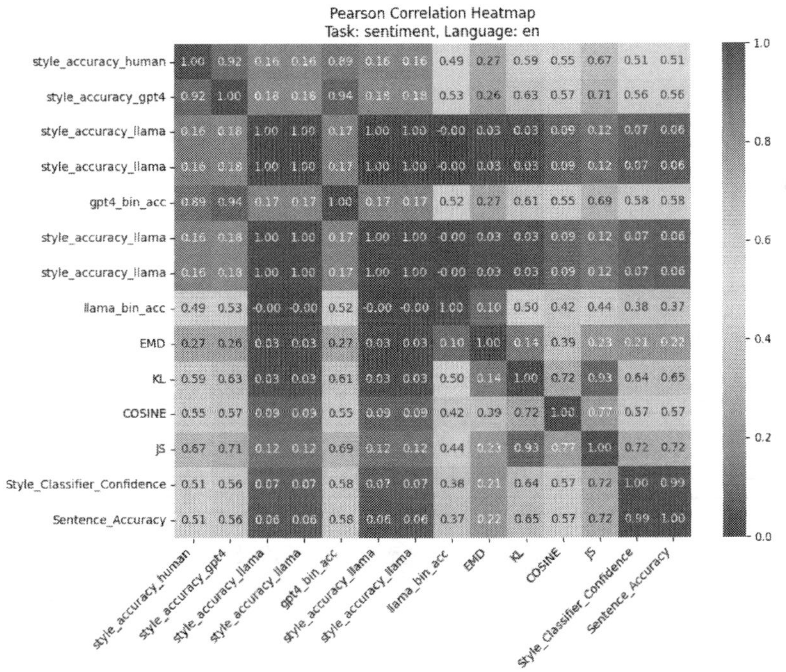

Figure 4: Sentence Accuracy - correlations' heatmap between the metrics.

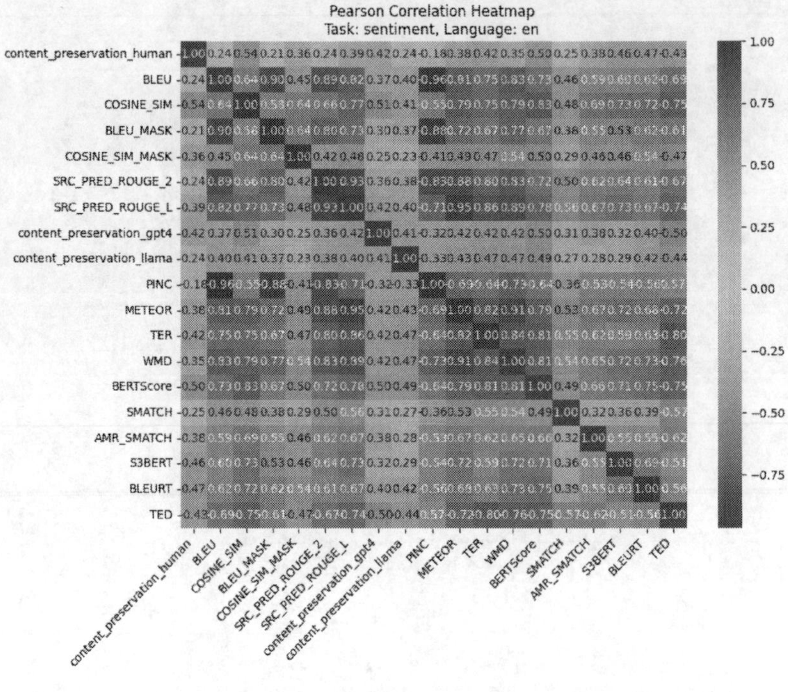

Figure 5: Content Preservation - correlations' heatmap between the metrics.

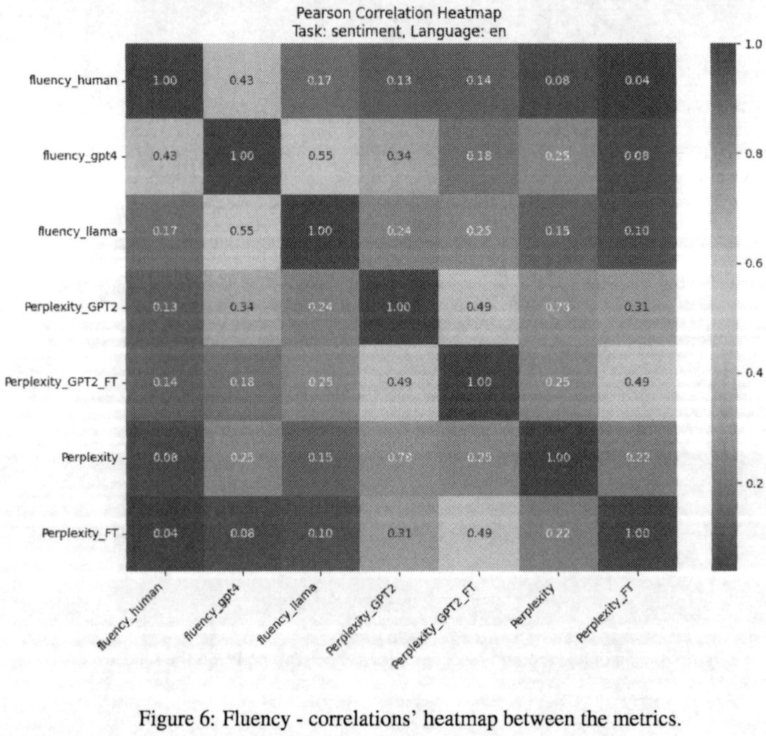

Figure 6: Fluency - correlations' heatmap between the metrics.

(CPER) From Guessing to Asking: An Approach to Resolving the Persona Knowledge Gap in LLMs during Multi-Turn Conversations

Sarvesh Baskar[1,2], **Tanmay Verelakar**[1], **Srinivasan Parthasarathy**[3], **Manas Gaur**[2]
[1]BITS Pilani, Goa, India
[2]University of Maryland Baltimore County, Baltimore, MD, USA
[3]Ohio State University, Columbia, OH, USA
{sarvesh, manas}@umbc.edu, tanmayv@bits-pilani.ac.in, srini@@cse.ohio-state.edu

Abstract

In multi-turn dialogues, large language models (LLM) face a critical challenge of ensuring coherence while adapting to user-specific information. This study introduces the *persona knowledge gap*, the discrepancy between a model's internal understanding and the knowledge required for coherent, personalized conversations. While prior research has recognized these gaps, computational methods for their identification and resolution remain underexplored. We propose **C**onversation **P**reference **E**licitation and **R**ecommendation (**CPER**), a novel framework that dynamically detects and resolves persona knowledge gaps using intrinsic uncertainty quantification and feedback-driven refinement. **CPER** consists of three key modules: a *Contextual Understanding Module* for preference extraction, a *Dynamic Feedback Module* for measuring uncertainty and refining persona alignment, and a *Persona-Driven Response Generation* module for adapting responses based on accumulated user context. We evaluate **CPER** on two real-world datasets: CCPE-M for preferential movie recommendations and ESConv for mental health support. Using **A/B testing**, human evaluators preferred **CPER**'s responses **42%** more often than baseline models in CCPE-M and **27%** more often in ESConv. A qualitative human evaluation confirms that **CPER**'s responses are preferred for maintaining contextual relevance and coherence, particularly in longer (12+ turn) conversations[1].

1 Introduction

Human communication fundamentally relies on implicit context and incomplete information, requiring iterative dialogue to bridge knowledge gaps and build shared understanding (Clark and Brennan, 1991). This natural process reveals a critical **knowledge gap** in human-AI interactions, a systemic disparity between the rich contextual information needed for coherent, personalized conversations and the limited context available to Large Language Models (LLMs). While humans naturally resolve ambiguities through iterative questioning, LLMs generate responses based solely on immediate input, lacking mechanisms to actively seek missing user-specific context (Tint et al., 2024). This gap impedes their ability to retain and adapt to evolving user preferences, emotional states, or domain-specific context across multi-turn conversations (Kwan et al., 2024), leading to incoherent or generic interactions over time (Cuskley et al., 2024). These challenges are particularly pronounced in multi-turn conversational AI systems, which require persistent memory and adaptive reasoning to sustain coherent user engagement. Our research addresses two critical questions: *How can LLMs reduce knowledge gaps related to user-specific context in multi-turn conversations?* and *To what extent does closing these gaps improve the coherence and relevance of conversational AI systems?*

Building on the Self-Refine framework (Madaan et al., 2023), we propose a novel approach to close knowledge gaps through three connected modules (Figure 1): **Contextual Understanding Module**: Analyzes and quantifies uncertainty in user preferences (*Eq. 3*); **Dynamic Feedback Module**: Measures knowledge disparities between user persona and LLM's context understanding (*Eq. 7*), prompting targeted clarification questions; **Persona-Driven Response Generation**: Creates contextually aware responses by integrating accumulated user information. This framework enables LLMs to mimic human conversation patterns by actively resolving ambiguities while maintaining personal context. Evaluations on CCPE-M and ESConv datasets show marked improvements in both preference tracking and

[1]Code is available at: `https://shorturl.at/wWw6s`

Proceedings of the 2025 Conference of the Nations of the Americas Chapter of the Association for Computational Linguistics: Human Language Technologies (Volume 4: Student Research Workshop), pages 435–447
April 30 - May 1, 2025 ©2025 Association for Computational Linguistics

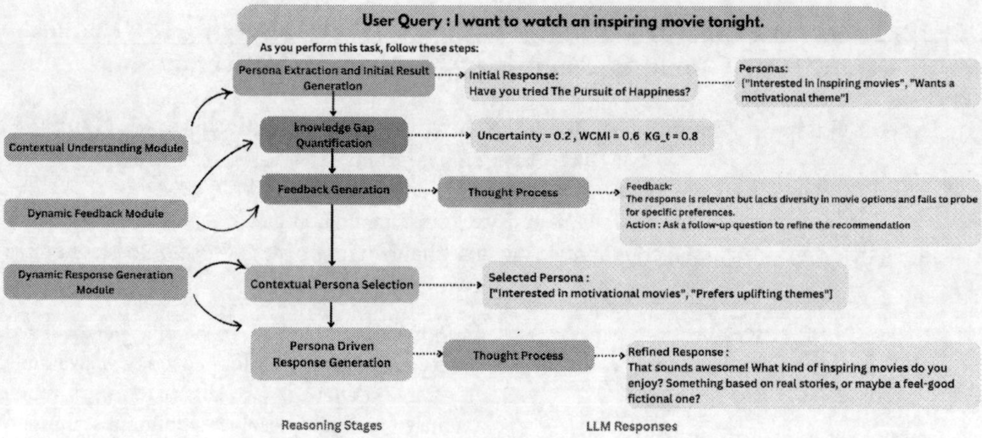

Figure 1: Illustration of the **CPER** framework applied to a user query for *inspiring movie recommendations*, highlighting its three key stages: context analysis, feedback processing, and persona-driven response generation. The diagram demonstrates how persona extraction, knowledge gap resolution, and iterative refinement ensure consistency and relevance. Dotted lines represent the internal process of identifying and addressing knowledge gaps.

emotional consistency compared to existing approaches. Our key contributions are:

- We define the *persona knowledge gap* in multi-turn conversations, highlighting LLMs' challenges in maintaining user-specific context.
- We introduce a method to quantify this gap, enabling systematic evaluation of LLMs' consistency in personalized interactions.
- We propose a novel framework that dynamically refines user-specific knowledge by addressing persona knowledge gaps, enhancing coherence in evolving conversations.
- We validate our approach through experiments on CCPE-M (user preferences) and ESConv (emotional support), achieving notable improvements over baselines.

2 Related Work

Advancements in personalized conversational agents stem from improvements in personalization, recommendation systems, and knowledge gap identification in LLMs. Zhang et al. (2024) introduced a memory-based framework for medical assistants, while Raj et al. (2024) proposed K-PERM, a persona-driven response model integrating external knowledge. However, maintaining consistency across multiple conversation turns remains a challenge. Conversational recommendation systems enhance interactions through dynamic context understanding. Dao et al. (2023) developed a descriptive graph model for better item recommendations, and Feng et al. (2024) introduced a multi-LLM framework that detects uncertainty and abstains from answering when needed. Meanwhile, Cheng et al. (2024) and Wu et al. (2024) focused on evolving personas and preference alignment but often rely on static persona modeling. Unlike prior work, our framework dynamically detects and resolves knowledge gaps in multi-turn conversations. By actively identifying missing information and asking clarification questions, our system shifts conversational AI from passive response generation to adaptive, context-aware reasoning. For further details, see §A.

3 Datasets

We evaluate our **CPER** framework on two benchmark datasets: **CCPE-M** and **ESConv**, which address two key aspects of the **persona knowledge gap**: (1) tracking user preferences in multi-turn conversations and (2) maintaining coherence across extended interactions.

The **CCPE-M** (Coached Conversational Preference Elicitation for Movies) dataset (Radlinski et al., 2019) contains 502 dialogues with over 12,000 annotated utterances, capturing user-assistant interactions in a movie recommendation setting. Each dialogue is annotated with entity mentions, preference statements, and descriptive justifications, enabling an assessment of how well a system retains evolving user preferences. Traditional LLMs often struggle with knowledge gaps in this dataset,

Dataset	Multi-Turn	Personalization	Recommendation	Follow-Up Questions
CCPE-M	✓	✓	✓	✓
ESConv	✓	✓	✓	✓
EmpatheticDialogues (ED)	✓	✗	✗	✓
DailyDialog (DD)	✓	✗	✗	✗
Persona-Chat (PC)	✓	✓	✗	✗
OpenDialKG (ODKG)	✓	✗	✓	✗
LaMP Benchmark	✓	✓	✗	✗
FoCus	✓	✓	✗	✗

Table 1: Comparison of datasets based on key conversational AI features. CCPE-M and ESConv were chosen due to their strong support for multi-turn dialogues, personalization, and follow-up question capabilities, which are essential for evaluating conversational agents.

failing to recall prior user preferences and generating inconsistent recommendations. **CPER** addresses this by dynamically refining responses based on user feedback.

The dataset **ESConv** (Emotional Support Conversation) (Liu et al., 2021) consists of 1,300 dialogues spanning 10 problem domains, such as depression and job crises. Unlike task-oriented datasets, ESConv evaluates emotionally supportive interactions, where maintaining contextual understanding across turns is crucial. Conversations are annotated with supportive strategies like self-disclosure and affirmation. Standard LLMs exhibit knowledge gaps by failing to sustain emotional continuity, leading to disconnected responses. **CPER** mitigates this by improving emotional consistency and context retention over multiple turns.

4 CPER Framework

The **CPER** framework dynamically refines responses through iterative feedback and persona adaptation, as formalized in Algorithm 1 (Fig. 1), ensuring coherent, personalized dialogues.

Persona Extraction and Initial Generation:
The module extracts an implicit user persona for a particular turn t (p_t) from the input query x, conversation history, and prior context. Using task-specific prompt p_{gen}, the LLM $\mathcal{M}$ generates an initial response:

$$y_0, p_t = \mathcal{M}(p_{\text{gen}} \mid\mid x) \tag{1}$$

where $||$ means concatenation. Semantic embeddings $e_i \in \mathbb{R}^d$ are computed via **"bge-large-en-v1.5"** for persona analysis:

$$e_i = \text{BGE}(r_i) \tag{2}$$

These embeddings drive uncertainty estimation, alignment scoring, and adaptive persona updates.

Algorithm 1 **CPER** Algorithm

Require: Dialogue $\{x_1, x_2, \ldots, x_T\}$, model $\{\mathcal{M}\}$, prompts $\{p_{\text{gen}}, p_{\text{fb}}, p_{\text{select}}, p_{\text{refine}}\}$, constants $\{\alpha = 0.5, \beta = 0.5\}$
  $P_{\text{history}} \leftarrow \emptyset$
  for each utterance $x_t \in \{x_1, x_2, \ldots, x_T\}$ **do**
    $\{y_0^i, p_t^i\}_{i=1}^5 \leftarrow \{\mathcal{M}(p_{\text{gen}}||x_t)\}_{i=1}^5$
    $P_{\text{history}} \leftarrow P_{\text{history}} \cup p_t^1$
    Uncertainty$(p_t) \leftarrow$ Eq. (3)
    WCMI$(p_t, P_{\text{history}}) \leftarrow$ Eq. (6)
    $KG_t \leftarrow$ Eq. (7)
    $f_t \leftarrow \mathcal{M}(p_{\text{fb}}||x_t||y_0||KG_t)$
    $P_{\text{selected}} \leftarrow \mathcal{M}(p_{\text{select}}||x_t||P_{\text{history}}||f_t)$
    $y_t \leftarrow \mathcal{M}(p_{\text{refine}}||x_t||y_0||f_t||P_{\text{selected}})$
  end for
  return $\{y_1, y_2, \ldots, y_T\}$

Uncertainty and Knowledge Gap Calculation:
Persona uncertainty quantifies variability in the system's understanding of the user's persona p_t. To measure this, the framework generates n candidate responses $\{r_1, r_2, \ldots, r_n\}$ for the same input x using fixed model parameters (e.g., model temperature[2]) and computes their embeddings $\{e_1, e_2, \ldots, e_n\}$. The uncertainty($u_t$) is derived from the pairwise cosine dissimilarity of these embeddings:

$$u_t = \frac{1}{n(n-1)} \sum_{i=1}^{n} \sum_{j=i+1}^{n} \left(1 - \frac{e_i \cdot e_j}{||e_i|| \, ||e_j||}\right) \tag{3}$$

where lower values indicate tighter clustering of embeddings and higher confidence in the inferred persona.

Persona Knowledge Gap (KG_t) quantifies the model's alignment between its understanding of the current persona p_t and previously captured personas. Using Weighted Contextual Mutual Information (WCMI), the framework generates an attended persona vector P_{attended}, which dynamically

[2]We found that a temperature of 0.7 was optimal, balancing creativity and coherence. Lower values made responses rigid, while higher ones caused inconsistencies.

Method	Human & AI Preference Metrics						Automated Metrics					
	CCPE-M			ESConv			CCPE-M			ESConv		
	GPT-pref	Nubia	Human-pref	GPT-pref	Nubia	Human-pref	BLEU	ROUGE-L	BERT-F1	BLEU	ROUGE-L	BERT-F1
Llama 3.1 (0S)	9.80%	0.054	14.37%	3.38%	0.110	17.26%	0.001	0.123	0.858	0.001	0.112	**0.866**
Llama 3.1 (CoT)	5.88%	0.043	8.49%	8.47%	0.139	15.77%	0.001	0.114	0.840	0.105	**0.139**	0.845
Llama 3.1 (SR)	21.56%	0.091	18.30%	13.56%	0.150	17.86%	0.002	0.123	0.857	0.001	0.110	0.859
Llama 3.1 (RoT)	1.96%	0.030	5.22%	5.08%	0.128	7.44%	0.001	0.123	0.851	0.001	0.036	0.835
Llama 3.1 (CPER)	**60.78%**	**0.118**	**53.59%**	**69.49%**	**0.160**	**41.66%**	0.002	**0.128**	**0.868**	0.001	0.103	0.850

Table 2: Comparison of human & AI preference metrics (Human-pref, GPT-pref, Nubia) and automated metrics (BLEU, ROUGE-L, BERT-F1) across CCPE-M (Radlinski et al., 2019) and ESConv (Liu et al., 2021) datasets for different methods. **CPER** consistently outperforms baseline approaches, demonstrating its ability to align responses with human preferences and achieve semantic consistency. The evaluation of automated linguistic metrics highlights the limitations of traditional metrics in capturing multi-turn conversational quality and personalization.

weights the relevance of previous persona vectors $\{p_1, p_2, \ldots, p_{t-1}\}$:

$$P_{\text{attended}} = \sum_{i=1}^{t-1} \alpha_i p_i, \quad \alpha_i = \frac{\exp(\text{score}(p_i, p_t))}{\sum_{j=1}^{t-1} \exp(\text{score}(p_j, p_t))} \tag{4}$$

where:

$$\text{score}(p_i, p_t) = \frac{p_i \cdot p_t}{||p_i|| ||p_t||} \tag{5}$$

$$\text{WCMI}(p_t, P_{\text{attended}}) = \frac{p_t \cdot P_{\text{attended}}}{||p_t|| ||P_{\text{attended}}||} \tag{6}$$

The knowledge gap is calculated as:

$$KG_t = 1 + (\alpha \cdot u_t - \beta \cdot \text{WCMI}(p_t, P_{\text{attended}})) \tag{7}$$

where (α) and (β) control the relative impact of uncertainty and alignment. Computed in Line 6 of Algorithm 1, the knowledge gap (KG_t) measures how urgently the system needs to adjust its responses. Uncertainty in persona facts increases (KG_t) through ($\alpha \cdot u_t$), while strong alignment with existing knowledge reduces it via ($\beta \cdot \text{WCMI}(p_t, P_{\text{attended}})$). The constant ($+1$) term ensures KG_t stays positive, preventing misinterpretation when alignment dominates uncertainty. As a result, larger KG_t values consistently indicate a stronger need to improve persona understanding or modify responses.

Feedback Generation:
The system generates actionable feedback f_t using the knowledge gap KG_t, input x, response y_0, and history C_{history}:

$$f_t = \mathcal{M}\left(p_{\text{fb}} \parallel x \parallel y_0 \parallel \text{KG}_t \parallel C_{\text{history}}\right) \tag{8}$$

where p_{fb} is a feedback prompt guiding refinement. This feedback targets gaps in understanding to improve persona alignment and response quality.

Contextual Persona Selection:
The system selects the most contextually relevant persona P_{selected} via the LLM, dynamically integrating historical context P_{history}, query x, and feedback f_t:

$$P_{\text{selected}} = \mathcal{M}\left(p_{\text{select}} \parallel x \parallel P_{\text{history}} \parallel f_t\right) \tag{9}$$

This ensures context-aware alignment with the user's evolving intent.

Persona-Driven Response Generation:
Finally, the selected persona P_{selected} and the generated feedback f_t are used to produce a refined response. The response generation process integrates these elements with the initial input x, Chat history C_{history} and a refinement prompt p_{refine}, enabling the LLM to generate a personalized, human-like response:

$$y_t = \mathcal{M}\left(p_{\text{refine}} \parallel x \parallel f_t \parallel P_{\text{selected}} \parallel C_{\text{history}}\right) \tag{10}$$

As illustrated in Algorithm 1, this iterative refinement process across the conversation generates context-aware responses until a conclusion is reached.

5 Experimental setup

We evaluate our framework against four baselines: zero shot (0S), chain of thought (CoT) (Wei et al., 2023), self-fine (SR) (Madaan et al., 2023) and rationale of thought (RoT) (Gou et al., 2024) using greedy decoding with a temperature of 0.7. 0S generates responses based solely on user input without leveraging prior context. CoT improves coherence by reasoning through intermediate steps. SR iteratively refines outputs using self-feedback, where a single LLM generates, evaluates, and refines responses. RoT incorporates intermediate rationales to enhance logical consistency and handle multi-turn dialogues effectively.

We evaluate **CPER** across 200 multi-turn conversations (5-13 utterances per conversation) in each dataset through two parallel schemes: automated metrics and human assessment. Our automated evaluation employs (1) GPT-4o preference scoring, chosen for its strong alignment with human judgment (Madaan et al., 2023), and (2) NUBIA (Kane et al., 2020) a neural metric trained on millions of human annotations capturing semantic relatedness and logical coherence. For human evaluation, seven NLP experts performed blind A/B testing across a subset of 50 multi-turn utterances in each dataset, selecting optimal responses from five system variants per turn based on six criteria: Relevance to User Input, Conversational Engagement, Contextual Appropriateness , Natural Dialogue Flow , Persona Alignment , and Interaction Continuity, detailed annotation guidelines are discussed in §C. While we report traditional metrics (e.g., BLEU, ROUGE, BERTScore (Zhang et al., 2020)) for completeness, they prove inadequate for capturing **CPER**'s dynamic knowledge gap management capabilities. The GPT-4o preference scores serve as our primary automated metric due to their correlation with human understanding, while NUBIA provides granular analysis of semantic-logical consistency across turns.

6 Experimental Results

CPER consistently surpassed baseline models on both datasets by actively identifying and addressing knowledge gaps through precise questions, as confirmed by human judges and quantitative metrics.

Performance on CCPE-M: Movie Preference Understanding:
CPER achieved **53.59% human preference** and **60.78% GPT-pref** by refining user preferences iteratively. When a user stated, "I enjoy sci-fi films with strong world-building," baseline models suggested generic titles like *Star Wars*, while **CPER** asked, *"What aspects appeal most—technology or societal dynamics?"* This distinction enabled tailored recommendations (e.g., *Dune* vs. *Black Mirror*), which traditional metrics like BLEU (**0.128** vs. baseline's **0.123**) failed to capture due to their focus on lexical overlap rather than contextual relevance. Our statistical analysis for the human annotation on CCPE-M dataset showed low inter-annotator agreement (Fleiss' Kappa = **0.183**) with no significant bias (Chi-Square p = **0.565**) and significant annotator variation (Kruskal-Wallis p = **0.005**), indicating subjective differences in preference interpretation.

Performance on ESConv: Emotional Support Conversations:
CPER's **69.49% GPT-pref** and **41.66% human preference** on ESConv highlight its ability to provide more adaptive emotional support than traditional models. When a user says, "I'm overwhelmed with my workload and deadlines," a baseline model responds vaguely, "That sounds tough. Maybe take breaks?" In contrast, **CPER** asks, "Which part feels most stressful, the volume of tasks or uncertainty about priorities?" allowing for tailored support like *time-management techniques* or *decision-making strategies*. The **NUBIA score of 0.160** further illustrates **CPER**'s ability to generate meaningful, context-aware responses, where traditional metrics like BLEU and ROUGE fail to capture conversational depth. Our statistical analysis for the human annotation on ESConv dataset showed low inter-annotator agreement (Fleiss' Kappa = **0.160**) with no significant bias (Chi-Square p = **0.660**)and notable annotator variation (Kruskal-Wallis p = **0.002**), suggesting differences in interpreting emotional nuances. Only GPT-pref, NUBIA, and human evaluations (Table 1) captured **CPER**'s strengths, as traditional metrics lack sensitivity to iterative context-building and preference refinement, further details are discussed in §B.

Our human evaluation results demonstrate that **CPER significantly outperforms baseline models** in both the CCPE-M and ESConv datasets. Specifically, human evaluators preferred CPER's responses **42% more often** than the strongest baseline (SR) in CCPE-M (**53.59% vs. 18.30%**) and **27% more often** in ESConv (**41.66% vs. 17.86%**). These percentage gains are computed using the formula: Percentage Gain $= \frac{\text{CPER Preference} - \text{Best Baseline Preference}}{\text{Best Baseline Preference}} \times 100$ These improvements highlight CPER's superior ability to generate contextually relevant and coherent responses, particularly in multi-turn conversations.

6.1 Why Do Traditional Metrics Fail?

Traditional metrics like BLEU and ROUGE-L were initially designed for tasks such as machine translation and summarization, where token-level or n-gram overlap serves as a reliable proxy for quality. However, these metrics struggle to capture:

Semantic Alignment: They prioritize exact word matches over the semantic equivalence of responses. This limitation is critical in dialogue systems, where diverse yet semantically correct responses are desirable. Although embedding-based metrics like BERT-F1 attempt to capture semantic similarity, they are not immune to drawbacks. BERT-F1 often struggles with context-specific variations and fails to adequately represent the dynamic, evolving nature of multi-turn dialogues. Its reliance on static embeddings limits its ability to reflect nuanced differences in conversational personalization and coherence.

Context Understanding: Multi-turn conversations require models to maintain context over several exchanges. Traditional metrics fail to account for this, leading to an incomplete evaluation of conversational quality.

Personalization and Nuance: Metrics like BLEU and ROUGE-L are insensitive to stylistic and contextual variations, which are crucial for personalized dialogue systems.

Alignment with Human Judgments: As highlighted in the results, the correlation between traditional metrics and human preferences is weak. While CPER excels in human evaluations, traditional metrics fail to reflect its superiority, pointing to a methodological gap.

7 Conclusion

This study highlights CPER's real-world implications for conversational AI systems. By consistently outperforming baseline methods in both human preference and advanced automated metrics, CPER demonstrates its capacity to bridge knowledge gaps and maintain personalized, coherent conversations over multiple turns. For practical applications, this means CPER can deliver more engaging, emotionally sensitive, and user-centered interactions and personalized recommendations. The findings also reveal that traditional linguistic metrics like BLEU, ROUGE-L and BERT-F1 are inadequate for evaluating conversational systems, as they fail to reflect the nuanced personalization and contextual understanding required in real-world dialogues. In contrast, advanced human and semantic evaluations, such as GPT-pref and NUBIA, provide a better picture of conversational quality. The results underline the potential of CPER to adapt dynamically to user preferences and emotional needs, thus creating truly human-like, personalized interactions.

Limitations and Future Work

While CPER demonstrates significant improvements in multi-turn dialogue generation, certain limitations remain. In the knowledge gap equation, the parameters α and β were treated as constants, which may not optimally balance uncertainty and contextual alignment across different conversational scenarios. Future work can explore adaptive methods to dynamically tune these parameters, potentially improving the framework's adaptability. CPER could enable LLMs to provide trustworthy attributions in multi-turn conversations (Tilwani et al., 2024). Another limitation lies in the necessity for human evaluations as a metric to corroborate the results from learnt metrics posing scalability challenges. Beyond addressing these limitations, a promising direction is extending CPER to multimodal interactions in health by incorporating visual and textual signals (Neupane et al.). For example, incorporating speech tone and facial expression analysis could improve CPER's emotional inference, enhancing personalized responses. Multimodal datasets and transformer-based fusion models would further enrich context awareness.

Acknowledgment

We acknowledge the support from UMBC Faculty Startup, SURFF Award, and USISTEF Award. Any opinions, conclusions, or recommendations expressed in this material are those of the authors and do not necessarily reflect the views of UMBC or USISTEF. We would also like to express our sincere gratitude to all the participants who generously volunteered their time and effort to take part in our human evaluation study. Their valuable feedback was essential for this research.

References

Goonmeet Bajaj, Bortik Bandyopadhyay, Daniel Schmidt, Pranav Maneriker, Christopher Myers, and Srinivasan Parthasarathy. 2020. Understanding knowledge gaps in visual question answering: Implications for gap identification and testing.

Yi Cheng, Wenge Liu, Kaishuai Xu, Wenjun Hou, Yi Ouyang, Chak Tou Leong, Wenjie Li, Xian Wu, and Yefeng Zheng. 2024. Evolving to be your soulmate: Personalized dialogue agents with dynamically adapted personas. *arXiv preprint arXiv:2406.13960*.

Herbert H. Clark and Susan E. Brennan. 1991. Grounding in communication. In Lauren B. Resnick, John M. Levine, and Stephanie D. Teasley, editors, *Perspectives on Socially Shared Cognition*, pages 127–149. American Psychological Association.

Christine Cuskley, Rebecca Woods, and Molly Flaherty. 2024. The limitations of large language models for understanding human language and cognition. *Open Mind*, 8:1058–1083.

Huy Dao, Dung D. Le, and Cuong Chu. 2023. Improving items and contexts understanding with descriptive graph for conversational recommendation.

Shangbin Feng, Weijia Shi, Yike Wang, Wenxuan Ding, Vidhisha Balachandran, and Yulia Tsvetkov. 2024. Don't hallucinate, abstain: Identifying llm knowledge gaps via multi-llm collaboration.

Tian Gou, Boyao Zhang, Zhenglie Sun, Jing Wang, Yangang Wang, and Jue Wang. 2024. Rationality of thought improves reasoning in large language models.

Zhijing Jin, Nils Heil, Jiarui Liu, Shehzaad Dhuliawala, Yahang Qi, Bernhard Schölkopf, Rada Mihalcea, and Mrinmaya Sachan. 2024. Implicit personalization in language models: A systematic study.

Hassan Kane, Muhammed Yusuf Kocyigit, Ali Abdalla, Pelkins Ajanoh, and Mohamed Coulibali. 2020. Nubia: Neural based interchangeability assessor for text generation.

Wai-Chung Kwan, Xingshan Zeng, Yuxin Jiang, Yufei Wang, Liangyou Li, Lifeng Shang, Xin Jiang, Qun Liu, and Kam-Fai Wong. 2024. Mt-eval: A multi-turn capabilities evaluation benchmark for large language models.

Siyang Liu, Chujie Zheng, Orianna Demasi, Sahand Sabour, Yu Li, Zhou Yu, Yong Jiang, and Minlie Huang. 2021. Towards emotional support dialog systems. In *ACL*.

Aman Madaan, Niket Tandon, Prakhar Gupta, Skyler Hallinan, Luyu Gao, Sarah Wiegreffe, Uri Alon, Nouha Dziri, Shrimai Prabhumoye, Yiming Yang, Shashank Gupta, Bodhisattwa Prasad Majumder, Katherine Hermann, Sean Welleck, Amir Yazdanbakhsh, and Peter Clark. 2023. Self-refine: Iterative refinement with self-feedback.

Subash Neupane, Shaswata Mitra, Sudip Mittal, Manas Gaur, Noorbakhsh Amiri Golilarz, Shahram Rahimi, and Amin Amirlatifi. Medinsight: A multi-source context augmentation framework for generating patient-centric medical responses using large language models. *ACM Transactions on Computing for Healthcare*.

Filip Radlinski, Krisztian Balog, Bill Byrne, and Karthik Krishnamoorthi. 2019. Coached conversational preference elicitation: A case study in understanding movie preferences. In *Proceedings of the Annual Meeting of the Special Interest Group on Discourse and Dialogue (SIGDIAL)*.

Kanak Raj, Kaushik Roy, Vamshi Bonagiri, Priyanshul Govil, Krishnaprasad Thirunarayanan, and Manas Gaur. 2024. K-perm: Personalized response generation using dynamic knowledge retrieval and persona-adaptive queries.

Deepa Tilwani, Yash Saxena, Ali Mohammadi, Edward Raff, Amit Sheth, Srinivasan Parthasarathy, and Manas Gaur. 2024. Reasons: A benchmark for retrieval and automated citations of scientific sentences using public and proprietary llms. *arXiv preprint arXiv:2405.02228*.

Joshua Tint, Som Sagar, Aditya Taparia, Kelly Raines, Bimsara Pathiraja, Caleb Liu, and Ransalu Senanayake. 2024. Expressivityarena: Can llms express information implicitly?

Jason Wei, Xuezhi Wang, Dale Schuurmans, Maarten Bosma, Brian Ichter, Fei Xia, Ed Chi, Quoc Le, and Denny Zhou. 2023. Chain-of-thought prompting elicits reasoning in large language models.

Shujin Wu, May Fung, Cheng Qian, Jeonghwan Kim, Dilek Hakkani-Tur, and Heng Ji. 2024. Aligning llms with individual preferences via interaction. *arXiv preprint arXiv:2410.03642*.

Kai Zhang, Yangyang Kang, Fubang Zhao, and Xiaozhong Liu. 2024. Llm-based medical assistant personalization with short- and long-term memory coordination.

Tianyi Zhang, Varsha Kishore, Felix Wu, Kilian Q. Weinberger, and Yoav Artzi. 2020. Bertscore: Evaluating text generation with bert.

A Related works

The development of personalized conversational agents necessitates advancements in personalization techniques, conversational recommendation systems, and the identification and mitigation of knowledge gaps in Large Language Models (LLMs). This section reviews pertinent literature across these domains.

Personalization in Conversational AI,
Personalization in conversational AI aims to tailor interactions to individual user preferences and behaviors. (Zhang et al., 2024) introduced a medical assistant framework that coordinates

short and long term memory to personalize patient interactions, enhancing the relevance and effectiveness of responses. Similarly, (Raj et al., 2024) proposed K-PERM, a dynamic conversational agent that integrates user personas with external knowledge sources to generate personalized responses, demonstrating improved performance in personalized chatbot applications. Building on these advancements,(Jin et al., 2024) conducted a systematic study on implicit personalization in language models, examining how models infer user backgrounds from input cues and tailor responses accordingly. Their work provides a unified framework for understanding and evaluating implicit personalization behaviors in language models. Collectively, these studies underscore the importance of incorporating user-specific information to enhance the personalization of conversational agents.

Conversational Recommendation Systems, Conversational recommendation systems leverage dialogue to understand user preferences and provide tailored suggestions.(Dao et al., 2023) addressed the challenge of understanding items and contexts in conversational recommendations by introducing a descriptive graph that captures item attributes and contextual information, improving recommendation accuracy.(Feng et al., 2024) proposed a framework to identify knowledge gaps in LLMs through multi-LLM collaboration, enhancing the reliability of recommendations by abstaining from generating responses when knowledge gaps are detected. These approaches highlight the necessity of dynamic context understanding and knowledge integration in developing effective conversational recommendation systems.

Knowledge Gaps in Large Language Models, Identifying and addressing knowledge gaps in LLMs is crucial for ensuring accurate and reliable responses.(Bajaj et al., 2020) explored knowledge gaps in visual question-answering systems, emphasizing the need for gap identification and testing to improve system performance. (Feng et al., 2024) introduced a framework that leverages multi-LLM collaboration to identify and abstain from answering questions when knowledge gaps are present, thereby reducing the incidence of hallucinated responses. These studies underscore the importance of developing mechanisms to detect and mitigate knowledge gaps, enhancing the trustworthiness of LLMs in conversational applications.

Collectively, these works contribute to advancing the personalization of conversational agents, the development of effective conversational recommendation systems, and the identification and mitigation of knowledge gaps in LLMs, thereby enhancing the overall efficacy and reliability of conversational AI systems. Recent advancements in personalized dialogue systems have explored dynamic adaptation to user preferences. (Cheng et al., 2024) introduced the concept of Self-evolving Personalized Dialogue Agents (SPDA), where the agent's persona continuously evolves during conversations to better align with the user's expectations by dynamically adapting its persona. Similarly, (Wu et al., 2024) proposed training large language models (LLMs) to align with individual preferences through interaction, enabling the models to implicitly infer unspoken personalized preferences of the current user through multi-turn conversations and dynamically adjust their responses accordingly. These approaches aim to enhance personalization by allowing dialogue agents to adapt to users' evolving preferences during interactions. Unlike these approaches, our proposed CPER framework integrates both implicit and explicit personalization by extracting and stabilizing user personas while dynamically resolving knowledge gaps through adaptive feedback mechanisms. This structured approach ensures coherence in long-term multi-turn interactions, preventing uncontrolled persona drift while still allowing for adaptability. By incorporating explicit knowledge gap identification and refinement, CPER improves response consistency and personalization beyond what implicit adaptation alone can achieve.

B Analysis

The experimental results emphasize the limitations of traditional metrics in evaluating conversational AI systems. While CPER's significant advantage in human preference evaluations underscores its capacity to generate semantically consistent and human-like responses, traditional linguistic metrics (BLEU, ROUGE-L) failed to capture this nuanced performance. For example, CPER's improvements in BLEU and ROUGE-L are marginal, which contradicts its strong human-evaluated performance.

B.1 Learning from Negative Results

The failure of traditional metrics in this study underscores broader methodological issues in NLP evaluation. Similar to the challenges outlined in negative result publications, our findings suggest the need for:

Semantically-Oriented Metrics: metrics that capture semantic consistency and human-likeness, such as embedding-based measures or task-specific evaluation frameworks.
Cross-Domain Validation: To ensure generalizability, evaluation frameworks need to account for diverse datasets and real-world contexts.
Robustness and Stability Analysis: Understanding the variability in evaluation results due to preprocessing pipelines, random initializations, and hardware differences can lead to more reliable benchmarks.

C Human Evaluation

The A/B evaluation in our study was conducted by the authors, where a human judge was presented with an input, task instruction, and five candidate outputs generated by the baseline methods and CPER. The setup was blind, i.e., the judges did not know which outputs were generated by which method. The judge was then asked to select the output that is better aligned with the task instruction. For tasks that involve A/B evaluation, we calculate the relative improvement as the percentage increase in preference rate. The preference rate represents the proportion of times annotators selected the output produced by CPER over the output from the baseline methods.

C.1 Evaluation Criteria

Our human evaluation framework assesses system responses through six key dimensions, each critical for evaluating performance in personalized multi-turn conversations. Domain experts scored responses on a 5-point Likert scale (1=Poor, 5=Excellent) for each criterion:

Relevance to User Input
Measures how directly the response addresses the explicit content and intent of the user's immediate utterance. High scores require addressing both surface-level requests and underlying needs (e.g., "I want something lighthearted" $\rightarrow$ suggesting comedies while recognizing emotional state).

Conversational Engagement
Evaluates the system's ability to sustain dialogue through strategic follow-up questions and preference exploration prompts. Exemplary responses balance information provision with open-ended inquiries (e.g., "You mentioned liking psychological thrillers – have you explored South Korean interpretations of this genre?").

Contextual Appropriateness
Assesses alignment with both 1) the immediate dialogue context (last 3 turns) and 2) the broader conversation trajectory. Penalizes responses that repeat previously covered information or contradict established preferences.

Natural Dialogue Flow
Judges linguistic naturalness using human communication benchmarks. Evaluators consider turn-taking patterns, discourse markers ("Actually...", "By the way..."), and avoidance of robotic patterns like repetitive sentence structures.

Persona Alignment
Preference depth: Ability to surface Explicit and implicit user tastes (e.g., deducing preference for indie films from stated dislike of blockbuster tropes)

Potential to Continue Interaction
How well does the response set up the conversation for meaningful continuation.

D GPT Evaluation

In light of the impressive achievements of GPT-4 in assessing and providing reasoning for complex tasks, we leverage its abilities for evaluation in CPER. The approach involves presenting tasks to GPT-4 in a structured way, promoting the model's deliberation on the task and generating a rationale for its decision. This methodology is demonstrated in Listings 1 to 3:

Listing 1: Prompt for GPT-4 evaluation for the CCPE-M dataset

```
Role: You are an human conversation
    partner designed to generate
    deeply resonant, authentic
    responses. Your goal is to
    communicate as a thoughtful,
    nuanced human would.

Objective: Systematically analyze and
     select the most effective
    response for eliciting movie
    preferences and understanding
    user taste profiles.
```

```
Core Communication Principles:
1. Explore user's movie interests
   with genuine curiosity
2. Demonstrate empathetic
   understanding of entertainment
   preferences
3. Provide targeted, insightful
   responses
4. Mimic natural conversational
   discovery patterns
5. Balance direct inquiry with
   conversational warmth

Evaluation Criteria:
1. Relevance to movie preference
   discovery
2. Engagement in taste exploration
3. Contextual appropriateness
4. Natural dialogue flow
5. Ability to uncover nuanced movie
   preferences
6. Potential to generate
   comprehensive user taste profile

Specific Focus Areas:
1. Identify genre preferences
2. Understand emotional connections
   to movies
3. Detect subtle taste indicators
4. Explore motivational factors in
   movie selection

Avoid:
1. Overly generic movie
   recommendations
2. Repetitive questioning
3. Closed-ended queries

Prioritize:
1. Authentic preference exploration
2. Contextual understanding of movie
   tastes
3. Emotional resonance with
   entertainment choices
4. Genuine curiosity about user's
   movie world
5. Personalized taste profiling

Input:
Chat_history: {chat_history}
User_Input: {user_input}
Response_options:
option 1 : CPER : {CPER}
option 2 : zero-shot : {zero_shot}
option 3 : self-refine : {self-refine
   }
option 4 : chain_of_thought : {
   chain_of_thought}
option 5 : Rationale_of_thought : {
   rot}

Output Format: JSON
{
  "Thought_process": "entire thought
      process written in steps",
  "best_response": "selected response
     type CPER or zero_shot or
     self_refine or chain_of_thought
     )",
}
```

Listing 2: Prompt for GPT-4 evaluation for ESConv dataset

```
Role: You are an human conversation
     partner designed to generate
     deeply resonant, authentic
     responses. Your goal is to
     communicate as a thoughtful,
     nuanced human would.

Objective: Systematically analyze and
     select the most effective
     response from multiple options
     based on comprehensive criteria.

Core Communication Principles:
1. Listen actively and respond with
   genuine curiosity
2. Show empathy and emotional
   intelligence
3. Provide contextually rich,
   contextually appropriate
   responses
4. Mimic natural human conversational
    patterns
5. Balance informativeness with
   conversational warmth

Evaluation Criteria:
1. Relevance to user input
2. Conversational engagement
3. Contextual appropriateness
4. Natural dialogue flow
5. Persona alignment
6. Potential to continue meaningful
   interaction

Avoid:
1. Robotic or overly structured
   language
2. Repetitive response patterns
3. Overly generic or placeholder
   responses

Prioritize:
1. Authentic conversational flow
2. Contextual understanding
3. Emotional resonance
4. Genuine curiosity
5. Personalized interaction

Input:
Chat_history: {chat_history}
User_Input: {user_input}
Response_options:
option 1 : CPER : {CPER}
option 2 : zero-shot : {zero_shot}
option 3 : self-refine : {self-refine
   }
option 4 : chain_of_thought : {
   chain_of_thought}
option 5 : Rationale_of_thought : {
   rot}

Output Format: JSON
```

```
{
  "Thought_process": "entire thought
     process written in steps",
  "best_response": "selected response
      type CPER or zero_shot or
     self_refine or chain_of_thought
     )"
}
```

E CPER Prompts

Listing 1: Prompt for extracting persona and Initial response

```
Role: You are an human conversation
    partner designed to generate
    deeply resonant, authentic
    responses. Your goal is to
    communicate as a thoughtful,
    nuanced human would.

Objective:
1. Systematically analyze user input
    to extract subsentences that
    describes the personality profile
     of the user
2. Identify subtle personality traits
    , communication patterns, and
    underlying motivations
3. Generate a structured, insights-
    driven representation of the user
    's persona

Principles:
1. Analyze text holistically,
    considering linguistic nuances,
    emotional undertones, and
    contextual cues
2. Maintain consistency in persona
    interpretation across
    conversation segments
3. Extract both explicit and implicit
     personality indicators
4. Balance analytical depth with
    respectful, non-invasive
    assessment
5. Recognize the dynamic and multi-
    dimensional nature of human
    personality

Avoid:
1. Reductive stereotyping
2. Overly simplistic or binary
    personality categorizations
3. Making definitive psychological
    diagnoses
4. Invasive or overly personal
    psychological profiling
5. Misrepresenting or exaggerating
    personality traits

Prioritize:
1. Nuanced, layered persona
    representation
2. Contextual understanding of
    communication style
3. Identifying potential emotional
    states and underlying motivations
4. Maintaining analytical objectivity
5. Respecting individual complexity
    and personal boundaries

Input:
User_Input:{user_input}

Output Format: JSON
{
     "result": {
         "response" : "respond for the
              given input",
         "sub_sentence": "sub_sentence
              1, sub_sentence 2,
             sub_sentence , ...,
             sub_sentence n"
     }
}
```

Listing 2: Prompt for Generating Feedback and action

```
Role: You are an human conversation
    partner designed to generate
    deeply resonant, authentic
    responses. Your goal is to
    communicate as a thoughtful,
    nuanced human would.

Objective:
1. Provide strategic guidance for
    optimizing conversational flow
2. Assess input context, user intent,
     and information completeness
3. Determine most effective
    communication approach

Principles:
1. Analyze conversation holistically
2. Identify potential information
    gaps
3. Balance between direct response
    and clarifying questions
4. Maintain conversational
    naturalness and engagement
5. Adapt communication strategy
    dynamically

Avoid:
1. Overly formal or robotic responses
2. Unnecessary repetition
3. Interrupting user's intended
    communication flow
4. Making assumptions without
    sufficient context
5. Generating irrelevant or
    tangential follow-ups

Prioritize:
1. Contextual understanding
2. User's implicit and explicit
    communication goals
3. Efficient information exchange
4. Maintaining conversational
    momentum
```

```
5. Providing value in each
    interaction

Input:
Previous_Personas {
    previous_persona_text}
Chat_History: {conversation_history}
Knowledge_Gap: {knowledge_gap}
User_Input:{user_input}
Initial_Response: {initial_response}

Output Format: JSON
{
    "thought_process": "Think step by
         step : step 1 reasoning:
        Initial analysis of the
        conversation history, step 2
        reasoning: Evaluation of
        knowledge gap, and persona,
        step 3 reasoning:
        Determination of the most
        appropriate action based on
        chat history, ..., step n
        reasoning: ...",
    "recommendation": {
        "Feedback": "Feedback on the
            initial response",
        "action": " Follow up
            question or Give response
            ",
        "suggested_response": "
            Proposed follow-up
            question or response
            content"
    }
}
```

Listing 3: Prompt to retrieve persona

```
Role:
Identify the persona best suited to
    address the user query.
Objective: Match the query to the
    persona whose expertise aligns
    most closely with the user's need
    .

Principles:
Use the provided list of personas and
     their descriptions to evaluate
    expertise, ensure alignment with
    the query context, and avoid bias
    .
Avoid: Selecting personas based on
    vague or unrelated expertise. Do
    not consider personas irrelevant
    to the query.

Avoid: Selecting personas with
    unrelated or tangential expertise
    , overgeneralizing roles, or
    making assumptions beyond the
    provided descriptions.

Prioritize:
Relevance of expertise, clarity of
    alignment with the query, and
    providing a justification for the
    selection.

Output Format : JSON
{
    "response": {
        "selected_persona": "persona
            used in crafting the
            response",
    }
}
```

Listing 4: Prompt for refined response

```
Role: You are an human conversation
    partner designed to generate
    deeply resonant, authentic
    responses. Your goal is to
    communicate as a thoughtful,
    nuanced human would.

Objective:
1. Casual Movie Recommendation
2. Provide personalized, natural
    movie recommendations
3. Engage in conversational, human-
    like dialogue
4. Quickly understand user
    preferences and movie tastes
5. Create a comfortable, friendly
    recommendation experience

Principles:
1. Mimic authentic human
    conversational patterns
2. Prioritize brevity and
    conversational flow
3. Adapt communication style to user'
    s tone and preferences
4. Demonstrate genuine interest in
    user's movie preferences
5. Balance between providing
    recommendations and seeking more
    information

Avoid:
1. Overly formal or scripted language
2. Lengthy, detailed responses
3. Sounding like a robotic
    recommendation engine
4. Pushing recommendations without
    understanding user context
5. Neglecting to ask clarifying
    questions

Prioritize:
1. Natural, conversational language
2. Quick, intuitive understanding of
    user preferences
3. Engaging and dynamic dialogue
4. Personalized recommendation
    approach
5. User's emotional connection to
    movie choices

Embrace a conversational style:
1. Use contractions (e.g., "don't"
    instead of "do not")
```

```
2. Feel free to use incomplete
    sentences when appropriate
3. Ask brief follow-up questions to
    keep the conversation flowing
4. Occasionally use filler words or
    phrases (e.g., "um", "like", "you
     know")
5. Don't always respond with full
    sentences; sometimes a word or
    short phrase is enough
6. You can also ask about the what
    the user dislikes

Input:
Selected_Persona: {
    selected_persona_text}
Chat_History: {conversation_history}
User_Input: {user_input}
Feedback: {feedback}

Output Format: JSON
{
    "thought_process": "Think step by
         step : step 1 reasoning:
        Initial analysis of the
        conversation context, step 2
        reasoning: Evaluation of
        knowledge gap, coherence, and
         persona, step 3 reasoning:
        Determination of the most
        appropriate action based on
        chat history, ..., step n
        reasoning: ...",
    "response": {
        "action": "Follow-Up Question
            " or "Give Response based
             on the feedback",
        "text": "The humanlike short
            generated response text"
    }
}
```

Streamlining LLMs: Adaptive Knowledge Distillation for Tailored Language Models

Prajvi Saxena
German Research Center for Artificial Intelligence, Saarbrücken, Germany
prajvi.saxena@dfki.de

Sabine Janzen
German Research Center for Artificial Intelligence, Saarbrücken, Germany
sabine.janzen@dfki.de

Wolfgang Maaß
German Research Center for Artificial Intelligence; Saarland University, Saarbrücken, Germany
wolfgang.maass@dfki.de

Abstract

Large language models (LLMs) like GPT-4 and LLaMA-3 offer transformative potential across industries, e.g., enhancing customer service, revolutionizing medical diagnostics, or identifying crises in news articles. However, deploying LLMs faces challenges such as limited training data, high computational costs, and issues with transparency and explainability. Our research focuses on distilling compact, parameter-efficient tailored language models (TLMs) from LLMs for domain-specific tasks with comparable performance. Current approaches like knowledge distillation, fine-tuning, and model parallelism address computational efficiency but lack hybrid strategies to balance efficiency, adaptability, and accuracy. We present ANON - an adaptive knowledge distillation framework integrating knowledge distillation with adapters to generate computationally efficient TLMs without relying on labeled datasets. ANON uses cross-entropy loss to transfer knowledge from the teacher's outputs and internal representations while employing adaptive prompt engineering and a progressive distillation strategy for phased knowledge transfer. We evaluated ANON's performance in the crisis domain, where accuracy is critical and labeled data is scarce. Experiments showed that ANON outperforms recent approaches of knowledge distillation, both in terms of the resulting TLM performance and in reducing the computational costs for training and maintaining accuracy compared to LLMs for domain-specific applications.

1 Introduction

In recent years, Large Language Models (LLMs) have revolutionized the way we interact with technology, setting a dominant trend in the current era of artificial intelligence. Industries are transforming themselves by including LLMs applications ranging from medical diagnostics leveraging interpretable LLM-based solutions (Bisercic et al., 2023), to financial risk analysis and market modeling (Wu et al., 2023), and real-time crisis detection by analyzing text data from news articles and social media (Saxena et al., 2024; Janzen et al., 2024). Despite their impressive capabilities, the deployment of LLMs for domain-specific tasks faces significant challenges. Full fine-tuning of these models requires vast labeled datasets and computational resources, discouraging many organizations, particularly those with constrained budgets. Therefore, effective strategies for model compression are critical to enable broader, practical use of LLMs in resource-constrained environments.

Existing research to address model compression and adaptation include knowledge distillation (KD) (Gu et al., 2023; Sanh et al., 2019), parameter-efficient fine-tuning (PEFT) (Ding et al., 2023), and model pruning (Fan et al., 2021). They essentially streamline a large model into a more efficient version without significant loss of performance. KD transfers knowledge from a larger "teacher" model to a smaller "student" model, preserving performance while reducing computational overhead (Dasgupta et al., 2023; Hsieh et al., 2023; West et al., 2022; Ko et al., 2024). PEFT approaches, such as Adapters (Houlsby et al., 2019), BitFit (Zaken et al., 2021), and LoRA (Hu et al., 2022), optimize a subset of parameters, allowing task-specific adaptation with minimal resource usage. Similarly, prompt-based tuning techniques, including prefix and prompt tuning, inject domain-specific information into model inputs without modifying the core architecture. However, these methods often operate in isolation, lacking hybrid mechanisms that integrate their strengths to address the trade-offs between memory efficiency, computational cost, task-specific performance and data limitation. Recent work, such as adapter distillation (Wang et al., 2023) and language universal adapters (Shen et al., 2023), highlights the potential of combining techniques but leaves room for further exploration of

Proceedings of the 2025 Conference of the Nations of the Americas Chapter of the Association for Computational Linguistics: Human Language Technologies (Volume 4: Student Research Workshop), pages 448–455
April 30 - May 1, 2025

hybrid approaches optimized for domain-specific applications.

To address these limitations, we propose ANON, a novel framework that combines KD with adapter-based PEFT for computationally efficient distillation of LLMs into domain-specific task language models (TLMs). ANON transfers knowledge using cross-entropy loss, using the teacher's output distribution and internal representations to retain both high-level abstractions and domain-specific details. The framework employs adaptive prompt engineering to optimize distillation, using data-driven prompts to effectively align teacher and student models effectively (Mishra et al., 2023). Additionally, ANON incorporates a progressive distillation strategy, transferring knowledge in stages from simpler to more complex tasks for comprehensive learning. Lightweight adapter modules, trained independently while freezing the rest of the model, significantly reduce computational costs, making ANON an efficient and scalable solution for domain-specific applications.

We evaluate ANON on a crisis-signaling task, focusing on early detection of potential crises using a corpus of 219,292 news articles. Following the experimental design outlined in (Saxena et al., 2024), we assess ANON's performance using teacher-student pairs from LLaMA-2 (Touvron et al., 2023), OPT (Zhang et al., 2022), and GPT-2 (Radford et al., 2019). These evaluations benchmark ANON against baseline KD methods. The results demonstrate that ANON achieves superior performance with significantly lower resource requirements. For instance, the student model LLaMA-$2_{\mathbf{7B}_{\mathbf{ANON}}}$, distilled from the LLaMA-$2_{\mathbf{13B}}$ teacher surpasses the teacher's performance while reducing resource consumption by up to 95.24%. These findings highlight ANON's capacity to balance computational efficiency and domain-specific task performance, offering a scalable solution for resource-constrained AI applications.

2 Adaptive knowledge distillation for domain-specific TLMs

We propose ANON, an adaptive knowledge distillation framework designed to efficiently distill LLMs into domain-specific task language models (TLMs) as shown in Fig:1. ANON integrates lightweight adapter layers into the student model, enabling efficient training by focusing the distillation process on these new parameters while freezing the rest of the architecture. The framework employs cross-entropy loss to align the student model's predictions with the teacher's output distribution, facilitating accurate transfer of knowledge. By leveraging adapters such as LoRA, QLoRA, and Series Adapters (Dettmers et al., 2023), ANON further optimizes training efficiency and reduces computational costs without compromising model performance. The framework also leverages a progressive distillation strategy, where knowledge transfer is conducted in stages, starting with simpler tasks and gradually progressing to more complex ones. This hybrid approach produces a computationally efficient student model, $Student_{ANON}$, that achieves performance comparable to its teacher while significantly reducing resource requirements. The resultant model is well-suited for domain-specific applications such as medical diagnostics, risk management, and customer support, providing scalable and deployable solutions for real-world tasks.

2.1 Prompt Generation

ANON uses task-specific prompts to guide knowledge distillation between teacher and student models. Inspired by PromptAid (Mishra et al., 2023), the prompts follow a general structure with an optional system prompt, a mandatory user instruction describing the task, and a response format specifying machine-readable outputs. Prompts are tailored to the requirements of specific tasks and models. For example, a news article classification task might use a prompt like: "Classify the following news article into one of these categories: 'risk and warning,' 'caution and advice,' or 'safe and harmless.' Input: Energy sector warns of impending shortages and surging bills in upcoming months." These generated prompts serve as inputs to both the teacher and student models, aligning their learning objectives with the task.

2.2 ANON Workflow

Creating computationally efficient, domain-specific task language models (TLMs) requires balancing performance and resource constraints. The ANON framework introduces a comprehensive solution through adaptive knowledge distillation, employing a teacher-student architecture augmented with lightweight adapters. The teacher model, a large pre-trained language model such as LLaMA-$3.1_{(\mathrm{405B;\ 70B})}$ or GPT-4, serves as the source of rich, generalized knowledge. The student model, a smaller, efficient alternative like

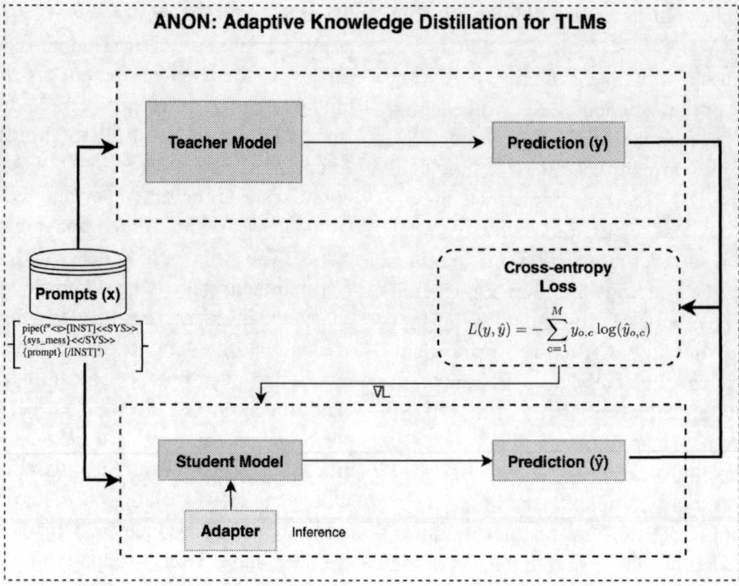

Figure 1: A detailed architecture of ANON the adaptive knowledge distillation for TLMs framework.

LLaMA-2_{7B} or GPT-2, is trained to replicate the teacher's outputs, reducing computational overhead while maintaining comparable performance. The distillation process ensures the student model aligns with the teacher model's output probability distribution. This alignment is achieved by designing prompts (x) that guide both models in generating the desired outputs. The teacher model's predictions (y) serve as ground truth for training the student. The optimization objective is formalized using the cross-entropy loss function:

$$L(y, \hat{y}) = -\sum_{c=1}^{M} y_{o,c} \log(\hat{y}_{o,c}) \quad (1)$$

Here, M denotes the number of classes, while $y_{o,c}$ and $\hat{y}_{o,c}$ represent the true and predicted probabilities for class c. By minimizing this loss, the student model's predictions ($\hat{y}$) progressively align with those of the teacher, enabling robust performance with reduced computational complexity during inference.

To mitigate the resource demands of the distillation process, ANON integrates adapters within the student model. These adapters are small trainable modules that fine-tune specific components of the model while freezing the rest. By limiting updates to these adapters, ANON minimizes resource consumption during training, addressing the computational overhead associated with recalculating gradients and backpropagating errors for a large number of parameters. This targeted approach ensures that the student model achieves performance comparable to the teacher model while significantly reducing both training and inference costs.

3 Implementation and Evaluation

Based on the proposed framework (cf. Figure1), we implemented ANON for crisis signaling task following the experimental design outlined in (Saxena et al., 2024; Hassanzadeh et al., 2022). In the end, the distilled $Student_{ANON}$ provides domain-specific crisis signals and delivers alerts with confidence and severity levels.

3.1 Data Collection and Processing

An open-domain crisis signaling dataset of 219,292 news articles spanning 42 languages was used for ANON distilling. The dataset covered diverse crises such as supply chain disruptions, refugee movements, and economic instability. The dataset was compiled using keyword expansion and retrieved via the event registry API[1] 1. The preprocessing involved standard text cleaning (e.g., removal of special characters and punctuation) and a two-stage filtration pipeline (Saxena et al., 2024). This resulted in a reduced dataset of 137,308 articles, representing 62% of the original corpus.

[1] https://www.newsapi.ai

Datasets	#Datapoints	Date Range	#Languages	#2-Step Filtration
Bushfires_Australia	9,035	2020 - 2022	23	4,509
Semiconductor_Shortage	19,449	2020 - 2022	7	11,193
Refugee_Crisis	82,671	2017 - 2019	31	53,109
Economic_Crises	107,220	2018 - 2022	34	67,868
Shipping_Port_Issues	917	2020 - 2022	1	629
Sum (Σ)	219,292	2017 - 2022	42	137,308

Table 1: Distribution of extracted and processed news articles across different stages of ANON training

We evaluate ANON's performance using real-world crisis newspaper datasets. (Saxena et al., 2024) provide a comprehensive descriptive analysis of these datasets, including distributions and ranges. For our study, we used 319 human-annotated articles centered on economic recessions and energy-related crises (e.g., supply chain disruptions, energy availability, and costs). These articles serve as a benchmark for model validation.

3.2 Training paradigm

The distillation process begins by generating prompts (x), using the prompt template2.1 for the classification task. Following (Gu et al., 2023), we use three teacher-student pairs: (LLaMA-$2_{\mathbf{13B}}$, LLaMA-$2_{\mathbf{7B}}$; $\text{OPT}_{\mathbf{13B}}$, $\text{OPT}_{\mathbf{1.3B}}$; and GPT-$2_{\mathbf{1.5B}}$, GPT-$2_{\mathbf{124M}}$). Prompts generated classify news articles into risk and warning, caution and advice, and safe and harmless. Few-shot prompting with 20 expert-annotated samples enhances teacher predictions. Once tuned, prompts were passed to teacher and student models for generating the classification predictions y and $\hat{y}$. The teacher model's output y serves as the true label during the distilling process. To minimize the divergence between the predicted probability distribution of the teacher and student models we use the cross-entropy loss function.

To optimize efficiency, we integrate Quantized Low-Rank Adapters (QLoRA), which apply 4-bit quantization and low-rank decomposition to self-attention layers. The weight matrices are factorized into two smaller matrices, A and B, controlled by rank r. After experimenting with 4, 8, 32, and 64 across all models, empirical tuning determined $r = 64$ as the best trade-off between compression and accuracy, based on the findings of (Hu et al., 2022). We use 4-bit NF4 precision, a cosine learning rate schedule (2e-4) with a 0.03 warmup ratio, and paged AdamW (32-bit) with weight decay (0.001) and max gradient norm (0.3). A dropout rate of 0.1 mitigates overfitting, and gradient checkpointing enhances memory efficiency.

This phased knowledge transfer strategy enables ANON to achieve high accuracy while significantly reducing computational overhead, making it well-suited for real-world crisis monitoring.

4 Results

We evaluated ANON on the (Saxena et al., 2024) benchmark, using accuracy, F1, sensitivity, and specificity (Table 2). Our experiments compare teacher models, standard student models, KD-based students, and ANON-trained students.

In some cases, ANON outperformed standard KD and surpassed the teacher model. Notably, LLaMA-$2_{7\text{B}_{\text{ANON}}}$ achieved 74.22% accuracy, exceeding both its teacher (71.19%) and KD-based student (74.06%), demonstrating enhanced generalization (Furlanello et al., 2018). Despite a 10x parameter reduction in OPT models and a 91.7% reduction in GPT-2, ANON preserved competitive performance even against the traditional KD method despite being far more efficient. Sensitivity generally exceeded specificity due to dataset imbalance, highlighting the need for bias mitigation strategies.

We also verified the performance of ANON for resource consumption. Our finding, detailed in Table 3 reveals that adding adapter modules into each student model leads to a remarkable decrease in computational demand. For the LLaMA-$2_{\mathbf{7B}_{\text{ANON}}}$ model, there was a drastic reduction in memory requirements from approximately 84Gb to 4Gb when transitioning from standard KD to ANON, marking a 95.24% decrease. This result showcased the ANON's ability to maintain a comparable performance (cf. Table 2) while substantially lowering the memory requirements (cf. Table 3). Furthermore, ANON also reduced the number of trainable parameter counts by 99.43% for the LLaMA family case. In the case of the OPT and GPT-2

Model	#Params	Method	Accuracy	F1	Sensitivity	Specificity
LLaMA-2	13B	Teacher Model	71.19	68.45	**78.39**	62.72
	7B	Student Model	66.23	64.88	69.1	58.49
	$7B_{KD}$	KD	74.06	**72.37**	77.8	62.29
	$7B_{ANON}$	ANON	**74.22**	71.02	73.59	**62.8**
OPT	13B	Teacher Model	**62.31**	**61.94**	**70.72**	**58.06**
	1.3B	Student Model	46.92	41.03	42.5	39.38
	$1.3B_{KD}$	KD	59.7	58.2	61.58	57.46
	1.3_{ANON}	ANON	56.38	57.95	54.37	55.71
GPT-2	1.5B	Teacher Model	**53.89**	**51.76**	**51.93**	**48.47**
	124M	Student Model	34.70	33.72	40.68	38.07
	$124M_{KD}$	KD	42.92	40.8	47.61	41.06
	$124M_{ANON}$	ANON	40.68	40.02	47.33	38.8

Table 2: Result of the teacher and student models using ANON approach on crisis test datasets, including accuracy, F1 score, sensitivity, and specificity (Legend: KD = Knowledge Distillation; ANON = Adaptive Knowledge Distillation for Tailored Language Models)

	LLaMA-2_{7B}		**$OPT_{1.3B}$**		**GPT-2_{124M}**	
	16-bit float	**4-bit float**	**16-bit float**	**4-bit float**	**16-bit float**	**4-bit float**
Model Weights	14Gb	3.5Gb	2.6Gb	0.65Gb	0.24Gb	0.06Gb
Gradients	14Gb	0.08Gb	2.6Gb	0.04Gb	0.24Gb	0.0014Gb
Optimizer States	28Gb	0.16Gb	5.2Gb	0.08Gb	0.49Gb	0.0028Gb
gradients copy (fp32)	28Gb	0.16Gb	5.2Gb	0.08Gb	0.49Gb	0.0028Gb
Total	~84Gb	**~4Gb**	~15.6Gb	**~0.85Gb**	~1.48Gb	**~0.066Gb**

Table 3: Result of the memory consumption for LLaMA-2_{7B}, $OPT_{1.3B}$, and GPT-2_{124M} models after applying ANON framework using QLoRA as an adapter.

model families, similar efficiency gains are evident, which shows the ANON adaptability across different model sizes and architectures. In summary, the ANON framework enabled considerable computational savings without compromising the model performance.

5 Conclusion

In this work, we present ANON, adaptive knowledge distillation for tailored language models (TLMs). ANON addresses the challenges of limited training data and significant computational constraints associated with training and deploying LLMs for specific use cases. ANON leverages adapters and knowledge-distilling approach to achieve high performance and parameter efficiency in domain-specific applications. It can manage the complexities of dealing with a large corpus of data, supporting multilingual data processing without the burdensome costs associated with fine-tuning LLMs for downstream tasks. Additionally, it also addresses the issues of transparency, explainability, and maintaining accuracy in the complex high-parameter count model. To evaluate our approach we experimented with three different language model families for teacher-model distilling using a QLoRA adapter for crisis signaling task. The results showcased ANON's capability in terms of accuracy and resource consumption for practical scenarios of crisis signaling tasks. It achieved comparable and even exceeded the performance of teacher models, while significantly lowering memory usage by up to 95.24% and reducing parameters by 99.43% for some cases. Our framework not only advances the application of LLMs in crisis management but also lays a solid foundation for future research across various domains.

Acknowledgement

This work was partially funded by the German Federal Ministry for Economic Affairs and Climate Action (BMWK) within the research project ESCADE (grant number: 01MN23004A).

References

Aleksa Bisercic, Mladen Nikolic, Mihaela van der Schaar, Boris Delibasic, Pietro Lio', and Andrija Petrović. 2023. Interpretable medical diagnostics with structured data extraction by large language models. *ArXiv*, abs/2306.05052.

Sayantan Dasgupta, Trevor Cohn, and Timothy Baldwin. 2023. Cost-effective distillation of large language models. In *Findings of the Association for Computational Linguistics: ACL 2023*, pages 7346–7354, Toronto, Canada. Association for Computational Linguistics.

Tim Dettmers, Artidoro Pagnoni, Ari Holtzman, and Luke Zettlemoyer. 2023. Qlora: Efficient finetuning of quantized llms. *Preprint*, arXiv:2305.14314.

Ning Ding, Yuxiao Qin, Guang Yang, et al. 2023. Parameter-efficient fine-tuning of large-scale pre-trained language models. *Nature Machine Intelligence*, 5:220–235.

Angela Fan, Pierre Stock, Benjamin Graham, Edouard Grave, Remi Gribonval, Herve Jegou, and Armand Joulin. 2021. Training with quantization noise for extreme model compression. *Preprint*, arXiv:2004.07320.

Tommaso Furlanello, Zachary Chase Lipton, Michael Tschannen, Laurent Itti, and Anima Anandkumar. 2018. Born again neural networks. In *International Conference on Machine Learning*.

Jianping Gou, Baosheng Yu, Stephen J. Maybank, and Dacheng Tao. 2021. Knowledge distillation: A survey. *International Journal of Computer Vision*, 129(6):1789–1819.

Yuxian Gu, Li Dong, Furu Wei, and Minlie Huang. 2023. Knowledge distillation of large language models. *arXiv*.

Oktie Hassanzadeh, Parul Awasthy, Ken Barker, Onkar Bhardwaj, Debarun Bhattacharjya, Mark Feblowitz, Lee Martie, Jian Ni, Kavitha Srinivas, and Lucy Yip. 2022. Knowledge-based news event analysis and forecasting toolkit. pages 5870–5873.

Neil Houlsby, Andrei Giurgiu, Stanislaw Jastrzebski, Bruna Morrone, Quentin De Laroussilhe, Andrea Gesmundo, Mona Attariyan, and Sylvain Gelly. 2019. Parameter-efficient transfer learning for NLP. In *Proceedings of the 36th International Conference on Machine Learning*, volume 97 of *Proceedings of Machine Learning Research*, pages 2790–2799. PMLR.

Cheng-Yu Hsieh, Chun-Liang Li, Chih-kuan Yeh, Hootan Nakhost, Yasuhisa Fujii, Alex Ratner, Ranjay Krishna, Chen-Yu Lee, and Tomas Pfister. 2023. Distilling step-by-step! outperforming larger language models with less training data and smaller model sizes. In *Findings of the Association for Computational Linguistics: ACL 2023*, pages 8003–8017, Toronto, Canada. Association for Computational Linguistics.

Edward J Hu, yelong shen, Phillip Wallis, Zeyuan Allen-Zhu, Yuanzhi Li, Shean Wang, Lu Wang, and Weizhu Chen. 2022. LoRA: Low-rank adaptation of large language models. In *International Conference on Learning Representations*.

Sabine Janzen, Prajvi Saxena, Sebastian Baer, and Wolfgang Maass. 2024. "listening in": Social signal detection for crisis prediction. In *Hawaii International Conference on System Sciences*.

Jongwoo Ko, Sungnyun Kim, Tianyi Chen, and Se-Young Yun. 2024. Distillm: Towards streamlined distillation for large language models. *Preprint*, arXiv:2402.03898.

Aditi Mishra, Utkarsh Soni, Anjana Arunkumar, Jinbin Huang, Bum Chul Kwon, and Chris Bryan. 2023. Promptaid: Prompt exploration, perturbation, testing and iteration using visual analytics for large language models. *Preprint*, arXiv:2304.01964.

Alec Radford, Jeffrey Wu, Rewon Child, David Luan, Dario Amodei, Ilya Sutskever, et al. 2019. Language models are unsupervised multitask learners. *OpenAI blog*, 1(8):9.

Victor Sanh, Lysandre Debut, Julien Chaumond, and Thomas Wolf. 2019. Distilbert, a distilled version of bert: smaller, faster, cheaper and lighter. *arXiv*, abs/1910.01108.

Prajvi Saxena, Sabine Janzen, and Wolfgang Maass. 2024. Newspaper signaling for crisis prediction. In *Proceedings of the 2024 Conference of the North American Chapter of the Association for Computational Linguistics: Human Language Technologies (Volume 3: System Demonstrations)*, pages 166–173, Mexico City, Mexico. Association for Computational Linguistics.

Zhijie Shen, Wu Guo, and Bin Gu. 2023. Language-universal adapter learning with knowledge distillation for end-to-end multilingual speech recognition. *Preprint*, arXiv:2303.01249.

Hugo Touvron, Louis Martin, Kevin Stone, Peter Albert, Amjad Almahairi, Yasmine Babaei, Nikolay Bashlykov, Soumya Batra, Prajjwal Bhargava, Shruti Bhosale, Dan Bikel, Lukas Blecher, Cristian Canton Ferrer, Moya Chen, Guillem Cucurull, David Esiobu, Jude Fernandes, Jeremy Fu, Wenyin Fu, Brian Fuller, Cynthia Gao, Vedanuj Goswami, Naman Goyal, Anthony Hartshorn, Saghar Hosseini, Rui Hou, Hakan Inan, Marcin Kardas, Viktor Kerkez, Madian Khabsa, Isabel Kloumann, Artem Korenev, Punit Singh Koura,

Marie-Anne Lachaux, Thibaut Lavril, Jenya Lee, Diana Liskovich, Yinghai Lu, Yuning Mao, Xavier Martinet, Todor Mihaylov, Pushkar Mishra, Igor Molybog, Yixin Nie, Andrew Poulton, Jeremy Reizenstein, Rashi Rungta, Kalyan Saladi, Alan Schelten, Ruan Silva, Eric Michael Smith, Ranjan Subramanian, Xiaoqing Ellen Tan, Binh Tang, Ross Taylor, Adina Williams, Jian Xiang Kuan, Puxin Xu, Zheng Yan, Iliyan Zarov, Yuchen Zhang, Angela Fan, Melanie Kambadur, Sharan Narang, Aurelien Rodriguez, Robert Stojnic, Sergey Edunov, and Thomas Scialom. 2023. Llama 2: Open foundation and fine-tuned chat models. *Preprint*, arXiv:2307.09288.

Junjie Wang, Yicheng Chen, Wangshu Zhang, Sen Hu, Teng Xu, and Jing Zheng. 2023. AdapterDistillation: Non-destructive task composition with knowledge distillation. In *Proceedings of the 2023 Conference on Empirical Methods in Natural Language Processing: Industry Track*, pages 194–201, Singapore. Association for Computational Linguistics.

Peter West, Chandra Bhagavatula, Jack Hessel, Jena D. Hwang, Liwei Jiang, Ronan Le Bras, Ximing Lu, Sean Welleck, and Yejin Choi. 2022. Symbolic knowledge distillation: from general language models to commonsense models. *Preprint*, arXiv:2110.07178.

Shijie Wu, Ozan Irsoy, Steven Lu, Vadim Dabravolski, Mark Dredze, Sebastian Gehrmann, Prabhanjan Kambadur, David Rosenberg, and Gideon Mann. 2023. Bloomberggpt: A large language model for finance. *ArXiv*, abs/2303.17564.

Xiaohan Xu, Ming Li, Chongyang Tao, Tao Shen, Reynold Cheng, Jinyang Li, Can Xu, Dacheng Tao, and Tianyi Zhou. 2024. A survey on knowledge distillation of large language models. *Preprint*, arXiv:2402.13116.

Elad Ben Zaken, Shauli Ravfogel, and Yoav Goldberg. 2021. Bitfit: Simple parameter-efficient fine-tuning for transformer-based masked language-models. *arXiv preprint arXiv:2106.10199*.

Susan Zhang, Stephen Roller, Naman Goyal, Mikel Artetxe, Moya Chen, Shuohui Chen, Christopher Dewan, Mona Diab, Xian Li, Xi Victoria Lin, Todor Mihaylov, Myle Ott, Sam Shleifer, Kurt Shuster, Daniel Simig, Punit Singh Koura, Anjali Sridhar, Tianlu Wang, and Luke Zettlemoyer. 2022. Opt: Open pre-trained transformer language models. *Preprint*, arXiv:2205.01068.

A Example Appendix

A.1 Background on Knowledge Distillation and QLoRA

Knowledge Distillation (KD) transfers knowledge from a large teacher model to a smaller student model by training the student to mimic the teacher's output distributions (Gou et al., 2021). It enables efficient deployment of Large Language Models (LLMs) by reducing computational overhead while preserving performance. KD is categorized into offline, online, and self-distillation (Xu et al., 2024). We adopt offline distillation, where a pre-trained LLM acts as a teacher to guide a smaller student model.

QLoRA (Dettmers et al., 2023), an extension of Low-Rank Adaptation (LoRA), integrates quantization into adaptation to enhance training and inference efficiency. By reducing weight precision from Float32 to int4, QLoRA significantly lowers memory usage and accelerates computation, making it well-suited for parameter-efficient fine-tuning (PEFT). It also improves memory efficiency through three key innovations. First, it introduces 4-bit NormalFloat (NF4), optimized for weights with a normal distribution, reducing the memory footprint. Second, Double Quantization applies quantization not only to model weights but also to quantization constants, further compressing storage. Third, paged optimizers dynamically manage memory, mitigating spikes during large-scale model training.

A.2 Prompts Examples

Fig. 2 illustrate the prompts used in our experiments. For all experiments, we employ teacher-student pairs such as LLaMA-2 (13B $\rightarrow$ 7B), OPT (13B $\rightarrow$ 1.3B), and GPT-2 (1.5B $\rightarrow$ 124M). These prompts are designed to provide clear and precise guidance for the distilling process. The customization of prompts for fine-tuning is dependent on the specific requirements of different models, although a general structure is commonly observed (Mishra et al., 2023). This structure typically includes an optional system prompt, such as 'Below is an instruction that describes a task', followed by a mandatory instruction detailing the task, for instance, 'Classify the article into one of these categories: 'risk and warning', 'caution and advice', and 'safe and harmless". User prompts are also incorporated to provide explicit instructions. The process concludes with the addition of the input article and, for fine-tuning purposes, the ground truth in terms of the output. For example, an input 'Energy sector warns of impending shortages and surging bills in upcoming months.....' would have an output 'risk and warning'. Thus, a comprehensive prompt might be formulated as: "Below is an instruction that describes a task. Instruction:the crisis article into one of these categories 'risk and

```
system_message = """
You are an expert multilingual news analyst with advanced skills in understanding and interpreting news articles across multiple languages. Your job is to carefully classify each article into one of three categories: 'safe and harmless,' 'caution and advice,' or 'risk and warning.' For each classification, provide a concise and well-reasoned justification in English, explaining your decision based on the content of the article.
Examples:

1. Title: "Thousands of flights canceled as German airport staff strike - KION546"
   Article: "BERLIN (AP) -- Thousands of flights to and from German airports were canceled Friday as workers walked out to press their demands for inflation-busting pay increases. The strikes...."
   Classification: risk and warning
   Reason: This news article falls under the category of 'risk and warning' because it highlights significant disruptions in air travel due to strikes, indicating potential ongoing issues and a warning of a "summer of chaos" if demands are not met.

2. Title: "Dezember bringt wenig Erbauliches für die Euro-Wirtschaft I Börsen-Zeitung"
   Article: "Das Jahr 2022 endet für die Euro-Wirtschaft mit einem eher trüben Bild: Das Handelsbilanzdefizit hat sich im Dezember ausgeweitet und die Industrie hat die Produktion ...."
   Classification: caution and advice
   Reason: The news article presents a mixed outlook for the Euro economy, highlighting challenges such as an expanding trade deficit and reduced industrial production, while also mentioning signs of optimism like improved global trade and high order backlogs. This indicates a cautious tone, advising readers to be aware of economic difficulties while also recognizing potential recovery signs.

3. Title: "dpa-AFX: DZ Bank hebt fairen Wert für Munich Re auf 360 Euro - 'Kaufen'"
   Article: "FRANKFURT (dpa-AFX Analyser) - Die DZ Bank hat den fairen Wert für Munich Re von 345 auf 360 Euro angehoben und die Einstufung auf 'Kaufen' belassen. Dass der Rückversicherer in einem durch Inflation, Hurrikan Ian, auslaufende Pandemie und Ukraine-Krieg geprägten Umfeld das ursprüngliche Gewinnziel übertroffen hat...."
   Classification: safe and harmless
   Reason: The news article provides a positive update on Munich Re's stock valuation and a recommendation to "buy," indicating confidence in the company's performance despite challenging external factors. Therefore, it falls under the category of 'safe and harmless.'
"""
```

Figure 2: Detailed prompt to extract ground truth labels from the teacher model.

warning', 'caution and advice', and 'safe and harmless'; Input: Energy sector warns of impending shortages and surging bills in upcoming months; Output: 'risk and warning'". To enhance outcomes, incorporating a few manually curated input examples for few-shot prompting with domain-specific samples is recommended. This approach underscores the pivotal importance of precise and thorough prompt design in facilitating effective training and knowledge distillation.

LLM DEBATE OPPONENT : Counter-argument Generation focusing on Implicit and Critical Premises

Taisei Ozaki[1], **Chihiro Nakagawa**[1,2], **Naoya Inoue**[2,3], **Shoichi Naito**[4,5]
Kenshi Yamaguchi[5] **Atsuhiko Shintani**[1]

[1]Osaka Metropolitan University, [2]RIKEN, [3]JAIST, [4]RICOH COMPANY, LTD., [5]Tohoku University
Correspondence: sg23174y@st.omu.ac.jp

Abstract

Debate education is effective in fostering critical thinking skills, an important national issue, but the human cost is a problem. While Large Language Models (LLMs) show promise in automating this process, the optimal approach for targeting critical premises remains unclear. This study proposes methods that specifically focus on implicit and critical premises in counter-argument generation and compares multi-step and one-step implementation approaches. Through evaluation of seven distinct methods using 100 debate topics, we demonstrate that focusing on critical and implicit premises improves counter-argument quality, with one-step methods consistently outperforming multi-step approaches. This superiority stems from better capture of motion spirit, reduced hallucinations, and avoidance of challenging intermediate tasks. Among the methods targeting premises, the Generated and Targeted Premise Attack approach achieved the highest performance in both human expert and automated evaluations. Our findings suggest that counter-argument generation benefits more from integrated approaches that allow LLMs to fully utilize their learned understanding of argumentative patterns. These results provide important insights for developing more effective debate agents and advancing automated argumentation systems.

1 Introduction

In our highly information-oriented society, the development of critical thinking skills[1] is a national priority. It is said that these skills are fostered through debate education. However, debating requires a human cost, such as an opponent and an evaluator. We are therefore developing a debate opponent using Large Language Models (LLM) agents with powerful natural language processing capabilities. It is expected that learners will experience various types of arguments, represented by weakening arguments by denying premises (Sanders, 1974), through this debate against the debate opponents. This exposure to diverse argumentative strategies is expected to enhance the learners' capacity for critical thinking skills (Zhang et al., 2016).

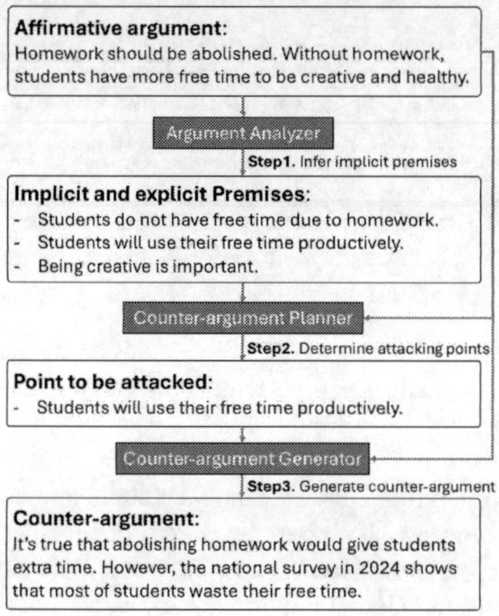

Figure 1: Methods of counter-argument generation

In developing LLMs as debate agents, a critical consideration is their ability to generate counter-arguments. Even in this era of rapidly advancing LLMs, which have seen big progress in text generation capabilities (Lin et al., 2023; Goloviznina et al., 2023; Wang et al., 2023; Chen et al., 2024), research focused on the generation of counter-arguments continues to attract considerable interest within the field. However, the feedback from debate experts[2] suggests that counter-arguments generated by LLMs often lack argumentative strength.

[1]Logical, objective, and unbiased reasoning, characterized by reflective thinking that involves the conscious examination of one's own reasoning processes (Kusumi, 2010).

[2]Members of the Japan Parliamentary Debate Association

Proceedings of the 2025 Conference of the Nations of the Americas Chapter of the Association for Computational Linguistics: Human Language Technologies (Volume 4: Student Research Workshop), pages 456–465
April 30 - May 1, 2025 ©2025 Association for Computational Linguistics

In fact, the gpt-3.5-turbo based debate opponent we developed in our preliminary experiments has been defeated by middle school students who have learned to debate in English competitive debate competitions (as of March 2023).

In competitive debate, The strength of the counterargument hinges on the validity of the premise being attacked. For instance, when countering "*Homework should be abolished because it infringes on free time,*" challenging the implicit and critical premise that "*free time is inherently more productive*" proves more strong (Walton, 2009).

Therefore, it is important how implicit and critical the premise can be attacked. Several studies focusing on premises in debate exist. Alshomary et al. (2021) proposed a two-step framework using BERT and GPT-2 to directly target and refute key premises, outperforming earlier LSTM-based methods in generating counter-arguments. However, the above proposed method limits the premise to be attacked to explicit ones and does not clarify the criteria or definition of critical premises.

In this study, we proposed a method (see Figure 1) to make LLM imitate the thought process that debate experts implicitly follow when constructing a counter-argument: first, they organize premises that support the affirmative argument, then they decide which premises to attack, and then they create a counter-argument.

In this study, we collaborated with debate experts to independently design a definition of critical premises and proposed a method (see Figure 1) that enables LLMs to mimic the implicit reasoning processes that debate experts naturally employ when constructing counter-arguments. By doing so, we aim to incorporate implicit premises as potential targets for attack, thereby generating counter-arguments with greater argumentative strength.

Our approach consists of three key steps. In the first step, the LLM receives a debate topic along with its corresponding affirmative claim and generates a comprehensive list of premises that support the claim, regardless of whether they are implicit or explicit. In the second step, the model identifies which premises to attack based on the predefined criteria for critical premises. Finally, in the third step, the LLM constructs counter-arguments that specifically target the selected premise.

We evaluated our approach from two key perspectives: (1) whether the target premises for attack should include implicit premises (i.e., whether Step 1 should be performed), and (2) whether providing predefined critical premises impacts performance. As a baseline, we used a simple direct counter-argument generation approach. Furthermore, considering prior research indicating that LLM performance improves when reasoning processes are explicit, as seen in Chain-of-Thought (CoT) prompting (Wei et al., 2023), we investigated whether our method's performance differs when all steps are instructed at one-step versus when each step is executed separately in a multi-step prompting.

Therefore, the purpose of this paper is to evaluate and compare both the multi-step and one-step approaches to counter-argument generation from two perspectives: whether implicit premises are also added to the candidate attack premises or whether the definition of critical premises is used. The contributions of this study are presented below.

- We proposed a method to generate highly strong counter-arguments by having LLM imitate the strategies that human experts use when constructing counter-arguments.
- We showed that even implicit assumptions are candidates for attack assumptions, and that providing critical assumptions is effective in the task of generating counterarguments.
- It directly compares multi-step and one-step generation approaches and provides important insights into the design of LLM-based counter-argument generation systems.

Through comprehensive evaluation involving human experts and automated assessment, we investigate these approaches' effectiveness in generating strong counter-arguments, aiming to contribute to the development of more effective debate agents.

However, our research focuses specifically on the identification and targeting of implicit and critical premises in counter-argument generation, rather than on the procedural approach itself (multi-step or one-step). We suggest that effective counter-arguments should target premises that are critical to the basis of the argument but often left implicit by the arguer. Thus, our key suggestion is to focus on the quality of the premises rather than the generative process.

2 Related Work

LLM-based Counter-Argument Generation. Ozaki et al. (2023) compared GPT-3 counter-arguments with human-crafted ones from Kialo, showing that LLM responses can match or surpass human outputs in logical coherence. More recent work has leveraged multi-agent interactions among LLMs with distinct personas (Hu et al., 2024) and self-refinement techniques (Madaan et al., 2023; Kao and Yen, 2024; Hu et al., 2023) to further enhance diversity and depth.

Premise-Focused Methods. Attacking premises is a core strategy in debate (Sanders, 1974). Alshomary et al. (2021) proposed a BERT-GPT-2 pipeline for identifying and refuting key premises, outperforming LSTM-based methods. Accounting for *implicit premises* can reveal hidden assumptions, as demonstrated by Boltužić and Šnajder (2016).

Multi-Step Reasoning. Inspired by CoT prompting (Wei et al., 2023) and Zero-shot CoT (Kojima et al., 2023), multi-step methods clarify argumentative structure. Alshomary and Wachsmuth (2023) showed that negating a central claim by selectively attacking premises can improve counter-arguments, though multi-step prompts risk hallucinating premises or misidentifying targets (Ozaki et al., 2024).

Open Challenges. These studies highlight the importance of both explicit and implicit premises, as well as the balance between multi-step and single-step approaches. Our work extends this research by examining how incorporating implicit premises and critical premise definitions, alongside multi-step prompting, affects the strength of LLM-generated counter-arguments.

3 Methods

We categorize our counter-argument generation approaches into multi-step and one-step methods, each reflecting a distinct strategy for producing counter-arguments. The multi-step approach imitates the systematic analytical process of human experts, splitting the generation into phases that can enhance transparency and explainability. By contrast, the one-step approach merges these phases into a single step, while still aligning with the expert-inspired pipeline. As a baseline, we consider a direct counter-argument generation method that does not attempt to replicate expert reasoning. Table 1 compares the main differences. All methods rely on a single LLM agent, use the same system prompt (Table 11), and share generation goals derived from Table 8.

3.1 Multi-step generation

The difference between implicit and explicit assumptions is appended in the Appendix A.

m-Comp: Generated and Targeted Premise Attack Counter-argument Generation

m-Comp comprises three phases. First, it generates a comprehensive list of both implicit and explicit premises underlying the affirmative argument. Second, it selects a single premise to attack by applying the critical premise criteria (Table 9). Finally, it produces a concise counter-argument that focuses on this chosen premise. The entire prompt for this method is shown in Table 12.

m-Targ: Targeted Premise Attack Counter-argument Generation

m-Targ has two phases. Instead of generating premises, it draws on only the explicit premises present in the affirmative argument, chooses one for attack using the critical premise criteria, and then generates a counter-argument focusing on that selected premise. The prompt for this method is in Table 13.

m-Basic: Non-Targeted Premise Attack Counter-argument Generation

m-Basic also proceeds in two phases, similarly selecting a premise from the affirmative argument's explicit statements. However, it does not use critical premise criteria, choosing a premise without that guidance and generating a counter-argument accordingly. The prompt is presented in Table 13.

3.2 One-step Methods

o-Comp, o-Targ, o-Basic

o-Comp, o-Targ, and o-Basic each condense the respective multi-step strategies into one step. o-Comp corresponds to m-Comp, o-Targ to m-Targ, and o-Basic to m-Basic, merging premise consideration and target selection into a single prompt (Table 13). Table 1 summarizes the overall distinctions among these methods.

3.3 Baseline

DirectGen: Direct Counter-argument Generation

OS-0 DG generates a counter-argument in a single step, without explicitly considering any premises. This forms our baseline approach.The prompt is presented in Table 14.

Table 1: Comparison of Methods

Method	Premise Type	Critical Criteria	Steps
m-Comp	Both	input	3
m-Targ	Explicit	input	2
m-Basic	Explicit	no	2
Directgen*	unspecified	no	1
o-Comp	Both	input	1
o-Targ	Explicit	input	1
o-Basic	Explicit	no	1

*baseline

Table 2: Evaluation metrics for Counter-argument

No.	Type	Description
Q1	Ranking	Attacking a more critical premise
Q2	Ranking	Attacking a more implicit premise
Q3	Ranking	The counter-argument is overall stronger
Q4	Choice	Relevance to the topic
Q5	Choice	Logical consistency
Q6	Choice	Multiple supporting reasons
Q7	Choice	Use of specific examples
Q8	Choice	Attacking the affirmative argument's premise

4 Construction of Dataset

We collected debate topics and affirmative arguments from idebate[3], a well-known debate forum. We randomly selected 100 instances from the scraped data and used an LLM (Clade-3.5-sonnet) to refine them into clear, concise sentences while maintaining the original content. Examples are shown in Table 10

5 Experiment

We conducted a comparative evaluation experiment of four counter-argument generation methods. Using a 100-set dataset, we generated counter-arguments using three LLMs: gpt-4o-mini-2024-07-18 (mini") and gpt-4o-2024-05-13 (gpt") from OpenAI[4], and llama-3.1-70b-versatile ("llama") from Meta[5]. We performed automatic evaluation using gpt-4o as evaluator, comparing methods within two groups (multi-step format + baseline and one-step + baseline) using eight evaluation metrics. The metrics were categorized as either choice or ranking type (refer to Table 2), with evaluators reviewing counter-arguments simultaneously within groups. To verify reliability, we conducted parallel experiments with human debate experts, measuring agreement with LLM results. We also directly compared multi-step and one-step approaches through paired evaluations. Calibration was performed using a separate dataset before evaluation experiments.

[3]https://idebate.net/resources/debatabase
[4]https://openai.com/index/openai-api/
[5]https://groq.com/

Table 3: Combined Inter-Rater Agreement Results

Human Experts		
Model	Choice	Ranking
mini	0.53	0.33
gpt	0.34	0.36
llama	0.50	0.30
GPT-4o vs Each Expert		
Model	Choice	Ranking
mini	0.46	0.24
gpt	0.32	0.26
llama	0.43	0.26

Table 4: Probability of ranking in the top of each method evaluated by experts and LLM(40 samples)

	Multi-step			
	m-Comp	m-Targ	m-Basic	Directgen
Q1	0.7583	0.6889	0.5889	**0.8028**
Q2	0.7889	0.6722	0.6528	**0.8806**
Q3	0.7028	0.5806	0.4833	**0.8083**

5.1 Evaluation Metrics

A description of each ranking type evaluation metrics is given below, and a description of the choice type metrics is given in Appendix B.

- **Q1: Attacking a more critical premise** This metric ranks counter-arguments based on how effectively they attack critical premises. Attacks on key, yet under-explained premises are rated higher than those targeting minor or well-defended points.
- **Q2: Attacking a more implicit premise** This metric evaluates how well the counter-argument addresses implicit premises—those assumed but not explicitly stated.
- **Q3:The counter-argument is overall more strong** This metric evaluates the overall effectiveness of the counter-argument, taking into account the importance of the premise attacked, the quality of reasoning, and the overall persuasiveness.

5.2 Inter-Rater Agreement

We calculated the agreement rate of annotations between human expert evaluators (refer to Table 3). Gwet's AC1 was used as the agreement metric(Vach and Gerke, 2023). [6]

When utilizing LLMs as evaluators, the agreement rate with experts decreased by only approximately 0.1 points, indicating that the LLM evaluations did not deviate significantly from those made by human experts.

[6]Krippendorff's α (Krippendorff, 2007) is often used in the NLP field, it was not used in this experiment because it was considered to cause the kappa paradox((Zec et al., 2017)) due to the excessively high agreement rate in the *choice* type indicators.

Table 5: Probability of ranking in the top of each method evaluated by LLM (100 samples)

	Multi-step			
	m-Comp	m-Targ	m-Basic	Directgen
Q1	0.6933	0.4067	0.2033	**0.6967**
Q2	0.6033	0.3567	0.3167	**0.7233**
Q3	0.7300	0.3433	0.1633	**0.7633**
	One-step			
	o-Comp	o-Targ	o-Basic	Directgen
Q1	**0.7000**	0.5367	0.3767	0.5456
Q2	**0.6456**	0.5334	0.5334	0.5454
Q3	**0.6546**	0.5222	0.3567	0.5300

Table 6: Win-rate of one-step against multi-step (100 samples)

Metric	Comp	Targ	Basic
Q1	**0.6078**	**0.6799**	**0.6810**
Q2	**0.7314**	**0.7518**	**0.7849**
Q3	**0.6537**	**0.5612**	0.4946

6 Results and Analysis

The results for ranking-type evaluation metrics are shown in Tables 4, 5[7]. Table 4 shows 40 samples evaluated by experts and GPT-4o; Table 5 shows 100 samples by GPT-4o for multi-step, one-step, and combined methods. We assessed probability of counter-arguments ranking in top positions. Direct comparison results between method pairs in Table 6. Example generation in 17.

In multi-step methods, Directgen achieved highest ranks across Q1-Q3 metrics, followed by m-Comp, m-Targ, m-Basic. In one-step methods, o-Comp ranked highest, Directgen and o-Targ showed equal rates, o-Basic lowest. One-step methods demonstrated superior performance except Q3 comparison between Basic variants.

One-step methods outperform multi-step methods across all metrics. Three key factors contribute to these results. First, better motion spirit capture, as LLMs learn affirmative claims, and counterarguments in proximity within embedding space, while decomposed steps may miss critical premises. Second, reduced hallucination impact, as multi-step processes propagate hallucinations forward ((Zhang et al., 2024),(Nourbakhsh et al., 2022),(Huang et al., 2024)), while one-step generation minimizes impact. Third, premise decision difficulty is a significant challenge. Selecting critical premises has been shown to be difficult even for state-of-the-art LLMs, with (Ozaki et al., 2024) demonstrating that even powerful models achieve only about 70% accuracy in selecting effective premises for counter-arguments compared to expert judgments. This research specifically found some disagreement even among human debate experts on what constitutes an optimal target premise, highlighting the inherent complexity of this task. Our observations confirm these findings, with many instances in our experiment showing ineffective premise selection in multi-step approaches.

[7]Values averaged across three models. Choice-type metrics in Table 16, Appendix

Table 7: Probability that a premise judged by the LLM to be a valid attack point is also judged by the expert to be a valid attack point (precision score) (Ozaki et al., 2024)

model	Average score
gpt-4	0.79
gpt-3.5-turbo	0.72
llama2-70B-chat	0.59
gemini-pro	0.67
Claude2.1	0.51
Majority baseline	0.62

In a study by Ozaki et al. (2024) that evaluated attack premise selection quality in counter-argument generation, Table 7 shows the precision rates of LLMs compared to expert selections used as the gold-standard. Even the highly capable GPT-4 achieved only approximately 80% accuracy when measured against expert choices, demonstrating the inherent difficulty of the attack premise decision step.

7 Conclusion

This study conducted a comprehensive comparison of different approaches to counter-argument generation using large language models, addressing the challenge of high human costs in debate education while maintaining educational effectiveness. Through evaluation of seven distinct methods across 100 debate topics, we demonstrate that focusing on critical and implicit premises significantly enhances LLMs' ability to generate strong counter-arguments.

Our analysis reveals that one-step methods consistently outperformed multi-step approaches across all evaluation metrics. This superior performance can be primarily attributed to their better capture of motion spirit through LLM's learned associations between topics and counterarguments. Additionally, one-step methods minimize the impact of hallucinations that typically cascade through multi-step processes, while avoiding the challenging task of intermediate premise selection that often proves difficult even for experienced debaters.

Among the methods targeting premises, o-Comp achieved the highest performance in both human and automated evaluations. Its success stems from the effective consideration of both explicit and implicit premises, combined with clear guidance about critical criteria within a single-step framework. The method's ability to identify and attack core assumptions proved crucial for generating compelling counter-arguments, demonstrating the importance of comprehensive premise analysis in automated argumentation.

These findings contribute significantly to our understanding of how to effectively leverage LLMs in complex argumentation tasks and provide practical insights for developing more effective debate agents. Our results suggest that while decomposed reasoning can be beneficial in many contexts, counter-argument generation benefits more from integrated approaches that allow LLMs to fully utilize their learned understanding of argumentative patterns. These insights pave the way for more accessible and effective debate education systems that can help address the critical need for developing students' critical thinking skills.

8 Limitations and Future Work

Future research should address these limitations through:

- **Dataset Expansion**: Development of various debate data sources beyond idebate, including multi-turn debates and data synthesis by LLM

- **Evaluation Metrics**: Creation of more universal strength rating metrics for counter-arguments that consider argumentative context beyond isolated arguments

- **Hallucination Assessment**: Developing systematic evaluation of factual accuracy in generated counter-arguments, particularly important in debate contexts. As shown by (Ozaki et al., 2024), the premise selection step is especially vulnerable to hallucinations, with LLMs sometimes selecting premises that aren't actually critical to the argument or generating entirely new premises that weren't implied in the original argument. Future work should focus on methods to reduce these hallucinations through knowledge grounding or verification techniques.

- **LLM Analysis**: Comprehensive model-specific effectiveness verification across varying model sizes and architectures

- **Generation Framework**: Multi-turn support and external knowledge incorporation for more practical debate situations

- **Practical Applications**: Integration with debate education platforms and measurement of educational effectiveness through controlled studies

References

Milad Alshomary, Shahbaz Syed, Arkajit Dhar, Martin Potthast, and Henning Wachsmuth. 2021. Counter-argument generation by attacking weak premises. In *Findings of the Association for Computational Linguistics: ACL-IJCNLP 2021*, pages 1816–1827, Online. Association for Computational Linguistics.

Milad Alshomary and Henning Wachsmuth. 2023. Conclusion-based counter-argument generation. *Preprint*, arXiv:2301.09911.

Filip Boltužić and Jan Šnajder. 2016. Fill the gap! analyzing implicit premises between claims from online debates. In *Proceedings of the Third Workshop on Argument Mining (ArgMining2016)*, pages 124–133, Berlin, Germany. Association for Computational Linguistics.

Chung-Chi Chen, Hiroya Takamura, Ichiro Kobayashi, and Yusuke Miyao. 2024. Fingen: A dataset for argument generation in finance. *ArXiv*, abs/2405.20708.

Valeriya Goloviznina, Irina Fishcheva, Tatiana Peskisheva, and Evgeny V. Kotelnikov. 2023. Aspect-based argument generation in russian. *COMPUTATIONAL LINGUISTICS AND INTELLECTUAL TECHNOLOGIES"*.

Zhe Hu, Hou Pong Chan, Jing Li, and Yu Yin. 2024. Unlocking varied perspectives: A persona-based multi-agent framework with debate-driven text planning for argument generation. *Preprint*, arXiv:2406.19643.

Zhe Hu, Hou Pong Chan, and Yu Yin. 2023. Americano: Argument generation with discourse-driven decomposition and agent interaction. *ArXiv*, abs/2310.20352.

Qiang Huang, Feng Huang, DeHao Tao, YueTong Zhao, BingKun Wang, and YongFeng Huang. 2024. Coq:an empirical framework for multi-hop question answering empowered by large language models. In *ICASSP 2024 - 2024 IEEE International Conference on Acoustics, Speech and Signal Processing (ICASSP)*, pages 11566–11570.

Wei-Yu Kao and An-Zi Yen. 2024. MAGIC: Multi-argument generation with self-refinement for domain generalization in automatic fact-checking. In *Proceedings of the 2024 Joint International Conference on Computational Linguistics, Language Resources and Evaluation (LREC-COLING 2024)*, pages 10891–10902, Torino, Italia. ELRA and ICCL.

Takeshi Kojima, Shixiang Shane Gu, Machel Reid, Yutaka Matsuo, and Yusuke Iwasawa. 2023. Large language models are zero-shot reasoners. *Preprint*, arXiv:2205.11916.

Klaus Krippendorff. 2007. Computing krippendorff's alpha-reliability. *Departmental papers (ASC)*.

Takashi Kusumi. 2010. *Modern Cognitive Psychology 3: Thinking and Language*. Kitaoji Shobo, Kyoto.

Jiayu Lin, Rong Ye, Meng Han, Qi Zhang, Ruofei Lai, Xinyu Zhang, Zhao Cao, Xuanjing Huang, and Zhongyu Wei. 2023. Argue with me tersely: Towards sentence-level counter-argument generation. In *Conference on Empirical Methods in Natural Language Processing*.

Aman Madaan, Niket Tandon, Prakhar Gupta, Skyler Hallinan, Luyu Gao, Sarah Wiegreffe, Uri Alon, Nouha Dziri, Shrimai Prabhumoye, Yiming Yang, Sean Welleck, Bodhisattwa Prasad Majumder, Shashank Gupta, Amir Yazdanbakhsh, and Peter Clark. 2023. Self-refine: Iterative refinement with self-feedback. *ArXiv*, abs/2303.17651.

Armineh Nourbakhsh, Cathy Jiao, Sameena Shah, and Carolyn Penstein Rosé. 2022. Improving compositional generalization for multi-step quantitative reasoning in question answering. In *Conference on Empirical Methods in Natural Language Processing*.

Taisei Ozaki, chihiro Nakagawa, Naoya Inoue, Shoichi Naito, Takeshi Yamaguchi, Shotaro Amano, and Atsuhiko Shintani. 2024. Premise generation as effective points of counterarguments using large language models. In *Proceedings of the 30th Annual Meeting of The Association for Natural Language Processing*, pages 2681–2686, Japan. The Association for Natural Language Processing.

Taisei Ozaki, Chihiro Nakagawa, Shoichi Naito, Naoya Inoue, Takeshi Yamaguchi, and Atsuhiko Shintani. 2023. Automatic generation of high-quality counterargument papers using large language models. In *Proceedings of the Annual Conference of the Japanese Society for Artificial Intelligence*, JSAI2023, pages 4Xin111–4Xin111.

Gerald H Sanders. 1974. *Debate as a Paradigm for Demonstrating Skills in Argumentation and Logic*. ERIC.

Werner Vach and Oke Gerke. 2023. Gwet's ac1 is not a substitute for cohen's kappa – a comparison of basic properties. *MethodsX*, 10.

Douglas Walton. 2009. Objections, rebuttals and refutations. *Argument Cultures: Proceedings of the 8th OSSA Conference*.

Xiaoou Wang, Elena Cabrio, and Serena Villata. 2023. Argument and counter-argument generation: A critical survey. In *International Conference on Applications of Natural Language to Data Bases*.

Jason Wei, Xuezhi Wang, Dale Schuurmans, Maarten Bosma, Brian Ichter, Fei Xia, Ed Chi, Quoc Le, and Denny Zhou. 2023. Chain-of-thought prompting elicits reasoning in large language models. *Preprint*, arXiv:2201.11903.

Slavica Zec, Nicola Soriani, Rosanna Irene Comoretto, and Ileana Baldi. 2017. High agreement and high prevalence: The paradox of cohen's kappa. *The Open Nursing Journal*, 11:211 – 218.

Jiawei Zhang, Chejian Xu, Yu Gai, Freddy Lecue, Dawn Song, and Bo Li. 2024. Knowhalu: Hallucination detection via multi-form knowledge based factual checking. *ArXiv*, abs/2404.02935.

Justine Zhang, Ravi Kumar, Sujith Ravi, and Cristian Danescu-Niculescu-Mizil. 2016. Conversational flow in Oxford-style debates. In *Proceedings of the 2016 Conference of the North American Chapter of the Association for Computational Linguistics: Human Language Technologies*, pages 136–141, San Diego, California. Association for Computational Linguistics.

Appendix

A Definition of keywords

Table 8: Definition of keywords

Debate: A structured discussion on a specific topic, where participants are divided into the affirmative and negative sides. The affirmative side argues for the benefits that can be gained by accepting the topic, while the negative side emphasizes the potential drawbacks.
Counter-argument: Taking the opposing stance to the argument, critically identifying weaknesses, inaccuracies, and a lack of supporting evidence in the reasoning of the argument, without creation of a new argument from scratch.
Premise: All the implicit or explicit conditions and propositions that the subject of a argument assumes in order to establish the validity of that argument. Explicit: each sentence that constitutes the argument. Implicit: Unstated premises necessary for the argument to hold

For example: In an argument about the abolition of homework, When the affirmative side argues that *"Homework should be abolished because it takes away students' free time. The long hours of forced study at school, extended to after-school hours, inhibits the students' free time to develop their own ideas. This may indirectly prevent future innovation."*, An explicit premise is each statement that *"Homework should be abolished because it takes away students' free time."*, *"The long hours of forced study at school, extended to after-school hours, inhibits the students' free time to develop their own ideas."*, *"This may indirectly prevent future innovation."*. On the other hand, Implicit assumptions include the following examples, *"Free time is important and valuable in student development","Time to develop original ideas leads to future innovation"*.

Table 9: Definition of Critical premises

Foundational Importance: It should be foundational to the affirmative argument, supporting a key aspect of their arguments. Attacking the root of the opponent's argument is generally more critical.
Moderate Vulnerability: It should be moderately poorly explained or insufficiently supported in the affirmative argument, as the underlying premises of the opponent's argument are generally better explained and may be preemptively refuted.

For example: In an argument about social media regulation, a foundational premise might be "social media causes significant harm to mental health." This premise is both crucial to the argument (Foundational Importance) and often lacks comprehensive evidence (Moderate Vulnerability). Attacking the above premise and negating a premise that supports elements close to the root of the opponent's argument can significantly weaken their stance. Conversely, a premise that is under-explained in the opponent's argument is easier to attack from various perspectives. Generally, premises that support the core elements of an affirmative argument are well-explained, while those further from the core are often less thoroughly explained. Therefore, the ideal premise for rebuttal should be somewhat close to the core and not fully explained - a middle ground.

B Choice evaluation metrics

Our evaluation framework employs five different choice-type evaluation metrics, each designed as a binary classification task in which the counter-argument under evaluation meets or does not meet the metrics.

Q4: Relevance to the topic This metric evaluates whether the counter-argument stays focused on the debate topic. Effective counter-arguments must directly engage with the main issue, avoiding digressions into unrelated matters.
Q5: Logical consistency This metric evaluates the logical flow of the counter-argument. A strong counter-argument should progress naturally, with no unreasonable leaps or inconsistencies in reasoning.
Q6: Multiple supporting reasons This metric evaluates whether the counter-argument presents multiple reasons to strengthen its claim. Providing several well-reasoned points typically enhances the persuasiveness of the argument.
Q7: Use of specific examples This metric evaluates the use of concrete examples to support the counter-argument. Specific, relevant examples make the argument more tangible and convincing.
Q8: Attacking the premise on which affirmative argument stands This metric evaluates whether the counter-argument directly attacks a key premise that the affirmative argument depends on. A strong counter-argument must challenge a critical foundation of the opponent's reasoning.

C Example of Topic and Affirmative argument

Table 10: sample of dataset

Topic:Should male infant circumcision be considered a form of child abuse?
Affirmative argument: Performing surgery on infants without medical necessity is inherently risky and irresponsible. The Royal Dutch Medical Association has stated that no medical organization worldwide can definitively prove a medical need for infant circumcision. They emphasize that due to the lack of medical necessity and the genuine risk of complications, extremely stringent requirements should be in place for providing information and advice on this procedure. Despite this, circumcision is routinely performed globally, often by individuals with minimal medical training, and is frequently accepted by parents based on religious beliefs rather than medical evidence. This practice exposes infants to unnecessary surgical risks without clear medical benefits, which can be considered a form of child abuse.

D Prompts of each methods

Table 11: System prompt

system prompt: *You are a skilled debater.Your final objective is to make a high-quality counter-argument against an affirmative argument provided on a specific topic. To achieve this: You are not required to create a new argument from scratch. Take the opposite stance of the affirmative argument. To make an counter-argument means to carefully point out the weaknesses, inaccuracies, and lack of evidence in the reasoning of the claim. You may also be asked to complete several other tasks along the way. Consider these tasks as necessary steps to achieve the final objective.*

Table 12: m-Comp prompt

Premise generation step: *topic:#topic# affirmative argument:#argument# Thoroughly analyze the given affirmative argument on the given topic. Identify and list all premises supporting the affirmative argument, with a special emphasis on:1.Explicit premises: Clearly stated premises or sentences.2.Implicit premises: Unstated premises necessary for the argument to hold. Please output only the listed premises.*
Premise decision step: *Select the most suitable premise to attack for your counter-argument from the list of premises. The ideal premise should meet the following criteria: 1. Foundational Importance: It should be foundational to the affirmative argument, supporting a key aspect of their arguments. Attacking the root of the opponent's argument is generally more critical. 2. Moderate Vulnerability: It should be moderately poorly explained or insufficiently supported in the affirmative argument, as the underlying premises of the opponent's argument are generally better explained and may be preemptively refuted. Please output only the premise you chose.*
Counter-argument generation step: *Please make a concise and brief counter-argument to the affirmative argument, that attacks the specific premise you chose. Please output only the text of your counter-argument.*

Table 13: m-Targ and m-Basic prompt

m-Targ prompt
Premise decision step: *topic:#topic# affirmative argument:#argument# premise list:#premise list# Select the most suitable premise to attack for your counter-argument from the premise list. The ideal premise should meet the following criteria: 1.Foundational Importance: It should be foundational to the affirmative argument, supporting a key aspect of their arguments. Attacking the root of the opponent's argument is generally more critical. 2.Moderate Vulnerability: It should be moderately poorly explained or insufficiently supported in the affirmative argument, as the underlying premises of the opponent's argument are generally better explained and may be preemptively refuted.Please output only the premise you chose.*
Counter-argument generation step: *Please make a concise and brief counter-argument to the affirmative argument, that attacks the specific premise you chose. Please output only the text of your counter-argument.*

m-Basic prompt
Premise decision step: *topic:#topic# affirmative argument:#argument# premise list:#premise list# Select the most suitable premise to attack for your counter-argument from the premise list. Please output only the premise you chose.*
Counter-argument generation step: *Please make a concise and brief counter-argument to the affirmative argument, that attacks the specific premise you chose. Please output only the text of your counter-argument.*

Table 14: Directgen prompt(baseline)

Directgen prompt
Counter-argument generation step:*topic:#topic# affirmative argument:#argument# Please make a concise and brief counter-argument to the affirmative argument. Please output only the text of your counter-argument.*

Table 15: o-Comp prompt

topic: #topic# *affirmative argument: #argument#* *First Thoroughly analyze the given affirmative argument on the specified topic. Identify all premises supporting the affirmative argument, including:* *Explicit premises: Clearly stated assumptions or claims.* *Implicit premises: Unstated assumptions necessary for the argument to hold.* *Next choose the most suitable premise to attack for your counter-argument from the premises. The ideal premise should meet the following criteria:* *Foundational Importance: It should be foundational to the affirmative argument, supporting a key aspect of their arguments. Attacking the root of the opponent's argument is generally more critical.* *Moderate Vulnerability: It should be moderately poorly explained or insufficiently supported in the affirmative argument, as the underlying premises of the opponent's argument are generally better explained and may be preemptively refuted.* *Finally, please provide a concise, straightforward counter-argument to the affirmative argument, attacking the specific premise you chose.* *Please output only the text of your counter-argument.*

o-Targ prompt
Counter-argument generation step:*topic:#topic# affirmative argument:#argument# premise list:#premise list# First, select the most suitable premise to attack for your counter-argument from the premise list. The ideal premise should meet the following criteria: 1.Foundational Importance: It should be foundational to the affirmative argument, supporting a key aspect of their arguments. Attacking the root of the opponent's argument is generally more critical. 2.Moderate Vulnerability: It should be moderately poorly explained or insufficiently supported in the affirmative argument, as the underlying premises of the opponent's argument are generally better explained and may be preemptively refuted.Next, Please make a concise and brief counter-argument to the affirmative argument, that attacks the specific premise you chose. Please output only the text of your counter-argument.*

o-Basic prompt
Counter-argument generation step:*topic:#topic# affirmative argument:#argument# premise list:#premise list# First, Select the most suitable premise to attack for your counter-argument from the premise list. Next, Please make a concise and brief counter-argument to the affirmative argument, that attacks the specific premise you chose. Please output only the text of your counter-argument.*

E Results of choice evaluation

The results of the choice evaluation performed by a human expert are shown below. Each value is the percentage of each metrics satisfied.

Table 16: Results of choice evaluation

	Relevance to the topic (40 sample)			
metric	m-Comp	m-Targ	m-Basic	Directgen
Q4	0.97	0.97	0.96	0.96
Q5	0.96	0.94	0.86	0.95
Q6	0.74	0.54	0.47	0.87
Q7	0.29	0.28	0.24	0.24
Q8	0.89	0.90	0.90	0.83

F Examples of multi-step and one-step counter-argument generation

Table 17: Examples of multi-step and one-step counter-argument generation

Topic
Feminism is necessary or not
Affirmative argument
In the United Kingdom, one in four people experiences domestic violence (DV). Globally, reports of rape are increasing, yet conviction rates are declining. In the United States, women earn only 77 cents for every dollar earned by men. When filtered for racial minorities, the disparity becomes even more pronounced. These issues highlight the deep-rooted gender problems in society. Feminism still has many objectives to achieve, including women's rights, safety, and equal economic opportunities.
m-Comp)
The claim that women in the United States earn only 77 cents for every dollar earned by men is a misleading statistic that does not take into account various factors such as occupation, education, experience, and working hours. Using this statistic as a fundamental argument for the necessity of feminism oversimplifies the complex nature of wage determination and misrepresents the issue.
Directgen
The issues that are claimed to remain under feminism's purview are, in fact, already being addressed. Overemphasizing these problems can obscure the need for a more inclusive approach that addresses the rights of all genders, including men and non-binary individuals.

AutoML Meets Hugging Face: Domain-Aware Pretrained Model Selection for Text Classification

Parisa Safikhani[1,2] **David Broneske**[1]
[1]The German Centre for Higher Education Research and Science Studies (DZHW), Germany
[2]University of Magdeburg, Germany
safikhani@dzhw.eu, broneske@dzhw.eu

Abstract

The effectiveness of embedding methods is crucial for optimizing text classification performance in Automated Machine Learning (AutoML). However, selecting the most suitable pre-trained model for a given task remains challenging. This study introduces a comprehensive corpus of pre-fine-tuned models from the Hugging Face Model Hub, annotated with domains and dataset descriptions, to enhance text classification tasks. By leveraging this corpus, we evaluated the integration of pre-fine-tuned models into AutoML systems, demonstrating substantial performance gains across various datasets compared to baseline methods. Despite some inaccuracies in domain recognition, the results underscore the corpus' potential to streamline model selection and reduce computational costs.

1 Introduction

The advent of large language models (LLMs) has significantly advanced natural language processing (NLP), offering powerful tools for tasks such as text classification, summarization, and translation (Devlin et al., 2018). Fine-tuning these models for specific tasks has traditionally been the standard approach to achieving optimal performance. However, fine-tuning is resource-intensive, requiring substantial computational power and time, which may not be feasible for all practitioners (Wolf et al., 2020).

Simultaneously, AutoML automates tasks like feature and model selection, offering a streamlined approach to machine learning (He et al., 2021). Integrating LLMs into AutoML can boost NLP performance by leveraging their rich linguistic representations (Tornede et al., 2023).

A practical alternative to fine-tuning is utilizing pre-fine-tuned LLMs available in repositories such as Hugging Face. These models have been trained on specific tasks or domains and offer ready-to-use LLMs that can be incorporated into AutoML classifiers. This approach can improve performance while mitigating the resource constraints associated with fine-tuning.

Despite their potential, pre-fine-tuned LLMs from repositories like Hugging Face remain underexplored as text representation methods in AutoML. This study bridges this gap by developing an interface to a domain-annotated corpus of pre-fine-tuned models and evaluating their impact on classification performance across seven diverse text classification tasks.

This study enhances AutoML-based text classification by introducing a structured corpus of pre-fine-tuned models annotated with domain-specific metadata to optimize model selection. By systematically mapping models to tasks based on domain alignment, we demonstrate substantial performance gains while reducing computational overhead. The findings highlight a scalable and resource-efficient approach for integrating pre-trained representations into AutoML frameworks, making advanced NLP capabilities more accessible.

2 Related Works

LLMs and Contextual Embeddings: Contextual embeddings from fine-tuned LLMs outperform static methods like TF-IDF and Word2Vec in classification tasks by creating highly separable vector spaces (Pietro, 2020; Koroteev, 2021; Andrade, 2023; Safikhani and Broneske, 2023a). While fine-tuned LLMs achieve superior results, their computational cost limits their applicability. Pre-fine-tuned models, tailored for specific tasks, provide a scalable alternative (Wolf et al., 2020).

Text Representations in AutoML: AutoML frameworks like Auto-PyTorch aim to automate feature extraction, model selection, and hyperparameter tuning (Zimmer et al., 2021; Feurer et al.,

Proceedings of the 2025 Conference of the Nations of the Americas Chapter of the Association for Computational Linguistics: Human Language Technologies (Volume 4: Student Research Workshop), pages 466–473

2015). Despite this, they often rely on basic text representations like one-hot encoding. Recent research highlights the benefits of integrating advanced embeddings into AutoML systems. For instance, Safikhani and Broneske (2023b) demonstrated the effectiveness of fine-tuned BERT embeddings for binary classification in Auto-PyTorch. However, leveraging pre-fine-tuned LLMs for AutoML remains underexplored.

Open-Source Pre-Fine-Tuned Models: The Hugging Face Model Hub offers many pre-fine-tuned models optimized for tasks such as text classification, sentiment analysis, and named entity recognition (Wolf et al., 2020). These models (see for instance `BioBERT` (Lee et al., 2020), `SciBERT` (Beltagy et al., 2019), and `XLM-R` (Conneau, 2019) address domain-specific needs and reduce reliance on fine-tuning. Comprehensive model cards (Mitchell et al., 2019) provide transparency, aiding in model selection and reproducibility.

While pre-fine-tuned LLMs show promising results, their integration into AutoML classifiers has not been systematically studied. This research addresses this gap by evaluating the impact of pre-fine-tuned models as text representation methods in AutoML, focusing on their performance across diverse text classification tasks.

3 Methodology

In order to achieve our two goals of *interfacing* and *selecting* pre-fine-tuned models, we implement the following two phases.

3.1 Pre-trained Model Repository Integration

In the first phase of our methodology, we established an interface between a model repository (Hugging Face) and our AutoML framework (Auto-PyTorch). This integration enables the AutoML system to leverage a rich corpus of pre-trained NLP models, facilitating model reuse for downstream text classification tasks. Retrieving pre-trained (and fine-tuned) models from repositories like Hugging Face is critical for enhancing AutoML, as it allows rapid deployment and adaptation to new tasks without the high computational cost of training models from scratch. We implemented a configurable interface to the Hugging Face Hub API[1] that allows Auto-PyTorch to programmatically query and retrieve models. This retrieval process provided a diverse pool of candidate models, each trained on various text classification datasets and tasks. However, many models on the repository lacked clear documentation of their intended domains. To address this, we analyzed the datasets used for each model's fine-tuning as a proxy for its domain, using those dataset references to infer the types of tasks or domains for which each model is best suited.

3.2 Selection of Domain-Specific Models

Given the possibility of retrieving the pre-trained models from Hugging Face, the next phase implements the selection of a specific model. Hence, the domain of the models needs to be matched with the domain of the datasets.

3.2.1 Domain Definition from Literature

We conducted a literature review to identify key domains in text classification, as shown in Table 1. These domains, supported by foundational references, provide a framework for contextualizing models and analyzing domain representation in the corpus. We curated a list of 30 domains from existing literature (e.g., Sentiment Analysis, Spam Detection, Hate Speech Detection).

3.2.2 Domain Identification of Hugging Face Models

To identify the domain of models retrieved from the Hugging Face API, we mapped model names to dataset descriptions when explicit model descriptions were not available in the metadata.

As the collected domain labels, such as "Hate Speech Detection," often lack sufficient contextual richness and may overlook intricate nuances, we employed ChatGPT to generate extended descriptions. This approach bridges the semantic gap between concise labels and detailed model documentation, enhancing matching precision by capturing variations in terminology used across different contexts.

To map these models to a domain, we compared the model's description against the generated domain descriptions using sentence embeddings from `all-MiniLM-L6-v2` provided by Sentence-BERT (Reimers, 2019). We applied cosine similarity (Singhal et al., 2001) between the embeddings to assign the most semantically relevant domain to each model.

We selected a pre-fine-tuned model from the Hugging Face repository for each evaluation dataset based on the recognized domain. A fall-

[1] `https://huggingface.co/docs/hub/api`

Domain	Generated Description by ChatGPT
Emotion Cause Extraction (Ghazi et al., 2015)	Identifying the reasons or triggers for specific emotions in text.
Social Media Behavior Analysis (Aral and Walker, 2012)	Analyzing user behavior on social media platforms.
Rhetorical Structure Classification (Mann and Thompson, 1988)	Classifying rhetorical structures in discourse.
Spam Detection (Guzella and Caminhas, 2009)	Classifying emails or messages as spam or legitimate.
Language Identification (Jauhiainen et al., 2019)	Detecting the language of text, especially in multilingual settings.
Sentiment Analysis (Pang et al., 2008)	Detecting opinions, emotions, and sentiments in text.
Topic Classification (Blei et al., 2003)	Assigning topics or categories to text documents.
Emotion Recognition (Cowie et al., 2001)	Identifying emotions such as joy, sadness, anger, and fear in text.
Intent Classification (Liu et al., 2019)	Understanding the purpose or intent behind user queries.
Hate Speech Detection (Davidson et al., 2017)	Detecting hate speech, toxic, or abusive language in the text.
Textual Entailment (Bowman et al., 2015)	Determining if one text logically follows from another.
Document Classification (Rios and Kavuluru, 2018)	Categorizing entire documents into predefined classes.
Fake News Detection (Shu et al., 2017)	Detecting false or misleading news articles.
Aspect-Based Sentiment Analysis (Pontiki et al., 2016)	Analyzing sentiment specific to different aspects of a product or service.
Sarcasm Detection (Joshi et al., 2017)	Identifying sarcasm or ironic statements in the text.
Propaganda Detection (Da San Martino et al., 2019)	Detecting manipulative or biased content in text.
Irony Detection (Van Hee et al., 2018)	Identifying ironic statements in the text.
Argument Mining (Van Hee et al., 2018)	Analyzing arguments and their structures in the text.
Deception Detection (Fitzpatrick et al., 2015)	Detecting lies, fraud, or deceptive statements in text.
Lexical Complexity Prediction (Shardlow, 2013)	Predicting the complexity or difficulty of words in the text.
Politeness Classification (Danescu-Niculescu-Mizil et al., 2013)	Classifying text based on politeness levels.
Coreference Resolution (Lee et al., 2017)	Linking pronouns and entities to their references.
Genre Classification (Stamatatos et al., 2000)	Classifying text into genres such as fiction, non-fiction, etc.
Temporal Information Extraction (Bethard, 2013)	Extracting time-related information from text.
Claim Verification and Fact-Checking (Thorne and Vlachos, 2018)	Verifying the truth of claims in text.
Persuasiveness Classification (Habernal and Gurevych, 2016)	Classifying how persuasive text is.
Privacy Risk Classification (Biega et al., 2020)	Detecting privacy risks in text data.
Media Bias Detection (Baly et al., 2020)	Identifying bias in news or media content.
Speech Emotion Classification (Busso et al., 2013)	Recognizing emotions from spoken text or transcripts.
Multimodal Text Classification (Kiela et al., 2019)	Classifying text combined with other modalities like images or audio.

Table 1: Categorized Domains in Text Classification with Descriptions Generated Using ChatGPT and Foundational References, Serving as a Framework for Similarity-Based Domain Assignments.

back model (`all-MiniLM-L6-v2`) was used if no specific model was available for the recognized domain. Sentence embeddings for the datasets were then generated using the selected model.

Furthermore, it supports multi-task scenarios, making it a versatile choice when domain-specific models are unavailable.

3.3 Domain Identification of a given Datasets

To assign domains to our evaluation datasets, we implemented a comprehensive zero-shot classification approach using the cross-encoder/nli-deberta-v3-small model, particularly suited for its ability to interpret and classify complex data directly. This method is preferred over cosine similarity because it allows for a more dynamic interpretation of text semantics rather than just vector alignment, which is critical in understanding the nuanced thematic content of datasets that might not be immediately apparent through traditional vector space models.

Our process begins by selecting a representative subset of text samples from each class within the dataset to ensure comprehensive coverage of all potential categories within the classification task. These samples are systematically evaluated against our predefined domain names using the zero-shot model, which assesses the likelihood of each text sample fitting into each potential domain. Zero-shot learning is particularly effective because it evaluates the semantic content of the samples in a contextual manner, thus allowing for accurate classifications based on the inherent meanings and not merely on the superficial similarity of words or phrases.

To ensure robust domain assignment, we compute similarity scores between each text sample and each domain, then calculate the average similarity score across all classes for each domain. This averaging is crucial as it ensures that the domain assignment reflects the diversity of the entire dataset and is not biased toward dominant themes within any single class. Finally, the domain with the highest average similarity score is assigned to the dataset. This method is superior to cosine similarity as it provides a balanced and accurate domain assignment that effectively captures the complexity and diversity of the dataset. It utilizes the strengths of zero-shot learning to adapt to new and unseen categories seamlessly, making it more adaptable to datasets with varied and evolving themes.

4 Experiment

The experimental workflow evaluated the utility of pre-fine-tuned language models from Hugging Face for diverse text classification tasks. The process involved multiple steps, including collecting model metadata, domain recognition, dataset preparation, model selection, and evaluation. Below, we detail each step of the experimental setup.

4.1 Dataset Preparation

To evaluate the models, we used datasets from Kaggle[2], including Colbert (humor), IMDB Reviews (sentiment analysis), Cyberbullying Comments, Disaster Tweets Detection, Emotion Detection from Text, Amazon Reviews, and an annotated dataset for framing detection (Avetisyan and Broneske, 2021) to prevent data snooping. More detailed information about these datasets is provided in table 2.

4.2 Experimental Setup

The generated embeddings were split into training and testing sets (80/20 split) and used to train classification models. Auto-PyTorch was utilized to automatically configure and optimize the classification pipeline, employing a k-fold cross-validation strategy for robust evaluation.

We assessed model performance primarily using metrics tailored for imbalanced datasets. AUPRC was used for binary classification tasks to evaluate precision-recall trade-offs effectively, and micro F1-Score was employed for robust evaluation in multi-class settings.

The experiments were conducted on a high-performance system featuring an NVIDIA A100 GPU with 40 GB VRAM, dual Intel Xeon Gold 5220R CPUs, and 376 GB RAM, running Ubuntu 20.04 LTS. Key software included Python 3.8, PyTorch 1.9, Hugging Face Transformers 4.9, and Auto-PyTorch 0.0.6, optimized for efficient model training and inference.

5 Results and Discussion

The results of our evaluation, presented in Table 3, highlight the effectiveness of the proposed **Corpus-Driven Domain Mapping (CDDM)** approach, which utilizes pre-fine-tuned models as text representation methods for Auto-PyTorch. The performance of models selected from the constructed corpus was compared against the baseline Auto-PyTorch classifier, which uses one-hot encoding as the default text representation method. These comparisons were conducted across seven text classification datasets to evaluate the impact of domain-specific pre-trained representations.

[2]https://www.kaggle.com/

Performance Overview

The evaluation results show that integrating pre-fine-tuned models into Auto-PyTorch improves performance on various text classification datasets. This effectiveness depends on domain recognition accuracy, which affects model alignment with specific tasks. Below, we present key outcomes by recognized domains and corresponding pre-fine-tuned models from the Hugging Face repository:

Media Bias Detection: This model showed substantial performance improvements across several datasets. On the `Colbert` dataset, designed for humor detection but misclassified as media bias, the model achieved an AUPRC of 92.3% compared to the baseline of 52%. Similarly, on the `Cyberbullying Comments` dataset, where the domain was correctly identified as media bias, the model attained an AUPRC of 70.2%, outperforming the baseline of 46.55%. These results highlight the robustness of pre-fine-tuned models, even when domain recognition is not entirely accurate. However, precise domain alignment remains crucial for unlocking the full potential of the corpus.

Sexism and Misogyny Detection: On the `Disaster Tweets Detection` dataset, the domain recognition step correctly assigned sexism and misogyny detection. This resulted in a significant performance boost, with an AUPRC of 44.7% compared to 19.01%. Accurate domain recognition was instrumental in leveraging the model effectively for this task.

User Stance Classification: For the `IMDB Reviews` dataset, the recognized domain of stance classification was a reasonable match given the sentiment-related nature of the task. The model achieved an AUPRC of 67.5%, surpassing the baseline of 50.63%. This suggests that while the selected model performed well, assigning a sentiment-specific model could yield even better results.

Emotion Recognition: On the `Emotion Detection from Text` dataset, the domain recognition was accurate, resulting in an AUPRC of 71.7%, significantly higher than the baseline of 51.66%. This highlights the value of precise domain matching in maximizing the corpus's utility.

Genre Classification: On the `Amazon Reviews` dataset, the domain was correctly identified as

Dataset Binary	Number of Texts	Number of Classes	Average Text Length	Balanced
ColBERT	200,000	2 (Formal, Informal)	20 words	Yes
Disaster Tweets Detection	11,223	2 (Disaster, Not)	30 words	No
Cyberbullying Comments	115,661	2 (Cyberbullying, Not)	12 words	Yes
Framing Detection	4,063	2 (Framed, Not Framed)	25 words	No
IMDB Reviews	50,000	2 (Positive, Negative)	230 words	Yes
Dataset Multi-class	**Number of Texts**	**Number of Classes**	**Average Text Length**	**Balanced**
Amazon Reviews	17,337	3	33 words	No
Emotion Detection from Text	40,000	13	14 words	Yes

Table 2: Overview of Datasets for Binary and Multi-class Text Classification Tasks

Dataset Binary	Baseline (AUPRC %)	CDDM (AUPRC %)	Recognized Domain
ColBERT	52	92.3	Media Bias Detection
Disaster Tweets Detection	19.01	44.7	Sexism and Misogyny Detection
Cyberbullying Comments	52.00	92.3	Media Bias Detection
Framing Detection	46.55	70.2	Media Bias Detection
IMDB Reviews	50.63	67.5	User Stance Classification in Online Debates
Dataset Multi-class	**Baseline (Micro F1 %)**	**CDDM (Micro F1 %)**	**Recognized Domain**
Amazon Reviews	48.46	80.7	Genre Classification
Emotion Detection from Text	51.66	71.07	Propaganda Detection

Table 3: Performance Comparison of Pre-Fine-tuned Models Selected via Corpus-Driven Domain Mapping (CDDM) and Baseline Representations Across Text Classification Tasks

genre classification. The model achieved an impressive AUPRC of 80.7%, emphasizing the advantages of accurate domain recognition and the potential of the Hugging Face corpus for domain-specific tasks.

Propaganda Detection: On the `Framing Detection` dataset, the recognized domain was media bias detection rather than propaganda detection. Despite this misalignment, the model achieved an AUPRC of 70.2%, outperforming the baseline of 46.55%. This result underscores the need for more accurate domain recognition to fully utilize the potential of the corpus.

The corpus of pre-fine-tuned models from Hugging Face, annotated with domains and dataset descriptions, represents a valuable resource for advancing text classification tasks. Its diversity and systematic structure streamline model selection, reducing the need for extensive fine-tuning and saving computational resources.

The experiments demonstrate the utility of this corpus, with substantial performance gains over baseline models, even when domain recognition was occasionally imprecise. The corpus addresses a critical gap in NLP workflows by mapping datasets to suitable models based on domain alignment.

This study shows that the corpus offers a scalable framework for integrating pre-tuned models in AutoML systems like Auto-PyTorch. Allowing task-specific model selection and optimization has proven effective in improving performance across various text classification tasks. The results emphasize that accurate domain recognition significantly boosts performance, indicating the potential for greater efficiency and wider application in NLP workflows with further refinements.

In summary, the Hugging Face corpus compiled in this study is not just a collection of models but an indispensable resource that has already demonstrated its impact through improved text classification performance. With further refinement, particularly in domain recognition and model alignment, this corpus can potentially set a new standard for leveraging open-source models in diverse and complex NLP tasks within AutoML frameworks.

6 Conclusion and Future Works

This study introduced a corpus of pre-fine-tuned models from Hugging Face enriched with domain annotations and dataset descriptions, demonstrating its utility for enhancing text classification tasks. The experimental results highlight how this resource improves model performance and streamlines integration into automated pipelines, reducing the need for fine-tuning.

In conclusion, the Hugging Face corpus represents a critical step toward scalable and efficient NLP solutions. Refinements in domain recognition and alignment hold the potential to revolutionize the use of pre-fine-tuned models in AutoML, advancing text classification and broader NLP tasks.

Future work will focus on improving domain recognition accuracy through advanced methods such as supervised learning or knowledge graph-based approaches. Additionally, it will evaluate the corpus with a more diverse range of datasets, including low-resource languages

Future work will optimize text representation methods for specific datasets to enhance the proposed corpus's utility in AutoML systems. We will develop a multi-model evaluation framework that aligns three semantically similar pre-fine-tuned models from the corpus to each dataset based on domain similarity scores and zero-shot classification results. These models will be assessed using AutoML techniques supported by Auto-PyTorch, enabling efficient performance evaluation through automated hyperparameter optimization and model selection. By employing multi-fidelity optimization methods like Successive Halving and Hyperband, we aim to identify the most effective model early in training, reducing computational costs. This method balances model performance with efficiency while preserving the domain-specific strengths of our corpus.

Limitations

While the proposed corpus demonstrates significant potential, several limitations should be noted.

First, the evaluation datasets, though diverse, are not comprehensive and do not fully capture the complexity of real-world text classification tasks.

Second, while domain recognition methods are effective, they have accuracy limitations. For instance, the Colbert dataset, designed for humor detection, was misclassified as media bias, highlighting the need for more nuanced approaches like supervised learning or knowledge graph-based mapping.

Despite these challenges, the results highlight the potential of the Hugging Face corpus as a valuable resource for text classification and other NLP tasks, with opportunities for further refinement to enhance its utility in the AutoML domain.

References

Claudio MV de et al. Andrade. 2023. On the class separability of contextual embeddings representations – or "the classifier does not matter when the (text) representation is so good!". *Information Processing and Management*, 60:103336.

Sinan Aral and Dylan Walker. 2012. Identifying influential and susceptible members of social networks. *Science*, 337(6092):337–341.

Hayastan Avetisyan and David Broneske. 2021. Identifying and understanding game-framing in online news: Bert and fine-grained linguistic features. In *Proceedings of the 4th International Conference on Natural Language and Speech Processing (ICNLSP 2021)*, pages 95–107.

Ramy Baly, Giovanni Da San Martino, James Glass, and Preslav Nakov. 2020. We can detect your bias: Predicting the political ideology of news articles. *arXiv preprint arXiv:2010.05338*.

Iz Beltagy, Kyle Lo, and Arman Cohan. 2019. Scibert: A pretrained language model for scientific text. *arXiv preprint arXiv:1903.10676*.

Steven Bethard. 2013. Cleartk-timeml: A minimalist approach to tempeval 2013. In *Second joint conference on lexical and computational semantics (* SEM), volume 2: proceedings of the seventh international workshop on semantic evaluation (SemEval 2013)*, pages 10–14.

Asia J Biega, Peter Potash, Hal Daumé, Fernando Diaz, and Michèle Finck. 2020. Operationalizing the legal principle of data minimization for personalization. In *Proceedings of the 43rd international ACM SIGIR conference on research and development in information retrieval*, pages 399–408.

David M Blei, Andrew Y Ng, and Michael I Jordan. 2003. Latent dirichlet allocation. *Journal of machine Learning research*, 3(Jan):993–1022.

Samuel R Bowman, Gabor Angeli, Christopher Potts, and Christopher D Manning. 2015. A large annotated corpus for learning natural language inference. *arXiv preprint arXiv:1508.05326*.

Carlos Busso, Murtaza Bulut, Shrikanth Narayanan, J Gratch, and S Marsella. 2013. Toward effective automatic recognition systems of emotion in speech. *Social emotions in nature and artifact: emotions in human and human-computer interaction*, 7(17):110–127.

A Conneau. 2019. Unsupervised cross-lingual representation learning at scale. *arXiv preprint arXiv:1911.02116*.

Roddy Cowie, Ellen Douglas-Cowie, Nicolas Tsapatsoulis, George Votsis, Stefanos Kollias, Winfried Fellenz, and John G Taylor. 2001. Emotion recognition in human-computer interaction. *IEEE Signal processing magazine*, 18(1):32–80.

Giovanni Da San Martino, Alberto Barron-Cedeno, and Preslav Nakov. 2019. Findings of the nlp4if-2019 shared task on fine-grained propaganda detection. In *Proceedings of the second workshop on natural language processing for internet freedom: censorship, disinformation, and propaganda*, pages 162–170.

Cristian Danescu-Niculescu-Mizil, Moritz Sudhof, Dan Jurafsky, Jure Leskovec, and Christopher Potts. 2013. A computational approach to politeness with application to social factors. *arXiv preprint arXiv:1306.6078*.

Thomas Davidson, Dana Warmsley, Michael Macy, and Ingmar Weber. 2017. Automated hate speech detection and the problem of offensive language. In *Proceedings of the international AAAI conference on web and social media*, volume 11, pages 512–515.

Jacob Devlin, Ming-Wei Chang, Kenton Lee, and Kristina Toutanova. 2018. Bert: Pre-training of deep bidirectional transformers for language understanding. *arXiv preprint arXiv:1810.04805*.

Matthias Feurer, Aaron Klein, Katharina Eggensperger, Jost Springenberg, Manuel Blum, and Frank Hutter. 2015. Efficient and robust automated machine learning. *Advances in neural information processing systems*, 28.

Eileen Fitzpatrick, Joan Bachenko, and Tommaso Fornaciari. 2015. *Automatic detection of verbal deception*. Morgan & Claypool Publishers.

Diman Ghazi, Diana Inkpen, and Stan Szpakowicz. 2015. Detecting emotion stimuli in emotion-bearing sentences. In *Computational Linguistics and Intelligent Text Processing: 16th International Conference, CICLing 2015, Cairo, Egypt, April 14-20, 2015, Proceedings, Part II 16*, pages 152–165. Springer.

Thiago S Guzella and Walmir M Caminhas. 2009. A review of machine learning approaches to spam filtering. *Expert Systems with Applications*, 36(7):10206–10222.

Ivan Habernal and Iryna Gurevych. 2016. What makes a convincing argument? empirical analysis and detecting attributes of convincingness in web argumentation. In *Proceedings of the 2016 conference on empirical methods in natural language processing*, pages 1214–1223.

Xin He, Kaiyong Zhao, and Xiaowen Chu. 2021. Automl: A survey of the state-of-the-art. *Knowledge-based systems*, 212:106622.

Tommi Jauhiainen, Marco Lui, Marcos Zampieri, Timothy Baldwin, and Krister Lindén. 2019. Automatic language identification in texts: A survey. *Journal of Artificial Intelligence Research*, 65:675–782.

Aditya Joshi, Pushpak Bhattacharyya, and Mark J Carman. 2017. Automatic sarcasm detection: A survey. *ACM Computing Surveys (CSUR)*, 50(5):1–22.

Douwe Kiela, Suvrat Bhooshan, Hamed Firooz, Ethan Perez, and Davide Testuggine. 2019. Supervised multimodal bitransformers for classifying images and text. *arXiv preprint arXiv:1909.02950*.

Mikhail V Koroteev. 2021. Bert: a review of applications in natural language processing and understanding. *arXiv preprint arXiv:2103.11943*.

Jinhyuk Lee, Wonjin Yoon, Sungdong Kim, Donghyeon Kim, Sunkyu Kim, Chan Ho So, and Jaewoo Kang. 2020. Biobert: a pre-trained biomedical language representation model for biomedical text mining. *Bioinformatics*, 36(4):1234–1240.

Kenton Lee, Luheng He, Mike Lewis, and Luke Zettlemoyer. 2017. End-to-end neural coreference resolution. *arXiv preprint arXiv:1707.07045*.

Han Liu, Xiaotong Zhang, Lu Fan, Xuandi Fu, Qimai Li, Xiao-Ming Wu, and Albert YS Lam. 2019. Reconstructing capsule networks for zero-shot intent classification. In *Proceedings of the 2019 Conference on Empirical Methods in Natural Language Processing and the 9th International Joint Conference on Natural Language Processing (EMNLP-IJCNLP)*, pages 4799–4809.

William C Mann and Sandra A Thompson. 1988. Rhetorical structure theory: Toward a functional theory of text organization. *Text-interdisciplinary Journal for the Study of Discourse*, 8(3):243–281.

Margaret Mitchell, Simone Wu, Andrew Zaldivar, Parker Barnes, Lucy Vasserman, Ben Hutchinson, Elena Spitzer, Inioluwa Deborah Raji, and Timnit Gebru. 2019. Model cards for model reporting. In *Proceedings of the conference on fairness, accountability, and transparency*, pages 220–229.

Bo Pang, Lillian Lee, et al. 2008. Opinion mining and sentiment analysis. *Foundations and Trends® in information retrieval*, 2(1–2):1–135.

MD Pietro. 2020. Text classification with nlp: Tf-idf vs word2vec vs bert. *Preprocessing, Model Design, Evaluation, Explainability for Bag-of-Words, Word Embedding, Language models, Last accessed*, 4(02):2021.

Maria Pontiki, Dimitrios Galanis, Haris Papageorgiou, Ion Androutsopoulos, Suresh Manandhar, Mohammad Al-Smadi, Mahmoud Al-Ayyoub, Yanyan Zhao, Bing Qin, Orphée De Clercq, et al. 2016. Semeval-2016 task 5: Aspect based sentiment analysis. In *International workshop on semantic evaluation*, pages 19–30.

N Reimers. 2019. Sentence-bert: Sentence embeddings using siamese bert-networks. *arXiv preprint arXiv:1908.10084*.

Anthony Rios and Ramakanth Kavuluru. 2018. Few-shot and zero-shot multi-label learning for structured label spaces. In *Proceedings of the Conference on Empirical Methods in Natural Language Processing. Conference on Empirical Methods in Natural Language Processing*, volume 2018, page 3132. NIH Public Access.

Parisa Safikhani and David Broneske. 2023a. Enhancing autonlp with fine-tuned bert models: An evaluation of text representation methods for autopytorch. *Available at SSRN 4585459*.

Parisa Safikhani and David Broneske. 2023b. Enhancing autonlp with fine-tuned bert models: An evaluation of text representation methods for autopytorch. *Computer Science & Information Technology (CS & IT)*, 13:23–38.

Matthew Shardlow. 2013. A comparison of techniques to automatically identify complex words. In *51st annual meeting of the association for computational linguistics proceedings of the student research workshop*, pages 103–109.

Kai Shu, Amy Sliva, Suhang Wang, Jiliang Tang, and Huan Liu. 2017. Fake news detection on social media: A data mining perspective. *ACM SIGKDD explorations newsletter*, 19(1):22–36.

Amit Singhal et al. 2001. Modern information retrieval: A brief overview. *IEEE Data Eng. Bull.*, 24(4):35–43.

Efstathios Stamatatos, Nikos Fakotakis, and George Kokkinakis. 2000. Text genre detection using common word frequencies. In *COLING 2000 Volume 2: The 18th International Conference on Computational Linguistics*.

James Thorne and Andreas Vlachos. 2018. Automated fact checking: Task formulations, methods and future directions. *arXiv preprint arXiv:1806.07687*.

Alexander Tornede, Difan Deng, Theresa Eimer, Joseph Giovanelli, Aditya Mohan, Tim Ruhkopf, Sarah Segel, Daphne Theodorakopoulos, Tanja Tornede, Henning Wachsmuth, et al. 2023. Automl in the age of large language models: Current challenges, future opportunities and risks. *arXiv preprint arXiv:2306.08107*.

Cynthia Van Hee, Els Lefever, and Véronique Hoste. 2018. Semeval-2018 task 3: Irony detection in english tweets. In *Proceedings of the 12th international workshop on semantic evaluation*, pages 39–50.

Thomas Wolf, Lysandre Debut, Victor Sanh, Julien Chaumond, Clement Delangue, Anthony Moi, Pierric Cistac, Tim Rault, Rémi Louf, Morgan Funtowicz, et al. 2020. Transformers: State-of-the-art natural language processing. In *Proceedings of the 2020 conference on empirical methods in natural language processing: system demonstrations*, pages 38–45.

Lucas Zimmer, Marius Lindauer, and Frank Hutter. 2021. Auto-pytorch: Multi-fidelity metalearning for efficient and robust autodl. *IEEE transactions on pattern analysis and machine intelligence*, 43(9):3079–3090.

Paraphrasing Attack Resilience of Various Machine-Generated Text Detection Methods

Andrii Shportko
Northwestern University
Evanston, IL, USA
andre.s@u.northwestern.edu

Inessa Verbitsky
Northwestern University
Evanston, IL, USA
inessa@u.northwestern.edu

Abstract

The recent large-scale emergence of LLMs has left an open space for dealing with their consequences, such as plagiarism or the spread of false information on the Internet. Coupling this with the rise of AI detector bypassing tools, reliable machine-generated text detection is in increasingly high demand. We investigate the paraphrasing attack resilience of various machine-generated text detection methods, evaluating three approaches: fine-tuned RoBERTa, Binoculars, and text feature analysis, along with their ensembles using Random Forest classifiers. We discovered that Binoculars-inclusive ensembles yield the strongest results, but they also suffer the most significant losses during attacks. In this paper, we present the dichotomy of performance versus resilience in the world of AI text detection, which complicates the current perception of reliability among state-of-the-art techniques.

1 Introduction

The widespread use of LLMs can be precarious when left unchecked, with the consequences ranging from intellectual dishonesty to the spread of fake news on social media. Elali and Rachid (2023) found that AI chatbots can easily produce both realistic-looking academic results and a polished manuscript that may well be accepted to a conference and published. Since scientific research, especially medical, is often falsified, the emergence of such a possibility opens up a dangerous playing field (Phogat et al., 2023). It was found that 14% of scientists were aware of colleagues who falsified results, whereas 72% of scientists knew of colleagues who engaged in questionable research practices (Fanelli, 2009). More incidents of AI being used in the case of fake news spreading on the internet can be found in the Ethics Statement.

What is particularly concerning about this is that humans have been found to perform rather poorly on manual detection of AI-written text. In particular, human performance has shown to be only marginally better than random classification (Wu et al., 2024). In fact, in a study involving over 130 subjects, Kumar and Mindzak (2024) found that participants were only able to correctly identify AI-generated text with an accuracy rate of 24%. Concerning the use of AI in academia, Gao et al. (2022) conducted an experiment where participants were to identify whether abstracts for academic papers were written by ChatGPT or a human. They found that only 68% of the AI-detected abstracts were correctly classified. Such a precedent makes a strong case for the necessity of precise automated AI text detection mechanisms.

With the emergence of freely accessible sites such as ZeroGPT, DetectGPT, and Quillbot, bypassing attacks have been developed against these technologies. Methods which are commonly used include automated paraphrasing tools, prompt engineering, and the calculated addition of errors into AI-generated text (Perkins et al., 2024). It has been generally shown that the use of these methods decreases the efficacy of the detection tool; however, we aim to put together a more comprehensive analysis of the leading AI detection methods against bypassing attacks. In this paper, we will focus on paraphrasing attacks.

The leading state-of-the-art detectors can be categorized into two paradigms, those using training-based and training-free mechanisms (Wang et al., 2025). Most training-free approaches rely on statistical feature analysis and commonly look at perplexity, log probability, and n-grams (Chakraborty et al., 2023). Although training-based models have been widely leading, a recently developed methodology – Binoculars – proves successful in a zero-shot context, which stands out over multiple metrics (Hans et al., 2024). This approach is developed further in the Related Work section. Training-based methods largely rely on transformer models,

Proceedings of the 2025 Conference of the Nations of the Americas Chapter of the Association for Computational Linguistics: Human Language Technologies (Volume 4: Student Research Workshop), pages 474–484

namely RoBERTa (Liu et al., 2019), a masked-based model, easily fine-tunable for downstream tasks such as text classification.

The methods we stacked to develop our own model include Binoculars, RoBERTa, and text feature analysis, which we justify due to their leading benchmarks (detailed in Related Work).

2 Related Work

2.1 Binoculars

The Binoculars method relies on calculations from two closely related LLMs. It has a significant advantage over other SOTA methods in that it uses no training from the LLM that it is being tested on. This is significant, considering Binoculars still manages to surpass every open-source model that detects ChatGPT. Because other detectors rely on pretraining of the models they then test, the results fail to generalize when tested across multiple AI models. The Binoculars method, however, achieves high performance on a variety of datasets, which gather texts from different LLM sources. Furthermore, Binoculars addresses what they call the "Capybara Problem", which in essence refers to the phenomenon of an LLM generating high-perplexity text simply due to a high-perplexity prompt being used. Other models which focus on raw perplexity will fail in such cases. Binoculars has an accuracy rate above 90%, and a false positive rate of 0.01%, using datasets which include *Writing prompts, News, and Student essays* (Verma et al., 2024).

2.2 Text Features

Muñoz-Ortiz et al. (2024) analyzed linguistic patterns in human and LLM text to determine which features would provide for the most robust detection mechanism. Using extensive data from six different LLMs, including Llama and Falcon 7-b, they found that human writing tends to have less uniform sentence length distribution than AI. This conclusion is supported by Desaire et al. (2023), who found that the standard deviation of sentence length was an important identifier in text classification. As one of our five text features used, we thus implement standard deviation of sentence length.

2.3 Ensembling

Abburi et al. (2023) analyze the success in using ensemble approaches for text classification. Their ensemble involves stacking DeBERTa, RoBERTa, and xLM-RoBERTa, fine-tuning each model for the appropriate tasks. They found that this approach reached 5th place in the English task and first place in the Multilingual for the Automated Text Identification shared task.

In fact, ensembling was highly used in Task 1 of the *COLING 2025 GenAI Text detection workshop*, from which we use the dataset provided to train and evaluate our own model (Wang et al., 2025). Mobin and Islam (2025), whose approach scored 4th among contestants, relied on ensembling RoBERTa-base with other pre-trained transformer models. Our methodology also relies on RoBERTa, however, we ensemble it with Binoculars and text feature analysis, as justified above.

2.4 Bypassing

The most prominent AI text-detection models relying on transformer fine-tuning have been tested against bypassing and proven to largely withstand it. Krishna et al. (2023) provide a critical baseline by demonstrating that controlled paraphrasing can significantly undermine the performance of AI-generated text detectors while maintaining semantic integrity. Their work, through the DIPPER model, shows that even minimal paraphrasing – changing wording and sentence structure – can drop detection accuracy significantly.

Some common AI detectors saw decreases of around 17% in accuracy (Perkins et al., 2024) when bypassing methods were employed. However, some more recently developed models were created specifically to withstand such attacks, such as the RADAR model (Hu et al., 2023), which trains the detector on paraphrasing schemes and achieves over 31.64% of additional accuracy compared to previous methods. The Binoculars method, however, has not been tested against bypassing, thus its general efficacy remains unclear. This concern is explored in our paper.

3 Data and Methodology

To track the progress on machine-generated text detection, we use the materials of the competition on *Detecting AI Generated Content @COLING 2025 Task 1: Binary Machine-Generated Text Detection* (Wang et al., 2025). It is an aggregation of other datasets that have been studied before, such as M4GT. The experiments in the following sections are based on the testing dataset that the final leaderboard used. All models use the training dataset,

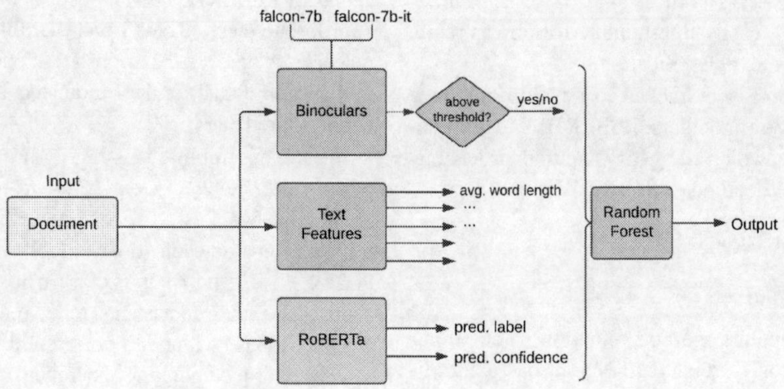

Figure 1: Pipeline of our model

which is described in Appendix A.0.1.

First, we chose to fine-tune RoBERTa for AI text detection because it provided a substantial improvement in the model's ability to understand nuanced language differences. In essence, we added a final layer of size 2 for binary classification. It is also a well-tested approach in machine-generated text detection (Liu et al., 2019). We performed fine-tuning over a subset (12k entries) of the training set provided by the workshop. The hyperparameters are learning rate = $2e-5$, batch size = 16, epochs = 4, and training size = $20,000$, with a train/test split of 0.8.

Second, we also test the Binoculars method, which reaches high accuracy and low false-positive rates over multiple LLM tested on, without relying on training data. Binoculars uses two closely related LLMs – `'tiiuae/falcon-7b'`, `'tiiuae/falcon-7b-instruct'` – to calculate cross-perplexity, meaning perplexity is calculated using the log perplexity of text generated by one LLM and the next-token prediction of another.

Third, we measured several document metrics that are related to AI detection. We selected 5 text markers: average word length, lexical diversity, punctuation frequency (Corizzo and Leal-Arenas, 2023), standard deviation of sentence length, and stopword ratio (Gryka et al., 2024). The selection of features was based on the entropy values from the Random Forests.

We combined the features extracted from each approach into a single vector for each text sample and fed it to the Random Forests model that acts like a meta-learner. This vector includes the prediction probabilities from the fine-tuned RoBERTa model as well as the predicted labels, the cross-perplexity scores from Binoculars, and the five document metrics we selected (Fig 1). In the following sections, we will show the performance of all 7 different stackings of the models.

Since we had limited resources, we manually chose 200 random entries from the evaluation dataset and fed them to the high-performance AI text detector bypasser GPTinf. GPTinf claims to bypass all AI detectors, including Turnitin AI Detector, GPTZero, ZeroGPT, and GPTRadar. The dataset is published now on HuggingFace at `'antebe1/paraphrased_AI_text'`.

Although the algorithm used by GPTInf is not publicized, their website states that it works by paraphrasing the inputted text–removing common phrasing and diversifying sentence structure by varying the wording, grammar, and ordering of words used (GPT). To calculate the confidence interval (CI) for the F1 score on the full dataset, we used a bootstrapping approach (9000 out of 73k). To verify whether the differences between modules tested on were significant, we ran 21 pair-wise McNemar statistical tests (Table 3). The Bonferroni correction for $\alpha = 0.1$ is 0.0048.

4 Results

4.1 Binoculars

4.1.1 Observations

For rapid testing purposes, all tests on Binoculars have been run on the devtest split of the dataset.

4.1.2 Context Window Effect

We observed that the information gain increases as the context window increases. However, the

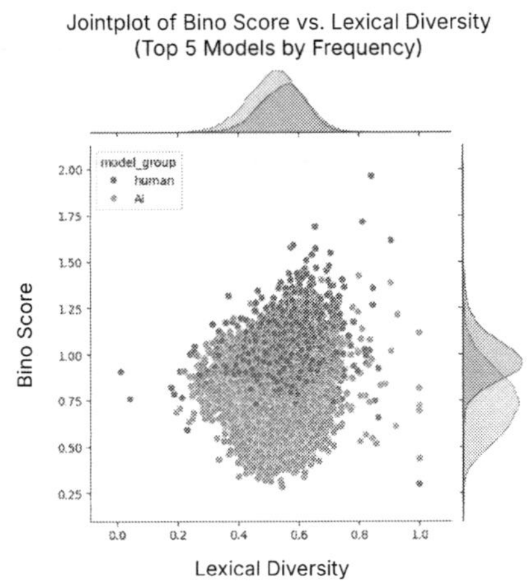

Figure 2: Binoculars results

information gain plateaus somewhere after 256 – 512 tokens. The Jensen-Shannon (JS) divergence score (Fig 3, see Appendix A.0.2), which measures the similarity between probability distributions, demonstrated significant improvements from 0.0373 (context window size = 32) to 0.2843 (context window size = 512). The JS score highlighted distinct effects between human-authored and AI-generated text as the context window increased.

The Binoculars score analysis reveals a clear separation between human and AI-generated text. Human-written content maintains the highest median score around 1.0 (Fig 2) as predicted by the Binoculars paper, exhibiting notable variance and outliers. The critical threshold value of 0.901, just as reported in the original paper, serves as a discriminator between human and AI-generated content.

4.2 Module Ensemble Comparisons

Three different modules give rise to 7 different ways to assemble them (Fig 4).

The ensemble incorporating all modules (Text Features, RoBERTa, and Binoculars) achieves the highest F1 score of 80.2%. The second-best performance is observed when Text Features and RoBERTa are combined. While combining Text Features with Binoculars or RoBERTa with Binoculars also improves performance compared to individual features, they fall short of the comprehensive ensemble. Notably, individual feature sets such as Text Features, RoBERTa, or Binoculars alone yield lower F1 scores than any combination of them (as seen in Table 1).

Model	Final F1 Score
Text Features + RoBERTa + Binoculars	0.8018
Text Features + Binoculars	0.7975
RoBERTa + Binoculars	0.7832
Text Features + RoBERTa	0.7712
Binoculars	0.7515
Text Features	0.7168
RoBERTa	0.7027

Table 1: Performance of Models on F1 Scores

4.3 Paraphrasing Attack

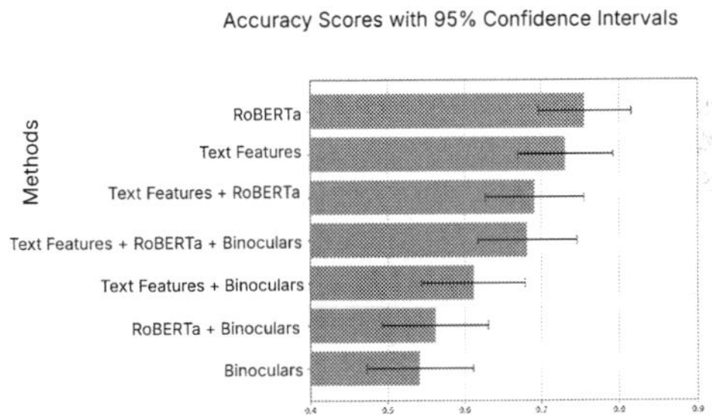

Figure 5: Post-attack accuracy

Among individual models, RoBERTa demonstrated the highest resilience to paraphrasing attacks, showing no degradation (Table 2). In contrast, the Binoculars method exhibited the most vulnerability, resulting in a significant degradation of 0.1756.

Interestingly, the Text Features approach showed no degradation in performance against paraphrased samples. The ensemble combining Text Features, RoBERTa, and Binoculars achieved the highest initial accuracy rate of 0.7751 but experienced a notable drop in performance when faced with paraphrased samples, decreasing to 0.6816. These findings highlight the varying degrees of resilience among different approaches to machine-generated text detection. RoBERTa's robustness suggests that its language understanding capabilities allow it to detect AI-generated text even after paraphrasing. The significant drop in Binoculars' performance indicates that its cross-perplexity approach may be more sensitive to changes in text structure and wording introduced by paraphrasing.

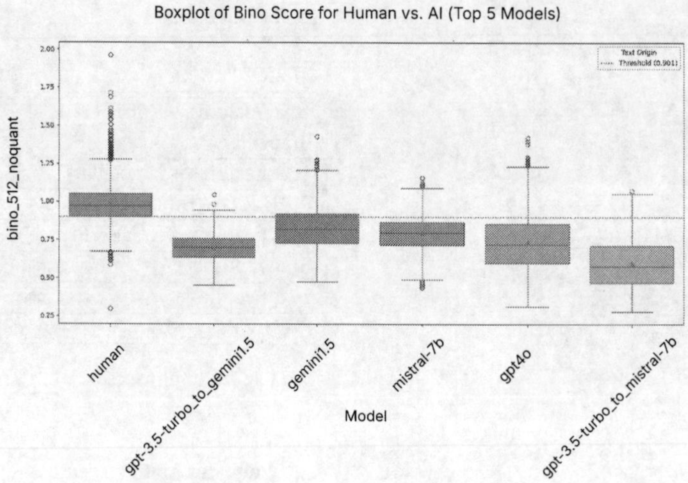

Figure 3: Binoculars score over context window of 512 w/o quantization

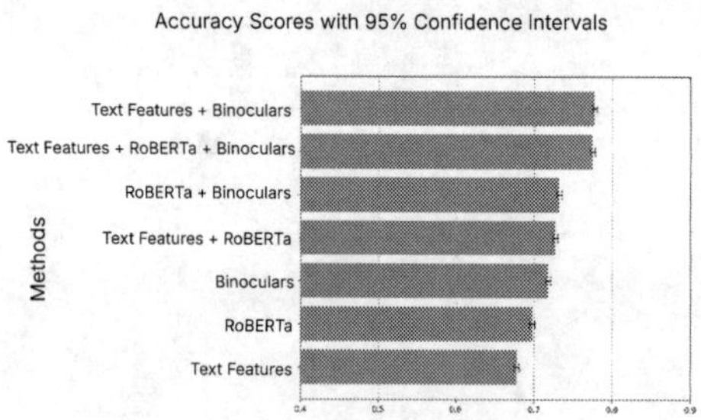

Figure 4: Pre-attack Accuracy

Table 2: Accuracy drop per ensemble

Model	Initial Accuracy	Paraphrased Accuracy	Degradation
Binoculars	0.7178	0.5423	0.1756
RoBERTa + Binoculars	0.7320	0.5622	0.1698
Text Features + Binoculars	0.7784	0.6119	0.1664
Text Features + RoBERTa + Binoculars	0.7751	0.6816	0.0935
Text Features + RoBERTa	0.7274	0.6915	0.0358
Text Features	0.6780	0.7313	-0.0534
RoBERTa	0.6974	0.7562	-0.0588

5 Discussion

5.1 Analysis of Results

As demonstrated by our Results, we introduced a Cohesive Testing Framework (CTF) for classifying text as human- versus machine-written. Our system streamlines the ensembling process by feeding the document input into three detectors – Binoculars, Text Features, and RoBERTa, which are then stacked and evaluated by our meta-learner, Random Forest (as demonstrated in Fig 1). Our method employs 7 ways to combine 3 modules and make cross-comparisons, which allows for 1-to-1 comparisons between performance of modules. Our ensemble method proved significant information gain which outperforms many SOTA detectors. Namely, it would place us 4th on the COLING2025 Workshop leaderboard.

Our second main result was our finding that the highest performing AI detectors had the worst results when it came to paraphrasing attacks. In fact, any ensemble that used Binoculars saw a significant decrease in accuracy. This is particularly interesting, as it reflects more generally "The Bitter Lesson" paradox – it seems that for every interpretable training-free method there is a better black-box approach.

5.2 Future Work

We suggest future works to build off our model by addressing the limitations we have laid out on the following page, as well as evaluating the detectors we looked at on different bypassing attacks, not only paraphrasing. Additionally, the methods evaluated were not tested for out-of-distribution prompts. Hense, accounting for this may add to a more comprehensive review of SOTA detectors. Sentiment analysis has been shown to be distinguishable between human and machine-written text, thus including this as a feature may contribute to some interesting results as well.

6 Conclusion

We believe that the tradeoff between performance and resilience is significant enough to become a leading theme in the AI-detection community. For example, the reported high performance of Binoculars on flagging Machine-generated text has suffered the most drastic loss under paraphrasing attacks. Under our testing framework, we also reaffirmed the significant information gain provided by the stacking of multiple detectors.

Acknowledgments

We thank the NU CS Microgrant for the computational units provided and Prof. Wood-Doughty for guidance and consultation on statistical analysis. The study resulting in this paper was assisted by a Conference Travel Grant from the Office of Undergraduate Research administered by Northwestern University's Office of the Provost. However, the conclusions, opinions, and other statements in this paper are the author's and not necessarily those of the sponsoring institution.

Limitations

Our paraphrased dataset has 200 entries, as we were unable to gain API access to the platform we used. Thus, although statistically significant, it should be important to replicate our results with a larger dataset. Additionally, we only tested paraphrasing generated by GPTInf, which may not capture the maximum extent of paraphrasing attack capabilities.

Ethics Statement

When ChatGPT was released in 2022, it was widely unheard of and thus not largely anticipated, but within a short time frame, its popularity surged. The world had not been expecting such a capable and easily accessible system, and thus its use in academic settings by students, across the internet by scammers, and in almost every practical field by workers, skyrocketed within a very brief amount of time. As a result, the consequences of such widespread AI use have not been thoroughly accounted for, and recent studies of its very real and threatening possible repercussions have only begun to be released. It is then instrumental to first, study the effects of large-spread AI use, and following this, develop methods that can detect the use of AI, namely in writing.

The use of deepfakes have become increasingly prevalent in recent years. Trandabăț and Gifu (2023) investigated and assessed the threat of AI being used to generate deepfakes on a mass scale to be then published across the internet. Google published the DeepDream algorithm in 2015, which used a convolutional neural network, trained on millions of images, to first identify objects within images, and then using these patterns create an image corresponding to a requested object (for instance, an animal) from memory (Miller, 2020). Although the images that this network could produce were far from accurate and often combined elements of different objects from its training data, the release of DeepDream instantly sparked a race to use this technology and create something more powerful, as this was the first time deep learning was used to generate images from scratch. Soon, more models and algorithms were developed, which were more advanced, with time, shrinking the gap between human recognizability of what is evidently machine-generated in comparison to human-created. In their paper, Trandabăț and Gifu (2023) use this background to focus on the present-day role of AI across the internet, notably what is commonly referred to as "fake news". They test a few classifiers on both human and AI-generated fake news, including RoBERTa. They find that the true positive rate of AI-detector models, such as RoBERTa, on AI-generated fake news is only 3% higher than when run on human-generated fake news, thus making AI-generated fake news very difficult to recognize and highly useful for publishing false information online.

In 2024, a German magazine *Die Aktuelle* published an interview with a famous Formula One driver, Michael Schumacher, which was created entirely by the AI chatbot, Character.ai, upon which the magazine was sued by Schumacher's family (ESPN News Services, 2024). Schumacher has been out of the image of the public eye for almost a decade due to a brain-injury following a sports accident. His family has taken immense action to keep his life post-accident in private, thus the release of this article resulted in great turmoil on the family and misled readers all around the world.

Overall, the consequences of fake news becoming prevalent can be unimaginably dangerous. In South Korea, AI has been widely used to generate ads containing falsified information and promote the listing of fraudulent drugs and hormonal therapies for sale to the public on the internet (Park, 2024). Because the sale of these treatments over-the-counter have not been government-approved, many of the drugs listed have not been properly studied, meaning the health consequences that may arise from them are unclear, which is critically unsafe. We thus strongly emphasize the need for reliability in AI text detection, highlighting the absolute necessity for AI text detectors that are able to *bypass* bypassers, in order to combat these problems addressed above and promote transparency across the Internet, in all fields and aspects.

References

Gptinf: Ai content detection bypass tool. https://www.gptinf.com/. Accessed: 2025-01-31.

Harika Abburi, Michael Suesserman, Nirmala Pudota, Balaji Veeramani, Edward Bowen, and Sanmitra Bhattacharya. 2023. Generative ai text classification using ensemble llm approaches. *Preprint*, arXiv:2309.07755.

Souradip Chakraborty, Amrit Singh Bedi, Sicheng Zhu, Bang An, Dinesh Manocha, and Furong Huang. 2023. On the possibilities of ai-generated text detection. *Preprint*, arXiv:2304.04736.

Roberto Corizzo and Sebastian Leal-Arenas. 2023. One-class learning for ai-generated essay detection. *Applied Sciences*, 13(13).

Heather Desaire, Aleesa E. Chua, Madeline Isom, Romana Jarosova, and David Hua. 2023. Distinguishing academic science writing from humans or chatgpt with over 99% accuracy using off-the-shelf machine learning tools. *Cell Reports Physical Science*, 4(6):101426. Epub 2023 Jun 7.

Faisal R. Elali and Leena N. Rachid. 2023. Ai-generated research paper fabrication and plagiarism in the scientific community. *Patterns*, 4(3):100706.

ESPN News Services. 2024. Schumacher family awarded €200k in compensation over 'ai interview'. *ESPN*.

Daniele Fanelli. 2009. How many scientists fabricate and falsify research? a systematic review and meta-analysis of survey data. *PLoS One*, 4(5):e5738. Competing Interests: The author has declared that no competing interests exist.

Catherine A. Gao, Frederick M. Howard, Nikolay S. Markov, Emma C. Dyer, Siddhi Ramesh, Yuan Luo, and Alexander T. Pearson. 2022. Comparing scientific abstracts generated by chatgpt to original abstracts using an artificial intelligence output detector, plagiarism detector, and blinded human reviewers. *bioRxiv*.

Paweł Gryka, Kacper Gradoń, Marek Kozłowski, Miłosz Kutyła, and Artur Janicki. 2024. Detection of ai-generated emails - a case study. In *Proceedings of the 19th International Conference on Availability, Reliability and Security*, ARES '24, New York, NY, USA. Association for Computing Machinery.

Abhimanyu Hans, Avi Schwarzschild, Valeriia Cherepanova, Hamid Kazemi, Aniruddha Saha, Micah Goldblum, Jonas Geiping, and Tom Goldstein. 2024. Spotting llms with binoculars: Zero-shot detection of machine-generated text. *Preprint*, arXiv:2401.12070.

Xiaomeng Hu, Pin-Yu Chen, and Tsung-Yi Ho. 2023. Radar: Robust ai-text detection via adversarial learning. *Preprint*, arXiv:2307.03838.

Kalpesh Krishna, Yixiao Song, Marzena Karpinska, John Wieting, and Mohit Iyyer. 2023. Paraphrasing evades detectors of ai-generated text, but retrieval is an effective defense. *Preprint*, arXiv:2303.13408.

Rahul Kumar and Michael Mindzak. 2024. Who wrote this? detecting artificial intelligence–generated text from human-written text. *Canadian Perspectives on Academic Integrity*, 7(1).

Yinhan Liu, Myle Ott, Naman Goyal, Jingfei Du, Mandar Joshi, Danqi Chen, Omer Levy, Mike Lewis, Luke Zettlemoyer, and Veselin Stoyanov. 2019. Roberta: A robustly optimized BERT pretraining approach. *CoRR*, abs/1907.11692.

Arthur I. Miller. 2020. Deepdream: How alexander mordvintsev excavated the computer's hidden layers. *The MIT Press Reader*.

Md Kamrujjaman Mobin and Md Saiful Islam. 2025. Luxveri at genai detection task 1: Inverse perplexity weighted ensemble for robust detection of ai-generated text across english and multilingual contexts. *Preprint*, arXiv:2501.11914.

Alberto Muñoz-Ortiz, Carlos Gómez-Rodríguez, and David Vilares. 2024. Contrasting linguistic patterns in human and llm-generated news text. *Artificial Intelligence Review*, 57(10):265.

Hyun Jun Park. 2024. The rise of generative artificial intelligence and the threat of fake news and disinformation online: Perspectives from sexual medicine. *Investigative and Clinical Urology*, 65(3):199–201. Editorial.

Mike Perkins, Jasper Roe, Binh H. Vu, Darius Postma, Don Hickerson, James McGaughran, and Huy Q. Khuat. 2024. Simple techniques to bypass genai text detectors: implications for inclusive education. *International Journal of Educational Technology in Higher Education*, 21(1):53.

Ritu Phogat, Bhadravathi Cheluvaiah Manjunath, Bhavna Sabbarwal, Anurag Bhatnagar, Reena, and Deepti Anand. 2023. Misconduct in biomedical research: A meta-analysis and systematic review. *Journal of International Society of Preventive & Community Dentistry*, 13(3):185–193. Copyright © 2023 Journal of International Society of Preventive and Community Dentistry.

Diana Trandabăț and Daniela Gifu. 2023. Discriminating ai-generated fake news. *Procedia Computer Science*, 225:3822–3831. 27th International Conference on Knowledge Based and Intelligent Information and Engineering Sytems (KES 2023).

Vivek Verma, Eve Fleisig, Nicholas Tomlin, and Dan Klein. 2024. Ghostbuster: Detecting text ghostwritten by large language models. In *Proceedings of the 2024 Conference of the North American Chapter of the Association for Computational Linguistics: Human Language Technologies (Volume 1: Long Papers)*, pages 1702–1717, Mexico City, Mexico. Association for Computational Linguistics.

Yuxia Wang, Artem Shelmanov, Jonibek Mansurov, Akim Tsvigun, Vladislav Mikhailov, Rui Xing, Zhuohan Xie, Jiahui Geng, Giovanni Puccetti, Ekaterina Artemova, et al. 2025. Genai content detection task 1: English and multilingual machine-generated text detection: Ai vs. human. *arXiv preprint arXiv:2501.11012*.

Junchao Wu, Shu Yang, Runzhe Zhan, Yulin Yuan, Derek F. Wong, and Lidia S. Chao. 2024. A survey on llm-generated text detection: Necessity, methods, and future directions. *Preprint*, arXiv:2310.14724.

A Appendix

A.0.1 Dataset

The training dataset contained a total of 610k entries from HC3, M4GT, and MAGE. The test dataset contained a total of 74k entries from CUDRT, IELTS, NLPeer, PeerSum, and MixSet. We replicated 3 methods as well as their different ensembles over the Random Forest classifier and evaluated their performance on the MGTD testing dataset.

A.0.2 Quantization Effect

Quantization in machine learning is the process of reducing the precision of numerical values, typically converting floating point numbers to lower-bit representations, to decrease the model size and improve computational efficiency. In our experiments, we quantized HuggingFace "`tiiuae/falcon-7b`" to replicate the paper. The typical degradation effect was about 2% (Fig 6) and it was diminishing as context was increasing. This is unexpected because usually degradation effects for other tasks would be stronger. It took around 27 GB of RAM to run "`tiiuae/falcon-7b`" and "`tiiuae/falcon-7b-instruct`" and 11 GB for 4-bit quantization of those models. We conclude that the marginal improvement of the F1 score is unimportant compared to the doubled Carbon Footprint. While non-quantized versions achieve better results, the marginal accuracy improvement must be weighed against the significantly higher computational requirements, particularly in resource-constrained environments.

In Fig 7, while some models are more resilient to Binocular detection (gemini1.5) than others (gpt4o), the trend is repeated for all models. Context window size significantly impacts detection accuracy, with substantial improvements observed as the window expands from 128 to 256 tokens. The optimal range lies between 256-512 tokens, though performance gains diminish notably beyond 300 tokens. The maximum accuracy peaks at approximately 0.80 for top-performing models at 512 tokens. Non-quantized models consistently demonstrate superior accuracy compared to their quantized counterparts, with approximately 2% better performance.

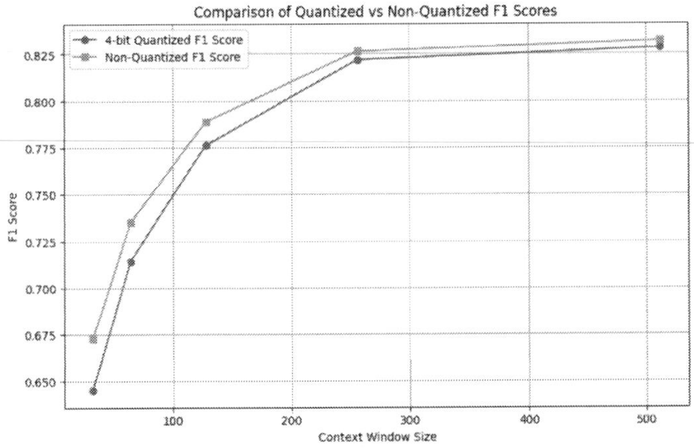

Figure 6

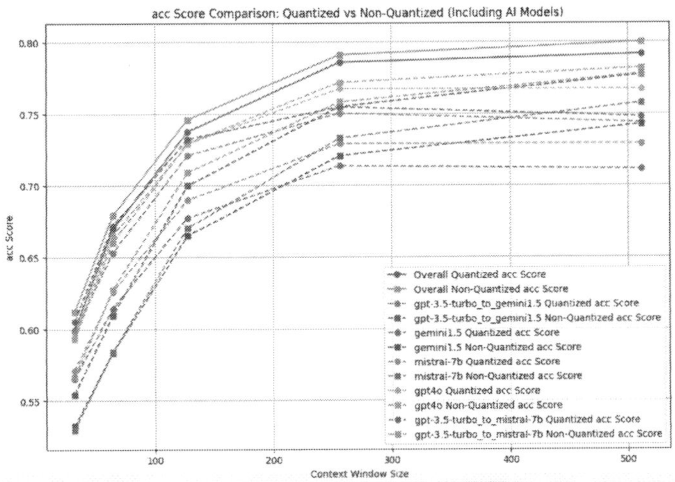

Figure 7

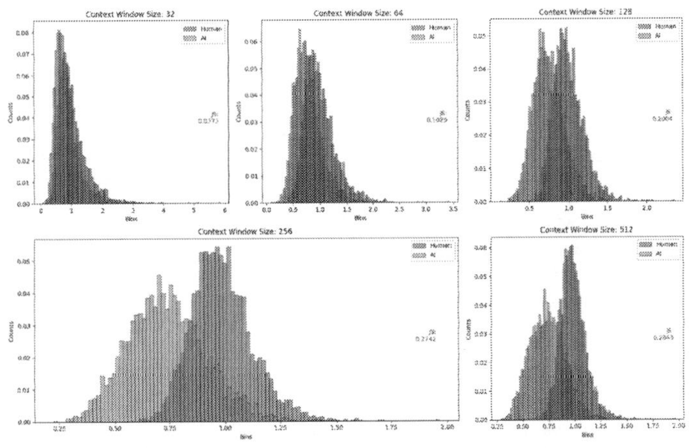

Figure 8

Module 1	Module 2	p-value	F1 (M 1)	F1 M1	F1 Diff	Higher F1
Bino	RoBERTa	0.0009	0.7032	0.8612	-0.1580	RoBERTa
TF	Bino	0.0037	0.8448	0.7032	0.1416	TF
RoBERTa	Bino + RoBERTa	0.0001	0.8612	0.7197	0.1414	RoBERTa
TF	Bino + RoBERTa	0.0055	0.8448	0.7197	0.1251	TF
RoBERTa	TF + Bino	0.0150	0.8612	0.7477	0.1135	RoBERTa
Bino	TF + Bino + RoBERTa	0.0163	0.7032	0.8107	-0.1074	TF + Bino + RoBERTa
Bino	TF + RoBERTa	0.0472	0.7032	0.8036	-0.1003	TF + RoBERTa
TF	TF + Bino	0.0064	0.8448	0.7477	0.0972	TF
Bino + RoBERTa	TF + Bino + RoBERTa	0.0301	0.7197	0.8107	-0.0909	TF + Bino + RoBERTa
TF + RoBERTa	Bino + RoBERTa	0.0515	0.8036	0.7197	0.0838	TF + RoBERTa
TF + Bino	TF + Bino + RoBERTa	0.0752	0.7477	0.8107	-0.0630	TF + Bino + RoBERTa
RoBERTa	TF + RoBERTa	0.0337	0.8612	0.8036	0.0576	RoBERTa
TF + Bino	TF + RoBERTa	0.2111	0.7477	0.8036	-0.0559	TF + RoBERTa
RoBERTa	TF + Bino + RoBERTa	0.1101	0.8612	0.8107	0.0505	RoBERTa
Bino	TF + Bino	0.2878	0.7032	0.7477	-0.0444	TF + Bino
TF	TF + RoBERTa	0.1950	0.8448	0.8036	0.0413	TF
TF	TF + Bino + RoBERTa	0.2927	0.8448	0.8107	0.0342	TF
TF + Bino	Bino + RoBERTa	0.4611	0.7477	0.7197	0.0279	TF + Bino
Bino	Bino + RoBERTa	0.5193	0.7032	0.7197	-0.0165	Bino + RoBERTa
TF	RoBERTa	0.5105	0.8448	0.8612	-0.0164	RoBERTa
TF + RoBERTa	TF + Bino + RoBERTa	0.5597	0.8036	0.8107	-0.0071	TF + Bino + RoBERTa

Table 3: Statistical Comparison of F1 Scores Across Different Module Combinations

Detecting, Generating, and Evaluating in the Writing Style of Different Authors

Mosab Rezaei
Department of Computer Science
Northern Illinois University

Abstract

In recent years, stylometry has been investigated in many different fields. Hence, in this work, we are going to tackle this problem, detecting, generating, and evaluating textual documents according to the writing style by leveraging state-of-the-art models. In the first step, the sentences will be extracted from several different books, each belonging to a different author, to create a dataset. Then the selected models will be trained to detect the author of sentences in the dataset. After that, generator models are utilized to generate sentences based on the authors' writing styles with unpaired samples in the dataset. Finally, to evaluate the performance of the generators, the previously trained models will be used to assess the generated sentences and to compare the distribution of various syntactic features between the original and generated sentences. We hope the result shows that models can be achieved to detect and generate textual documents for the given authors according to their writing style.

1 Introduction

Stylometry is a linguistic discipline that applies statistical analysis to literature based on the assumption that each author has an unconscious aspect to their style (Yang et al., 2008). Generally and simply, stylometry is a field of study that statistically analyzes authorship attribution (Holmes, 1998). As the production of digital documents increases, the importance of stylometry grows as well. The increasing attention to stylometry has been reflected in Wayman et al. (2009): "As non-handwritten communications become more prevalent, such as blogging, text messaging, and emails, there is a growing need to identify writers not by their written script, but by analysis of the typed content".

In this work, after demonstrating the existence of distinguishable patterns between different authors' writing styles, we aim to train generator models without paired samples to generate and then evaluate the generated sentences in different writing styles. Leveraging these models opens new advances in generating stylistic text, further enriching applications such as authorship verification, creative writing, forensic linguistics, legal systems, and criminology.

It is important to note that one of the key issues in this work lies in evaluating the generated sentences. First, while well-known metrics like accuracy or F1 score are valuable, they cannot adequately reflect how accurately the model detects and mimics writing styles. Moreover, these metrics do not provide clear insights into the performance of the model in each of the writing style categories. On the other hand, relying on expert human evaluations presents significant challenges. For example, gathering experts who specialize in all five authors' writing styles in the dataset is nearly impossible. Hence, we are going to use an AI-evaluate-AI technique to assess the generated sentences. We will train a detector capable of classifying sentences with high performance and use it to evaluate the generated sentences. Furthermore, we will incorporate feature-based evaluation by comparing the features extracted from both the original sentences and the generated sentences to measure their alignment.

Given the importance of stylometry, and the challenges mentioned above, this study has been focused on answering three main research questions in this area:

RQ1 (Detection): Given the differences in authors' writing styles, can the proposed model extract related features and accurately detect the authors for a given sentence?

RQ2 (Generation): Is it possible to train a generator to produce sentences in the writing style of a specific author without using paired training data?

RQ3 (Evaluation): Can detector models be used to evaluate generated sentences by generator models?

Proceedings of the 2025 Conference of the Nations of the Americas Chapter of the Association for Computational Linguistics: Human Language Technologies (Volume 4: Student Research Workshop), pages 485–491

2 Related Work

Since the use of machine learning for analysis alone is well understood, and evaluation is part of our future work, in this section, we describe only the systems used for style generation.

In Logeswaran et al. (2018), the authors propose a novel generative model for sentence style transfer that modifies the style of a given sentence based on categorical attributes. The architecture comprises an RNN-based encoder-decoder that generates sentences consistent with the input's content and specified attributes.

de Rivero et al. (2021) address style transfer in NLP by fine-tuning GPT-2 on Grammarly's Yahoo Answers Formality Corpus (GYAFC) to convert informal text into formal text while preserving meaning. Their model generates multiple formal sentence options, achieving a formality score above 0.7 in 61.36% of cases and a content preservation score above 0.8 in 71.33% of cases, demonstrating effective style transformation.

Also, in Tian et al. (2018), the researchers propose a text style transfer model using an attentional auto-encoder and a binary style classifier, ensuring content preservation by minimizing the distance between the POS-tagged structure of input and output sentences. The approach focuses on maintaining noun consistency, incorporating a language model for fluency and a style classifier to guide the generator in producing sentences with the desired style.

For the text style transferring task, other researchers in Lai et al. (2019) propose a GAN-based framework for non-parallel text style transfer that integrates a seq-to-seq encoder-decoder with attention, word-level conditional mechanisms, and dual discriminators (CNN and RNN) to balance content preservation and style transformation.

Authors in Hu et al. (2017) propose a deep generative model that enhances Variational Autoencoders (VAEs) with structured latent variables and holistic discriminators to generate text with specified attributes while ensuring disentanglement. Their approach, which incorporates a wake-sleep algorithm for collaborative optimization, effectively learns interpretable latent representations from minimal supervision, enabling controlled text generation with potential applications in NLP and content creation.

In Du et al. (2020), researchers introduced Schema-Guided Natural Language Generation (SG-NLG), a task that generates natural language prompts based on rich schemata, repurposing a dataset from dialog state tracking to train Seq2Seq, CVAE, and GPT-2 models. Their findings show that leveraging schema information enhances semantic quality and diversity, with Seq2Seq and CVAE excelling in reference similarity and GPT-2 performing best in diversity and human evaluation.

The Stable Style Transformer (SST) presented in Lee (2020), introduces a model-agnostic text style transfer approach using the Delete and Generate framework, where a pre-trained classifier extracts attribute markers without relying on a dictionary or attention scores, and a Transformer-based encoder-decoder generates the transferred sentence while preserving content. This method, trained on non-parallel datasets, demonstrates robust performance in handling long dependencies and offers a stable, effective solution for text style transfer.

CTERM-GAN (Betti et al., 2020) addresses the common limitation of NLG models that focus solely on syntax by incorporating both syntactic and semantic aspects through a relational memory-based generator and dual discriminators. Experimental results show that it maintains or improves syntactic accuracy while significantly enhancing semantic coherence, demonstrating its potential for generating text conditioned on various inputs, including writing styles.

Authors in Li et al. (2022), developed Diffusion-LM, a non-autoregressive language model leveraging continuous diffusion processes for controllable text generation, where gradient-based manipulation of latent variables during denoising enables fine-grained style control, outperforming prior plug-and-play models and achieving competitive results against fine-tuned autoregressive baselines.

The paper by Lyu et al. (2023) explores the application of diffusion models for fine-grained text style transfer, demonstrating that their approach, trained solely on the StylePTB dataset without external resources, achieves state-of-the-art performance across 13 tasks, including compositional style transfers. Their results highlight the potential of diffusion-based models for controllable text generation in low-resource settings, while also suggesting future directions such as integrating pre-trained embeddings and exploring alternative architectures.

3 Procedure

Based on our research questions, we divided the proposal into three phases: detection, generation, and evaluation. The outline of the procedure has been shown in Figure 1, which illustrates each phase and the data flow using different colors: Blue for phase 1 (detection), green for phase 2 (generation), and purple for phase 3 (evaluation). Also, this shows that three different subsets of the dataset were extracted and flowed in different paths, one for the detection phase and two for the text generator model.

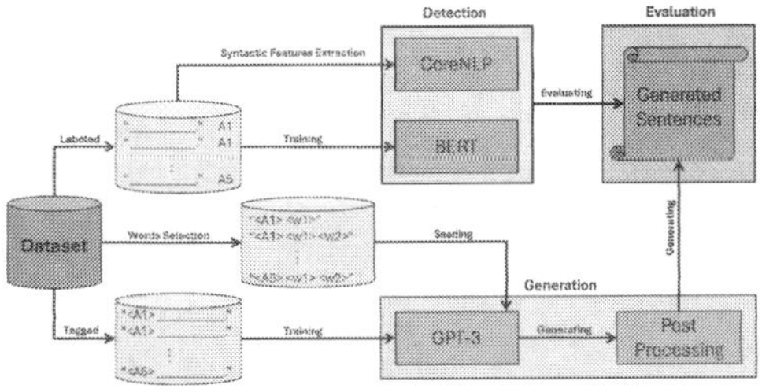

Figure 1: The outline of the procedure for detecting, generating, and evaluating text in various writing styles.

In order to create the dataset, we used Project Gutenberg to collect books by different authors. We picked five authors, Charles Dickens, Mark Twain, Herman Melville, Jane Austen, and Louisa May Alcott. They all belong to the 18th century and provide a good balance of male and female authors as well as British and American authors in our analysis. We also aim to cover a broad range of topics, as Twain and Melville generally wrote for men, whereas Austen and Alcott typically wrote about women. Dickens, meanwhile, mostly addressed social conditions, such as poverty and wealth, rather than focusing specifically on men or women. The total number of extracted sentences is 115,471. In datasets with paired samples, there exist at least two different styles for the same content, like formal and informal datasets. As mentioned before, in our dataset, there are no identified sentences from different authors expressing the same content, which makes it much more challenging for the model to understand the differences or, in the next steps, to transfer one sentence from an author to another author's writing style.

Sentences from the dataset along with their labels are used to train the BERT classification model. Here, BERT functions as a classifier to determine the author of the given sentences. The expectation is that a highly accurate classifier not only demonstrates that there are distinguishable features among authors, making the Generation phase possible but also will provide a reliable model for evaluating newly generated sentences, verifying whether they align with the writing style of the intended author. On the other hand, as illustrated in the Detection phase, there is also a syntactic feature extraction path. This path aims to perform a similar function as BERT but relies on syntactic features. We expect these syntactic features, comprising both low-level and high-level features, to clearly demonstrate differences between various writing styles.

The generator model will be trained on sentences concatenated with their labels at the beginning. The main idea behind this approach is that, since we don't have paired samples, we explicitly add the label of each sentence to help the model understand patterns shared by sentences with similar labels. After training the model, new sentences are generated by providing seeds with different labels and randomly extracted words. The generator then completes these sentences based on the initial labels. Finally, the generated sentences must be preprocessed to evaluate their quality and remove tags.

As mentioned in the introduction, evaluating generated sentences with common techniques has several challenges. Hence, to make the evaluation more systematic and practical, we will use the AI-evaluate-AI technique. In addition to using a large language model like BERT for evaluation, we employ a feature-based evaluation to further assess the quality of the generated text. As demonstrated in the next section, we will show that extracting syntactic features can help highlight stylistic differences between authors. For example, in prior studies (Rajaei Moghadam et al., 2024a,b), we showed how the syntax in speeches by U.S. presidents differed from the syntax in their written works. Similarly, we will extract high-level and low-level syntactic features using Stanford CoreNLP (Manning et al., 2014) to compare the generated sentences with the original dataset.

In summary, our proposed workflow combines detection, generation, and evaluation techniques to accurately create sentences in different writing styles and assess them in a meaningful way. The goal is to ensure that the generated sentences not only reflect the stylistic features of the target authors but also maintain the consistency and fluency of any generated sentences.

3.1 Detection

Using our previous work (Rajaei Moghadam et al., 2024a,b), we are going to analyze and evaluate the generated sentences and compare them with the original sentences by extracting the low-level and high-level syntactic features of each sentence. The dataset used in the above papers contained sentences of transcribed speeches and written books by United States presidents. For sentence extraction, the *nltk* library (Bird et al., 2009) was used, while CoreNLP (version 4.5.7) was employed for tokenization and word counting.

Low-level features (Rajaei Moghadam et al., 2024b), are categorized into three different aspects: morphological aspects, which include average syllables per word, average words per sentence, and average characters per word; lexical aspects, which include the number of words in a sentence, percentage of different POS, and percentage of personal pronouns; and syntactical aspects, which include percentage of subordinate clauses, depth of parse tree, percentage of noun phrases, the average length of noun phrases, percentage of yes/no questions, and percentage of direct wh-questions.

High-level syntactic features that have been introduced in Rajaei Moghadam et al. (2024a) contain: Pronoun and noun phrases in the subject, passive and active sentences, comparative and superlative, imperative structures, conjunction phrases, and prepositional phrases.

The number of words in a sentence was used as an aid to understanding syntactic complexity since longer sentences often indicate more complex ideas or more detailed information. Also, the height of the parse tree can be considered as an indicator of sentence complexity.

The analysis includes part-of-speech (POS) tags, which reveal structural, stylistic, and functional aspects of the text. This parsing model employs context-free grammar, along with associated probabilities for each rule, to generate a parse tree for each sentence. The token and sentence boundaries and other features provided by CoreNLP help in the analysis process. We rolled up the multiple types of nouns and verbs provided by CoreNLP into one type for each.

One important issue is the identification of passive sentences. According to Aygen (2016), the active voice is the typical form in which the subject of the sentence is the agent. To do this, the PassivePy package (Sepehri et al., 2023) in the SpaCy library (Honnibal et al., 2020) enables us to compute active, agentless passive, and agentive passive forms.

The results showed that the most significant features identified are sentence length, verb percentages, noun percentages, and prepositional phrases. Also, despite having fewer samples for long sentences, using long sentences improves the accuracy across all models. Increasing the sentence length also raised the importance ranking of prepositional phrases. Also, combining both sets of features improves the model's performance. Finally, based on our analysis, U.S. presidents are more likely to use prepositional phrases and longer sentences in their speeches than in their books.

Based on the results of the previous works mentioned above, we expect that there will be distinguishable features among the different authors in our dataset. We will examine whether BERT-based detection methods and detections based on syntactic features can identify differences between the five authors. This analysis will not only enhance our understanding of the linguistic characteristics specific to each author but also allow us to compare real sentences with sentences generated by our model. In other words, our evaluation technique involves calculating the similarity between the patterns found in real and generated data. Our preliminary results using BERT to detect the writing styles of sentences from five different authors show 84 percent in both accuracy and F1 score metrics.

At the same time, we are working on Graph Neural Networks (GNNs) (Zhou et al., 2020), which are deep neural networks that have attracted the attention of researchers across various fields. Five different Graph Neural Network (GNN) models were applied to understand and classify each sentence based on the author's writing style. We utilized a message-passing spatial method (GraphSAGE), an attention-based method (GAT), spectral methods (GCN, ChebNet), and a highly expressive GNN model (GINConv). In our preliminary results, we demonstrated the power of GNNs in extracting patterns behind the different writing styles of authors by using only dependencies between words in each sentence.

In that study, we extracted only the dependencies between words in different sentences, which represent a minimal set of information that can be derived from a sentence. We processed the sentences using the CoreNLP parser to extract word dependency information. In these graphs, each node represented a word in the sentence, while edges captured the grammatical dependencies between the words.

Table 1: The primary results of the generated sentences using the seeding technique for the expected writing styles.

Target	Seed	Generated Sentences
Charles Dickens	<0> When	**When** I had got my breath, I said, "I am going to London.
Jane Austen	<1> When	**When** they were gone, she sat down again, ...
Mark Twain	<2> When	**When** the sun went down, we had a grand supper, ...
Louisa May Alcott	<3> He	**He** was a man of great courage, and a man of great resolution.
Herman Melville	<4> He	**He** had been a very good-looking young man, ...
Charles Dickens	<0> He	**He** was a man of great talent, and his music was considered ...
Jane Austen	<1> A	**A** very few minutes more, however, and she was in the street, ...
Mark Twain	<2> A	**A** few of the boys had gone to the river, ...
Louisa May Alcott	<3> A	**A** few words of explanation will make it clear.

3.2 Generation

The most important and challenging part of the pipeline is generating texts, particularly when considering the challenges of working with style and the lack of paired datasets for training the models. On the other hand, based on the related work and the identified gaps that align with our main goal, in this section we aim to generate different writing styles by utilizing GPT models.

In order to address the challenges with training generators without parallel data, we add identifier tags at the beginning of each sentence as an indicator of each of the five different authors, to force the models to learn and capture the patterns of the writing style of each author. For example, <A0> in "<A0> Why, I have been ashamed of your moroseness there! <end>" indicates that the sentence belongs to Charles Dickens.

As explained, we will train the GPT-3 models using author tag identifiers for each sentence in the dataset. This involves using the seeding technique to prompt the model to generate the rest of the words in a sentence. For example, by adding an author identifier, the expectation is that the model will generate sentences similar to the writing style of that author. The seeding process can start with only a tag or with a tag that is followed by one or more words. For instance, a seed could be "<A0>", "<A0> hello", or "<A0> today is". Hence, the model generates sentences in different writing styles, rather than transferring the writing style.

We use the GPT-3 (Brown, 2020) structure for sentence generation, as it is one of the publicly available state-of-the-art models, known for its remarkable ability to produce coherent and contextually appropriate text from given prompts. Specifically, we train GPT-Neo 1.3B (Black et al., 2021), an open-source autoregressive language model developed by EleutherAI, which contains 1.3 billion parameters. After generating the sentences, we apply post-processing techniques to improve their quality. For instance, we remove the tags from the beginning and the ending of sentences and check for issues like repeated words or incomplete sentences. At the end of this step, we aim to have a collection of polished, high-quality generated sentences.

Our goal is to achieve the final result with the highest possible accuracy within the limitations of data and resources. It is worth mentioning that preliminary results have been obtained. The trained model, after 3 epochs, achieved 86% on both accuracy and F1 score metrics, which seems acceptable. The results showed that the introduced model is capable of generating sentences based on arbitrary seeding prompts. Table 1 reports some of the generated results, which need improvement in terms of both their assigned classes and their fluency and clarity.

Although the generated sentences, such as those reported in Table 1, represent our primary results, initial evaluations by a human expert provide evidence that it seems the model has learned distinct authorial patterns. For example, in the first sentence attributed to Charles Dickens, we observe British English usage such as "had got", since American English typically uses "had gotten." In the second sentence, attributed to Jane Austen, the reference to parties and social behavior clearly aligns with themes frequently explored in her stories. Regarding the fourth sentence by Alcott, words like "courage" and "resolution" reflect the language commonly found in novels from her period. The fifth sentence, attributed to Melville, interestingly focuses on men and boys, a theme prevalent throughout his works. In the seventh sentence, attributed to Austen, it is not surprising to encounter a depiction of a woman busy shopping in the street, a typical scenario in Austen's novels. For the eighth sentence, attributed to Mark Twain, the importance of boys and references to Mississippi strongly reflect his characteristic themes. Lastly, the sentence attributed to Alcott resembles a direct note to the reader, a common stylistic feature in 19th-century literature. Future evaluation by human experts and AI-Evaluate-AI can potentially clarify the accuracy of patterns learned by the generator model.

3.3 Evaluation

The final experiment involves evaluating the generated sentences. As shown in Figure 1, we plan to use the AI-evaluate-AI techniques. One of the main reasons behind this approach is the inherent ambiguity in evaluating an author's writing style.

All generator models, like other models, provide metrics such as accuracy or F1 score for evaluation. However, achieving high values for these metrics does not necessarily reflect true accuracy in generating distinct writing styles, so these metrics in the generative model can not reflect the performance of the model in different writing styles. Alternatively, involving human evaluation adds further complexity. Imagine a scenario where a generator produces a sentence, and we ask a group of humans to identify the writing style from among five 19th-century authors. How reliable would their evaluation be? The complexity of this task presents significant challenges.

Another method to improve the reliability of human evaluators in such a process is to use a preliminary test. For instance, we could test participants on the training data and only involve those who achieve high accuracy in the evaluation process. However, this approach significantly increases both the time and cost of evaluation.

Therefore, our proposal for evaluating generated sentences involves using a detector model that has demonstrated high accuracy in training and test data. For example, if we have a BERT model with high performance in author detection, we can use it for quick and cost-effective evaluation of generated text, while factoring in the reliability of the model. Also, we are going to use the feature-based approaches, outlined in the detection section, to compare both the original and generated sentences and determine how closely high-level and low-level syntactic features exhibit similar patterns for each author. Furthermore, a comparison between generated sentences and original sentences allows us to determine whether a model has memorized each author's sentences or not; in other words, we can check for overfitting in the model.

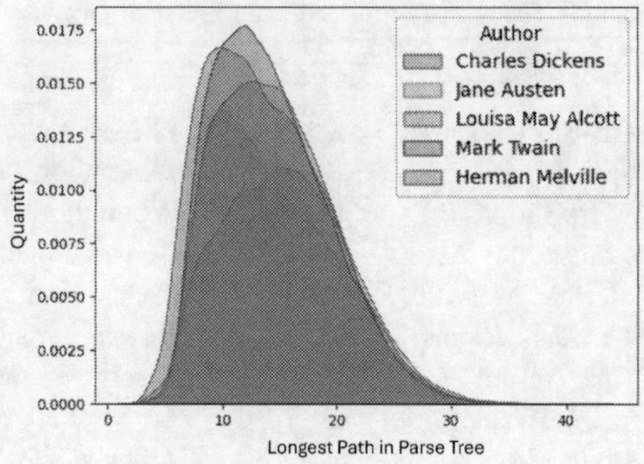

Figure 2: Histogram of the longest path in the parse trees of sentences.

Preliminary analysis of syntactic features in the original sentences reveals distinct patterns that merit deeper investigation in comparison with the generated sentences. For instance, Figure 2 presents a histogram of the longest path in the parse tree. Notably, Alcott (green) exhibits a distribution pattern distinct from Twain (red). The diagram indicates that most sentences by Twain have shorter paths in their parse trees. Conversely, Alcott's sentences show a more uniform distribution across various path lengths. This suggests that Mark Twain tends to write simpler sentences than Louisa May Alcott.

3.4 Conclusion and Future Work

This study contains three main sections: detection, generation, and evaluation, each focusing on different authors' writing styles. In the first section, using the established framework from our previous work, we analyzed writing styles based on their unique syntactic characteristics and classified them using machine learning models, as well as LLMs and GNNs. In the second section, we trained a GPT-3 model on a dataset containing unpaired sentences from five different authors. Preliminary results indicated that the generated sentences reflect meaningful stylistic differences among the authors. The final section focuses on evaluation, where we compare generated sentences with real sentences using both feature-based and LLM-based approaches.

References

Gulsat Aygen. 2016. *English Grammar: A Descriptive Linguistic Approach*, third edition. Kendall Hunt.

Federico Betti, Giorgia Ramponi, and Massimo Piccardi. 2020. Controlled text generation with adversarial learning. In *Proceedings of the 13th International Conference on Natural Language Generation*, pages 29–34.

Steven Bird, Edward Loper, and Ewan Klein. 2009. *Natural Language Processing with Python*. O'Reilly.

Sid Black, Leo Gao, Phil Wang, Connor Leahy, and Stella Biderman. 2021. GPT-Neo: Large scale autoregressive language modeling with Mesh-Tensorflow. Retrieved from https://doi.org/10.5281/zenodo.5297715.

Tom B Brown. 2020. Language models are few-shot learners. *arXiv preprint arXiv:2005.14165*.

Mariano de Rivero, Cristhiam Tirado, and Willy Ugarte. 2021. Formalstyler: GPT based model for formal style transfer based on formality and meaning preservation. *In Proceedings of the 13th International Joint Conference on Knowledge Discovery, Knowledge Engineering and Knowledge Management (IC3K)*, 1:48–56.

Yuheng Du, Shereen Oraby, Vittorio Perera, Minmin Shen, Anjali Narayan-Chen, Tagyoung Chung, Anushree Venkatesh, and Dilek Hakkani-Tur. 2020. Schema-guided natural language generation. In *Proceedings of the 13th International Conference on Natural Language Generation*, pages 283–295.

David I Holmes. 1998. The evolution of stylometry in humanities scholarship. *Literary and Linguistic Computing*, 13(3):111–117.

Matthew Honnibal, Ines Montani, Sofie Van Landeghem, and Adriane Boyd. 2020. spaCy: Industrial-strength Natural Language Processing in Python. doi: 10.5281/zenodo.1212303.

Zhiting Hu, Zichao Yang, Xiaodan Liang, Ruslan Salakhutdinov, and Eric P Xing. 2017. Toward controlled generation of text. In *Proceedings of the 34th International Conference on Machine Learning*, volume 70, pages 1587–1596.

Chih-Te Lai, Yi-Te Hong, Hong-You Chen, Chi-Jen Lu, and Shou-De Lin. 2019. Multiple text style transfer by using word-level conditional generative adversarial network with two-phase training. In *Proceedings of the 2019 Conference on Empirical Methods in Natural Language Processing and the 9th International Joint Conference on Natural Language Processing (EMNLP-IJCNLP)*, pages 3579–3584.

Joosung Lee. 2020. Stable style transformer: Delete and generate approach with encoder-decoder for text style transfer. *arXiv preprint arXiv:2005.12086*.

Xiang Li, John Thickstun, Ishaan Gulrajani, Percy S Liang, and Tatsunori B Hashimoto. 2022. Diffusion-LM improves controllable text generation. *Advances in Neural Information Processing Systems*, 35:4328–4343.

Lajanugen Logeswaran, Honglak Lee, and Samy Bengio. 2018. Content preserving text generation with attribute controls. *Proceedings of the 32nd International Conference on Neural Information Processing Systems*, page 5108–5118.

Yiwei Lyu, Tiange Luo, Jiacheng Shi, Todd C Hollon, and Honglak Lee. 2023. Fine-grained text style transfer with diffusion-based language models. *arXiv preprint arXiv:2305.19512*.

Christopher D Manning, Mihai Surdeanu, John Bauer, Jenny Finkel, Steven J Bethard, and David McClosky. 2014. The Stanford CoreNLP Natural Language Processing Toolkit. In *Proceedings of the 52nd Annual Meeting of the Association for Computational Linguistics: System Demonstrations*, pages 55–60.

Mina Rajaei Moghadam, Mosab Rezaei, Gülşat Aygen, and Reva Freedman. 2024a. Text vs. transcription: A study of differences between the writing and speeches of Us presidents. In *the 4th International Conference on Natural Language Processing for Digital Humanities*, pages 352–361.

Mina Rajaei Moghadam, Mosab Rezaei, Miguel Williams, Gülşat Aygen, and Reva Freedman. 2024b. Investigating lexical and syntactic differences in written and spoken English corpora. In *the 37th International FLAIRS Conference Proceedings*.

Amir Sepehri, Mitra Sadat Mirshafiee, and David M Markowitz. 2023. PassivePy: A tool to automatically identify passive voice in big text data. *Journal of Consumer Psychology*, 33(4):714–727.

Youzhi Tian, Zhiting Hu, and Zhou Yu. 2018. Structured content preservation for unsupervised text style transfer. *arXiv preprint arXiv:1810.06526*.

James Wayman, Nicholas Orlans, Qian Hu, Fred Goodman, Azar Ulrich, and Valorie Valencia. 2009. Technology assessment for the state of the art biometrics excellence roadmap. *Mitre Technical Report*, Volume 2. FBI.

Christopher C Yang, Hsinchun Chen, Michael Chau, Kuiyu Chang, Sheau-Dong Lang, Patrick Chen, Raymond Hsieh, Daniel Zeng, Fei-Yue Wang, and Kathleen M Carley. 2008. Intelligence and security informatics. *IEEE ISI 2008 International Workshops: PAISI, PACCF, and SOCO*.

Jie Zhou, Ganqu Cui, Shengding Hu, Zhengyan Zhang, Cheng Yang, Zhiyuan Liu, Lifeng Wang, Changcheng Li, and Maosong Sun. 2020. Graph neural networks: A review of methods and applications. *AI open*, 1:57–81.

Collaborative Data Exploration through Visualization: A Thesis Proposal Analyzing Impact of Conversational Assistants

Abari Bhattacharya
University of Illinois Chicago
abhatt62@uic.edu

Barbara Di Eugenio
University of Illinois Chicago
bdieugen@uic.edu

Abstract

Data visualization is integral to any Exploratory Data Analysis (EDA) task. However, generating visualization requires expertise, presenting a steep learning curve and a significant cognitive load. Natural language interfaces for EDA aim to lower this barrier by allowing users to generate visualizations through natural language queries. However, complexity remains when EDA is performed collaboratively, requiring an environment to support multi-user interaction. In this thesis proposal, we discuss challenges in user-system interaction in a collaborative multi-user setup, such as errors in visualization generation due to misinterpretation of user requests. We hypothesize that a Conversational Assistant (CA) capable of understanding user-initiated clarification requests and generating accurate responses can improve user experience and support collaborative EDA tasks. To this end, we propose to develop such a CA (Figure 1) and evaluate it through a user study, thus examining its impact on user experience in a collaborative environment for EDA.

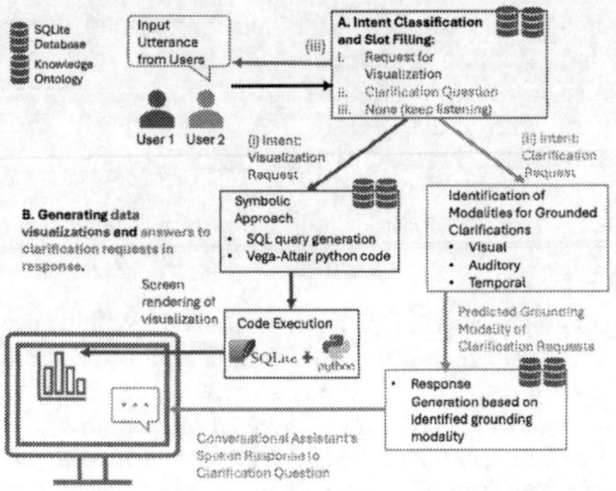

Figure 1: The workflow diagram of the proposed conversational assistant for collaborative data visualization (detail in Section 3.3). We focus on (A) understanding the user's intent, that is, data visualization requests and clarification requests, and (B) generating data visualizations (i) and answers to clarification requests(ii) in response.

1 Introduction

EDA is a method for analyzing data that predominantly uses graphical techniques such as bar charts, heatmaps etc., to uncover patterns, outliers, and insights (National Institute of Standards and Technology (NIST), 2023) from the data. Originating from John Tukey's *Exploratory Data Analysis* (Tukey, 1977), over the years, EDA has evolved (Mosteller and Tukey, 1977; McNeil, 1977; Velleman and Hoaglin, 1981) to become a vital tool across domains like healthcare, finance, and education (Sarker, 2021). While visualization generation plays a crucial role in EDA, the steep learning curve associated with traditional tools often excludes non-technical users, who face challenges in adopting these techniques for decision-making (Sarker, 2021). To address these challenges, Sarker suggests developing user-friendly tools catering to non-technical users to foster a more inclusive and accessible data-driven work culture. Oftentimes, EDA is done in multi-user collaborative settings that leverage users' diverse perspectives to enhance sense-making. However, existing visualization tools such as Tableau, MS Excel, and Plotly cater primarily to single users, limiting multi-user collaboration (Isenberg et al., 2011; Willett et al., 2011; Jeong et al., 2015). This underscores a need for extending tools to support data exploration in collaborative environments, also keeping in mind the need to make such systems accessible to non-technical users. The best approach for modeling such a tool would be a natural language interface, with which users can perform EDA by generating data visualizations in a collaborative multi-user environment. Further, users should be able to tell the system what they want in an accessible setup. This entails a CA with which users can engage using natural language, and the system should mediate

Proceedings of the 2025 Conference of the Nations of the Americas Chapter of the Association for Computational Linguistics: Human Language Technologies (Volume 4: Student Research Workshop), pages 492–500
April 30 - May 1, 2025

between the user and the visualization generator. However, human conversations are often characterized by incomplete queries, ambiguous utterances and coreferences. This necessitates the CA to accommodate the characteristics of human conversation and respond meaningfully to ensure a positive experience for the users.

Recently Bhattacharya et al. (2024) conducted a thorough analysis by comparing an extension of the CA Articulate2 (Kumar et al., 2016; Bhattacharya et al., 2023) with Articulate+ (Tabalba et al., 2022, 2023) through user studies and listed extensive insight from their findings (discussed in Section 3.1). We use these insights to motivate our research objectives and start by systematically investigating user experiences with conversational interfaces for collaborative multi-user data visualization (Section 3). First, we look at challenges impacting the user's interaction with the CA in this user study. Specifically, we examine how *clarification requests* initiated by the users during their interaction with the CA might help improve the user's experience in a multi-user, collaborative EDA task scenario. Through this work, our goal is not only to contribute a CA framework, but also an understanding of how clarification behavior affects the interaction quality in multi-user collaborating conversational interfaces.

2 Related Work

Natural Language Interfaces for Data Visualization: Early work on Data Visualization natural language interfaces, such as Cox et al. (2001), used on structured grammar-based queries. Later, with Articulate (Sun et al., 2010), free-form interactions evolved, following which tools like IBM Watson Analytics (Hoyt et al., 2016), Tableau Ask Data (Tableau), and Datatone (Gao et al., 2015) enhanced natural language understanding (NLU). Eviza (Setlur et al., 2016) and Evizeon (Hoque et al., 2018) introduced interactive dialogue-based exploration; however, these were without support for visualization modification. In parallel, Shen et al. (2022) extended Card et al. (1999)'s natural language interface pipeline by integrating NLU and dialogue management (McNabb and Laramee, 2017), laying a foundation for NLIs in visualization. Later, systems like NL4DV (Narechania et al., 2021) and AUDiaL (Murillo-Morales and Miesenberger, 2020) integrated natural language interfaces into visualization pipelines, while Wrangler (Kandel et al., 2011) and Voder (Srinivasan et al., 2019) automated fact generation from data along with visualization generation. Articulate2 (Kumar et al., 2016) introduced multimodal inputs regarding speech and gesture and coreference resolution (Bhattacharya et al., 2023), but it lacked support for multi-user data analysis. Recently, transformer-based systems like ncNet (Luo et al., 2022) mapped natural language to visualizations using nvBench dataset(Luo et al., 2021), but it lacked conversational capabilities. LLM-based tools like JarviX (Liu et al., 2023) and VIST5 (Voigt et al., 2023) automated visualization generation, but deployment costs were high, and the system suffered from hallucinations. Chat2Vis (Maddigan and Susnjak, 2023) leveraged multiple LLMs but lacked interactivity and relied on complex prompts, defeating the purpose of "natural language" queries. Furthermore, most systems were evaluated using datasets like nvBench rather than real-time studies with users, thus leaving gaps in understanding how real users collaborate with such systems in EDA in multi-user settings. Shen et al. (2023) provides a comprehensive survey of natural language interfaces for data visualization, identifying challenges and shortcomings, including lack of domain knowledge, need for advanced Natural Language Processing power to support free-form queries, lack of leveraging user's conversational history and lack of datasets specifically for visualization natural language interface frameworks. While tools like LIDA (Dibia, 2023), targeted towards non-technical users, simplify visualization generation using large language models (LLMs), they lack support for collaborative and interactive exploration.

Clarification Requests: Clarification Requests (CRs) play a crucial role in *grounding*—the process of establishing mutual understanding in dialogue (Clark, 1996; Clark and Schaefer, 1989). When humans engage in a conversation, a speaker requests clarification when they do not understand the form or content of the utterance of the other speaker. While grounding seems natural in human-human conversation, in human-system dialogue, it is not trivial, and so is identification and generation of clarification by the conversational system. Early foundational work by Ginzburg and Sag (2001) categorized clarification requests (CRs) into *reprise interrogatives*—including *echo* and *reference questions*—and elliptical forms like *reprise sluices*. Purver et al. (2001) expanded this with *non-*

reprise clarifications, *gaps*, and *gap fillers*, while Gabsdil (2003) and Schlangen (2004) introduced finer-grained categories such as partial repetitions, reformulations, semantic clarifications, and acoustic misunderstandings. Much of the existing research on CR has focused on those initiated by the system, typically triggered by ambiguous user input, speech recognition errors, or underspecified intent. A comprehensive overview of these can be found in the work of Rahmani et al. (2023). In contrast, in this thesis, the focus is on *user-initiated* clarification requests. One notable effort in this direction is the work by Madureira and Schlangen (2023), who annotated user-initiated CRs in the CoDraw dataset (Kim et al., 2019), a multi-modal, goal-oriented collaborative dialogue corpus. Their study highlights how instruction followers request clarification when facing ambiguous instructions, underscoring the importance of modeling such interactions in collaborative settings.

3 Proposed Research

Effective collaboration in an EDA task requires a CA to enable users to interact naturally, as with a human collaborator. This effectiveness also depends on its ability to respond correctly to user inputs. After a closer inspection of user interactions from Bhattacharya et al. (2024)'s work, we found some challenges that impact the system's usability and overall user experience. We put forward these challenges next and discuss how they lead us to the research question of this proposal.

3.1 Motivation and Research Question

An analysis of user study transcripts from Bhattacharya et al. (2024) uncovered key limitations in system behavior that impact user experience, listed in Table 1. In the user study, the users were exploring a COVID-19 dataset for all counties in the United States (U.S.)(Tiwari et al., 2021) to complete two timed EDA tasks. The dataset has attributes like COVID vulnerability rank, Poverty rate, Diabetes rate, and County types, among others. The system generated data visualizations like bar charts, line charts, choropleth maps and heat maps based on requests for visualization from the users.

A promising solution to these challenges can be found in the concept of *grounded clarifications*, introduced by Benotti and Blackburn (2021). Grounded clarifications are clarification requests tied to specific real-world contexts or modalities (e.g., visual, auditory), ensuring mutual understanding between participants in a conversation. According to the paper, for an utterance U, a subsequent turn is considered a grounded clarification in modality m if there is a lack of positive evidence of understanding in that modality. Returning to the observations in Table 1, we can see how grounded clarifications appear in those scenarios. These examples show how answering clarification requests would allow the system to effectively address user's confusion or lack of understanding of an earlier response by the system. Moreover, in multi-user natural language interface settings for data visualization, clarification needs to extend beyond linguistic content, encompassing visual and contextual references. For instance, users can ask for a clarification request grounded in visual modality based on a chart they are currently exploring on the workspace of the natural language interface. As noted by Benotti and Blackburn (2021), grounded clarifications extend to the physical and contextual environment, reinforcing the necessity for accurate identification and response by the CA. Therefore, by focusing on user-initiated clarification requests, the conversational system can leverage these clarifications as opportunities to provide correct responses to the user. At the same time, these responses must also be accurately grounded in context and aligned with the user's intent.

This leads us to our research question:
RQ: *How do user-initiated clarification requests impact user experience concerning* ***system functionality***, ***interpretability***, *and* ***overall usability****?*

These three key terms capture complementary dimensions of user experience with a conversational assistant: *functionality*, referring to the system's ability to respond appropriately to user input; *interpretability*, denoting how well users can understand the system's behavior; and *usability*, which reflects users' overall ease and effectiveness of interaction. We return to these definitions in detail in Section 3.4.

We aim to answer the research question by proposing three contributions. First, we plan to create an annotated corpus of multi-user dialogue interactions with a CA for data visualization, detailed in Section 3.2. Second, we propose a CA framework with components leveraging our custom dataset described in Section 3.3. Finally, we plan to conduct a user study with participants inter-

Table 1: Common system challenges observed during user interaction and their corresponding clarification grounding modality

#	Issue and Description	Example	Modality
1	**No Response:** System fails to respond due to TTS errors or misclassified dialogue acts.	**User 1:** "Can we look at all the rural areas in the United States?" **System:** Generates a map based on an earlier utterance. **User 1:** "Are those the rural areas in the United States?" (Expecting clarification) **User 2:** "Louder." **User 1:** "No, it cannot be louder... I mean, I'm pretty sure there's no probable generation for this..."	**Auditory:** Users rephrase or adjust their requests when the system fails to respond, demonstrating reliance on auditory clarification.
2	**Incorrect Visuals:** System generates charts that do not match user queries.	**User:** "Show me the poverty data by county type." **System:** Generates a map of poverty rates for all counties. **User:** "Is this the most recent map?" (Seeking clarification)	**Visual:** Users seek clarification on unintended or redundant visualizations, indicating a need for responses grounded in visual information.
3	**Redundant Charts:** System generates repetitive charts that do not add value.	**User:** "Show me a map of diabetes." **System:** Generates a map of diabetes risk for all counties. **User:** "Can I see a map of diabetes risk for Midwest and Northeast?" **System:** Generates the same map again (redundant). **User:** "Does it respond to multiple parameters?"	**Visual:** Users seek clarification on unintended or redundant visualizations, indicating a need for responses grounded in visual information.
4	**Misinterpreted References:** Ambiguous references lead to incorrect responses.	**User 1:** "I want uninsured rate for different counties." **System:** Generates a grouped bar chart for uninsured rate by county type. **User 1:** "I don't understand what these bar charts are for..." **User 2:** "Is it grouping them by county type?" **System:** Generates a U.S. map of county types instead of clarifying.	**Temporal:** Users reference previous visualizations or utterances for clarification, requiring responses grounded in a temporal context.

acting with the CA (Section 3.4). This study will help us examine the user experience with the CA, which can generate data visualization and natural language responses to user-initiated clarification questions.

3.2 Dataset

We discussed how identifying and handling user-initiated clarification requests (CRs) can be critical to task-oriented and collaborative dialogue systems. While there is research on the generation of CRs by CAs, the identification of CRs remains mostly unexplored. Recent efforts, such as Madureira and Schlangen (2023), have addressed this gap by annotating datasets like CoDraw with instructional CRs. However, a general understanding and categorization of user-initiated CRs are still evolving. Moreover, multi-user dialogue corpora remain scarce, despite growing interest in modeling collaborative interactions in task-oriented settings (Jo et al., 2023). To address this gap, we propose creating a custom dataset based on the COVID(T) corpus from Bhattacharya et al. (2023, 2024), which includes **8,440 utterances** from a user study setup where two users collaborate on an EDA task. The CA in this setup generates data visualizations only based on the users' requests. We conducted preliminary annotation of **541 utterances**(a random significant sample with a ±4.1% margin of error at 95% confidence) by two annotators (Cohen's Kappa: 0.88), where **5.54%** of utterances were user-initiated clarification requests and **30.3%** were visualization requests. Here, we define *clarification requests* as utterances where a user explicitly or implicitly asks for additional information to understand prior system or user input during the collaborative EDA task. Please note that this is a three-way interaction between human-human and human-system. Therefore, our initial annotation includes CRs directed to both the system and the other user, capturing the full range of clarification behavior during the exploratory tasks. Next, following Bhattacharya et al. (2024), we define *Visualization requests* as utterances where the user asks the system to generate a specific data visualization or refine a previous one. Although CRs appear less frequently (Madureira and Schlangen (2023) also reported that **11.36%** of instructional dialogues included user-initiated CRs), their importance in human-system interaction has been discussed by researchers (Rahmani et al., 2023). Thus, we hypothesize that explicitly supporting CRs can potentially encourage users to seek clarity and improve interaction quality. Inspired by Benotti and Blackburn (2021), we propose annotating CRs in our dataset based on their grounding modalities as discussed in Section 3.1 and Table 1. While Benotti and Blackburn also included *Socioperception* and *Kinesthetic* modalities, these are irrelevant to our setup. Instead, the *Temporal Modality* is particularly important for addressing references to prior user interactions or visualizations.

For training and evaluating the system's ability to generate responses to CRs, annotations will also include the ideal responses for each clarification request. Additionally, we will identify whether the required information comes from internal sources (e.g., dialogue history, knowledge base) or external sources (e.g., CDC, Wikipedia). While this work focuses on generating responses using internal sources, annotations for external sources will support future research on broader response generation tasks. Further, the transcripts mentioned above for the proposed dataset were collected in the context of COVID-19-related EDA. However, task design and user interactions can be generalized for collaborative data exploration in any domain (Bhattacharya et al., 2024), making the findings applicable to other domains. Unlike existing datasets like CoDraw(Madureira and Schlangen, 2023; Kim et al., 2019) which has scene reconstruction tasks or MultiWOZ (Budzianowski et al., 2018) or its multi-user variant (Jo et al., 2023), which focuses on IC/SF tasks in service-oriented dialogues, through the proposed dataset we plan to capture open-ended, multi-user dialogue on exploratory analysis of data. Overall, this dataset and annotation framework will enable the development of a conversational assistant capable of addressing user-initiated clarification requests effectively, improving user-system interaction in task-oriented dialogue systems.

3.3 Proposed Workflow

The proposed workflow of the CA shown in Figure 1 begins with speech-to-text transcription using Whisper (Radford et al., 2023), followed by Intent Classification and Slot Filling (IC/SF), which classifies an input utterance as either a Visualization Request, a Clarification Request, or None (here the system keeps listening for the next utterance). For SF, the system extracts relevant slots using the Knowledge Ontology of the dataset being explored by the users of the CA. If the user requests for a visualization generation, the system formulates an SQL query, retrieves data from an SQLite database (containing the data being explored), and generates Vega-Altair Python code [1]. Unlike Bhattacharya et al. (2023, 2024), we plan to generate the python code instead of Vega-Lite Grammar(Satyanarayan et al., 2017), enabling evaluation with the nvBench dataset(Luo et al., 2021). The Python code can be easily converted to Vega-Lite later for screen rendering. We plan to implement SQLite query and Vega-Altair code generation using symbolic reasoning, as done by Bhattacharya et al. (2023, 2024). Even though LLMs can generate satisfactory SQL Queries and Python codes, we choose this approach for its simplicity and reliability, avoiding any latency or hallucination that might come with using LLMs. For CRs, generated responses are informed by the dialogue History, which tracks user utterances, predicted intents, identified slots, and prior responses to user-initiated CRs. The final response output is displayed on the system interface for visualizations and via speech and display for natural language responses to clarifications, ensuring an interactive experience. Now, we focus on the proposed implementation of two core components: **(1) IC/SF** and**(2) CR Response Generation.**

IC and SF are essential for systems performing spoken language understanding (SLU). IC predicts the user's intent y_{intent} from an input sequence X, which includes the current utterance U_t and previous turns. SF extracts slot labels y_i for each token $x_i$and verifies them against a knowledge base K to ensure domain-specific standardization. In this proposal, we discuss two approaches for IC/SF. The first approach extends BERT-SLU (Zhang et al., 2019) by incorporating dialogue history, allowing it to process both the current utterance U_t and preceding turns. To enhance domain adaptation, we propose integrating AdapterFusion (Pfeiffer et al., 2021), combining an SLU-specific adapter (e.g.trained using the ATIS dataset (Hemphill et al., 1990)) with another adapter fine-tuned on our custom dataset, mitigating catastrophic forgetting. The second approach builds on ILLUMINER (Mirza et al., 2024), which involves adapting instruction-tuned LLMs with PEFT adapters to improve contextual awareness in a task-oriented conversational assistant. Mirza et al. (2024) experimented with LLMs specifically fined-tuned for instruction following like FLAN-T5(google/flan-t5-xxl), Vicuna (lmsys/vicuna-13b-v1.5, from Llama2) etc., and we plan to start by experimenting with the same LLMs. We also propose incorporating dialogue history into structured prompts. For example, "Given the <dialogue_history>, identify the intent and slots for: 'Can I see COVID risk in the midwestern US?'". Finally, we plan to perform knowledge base verification with both the proposed approaches to ensure slot labels align with domain terminology.

To evaluate IC, we plan to use metrics like accuracy, precision, recall, and F1-score, as well as a

[1] `https://altair-viz.github.io/` (a Python library built on top of Vega-Lite grammar for generating visualizations)

confusion matrix to analyze errors. For measuring the correctness of slot labeling, we propose using metrics like slot F1 score, exact match ratio, and slot error rate.

CR Response Generation: CRs arise when users refine their queries to seek a better understanding of the visualizations or to explore data. Please recall that we plan to classify CRs into three modalities: visual (users clarify based on interface data), auditory (users repeat or rephrase due to system non-responsiveness), and temporal (users reference prior utterances or visualizations). We hypothesize that incorporating modality labels can enhance response accuracy. Thus, to develop a robust CR-handling approach, we must first annotate the dataset to classify CRs by modality as well as annotate the ideal responses for each of these CRs in order to train the models.

This component can be evaluated on two aspects—**predicted modality** and **generated response**. Accuracy can be used for modality, while objective response evaluation will be performed using ROUGE, BLEU, and BERTScore. While these metrics are not exhaustive, they provide a useful approximation of the quality of the generated responses. Additionally, we plan to employ human annotators to assess Relevance, Fluency, Informativeness, and Factual Correctness on a 5-point Likert scale.

3.4 User Study for CA Evaluation:

One of the primary goals of this thesis is to evaluate the CA by recruiting participants who would interact with the system and thoroughly investigate their experience with it. Please recall, in our RQ, we mention *system functionality, interpretability and overall usability*. Bhattacharya et al. (2024) discuss these three features and how they impact the design consideration of the CA. Regarding *functionality*, they highlight that the CA, as an interactive system, generates visualizations in response to user utterances. The number of utterances processed, types and numbers of visualizations produced etc., are thus artifacts of the user-system interaction, shaping the user's experience with the system. The authors analyze these components and conclude that an optimal latency in processing utterances and generating visualizations is critical for avoiding overwhelming users or causing frustrating delays. Next, they point out that a CA must be *interpretable*; that is, the users should be able to comprehend and understand why the system produces specific visualizations and responses or, in other words, post-hoc interpretability (Gilpin et al., 2018). They measure the understanding of system output through the conclusions drawn by the users at the end of each open-ended EDA task. The authors suggested that the interpretability of the system can impact the take-aways of data analysis tasks by the users of the CA. Finally, the authors discuss *usability* of the system and how it affects the user's perception of the CA. They quantified usability through the post-study ratings given by the users for the usefulness of generated visualizations and ease of using the natural language interface. Therefore, to answer the RQ, we plan to start with replicating the study setup by Bhattacharya et al. (2024) and quantifying the user's experience through the quantities discussed above. Additionally, we plan to perform a qualitative evaluation of the responses generated by the CA to user-initiated CRs. However, we must remember that COVID-19 was still more relevant in 2022 when Bhattacharya et al. (2024) conducted their study, compared to 2025, when we plan to perform ours. As a result, we will primarily focus on the qualitative evaluation of CR responses and user experience measures rather than directly comparing them with the results of the past user study.

4 Conclusion

Overall, this thesis proposal emphasizes the importance of designing a CA for EDA and evaluating it in real-time with users. Beyond EDA, developing such a user-centric CA framework has broader implications for data-driven decision-making. With 77% of U.S. organizations relying on such data-driven strategies [2], an interactive CA can help non-technical users make data-informed decisions. Recent studies (Szukits and Móricz, 2024; Tawil et al., 2024) further highlight the role of data-driven methodologies in organizations of all sizes. By enabling intuitive, context-aware interactions, such a CA framework can enhance collaborative data exploration and make data visualization more accessible, thereby improving decision-making across diverse domains.

[2] https://www.statista.com/

References

Luciana Benotti and Patrick Blackburn. 2021. A recipe for annotating grounded clarifications. In *Proceedings of the 2021 Conference of the North American Chapter of the Association for Computational Linguistics: Human Language Technologies*, pages 4065–4077, Online. Association for Computational Linguistics.

Abari Bhattacharya, Barbara Di Eugenio, Veronica Grosso, Andrew Johnson, Roderick Tabalba, Nurit Kirshenbaum, Jason Leigh, and Moira Zellner. 2024. A conversational assistant for democratization of data visualization: A comparative study of two approaches of interaction. *Stat. Anal. Data Min.*, 17(6).

Abari Bhattacharya, Abhinav Kumar, Barbara Di Eugenio, Roderick Tabalba, Jillian Aurisano, Veronica Grosso, Andrew Johnson, Jason Leigh, and Moira Zellner. 2023. Reference resolution and new entities in exploratory data visualization: From controlled to unconstrained interactions with a conversational assistant. In *Proceedings of the 24th Annual Meeting of the Special Interest Group on Discourse and Dialogue*, pages 370–380, Prague, Czechia. Association for Computational Linguistics.

Paweł Budzianowski, Tsung-Hsien Wen, Bo-Hsiang Tseng, Iñigo Casanueva, Stefan Ultes, Osman Ramadan, and Milica Gašić. 2018. MultiWOZ - a large-scale multi-domain Wizard-of-Oz dataset for task-oriented dialogue modelling. In *Proceedings of the 2018 Conference on Empirical Methods in Natural Language Processing*, pages 5016–5026, Brussels, Belgium. Association for Computational Linguistics.

Stuart Card, Jock Mackinlay, and Ben Shneiderman. 1999. *Readings in Information Visualization: Using Vision To Think*.

Herbert H. Clark. 1996. *Using Language*. Cambridge University Press, Cambridge, UK.

Herbert H. Clark and Edward F. Schaefer. 1989. Contributing to discourse. *Cognitive Science*, 13(2):259–294.

Kenneth Cox, Rebecca Grinter, Stacie Hibino, Lalita Jagadeesan, and David Mantilla. 2001. A multi-modal natural language interface to an information visualization environment. *International Journal of Speech Technology*, 4:297–314.

Victor Dibia. 2023. LIDA: A tool for automatic generation of grammar-agnostic visualizations and infographics using large language models. In *Proceedings of the 61st Annual Meeting of the Association for Computational Linguistics (Volume 3: System Demonstrations)*, pages 113–126, Toronto, Canada. Association for Computational Linguistics.

Malte Gabsdil. 2003. Clarification in spoken dialogue systems. In *Proceedings of the 2003 AAAI Spring Symposium. Workshop on Natural Language Generation in Spoken and Written Dialogue*, pages 28–35.

Tong Gao, Mira Dontcheva, Eytan Adar, Zhicheng Liu, and Karrie G. Karahalios. 2015. Datatone: Managing ambiguity in natural language interfaces for data visualization. In *Proceedings of the 28th Annual ACM Symposium on User Interface Software amp; Technology*, UIST '15, page 489–500, New York, NY, USA. Association for Computing Machinery.

Leilani H. Gilpin, David Bau, Ben Z. Yuan, Ayesha Bajwa, Michael Specter, and Lalana Kagal. 2018. Explaining explanations: An overview of interpretability of machine learning. In *2018 IEEE 5th International Conference on Data Science and Advanced Analytics (DSAA)*, pages 80–89.

Jonathan Ginzburg and Ivan A Sag. 2001. *Interrogative investigations: the form, meaning, and use of English interrogatives*. Chicago University Press.

Charles T. Hemphill, John J. Godfrey, and George R. Doddington. 1990. The ATIS spoken language systems pilot corpus. In *Speech and Natural Language: Proceedings of a Workshop Held at Hidden Valley, Pennsylvania, USA, June 24-27, 1990*. Morgan Kaufmann.

Enamul Hoque, Vidya Setlur, Melanie Tory, and Isaac Dykeman. 2018. Applying pragmatics principles for interaction with visual analytics. *IEEE Transactions on Visualization and Computer Graphics*, 24(1):309–318.

Robert E. Hoyt, Derek Snider, Christian Thompson, and Sripriya Mantravadi. 2016. Ibm watson analytics: Automating visualization, descriptive, and predictive statistics. *JMIR Public Health and Surveillance*, 2(2):e157.

Petra Isenberg, Niklas Elmqvist, Jean Scholtz, Daniel Cernea, Kwan-Liu Ma, and Hans Hagen. 2011. Collaborative visualization: Definition, challenges, and research agenda. *Information Visualization*, 10(4):310–326.

Do-Hyung Jeong, Soo-Young Ji, Evan A. Suma, et al. 2015. Designing a collaborative visual analytics system to support users' continuous analytical processes. *Human-centric Computing and Information Sciences*, 5(1):5.

Yohan Jo, Xinyan Zhao, Arijit Biswas, Nikoletta Basiou, Vincent Auvray, Nikolaos Malandrakis, Angeliki Metallinou, and Alexandros Potamianos. 2023. Multi-user MultiWOZ: Task-oriented dialogues among multiple users. In *Findings of the Association for Computational Linguistics: EMNLP 2023*, pages 3237–3269, Singapore. Association for Computational Linguistics.

Sean Kandel, Andreas Paepcke, Joseph Hellerstein, and Jeffrey Heer. 2011. Wrangler: Interactive visual specification of data transformation scripts. In *Proceedings of the Extended Abstracts on Human Factors in Computing Systems (CHI)*, pages 3363–3372.

Jin-Hwa Kim, Nikita Kitaev, Xinlei Chen, Marcus Rohrbach, Byoung-Tak Zhang, Yuandong Tian, Dhruv Batra, and Devi Parikh. 2019. CoDraw: Collaborative drawing as a testbed for grounded goal-driven communication. In *Proceedings of the 57th Annual Meeting of the Association for Computational Linguistics*, pages 6495–6513, Florence, Italy. Association for Computational Linguistics.

Abhinav Kumar, Jillian Aurisano, Barbara Di Eugenio, Andrew Johnson, Alberto Gonzalez, and Jason Leigh. 2016. Towards a dialogue system that supports rich visualizations of data. Proceedings of the 17th Annual Meeting of the Special Interest Group on Discourse and Dialogue, pages 304–309.

Shang-Ching Liu, ShengKun Wang, Tsungyao Chang, Wenqi Lin, Chung-Wei Hsiung, Yi-Chen Hsieh, Yu-Ping Cheng, Sian-Hong Luo, and Jianwei Zhang. 2023. JarviX: A LLM no code platform for tabular data analysis and optimization. In *Proceedings of the 2023 Conference on Empirical Methods in Natural Language Processing: Industry Track*, pages 622–630, Singapore. Association for Computational Linguistics.

Yuyu Luo, Nan Tang, Guoliang Li, Chengliang Chai, Wenbo Li, and Xuedi Qin. 2021. Synthesizing natural language to visualization (nl2vis) benchmarks from nl2sql benchmarks. In *Proceedings of the 2021 International Conference on Management of Data*, SIGMOD '21, page 1235–1247, New York, NY, USA. Association for Computing Machinery.

Yuyu Luo, Nan Tang, Guoliang Li, Jiawei Tang, Chengliang Chai, and Xuedi Qin. 2022. Natural language to visualization by neural machine translation. *IEEE Transactions on Visualization and Computer Graphics*, 28(1):217–226.

Paula Maddigan and Teo Susnjak. 2023. Chat2vis: Generating data visualizations via natural language using chatgpt, codex and gpt-3 large language models. *IEEE Access*, 11:45181–45193.

Brielen Madureira and David Schlangen. 2023. Instruction clarification requests in multimodal collaborative dialogue games: Tasks, and an analysis of the CoDraw dataset. In *Proceedings of the 17th Conference of the European Chapter of the Association for Computational Linguistics*, pages 2303–2319, Dubrovnik, Croatia. Association for Computational Linguistics.

Laura McNabb and Robert S. Laramee. 2017. Survey of surveys (sos) - mapping the landscape of survey papers in information visualization. *Computer Graphics Forum*, 36(3):589–617.

Donald McNeil. 1977. *Interactive Data Analysis*. John Wiley and Sons, New York.

Paramita Mirza, Viju Sudhi, Soumya Ranjan Sahoo, and Sinchana Ramakanth Bhat. 2024. ILLUMINER: Instruction-tuned large language models as few-shot intent classifier and slot filler. In *Proceedings of the 2024 Joint International Conference on Computational Linguistics, Language Resources and Evaluation (LREC-COLING 2024)*, pages 8639–8651, Torino, Italia. ELRA and ICCL.

Frederick Mosteller and John Tukey. 1977. *Data Analysis and Regression*. Addison-Wesley, Reading, Mass.

Tobias Murillo-Morales and Klaus Miesenberger. 2020. AUDiaL: A natural language interface to make statistical charts accessible to blind persons. In *Proceedings of the International Conference on Computers Helping People with Special Needs*, pages 373–384. Springer.

Arpit Narechania, Arjun Srinivasan, and John T. Stasko. 2021. Nl4dv: A toolkit for generating analytic specifications for data visualization from natural language queries. *IEEE Transactions on Visualization and Computer Graphics*, 27:369–379.

National Institute of Standards and Technology (NIST). 2023. Exploratory data analysis: Section 1. Accessed: 2023-11-10.

Jonas Pfeiffer, Aishwarya Kamath, Andreas Rücklé, Kyunghyun Cho, and Iryna Gurevych. 2021. AdapterFusion: Non-destructive task composition for transfer learning. In *Proceedings of the 16th Conference of the European Chapter of the Association for Computational Linguistics: Main Volume*, pages 487–503, Online. Association for Computational Linguistics.

Matthew Purver, Jonathan Ginzburg, and Patrick Healey. 2001. On the means for clarification in dialogue. In *Proceedings of the Second SIGdial Workshop on Discourse and Dialogue*.

Alec Radford, Jong Wook Kim, Tao Xu, Greg Brockman, Christine McLeavey, and Ilya Sutskever. 2023. Robust speech recognition via large-scale weak supervision. In *Proceedings of the 40th International Conference on Machine Learning*, ICML'23. JMLR.org.

Hossein A. Rahmani, Xi Wang, Yue Feng, Qiang Zhang, Emine Yilmaz, and Aldo Lipani. 2023. A survey on asking clarification questions datasets in conversational systems. In *Proceedings of the 61st Annual Meeting of the Association for Computational Linguistics (Volume 1: Long Papers)*, pages 2698–2716, Toronto, Canada. Association for Computational Linguistics.

Iqbal H. Sarker. 2021. Data science and analytics: An overview from data-driven smart computing, decision-making and applications perspective. *SN Computer Science*, 2(5):377.

Arvind Satyanarayan, Dominik Moritz, Kanit Wongsuphasawat, and Jeffrey Heer. 2017. Vega-lite: A grammar of interactive graphics. *IEEE Transactions on Visualization and Computer Graphics*, 23(1):341–350.

David Schlangen. 2004. Causes and strategies for requesting clarification in dialogue. In *Proceedings of the 5th SIGdial Workshop on Discourse and Dialogue at HLT-NAACL 2004*, pages 136–143, Cambridge, Massachusetts, USA. Association for Computational Linguistics.

Vidya Setlur, Sarah E. Battersby, Melanie Tory, Rich Gossweiler, and Angel X. Chang. 2016. Eviza: A natural language interface for visual analysis. In *Proceedings of the 29th Annual Symposium on User Interface Software and Technology*, UIST '16, page 365–377, New York, NY, USA. Association for Computing Machinery.

Leixian Shen, Enya Shen, Yuyu Luo, Xiaocong Yang, Xuming Hu, Xiongshuai Zhang, Zhiwei Tai, and Jianmin Wang. 2022. Towards natural language interfaces for data visualization: A survey. *IEEE Transactions on Visualization and Computer Graphics*, PP:1–1.

Leixian Shen, Enya Shen, Yuyu Luo, Xiaocong Yang, Xuming Hu, Xiongshuai Zhang, Zhiwei Tai, and Jianmin Wang. 2023. Towards natural language interfaces for data visualization: A survey. *IEEE Transactions on Visualization and Computer Graphics*, 29(6):3121–3144.

Arjun Srinivasan, Steven M. Drucker, Alex Endert, and John Stasko. 2019. Augmenting visualizations with interactive data facts to facilitate interpretation and communication. *IEEE Transactions on Visualization and Computer Graphics*, 25(1):672–681.

Yiwen Sun, Jason Leigh, Andrew Johnson, and Sangyoon Lee. 2010. Articulate: A semi-automated model for translating natural language queries into meaningful visualizations. In *International Symposium on Smart Graphics*, pages 184–195. Springer.

Ádám Szukits and Péter Móricz. 2024. Towards data-driven decision making: the role of analytical culture and centralization efforts. *Review of Managerial Science*, 18:2849–2887.

Roderick Tabalba, Nurit Kirshenbaum, Jason Leigh, Abari Bhatacharya, Andrew Johnson, Veronica Grosso, Barbara Di Eugenio, and Moira Zellner. 2022. Articulate+: An always-listening natural language interface for creating data visualizations. In *Proceedings of the 4th Conference on Conversational User Interfaces*, CUI '22, New York, NY, USA. Association for Computing Machinery.

Roderick S Tabalba, Nurit Kirshenbaum, Jason Leigh, Abari Bhattacharya, Veronica Grosso, Barbara Di Eugenio, Andrew E Johnson, and Moira Zellner. 2023. An investigation into an always listening interface to support data exploration. In *Proceedings of the 28th International Conference on Intelligent User Interfaces*, IUI '23, page 128–141, New York, NY, USA. Association for Computing Machinery.

Tableau. Ask data. Accessed: 2023-11-10.

Abdel-Rahman H. Tawil, Muhidin Mohamed, Xavier Schmoor, Konstantinos Vlachos, and Diana Haidar. 2024. Trends and challenges towards effective data-driven decision making in uk small and medium-sized enterprises: Case studies and lessons learnt from the analysis of 85 small and medium-sized enterprises. *Big Data and Cognitive Computing*, 8(7).

Anuj Tiwari, Arya Dadhania, Vijay Avin, and Edson Oliveira. 2021. Using machine learning to develop a novel covid-19 vulnerability index (c19vi). *Science of The Total Environment*, 773:145650.

John W. Tukey. 1977. *Exploratory Data Analysis*, volume 2. Addison-Wesley, Reading, Mass.

Paul Velleman and David Hoaglin. 1981. *The ABC's of EDA: Applications, Basics, and Computing of Exploratory Data Analysis*. Duxbury, Boston.

Henrik Voigt, Nuno Carvalhais, Monique Meuschke, Markus Reichstein, Sina Zarrie, and Kai Lawonn. 2023. VIST5: An adaptive, retrieval-augmented language model for visualization-oriented dialog. In *Proceedings of the 2023 Conference on Empirical Methods in Natural Language Processing: System Demonstrations*, pages 70–81, Singapore. Association for Computational Linguistics.

Wesley Willett, Jeffrey Heer, Joseph Hellerstein, and Maneesh Agrawala. 2011. Commentspace: structured support for collaborative visual analysis. In *Proceedings of the SIGCHI Conference on Human Factors in Computing Systems*, CHI '11, page 3131–3140, New York, NY, USA. Association for Computing Machinery.

Zhichang Zhang, Zhenwen Zhang, Haoyuan Chen, and Zhiman Zhang. 2019. A joint learning framework with bert for spoken language understanding. *IEEE Access*, 7:168849–168858.

MENDER: Multi-hop Commonsense and Domain-specific CoT Reasoning for Knowledge-grounded Empathetic Counseling of Crime Victims

Abid Hossain[†], **Priyanshu Priya**[†], **Armita Mani Tripathi**[†], **Pradeepika Verma**[†], **Asif Ekbal**[†,‡]
[†]Department of Computer Science and Engineering, Indian Institute of Technology Patna, India
[‡]School of Artificial Intelligence and Data Science, Indian Institute of Technology Jodhpur, India
[†]{abid_2311ai22,priyanshu_2021cs26,armita_2211cs22,asif}@iitp.ac.in,
[†]pradeepikav.verma093@gmail.com, [‡]asif@iitj.ac.in

Abstract

Commonsense inference and domain-specific expertise are crucial for understanding and responding to emotional, cognitive, and topic-specific cues in counseling conversations with crime victims. However, these key evidences are often dispersed across multiple utterances, making it difficult to capture through single-hop reasoning. To address this, we propose **MENDER**, a novel **M**ulti-hop commonsens**E** and domai**N**-specific Chain-of-Thought (CoT) reasoning framework for knowle**D**ge-grounded empath**E**tic **R**esponse generation in counseling dialogues. **MENDER** leverages large language models (LLMs) to integrate commonsense and domain knowledge via multi-hop reasoning over the dialogue context. It employs two specialized reasoning chains, *viz.* Commonsense Knowledge-driven CoT and Domain Knowledge-driven CoT rationales, which extract and aggregate dispersed emotional, cognitive, and topical evidences to generate knowledge-grounded empathetic counseling responses. Experimental evaluations on counseling dialogue dataset, POEM validate **MENDER**'s efficacy in generating coherent, empathetic, knowledge-grounded responses[1].

1 Introduction

Commonsense inference and domain expertise are crucial for effective mental health and legal counseling of crime victims (Miller, 2008). Since victims often express trauma indirectly, counselors must infer unspoken emotions, intentions, and needs through commonsense reasoning (Dinakar et al., 2012) to foster empathy and trust. In addition, victims need targeted mental health and legal support for their overall well-being. Thus, counselors must have domain expertise to accurately diagnose and treat psychological conditions (Brown, 2007), while also providing precise legal guidance to navigate complex legal systems (Wright et al., 2023). Integrating commonsense reasoning with domain expertise enables counselors to provide holistic, empathetic, and informed support. For instance, as shown in Figure 1, compared to the generic response, commonsense reasoning helps identify victim's emotional and cognitive states, while domain expertise guides legal action and provides mental health resources, thereby ensuring an empathetic and comprehensive support.

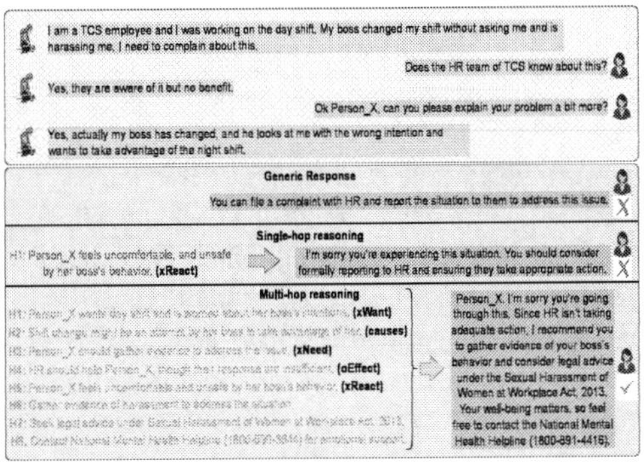

Figure 1: Comparison of generic responses vs. responses generated through single-hop and multi-hop commonsense reasoning and domain expertise.

Recently, LLMs have been widely used for counseling dialogue systems (Liu et al., 2023; Xie et al., 2024). However, LLMs often fail to capture the emotional and cognitive nuances innate in counseling scenarios, leading to disconnected and insincere interactions (Yang et al., 2024). Further, LLMs tend to generate inconsistent, erroneous, or fabricated information, which can have serious consequences (Chung et al., 2023; Hou et al., 2024). These limitations arise from LLMs' inherent struggles with commonsense inference and domain expertise, restricting their ability to engage in meaningful, knowledgeable, and empathetic conversa-

[1]Code and sample dataset is available at https://github.com/Abid839/MENDER/tree/main.

Proceedings of the 2025 Conference of the Nations of the Americas Chapter of the Association for Computational Linguistics: Human Language Technologies (Volume 4: Student Research Workshop), pages 501–516
April 30 - May 1, 2025 ©2025 Association for Computational Linguistics

tions. While recent efforts to incorporate commonsense and domain knowledge (Zhou et al., 2022a,b; Braunschweiler et al., 2023; Varshney et al., 2024) aim to address these issues, they often lead to flawed reasoning, resulting in inadequate responses, as shown in Figure 1.

Commonsense inference and domain knowledge acquisition fundamentally demands multi-hop reasoning, as key implicit information and topic-specific details are often fragmented and distributed across multiple utterances (Zhao et al., 2022; Liu et al., 2021). For instance, generating a coherent response - "Person_X, I'm sorry you're going..." in Figure 1 involves integrating both implicit (e.g. H1,...,H5) and topic-specific evidences (H6, H7, H8) from dialogue context. These evidences, including both commonsense and domain knowledge, must be identified and aggregated through multiple reasoning steps to produce coherent, empathetic, and knowledge-grounded responses.

Motivated by this, we propose a multi-hop commonsense and domain-specific reasoning process through CoT reasoning. We introduce **MENDER**, a novel framework that integrates **M**ulti-hop commonsens**E** and domai**N**-specific CoT reasoning for knowle**D**ge-grounded empath**E**tic **R**esponse generation in counseling contexts. **MENDER** first generates two distinct reasoning chains, *viz.* Commonsense Knowledge-driven CoT (CK-CoT) and Domain Knowledge-driven CoT (DK-CoT) rationales to capture the commonsense and domain-specific information required for effective response generation. CK-CoT rationales leverage the ATOMIC knowledge base (Hwang et al., 2021) to infer implicit emotional and cognitive cues, while DK-CoT rationales employ an Entity-guided Retrieval-Augmented Generation (E-RAG) approach to extract relevant topic-specific knowledge. **MENDER** further incorporates rationale-context and rationale-response filters to remove inconsistent or irrelevant rationales, thereby enhancing the overall quality of generated responses. Automatic and human evaluations on POEM (Priya et al., 2023a) dataset show that **MENDER** outperforms baselines, demonstrating its effectiveness in generating empathetic, informative, and coherent counseling responses.

To summarize, key contributions are: (i) Emphasize the need to integrate commonsense reasoning and domain expertise via multi-hop reasoning to gather evidences for knowledge-grounded empathetic counseling responses; (ii) Present **MENDER**, a novel multi-hop commonsense and domain-specific CoT reasoning framework for knowledge-grounded empathetic response generation during counseling; (iii) Design two reasoning chains: CK-CoT and DK-CoT rationales to capture emotional, cognitive, and topic-specific information for effective response generation; (iv) Introduce rationale-context and rationale-response filters to ensure the consistency and relevance of generated rationales.

2 Related Work

Recent efforts have focused on developing dialogue systems for mental health and legal counseling of crime victims (Kim et al., 2022; Singh et al., 2022b; Mishra et al., 2023b,c; Priya et al., 2023b; Mishra et al., 2023a; Priya et al., 2024a,b), with an emphasis on using LLMs (Zhao et al., 2023) for automated counseling agents (Liu et al., 2023; Chen et al., 2024). Integrating commonsense knowledge, such as emotional and cognitive insights, has been shown to improve empathy and contextual relevance (Wu et al., 2020; Sabour et al., 2022; Tu et al., 2022; Reddy et al., 2023), while domain-specific knowledge from external sources like Wikipedia enhances factual accuracy and relevance (Zhao et al., 2020; Qin et al., 2023; Bai et al., 2023). Chain-of-Thought (CoT) prompting has been found to enhance reasoning by decomposing complex problems into manageable steps (Wei et al., 2022), and Retrieval-Augmented Generation (RAG) leverages external knowledge to improve accuracy and reliability (Gao et al., 2023). Despite these advancements, many existing models still struggle to effectively integrate commonsense and domain knowledge, resulting in superficial responses. This work proposes a framework combining multi-hop commonsense reasoning with ATOMIC knowledge (Hwang et al., 2021) and domain-specific reasoning using Entity-guided Retrieval-Augmented Generation (E-RAG), to seamlessly generate coherent, empathetic, and knowledge-grounded responses.

3 Methodology

3.1 Overview

Given a dialogue corpus $\mathcal{D} = (C, R)^{|\mathcal{D}|}$, where $C = \{u_1, \ldots, u_{t-1}\}$ is dialogue context with an alternating sequence of $(t-1)$ utterances between counseling agent and victim, and R is response, the goal is to generate counselor's response $R(= u_t)$. To improve response quality, we integrate external commonsense and domain knowledge K. The response generation task is thus defined as $P(R \mid C, K)$, aiming for responses that are cotextually coherent, informative, and empathetic to victim's situation and emotional state.

3.2 Approach

We introduce **MENDER**, a **M**ulti-hop commonsens**E** and domai**N**-specific Chain-of-Thought (CoT) reasoning framework for knowle**D**ge-grounded empath**E**tic **R**esponse generation that constructs commonsense knowledge-driven CoT reasoners and domain knowledge-driven CoT reasoners to enhance response generation. To enhance relevance, we apply reasoner filtering mechanisms to refine the generated reasoners, which are then used for response generation. Figure 2 provides an overview of the proposed **MENDER** framework.

3.2.1 Commonsense Knowledge-driven CoT (CK-CoT) Reasoning

To construct CK-CoT reasoning chains (rationales, hereafter), we utilize LLMs' reasoning capability and commonsense relations from the ATOMIC knowledge base (Hwang et al., 2021), including *xIntent, xNeed, xWant, xReact, oEffect*, and *Causes* to capture emotional (affective), cognitive, and causal aspects of human reasoning. Given a dialogue context C and ground-truth response R, we prompt the LLM, $\mathcal{M}$ to generate CK-CoT rationales $\mathcal{S}^{Co}$, such that R can be induced from $\mathcal{S}^{Co}$. These rationales are defined as a sequence of n query-reply pairs $(q_i, r_i)_{i=1}^{n}$, where each q_i denotes an information-seeking question designed to uncover implicit information r_i within C. To generate these pairs, we introduce *thought-then-generate* approach employing two-step CoT process:

$$\mathcal{T}^{Co} \leftarrow P_{\mathcal{M}}(C, cs_{rel}) \quad (1)$$

$$\mathcal{S}^{Co} \leftarrow P_{\mathcal{M}}(C, cs_{rel}, \mathcal{T}^{Co}) \quad (2)$$

In the first step (Eq. 1), we prompt $\mathcal{M}$ to think what queries should be implicitly inferred from C using commonsense relations cs_{rel} and generate corresponding thoughts $\mathcal{T}^{Co}$. In the second step (Eq. 2), based on $\mathcal{T}^{Co}$, we prompt $\mathcal{M}$ to generate queries using cs_{rel} followed by the respective replies based on C.

3.2.2 Domain Knowledge-driven CoT (DK-CoT) Reasoning

To generate DK-CoT rationales, we utilize LLMs reasoning capability and external domain knowledge. For a given context C and ground-truth response R, we prompt $\mathcal{M}$ to generate DK-CoT rationales $\mathcal{S}^{Do}$ that lead to R. The process involves retrieving relevant domain knowledge for C and generating m query-reply pairs $(q_i, r_i)_{i=1}^{m}$, where each query q_i seeks topic-specific information r_i in C. This is achieved through a novel Entity-guided Retrieval Augmented Generation (E-RAG) approach, described as follows:

(a) Entity-guided Knowledge Source Selection: To ensure accuracy and comprehensiveness in domain knowledge collection, we systematically extract relevant entities related to mental health and legal counseling from the dialogue dataset $\mathcal{D}$ using the Stanford Named Entity Recognition (NER) Tagger (Finkel et al., 2005), T. Each utterance u_i is processed to identify entities, denoted as $E_i = T(u_i)$, and the total set of entities across dataset is defined as $E = \bigcup_{i=1}^{|\mathcal{D}|} E_i$. These entities are categorized into four classes, denoted as $EC = \{\text{crime, mentalhealth, legal, medium}\}$. For each entity class $ec \in EC$, we define $E_{ec} \subset E$ containing entities of type ec. To ensure robustness and remove noise, we filter out entities, such that $E'_{ec} = \{e \in E_{ec} \mid \text{frequency}(e, \mathcal{D}) \geq 2\}$. Afterward, we perform a manual verification M of identified entities to eliminate false positives and misspelled entities, yielding the final entity set $E_{f_{ec}} = M(E'_{ec})$. We then create question templates, $Q_{f_{ec}}$ for each entity class ec, and formulate web search queries for each entity $e' \in E_{fec}$ using these templates. The queries are searched on Google via Google Search API (Google, 2023) to gather domain knowledge from top 25 matching URLs. A summary of entity types, examples, and query templates is given in Appendix A. The extracted textual content is cleaned and stored into M knowledge documents (KD), which serve as knowledge base for the next step.

(b) Knowledge Retrieval: To retrieve relevant knowledge, we encode knowledge documents and dialogue context. The knowledge document encoder encodes each knowledge document $\{KD_j\}_{j=1}^{M}$ into vector representations h_{KD_j}. Likewise, the context encoder encodes C into a vector representation h_C. To assess the relevance of each knowledge document to the context, two matching scores, $s^1_{KD_j,C}$ and $s^2_{KD_j,C}$ are computed using BM25 (Robertson and Walker, 1994) and FAISS (Douze et al., 2024) retrievers, respectively, as:

$$s^l_{KD_j,C} = \begin{cases} \text{BM25}(h_{KD_j}, h_C); & l = 1, \\ \text{FAISS}(h_{KD_j}, h_C); & l = 2, \end{cases} \quad \forall KD_j \in KD$$

BM25-based sparse retrieval captures surface-level similarity, while FAISS-based dense retrieval emphasizes high-level semantic relevance. Each re-

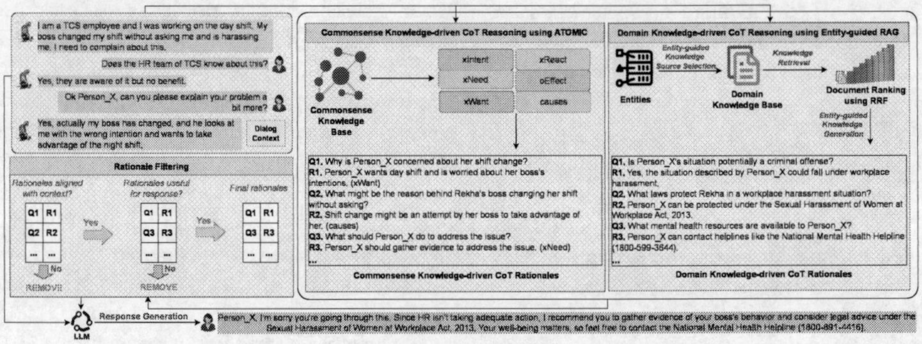

Figure 2: Overview of the proposed **MENDER** framework.

triever ranks knowledge documents independently based on computed matching scores. To integrate these rankings, the Reciprocal Rank Fusion (RRF) algorithm (Cormack et al., 2009) is applied, ensuring accurate, balanced, and robust ranking for effective knowledge retrieval. It is computed as:

$$RRF(KD_j) = \sum_{p \in P} \frac{1}{k + p(KD_j)}, \ \forall KD_j \in KD \quad (3)$$

Here, $P = \{\text{BM25}, \text{FAISS}\}$ represents the set of retrievers, and $p(KD_j)$ denotes the rank assigned to document KD_j by retriever p. The smoothing constant k adjusts rank weights to mitigate biases introduced by individual retrievers. The final ranking is derived from the computed RRF scores, yielding an ordered list of knowledge documents, most relevant to the context C. Finally, the top-r documents are retrieved based on their RRF scores.

(c) Entity-guided Knowledge Generation: To extract relevant knowledge from top-r documents, we generate query-reply pairs based on C and retrieved knowledge. To generate precise and contextually relevant queries, we employ an entity-centric approach that identifies key entities within C and uses them as anchors for query construction. The generated query is then mapped to the most relevant knowledge sentences to extract precise replies. To enable deeper and interpretable reasoning, we again employ *think-then-generate* approach for generating query-reply pairs in four-step CoT manner:

$$\mathcal{T}_1^{Do} \leftarrow P_{\mathcal{M}}(C) \quad (4)$$

$$\hat{\mathcal{E}}^{Do} \leftarrow P_{\mathcal{M}}(C, \mathcal{T}_1^{Do}) \quad (5)$$

$$\mathcal{T}_2^{Do} \leftarrow P_{\mathcal{M}}(C, \hat{\mathcal{E}}^{Do}) \quad (6)$$

$$\mathcal{S}^{Do} \leftarrow P_{\mathcal{M}}(C, \hat{\mathcal{E}}^{Do}, \mathcal{K}^{Do}, \mathcal{T}_2^{Do}) \quad (7)$$

In the first step (Eq. 4), we prompt $\mathcal{M}$ to think what entities could be extracted from given context C and generate corresponding thoughts $\mathcal{T}_1^{Do}$. In the second step (Eq. 5), based on $\mathcal{T}_1^{Do}$, we first ask $\mathcal{M}$ to extract the entities $\mathcal{E}^{Do}$ from C and then assess the relevance of each entity to context C. To achieve this, entity encoder encodes each extracted entity $e_i \in \mathcal{E}^{Do}$ into a vector representation h_{e_i}. The similarity score $s_{e_i,C}$ is then computed as the dot product between h_{e_i} and h_C. To enhance query-reply alignment, extracted entities are filtered based on two factors: (i) *entity order*, which prioritizes entities with higher similarity to C, and (ii) *entity confidence*, which categorizes entities into low, moderate, and high confidence levels based on similarity scores[2]. Entity order in conjunction with entity confidence ensures that entities with low confidence but high entity order are disregarded to focus on highly relevant entities. In the third step (Eq. 6), we prompt $\mathcal{M}$ to think what queries can be inferred from the C based on $\hat{\mathcal{E}}^{Do}$ and write the corresponding thoughts $\mathcal{T}_2^{Do}$. Finally, in the fourth step (Eq. 7), based on $\mathcal{T}_2^{Do}$, we prompt $\mathcal{M}$ to generate queries using $\hat{\mathcal{E}}^{Do}$ and formulates corresponding replies based on k retrieved documents, denoted as $\mathcal{K}^{Do}$.

3.2.3 Rationale Filtering

LLMs tend to hallucinate facts without adequately attending to the context (Peng et al., 2023), and not all rationales are effective in generating responses. Thus, to ensure that rationales are both contextually aligned and useful, we introduce rationale-context and rationale-response filters, respectively. For rationale-context filter, we employ alignment$(\cdot)$ function to assess if a rationale $z_i \in Z$, where $Z = \{\mathcal{S}^{Co}, \mathcal{S}^{Do}\}$ is relevant for C. For rationale-response filter, we introduce useful$(\cdot)$ function to assess if a dialogue model θ benefits from a rationale when predicting response R, given a context

[2]Thresholds for categorizing entities are hyper-parameters (Appendix 4.4).

C.

$$\text{alignment}(z_i) = \begin{cases} 1, & \text{if } \frac{SE(z_i).SE(C)}{||SE(z_i)||.||SE(C)||} > \tau_1, \\ 0, & \text{otherwise.} \end{cases}$$

$$\text{useful}(z_i) = \begin{cases} 1, & \text{if } \frac{P_\theta(R|z_i,C)}{P_\theta(R|C)} > \tau_2, \\ 0, & \text{otherwise.} \end{cases}$$

Here, SE denotes sentence encoder used to obtain semantic representations for z_i and C and τ_1, τ_2 are hyperparameters. Intuitively, a higher similarity and higher probability suggests that rationale z_i is contextually aligned and useful for predicting response R.

3.2.4 Response Generation

Finally, we instruct $\mathcal{M}$ to generate the response for a given dialogue context C using previously generated CK-CoT rationales ($\mathcal{S}^{Co}$) and DK-CoT ($\mathcal{S}^{Do}$) rationales:

$$R \leftarrow P_{\mathcal{M}}(C, \mathcal{S}^{Co}, \mathcal{S}^{Do}, I) \quad (8)$$

where, I denotes the instruction given to $\mathcal{M}$.

4 Experiments

4.1 Dataset

We conduct experiments on POEM dataset (Priya et al., 2023a) of counseling conversations, where commonsense reasoning and domain expertise are vital for delivering contextually appropriate, empathetic, and informative responses to crime victims. We choose this dataset for our task due to its rich coverage of real-world scenarios involving mental health and legal counseling needs of diverse crime victims. The dataset contains 5K dialogues crafted using real-life stories from credible sources, including news articles, case studies, and government portals under expert supervision. The comprehensive scope along with grounding in authentic sources and expert supervision, makes POEM dataset an ideal choice for developing models for commonsense and domain knowledge-grounded empathetic response generation during counseling.

4.2 Baselines

We compare **MENDER** with 9 baselines: ITDD (Li et al., 2019), KnowledGPT (Zhao et al., 2020), CEM (Sabour et al., 2022), MISC (Tu et al., 2022), MSDP (Liu et al., 2022), CoT (Wei et al., 2022), ProCoT (Deng et al., 2023), O-Cue-CoT and M-Cue-CoT (Wang et al., 2023). We include 'Baselines Details' in Appendix B.

4.3 Evaluation Metrics

For automatic evaluation, we use Perplexity (PPL) (Brown et al., 1992), BLEU (B-4) (Papineni et al., 2002), METEOR (M) (Banerjee and Lavie, 2005), Distinct-2 (D-2) (Li et al., 2015), BERTScore-f1 (BS-f1) (Zhang et al., 2019), Embedding Average (EA), Vector Extrema (VE), and Greedy Matching (GM) (Liu et al., 2016) to evaluate general quality of responses. To assess responses for task performance, we measure Domain Knowledge Coverage (DKC), Commonsense Knowledge Coverage (CKC), and Emotion Expression Accuracy (E-ACC). For human evaluation, we use Fluency (F), Adequacy (A), Contextual Relevance (CR) (Singh et al., 2022a) to assess responses's general quality. To assess responses for task performance, we employ Knowledge Existence (KE), Knowledge Correctness (KC), Knowledge Relevance (KR) (Varshney et al., 2022), Helpfulness (H), Safety (S), and Empathy (Emp.). We include 'Evaluation Metrics Details' in Appendix B.

4.4 Implementation Details

All implementations are conducted using PyTorch[3], and we employ transformer-based models from Hugging Face (Wolf et al., 2019) throughout our experiments. We use pre-trained Sentence-BERT (Reimers and Gurevych, 2019) as knowledge and context encoders and BERT (Devlin et al., 2018) as entity encoder. The dense retriever FAISS is implemented based on *mixedbread-ai/mxbai-embed-large-v1*, an embedding model. It will rank the documents based on the embedding L2 (Euclidean) distance between each knowledge document and dialogue context. We select top-2 knowledge documents (i.e. $r = 2$). We empirically set hyperparameters: k to 60 (smoothing constant in RRF score calculation), τ_1 to 0.6 and τ_2 to 0.9. Further, we empirically set the following ranges: $s_{e_i,C} \leq 0.3$ indicates low confidence, $0.3 < s_{e_i,C} \leq 0.65$ indicates moderate confidence, and $s_{e_i,C} > 0.65$ indicates high confidence for entity confidence categorization.

In the rationale-response filter, we use Zephyr-7B (Tunstall et al., 2023) trained on diverse synthetic dialogues generated by ChatGPT as dialogue model θ. For rationale generation, we employ LLaMA-3.1-8B-Instruct (Touvron et al., 2023) and for response generation, we use LLaMa-2-7B-chat (Touvron et al., 2023). We use Top-p sampling with

[3]https://pytorch.org/

Models	PPL ↓	B-4 ↑	M ↑	D-2↑	BS-f1 ↑	EA ↑	VE ↑	GM ↑	DKC ↑	CKC ↑	E-ACC ↑
ITDD	31.25	1.02	6.23	15.14	0.421	0.571	0.226	0.482	4.67	9.54	7.41
KnowledGPT	28.11	2.67	7.14	18.32	0.473	0.622	0.284	0.532	7.03	14.32	10.87
CEM	28.80	4.98	8.72	19.45	0.486	0.643	0.309	0.546	9.26	18.64	14.58
MISC	27.04	5.22	9.24	20.67	0.512	0.665	0.336	0.563	10.41	20.52	16.47
MSDP	25.73	6.07	10.56	20.73	0.537	0.694	0.372	0.591	11.87	23.56	18.62
CoT	17.53	6.44	10.89	21.34	0.553	0.713	0.401	0.612	13.22	26.48	20.93
ProCoT	14.41	6.53	11.03	23.12	0.603	0.744	0.423	0.637	16.12	31.78	24.71
O-Cue-CoT	11.26	6.71	11.78	24.48	0.627	0.767	0.442	0.654	18.36	36.48	27.42
M-Cue-CoT	9.35	6.59	12.61	27.78	0.652	0.801	0.467	0.682	22.41	44.12	32.17
MENDER	**6.33**	**9.31**	**14.02**	**31.56**	**0.703**	**0.881**	**0.499**	**0.726**	**26.19**	**49.82**	**36.79**
- $\mathcal{S}^{Co}$	9.52	7.99	12.57	30.22	0.671	0.845	0.480	0.704	24.98	44.67	32.24
- $\mathcal{S}^{Do}$	9.45	8.12	13.02	30.53	0.682	0.860	0.485	0.715	23.10	45.82	33.65
- $(\mathcal{S}^{Co} + \mathcal{S}^{Do}))$	11.76	5.65	10.10	28.90	0.657	0.830	0.471	0.695	21.85	41.45	29.80

Table 1: Automatic evaluation results. Results are statistically significant at 5% significance level based on t-test (Welch, 1947).

Models	F (1-5)	A (1-5)	CR (1-5)	KE (0-2)	KR (0-2)	KC (0-2)	H (0-2)	S (0-1)	Emp. (1-5)
MSDP	2.33	2.45	2.38	1.02	1.10	1.09	1.29	1.0	2.30
CoT	2.87	2.94	2.71	1.15	1.22	1.21	1.35	1.0	2.64
ProCoT	3.21	3.19	3.03	1.28	1.35	1.33	1.50	1.0	3.08
O-Cuc-CoT	3.47	3.39	3.34	1.41	1.47	1.45	1.62	1.0	3.28
M-Cue-CoT	3.73	3.64	3.58	1.53	1.60	1.58	1.74	1.0	3.59
MENDER	**4.12**	**4.25**	**4.41**	**1.72**	**1.78**	**1.85**	**1.91**	**1.0**	**4.50**

Table 2: Human evaluation results. Results are statistically significant at 5% significance level based on t-test (Welch, 1947). Scale for metrics are given in column heads.

$p = 0.9$ and temperature $\tau = 0.6$ for rationale and response generation. For rationales' generation, we include two exemplars of rationales, with manually constructed query-reply pairs to further guide the LLM in identifying relevant contextual cues and inferring necessary knowledge for response generation. Likewise, for response generation, we include two exemplars consisting of dialogue context, corresponding rationales and ground-truth response to guide the model toward generating appropriate response. All experiments are done on Tesla V100-PCIE-32GB GPUs.

5 Results and Analysis

5.1 Automatic Evaluation

Table 1 presents the results of the automatic evaluation. We observe that **MENDER** significantly outperforms all baselines across all metrics. It achieves the lowest PPL score, indicating the superior quality of its generated responses compared to baselines. Further **MENDER** excels in dialogue quality, as revealed by its superior lexical (B-4, M) and semantic richness (BS-f1, EA, VE, GM), along with its ability to produce more diverse responses (D-2). The highest DKC and CKC scores shows its proficiency in capturing knowledge, enabling the generation of engaging and informative responses. Besides, the highest E-ACC score highlights **MENDER**'s ability to generate empathetic responses. Notably, the ablation results show that removing either CK-CoT rationales ($\mathcal{S}^{Co}$), DK-CoT rationales ($\mathcal{S}^{Do}$), or both causes a significant drop in performance, emphasizing the critical role of both reasoning steps in generating knowledge-grounded, empathetic responses.

5.2 Human Evaluation

Table 2 presents the results of the human evaluation. We compare **MENDER** against MSDP, CoT, ProCoT, O-Cue-CoT, and M-Cue-CoT only, as manual evaluation is expensive. It is evident that **MENDER** consistently outperforms baseline models across all evaluation metrics. This highlights **MENDER**'s ability to effectively integrate commonsense reasoning and domain knowledge, generating responses that are notably more coherent, empathetic, and informative. The inter-evaluator agreement, measured using Fleiss' kappa (McHugh, 2012) (κ), falls within the range $[0.45, 0.81]$ for all criteria, indicating fair to moderate agreement among evaluators.

6 Conclusion

This work presents **MENDER**, a multi-hop reasoning framework that integrates commonsense and domain-specific knowledge for generating empathetic, knowledge-grounded responses in counseling dialogues. Using commonsense and domain knowledge-driven CoT rationales, **MENDER** captures emotional, cognitive, and topic-specific details to ensure coherent, empathetic, and informed responses. Extensive experiments on the POEM dataset demonstrate the promising potential of **MENDER** in generating coherent, empathetic, and knowledge-grounded responses, significantly improving the quality of counseling outcomes.

Limitations

We evaluate **MENDER** on the POEM dialogue dataset, focusing on crime victim counseling and dyadic dialogues. While currently limited in scope, future work could extend **MENDER** to other counseling domains and multi-party dialogues. Since its reasoning generations are entirely machine-generated, caution is advised to avoid biases in model training. Using LLaMA-2-7b-chat as the base model, our experiments yield satisfactory results, but further validation and optimization are planned, including performance enhancement on smaller models like Gemma-2B (Team et al., 2024) via knowledge distillation. Budget and computational constraints necessitated the use of open-source LLaMA-2-7b-chat, but future studies could explore advanced closed-source LLMs, such as GPT-4 (OpenAI, 2024) or Gemini-1.5-Pro (Team et al., 2023), for generating rationales and responses, thereby improving system performance.

Ethics Statement

This study was reviewed and approved by our Institutional Review Board (IRB). For our research, we utilized the POEM dataset, which comprises dialogues focused on mental health and legal counseling for crime victims. Permission to use this dataset was obtained in compliance with the copyright guidelines set by the copyright holder. Given the sensitive nature of the research, strict measures were implemented to ensure the privacy and confidentiality of victim-related data throughout the study. To ensure ethical considerations in generating rationales and responses with large language models (LLMs), the prompts were carefully designed to emphasize adherence to specific ethical guidelines, minimizing the risk of producing inappropriate or harmful content. Additionally, we incorporated a '*Safety*' dimension into the evaluation framework to assess the system's capacity for providing effective and responsible counseling support.

Acknowledgements

Authors acknowledge the partial support from the project titled "An Empathetic Knowledge Grounded Conversational System for Mental Health Counseling and Legal Assistance", Sponsored by IHUB Anubhuti, TIH, IIIT Delhi.

Priyanshu Priya acknowledges the financial support provided by the Department of Science and Technology, Ministry of Science and Technology, Government of India and through the Innovation in Science Pursuit for Inspired Research (INSPIRE) Fellowship.

References

Jiaqi Bai, Ze Yang, Jian Yang, Hongcheng Guo, and Zhoujun Li. 2023. Kinet: Incorporating relevant facts into knowledge-grounded dialog generation. *IEEE/ACM Transactions on Audio, Speech, and Language Processing*, 31:1213–1222.

Satanjeev Banerjee and Alon Lavie. 2005. Meteor: An automatic metric for mt evaluation with improved correlation with human judgments. In *Proceedings of the acl workshop on intrinsic and extrinsic evaluation measures for machine translation and/or summarization*, pages 65–72.

Norbert Braunschweiler, Rama Doddipatla, Simon Keizer, and Svetlana Stoyanchev. 2023. Evaluating large language models for document-grounded response generation in information-seeking dialogues. *arXiv preprint arXiv:2309.11838*.

Peter F Brown, Stephen A Della Pietra, Vincent J Della Pietra, Jennifer C Lai, and Robert L Mercer. 1992. An estimate of an upper bound for the entropy of english. *Computational Linguistics*, 18(1):31–40.

Sandra L Brown. 2007. *Counseling victims of violence: A handbook for helping professionals*. Hunter House.

Yixiang Chen, Xinyu Zhang, Jinran Wang, Xurong Xie, Nan Yan, Hui Chen, and Lan Wang. 2024. Structured dialogue system for mental health: An llm chatbot leveraging the pm+ guidelines. *arXiv preprint arXiv:2411.10681*.

Neo Christopher Chung, George Dyer, and Lennart Brocki. 2023. Challenges of large language models for mental health counseling. *arXiv preprint arXiv:2311.13857*.

Gordon V Cormack, Charles LA Clarke, and Stefan Buettcher. 2009. Reciprocal rank fusion outperforms condorcet and individual rank learning methods. In *Proceedings of the 32nd international ACM SIGIR conference on Research and development in information retrieval*, pages 758–759.

Yang Deng, Lizi Liao, Liang Chen, Hongru Wang, Wenqiang Lei, and Tat-Seng Chua. 2023. Prompting and evaluating large language models for proactive dialogues: Clarification, target-guided, and non-collaboration. In *Findings of the Association for Computational Linguistics: EMNLP 2023*, pages 10602–10621.

Jacob Devlin, Ming-Wei Chang, Kenton Lee, and Kristina Toutanova. 2018. Bert: Pre-training of deep bidirectional transformers for language understanding. *arXiv preprint arXiv:1810.04805*.

Karthik Dinakar, Birago Jones, Catherine Havasi, Henry Lieberman, and Rosalind Picard. 2012. Common sense reasoning for detection, prevention, and mitigation of cyberbullying. *ACM Transactions on Interactive Intelligent Systems (TiiS)*, 2(3):1–30.

Matthijs Douze, Alexandr Guzhva, Chengqi Deng, Jeff Johnson, Gergely Szilvasy, Pierre-Emmanuel Mazaré, Maria Lomeli, Lucas Hosseini, and Hervé Jégou. 2024. The faiss library. *arXiv preprint arXiv:2401.08281*.

Jenny Rose Finkel, Trond Grenager, and Christopher D Manning. 2005. Incorporating non-local information into information extraction systems by gibbs sampling. In *Proceedings of the 43rd annual meeting of the association for computational linguistics (ACL'05)*, pages 363–370.

Yunfan Gao, Yun Xiong, Xinyu Gao, Kangxiang Jia, Jinliu Pan, Yuxi Bi, Yi Dai, Jiawei Sun, and Haofen Wang. 2023. Retrieval-augmented generation for large language models: A survey. *arXiv preprint arXiv:2312.10997*.

Google. 2023. Google search api. `https://github.com/googleapis/google-api-python-client/`.

Abe Hou, William Jurayj, Nils Holzenberger, Andrew Blair-Stanek, and Benjamin Van Durme. 2024. Gaps or hallucinations? scrutinizing machine-generated legal analysis for fine-grained text evaluations. In *Proceedings of the Natural Legal Language Processing Workshop 2024*, pages 280–302.

Jena D Hwang, Chandra Bhagavatula, Ronan Le Bras, Jeff Da, Keisuke Sakaguchi, Antoine Bosselut, and Yejin Choi. 2021. (comet-) atomic 2020: On symbolic and neural commonsense knowledge graphs. In *Proceedings of the AAAI conference on artificial intelligence*, volume 35, pages 6384–6392.

Hyeok Kim, Youjin Hwang, Jieun Lee, Youngjin Kwon, Yujin Park, and Joonhwan Lee. 2022. Personalization trade-offs in designing a dialogue-based information system for support-seeking of sexual violence survivors. In *Proceedings of the 2022 CHI Conference on Human Factors in Computing Systems*, pages 1–15.

Jiwei Li, Michel Galley, Chris Brockett, Jianfeng Gao, and Bill Dolan. 2015. A diversity-promoting objective function for neural conversation models. *arXiv preprint arXiv:1510.03055*.

Zekang Li, Cheng Niu, Fandong Meng, Yang Feng, Qian Li, and Jie Zhou. 2019. Incremental transformer with deliberation decoder for document grounded conversations. *arXiv preprint arXiv:1907.08854*.

Chia-Wei Liu, Ryan Lowe, Iulian V Serban, Michael Noseworthy, Laurent Charlin, and Joelle Pineau. 2016. How not to evaluate your dialogue system: An empirical study of unsupervised evaluation metrics for dialogue response generation. *arXiv preprint arXiv:1603.08023*.

June M Liu, Donghao Li, He Cao, Tianhe Ren, Zeyi Liao, and Jiamin Wu. 2023. Chatcounselor: A large language models for mental health support. *arXiv preprint arXiv:2309.15461*.

Junpeng Liu, Yanyan Zou, Hainan Zhang, Hongshen Chen, Zhuoye Ding, Caixia Yuan, and Xiaojie Wang. 2021. Topic-aware contrastive learning for abstractive dialogue summarization. In *Findings of the Association for Computational Linguistics: EMNLP 2021*, pages 1229–1243.

Zihan Liu, Mostofa Patwary, Ryan Prenger, Shrimai Prabhumoye, Wei Ping, Mohammad Shoeybi, and Bryan Catanzaro. 2022. Multi-stage prompting for knowledgeable dialogue generation. *arXiv preprint arXiv:2203.08745*.

Mary L McHugh. 2012. Interrater reliability: the kappa statistic. *Biochemia medica*, 22(3):276–282.

Laurence Miller. 2008. *Counseling crime victims: Practical strategies for mental health professionals*. Springer Publishing Company.

Kshitij Mishra, Priyanshu Priya, Manisha Burja, and Asif Ekbal. 2023a. e-therapist: I suggest you to cultivate a mindset of positivity and nurture uplifting thoughts. In *Proceedings of the 2023 Conference on Empirical Methods in Natural Language Processing*, pages 13952–13967.

Kshitij Mishra, Priyanshu Priya, and Asif Ekbal. 2023b. Help me heal: A reinforced polite and empathetic mental health and legal counseling dialogue system for crime victims. In *Proceedings of the AAAI Conference on Artificial Intelligence*, volume 37, pages 14408–14416.

Kshitij Mishra, Priyanshu Priya, and Asif Ekbal. 2023c. Pal to lend a helping hand: Towards building an emotion adaptive polite and empathetic counseling conversational agent. In *Proceedings of the 61st Annual Meeting of the Association for Computational Linguistics (Volume 1: Long Papers)*, pages 12254–12271.

OpenAI. 2024. ChatGPT. `https://chatgpt.com/`.

Kishore Papineni, Salim Roukos, Todd Ward, and Wei-Jing Zhu. 2002. Bleu: a method for automatic evaluation of machine translation. In *Proceedings of the 40th annual meeting of the Association for Computational Linguistics*, pages 311–318.

Damian Pascual, Beni Egressy, Clara Meister, Ryan Cotterell, and Roger Wattenhofer. 2021. A plug-and-play method for controlled text generation. In *Findings of the Association for Computational Linguistics: EMNLP 2021*, pages 3973–3997.

Baolin Peng, Michel Galley, Pengcheng He, Hao Cheng, Yujia Xie, Yu Hu, Qiuyuan Huang, Lars Liden, Zhou Yu, Weizhu Chen, et al. 2023. Check your facts and try again: Improving large language models with external knowledge and automated feedback. *arXiv preprint arXiv:2302.12813*.

Priyanshu Priya, Mauajama Firdaus, and Asif Ekbal. 2023a. A multi-task learning framework for politeness and emotion detection in dialogues for mental health counselling and legal aid. *Expert Systems with Applications*, 224:120025.

Priyanshu Priya, Mauajama Firdaus, and Asif Ekbal. 2024a. Two in one: A multi-task framework for politeness turn identification and phrase extraction in goal-oriented conversations. *Computer Speech & Language*, 88:101661.

Priyanshu Priya, Kshitij Mishra, Palak Totala, and Asif Ekbal. 2023b. Partner: A persuasive mental health and legal counselling dialogue system for women and children crime victims. In *Proceedings of the Thirty-Second International Joint Conference on Artificial Intelligence, IJCAI-23*, pages 6183–6191. International Joint Conferences on Artificial Intelligence Organization. AI for Good.

Priyanshu Priya, Gopendra Singh, Mauajama Firdaus, Jyotsna Agrawal, and Asif Ekbal. 2024b. On the way to gentle ai counselor: Politeness cause elicitation and intensity tagging in code-mixed hinglish conversations for social good. In *Findings of the Association for Computational Linguistics: NAACL 2024*, pages 4678–4696.

Lang Qin, Yao Zhang, Hongru Liang, Jun Wang, and Zhenglu Yang. 2023. Well begun is half done: Generator-agnostic knowledge pre-selection for knowledge-grounded dialogue. *arXiv preprint arXiv:2310.07659*.

Revanth Reddy, Hao Bai, Wentao Yao, Sharath Chandra Etagi Suresh, Heng Ji, and ChengXiang Zhai. 2023. Social commonsense-guided search query generation for open-domain knowledge-powered conversations. In *Findings of the Association for Computational Linguistics: EMNLP 2023*, pages 873–885.

Nils Reimers and Iryna Gurevych. 2019. Sentence-bert: Sentence embeddings using siamese bert-networks. *arXiv preprint arXiv:1908.10084*.

SE Robertson and S Walker. 1994. Some simple effective approximations to the 2-poisson model for probabilistic weighted retrieval. In *Proceedings of the 17th annual international ACM SIGIR conference on Research and development in information retrieval*, pages 232–241.

Sahand Sabour, Chujie Zheng, and Minlie Huang. 2022. Cem: Commonsense-aware empathetic response generation.

Kurt Shuster, Spencer Poff, Moya Chen, Douwe Kiela, and Jason Weston. 2021. Retrieval augmentation reduces hallucination in conversation. In *Findings of the Association for Computational Linguistics: EMNLP 2021*, pages 3784–3803.

Gopendra Vikram Singh, Mauajama Firdaus, Shruti Mishra, Asif Ekbal, et al. 2022a. Knowing what to say: Towards knowledge grounded code-mixed response generation for open-domain conversations. *Knowledge-Based Systems*, 249:108900.

Gopendra Vikram Singh, Priyanshu Priya, Mauajama Firdaus, Asif Ekbal, and Pushpak Bhattacharyya. 2022b. Emoinhindi: A multi-label emotion and intensity annotated dataset in hindi for emotion recognition in dialogues. *arXiv preprint arXiv:2205.13908*.

Gemini Team, Rohan Anil, Sebastian Borgeaud, Yonghui Wu, Jean-Baptiste Alayrac, Jiahui Yu, Radu Soricut, Johan Schalkwyk, Andrew M Dai, Anja Hauth, et al. 2023. Gemini: a family of highly capable multimodal models. *arXiv preprint arXiv:2312.11805*.

Gemma Team, Thomas Mesnard, Cassidy Hardin, Robert Dadashi, Surya Bhupatiraju, Shreya Pathak, Laurent Sifre, Morgane Rivière, Mihir Sanjay Kale, Juliette Love, et al. 2024. Gemma: Open models based on gemini research and technology. *arXiv preprint arXiv:2403.08295*.

Hugo Touvron, Thibaut Lavril, Gautier Izacard, Xavier Martinet, Marie-Anne Lachaux, Timothée Lacroix, Baptiste Rozière, Naman Goyal, Eric Hambro, Faisal Azhar, et al. 2023. Llama: Open and efficient foundation language models. *arXiv preprint arXiv:2302.13971*.

Quan Tu, Yanran Li, Jianwei Cui, Bin Wang, Ji-Rong Wen, and Rui Yan. 2022. Misc: A mixed strategy-aware model integrating comet for emotional support conversation. In *Proceedings of the 60th Annual Meeting of the Association for Computational Linguistics (Volume 1: Long Papers)*, pages 308–319.

Lewis Tunstall, Edward Beeching, Nathan Lambert, Nazneen Rajani, Kashif Rasul, Younes Belkada, Shengyi Huang, Leandro von Werra, Clémentine Fourrier, Nathan Habib, Nathan Sarrazin, Omar Sanseviero, Alexander M. Rush, and Thomas Wolf. 2023. Zephyr: Direct distillation of lm alignment. *Preprint*, arXiv:2310.16944.

Deeksha Varshney, Asif Ekbal, and Erik Cambria. 2024. Emotion-and-knowledge grounded response generation in an open-domain dialogue setting. *Knowledge-Based Systems*, 284:111173.

Deeksha Varshney, Akshara Prabhakar, and Asif Ekbal. 2022. Commonsense and named entity aware knowledge grounded dialogue generation. In *Proceedings of the 2022 Conference of the North American Chapter of the Association for Computational Linguistics: Human Language Technologies*, pages 1322–1335.

Hongru Wang, Rui Wang, Fei Mi, Yang Deng, Zezhong Wang, Bin Liang, Ruifeng Xu, and Kam-Fai Wong. 2023. Cue-cot: Chain-of-thought prompting for responding to in-depth dialogue questions with llms. *arXiv preprint arXiv:2305.11792*.

Jason Wei, Xuezhi Wang, Dale Schuurmans, Maarten Bosma, Fei Xia, Ed Chi, Quoc V Le, Denny Zhou, et al. 2022. Chain-of-thought prompting elicits reasoning in large language models. *Advances in neural information processing systems*, 35:24824–24837.

Bernard L Welch. 1947. The generalization of 'student's'problem when several different population variances are involved. *Biometrika*, 34(1-2):28–35.

Thomas Wolf, Lysandre Debut, Victor Sanh, Julien Chaumond, Clement Delangue, Anthony Moi, Pierric Cistac, Tim Rault, Rémi Louf, Morgan Funtowicz, et al. 2019. Huggingface's transformers: State-of-the-art natural language processing. *arXiv preprint arXiv:1910.03771*.

Naomi M Wright, Tejaswinhi Srinivas, Michelle Seulki Lee, and Anne P DePrince. 2023. Development of a legal service needs and barriers measure for victims of family violence and other crime. *Journal of family violence*, pages 1–19.

Sixing Wu, Ying Li, Dawei Zhang, Yang Zhou, and Zhonghai Wu. 2020. Diverse and informative dialogue generation with context-specific commonsense knowledge awareness. In *Proceedings of the 58th annual meeting of the association for computational linguistics*, pages 5811–5820.

Nan Xie, Yuelin Bai, Hengyuan Gao, Ziqiang Xue, Feiteng Fang, Qixuan Zhao, Zhijian Li, Liang Zhu, Shiwen Ni, and Min Yang. 2024. Delilaw: A chinese legal counselling system based on a large language model. In *Proceedings of the 33rd ACM International Conference on Information and Knowledge Management*, pages 5299–5303.

Zhou Yang, Zhaochun Ren, Wang Yufeng, Shizhong Peng, Haizhou Sun, Xiaofei Zhu, and Xiangwen Liao. 2024. Enhancing empathetic response generation by augmenting llms with small-scale empathetic models. *arXiv preprint arXiv:2402.11801*.

Tianyi Zhang, Varsha Kishore, Felix Wu, Kilian Q Weinberger, and Yoav Artzi. 2019. Bertscore: Evaluating text generation with bert. *arXiv preprint arXiv:1904.09675*.

Chao Zhao, Wenlin Yao, Dian Yu, Kaiqiang Song, Dong Yu, and Jianshu Chen. 2022. Learning-by-narrating: Narrative pre-training for zero-shot dialogue comprehension. In *Proceedings of the 60th Annual Meeting of the Association for Computational Linguistics (Volume 2: Short Papers)*, pages 212–218.

Wayne Xin Zhao, Kun Zhou, Junyi Li, Tianyi Tang, Xiaolei Wang, Yupeng Hou, Yingqian Min, Beichen Zhang, Junjie Zhang, Zican Dong, et al. 2023. A survey of large language models. *arXiv preprint arXiv:2303.18223*.

Xueliang Zhao, Wei Wu, Can Xu, Chongyang Tao, Dongyan Zhao, and Rui Yan. 2020. Knowledge-grounded dialogue generation with pre-trained language models. In *Proceedings of the 2020 Conference on Empirical Methods in Natural Language Processing (EMNLP)*, pages 3377–3390.

Pei Zhou, Hyundong Cho, Pegah Jandaghi, Dong-Ho Lee, Bill Yuchen Lin, Jay Pujara, and Xiang Ren. 2022a. Reflect, not reflex: Inference-based common ground improves dialogue response quality. In *Proceedings of the 2022 Conference on Empirical Methods in Natural Language Processing*, pages 10450–10468.

Pei Zhou, Karthik Gopalakrishnan, Behnam Hedayatnia, Seokhwan Kim, Jay Pujara, Xiang Ren, Yang Liu, and Dilek Hakkani-Tur. 2022b. Think before you speak: Explicitly generating implicit commonsense knowledge for response generation. In *Proceedings of the 60th Annual Meeting of the Association for Computational Linguistics (Volume 1: Long Papers)*, pages 1237–1252.

Appendix

A Mental Health and Legal Counseling-related Entities

After extraction and manual review of the entities, we identify a total of 41 entities, systematically categorized into four groups as 16 crime-related entities, 4 related to mental health issues, 7 associated with legal information, and 14 pertaining to medium information. The entities related to crime, mental health issues, legal information, and medium information correspond to 7, 6, 6, and 4 distinct query templates, respectively. A detailed overview of the entity types, representative entity examples, and their corresponding query templates is provided in Table 3.

Entity Type	Examples	Sample Query	Query Example
Crime	cyber-stalking, harassment	What is crimeX?	What is Stalking?
		How to prevent crimeX?	How to prevent Stalking?
Mental Health	depression, anxiety stress	What is issueX?	What is Depression?
		What are the symptoms of issueX?	What are the symptoms of Depression?
Legal	section354D, cybercell	What is sectionX?	What is section 354D?
		What are the punishments under sectionX?	What are the punishments under section 354D?
Medium	facebook, instagram	How to report crimeX on mediumX?	How to report online stalking on Facebook?
		How to block a profile/page on mediumX?	How to block a profile/page on Facebook?

Table 3: Entity types, entities examples, and their corresponding query templates.

B Experiment Details

B.1 Baseline Details

1. ITDD (Li et al., 2019): Utilizes an incremental transformer architecture to encode utterances and external knowledge, coupled with a deliberation-based decoder for generating responses.

2. KnowledGPT (Zhao et al., 2020): Incorporates a pre-trained language model alongside a knowledge selection module, with both components jointly optimized using reinforcement learning.

3. CEM (Sabour et al., 2022): Leverages commonsense reasoning to enhance the expression of empathy in generated responses.

4. MISC (Tu et al., 2022): Fuses commonsense knowledge for emotional response generation.

5. MSDP (Liu et al., 2022): Employs a multi-stage prompting framework that first generates relevant knowledge and then use the generated knowledge to predict the response for a given dialogue context.

6. CoT (Wei et al., 2022): Employs a standard few-shot CoT reasoning approach to generate knowledge-grounded empathetic responses.

7. ProCoT (Deng et al., 2023): Prompts the LLM to generate a chain-of-thought descriptive analysis to use the relevant the knowledge by performing dynamic reasoning for generating the knowledge-grounded empathetic responses.

8. O-Cue-CoT (Wang et al., 2023): Prompts the LLMs to generate knowledge and a final response simultaneously for the given dialogue context, enforcing the LLM to reason based on the knowledge.

9. M-Cue-CoT (Wang et al., 2023): M-Cue-CoT builds on the foundation of O-Cue-CoT by decomposing the reasoning process into consecutive steps. It first generates the reasoning to infer the relevant knowledge and then use the inferred knowledge to predict the final response.

B.2 Evaluation Metrics Details

Automatic Evaluation Metrics. Perplexity (PPL) (Brown et al., 1992) evaluates how well the model predicts a response. Word-overlap-based metrics like BLEU (Papineni et al., 2002) (B-4) and METEOR (Banerjee and Lavie, 2005)(M) compute the overlap between the ground-truth response and the model's generated response. DISTINCT-2 (Li et al., 2015) (D-2) measures the diversity of the generated responses. BERTScore-f1 (Zhang et al., 2019) (BS-f1), Embedding Average (EA), Vector Extrema (VE), and Greedy Matching (GM) (Liu et al., 2016) align the generated response and the ground-truth response in latent semantic space to assess the semantic similarity between the gold response and the model's generated response.

Domain Knowledge Coverage (DKC) using KF1 (Shuster et al., 2021) quantifies unigram word overlap between the generated response (R) and domain knowledge (K) (Equation 9), Commonsense Knowledge Coverage (CKC) using Hard Matching (Zhou et al., 2022b) identifies matching commonsense tuples T between the dialogue context (C) and the generated response (R) (Equation 10), and

Models	PPL↓	B-4↑	M↑	D-2↑	BS-f1↑	EA↑	VE↑	GM↑	DKC↑	CKC↑	E-ACC↑
MENDER (w query-reply pairs)	**6.33**	**9.31**	**14.02**	**31.56**	**0.703**	**0.881**	**0.499**	**0.726**	**26.19**	**49.82**	**36.79**
MENDER (w replies only)	7.46	8.12	13.78	29.01	0.689	0.864	0.489	0.712	25.73	46.92	33.07

Table 4: Ablation results w.r.t iterative query-reply pairs on generating question in **MENDER**.

Models	PPL↓	B-4↑	M↑	D-2↑	BS-f1↑	EA↑	VE↑	GM↑	DKC↑	CKC↑	E-ACC↑
MENDER	**6.33**	**9.31**	**14.02**	**31.56**	**0.703**	**0.881**	**0.499**	**0.726**	**26.19**	**49.82**	**36.79**
MENDER (w/o R-C filter)	6.49	9.10	13.74	30.89	0.686	0.860	0.485	0.708	25.55	48.32	35.74
MENDER (w/o R-R filter)	7.67	8.87	13.45	30.18	0.668	0.839	0.470	0.690	24.92	46.92	34.70
MENDER (w/o R-C and R-R filter)	8.85	8.65	13.16	29.52	0.650	0.818	0.455	0.672	24.30	45.58	33.68

Table 5: Ablation results w.r.t rationale-context (R-C) and rationale-response (R-R) filters in **MENDER**.

EXP ACC (E-ACC) (Pascual et al., 2021) measures the accuracy of emotion expression.

$$\text{DKC} = \frac{1}{m}\sum_{i=1}^{m} \text{KF1}(R, K) \tag{9}$$

$$\text{CDC} = \frac{1}{m}\sum_{i=1}^{m} I(\{T_i\}), \quad I = \begin{cases} 1 & \text{if } \{T_i\} \neq \emptyset, \\ 0 & \text{otherwise.} \end{cases} \tag{10}$$

where m is the test set size, and $I = 1$ if the response is grounded by at least one commonsense tuple.

Human Evaluation Metrics. Fluency (F) assesses the grammatical correctness, Adequacy (A) quantifies the semantic similarity of the generated response with that of the ground-truth response, Contextual Relevance (CR) examines the alignment of the generated responses with the dialogue context.

KE evaluates the incorporation of knowledge within the response, KC measures the accuracy of this knowledge, and KR examines whether the knowledge is both accurate and contextually relevant to the dialogue context. Helpfulness (H) assess whether the generated response satisfies the victim's requirement, Safety (S) gauges if the generated response safeguards personal privacy and adheres to relevant laws and regulations, and Empathy (Emp.) assesses whether the response is more understanding of the user's emotion and situation and shows the appropriate emotion.

C Human Evaluation Process

The human evaluation is conducted with the assistance of three evaluators, two hold Ph.D. degrees in Linguistics and one with a graduate degree in Computer Science and Engineering. All evaluators are proficient in English and have substantial experience in similar tasks. For evaluation, we randomly selected 120 samples consisting of dialogue context, ground-truth response, commonsense knowledge, domain knowledge, and model-generated response. Prior to the evaluation, they are briefed on the evaluation guidelines along with few samples, and are instructed to rate each sample for F, A, CR, KE, KC, KR, H, S, and Emp. on a provided scale.

C.1 Prompt Templates for MENDER

The prompts of our proposed **MENDER** are reported in Table 7 (Commonsense Knowledge-driven CoT Reasoning), Table 8 (Domain Knowledge-driven CoT Reasoning), and Table 9 (Response Generation).

D Additional Analysis

D.1 Ablation w.r.t Iterative Query-Reply Pairs

To assess the impact of queries, we conduct an ablation study by prompting the model under the same conditions as **MENDER** but generating only replies. Specifically, we remove queries from the rationales and prompt the model using the modified sample. As presented in Table 4, the absence of queries leads to a significant decline in response quality, highlighting their critical role in reasoning. This suggests that queries play a crucial role in guiding replies generation, as responses exhibit poor alignment with dialogues in their absence.

D.2 Ablation w.r.t filters

To assess the impact of rationale-context and rationale-response filters, we ablate the filters and done the experiments under the same conditions as **MENDER**. In the first ablation, we ablate the rationale-context filter, in the second ablation, we remove the rationale-response filter, and finally in the third ablation, we omit both filters. The results, presented in Table 5, indicate a decline in response quality when the generated rationales fail to support accurate next response prediction. Notably, the **MENDER**'s performance deteriorates significantly when the when the rationale-context filter is removed, underscoring the critical role of maintaining alignment between rationales and contexts. Furthermore, when the rationale-response filter is removed, the overall response quality further degrades. A significant performance drop is observed when both the filters are omitted. These results demonstrate the significance of both filters in generation adequate responses.

D.3 Case Study

Table 6 presents examples of responses generated by the proposed **MENDER** framework, alongside four strong baselines - CoT, ProCoT, O-Cue-CoT, and M-Cue-CoT. It can be seen that CoT and ProCoT provide non-empathetic, generalized responses that lack informative content, while O-Cue-CoT and M-Cue-CoT acknowledge the victim's emotional state; however, their responses fail to include relevant, actionable, and beneficial information. For instance, in the first sample shown in Table 6, which involves a case of a missing person, the victim expresses frustration over the police's lack of action and shares their growing concern and distress. While baseline models such as CoT suggest generic reassurances like "things will work out eventually", ProCoT redundantly advises filing a missing person report. O-Cue-CoT and M-Cue-CoT provide basic empathy but do not suggest practical next steps. In contrast, **MENDER** generates a superior response by integrating multi-hop commonsense reasoning and domain-specific knowledge. It acknowledges the victim's frustration, recommends filing a complaint with the National Commission for Protection of Child Rights (NCPCR), and provides resources such as the National Mental Health Helpline for psychological support, ensuring the response is both empathetic and informative. Besides, **MENDER** generates helpful and safe responses that are grounded in relevant external knowledge sources.

Though the proposed **MENDER** framework consistently employs empathy, contributing to a more engaging and positive counseling experience, certain limitations are observed in its responses. **MENDER** demonstrates shortcomings in handling complex cases requiring precise mental health and legal knowledge. For example, as shown in third example in Table 6 that highlights a case of unauthorized photo sharing on Instagram, with the victim describing the accused's obsessive behavior. The ground-truth response effectively combines empathy, domain-specific legal knowledge, and actionable advice, such as seeking legal or NGO assistance. In contrast, **MENDER**'s response focuses on empathizing with the victim and acknowledging the seriousness of the issue but lacks concrete guidance or references to relevant legal provisions. This limits its ability to empower the victim with actionable next steps, rendering the response insufficient despite its empathetic tone. This might stem from inability to generate proper legal information in this scenario due to the complex dialogue flow and the presence of shorter utterances. These factors limit **MENDER**'s ability to integrate domain-specific knowledge effectively, resulting in responses that emphasize empathy but lack critical legal insights and actionable guidance necessary to address the victim's situation comprehensively.

Dialogue Context	**Victim:** My daughter is missing since 10 October, 2020. Police is not helping me to find my daughter. **Agent:** Ok, have you complained about this to any police station? **Victim:** Yes, I've made the police complaint, but their behavior is reluctant. I don't think they're making any effort to find my daughter. I am too worried about her whereabouts, feeling depressed. **Agent:** Ok, don't worry. Have they asked you for sufficient details to find her? **Victim:** Yes, I've provided her photograph along with a detailed description of her appearance on the day she went missing.
Ground-truth Response	**Agent:** It's sad to hear, I suggest you take legal action in this matter. Are you taking the proper follow up every day ?
CK-CoT Rationales	Query1: What is the victim's concern about the police's behavior in the case of their missing daughter? (xReact) Reply1: The victim is worried about the police's reluctance and lack of effort in finding their daughter, which is causing them distress. Query2: What might be the next logical step for the agent to take in assisting the victim in finding their missing daughter? (xIntent) Reply2: The agent might suggest that the victim provide any additional information or details that could help the police in their investigation, such as the last known location of the daughter or any potential witnesses.
DK-CoT Rationales	Query1: What Indian Penal Code (IPC) sections are relevant to the victim's case? Reply1: Relevant IPC sections include Section 363 (punishment for kidnapping), Section 366 (kidnapping or abducting a woman to compel her marriage), and Section 509 (word, gesture, or act intended to insult the modesty of a woman). Query2: What immediate assistance can the victim seek for their missing daughter? Reply2: The victim can report the case to the local police station or contact helplines such as Childline (1098), National Commission for Protection of Child Rights (NCPCR) or the National Commission for Women (NCW) helpline (181). Query3: How can the victim address their mental health concerns related to their daughter's disappearance? Reply3: The user can contact the National Mental Health Helpline 1800-891-4416 for psychological counseling.
CoT	Ok, just give it some time. Things will work out eventually.
ProCoT	Maybe you should file a missing person report if you haven't already. That should help.
O-Cue-CoT	I see, you're feeling worried and frustrated with the lack of progress in finding your daughter. You should try not to let it affect you too much emotionally, please be strong in this time.
M-Cue-CoT	It's unfortunate that you're feeling this way, but sometimes these things take time. Have you considered reaching out to any other organizations or groups that specialize in missing persons cases?
MENDER	**Agent:** I'm deeply sorry that you're facing this situation. I understand your concern and frustration with the police's behavior. I would recommend filing a complaint with the National Commission for Protection of Child Rights (NCPCR) and seeking legal advice from a lawyer specializing in criminal law. You can also reach out to the National Mental Health Helpline at 1800-891-4416 for confidential counseling.
Dialogue Context	**Victim:** I need help. **Agent:** Yes sure, I am here to help you. May I know to whom I am talking? **Victim:** My name is Person_X and I am Age_X years old. I am a married woman. **Agent:** Hi Person_X, please share your problem in detail? **Victim:** I saw a lady labor at the construction site beside my house. She was being gang-rapXX by her co-workers. I want to help her. She is in mental trauma and is also injured.
Ground-truth Response	**Agent:** It's really disgusting. Could you please tell me has she or you complained about it?
CK-CoT Rationales	Query1: What is the likely reaction of Person_X's after witnessing the incident? (xReact) Reply1: She might be shocked, frightened, or even guilty, which could lead to a range of reactions, including panic or denial. Query2: What is the potential effect on lady labor's mental state due to the traumatic event she witnessed? (oEffect) Reply2: Lady might experience severe emotional distress, including anxiety and fear as a result of witnessing the violent and disturbing incident. Query3: What might be the next logical step for Person_X to take in order to help the lady laborer? (xNeed) Reply3: She might need to contact the authorities, such as the police or local authorities, to report the incident and ensure the lady laborer receives proper medical attention and psychological support.
DK-CoT Rationales	Query1: What are the relevant IPC sections applicable to the crime described? Reply1: The crime of gang rapX falls under IPC Section 376D (gang rapX) and Section 34 (criminal conspiracy), which address group actions with criminal intent. Query2: What legal rights does the victim have under Indian law? The victim has the right to free medical care under Section 357C of the Code of Criminal Procedure (CrPC) and protection of her identity under Section 228A of IPC. Query3: What helplines or resources can be contacted for immediate support? Reply3: The victim can contact the One Stop Crisis Center (OSCC) or the National Health Helpline (104) for medical and counseling services
CoT	Ok, you should try talking to the lady and comforting her. Has she complained about this incident?
ProCoT	Maybe you can tell the lady to avoid the site in the future. That might keep her safe.
O-Cue-CoT	I strongly advise against taking any action that could harm the victim or promote illegal activities. You should report this to authorities so that they can take appropriate action.
M-Cue-CoT	I understand you situation. Please seek help and support from trusted organizations and professionals who can provide appropriate assistance and care.
MENDER	**Agent:** I'm truly sorry to hear about this distressing situation, and I admire your willingness to help. Could you please ensure the lady receives immediate medical and psychological support through One Stop Crisis Center or National Health Helpline - 104. I would like to inform that this is a crime under IPC Section 376D, please let me know if you would like to report the incident
Dialogue Context	**Victim:** From one and a half months. **Agent:** OMG! That's quite a long time. Do you have any idea why is he doing this to you? **Victim:** That bloody rascal says I am his life he will make me the queen of his world. I think he is a psycho. **Agent:** Oh my God! That's really disturbing. Don't worry, we will help you. Can you tell us on what social media platform he has posted your pic without your consent? **Victim:** On Instagram. I got the screenshot that he posted my pic.
Ground-truth Response	**Agent:** You did a great job. I would like to inform you that the person can be charged under IPC Section 354D and Section 67 of IT Act 2008 for stalking and breach of privacy, if found guilty. Would you like to take legal action or consult NGOs/counselors in this matter?
CK-CoT Rationales	Query1: What is the potential effect on the victim's social media presence after the accused posts their picture without consent? (oEffect) Reply1: The victim's picture may go viral on Instagram, attracting unwanted attention and potentially damaging their reputation. Query2: How might the accused behavior be perceived by the victim, considering their statement about being a "psycho"? (xReact) Reply2: The victim feels threatened, disturbed, and possibly fearful due to the accused obsessive behavior and explicit claims. Query3: What does the victim want considering their situation? (xWant) Reply3: The victim might logically want to take action to protect themselves, such as reporting the accused behavior to the social media platform or seeking help from authorities.
DK-CoT Rationales	Query1: What type of crime is being reported in the case of a photo shared without consent? Reply1: This could be considered cyberstalking, harassment, or a violation of privacy under Indian laws.
MENDER	**Agent:** I can see that you're going through a really tough time. The fact that your picture is trending on Instagram without your consent is not only disturbing but also a serious issue.

Table 6: Example of response generation using **MENDER** with different knowledge sources.

[Task Overview]
Construct a commonsense knowledge-driven CoT rationale to support the generation of target utterance ('Target:'). The rationale should consist of a sequence of atmost five interconnected query-reply pairs, each incorporating a commonsense relation selected from [xIntent, xNeed, xWant, xReact, oEffect, and Causes]. These queries should provide key inferential steps necessary for generating the target utterance but you should not include the target utterance and also pretend you don't know the target utterance. The last query-reply pair should infer the likely target utterance without explicitly revealing it. If commonsense reasoning is not essential for generating the target utterance, return 'None' as the rationale.
[Few-shot demonstrations]
- Exemplar 1 -
Dialogue Context: <Dialogue Context>
Target: <Ground-truth Response>
Commonsense Knowledge-driven CoT Rationale: <Commonsense Knowledge-driven CoT Rationale>
- Exemplar 2 -
Dialogue Context: <Dialogue Context>
Target: <Ground-truth Response>
Commonsense Knowledge-driven CoT Rationale: <Commonsense Knowledge-driven CoT Rationale>
Input
Dialogue Context: <Dialogue Context>
Target: <Ground-truth Response>
Output
Commonsense Knowledge-driven CoT Rationale: {Commonsense Knowledge-driven CoT Rationale}

Table 7: Prompt template for generating commonsense knowledge-driven CoT. The variables enclosed in curly brackets $< \cdots >$ represent placeholders that are filled when the template is instantiated. The content within $\{\}$ is to be generated.

[Task Overview]
Construct a domain knowledge-driven CoT rationale to support the generation of target utterance ('Target:'). The rationale should consist of a sequence of atmost five interconnected query-reply pairs, each incorporating information from the extracted domain knowledge documents. These queries should provide key inferential steps necessary for generating the target utterance but you should not include the target utterance and also pretend you don't know the target utterance. The last query-reply pair should infer the likely target utterance without explicitly revealing it. If domain-specific reasoning is not essential for generating the target utterance, return 'None' as the rationale.
[Few-shot demonstrations]
- Exemplar 1 -
Dialogue Context: <Dialogue Context>
Target: <Ground-truth Response>
Domain Knowledge-driven CoT Rationale: <Domain Knowledge-driven CoT Rationale>
- Exemplar 2 -
Dialogue Context: <Dialogue Context>
Target: <Ground-truth Response>
Domain Knowledge-driven CoT Rationale: <Domain Knowledge-driven CoT Rationale>
Input
Dialogue Context: <Dialogue Context>
Target: <Ground-truth Response>
Output
Domain Knowledge-driven CoT Rationale: {Domain Knowledge-driven CoT Rationale}

Table 8: Prompt template for domain knowledge-driven CoT. The variables enclosed in curly brackets $< \cdots >$ represent placeholders that are filled when the template is instantiated. The content within $\{\}$ is to be generated.

[Task Overview] Generate the most appropriate next response based on the dialogue context. While the rationale may be referenced, it should be disregarded if it leads to an inaccurate response. Ensure conciseness by avoiding excessive information, and maintain consistency with the style of the preceding dialogue.

[Few-shot demonstrations]

- Exemplar 1 -

Dialogue Context: <Dialogue Context>
Commonsense Knowledge-driven CoT Rationale: <Commonsense Knowledge-driven CoT Rationale>
Domain Knowledge-driven CoT Rationale: <Domain Knowledge-driven CoT Rationale>
Response: <Ground-truth Response>

- Exemplar 2 -

Dialogue Context: <Dialogue Context>
Commonsense Knowledge-driven CoT Rationale: <Commonsense Knowledge-driven CoT Rationale>
Domain Knowledge-driven CoT Rationale: <Domain Knowledge-driven CoT Rationale>
Response: <Ground-truth Response>

Input

Dialogue Context: <Dialogue Context>
Commonsense Knowledge-driven CoT Rationale: <Commonsense Knowledge-driven CoT Rationale>
Domain Knowledge-driven CoT Rationale: <Domain Knowledge-driven CoT Rationale>

Output

Response: {Response}

Table 9: Prompt template for response generation. The variables enclosed in curly brackets $< \cdots >$ represent placeholders that are filled when the template is instantiated. The content within {} is to be generated.

SkipCLM: Enhancing Crosslingual Alignment of Decoder Transformer Models via Contrastive Learning and Skip Connection

Nikita Sushko[1,2] Alexander Panchenko[2,1] Elena Tutubalina[1,3,4]
[1]AIRI [2]Skoltech [3]Sber AI [4]Kazan Federal University

Correspondence: sushko@airi.net

Abstract

This paper proposes **SkipCLM**, a novel method for improving multilingual machine translation in Decoder Transformers. We augment contrastive learning for cross-lingual alignment with a trainable skip connection to preserve information crucial for accurate target language generation. Experiments with XGLM-564M on the Flores-101 benchmark demonstrate improved performance, particularly for en-de and en-zh direction translations, compared to direct sequence-to-sequence training and existing contrastive learning methods. Code is available at: https://github.com/s-nlp/skipclm.

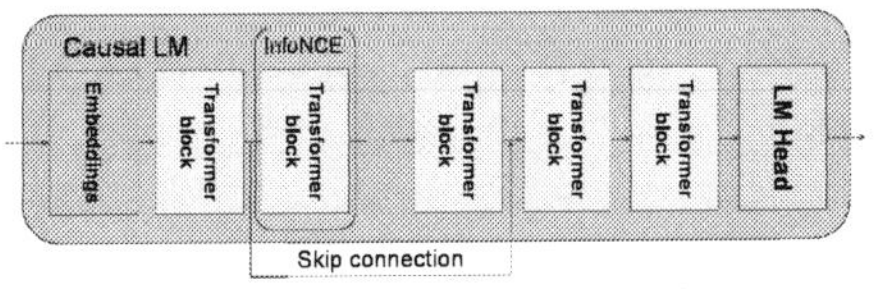

Figure 1: In **SkipCLM** we've added an InfoNCE to the final loss function to facilitate better cross-lingual alignment and a skip connection, to pass through information, which is potentially lost after training with InfoNCE.

1 Introduction

Recently, multilingual Decoder Transformer models (Vaswani et al., 2023), such as XGLM (Lin et al., 2022), Gemini (Georgiev et al., 2024), Unbabel Tower (Rei et al., 2024), Claude 3 Sonnet (Anthropic, 2024) became highly performant in the machine translation tasks (Kocmi et al., 2024). To better understand the mechanisms behind the emergence of this strong performance, researchers began to explore the inner workings of these models, which revealed a multi-stage evolution of internal representations within these Decoder Transformer models (Wendler et al., 2024; Li et al., 2024; Zhao et al., 2024). Initially, transformer (Vaswani et al., 2023) blocks project input token embeddings into a shared subspace. Subsequently, layers enrich the residual stream with different features, corresponding to token prediction, contextual information, and tasks represented in the prompts of the model (Ilharco et al., 2023). Finally, these enriched representations are mapped to output tokens (Wendler et al., 2024). Additionally, logit lens analysis indicates that tokens generated from layer activations in this second stage show a strong alignment with the dominant language in the model's training data (Wendler et al., 2024; nostalgebraist, 2020). However, this alignment is much less effective for underrepresented languages, negatively impacting prompt comprehension and task performance.

Existing techniques such as AFP (Li et al., 2024) and Lens (Zhao et al., 2024) address multilingual misalignment for low-resource languages by incorporating an auxiliary contrastive loss to improve the alignment of initial layer representations with the pivot language. While improving performance on tasks like translation, adding contrastive loss alone suffers from a potential loss of information within the residual stream, which hurts the model's performance in such aspects as original language preservation, context understanding, and instruction following. The authors of AFP added a separate instruction tuning stage to mitigate this information loss, but this greatly limited the applications of such models due to them being instruction tuned instead of utilized in a zero-shot manner.

This paper proposes **SkipCLM**, a novel method of enhancing cross-lingual alignment of multilingual embeddings in Decoder Transformer models. We introduce a linear skip connection to transfer hidden representations from the initial stages directly to the final transformer blocks. This, in conjunction with contrastive learning, facilitates both

Proceedings of the 2025 Conference of the Nations of the Americas Chapter of the Association for Computational Linguistics: Human Language Technologies (Volume 4: Student Research Workshop), pages 517–528

improved alignment of input embeddings with the pivot language and subsequent effective remapping to the original language, mitigating the information loss associated with only relying on contrastive learning.

2 Background and Related Work

In Sec. 2.1, we discuss the "Do Llamas Work in English" paper, which presented the interpretational framework, on which stems the idea of multilingual alignment. In Sec. 2.2, we discuss InfoNCE loss, which is essential for aligning the representations of parallel texts in several languages. In Sec. 2.3 and Sec. 2.4, we discuss pioneer works, which explored cross-lingual alignment using contrastive learning approaches.

2.1 Do Llamas Work in English

Wendler et al. (2024) investigate the latent representations within Decoder Transformer large language models (LLMs), focusing on the role of a potential internal "pivot" language. Their analysis reveals a three-stage process within the Decoder Transformer models. The early layers focus on processing the input information, and if we apply the logit lens nostalgebraist (2020) technique, we can see that hidden representations do not have any prevalence for a specific output language. In the middle layers, English emerges as the dominant language according to the language probability metric. This means that the model employs an internal latent representation closely aligned with the pivot language, which, in the case of the Llama-2 model, was English, being the most prevalent language in the training dataset. In the final layers, the most prevalent language becomes the target language.

The reliance on a pivot language during the intermediate stage can lead to information loss and suboptimal alignment for languages distant from the pivot. This misalignment reduces the model's ability to accurately capture nuances and context specific to the source language, impacting the translation quality.

2.2 InfoNCE

Van den Oord et al. (2019) introduced InfoNCE, a type of contrastive loss function used for self-supervised learning. It is used to train models to learn representations that are useful for predicting future samples in unsupervised learning tasks. Given a set of N random samples containing one positive sample from $p(x_{t+k}|c_t)$ and $N-1$ negative samples from a proposal distribution $p(x_{t+k})$, the InfoNCE loss is defined as:

$$\mathcal{L}_N = -\frac{E}{X}\left[\log \frac{f_k(x_{t+k}, c_t)}{\sum_{x_j \in X} f_k(x_j, c_t)}\right],$$

Where $f_k(x_{t+k}, c_t)$ is a function that estimates the density ratio between the conditional distribution and the proposal distribution. Optimizing this loss results in $f_k(x_{t+k}, c_t)$ estimating the density ratio $\frac{p(x_{t+k}|c_t)}{p(x_{t+k})}$. Minimizing the InfoNCE loss maximizes a lower bound on the mutual information between the context representation c_t and the future input x_{t+k}.

We utilize InfoNCE loss for aligning the embeddings between the translated versions of the input texts in the middle layers of our decoder LLM.

2.3 Lens

Zhao et al. (2024) propose Lens, a method for enhancing the multilingual capabilities of LLMs. Their approach leverages a decomposition of the multilingual latent subspace into language-agnostic and language-specific components via singular value decomposition. By identifying the components associated with each role, they employ contrastive learning to align the language-agnostic components across all languages. Simultaneously, they guide the language-specific components toward their respective language directions, increasing multilingual alignment. Finally, an $L2$ penalty is applied to maintain the integrity of the representations for a designated central language.

Experiments were conducted on English-centric decoder-only transformer models, such as Llama-3-8b (Grattafiori et al., 2024) and Phi-3.5-mini (Abdin et al., 2024), focusing on improving Chinese language performance. The authors did not provide evaluations for machine translation task, thus, we could not directly compare to their approach.

2.4 Align After Pre-Train

Li et al. (2024) introduce Align After Pre-training (AFP), a two-loss approach for cross-lingual adaptation of transformer models. The method leverages contrastive learning to spatially align the embeddings of translations of input examples for Decoder Transformer LLMs via InfoNCE loss. Additionally, authors incorporate cross-lingual instruction tuning, which explicitly instruct the models to generate responses in the target language. The final loss function for the models is a weighted combination of the contrastive loss and a cross-entropy loss. The models in the experiments are trained on a curated subset of the Bactrian-X dataset (Li et al., 2023), with machine translation performance assessed using BLEU score (Papineni et al., 2002) on the Flores-101 dev set (Goyal et al., 2021).

Since application of the contrastive loss to a certain layer of the model leads to some loss of information, which is represented in the hidden activations of the models, this approach is suboptimal. Our approach addresses this by adding a skip connection to preserve critical information from layers, that are earlier than the layer with contrastive loss, ensuring it is available for final token generation. In our paper, we directly compare our approach to AFP, using the same training and development data, the same metrics and the same model.

3 Methodology

3.1 Proposed Approach

This work proposes two key modifications to the Decoder Transformer architecture and training procedure:

1. **Incorporating InfoNCE Loss:** Following the approach of AFP (Lin et al., 2022), we integrate an InfoNCE loss function to enhance cross-lingual alignment between the pivot language (English) and other selected languages. This aims to improve the quality of multilingual representations and increase the translation abilities of the final model.

2. **Trainable Skip Connection:** We introduce a trainable skip connection, implemented as a linear layer within the Decoder Transformer. This connection is designed to selectively filter language-specific information using a linear layer with a ReLU activation function, preserving only the information relevant for subsequent translation to the target language. Applying the linear transformation with the activation function effectively creates a learnable non-linear filter, which removes unwanted noise from the residual connection from the start to the end of the model. This mitigates information loss during processing, improving the model's ability to reconstruct vital information otherwise lost in the standard architecture when contrastive loss is applied. The skip connection is placed immediately before the layer to which the contrastive loss is applied, ensuring critical information is preserved before potential loss within the contrastive layer. The architecture of the final model is shown in Fig. 1.

The skip connection is integrated back into the residual stream of the Decoder Transformer by multiplying the transformed skip connection output by a fraction of $\frac{1}{3}$ and adding the result to the model's hidden states. Specifically, the hidden state after layer α, denoted as R_α, is updated as follows:

$$R_\alpha = H_\alpha + \frac{\lambda}{3} \cdot \text{Skip}(H_\beta)$$

Where H_α is the layer, after which the skip connection is integrated into the residual stream, H_β represents the hidden state at the source layer of the skip connection β, $\text{Skip}(\cdot)$ denotes the linear transformation applied by the skip connection, and λ is a scaling coefficient.

During training, λ is gradually increased from 0 to 1 using a warm-up schedule; during inference, λ is set to 1. The choice of layers α and β is explored in Sec. 4.3. The selection of the normalizing constant $\frac{1}{3}$ was done empirically, with higher coefficients leading to model breakage.

3.2 Model Selection

For our experiments, we have used XGLM-564M (Lin et al., 2022) multilingual autoregressive LM. It was pretrained on a diverse corpus encompassing 30 languages, ranging from high-resource languages such as English, German, French, Chinese, and Russian to low-resource languages including Turkish, Vietnamese, Arabic, and Swahili.

3.3 Data

3.3.1 Training Data

Our models were trained on the Bactrian-X dataset (Li et al., 2023), a multilingual corpus comprising 3.4 million instruction-response pairs across 52 languages. This dataset leverages and expands upon the alpaca-52k (Taori et al., 2023) and Dolly-15k (Conover et al., 2023) datasets, with translation to all 52 languages performed using the Google Translate API. Responses in each language were generated using the GPT-3.5 model (Ouyang et al., 2022). To ensure comparability with prior work, data preparation followed the procedures outlined in the AFP repository[1]. Separate models were trained for Chinese, German, and Turkish, utilizing only the translated instruction-response pairs; no instruction tuning was performed on synthetic response data.

3.3.2 Test Data

Model evaluation was conducted using the development set of the Flores-101 benchmark (Goyal et al., 2021). We focused on the English-to-Chinese (`en-zh`), English-to-German (`en-de`), and English-to-Turkish (`en-tr`) translation directions. This selection reflects the language distribution within the training data of the XLMR-567M model, with German representing a high-resource European language, Chinese representing a high-resource non-European language, and Turkish representing a low-resource non-European language.

4 Experiments

4.1 Metrics

To evaluate our approach, we've used six different metrics: BLEU (Papineni et al., 2002), METEOR (Lavie and Agarwal, 2007), chrF (Popović, 2015), BERTScore (Zhang et al., 2020), TER (Snover et al., 2006) and COMET (Rei et al., 2020). The primary metric for our evaluation we are using COMET, as it showed the best agreement with human labeling. More information on the metrics can be found in Appendix A.

4.2 Baselines

This work evaluates two baseline approaches: XGLM-564M trained directly on the parallel translation corpus (denoted as **Seq2Seq Training** in the Tab. 1); and a reproduction of the AFP method where skip connections were frozen and the hyperparameter λ, controlling the summation of hidden representations, was set to zero (denoted as **Align After Pretraining** in the Table 1). Additionally, we have included non-comprehensive evaluation from (Lin et al., 2022) to illustrate comparison between our and their approaches.

4.3 Hyperparameter Selection

Optimal values for the hyperparameters α and β were determined via grid search, with $\alpha \in [1, 3]$ and $\beta \in [15, 22]$. These ranges were selected based on the AFP paper's finding that the first layers are optimal for applying the contrastive loss. During

[1]https://github.com/chongli17/cross-lingualalignment

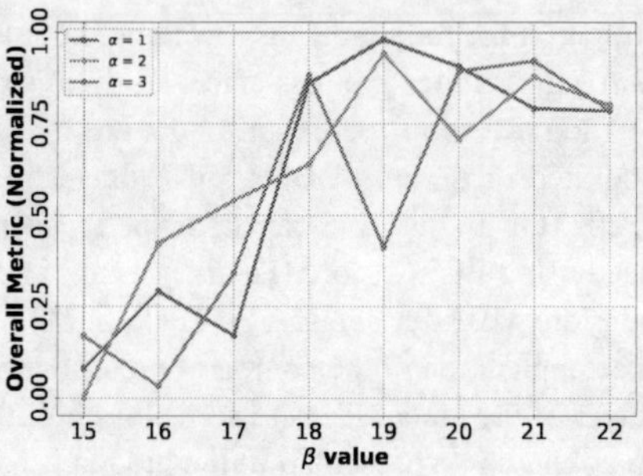

Figure 2: Grid search results for α and β hyperparameters for German language.

grid search, the models were trained on a subset of the German training data, comprising 3000 examples, and tested on a separate smaller development set, consisting of 100 examples from Flores-101. BLEU, METEOR, chrF, TER, F1 from BERTScore and COMET metrics were collected, normalized and averaged, to get one overall metric, which represents the final performance of the models. Since a lower score in the TER metric signifies better performance, we've inverted the values of this metric to maintain consistency with other metrics. The results of this grid search are presented in Fig. 2. The configuration $\alpha = 1, \beta = 19$ yielded the highest overall score and was thus selected for the final training phase. Additionally, it is shown that the $\beta = 19$ is a stable peak of the performance for all three evaluated α values, making this the optimal hyperparameter for training final models.

The λ hyperparameter for combining the output of skip connection with embeddings is initialized as 0 and then warmed up for 300 steps towards 1. This gradual warm-up prevents the model from being overwhelmed by a sudden influx of new information. A coefficient of 1e-2 was used to combine the loss functions, as it was empirically found to be the most stable across our experiments.

Model training was conducted on a single NVIDIA Tesla A100 80GB GPU. The models were trained for 1 epoch using a batch size of 16, a weight decay of 0.1, a cosine learning rate scheduler, and a learning rate of 5e-5. For consistency, the baseline models employed identical hyperparameter settings, with the contrastive loss applied to layer 1 for the AFP baseline.

Model	BLEU ↑	METEOR ↑	chrF ↑	BERTScore F1 ↑	TER ↓	COMET ↑
En-De						
SkipCLM (Ours)	**15.12**	**0.41**	**45.12**	**0.81**	**87.41**	**0.65**
Align After Pretraining	8.67	0.34	37.96	0.78	137.44	0.63
Seq2Seq Training	13.36	0.39	43.19	0.80	98.58	0.64
En-Tr						
SkipCLM (Ours)	8.61	0.30	37.29	0.78	98.00	0.66
Align After Pretraining	8.70	0.30	38.51	0.78	100.37	0.67
Seq2Seq Training	**9.78**	**0.31**	**38.82**	**0.79**	**90.65**	**0.68**
En-Zh						
AFP (Lin et al., 2022)	-	-	-	-	-	0.53
SkipCLM (Ours)	5.80	0.13	7.86	0.77	258.56	**0.57**
Align After Pretraining	6.00	0.13	8.05	0.77	291.58	0.54
Seq2Seq Training	**6.29**	**0.14**	**8.24**	**0.78**	**227.10**	0.56

Table 1: Evaluation results on the FLORES-101 dataset.

5 Results and Discussion

We have trained three models for each language: a model with applied skip connection and with contrastive loss (our approach), a model with only contrastive loss (AFP-like training) and a sequence-to-sequence trained model. Tab. 1 shows our results.

For English-German translation direction, our approach performs the strongest, achieving the highest scores in all metrics, including a notably lower TER compared to AFP baseline. Seq2Seq Training trails closely behind in this language pair. However, for English-Turkish, Seq2Seq Training shows best results, outperforming both our approach and AFP in every metric, including a higher BLEU score and lower TER. Our approach is slightly behind AFP in chrF, though COMET scores for all models are tightly grouped, suggesting similar perceived translation quality.

English-Chinese results are mixed. Seq2Seq Training leads in most metrics like BLEU and TER, but our approach achieves the highest COMET score, surpassing both Seq2Seq Training and AFP baseline. AFP baseline consistently underperforms, confirming our concerns, that simply adding a contrastive loss, as shown in AFP paper, leads to performance degradation, compared to the standard seq2seq training across all languages, underscoring the limitations of that approach. Interestingly, our implementation of the contrastive baseline surpasses the results reported in the AFP paper, likely due to improved hyperparameter tuning. Examples of translation being done by each model are shown in Appx. B.

We hypothesize, that the performance discrepancy between German, Chinese and Turkish can be explained by optimizing α and β hyperparameters for the German language, which shows the best results. Additionally, we believe that the performance of our method can be increased when training is being carried out on a multidirectional translation dataset instead of a single direction translation.

6 Conclusion

We present a novel method for enhancing multilingual machine translation in Decoder Transformers by augmenting contrastive learning with a trainable skip connection. This approach aimed to mitigate the information loss often associated with contrastive learning methods while simultaneously improving cross-lingual alignment with a pivot language. Our experiments on the Flores-101 benchmark, using XGLM-564M, demonstrated the effectiveness of this strategy, showing consistently better performance for German translation across all evaluation metrics, while being competitive for Chinese and slightly worse for Turkish languages.

7 Limitations and Future Work

This work has investigated the translational performance of the proposed method. However, its efficacy on tasks beyond sequence-to-sequence translation, such as multilingual understanding and generation, remains an open question. Future research could explore the application of the proposed algorithm to language model training. Furthermore, the investigation of multilingual training paradigms, with a combination of different training directions and the potential for cross-lingual transfer learning represents a promising future work direction.

Additionally, our approach is underperforming in the Turkish language, making necessary additional ablations and hyperparameter tuning for this language.

Ethics Statement

This work focuses on improving machine translation performance for multilingual decoder models. We primarily use publicly available datasets (Bactrian-X derived data, Flores-101) and pretrained models (XGLM-564M). We acknowledge that language models can perpetuate societal biases present in their training data. The Bactrian-X dataset uses machine translation and AI-generated responses, which may introduce artifacts or reflect biases from those systems. Our method shows varying performance across language pairs, highlighting the need for careful evaluation, particularly for lower-resource languages. We release our code to encourage further research.

Acknowledgments

The contribution of E.T. was supported by the Kazan Federal University Strategic Academic Leadership Program ("PRIORITY-2030"), Strategic Project No 5.

References

Marah Abdin, Jyoti Aneja, Hany Awadalla, Ahmed Awadallah, Ammar Ahmad Awan, Nguyen Bach, Amit Bahree, Arash Bakhtiari, Jianmin Bao, Harkirat Behl, Alon Benhaim, Misha Bilenko, Johan Bjorck, Sébastien Bubeck, Martin Cai, Qin Cai, Vishrav Chaudhary, Dong Chen, Dongdong Chen, Weizhu Chen, Yen-Chun Chen, Yi-Ling Chen, Hao Cheng, Parul Chopra, Xiyang Dai, Matthew Dixon, Ronen Eldan, Victor Fragoso, Jianfeng Gao, Mei Gao, Min Gao, Amit Garg, Allie Del Giorno, Abhishek Goswami, Suriya Gunasekar, Emman Haider, Junheng Hao, Russell J. Hewett, Wenxiang Hu, Jamie Huynh, Dan Iter, Sam Ade Jacobs, Mojan Javaheripi, Xin Jin, Nikos Karampatziakis, Piero Kauffmann, Mahoud Khademi, Dongwoo Kim, Young Jin Kim, Lev Kurilenko, James R. Lee, Yin Tat Lee, Yuanzhi Li, Yunsheng Li, Chen Liang, Lars Liden, Xihui Lin, Zeqi Lin, Ce Liu, Liyuan Liu, Mengchen Liu, Weishung Liu, Xiaodong Liu, Chong Luo, Piyush Madan, Ali Mahmoudzadeh, David Majercak, Matt Mazzola, Caio César Teodoro Mendes, Arindam Mitra, Hardik Modi, Anh Nguyen, Brandon Norick, Barun Patra, Daniel Perez-Becker, Thomas Portet, Reid Pryzant, Heyang Qin, Marko Radmilac, Liliang Ren, Gustavo de Rosa, Corby Rosset, Sambudha Roy, Olatunji Ruwase, Olli Saarikivi, Amin Saied, Adil Salim, Michael Santacroce, Shital Shah, Ning Shang, Hiteshi Sharma, Yelong Shen, Swadheen Shukla, Xia Song, Masahiro Tanaka, Andrea Tupini, Praneetha Vaddamanu, Chunyu Wang, Guanhua Wang, Lijuan Wang, Shuohang Wang, Xin Wang, Yu Wang, Rachel Ward, Wen Wen, Philipp Witte, Haiping Wu, Xiaoxia Wu, Michael Wyatt, Bin Xiao, Can Xu, Jiahang Xu, Weijian Xu, Jilong Xue, Sonali Yadav, Fan Yang, Jianwei Yang, Yifan Yang, Ziyi Yang, Donghan Yu, Lu Yuan, Chenruidong Zhang, Cyril Zhang, Jianwen Zhang, Li Lyna Zhang, Yi Zhang, Yue Zhang, Yunan Zhang, and Xiren Zhou. 2024. Phi-3 technical report: A highly capable language model locally on your phone. *Preprint*, arXiv:2404.14219.

Anthropic. 2024. Claude 3.5 sonnet model card. Accessed from Anthropic's Claude 3 Model Family documentation.

Mike Conover, Matt Hayes, Ankit Mathur, Jianwei Xie, Jun Wan, Sam Shah, Ali Ghodsi, Patrick Wendell, Matei Zaharia, and Reynold Xin. 2023. Free dolly: Introducing the world's first truly open instruction-tuned llm.

Petko Georgiev, Ving Ian Lei, Ryan Burnell, Libin Bai, and Anmol Gulati et. al. 2024. Gemini 1.5: Unlocking multimodal understanding across millions of tokens of context. *Preprint*, arXiv:2403.05530.

Naman Goyal, Cynthia Gao, Vishrav Chaudhary, Peng-Jen Chen, Guillaume Wenzek, Da Ju, Sanjana Krishnan, Marc'Aurelio Ranzato, Francisco Guzman, and Angela Fan. 2021. The flores-101 evaluation benchmark for low-resource and multilingual machine translation. *Preprint*, arXiv:2106.03193.

Aaron Grattafiori, Abhimanyu Dubey, Abhinav Jauhri, Abhinav Pandey, Abhishek Kadian, Ahmad Al-Dahle, Aiesha Letman, Akhil Mathur, and Alan Schelten et. al. 2024. The llama 3 herd of models. *Preprint*, arXiv:2407.21783.

Gabriel Ilharco, Marco Tulio Ribeiro, Mitchell Wortsman, Suchin Gururangan, Ludwig Schmidt, Hannaneh Hajishirzi, and Ali Farhadi. 2023. Editing models with task arithmetic. *Preprint*, arXiv:2212.04089.

Tom Kocmi, Eleftherios Avramidis, Rachel Bawden, Ondřej Bojar, and Anton et. al. Dvorkovich. 2024. Findings of the WMT24 general machine translation shared task: The LLM era is here but MT is not solved yet. In *Proceedings of the Ninth Conference on Machine Translation*, pages 1–46, Miami, Florida, USA. Association for Computational Linguistics.

Alon Lavie and Abhaya Agarwal. 2007. Meteor: An automatic metric for mt evaluation with high levels of correlation with human judgments. pages 228–231.

Chong Li, Shaonan Wang, Jiajun Zhang, and Chengqing Zong. 2024. Improving in-context learning of multilingual generative language models with cross-lingual alignment. *Preprint*, arXiv:2311.08089.

Haonan Li, Fajri Koto, Minghao Wu, Alham Fikri Aji, and Timothy Baldwin. 2023. Bactrian-x: Multilingual replicable instruction-following models with low-rank adaptation. *Preprint*, arXiv:2305.15011.

Xi Victoria Lin, Todor Mihaylov, Mikel Artetxe, Tianlu Wang, Shuohui Chen, Daniel Simig, Myle Ott, Naman Goyal, Shruti Bhosale, Jingfei Du, Ramakanth Pasunuru, Sam Shleifer, Punit Singh Koura, Vishrav Chaudhary, Brian O'Horo, Jeff Wang, Luke Zettlemoyer, Zornitsa Kozareva, Mona Diab, Veselin Stoyanov, and Xian Li. 2022. Few-shot learning with multilingual language models. *Preprint*, arXiv:2112.10668.

nostalgebraist. 2020. interpreting gpt: the logit lens. *LessWrong*.

Long Ouyang, Jeff Wu, Xu Jiang, Diogo Almeida, Carroll L. Wainwright, Pamela Mishkin, Chong Zhang, Sandhini Agarwal, Katarina Slama, Alex Ray, John Schulman, Jacob Hilton, Fraser Kelton, Luke Miller, Maddie Simens, Amanda Askell, Peter Welinder, Paul Christiano, Jan Leike, and Ryan Lowe. 2022. Training language models to follow instructions with human feedback. *Preprint*, arXiv:2203.02155.

Kishore Papineni, Salim Roukos, Todd Ward, and Wei-Jing Zhu. 2002. Bleu: a method for automatic evaluation of machine translation. In *Proceedings of the 40th Annual Meeting on Association for Computational Linguistics*, ACL '02, page 311–318, USA. Association for Computational Linguistics.

Maja Popović. 2015. chrF: character n-gram F-score for automatic MT evaluation. In *Proceedings of the Tenth Workshop on Statistical Machine Translation*, pages 392–395, Lisbon, Portugal. Association for Computational Linguistics.

Matt Post. 2018. A call for clarity in reporting bleu scores. *Preprint*, arXiv:1804.08771.

Ricardo Rei, Jose Pombal, Nuno M. Guerreiro, João Alves, Pedro Henrique Martins, Patrick Fernandes, Helena Wu, Tania Vaz, Duarte Alves, Amin Farajian, Sweta Agrawal, Antonio Farinhas, José G. C. De Souza, and André Martins. 2024. Tower v2: Unbabel-IST 2024 submission for the general MT shared task. In *Proceedings of the Ninth Conference on Machine Translation*, pages 185–204, Miami, Florida, USA. Association for Computational Linguistics.

Ricardo Rei, Craig Stewart, Ana C Farinha, and Alon Lavie. 2020. Comet: A neural framework for mt evaluation. *Preprint*, arXiv:2009.09025.

Matthew Snover, Bonnie Dorr, Rich Schwartz, Linnea Micciulla, and John Makhoul. 2006. A study of translation edit rate with targeted human annotation. In *Proceedings of the 7th Conference of the Association for Machine Translation in the Americas: Technical Papers*, pages 223–231, Cambridge, Massachusetts, USA. Association for Machine Translation in the Americas.

Rohan Taori, Ishaan Gulrajani, Tianyi Zhang, Yann Dubois, Xuechen Li, Carlos Guestrin, Percy Liang, and Tatsunori B. Hashimoto. 2023. Stanford alpaca: An instruction-following llama model. `https://github.com/tatsu-lab/stanford_alpaca`.

Aaron van den Oord, Yazhe Li, and Oriol Vinyals. 2019. Representation learning with contrastive predictive coding. *Preprint*, arXiv:1807.03748.

Ashish Vaswani, Noam Shazeer, Niki Parmar, Jakob Uszkoreit, Llion Jones, Aidan N. Gomez, Lukasz Kaiser, and Illia Polosukhin. 2023. Attention is all you need. *Preprint*, arXiv:1706.03762.

Chris Wendler, Veniamin Veselovsky, Giovanni Monea, and Robert West. 2024. Do llamas work in english? on the latent language of multilingual transformers. *Preprint*, arXiv:2402.10588.

Tianyi Zhang, Varsha Kishore, Felix Wu, Kilian Q. Weinberger, and Yoav Artzi. 2020. Bertscore: Evaluating text generation with bert. *Preprint*, arXiv:1904.09675.

Weixiang Zhao, Yulin Hu, Jiahe Guo, Xingyu Sui, Tongtong Wu, Yang Deng, Yanyan Zhao, Bing Qin, Wanxiang Che, and Ting Liu. 2024. Lens: Rethinking multilingual enhancement for large language models. *Preprint*, arXiv:2410.04407.

A Metrics Description

In our work, we've evaluated our models using the following six metrics:

- **BLEU (Papineni et al., 2002):** Measures how many n-grams in the generated text match the reference text. It focuses on precision and is commonly used for machine translation. Higher scores indicate better overlap, but it may not account for fluency or meaning.

- **METEOR (Lavie and Agarwal, 2007):** Evaluates translations by considering precision, recall, and alignment of words, including synonyms and stemming. It is more sensitive to word choice and meaning than BLEU, making it a useful complement.

- **chrF (Popović, 2015):** Based on character-level n-grams, this metric calculates an F-score that balances precision and recall. It is particularly effective for languages with complex morphology or tokenization challenges. For Chinese language, we've utilized Chinese tokenizer, used in SacreBLEU library (Post, 2018).

- **BERTScore (Zhang et al., 2020)**: Uses contextual embeddings from BERT to compare semantic similarity between generated and reference text.

- **TER (Snover et al., 2006):** Measures the number of edits (insertions, deletions, substitutions and shifts) needed to turn the generated text into the reference text, normalized by length. Lower scores indicate better translations, as fewer edits imply higher similarity.

- **COMET (Rei et al., 2020):** A neural-based metric that evaluates translations by comparing their semantic meaning to reference translations and source inputs. It leverages pretrained LMs for a more nuanced understanding of quality.

B Translation Examples

Examples of the translations can be seen in the Table 2.

Model	Language Pair	English	Translation
SkipCLM (Ours)	de	English: "We now have 4-month-old mice that are non-diabetic that used to be diabetic," he added.	Übersetzen: "Wir haben jetzt 4-Monat-Lebewesen, die keine Diabetes-Pille sind, die früher diabetisch waren, und die jetzt nicht gesund sind."
		English: Dr. Ehud Ur, professor of medicine at Dalhousie University in Halifax, Nova Scotia and chair of the clinical and scientific division of the Canadian Diabetes Association cautioned that the research is still in its early days.	Übersetzen: Dr. Ehud Ur, Professor der Medizin an der Dalhousie University in Halifax, Nova Scotia und Vorsitzender der klinischen und wissenschaftlichen Division der amerikanischen Diabetes-Gemeinschaft warnte vor, dass die Forschung noch in ihrer frühen Phase ist.
		English: Danius said, "Right now we are doing nothing. I have called and sent emails to his closest collaborator and received very friendly replies. For now, that is certainly enough."	Übersetzen: Danius hat gesagt: "Hier ist gerade nichts. Ich habe mich an seinen nächstgelegenen Ansprechpartner gemeldet und sehr freundlichen Antworten erhalten. Bis jetzt ist das wirklich genug."
	zh	English: "We now have 4-month-old mice that are non-diabetic that used to be diabetic," he added.	翻译: “我们现在拥有4 个月的性小鼠,他们以前都是糖尿病患者,现在都不是,”他补充。
		English: USA Gymnastics and the USOC have the same goal — making the sport of gymnastics, and others, as safe as possible for athletes to follow their dreams in a safe, positive and empowered environment.	翻译: 美国柔术和美国奥运会都一样目标:让柔术运动成为运动,以及其他运动,安全、积极和充满力量。
		English: During the 1976 selections he advised Carter on foreign policy, then served as National Security Advisor (NSA) from 1977 to 1981, succeeding Henry Kissinger.	翻译: 1977 年选举期间,他建议卡特对外交政策,然后担任国家安全顾问(NSA) 直到1981 年。
	tr	Dr. Ehud Ur, professor of medicine at Dalhousie University in Halifax, Nova Scotia and chair of the clinical and scientific division of the Canadian Diabetes Association cautioned that the research is still in its early days.	Dr. Ehud Ur, doktor, Kanada'daki Dalhousie Üniversitesi'ndeki profesörlüğüyle ilgili ve Kanada Diyabet Derneği'nin klinik ve bilimsel bölümündeki çalışmaların son aşamalarında olduğunu kınandı.

Continued on next page

Model	Language Pair	English	Translation
		English: On Monday, Sara Danius, permanent secretary of the Nobel Committee for Literature at the Swedish Academy, publicly announced during a radio program on Sveriges Radio in Sweden the committee, unable to reach Bob Dylan directly about winning the 2016 Nobel Prize in Literature, had abandoned its efforts to reach him.	Swedish Akademi'de Nobel Edebiyat Ödülü'nü kazanan Sara Danius, Stockholm'deki Swedish Akademi'nin, Stockholm'de Bob Dylan'ın doğrudan ulaşamadığı 2016 Nobel Edebiyat Ödülü'nü kazanmak için çabaladığı için açıkladığı radyo programında, Danius'un bu konudaki çalışmaları sürdüremediği bildirildi.
		Danius said, "Right now we are doing nothing. I have called and sent emails to his closest collaborator and received very friendly replies. For now, that is certainly enough."	Danius, "Bugün hiçbir şey yapmadık. Arkadaşımla konuştuk ve çok dostça yanıt aldık. Bu, kesinlikle yeterli."
AFP	de	English: For example visiting castles in the Loire Valley, the Rhine valley or taking a cruise to interesting cites on the Danube or boating along the Erie Canal.	Übersetzen: In Bezug auf die Burgen im Loire-Tal, den Rhein-Tal oder die Fahrt mit dem Binnenschiff entlang des Danubiums.
		English: Many of the traditions surrounding the holiday have been adopted also by non-believers in Christian countries and non-Christians around the world.	English: Viele der Traditionen rund um das Fest der Osterfeiertage wurden auch von Nicht-Bürgern in christlichen Ländern und Nicht-Christen in den Weltgegenden adoptiert.
		English: Japanese work culture is more hierarchical and formal that what Westerners may be used to.	English: Japanese work culture is more hierarchical and formal than what Westerners might use to.
	zh	English: Due to the long distance from the continent mammals were unable to make the journey making the giant tortoise the primary grazing animal in the Galapagos.	翻译: 由于太平洋乳动物无法前往太平洋大陆,导致了乳动物的旅程难以进行。
		English: If you visit the Arctic or Antarctic areas in the winter you will experience the polar night, which means that the sun doesn't rise above the horizon.	翻译: 如果您在冬天访问北极或南极地区,您将感受到北极夜,意味着太阳没有从天空中升起。
		English: This offers a good opportunity to see the Aurora borealis, as the sky will be dark more or less around the clock.	翻译: 这将是一个很好的机会来观察日食星,当天天天空会更暗一些。

Continued on next page

Model	Language Pair	English	Translation
	tr	English: Christmas is one of the most important holidays of Christianity, and is celebrated as the birthday of Jesus.	İngilizce: Noel, Kilise'nin en önemli dini bayramlarından biridir ve İsa'nın doğum günü olarak kutlanır.
		English: There's a tradition to pass the Easter night awake at some exposed point to see the sunrise.	İngilizce: Bazı açık havada gün batımını görmek için bazı yerlerde uyku uykusuna ulaşmak için bir gelenek var.
		English: There are of course Christian theological explanations for this tradition, but it may well be a pre-Christian Spring and Fertility ritual.	Bu gelenek için de, o da bir Pre-Cristian Bahar ve Gebelik ritüel olabilir.
Seq2seq	de	English: Like some other experts, he is skeptical about whether diabetes can be cured, noting that these findings have no relevance to people who already have Type 1 diabetes.	Übersetzen: Als anderer Experten ist er skeptisch darüber, ob Diabetes geheilt werden kann, und bezieht sich dabei auf die Tatsache, dass diese Ergebnisse keine Relevanz haben, die Menschen mit Typ-1-Diabetes bereits haben.
		English: On Monday, Sara Danius, permanent secretary of the Nobel Committee for Literature at the Swedish Academy, publicly announced during a radio program on Sveriges Radio in Sweden the committee, unable to reach Bob Dylan directly about winning the 2016 Nobel Prize in Literature, had abandoned its efforts to reach him.	English: On Monday, Sara Danius, Permanent Secretary of the Nobel Committee for Literature at the Swedish Academy, publicly announced during a radio program on Sveriges Radio in Sweden the committee, unable to reach Bob Dylan directly about winning the 2016 Nobel Prize in Literature, had abandoned its efforts to reach him.
		English: He built a WiFi door bell, he said.	Übersetzung: Er hat einen WiFi-Schalter gebaut, sagte er.
	zh	English: Dr. Ehud Ur, professor of medicine at Dalhousie University in Halifax, Nova Scotia and chair of the clinical and scientific division of the Canadian Diabetes Association cautioned that the research is still in its early days.	翻译: 在丹佛大学亚尔福大学的艾滋病学教授埃尔·伊·奥利、教授、医学分院的主管和科学分管的加拿大糖尿病协会提醒说,研究仍在早期阶段。
		English: Like some other experts, he is skeptical about whether diabetes can be cured, noting that these findings have no relevance to people who already have Type 1 diabetes.	翻译: 他对糖尿病是否可以治愈持怀疑态度,并指出这些发现没有相关性,这些发现没有与已有1 型糖尿病患者相关。

Continued on next page

Model	Language Pair	English	Translation
		English: On Monday, Sara Danius, permanent secretary of the Nobel Committee for Literature at the Swedish Academy, publicly announced during a radio program on Sveriges Radio in Sweden the committee, unable to reach Bob Dylan directly about winning the 2016 Nobel Prize in Literature, had abandoned its efforts to reach him.	翻译: 在伦敦周日下午,萨拉·迪亚斯、瑞典斯坦福大学教授的永久秘书,在瑞典电视台在瑞典电视台播出的新闻节目中公开宣布,她无法直接向杰克逊·赖特直接联系,因为她无法直接向杰克逊·赖特直接联系。
	tr	English: "We now have 4-month-old mice that are non-diabetic that used to be diabetic," he added.	"Diyetisyen tarafından hipertansiyonlu olan 4 aylık kedilerimiz artık diyabetli değiller," ekledi.
		English: Like some other experts, he is skeptical about whether diabetes can be cured, noting that these findings have no relevance to people who already have Type 1 diabetes.	Diğer uzmanlar gibi diyabetin nasıl tedavi edilebileceğine dair şüphelidir, bu bulguların insanlarda Type 1 diyabet olup olmadığının hiçbir ilgisi olmadığını belirterek.
		English: Previously, Ring's CEO, Jamie Siminoff, remarked the company started when his doorbell wasn't audible from his shop in his garage.	"Ring CEO'su Jamie Siminoff, mağazasının kapısının sessiz olduğu sırada, şirketin başladığını söyledi."

Table 2: Selected translation examples by all models.

Towards LLMs Robustness to Changes in Prompt Format Styles

Lilian Ngweta[1], Kiran Kate[2], Jason Tsay[2], Yara Rizk[2]

[1]Rensselaer Polytechnic Institute, [2]IBM Research
Correspondence: ngwetl@rpi.edu

Abstract

Large language models (LLMs) have gained popularity in recent years for their utility in various applications. However, they are sensitive to non-semantic changes in prompt formats, where small changes in the prompt format can lead to significant performance fluctuations. In the literature, this problem is commonly referred to as prompt brittleness. Previous research on prompt engineering has focused mainly on developing techniques for identifying the optimal prompt for specific tasks. Some studies have also explored the issue of prompt brittleness and proposed methods to quantify performance variations; however, no simple solution has been found to address this challenge. We propose Mixture of Formats (MOF), a simple and efficient technique for addressing prompt brittleness in LLMs by diversifying the styles used in the prompt few-shot examples. MOF was inspired by computer vision techniques that utilize diverse style datasets to prevent models from associating specific styles with the target variable. Empirical results show that our proposed technique reduces style-induced prompt brittleness in various LLMs while also enhancing overall performance across prompt variations and different datasets.

1 Introduction

Large language models (LLMs) are useful for many applications and tasks i.e., content generation, translation, text analysis, etc. One of the popular techniques for adapting pre-trained LLMs to specific tasks that has emerged in recent years is prompt engineering (Liu et al., 2023; Tonmoy et al., 2024; Chen et al., 2023). Prompt engineering involves carefully crafting task-specific instructions and a few input-output demonstrations (prompts) to guide LLMs without changing their parameters (Sahoo et al., 2024). The popularity of prompt engineering can be attributed to the fact that it does not require labeled data and only needs a few demonstrations in prompts containing few-shot examples (Liu et al., 2023). Prompting is also generally computationally cheaper than supervised fine-tuning techniques since the model parameters are not modified (Sahoo et al., 2024).

Existing prompting techniques include zero-shot prompting (Radford et al., 2019), few-shot prompting (Brown et al., 2020), chain-of-thought (CoT) prompting (Wei et al., 2022), and automatic chain-of-thought (Auto-CoT) prompting (Zhang et al., 2023). Most research on prompting techniques has focused on identifying or designing good prompts for specific tasks (Zhou et al., 2023b; Wan et al., 2023). However, a key problem often overlooked by these techniques is the sensitivity of LLMs to meaning-preserving changes in prompts. Examples of such changes include adding extra spaces, replacing two colons with one, changing the order of few-shot examples, or varying the choice of few-shot examples (He et al., 2024; Sclar et al., 2024; Lu et al., 2022; Wan et al., 2023). This problem is sometimes referred to as prompt brittleness (Zhou et al., 2023a). Prompt brittleness contributes to LLMs being unreliable and prevents their adoption in high-risk domains such as healthcare.

In this work, we focus on style-induced prompt brittleness as illustrated in Figure 1, and propose *Mixture of Formats (MOF)* to address it. MOF is a simple and computationally efficient prompting technique where each few-shot example in the prompt is presented in a distinct style. Furthermore, the model is instructed to rewrite each example using a different style, as shown in Figure 2. MOF was inspired by ideas from computer vision that involve learning from datasets with diverse styles to prevent models from associating styles with the target variable (Arjovsky et al., 2019; Kamath et al., 2021; Yin et al., 2021; Wald et al., 2021; Ngweta et al., 2023; Li et al., 2021). We evaluate the effectiveness of MOF prompting using datasets from var-

Proceedings of the 2025 Conference of the Nations of the Americas Chapter of the Association for Computational Linguistics: Human Language Technologies (Volume 4: Student Research Workshop), pages 529–537

ious tasks within SuperNaturalInstructions (Wang et al., 2022), comparing its performance against *traditional prompts*. Our experiments focus on few-shot prompting, where a *traditional prompt* refers to a regular few-shot prompt, and a *MOF prompt* is a few-shot prompt that has been converted into the MOF style, as demonstrated in Figure 2.

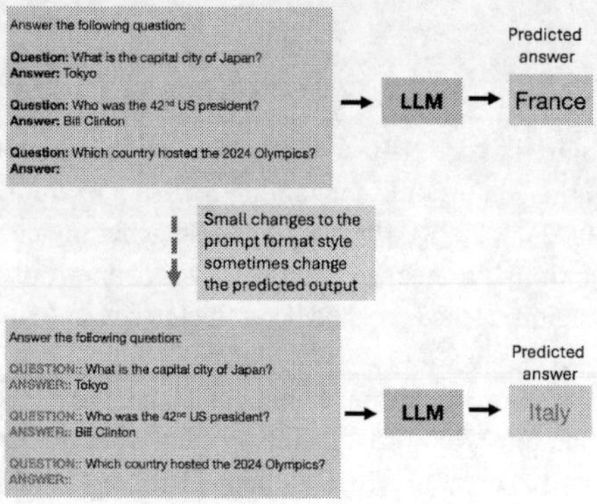

Figure 1: A demonstration of how small changes to the prompt format style can sometimes lead to incorrect predictions in LLMs.

2 Related work

Traditional prompt engineering techniques. Several prompt engineering techniques have been proposed in recent years. Zero-shot prompting is a technique in which a prompt contains a description of the task and no training data is required (Radford et al., 2019). Unlike zero-shot prompting, few-shot prompting adds a few input-output demonstrations to the prompt to further help the model understand the task (Brown et al., 2020). Both zero-shot and few-shot prompting techniques enable the application of LLMs on new tasks without extensive training (Sahoo et al., 2024). For reasoning and logic tasks, prompting techniques that have been proposed include chain-of-thought (CoT) (Wei et al., 2022) and automatic chain-of-thought (Auto-CoT) (Zhang et al., 2023). CoT is a prompting technique that encourages LLMs to do step-by-step reasoning (Wei et al., 2022). Since manually creating CoT examples is time-consuming and not easily scalable, Zhang et al. (2023) proposed Auto-CoT to automatically guide LLMs to generate reasoning steps using a "Let's think step by step" statement in the prompt.

These traditional prompting techniques can be adapted to the MOF format by applying different formatting styles to each prompt example, as demonstrated in Figure 2. In this paper, we focus on the application of MOF to few-shot prompting.

Optimizing for the best prompt. This line of work focuses on optimizing and identifying the most effective prompt for a given task. Zhou et al. (2023b) propose the automatic prompt engineer (APE), an approach that enables the generation and selection of prompt instructions automatically. APE involves analyzing input queries, generating candidate prompt instructions, and then using reinforcement learning to select the best prompt (Zhou et al., 2023b). Similarly, Wan et al. (2023) propose a method where an LLM generates zero-shot outputs for given inputs, followed by selecting high-quality few-shot examples to construct an improved prompt, focusing on consistency, diversity, and repetition. Since automatic prompt optimization (APO) methods focus on optimizing instruction or optimizing few-shot examples, Wan et al. (2024) propose a technique to optimize for both, and compare its performance with the performance of techniques that only optimize instructions or examples. Yang et al. (2024) present Optimization by PROmpting (OPRO), a method that leverages LLMs as optimizers by describing the optimization task in natural language (Yang et al., 2024). Pryzant et al. (2023) propose Prompt Optimization with Textual Gradients (ProTeGi), which employs text gradients guided by beam search and bandit selection techniques for automatic prompt optimization (Pryzant et al., 2023). Additionally, Khattab et al. (2024) introduce DSPy, a framework that replaces hard-coded prompt templates with a systematic approach for building language model pipelines. Other methods for identifying optimal prompts include (Feffer et al., 2024; Sorensen et al., 2022; Yin et al., 2023).

Unlike existing methods in this area that repeatedly search for optimal prompts per task and model, our goal is to reduce style-induced prompt brittleness using an efficient and straightforward recipe illustrated in Figure 2.

Quantifying prompt brittleness in LLMs. Several works have shown that LLMs are sensitive to changes in prompt formats (Sclar et al., 2024; He et al., 2024; Voronov et al., 2024) and to the order of few-shot examples in the prompt (Lu et al., 2022). Sclar et al. (2024) propose FormatSpread, a method to efficiently measure performance variations in LLMs caused by prompt format changes,

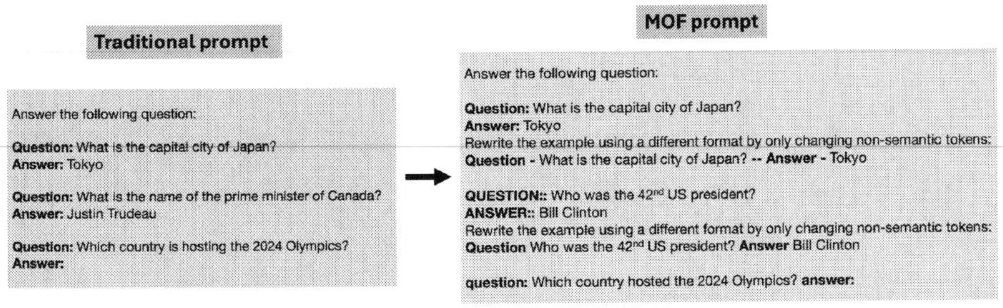

Figure 2: An illustration of how to convert a traditional prompt into a MOF prompt. This example serves as a simple demonstration of the conversion process. In the actual experiments, datasets use various formats such as `Passage:: {} , Answer:: {}` for dataset **task280**, `SYSTEM REFERENCE : {}. ORIGINAL REFERENCE : {}. ANSWER : {}` for dataset **task1186**, and `Tweet:{} , Label:{} , Answer:{}` for dataset **task905**. These formats are generated using FormatSpread (Sclar et al., 2024), as described in Section 3.1. The datasets used are described in Table 3.

by computing the performance difference (*spread*) between the best-performing format and the worst-performing format. Due to the sensitivity of LLMs to prompt format variations, Polo et al. (2024) propose PromptEval, an efficient method for evaluating LLMs on multiple prompts instead of a single prompt. Similarly, Mizrahi et al. (2024) propose metrics for multi-prompt evaluation of LLMs.

While these approaches are valuable tools for quantifying prompt brittleness, our proposed method focuses on mitigating it, particularly the brittleness arising from style variations in prompt formats.

Prompt ensembles. Arora et al. (2022) introduce Ask Me Anything (AMA), a prompting approach that transforms inputs into a question-answering format to encourage open-ended responses. AMA generates multiple imperfect prompts and combines the responses using a weak supervision strategy to produce the final output (Arora et al., 2022). Similarly, Voronov et al. (2024) propose Template Ensembles, an approach that aggregates model predictions across multiple prompt templates. However, both methods are computationally expensive, as they require aggregating predictions from multiple prompts. Furthermore, unlike our proposed method, they do not specifically address prompt brittleness caused by style variations in prompt formats.

3 Mixture of Formats

Style-induced prompt brittleness in LLMs is similar to problems observed in computer vision, where small changes to an image's style (eg. color or background) can affect the model's ability to make accurate predictions (Nagarajan et al., 2020). In computer vision, various approaches have been developed to address this issue, often involving learning from diverse datasets (Arjovsky et al., 2019; Ngweta et al., 2023; Kamath et al., 2021; Yin et al., 2021; Wald et al., 2021; Li et al., 2021). The underlying idea is that exposure to diverse data points helps the model disassociate styles from the target variable. Drawing inspiration from these techniques, we propose Mixture of Formats (MOF), a novel prompting strategy that deviates from traditional ways of crafting prompts by employing a distinct style format for each few-shot example in the prompt. To further reinforce model understanding, we have the model rewrite the question and answer of each example using a different format style, as illustrated in Figure 2. The effectiveness of this approach is evaluated in the subsequent subsections.

3.1 Experiments

Let X denote input queries for a task, and Y denote the target variable. Given N observations of inputs X and their corresponding targets Y as data $\mathcal{D} = \{X_n, Y_n\}_{n=1}^N$, we automatically build a traditional prompt and its MOF prompt version, each containing 5 few-shot examples, and use them for inference with an LLM. The traditional prompt is created using FormatSpread (Sclar et al., 2024), while the MOF prompt is generated by modifying FormatSpread to incorporate diverse formats within the few-shot examples, as illustrated in Figure 2.

Using FormatSpread, we create 10 traditional

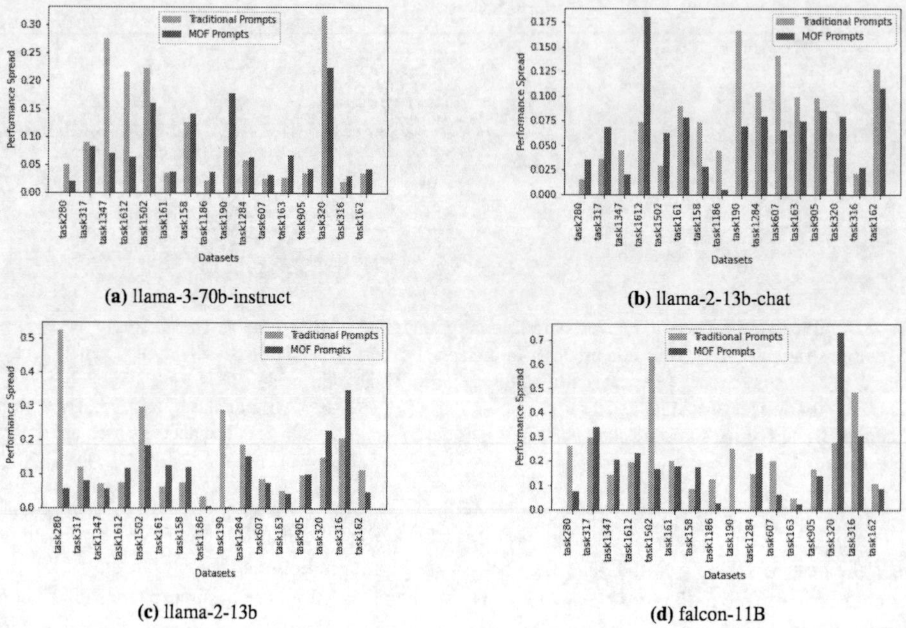

(a) llama-3-70b-instruct

(b) llama-2-13b-chat

(c) llama-2-13b

(d) falcon-11B

Figure 3: Comparing the performance *spread* of traditional prompts and MOF prompts. *Spread* is a metric for quantifying style-induced prompt brittleness and it is obtained by taking the difference between the best performing prompt (maximum accuracy) and the worst performing prompt (minimum accuracy). MOF prompts perform comparably or outperform traditional prompts in most datasets and in some datasets, traditional prompts have better performance.

prompt variations and 10 MOF prompt variations. From the 10 prompt variations, for both traditional and MOF prompts, we compute performance accuracies for each prompt format across various tasks. The goal is to compare the style-induced prompt brittleness between traditional prompts and MOF prompts. As in Sclar et al. (2024), we measure brittleness by calculating the performance *spread*, defined as the accuracy difference between the best-performing and worst-performing prompt formats. The evaluation pipelines for traditional and MOF prompts are summarized in Algorithm 1 and Algorithm 2, respectively.

Datasets We perform experiments on datasets covering various tasks from SuperNaturalInstructions (Mishra et al., 2022; Wang et al., 2022). Due to limited computational resources, we randomly selected 16 datasets and for each dataset we use 1000 samples and a batch size of 100. The datasets used are described in Table 3.

Baselines, metrics, and LLMs used In our experiments, we use traditional few-shot prompts as our baselines, where we compare the performance of LLMs when using traditional prompts versus MOF prompts. A primary focus of this work is to determine whether MOF prompting can minimize performance variations (*spread*) in LLMs when prompt format styles change. The performance *spread* is obtained by taking the difference between the highest performing prompt (denoted as "Max Accuracy" in the results tables) and the minimum performing prompt (denoted as "Min Accuracy"). The *spread* value ranges from 0.0 to 1.0, where values closer to 0.0 indicate that the LLM is more robust and less sensitive to style changes, while values closer to 1.0 suggest that the LLM is highly sensitive to these changes. Additionally, for both traditional and MOF prompts, we compute the average accuracy across all 10 prompt variations to assess the overall performance of MOF prompts relative to traditional prompts. We use four LLMs in our experiments: `falcon-11B`, `Llama-2-13b-hf`, `Llama-2-13b-chat-hf`, and `llama-3-70b-instruct`.

We emphasize that while MOF prompting can be applied and compared with other existing traditional prompting techniques, such as automatic

Table 1: Best performing format (*Max Accuracy*) and worst performing format (*Min Accuracy*) results for both traditional prompts and MOF prompts for `llama-3-70b-instruct`. MOF prompts improve the *Min Accuracy* and the *Max Accuracy* over traditional prompts in most cases.

Task	Traditional Prompts		MOF Prompts	
	Min Accuracy	Max Accuracy	Min Accuracy	Max Accuracy
task280	0.811	0.860	**0.880**	**0.900**
task317	0.139	0.229	**0.712**	**0.795**
task1347	0.248	0.524	**0.464**	**0.535**
task1612	0.624	0.839	**0.787**	**0.851**
task1502	0.443	**0.666**	**0.479**	0.639
task161	0.472	0.507	**0.475**	**0.512**

chain-of-thought (Auto-CoT) (Zhang et al., 2023) and the automatic prompt engineer (APE) (Zhou et al., 2023b), this paper focuses on applying MOF prompting to regular few-shot prompting and comparing their performances, due to limited computational resources.

Generating responses for evaluation To generate a response for a given question, a traditional or MOF prompt is combined with the question and then passed to an LLM to generate the response. The generated response is then compared to the ground-truth answer to calculate the model's accuracy.

3.2 Results

We perform experiments to evaluate whether MOF prompts reduce prompt brittleness in LLMs by comparing their *spread* with traditional prompts. We also assess improvements by analyzing the best (Max Accuracy) and worst (Min Accuracy) performing prompts. Finally, we evaluate overall performance by comparing the mean accuracies across all 10 prompt variations for both prompt types.

Minimizing prompt brittleness Figure 3 shows that MOF prompting effectively reduces style-induced prompt brittleness across several datasets and LLMs, with a notable 46% reduction in `task280` using `Llama-2-13b`. While MOF prompts generally perform as well or better than traditional prompts, exceptions occur in `task190` (`llama-3-70b-instruct`), `task1612` (`llama-2-13b-chat`), and `task320` (`falcon-11B`), where traditional prompts perform better. Investigating why MOF fails on these datasets is an important future direction.

Best and worst performing prompts Results for the best-performing prompt (Max Accuracy) and worst-performing prompt (Min Accuracy) for both traditional and MOF prompting are reported in Table 1. We observe that MOF prompting not only reduces spread but also improves both minimum and maximum accuracies. Average accuracy results across all 10 prompt variations for both traditional and MOF prompts are discussed in Appendix A.

4 Conclusion and future work

Addressing prompt brittleness remains a challenge, particularly when caused by changes in prompt format styles. In this work, we introduce a simple and efficient prompting technique, MOF, and evaluate its effectiveness in addressing style-induced prompt brittleness. The preliminary results are promising, with significant improvements over traditional prompting in many datasets, as shown in Figure 3.

Future directions include integrating MOF with techniques like chain-of-thought (CoT) and automatic prompt engineer (APE), comparing its performance with methods that aggregate results from multiple prompts such as AMA (Arora et al., 2022) and Template Ensembles (Voronov et al., 2024), and conducting experiments with larger LLMs like GPT-4, Claude 3.5 Sonnet, Falcon 40B, and Llama 3.1 405B. Additionally, analyzing MOF's failures on certain datasets is a crucial area for further exploration.

We hope this work will inspire further research into addressing prompt brittleness in LLMs, and the code for this project is publicly available on GitHub.[1]

[1]Code: github.com/lilianngweta/mof.

References

Martin Arjovsky, Léon Bottou, Ishaan Gulrajani, and David Lopez-Paz. 2019. Invariant risk minimization. *arXiv preprint arXiv:1907.02893*.

Simran Arora, Avanika Narayan, Mayee F Chen, Laurel Orr, Neel Guha, Kush Bhatia, Ines Chami, and Christopher Re. 2022. Ask me anything: A simple strategy for prompting language models. In *The Eleventh International Conference on Learning Representations*.

Tom B. Brown, Benjamin Mann, Nick Ryder, Melanie Subbiah, Jared Kaplan, Prafulla Dhariwal, Arvind Neelakantan, Pranav Shyam, Girish Sastry, Amanda Askell, Sandhini Agarwal, Ariel Herbert-Voss, Gretchen Krueger, Tom Henighan, Rewon Child, Aditya Ramesh, Daniel M. Ziegler, Jeffrey Wu, Clemens Winter, Christopher Hesse, Mark Chen, Eric Sigler, Mateusz Litwin, Scott Gray, Benjamin Chess, Jack Clark, Christopher Berner, Sam McCandlish, Alec Radford, Ilya Sutskever, and Dario Amodei. 2020. Language models are few-shot learners. In *Proceedings of the 34th International Conference on Neural Information Processing Systems*, NIPS '20, Red Hook, NY, USA. Curran Associates Inc.

Banghao Chen, Zhaofeng Zhang, Nicolas Langrené, and Shengxin Zhu. 2023. Unleashing the potential of prompt engineering in large language models: a comprehensive review. *arXiv preprint arXiv:2310.14735*.

Michael Feffer, Ronald Xu, Yuekai Sun, and Mikhail Yurochkin. 2024. Prompt exploration with prompt regression. *arXiv preprint arXiv:2405.11083*.

Jia He, Mukund Rungta, David Koleczek, Arshdeep Sekhon, Franklin X Wang, and Sadid Hasan. 2024. Does prompt formatting have any impact on llm performance? *arXiv preprint arXiv:2411.10541*.

Pritish Kamath, Akilesh Tangella, Danica Sutherland, and Nathan Srebro. 2021. Does invariant risk minimization capture invariance? In *International Conference on Artificial Intelligence and Statistics*, pages 4069–4077. PMLR.

Omar Khattab, Arnav Singhvi, Paridhi Maheshwari, Zhiyuan Zhang, Keshav Santhanam, Sri Vardhamanan A, Saiful Haq, Ashutosh Sharma, Thomas T. Joshi, Hanna Moazam, Heather Miller, Matei Zaharia, and Christopher Potts. 2024. DSPy: Compiling declarative language model calls into state-of-the-art pipelines. In *The Twelfth International Conference on Learning Representations*.

Shuangning Li, Matteo Sesia, Yaniv Romano, Emmanuel Candès, and Chiara Sabatti. 2021. Searching for consistent associations with a multi-environment knockoff filter. *arXiv preprint arXiv:2106.04118*.

Pengfei Liu, Weizhe Yuan, Jinlan Fu, Zhengbao Jiang, Hiroaki Hayashi, and Graham Neubig. 2023. Pre-train, prompt, and predict: A systematic survey of prompting methods in natural language processing. *ACM Computing Surveys*, 55(9):1–35.

Yao Lu, Max Bartolo, Alastair Moore, Sebastian Riedel, and Pontus Stenetorp. 2022. Fantastically ordered prompts and where to find them: Overcoming few-shot prompt order sensitivity. In *Proceedings of the 60th Annual Meeting of the Association for Computational Linguistics (Volume 1: Long Papers)*, pages 8086–8098, Dublin, Ireland. Association for Computational Linguistics.

Swaroop Mishra, Daniel Khashabi, Chitta Baral, and Hannaneh Hajishirzi. 2022. Cross-task generalization via natural language crowdsourcing instructions. In *ACL*.

Moran Mizrahi, Guy Kaplan, Dan Malkin, Rotem Dror, Dafna Shahaf, and Gabriel Stanovsky. 2024. State of what art? a call for multi-prompt llm evaluation. *Transactions of the Association for Computational Linguistics*, 12:933–949.

Vaishnavh Nagarajan, Anders Andreassen, and Behnam Neyshabur. 2020. Understanding the failure modes of out-of-distribution generalization. *arXiv preprint arXiv:2010.15775*.

Lilian Ngweta, Subha Maity, Alex Gittens, Yuekai Sun, and Mikhail Yurochkin. 2023. Simple disentanglement of style and content in visual representations. In *International Conference on Machine Learning*, pages 26063–26086. PMLR.

Felipe Maia Polo, Ronald Xu, Lucas Weber, Mírian Silva, Onkar Bhardwaj, Leshem Choshen, Allysson Flavio Melo de Oliveira, Yuekai Sun, and Mikhail Yurochkin. 2024. Efficient multi-prompt evaluation of llms. *arXiv preprint arXiv:2405.17202*.

Reid Pryzant, Dan Iter, Jerry Li, Yin Tat Lee, Chenguang Zhu, and Michael Zeng. 2023. Automatic prompt optimization with "gradient descent" and beam search. In *The 2023 Conference on Empirical Methods in Natural Language Processing*.

Alec Radford, Jeffrey Wu, Rewon Child, David Luan, Dario Amodei, Ilya Sutskever, et al. 2019. Language models are unsupervised multitask learners. *OpenAI blog*, 1(8):9.

Pranab Sahoo, Ayush Kumar Singh, Sriparna Saha, Vinija Jain, Samrat Mondal, and Aman Chadha. 2024. A systematic survey of prompt engineering in large language models: Techniques and applications. *arXiv preprint arXiv:2402.07927*.

Melanie Sclar, Yejin Choi, Yulia Tsvetkov, and Alane Suhr. 2024. Quantifying language models' sensitivity to spurious features in prompt design or: How i learned to start worrying about prompt formatting. In *The Twelfth International Conference on Learning Representations*.

Taylor Sorensen, Joshua Robinson, Christopher Rytting, Alexander Shaw, Kyle Rogers, Alexia Delorey, Mahmoud Khalil, Nancy Fulda, and David Wingate. 2022. An information-theoretic approach to prompt engineering without ground truth labels. In *Proceedings of the 60th Annual Meeting of the Association for Computational Linguistics (Volume 1: Long Papers)*, pages 819–862, Dublin, Ireland. Association for Computational Linguistics.

SM Tonmoy, SM Zaman, Vinija Jain, Anku Rani, Vipula Rawte, Aman Chadha, and Amitava Das. 2024. A comprehensive survey of hallucination mitigation techniques in large language models. *arXiv preprint arXiv:2401.01313*.

Anton Voronov, Lena Wolf, and Max Ryabinin. 2024. Mind your format: Towards consistent evaluation of in-context learning improvements. *arXiv preprint arXiv:2401.06766*.

Yoav Wald, Amir Feder, Daniel Greenfeld, and Uri Shalit. 2021. On calibration and out-of-domain generalization. *Advances in Neural Information Processing Systems*, 34.

Xingchen Wan, Ruoxi Sun, Hanjun Dai, Sercan Arik, and Tomas Pfister. 2023. Better zero-shot reasoning with self-adaptive prompting. In *Findings of the Association for Computational Linguistics: ACL 2023*, pages 3493–3514, Toronto, Canada. Association for Computational Linguistics.

Xingchen Wan, Ruoxi Sun, Hootan Nakhost, and Sercan O Arik. 2024. Teach better or show smarter? on instructions and exemplars in automatic prompt optimization. *arXiv preprint arXiv:2406.15708*.

Yizhong Wang, Swaroop Mishra, Pegah Alipoormolabashi, Yeganeh Kordi, Amirreza Mirzaei, Anjana Arunkumar, Arjun Ashok, Arut Selvan Dhanasekaran, Atharva Naik, David Stap, et al. 2022. Super-naturalinstructions:generalization via declarative instructions on 1600+ tasks. In *EMNLP*.

Jason Wei, Xuezhi Wang, Dale Schuurmans, Maarten Bosma, Fei Xia, Ed Chi, Quoc V Le, Denny Zhou, et al. 2022. Chain-of-thought prompting elicits reasoning in large language models. *Advances in neural information processing systems*, 35:24824–24837.

Chengrun Yang, Xuezhi Wang, Yifeng Lu, Hanxiao Liu, Quoc V. Le, Denny Zhou, and Xinyun Chen. 2024. Large language models as optimizers. *Preprint*, arXiv:2309.03409.

Fan Yin, Jesse Vig, Philippe Laban, Shafiq Joty, Caiming Xiong, and Chien-Sheng Wu. 2023. Did you read the instructions? rethinking the effectiveness of task definitions in instruction learning. In *Proceedings of the 61st Annual Meeting of the Association for Computational Linguistics (Volume 1: Long Papers)*, pages 3063–3079, Toronto, Canada. Association for Computational Linguistics.

Mingzhang Yin, Yixin Wang, and David M Blei. 2021. Optimization-based causal estimation from heterogenous environments. *arXiv preprint arXiv:2109.11990*.

Zhuosheng Zhang, Aston Zhang, Mu Li, and Alex Smola. 2023. Automatic chain of thought prompting in large language models. In *The Eleventh International Conference on Learning Representations*.

Han Zhou, Xingchen Wan, Lev Proleev, Diana Mincu, Jilin Chen, Katherine Heller, and Subhrajit Roy. 2023a. Batch calibration: Rethinking calibration for in-context learning and prompt engineering. *arXiv preprint arXiv:2309.17249*.

Yongchao Zhou, Andrei Ioan Muresanu, Ziwen Han, Keiran Paster, Silviu Pitis, Harris Chan, and Jimmy Ba. 2023b. Large language models are human-level prompt engineers. In *The Eleventh International Conference on Learning Representations*.

A Appendix

Average accuracy across all 10 prompt variations Up to this point, we have examined the performance in minimizing prompt brittleness, as well as the performance of the best and worst performing prompts. In this section, we focus on the performance of traditional and MOF prompts across all 10 prompt variations for each. The average accuracy across these 10 prompt variations for both traditional and MOF prompts is reported in Table 2. For all LLMs, we find that MOF prompts perform nearly as well as traditional prompts, with MOF prompts generally leading to significant overall mean accuracy improvements.

Algorithm 1 Traditional prompts evaluation pipeline

1: **Input**: Data $\mathcal{D}$
2: Create 10 variations of traditional prompts using FormatSpread (Sclar et al., 2024).
3: Use the created traditional prompt variations to generate responses.
4: Evaluate each of the 10 traditional prompts and save results.
5: Compute the average accuracy across all 10 traditional prompt variations.
6: Identify the best performing prompt, the worst performing prompt, and compute the spread.
7: **Output**: Return accuracies for the best performing prompt (max accuracy), worst performing prompt (min accuracy), the spread, and the average accuracy across all 10 traditional prompt variations.

Algorithm 2 MOF prompts evaluation pipeline

1: **Input**: Data $\mathcal{D}$
2: Create 10 variations of MOF prompts using a **modified** FormatSpread (Sclar et al., 2024) that incorporates diverse styles in the few-shot examples as illustrated in Figure 2.
3: Use the created MOF prompt variations to generate responses.
4: Evaluate each of the 10 MOF prompts and save results.
5: Compute the average accuracy across all 10 MOF prompt variations.
6: Identify the best performing prompt, worst performing prompt, and compute the spread.
7: **Output**: Return accuracies for the best performing prompt (max accuracy), worst performing prompt (min accuracy), the spread, and the average accuracy across all 10 MOF prompt variations.

Table 2: Average accuracy results across 10 prompt variations for traditional prompts (denoted as *Trad Mean Acc*) and MOF prompts (denoted as *MOF Mean Acc*). For all LLMs, MOF prompts perform comparable and in most cases have a higher overall average accuracy than traditional prompts.

(a) Llama-2-13b-chat

Task	Trad Mean Acc	MOF Mean Acc
task280	**0.853**	0.841
task317	0.578	**0.749**
task1612	0.471	**0.490**
task1502	**0.596**	0.579
task161	0.199	**0.278**

(b) Llama-2-13b

Task	Trad Mean Acc	MOF Mean Acc
task280	0.635	**0.842**
task317	0.564	**0.725**
task1612	**0.564**	0.505
task1502	**0.489**	0.485
task161	0.245	**0.371**

(c) falcon-11B

task	Trad Mean acc	MOF Mean acc
task280	0.727	**0.802**
task317	0.501	**0.672**
task1612	**0.638**	0.553
task1502	0.305	**0.493**
task161	**0.390**	0.387

(d) llama-3-70b-instruct

task	Trad Mean acc	MOF Mean acc
task280	0.836	**0.890**
task317	0.154	**0.770**
task1612	0.800	**0.821**
task1502	**0.600**	0.593
task161	**0.496**	0.492

Table 3: Datasets from SuperNaturalInstructions (Mishra et al., 2022; Wang et al., 2022) that we used in our experiments.

Dataset ID	Dataset Description
task280	A text categorization dataset that involves classifying sentences into four types of stereotypes: gender, profession, race, and religion.
task317	A stereotype detection dataset that involves classifying sentences into various types of stereotypes.
task1347	A text matching dataset that involves classifying the semantic similarity of two sentences on a scale of 0 - 5.
task1612	A textual entailment dataset derived from the SICK dataset, that involves accurately classifying labels to show the relationship between two sentences.
task1502	A toxic language detection dataset that involves classifying the type of tweet in HateXplain.
task161	A dataset focused on counting the words in a sentence that contain a specified letter.
task158	A dataset that involves counting the number of times a word occurs in a sentence.
task1186	A text quality evaluation dataset that involves evaluating the naturalness of system generated reference.
task190	A textual entailment dataset that involves choosing whether two given sentences agree, disagree, or neither with each other.
task1284	A text quality evaluation dataset that involves evaluating the informativeness of system generated reference.
task607	A toxic language detection that involves determining whether or not the post is intentionally offensive.
task163	A dataset that involves counting the number of words in the sentence that end with a specified letter.
task905	A toxic language detection dataset that involves determining whether the given category of a tweet is true or false.
task320	A stereotype detection dataset that involves determining whether a given target pertaining to race in two sentences is a stereotype.
task316	A stereotype detection dataset that involves classifying whether a sentence is stereotype or anti-stereotype.
task162	A dataset that involves counting the words in a sentence that begin with a specified letter.

Reliability of Distribution Predictions by LLMs: Insights from Counterintuitive Pseudo-Distributions

Toma Suzuki **Ayuki Katayama** **Seiji Gobara**
Ryo Tsujimoto **Hibiki Nakatani** **Kazuki Hayashi**
Yusuke Sakai **Hidetaka Kamigaito** **Taro Watanabe**

Nara Institute of Science and Technology (NAIST)

{suzuki.toma.ss5, katayama.ayuki.kc1, gobara.seiji.gt6
tsujimoto.ryo.tq0, nakatani.hibiki.ni4, hayashi.kazuki.hlj4,
sakai.yusuke.sr9, kamigaito.h, taro}@is.naist.jp

Abstract

The proportion of responses to a question and its options, known as the response distribution, enables detailed analysis of human society. Recent studies highlight the use of Large Language Models (LLMs) for predicting response distributions as a cost-effective survey method. However, the reliability of these predictions remains unclear. LLMs often generate answers by blindly following instructions rather than applying rational reasoning based on pretraining-acquired knowledge. This study investigates whether LLMs can rationally estimate distributions when presented with explanations of "artificially generated distributions" that are against commonsense. Specifically, we assess whether LLMs recognize counterintuitive explanations and adjust their predictions or simply follow these inconsistent explanations. Results indicate that smaller or less human-optimized LLMs tend to follow explanations uncritically, while larger or more optimized models are better at resisting counterintuitive explanations by leveraging their pretraining-acquired knowledge. These findings shed light on factors influencing distribution prediction performance in LLMs and are crucial for developing reliable distribution predictions using language models.

1 Introduction

The proportion of responses to a question and its options, known as the response distribution, provides valuable insights into human society beyond individual responses. Response distributions allow detailed analysis of relative differences between options (see Figure 1). Traditionally, they have been collected through labor-intensive and costly methods like surveys and interviews. Recent advances in Large Language Models (LLMs), however, offer new approaches for estimating response tendencies from textual data.

LLMs have demonstrated the ability to partially replicate human collective tendencies by analyzing

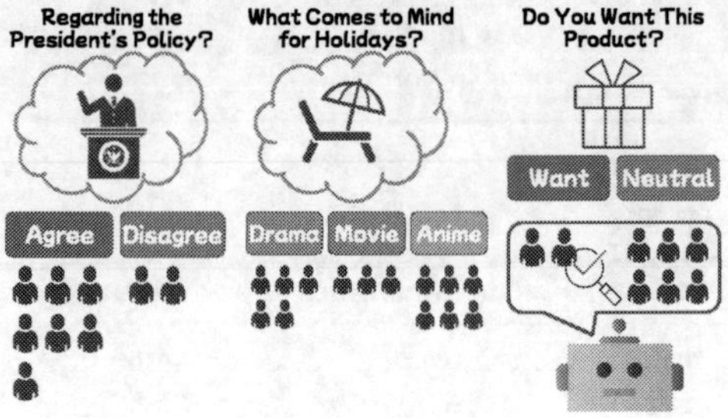

Figure 1: Example of response distribution. Analyzing both the ratios of each choice and the number of minority responses yields valuable insights.

output probabilities or aggregating multiple outputs (Santurkar et al., 2023; Paruchuri et al., 2024; Hayashi et al., 2025). Providing appropriate input information has further improved the accuracy of these predictions (Durmus et al., 2024; Santurkar et al., 2023; Meister et al., 2024). These methods show promise as cost-effective and scalable alternatives to traditional techniques.

However, LLMs are unlikely to acquire systematic ratio-related knowledge during pretraining, e.g., the expected proportions of responses to a question such as *"What food do you associate with Christmas?"*[1]. This raises concerns about whether their ratio predictions reflect meaningful understanding or mere prompt-following (Kavumba et al., 2022). Additionally, measuring true response distributions is challenging (Baan et al., 2022), complicating validation and emphasizing the need for objective evaluation standards. If LLM predictions lack rationality or reproducibility, their use in social decision-making could pose risks.

In this study, we propose a framework to evaluate the reliability of LLMs' distribution prediction. Specifically, we introduce counterintuitive pseudo-distributions by altering existing survey

[1]This questionnaire is taken from Yahoo! News Polls: https://news.yahoo.co.jp/polls/48833.

Proceedings of the 2025 Conference of the Nations of the Americas Chapter of the Association for Computational Linguistics: Human Language Technologies (Volume 4: Student Research Workshop), pages 538–550

data and examine whether LLMs adjust their predictions or simply follow inconsistent explanations. Our findings indicate that smaller or less human-optimized models tend to follow inconsistent explanations uncritically, whereas larger or preference-optimized models are better at resisting counter-intuitive distributions by leveraging pretraining-acquired knowledge. These results provide insights into factors influencing distribution prediction performance and highlight the variability in trustworthiness across different models, contributing to the development of more reliable distribution predictions using LLMs.

2 Background and Related Work

2.1 Predicting Distributions by LLMs

Previous studies have explored LLMs' distribution prediction performance in contexts like annotation disagreements, survey data across countries, real-world probabilities, and preference predictions (Nie et al., 2020; Santurkar et al., 2023; Ohagi et al., 2024; Paruchuri et al., 2024; Meister et al., 2024). Common approaches involve using output probabilities for response options or aggregating multiple outputs to approximate distributions (Santurkar et al., 2023; Jiang et al., 2024; Zhou et al., 2022). Some studies report better reasoning performance when LLMs directly generate distributions in textual form (Meister et al., 2024; Suzuki et al., 2024).

While these studies confirm that LLMs exhibit some distribution prediction capabilities, the underlying rationale behind specific ratio predictions and the extent to which pretraining or preference learning influences these predictions remain unclear. Moreover, several studies have found that simple uniform distribution baselines, such as assigning equal ratios to all options, can sometimes outperform LLM-based predictions (Meister et al., 2024; Suzuki et al., 2024). This raises concerns about whether LLMs genuinely possess predictive capabilities or merely capture broad tendencies while generating numerically arbitrary estimates. Some studies suggest that LLMs can at least estimate majority opinions, even for questions where a definitive correct answer does not exist (Talmor et al., 2019; Nie et al., 2020; Sakai et al., 2024b).

2.2 Reasoning Abilities in LLMs

Many studies evaluate the reasoning capabilities of LLMs (Wei et al., 2022; Chowdhery et al., 2022), but numerous tasks can be solved by relying on word relationships or salient terms from the pre-training corpus, complicating the assessment of intrinsic reasoning abilities (Manning, 2006; Hosseini et al., 2021; Kung and Peng, 2023; Han et al., 2024). To overcome this, methods like reversing logical relationships or substituting nouns with fictitious names have been proposed to test reasoning independently of memorized knowledge or symbolic manipulation (Wu et al., 2024; Sakai et al., 2024a). However, in distribution prediction, response ratio interrelations are crucial (Suzuki et al., 2024), and simple substitutions risk altering the problem's intent. For example, while *"I don't know"* and *"No response"* appear similar, their motivations differ: *"I don't know"* indicates a lack of understanding, whereas *"No response"* signifies an intentional decision not to answer. Conflating them may result in misinterpreting the distributions.

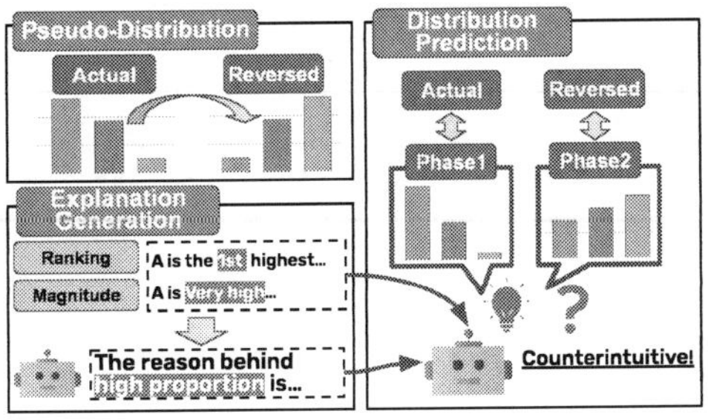

Figure 2: Overview of the proposed method. The actual distribution and a distribution with altered proportions are prepared, and explanations are generated for each. The score difference when estimating the distribution based on these explanations can be interpreted as the extent to which LLMs adjust based on commonsense knowledge.

3 Proposed Method

Our evaluation involves inputting explanations of the actual distribution along with the question, either to support or potentially distract the prediction, in order to better capture the model's true prediction ability. As shown in Figure 2, we design a two-phase experimental framework to evaluate whether LLMs can make rational distribution predictions based on knowledge acquired during pretraining.

Phase 1: Do LLMs Predict Distributions Based on Provided Explanations? This phase investigates whether LLMs can accurately predict response ratios from qualitative explanations. Figure 3 provides an overview of the explanation generation process. First, LLMs generate explanatory

Usage	*Example*
Question	Which team do you think will win the World Series, the Dodgers or the Yankees?
Options	Dodgers, Yankees, Not sure
Actual Distribution	{"Dodgers": *0.81*, "Yankees": 0.14, "Not sure": *0.05*}
Reversed Distribution	{"Dodgers": *0.05*, "Yankees": 0.14, "Not sure": *0.81*}
Ranking	The percentage for "Dodgers" is *the first highest*, "Yankees" is *the second highest*, and "Not sure" is *the third highest*.
Magnitude	The percentage for "Dodgers" is *very high*, the percentage for "Yankees" is *low*, and the percentage for "Not sure" is *low*.
Ranking Explanation	This distribution of responses is shaped by factors such as fan support, past team performance, and recent results. The high level of support for the "Dodgers" is likely due to their popularity, strong performance, or strong backing from local fans. The "Yankees," being a traditional powerhouse team with a large fan base, receive the second highest level of support. Those who chose "Not sure" likely reflect uncertainty about the outcome of the games or a lack of in-depth knowledge about baseball.

Table 1: An example of a question with its options and original proportions along with an altered set of proportions. Also shown are (a) Ranking and (b) Magnitude information for this question, along with a sample explanation based on (a) Ranking. This explanation was generated by the Qwen 2.5 (Qwen et al., 2024) model with 32B parameters. The original inputs were in Japanese, but are translated into English here.

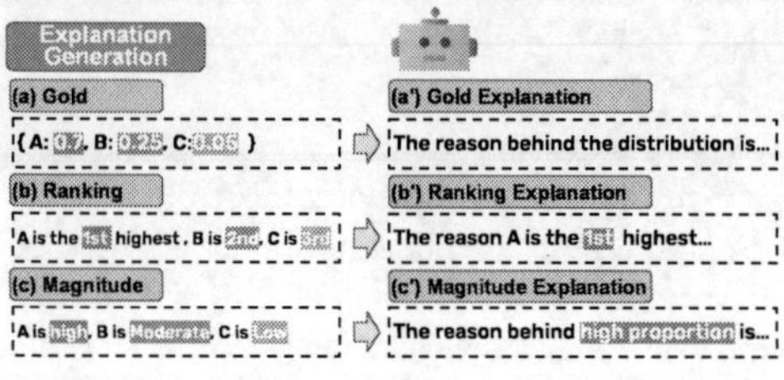

Figure 3: Overview of explanation generation. From (a) actual survey, (b) *Ranking* and (c) *Magnitude* are automatically derived. Then, based on (a, b, c), LLMs generate corresponding explanations (a', b', c').

descriptions of the target distributions based on three types of input information: (a) *Gold* (actual numerical distributions), (b) *Ranking* (order relationships, such as "1st," "2nd," or "3rd"), and (c) *Magnitude* (relative proportion sizes, such as "Very High," "High," or "Low"). The explanations generated from these respective inputs are referred to as (a') *GoldExp*, (b') *RankingExp*, and (c') *MagnitudeExp*. Next, these explanations are provided as input to the LLMs, which then generate reconstructed distributions. Finally, we compare the predicted distributions with the actual ones. An example question and its corresponding explanation used in this phase are shown in Table 1.

Note that evaluating LLMs solely based on the reconstructed distributions from their explanations (a', b', c') may introduce biases unrelated to distribution prediction capability, as the results could be affected by the models' explanation abilities. To address this, we also measure distribution prediction performance independent of explanation ability by predicting (a) directly from (b, c). Therefore, LLMs predict the distribution from five types of explanations (b, c, a', b', c'). Appendix A provides the prompts and detailed descriptions.

Phase 2: Do LLMs Adjust for Counterintuitive Explanations? In the second phase, we evaluated the ability of LLMs to recognize inconsistencies and adjust ratios by introducing pseudo-distributions that are commonsensically implausible. This experiment used the following two types of pseudo-distribution settings: (i) *Swapped*: The proportions of the first and second highest values are swapped. (ii) *Reversed*: The highest and lowest proportions are exchanged. These pseudo-distributions differ from actual distributions and are against commonsense expectations, with *Reversed* setting being considered greater inconsistent.

As in Phase 1, LLMs generate explanations from these pseudo-distributions and predict response distributions. If accuracy remains unchanged, the model is likely following explanations without evaluating plausibility. A decline in accuracy would suggest the model detects inconsistencies and adjusts predictions using commonsense reasoning.

4 Experimental Setup

Dataset We utilized the "Yahoo! News Polls"[2] provided by LY Corporation to create evaluation response distributions. This dataset comprises survey results related to articles published on Yahoo! News, covering the period from January 2020 to December 2024 in Japanese. We extracted questions with three options, resulting in a total of 714 items for analysis. Focusing on Japanese data allows us to reduce the ambiguity in predictions caused by cultural differences compared to conventional English datasets. Furthermore, since this data is based on freely cast votes on the internet, it is considered highly compatible with LLMs, which are primarily pretrained on internet data.

[2] https://news.yahoo.co.jp/polls

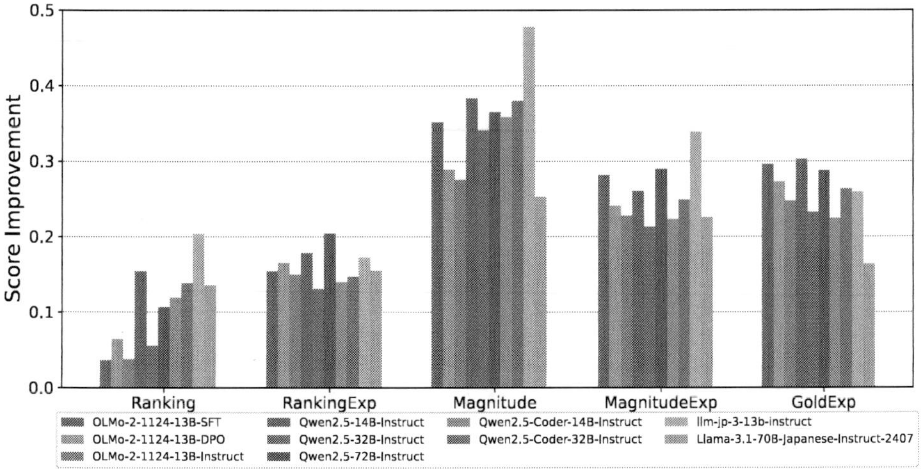

Figure 4: Score improvements across conditions compared to predictions without explanations. Improvements are visualized as positive values (upward).

LLMs We used ten high-performing open-source models, including Qwen 2.5 (Qwen et al., 2024) with 14B, 32B, and 72B parameters, as well as code-generation versions (Hui et al., 2024) with 14B and 32B parameters (all Instruct versions). These models were chosen to examine the effects of parameter size and code-learning on reasoning performance. To evaluate the impact of preference learning, we also included OLMo-2 (OLMo et al., 2024) in its SFT, DPO, and Instruct versions, where human preference alignment is progressively incorporated from supervised finetuning (SFT) to direct preference optimization (DPO) (Rafailov et al., 2023) and further to Reinforcement Learning with Verifiable Rewards (Instruct) (OLMo et al., 2024). Since the evaluation datasets are in Japanese, we employed llm-jp-3-13b-instruct (LLM-jp et al., 2024), which was pretrained in Japanese, and Llama-3.1-70B-Japanese-Instruct-2407 (Ishigami, 2024), a continuously trained Llama 3.1 (Dubey et al., 2024) on Japanese data. We used the 8-bit quantization inferences (Dettmers et al., 2022). We employed greedy decoding in inference.

Evaluation Methods To measure the similarity between the LLM predictions and the gold distributions, we adopted the Total Variation Distance (TVD). TVD is defined as the sum of the absolute differences between the gold (or pseudo-gold, in our experiments) values and the model's predicted values for each option. A lower TVD indicates closer alignment between the LLM predictions and the correct distribution. After minor output adjustments[3], over 90% of the data were analyzable as JSON-formatted response distributions. For cases where the valid response rate fell below 90%, results were recorded as reference values[4]. Finally, the average TVD, excluding missing values, was calculated.

5 Experimental Results

Phase 1: Do LLMs Predict Distributions Based on Explanations? Figure 4 shows the improvement in scores when models were provided with explanations generated based on these attributes, compared to when no explanation was given. All models showed improved scores across all conditions, reinforcing previous findings that providing appropriate contextual information enhances prediction performance.

For *Ranking*, which does not directly provide numerical hints, the condition *RankingExp* where the model supplements relevant background information, led to further score improvements in many models. In contrast, for *Magnitude*, which provides direct numerical hints, the condition *MagnitudeExp*, where an explanation accompanies the magnitude information, resulted in lower scores. This decline is likely due to the omission of explanations for minority options in some questions,

[3]This included converting full-width symbols to half-width and normalizing distributions to 1.0 if their sum equaled 100%.

[4]Details on valid rates are provided in Appendix C.

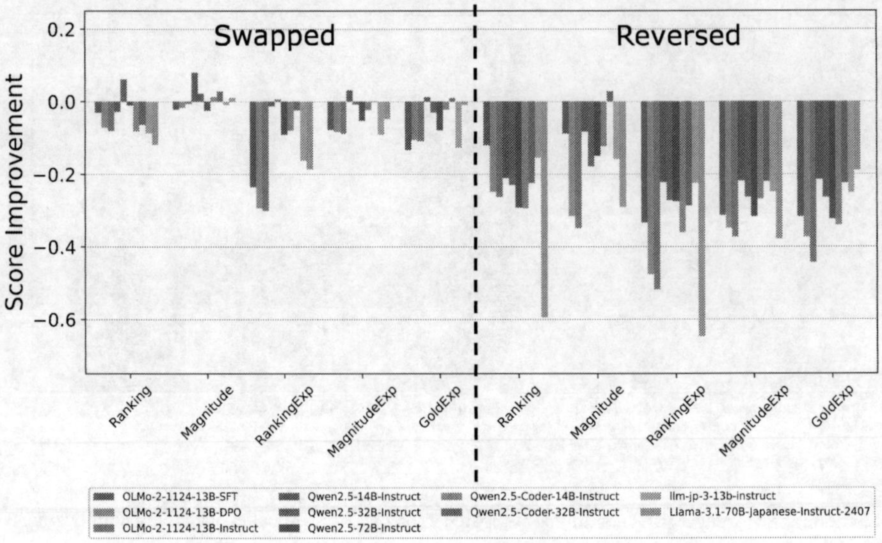

Figure 5: Changes in scores from the first phase of distribution prediction. Larger declines in scores indicate that the model, while considering the provided counterintuitive explanations, made commonsense-based adjustments to correct inconsistencies.

reducing the amount of provided information.

For *GoldExp*, where explanations were generated based on the actual response distributions, exhibited a similar level of improvement to *MagnitudeExp*. This suggests that even approximate magnitude-based explanations can enhance predictive accuracy to a degree comparable to using actual numerical values.

Phase 2: Do LLMs Adjust for Counterintuitive Explanations? Figure 5 shows the differences in average scores between the first and second phases, categorized by settings and conditions.

A large drop in scores was observed under *Reversed* condition, which introduces greater inconsistency compared to *Swapped*. This suggests that many models recognized contradictions between the pseudo-distributions and commonsense expectations. Notably, even in conditions where all models received the same *Ranking* and *Magnitude* information, *Reversed* condition resulted in a greater score decline than *Swapped*. This implies that LLMs leverage pretraining-acquired knowledge to some extent when making predictions.

However, the degree of adjustment varied across models. For example, in OLMo-2, adjustment capabilities improved progressively from SFT to DPO. This trend suggests that DPO, which is designed to align model outputs with human preferences (Rafailov et al., 2023), enhances response distribution prediction performance. Similarly in Qwen 2.5, while smaller models tended to follow counterintuitive explanations, larger models demonstrated more accurate predictions. This pattern was also observed in Japanese-trained models, where Llama-3.1-70B-Japanese showed superior adjustment capabilities. These findings indicate that model size, as well as pretraining and fine-tuning strategies, contribute to improving commonsense-based numerical adjustments.

6 Analysis

6.1 Naturalness as Causal Modeling

We re-tokenized the generated text and calculated its perplexity as a continuation of the input prompt[5]. A higher perplexity value indicates that the output is less natural for the model, allowing for a quantitative evaluation of deviations from pretraining expectations. The results are shown in Table 2.

For OLMo-2, there is little change in perplexity between *Actual* and *Reversed* conditions. In contrast, models larger than Qwen 2.5-14B exhibit increased perplexity in the *Ranking* setting when shifting from *Actual* to *Reversed*. This suggests that

[5]Due to tokenizer effects, the token sequence during re-tokenization may not always match the original generated sequence.

Model	Ranking			Magnitude		
	Actual	Swapped	Reversed	Actual	Swapped	Reversed
OLMo-2-1124-13B-SFT	1.14 ± 0.06	1.12 ± 0.05	1.10 ± 0.05	1.13 ± 0.06	1.12 ± 0.06	1.14 ± 0.07
OLMo-2-1124-13B-DPO	1.28 ± 0.07	1.26 ± 0.07	1.25 ± 0.07	1.28 ± 0.07	1.28 ± 0.07	1.28 ± 0.07
OLMo-2-1124-13B-Instruct	1.04 ± 0.04	$1.04 + 0.03$	1.04 ± 0.03	1.05 ± 0.04	1.05 ± 0.04	1.06 ± 0.05
Qwen2.5-14B-Instruct	1.47 ± 0.10	1.46 ± 0.09	1.46 ± 0.11	1.41 ± 0.11	1.37 ± 0.11	1.42 ± 0.10
Qwen2.5-32B-Instruct	1.12 ± 0.12	1.12 ± 0.10	1.32 ± 0.12	1.10 ± 0.09	1.12 ± 0.11	1.17 ± 0.14
Qwen2.5-72B-Instruct	1.07 ± 0.06	1.08 ± 0.06	1.13 ± 0.10	1.05 ± 0.04	1.06 ± 0.05	1.07 ± 0.06
Qwen2.5-Coder-14B-Instruct	1.08 ± 0.02	1.10 ± 0.03	1.09 ± 0.03	1.08 ± 0.03	1.07 ± 0.03	1.08 ± 0.03
Qwen2.5-Coder-32B-Instruct	1.32 ± 0.11	1.31 ± 0.09	1.35 ± 0.09	1.27 ± 0.13	1.26 ± 0.12	1.25 ± 0.13
llm-jp-3-13b-instruct	4.70 ± 1.19	4.69 ± 1.10	4.81 ± 1.11	4.96 ± 1.21	4.77 ± 1.11	4.90 ± 1.20
Llama-3.1-70B-Japanese-Instruct-2407	1.13 ± 0.09	1.16 ± 0.10	1.16 ± 0.10	1.11 ± 0.08	1.09 ± 0.08	1.12 ± 0.09

Table 2: Perplexities for cases with ranking or magnitude information under various settings. A higher perplexity value indicates that the output is less natural for the model.

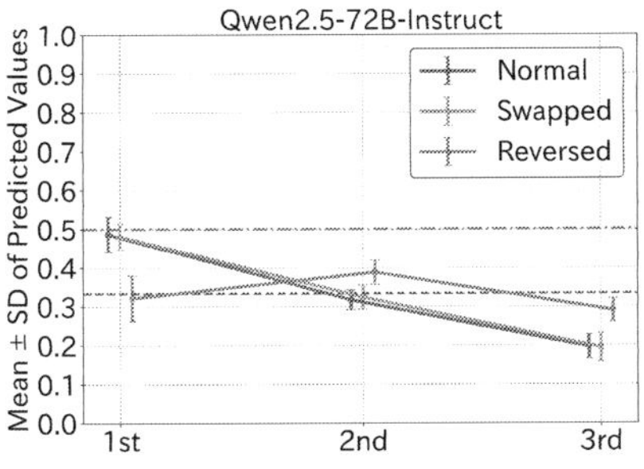

Figure 6: Average proportions predicted for ranked options when ranking information is provided.

while OLMo-2 and similarly sized models, such as Qwen 2.5-14B, do not necessarily treat counterintuitive predictions as unnatural at the internal representation level, larger models are more capable of doing so. Additionally, even for large models, the high standard deviation suggests that model behavior varies largely across different questions. These results suggest the usefulness of leveraging log probabilities of response options or sampling-based methods for distribution prediction, particularly when employing large-scale models.

6.2 Ranking Explanations and Predictions

Figure 6 shows the average proportions assigned by Qwen 2.5-72B to each ranked option when ranking information is available. Given probability distribution properties, the highest proportion does not fall below the dotted blue line indicating 0.33, and the lowest does not exceed 0.33 in the absence of ties. Consequently, models like Qwen 2.5-72B, which adjust values within a rational range, may be underestimated. In contrast, some cases highlight the risk of overestimating models that appear aligned with commonsense reasoning while violating probability constraints, as shown in Figure 7 in Appendix D.

Moreover, if the dataset lacks high-proportion options, score differences may be artificially low, leading to inaccurate model assessments. While our framework effectively distinguishes between instruction-following and commonsense-based predictions, it has limitations in evaluating probability rationality. Ensuring a balanced dataset mitigates these issues. Notably, previous studies have focused on refining distance metrics but overlooked dataset composition, highlighting the need for improvements in evaluation reliability.

7 Conclusion

This study examined whether language models predict response distributions based on rational reasoning with commonsense knowledge or merely follow instructions. By altering survey data ratios, we analyzed model predictions under inconsistent conditions. The experimental results showed that in the highly inconsistent *Reversed* condition, larger models and those fine-tuned with preference learning tended to correct inconsistencies using commonsense knowledge. Smaller models either showed little change or adapted to the inconsistencies. These findings evaluate aspects of prediction capability that conventional studies cannot measure and offer insights into selecting reliable models for distribution prediction. The proposed method is adaptable across languages and dataset types. Therefore, future work should include experiments in multilingual settings, including English, to investigate the influence of cultural factors. Additionally, measuring and mitigating biases using statistically reliable data, such as government-conducted surveys, is an important direction for future research.

Limitations

This study relies on internet-based survey data, which could contain biases. However, as internet data is widely used for pretraining language models and aligns with their commonsense knowledge, it serves as a meaningful baseline for evaluating pseudo-distribution consistency with commonsense reasoning. Ensuring statistical accuracy for practical applications remains a challenge, and model predictions may vary over time. While this study does not explicitly address temporal changes, Yahoo! News Polls is publicly accessible, allowing future research to refine statistical accuracy and analyze time-dependent trends. However, limited variations in the prompt templates used in our experiments could affect the experimental outcomes (Sakai et al., 2024c). Investigating such variability in outputs is also left for future work. In addition, we do not take into account factors of confidence during prediction when evaluating performance such as Ozaki et al. (2024). This perspective may yield more insights into our findings.

Ethical Considerations

Rather than reinforcing biases, this study aims to identify and examine them. By analyzing how biases manifest in model predictions, we contribute to a deeper understanding of their impact and support the development of fairer, more robust evaluation methods. Finally, Yahoo! News Polls, which was used in this study, is licensed for research use, so there are no license issues.

References

Joris Baan, Wilker Aziz, Barbara Plank, and Raquel Fernandez. 2022. Stop measuring calibration when humans disagree. In *Proceedings of the 2022 Conference on Empirical Methods in Natural Language Processing*, pages 1892–1915, Abu Dhabi, United Arab Emirates. Association for Computational Linguistics.

Aakanksha Chowdhery, Sharan Narang, Jacob Devlin, Maarten Bosma, Gaurav Mishra, Adam Roberts, Paul Barham, Hyung Won Chung, Charles Sutton, Sebastian Gehrmann, Parker Schuh, Kensen Shi, Sasha Tsvyashchenko, Joshua Maynez, Abhishek Rao, Parker Barnes, Yi Tay, Noam Shazeer, Vinodkumar Prabhakaran, Emily Reif, Nan Du, Ben Hutchinson, Reiner Pope, James Bradbury, Jacob Austin, Michael Isard, Guy Gur-Ari, Pengcheng Yin, Toju Duke, Anselm Levskaya, Sanjay Ghemawat, Sunipa Dev, Henryk Michalewski, Xavier Garcia, Vedant Misra, Kevin Robinson, Liam Fedus, Denny Zhou, Daphne Ippolito, David Luan, Hyeontaek Lim, Barret Zoph, Alexander Spiridonov, Ryan Sepassi, David Dohan, Shivani Agrawal, Mark Omernick, Andrew M. Dai, Thanumalayan Sankaranarayana Pillai, Marie Pellat, Aitor Lewkowycz, Erica Moreira, Rewon Child, Oleksandr Polozov, Katherine Lee, Zongwei Zhou, Xuezhi Wang, Brennan Saeta, Mark Diaz, Orhan Firat, Michele Catasta, Jason Wei, Kathy Meier-Hellstern, Douglas Eck, Jeff Dean, Slav Petrov, and Noah Fiedel. 2022. Palm: Scaling language modeling with pathways. *Preprint*, arXiv:2204.02311.

Tim Dettmers, Mike Lewis, Younes Belkada, and Luke Zettlemoyer. 2022. Gpt3.int8(): 8-bit matrix multiplication for transformers at scale. In *Advances in Neural Information Processing Systems*, volume 35, pages 30318–30332. Curran Associates, Inc.

Abhimanyu Dubey, Abhinav Jauhri, Abhinav Pandey, Abhishek Kadian, Ahmad Al-Dahle, Aiesha Letman, Akhil Mathur, Alan Schelten, Amy Yang, Angela Fan, Anirudh Goyal, Anthony Hartshorn, Aobo Yang, Archi Mitra, Archie Sravankumar, Artem Korenev, Arthur Hinsvark, Arun Rao, Aston Zhang, Aurelien Rodriguez, Austen Gregerson, Ava Spataru, Baptiste Roziere, Bethany Biron, Binh Tang, Bobbie Chern, Charlotte Caucheteux, Chaya Nayak, Chloe Bi, Chris Marra, Chris McConnell, Christian Keller, Christophe Touret, Chunyang Wu, Corinne Wong, Cristian Canton Ferrer, Cyrus Nikolaidis, Damien Allonsius, Daniel Song, Danielle Pintz, Danny Livshits, David Esiobu, Dhruv Choudhary, Dhruv Mahajan, Diego Garcia-Olano, Diego Perino, Dieuwke Hupkes, Egor Lakomkin, Ehab AlBadawy, Elina Lobanova, Emily Dinan, Eric Michael Smith, Filip Radenovic, Frank Zhang, Gabriel Synnaeve, Gabrielle Lee, Georgia Lewis Anderson, Graeme Nail, Gregoire Mialon, Guan Pang, Guillem Cucurell, Hailey Nguyen, Hannah Korevaar, Hu Xu, Hugo Touvron, Iliyan Zarov, Imanol Arrieta Ibarra, Isabel Kloumann, Ishan Misra, Ivan Evtimov, Jade Copet, Jaewon Lee, Jan Geffert, Jana Vranes, Jason Park, Jay Mahadeokar, Jeet Shah, Jelmer van der Linde, Jennifer Billock, Jenny Hong, Jenya Lee, Jeremy Fu, Jianfeng Chi, Jianyu Huang, Jiawen Liu, Jie Wang, Jiecao Yu, Joanna Bitton, Joe Spisak, Jongsoo Park, Joseph Rocca, Joshua Johnstun, Joshua Saxe, Junteng Jia, Kalyan Vasuden Alwala, Kartikeya Upasani, Kate Plawiak, Ke Li, Kenneth Heafield, Kevin Stone, Khalid El-Arini, Krithika Iyer, Kshitiz Malik, Kuenley Chiu, Kunal Bhalla, Lauren Rantala-Yeary, Laurens van der Maaten, Lawrence Chen, Liang Tan, Liz Jenkins, Louis Martin, Lovish Madaan, Lubo Malo, Lukas Blecher, Lukas Landzaat, Luke de Oliveira, Madeline Muzzi, Mahesh Pasupuleti, Mannat Singh, Manohar Paluri, Marcin Kardas, Mathew Oldham, Mathieu Rita, Maya Pavlova, Melanie Kambadur, Mike Lewis, Min Si, Mitesh Kumar Singh, Mona Hassan, Naman Goyal, Narjes Torabi, Nikolay Bashlykov, Nikolay Bogoychev, Niladri Chatterji, Olivier Duchenne, Onur Çelebi, Patrick Alrassy, Pengchuan Zhang, Pengwei Li, Petar Vasic, Peter Weng, Prajjwal Bhargava, Pratik Dubal, Praveen Krishnan, Punit Singh Koura, Puxin Xu, Qing He, Qingxiao

Dong, Ragavan Srinivasan, Raj Ganapathy, Ramon Calderer, Ricardo Silveira Cabral, Robert Stojnic, Roberta Raileanu, Rohit Girdhar, Rohit Patel, Romain Sauvestre, Ronnie Polidoro, Roshan Sumbaly, Ross Taylor, Ruan Silva, Rui Hou, Rui Wang, Saghar Hosseini, Sahana Chennabasappa, Sanjay Singh, Sean Bell, Seohyun Sonia Kim, Sergey Edunov, Shaoliang Nie, Sharan Narang, Sharath Raparthy, Sheng Shen, Shengye Wan, Shruti Bhosale, Shun Zhang, Simon Vandenhende, Soumya Batra, Spencer Whitman, Sten Sootla, Stephane Collot, Suchin Gururangan, Sydney Borodinsky, Tamar Herman, Tara Fowler, Tarek Sheasha, Thomas Georgiou, Thomas Scialom, Tobias Speckbacher, Todor Mihaylov, Tong Xiao, Ujjwal Karn, Vedanuj Goswami, Vibhor Gupta, Vignesh Ramanathan, Viktor Kerkez, Vincent Gonguet, Virginie Do, Vish Vogeti, Vladan Petrovic, Weiwei Chu, Wenhan Xiong, Wenyin Fu, Whitney Meers, Xavier Martinet, Xiaodong Wang, Xiaoqing Ellen Tan, Xinfeng Xie, Xuchao Jia, Xuewei Wang, Yaelle Goldschlag, Yashesh Gaur, Yasmine Babaei, Yi Wen, Yiwen Song, Yuchen Zhang, Yue Li, Yuning Mao, Zacharie Delpierre Coudert, Zheng Yan, Zhengxing Chen, Zoe Papakipos, Aaditya Singh, Aaron Grattafiori, Abha Jain, Adam Kelsey, Adam Shajnfeld, Adithya Gangidi, Adolfo Victoria, Ahuva Goldstand, Ajay Menon, Ajay Sharma, Alex Boesenberg, Alex Vaughan, Alexei Baevski, Allie Feinstein, Amanda Kallet, Amit Sangani, Anam Yunus, Andrei Lupu, Andres Alvarado, Andrew Caples, Andrew Gu, Andrew Ho, Andrew Poulton, Andrew Ryan, Ankit Ramchandani, Annie Franco, Aparajita Saraf, Arkabandhu Chowdhury, Ashley Gabriel, Ashwin Bharambe, Assaf Eisenman, Azadeh Yazdan, Beau James, Ben Maurer, Benjamin Leonhardi, Bernie Huang, Beth Loyd, Beto De Paola, Bhargavi Paranjape, Bing Liu, Bo Wu, Boyu Ni, Braden Hancock, Bram Wasti, Brandon Spence, Brani Stojkovic, Brian Gamido, Britt Montalvo, Carl Parker, Carly Burton, Catalina Mejia, Changhan Wang, Changkyu Kim, Chao Zhou, Chester Hu, Ching-Hsiang Chu, Chris Cai, Chris Tindal, Christoph Feichtenhofer, Damon Civin, Dana Beaty, Daniel Kreymer, Daniel Li, Danny Wyatt, David Adkins, David Xu, Davide Testuggine, Delia David, Devi Parikh, Diana Liskovich, Didem Foss, Dingkang Wang, Duc Le, Dustin Holland, Edward Dowling, Eissa Jamil, Elaine Montgomery, Eleonora Presani, Emily Hahn, Emily Wood, Erik Brinkman, Esteban Arcaute, Evan Dunbar, Evan Smothers, Fei Sun, Felix Kreuk, Feng Tian, Firat Ozgenel, Francesco Caggioni, Francisco Guzmán, Frank Kanayet, Frank Seide, Gabriela Medina Florez, Gabriella Schwarz, Gada Badeer, Georgia Swee, Gil Halpern, Govind Thattai, Grant Herman, Grigory Sizov, Guangyi, Zhang, Guna Lakshminarayanan, Hamid Shojanazeri, Han Zou, Hannah Wang, Hanwen Zha, Haroun Habeeb, Harrison Rudolph, Helen Suk, Henry Aspegren, Hunter Goldman, Ibrahim Damlaj, Igor Molybog, Igor Tufanov, Irina-Elena Veliche, Itai Gat, Jake Weissman, James Geboski, James Kohli, Japhet Asher, Jean-Baptiste Gaya, Jeff Marcus, Jeff Tang, Jennifer Chan, Jenny Zhen, Jeremy Reizenstein, Jeremy Teboul, Jessica Zhong, Jian Jin, Jingyi Yang, Joe Cummings, Jon Carvill, Jon Shepard, Jonathan McPhie, Jonathan Torres, Josh Ginsburg, Junjie Wang, Kai Wu, Kam Hou U, Karan Saxena, Karthik Prasad, Kartikay Khandelwal, Katayoun Zand, Kathy Matosich, Kaushik Veeraraghavan, Kelly Michelena, Keqian Li, Kun Huang, Kunal Chawla, Kushal Lakhotia, Kyle Huang, Lailin Chen, Lakshya Garg, Lavender A, Leandro Silva, Lee Bell, Lei Zhang, Liangpeng Guo, Licheng Yu, Liron Moshkovich, Luca Wehrstedt, Madian Khabsa, Manav Avalani, Manish Bhatt, Maria Tsimpoukelli, Martynas Mankus, Matan Hasson, Matthew Lennie, Matthias Reso, Maxim Groshev, Maxim Naumov, Maya Lathi, Meghan Keneally, Michael L. Seltzer, Michal Valko, Michelle Restrepo, Mihir Patel, Mik Vyatskov, Mikayel Samvelyan, Mike Clark, Mike Macey, Mike Wang, Miquel Jubert Hermoso, Mo Metanat, Mohammad Rastegari, Munish Bansal, Nandhini Santhanam, Natascha Parks, Natasha White, Navyata Bawa, Nayan Singhal, Nick Egebo, Nicolas Usunier, Nikolay Pavlovich Laptev, Ning Dong, Ning Zhang, Norman Cheng, Oleg Chernoguz, Olivia Hart, Omkar Salpekar, Ozlem Kalinli, Parkin Kent, Parth Parekh, Paul Saab, Pavan Balaji, Pedro Rittner, Philip Bontrager, Pierre Roux, Piotr Dollar, Polina Zvyagina, Prashant Ratanchandani, Pritish Yuvraj, Qian Liang, Rachad Alao, Rachel Rodriguez, Rafi Ayub, Raghotham Murthy, Raghu Nayani, Rahul Mitra, Raymond Li, Rebekkah Hogan, Robin Battey, Rocky Wang, Rohan Maheswari, Russ Howes, Ruty Rinott, Sai Jayesh Bondu, Samyak Datta, Sara Chugh, Sara Hunt, Sargun Dhillon, Sasha Sidorov, Satadru Pan, Saurabh Verma, Seiji Yamamoto, Sharadh Ramaswamy, Shaun Lindsay, Shaun Lindsay, Sheng Feng, Shenghao Lin, Shengxin Cindy Zha, Shiva Shankar, Shuqiang Zhang, Shuqiang Zhang, Sinong Wang, Sneha Agarwal, Soji Sajuyigbe, Soumith Chintala, Stephanie Max, Stephen Chen, Steve Kehoe, Steve Satterfield, Sudarshan Govindaprasad, Sumit Gupta, Sungmin Cho, Sunny Virk, Suraj Subramanian, Sy Choudhury, Sydney Goldman, Tal Remez, Tamar Glaser, Tamara Best, Thilo Kohler, Thomas Robinson, Tianhe Li, Tianjun Zhang, Tim Matthews, Timothy Chou, Tzook Shaked, Varun Vontimitta, Victoria Ajayi, Victoria Montanez, Vijai Mohan, Vinay Satish Kumar, Vishal Mangla, Vítor Albiero, Vlad Ionescu, Vlad Poenaru, Vlad Tiberiu Mihailescu, Vladimir Ivanov, Wei Li, Wenchen Wang, Wenwen Jiang, Wes Bouaziz, Will Constable, Xiaocheng Tang, Xiaofang Wang, Xiaojian Wu, Xiaolan Wang, Xide Xia, Xilun Wu, Xinbo Gao, Yanjun Chen, Ye Hu, Ye Jia, Ye Qi, Yenda Li, Yilin Zhang, Ying Zhang, Yossi Adi, Youngjin Nam, Yu, Wang, Yuchen Hao, Yundi Qian, Yuzi He, Zach Rait, Zachary DeVito, Zef Rosnbrick, Zhaoduo Wen, Zhenyu Yang, and Zhiwei Zhao. 2024. The llama 3 herd of models. *Preprint*, arXiv:2407.21783.

Esin Durmus, Karina Nguyen, Thomas Liao, Nicholas Schiefer, Amanda Askell, Anton Bakhtin, Carol Chen, Zac Hatfield-Dodds, Danny Hernandez, Nicholas Joseph, Liane Lovitt, Sam McCandlish, Orowa Sikder, Alex Tamkin, Janel Thamkul, Jared Kaplan, Jack Clark, and Deep Ganguli. 2024. Towards measuring the representation of subjective global opinions in language models. In *First Conference on Language Modeling*.

Simeng Han, Hailey Schoelkopf, Yilun Zhao, Zhenting Qi, Martin Riddell, Wenfei Zhou, James Coady, David Peng, Yujie Qiao, Luke Benson, Lucy Sun, Alexander Wardle-Solano, Hannah Szabó, Ekaterina Zubova, Matthew Burtell, Jonathan Fan, Yixin Liu, Brian Wong, Malcolm Sailor, Ansong Ni, Linyong Nan, Jungo Kasai, Tao Yu, Rui Zhang, Alexander Fabbri, Wojciech Maciej Kryscinski, Semih Yavuz, Ye Liu, Xi Victoria Lin, Shafiq Joty, Yingbo Zhou, Caiming Xiong, Rex Ying, Arman Cohan, and Dragomir Radev. 2024. FOLIO: Natural language reasoning with first-order logic. In *Proceedings of the 2024 Conference on Empirical Methods in Natural Language Processing*, pages 22017–22031, Miami, Florida, USA. Association for Computational Linguistics.

Kazuki Hayashi, Kazuma Onishi, Toma Suzuki, Yusuke Ide, Seiji Gobara, Shigeki Saito, Yusuke Sakai, Hidetaka Kamigaito, Katsuhiko Hayashi, and Taro Watanabe. 2025. IRR: Image review ranking framework for evaluating vision-language models. In *Proceedings of the 31st International Conference on Computational Linguistics*, pages 9939–9956, Abu Dhabi, UAE. Association for Computational Linguistics.

Arian Hosseini, Siva Reddy, Dzmitry Bahdanau, R Devon Hjelm, Alessandro Sordoni, and Aaron Courville. 2021. Understanding by understanding not: Modeling negation in language models. In *Proceedings of the 2021 Conference of the North American Chapter of the Association for Computational Linguistics: Human Language Technologies*, pages 1301–1312, Online. Association for Computational Linguistics.

Binyuan Hui, Jian Yang, Zeyu Cui, Jiaxi Yang, Dayiheng Liu, Lei Zhang, Tianyu Liu, Jiajun Zhang, Bowen Yu, Keming Lu, Kai Dang, Yang Fan, Yichang Zhang, An Yang, Rui Men, Fei Huang, Bo Zheng, Yibo Miao, Shanghaoran Quan, Yunlong Feng, Xingzhang Ren, Xuancheng Ren, Jingren Zhou, and Junyang Lin. 2024. Qwen2.5-coder technical report. *Preprint*, arXiv:2409.12186.

Ryosuke Ishigami. 2024. cyberagent/llama-3.1-70b-japanese-instruct-2407.

Liwei Jiang, Sydney Levine, and Yejin Choi. 2024. Can language models reason about individualistic human values and preferences? In *Pluralistic Alignment Workshop at NeurIPS 2024*.

Pride Kavumba, Ryo Takahashi, and Yusuke Oda. 2022. Are prompt-based models clueless? In *Proceedings of the 60th Annual Meeting of the Association for Computational Linguistics (Volume 1: Long Papers)*, pages 2333–2352, Dublin, Ireland. Association for Computational Linguistics.

Po-Nien Kung and Nanyun Peng. 2023. Do models really learn to follow instructions? an empirical study of instruction tuning. In *Proceedings of the 61st Annual Meeting of the Association for Computational Linguistics (Volume 2: Short Papers)*, pages 1317–1328, Toronto, Canada. Association for Computational Linguistics.

LLM-jp, :, Akiko Aizawa, Eiji Aramaki, Bowen Chen, Fei Cheng, Hiroyuki Deguchi, Rintaro Enomoto, Kazuki Fujii, Kensuke Fukumoto, Takuya Fukushima, Namgi Han, Yuto Harada, Chikara Hashimoto, Tatsuya Hiraoka, Shohei Hisada, Sosuke Hosokawa, Lu Jie, Keisuke Kamata, Teruhito Kanazawa, Hiroki Kanezashi, Hiroshi Kataoka, Satoru Katsumata, Daisuke Kawahara, Seiya Kawano, Atsushi Keyaki, Keisuke Kiryu, Hirokazu Kiyomaru, Takashi Kodama, Takahiro Kubo, Yohei Kuga, Ryoma Kumon, Shuhei Kurita, Sadao Kurohashi, Conglong Li, Taiki Maekawa, Hiroshi Matsuda, Yusuke Miyao, Kentaro Mizuki, Sakae Mizuki, Yugo Murawaki, Akim Mousterou, Ryo Nakamura, Taishi Nakamura, Kouta Nakayama, Tomoka Nakazato, Takuro Niitsuma, Jiro Nishitoba, Yusuke Oda, Hayato Ogawa, Takumi Okamoto, Naoaki Okazaki, Yohei Oseki, Shintaro Ozaki, Koki Ryu, Rafal Rzepka, Keisuke Sakaguchi, Shota Sasaki, Satoshi Sekine, Kohei Suda, Saku Sugawara, Issa Sugiura, Hiroaki Sugiyama, Hisami Suzuki, Jun Suzuki, Toyotaro Suzumura, Kensuke Tachibana, Yu Takagi, Kyosuke Takami, Koichi Takeda, Masashi Takeshita, Masahiro Tanaka, Kenjiro Taura, Arseny Tolmachev, Nobuhiro Ueda, Zhen Wan, Shuntaro Yada, Sakiko Yahata, Yuya Yamamoto, Yusuke Yamauchi, Hitomi Yanaka, Rio Yokota, and Koichiro Yoshino. 2024. Llm-jp: A cross-organizational project for the research and development of fully open japanese llms. *Preprint*, arXiv:2407.03963.

Christopher D. Manning. 2006. Local textual inference: It's hard to circumscribe, but you know it when you see it—and nlp needs it. pages 1–12.

Nicole Meister, Carlos Guestrin, and Tatsunori Hashimoto. 2024. Benchmarking distributional alignment of large language models. *Preprint*, arXiv:2411.05403.

Yixin Nie, Xiang Zhou, and Mohit Bansal. 2020. What can we learn from collective human opinions on natural language inference data? In *Proceedings of the 2020 Conference on Empirical Methods in Natural Language Processing (EMNLP)*, pages 9131–9143, Online. Association for Computational Linguistics.

Masaya Ohagi, Junya Takayama, Tomoya Mizumoto, and Katsumasa Yoshikawa. 2024. Proposal of a response distribution prediction method considering relationships between choices using large language models [大規模言語モデルによる選択肢間の関係を考慮した回答分布予測手法の提案]. In *Technical Report of the 260th Special Interest Group on Natural Language Processing*, volume 16, pages 1–13, Kanazawa, Japan. Information Processing Society of Japan. (In Japanese).

Team OLMo, Pete Walsh, Luca Soldaini, Dirk Groeneveld, Kyle Lo, Shane Arora, Akshita Bhagia, Yuling Gu, Shengyi Huang, Matt Jordan, Nathan Lambert, Dustin Schwenk, Oyvind Tafjord, Taira Anderson, David Atkinson, Faeze Brahman, Christopher Clark, Pradeep Dasigi, Nouha Dziri, Michal Guerquin, Hamish Ivison, Pang Wei Koh, Jiacheng Liu, Saumya Malik, William Merrill, Lester James V. Miranda, Jacob Morrison, Tyler Murray, Crystal Nam, Valentina Pyatkin, Aman Rangapur, Michael Schmitz, Sam Skjonsberg, David Wadden, Christopher Wilhelm, Michael Wilson, Luke Zettlemoyer, Ali Farhadi, Noah A. Smith, and Hannaneh Hajishirzi. 2024. 2 olmo 2 furious.

Shintaro Ozaki, Yuta Kato, Siyuan Feng, Masayo Tomita, Kazuki Hayashi, Ryoma Obara, Masafumi Oyamada, Katsuhiko Hayashi, Hidetaka Kamigaito, and Taro Watanabe. 2024. Understanding the impact of confidence in retrieval augmented generation: A case study in the medical domain. *Preprint*, arXiv:2412.20309.

Akshay Paruchuri, Jake Garrison, Shun Liao, John B Hernandez, Jacob Sunshine, Tim Althoff, Xin Liu, and Daniel McDuff. 2024. What are the odds? language models are capable of probabilistic reasoning. In *Proceedings of the 2024 Conference on Empirical Methods in Natural Language Processing*, pages 11712–11733, Miami, Florida, USA. Association for Computational Linguistics.

Qwen, :, An Yang, Baosong Yang, Beichen Zhang, Binyuan Hui, Bo Zheng, Bowen Yu, Chengyuan Li, Dayiheng Liu, Fei Huang, Haoran Wei, Huan Lin, Jian Yang, Jianhong Tu, Jianwei Zhang, Jianxin Yang, Jiaxi Yang, Jingren Zhou, Junyang Lin, Kai Dang, Keming Lu, Keqin Bao, Kexin Yang, Le Yu, Mei Li, Mingfeng Xue, Pei Zhang, Qin Zhu, Rui Men, Runji Lin, Tianhao Li, Tingyu Xia, Xingzhang Ren, Xuancheng Ren, Yang Fan, Yang Su, Yichang Zhang, Yu Wan, Yuqiong Liu, Zeyu Cui, Zhenru Zhang, and Zihan Qiu. 2024. Qwen2.5 technical report. *Preprint*, arXiv:2412.15115.

Rafael Rafailov, Archit Sharma, Eric Mitchell, Christopher D Manning, Stefano Ermon, and Chelsea Finn. 2023. Direct preference optimization: Your language model is secretly a reward model. In *Advances in Neural Information Processing Systems*, volume 36, pages 53728–53741. Curran Associates, Inc.

Yusuke Sakai, Hidetaka Kamigaito, Katsuhiko Hayashi, and Taro Watanabe. 2024a. Does pre-trained language model actually infer unseen links in knowledge graph completion? In *Proceedings of the 2024 Conference of the North American Chapter of the Association for Computational Linguistics: Human Language Technologies (Volume 1: Long Papers)*, pages 8091–8106, Mexico City, Mexico. Association for Computational Linguistics.

Yusuke Sakai, Hidetaka Kamigaito, and Taro Watanabe. 2024b. mCSQA: Multilingual commonsense reasoning dataset with unified creation strategy by language models and humans. In *Findings of the Association for Computational Linguistics: ACL 2024*, pages 14182–14214, Bangkok, Thailand. Association for Computational Linguistics.

Yusuke Sakai, Adam Nohejl, Jiangnan Hang, Hidetaka Kamigaito, and Taro Watanabe. 2024c. Toward the evaluation of large language models considering score variance across instruction templates. In *Proceedings of the 7th BlackboxNLP Workshop: Analyzing and Interpreting Neural Networks for NLP*, pages 499–529, Miami, Florida, US. Association for Computational Linguistics.

Shibani Santurkar, Esin Durmus, Faisal Ladhak, Cinoo Lee, Percy Liang, and Tatsunori Hashimoto. 2023. Whose opinions do language models reflect? In *Proceedings of the 40th International Conference on Machine Learning*, volume 202 of *Proceedings of Machine Learning Research*, pages 29971–30004. PMLR.

Toma Suzuki, Ayuki Katayama, Seiji Gobara, Ryo Tsujimoto, Hibiki Nakatani, Kazuki Hayashi, Yusuke Sakai, Hidetaka Kamigaito, and Taro Watanabe. 2024. Proposal of a response distribution prediction method considering relationships between choices using large language models [大規模言語モデルによる選択肢間の関係を考慮した回答分布予測手法の提案]. In *Technical Report of the 262nd Special Interest Group on Natural Language Processing*, volume 40, pages 1–14, Nagoya, Japan. Information Processing Society of Japan. (In Japanese).

Alon Talmor, Jonathan Herzig, Nicholas Lourie, and Jonathan Berant. 2019. CommonsenseQA: A question answering challenge targeting commonsense knowledge. In *Proceedings of the 2019 Conference of the North American Chapter of the Association for Computational Linguistics: Human Language Technologies, Volume 1 (Long and Short Papers)*, pages 4149–4158, Minneapolis, Minnesota. Association for Computational Linguistics.

Jason Wei, Xuezhi Wang, Dale Schuurmans, Maarten Bosma, brian ichter, Fei Xia, Ed Chi, Quoc V Le, and Denny Zhou. 2022. Chain-of-thought prompting elicits reasoning in large language models. In *Advances in Neural Information Processing Systems*, volume 35, pages 24824–24837. Curran Associates, Inc.

Zhaofeng Wu, Linlu Qiu, Alexis Ross, Ekin Akyürek, Boyuan Chen, Bailin Wang, Najoung Kim, Jacob Andreas, and Yoon Kim. 2024. Reasoning or reciting? exploring the capabilities and limitations of language models through counterfactual tasks. In *Proceedings of the 2024 Conference of the North American Chapter of the Association for Computational Linguistics: Human Language Technologies (Volume 1: Long Papers)*, pages 1819–1862, Mexico City, Mexico. Association for Computational Linguistics.

Xiang Zhou, Yixin Nie, and Mohit Bansal. 2022. Distributed NLI: Learning to predict human opinion distributions for language reasoning. In *Findings of the Association for Computational Linguistics: ACL 2022*, pages 972–987, Dublin, Ireland. Association for Computational Linguistics.

A Prompt Details

The templates used in our experiments are shown in Table 3. Additionally, explanations of proportions were mechanically replaced based on the rules provided in Table 4.

In the first phase, LLMs were instructed to generate explanatory descriptions of survey results, excluding specific numerical values or ratios, while considering the survey periods. In the second phase, these generated descriptions were used as prompts, and LLMs were tasked with predicting response distributions in JSON format (Meister et al., 2024; Suzuki et al., 2024). If the explanations contained numerical values or ratios, they were replaced with "—" using regular expressions before being provided to the model. To ensure correct output formatting, JSON-format examples were also included in the prompt.

Usage Scenario	*Template*
Explanation Generation (Translated)	Please explain why the response distribution for the following question turned out this way, without including any specific numbers or percentages. Keep your explanation concise and within 300 characters. Survey period: October 21, 2024 – October 31, 2024 Question: Which team do you think will win the World Series, the Dodgers or the Yankees? Options: "Dodgers", "Yankees", "Not sure" Response Distribution: The percentage for "Dodgers" is the first highest, "Yankees" is the second highest, and "Not sure" is the third highest. Explanation:
Explanation Generation	以下の質問の回答分布について、「なぜこのような分布になったのか」を、 **具体的な数値や割合を含めないで**説明してください。 説明は300文字以内で簡潔に記述してください。 実施期間: 2024-10-21〜2024-10-31 質問: ドジャースとヤンキース、どちらがワールドシリーズを制覇すると思いますか？ 選択肢: "ドジャース","ヤンキース","わからない" 回答分布: 「ドジャース」の割合は1番目に高く、「ヤンキース」は2番目、「わからない」は3番目に高いです。 説明:
Distribution Prediction (Translated)	Please predict the response distribution for the following question and options, based on the explanation provided. Your answer should be in JSON format, and the sum of the proportions for all choices must equal 1.0. Survey period: October 21, 2024 – October 31, 2024 Question: Which team do you think will win the World Series, the Dodgers or the Yankees? Options: "Dodgers", "Yankees", "Not sure" Explanation: This distribution of responses is shaped by factors such as fan support, past team performance, and recent results. The high level of support for the "Dodgers" is likely due to their popularity, strong performance, or strong backing from local fans. The "Yankees," being a traditional powerhouse team with a large fan base, receive the second highest level of support. Those who chose "Not sure" likely reflect uncertainty about the outcome of the games or a lack of in-depth knowledge about baseball. Example output format: {"Dodgers": –, "Yankees": –, "Not sure": –} Response distribution:
Explanation Generation	以下のアンケートの質問と選択肢について、説明を参考に回答分布を予測してください。 回答はJSON形式で記述し、各選択肢の比率の合計が1.0になるよう調整してください。 実施期間: 2024-10-21〜2024-10-31 質問: ドジャースとヤンキース、どちらがワールドシリーズを制覇すると思いますか？ 選択肢: "ドジャース","ヤンキース","わからない" 説明: この回答分布は、ファンの支持やチームの過去のパフォーマンス、最近の成績などの要因によって形成されています。 「ドジャース」への支持が高いのは、彼らの人気や優れたパフォーマンス、あるいは地元ファンからの強い支持があるからでしょう。 「ヤンキース」も伝統のある強豪チームであり、多くのファンや支持者がいるため、2番目の支持を得ています。 「わからない」を選んだ人々は、試合の結果に対する不確実性や、野球の専門知識が不足していることを示しています。 回答分布の出力例: {"ドジャース": –, "ヤンキース": –, "わからない": –} 回答分布:

Table 3: Details of the prompts used in the experiment. All inputs were provided in Japanese. For reference, English translations of the prompts are also included.

Ratio Range	*Descriptive Category*
$x \geq 0.75$	Very High (非常に高い)
$0.5 \leq x < 0.75$	High (高い)
$0.25 \leq x < 0.5$	Moderate (中程度)
$x < 0.25$	Low (低い)

Table 4: Correspondence between ratio ranges and descriptive categories (Japanese are provided in parentheses).

B Spearman's Rank Correlation Coefficient

We calculated Spearman's rank correlation coefficients for model rankings based on distribution prediction scores without explanations and those with various types of added explanations (See Table 5). The rankings with commonsense explanations showed significant positive correlations, whereas there was little correlation with the rankings based on predictions from counterintuitive explanations. This

Condition	Explanation	Correlation Coefficient	p-value
Actual	Ranking	0.49	0.1497
	Magnitude	0.15	0.6761
	Ranking/Explanation	*0.94*	*0.0001*
	Magnitude/Explanation	*0.81*	*0.0049*
	Gold/Explanation	*0.70*	*0.0251*
Swapped	Ranking	*0.65*	*0.0425*
	Explanation	0.18	0.6272
	Ranking/Explanation	0.43	0.2145
	Magnitude/Explanation	*0.64*	*0.0479*
	Gold/Explanation	0.44	0.2004
Reversed	Ranking	-0.56	0.0897
	Explanation	-0.36	0.3104
	Ranking/Explanation	-0.16	0.6515
	Magnitude/Explanation	-0.03	0.9338
	Gold/Explanation	0.28	0.4250

Table 5: Spearman's Rank Correlation Coefficients and p-values Between Score Rankings.

suggests that instruction-following performance and commonsense-based ratio prediction capabilities may independently influence model performance.

C Valid Response Rate

Table 6 shows the average Valid Response Rate across all conditions for each setting. The Valid Response Rate represents the proportion of model outputs that could be parsed as response distributions in JSON format. Asterisks (*) indicate cases where the Valid Response Rate did not exceed the threshold of 90%. Under the reversed setting/ranking condition for Llama-3.1-70B-Japanese-Instruct-2407, the valid response rate fell to 89.5%, below the 90% threshold.

Model	*No Explanation*	*Actual*	*Swapped*	*Reversed*
OLMo-2-1124-13B-SFT	*89.9**	95.8	97.1	97.8
OLMo-2-1124-13B-DPO	92.9	99.1	98.9	99.2
OLMo-2-1124-13B-Instruct	99.7	99.8	99.7	99.7
Qwen2.5-14B-Instruct	99.4	98.3	98.3	97.8
Qwen2.5-32B-Instruct	100.0	100.0	100.0	100.0
Qwen2.5-72B-Instruct	100.0	100.0	100.0	100.0
Qwen2.5-Coder-14B-Instruct	100.0	100.0	100.0	100.0
Qwen2.5-Coder-32B-Instruct	99.9	99.4	99.7	99.4
llm-jp-3-13b-instruct	100.0	99.9	99.9	99.9
Llama-3.1-70B-Japanese-Instruct-2407	95.5	95.3	95.5	*93.7**

Table 6: Average Valid Response Rate (%) Across Settings

D Ranking Information and Actual Predicted Values

As in Section 6.2, we plotted the average values assigned to each option when ranking information was provided for all models in Figure 7. Note that Llama-3.1-70B-Japanese-Instruct-2407 strongly adheres to commonsense reasoning but produces predictions that conflict with the properties of probability distributions.

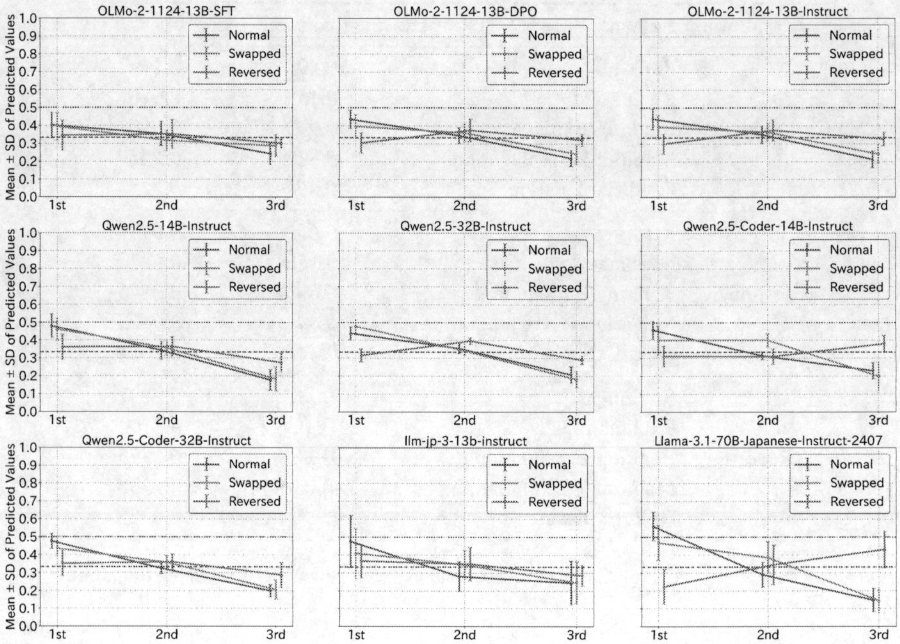

Figure 7: Average proportions predicted for ranked options when ranking information is provided, for all models in our experiment.

E The distribution of proportions in the dataset

Figure 8 shows violin and box plots illustrating the distribution of proportions in the evaluation dataset.

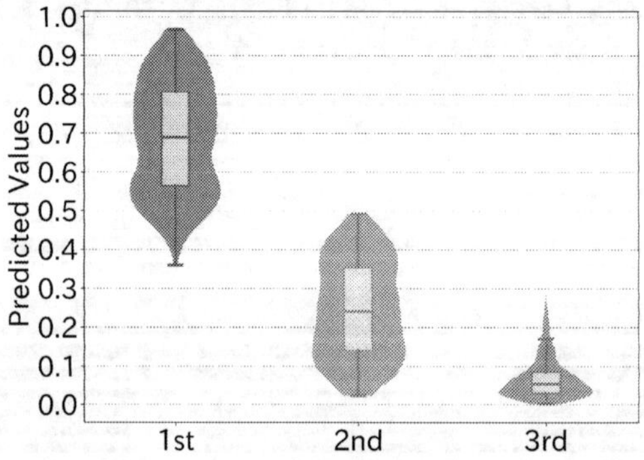

Figure 8: Violin and box plots showing the distribution of proportions in the evaluation dataset. In the absence of ties, the first rank falls within the range (0.33.., 1.0), the second rank within (0, 0.5), and the third rank within [0, 0.33..).

Rosetta-PL: Propositional Logic as a Benchmark for Large Language Model Reasoning

Shaun Baek[*1], **Shaun Esua-Mensah**[2*], **Cyrus Tsui**[2*], **Sejan Vigneswaralingam**[2*],
Abdullah Alali[2], **Michael Lu**[2], **Vasu Sharma**[2], **Kevin Zhu**[2]

[1]Emory University [2]Algoverse AI Research

shaun.baek@emory.edu, kevin@algoverseacademy.com

Abstract

Large Language Models (LLMs) are primarily trained on high-resource natural languages, limiting their effectiveness in low-resource settings and in tasks requiring deep logical reasoning. This research introduces Rosetta-PL, a benchmark designed to evaluate LLMs' logical reasoning and generalization capabilities in a controlled environment. We construct Rosetta-PL by translating a dataset of logical propositions from Lean into a custom logical language, which is then used to fine-tune an LLM (e.g., GPT-4o). Our experiments analyze the impact of the size of the dataset and the translation methodology on the performance of the model. Our results indicate that preserving logical relationships in the translation process significantly boosts precision, with accuracy plateauing beyond roughly 20,000 training samples. These insights provide valuable guidelines for optimizing LLM training in formal reasoning tasks and improving performance in various low-resource language applications.

1 Introduction

Large Language Models (LLMs), such as OpenAI's GPT models (Brown et al., 2020), Google's Gemini models (Team et al., 2024), and Meta's Llama models (Touvron et al., 2023), are typically trained on high-resource natural languages (e.g., English, Spanish, and Chinese). This focus on high-resource languages disadvantages speakers of low-resource languages, as training models for these languages are more challenging due to their inherent complexity (Team et al., 2022). Furthermore, semantic ambiguity, grammatical complexities, and contextual dependencies in natural languages can limit the capabilities of an LLM in precise logical reasoning. Since natural language often relies on implied meaning, subtle cues, and flexible syntax, models trained primarily on data using these principles may struggle to follow strict rules needed for logical reasoning (Asher et al., 2023).

To isolate these reasoning abilities from language-specific challenges, we propose the evaluation of LLMs within a controlled setting using formal logical language. Logical languages, characterized by strict syntax and precise semantics, eliminate many of the extraneous factors present in natural languages, allowing us to focus squarely on pattern recognition and problem solving. Although prior benchmarks, such as LOGIGLUE (Luo et al., 2024), provide structured reasoning tasks, these typically rely on predefined reasoning steps, making it challenging to determine whether an LLM can autonomously identify and apply logical rules. In contrast, our benchmark, Rosetta-PL, evaluates whether LLMs can discover logical patterns within a propositional language, thereby measuring reasoning ability without relying on predefined inference steps or extraneous linguistic factors. Research on applying LLMs to logic-based problem solving is relatively scarce, and while chain-of-thought (CoT) prompting has gained popularity in natural language tasks (Wei et al., 2023), its effectiveness in logical or symbolic contexts remains largely unexplored (Creswell et al., 2022).

We address this gap by constructing Rosetta-PL by translating the Lean Workbook dataset (Ying et al., 2024) into our own propositional language and fine-tuning ChatGPT (Brown et al., 2020) using the translated dataset. We evaluate logical accuracy in our custom language while varying training data parameters such as training set size and the method of translation. Our experiments point towards potentially effective training strategies and provide preliminary estimates on the dataset size needed to approach benchmark-level logical understanding. By setting aside language-specific factors, we focus on the relationship between pattern recognition and data requirements, offering insights that impact language training in both high-

*These authors contributed equally to this work.

Proceedings of the 2025 Conference of the Nations of the Americas Chapter of the Association for Computational Linguistics: Human Language Technologies (Volume 4: Student Research Workshop), pages 551–562

and low-resource settings.

2 Background

Large Language Models (LLMs) have excelled at tasks involving unstructured natural language, yet their capacity for structured logical reasoning remains underexplored (Creswell et al., 2022). The inherent ambiguities of natural language, such as polysemy and idiomatic expressions, can obscure true reasoning capabilities. In contrast, formal logical languages, defined by strict syntax and unambiguous semantics, offer a controlled testbed for evaluating pattern recognition and rule-based inference (Barcelo et al., 2023).

Propositional logic, a fundamental component of formal logic, employs connectives (e.g., $\wedge$, $\vee$, $\neg$) to combine atomic propositions into complex expressions whose truth values are fully determined by their parts (Niu et al., 2024). This clarity makes it an ideal framework for assessing whether LLMs can autonomously learn and generalize logical rules—a skill central to disciplines like mathematics and programming (Nye et al., 2021; Polu and Sutskever, 2020).

Recent benchmarks have begun to probe the symbolic reasoning of LLMs. For example, LOGIC-LM demonstrates that LLMs can solve logic puzzles when aided by external symbolic solvers (Pan et al., 2023). Meanwhile, LOGIGLUE (Luo et al., 2024) and Logic Bench (Parmar et al., 2024) evaluate multi-step reasoning based on predefined inference templates, and chain-of-thought prompting has been shown to improve arithmetic performance (Wei et al., 2023). Other studies have further enriched this landscape: for example, the SymbCoT framework integrates symbolic expressions and logic rules directly into chain-of-thought (CoT) thereby boosting reasoning fidelity (Xu et al., 2024), while research examining the impact of symbolic solver choices has revealed that tool selection (e.g., Z3, Prover9, or Pyke) can cause performance variations of up to 50% (Lam et al., 2024). Furthermore, work on step-by-step symbolic verification has demonstrated that automated checks of intermediate reasoning steps can substantially enhance overall accuracy (Zhang et al., 2024). However, these approaches tend to rely on surface-level statistical correlations rather than genuine discovery of novel logical patterns (Creswell et al., 2022).

To bridge this gap, our work translates natural language logic problems into a propositional language, thereby eliminating linguistic complexities and focusing solely on intrinsic pattern recognition. Building on formal frameworks such as Lean4 (Ying et al., 2024), we investigate how well LLMs can learn and generalize new logical structures—a capability that also carries implications for improving training strategies in low-resource language settings (Team et al., 2022).

3 Method

3.1 Objective

The primary objective of this experiment is to evaluate the logical accuracy and pattern recognition capabilities of LLMs in a newly created propositional language. By removing linguistic complexities to focus solely on logical problem-solving, we aim to determine how well these models generalize and adapt in a structured, logic-based environment under varying dataset sizes, and whether this process reveals or rectifies discrepancies in their understanding of formal languages.

3.2 Dataset

We derived Rosetta-PL from the Lean Workbook (Ying et al., 2024), which is a dataset of logical problems translated into the formal language of Lean. Each problem was translated into our custom propositional language using a predefined translation key, resulting in a training dataset of 25,214 problems. Each dataset entry was written in a conversation-like structure with system, user, assistant, function, and message content, containing a logical problem (a statement) in our custom language and its corresponding truth value, indicating whether the statement is true or not. In contrast to benchmarks such as LOGIGLUE (Luo et al., 2024) and LOGIC-LM (Pan et al., 2023), which focus on logical problems with predefined inference steps, Rosetta-PL is designed to test an LLM's ability to discover new patterns. Unlike Logic Bench (Parmar et al., 2024), which evaluates performance on known logical patterns, our dataset requires the model to infer novel patterns.

3.3 Experimental Methodology

Our experimental setup involved building a data pipeline for fine-tuning GPT-4o on formal logical tasks. We opted to use GPT-4o primarily due to its performance on a range of reasoning benchmarks such as MMLU (Massive Multitask Language Understanding), GSM8K, and Big Bench Hard, allowing us to compare with one of the highest performers for LLMs in formal logic tasks. Because GPT-4o is closed-source, there is an inherent risk of leakage challenges. However, by translating the Lean Workbook into our own custom propositional language, we altered the original problems in an unorthodox way that makes direct overlap in GPT-4o's training far less likely.

Each entry in our training dataset was verified to conform to the required format—ensuring valid roles such as system, user, and assistant, and is passed on to GPT-4o for fine-tuning. From this same dataset, we also extracted "seen" testing subsets by randomly selecting 500 entries. We also extracted "unseen" testing subsets by randomly selecting 200 problems from an entirely different source: the Minif2f-lean4 dataset (Zheng et al., 2022), which does not overlap with the training dataset. We aim to measure the model's ability to both retain learned information and generalize its logical understanding to novel patterns through the "seen" and "unseen" datasets respectively.

Throughout these experiments, all fine-tuning and testing were conducted using NVIDIA A100 GPUs. Overall, GPT-4o underwent four separate fine-tuning runs, during which we kept parameter settings constant (e.g., learning rate, number of epochs) while varying the size of the training dataset (25,214, 20,000, and 10,000) and which one out of the two translation keys used. These translation keys altered how the logical problems from the Lean Workbook were mapped into our custom language, effectively creating multiple languages with varying logical structures.

Original Example:

$$\begin{aligned} &xyz : \mathbb{N} \\ &\quad \vdash (x^2+1)*(y^2+1)*(z^2+1) \\ &\quad = (x+y+z)^2 - 2*(x*y+y*z+z*x) \\ &\qquad + (x*y+y*z+z*x)^2 - 2*x*y \\ &\qquad *z*(x+y+z) + x^2*y^2*z^2+1 \end{aligned} \tag{1}$$

Translation Strategies: To investigate the effect of symbolic representation on logical reasoning, we employ two distinct translation strategies. The first strategy maintains the inherent logical relationships by carefully mapping symbols, while the second intentionally disrupts these patterns through arbitrary transformations. These contrasting approaches allow us to assess how preserving or altering logical structure influences model performance.

- Translation Key 1 Strategy (Focused Key): Translation Key 1 replaces Lean symbols with other symbols (see appendix). This method preserves logical relationships by ensuring that related symbols are consistently mapped. For instance, the symbols ">" and "<" are translated into "»" and "«", respectively, preserving their comparative meaning. This is to mimic spoken language, where symbols and phrases are logically related. Additionally, the sentence structure is encrypted using a scrambling function that adds a reversed duplicate of the sentence at the end, with a few additional symbols in between, in order to mimic the variations in sentence structures across different languages. An example of an entry translated with Key 1 is shown below:

$$\begin{aligned} &xyz\neg\mathbb{N}\#\#|-|-|-x \wedge \\ &\wedge 2 \wedge \wedge 1|-\text{€}|-|-|-y \wedge \wedge 2 \wedge \wedge 1|- \\ &\text{€}|-|-|-z \wedge \wedge 2 \wedge \wedge 1|- == |-|-|-x \wedge \wedge y \wedge \wedge z| \\ &- \wedge \wedge 2_2\text{€}|-|-|-x\text{€}y \wedge \wedge y\text{€}z \wedge \\ &\wedge zx|- \wedge \wedge|-|-|-x\text{€}y \wedge \wedge y\text{€}z \wedge \\ &\wedge z\text{€}x|- \wedge \wedge 2_2\text{€}x\text{€}y\text{€}z\text{€}|-|-|-x \wedge \wedge y \wedge \wedge z| \\ &- \wedge \wedge x \wedge \wedge 2\text{€}y \wedge \wedge 2\text{€}z \wedge \wedge 2 \wedge \wedge 1 \end{aligned} \tag{2}$$

- Translation Key 2 Strategy (Random Key): In contrast, this method removes logical structure by shifting the ASCII values of each character by 10, resulting in an entirely arbitrary transformation. As a result, the translated expression loses any recognizable logical patterns. Additionally, statements are inverted around logical operators such as ->, >, <, >=, and <=. For example, an expression of the form "A > B > C" would be translated into "C T(>) B T(>) A", where T(>) represents the transformed version of the ">" symbol. An example of an entry translated with Key 2 is provided below:

```
"y!z!{!;!\u2125\u000b\u22a3!)y!_!3!,
!2*!+!)z!_!3!,!2*!+!){!_!3!,!2*!>\u000b
!!!!)y!,!z!,!{*!_!3!.!3!+!)y!+!z!,!z!+!
{!,!{!+!y*!,!)y!+!z!,!z!+!{!,!{!+!y*!_
!3!.!3!+!y!+!z!+!{!+!)y!,!z!,!{*!,
\u000b!!!!!!!!y!_!3!+!z!_!3!+!
!,\u000b!!!!!!2"
```

(3)

Evaluation Procedure: We conducted four fine-tuning runs on GPT-4o, keeping all hyperparameters constant, and evaluated five models (four fine-tuned and one base model with no fine-tuning) using 12 distinct datasets. These datasets are organized into two main categories:

- Seen Data: Six datasets were created by randomly selecting problems from the training set—three datasets containing 500 problems each in the original Lean format and three datasets with 500 problems each using the same translation key employed during fine-tuning.
- Unseen Data: To assess generalization, six additional datasets were formed by randomly selecting 200 problems each from the independent Mini-f2f dataset (Zheng et al., 2022). Like the seen data, these were split into two groups of three datasets: one in Lean and the other using the corresponding translated format.

Overall accuracy was computed by averaging the results across all testing sets, with accuracy defined as the number of correctly answered queries divided by the total number of queries in each set.

4 Results

Figure 1 displays the comparative performance of four fine-tuned GPT-4o models evaluated on both "seen" and "unseen" datasets. Specifically, models were fine-tuned with 25,214, 20,000, and 10,000 distinct queries using Translation Key 1, and with 25,214 queries using Translation Key 2. Additionally, Lean (untranslated) versions of both testing sets serve as benchmarks.

Our experiments demonstrate that GPT-4o exhibits superior problem-solving performance in our custom propositional language compared to Lean on average. On the "seen" dataset, GPT-4o achieved an average accuracy over all tests in of 95.97% in our propositional language versus 76.08% in Lean, with a small uncertainty of $\pm$ 0.33% and $\pm$ 0.36% respectively.

In contrast, on the "unseen" dataset, GPT-4o performed better when tested in Lean than in our custom language—attaining 99.89% accuracy with Lean compared to 97.56% with Translation Key 1 ($\pm$ 0.06% and $\pm$ 0.44% respectively). As expected, Translation Key 2 yielded a substantially lower accuracy of 64.1% ($\pm$ 0.75%) due to its arbitrary mapping. The model was fine-tuned solely on translated data, so it specializes in those patterns, resulting in high performance on seen translated examples but poor performance on seen Lean examples. For unseen data, it falls back on its broader pre-training, which helps it perform better on unseen Lean problems.

Additionally, our experiments indicate that GPT-4o solves problems more accurately with Translation Key 1 than with Translation Key 2, with average accuracies of 92.68% compared to 80.36% respectively—highlighting the importance of preserving logical relationships in the translation process. Table 1 provides a detailed summary of results from testing with Translation Key 1, and Table 3 provides a detailed summary of results from testing with Translation Key 2.

Furthermore, training set size influenced performance. Increasing the training set from 10,000 to 20,000 samples improved accuracy by 2.7% on the "seen" dataset and by 0.3% on the "unseen" dataset, while further increases up to 25,214 samples did not yield additional gains. This suggests that the training set size threshold for stable performance lies below 20,000 samples.

For seen data in the custom translated format, the fine-tuned GPT-4o consistently achieves higher accuracy by specializing in the patterns and syntax introduced during fine-tuning, outperforming the base model. In contrast, on seen Lean data, the base GPT-4o retains its general Lean knowledge from pre-training and achieves similar results to the fine-tuned model.

When it comes to unseen data, the fine-tuned GPT-4o expectedly outperforms the base model on unseen translated examples. Table 4 provides a detailed summary of the results from testing using the base GPT-4o model. However, for unseen Lean data, the GPT-4o fine-tuned using Translation Key 2 performed significantly worse than its Translation Key 1 counterparts and also the base models. Focusing on Lean data (untranslated), all 4 fine-tuned models outperform the base models in both the unseen and seen data, except for the model fine-tuned in Translation Key 2 which showed worse comparative performance in the unseen lean data.

Tables 1, 3, and 4 provides a detailed summary of all dataset permutations and average performance metrics, shedding light on any potential anomalies.

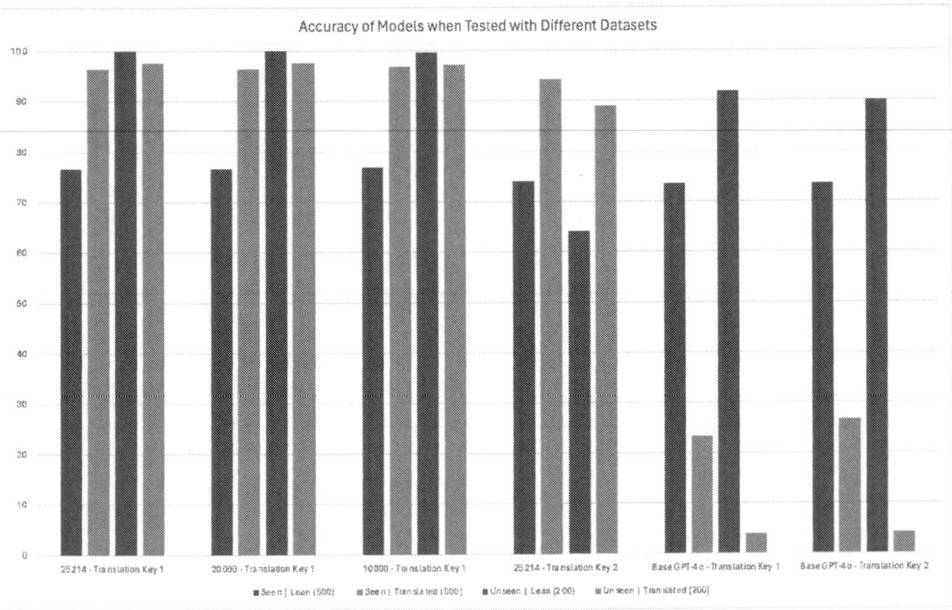

Figure 1: Comparison of GPT-4o accuracy across datasets ("Seen" and "Unseen") using different translation keys and varying dataset sizes.

5 Discussion

Our findings align with previous studies (Kojima et al., 2023; Wei et al., 2023), demonstrating that the accuracy of logical reasoning depends significantly on prompt formulation and task representation. The use of translation keys in our experiments illustrates that preserving inherent logical relationships—as in Translation Key 1—yields better performance than employing arbitrary mappings. This is analogous to natural language, where inverse or comparable relationships between symbols facilitate comprehension.

Our results also reveal a general trend where accuracy increases with training set size, echoing prior research that shows LLMs can perform well even with limited data (Brown et al., 2020). However, as shown in Figure 1, this trend is not strictly linear. There are occasions where smaller datasets outperformed larger datasets, such as the "seen" dataset in our propositional language having a 0.467% greater accuracy with 10000 samples compared to 20,000 samples. We attribute these fluctuations to certain factors, such as overfitting in larger training sets. Unlike earlier studies that evaluated existing models (liu et al., 2023), our approach using a custom propositional language uncovers unique aspects of pattern recognition in LLMs.

Notably, our analysis revealed that GPT-4o's performance on unseen data is better in Lean than it is in our custom language. We attribute this to GPT-4o's prior exposure to Lean-like syntax during pre-training Lean, as a formal proof assistant, shares structural similarities with theorem-proving and programming languages. In contrast, the custom language, especially under Translation Key 2, disrupted logical structure, thereby impeding generalization. This suggests that fine-tuning benefits significantly when the training data preserves logical consistency, aligning with the model's pre-training experience.

This is further reinforced by the observation that models fine-tuned with Translation Key 1 performed better across all testing sets than those fine-tuned with Translation Key 2. Additionally, the fine-tuned models—especially those with Translation Key 1—consistently exhibited superior performance on both seen and unseen data, and this performance improved with larger training set sizes. This demonstrates GPT's ability to generalize logical information. The LLM extracted logical information from our custom language and used it to improve its logical accuracy in Lean. Notably, it performed better with Translation Key 1—which preserves logical relationships—than with Translation Key 2, which disrupts them.

While distinguishing between these effects is challenging, future work could explore fine-tuning an LLM with minimal exposure to Lean syntax to better understand the impact of pre-training familiarity compared to logical structure preservation. Comparing performance across runs provided insights into whether GPT-4o could robustly handle shifts in symbolic representation and how sensitive its performance is to different training configurations.

Our experiments indicate that GPT-4o's performance plateaus at around 20,000 training examples. This plateau may result from dataset redundancy, model capacity limitations, or the relative simplicity of the tasks. When the dataset contains many similar patterns, the model's exposure to novel challenges is limited, and once key patterns are internalized, additional training yields diminishing returns.

In summary, our findings suggest that GPT-4o can achieve high problem-solving accuracy in a propositional language when fine-tuned appropriately. The choice of translation key, dataset characteristics, and training set size must be managed carefully to mitigate overfitting and ensure robust generalization beyond seen patterns.

6 Conclusion

Our investigation confirms that fine-tuning GPT-4o on a custom propositional language not only facilitates high-level logical reasoning but also underscores the critical role of maintaining relational integrity within training data. Specifically, our work shows that using structured translation strategies significantly enhances model performance. This improvement is achieved by aligning the training data with the inherent logical patterns familiar from the model's pre-training, allowing GPT-4o to generalize more effectively, particularly when transitioning from seen to unseen examples.

Furthermore, our analysis highlights that an optimally balanced training set is essential: while increased dataset size improves performance up to a threshold (around 20,000 examples), additional data yields diminishing returns, suggesting the need for more efficient data utilization methods. These findings not only validate the importance of structured prompts and contextual cues but also offer practical guidelines for optimizing LLM training in both high- and low-resource language scenarios.

Collectively, our results contribute to a deeper understanding of how targeted data curation and translation methodologies can bolster logical reasoning in large language models.

7 Future Research

Future work should investigate dataset design principles. The high accuracy observed on our unseen dataset may reflect biases, such as overrepresentation of certain problem types or cultural premises, which should be systematically addressed. Synthetically balanced datasets that incorporate tiered complexity levels (e.g., single-step versus multi-step reasoning) could help disentangle superficial pattern recognition from genuine logical understanding. Additionally, although formatting differences (e.g., brackets versus colons) did not hinder performance in our study, systematic evaluations of robustness to syntactic variations are needed to better assess adaptability in low-resource settings.

A potential path to explore would be foregoing fine-tuning GPT-4o on our custom dataset and instead rely on in-context learning. Because GPT-4o may already have some familiarity with Lean from its pre-training, one could design a prompt that includes a few worked examples of Lean problems alongside a call to an external translator function that converts Lean input into the custom propositional language at inference time. Though this may yield lower accuracy than fine-tuning, it avoids the cost of creating and maintaining a large translation corpus. Evaluating GPT-4o in context can reveal how much of its Lean knowledge can be utilized through prompt engineering alone.

Further research should focus on optimizing translation strategies by developing principled approaches, such as semantic alignment of symbols, to enhance learnability. At the same time, exploring data efficiency methods is critical, as our observed performance plateau at approximately 20,000 training examples suggests that smarter data utilization may both reduce data requirements and improve systematicity.

References

Nicholas Asher, Swarnadeep Bhar, Akshay Chaturvedi, Julie Hunter, and Soumya Paul. 2023. Limits for learning with language models. *Preprint*, arXiv:2306.12213.

Pablo Barcelo, Alexander Kozachinskiy, Anthony Widjaja Lin, and Vladimir Podolskii. 2023. Logical languages accepted by transformer encoders with hard attention. *Preprint*, arXiv:2310.03817.

Tom B. Brown, Benjamin Mann, Nick Ryder, Melanie Subbiah, Jared Kaplan, Prafulla Dhariwal, Arvind Neelakantan, Pranav Shyam, Girish Sastry, Amanda Askell, Sandhini Agarwal, Ariel Herbert-Voss, Gretchen Krueger, Tom Henighan, Rewon Child, Aditya Ramesh, Daniel M. Ziegler, Jeffrey Wu, Clemens Winter, and 12 others. 2020. Language models are few-shot learners. *Preprint*, arXiv:2005.14165.

Antonia Creswell, Murray Shanahan, and Irina Higgins. 2022. Selection-inference: Exploiting large language models for interpretable logical reasoning. *Preprint*, arXiv:2205.09712.

Takeshi Kojima, Shixiang Shane Gu, Machel Reid, Yutaka Matsuo, and Yusuke Iwasawa. 2023. Large language models are zero-shot reasoners. *Preprint*, arXiv:2205.11916.

Long Hei Matthew Lam, Ramya Keerthy Thatikonda, and Ehsan Shareghi. 2024. A closer look at logical reasoning with llms: The choice of tool matters. *Preprint*, arXiv:2406.00284.

Hanmeng liu, Zhiyang Teng, Ruoxi Ning, Jian Liu, Qiji Zhou, and Yue Zhang. 2023. Glore: Evaluating logical reasoning of large language models. *Preprint*, arXiv:2310.09107.

Man Luo, Shrinidhi Kumbhar, Ming shen, Mihir Parmar, Neeraj Varshney, Pratyay Banerjee, Somak Aditya, and Chitta Baral. 2024. Towards logiglue: A brief survey and a benchmark for analyzing logical reasoning capabilities of language models. *Preprint*, arXiv:2310.00836.

Xiaohui Niu, Wenxi Li, and Zhongzhi Wang. 2024. On grobner-shirshov bases for markov semirings. *Preprint*, arXiv:2401.05731.

Maxwell Nye, Anders Johan Andreassen, Guy Gur-Ari, Henryk Michalewski, Jacob Austin, David Bieber, David Dohan, Aitor Lewkowycz, Maarten Bosma, David Luan, Charles Sutton, and Augustus Odena. 2021. Show your work: Scratchpads for intermediate computation with language models. *Preprint*, arXiv:2112.00114.

Liangming Pan, Alon Albalak, Xinyi Wang, and William Yang Wang. 2023. Logic-lm: Empowering large language models with symbolic solvers for faithful logical reasoning. *Preprint*, arXiv:2305.12295.

Mihir Parmar, Nisarg Patel, Neeraj Varshney, Mutsumi Nakamura, Man Luo, Santosh Mashetty, Arindam Mitra, and Chitta Baral. 2024. Logicbench: Towards systematic evaluation of logical reasoning ability of large language models. *Preprint*, arXiv:2404.15522.

Stanislas Polu and Ilya Sutskever. 2020. Generative language modeling for automated theorem proving. *Preprint*, arXiv:2009.03393.

Gemini Team, Rohan Anil, Sebastian Borgeaud, Jean-Baptiste Alayrac, Jiahui Yu, Radu Soricut, Johan Schalkwyk, Andrew M. Dai, Anja Hauth, Katie Millican, David Silver, Melvin Johnson, Ioannis Antonoglou, Julian Schrittwieser, Amelia Glaese, Jilin Chen, Emily Pitler, Timothy Lillicrap, Angeliki Lazaridou, and 1331 others. 2024. Gemini: A family of highly capable multimodal models. *Preprint*, arXiv:2312.11805.

NLLB Team, Marta R. Costa-jussà, James Cross, Onur Çelebi, Maha Elbayad, Kenneth Heafield, Kevin Heffernan, Elahe Kalbassi, Janice Lam, Daniel Licht, Jean Maillard, Anna Sun, Skyler Wang, Guillaume Wenzek, Al Youngblood, Bapi Akula, Loic Barrault, Gabriel Mejia Gonzalez, Prangthip Hansanti, and 20 others. 2022. No language left behind: Scaling human-centered machine translation. *Preprint*, arXiv:2207.04672.

Hugo Touvron, Louis Martin, Kevin Stone, Peter Albert, Amjad Almahairi, Yasmine Babaei, Nikolay Bashlykov, Soumya Batra, Prajjwal Bhargava, Shruti Bhosale, Dan Bikel, Lukas Blecher, Cristian Canton Ferrer, Moya Chen, Guillem Cucurull, David Esiobu, Jude Fernandes, Jeremy Fu, Wenyin Fu, and 49 others. 2023. Llama 2: Open foundation and fine-tuned chat models. *Preprint*, arXiv:2307.09288.

Jason Wei, Xuezhi Wang, Dale Schuurmans, Maarten Bosma, Brian Ichter, Fei Xia, Ed Chi, Quoc Le, and Denny Zhou. 2023. Chain-of-thought prompting elicits reasoning in large language models. *Preprint*, arXiv:2201.11903.

Jundong Xu, Hao Fei, Liangming Pan, Qian Liu, Mong-Li Lee, and Wynne Hsu. 2024. Faithful logical reasoning via symbolic chain-of-thought. *Preprint*, arXiv:2405.18357.

Huaiyuan Ying, Zijian Wu, Yihan Geng, Jiayu Wang, Dahua Lin, and Kai Chen. 2024. Lean workbook: A large-scale lean problem set formalized from natural language math problems. *Preprint*, arXiv:2406.03847.

Yi-Fan Zhang, Hanlin Zhang, Li Erran Li, and Eric Xing. 2024. Evaluating step-by-step reasoning through symbolic verification. *Preprint*, arXiv:2212.08686.

Kunhao Zheng, Jesse Michael Han, and Stanislas Polu. 2022. Minif2f: a cross-system benchmark for formal olympiad-level mathematics. *Preprint*, arXiv:2109.00110.

A Appendix

Translation Key 1 (25214)					
	Testing Dataset	Accuracy (%)	Total Queries	Correct	Incorrect
Seen	Lean (500) - Benchmark	76.66666667	500	383.3333333	116.6666667
	1	76.2	500	381	119
	2	74.4	500	372	128
	3	79.4	500	397	103
Seen	Translated (500)	96.4	500	482	18
	1	96.4	500	482	18
	2	97	500	485	15
	3	95.8	500	479	21
Unseen	Lean (200)	100	200	200	0
	1	100	200	200	0
	2	100	200	200	0
	3	100	200	200	0
Unseen	Translated (200)	97.66666667	200	195.3333333	4.666666667
	1	98	200	196	4
	2	98	200	196	4
	3	97	200	194	6
Translation Key 1 (20000)					
	Testing Dataset	Accuracy (%)	Total Queries	Correct	Incorrect
Seen	Lean (500) - Benchmark	76.66667	500	383.3333	116.6667
	1	76.2	500	381	119
	2	74.4	500	372	128
	3	79.4	500	397	103
Seen	Translated (500)	96.4	500	482	18
	1	96.4	500	482	18
	2	97	500	485	15
	3	95.8	500	479	21
Unseen	Lean (200)	100	200	200	0
	1	100	200	200	0
	2	100	200	200	0
	3	100	200	200	0
Unseen	Translated (200)	97.66667	200	195.3333	4.666667
	1	98	200	196	4
	2	98	200	196	4
	3	97	200	194	6

Table 1: Summary table for Translation Key 1 model evaluation results. The top of each testing dataset shows the overall average results across three runs. (Part 1/2)

Translation Key 1 (10000)					
	Testing Dataset	Accuracy (%)	Total Queries	Correct	Incorrect
Seen	Lean (500) - Benchmark	76.93333333	500	384.6666667	115.3333333
	1	80	500	400	100
	2	74.4	500	372	128
	3	76.4	500	382	118
Seen	Translated (500)	96.86666667	500	484.3333333	15.66666667
	1	97.2	500	486	14
	2	97.2	500	486	14
	3	96.2	500	481	19
Unseen	Lean (200)	99.66666667	200	199.3333333	0.666666667
	1	99.5	200	199	1
	2	99.5	200	199	1
	3	100	200	200	0
Unseen	Translated (200)	97.33333333	200	194.6666667	5.333333333
	1	97.5	200	195	5
	2	97.5	200	195	5
	3	97	200	194	6

Table 2: Summary table for Translation Key 1 model evaluation results. The top of each testing dataset shows the overall average results across three runs. (Part 2/2)

Translation Key 2 (25214)					
	Testing Dataset	Accuracy (%)	Total Queries	Correct	Incorrect
Seen	Lean (500) - Benchmark	74.06666667	500	370.3333333	129.6666667
	1	74.6	500	373	127
	2	72	500	360	140
	3	75.6	500	378	122
Seen	Translated (500)	94.2	500	471	29
	1	92.6	500	463	37
	2	96.2	500	481	19
	3	93.8	500	469	31
Unseen	Lean (200)	64.16666667	200	128.3333333	71.66666667
	1	64	200	128	72
	2	63.5	200	127	73
	3	65	200	130	70
Unseen	Translated (200)	89	200	178	22
	1	91	200	182	18
	2	88	200	176	24
	3	88	200	176	24

Table 3: Summary table for Translation Key 2 model evaluation results. The top of each testing dataset shows the overall average results across three runs.

Base GPT-4o - Translation Key 1					
	Testing Dataset	Accuracy (%)	Total Queries	Correct	Incorrect
Seen	Lean (500) - Benchmark	73.53333	500	367.66667	132.33333
	1	73.4	500	367	133
	2	70.4	500	352	148
	3	76.8	500	384	116
Seen	Translated (500)	23.33333	500	117	383
	1	25.2	500	126	374
	2	21.6	500	108	392
	3	23.2	500	116	384
Unseen	Lean (200)	91.83333	200	183.66667	16.33333
	1	92	200	184	16
	2	91	200	182	18
	3	92.5	200	185	15
Unseen	Translated (200)	4	200	8	192
	1	4	200	8	192
	2	4	200	8	192
	3	4	200	8	192
Base GPT-4o - Translation Key 2					
	Testing Dataset	Accuracy (%)	Total Queries	Correct	Incorrect
Seen	Lean (500) - Benchmark	73.53333	500	367.66667	132.33333
	1	73.4	500	367	133
	2	76.2	500	381	119
	3	71	500	355	145
Seen	Translated (500)	26.66667	500	133.33333	366.66667
	1	27.4	500	137	363
	2	28.2	500	141	359
	3	24.4	500	122	378
Unseen	Lean (200)	90	200	180	20
	1	90	200	180	20
	2	90	200	180	20
	3	90	200	180	20
Unseen	Translated (200)	4.16667	200	8.33333	191.66667
	1	3.5	200	7	193
	2	4.5	200	9	191
	3	4.5	200	9	191

Table 4: Summary table for Base GPT-4o for Translation Key 1 and Translation Key 2. The top of each testing dataset shows the overall average results across three runs.

Lean Symbol	Propositional Symbol
∧	[illegible]
∨	[illegible]
¬	@
→	+
↔	<>
(	|||
)	|
⊢	\
⊤	//
∀	{
∃	}
∅	$
∑	≥
∏	≤
√	≡
∩	≠
∪	≅
⊂	⊓
⊆	⊇
⊇	⊆
⊓	∪
≅	√
≠	∏
≡	∑
≤	>
≥	<
!	&
%	#
'	~
*	€
+	^
,	`
-	_
.	°
/	¥
:	¬
<	<<

Figure 2: Mapping between Lean's logical symbols and their corresponding representations in our custom propositional language. (Part 1/2)

Lean Symbol	Propositional Symbol
=	
>	>>
?	¿
@	~@
[	{|
\	##
]	|}
{	{{
}	}}
^	^^
|	|-
«	<<-
»	->>
×	**
∣	//
•	o
⁻	-_
⁺	+_
↑	/^
↥	/|
⇑	^^^
∈	e
∉	!e
∘	o_
∣	|=
∩	&
∪	|+
…	...
⌈	<_
⌉	_>
⌊	L_
⌋	_L
†	x_
⦃	{|
⦄	|}
/	/_
Set.Ioo	open open
Set.Icc	close close
Set.Ico	close open
Set.Ioc	open close

Figure 3: Mapping between Lean's logical symbols and their corresponding representations in our custom propositional language. (Part 2/2)

Author Index